P9-CUK-437

Here are your

2002 Year Book Cross-Reference Tabs

For insertion in your WORLD BOOK set

Put these Tabs in the appropriate volumes of your **World Book Encyclopedia** now. Then, when you later look up some topic in **World Book** and find a Tab near the article, you will know that one of your **Year Books** has newer or more detailed information about that topic.

How to use these Tabs

First, remove this page from **THE YEAR BOOK**.

Begin with the first Tab, **ARCHITECTURE,** of your **World Book** set and find the **ARCHITECTURE** article in it. Moisten the **ARCHITECTURE** Tab and affix it to that page.

Glue all the other Tabs in the appropriate **World Book** volume.

Special Report
ARCHITECTURE
2002 Year Book, p. 68

New World Book Article
BUSH, GEORGE W.
2002 Year Book, p. 450

New World Book Article
CHENEY, RICHARD BRUCE
2002 Year Book, p. 455

New World Book Article
CLASSICAL MUSIC
2002 Year Book, 456

Special Report
COLOMBIA
2002 Year Book, p. 284

Special Report
COPYRIGHT
2002 Year Book, p. 258

Special Report
CRIME
2002 Year Book, p. 158

Special Report
ENERGY SUPPLY
2002 Year Book, p. 198

Special Report
GLOBAL WARMING
2002 Year Book, p. 230

New World Book Article
INTERNET
2002 Year Book, p. 466

Special Report
LATIN AMERICA
2002 Year Book, p. 284

New World Book Article
MONTREAL
2002 Year Book, p. 472

New World Book Article
NEW ZEALAND
2002 Year Book, p. 484

New World Book Article
POSTAL SERVICES
2002 Year Book, p. 495

Special Report
SPACE EXPLORATION
2002 Year Book, p. 374

New World Book Article
SPANISH CIVIL WAR
2002 Year Book, p. 502

Special Report
TERRORISM
2002 Year Book, p. 38

Special Report
UNITED STATES, GOVERNMENT OF
2002 Year Book, p. 426

New World Book Article
VIETNAM
2002 Year Book, p. 504

Special Report
WRIGHT, FRANK LLOYD
2002 Year Book, p. 68

The 2002 World Book

YEAR BOOK

The Annual Supplement to The World Book Encyclopedia

▪▪▪ A REVIEW OF THE EVENTS OF 2001 ▪▪▪

World Book, Inc.
a Scott Fetzer company
Chicago

www.worldbook.com

World Book, Inc.
233 N. Michigan Ave.
Chicago, IL 60601

ISBN: 0-7166-0453-1
ISSN: 0084-1439
Library of Congress Control Number: 62004818

Printed in the United States of America.

Staff

EDITORIAL

Editor in Chief
Darlene R. Stille

Managing Editor
Scott Thomas

Assistant Managing Editor
Alfred J. Smuskiewicz

Senior Editors
Timothy D. Frystak
Kristina Vaicikonis

Staff Editors
Dan Blunk
Tabitha A. Hostetler

Editorial Assistant
Ethel Matthews

Cartographic Services
H. George Stoll, Head
Wayne K. Pichler, Manager, Cartographic Database
Kari Burnett, Staff Cartographer

Indexing Services
David Pofelski, Head
Tina Trettin, Staff Indexer

Statistical Services
Ken Shenkman, Head

Permissions Editor
Janet T. Peterson

ART

Executive Director
Roberta Dimmer

Design
Brenda B. Tropinski, Senior Designer, Year Book
Cari L. Biamonte Senior Designer
Don Di Sante, Senior Designer
John Horvath, Designer

Photography
Sandra M. Dyrlund Photography Manager
Sylvia Ohlrich Photographs Editor
Laurie Schuh Assistant Photographs Editor

Art Production Assistant
John Whitney

RESEARCH SERVICES

Executive Director, Research Services and Product Development
Paul A. Kobasa

Researchers
Madolynn H. Cronk
Karen A. McCormack
Thomas Ryan Sullivan

Library Services
Jon Fjortoft, Head

PRODUCTION

Manufacturing/Pre-Press
Carma Fazio, Director, Manufacturing and Pre-Press
Barbara Podczerwinski, Manufacturing Manager
Madelyn S. Underwood Senior Production Manager
Jared Svoboda, Production Manager

Proofreaders
Anne Dillon
Chad Rubel

Text Processing
Curley Hunter
Gwendolyn Johnson

EXECUTIVE VICE PRESIDENT AND PUBLISHER

Michael Ross

Contributors

Contributors not listed on these pages are members of the editorial staff.

- **ANDREWS, PETER J.,** B.A., M.S.; Free-lance writer. **[Chemistry]**
- **APPLEBY, R. SCOTT,** A.B., M.A., Ph.D.; Professor of History and Director of The Joan B. Kroc Institute for International Peace Studies, University of Notre Dame. [Special Feature: **Terrorism: America's New Enemy]**
- **APSELOFF, MARILYN FAIN,** B.A., M.A.; Professor of English, Kent State University, Ohio. **[Literature for children]**
- **ASKER, JAMES R.,** B.A.; Washington bureau chief, *Aviation Week & Space Technology* magazine. **[Space exploration]**
- **BARNHART, BILL,** B.A., M.S.T., M.B.A.; Financial markets columnist, *Chicago Tribune.* **[Stocks and bonds]**
- **BARRETT, NORMAN,** M.A.; Free-lance writer. **[Soccer]**
- **BAYNHAM, SIMON,** B.A., M.A., Ph.D.; Senior research associate, Centre for Defence & International Security Studies, University of Lancaster, U.K. **[Africa and African country articles]**
- **BERGER, ERIC R.** B.A, M.A.; Science writer, *Houston Chronicle.* **[Houston]**
- **BOULDREY, BRIAN,** B.A., M.F.A.; Visiting Assistant Professor of English, Northwestern University. **[Literature, world; Poetry; Prison; Pulitzer Prizes; San Francisco]**
- **BOYD, JOHN D.,** B.S.; News editor, *Transport Topics.* **[Economics; International trade; Manufacturing]**
- **BRADSHER, HENRY S.,** A.B., B.J.; Foreign affairs analyst. **[Asia and Asian country articles]**
- **BRETT, CARLTON E.,** B.A., M.S., Ph.D.; Professor of geology, University of Cincinnati. **[Paleontology]**
- **BUERKLE, TOM,** B.A.; European editor, *Institutional Investor.* **[Europe and Western European nation articles]**
- **CAMPBELL, GEOFFREY A.,** B.J.; Free-lance writer. **[U.S. government** Special Report: **The Changing Profile of America: The 2000 Census; U.S. government articles]**
- **CARDINALE, DIANE P.,** B.A.; Public information manager, Toy Industry Association, Incorporated. **[Toys and games]**
- **CASEY, MIKE,** B.S., M.A.; Assistant editor, *Kansas City Star.* **[Automobile]**
- **CICERONE, RALPH J.,** B.S., M.S. Ph.D.; Aldrich Professor of Earth System Science and Chemistry, and Chancellor, University of California at Irvine. **[Global Warming** Special Report: **What We Know About Global Warming]**
- **DeFRANK, THOMAS M.,** B.A., M.A.; Washington bureau chief, *New York Daily News.* **[Armed forces]**
- **DILLON, DAVID,** B.A., M.A., Ph.D.; Architecture and design editor, *The Dallas Morning News.* **[Architecture]**
- **DUCKHAM, DAVID,** Free-lance writer, marketing consultant, and former professional rugby player. **[Rugby football]**
- **ELLIS, GAVIN,** Editor in chief, *The New Zealand Herald & Weekend Herald.* **[New Zealand]**
- **FARR, DAVID M. L.,** D.Phil.; Professor emeritus of history, Carleton University. **[Canada; Canada, Prime Minister of; Canadian provinces; Canadian territories]**
- **FISHER, ROBERT W.,** B.A., M.A.; Free-lance writer. **[Labor and employment]**
- **FITZGERALD, MARK,** B.A.; Editor at large, *Editor & Publisher* magazine. **[Magazine; Newspaper]**
- **FOX, THOMAS C.,** B.A., M.A.; Publisher, *The National Catholic Reporter.* **[Roman Catholic Church]**
- **FRIEDMAN, EMILY,** B.A.; Health policy and ethics analyst. **[Health care issues]**
- **GADOMSKI, FRED,** B.S., M.S.; Meteorologist, Pennsylvania State University. **[Weather]**
- **GATTY, ROBERT C.,** Vice president of communications and marketing, Food Distributors International. **[Food]**
- **GOLDEN, JONATHAN J.,** B.A., M.J.; Ph.D. candidate, Brandeis University. **[Judaism]**
- **GOLDNER, NANCY,** B.A.; Free-lance dance critic. **[Dance]**
- **HALES, DIANNE,** B.A., M.A.; Free-lance writer. **[Crime** Special Report: **Juvenile Violence]**
- **HARAKAS, STANLEY SAMUEL,** B.A., B. Th., Th.D.; Archbishop Iakovos Professor (Emeritus) of Orthodox Theology, Holy Cross Greek Orthodox School of Theology. **[Eastern Orthodox Churches]**
- **HAVERSTOCK, NATHAN A.,** A.B.; Affiliate scholar, Oberlin College. **[Latin America** Special Report: **Drugs, Guns, and Money: The Conflict in Colombia; Latin America and Latin American country articles]**
- **HELMS, CHRISTINE,** B.A., Ph.D.; Writer and Middle East analyst. **[Middle East and Middle Eastern country articles; North African country articles]**
- **HENDERSON, HAROLD,** B.A.; Staff writer, Chicago *Reader.* **[Chicago]**
- **HOFFMAN, ANDREW J.,** B.S., M.S., Ph.D.; Assistant professor of organizational behavior, Boston University. **[Environmental pollution]**
- **ISENBERG, DOUG,** A.B. J.D.; Founder, GigaLaw.com. **[Internet** Special Report: **The Internet, Copyright, and You]**
- **JOHANSON, DONALD C.,** B.S., M.A., Ph.D.; Director and professor, Institute of Human Origins, Arizona State University. **[Anthropology]**
- **JOHN, NANCY R.,** A.B., M.L.S.; Assistant university librarian, University of Illinois at Chicago. **[Library]**
- **JOHNSON, CHRISTINA S.,** B.A., M.S.; Free-lance science writer. **[Ocean]**
- **KATES, MICHAEL,** B.S.J.; Associate sports editor, *Chicago Tribune.* **[Sports articles]**
- **KENNEDY, BRIAN,** M.A.; Free-lance writer. **[Australia; Australia, Prime Minister of; Australian rules football]**

- **KILGORE, MARGARET,** B.A., M.B.A.; Free-lance writer, Kilgore and Associates. **[Los Angeles]**

- **KING, MIKE,** Reporter, *The* (Montreal) *Gazette.* **[Montreal]**

- **KLINTBERG, PATRICIA PEAK,** B.A.; Office of Communications, U.S. Department of Agriculture. **[Agriculture]**

- **KNIGHT, ROBERT,** B.A., M.M.; Free-lance writer. **[Nobel Prizes; People in the news]**

- **KRONHOLZ, JUNE,** B.S.J.; Staff reporter, *The Wall Street Journal.* **[Education]**

- **LAWRENCE, ALBERT,** B.A., M.A., M.Ed.; President, OutExcel! **[Chess]**

- **LEWIS, DAVID C.,** M.D.; Professor of medicine and community health, Brown University. **[Drug abuse]**

- **LIEBENSON, DONALD,** B.A.; Free-lance writer. **[Popular music; Television]**

- **LYE, KEITH,** B.A., F.R.G.S.; Free-lance writer and editor. **[Cricket]**

- **MARCH, ROBERT H.,** A.B., M.S., Ph.D.; Professor emeritus of physics and liberal studies, University of Wisconsin at Madison. **[Physics]**

- **MARSCHALL, LAURENCE A.,** B.S., Ph.D.; Professor of physics, Gettysburg College. **[Astronomy]**

- **MARTY, MARTIN E.,** Ph.D.; Fairfax M. Cone Distinguished Service Professor Emeritus, University of Chicago. **[Protestantism]**

- **MAUGH, THOMAS H., II,** Ph.D.; Medical writer, *Los Angeles Times.* **[Biology]**

- **MAY, SALLY RUTH,** B.A, M.A.; Free-lance art writer. **[Art]**

- **McWILLIAM, ROHAN,** B.A., M.A. D. Phil; Senior lecturer in history, Anglia Polytechnic University, Cambridge, U.K. **[Ireland; Northern Ireland; United Kingdom; United Kingdom, Prime Minister of]**

- **MESSENGER, ROBERT,** B.A.; Editor, *New Criterion.* **[City; Crime; Literature, American; Washington, D.C.]**

- **MINER, TODD J.,** B.S., M.S.; Meteorologist, Pennsylvania State University. **[Weather]**

- **MORITZ, OWEN,** B.A.; Urban-affairs editor, *New York Daily News.* **[New York City]**

- **MORRIS, BERNADINE,** B.A., M.A.; Free-lance fashion writer. **[Fashion]**

- **MULLINS, HENRY T.,** B.S., M.S., Ph.D.; Professor of geology, Syracuse University. **[Geology]**

- **NGUYEN, J. TUYET,** M.A.; United Nations correspondent, Deutsche Presse-Agentur. **[Population; United Nations]**

- **OGAN, EUGENE,** B.A., Ph.D.; Professor emeritus of anthropology, University of Minnesota. **[Pacific Islands]**

- **PAETH, GREGORY,** B.A.; Television and radio writer, *The Cincinnati Post.* **[Radio]**

- **REINHART, A. KEVIN,** B.A., M.A., Ph.D.; Associate professor of religious studies, Dartmouth College. **[Islam]**

- **ROSE, MARK J.,** B.A., M.A., Ph.D.; Executive editor, *Archaeology* magazine. **[Archaeology]**

- **RUBENSTEIN, RICHARD E.,** B.A., M.A., J.D.; Professor of conflict resolution and public affairs, George Mason University. **[Terrorism]**

- **SARNA, JONATHAN D.,** Ph.D.; Joseph H. & Belle R. Braun Professor of American Jewish History, Brandeis University. **[Judaism]**

- **SAVAGE, IAN,** B.A., Ph.D.; Assistant professor of economics and transportation, Northwestern University. **[Aviation; Transportation]**

- **SHAPIRO, HOWARD,** B.S.; Travel editor, *The Philadelphia Inquirer.* **[Philadelphia]**

- **SOLNICK, STEVEN L.,** B.A., M.A., Ph.D.; Associate professor of political science, Columbia University. **[Russia and other former Soviet republic articles]**

- **STEIN, DAVID LEWIS,** B.A., M.S.; Former urban affairs columnist, *The Toronto Star.* **[Toronto]**

- **STOCKER, CAROL M.,** B.A.; Reporter, *The Boston Globe.* **[Gardening]**

- **STUART, ELAINE,** B.A.; Senior managing editor, Council of State Governments. **[State government]**

- **TANNER, JAMES C.,** B.J.; Former news editor—energy, *The Wall Street Journal.* **[Energy supply** Special Report: **The 2001 Energy Crunch—Crisis or Wake-up Call?; Energy supply]**

- **TATUM, HENRY K.,** B.A.; Associate editor, *The Dallas Morning News.* **[Dallas]**

- **THOMAS, PAULETTE,** B.A.; Staff writer, *The Wall Street Journal.* **[Bank]**

- **VAN, JON,** B.A., M.A.; Technology writer, *Chicago Tribune.* **[Telecommunications]**

- **von RHEIN, JOHN,** B.A.; Classical music critic, *Chicago Tribune.* **[Classical music]**

- **WALTER, EUGENE J., Jr.,** B.A.; Free-lance writer. **[Conservation; Zoos]**

- **WILSON, DAVE,** B.A.; Technology columnist, *Los Angeles Times.* **[Internet]**

- **WOLCHIK, SHARON L.,** B.A., M.A., Ph.D.; Professor of political science and international affairs, George Washington University. **[Eastern European country articles]**

- **WOODS, MICHAEL,** B.S.; Science editor, *The Toledo* (Ohio) *Blade* and *Pittsburgh Post-Gazette.* **[AIDS; Computer; Drugs; Electronics; Medicine; Mental health; Public health and safety]**

- **WRIGHT, ANDREW G.,** B.A.; Managing editor, *Design-Build* magazine. **[Building and construction]**

- **WUNTCH, PHILIP,** B.A.; Film critic, *The Dallas Morning News.* **[Motion pictures]**

- **YEZZI, DAVID,** B.A., M.A.; Free-lance theater critic. **[Theater]**

Contents

Cross-Reference Tabs

A tear-out page of Cross-Reference Tabs for insertion in *The World Book Encyclopedia* appears before page 1.

▲ Page 227

▼ Page 270

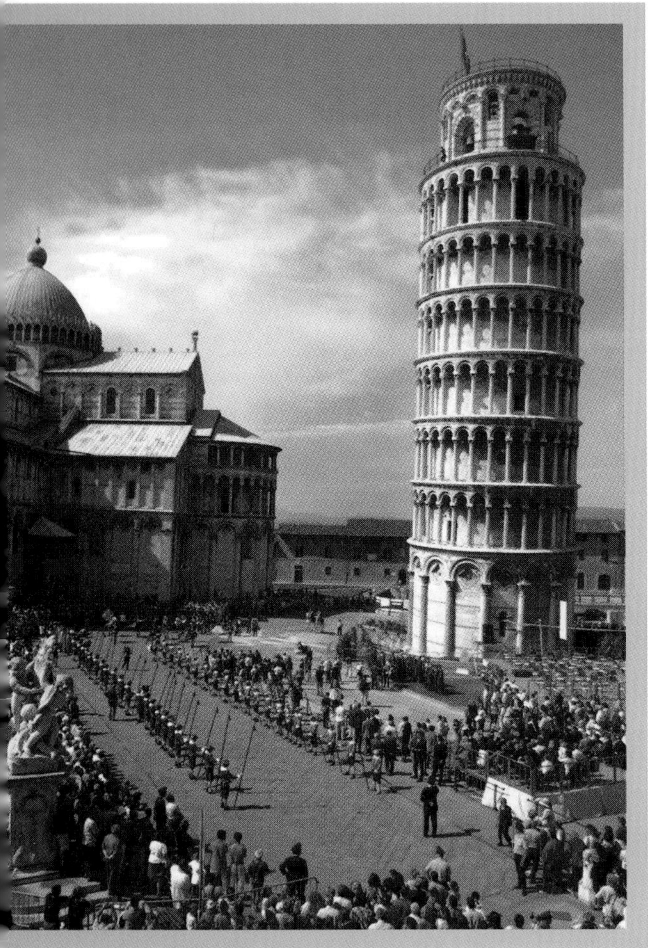

▼ Page 65

World Book Supplement 449

Nine new or revised articles are reprinted from the 2002 edition of *The World Book Encyclopedia.*

Index 513

A 15-page cumulative index covers the contents of the 2000, 2001, and 2002 editions of *The Year Book.*

▼ Page 389

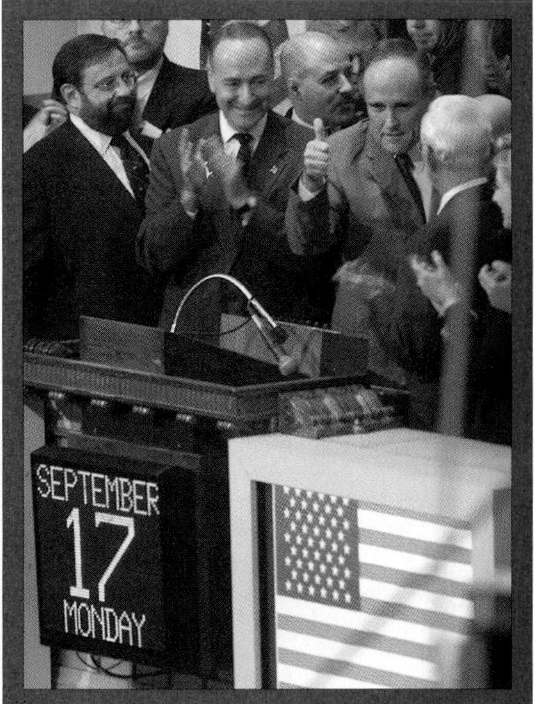

2001 The Year's Major News Stories

From the terrorist attacks on the United States on September 11 to the military strikes against Afghanistan in October and the stepped up violence in the Middle East, 2001 was a year of extraordinary events. On these three pages are stories the editors picked as some of the most important of the year, along with details on where to find more information about them in this volume.
The Editors

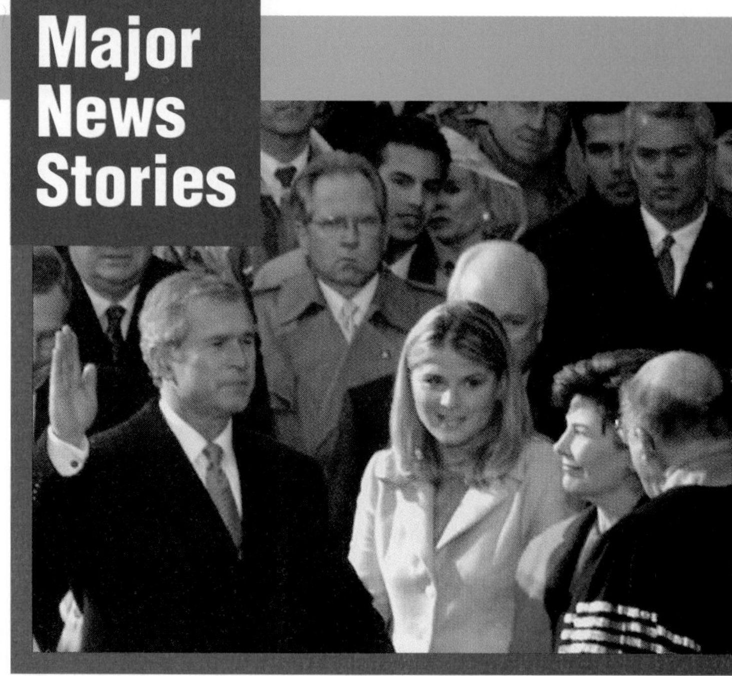

The 43rd president sworn in

George W. Bush, standing with his daughter Jenna and wife Laura, is sworn in as the 43rd president of the United States on January 20. See **Republican Party**, page 357; **United States, Government of the,** page 422; **United States, President of the,** page 438.

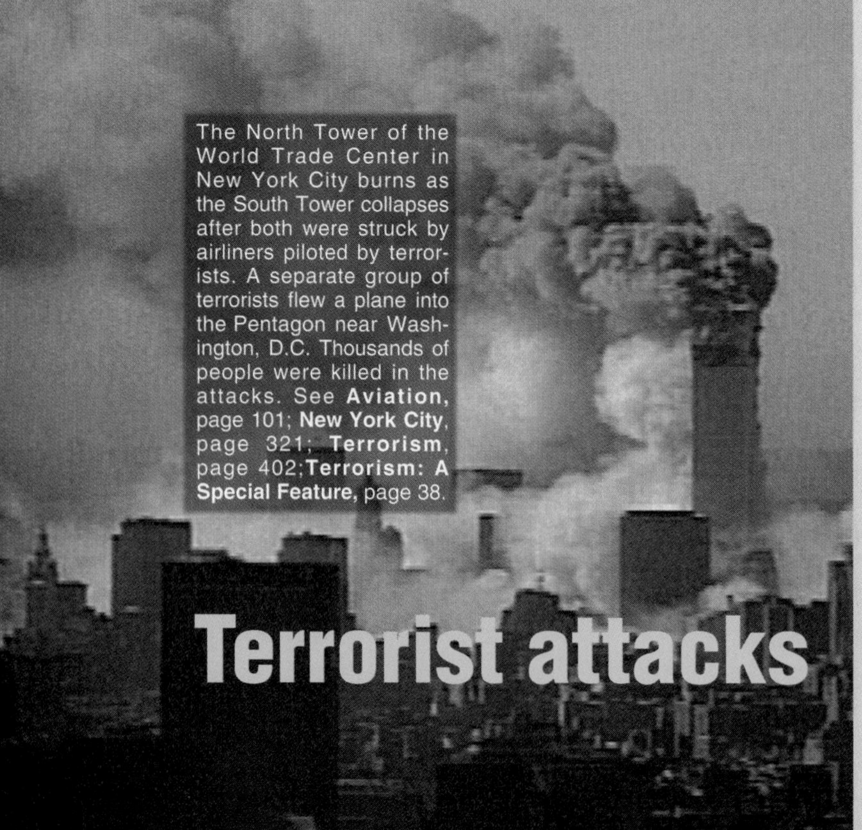

Terrorist attacks

The North Tower of the World Trade Center in New York City burns as the South Tower collapses after both were struck by airliners piloted by terrorists. A separate group of terrorists flew a plane into the Pentagon near Washington, D.C. Thousands of people were killed in the attacks. See **Aviation,** page 101; **New York City,** page 321; **Terrorism,** page 402; **Terrorism: A Special Feature,** page 38.

Artificial heart

The first completely self-contained artificial heart was successfully implanted into a human patient on July 2. The heart, called the Abiocor Implantable Replacement Heart, operated on an internal battery, eliminating the need for heavy support equipment. See **Medicine**, page 307.

Intifada in Israel

The Palestinian uprising, or intifada, which began in September 2000, claimed hundreds of lives in 2001 and greatly complicated international efforts to broker a peace agreement. See **Israel,** page 268; **Middle East,** page 312.

Power crisis in California

In March, California's two biggest electric utilities responded to widespread shortages of electricity by ordering rolling blackouts, leaving millions of customers without power. The shortages drove up the wholesale price of electricity, forcing California regulators to pass the biggest rate hike in state history. See **Energy supply** page 197**; Energy supply: A Special Report,** page 198; **State government,** page 386.

Military presence in Afghanistan

A U.S. Special Forces soldier stands guard in Afghanistan after the United States in October launched Operation Enduring Freedom, a series of air strikes and military deployments in Afghanistan. The operation removed the Taliban from power and destroyed the al-Qaida terrorist network in Afghanistan. See **Afghanistan,** page 52; **Armed forces,** page 80; **United States, Government of the,** page 422.

Economy declines

The U.S. economy lost steam in 2001, ending the longest economic expansion in U.S. history, dating back to 1991. In November 2001, the National Bureau of Economic Research reported that the U.S. economy had actually been in recession since March. See **Bank,** page 104; **Economy,** page 190; **Labor and employment,** page 277; **Stocks and bonds,** page 388; **United States, Government of the,** page 422.

Foot-and-mouth disease

In 2001, farmers throughout Europe were forced to destroy about 4 million cattle, sheep, and pigs to prevent the spread of highly contagious foot-and-mouth disease. The exportation of meat from European Union countries was banned to prevent the disease from spreading into other countries. See **Agriculture,** page 59; **Europe,** page 212.

Labour Party wins election

The United Kingdom's Labour Party, led by Prime Minister Tony Blair, won a resounding victory in parliamentary elections in June. The party will serve two full terms for the first time in its history. See **Europe**, page 212; **United Kingdom**, page 414; **United Kingdom, Prime Minister of**, page 420.

Anthrax scare

Guards in biohazard suits patrol the U.S. Capitol in Washington, D.C., in October after letters contaminated with anthrax spores were found in government offices. See **Congress of the United States,** page 147; **New York City,** page 321; **Public health and safety,** page 354; **Terrorism: A Special Feature,** page 38; **United States, Government of the,** page 422.

Democrats take control of Senate

In May, Senator James R. Jeffords of Vermont announced that he was leaving the Republican Party over disagreements with party leaders, including U.S. President George Bush. Jeffords's decision to become an independent aligned with the Democratic Party gave the Democrats control of the Senate for the first time since 1994. See **Congress of the United States,** page 147**; Democratic Party,** page 182; **Republican Party,** page 357; **United States, Government of the,** page 422.

2001 YEAR IN BRIEF

A month-by-month listing of the most significant world events that occurred during 2001.

October
November
December

JANUARY

2001 YEAR IN BRIEF

George W. Bush, with his daughter Jenna and wife Laura beside him, is sworn in as the 43rd president of the United States on January 20. Bush, the son of George Herbert Walker Bush, the 41st president, was only the second son of a U.S. president to also win that office.

1 **At least 50 people** drown when the front section of a cargo ship sinks after the vessel breaks apart during a storm along Turkey's southern Mediterranean coast.

2 **President-elect George W. Bush** nominates several people for Cabinet positions, including Spencer Abraham for the Department of Energy; Linda Chavez for the Department of Labor; and Norman Mineta for secretary of the Department of Transportation.

3 **The Federal Reserve Bank** (the Fed), the central bank of the United States, cuts short-term interest rates from 6.5 percent to 6 percent. Short-term rates refer to the interest rate banks charge each other for overnight loans.

4 **A Yemeni government official** announces that authorities have uncovered evidence that six people currently in custody in Sana, the capital, were involved in the Oct. 12, 2000, bombing attack on the U.S.S. *Cole*, which left 17 U.S. sailors dead and 30 others injured.

5 **United States President** Bill Clinton issues a presidential order placing more than 50 million acres (23.5 million hectares) in 39 states permanently off-limits to road building, logging, and oil and gas development.

6 **Members of the U.S. Congress** ratify the tally of the Dec. 18, 2000, Electoral College presidential election vote. Texas Governor George W. Bush receives 271 votes, one vote more than the 270 he needed to defeat Vice President Al Gore.

8 **California Governor** Gray Davis proposes that California reassert control over the state's electrical utilities, which were deregulated in 1996. The deregulation law mandated that utilities buy power on the open market at market prices but barred passing increases on to customers until 2002.

9 **The discovery of** what may be the largest concentration of galaxies and quasars in the observable universe is reported at a meeting of the American Astronomical Society. Astronomers estimate that the giant cluster is about 500 million light-years across and includes at least 11 galaxies and as many as 18 quasars.

11 **The Federal Communications Commission** (FCC), an independent U.S. government agency that regulates communication by wire, cable, radio, and television, unanimously approves the merger of America Online, Incorporated, of Dulles, Virginia, with Time Warner, Incorporated, a New York

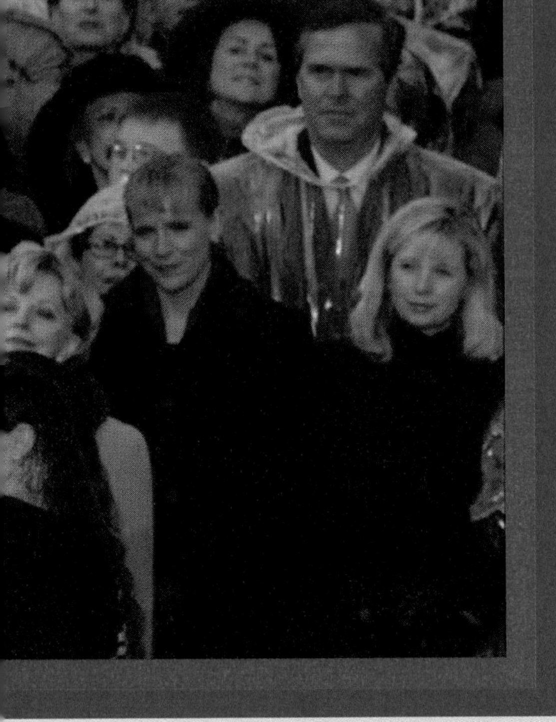

City-based media corporation. AOL is the world's largest Internet service provider, with more than 22 million subscribers. Time Warner is the world's largest media conglomerate, with operations in publishing; cable television systems and channels; and the film and record industries.

13 **A 7.6-magnitude earthquake** along El Salvador's Pacific coast kills more than 800 people in and around San Salvador, the capital. In one neighborhood, the quake sets off a landslide that buries between 200 and 300 houses, trapping hundreds of residents.

15 **Israel** cancels peace talks with Palestinian leaders and seals off Gaza in response to the killing of an Israeli settler, allegedly by militants affiliated with the extremist Islamic group Hamas. At least 360 people, the vast majority of them Palestinians, have been killed since the Palestinian uprising began in September 2000.

17 **Electrical power shortages** in California force state officials to authorize rolling blackouts in an area stretching from the Oregon border to Bakersfield, in the central part of the state. The cutoffs, arranged in checkerboard patterns to avoid blacking out whole cities at a time, leave hundreds of thousands of houses and businesses without power for periods of 60 to 90 minutes.

18 **A spokesperson** for the government of Congo (Kinshasa) confirms that President Laurent Kabila is dead. Kabila was shot on January 16 during a disturbance at the presidential palace in Kinshasa, the capital.

20 **George W. Bush**, son of former President George H. W. Bush, is sworn in as the 43rd president of the United States. The inauguration ceremony takes place on the west side of the U.S. Capitol in Washington, D.C.

22 **Bush administration officials** warn the government of Iraq that the United States expects Iraqi President Saddam Hussein to honor his agreement to end nuclear, biological, and chemical weapons programs.

26 **A powerful earthquake** of 7.9 magnitude strikes northwest India, killing more than 14,000 people and injuring 166,000 others. The epicenter is in the state of Gujarat, near the city of Bhuj, which is devastated.

28 **The Baltimore Ravens** win Super Bowl XXXV by beating the New York Giants 34-7 at Raymond James Stadium in Tampa, Florida.

29 **The U.S. Senate** confirms Elaine Chao as secretary of the Department of Labor. Chao was nominated after Linda Chavez withdrew as Bush's nominee for secretary of labor.

31 **The Federal Reserve** lowers interest rates for the second time in less than one month, dropping the federal funds target rate on overnight loans between banks from 6 to 5.5 percent. Economists describe the cut as another attempt to stimulate the U.S. economy.

Three Scottish judges find Libyan defendant Abdelbaset Ali Mohmed al-Megrahi guilty of murder in the 1988 terrorist bombing of Pan Am Flight 103 from London to New York City. The judges rule that Megrahi hid the bomb that killed the 270 passengers and crew members aboard the jet.

1 **The United States Senate** confirms John Ashcroft, President George W. Bush's nominee for attorney general, to head the U.S. Department of Justice. Ashcroft served as governor of Missouri from 1985 to 1993 and as a U.S. senator from 1995 to 2001.

The Indonesian parliament censures President Abdurrahman Wahid on charges of official corruption. He is alleged to have been involved in the theft of more than $4 million from the government's food-distribution agency and for failing to pay taxes.

2 **The unemployment rate** in the United States rose from 4 percent in December 2000 to 4.2 percent in January 2001, the highest rate in 16 months.

5 **The percentage of young gay men** in urban America infected with HIV, the virus that causes AIDS, increased from 7 percent to 12.3 percent between the mid-1990's and the late 1990's, reports the Centers for Disease Control and Prevention, based in Atlanta, Georgia.

6 **Likud Party leader** Ariel Sharon is elected prime minister of Israel with the largest margin in that country's history—63 percent of the vote. Sharon served as a field commander in the Israeli army before entering politics.

8 **U.S. President George W. Bush** sends a plan outlining $1.6 trillion in tax cuts to the U.S. Congress. According to the president, future budget surpluses will cover the reduction in federal income caused by the tax cuts. The White House Office of Management and Budget projects that surpluses will total nearly $5 trillion by 2011.

9 **The space shuttle** Atlantis docks with the International Space Station, 225 miles (360 kilometers) above Earth. The shuttle carries the $1.4-billion Destiny science laboratory, which is designed to enable residents aboard the station to conduct experiments.

A U.S. nuclear-powered submarine, the U.S.S. *Greeneville,* collides with the *Ehime Maru*, a Japanese fishing vessel, as the submarine surfaces 9 miles (14 kilometers) off Honolulu, Hawaii. Nine of the 35 people aboard the *Ehime Maru* are killed, including high school students from Japan.

10 **The first analysis** of the human genome—the 3 billion chemical subunits that make up the human genetic blueprint—reveals that humans have far fewer genes than scientists previously believed. Scientists at Celeras Genomics Corporation of Rockville, Maryland, and the International Human Genome Project, a group of academic centers, report that humans have only 30,000 genes, some 70,000 genes fewer than many scientists thought.

12 **The U.S. Appeals Court** for the Ninth Circuit, meeting in San Francisco, upholds a lower court ruling that the Internet company Napster, Inc., must suspend its online music-sharing service. The service allows users to make free copies of copyrighted music recordings.

The spacecraft NEAR (Near Earth Asteroid Rendezvous)–Shoemaker lands on the asteroid Eros under the remote control of scientists at the Johns Hopkins University Applied Physics Laboratory in Laurel, Maryland. The landing is the first controlled descent of an unmanned craft onto an asteroid.

13 **Two Israeli helicopter gunships,** flying over northern Gaza, launch missiles into the car of a top Palestinian official, instantly killing Massoud Ayyad, who Israeli officials say was a terrorist.

15 **The crew of the space shuttle** Atlantis sends the International Space Station into higher orbit, completing its final task before beginning its return to Earth. The astronauts had completed work on the computer and laboratory systems and outfitted the space station's new science laboratory, Destiny.

16 **U.S. and British military pilots** bomb radar stations and military command centers in Iraq. The strikes are the first in two years against targets north of the no-fly zone over southern Iraq, which American and British planes have patrolled since 1992.

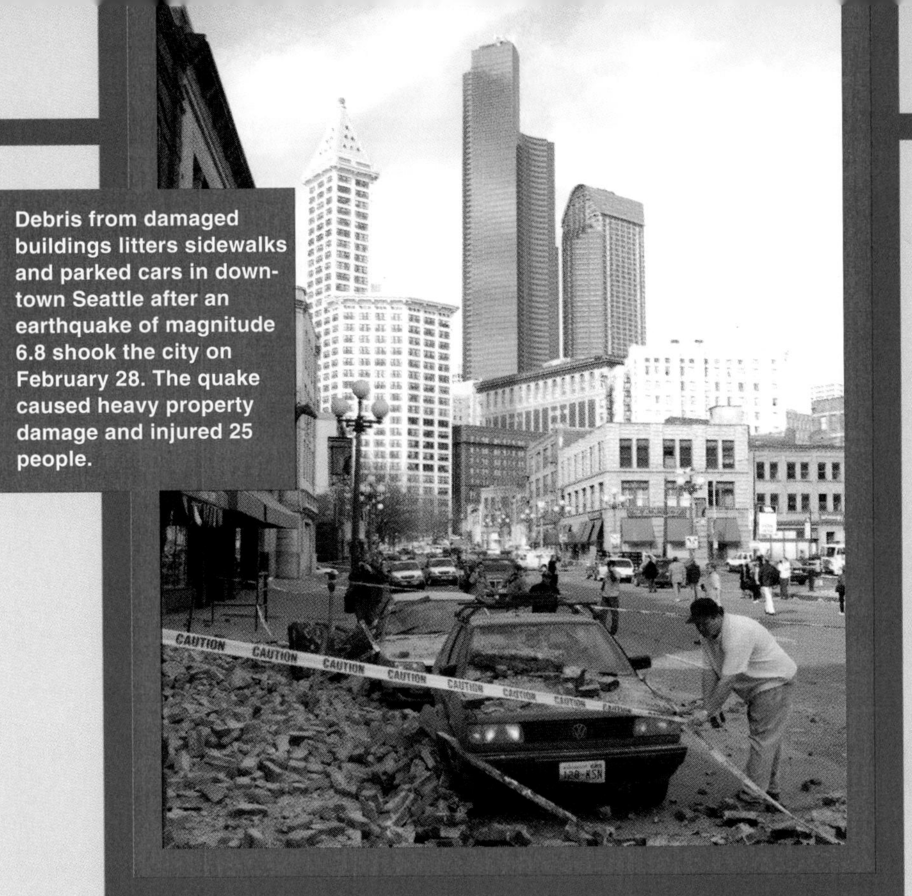

Debris from damaged buildings litters sidewalks and parked cars in downtown Seattle after an earthquake of magnitude 6.8 shook the city on February 28. The quake caused heavy property damage and injured 25 people.

18 **Rioting prisoners** in Brazil's Carandiru prison, the largest penal institution in Latin America, take some 8,000 people hostage, including 72 guards. Most of the hostages are wives and children visiting inmates in the prison.

19 **Global warming** is creating climate changes that could affect nations worldwide for hundreds of years, announce scientists with the Intergovernmental Panel on Climate Change (IPCC). The IPCC is an organization, based in Switzerland, that works with the United Nations to advise governments on climatic change.

21 **The U.S. Supreme Court** rules 5 to 4 that states cannot be sued by state employees for violation of the Americans with Disabilities Act, a federal law that prohibits discrimination against the disabled. Approximately 4.5 million people in the United States are employed by state governments.

25 **British officials** confirm that the outbreak of foot-and-mouth disease among livestock on British farms continues to spread. The disease is a highly contagious viral infection that affects animals with *cloven* (divided) hoofs, such as cattle, hogs, and sheep.

27 **World population** will increase by 3 billion people in the next 50 years—from 6.1 billion people in 2001 to 9.3 billion in 2050—report officials with the United Nations. According to a study released by the United Nations Population Division, most of the increase will occur in developing nations in Africa and Asia.

28 **A 6.8-magnitude earthquake,** centered 35 miles (56 kilometers) southwest of Seattle, near Washington's capital, Olympia, shakes the Pacific Northwest and is felt as far south as Portland, Oregon. Officials report that more than 150 people are injured and estimate that the cost of repairing the city could exceed $2 billion.

MARCH

3 **The Afghani army** begins destroying the Bamiyan Buddhas, two figures that stand 175 feet (53 meters) and 120 feet (36 meters) tall. The statues were carved into the side of a mountain between A.D. 200 and 500. The commander of the Taliban, an organization of Islamic extremists in control of much of Afghanistan, ordered their demolition, saying the statues were idolatrous.

A military transport plane assigned to the U.S. Army Air National Guard crashes in central Georgia, killing all 21 people aboard—3 Army crew members and 18 members of the Virginia Air National Guard.

4 **Sheep on nine French farms** test positive for the virus that causes foot-and-mouth disease, announce French agricultural officials. Foot-and-mouth disease, also known as hoof-and-mouth disease, is a highly contagious viral infection to which animals with divided hoofs, such as cattle, hogs, and sheep, are subject. French officials remain unsure whether the sheep, all of which were imported from the United Kingdom, merely carry the virus or had actually developed the disease and contaminated other animals.

6 **European Union** (EU) agricultural officials order the 15 EU member nations to close all livestock markets for two weeks in an effort to contain the spread of foot-and-mouth disease.

7 **Ariel Sharon** is sworn in as Israel's fifth prime minister in six years. In his inaugural address, Sharon, a former general of the Israeli Army, announces that his primary goal is to provide security to Israel and combat terrorism.

9 **President George W. Bush** issues an executive order forbidding mechanics at Northwest Airlines to go on strike. Speaking to a crowd at an airport in Sioux Falls, South Dakota, the president announces that he will not allow workers at any major U.S. airline to use a strike to disrupt air service.

An international team of fertility experts, meeting in Rome, announces that they plan to clone a human being. The work is scheduled to begin in October in an unidentified Mediterranean country. The scientists describe the project as therapeutic, saying that it may eventually lead to finding cures to a range of degenerative diseases.

11 **A crowd of 100,000 people** in Mexico City cheer the arrival of Zapatista rebels after a 2,000-mile (3,200-kilometer) journey from their hideout in the jungles of Chiapas. The rebels sought to focus attention on the failure of the Congress to ratify the San Andres Accords, which guarantee full civil rights to Mexico's 10 million Indians.

14 **President Yoweri Museveni** is re-elected president of Uganda with 69.3 percent of the vote. His challenger, Kizza Besigye, receives 27.8 percent.

19 **The sudden failure** of two large power plants in California forces the state's two main electrical utility companies to order rolling blackouts. The blackouts, which last for up to two hours, leave at least 1 million people without electricity in an area stretching from San Francisco to Los Angeles. Utility company officials blame the power failure on a transformer fire coupled with high demand for air-conditioning because of unusually warm temperatures.

A French farmer mourns the loss of her flock of 800 lambs, which were killed in March to prevent the spread of foot-and-mouth disease. Farmers across Europe slaughtered millions of animals to prevent the spread of the contagious disease.

20 **The world's largest oil platform,** owned by the Brazilian state oil company Perturbs, tumbles into the Atlantic Ocean off the coast of Brazil. A series of explosions ripped through the 40-story rig on March 15, killing at least 10 workers and damaging an underwater support column.

Twenty-five percent of all adults in South Africa—4.7 million people—are infected with HIV, the virus that causes AIDS, report government officials in Pretoria, the country's administrative capital. However, officials said the rate of infection is slowing.

21 **Paleoanthropologist Meave Leakey** announces that a 3.5-million-year-old skull found in Kenya in 1999 may present a new view of human origins. Leakey announces that the skull is from an entirely new branch of the early human family.

22 **Officials in Dublin** confirm that foot-and-mouth disease has been diagnosed in Ireland. A veterinarian found a single diseased sheep on a farm near the border with Northern Ireland, where a case was diagnosed earlier in March.

23 **The Russian space station** Mir breaks apart as it reenters Earth's atmosphere and crashes into the Pacific Ocean in a remote area approximately 1,800 miles (2,900 kilometers) east of New Zealand. Personnel at Mission Control outside Moscow guided the craft's descent to Earth, ending a record-breaking 15 years in space.

24 **Car bombs** explode simultaneously in three Russian towns, Mineralnye Vody, Adygek-Khabl, and Yessentuk. Russian officials blame the explosions, which kill at least 21 people and injure 90 others, on insurgents from Chechnya.

26 **A fire in a school dormitory** filled with sleeping boys in Machakos, Kenya, leaves 67 teen-aged students dead and more than 20 others seriously injured. Many of the victims were crushed as they attempted to escape. Police claim the fire had been set by students accused of cheating on their college entrance examinations.

27 **The California Public Utilities** Commission passes the largest rate hike in state history, boosting the price of electricity by up to 46 percent. Members of the commission claim that the increase is needed to avoid more rolling blackouts and to keep utility companies from going bankrupt.

30 **Serb riot police** storm the Belgrade residence of Slobodan Milosevic and exchange gunfire with his bodyguards. Yugoslav officials say the former Yugoslav president refuses to accept a warrant for his arrest on charges of abuse of power and corruption.

Ten Islamic militants are arrested in Yemen in connection with the Oct. 12, 2000, bombing of the U.S.S. *Cole*, which left 17 U.S. sailors dead and 30 others wounded. Yemeni officials are holding eight other men, who are to be tried for their suspected roles in the bombing.

2001 YEAR IN BRIEF APRIL

1 **Serbian special police** arrest former Yugoslav President Slobodan Milosevic on charges of abuse of power and official corruption. The arrest follows a 26-hour stand-off outside Milosevic's villa in Belgrade, the capital.

The pilot of a U.S. Navy intelligence plane is forced to make an emergency landing on the Chinese island of Hainan after colliding with one of two Chinese fighter jets that were tailing the U.S. aircraft. The aircraft, with a crew of 24 people, was on a surveillance patrol over the South China Sea.

4 **U.S. Secretary of State** Colin Powell expresses regret for the collision on April 1 of a U.S. Navy electronic surveillance plane and a Chinese fighter jet but stops short of issuing an apology. The president of China, Jiang Zemin, insists that the government of the United States must apologize before the crew is released.

5 **The discovery** of 11 planets beyond Earth's solar system is announced by an international team of astronomers. One of the planets is the first ever found in an Earthlike orbit around a sunlike star. However, the planet is a gaseous giant at least as large as Jupiter and is unlikely to support life.

8 **Alejandro Toledo** receives the most votes in Peru's presidential election but falls short of taking the 50 percent required to avert a runoff election. Toledo will face a former president of Peru, Alan Garcia, in the runoff.

11 **At least 43 people** are crushed to death when a crowd pushing into a stadium in Johannesburg, South Africa, stampedes at the start of a professional soccer match. Officials believe that as many as 120,000 people were admitted through the gates of a stadium designed to hold 70,000 spectators.

12 **China** ends a tense 11-day standoff with the United States with the release of all 24 crew members of a U.S. Navy intelligence plane that was forced to land on the Chinese island of Hainan on April 1.

The mayor of Cincinnati, Ohio, orders an 8 p.m.-to-6 a.m. curfew following four days of violent demonstrations, looting, and vandalism in which more than 70 people are injured. The rioting was sparked by the fatal shooting of an unarmed black teen-ager by a white police officer, the 15th such death since 1995.

14 **The price of a gallon** of unleaded, regular gasoline tops $2 in Chicago after a 25-percent price increase in less than two weeks. Gas prices in Chicago were the highest in the United States.

16 **Israel** bombs a Syrian radar station in Lebanon, killing three soldiers. The air strike is made in response to the April 14 death of an Israeli soldier killed during a missile attack by Syrian-backed Hezbollah guerrillas.

18 **The United States Federal Reserve,** the nation's central bank, cuts the interest rate on overnight loans between banks from 5 percent to 4.5 percent. The reduction is the fourth cut in short-term interest rates in 2001.

19 **Space shuttle Endeavour** blasts off from the Kennedy Space Center at Cape Canaveral, Florida, for the International Space Station. The shuttle carries a massive robotic arm, which the shuttle crew will install on the international outpost.

20 **A Peruvian Air Force pilot** shoots down a civilian aircraft over the Amazon jungle close to the Peru-Brazil border, killing a U.S. missionary and her infant daughter. According to U.S. officials in Peru, the pilot apparently mistook the small plane for a drug-running aircraft.

24 **President George W. Bush** approves the sale of several sophisticated weapons, including eight diesel submarines, to Taiwan. China has long attempted to block the sale of such weapons to Taiwan, which China claims is a renegade province.

24 **The Mississippi River** crests at 22 feet (6.8 meters) at Davenport, Iowa, some 7 feet (2 meters) above flood stage. Flooding along the Mississippi in Min-

A U.S. Coast Guard helicopter mechanic surveys a baseball stadium in Davenport, Iowa, that is nearly covered by floodwaters from the Mississippi River in April. Flooding along the Mississippi River in 2001 was the second-worst on record.

nesota, Wisconsin, Iowa, and Illinois is the second worst on record.

24 **Japan's Liberal Democratic Party** elects Junichiro Koizumi party president, putting him in line to become Japan's next prime minister.

26 **Ukraine's parliament** votes overwhelmingly to dismiss Prime Minister Viktor Yushchenko and his Cabinet. Foreign affairs specialists see the dismissal as a major setback to economic reform.

27 **The U.S. economy** grew by 2 percent in the first three months of 2001, report officials with the U.S. Treasury Department. The announcement surprises many economists, who had predicted that the economy had slowed to near zero growth.

28 **A Russian Soyuz rocket** lifts off from Kazakhstan for the International Space Station, in orbit approximately 225 miles (360 kilometers) above Earth. The rocket carries two Russian cosmonauts and U.S. businessman Dennis Tito. Tito, a former NASA engineer, is paying $20 million to the Russian space agency to became the first "space tourist."

29 **Uganda** withdraws from a United Nations-brokered peace agreement designed to bring the civil war in Congo (Kinshasa) to an end. Ugandan President Yoweri Museveni said Ugandan troops may return to Congo if the "chaos in the region" continues.

30 **U.S. Vice President Dick Cheney** outlines details of the Bush administration's energy policy. President Bush will push for the passage of legislation that would provide private companies with incentives to explore for new sources of oil and gas within the United States. Under the policy, protected areas, such as the Arctic National Wildlife Refuge in Alaska, would be opened to oil and gas exploration.

MAY

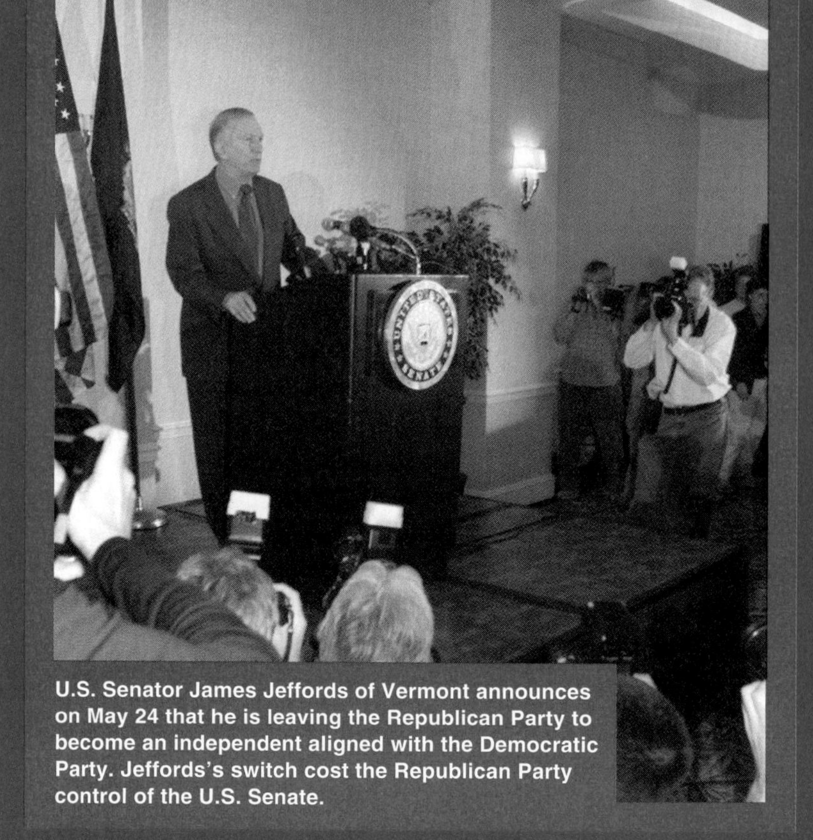

U.S. Senator James Jeffords of Vermont announces on May 24 that he is leaving the Republican Party to become an independent aligned with the Democratic Party. Jeffords's switch cost the Republican Party control of the U.S. Senate.

1 **The government of the Philippines** declares a state of rebellion, giving President Gloria Macapagal-Arroyo the power to order the Philippine military into the streets of Manila, the capital, to help police put down protests.

2 **Rioting Slavs** in Macedonia's capital, Skopje, attack the city's ethnic Albanian minority. Rioters, armed with automatic weapons and baseball bats, kill at least one shop owner and loot and burn Albanian-owned businesses.

3 **The United States Coast Guard** seizes approximately 13 tons (12 metric tons) of cocaine from a fishing vessel registered in Belize with a Russian and Ukrainian crew. The seizure is the largest in U.S. maritime history.

5 **The prime minister of Macedonia,** Ljubco Georgievski, announces that he plans to ask parliament to declare a state of war as government troops use heavy artillery to hammer villages occupied by ethnic Albanian rebels along the Macedonian-Yugoslav border.

9 **More than 125 people** are killed in a stampede at the end of a soccer match in Accra, the capital of Ghana. According to reports, police triggered the stampede by firing tear gas into a crowd of rioting soccer fans.

10 **The Palestinian Authority** declares a state of emergency after its headquarters in Gaza City and the office of Yasir Arafat's Fatah faction are hit by Israeli surface-to-surface missiles. Experts on political affairs in the Middle East suggest that Israel launched the attacks in response to the murder of two teenage Israeli boys, who had been stoned to death by a crowd of Palestinians on May 9.

11 **A third year of drought** across southwestern Asia is forcing tens of thousands of people in Afghanistan out of the countryside. According to United Nations officials conducting a worldwide survey of displaced people, the migration in Afghanistan is the "fastest growing displacement crisis anywhere."

15 **A panel** sponsored by the National Institutes of Health recommends that U.S. physicians treat people at risk for heart disease more aggressively. The recommendations could increase the number of adults taking cholesterol-lowering drugs from 13 million to 36 million.

17 **President George W. Bush** outlines details of his administration's national long-range energy strategy. The president promises to increase the supply of fossil fuels by providing private companies with incentives to explore for new sources of oil and gas within the United States. The president also proposes offering tax credits to utility companies that utilize renewable fuels.

20 **Israeli Prime Minister** Ariel Sharon defends his decision to use F-16 fighter jets against Palestinian targets, telling reporters that "[Israel] will do everything necessary . . . to protect Israeli citizens."

21 **Ethnic Albanian rebels** in northwestern Macedonia launch a mortar attack on government troops after several days of cease-fire. The attack triggers intense fighting above the town of Tetovo, where government forces are responding with heavy artillery fire.

Authorities in Sichuan Province in southwestern China order all small coal mines temporarily closed for safety checks. At least 50 miners in the province were killed in three separate accidents on May 18 and May 19.

22 **The defense minister of Israel** announces a cease-fire in the current Israeli-Palestinian violence. Israeli troops are ordered not to fire on Palestinians except when the lives of Israeli soldiers are threatened. Prior to the announcement, Israeli Prime Minister Ariel Sharon declared on television that Israel would resume peace negotiations when the Palestinians called a halt to the violence.

The Taliban orders Hindus in Afghanistan to wear identification labels on their clothing to differentiate them from the Muslim majority. A Taliban spokesman said that the order is to safeguard Hindus from religious police who enforce Taliban rulings governing Islamic behavior in Afghanistan.

23 **The government of China** formally protests that U.S. President George W. Bush met earlier in the day with the Dalai Lama, Tibet's exiled spiritual leader. During the meeting, which took place on the 50th anniversary of China's annexation of Tibet, the Dalai Lama asked President Bush to assure the Chinese government that the Dalai Lama did not seek independence for Tibet, but rather *autonomy* (freedom of self-rule).

24 **United States Senator** James Jeffords of Vermont announces that he is leaving the Republican Party to become an independent aligned with the Democratic Party. The move reduces the number of Senate seats held by the Republicans from 50 to 49, shifting control to the Democrats.

26 **The U.S. Congress** passes legislation that cuts income taxes by $1.35 trillion over the next 10 years. Individual taxpayers are each set to receive refunds of approximately $300.

28 **Racial violence** between white and Asian youths in Oldham, England, a former mill town outside Manchester, continues for a third straight night. On May 27, police in full riot gear battled as many as 500 men and boys armed with firebombs and bricks for control of the streets. English authorities blame white supremacist groups for inciting the violence.

29 **California Governor** Gray Davis announces that he intends to file a suit in federal court to force the Federal Energy Regulatory Commission to impose limits on the rates that wholesale energy suppliers charge California utility companies.

30 **The German parliament,** the Bundestag, votes to establish a $4.5-billion fund to compensate people forced to work as slave laborers during World War II (1939–1945). German corporations that used slave labor are to provide half of the funding. Payments are scheduled to begin in mid-June.

2001 YEAR IN BRIEF — JUNE

1 **A Palestinian suicide bomber** detonates an explosive device outside a crowded disco in Tel Aviv, Israel, killing himself and 20 young Israelis.

King Birendra Bir Birkram Shah Dev of Nepal is shot to death at the royal palace at Katmandu, the capital. According to witnesses, the king and eight members of his family are murdered by Crown Prince Dipendra.

3 **Alejandro Toledo** defeats former president Alan Garcia to become president of Peru. Toledo initially ran for president in 2000 but refused to participate in a runoff, claiming that the incumbent, Alberto Fujimori, had compromised the election.

5 **The Democratic Party** regains control of the U.S. Senate for the first time since 1995. The power shift was triggered by Vermont Senator James Jeffords's May 24 resignation from the Republican Party, which reduced the number of Republican seats from 50 to 49.

6 **A panel of atmospheric scientists** representing the National Academy of Sciences conclude in a report to the Bush administration that the Earth's atmosphere is gradually getting warmer and that human activity is largely responsible.

7 **British voters** give Prime Minister Tony Blair's Labour Party a resounding victory in parliamentary elections. Labour enjoys the biggest parliamentary majority that any British party has ever held going into a second term.

8 **A man armed with a kitchen knife** attacks students in an elementary school in Ikeda, Japan, killing 8 children and wounding 15 others.

9 **Iranian President** Mohammad Khatami is declared the winner in Iran's June 8 presidential election with 77 percent of the vote. Experts on Iranian politics describe the election as a referendum on Khatami's attempts to reform the government, which is a constitutional theocracy largely controlled by fundamentalist Islamic clergy.

10 **Officials in Texas and Louisiana** announce that 16 people have died as a result of Tropical Storm Allison, which has caused at least $1 billion in damages since coming ashore on June 5. The slow-moving storm inundated southeast Texas with as much as 28 inches (71 centimeters) of rain.

11 **Timothy McVeigh** is executed at the Federal Penitentiary at Terre Haute, Indiana, for the 1995 bombing of the Murrah Federal Building in Oklahoma City, Oklahoma, which killed 168 people. The execution is the first to be carried out by the federal government since 1963.

13 **Days of heavy rains** in Ecuador's Andes Mountains trigger a landslide of mud and rock that buries 31 people who had taken refuge in a shack some 30 miles (48 kilometers) east of Quito, the capital. The victims were motorists stranded in the mountains when an earlier avalanche blocked the highway.

17 **Syria begins** pulling troops out of Lebanon's capital, Beirut, after 25 years of occupation. According to security officials, the withdrawal is to be complete within 48 hours. The pullback, which began in the Lebanese countryside on June 14, came in response to a massive campaign by Lebanese Christians against Syria's military and political domination of Lebanon.

18 **Russian President Vladimir Putin** announces that Russia will begin upgrading its strategic nuclear arsenal if the United States proceeds with its plans to construct a missile defense shield. An increase in the nuclear arsenal would reverse years of arms control between the world's nuclear powers.

20 **Pakistan's military ruler,** General Pervez Musharraf, declares himself president and head of state after dismissing the former figurehead president, Rafiq Tara. The new president announces that he has scheduled an election for October 2002 that will return Pakistan to civilian rule.

22 **At least 57 people are killed** and 300 others wounded when the Mangalore-Chennai Mail Train derails on a bridge spanning the Kadalundi River in the state of Kerala in southern India. The three last cars on the train plunge 100 feet (30 meters) into the river where it flows into the Arabian Sea.

23 **An earthquake** of 8.1 magnitude rocks southern Peru, killing at least 100 people, injuring 1,300 others, and leaving more than 45,000 people homeless.

24 **Typhoon Chebi** leaves at least 70 people dead and more than 80 people missing in the province of Fujian in southeastern China. Most of the victims lived in Fuzhou, the provincial capital.

25 **Thousands of Macedonians** march on the parliament in Skopje, the capital, protesting the removal of several hundred armed ethnic Albanian rebels from a village northeast of Skopje by North Atlantic Treaty Organization (NATO) forces.

28 **A U.S. federal appeals court** reverses an order to break up Microsoft Corporation of Redmond, Washington. In a unanimous decision, the U.S. Court of Appeals for the District of Columbia concludes that the judge who tried Microsoft in 2000 on antitrust charges appeared to be biased against the software maker.

29 **The Yugoslav cabinet,** a coalition that combines prodemocracy forces with allies of former President Slobodan Milosevic, collapses when the prime minister, Zoran Zizic, resigns to protest the June 28 transfer of Milosevic to the custody of the United Nations International Criminal Tribunal in The Hague, the Netherlands. Yugoslavia's president, Vojislav Kostunica, denounced the transfer. Experts speculate that the collapse could lead to Montenegro opting out of the federation with Serbia.

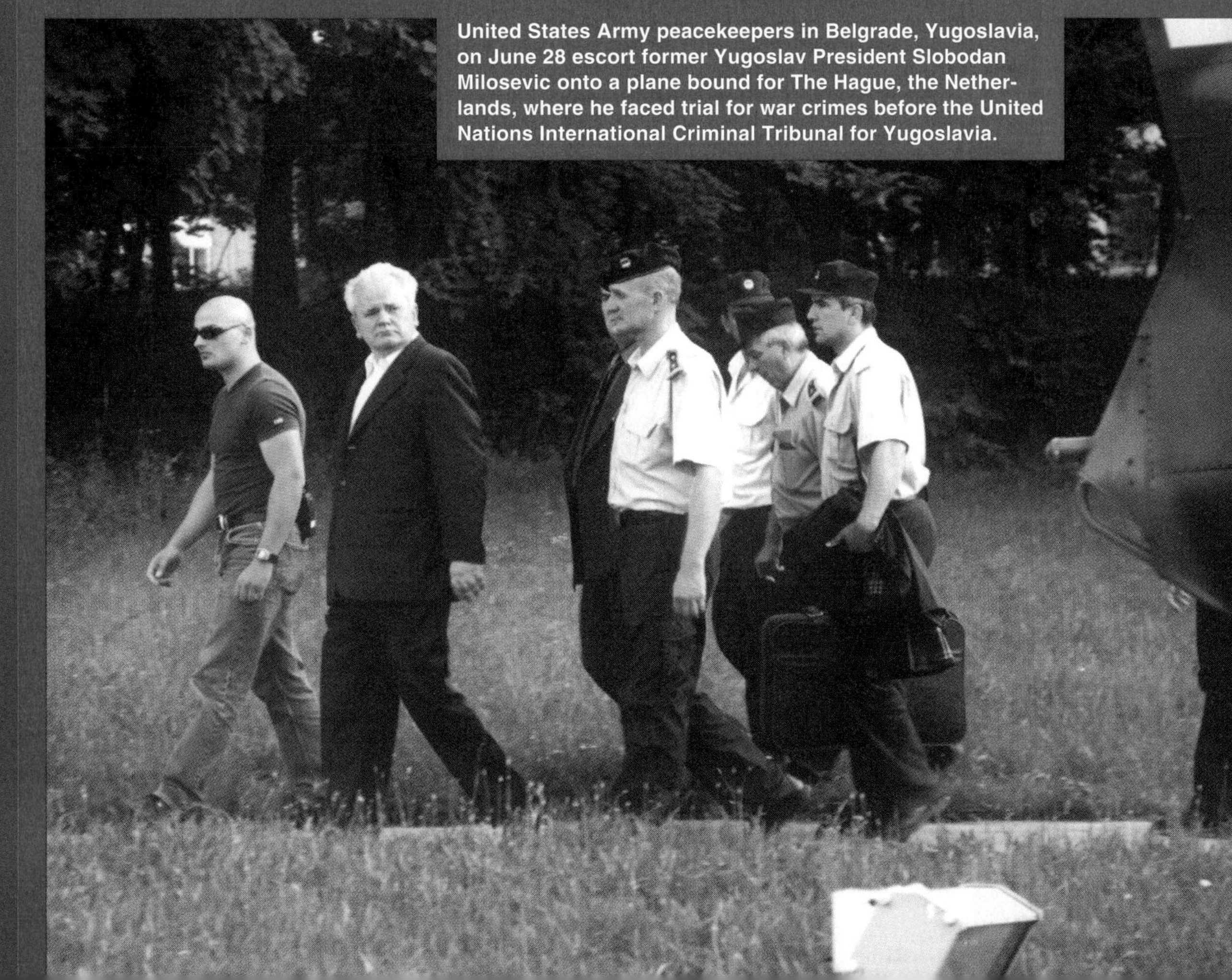

United States Army peacekeepers in Belgrade, Yugoslavia, on June 28 escort former Yugoslav President Slobodan Milosevic onto a plane bound for The Hague, the Netherlands, where he faced trial for war crimes before the United Nations International Criminal Tribunal for Yugoslavia.

JULY

1 **Northern Ireland First Minister** David Trimble resigns after the Northern Ireland independent disarmament commission confirmed that the Irish Republican Army (IRA) had failed to relinquish its weapons. Trimble's resignation fulfills the threat he had made in May 2000 to resign his post if the IRA continued to ignore its pledge to disarm.

2 **The world's first** self-contained artificial heart is implanted in the chest of a man suffering from heart failure. Surgeons from the University of Louisville perform the operation at Jewish Hospital in Louisville, Kentucky. The device—developed by Abiomed Inc. of Danvers, Massachusetts—is powered by a rechargeable battery.

3 **The European Union's** chief antitrust regulator, EU Commissioner Mario Monti, blocks General Electric's $42-billion takeover of Honeywell International. The decision marks the first time a European official has stopped a merger of companies in the United States previously approved by U.S. antitrust regulators.

5 **Macedonian government officials** announce that ethnic Albanian insurgents have agreed to a cease-fire in their four-month rebellion.

6 **U.S. employers** cut 114,000 jobs in June, primarily in the manufacturing sector, announce officials at the U.S. Department of Labor. The rate of unemployment rose from 4.4 percent in May to 4.5 percent in June.

9 **Goran Ivanisevic** of Croatia beats Patrick Rafter of Australia 6-3, 3-6, 6-3, 2-6, 9-7 to win the men's championship at Wimbledon. Ivanisevic, who entered the tournament ranked number 125 in the world, is the first wild-card entrant to ever win a Grand Slam title.

10 **Justices of the Philippines'** top anti-corruption court, the Sandiganbayan, formally charge former President Joseph Estrada with accepting millions of dollars in bribes and kickbacks during his 31 months in office. Estrada, on the advice of his lawyers, refuses to respond to the charges.

12 **Fossilized fragments of bones** and teeth of a chimpanzee-sized hominid, who lived in African forests between 5.8 million and 5.2 million years ago, have been discovered in the Middle Awash River Valley of Ethiopia, announce paleontologists at the University of California (UC) at Berkeley. Hominids make up the scientific family that consists of human beings and early humanlike creatures. Paleontologists at UC Berkeley said the fossils were close in time to when the evolutionary lines of humans and chimps split.

The Bulgarian parliament votes to approve Simeon Saxe-Coburg-Gotha prime minister of Bulgaria. Saxe-Coburg-Gotha is Bulgaria's exiled king, Simeon II, who was forced from the throne in 1946, when he was nine years old. In June 2001, Simeon led his own political party, the National Movement for Simeon II, to a huge victory in national elections.

13 **The president** of the International Olympic Committee, Juan Antonio Samaranch, announces in Moscow that the games of the 29th Olympiad, which are scheduled for 2008, will take place in the Chinese capital of Beijing.

16 **A summit meeting** between President Pervez Musharraf of Pakistan and Prime Minister Atal Behari Vajpayee of India collapses when the two leaders are unable to agree to the wording of a joint resolution on ways to reduce the risks of nuclear war.

18 **Alan Greenspan,** the chairman of the Federal Reserve (the Fed), the nation's central bank, reports to Congress that the U.S. economy may be approaching the bottom of the current business cycle and could be on its way to recovery. The Fed chairman notes, however, that the economy is "not yet out of the woods."

21 **Firefighters in Baltimore** reach the center of a railroad tunnel that is blocked by four burning freight cars, the remains of a 62-car train that derailed on July 18. Smoke from the cars, burning 60 feet (18 meters) below ground, has billowed through the city's downtown for three days, as firefight-

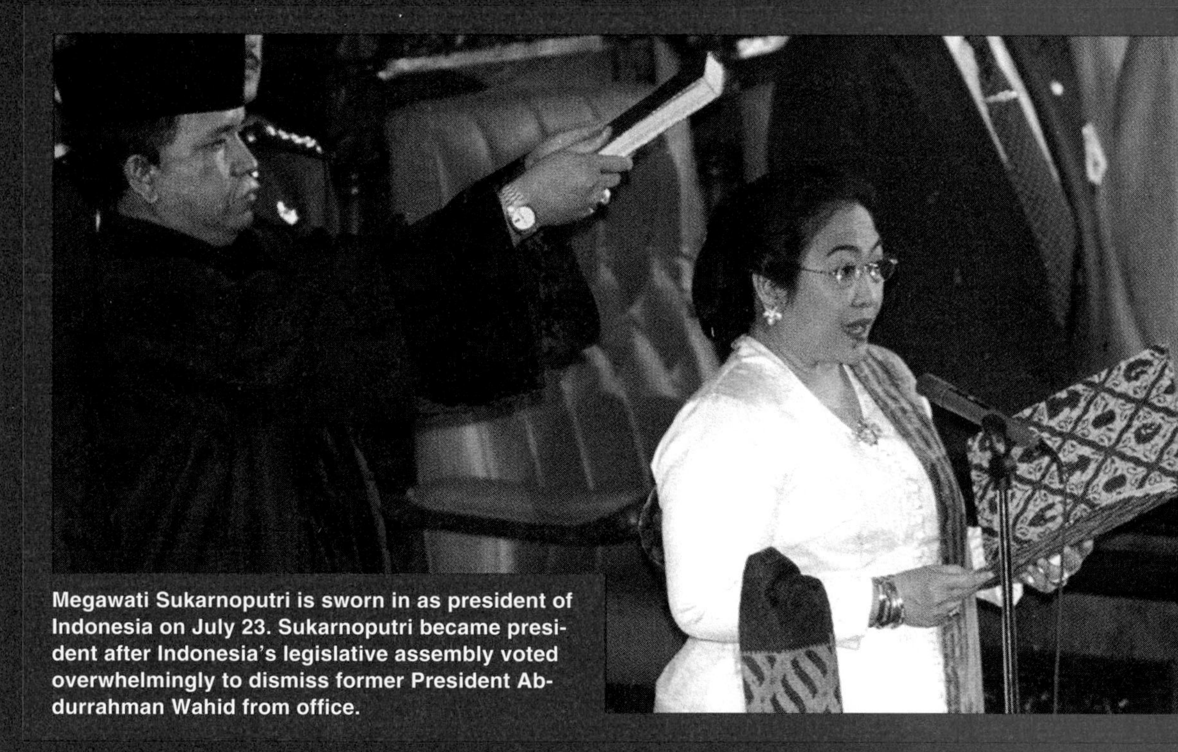

Megawati Sukarnoputri is sworn in as president of Indonesia on July 23. Sukarnoputri became president after Indonesia's legislative assembly voted overwhelmingly to dismiss former President Abdurrahman Wahid from office.

ers climbed down manholes, attempting to reach the source of the fire with water hoses.

23 **Vice President Megawati** Sukarnoputri becomes president of Indonesia after the legislative assembly votes overwhelmingly to dismiss Abdurrahman Wahid from office.

Representatives of 178 countries, meeting in Bonn, Germany, agree to a revision of the 1997 Kyoto Protocol. The revised accord gives participating industrialized countries more flexibililty in reducing emissions of greenhouse gases, such as carbon dioxide, by 2012. The agreement does not require reductions from developing countries. Officials from the United States, which will not participate in the protocol, described the accord as flawed.

At least 200 people drown when torrential rains in Pakistan trigger flash floods that destroy dozens of houses and other structures. In Islamabad, the capital, 24 inches (61 centimeters) of rain falls in less than 24 hours. It is the city's heaviest downpour in the 100 years that weather records have been kept in Pakistan.

29 **Clouds of ash** from an erupting volcano on the Caribbean island of Montserrat force airlines to cancel all flights in and out of Puerto Rico and the U.S. Virgin Islands, which are located more than 200 miles (320 kilometers) to the northwest. About half of the land mass of Montserrat has been lost since the Soufriere Hills Volcano began erupting in 1995.

30 **Ten freezer trucks** containing the remains of as many as 1,000 people have been discovered in Serbia, announce police in the capital, Belgrade. Trucks have been found in the Danube River and in a reservoir southwest of Belgrade. Authorities believe the bodies were those of ethnic Albanian victims of Serb security forces fighting in Kosovo in 1999.

AUGUST

1 **The skulls** of two rare titanosaurs—huge, plant-eating dinosaurs—have been unearthed in Madagascar, announce scientists from the State University of New York (SUNY) at Stony Brook. The paleontologists uncovered the fossilized skulls on an expedition in 1995. The skulls date to between 70 million and 65 million years old.

4 **North Korean leader** Kim Chong Il, meeting with Russian President Vladimir Putin in Moscow, Russia's capital, announces that the North Korean missile program poses no threat to any nation. Kim repeats his promise to suspend all ballistic-missile launches until 2003.

5 **Ayatollah Khamenei,** who heads Iran's Guardian Council, blocks the inauguration of Mohammad Khatami, who was to have been sworn in as the president of Iran for a second term. According to foreign affairs experts, the Ayatollah canceled the ceremony because he is furious that the parliament failed to approve the new members he wants appointed to the council.

9 **U.S. President George W. Bush** announces that taxpayer money could be

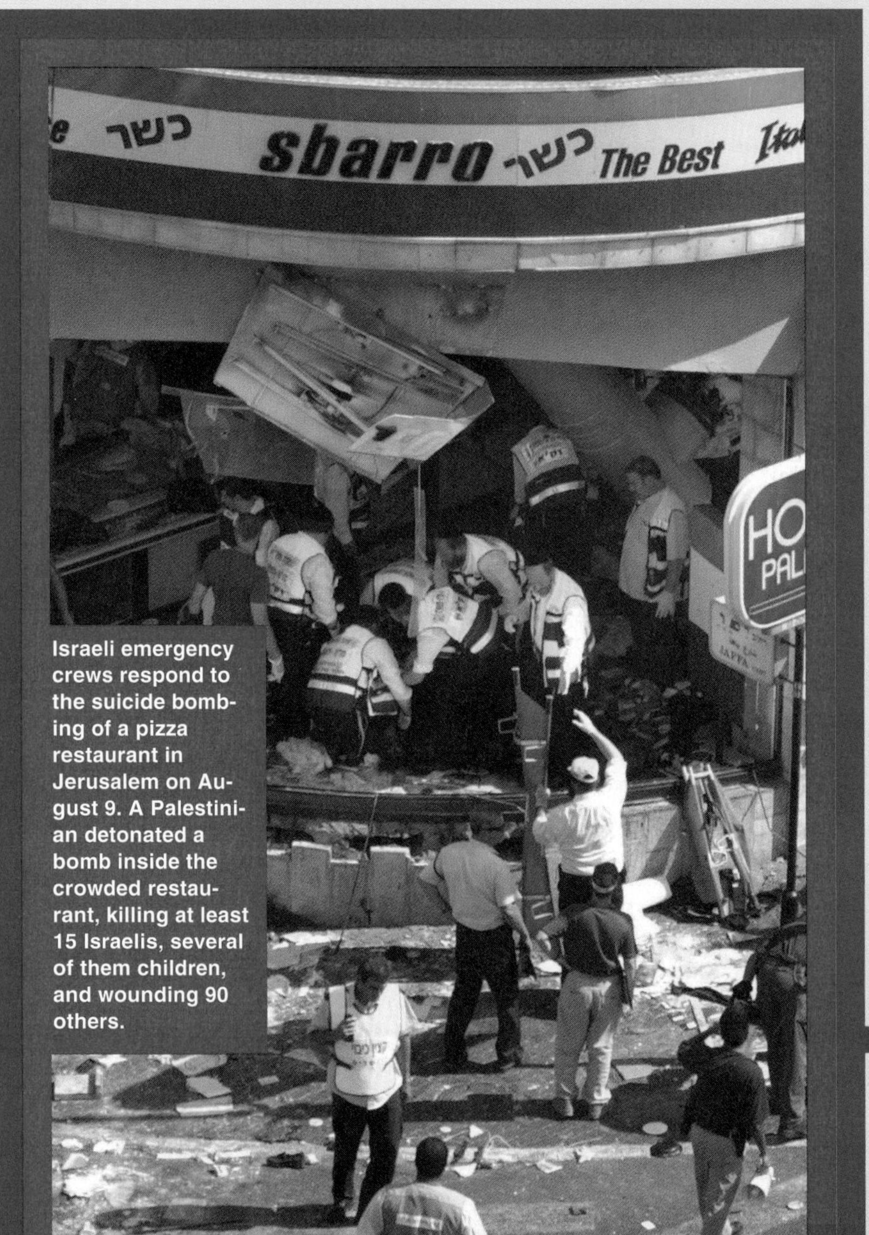

Israeli emergency crews respond to the suicide bombing of a pizza restaurant in Jerusalem on August 9. A Palestinian detonated a bomb inside the crowded restaurant, killing at least 15 Israelis, several of them children, and wounding 90 others.

used to fund research using stem cells, which can be grown into any type of cell or tissue, from human embryos. The president says that such funding must be limited to research on existing lines of stem cells and cannot be used in the destruction of embryos.

Fifteen Israelis, 6 of them children, are killed and more than 90 people are injured when a Palestinian suicide bomber detonates an explosive device packed with nails in a crowded restaurant in the heart of Jerusalem.

11 **Flash floods** set off by heavy rains roar down mountainsides in Thailand's northern province of Phetchabun, killing at least 85 people.

12 **Iranian officials** in Tehran, the capital, confirm that an estimated 200 people were killed in flash floods and mudslides triggered by a series of severe rainstorms that began on August 10. The storms ended three years of severe drought in the region.

13 **An aircraft** that consists of a flying wing driven by 14 propellers—the Helios Prototype—sets altitude records for a propeller-driven aircraft and for a nonrocket craft by climbing to 85,100 feet (26,000 meters) in tests off Hawaii.

15 **NATO ambassadors,** meeting in Brussels, Belgium, authorize moving an initial peacekeeping force of 400 troops, all British, into Macedonia. If the current cease-fire holds, a multinational force of 3,500 soldiers, which would include Americans, will be deployed to collect weapons from the ethnic Albanian rebels, who agreed to disarm as part of the peace agreement signed on August 13.

The first planetary system in which planets orbit a star in a nearly circular path similar to Earth's orbital path around the Sun has been discovered, announce astronomers at the University of California at Berkeley. The scientists discovered the solar system, which is nearly 45 light-years from Earth, in the Big Dipper, or Ursa Major, constellation. One planet is approximately the size of Jupiter. The other is two and one-half times larger than Jupiter.

18 **The Brazilian Congress** passes a new legal code that grants women the same rights as men, ending 26 years of debate on the measure.

19 **At least 36 miners** are killed and more than 40 more are injured when a methane gas explosion ignites an underground fire in Ukraine's largest coal mine, which is located near the eastern city of Donetsk.

20 **More than 430 cattle** are sold in the first livestock auction to be held in the United Kingdom since the outbreak of foot-and-mouth disease in February. The auction in Kirkwall, capital of northern Scotland's Orkney Islands, is conducted with disease-prevention measures as a trial run for future sales.

23 **U.S. President George W. Bush** announces that the United States will withdraw from the Antiballistic Missile (ABM) Treaty at its convenience at some unspecified time. The ABM treaty, signed by President Richard M. Nixon of the United States and Communist leader Leonid Brezhnev of the Soviet Union in 1972, is a major arms control pact that limits each country's defensive missile systems.

27 **British soldiers** taking part in NATO's 30-day disarmament mission in Macedonia begin collecting weapons from ethnic Albanian rebels. The disarmament program is part of a NATO-brokered cease-fire to end an insurgency that threatened to spiral into the fifth civil war in the Balkans in the last 10 years.

29 **The U.S. gross domestic product** (GDP), the value of all goods and services produced in a given year, grew 0.2 percent in the second quarter of 2001, the smallest percentage in eight years, report officials with the U.S. Commerce Department.

30 **More than 90 percent** of all eligible voters in East Timor turn out to elect an 88-member assembly in the nation's first democratic election. The assembly is to write East Timor's constitution. East Timor gained its independence from Indonesia in 1999 after a long and violent struggle.

3 **St. Louis Cardinals** pitcher Bud Smith throws a no-hitter as the Cardinals defeat the San Diego Padres 4-0 in San Diego. Smith becomes the 16th rookie in modern baseball history to not allow a hit during a nine-inning game.

5 **Protestant extremists** in Belfast, Northern Ireland, hurl a homemade fire bomb at girls crossing into a Protestant area on their way to a Roman Catholic grammar school. The explosion seriously injures four police officers escorting the children.

8 **Venus Williams** successfully defends her United States Open women's tennis championship by defeating her sister Serena 6-2, 6-4.

9 **Aleksandr Lukashenko** claims victory with more than 75 percent of the vote in his bid for reelection as president of Belarus. International monitors and Lukashenko's opponent accuse Lukashenko and his followers of rigging the vote.

A suicide bomber, disguised as a journalist carrying a television camera that is packed with explosives, assassinates Ahmed Shah Massoud, leader of Afghanistan's Northern Alliance, which opposes the ruling Taliban.

11 **Terrorists crash** two hijacked commercial airliners into the twin towers of the World Trade Center in New York City, causing both of the 110-story buildings to collapse. A third hijacked airliner dives into the Pentagon Building, the Arlington, Virginia, headquarters of the U.S. Department of Defense, triggering a massive fire and the collapse of a section of the huge five-sided structure. A fourth hijacked airliner crashes into a field in western Pennsylvania after an apparent uprising among the passengers.

13 **Federal authorities** announce that they have identified most of the hijackers responsible for the September 11 terrorist attacks in the United States. Investigators believe that some of the suspected hijackers had ties to the organization of Osama bin Laden, an exiled Saudi millionaire accused of backing many large-scale terrorist activities. Authorities believe bin Laden's organization works out of Afghanistan, where the ruling Taliban has granted him asylum.

More than 5,300 people are missing or are thought to be dead from the September 11 attacks on the World Trade Center, announces New York City Mayor Rudolph Giuliani. Pentagon officials estimate that approximately 200 people died in the attack on the Defense Department headquarters in Arlington, Virginia. United Airlines and American Airlines officials believe there were 265 people killed aboard the four planes hijacked on September 11.

16 **The president of Pakistan,** General Pervez Musharraf, agrees to send a team of military officers to Afghanistan to relay an ultimatum from U.S. President George W. Bush. The government of the United States demands that the Taliban, the fundamentalist Islamic organization that controls most of Afghanistan, hand over Osama bin Laden and his top associates or face almost certain U.S. military action. U.S. officials believe bin Laden masterminded and funded the September 11 terrorist attacks on the World Trade Center in New York City and the Pentagon Building outside Washington, D.C.

17 **The Dow Jones industrial average** of 30 companies listed on the New York Stock Exchange closes down 684.81 points on the first day of trading since the September 11 attack on the World Trade Center. The one-day point loss is the largest in the history of the New York Stock Exchange.

20 **United States President George W. Bush,** addressing a joint session of Congress, demands that the leaders of Afghanistan's ruling Taliban regime turn over Osama bin Laden and other members of bin Laden's terrorist organization, al-Qaida ("The Base" in Arabic). President Bush notes that Afghanistan faces certain military attack by the United States and its allies if the Taliban leaders refuse to comply with U.S. demands.

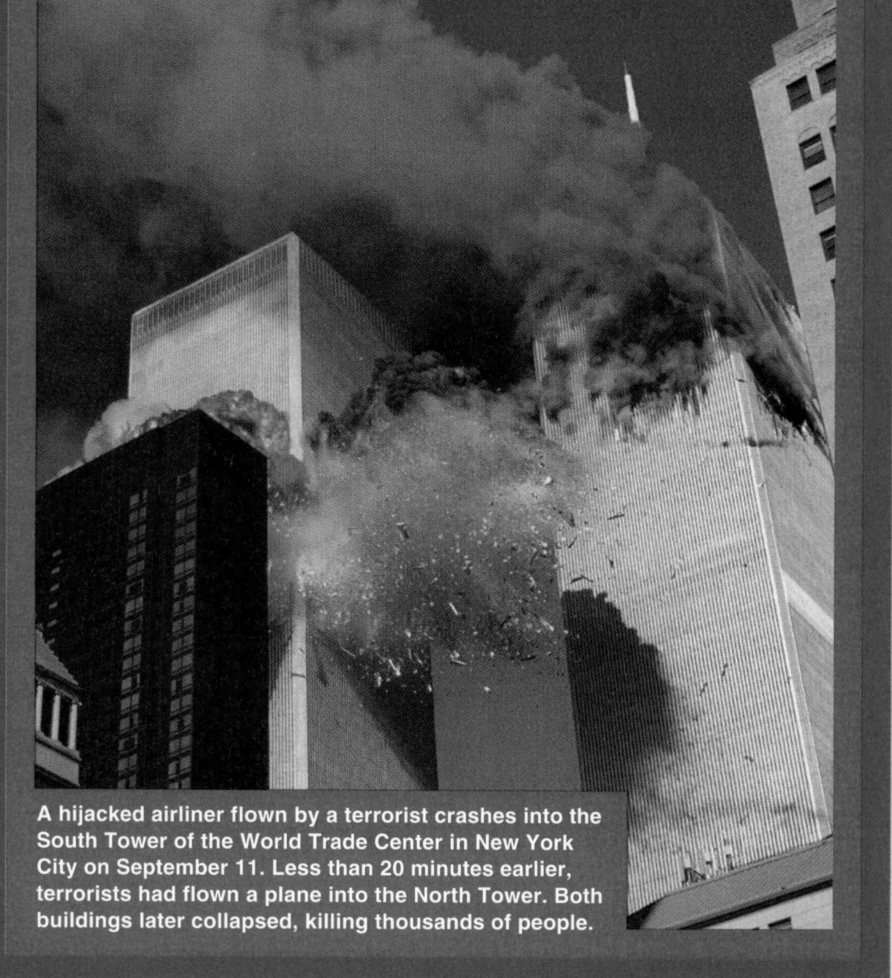

A hijacked airliner flown by a terrorist crashes into the South Tower of the World Trade Center in New York City on September 11. Less than 20 minutes earlier, terrorists had flown a plane into the North Tower. Both buildings later collapsed, killing thousands of people.

23 **Condoleezza Rice,** national security adviser, announces that government investigators have uncovered "very good evidence" linking men associated with the al-Qaida terrorist network with the September 11 terrorist attacks on the United States.

25 **NASA scientists** announce that an unmanned space probe, Deep Space 1, traveled within 1,400 miles (2,250 kilometers) of the comet Borrelly, located 136 million miles (219 million kilometers) from Earth. Photographs taken from the probe are providing scientists with their first close-up image of the core, or nucleus, of a comet.

Michael Jordan, who led the Chicago Bulls to six National Basketball Association titles, announces he will come out of retirement to play for the Washington Wizards.

27 **Afghanistan's ruling Taliban** claims to have located Osama bin Laden, the prime suspect in the September 11 terrorist attacks on the United States, and asked him to leave the country. According to Afghanistan's ambassador to Pakistan, the Taliban's spiritual leader, Mullah Mohammed Omar, has endorsed a decision by the council of religious scholars to inform bin Laden that he is no longer welcome and should leave Afghanistan voluntarily.

29 **The observation deck** at the Empire State Building, once again New York City's tallest skyscraper, reopens after being closed for security reasons in the wake of the September 11 attack on the World Trade Center. All visitors to the observation platform must pass through an X-ray machine before entering an elevator to the 86th floor.

1 **The U.S.S. *Kitty Hawk*** leaves its home port in Yokosuka, Japan, for the Arabian Sea. The *Kitty Hawk* is the third U.S. aircraft carrier to be ordered into the Arabian Sea or Persian Gulf. Military experts believe the carriers could be used as secure bases of operations from which American troops could be sent into Afghanistan.

2 **The Federal Reserve,** the central bank of the United States, cuts short-term interest rates for the ninth time in 2001.

5 **U.S. companies** cut 199,000 jobs in September, announce officials with the U.S. Department of Labor. The reduction is the largest in a single month since February 1991, when the United States was last in a recession.

Barry Bonds of the San Francisco Giants hits his 71st and 72nd home runs of the 2001 baseball season, breaking Mark McGwire's 1998 record of 70 home runs in a season.

7 **U.S. and British forces** launch air and missile strikes against Afghanistan. The strikes, the first in a campaign that military experts believe will be long and difficult, are aimed specifically at the ruling Taliban and terrorists harbored by the Taliban.

Osama bin Laden, whom U.S. officials believe masterminded the September 11 terrorist attacks on the United States, appears on television on a popular Arabic satellite channel minutes after the start of the U.S. and British bombing of Afghanistan. In a videotaped speech, bin Laden calls on all Muslims to join a jihad, or holy war, against the United States.

8 **Federal Bureau of Investigation** (FBI) agents are investigating anthrax contamination in South Florida, announces U.S. Attorney General John Ashcroft. The FBI sealed off the offices of American Media Inc., of Boca Raton, Florida, after a second American Media employee was found to have been exposed to anthrax spores. Another American Media employee died of the rare disease on October 5.

10 **U.S. long-range bombers** and fighter jets pound barracks, garrisons, and encampments across Afghanistan in the heaviest airstrikes yet against Taliban ground forces. The U.S. aircraft also target Kabul, the capital, and Qandahar (Kandahar), a Taliban stronghold.

11 **The Federal Bureau of Investigation** (FBI) alerts all local law enforcement agencies in the United States to be on the highest alert for the possibility of another terrorist attack. Citizens also are asked to be on the alert and to immediately notify law enforcement agencies of any suspicious activity.

16 **Anthrax *spores*** (an inactive form of the bacteria) mailed in a letter to the office of Senate Majority Leader Tom Daschle are of a highly potent, airborne strain that Federal Bureau of Investigation officers describe as "weapons grade" and so "fine and pure" that it dispersed invisibly through the senator's office.

17 **Gunmen** assassinate Rehavam Zeevi, an ultranationalist member of Prime Minister Ariel Sharon's Cabinet, at the Hyatt Hotel in Jerusalem. The Popular Front for the Liberation of Palestine claims responsibility.

18 **The government of China** welcomes U.S. President George W. Bush to Shanghai by issuing a statement strongly supporting the United States in its war on terrorism.

22 **Two postal employees** in Washington, D.C., have died of pulmonary-type anthrax, announce federal officials. The officials believe the two victims were exposed to the bacterium when a letter carrying anthrax spores addressed to Senate Majority Leader Tom Daschle passed through the main post office.

25 **The U.S. Senate** votes 98 to 1 in favor of an antiterrorism bill that expands the ability of the government to conduct electronic surveillance and relaxes the conditions under which judges authorize wiretaps. The bill gives the government the power to jail immigrants for limited periods without charging them with crimes.

26 **The U.S. Department of Defense** awards the largest defense contract in U.S. history, $200 billion for the production of the Joint Strike Fighter jet, to Lockheed Martin Corp., the Bethesda, Maryland-based manufacturer of aeronautical and space systems.

28 **Islamic extremists,** armed with automatic assault rifles, break into a Christian church in Behwalpur, Pakistan, and open fire on the congregation during Sunday services. At least 16 people, including 4 children, are killed.

29 **U.S. Attorney General** John Ashcroft issues a "terrorist threat advisory" to 18,000 state and local law enforcement agencies in the United States and warns the public that Federal Bureau of Investigation (FBI) officials believe they have credible evidence that new terrorist attacks could be launched during the next week.

30 **Limited numbers of U.S. and British troops** are being deployed in Afghanistan to coordinate air strikes against the Taliban and to serve as communication links between U.S. commanders and leaders of Northern Alliance opposition forces.

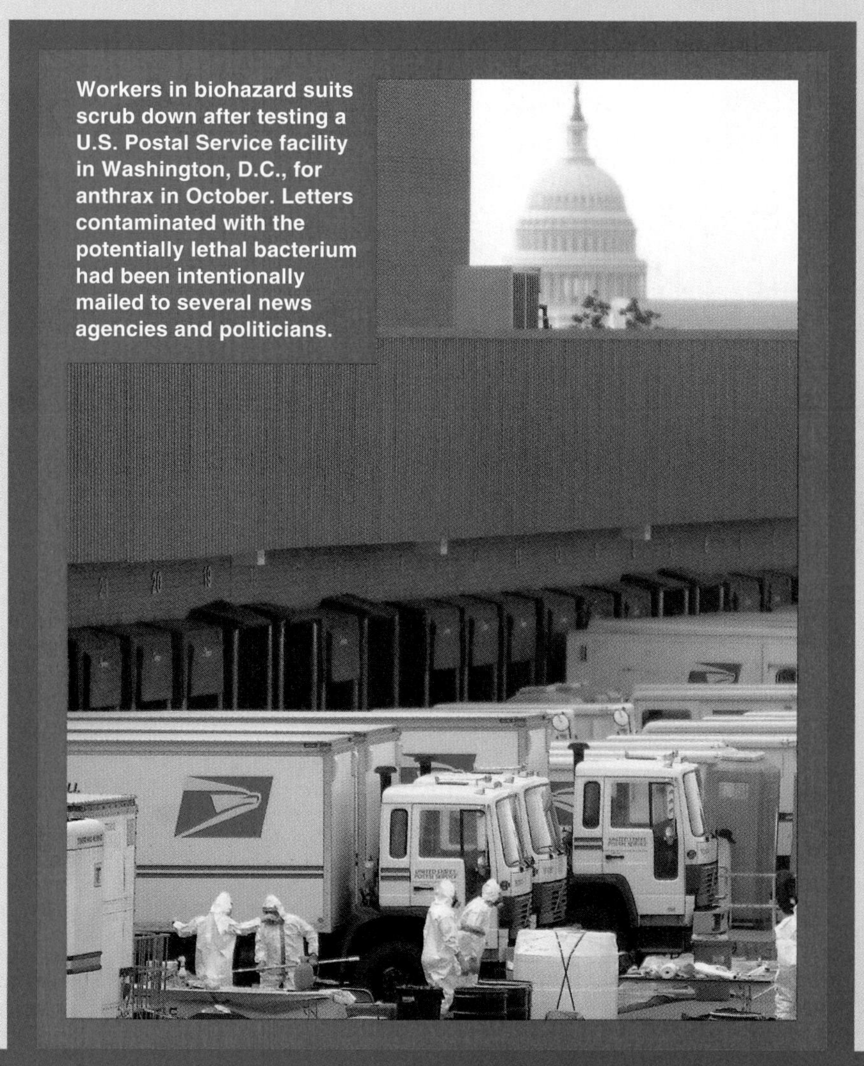

Workers in biohazard suits scrub down after testing a U.S. Postal Service facility in Washington, D.C., for anthrax in October. Letters contaminated with the potentially lethal bacterium had been intentionally mailed to several news agencies and politicians.

NOVEMBER

2001 YEAR IN BRIEF

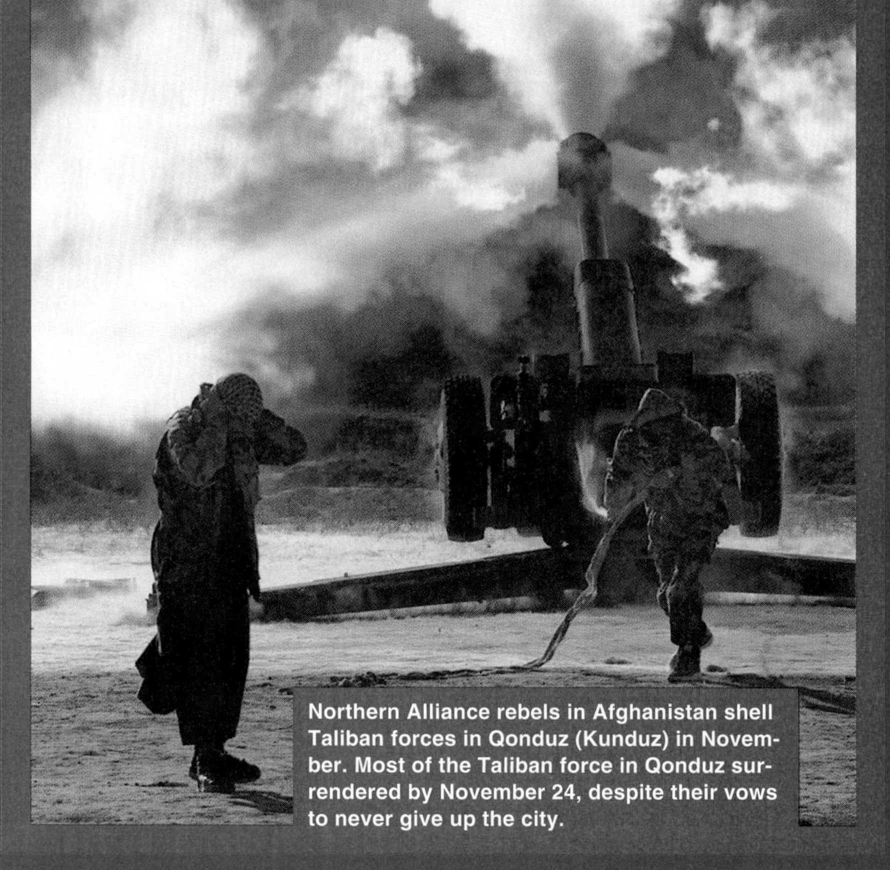
Northern Alliance rebels in Afghanistan shell Taliban forces in Qonduz (Kunduz) in November. Most of the Taliban force in Qonduz surrendered by November 24, despite their vows to never give up the city.

1 **UAL Corp.,** the parent company of United Airlines of Elk Grove Township, Illinois, lost $1.6 billion in the third quarter of 2001, announces the company's new chairman and chief executive officer, John Creighton. Company officials cite reduced travel after the terrorist attacks on September 11 as the reason.

2 **The rate of unemployment** in the United States jumped from 4.9 percent in September to 5.4 percent in October, the largest increase in a single month since 1980, according to officials with the U.S. Department of Labor.

4 **The Arizona Diamondbacks** capture the 2001 World Series by beating the New York Yankees 3-2 in game 7 of the series, played in Phoenix.

5 **Enrique Bolanos** is elected president of Nicaragua, taking 53.7 percent of the vote against Daniel Ortega. Ortega, who led the Sandinista National Liberation Front that overthrew the government of Anastasio Somoza Debayle in 1979, ruled Nicaragua until 1990.

6 **Republican candidate** Michael R. Bloomberg is elected mayor of New York City, narrowly defeating the Democratic challenger, Mark Green.

9 **Northern Alliance** opposition forces claim to have broken through Taliban defenses and entered Mazar-e Sharif, a key Taliban stronghold in northern Afghanistan.

10 **China** joins the World Trade Organization (WTO), ending 15 years of negotiations. The WTO, which is located in Geneva, Switzerland, arbitrates trade disputes among member countries.

12 **American Airlines Flight 587** crashes after taking off from John F. Kennedy International Airport in New York City, killing all 260 people on board and 5 people on the ground. Officials with the U.S. Department of Transportation suggest that the crash is more likely the result of a "catastrophic engine event" than a terrorist attack.

13 **Northern Alliance rebels** in Afghanistan enter Kabul, the capital, meeting little resistance from Taliban forces, who are abandoning the city in large numbers. Reporters and U.S. soldiers accompanying the rebels describe the city's civilian population as jubilant at being freed from Taliban rule.

16 **The U.S. Senate** and House of Representatives pass legislation designed to improve airport security in the wake of the September 11 terrorist attacks on the United States. The bill creates a new division—the Transportation Safety Administration—within the Department of Transportation (DOT) and requires that DOT hire 28,000 employees to conduct security screening of travelers and baggage at airports across the United States.

A letter addressed to Senator Patrick J. Leahy of Vermont containing anthrax spores is discovered among more than 250 barrels of unopened congressional mail by Federal Bureau of Investigation (FBI) officials.

17 **Arab, Pakistani, and Chechen** soldiers fighting with the Taliban are in control of the city of Qonduz (Kunduz), which is under siege by Afghanistan's Northern Alliance rebels. Refugees from the city claim that the foreign soldiers are killing any Afghan soldier who attempts to defect from the Taliban cause.

19 **The United States military** begins broadcasting radio messages in Afghanistan announcing that the U.S. government is offering a $25-million cash reward for information on the whereabouts of Osama bin Laden.

21 **A 94-year-old woman** dies of anthrax in her house in Oxford, Connecticut. She is the fifth victim to die of anthrax since the first diagnosis was made in Florida in early October. Public health officials are unable to explain how the woman, who neighbors describe as a shut-in, contracted the disease.

24 **Taliban soldiers** pour out of the besieged city of Qonduz (Kunduz), the Taliban's last stronghold in northern Afghanistan, to surrender by the hundreds to Northern Alliance rebels.

Economists at the Organization for Economic Cooperation and Development (OECD) estimate that the global economy has entered a recession.

25 **More than 1,000 U.S. Marines** land at a makeshift airfield near Qandahar (Kandahar) in southern Afghanistan in the first major deployment of American ground troops in the war. Officials with the U.S. Defense Department describe the arrival of the Marines as the first step in a sustained assault on Taliban forces and members of the al-Qaida terrorist network.

26 **U.S. President George W. Bush** demands that Saddam Hussein allow United Nations weapons inspectors into Iraq to verify that the Iraqi military is not developing weapons of mass destruction. Asked what would happen if Hussein refused to comply, the president responds, "He'll find out."

28 **Enron Corp.,** an energy-trading company located in Houston, collapses when Dynegy, Inc., another Houston-based energy trader, withdraws an offer to buy Enron for $9 billion in stock plus assumption of debts. According to financial experts, Enron, the seventh largest corporation in the United States, will be the biggest American company ever to go bankrupt.

29 **A Palestinian suicide bomber** detonates a bomb on a bus outside Hadera, a city along Israel's Mediterranean coast, killing three Israelis and wounding nine other passengers. The attack is the third suicide bombing in Israel in four days.

30 **Health officials in Japan** diagnose a third case of bovine spongiform encephalopathy, or mad cow disease. Japan's first case was discovered in September. Japan is the only country in Asia with herds affected by the disease, which badly hurt the beef industry in Europe, particularly in Great Britain.

1 **A car bomb** explodes a block away from Jerusalem's Ben Yahuda mall. Minutes earlier, two Palestinian suicide bombers blew themselves up at each end of the pedestrian mall. Eleven Israelis are killed in the blasts and at least 150 other people are wounded.

2 **A suicide bomber** in Haifa, Israel, detonates a bomb in a city bus, killing himself and 15 Israelis. The bombing is the third in Israel in just over 12 hours.

3 **Prime Minister Ariel Sharon** of Israel declares war on Palestinian terrorism minutes after Israeli helicopter gunships attack Yasir Arafat's Gaza headquarters, destroying part of the compound, including the helicopter pad and two of the Palestinian leader's personal helicopters.

4 **Israel** launches wide-ranging attacks on Palestinian targets on the West Bank and the Gaza Strip. Israeli helicopters fire missiles into the personal compound of Yasir Arafat, leader of the Palestinian Authority, punching a hole in a stone wall less than 300 feet (91 meters) from Arafat's office.

5 **U.S. Attorney General John Ashcroft** refuses to give Federal Bureau of Investigation (FBI) officials access to background-check records on people who have purchased guns. The FBI requested the records to determine if any of the 1,200 people detained after the terrorist attacks on September 11 had bought guns in the United States.

6 **Leaders of the Taliban militia** agree to surrender Qandahar (Kandahar), the last Taliban stronghold in Afghanistan. U.S. military officers in Afghanistan, however, are uncertain as to the whereabouts of the Taliban regime's spiritual leader, Mullah Mohammed Omar.

9 **Health officials** have diagnosed Ebola, one of the most virulent of viral diseases, in Gabon in West Africa, announce officials with the World Health Organization, a United Nations agency that helps build better health systems in developing countries. Ebola, which is passed through contact with bodily fluids, is fatal in 50 percent to 90 percent of all cases.

10 **The Taliban regime** in Afghanistan is defeated, announces Deputy Defense Secretary Paul Wolfowitz at the Pentagon outside Washington, D.C. The collapse of the Taliban comes three months after the terrorist attacks on the United States on September 11.

11 **The forces** of the al-Qaida terrorist network in Afghanistan are retreating into the mountains of Afghanistan's rugged Tora Bora region, southeast of Jalalabad. U.S. jets attack mountain tops as opposition fighters and U.S. troops shell caves, where U.S. intelligence officials believe al-Qaida leader Osama bin Laden may be hiding.

12 **The highly lethal** powdered form of anthrax that was mailed to various government officials and to news departments in Washington, D.C., New York City, and Boca Raton, Florida, in September and October matches an anthrax strain developed by U.S. Army scientists, announce officials at Dugway Proving Ground in Utah.

13 **The government of Israel** breaks off communications with Yasir Arafat, leader of the Palestinian Authority. Experts on foreign relations in the Middle East equate Israel's severance of ties with Arafat as the complete abandonment of the Oslo Accords, the series of peace agreements between Israel and the Palestine Liberation Organization (PLO) that were brokered in 1993.

U.S. President George W. Bush announces that the United States will nullify the Antiballistic Missile (ABM) Treaty in 2002. The treaty, signed in 1972 by U.S. and Soviet officials, allows testing of ground-based systems but forbids the deployment of airborne laser interceptors and sea-launched missiles that would form the basis of the missile defense shield the Bush administration intends to build.

Five gunmen storm India's Parliament in New Delhi, the capital, killing nine people before being killed by security guards. No organization claims responsibility for the attack.

16 **The al-Qaida** terrorist network has been destroyed in Afghanistan, an-

nounces U.S. Secretary of State Colin L. Powell.

20 **The president** of Argentina, Fernando de la Rua, resigns two years into a four-year term, in the face of a widening economic crisis.

21 **A government spokesperson** in India's capital, New Delhi, announces that India is recalling its ambassador to Pakistan. The spokesperson claims that India has shown the United States and other governments involved in the U.S.-led war on terrorism evidence that proves that one of two Pakistan-based Islamic groups was responsible for the attack on the Indian Parliament on December 13.

Hamid Karzai addresses the media after taking office as interim prime minister of Afghanistan on December 22. Karzai chaired a 30-person Cabinet that was to administer Afghanistan for six months as part of a political transition organized by the United Nations.

22 **An interim government,** headed by the Afghan tribal leader Hamid Karzai, assumes power in Afghanistan as chairman of a 30-person Cabinet. Under terms brokered by the United Nations (UN), the Cabinet is to administer Afghanistan for six months in what UN officials call the first phase of a political transition.

25 **Brush fires** burn out of control across the Australian state of New South Wales, forcing state officials to close highways and railroads and local residents to evacuate burning houses. More than 5,000 firefighters are battling the fires, which broke out on December 20.

26 **The governments of India and Pakistan** amass troops along their shared 1,800 miles (2,895 kilometers) of border and place their missile systems on full alert.

28 **Buffalo, New York,** receives 33.6 inches (85 centimeters) of snow in 24 hours, bringing the total amount of snow that has fallen on the city since December 24 to at least 81.5 inches (207 centimeters) or nearly 7 feet (2 meters), a city record.

2001 UPDATE

Stocks and bonds
Conservation
Australia
Classical music

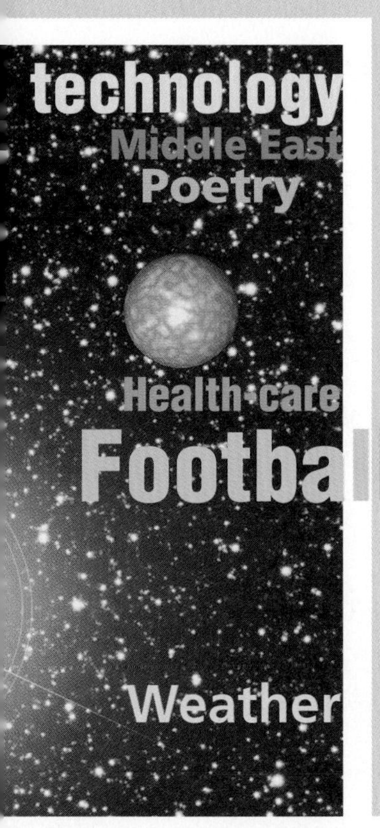

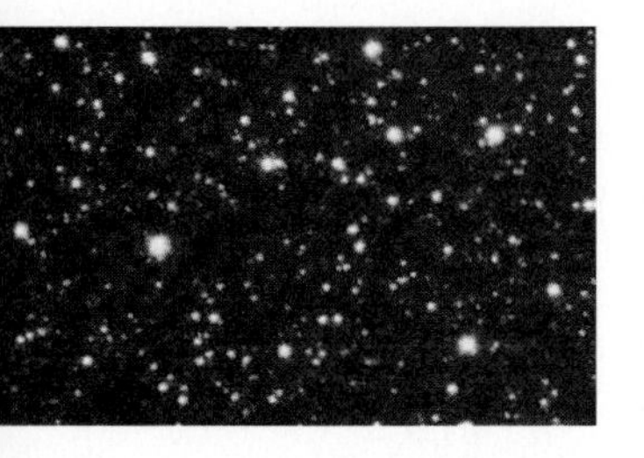

The major events of 2001 are summarized in more than 250 alphabetically arranged articles, from "Afghanistan" to "Zoos." Included are Special Reports that offer in-depth looks at subjects ranging from the terrorist attacks on the United States on September 11 to global warming. The Special Reports can be found on the following pages.

TERRORISM:

On Tuesday, Sept. 11, 2001, the world changed forever. The United States, the world's only superpower, sustained a devastating attack on its own soil by a foreign enemy whose agents had infiltrated American society. The ferocity and scale of the attack shook most Americans' sense of security and awakened them to the threat of deadly terrorist violence. The enemy was not a rival nation, as had been the case in wars of the 20th century, but a shadowy, multinational movement whose members were highly motivated and technologically sophisticated. The members of this enemy movement claimed to be fighting the United States in defense of their religion, Islam, in a great struggle between good and evil.

Shortly before 9:00 a.m. in New York City that September morning, American Airlines Flight 11, a Boeing 767, slammed into the north tower of the World Trade Center in New York

Sept. 11, 2001, became a new date that will live in infamy when Islamic fundamentalist terrorists attacked symbols of economic and military power in the United States, killing thousands of people.

AMERICA'S NEW ENEMY

By R. Scott Appleby

City. Less than 20 minutes later, United Airlines Flight 175, also a Boeing 767, crashed into the south tower. Both planes had been hijacked after taking off from Boston's Logan International Airport. Less than two hours later, the twin 110-story skyscrapers collapsed into a massive, smoldering pile of rubble.

The dramatic attack on the twin towers in the financial heart of the United States was only the beginning of the nightmare. At approximately 9:40 a.m., a hijacked American Airlines Boeing 757 out of Dulles International Airport in Herndon, Virginia, plowed into the Pentagon Building, the headquarters of the U.S. Department of Defense, just outside Washington, D.C. A fourth plane, United Airlines Flight 93, a Boeing 757 scheduled to fly from Newark, New Jersey, to San Francisco, was taken over by hijackers and redirected toward Washington, D.C. Officials with the Federal Bureau of Investigation (FBI) later speculated that the

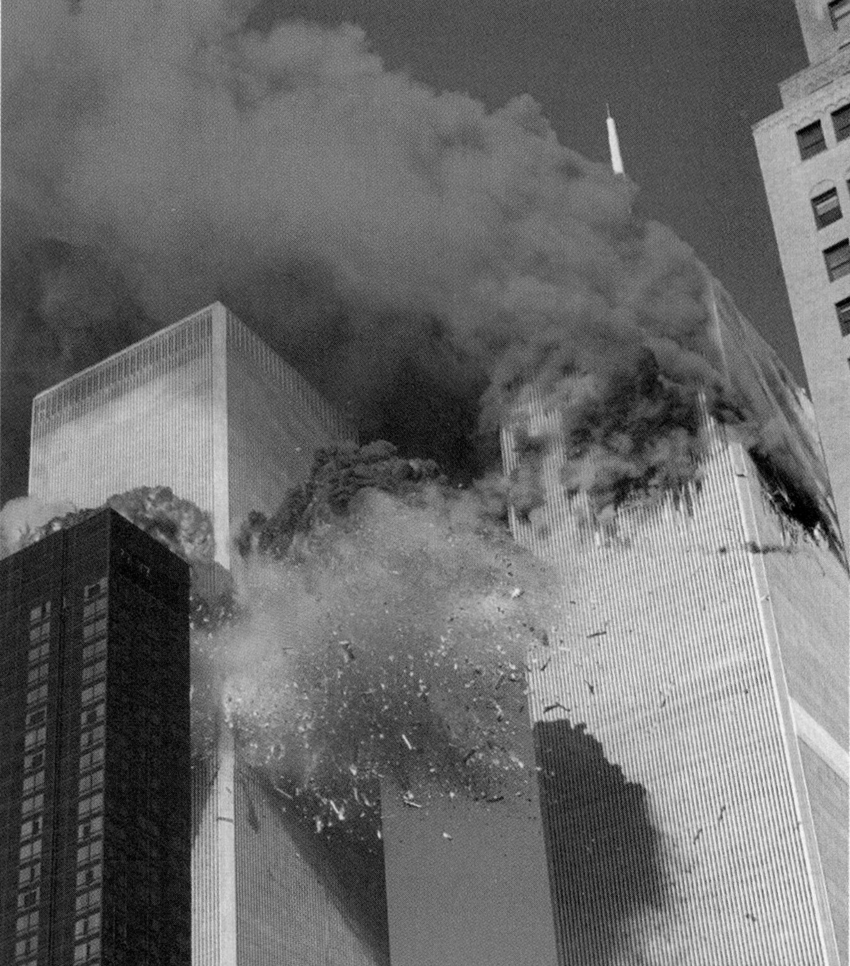

The South Tower of the World Trade Center in New York City explodes into flames after a hijacked airliner slammed into it the morning of Sept. 11, 2001. At the same time, smoke billows from the North Tower, which had been struck by another hijacked plane about 18 minutes earlier. Less than two hours after being hit, both of the 110-story buildings collapsed.

hijackers intended to crash the plane into the White House or Capitol. However, at about 10:00 a.m., the plane went down in a field in Pennsylvania. Passengers on board, after learning of the other suicide hijackings from cellular telephone calls, apparently overpowered the hijackers and forced the plane to crash.

Thousands of people were killed in the carnage of September 11. By the end of 2001, hundreds of bodies were still missing at the site of the World Trade Center wreckage, and the precise number of people who died there remained unknown. Estimates placed the number at approximately 3,000. This number included more than 300 firefighters who rushed to the burning buildings to save other people, only to be killed themselves when the structures collapsed. One hundred and eighty-nine people died in the crash at the Pentagon, and 44 were killed in the Pennsylvania crash. The September 11 attacks killed more people than the Japanese attack on Pearl Harbor on Dec. 7, 1941, and were the most devastating assault on the U.S. mainland since the British burned Washington, D.C., in the War of 1812.

U.S. officials soon concluded that the planes involved in the attacks had been commandeered by 19 hijackers from Saudi Arabia, Egypt, Algeria, and other parts of the Arab world. The hijackers belonged to a network of Islamic fundamentalist terror-

The author:
R. Scott Appleby is a Professor of History and Director of The Joan B. Kroc Institute for International Peace Studies at the University of Notre Dame in Indiana.

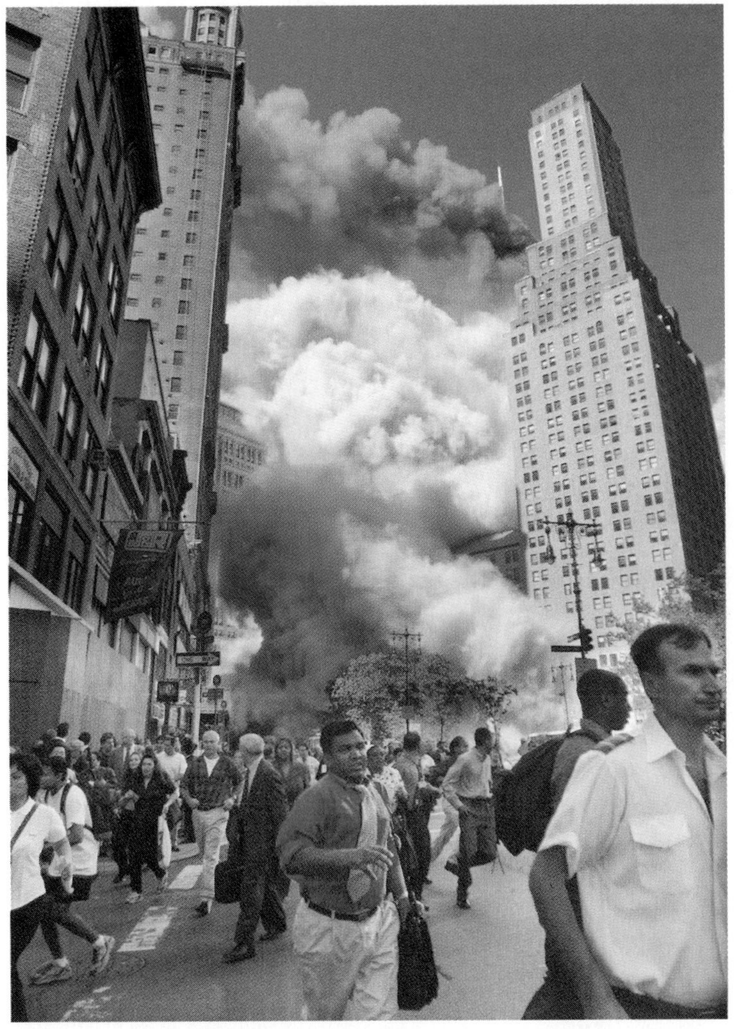

The collapse of the World Trade Center towers generated huge clouds of dust and ash that raced through the skyscraper canyons of New York City, causing frightened pedestrians to run through the streets seeking shelter.

ists known as al-Qaida ("the Base" in Arabic), which had begun to take shape in the 1980's. The leader of al-Qaida was an exiled Saudi Arabian named Osama bin Laden. Bin Laden exhorted his terrorists to wage a holy war against any nation that he perceived to be an enemy of Islam, especially the United States.

By 2001, al-Qaida could boast several thousand members living in dozens of countries. Terrorists affiliated with the network were suspects in several attacks against U.S. interests, including the 1993 murders of 18 U.S. Army Rangers in Somalia; the 1998 bombings of the U.S. embassies in Kenya and Tanzania; and the 2000 bombing of the Navy destroyer USS *Cole* in Yemen.

Americans were shocked and confused by the sweeping events that created a suddenly frightening world after September 11. Why did fundamentalist Islamic groups in other countries hate the United States? What were the roots of Islamic fundamentalism?

Why did the Islamic view of society differ so greatly from the Western view, accepted in Europe and America? To discover answers to these questions, Westerners began seeking an understanding of Islam, the world's second largest religion, after Christianity.

Searching for answers in Islam

In 2001, there were some 1.2 billion Muslims, or followers of Islam, in the world, spanning many different ethnic groups. Most Muslims were concentrated in the Middle East, Africa, and southern Asia.

The main texts of Islam are the Quran, the Muslim holy book, and the hadith, which contains the *Sunna,* examples of the words and practices of the Prophet Muhammad, whom Muslims believe was the final messenger from God. All Muslims believe the Quran

The day after the attack, rescue workers from the Fire Department of New York City search for survivors in the mangled wreckage of the World Trade Center towers. Few survivors were found.

Rescue workers carry the body of the Reverend Mychal Judge, chaplain of the Fire Department of New York City, from the ruins of the twin towers on September 11. Reverend Judge was killed by falling debris while he was administering the last rites to an injured firefighter.

to be "the recitation" of God, or Allah, as revealed to Muhammad by the angel Gabriel in the A.D. 600's. But there are several divisions within Islam.

Most Muslims belong to one of two major branches of Islam—Sunni or Shiah. About 90 percent of Muslims are Sunnis. In Sunni tradition, the political ruler of a Muslim country must govern within the framework of the *Sharia* (Islamic law). The Sharia, in turn, is derived from the Quran and the Sunna.

Shiites, followers of the Shiah branch of Islam, make up roughly 10 percent of the world's Muslim population and are concentrated in Iran, southern Iraq, Lebanon, and some regions of southwest Asia. Unlike Sunni Muslims, Shiites traditionally do not expect justice to be upheld by earthly rulers. Instead, they look forward to the return of the Hidden Imam, a great religious scholar who will lead the Shiites to victory over their many persecutors.

Although the Sunni and Shiite branches do not share the same religious beliefs, there are radical Islamic fundamentalists in both branches who share the same basic world-view. Most Islamic fundamentalists believe that Western culture encourages individuals to abandon what they regard as traditional values, such as the primary importance of the family; the authority of the father; and the sanctity of religion. The fundamentalists resent the influence of Western businesses, consumer goods, missionaries, and such cultural ideas as individualism and *secular* (nonreligious) government. The fundamentalists especially resent the presence of Western troops in Saudi Arabia, which is home to Islam's two holiest sites—Mecca and Medina. And they condemn what they regard as widespread corruption in the Saudi government, which they believe the West supports in its dependence on Saudi oil.

Radical Islamic fundamentalists also deeply resent the presence of the Jewish nation of Israel in the Middle East. They accuse Israel of harsh treatment of the Palestinian people, many of whom became refugees after Israel was created in 1948. The United States' strong support of Israel has been a thorn in the side of Muslim extremists for decades.

Islamic militants have charged the West with hypocrisy regarding Islam and the Arab world. They claim that despite the U.S. rhetoric about freedom and human rights, the United States has propped up governments throughout the Islamic world that the fundamentalists regard as corrupt and dictatorial.

Most Americans first became aware of radical Islamic fundamentalism during the 1978-1979 Islamic revolution in Iran. This Shiite revolution toppled the Shah of Iran, who was a strong ally of the United States. Ruhollah Khomeini, an *ayatollah* (religious scholar) who denounced the United States as "the great Satan," replaced the shah as head of Iran in 1979. Revolutionaries in Tehran, Iran's capital, seized a group of Americans at the U.S. embassy in November 1979 and held them hostage until January 1981.

Most Western governments regarded the Islamic Republic of Iran as a repressive state that fostered terrorist groups dedicated to spreading the Iranian revolution. However, Khomeini's brand of Islamic fundamentalism had a limited influence in the Islamic world, primarily because it appealed to a relatively small number of Shiite Muslims. In the larger Sunni world, fundamentalism took on different characteristics inspired by two visionary scholars.

The roots of a violent vision

The father of Sunni extremism was an Egyptian schoolteacher, Sayyid Qutb, who was born in 1906. After studying for three years in the United States, Qutb returned to Egypt in 1951 and joined the Muslim Brotherhood, a leading Egyptian opposition movement of the day. The goal of the brotherhood was to expel British forces, which had effectively controlled Egypt since the late 1800's, and bring Egyptian society directly under the rule of Islamic law. While imprisoned for being a threat to the government in the early 1960's, Qutb wrote *Signposts Along the Road,* which soon became the *manifesto* (proclamation of intent) of Sunni extremism. In his manifesto, Qutb introduced the basic elements of Islamic fundamentalist ideology, including alarm over the loss of Islamic religious values; a refusal to compromise with outsiders; a sense of crisis and approaching intervention by God; disgust at what he regarded as the immoral excesses of secular society; and a desire to build a religious alternative to secularism.

Qutb also developed his own interpretation of jihad, a Quranic concept traditionally interpreted as an internal struggle against one's tendencies toward disobedience. Qutb promoted a militant interpretation of jihad as Islamic holy war against nonbelievers. He wrote, "This movement uses the methods of preaching and persuasion for reforming ideas and beliefs, and it uses physical

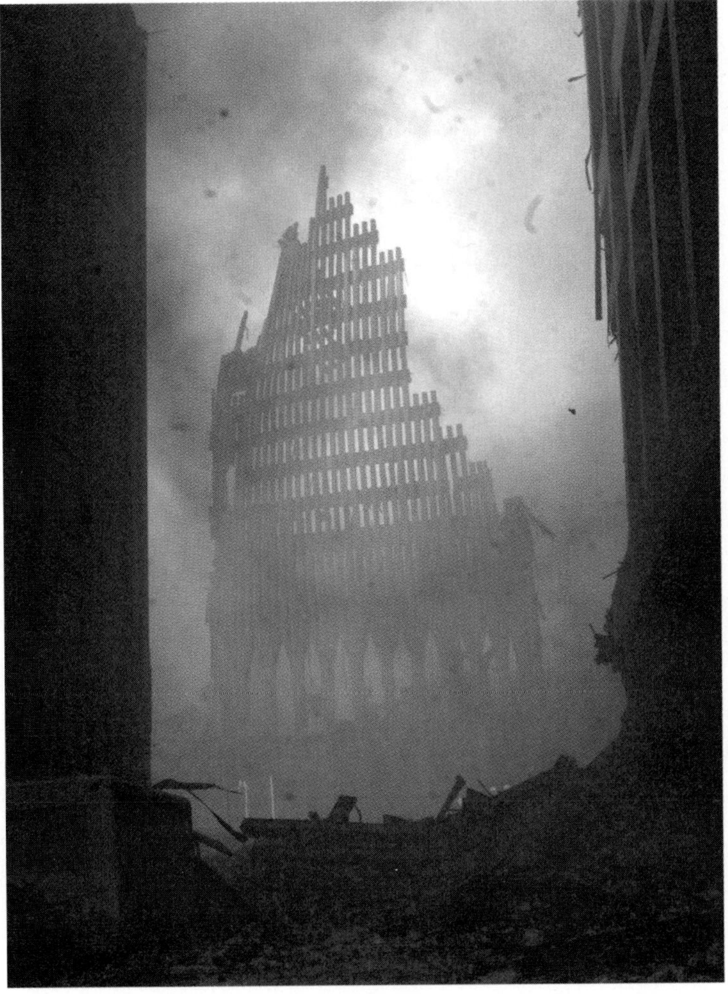

The ghostly, skeletal remains of one of the World Trade Center towers stands amid the smoking rubble. The seven-story fragment of metal facade, which served as a powerful symbol of the attack, was later dismantled but saved for a possible future memorial structure.

power and jihad for abolishing the organizations and authorities of the (secular world)."

The Egyptian government executed Qutb in 1966 for "crimes against the nation." But long after his death, Qutb continued to exert influence through his ideological heirs, including bin Laden; Omar Abdel Rahman, the blind sheik who was convicted of bombing the World Trade Center in 1993; and Ayman al-Zawahiri, head of the radical Egypt-based movement, Islamic Jihad. Qutb's legacy also included the Taliban of Afghanistan; the Harkat *Mujahideen* (Holy Warriors) of Pakistan; and the Armed Islamic Group of Algeria.

Theocracy versus democracy

Qutb was influenced by the teachings of Abu al-Ala Maududi, a writer, orator, and politician who was born in India in 1903 and died in 1979. In 1941, Maududi founded Jamaat-i-Islami, an Is-

Less than an hour after the attack on the World Trade Center, a hijacked airliner crashed into the Pentagon Building just outside Washington, D.C. The crash resulted in the deaths of 189 people, including 64 on the plane.

lamic organization that is still active in Pakistan and southern Asia. His core concept is based on the traditional idea of Islam as a comprehensive way of life—the total obedience of society and government to the authority of traditional Islamic law.

Maududi envisioned a theocratic state in which God is recognized as the supreme civil ruler and in which religious authorities rule as God's representatives. This idea stands in direct opposition to a basic tenet of the U.S. system of government: the separation of church and state. That tenet is spelled out in the first sentence of the first amendment to the U.S. Constitution.

The framers of the U.S. Constitution, who were largely of English ancestry, were well aware of what happens to a society when its citizens go to war over the relationship between religion and government. In 1534, England's Parliament separated the Church of England from the Roman Catholic Church and made King Henry VIII—rather than the Pope—supreme head of the English church, setting off more than 150 years of trouble. Thousands of people died in religious persecutions, foreign invasions, civil war, and revolution. At one point, England became a dictatorship un-

der the Puritan Oliver Cromwell, who demanded that people follow rigid moral standards. When England tired of Puritan rule, the monarchy was restored. During the same period, Puritans from England established the Massachusetts Bay Colony, where they permitted no religion except their own. Nonconformists were expelled, or they left to colonize other parts of New England.

Their descendants did not forget the effects of religious intolerance when in 1789 they demanded that the new U.S. Constitution be amended to read: "Congress shall make no law respecting an establishment of religion, or prohibiting the free exercise thereof." While Americans have argued for more than 200 years over exactly what that phrase means, few would argue its importance. Yet, it is exactly that phrase, and the government and culture it fosters, that the Islamic fundamentalists regard as evil and dangerous. And Osama bin Laden emerged in the 1990's as a chief proponent of this anti-American view.

The rise of Osama bin Laden

Bin Laden was born in Saudi Arabia to a life of riches and privilege. His father was a wealthy contractor, and bin Laden became a multimillionaire by inheriting part of the family fortune. Bin Laden was influenced by the anti-Western ideas of Qutb and Maududi as well as by the conservative Wahhabism movement, the dominant form of Sunni Islam in Saudi Arabia. Wahhabis believe that any ideas not found in a literal reading of the Quran should be abandoned, and that Muslims must free themselves of any non-Islamic influence. In the 1980's, bin Laden used his wealth to recruit and train young Muslim Arabs to fight against Soviet troops who had invaded Afghanistan, another Muslim country. Bin Laden and the Muslim warriors, supported by the United States, succeed in ousting the Soviets from Afghanistan in 1989, and bin Laden returned to Saudi Arabia. Bin Laden's recruitment of Arab troops, however, marked the beginning of al-Qaida.

The chain of events that eventually led to the attacks on America in 2001 began during the Persian Gulf War of 1991, when King Fahd of Saudi Arabia allowed U.S. forces to use Saudi territory for launching air strikes against Iraqi troops who had invaded neighboring Kuwait. This decision enraged bin Laden, who believed Islamic law required the Saudis to support their fellow Muslims, the Iraqis. Bin Laden's outspoken opposition to the Saudi-U.S. alliance caused Saudi authorities to place him under house arrest. However, bin Laden fled to Sudan, where he lived from 1991 to 1996. While in Sudan, he built up the al-Qaida network and began to turn it against the United States. In 1996, the government of Sudan, under pressure from the United States, expelled bin Laden, and he moved his terrorist-training operations to Afghanistan, which was coming under the control of an extremist Islamic militia called the Taliban. The Taliban and al-Qaida soon formed a mutually supportive relationship.

Bin Laden had set as his goals expelling the Western presence

After the terrorist attacks on the United States, more than 1 million people fled cities in Afghanistan for safer areas in the country or for refuge in neighboring nations. The refugees feared both U.S. retaliatory strikes against Afghanistan and conscription by Afghanistan's ruling Taliban, which the United States accused of harboring the terrorists responsible for the September attacks.

from Islamic lands, abolishing boundaries between Muslim nations, and creating a multiethnic Islamic society ruled by a restored *Caliphate* (the title of Islamic governments during Medieval times). Working toward these goals, bin Laden and his compatriots supported Muslim rebel forces in Chechnya (a republic in southwestern Russia); Kosovo (a province in Yugoslavia); Bosnia-Herzegovina; Tajikistan; Somalia; and Yemen. Al-Qaida also trained members of terrorist organizations from such diverse countries as the Philippines, Algeria, and Eritrea.

Fundamentalist inspiration for terrorists

At the same time, Islamic fundamentalism was thriving, in part, because the mass media had increased awareness of the social, economic, and political injustices common in many Muslim societies. The media also made people more aware of the corruption and mismanagement that plagues many Muslim governments. This media exposure created a growing sense that many Muslims are deprived, compared with people in other societies. Islamic fundamentalists gained support in this environment by blaming the failures of society on the abandonment of strict Islam.

In many Islamic countries, fundamentalist "laymen" gained more respect among citizens than mainstream Islamic scholars. This may be because they often demonstrate greater concern than the mainstream leaders for the oppressed and needy of their nations. The fundamentalists are also militantly dedicated to their cause. While many Western, as well as Islamic, scholars may find fundamentalist leaders simplistic in their use of Islamic ideas, their message is effective among large numbers of Muslims. The fundamentalists know how to inspire an audience to believe in their interpretation of Islam. Under their guidance, the radical faithful accept the promise of paradise for martyrs who die in the cause of Islam, and this becomes an advertisement for would-be suicide bombers.

Declaring war against terrorism

United States President George W. Bush responded to the attacks of Sept. 11, 2001, by launching a worldwide "war against terrorism." Bush urged all countries to join a coalition against terrorism by freezing the financial assets of suspected terrorist organizations, apprehending suspects, sharing intelligence information about terrorists, or cooperating in military efforts to root out terrorists and their supporters. Many nations, including such Muslim countries as Turkey, Jordan, and Saudi Arabia, agreed to help the United States in one or more of these areas. On October 7, U.S. and British forces began bombing targets in Afghanistan associated with al-Qaida and the Taliban. By December, the intense bombing campaign had allowed Afghan anti-Taliban forces to gain control of most of Afghanistan. Furthermore, a number of senior al-Qaida and Taliban figures had reportedly been killed or captured.

On the home front, the U.S. Congress gave the FBI and other law enforcement agencies greater powers to monitor the communica-

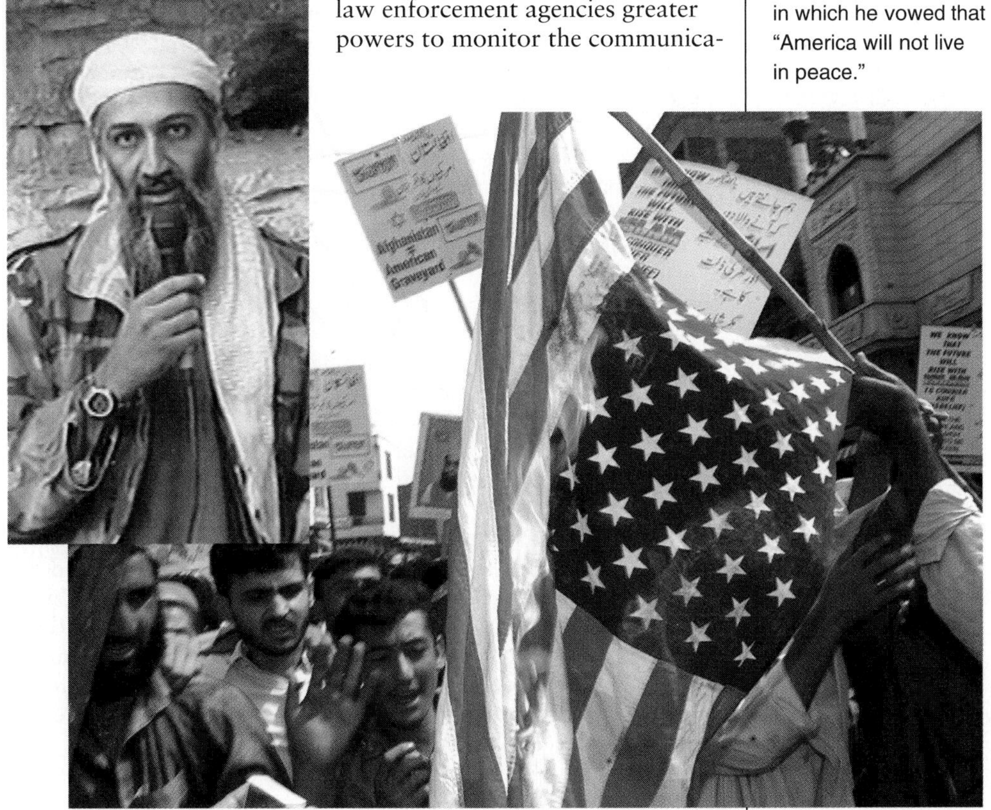

Islamic militants in Pakistan (below) burn an American flag in late September during a demonstration against expected U.S. military strikes on Afghanistan. After the U.S. bombing campaign began on October 7, Osama bin Laden (left), the leader of the terrorist network believed to have carried out the attacks on the United States, released a videotape in which he vowed that "America will not live in peace."

tion and behavior of, and detain for questioning, people suspected of having links to terrorism. In addition, President Bush announced a crackdown on foreigners who overstayed their visas and the establishment of military courts in which noncitizens accused of terrorism could be tried in secret.

The threat of more terrorism and the need to protect U.S. citizens raised a basic question and started a public debate: How can the United States preserve its founding principles of freedom and equal protection under the law in the dangerous world that violent Islamic fundamentalism thrust upon it on September 11? Bush administration officials and most Americans, as revealed by public opinion polls, supported strong security measures as an effective way to thwart an unseen and dangerous enemy. However, civil libertarians and some members of Congress warned that the government should be cautious about curtailing personal liberties in exchange for security. They pointed out that if the United States turns into a security state, the terrorists win, because Islamic fundamentalists seek a society in which personal liberty is limited and dependent upon the needs of the state. The use of law to dictate behavior in areas Americans regard as protected—such as the freedoms of assembly, speech, and worship—would undermine the U.S. Constitution, they argued.

Such drastic consequences seemed unlikely to happen in 2001. A greater danger, however, was that Americans might lose their love of diversity and tolerance for those who do not conform to the "mainstream." Suspicion of people who appear to be "different" could ultimately prove highly destructive, particularly of the inventiveness and creativity that is the glory of U.S. society and its technology-driven economy. President Bush and other political leaders counseled Americans not to make this mistake, especially in regard to peace-loving Muslims.

Defeating the violent vision

Despite bin Laden's efforts, the violent vision of Islamic jihad appeals only to a minority of Muslims. Islam is a vast religion, and in 2001 relatively few of its believers belonged to, or supported, Islamic terrorist organizations. Moreover, not all of the Islamic fundamentalist movements in 2001 were violent. The Muslim Brotherhood organizations in Egypt and Jordan, for example, renounced violence to pursue power through political means. Moderate Muslims all over the world reacted with shock and horror to the events of September 11.

U.S. National Guard troops patrol Ronald Reagan Washington National Airport near Washington, D.C., in October 2001. The terrorist attacks of September 11 prompted federal officials to increase the security forces in airports to protect travelers.

In this atmosphere, many experts in international affairs believed that the United States and its Western allies should go on the offensive to counter the terrorist threat—not just a military offensive, but also a cultural and educational offensive to win hearts and minds. They urged the U.S. government to address why the Islamic world produces violent fundamentalist movements and how the United States might draw on its historic tradition of generosity to help solve the problems that are the root causes of Islamic militancy. Taking this approach in the years after World War II (1939-1945), the United States transformed two of its greatest enemies, Germany and Japan, into two of its strongest allies. In the same way, the United States might turn Arab enemies into allies by giving greater support to broad-based economic development, widespread education, and participatory forms of government in key regions of the Islamic world.

Extremist Islam will fail if and when an effective social alternative is provided. Many international leaders believe that the United States has the capacity to contribute to the development of such an alternative. Efforts to address the economic and educational problems fueling Islamic fundamentalism may come at a considerable financial cost to the United States, they say, but this price may be preferable to closing off U.S. borders and diminishing the diversity that has been the greatest strength of American society. ■■■

Afghanistan. A coalition of military forces led by the United States launched a campaign against Afghanistan in 2001 that toppled the ruling Taliban regime in December. The Taliban was an Islamic fundamentalist movement that had controlled most of Afghanistan since 1996. The U.S.-led military action came in the wake of terrorist attacks on the United States on Sept. 11, 2001, which killed thousands of people. U.S. intelligence agents claimed that Osama bin Laden, a Saudi-born exile living in Afghanistan, was behind the terrorist attacks, as well as other attacks, such as the bombing of two U.S. embassies in Africa in 1998. U.S. President George W. Bush demanded that the Taliban turn over bin Laden to U.S. officials. The Taliban leaders refused, claiming that U.S. officials had offered no evidence that he was involved.

War. Armed forces from the United States and the United Kingdom launched air strikes against Afghanistan on Oct. 7, 2001. The objective was to destroy both the Taliban, which harbored bin Laden, and bin Laden's terrorist network, al-Qaida ("The Base" in Arabic). In addition to the air strikes, U.S. armed forces supported the Northern Alliance, a group of anti-Taliban rebels, in its ground attacks against Taliban forces.

U.S. bombers and fighter jets attacked Taliban ground troops, barracks, and troop encampments across Afghanistan throughout October, November, and early December. The U.S. military also targeted Kabul, the capital, and Qandahar (Kandahar), a Taliban stronghold. On October 21, jet fighter pilots bombed a series of Taliban trenches, bunkers, and minefields approximately 35 miles (56 kilometers) north of the capital, which had separated Taliban forces from the rebels.

On November 9, rebel forces broke through Taliban defenses and entered Mazar-e Sharif, a strategically important Taliban stronghold in northern Afghanistan. On November 13, Taliban forces offered little resistance as Northern Alliance rebels took Kabul.

Dozens of U.S. Special Operations troops moved into Afghanistan in mid-November to pursue bin Laden, al-Qaida members, and Taliban leaders. By late November, Taliban soldiers were fleeing the besieged city of Qonduz (Kunduz), the Taliban's last stronghold in the north, and surrendered by the hundreds. Rebel leaders captured Qonduz on November 25.

Leaders of the Taliban militia surrendered Qandahar, the last Taliban stronghold, on December 6. On December 10, officials with the U.S. Department of Defense announced that Afghanistan's Taliban had been defeated. By mid-December, the forces of al-Qaida had retreated into the mountains of Afghanistan's rugged Tora Bora region southeast of Jalalabad, where U.S. intelligence officials believed that bin Laden and other al-Qaida leaders also had taken refuge. U.S. jets bombarded the region to disable the terrorist network. Although hundreds of al-Qaida members were killed or captured, U.S. officials theorized that others continued to hide in complex cave systems in the re-

Battlegrounds in Afghanistan, 2001

gion or had escaped over the border into Pakistan. On December 16, U.S. Secretary of State Colin Powell announced that al-Qaida had been destroyed in Afghanistan. However, neither bin Laden nor Mullah Mohammed Omar, the spiritual leader of the Taliban, had been located by the end of 2001.

Interim government. Afghan tribal leader Hamid Karzai assumed power in Afghanistan as chairman of a 30-person cabinet on December 22. Karzai was sworn into office in Kabul before an array of Afghan leaders and U.S. government and military officials. After taking office, Karzai presided over the swearing in of the members of his cabinet. Under terms brokered by the United Nations (UN), the cabinet was to administer an interim government in Afghanistan for six months in what UN officials called the first phase of a political transition. The transition was scheduled to culminate in national elections by 2004.

Peacekeeping. On Dec. 19, 2001, the UN Security Council authorized the United Kingdom to lead an international peacekeeping force in Afghanistan. The force was to support Afghanistan's newly formed interim government. Bangladesh, Canada, France, Germany, Italy, Jordan, and Turkey also made commitments to the operation.

Refugees. Western bombing and intensified fighting between the Taliban and the Northern Alliance caused thousands of Afghans to flood into neighboring Pakistan and Iran, despite efforts by those countries to keep the Afghans out. The refugees joined thousands of other Afghans who already had fled Afghanistan, which in 2001 suffered a third consecutive year of drought, which resulted in widespread famine. The World Food Program, a UN agency that combats hunger, reported in July that approximately 5 million Afghans, "have little or no access to food" and that malnutrition due to lack of food was common across Afghanistan.

Western aid, including $105 million in wheat and other supplies from the United States, was channeled to Afghanistan between August 2000 and September 2001. As the Taliban began to lose control in October, Western troops rushed more food into the country. U.S. aircrews in C-17 cargo planes air-dropped food, winter clothing, and other relief supplies into Afghanistan.

Statues destroyed. In February, Taliban leaders ordered that all statues and carvings of humans and animals be destroyed in Afghanistan. Taliban leaders claimed that the statues were idolatrous and contrary to the teachings of Islam. Despite worldwide protests over the destruction of a cultural heritage, Taliban workers smashed relics of Afghanistan's Buddhist period, and in March, the Afghan army blew up two 1,400-year-old Buddhas. The two statues, the largest of which was 175 feet (53 meters) high, had been carved into a cliff in the central province of Bamiyan, 70 miles (113 kilometers) west of Kabul.

☐ Henry S. Bradsher

See also **Armed forces; Asia; Pakistan; People in the news** (bin Laden, Osama); **Terrorism: A Special Feature,** p. 38; **United States, Government of the.**

A U.S. fighter jet takes off from the U.S.S. *Enterprise* on October 9. U.S.-led armed forces bombed Taliban and al-Qaida positions in Afghanistan for three months beginning in October.

On Nov. 13, 2001, Afghans cheer the arrival of Northern Alliance rebels in Kabul, the capital, following the retreat and surrender of Taliban forces in the city.

Africa

United Nations (UN) Secretary-General Kofi Annan urged more than 40 African heads of state at the July 2001 summit of the Organization of African Unity (OAU) in Lusaka, Zambia, to depart from the "ways of the past" and create a stable, democratic, and prosperous continent. He said they needed courage and leadership to rebuild Africa, a task he compared with the reconstruction of Europe after World War I (1914-1918) and World War II (1939-1945).

African Union. The OAU—an association of more than 50 African nations—was scheduled to be renamed the African Union (AU) during a one-year transition following the July 2001 summit. The charter for the new organization proposed a single currency, a continental parliament, and a multinational African court of justice to uphold human rights. Critics had long dismissed the OAU, founded in 1963, as a "talking shop," which lacked the will or power to address poverty, corruption, and violent conflicts that afflict many African nations.

The transformation from OAU to AU—sponsored mainly by Libyan leader Muammar Muhammad al-Qadhafi—was to proceed according to a plan called the African Initiative. The plan called on the world's wealthiest nations to cancel the African nations' indebtedness of $330 billion and increase foreign investment aimed at achieving an average annual growth rate of 7 percent by

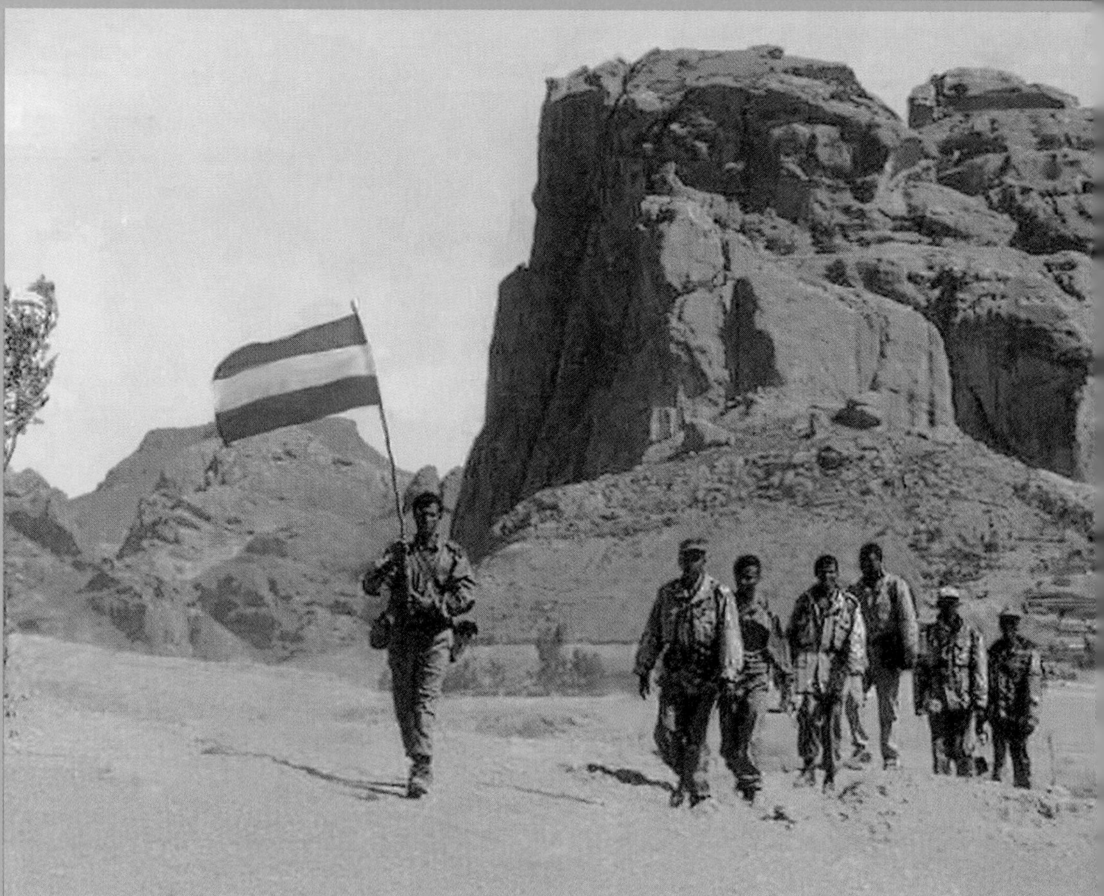

2016. Forecasts by economists at international lending agencies, however, suggested a growth rate in 2001 and 2002 of no more than 3.5 percent. Independent observers warned that Africa would have to solve its many armed conflicts in order to have any chance of meeting the AU growth target.

Western Africa. On Jan. 7, 2001, Ghana's outgoing president, Jerry Rawlings, handed over power to New Patriotic Party leader John Agyekum Kufuor. Kufuor had won the presidential runoff on Dec. 28, 2000, with 57 percent of the vote against Rawlings's chosen National Democratic Congress candidate, John Atta Mills, who became vice president. Rawlings, a former fighter pilot, had ruled Ghana since seizing power from a civilian government in 1981.

Violence between Christians and Muslims in northern and central Nigeria during 2001 left at least 800 people dead. Most of the violence was sparked by disputes involving the introduction of *Sharia* (Islamic law) in many central and northern states of Nigeria and communities of the region. Northern Nigeria is predominantly Muslim, while the south is mainly Christian.

An Ethiopian soldier, bearing his nation's flag, leads an orderly withdrawal from Eritrean territory in February 2001. The withdrawal was part of a United Nations- (UN) supervised cease-fire between Ethiopia and Eritrea, which went to war in May 1998 over disputed territory along their joint border. UN peacekeepers patrolled a security zone between the two countries for most of 2001.

Supporters of President Olusegun Obasanjo said that some of the violence was instigated by exmilitary officials, who had ruled Nigeria for nearly 16 years until Obasanjo's election in 1996.

In Cote d'Ivoire, at least eight people died on the night of Jan. 7, 2001, when troops stopped a *coup* (overthrow) attempt against the government of Laurent Gbagbo, the head of state. The attempted coup was the latest in a series of rebellions that began in December 1999, when General Robert Guei seized power in a military coup that was the first violent change of government since Cote d'Ivoire achieved independence from France in 1960. General Guei had attempted to retain power after an October 2000 election gave Gbagbo power, but he was overthrown by a popular uprising.

Security in Sierra Leone improved dramatically in 2001 following a May 15 cease-fire agreement between the democratically elected government of President Ahmad Tejan Kabbah and rebel forces. The pact paved the way for the deployment in Sierra Leone of some 17,500 UN peacekeepers by late 2001 in preparation for presidential and parliamentary elections scheduled for May 2002.

In March 2001, a UN report had warned African governments that the activities of loosely allied rebel groups in Sierra Leone and Guinea seriously undermined peace efforts in the West African region. An October UN report blamed Liberian President Charles Taylor with fueling the crisis by providing the Sierra Leone rebels with weapons and training.

Central Africa. The assassination of Congo (Kinshasa) President Laurent Kabila by a bodyguard on January 16 rocked the Great Lakes region of central Africa. His death was followed by the installation as president of his 31-year-old son, Joseph Kabila, on January 26. UN officials expressed hope that the younger Kabila would work to ensure implementation of a cease-fire agreement, brokered in 2000, between the government and rebel groups. Angola, Zimbabwe, and Namibia backed the government. Rwanda and Uganda backed the rebels. The withdrawal of foreign troops, who had intervened in Congo (Kinshasa) soon after renewal of the country's civil war in 1998, remained a sticking point in 2001.

On July 23, Tutsi troops staged an unsuccessful coup in Burundi. Tutsis were angered by President Pierre Buyoya's plans to share power with the country's majority Hutus. Ethnic civil war between Tutsis and Hutus had claimed more than 200,000 lives in Burundi since 1993. In November 2001, a new three-year power-sharing transitional government was inaugurated in Bujumbura,

Facts in brief on African political units

Country	Population	Government	Monetary unit*	Foreign trade (million U.S.$) Exports†	Imports†
Algeria	32,813,000	President Abdelaziz Bouteflika; Prime Minister Ali Benflis	dinar (75.49 = $1)	19,600	9,200
Angola	13,684,000	President Jose Eduardo dos Santos	readj. kwanza (18.25 = $1)	7,800	2,500
Benin	6,422,000	President Mathieu Kerekou	CFA franc (713.78 = $1)	374	600
Botswana	1,661,000	President Festus Mogae	pula (6.08 = $1)	2,600	2,200
Burkina Faso	12,600,000	President Blaise Compaore	CFA franc (713.78 = $1)	210	618
Burundi	7,044,000	President Pierre Buyoya	franc (833.90 = $1)	50	148
Cameroon	15,855,000	President Paul Biya	CFA franc (713.78 = $1)	1,594	1,313
Cape Verde	447,000	President Pedro Pires; Prime Minister Jose Maria Pereira Neves	escudo (119.75 = $1)	40	250
Central African Republic	3,746,000	President Ange Patasse	CFA franc (713.78 = $1)	166	154
Chad	8,081,000	President Idriss Deby	CFA franc (713.78 = $1)	183	291
Comoros	582,000	Head of State Assoumani Azzali	franc (537.11 = $1)	8	55
Congo (Brazzaville)	3,105,000	President Denis Sassou-Nguesso	CFA franc (713.78 = $1)	1,555	820
Congo (Kinshasa)	54,768,000	President Joseph Kabila	Congolese franc (315.00 = $1)	960	660
Cote d'Ivoire (Ivory Coast)	15,417,000	Head of State Laurent Gbagbo	CFA franc (713.78 = $1)	3,988	3,079
Djibouti	665,000	President Ismail Omar Guelleh; Prime Minister Mohamed Dilleita Dilleita	franc (172.00 = $1)	260	440
Egypt	70,818,000	President Hosni Mubarak; Prime Minister Atef Mohammed Obeid	pound (4.26 = $1)	4,691	14,010
Equatorial Guinea	475,000	President Teodoro Obiang Nguema Mbasogo; Prime Minister Candido Muatetema Rivas	CFA franc (713.78 = $1)	407	28
Eritrea	4,044,000	President Isaias Afworki	nafka (9.50 = $1)	26	560
Ethiopia	65,579,000	President Girma Wolde-Giorgis	birr (8.42 = $1)	460	1,250
Gabon	1,280,000	President El Hadj Omar Bongo; Prime Minister Jean-François Ntoutoume-Emane	CFA franc (713.78 = $1)	3,400	1,000
Gambia	1,372,000	Head of State Yahya Jammeh	dalasi (16.60 = $1)	7	192
Ghana	21,318,000	President John Agyekum Kufuor	cedi (7,260.00 = $1)	1,600	2,200
Guinea	7,794,000	President Lansana Conte	franc (1,965.40 = $1)	820	634
Guinea-Bissau	1,264,000	President Kumba Yala	CFA franc (713.78 = $1)	80	55
Kenya	31,069,000	President Daniel T. arap Moi	shilling (78.85 = $1)	1,734	3,105
Lesotho	2,237,000	King Letsie III; Prime Minister Pakalitha Mosisili	maloti (9.20 = $1)	175	700
Liberia	3,385,000	President Charles Taylor	dollar (1 = $1)	55	170

*Exchange rates as of Oct. 5, 2001, or latest available data. †Latest available data.

Country	Population	Government	Monetary unit*	Foreign trade (million U.S.$) Exports†	Imports†
Libya	5,869,000	Leader Muammar Muhammad al-Qadhafi; General People's Committee Secretary (Prime Minister) Mubarak Abdullah Al-Shamikh	dinar (0.64 = $1)	13,900	7,600
Madagascar	16,811,000	President Didier Ratsiraka	franc (6,177.00 = $1)	241	511
Malawi	11,449,000	President Bakili Muluzi	kwacha (61.50 = $1)	442	697
Mali	11,810,000	President Alpha Oumar Konare; Prime Minister Mande Sidibe	CFA franc (713.78 = $1)	520	689
Mauritania	2,814,000	President Maaouya Ould Sid Ahmed Taya	ouguiya (257.73 = $1)	333	305
Mauritius	1,177,000	President Sir Cassam Uteem; Prime Minister Sir Anerood Jugnauth	rupee (29.90 = $1)	1,554	2,247
Morocco	29,248,000	King Mohamed VI; Prime Minister Abderrahmane Youssoufi	dirham (11.24 = $1)	7,417	11,484
Mozambique	20,367,000	President Joaquim Alberto Chissano; Prime Minister Pascoal Manuel Mocumbi	metical (22,700.00 = $1)	263	1,139
Namibia	1,768,000	President Sam Nujoma; Prime Minister Hage Geingob	dollar (9.35 = $1)	1,400	1,600
Niger	11,395,000	President Mamadou Tandja; Prime Minister Hama Amadou	CFA franc (713.78 = $1)	254	362
Nigeria	128,886,000	President Olusegun Obasanjo	naira (111.50 = $1)	9,729	10,002
Rwanda	8,063,000	President Paul Kagame	franc (438.00 = $1)	53	213
São Tomé and Príncipe	153,000	President Fradique de Menezes	dobra (8,937.20 = $1)	3	40
Senegal	9,969,000	President Abdoulaye Wade; Prime Minister Madior Boye	CFA franc (713.78 = $1)	997	1,364
Seychelles	79,000	President France Albert Rene	rupee (5.62 = $1)	145	434
Sierra Leone	5,067,000	President Ahmad Tejan Kabbah	leone (1,943.00 = $1)	13	149
Somalia	10,837,000	Interim President Abdikassim Salad Hassan; Interim Prime Minister Hassan Abshir Farah	shilling (2,620.00 = $1)	186	314
South Africa	40,952,000	President Thabo Mvuyelwa Mbeki	rand (9.23 = $1)	29,267	28,980
Sudan	30,742,000	President Umar Hasan Ahmad al-Bashir	dinar (258.70 = $1) pound (2,587.00 = $1)	616	1,988
Swaziland	1,064,000	King Mswati III; Prime Minister Barnabas Sibusiso Dlamini	lilangeni (9.20 = $1)	881	928
Tanzania	35,090,000	President Benjamin William Mkapa; Prime Minister Frederick Sumaye	shilling (892.00 = $1)	663	1,522
Togo	4,865,000	President Gnassingbe Eyadema	CFA franc (713.78 = $1)	333	542
Tunisia	9,845,000	President Zine El Abidine Ben Ali; Prime Minister Mohamed Ghannouchi	dinar (1.42 = $1)	5,850	8,560
Uganda	23,199,000	President Yoweri Kaguta Museveni; Prime Minister Apollo Nsibambi	shilling (1,770.00 = $1)	516	1,341
Zambia	9,549,000	President Levy Mwanawasa	kwacha (3,650.00 = $1)	928	1,050
Zimbabwe	11,896,000	President Robert Mugabe	dollar (55.45 = $1)	1,800	1,300

Burundi's capital, with Buyoya, a Tutsi, as president, and Domitien Ndayizeye, a Hutu, as vice president. The two men were to switch roles at the end of 18 months, the halfway point in the administration.

Elsewhere in the region, a civil war that began in Angola in 1992 continued in 2001. Attacks between the soldiers of President Jose Eduardo dos Santos and rebel forces of Jonas Savimbi intensified throughout the year.

President Ange Patasse of the Central African Republic declared victory on June 3 over mutinous troops who tried to overthrow him on May 28. Dozens of people were killed in six days of fighting in the capital, Bangui.

Eastern Africa and the Horn. Clashes between security forces and opposition groups protesting alleged election fraud left scores of people dead and hundreds of others injured on the Tanzanian island of Zanzibar in late January. Western diplomats condemned the authorities' "excessive force" and threatened to withhold financial aid from Tanzania. The violence was the worst on record in Zanzibar since 1964 when 17,000 people died in clashes between Africans and Arabs.

On March 15, 2001, and again on September 15, the UN Security Council extended for six months a 4,200-strong UN peacekeeping mission to monitor a December 2000 peace agreement between Ethiopia and Eritrea. The pact ended a border conflict that broke out in May 1998. Fighting between Ethiopia and Eritrea left 100,000 people dead and caused massive economic damage to two of the world's poorest nations.

A referendum in May 2001 in the self-declared independent nation of Somaliland showed that 97 percent of voters supported the territory's secession in May 1991 from strife-ridden Somalia. However, Somaliland's leader, Muhammad Ibrahim Egal, failed again in 2001 to receive formal international recognition of his country's independence. Somaliland, a former British colony, had merged with Somalia, a former Italian colony, in 1960.

Southern Africa. In 2001, the political crisis in Zimbabwe threatened the security and economic well-being of all of southern Africa. In February 2000, President Robert Mugabe's ruling Zimbabwe African National Union-Patriotic Front (ZANU-PF) had launched a terror campaign to intimidate the mainly black opposition Movement for Democratic Change (MDC) and force white farmers off their land. That campaign intensified in 2001, resulting in dozens of deaths, hundreds of injuries, and major food shortages.

South Africa's President, Thabo Mbeki, faced several major challenges to his authority during 2001. In April, news sources announced that several top members of President Mbeki's party, the African National Congress (ANC), were under investigation in connection with an alleged conspiracy to topple, and perhaps kill Mbeki. The ANC is the ruling party in South Africa. The arrest of senior ANC official Tony Yengeni on corruption charges on October 3 plunged the party further into controversy.

In a blow to Zambia's reputation as one of Africa's more stable states, Paul Tembo, a former aide to President Frederick Chiluba, was murdered on July 6, in what opposition politicians called a political assassination. Tembo was slated to present evidence supporting allegations of corruption against President Chiluba. The killing followed months of turmoil sparked by Chiluba's unsuccessful campaign to strip the constitution of presidential term limits. On December 27, Chiluba's handpicked successor, Levy Mwanawasa, was elected president but with only 27 percent of the vote. He took office on January 2 in the face of widespread opposition and allegations of vote fraud.

Race summit. Thousands of delegates from 170 countries gathered at the UN World Conference Against Racism, held in Durban, South Africa, from Aug. 30, 2001, through September 8. What UN organizers had envisioned as a historic opportunity to forge a global antiracism alliance turned into a forum for argument and controversy. Arab and other Islamic countries condemned Israel as "a racist state" for its treatment of Palestinians. In response, the United States and Israel withdrew from the conference, protesting what they called a "campaign of hate" against Israel.

The conference also divided over the issue of the transatlantic slave trade from the 1500's to the mid-1800's. Many Africans and African Americans demanded an apology and financial reparations from Western nations. Conference officials eventually adopted a compromise declaration stating that the slave trade was a crime against humanity, but officials from European Union countries and the United States said that they could not be held responsible for actions of governments centuries ago.

Child exploitation. In April 2001, world media focused international attention on a "slave ship," the MV *Etireno*, believed to be carrying children into forced labor. On April 17, the vessel docked at Benin's main port, Cotonou, where authorities discovered dozens of migrant laborers, including 23 unaccompanied children who were taken into custody. The episode served to focus attention on the trafficking of children as young as 9 years old who were kidnapped or sold into slavery from countries such as Benin, Togo, and Mali. The UN Children's Fund (UNICEF) alleged in 2001 that there were 200,000 child slaves in western and central Africa, thousands of whom labored as "chocolate slaves" in Cote d'Ivoire, the world's top cocoa producer. Slavery is banned worldwide, but there have been many reports since the 1960's of child slavery in war-ravaged regions of Africa and other parts of the world.

On June 12, 2001, the Coalition to Stop the Use of Child Soldiers, an international alliance of peace and human rights organizations, released a report calling for a worldwide ban on the recruitment of child soldiers. According to the report, 500,000 or more soldiers between the ages of 7 and 18 were serving in various armed forces worldwide, and as many as 120,000 children were being used as soldiers in sub-Saharan Africa.

AIDS in Africa. UN Secretary-General Annan, speaking at the first African summit on AIDS in Nigeria's capital, Abuja, on April 26, proposed the creation of an annual global war chest of $7 billion to $10 billion to help fight against the AIDS epidemic in Africa. Annan also called on pharmaceutical companies to continue to cut the price of expensive drugs to combat AIDS on the African continent. In 2001, Africa was home to 75 percent of the world's 36 million people infected with the human immunodeficiency virus (HIV), which causes AIDS. Sixteen million of the more than 22 million people who died of AIDS between 1981 and 2001 were Africans.

Sports. On April 11, 43 spectators were crushed to death at a soccer match in Johannesburg, South Africa, when 15,000 fans surged into a stadium already packed with 60,000 people. On April 29, 10 people were killed when police used tear gas on bottle-throwing fans, unleashing panic at a soccer match in Lubumbashi, in southern Congo (Kinshasa).

Tragedy struck again at a soccer match in Ghana's capital, Accra, on May 9. Again, spectators fled from tear gas fired by police to quell a fight, setting off a stampede. At least 125 died in Africa's worst sporting disaster. In early May, clashes between soccer fans and police in Cote d'Ivoire left one person dead and 40 others injured. A spokesperson for Federation Internationale de Football Association announced in May that the string of tragedies would not eliminate Africa from the running to host the 2010 World Cup soccer championships.

At the World Track and Field Championships, held in August 2001 at Edmonton, Alberta, in Canada, African athletes from eight countries won 24 medals, 10 of them gold. In the grueling 10,000-meter women's race, Ethiopia's Derartu Tulu, Berhane Adere, and Gete Wami made a clean sweep of gold, silver, and bronze medals, rewriting the record books in the process.

☐ Simon Baynham

See also **AIDS; United Nations;** and the various African country articles.

Agriculture. The world's farmers harvested bumper crops for a sixth consecutive year in 2001. However, the size of crops masked fluctuations in individual countries. Livestock producers were less fortunate, battling an epidemic of foot-and-mouth disease (FMD) in the United Kingdom, Ireland, the Netherlands, and France. FMD is a highly contagious viral infection of cattle, sheep, hogs, and other animals with *cloven* (divided) hoofs.

World crop production. According to a U.S. Department of Agriculture (USDA) report released in December, the global harvest of small grains, which includes corn, rye, sorghum, barley, oats, and millet, totaled 873 million metric tons—2 percent more than in 2000. Larger crops in Ukraine and Eastern Europe offset falling corn production in Argentina and the European Union (EU).

Production of oilseeds—soybeans, sunflower seeds, cottonseed, and peanuts—hit a record high of 323 million metric tons in 2001, 6 percent above 2000. Larger soybean crops in the United States, Argentina, and Brazil offset smaller sunflower seed crops in Argentina and Turkey.

Cotton production in 2001 was up 8 percent at 96 million bales. (One bale is equivalent to 480 pounds [218 kilograms] of cotton.) The USDA attributed the increase to larger crops in the United States, China, Egypt, central Asia, and Turkey.

In 2001, the rice harvest was down 1 percent at 393 million metric tons. Bumper crops in India, Brazil, the Philippines, and South Korea were offset by reduced production in Italy, Bangladesh, Vietnam, and Japan. World wheat production totaled 577 million metric tons in November, 2 percent less than in 2000. Smaller wheat crops in Canada and the United States were offset by large harvests in Ukraine and Russia.

U.S. crop production. In 2001, U.S. farmers harvested 9.5 billion bushels of corn, 4 percent less than the 2000 harvest. The 2001 wheat harvest also declined, falling 12 percent from 2000. Production of soybeans, cotton, and rice rose in 2001.

Soybean production was up 6 percent, to 2.92 billion bushels. Cotton production hit a record high of 20.1 million bales, up 17 percent over 2000 production. The 2001 rice crop stood at 6.56 million metric tons, up 11 percent over 2000.

GM crops. U.S. farmers increased the number of acres of genetically modified (GM) crops in 2001. GM plants, also called transgenic crops, contain genes, often from other species that confer new traits on the crops, such as pest resistance and greater productivity. Acreage planted in GM soybeans increased from 54 percent in 2000 to 68 percent in 2001. GM corn acreage increased from 18 percent to 26 percent, while GM cotton rose from 61 percent to 69 percent in 2001.

Biotechnology. On October 16, the U.S. Environmental Protection Agency (EPA) approved the planting for several more years of GM corn containing a gene from the bacterium *Bacillus Thurigniensis* (BT), that enables the corn to resist the corn borer. The agency reported that GM corn poses no risk to humans or the environment.

In October, the European Commission issued a report concluding that GM foods do not "pose any new risks to human health or the environment." Despite the commission's ruling, the EU decided to label food and animal feed derived from GM crops and to create a system to trace the raw ingredients of food and feed products back to the manufacturer and the farm where it originated. In 2001, the EU refused to lift a ban that had been in place since 1998 on new varieties of GM crops.

In June 2001, China announced it would adopt new regulations governing imports of GM crops. The policy stalled Chinese imports of U.S. soybeans until October, when officials agreed to allow trade to continue until the regulations were in place.

In October, New Zealand lifted a ban on research and development of GM crops. The New Zealand government did, however, issue a two-year ban on the commercial release of any genetically engineered foods.

Crop uses. In August, textile manufacturers unveiled fabrics made of corn at the Outdoor Retailer Summer Market in Salt Lake City, Utah. The fabrics were made with corn polymers. A polymer is a large molecule formed by the chemical linking of many smaller molecules into a long chain. Manufacturers predicted that they would be using nearly 40,000 bushels of corn a day in 2002 to make polymers for furniture and fabric.

World Trade Organization. In November 2001, officials from the 142 member countries of the World Trade Organization (WTO) met in Doha, Qatar. The WTO arbitrates trade disputes among member countries. WTO members agreed to launch a new round of international trade negotiations aimed at reducing barriers to commerce among member nations. The United States sought to reduce agricultural export subsidies and tariffs imposed on imports of U.S. products.

Administration. On January 20, Ann M. Veneman was sworn in as the 27th secretary of agriculture and the first woman to hold the position. She had served as the deputy secretary of agriculture in the administration of President George H. W. Bush. Veneman also was secretary of the California Department of Food and Agriculture between 1995 and 1999.

Farm bill debate. On Aug. 13, 2001, President George W. Bush signed a bill providing $5.5 billion in direct payments to U.S. farmers. The need to provide additional assistance for the fourth year in a row, above funds already provided by 1996 legislation, renewed calls for a new law. The 1996 law enabled farmers to choose the crops they planted based on market trends, in return for direct government payments.

In December 2001, the U.S. Congress negotiated a farm bill that agriculture advocates hoped would incorporate the direct payments of the 1996 law with a new "income safety net." The new program would provide additional money for farmers who stressed conservation, promotion of wind energy and ethanol, and rural development.

Exports and food aid. In 2001, exports of U.S. agricultural products totaled $53 billion, an increase of $2.1 billion from 2000. The U.S. exported more than 110 million tons (100 million metric tons) of bulk commodities and high-value products, such as meat. Nearly 6.6 million tons (6 million metric tons) of the exports were aid to foreign countries. In 2001, the U.S. provided $184 million in food aid to Afghanistan.

Animal diseases and food safety. On February 20, the British government reported its first case of foot-and-mouth disease (FMD) since the 1980's. FMD turned up in France and the Netherlands in March 2001. To prevent the spread of the disease, more than 3.8 million cattle, sheep, and hogs were destroyed in Great Britain alone. FMD dealt an enormous economic blow to the British livestock industry in 2001, coming on the heels of its struggle in 2000 with outbreaks of mad cow disease, a fatal brain disease in cattle.

In early 2001, U.S. officials banned meat imports from EU countries affected by FMD to protect the U.S. livestock industry. The United States also increased monitoring of international travelers to prevent the inadvertent spread of FMD.

Concerns over FMD and possible *bioterrorism* (the use of biological or chemical agents to carry out terrorist attacks) in the wake of the September 11 terrorist attacks on the United States prompted the USDA to tighten security in food processing plants and on the farm. In 2001, the USDA spent nearly $80 million in emergency safety efforts.

On Sept. 10, 2001, the Japanese government announced that health officials had diagnosed Japan's first case of mad cow disease in a Tokyo suburb. As a result, October beef sales in Japan fell 20 percent, as many consumers turned to fish, chicken, and pork, to avoid beef. In December, Finland reported its first case of mad cow disease.

U.S. livestock producers were relieved in 2001 after a three-year study conducted by Harvard University found a "very low" risk of BSE occurring in the U.S. cattle herd. The November report found preventative actions—the 1989 ban on imports of live cattle, sheep, and goats from countries with BSE-infected herds and the 1997 ban on feeding animal byproducts to sheep and cattle—responsible for reducing the risk of BSE in the United States. ☐ Patricia Peak Klintberg

See also **Food; United Kingdom.**

AIDS. The year 2001 was the 20th anniversary of the first diagnosed case of acquired immune deficiency syndrome (AIDS). In May, the United States Centers for Disease Control and Prevention (CDC), a federal agency based in Atlanta, Georgia, announced that nearly 775,000 AIDS cases had been reported and almost 450,000 AIDS-related deaths had occurred in the United States between 1981 and 2000.

At an AIDS conference at the United Nations in June 2001, representatives of several nations called for a dramatic increase in AIDS spending in countries with low and middle incomes. Health organizations spent $1.8 billion on AIDS programs in poor countries in 2001. However, officials have estimated that poor nations needed $7 billion to $10 billion per year to fight AIDS.

Affordable AIDS drugs. Drugs to combat AIDS became available at low costs in poor countries in April when a group of pharmaceutical companies dropped a lawsuit against the South African government. South African legislators had passed a law in 1997 that allowed the importation and manufacture of cheap versions of AIDS drugs without the consent of companies that owned patents on the drugs. A group of 39 companies sued to protect their patents.

Almost 90 percent of people infected with HIV, the virus that causes AIDS, lived in developing countries in 2001. Most of those patients could not afford patented AIDS drugs, which cost $10,000 to $15,000 per person per year in the United States. After the companies dropped the lawsuit, South Africa and other developing nations were able to import AIDS drugs at a cost of about $200 per patient per year.

New statistics. Deaths from HIV infection dropped in the United States by approximately 4 percent in 1999 after declining by more than 70 percent between 1996 and 1998, CDC officials reported in June 2001. The slower rate of decline in 1999 raised the possibility that prevention programs and antiviral drugs might be losing effectiveness. CDC officials expressed concern that increasing numbers of young homosexual men, who are at high risk for HIV, were not taking precautions to prevent infection.

Prevention strategy. Antiviral drugs curb the high levels of HIV that appear in body fluids after infection, medical researchers at the University of North Carolina at Chapel Hill reported in May 2001. Individuals could slow the spread of HIV if they take antiviral drugs shortly after becoming infected, said the researchers.

☐ Michael Woods

Air pollution. See Environmental pollution.

Alabama. See State government.

Alaska. See State government.

Albania. The ruling Socialist Party won a majority in the Albanian parliament in elections in June and July 2001. The party, headed by Prime Minister Ilir Meta, captured 73 of 140 seats. The opposition Democratic Party, which took 46 seats, boycotted the new parliament after accusing the Socialists of rigging the vote. Delegates of the European Parliament (EP), the legislative body of the European Union, met with Albanian government officials on October 11 to receive a report on the post election controversy, which remained unresolved. The EP representatives expressed concern that political instability might threaten the economic gains made by Albania since 1999.

Officials at the Bank of Albania said they expected Albania to post a growth rate of 7.3 percent in 2001, compared with 7-percent growth in 2000. Unemployment, which stood at 16.6 percent in 2000, fell to 13.3 percent in July 2001. Inflation, however, climbed to 5.6 percent by July 2001, compared with 2.4 percent in 2000.

Albanian President Rexhep Meidani announced in March 2001 that Albania had no aspirations to increase its territory. The announcement came after fighting erupted in early 2001 in neighboring Macedonia between ethnic Albanian guerrillas and government troops.

☐ Sharon L. Wolchik

See also **Europe; Macedonia.**

Algeria. The worst civil unrest in Algeria since it gained independence in 1962 stunned the military-backed government of President Abdelaziz Bouteflika in 2001. The unrest overshadowed the government's war against Islamic militants, which claimed the lives of more than 100,000 Algerians between 1992 and 2001.

Berber riots. The death of a Berber teenager in police custody on April 18 triggered riots between Algerian Berbers and police that left at least 56 people dead and 2,300 others wounded. Berbers are an ethnic group of northwest Africa and the Sahara. Many live in the Kabylia region of northern Algeria.

On June 14, nearly 1 million Berbers and Arabs joined in a "march for democracy" in Algiers, the capital. They condemned the government for what they claimed was abuse of power and unjust economic policies. At least six people died in violent incidents during the march.

Berber concessions. Prime Minister Ali Benflis announced on October 4 that Algeria's constitution would be amended to include the Berber language as a national language. Previously, Arabic had been the only official language in Algeria. Benflis also said the government would investigate reports of excessive police force in Kabylia.

Islamic militancy. An upsurge in violence by Islamic extremists left more than 300 civilians dead in August and September. The violence included a series of attacks against young couples and the first bombing in Algiers in two years.

In late September, French authorities arrested at least 11 suspected Islamic militants. The authorities said some of the arrested men were part of a terrorist cell headed by Djamel Beghal, a French-Algerian who allegedly had planned to attack U.S. interests in France. Beghal was arrested in the United Arab Emirates in July and extradited to France on September 30.

In a November meeting with U.S. President George W. Bush in Washington, D.C., President Bouteflika affirmed his commitment to an international coalition against terrorism. The Bush administration formed the coalition in the wake of the September 11 terrorist attacks on the United States.

Flash foods caused mudslides that killed more than 700 people in Algiers in early November. Angry residents said the disaster was worsened by the government, which they accused of blocking drains to prevent Islamic militants from using them as hideouts. Officials in Algiers denied the charge. ☐ Christine Helms

See also **Africa; Middle East; Terrorism: A Special Feature,** p. 38.

Angola. See **Africa.**

Animal. See **Biology, Conservation, Zoos.**

Anthropology. In March 2001, paleoanthropologist Meave Leakey of the National Museums of Kenya announced the discovery of a 3.5-million-year-old skull from the western side of Lake Turkana in northern Kenya. Because the skull has a unique combination of structural features, Leakey classified it as not only a new species but also as a new *genus* (group of related species). She named it *Kenyanthropus platyops,* which means "flat-faced man of Kenya."

The skull has a small braincase similar to the braincase of *Australopithecus afarensis* (best known from a specimen called "Lucy"), a species that lived at the same time as *Kenyanthropus.* However, the *Kenyanthropus* specimen has a flatter face, smaller teeth, and a taller cheek region than *A. afarensis.* Anthropologists said these differences revealed that more than one line of *hominid* (human ancestors and their relatives) lived between 3 million and 4 million years ago. Anthropologists were not sure which line led to modern humans. The position of *K. platyops* on the human family tree, therefore, remained uncertain.

Insights into the human-chimp split. In July 2001, Yohannes Haile-Selassie, a paleoanthropology graduate student at the University of California at Berkeley, reported the discovery of 11 fossils of a possible human ancestor dating

The flat face, small teeth, and tall cheek region of a 3.5-million-year-old skull differentiates it from *Australopithecus afarensis,* a previously known *hominid* (human ancestor) species of the same era. Paleoanthropologist Meave Leakey announced her discovery of the new species, *Kenyanthropus platyops,* in March.

from between 5.8 million and 5.2 million years ago. The dates of the fossils were very close in time to when the evolutionary lines of humans and chimpanzees split, thought to be approximately 6 million years ago. Thus, the fossils were one of the earliest possible links to humans.

Haile-Selassie discovered the teeth, jaw, hand, arm, and foot fossils in five different locations in the Middle Awash region of central Ethiopia. He classified the fossils as *Ardipithecus ramidus kadabba,* a subspecies of *Ardipithecus ramidus*, a hominid previously known from 4.4-million-year-old remains discovered in Ethiopia in 1994.

The shape of a toe bone suggested that *A. ramidus kadabba,* which lived in a forested area, may have been capable of walking upright. However, anthropologists who believe that upright walking did not evolve until hominids moved to savannas said more evidence was needed to clarify how *A. ramidus kadabba* walked.

Oldest human ancestor? In February 2001, two researchers in France announced the discovery of several 6-million-year-old fossils that they claimed represented the oldest human ancestor. Geologist Martin Pickford of the Collegge de France and paleontologist Brigitte Senut of the National Museum of Natural History discovered 13 specimens of teeth, jaw bones, and leg bones in the Tugen Hills of central Kenya. The scientists classified their find as *Orrorin tugenensis.*

The *O. tugenensis* fossils show a unique mixture of apelike and humanlike features. The teeth, especially the long canines, are apelike. However, the structure of the leg bones indicated to the French researchers that these creatures walked upright like hominids. Although the researchers believed that *O. tugenensis* was a human ancestor, many anthropologists said the fossils were too fragmentary for scientists to reach this conclusion.

Neanderthal hands and tools. Neanderthals were not capable of making the range of finger movements that modern humans are capable of making, anthropologist Wesley A. Niewoehner of the University of New Mexico in Albuquerque reported in February. This finding implied that Neanderthal tool use was limited.

Neanderthals were a type of human who lived from approximately 130,000 to 30,000 years ago. Modern humans also lived during this time. Both types of humans made stone tools that appear to be virtually identical. However, after comparing hand bones of Neanderthals with hand bones of modern humans, Niewoehner concluded that modern human hands were capable of a more precise manipulation of tools. He said this ability allowed humans to eventually develop more sophisticated tools. ☐ Donald C. Johanson

See also **Archaeology.**

Archaeology.

"Otzi the Iceman," whose 5,300-year-old frozen body was found in the Otztaler Alps on the Austria-Italy border in 1991, was killed by an arrow, according to a July 2001 announcement by scientists at Italy's South Tyrol Museum of Archaeology. Scholars had previously suspected that the man froze to death during a heavy snowstorm.

Archaeologists at the museum discovered an arrowhead buried in Otzi's left shoulder when they examined his body with both conventional X rays and *computed tomography* (an X-ray system used to produce cross-sectional images). The scientists said the arrowhead, which is 0.83 inch (2.1 centimeters) long, passed through the left shoulder blade, cutting blood vessels and nerves. Otzi probably bled to death.

Ancient shipwreck. Explorers searching for an Israeli submarine that sank in the eastern Mediterranean Sea in 1968 discovered a Greek shipwreck from the 200's B.C. Researchers from Nauticos Corporation, an ocean-exploration company in Hanover, Maryland, announced the discovery of the ship in March 2001.

Archaeologists working with Nauticos detected the ancient ship with a remotely operated camera, which produced images of the ship's lead anchors and cargo. The cargo consisted of some 2,500 *amphorae,* pottery vessels used to hold wine or other liquids. The ship rested on the seafloor nearly 10,000 feet (3,048 meters) below the surface, making it the deepest ancient shipwreck ever discovered. The ship's location, between the important ancient trading centers of Alexandria, Egypt, and the island of Rhodes, suggested to the archaeologists that ancient mariners crossed long distances of open water. This contradicted previous beliefs that ancient ships sailed primarily along the relative safety of coastlines.

Cussac cave. French archaeologists announced in July 2001 the discovery of a cave in the Cussac region of southern France that is decorated with more than 200 prehistoric engravings of horses, bison, mammoths, deer, people, and other figures. The engravings were deeply carved with sharp flint chisels. The style of the figures, as well as stone tools recovered from an excavation near the cave, suggested to archaeologists at the French Ministry of Culture that the art gallery is 28,000 to 22,000 years old. The archaeologists said the large size of the figures—some as long as 13 feet (4 meters)—and the depiction of birds and women in silhouette make the cave's engravings highly unusual compared with previously discovered cave art.

An amateur explorer discovered the engravings in September 2000 after widening a crevice that led deep into the cave. The archaeologists, during their later exploration of the site, found the remains of several people who had been laid to rest on the cave floor. The scientists hoped further study would enable them to determine if the human remains are from the same period as the engravings.

Grave of Genghis Khan? In August 2001, archaeologists with an American-Mongolian expedition searching for the tomb of the Mongol conqueror Genghis Khan announced that they had discovered a walled burial ground 200 miles (322 kilometers) northeast of Ulan Bator, Mongolia. The site is near where historians believe Genghis Khan was born in 1162. At the time of his death in 1227, Genghis Khan had conquered and controlled an empire that stretched from present-day Beijing in China to the Caspian Sea in western Asia.

Archaeologists, led by historian John Woods of the University of Chicago, discovered a stone wall that is 2 miles (3.2 kilometers) long and up to 12 feet (3.6 meters) high. The wall surrounds a site containing two levels of tombs. In the upper level, the team found at least 20 unopened tombs, perhaps of high-status individuals. Forty more unopened tombs were found in the lower area.

Historians have long sought to locate the tomb of Genghis Khan, who they believe was buried with a treasure trove of silver and gold. Woods called the find "exciting" but said his team did not know if the site contained the tomb of the great conqueror. The expedition hoped to return to the site in 2002 to begin excavations.

***Hunley* discoveries.** Officials at the Washington, D.C.-based Naval Historical Center began exploring the inside of the Confederate submarine *H.L. Hunley* in February 2001. The *Hunley,* which sank in 1864 after sinking the U.S.S. *Housatonic* during the U.S. Civil War (1861-1865), was raised from the Atlantic Ocean off the coast of Charleston, South Carolina, in August 2000.

The archaeologists discovered partial remains of all nine crewmembers along with a number of artifacts, including pencils, pocketknives, and clothing. They also found a gold coin that the *Hunley's* captain, George E. Dixon, carried for good luck. As an infantry officer at the Battle of Shiloh in 1862, Dixon's life had been saved when the coin stopped a bullet. The coin, a gift from Dixon's fiancee, was inscribed, "My Life Preserver." The archaeologists also found a dog tag with the name of Union soldier Ezra Chamberlin around the neck of one of the crew. The researchers suspected that the Union tag was a souvenir kept by the Confederate crewmember, who served in an artillery unit in the 1863 battle in which Chamberlin was killed. ☐ Mark Rose

See also **Anthropology**.

A French underwater archaeologist (above) examines a statue of Hapi, the ancient Egyptian god of flooding, in May 2001. Divers discovered the statue next to the sunken ruins of a large temple.

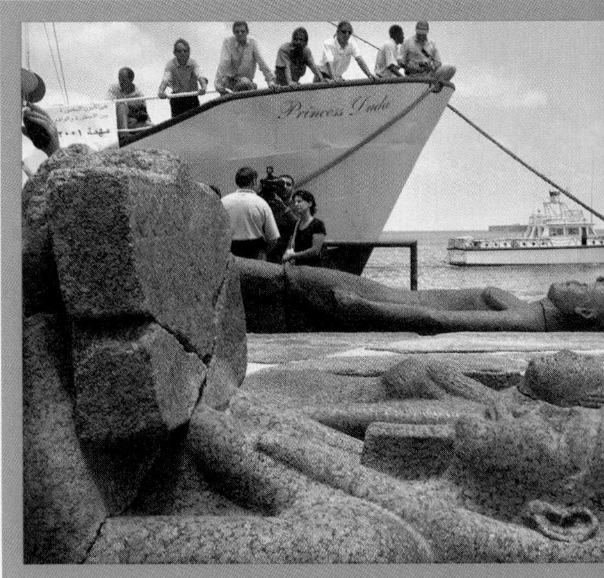

FOCUS ON

Archaeologists in 2001 explored the wonders of the ancient Egyptian port city of Herakleion, which sank into the Mediterranean Sea after an earthquake 1,200 years ago.

An archaeologist (above) inspects hieroglyphics carved on a *stele*, an upright slab bearing an inscription, submerged off the Egyptian coast near Alexandria. Later in 2001, scientists dated the stele to 380 B.C.

Three huge statues (left) lie on a ship's deck anchored off Alexandria, Egypt, in June 2001, French archaeologists, led by Franck Goddio, raised them from the Mediterranean Sea.

Architecture. The biggest architecture story of 2001 was the destruction of the World Trade Center towers in New York City by terrorists. Both of the 110-story skyscrapers, which were completed in 1972, collapsed on Sept. 11, 2001, after two hijacked airliners crashed into their upper floors and exploded like bombs. Fires fed by thousands of gallons of jet fuel caused the steel frames of the buildings to bend. This, in turn, caused the external walls to buckle, leading to the floor-by-floor collapse of the structures. In less than two hours, both buildings had been reduced to enormous piles of smoking rubble. The 102-story Empire State Building, completed in 1931, was once again New York City's tallest building.

The collapse of the two structures provoked profound soul-searching among architects over nearly every aspect of skyscraper design, from structural technology to building security. Some architects expressed doubts about the wisdom of continuing to design such tall buildings. However, at a symposium at the National Building Museum in New York City in November 2001, an architectural panel agreed that skyscrapers were here to stay.

Milwaukee Art Museum. The expanded Milwaukee Art Museum, by Spanish architect and engineer Santiago Calatrava, opened in October 2001. The centerpiece of the museum is a soaring glass pavilion featuring a curved, steel *brise soleil* (architectural sunshade) that opens and closes like a pair of butterfly wings to regulate temperature and light. From certain angles, the lakefront museum resembles a docked ocean liner with a bold *prow* (front part of ship), long vaulted galleries to port and starboard, and a cabled footbridge linking the building to downtown Milwaukee.

The Pulitzer Foundation for the Arts opened its new museum and study center in St. Louis, Missouri, in October. The center features public galleries containing paintings and sculptures collected by the late publisher Joseph Pulitzer, Jr., and his wife, Emily. Designed by Japanese architect Tadao Ando, the building has a stark concrete exterior with two long, narrow wings framing a shallow reflecting pool. The pool casts dramatic light and shadow patterns throughout the building.

The American Folk Art Museum, which had occupied several temporary locations in New York City since its founding in 1961, finally opened a permanent home in December 2001. The Manhattan museum, designed by the New York firm of Tod Williams Billie Tsien and Associates is a nearly windowless tower covered in white bronze panels. The roof of the eight-story building has a large glass skylight that sends daylight cascading into staircases, lobbies, and galleries. The structure was the first new art museum in New York City since 1966.

The Kimmel Center for the Performing Arts, designed by Uruguay-born architect Rafael Vinoly, opened in Philadelphia in December 2001. The center, home of the Philadelphia Orchestra and seven other arts institutions, contains the 2,500-seat Verizon Hall and the 650-seat Perelman Theater. A vaulted glass roof and a lush interior garden connect the hall and theater. The $265-million structure was one of several major performing arts centers under construction in 2001 in U.S. cities.

Friends meeting house. In January, the Religious Society of Friends, or Quakers, opened the Live Oak Friends Meeting House in Houston. Designed by Leslie Elkins Architects of Houston, the

Santiago Calatrava's expanded Milwaukee Art Museum in Wisconsin features a huge *brise soleil* (architectural sunshade) that opens and closes like the wings of a butterfly to regulate temperature and light. The museum opened in October.

meeting house resembles a simple Texas ranch building with concrete walls and a broad overhanging roof. Inside the structure, however, is a "skyspace" designed by Arizona light artist James Turrell, himself a Quaker. It features a 12-foot- (3.6-meter-) wide square opening in the ceiling that draws the eye up from the simple meeting room toward the heavens.

Retrospectives. In May, the Guggenheim Museum in New York City opened a retrospective on the work of Frank Gehry, the renowned California-based architect known for pushing the limits of architectural design with buildings of swirling organic form. The show included models, drawings, and photographs of Gehry's work.

Two exhibitions in New York City in 2001 focused on Ludwig Mies van der Rohe, one of the major figures of the "less-is-more" modernism movement of the 20th century. "Mies in Berlin," at the Whitney Museum of American Art, presented the architect's designs in Germany from 1905 until his immigration to the United States in 1938. "Mies in America," at the Museum of Modern Art, concentrated on his later work, including the famous Seagram Building in Manhattan.

Awards. The 2001 Gold Medal of the American Institute of Architects was awarded to architect Michael Graves of Princeton, New Jersey. His Portland Municipal Building in Oregon became an icon of postmodernism in the early 1980's.

The 2001 Pritzker Prize, considered the most prestigious award in architecture, went to partners Jacques Herzog and Pierre de Meuron of Switzerland. Their projects, such as the Tate Museum Gallery of Modern Art in London, refined the traditions of modernism to elemental simplicity while experimenting with new materials and unusual textures. ☐ David Dillon

See also **Building and construction; Terrorism: A Special Feature,** p. 38.

FRANK LLOYD WRIGHT'S PRAIRIE HOUSE: BIRTH OF THE MODERN AMERICAN HOUSE

BY SCOTT THOMAS

The year 2001 was the 100th anniversary of a revolutionary development in American architecture—the birth of Frank Lloyd Wright's prairie house. In February 1901, the Curtis Publishing Company of Philadelphia published a set of house plans specifically commissioned for its widely read magazine, *The Ladies' Home Journal*. The article, "A Home in a Prairie Town," included exterior and interior drawings, floor plans, and the architect's description of a house that was radical in appearance and layout.

The exterior of the house was dominated by a long, low roof, unlike the high peaked roofs of the Victorian houses then popular. The prairie house sat low to the ground on a slab, rather than up on a basement, and the front door opened at ground level, rather than at the top of a flight of stairs.

Inside, the public rooms formed a single, open space that was irregular in shape. The typical house of 1900 was divided into separate rooms with highly defined functions, such as

The Curtis Publishing Company of Philadelphia unveiled the first prairie house (above) in the February 1901 issue of *The Ladies' Home Journal.* The self-portrait of Frank Lloyd Wright (at far left) was made during the prairie house period (1901-1909).

front parlors for company and back parlors for family. In the prairie house, as it came to be called, there were no special rooms for company and no doors to keep family spaces out of sight.

While the prairie house was radical, it was also old-fashioned, with details reminiscent of houses in colonial New England. Like colonial houses, the main chimney, around which all members of the family met, was located at the center of the house to conserve heat. The walls, woodwork, and furniture were simple and straightforward. Nothing was made to look like something it was not. The plaster was left uncovered. Woodwork was plain and without decoration. Even the windows in the prairie house—casements made up of small panes of diamond-shaped glass leaded together—harkened back to the windows in New England colonial houses.

FRANK LLOYD WRIGHT'S PRAIRIE HOUSES, WHICH BURST ON THE AMERICAN SCENE 100 YEARS AGO, CHANGED HOW AMERICANS LIVE.

Reaction to the Industrial Revolution

The prairie house was part of two distinct, but related movements—the Arts and Crafts Movement and the Progressive Era—that helped shape the United States at the turn of the last century.

William Morris, an English architectural critic and designer, launched the Arts and Crafts Movement in Great Britain in the mid-1800's in response to the poor artistic quality of the machine-made products of the Industrial Revolution. (The Industrial Revolution during the 1800's was the change from an agrarian to an industrial society, when the manufacture of products moved from being home-based to factory-based.) Morris wanted to replace the mass-produced objects of his time with the beauty and individuality that he found in the art and handmade crafts of medieval Europe. Morris founded a company that produced furniture, wallpaper, stained glass, tapestries, and other decorative articles for the home. His writings and example encouraged a new artistic freedom and spirit of experimentation that flowered in Europe and in the United States from the 1890's until the outbreak of World War I. In the United States, the movement included a variety of architects, designers, and artists: Frank Lloyd Wright and the other architects identified with the Prairie School of Architecture; the brothers Charles and Henry Greene whose California houses helped launch the popularity of the *bungalow* (a generally small, story-and-a-half house popular between 1900 and 1930); furniture makers Gustav Stickley and his brothers, who popularized a style that came to be called "mission"; and hundreds of artists and craftspersons whose paintings, pottery, and metal work enjoyed a wide audience among the American middle class.

The Progressive Era in America

The Progressive Era was a political movement that was an outgrowth of the Industrial Revolution. Between 1840 and 1900, the United States changed from an agrarian nation to the largest industrial country in the world. Rapid industrialization produced enormous social change. American cities exploded in size. Chicago, for example, grew from 4,000 people in 1837 to 300,000 people in 1870 to more than 1.6 million people in 1900. Such explosive growth bred crime and social unrest. The power of big business, corruption in government, violent strikes, and the rise of socialism seemed to threaten democracy. Rapid industrialization also produced extremes of poverty and wealth. The owners of the fortunes of the era—families such as the Vanderbilts—often imitated the lifestyle and manners of European royalty and built summer palaces for themselves in Newport, Rhode Island, and other resorts on the East Coast. Such "conspicuous consumption," a term coined in that period, in the face of widespread poverty troubled many Americans. They questioned the justice of a society that tolerated such extremes. Many people demanded reform. The political response to these demands by such leaders as Presidents Theodore Roosevelt and Woodrow Wilson defined the Progressive Era.

The prairie house was part of this reform movement. Designed to foster an "old-fashioned," family-oriented lifestyle, the house offered an alternative to the conspicuous consumption of the period. It also provided a sense of individuality in the face of a government and economy that many people of the era believed was under the control of those "unseen forces" that Theodore Roosevelt characterized as "malefactors of great wealth." Wright's clients, for the most part, understood this. To commission and live in a house by Frank Lloyd Wright was a public statement, both artistic and political.

The author, Scott Thomas, is the managing editor of *The Year Book.*

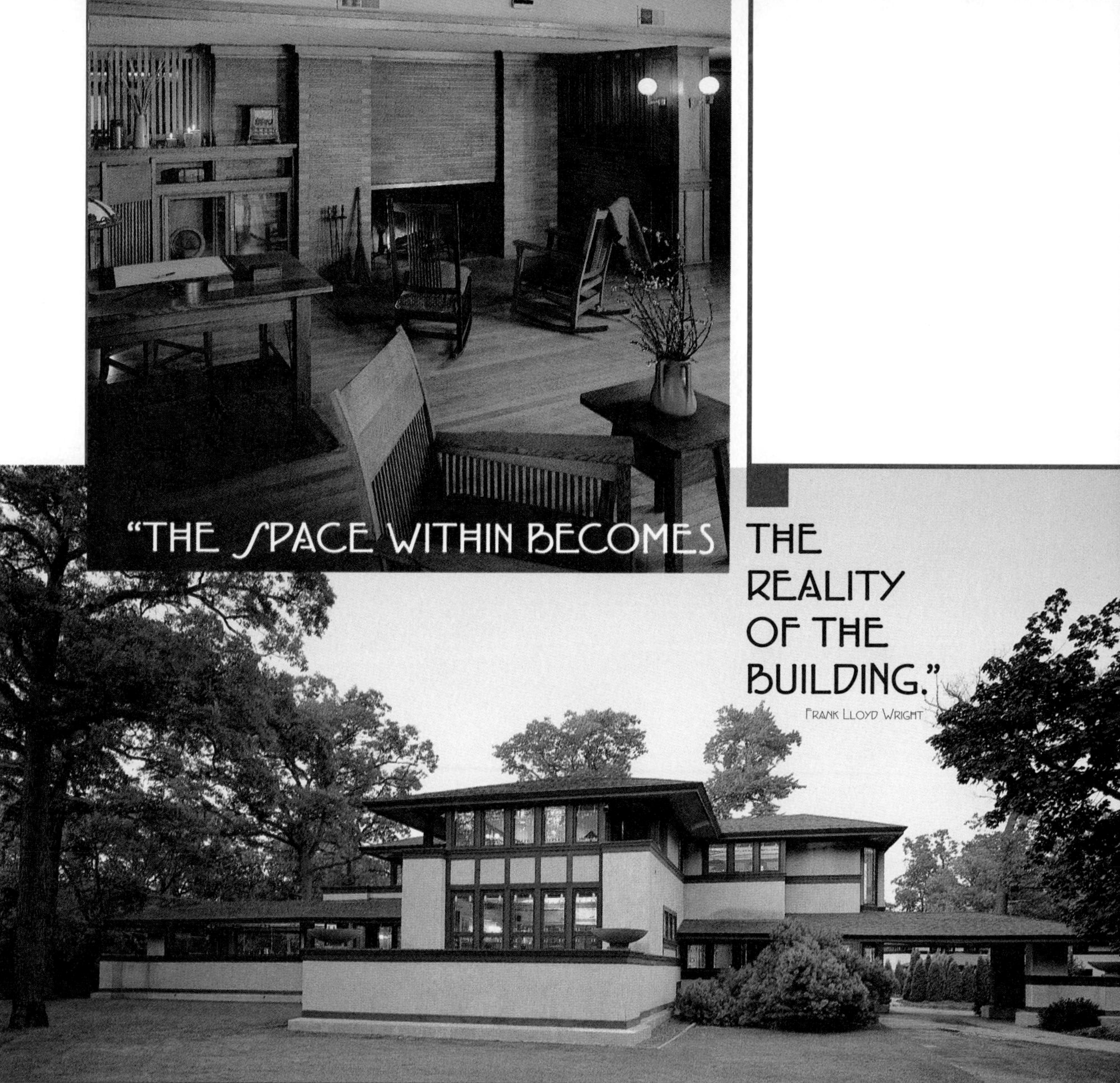

"THE SPACE WITHIN BECOMES THE REALITY OF THE BUILDING."
FRANK LLOYD WRIGHT

Wright's early life

Frank Lloyd Wright was born in 1867, a time when the Industrial Revolution in America was just beginning and the United States was still largely rural. His father, William C. Wright, was an itinerant preacher and musician who never had much success earning a living, and Wright's childhood was largely rootless. The elder Wright moved his family from Wisconsin to Iowa; on to Rhode Island and Massachusetts; and back to Wisconsin. Stability in the family came from Wright's mother, Anna Lloyd-Jones Wright, and from her family. The Lloyd-Joneses were successful farmers who owned much of the Wyoming Valley outside Spring Green, Wisconsin. Young Wright spent his summers in the valley, working on his uncles' farms. The fiercely independent Lloyd-Jones family

The 1901 Ward Willits House in Highland Park, Ill. (above), exemplifies the prairie house style. The tension between horizontal and vertical elements lends energy and movement to the exterior. Interiors (top) flow around a central fireplace that provides warmth and a sense of shelter. Wright designed all aspects of the house, including the furniture.

The Frederick Robie House, completed in Chicago in 1909, is one of the undisputed masterpieces of Wright's prairie period and among the most influential buildings of the 20th century. Neighbors compared the horizontal exterior with an ocean liner straining to take off.

instilled in Wright the importance of hard work and self-reliance; an appreciation of a close-knit family life; and a reverence for the land and nature. (Wright later returned to the valley to build a country estate, Taliesan.)

In 1885, William Wright abandoned his family, and Frank, who never saw his father again, dropped out of school to support his mother and two sisters. The following year, he returned to school as a part-time civil engineering student at the University of Wisconsin in Madison.

Wright moves to Chicago

Wright left school in 1887 and moved to Chicago, which did not impress the young man. Wright was horrified by the squalor and disorder of industrial America and by urban life in general, which he saw as driven primarily by greed. Wright initially found a job in the office of architect J. L. Silsbee. Before the end of the year, he landed a job as a draftsman in the offices of Dankmar Adler and Louis Sullivan. The firm of Adler & Sullivan had just been chosen to design the Chicago Auditorium, an opera house, hotel, and office block within a single structure. The job was stupendous, and Wright proved highly valuable to Sullivan, the chief designer. Sullivan named

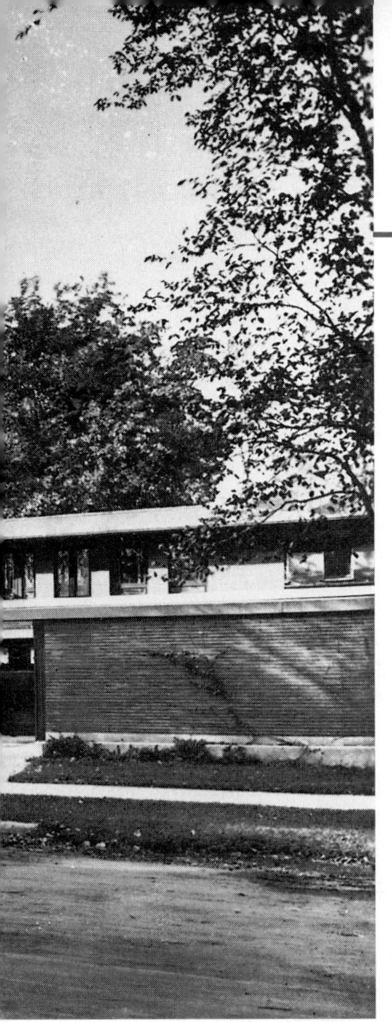

"WITHOUT AN ARCHITUCTURE OF OUR OWN WE HAVE NO SOUL OF OUR OWN CIVILIZATION."

FRANK LLOYD WRIGHT

Frank Lloyd Wright, as he then began calling himself, chief assistant architect on the largest structure ever built in the United States up to that time. Wright was 21 years old.

In June 1889, Wright married Catherine Tobin. The couple, who would have six children, purchased land in the Chicago suburb of Oak Park, Illinois, where Wright built a house of his own design.

Wright borrowed the money for the house from Sullivan. Throughout his life, Wright acknowledged Sullivan's influence and referred to the older man as "Lieber Meister" or "beloved teacher." Wright spent many late nights at the office listening to Sullivan's theories, including America's need for a new architecture that befitted a democratic nation.

Wright's apprenticeship as an architect

As chief assistant, Wright was expected to take on any commissions for houses that came into the firm and to complete them on his own time. Sullivan, who specialized in skyscrapers and other large commercial structures, had little interest in or aptitude for designing houses. This provided Wright with an opportunity to develop a style independent of Sullivan's. Eventually, clients bypassed Sullivan and went directly to Wright. Although under exclusive contract, Wright—an extravagant man who was always short of money—began "moonlighting." In 1893, Sullivan happened on one of these "bootlegged" houses, as Wright came to call them, and immediately recognized the hand of his assistant. A terrible row ensued, and Wright walked out on Sullivan to establish his own practice.

The prairie house exterior

At the time of the publication of "A Home in a Prairie Town," Wright had a number of such dwellings on the drawing boards. One—the Ward Willits House, completed in 1901 in the Chicago suburb of Highland Park, Illinois—would prove to be what many critics consider the first masterpiece of Wright's prairie period.

The Willits House offers a synthesis of all the components associated with the prairie house. The exterior is relentlessly horizontal, which makes the two-story house appear to hug the ground. Its walls rise from a concrete slab, which Wright called a "water table." Gently sloping hip roofs with broad, overhanging eaves shelter the main structure and porches. The roofs are cantilevered well beyond the understructure, giving the house a sense of dynamic movement. (A cantilever is a structure supported at one end by a downward force; the other end projects into space without support.) Vertical elements—the low, broad chimney stack and a series of dark, vertical wooden bands running between lower and upper windows—break the horizontal lines and seem to root the house to the ground. Critics point out that the contrast between the horizontal and vertical in Wright's prairie houses create a tension that suggests energy under constraint. Ordinary people simply liken the houses to ships or airplanes straining to take off.

The prairie house interior

According to Wright, the reality of a building is not the exterior, but the space within. Getting in, however, is never a straightforward journey. Passage into the Willits House involves climbing two short flights of stairs and making five 90-degree turns. The destination is the living room fireplace, a broad open hearth in a cavelike alcove that anchors the center of the house.

The reception, living, and dining rooms in the Willits House make up a single, flowing space. Wright described this feature as "breaking out of the box." Architects now call it the open floor plan. Space is defined not by walls into which doorways are cut, but by free-standing *piers* (large, solid supports that bear pressure from above), fireplaces, and built-in furniture. The space is informal. With the exception of the built-ins, the furniture was designed to be rearranged to suit the all-purpose nature of the space. Near the ceiling, bands of wood carry the eye to French doors that lead to a terrace from which the outside world can be viewed from a sheltered, secure vantage point. Atop the terrace walls, oversized urns raise the level of the garden to the level of the first floor, bringing nature inside.

The Ward Willits dining room is as formal as the living room is informal. A massive table and sideboard are highly architectural and echo the exterior of the house. The dining chairs are straight with high backs so severe that critics complain that prairie house dining room ensembles are better suited to a monastery than a home. Social historians respond that this formality reflected the formality of upper middle-class life in the period before World War I (1914-1918). At the time, socializing revolved around highly ritualized dinners, making the dining room the central space of a house. Architects argue that these chairs provided Wright with yet another way to define space. Their high backs create a "wall" or room within a room that provides diners with a sense of intimacy and enclosure.

In the Willits House, space flows vertically as well as horizontally. From the entrance with its reception area, visitors climb to the living and dining spaces; up a second half flight to an area devoted to books and reading; and finally up to the second-floor bedrooms. In most prairie houses, bedrooms are not particularly large. Typically, there are built-in cabinets and good-sized closets, amenities that were atypical at the time. More often than not, master bedrooms have fireplaces.

Integral ornament

Frank Lloyd Wright preached that ornament should be "integral," meaning that it should be an outgrowth of the plan, rather than something foreign plastered on. In the prairie houses, the bands of leaded windows are the single most

Mr. and Mrs. Avery Coonley pose with their daughter before their prairie house (below) soon after the Coonley estate was completed in Riverside, Illinois, in 1909. The repose of the garden facade contrasts sharply with the dynamic exterior of Wright's city houses, like Robie, which were designed to fit into an urban street grid. Wright considered Coonley his best work of the period.

"STUDY NATURE, LOVE NATURE,
STAY CLOSE TO NATURE.
IT WILL NEVER FAIL YOU."
FRANK LLOYD WRIGHT

decorative feature, inside and out. The windows typically are made of hundreds of pieces of clear and colored glass leaded into intricate patterns. Wright often created dozens of unique window patterns for each prairie house. In the early houses, he based window designs on natural plant forms, such as sumac and wisteria. Over time, his patterns grew more abstract as he began extracting designs from the geometry of the house.

Shadows cast by long, overhanging eaves cool the1908 Meyer May House (top) in Grand Rapids, Michigan, in summer and protect its walls from harsh weather in winter. On the interior of the May House (above), Wright "breaks out of the box" by dissolving corners with bands of windows and skylights that bring the outside in.

Light provided another important element of Wright's "integral" decoration. Because two pieces of glass cannot be leaded together evenly, each reflects light at a slightly different angle. Sunlight sparkles off the hundreds of pieces of glass that made up a single window as it does off water. In daylight, the sparkle enlivens the exterior and blocks passers-by from seeing in. On the interior, squares of light, colored by the window glass, dance across rooms, creating more "integral" decoration.

The Wright scale

The prairie house style proved highly adaptable, and in the first decade of the 1900's Wright built more than 100 houses. They ranged in size from inexpensive stucco and wood-trimmed "cottages" to luxurious country estates. Regardless of size, all of Wright's buildings share a unique characteristic, their scale.

In architecture, scale refers to the relationships between the size of a building, its interior and furnishings, and the size of the people who use it. Wright based the scale of his houses on the human figure, usually his own. He was 5 feet, 8.5 inches (1.5 meters) tall. Every aspect of his building—from the heights of ceilings, to the distance between walls and size of the furniture—was based on a single, predetermined scale. The result is a structure perfectly suited to the human figure, if that figure is average in size. People who are short or of medium height tend to find the scale of Wright's prairie houses aesthetically pleasing and psychologically reassuring. Tall people often find the scale oppressive, particularly when the ceilings are just over their heads. Wright admitted that if he had been a taller man, the scale of his houses might have been different.

Wright's application of human scale to large buildings produces interesting effects. His *masonry* (brick and stone) prairie houses, which rest on substantial concrete pads and are trimmed with heavy stone

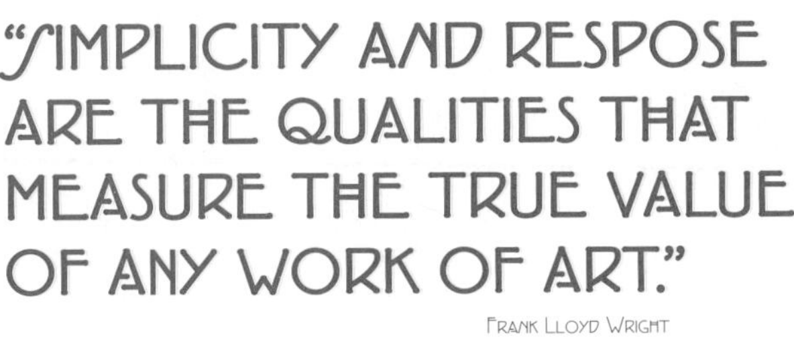

"SIMPLICITY AND RESPOSE ARE THE QUALITIES THAT MEASURE THE TRUE VALUE OF ANY WORK OF ART."
FRANK LLOYD WRIGHT

Wright's bands of windows, such as in the Meyer May House (below), bring light into the interior and help cool the house through sultry Midwestern summers. The hundreds of pieces of glass (insert) leaded into unique patterns provide privacy and what Wright called "integral ornament."

"THE ROOM WITHIN IS THE GREAT FACT ABOUT THE BUILDING."

FRANK LLOYD WRIGHT

copings and sills, are monumental yet playful. The effect on visitors is rather like what a child feels upon entering an elaborate playhouse—enchantment. This quality is particularly evident in such residences as the Dana House (1902) in Springfield, Illinois, and the Robie House (1909) in Chicago.

The close of Wright's prairie house period

For Frank Lloyd Wright, the era of the prairie house came to an abrupt end in 1909. In that year, he abandoned his wife and family, like his father before him. He left Chicago and sailed for Europe. Already one of the most famous architects in the country, Wright was recognized by a reporter, who realized that the architect was traveling with a woman other than his wife. Details were published on the front pages of newspapers across the country. The after effects were disastrous for a man who had portrayed himself as a reformer whose work embodied the "family values" of the day. His career, while not destroyed, was severely compromised.

His ambition had been nothing less than to create a new architecture that reflected the spirit of the country and its democratic system. In some ways, he succeeded. While he would never convince Americans to relinquish their fondness for picturesque buildings based on European styles, he did change how they lived.

The prairie house changes how Americans live

Wright's open floor plan provided the basis for how most subsequent houses in the United States were laid out. The public rooms of nearly all bungalows are single, open spaces defined not by walls, but by such architectural elements as shoulder-high, built-in bookcases and cabinets. In the 1920's, architects, scrambling for ways to express a new, less formal lifestyle, turned to Wright for inspiration. While they ignored his scale and the style of his work, they appropriated the open floor plan. Soon, city apartments and suburban houses with Tudor or Georgian facades had interiors that flowed.

During the Great Depression (the worldwide business slump of the 1930's), Wright adopted the prairie house to changing economic times. The result was an inexpensive house designed to be run without servants. The Usonian, as he called it, is one story in height and has a "car port," rather than garage. Inside, the dining table has moved into the living area and the kitchen hides behind the living room fireplace. After World War II (1939-1945), the Usonian House provided architects with the basic elements of the Ranch House, which filled suburban subdivisions from Long Island in New York state to the San Fernando Valley in California.

The open floor plan showed up again in the 1980's and 1990's in the "great room," an indefinable space that incorporates living, dining, and cooking spaces. Ironically, these great rooms were often attached to the kind of unused ceremonial living and dining rooms that Wright tried to banish.

In the 100 years since the publication of "A Home in a Prairie Town," the scope of Wright's accomplishment has become even more apparent. Nearly all architects acknowledge his enormous influence and credit Wright and Sullivan as founders of modern architecture. Most critics acknowledge Wright's importance as an artist of a stature equal to any American artist. And many people acknowledge Wright as a source of inspiration and direction in yet another period of enormous social change. Time has allowed Wright to regain his place as a reformer, a radical in defense of what he called the "cause conservative," the individual and family in America. ■■■

Wright's prairie house dining rooms, such as in the Meyer May House (left), were formal, ceremonial spaces designed to lend a sense of occasion to family meals and formal entertaining. Wright's high-back dining chairs create "a room within a room" that provides diners with a sense of intimacy. To create harmonious interior spaces, the architect oversaw every element, down to floor rugs and table runners.

Argentina was thrown into political chaos following the Dec. 20, 2001, resignation of President Fernando de la Rua, who was forced out of office by violent protests over his failure to end nearly four years of recession. The opposition Peronist Party struggled to form a stable government as the year drew to a close.

Austerity measures. On March 29, 2001, the Argentine Congress had approved the requests of Economy Minister Domingo Cavallo for emergency financial powers. The powers enabled Cavallo to raise tariffs on imported consumer goods to protect Argentine industries and lower tariffs on capital goods to encourage investment. Cavallo also eliminated many government regulations on businesses and cracked down on tax evasion. In July, Cavallo announced increases in taxes and decreases of up to 13 percent in government salaries and pensions. He said the added revenue and savings would help cut $1.5 billion in projected fiscal deficits.

Growing protests. On July 14, employees of a bankrupt airline pelted Cavallo and his daughter with eggs outside a church in Buenos Aires, the capital, where she was about to be married. The incident marked the beginning of a series of nationwide protests by unemployed workers and others opposed to austerity measures.

Conditions worsen. The International Monetary Fund (IMF), a United Nations-affiliated organization that assists nations in financial difficulties, announced in August that it would provide up to $8 billion in emergency aid to stabilize the Argentine economy. However, much of the aid was contingent upon Argentina reducing its $132-billion public debt.

Despite the financial assistance, economic conditions worsened in Argentina and spread to neighboring countries, especially Brazil. Between July and November 2001, the value of stocks listed on the Merval index, Argentina's main stock index, declined by about 44 percent. Foreign investment declined by 45 percent between January and September, as unemployment approached 20 percent. In November, the economy ministry projected a 2001 fiscal deficit of more than $7 billion.

Debt deal. Cavallo announced a plan in November to reduce Argentina's debt burden. He said the government would seek to restructure much of the public debt, offering investors new government bonds at lower interest rates. The central government also reached an agreement with governors to cut federal payments to their provinces to help bring the debt under control.

Amid growing fears that Argentina might be forced to default on its international debts or devalue its currency, Cavallo sought in December to demonstrate to the IMF that he could trim another 10 percent from Argentina's 2002 budget.

Crisis climax. Riots prompted by austerity measures unveiled in mid-December 2001 resulted in the deaths of more than 25 people and the resignations of both Cavallo and de la Rua. On December 23, Interim President Adolfo Rodriguez Saa announced a suspension of payments of the public debt and other emergency measures. After further unrest, Saa announced his resignation on December 30. On Jan. 1, 2002, Congress selected Senator Eduardo Duhalde to fill out de la Rua's term, scheduled to end in December 2003.

Former leaders indicted. On July 4, 2001, an Argentine court indicted former President Carlos Saul Menem on charges of conspiracy to smuggle 6,500 tons (5,900 metric tons) of weapons to Ecuador and Croatia between 1991 and 1995. On July 10, 2001, General Jorge Rafael Videla, who led a military dictatorship in Argentina from 1976 to 1981, was indicted in an Argentine court for his alleged involvement in the so-called Condor Plan. This plan was an operation in which several South American military rulers conspired across borders to abduct and kill left-wing political opponents in the 1970's and 1980's.

☐ Nathan A. Haverstock

See also **Brazil; Latin America.**

Arizona. See **State government.**

Arkansas. See **State government.**

Armed forces. The armed forces of the United States launched a military action against terrorism after an airliner hijacked by terrorists crashed into the Pentagon Building, the headquarters of the United States Department of Defense, outside Washington, D.C., on Sept. 11, 2001. The attack killed 189 people.

American Airlines Flight 77 was on a flight from Dulles International Airport in Herndon, Virginia, to Los Angeles but was diverted shortly after takeoff by five men. The Boeing 757 jet crashed into the Pentagon, creating a 100-foot- (30-meter) wide gap that extended through three of the Pentagon's five rings of offices. The damaged segment contained U.S. Army and U.S. Navy offices.

The attack was part of a coordinated assault—the worst in U.S. history—in which 19 men hijacked four commercial airliners in flight over the eastern United States. The hijackers crashed two of the aircraft into the twin towers of the World Trade Center in New York City, killing thousands of people. The fourth airliner crashed into a field in western Pennsylvania.

Federal officials reported that one-third of the Pentagon Building was left unusable. Repairs were expected to take two years to complete and were estimated to cost more than $100 million.

A war on terrorism. U.S. President George W. Bush responded to the attacks by placing the U.S.

armed forces on heightened readiness. On September 20, he declared a sustained war against terrorism during an address before a joint session of Congress. On September 14, the Senate and the House of Representatives had passed a resolution that authorized the president to use force against any nation, organization, or person he determined had planned, authorized, committed, or aided in the terrorist attacks. The measure also allowed President Bush to use force against any person or nation that harbored terrorists. The president described the war on terrorism as broad-based, including not only military responses but also diplomacy, espionage, and financial pressure.

U.S. response. U.S. intelligence agents quickly discovered evidence that Osama bin Laden, a Saudi-born exile living in Afghanistan, had masterminded the September 11 attacks. Bin Laden was a fundamentalist Muslim who was suspected of other acts of terrorism, including the bombing of U.S. embassies in Africa in 1998 and the October 2000 attack on the destroyer U.S.S. *Cole* in Yemen. U.S. officials in 2001 demanded that Afghanistan's ruling Taliban turn over bin Laden in connection with the attacks. Taliban leaders, who had been providing bin Laden with asylum, refused, claiming that the United States offered no proof that he was connected to the attacks.

On October 7, the United States and the United Kingdom launched air strikes against Afghanistan, with the purpose of destroying bin Laden's terrorist network, al-Qaida ("The Base" in Arabic), and crippling the military systems of the Taliban. U.S. armed forces supported the Northern Alliance, a group of anti-Taliban rebels, in its ground attacks against the Taliban.

U.S. long-range bombers and fighter jets pounded Taliban ground troops, barracks, garrisons, and troop encampments across Afghanistan with heavy airstrikes throughout October, November, and early December. U.S. aircraft also targeted the cities of Kabul, the capital, and Qandahar (Kandahar), a Taliban stronghold. On October 21, U.S. war planes attacked the front line of the Taliban's ground forces in Afghanistan. The line, consisting of a series of trenches, bunkers, and minefields some 35 miles (56 kilometers) north of Kabul, separated Taliban forces from the Northern Alliance.

On November 9, Northern Alliance forces broke through Taliban defenses and entered Mazar-e Sharif, a strategically important Taliban stronghold in northern Afghanistan. By November 13, Northern Alliance rebels entered Kabul after meeting little resistance from Taliban forces. U.S. soldiers who accompanied the rebels described the city's civilian population as jubilant at being freed from the Taliban's extreme Islamic fundamentalist rule. The next day, outside Kabul, U.S. warplanes bombed convoys of trucks loaded with Taliban soldiers moving south.

U.S. Defense Department officials reported on November 18 that dozens of U.S. Special Operations troops had moved into Afghanistan to pursue bin Laden, other al-Qaida members, and Taliban leaders. By November 24, Taliban soldiers were pouring out of the besieged city of Qonduz (Kundez) , the Taliban's last stronghold in northern Afghanistan, to surrender by the hundreds to Northern Alliance rebels. Rebel leaders captured Qonduz the next day.

Leaders of the Taliban militia agreed to surrender Qandahar, the last Taliban stronghold, on December 6. U.S. military officers were uncertain as to the whereabouts of the Taliban regime's spiritual leader, Mullah Mohammed Omar. U.S. Secretary of Defense Donald Rumsfeld insisted that Omar must be turned over to the United States for trial as an accomplice in global terrorism for harboring bin Laden. That same day, three U.S. Army Special Forces soldiers were killed when a bomb dropped from an Air Force B-52 bomber missed its target and landed 100 yards (91 meters) from the soldiers.

On December 10, Deputy Defense Secretary Paul Wolfowitz announced that the Taliban had been defeated, but that the war on terrorism was not over. Wolfowitz admitted that it could take months before the United States was able to find bin Laden and leaders of al-Qaida.

By mid-December, al-Qaida forces had retreated into the mountains of Afghanistan's rugged Tora Bora region, southeast of Jalalabad. U.S. jets bombed mountain tops as opposition fighters and U.S. troops shelled cave complexes on mountainsides, where U.S. intelligence officials believed bin Laden was hiding. On December 16, Secretary of State Colin Powell announced that al-Qaida had been destroyed in Afghanistan, but armed forces continued to search Tora Bora and elsewhere for bin Laden.

Surveillance plane incident. A U.S. Navy electronic surveillance plane and a Chinese air force fighter jet collided over the South China Sea on April 1. The Chinese F-8 interceptor crashed into the sea and its pilot was killed. The U.S. plane was badly damaged and made an emergency landing at a Chinese military airfield on Hainan Island, where the 24 crew members were detained.

On April 10, the Bush administration sent the Chinese government a statement of regret for the loss of their pilot and for landing in China without permission. Chinese officials agreed to release the crew on April 12. Crew members reported that most of the sensitive intelligence data on-board the plane had been destroyed before it landed in China. The plane was dismantled and returned to the United States in July.

Submarine accident. A U.S. Navy nuclear-powered submarine struck a Japanese fishing vessel south of Honolulu, Hawaii, on February 9, sinking the Japanese vessel and triggering an international incident. Nine people aboard the Japanese ship, *Ehime Maru,* were killed.

The U.S.S. *Greeneville* was demonstrating a rapid-surface maneuver for a group of civilians on board when it rammed the trawler passing above. Navy crew members later said that two civilians—part of a group of 16 civilians aboard the ship participating in a Navy community relations program—were at the controls of the submarine at the moment of the crash.

A naval board of inquiry on April 23 ruled against court-martialing Commander Scott Waddle, the submarine's commanding officer, and several sailors, concluding there was no evidence of criminal intent or deliberate misconduct. The board found Waddle guilty of dereliction of duty. He received a letter of reprimand and was barred from future command, ending his naval career. Waddle retired in October with an honorable discharge and full pension. Four crew members received letters of admonition.

Missile defense. A controversy over the Bush administration's plans to develop and deploy a missile defense system intensified during 2001 as the Department of Defense increased spending for the system designed to protect U.S. cities from a missile attack.

The Department of Defense planned to spend $8 billion on missile defense in fiscal year 2002, which began Oct. 1, 2001. Pentagon officials admitted in July that the program would violate the 1972 antiballistic missile treaty with Russia. The ABM treaty allows testing of ground-based systems but forbids the deployment of airborne laser interceptors and sea-launched missiles envisioned by the Bush administration plan. In December

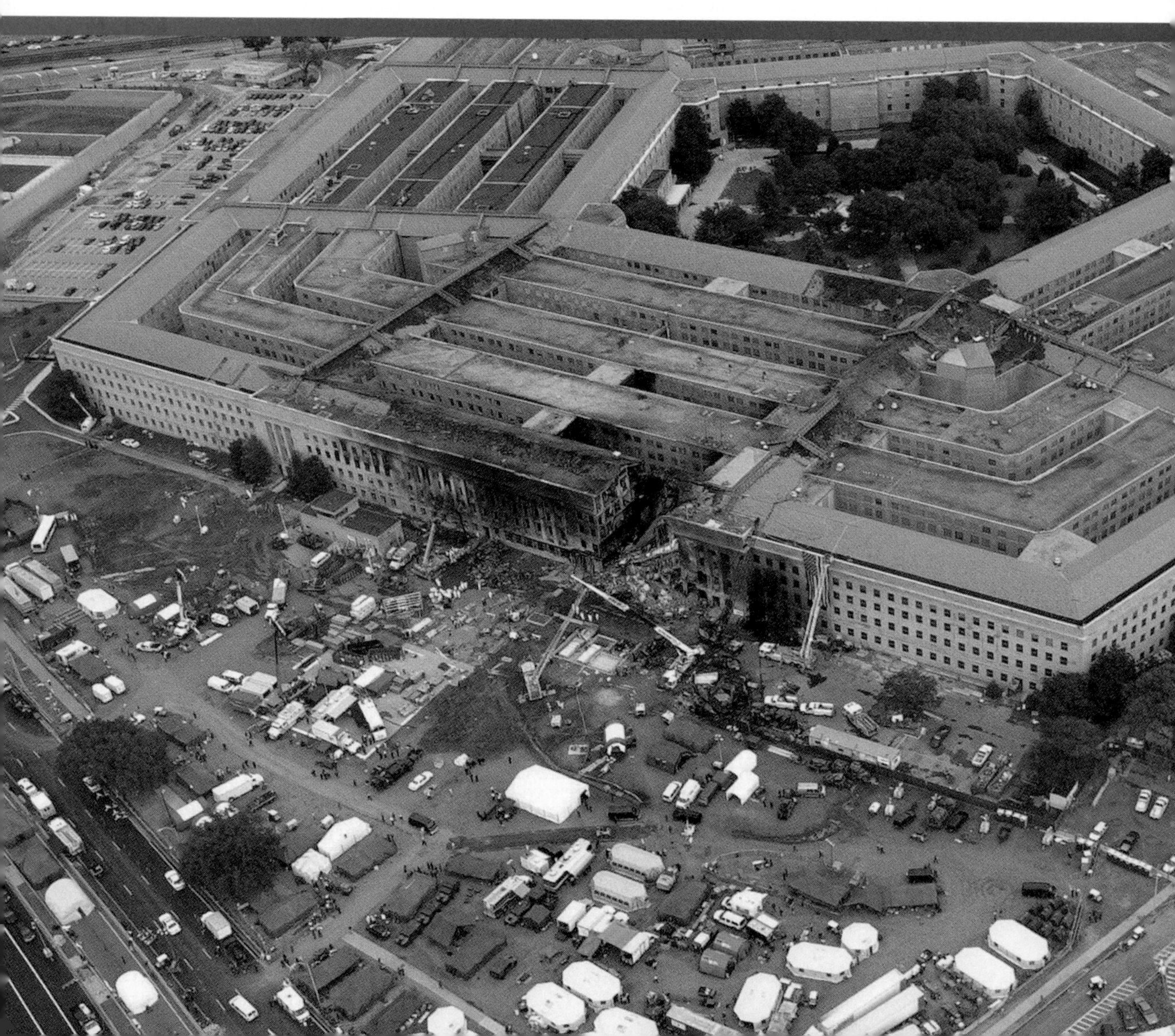

2001, the Bush administration notified Russia that it planned to withdraw from the ABM treaty so that the administration could continue testing its missile defense system.

Osprey. The U.S. Marine V-22 program remained plagued by controversy in 2001. The tilt-rotor plane, which can take off and land like a helicopter but fly like a conventional aircraft, had been grounded since December 2000 because of maintenance problems and two crashes.

On Aug. 17, 2001, the Marine Corps charged eight officers with dereliction of duty for allegedly falsifying maintenance records of the aircraft. Charges against most of the officers were dropped in September. However, the Osprey group and squadron commanders received letters of reprimand that ended their careers.

U.S. military strength at the end of 2001 stood at 1.35 million soldiers, a slight decline from 2000. U.S. armed forces were involved in peacekeeping or humanitarian operations in several countries. A decade after the Persian Gulf War (1991), approximately 16,000 U.S. troops remained stationed in the region. About 6,000 troops were on peacekeeping duty in the Yugoslav province of Kosovo and another 4,000 soldiers were stationed in the former Yugoslav republic of Bosnia-Herzegovina.

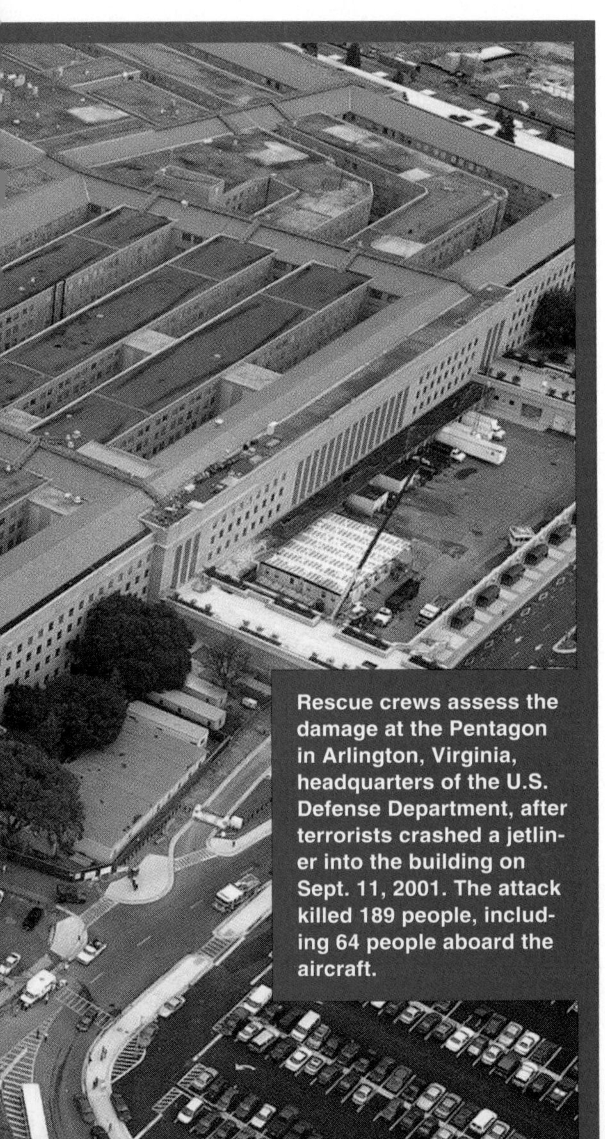

Rescue crews assess the damage at the Pentagon in Arlington, Virginia, headquarters of the U.S. Defense Department, after terrorists crashed a jetliner into the building on Sept. 11, 2001. The attack killed 189 people, including 64 people aboard the aircraft.

Defense budget. President Bush ordered a review of U.S. defense strategy and deferred many major spending decisions until its completion. As a result, the defense budget for fiscal year 2002 remained at $310 billion, the amount approved by President Bill Clinton in 2000. On June 22, 2001, Bush asked Congress for an additional $18.4 billion for defense.

On December 13, Congress approved a $343.3-billion defense authorization bill, adding $15 billion to help fund the added costs of antiterrorism operations and the war in Afghanistan. The bill also created an independent commission to recommend a list of bases to be closed by 2005. Defense department officials had wanted a new round of base closings to begin in 2003.

☐ Thomas M. DeFrank

See also **Afghanistan; China; Congress of the United States; People in the news** (Rumsfeld, Donald); **Russia; Terrorism; Terrorism: A Special Feature,** p. 38; **United States, Government of the.**

Art. Governments and museums in Europe and the United States continued in 2001 to struggle with questions concerning art stolen during World War II (1939–1945). Germany's Nazi government had seized much of the art from Jewish collectors, many of whom were killed during the Holocaust (the systematic execution of millions of Jews and other people considered undesirable by the Nazis). Throughout the 1990's, many American and European institutions tried to identify Nazi-looted art and return it to its rightful owners. In 2000 and 2001, a number of museums published Internet lists of artwork with questionable histories. Heirs of Holocaust victims continued to take legal action to recover lost property.

The Presidential Advisory Commission on Holocaust Assets in the United States, which had been created by the U.S. Congress in 1988, issued its final report in January 2001. The report outlined standards for the disclosure of information to aid in the identification of looted objects in museum collections. The report recommended the creation of a foundation that would provide a centralized database of collections information and assist institutions and individuals in resolving restitution issues. The American Association of Museums and the Association of Art Museum Directors (professional organizations that represent more than 3,000 museums and 170 museum directors in North America), endorsed the report.

In February, the Kiyomizu Sannenzaka Museum in Kyoto, Japan, voluntarily returned a painting by Swiss artist Paul Klee to Jen Lissitsky, son of the collector from whom it had been seized by the Nazis in 1937. Still pending in 2001 was the outcome of Lissitsky's suit against the Beyeler Foundation in Basel, Switzerland, to recover a painting by Russian artist Wassily Kandinsky that also had been taken by the Nazis in 1937.

In May 2001, the only surviving heir of Dutch Jewish art collector Jacques Goudstikker received the first of some 1,400 Goudstikker collection paintings plundered by the Nazis during World War II. The estate of Hertha Katz, which had consigned the painting for sale in January at the auction house Christie's, returned it after discovering that it had been stolen.

Bloch-Bauer claim. A U.S. federal district court in Los Angeles ruled in May that the niece of Austrian industrialist Ferdinand Bloch-Bauer could sue Austria in a U.S. court for the return of six paintings by Austrian painter Gustav Klimt seized by the Nazis in 1938. The court ruled that Austria had violated international law when it refused to return the works to the heirs after World War II. The lawyer representing Austria appealed the decision.

Trophy art. In June 2001, Germany and Russia agreed to make their first exchange of cash for trophy art, works that each country had stolen from the other during and after World War II. Russia was to return a set of stained-glass windows from the 1300's that had been stolen from Germany in 1945. In return, a German oil and gas company had pledged to pay Russia $1.5 million.

In July 2001, the United States returned 12 drawings to Germany that Soviet troops had stolen during World War II. The drawings, among them works by Dutch artist Rembrandt van Rijn and German artist Albrecht Durer, had been given to a museum in Azerbaijan but were stolen again in 1993. U.S. Customs officials recovered the drawings in New York City in 1997.

International conflict. In May 2001, representatives from Yad Vashem, Israel's main Holocaust museum, provoked controversy by removing portions of a mural in Drogobych, a city in Ukraine that was part of Poland during World War II. Bruno Schulz, the Polish Jewish writer and artist who made the mural to decorate the nursery of a Gestapo officer's son, was killed by Nazis. Spokespersons from Yad Vashem justified the museum's action by claiming a "moral right" to the property of Jewish Holocaust victims. Both Poland and Ukraine protested the legality of the action and filed formal inquiries with the Israeli government.

Rediscovered Italian art. Two paintings by Italian artist Giotto came to light in June 2001. The paintings, believed to have been created between 1320 and 1330, were known only to a few people until they were reported to have disappeared from a private collection in Florence during an inheritance dispute in 1999. They were recovered in Florence, along with other pictures stolen from the collection, during an investigation of illegal marketing of artworks.

In July 2001, the London auction house Sotheby's sold a newly discovered drawing by Renaissance artist Michelangelo for over $8.3 million.

Globalization. In January, the Solomon R. Guggenheim Foundation in New York City added the Kunsthistorisches Museum in Vienna, Austria, to its existing collaboration with the State Hermitage Museum in St. Petersburg, Russia. The partnership was expected to include sharing of resources in existing and planned museum sites. Later in 2001, the three partners were joined by the Albertina in Vienna and the Center for Art and Media in Karlsruhe, Germany, in the launch of Guggenheim.com, a for-profit Web site.

Las Vegas art. Several major museums staged exhibits or opened branches in Las Vegas, Nevada, in 2001. The Phillips Collection of Washington, D.C., exhibited European art at the Bellagio Gallery of Fine Art through March. In October, the Guggenheim Foundation opened two museums at the Venetian Resort-Hotel-Casino: the Guggenheim Las Vegas and, in partnership with the Hermitage, the smaller Guggenheim Hermitage Museum.

New York City museums. In November 2001, the Neue Galerie opened with a selection of German and Austrian art from the early 1900's. The renamed American Folk Art Museum opened in December in a new, eight-story building that quadrupled the museum's gallery space.

Major exhibitions. The Smithsonian American Art Museum in Washington, D.C., which had closed in 2000 for a four-year renovation, continued in 2001 to circulate within the U.S. eight exhibitions featuring over 500 of its most celebrated works. An exhibition of presidential portraits from the Smithsonian Institution's National Portrait Gallery, which was closed in 2000 for a three-year renovation, began traveling in 2001.

The San Francisco Museum of Modern Art launched the New Year with the online exhibition "010101: Art in Technological Times," which the museum later expanded with works displayed in its galleries. The Whitney Museum of American Art in New York City opened two exhibitions of art made with digital technology, "BitStreams" and "Data Dynamics," in its galleries and on its Web site. Other exhibitions exploring art and technology in 2001 included "Art Now: Art and Money Online," at Tate Britain in London, and "TimeStream," by artist Tony Oursler, presented by the Museum of Modern Art in New York City.

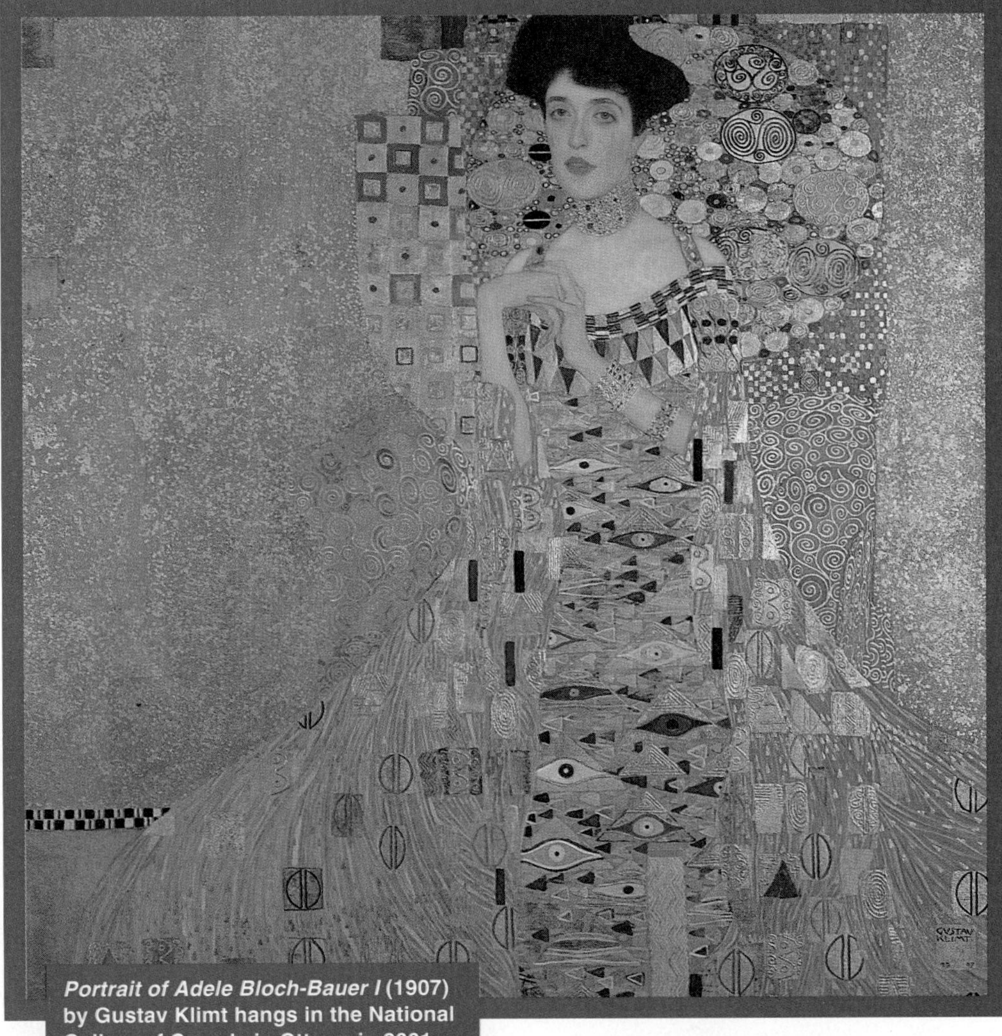

Portrait of Adele Bloch-Bauer I (1907) by Gustav Klimt hangs in the National Gallery of Canada in Ottawa in 2001 during the first North American retrospective of Klimt's work. Klimt, an Austrian artist, was a leader of the Vienna Secession, a group of artists who created the Austrian version of French art nouveau in painting and the decorative arts.

The Metropolitan Museum of Art in New York City presented "Vermeer and the Delft School," a showcase of Dutch arts from the 1600's. "Van Gogh and Gauguin: The Studio of the South" at The Art Institute of Chicago examined the two artists' brief collaboration. In Washington, D.C., "Virtue and Beauty: Leonardo's Ginevra de' Benci and Renaissance Portraits of Women" was presented at the National Gallery of Art. Sculptor Robert Gober represented the U.S. at the 49th Venice Biennale in Italy, while the 4th International Biennial at Site Santa Fe in New Mexico featured works by 29 artists.

Photography of the 1900's was surveyed during 2001 with exhibitions of the work of Walker Evans at the J. Paul Getty Museum in Los Angeles; "Ansel Adams at 100" at the San Francisco Museum of Modern Art; and "The Photography of Alfred Stieglitz: Georgia O'Keeffe's Enduring Legacy" at the Norton Museum of Art in West Palm Beach, Florida.

Museum cutbacks. Terrorist attacks on the United States on September 11 profoundly depressed tourism in the United states, which in turn affected museum attendance. In New York City, attendance at the Guggenheim, a museum dependent on admission fees, dropped 60 percent in October, forcing the museum to lay off 80 employees. The Whitney Museum of American Art in New York City was also forced to cut its staff to stem financial disaster. □ Sally Ruth May

Asia

An international war against terrorism rocked the political and economic stability of many Asian countries in 2001. The war, which began after terrorists crashed commercial airliners into the World Trade Center in New York City and the Pentagon Building in Arlington, Virginia, on September 11 brought worldwide attention to fundamentalist Islamic terrorist groups based in Asia, as well as to the plight of the poor in Afghanistan and other Asian countries.

The United States launched the war on terrorism after U.S. officials found evidence that Osama bin Laden, a Saudi-born millionaire and radical Islamic leader based in Afghanistan, had orchestrated the attacks on September 11. United States officials put together an international coalition to destroy terrorist bases in Afghanistan. The United States led a military campaign in Afghanistan that by December had defeated the ruling Taliban, a militant Islamic group that protected bin Laden and his terrorist network. U.S. officials also warned other Asian nations, such as the Philippines, to crack down on terrorist cells in their countries.

The U.S.-led coalition created new political alignments in Asia. Pakistani President Pervez Musharraf announced that Pakistan would cooperate with the United States, despite the protests of many Pakistanis who supported the Taliban. Uzbekistan, where the Islamic Movement of Uzbekistan is linked to bin Laden, also cooperated with the United States.

Economic problems that were already apparent before the terrorist attacks on the United States worsened after September 11. The economies of Taiwan and Singapore, as well as other Asian countries, fell into a recession during 2001. After the collapse of many economies in Asia in 1997 and 1998, many Asian countries began economic reform projects, such as restructuring bad debts and reducing dependence on exports. These efforts were beginning to pay off by 2001, but the worldwide economic slowdown derailed Asian recovery. Countries highly dependent on exporting high-technology equipment to the United States were especially hard hit in 2001.

Many Asian countries also worried about competition from China. In 2001, China was still burdened by internal economic problems, including unemployment and unprofitable state-owned industries. However, China was taking steps to reform its business relations with the West and update its technology sector. In addition, the country's young population and cheap labor attracted foreign investors, which increased exports. China's stature in the international community rose in November when it was admitted into the World Trade Organization, which regulates trade among member nations.

Droughts, floods, and storms caused misery across Asia's broad expanse in 2001. The third year of a devastating drought in Afghanistan resulted in some 500,000 people becoming refugees in search of food and water. People died of cold as well as hunger. Millions of Afghans were dependent on relief supplies from foreign countries. Foreign aid efforts were complicated by the Taliban, which placed restrictions on foreign aid projects. Following the start of the U.S.-led military campaign against the Taliban, U.S. military planes dropped thousands of food packages into Afghanistan. The United Nations and other relief groups also set up camps to provide food and shelter for Afghan refugees.

The bodies of King Birendra of Nepal, Queen Aiswarya, and seven other members of the royal family are cremated along the banks of the Bagmati River in Katmandu, the capital, on June 2. Birendra's son, Crown Prince Dipendra, shot and killed his father and members of the royal family before shooting himself.

In northeast China's Inner Mongolia region and in the adjacent nation of Mongolia, the most severe winter in living memory killed hundreds of thousands of head of livestock. Temperatures reached lows of -50 °F (-45 °C). A second summer of drought followed the brutal winter, threatening more livestock. Animals and animal products are the backbone of the Mongolian economy.

Typhoon Utor hit the Philippines in July, killing more than 160 people and displacing nearly 1 million others. In Vietnam, Typhoon Durian dropped 17 inches (440 millimeters) of rain in a 48-hour period. Taiwan was hit by eight typhoons in 2001, the most since 1914. The storms killed more than 300 people in 2001 and caused extensive damage.

Elections. Popular elections in Thailand and Bangladesh resulted in leadership changes in 2001. In Thailand, a political party that Thaksin Chinnawat , a billionaire businessman, had put together in 1998 carried him into office as prime minister. Shinawatra's Thai Rak Thai party and two allied parties won the largest voter mandate in modern Thai history. In Bangladesh, Khaleda Zia became prime minister after winning parliamentary elections by campaigning against lawlessness and corruption.

Changing governments. Political maneuvering led to leadership changes in Japan and Nepal in 2001. The Liberal Democratic Party (LDP) in Japan forced Prime Minister Yoshiro Mori to resign and selected Junichiro Koizumi to succeed him. Koizumi then led the LDP to an unexpected victory in elections for seats in the upper house of parliament in July.

In June, Nepal's King Birendra Bir Bikram Shah Dev and most of the royal family were murdered by his son, Crown Prince Dipendra, who then shot himself. Birendra's brother, Gyanendra Bir Bikram Shah, became king following the massacre.

Nepal's Congress Party replaced Girija Prasad Koirala with Sher Bahadur Deuba as prime minister in July. The prime minister governs Nepal, which has a revered but powerless king. The Congress Party blamed Koirala for allowing Maoist guerrillas, who controlled some remote villages in the western Himalaya, to expand their area of control. Koirala was also blamed for not protecting the royal family while he was in office.

The presidents of the Philippines and Indonesia were ousted in 2001. Gloria Macapagal-Arroyo became president of the Philippines in January, after

Facts in brief on Asian countries

Country	Population	Government	Monetary unit*	Foreign trade (million U.S.$) Exports†	Imports†
Afghanistan	24,977,000	provisional government under United Nations sponsorship	afghani (4,750.00 = $1)	80	150
Armenia	3,543,000	President Robert Kocharian	dram (554.07 = $1)	294	882
Australia	19,231,000	Governor General Peter Hollingworth; Prime Minister John Howard	dollar (1.97 = $1)	63,877	71,537
Azerbaijan	7,854,000	President Heydar A. Aliyev	manat (4,670.00 = $1)	606	1,077
Bangladesh	133,557,000	President A.Q.M. Badruddoza; Chowdhury Prime Minister Khaleda Zia	taka (56.95 = $1)	3,919	7,685
Bhutan	2,238,000	King Jigme Singye Wangchuck	ngultrum (47.87 = $1)	154	269
Brunei	340,000	Sultan Sir Hassanal Bolkiah	dollar (1.78 = $1)	2,058	1,552
Cambodia (Kampuchea)	12,269,000	King Norodom Sihanouk; Prime Minister Hun Sen	riel (3,835.00 = $1)	942	1,300
China	1,303,875,000	Communist Party General Secretary and President Jiang Zemin; Premier Zhu Rongji	renminbi yuan (8.28 = $1)	249,297	206,132
Georgia	4,969,000	President Eduard Shevardnadze	lari (1.98 = $1)	372	898
India	1,042,249,000	President Kocheril Raman Narayanan; Prime Minister Atal Behari Vajpayee	rupee (48.00 = $1)	42,194	51,868
Indonesia	217,314,000	President Megawati Sukarnoputri; Vice President Hamzah Haz	rupiah (9,865.00 = $1)	64,700	40,400
Iran	69,049,000	Supreme Leader Ayatollah Ali Hoseini-Khamenei; President Mohammed Khatami-Ardakani	rial (1,750.00 = $1)	25,000	15,000
Japan	127,018,000	Emperor Akihito; Prime Minister Junichiro Koizumi	yen (120.48 = $1)	479,175	379,450
Kazakhstan	16,191,000	President Nursultan Nazarbayev	tenge (148.02 = $1)	9,140	5,052
Korea, North	24,585,000	Korean Workers' Party General Secretary Kim Chong-il	won (2.20 = $1)	520	960
Korea, South	47,521,000	President Kim Dae-jung; Prime Minister Lee Han-dong	won (1,307.00 = $1)	172,268	160,481
Kyrgyzstan	4,784,000	President Askar Akayev	som (48.70 = $1)	454	600
Laos	5,709,000	President Khamtai Siphandon; Prime Minister Boungnang Volachit	kip (7,600.00 = $1)	323	540
Malaysia	23,002,000	Paramount Ruler Sultan Syed Sirajuddin Syed Putra Jamalullail; Prime Minister Mahathir bin Mohamad	ringgit (3.80 = $1)	98,136	82,199

massive public demonstrations forced Joseph Estrada from office. The protests came after the government abandoned an impeachment trial against Estrada. Macapagal-Arroyo had served as vice president under Estrada.

In Indonesia, the People's Consultative Assembly voted the erratic President Abdurrahman Wahid out of office in July. Wahid had attempted to disband the assembly in order to prevent a vote against him. Vice President Megawati Sukarnoputri, the daughter of Indonesia's first president, Sukarno, succeeded Wahid.

The ruling Communist party in Vietnam forced Le Kha Phieu out as its secretary-general, the nation's top job, and named Nong Duc Manh to replace Phieu. Phieu had refused to implement reforms that his colleagues encouraged. Party members regarded his replacement, Manh, as a progressive reformer.

East Timor took a big step toward becoming an independent nation in 2001 by holding elections on August 30. In 1999, the people of East Timor had voted against remaining part of Indonesia, which had seized the former Portuguese colony in 1975. The United Nations, which helped East Timor overcome violence and destruction by

Country	Population	Government	Monetary unit*	Foreign trade (million U.S.$) Exports†	Imports†
Maldives	302,000	President Maumoon Abdul Gayoom	rufiyaa (11.77 = $1)	76	389
Mongolia	2,455,000	President Natsagiyn Bagabandi; Prime Minister Namburiin Enkhbayar	tugrik (1,100.00 = $1)	233	426
Myanmar (Burma)	46,648,000	Prime Minister, State Peace and Development Council Chairman Than Shwe	kyat (6.61 = $1)	1,402	2,371
Nepal	25,009,000	King Gyanendra Bir Bikram Shah; Prime Minister Girija Prasad Koirala	rupee (76.24 = $1)	804	1,572
New Zealand	3,930,000	Governor General Dame Silvia Cartwright; Prime Minister Helen Clark	dollar (2.41 = $1)	13,267	13,906
Pakistan	144,135,000	President and Chief Executive General Pervez Musharraf	rupee (62.55 = $1)	9,174	11,050
Papua New Guinea	5,015,000	Governor General Sir Silas Atopare; Prime Minister Sir Mekere Morauta	kina (3.53 = $1)	2,100	1,100
Philippines	78,850,000	President Gloria Macapagal-Arroyo	peso (51.53 = $1)	39,783	33,808
Russia	146,376,000	President Vladimir Putin	ruble (29.51 = $1)	104,836	49,125
Singapore	3,641,000	President Sellapan Rama Nathan; Prime Minister Chok Tong Goh	dollar (1.79 = $1)	137,876	134,546
Sri Lanka	19,415,000	President Chandrika Kumaratunga; Prime Minister Ratnasiri Wickramanayake	rupee (90.10 = $1)	5,120	6,850
Taiwan	22,735,000	President Chen Shui-bian; Vice President Lu Annette	dollar (34.55 = $1)	148,380	140,010
Tajikistan	6,347,000	President Emomali Rahmonov; National Assembly Chairman Makhmadsaid Ubaydulloyev	somoni (2.20 = $1)	689	664
Thailand	62,422,000	King Phumiphon Adunyadet; Prime Minister Thaksin Chinnawat	baht (44.75 = $1)	69,055	61,922
Turkmenistan	4,605,000	President Saparmurat Niyazov	manat (5,200.00 = $1)	2,400	1,650
Uzbekistan	25,355,000	President Islam Karimov	som (325.00 = $1)	2,900	2,600
Vietnam	79,387,000	Communist Party General Secretary Nong Duc Manh; President Tran Duc Luong; Prime Minister Phan Van Khai	dong (15,037.00 = $1)	14,300	15,200

*Exchange rates as of Oct. 5, 2001, or latest available data.
†Latest available data.

Indonesia's supporters after the 1999 vote, reported in July 2001 that the population of East Timor, which stood at 737,811 people, had declined by about 60,000 people since the violence began there in the mid 1990's.

In August 2001 elections, East Timorese voters chose an 88-member assembly, which was charged with the task of writing a constitution for the region. The National Front for East Timorese Resistance, a political party known as Fretilin, won 55 seats in the assembly. One of the Fretilin leaders, Mari Alkatiri, became head of an interim cabinet. Political experts expected the UN to recognize East Timor as an independent nation in May 2002.

East Timor faced a difficult economic future in 2001. The area is prone to drought, has little industry, and scant resources. However, East Timorese and Australian officials agreed in August that East Timor would receive 90 percent of the royalties from undersea oil and gas fields lying between the two neighbors. The royalties were expected to provide East Timor with $180 million a year.

Mongolia. President Natsagiyn Bagabandi was reelected for a second four-year term on May 20 by a large majority. Bagabandi headed the Mongolian People's Revolutionary Party (MPRP). The

MPRP, the former Communist Party that controlled Mongolia during the 70 years it was a Soviet satellite, won control of parliament in 2000. Democratic parties had been unable to provide stability and solve economic problems.

Laos. In March 2001, the aging leadership of the ruling Communist party, Lao People's Revolutionary Party, reappointed itself. The 77-year-old party president, Khamtai Siphandon, began another five-year term. The National Assembly, run by Siphandone's party, named former Finance Minister Boungnang Volachit to succeed Sisavat Keobounphan as prime minister on March 27. Sisavat's term as prime minister had been rife with economic instability and corruption.

Wild elephants became a problem in South Asia in 2001 as the growing human population expanded into jungles, reducing the area left for animals. In the jungles of the Chittagong Hill Tracts in Bangladesh, elephants trampled two villagers to death in August. In nearby Assam, in northeast India, where 5,500 of the country's 30,000 elephants lived in 2001, villagers complained that the animals had trampled rice fields and destroyed houses while searching for food. In September, forest guards found 15 dead elephants, apparently poisoned by angry villagers. □ Henry S. Bradsher

See also **Armed forces; Terrorism: A Special Feature,** p. 38; the various Asian country articles.

Astronomy. In 2001, scientists with the National Aeronautics and Space Administration (NASA) flew a spacecraft close to a comet and landed another on an asteroid. Astronomers for the first time detected an atmosphere around a planet outside the solar system. They also discovered an extremely ancient galaxy, which could be one of the building blocks of the universe, and the most distant *supernova* (exploded star) ever recorded.

NEAR lands on Eros. On Feb. 12, 2001, NEAR-Shoemaker, a spacecraft designed and built by NASA scientists, touched down on the surface of the asteroid Eros. The landing was the first on the surface of an asteroid. NEAR-Shoemaker, launched in 1996, had spent nearly a year in orbit around Eros, photographing the 21-mile- (34-kilometer-) long asteroid and measuring its physical properties. As the mission ended, NASA engineers attempted the risky landing even though the craft had not been designed to land.

As it descended, NEAR-Shoemaker took close-up pictures of the asteroid, the last showing pebbles less than 1 inch (2.5 centimeters) across. Even though the camera ceased operating after the landing, an on-board device called a gamma-ray spectrometer continued to send back data on the chemical composition of Eros.

Scientists reported that Eros is about 4.5 billion years old, nearly as old as the solar system. Its surface is blanketed with finely powdered rock. Scientists believe that Eros was struck by at least one meteorite or small comet about 1 billion years ago. As a result of that impact, thousands of house-sized boulders are strewn over the surface.

Comet fly-by. Astronomers gained a wealth of data about comets when a NASA spacecraft flew within 1,400 miles (2,250 kilometers) of comet Borrelly on Sept. 22, 2001. The craft, Deep Space 1, took high-quality close-up photographs and measurements of particles in the tail of the comet.

Deep Space 1 had been testing advanced propulsion and other technologies, but scientists realized that the craft was close enough to attempt the fly-by. The craft became the first to visit a comet since a fleet of probes studied Halley's Comet in 1986. Astronomers are using the Borrelly data to identify the comet's chemical makeup.

Extraterrestrial atmosphere. On Nov. 27, 2001, astronomers announced they had detected and studied the first atmosphere of a planet outside the solar system. The astronomers, with the California Institute of Technology in Pasadena and the National Center for Atmospheric Research in Boulder, Colorado, used the Hubble Space Telescope to study the planet as it passed between its

An image taken in 2001 with the Hubble Space Telescope reveals the irregular-shaped galaxy ESO 510-13, which astronomers theorize is twisted because of gravitational effects that occurred when it absorbed a smaller galaxy.

Clouds of dust are forming new planets in the Orion Nebula (above), 1,500 light-years from Earth. Radiation emitted by a young star blows apart a *planetary disc* (planetary building blocks) orbiting the star (right) in the Orion Nebula. Both images were taken with the Hubble Space Telescope in 2001.

star and Earth. They studied the light reflected by the Jupiter-sized planet to detect its atmosphere. The planet orbits a star that is about 150 light-years from Earth. A light-year is the distance that light travels in one year—approximately 5.9 trillion miles (9.5 trillion kilometers). Although the planet is far too hot to support life, the discovery was heralded as a breakthrough in planetary exploration.

Familiar-looking solar system. In August 2001, astronomers from several U.S. institutions announced finding the first solar system similar to the sun's. The group, led by Debra Fischer and Geoffrey Marcy of the University of California at Berkeley, Paul Butler of the Carnegie Institution of Washington, D.C., and others, found the system in orbit around the star 47 Ursa Majoris.

The 47 Ursa Majoris system resembles our own solar system in that the two known giant planets are in nearly circular orbits and are relatively far from their star, which is similar in size and age to the sun. The star could be orbited by an Earth-sized planet on which life might evolve.

Until the discovery of 47 Ursa Majoris, astronomers were unsure whether our solar system was typical. Now that at least one similar system has been discovered, astronomers think that others like it will be discovered in the future.

Baby galaxy. In October 2001, a team of astronomers led by Richard Ellis of the California Institute of Technology in Pasadena reported finding a small, faint galaxy that is 13.4 billion light-years from Earth.

The astronomers speculated that the galaxy may be a "baby galaxy," one of the building blocks of the universe. It has about 100,000 times less mass than our own Milky Way Galaxy. Present-day galaxies may have formed when these smaller baby galaxies merged.

Distant supernova. In April 2001, a team of astronomers led by Adam Reiss of the Space Telescope Science Institute in Baltimore announced the discovery of the most distant supernova ever observed. The object is about 10 billion light-years from Earth.

The supernova was not as bright as it should have been if the universe had been expanding at a constant rate. Astronomers theorized that shortly after the *big bang* (the violent explosion that most astronomers think gave rise to the universe), the expansion of the universe slowed. However, when the universe was about half its present age, it began to expand faster.

To explain this change in speed, some scientists have suggested that space is filled with a type of "dark energy" that is powering the expansion. However, no one is certain of the source of this energy. ☐ Laurence A. Marschall

See also **Space exploration.**

Australia

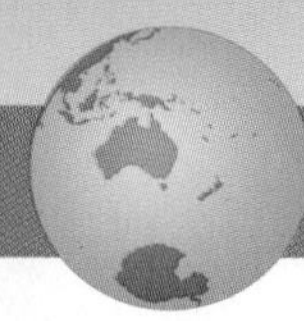

Prime Minister John Howard and his conservative coalition government won a historic third term in November 2001 in national elections that focused on immigration issues. Howard's Liberal Party won 67 seats in the 150-seat lower house of Parliament, and its coalition partner, the National Party, won 12 seats. The rival Australian Labor Party, led by Kim Beazley, won 65 seats. Political experts credit Howard's hard-line stance against illegal immigration and support for the United States-led war in Afghanistan for his popularity among voters.

In early 2001, the Liberal-National Party coalition government had trailed the Labor Party in the polls. The government was unpopular because of such issues as a goods and services tax, which was introduced by the government in 2000. The government's popularity improved in August 2001, after Howard took a firm line on refusing entry to asylum seekers from the Middle East arriving in Australia illegally by boat from Indonesia. After the terrorist attacks on the United States in September, Howard's strict immigration policy was praised by most Australians.

Immigration. Australia typically accepts about 12,000 refugees a year. In early 2001, some Australians urged the government to take more refugees because of the increased number of people seeking asylum from both Asia and the Middle East. Many of the illegal immigrants arrived on boats from Indonesia. Smugglers, who used dilapidated and overloaded boats to get asylum seekers into the country, stepped up their operations in 2001. Between 1996 and 1997, Australian immigration officials estimated 365 unauthorized immigrants entered the country on 13 boats. Between July 1, 1999, and June 30, 2001, officials estimated that nearly 10,000 unauthorized immigrants arrived in Australia on about 135 boats.

Most illegal immigrants were detained in special facilities in remote parts of Australia while immigration officials assessed their claims for refugee status. The majority of these immigrants were eventually accepted into Australia as genuine refugees. Some Australians criticized the government for accepting these asylum seekers, because it kept other people who had been waiting in overseas refugee camps out of Australia. People sympathetic to the illegal refugees criticized living conditions in the Australian detention centers. In 2001, the Australian media reported riots, hunger strikes, and attempted escapes from these camps.

The controversy took on international dimensions on August 26, when an Indonesian boat carrying more than 430 asylum seekers from Afghanistan sank in international waters off Christmas Island. Christmas Island is an Australian territory in the Indian Ocean south of Java. The survivors were taken aboard a Norwegian freighter, but the Australian government refused to allow the boat to land at Christmas Island. The decision provoked international criticism. However, opinion polls showed that more than 70 percent of Australians supported Howard's decision.

Australian immigration officials demanded that the illegal immigrants be returned to Indonesia. However, Indonesia refused to accept them. The standoff was resolved on September 1, when New Zealand agreed to take some of the immigrants. The tiny island of Nauru, in exchange for a financial package from Australia, temporarily accepted some of the people while their claims for asylum were assessed.

In October, more than 350 people from the Middle East drowned when an Indonesian vessel taking them to Christmas Island sank in the Java Sea. Sources in Indonesia reported that there were more Middle Eastern asylum seekers who had entered Indonesia legally in 2001 and were waiting for smugglers to take them to Australia.

Support for the United States. Howard's prompt commitment to the U.S. campaign against terrorism also won him voter support. Howard, who was in the United States on September 11, immediately offered support to the United States. He committed Australia's Special Air Service troops and air-to-air refueling aircraft to the war effort.

Howard also announced antiterrorism measures within Australia. These measures included armed guards on airplanes and a doubling of the Australian Defense Forces counter-terrorism capability. Howard also promised to introduce new laws on terrorism with penalties that included life imprisonment.

Centenary of Federation. On May 9, Australia marked the 100th anniversary of the opening of the first federal Parliament. More than 7,000 guests attended the ceremony at the Royal Exhibition Hall in Melbourne, where the first Parliament met in 1901. Six Australian colonies joined together in 1901 to create the Commonwealth of Australia.

State elections. In February 2001, the Australian Labor Party candidates made a strong showing in state elections. In Western Australia, voters elected Geoff Gallop as the new Labor premier, ousting the long-serving Liberal leader Richard Court. Carol Martin, the ALP candidate for Kimberley in Western Australia, became the first

Fireworks fill the sky over Sydney Harbor Bridge on Jan. 1, 2001, in celebration of the launch of the centenary of the Federation of Australia. Officials estimated that as many as 1 million people attended the opening event of Australia's year-long "birthday celebration."

female Aborigine ever to be elected to an Australian Parliament. Despite scandals about irregular voting procedures, Queenslanders reelected Labor Premier Peter Beattie on February 17.

In April, Natasha Stott Despoja replaced Meg Lees as head of the Australian Democrats, and Aden Ridgeway became deputy leader. At the age of 31, Stott Despoja was the youngest person to become leader of a major political party in Australia. Ridgeway became the first Aborigine to hold a leadership post in a political party.

In June, Sir William Deane retired from his position as governor-general of Australia. The governor-general is the representative of Queen Elizabeth II, who is the official head of state in Australia. Peter Hollingworth, the former Anglican archbishop of Brisbane, replaced Deane.

On August 18, voters in the sparsely inhabited Northern Territory ended the Liberal Party's 26-year tenure in office by electing Labor's Claire Martin as chief minister. Martin promised to end mandatory sentencing, which compelled judges to jail repeat offenders of petty theft and property offenses. Political observers believed that the regulation discriminated against the many unemployed and homeless Aborigines in the territory.

In October, John Olsen, Australia's only remaining Liberal state premier, was forced to resign after an inquiry accused him of dishonesty involving a telecommunications contract. Fellow Liberal Rob Kerin replaced Olsen.

The economy. Australia's economic growth slowed noticeably during 2001 with the tourist industry being hard hit by the collapse of Ansett Airlines and the events of September 11. But in general, the Australian economy fared better than that of most comparable countries, and most bank and other blue chip stocks largely retained their value on the stock exchange. However, several large Australian companies collapsed in 2001.

Treasurer Peter Costello introduced his 2002 budget on May 22, 2001. He forecast an unemployment rate of 7 percent, an inflation rate of about 2 percent, and a growth rate of 3 percent. He predicted a surplus of $1.5 billion (all amounts in Australian dollars). The primary beneficiaries of the 2002 budget were elderly Australians who received spending increases of more than $3 billion.

In March 2001, the value of the Australian dollar sank to below U.S. $0.50 for the first time. In early April, it dropped to U.S. $0.47 before returning to a level of around U.S. $0.50. Commentators attributed the fall of the Australian dollar to the strength of the U.S. currency, rather than to any fundamental weakness in the Australian economy.

Business. Several large Australian companies collapsed in 2001. On March 15, HIH Insurance Ltd., one of Australia's largest insurance companies, went into provisional liquidation. The collapse was one of the largest in Australia's corporate history. The company held nearly 15 percent of the country's insurance market. The government promised to assist Australian citizens and small businesses affected by the collapse and initiated an investigation into the company's finances.

In May, One.Tel, Australia's fourth largest telecommunications company, was declared insolvent with debts of $180 million. The collapse caused embarrassment to Australia's two leading media-owners, Kerry Packer and Rupert Murdoch, whose sons, Jamie Packer and Lachlan Murdoch, were the directors of One.Tel. Both young men claimed they had been misinformed about the company's financial position.

In September, Melbourne-based Pasminco, the world's largest producer of lead and zinc, went into provisional liquidation with debts estimated at $2.6 billion.

In April, Dairy Farm International, the Hong Kong-based owners of Australia's third largest grocery chain, Franklins, announced that it would sell the chain. Woolworths, Australia's largest grocer, bought 80 of the 287 Franklins stores. In September, the Japanese retailer Daimaru announced that it was closing its Melbourne and Gold Coast department stores. Company officials reported that the Melbourne store had lost $11.9 million between July 2000 and July 2001.

Not all Australian companies were struggling however. On March 19, the directors of the long-established mining company BHP announced a merger with Billiton, a metal producing company based in the United Kingdom. BHP directors said that the newly merged company, known as BHP Billiton, would be among the world's largest metal and mining organizations.

Airline companies also struggled in 2001. Two new Australian-based airlines, Impulse and Virgin Blue, began offering heavily discounted fares to challenge Australia's two largest airlines, Qantas Airways Ltd. and Ansett Airlines. In May, Qantas absorbed the cash-strapped Impulse airline.

Australia's second largest airline, Ansett, a division of Air New Zealand, also ran into financial trouble in 2001. In April, the Civil Aviation Authority grounded Ansett's aging fleet, citing safety concerns. Even after Ansett resumed flights, increased competition and mechanical problems plagued the airline. By September, Ansett officials reported losses of more than $1 million a day. On September 14, Ansett canceled all of its flights, leaving nearly 47,000 passengers stranded. The 65-year-old airline's closure resulted in the biggest mass layoff in Australian history, leaving more than 16,000 people without jobs.

The closure also left many remote areas of Australia without airline service. On September 30, after the Australian government had provided fi-

Members of the Australian House of Representatives

The House of Representatives of the 40th Parliament was elected on Nov. 10, 2001. As of Dec. 5, 2001, the House of Representatives consisted of the following members: 68 Liberal Party of Australia, 65 Australian Labor Party, 13 National Party of Australia, 3 independents, and 1 Country Liberal Party. This table shows each legislator and party affiliation. An asterisk (*) denotes those who served in the 39th Parliament.

Australian Capital Territory
Annette Ellis, A.L.P.*
Bob McMullan, A.L.P.*

New South Wales
Tony Abbott, L.P.*
Anthony Albanese, A.L.P.*
John Anderson, N.P.*
Peter Andren, Ind.*
Larry Anthony, N.P.*
Bruce Baird, L.P.*
Bob Baldwin, L.P.
Kerry Bartlett, L.P.*
Bronwyn Bishop, L.P.*
Laurie Brereton, A.L.P.*
Alan Cadman, L.P.*
Ross Cameron, L.P.*
Ian Causley, N.P.*
John Cobb, N.P.
Janice Crosio, A.L.P.*
Patrick Farmer, L.P.
Laurie Ferguson, A.L.P.*
Joel Fitzgibbon, A.L.P.*
Joanna Gash, L.P.*
Jennie George, A.L.P.
Sharon Grierson, A.L.P.
Jill Hall, A.L.P.*
Luke Hartsuyker, N.P.
Michael Hatton, A.L.P.*
Kelly Hoare, A.L.P.*
Joe Hockey, L.P.*
John Howard, L.P.*
Kay Hull, N.P.*
Julia Irwin, A.L.P.*
Jackie Kelly, L.P.*
Peter King, L.P.
Mark Latham, A.L.P.*
Sussan Ley, L.P.
Jim Lloyd, L.P.*
Stephen Martin, A.L.P.*
Robert McClelland, A.L.P.*
Leo McLeay, A.L.P.*
Daryl Melham, A.L.P.*
Frank Mossfield, A.L.P.*
John Murphy, A.L.P.*
Gary Nairn, L.P.*
Brendan Nelson, L.P.*
Tanya Plibersek, A.L.P.*
Roger Price, A.L.P.*
Philip Ruddock, L.P.*
Alby Schultz, L.P.*
Kenneth Ticehurst, L.P.
Mark Vaile, N.P.*
Danna Vale, L.P.*
Tony Windsor, Ind.

Northern Territory
Warren Snowdon, A.L.P.*
David Tollner, C.L.P.

Queensland
Arch Bevis, A.L.P.*
Mal Brough, L.P.*
Steven Ciobo, L.P.
Peter Dutton, L.P.
Kay Elson, L.P.*
Craig Emerson, A.L.P.*
Warren Entsch, L.P.*
Teresa Gambaro, L.P.*
Gary Hardgrave, L.P.*
Michael Johnson, L.P.
David Jull, L.P.*
Robert Katter, Ind.*
De-Anne Kelly, N.P.*
Peter Lindsay, L.P.*
Kirsten Livermore, A.L.P.*
Ian Macfarlane, L.P.*
Margaret May, L.P.*
Paul Neville, N.P.*
Bernie Ripoll, A.L.P.*
Kevin Rudd, A.L.P.*
Con Sciacca, A.L.P.*
Bruce Scott, N.P.*
Peter Slipper, L.P.*
Alexander Somlyay, L.P.*
Wayne Swan, A.L.P.*
Cameron Thompson, L.P.*
Warren Truss, N.P.*

South Australia
Neil Andrew, L.P.*
David Cox, A.L.P.*
Alexander Downer, L.P.*
Trish Draper, L.P.*
Martyn Evans, A.L.P.*
Christine Gallus, L.P.*
Christopher Pyne, L.P.*
Rodney Sawford, A.L.P.*
Patrick Secker, L.P.*
Andrew Southcott, L.P.*
Barry Wakelin, L.P.*
Trish Worth, L.P.*

Tasmania
Dick Adams, A.L.P.*
Duncan Kerr, A.L.P.*
Michelle O'Byrne, A.L.P.*
Harry Quick, A.L.P.*
Sid Sidebottom, A.L.P.*

Victoria
Kevin Andrews, L.P.*
Fran Bailey, L.P.*
Phillip Barresi, L.P.*
Bruce Billson, L.P.*
Anna Burke, A.L.P.*
Anthony Byrne, A.L.P.*
Bob Charles, L.P.*
Ann Corcoran, A.L.P.*
Peter Costello, L.P.*
Simon Crean, A.L.P.*
Michael Danby, A.L.P.*
Martin Ferguson, A.L.P.*
John Forrest, N.P.*
Petro Georgiou, L.P.*
Steve Gibbons, A.L.P.*
Julia Gillard, A.L.P.*
Alan Griffin, A.L.P.*
David Hawker, L.P.*
Greg Hunt, L.P.
Harry Jenkins, A.L.P.*
David Kemp, L.P.*
Catherine King, A.L.P.
Jenny Macklin, A.L.P.*
Stewart McArthur, L.P.*
Peter McGauran, N.P.*
Brendan O'Connor, A.L.P.
Gavan O'Connor, A.L.P.*
Sophie Panopoulos, L.P.
Chris Pearce, L.P.
Nicola Roxon, A.L.P.*
Bob Sercombe, A.L.P.*
Tony Smith, L.P.
Sharman Stone, L.P.*
Lindsay Tanner, A.L.P.*
Kelvin Thomson, A.L.P.*
Maria Vamvakinou, A.L.P.
Christian Zahra, A.L.P.*

Western Australia
Kim Beazley, A.L.P.*
Julie Bishop, L.P.*
Graham Edwards, A.L.P.*
Barry Haase, L.P.*
Sharryn Jackson, A.L.P.
Carmen Lawrence, A.L.P.*
Jann McFarlane, A.L.P.*
Judi Moylan, L.P.*
Geoffrey Prosser, L.P.*
Don Randall, L.P.
Stephen Smith, A.L.P.*
Wilson Tuckey, L.P.*
Mal Washer, L.P.*
Kim Wilkie, A.L.P.*
Daryl Williams, L.P.*

The Ministry of Australia*

John Howard—prime minister

John Anderson—minister for transport and regional services; deputy prime minister

Peter Costello—treasurer

Mark Vaile—minister for trade

Robert Hill—minister for defense; leader of the government in the Senate

Richard Alston—minister for communications and information technology; deputy leader of the government in the Senate

Alexander Downer—minister for foreign affairs

Tony Abbott—minister for employment and workplace relations

Philip Ruddock—minister for immigration and multicultural and indigenous affairs

David Kemp—minister for environment and heritage

Daryl Williams—attorney-general

Nick Minchin—minister for finance and administration

Warren Truss—minister for agriculture, fisheries, and forestry

Amanda Vanstone—minister for family and community services

Brendan Nelson—minister for education, science, and training

Kay Patterson—minister for health and aging

Ian Macfarlane—minister for industry, tourism, and resources

*As of Nov. 28, 2001.

Premiers of Australian states

State	Premier
New South Wales	Bob Carr
Queensland	Peter Beattie
South Australia	Rob Kerin
Tasmania	Jim Bacon
Victoria	Steve Bracks
Western Australia	Geoff Gallop

Government leaders of Australian mainland territories

Australian Capital Territory	Jon Stanhope
Northern Territory	Clare Martin

nancial assistance, Ansett resumed service between Sydney and Melbourne. In November, two well-known Melbourne millionaires, retailer Solomon Lew and transportation entrepreneur Lindsay Fox, announced they would purchase the airline. The new company was expected tobe much smaller and would concentrate on profitable routes between the state capital cities of Australia.

Railroad. On July 17, Prime Minister Howard fulfilled a promise made by many of his predecessors when he inaugurated the construction of the $1.3-billion Alice Springs to Darwin rail line. The first rail link between Adelaide and Alice Springs was begun in 1878, but the track between Alice Springs in central Australia and Darwin on the north coast was never built. The rail project was intended to capitalize on Australia's growing trade with Asia. Construction on the new 875-mile (1,400-kilometer) track created an estimated 1,300 jobs and was scheduled for completion in 2004.

Motion pictures. In March, New Zealand-born, Australian-trained actor Russell Crowe won the Academy Award for best actor for his role in *Gladiator*. In May, *Moulin Rouge*, directed by Australia's Baz Luhrmann, opened France's Cannes Film Festival. The film's opening weekend in Australia collected $3,600,596, the most ever for an Australian film.

Dingo attack. In April, two *dingoes* (wild dogs) on Fraser Island attacked and killed a 9-year-old boy, Clinton Gage. Queensland Premier Peter Beattie ordered the staff at all wildlife parks to begin culling the animals. Some animal experts believed that the dingoes were starving and had attacked the boy for food. In May, an autopsy showed the dingoes were not starving but were, in fact, well fed.

Wild fires. In late December, some 75 brush fires burned out of control in New South Wales, forcing state officials to close highways and railroads and local residents to evacuate burning houses. The fires were fanned by 55 mile- (88 kilometer-) per-hour winds that blew smoke into the center of Sydney. More than 5,000 firefighters battled the wild fires, which burned across thousands of acres, killing large numbers of sheep and cattle.

Death. Australian cricketer Sir Donald Bradman, who was revered as the finest batsman in the world, died on February 25 at the age of 92. During his career, Bradman scored 6,996 runs at an average of 99.94, an achievement no other player has come close to breaking. His memory was honored in March in a nationally televised service at St. Peter's Cathedral in Adelaide. The Governor-General, Sir William Deane, and many cricket celebrities attended the memorial service. ☐ Brian Kennedy

See also **Australia, Prime Pinister of; Cricket; People in the news** (Crowe, Russell); **Terrorism: A Special Feature,** p. 38.

Australia, Prime Minister of.

Prime Minister John Howard was reelected to a third term in November 2001 general parliamentary elections. Howard refused to guarantee that he would serve out the full three-year term, saying he would reconsider his position as prime minister after his 64th birthday in July 2003.

In June 2001, Indonesian President Abdurrahman Wahid went to Australia to meet with Howard. The trip was the first visit to Australia by an Indonesian leader since 1975. Relations between Australia and Indonesia had been strained since Indonesia invaded East Timor in 1975. Australia had supported East Timor's independence.

Soon after the visit, Wahid was removed from office and succeeded by Vice President Megawati Sukarnoputri. In August 2001, Howard went to Jakarta, Indonesia's capital, to establish relations with Megawati. The two leaders agreed on the importance of mutual cooperation in dealing with immigration issues.

In September, Howard visited the United States to discuss trade issues with President George W. Bush and was in Washington, D.C., on the day terrorists attacked the United States. Howard quickly pledged support for the United States in its war against terrorism. ☐ Brian Kennedy

See also **Australia; Indonesia; Terrorism: A Special Feature,** p. 38.

Australian rules football.

The Brisbane Lions defeated the Essendon Bombers by 26 points in the Australian Football League (AFL) 2001 Grand Final at the Melbourne Cricket Ground on September 29. Essendon led by 14 points at half-time, but Brisbane dominated the final. The final score was Brisbane 15 goals 18 behinds (108 points) to Essendon's 12 goals 10 behinds (82 points). The 2001 season capped a remarkable turnaround for the Lions, which had finished in last place in the league in 1998.

The Lions' Grand Final win, the first for a Queensland side, was a triumph for captain Michael Voss and coach Leigh Matthews. Brisbane's Shaun Hart won the Norm Smith Medal for the best player on the ground. Brisbane's Jason Akermanis won the Brownlow Medal for best and fairest player of the season.

Local competitions. The Brisbane Lions Reserves won the Queensland State League premiership title, defeating Southport by 13.2 (98) to 13.8 (86). In the Western Australian Football League Grand Final, East Perth beat South Fremantle 17.18 (120) to 5.8 (38). Clarence won the Southern Football League Grand Final over Glenorchy 17.19 (121) to 11.11 (77). In the South Australia National Football League, Central Districts defeated the Woodville-West Torrens Eagles 10.11 (71) to 4.8 (32). ☐ Brian Kennedy

Austria.

The far-right Freedom Party suffered a setback in 2001 after a decade of political advancement. The party won just 20 percent of the vote in elections in Vienna on March 25, down from 28 percent in the previous city election in 1996 and the party's 28 percent share of the vote in national elections in 1999. The 1999 election enabled the Freedom Party to enter government for the first time by forming a coalition with the People's Party of Chancellor Wolfgang Schuessel.

The city election followed a bitter campaign in which Joerg Haider, the Freedom Party's most prominent figure, criticized the leader of Vienna's Jewish community as well as Stanley Greenberg, a political consultant from the United States who advised Vienna's Social Democratic mayor during the campaign. Many Austrians regarded Haider's comments as anti-Semitic. The Freedom Party had aroused concern across Europe because of its anti-immigrant stance and because of previous inflammatory comments by Haider.

The Social Democrats won 47 percent of the vote in the Vienna elections, while the Green Party's share rose to more than 12 percent, up from 8 percent in 1996. The result raised the prospect that the Social Democrats, who were thrown out of the national government in 2000 after more than 30 years in power, could return in 2003 by forming an alliance with the Greens.

Economy. The Austrian government's goal to balance the budget by 2002 was cast in doubt in 2001, when the country experienced the same slowdown in growth that affected other European Union nations. In the wake of the terrorist attacks on the United States on September 11, Bank Austria, the country's leading bank, forecast that Austria's economy would grow by 1.4 percent in 2001, down from 3 percent in 2000.

Several leading Austrian companies suffered management turmoil in 2001. The turmoil stemmed from OIAG, the entity that oversees the government's stakes in former state-owned companies. The Schuessel government had promised to end the practice of awarding top business jobs to executives loyal to the governing parties. However, complaints of political influence—especially by Johannes Ditz, a former People's Party politician who was appointed chief executive of OIAG in 2000—continued. In September 2001, the OIAG supervisory board announced that it would cancel the remainder of Ditz's contract.

Vienna's arts scene gained a major new attraction in June with the opening of the MuseumsQuartier, a complex of art galleries and theaters in the center of the city. The new complex is housed in the Baroque buildings of the former Imperial Riding Stables, which were converted in a redevelopment project. ☐ Tom Buerkle

See also **Europe.**

FOCUS ON AUTOMOBILE

Ford takes a page from the past in 2001 and revives the Thunderbird the same year that General Motors announces the end of two of its sportiest models, the Chevrolet Camaro and the Pontiac Firebird.

Ford Motor Company in 2001 reintroduced the Ford Thunderbird. The styling of the 2002 model (above), which was virtually sold out by the end of 2001, was reminiscent of the original Thunderbird (top), introduced in 1955.

Automobile. The United States automobile industry posted positive sales totals in 2001. Yet sales failed to reach the levels they did in 2000, hurt by a sluggish economy that made consumers reluctant to buy big-ticket items. The 2001 terrorist attacks on the United States also depressed automotive sales in September.

Automobile analysts predicted that 2001 would be one of the auto industry's best years with U.S. sales of around 17 million cars and light trucks. However, the total trailed the record sales year reached in 2000, when the industry sold 17.4 million cars and light trucks. To reach 2001's sales total, automakers were forced to offer special deals, including interest-free financing on new car loans, to entice customers into showrooms. Analysts noted that such incentives and the weak U.S. economy lowered automakers' profits in 2001.

Top sellers. Ford and Honda outsold all other car manufacturers in the United States during the 2001 model year. Ford held the light-truck title with its 2001 F-series truck, which sold more than 844,000 units. The Honda Accord captured the car sales title, replacing the Toyota Camry, which had been the top-selling car for two consecutive years. Honda sold more than 412,000 Accords in 2001.

Capturing market share. Through the end of September 2001, sales of new cars and light trucks totaled 12.8 million vehicles, 5.7 percent below the same period in 2000. Sales figures for the first nine months of 2001 showed the continuation of a lower market share for the largest U.S. automakers. Officials at General Motors Corporation (GM) of Detroit, Ford Motor Company of Dearborn, Michigan, and the U.S. division of DaimlerChrysler AG of Germany reported a total market share of 64.3 percent through September, 3 percentage points lower than the first nine months of 2000.

Asian automakers reported that their market share rose to 30.5 percent in the first nine months of 2001, 2.5 percentage points higher than for the same period in 2000. European automakers

General Motors (GM) introduced a special 2002 Collector Edition of the Pontiac Firebird Trans AM (top) and a 35th-Anniversary Edition of the Chevrolet Camaro (bottom) in 2001 to mark the final year that both cars would be produced. GM officials announced the end of the two sporty models in September.

gained market share, capturing 5.2 percent of the market through September 2001, compared with 4.7 percent for the first nine months of 2000.

Domestic auto companies. GM, the number-one automaker in the United States, saw its market share decline again in 2001. Through September, the company's market share stood at 28.1 percent, compared with 28.4 percent in the first nine months of 2000. GM's sales dropped 6.9 percent to 3.6 million vehicles in the first three quarters of 2001. Through September 2001, the company earned $346 million, compared with $4.4 billion in 2000.

Declining sales of the Chevrolet Camaro and Pontiac Firebird prompted the automaker to announce that it would discontinue production of the performance cars at the end of the 2002 model year. The move was to result in the closing of an assembly plant in Ste. Therese, Canada.

One of GM's successful products in 2001 was the Silverado pickup truck. Sales of the Silverado improved 20 percent to 490,378 units through the first nine months of the year.

Ford Motor Company, the second-largest automaker in the United States, weathered a difficult year in 2001. Ford continued to deal with problems stemming from its use of Firestone tires that became the focus of a federal safety investigation in 2000. Officials said the tires could shred at high or low speeds. Officials at Bridgestone/Firestone, Inc., a Japanese-owned tire company located in Nashville, Tennessee, recalled 6.5 million tires. The tires were installed as original equipment on Ford light trucks and sport utility vehicles (SUV's).

In May 2001, Ford officials announced they would replace an additional 13 million tires on Ford vehicles as a precaution after the company tested the performance of Firestone Wilderness tires against the performance of other tire brands.

The Ford announcement followed an announcement by Bridgestone/Firestone that the company would no longer supply tires to Ford. The tire company claimed that the safety problems were caused by deficiencies in Ford vehicles, not by the tires.

Ford Company Chairman William Clay Ford, Jr., the great-grandson of company founder Henry Ford, announced in October that he was replacing Jacques Nasser as Ford's chief executive officer following Nasser's sudden resignation. Ford said that the terrorist attacks on the United States on September 11 had worsened an already bleak outlook for the auto industry and accelerated the need for change. Automotive analysts viewed the move as a rejection of Nasser's leadership.

Through September 2001, Ford recorded a net loss of $385 million compared with a net gain of $2.4 billion in 2000. In the first nine months of 2001, Ford's share of the U.S. market dropped to 22.8 percent, compared with 24.3 percent for the previous nine months. The automaker's sales fell to 2.9 million units for the first nine months of 2001, 11.3 percent lower than in 2000.

Reflecting the drop, sales of the Explorer totaled 303,455 vehicles through September 2001, 14.4 percent lower than for the same period in 2000. However, Ford's Escape posted strong sales of 115,566 vehicles. Production of the reintroduced Thunderbird was virtually sold out by the end of 2001.

DaimlerChrysler officials also suffered setbacks in 2001. The company posted a market share of 13.4 percent through the first nine months of 2001, compared with 14.6 percent in 2000. Sales declined to 1.7 million vehicles through September 2001, 13.5 percent lower than the first nine months of 2000.

Sales of the Dodge Caravan minivan dropped by 22 percent and Jeep Grand Cherokee sales fell 25 percent in 2001. However, sales of the PT Cruiser rose to 105,363 units through September for an increase of 85 percent over 2000. The Chrysler Group moved to capture its share of the small sport utility segment with the Jeep Liberty. Through September, DaimlerChrysler recorded a net loss of $659 million, compared with a net income of $5.8 billion in the previous year's first three quarters.

Japanese companies captured increased market share in 2001. Honda reported a market share of 7.2 percent in the first nine months of 2001, compared with 6.7 percent for the same period in 2000. Toyota executives reported that their market share rose to 10.1 percent through September 2001 from 9.1 percent for the first nine months of 2000.

Toyota continued its expansion in the United States with an announcement in February 2001 that it would build its first V-8 engine factory outside of Japan in Huntsville, Alabama. Nissan announced in September that production of the new Maxima would start at its Smyrna, Tennessee, assembly plant in 2003. ☐ Mike Casey

Automobile racing. Safety issues cast a long shadow over professional automobile racing in 2001. Racing legend Dale Earnhardt was killed on February 18 in a crash on the final lap of the Daytona 500 at Daytona International Speedway in Daytona Beach, Florida. Earnhardt's death, combined with the death in October of Blaise Alexander, fueled the debate over whether NASCAR officials were taking proper safety precautions.

A legend dies. Dale Earnhardt, who won seven Winston Cup championships, died when his car slammed into the wall during the final lap of the Daytona 500. Earnhardt, known as "the Intimidator" because of his aggressive driving style,

was attempting to prevent other racers from catching his teammate, Michael Waltrip, who won the race moments after the crash. The crash occurred when another racer tapped Earnhardt's car from behind, forcing him into the concrete wall at about 180 miles (290 kilometers) per hour.

Shortly after the crash, NASCAR officials announced that they had found a broken seat belt in Earnhardt's car. However, a paramedic who tended to Earnhardt after the crash reported he had not seen a broken seat belt. An independent expert who was appointed by a Florida Circuit Court to examine photos taken during Earnhardt's autopsy determined that even if the belt had broken during the crash, it happened after Earnhardt's fatal injury occurred. Earnhardt died from head trauma caused when his head snapped forward violently.

Additional safety questions were raised on October 4, when Blaise Alexander, 25, died in a crash after sustaining injuries similar to Earnhardt's. Both drivers had opted not to wear a Head and Neck Safety (HANS) device, a system of helmet tethers anchored to a collar made of a carbon-fiber composite. On October 17, NASCAR officials said all drivers must immediately begin wearing either the HANS device or the "Hutchens," another head-restraint system.

NASCAR. Jeff Gordon took the Winston Cup Series Championship when he finished sixth at the Napa 500 on November 18. It was Gordon's fourth Winston Cup title, putting him third on the all-time list. Tony Stewart finished second in the Winston Cup standings, 22 points ahead of Sterling Marlin.

IRL. Sam Hornish, Jr., took the Indy Racing League (IRL) title on October 6, winning the Chevy 500 at Texas Motor Speedway in Fort Worth. The race was the closest in IRL history, with Hornish coming from behind to edge Scott Sharp by a mere 0.0188 second.

CART. Gil de Ferran edged out Kenny Brack in a hotly contested race for the 2001 CART championship. De Ferran won the title with his fourth-place finish at the Honda Indy 300 in Queensland, Australia. He finished with 199 points, 36 more than Brack.

Racing legend Dale Earnhardt, (inset), died on Feb. 18, 2001, in a crash at the Daytona 500 in Daytona Beach, Florida. Earnhardt, in car number 3, was blocking for teammate Michael Waltrip when he was tapped from behind and hit the wall. He died from head injuries.

Indianapolis 500. Helio Castroneves of Brazil took the checkered flag at the Indianapolis 500 on May 27. Drivers from the rival CART circuit claimed the top five positions in the race, which is the IRL's highest-profile race. Castroneves averaged 153.601 miles (247.196 kilometers) per hour and was the eighth rookie to win the Indy 500.

Formula One. Michael Schumacher of Germany claimed the world driver's title for the second straight year. Schumacher won 7 of the first 13 races of the 17-race Formula One season, clinching the title on August 19 by winning the Grand Prix of Hungary.

Endurance. In the Rolex 24-hour race on February 4 in Daytona Beach, Florida, Americans Chris Kneifel and Johnny O'Connell, Canadian Ron Fellows, and France's Franck Freon drove a Chevrolet C-5 Corvette to victory. On June 17, the Audi team of Frank Biela of Germany, Tom Kristensen of Denmark, and Emanuele Pirro of Italy captured the 24 Hours of Le Mans.

Dragsters. Kenny Bernstein won the 2001 National Hot Rod Association top fuel championship; John Force won the funny car division; and Warren Johnson won the pro stock division. ☐ Michael Kates

See also **Sports.**

Aviation. On Sept. 11, 2001, in one of the worst aviation disasters in history, hijackers took control of four commercial jetliners flying from the East Coast of the United States to California. After overpowering the pilots, the hijackers intentionally flew jets into the World Trade Center towers in New York City and the Pentagon Building outside Washington, D.C.

Tragedy strikes. Shortly before 9:00 Eastern Daylight Time on September 11, hijackers purposely crashed an American Airlines Boeing 767 into the north tower of the World Trade Center. The plane had been en route from Boston to Los Angeles. About 20 minutes later, a second group of hijackers crashed a United Airlines Boeing 767, also en route from Boston to Los Angeles, into the south tower.

Just before 10:00, a third group of hijackers, who had taken control of an American Airlines Boeing 757 on its way from Dulles International Airport in Herndon, Virginia, to Los Angeles, crashed the plane into the Pentagon, the headquarters of the U.S. Department of Defense, in Arlington, Virginia. The fourth hijacked plane, a United Airlines Boeing 757 en route from Newark, New Jersey, to San Francisco, crashed outside Pittsburgh in rural Pennsylvania. Federal investigators concluded that the plane crashed after several passengers attempted to regain con-

An employee at McCarran International Airport in Las Vegas, Nevada, sorts knives and other potentially dangerous objects confiscated from boarding passengers in the first 72 hours after commercial flights resumed following the September 11 terrorist attacks on the United States.

trol of the aircraft from the hijackers.

Security. Less than an hour after the first terrorist attack, officials with the Federal Aviation Administration (FAA) grounded all U.S. air traffic to prevent further attacks, an unprecedented action. When air travel resumed, the FAA stepped up security checks on passengers and made changes in airport security procedures.

Before the new rules, passengers had been allowed to carry small knives, and the hijackers apparently used boxcutting tools as weapons when they took control of the planes. After the attacks, the FAA outlawed knives and blades of any kind on commercial flights. The FAA also announced armed federal marshals would be assigned to travel undercover on some flights. All of the major airlines announced that more-secure cockpit doors would be installed in planes.

In the weeks following the attacks, Argenbright Security, Inc., of Atlanta, Georgia, the nation's largest airport security firm, came under fire for several airport security lapses. In some cases, Argenbright screeners failed to notice concealed knives when carry-on bags were X-rayed at security checkpoints. On November 19, U.S. President George W. Bush signed a law mandating that airport security be carried out by federal employees by late 2002. After three years of this system, airports can choose to hire private security companies. The law also included a provision for the increased presence of armed federal marshals on domestic flights to prevent hijackings.

Airline industry nosedives. Many people were reluctant to fly in the wake of the attacks, which shook the airline industry worldwide. The drop in airline revenues compounded a decline in air travel that had begun earlier in 2001 because of a slowdown in the economies of the United States and other countries. Airlines had responded by cutting prices to attract passengers. After the attacks, airlines slashed expenses by reducing flights by about 20 percent and by laying off more than 100,000 employees.

On September 22, President Bush signed into law a $15-billion federal bailout package for the U.S. airline industry. The plan provided $5 billion in immediate cash grants to the airlines to compensate for the three-to-four day loss of income during the FAA-ordered grounding of flights. The bailout package also included $10 billion in government-guaranteed loans.

Bankruptcies. The economic slowdown, coupled with the fallout from the attacks, compounded the financial problems that many airlines were already experiencing because of unwise acquisitions and expansion in the mid-1990's. In October 2001, the government of New Zealand retook control of Air New Zealand 12 years after the airline was privatized. The government acted in part because of financial problems stemming from the bankruptcy of an Air New Zealand subsidiary.

The Swissair Group, a holding company based in Zurich, Switzerland, that owned several airlines, including Swiss-based Swissair, filed for bankruptcy protection on October 1. The Swiss government and large corporations provided funds for Swissair to continue operating until the end of March 2002, when many of the company's services were to be transferred to a Swissair subsidiary, Crossair.

On Nov. 7, 2001, Sabena SA of Brussels, the national airline of Belgium, ceased operations as a direct result of the collapse of Swissair. Two days later, Canada 3000, Inc. of Toronto, Canada's second-largest airline, ceased operations due to reduced demand after the September 11 attacks.

Crash. On November 12, an American Airlines Airbus A-300 crashed in a New York City neighborhood minutes after taking off from John F. Kennedy International Airport, killing all 260 people on-board and 5 people on the ground. After the crash, investigators focused on the tail of the aircraft, which had sheared off, apparently after encountering strong turbulence created by the wake of another aircraft. ☐ Ian Savage

See also **Armed forces; New York City; Terrorism; Terrorism: A Special Feature**, p. 38.

Azerbaijan. The contested enclave of Nagorno-Karabakh dominated relations between Azerbaijan and Armenia in 2001. Nagorno-Karabakh, a mountainous region with an ethnic Armenian majority, seceded from Azerbaijan in 1988, sparking a six-year war between Azerbaijan and Armenia. Since a 1994 cease-fire, Nagorno-Karabakh has been occupied by Armenia, while Azerbaijan continued to claim it.

In April 2001, Azerbaijan's President Heydar Aliyev met with Armenian President Robert Kocharian in Florida for peace talks. The presidents reported a "narrowing of differences" over Nagorno-Karabakh but failed to reach an agreement. In late May, they indefinitely postponed plans to hold a further round of talks in Geneva, Switzerland. In October, Aliyev warned that Azerbaijan would resort to "military means" to retake the enclave unless Armenian troops withdrew.

Azerbaijan completed its transition from the Cyrillic to the Latin alphabet in August. The Cyrillic alphabet is used in Russian and other Slavic languages. Leaders had initiated the transition in 1992 to emphasize Azerbaijan's independent post-Soviet identity. ☐ Steven L. Solnick

See also **Asia**.

Bahamas. See **West Indies.**
Bahrain. See **Middle East.**
Ballet. See **Dance.**

Bangladesh. Khaleda Zia became prime minister on Oct. 10, 2001, after her Bangladesh Nationalist Party (BNP) and a small allied Islamic party won 201 of the 300 seats available in parliament. Local observers reported that voters backed the BNP in response to a breakdown of law and order and increased corruption while Sheikh Hasina Wajed of the Awami League (AL) was prime minister.

A political duel between the two women had disrupted Bangladeshi life for a decade. Zia, the widow of a murdered Bangladeshi president, first became prime minister in 1991. Hasina, daughter of Bangladesh's independence leader, refused to accept her party's loss. She led years of strikes and protests, until Zia resigned in 1996, and the AL won the subsequent parliamentary elections.

Zia then began strikes against the AL government. Since 1996, the BNP had called almost 100 days of strikes, which analysts estimate cost the economy some $6 billion. The strikes did not force Hasina from power, and she became Bangladesh's first leader to serve a full five-year term.

Hasina turned the government over to a neutral, caretaker regime to conduct the 2001 election. The campaign focused on the two women's feud, rather than on any principles or policy issues. The BNP won 185 seats in parliament by capturing 36 percent of the 56 million votes cast. The AL

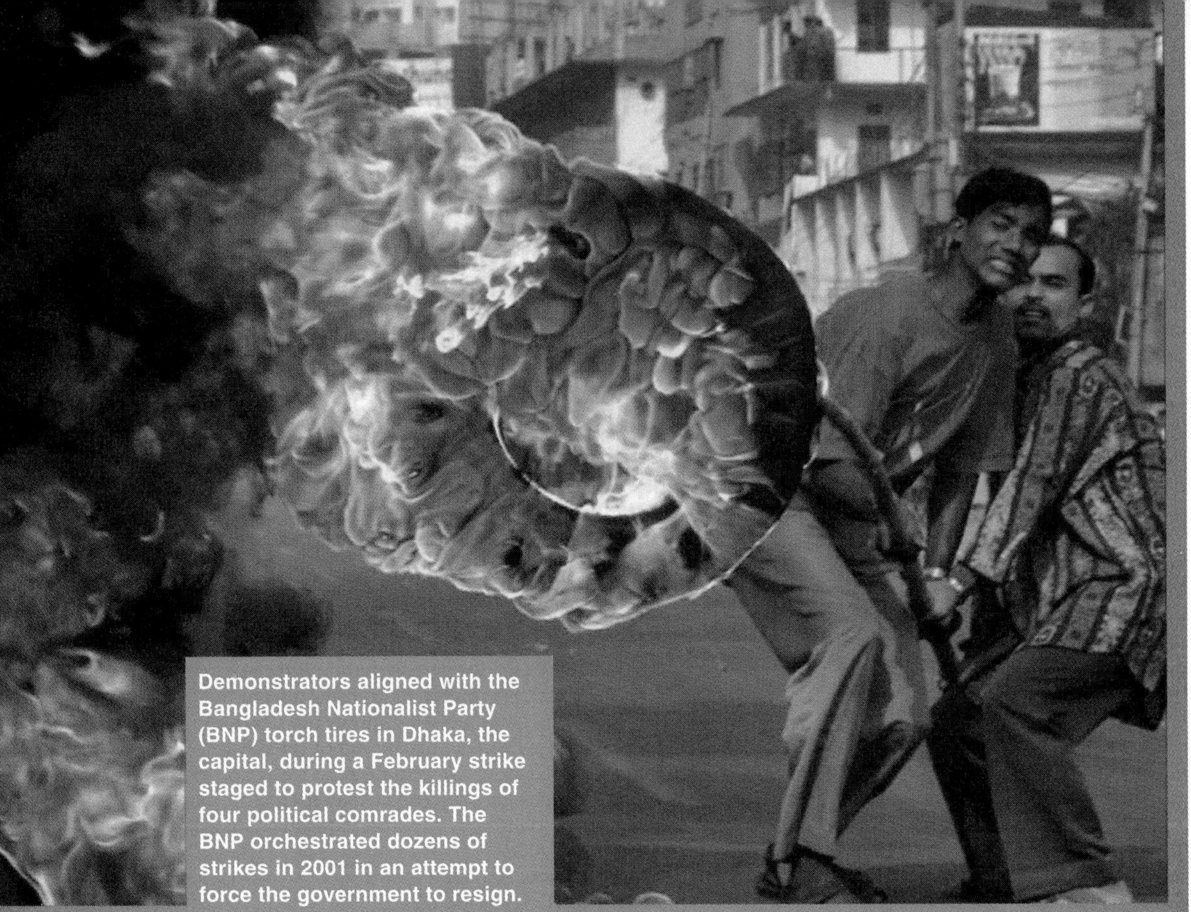

Demonstrators aligned with the Bangladesh Nationalist Party (BNP) torch tires in Dhaka, the capital, during a February strike staged to protest the killings of four political comrades. The BNP orchestrated dozens of strikes in 2001 in an attempt to force the government to resign.

took 63 seats with 40.5 percent of the ballots.

International observers called the election free and fair, despite the more than 300 murders associated with the campaign. Hasina, however, claimed that the results were fixed and briefly threatened strikes unless new elections were held.

Economic problems. The World Bank, a United Nations agency that provides loans to countries for development, blamed Bangladesh's confrontational politics for blocking the reforms needed for economic growth. A March 2001 World Bank report noted that economic and social well-being had improved steadily in the past decade, but inequality and massive poverty, especially in rural areas, persisted. The report described Bangladesh's economic growth, which averaged 5.5 percent in 2001, as below the country's potential and cited poor government and weak institutions for making nearly $2 billion a year in aid less effective than it should be.

Border incidents occurred after Bangladeshi soldiers seized a disputed village on the Indian border in April. When Indian troops tried to recapture the village, 16 Indian and 3 Bangladeshi soldiers were killed. In July, Bangladesh officials accused Indian officials of killing 17 people who were farming or fishing on the Bangladeshi side of the border. □ Henry S. Bradsher

See also **Asia; India.**

Bank.

United States banks in 2001 played a major role in boosting the nation's weakening economy. They also contributed to antiterrorist measures taken by the U.S. government after the September 11 terrorist attacks on the World Trade Center in New York City and the Pentagon Building near Washington, D.C.

Interest rate cuts. As economic growth slowed, the U.S. Federal Reserve System (the Fed), an independent government agency that oversees the U.S. banking system, reduced interest rates 11 times in 2001. The Fed cut its federal funds rate (the rate the Fed's member banks charge one another for overnight loans) a total of 4.75 percentage points, ending with a quarter-point rate cut on December 11. After the final rate cut, the federal funds rate stood at 1.75 percent, the lowest since 1961. Mortgage rates fell to about 6 percent by early November 2001.

The Federal Reserve lowers interest rates on the economic theory that businesses will borrow money to expand if they can do so relatively cheaply. In 2001, the Fed was responding to evidence that the economy was slowing for the first time in a decade. In the third quarter of 2001, the *gross domestic product* (GDP—the measure of all goods and services produced in a country in a given period) fell by 0.4 percent. Even in the second quarter, the GDP had flattened out, posting a rise of just 0.2 percent. Few economists doubted that the September 11 terrorist attacks added strains to the already burdened economy.

Antiterrorism efforts. Banks played several important roles in the antiterrorism campaign that the U.S. government launched following the terrorist attacks on the United States on September 11. On September 24, U.S. President George W. Bush ordered banks to freeze assets in the United States held by suspected terrorist groups. Under the order, the holders of those accounts could not withdraw their funds. In the executive order, President Bush also said that any foreign banks that did not cooperate with U.S. investigators could be cut off from doing business in the United States. The executive order froze assets of 27 individuals and organizations with links to Osama bin Laden, the Afghanistan-based Saudi whom U.S. intelligence officials suspected of organizing the attacks.

In the wake of the attacks, the U.S. Congress passed sweeping antiterrorist legislation, which President Bush signed into law on October 26. The new law included the International Money Laundering Abatement and Anti-Terrorist Financing Act of 2001. Among other provisions, it allowed the U.S. Treasury Department to block U.S. banks from dealing with questionable foreign banks. The law also required U.S. banks to attempt to determine the sources of deposits from foreign countries and to turn away those it deemed questionable.

The new law required the treasury secretary to adopt regulations to encourage cooperation among banks, their regulatory authorities, and law enforcement authorities. The purpose was to encourage bank regulators—such as officials of the Fed or the Federal Deposit Insurance Corporation (FDIC), a government agency that insures deposits at financial institutions in the United States—to share information about suspected terrorists with banks.

The law also established U.S. jurisdiction over foreign money launderers, including their assets held in the United States and money that is *laundered* (made to appear legitimate) through a foreign bank. The legislation amended a previous law, the Right to Financial Privacy Act, to permit the transfer of banking records to U.S. law enforcement agencies if the records were relevant to international terrorism.

Help for damaged banks. In the aftermath of the September terrorist attacks, the Federal Reserve pumped an extra $45 billion into the U.S. banking system to help banks that had suffered damage from the attacks. Some New York City banks in the vicinity of "ground zero" in lower Manhattan sustained damage to their facilities and had difficulties processing trades in government bonds. The extra liquidity provided by the Fed enabled these banks to sell treasury securities back to the government in order to raise funds to meet their obligations.

Profitability. Despite the slowing economy, banks stayed profitable in 2001. For the first half of 2001, U.S. commercial banks posted earnings of $39.98 billion, a record for the period. The banks' assets totaled $6.36 trillion.

The second quarter, April through June, was the fifth most profitable quarter the U.S. banking industry had ever reported. However, fewer than half of all banks—just 49.4 percent—reported quarterly earnings higher than one year ago, according to the FDIC.

The industry's return on assets (ROA), a standard measure of profitability, dropped to 1.21 percent in the second quarter, down from 1.27 percent in the first quarter. A majority of banks reported lower ROA's in 2001, compared with a year ago.

Total noncurrent loans, another important measure of banking health, increased by $2.7 billion (5.8 percent) during the second quarter of 2001. At mid-year, 1.26 percent of commercial banks' loans were noncurrent, the highest level in six years.

Mergers. The rapid pace of industry consolidation seen in previous years slowed in 2001. In the first half of the year, 211 banks and savings institutions were absorbed by mergers. In 2000, 499 banks and savings institutions merged. In 1999, there were 513 mergers.

FDIC. In April 2001, FDIC officials recommended ways for Congress to revise the system of insuring bank deposits. Under laws that date back to the 1930's, deposits are safe, even if a bank fails. The limit on deposit insurance in 2001 was $100,000 per account. FDIC officials wanted to change the rules so that banks that make riskier loans would pay more for deposit insurance. However, Federal Reserve Chairman Alan Greenspan, testifying before Congress on May 10, advised policymakers to be cautious in revising deposit insurance rules. FDIC rules remained unchanged at the end of 2001.

In July, the U.S. Senate confirmed Donald E. Powell as 18th chairman of the FDIC. Powell was sworn in at a ceremony on August 28. He replaced John Reich, who had served as acting FDIC chairman. Powell served as president and chief executive officer of the First National Bank of Amarillo in Texas, before taking the FDIC post.

Bank failures. The pace of bank failures also slowed in 2001. Just two banks insured by the FDIC failed in 2001. Eight FDIC-insured banks had failed in 2000. ☐ Paulette Thomas

See also **Economics; Terrorism.**

Arizona Diamondbacks pitchers Curt Schilling (left) and Randy Johnson (right) congratulate each other after the Diamondbacks won the 2001 World Series. Schilling and Johnson were named Most Valuable Players of the series.

Baseball. Fans in 2001 witnessed one of the most dramatic World Series in the history of Major League Baseball (MLB) and saw major individual and team records broken. The fledgling Arizona Diamondbacks of the National League (NL) defeated the New York Yankees of the American League (AL) in the World Series in seven games, three of which were decided in extra innings or in the ninth. Because of a six-day delay in the regular season prompted by the September 11 terrorist attacks on the United States, World Series games were played in November for the first time.

Barry Bonds of the San Francisco Giants established new single-season records for home runs (73), slugging percentage (.863), and walks (177). Sammy Sosa of the Chicago Cubs hit 64 home runs, becoming the first player to hit 60 or more home runs in three seasons.

Contraction. On November 6, MLB team owners voted to eliminate two teams for the 2002 season because of financial pressures. MLB officials said that the Minnesota Twins and the Montreal Expos might be eliminated. The players' union, however, fought the move and a hearing was set for early January 2002 to decide whether teams would be eliminated in 2002 or 2003.

World Series. On Nov. 4, 2001, the Arizona Diamondbacks won the World Series, defeating the New York Yankees in seven games. The Diamondbacks won the seventh game 3-2 with a bottom-of-the-ninth, two-run rally against premier Yankee reliever Mariano Rivera. Rivera had been credited with 23 consecutive post-season saves dating back to 1997.

Arizona won the first two games in Phoenix, but the Yankees took all three games in New York City, the last two in thrilling fashion. Trailing 3-1 with two outs in the bottom of the ninth of game 4 on Oct. 31, 2001, the Yankees' Tino Martinez clubbed a two-run homer to tie the game. Derek Jeter hit a solo homer in the 10th inning to give New York a 4-3 win and tie the series. The Yan-

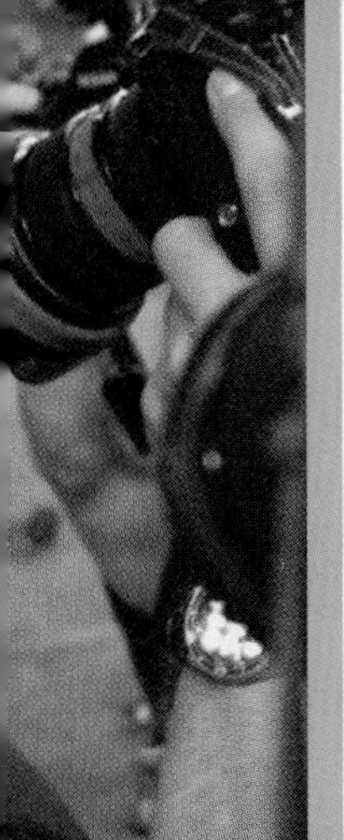

kees then duplicated the feat the next night in game 5. Trailing 2-0 with two outs in the bottom of the ninth, the Yankees' Scott Brosius belted a two-run homer to tie the game. The Yankees won in the 12th inning, 3-2. Back in Phoenix for game 6, the Diamondbacks blasted the Yankees 15-2, setting a World Series record for hits with 22. The Diamondbacks, founded in 1998, became the youngest franchise to win the crown.

Arizona pitchers Randy Johnson and Curt Schilling were named co-Most Valuable Players (MVP) of the World Series. Schilling started three games and posted a 1-0 record with a 1.69 earned run average (ERA). Johnson started two World Series games and won them both. After pitching game 6, he pitched the final four outs of game 7 in relief of Schilling to finish the Series with a 3-0 record and an ERA of 1.04.

Play-offs. The Yankees beat the Oakland Athletics in the first round of the play-offs 3 games to 2, becoming the first team to win a best-of-five series after dropping the first two games at home. The Yankees then toppled the

Final standings in Major League Baseball

American League

American League champions—
New York Yankees (defeated Seattle Mariners, 4 games to 1)

Eastern Division	W.	L.	Pct.	G.B.
New York Yankees	95	65	.594	—
Boston Red Sox	82	79	.509	13½
Toronto Blue Jays	80	82	.494	16
Baltimore Orioles	63	98	.391	32½
Tampa Bay Devil Rays	62	100	.383	34
Central Division				
Cleveland Indians	91	71	.562	—
Minnesota Twins	85	77	.525	6
Chicago White Sox	83	79	.512	8
Detroit Tigers	66	96	.407	25
Kansas City Royals	65	97	.401	26
Western Division				
Seattle Mariners	116	46	.716	—
Oakland Athletics*	102	60	.630	14
Anaheim Angels	75	87	.463	41
Texas Rangers	73	89	.451	43

Offensive leaders

Batting average	Ichiro Suzuki, Seattle	.350
Runs scored	Alex Rodriguez, Texas	133
Home runs	Alex Rodriguez, Texas	52
Runs batted in	Bret Boone, Seattle	141
Hits	Ichiro Suzuki, Seattle	242
Stolen bases	Ichiro Suzuki, Seattle	56
Slugging percentage	Jason Giambi, Oakland	.660

Leading pitchers

Games won	Mark Mulder, Oakland	21
Earned run average (162 or more innings)—	Freddy Garcia, Seattle	3.05
Strikeouts	Hideo Nomo, Boston	220
Saves	Mariano Rivera, New York	50
Shut-outs	Mark Mulder, Oakland	4
Complete games	Steve Sparks, Detroit	8

Awards†

Most Valuable Player ....Ichiro Suzuki, Seattle
Cy Young............................Roger Clemens, New York
Rookie of the Year......................Ichiro Suzuki, Seattle
Manager of the Year.....................Lou Piniella, Seattle

*Qualified for wild-card play-off spot.
†Selected by the Baseball Writers Association of America.

National League

National League champions—
Arizona Diamondbacks (defeated Atlanta Braves, 4 games to 1)
World Series champions—
Arizona Diamondbacks (defeated New York Yankees, 4 games to 3)

Eastern Division	W.	L.	Pct.	G.B.
Atlanta Braves	88	74	.543	—
Philadelphia Phillies	86	76	.531	2
New York Mets	82	80	.506	6
Florida Marlins	76	86	.469	12
Montreal Expos	68	94	.420	20
Central Division				
Houston Astros	93	69	.574	—
St. Louis Cardinals*	93	69	.574	—
Chicago Cubs	88	74	.543	5
Milwaukee Brewers	68	94	.420	25
Cincinnati Reds	66	96	.407	27
Pittsburgh Pirates	62	100	.383	31
Western Division				
Arizona Diamondbacks	92	70	.568	—
San Francisco Giants	90	72	.556	2
Los Angeles Dodgers	86	76	.531	6
San Diego Padres	79	83	.488	13
Colorado Rockies	73	89	.451	19

Offensive leaders

Batting average	Larry Walker, Colorado	.350
Runs scored	Sammy Sosa, Chicago	146
Home runs	Barry Bonds, San Francisco	73
Runs batted in	Sammy Sosa, Chicago	160
Hits	Rich Aurilia, San Francisco	206
Stolen bases	Juan Pierre, Colorado; Jimmy Rollins, Philadelphia	46 (tie)
Slugging percentage	Barry Bonds, San Francisco	.863

Leading pitchers

Games won	Matt Morris, St. Louis; Curt Schilling, Arizona	22 (tie)
Earned run average	(162 or more innings)— Randy Johnson, Arizona	2.49
Strikeouts	Randy Johnson, Arizona	372
Saves	Rob Nen, San Francisco	45
Shut-outs	Greg Maddux, Atlanta; Javier Vazquez, Montreal	3 (tie)
Complete games	Curt Schilling, Arizona	6

Awards†

Most Valuable Player..........Barry Bonds, San Francisco
Cy Young................................Randy Johnson, Arizona
Rookie of the Year.....................Albert Pujols, St. Louis
Manager of the Year................Larry Bowa, Philadelphia

Seattle Mariners 4 games to 1 to advance to the World Series. The Mariners had defeated the Cleveland Indians 3 games to 2.

In the NL play-offs, Arizona edged the St. Louis Cardinals 3 games to 2 in the first round and won the NL pennant 4 games to 1 over the Atlanta Braves.

Regular season. The Seattle Mariners tied the 1906 Chicago Cubs for most wins in a season with 116. The Mariners surprised many fans by winning 47 of their first 59 games, the second-best start since 1900. The Mariners finished the 2001 season with a record of 116-46. They clinched a play-off berth on Sept. 3, 2001, and won the AL West Division on September 19. Oakland finished 102-60 to win the wild-card berth. The Yankees won the AL East with a record of 95-65, and the Cleveland Indians took the AL Central Division title with 91 wins and 71 losses.

In the National League, all three divisional races came down to the final week of the season. The Atlanta Braves won the NL East with a record of 88-74; the Arizona Diamondbacks claimed the NL West with a 92-70 mark; and the Houston Astros upended the St. Louis Cardinals on the final day of the season to win the NL Central with a record of 93-69. The Cardinals netted the wild-card berth with their 93-69 record but lost the division crown to Houston because of Houston's 9-7 advantage in games against St. Louis.

Ichiro. Seattle rookie Ichiro Suzuki led the MLB in hits (242), batting average (.350), and stolen bases (56). He had more hits than any player since 1930, breaking "Shoeless" Joe Jackson's 1911 rookie mark of 233. Ichiro was the first rookie since Jackie Robinson in 1949 to win a batting title and stolen-base crown in the same season. Ichiro also set a rookie record for singles with 192.

Milestones. On Oct. 7, 2001, Rickey Henderson of the San Diego Padres became only the 25th player to get 3,000 hits. In April, Henderson broke Babe Ruth's career walks record (2,062), and in October, he broke Ty Cobb's career record for runs (2,246). On September 19, Roger Clemens of the New York Yankees became the first pitcher ever to win 20 of 21 starts.

Going, going, gone. San Diego Padres hitting star Tony Gwynn ended his illustrious 20-year career with the club on October 7, finishing with eight NL batting titles, a .338 lifetime average, and 3,141 hits—17th on the all-time list.

Cal Ripken, Jr., of the Baltimore Orioles, the record-holder for consecutive games played with 2,632, retired on October 6. Fans selected Ripken to start in the 2001 All-Star Game and he responded by smacking a home run and being named MVP.

On November 11, St. Louis Cardinals slugger Mark McGwire announced his retirement, saying injuries were affecting his performance. McGwire is best known for his 1998 season when he belted 70 home runs, smashing Roger Maris's 1961 single-season record of 61.

Hall of Fame. On Aug. 5, 2001, former Minnesota Twins center fielder Kirby Puckett; veteran slugger Dave Winfield, who played for six teams including New York and San Diego; Pittsburgh Pirates second baseman Bill Mazeroski; and Negro leagues pitcher Hilton Smith were inducted into the Baseball Hall of Fame in Cooperstown, New York.

College. On June 16, the University of Miami Hurricanes defeated the Stanford Cardinals 12-1 in Omaha, Nebraska, to take their second National Collegiate Athletic Association title in three years.

Youth. On August 26, Tokyo Kitasuna from Japan defeated the team from Apopka, Florida, 2-1, to win the Little League World Series.

☐ Michael Kates

See also **People in the news** (Ripken, Cal, Jr.); **Sports.**

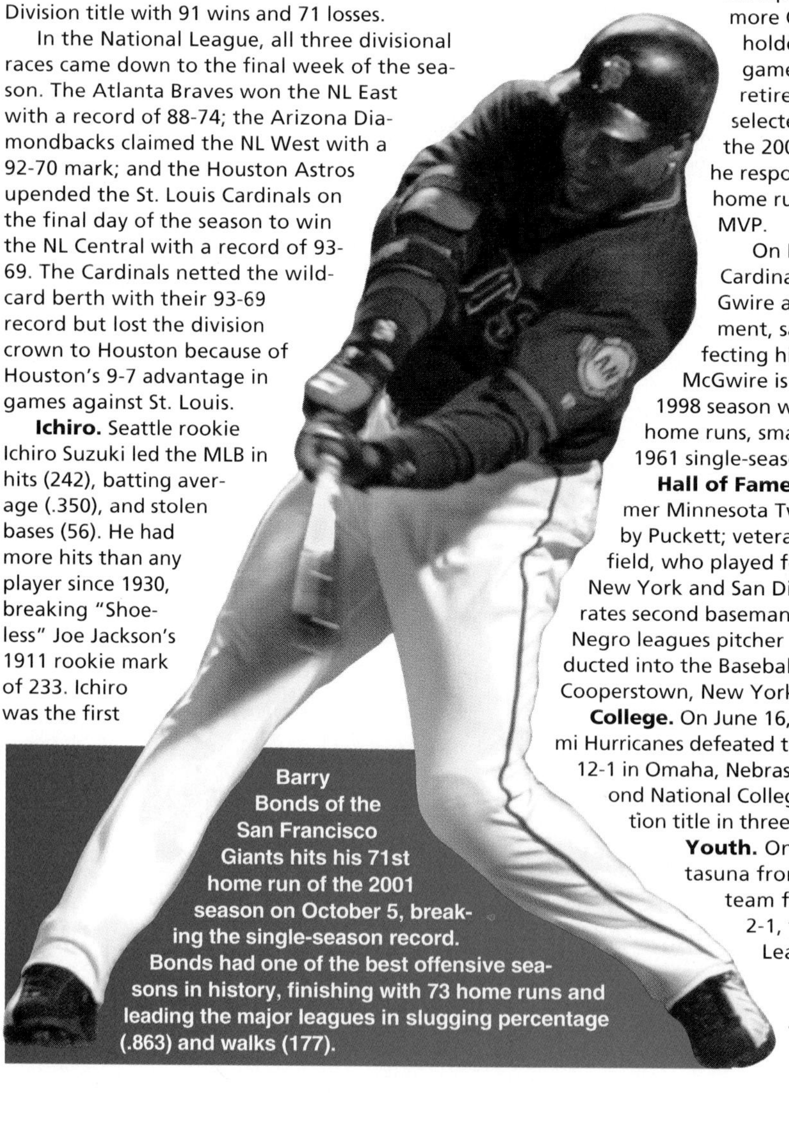

Barry Bonds of the San Francisco Giants hits his 71st home run of the 2001 season on October 5, breaking the single-season record. Bonds had one of the best offensive seasons in history, finishing with 73 home runs and leading the major leagues in slugging percentage (.863) and walks (177).

Basketball. The Los Angeles Lakers overcame a rocky regular season to retain the National Basketball Association (NBA) championship title in 2001, romping over the Philadelphia 76ers 4 games to 1. The Lakers went 15-1 in the play-offs, setting an NBA record for the highest postseason winning percentage (0.938). In women's professional basketball, the Los Angeles Sparks in 2001 became the first team other than the Houston Comets to win a Women's National Basketball Association (WNBA) championship in the league's five-year history. In college, Duke University lived up to its top ranking, winning the National Collegiate Athletic Association (NCAA) men's title. Notre Dame's women's team made two dramatic comebacks to win its first NCAA basketball title.

Michael Jordan announced in 2001 that he was returning to professional basketball as a player. After spending 13 spectacular seasons in the NBA with the Chicago Bulls, Jordan retired in 1998 to become the general manager and part-owner of the NBA's Washington Wizards. However, in the summer of 2001, Jordan began practicing against NBA players, spurring rumors that he was getting in shape to return in the 2001-2002 season. Jordan announced on September 25 that he was suiting up for the Wizards.

Professional men. The Philadelphia 76ers created a buzz throughout the 2000-2001 NBA season. Although the clashing personalities of coach Larry Brown and star guard Allen Iverson triggered feuding in the locker room, the team managed to finish the season with a record of 56 wins and 26 losses, the best in the Eastern Conference. The San Antonio Spurs posted the best record at 58-24, two games better than the Los Angeles Lakers in the Western Conference. The Lakers also struggled with injuries and squabbles between stars Shaquille O'Neal and Kobe Bryant. Both Bryant and O'Neal missed games during the regular season.

In the play-offs, the Lakers put aside any infighting and got to work, setting a new NBA record by winning eight consecutive play-off games on the road. The Lakers swept Portland in three games in the first round; Sacramento in four games in the Western Conference semifinals; and San Antonio in four games in the conference finals. The 76ers struggled after ousting the Indiana Pacers 3 games to 1 in the first round of the

National Basketball Association standings

Eastern Conference

Atlantic Division	W.	L.	Pct.	G.B.
Philadelphia 76ers*	56	26	.683	—
Miami Heat*	50	32	.610	6
New York Knicks*	48	34	.585	8
Orlando Magic*	43	39	.524	13
Boston Celtics	36	46	.439	20
New Jersey Nets	26	56	.317	30
Washington Wizards	19	63	.232	37
Central Division				
Milwaukee Bucks*	52	30	.634	—
Toronto Raptors*	47	35	.573	5
Charlotte Hornets*	46	36	.561	6
Indiana Pacers*	41	41	.500	11
Detroit Pistons	32	50	.390	20
Cleveland Cavaliers	30	52	.366	22
Atlanta Hawks	25	57	.305	27
Chicago Bulls	15	67	.183	37

Western Conference

Midwest Division	W.	L.	Pct.	G.B.
San Antonio Spurs*	58	24	.707	—
Utah Jazz*	53	29	.646	5
Dallas Mavericks*	53	29	.646	5
Minnesota Timberwolves*	47	35	.573	11
Houston Rockets	45	37	.549	13
Denver Nuggets	40	42	.488	18
Memphis Grizzlies	23	59	.280	35
Pacific Division				
Los Angeles Lakers*	56	26	.683	—
Sacramento Kings*	55	27	.671	1
Phoenix Suns*	51	31	.622	5
Portland Trail Blazers*	50	32	.610	6
Seattle Supersonics	44	38	.537	12
Los Angeles Clippers	31	51	.378	25
Golden State Warriors	17	65	.207	39

Individual leaders

Scoring	G.	F.G.	F.T.	Pts.	Avg.
Allen Iverson, Philadelphia	71	762	585	2,207	31.1
Jerry Stackhouse, Detroit	80	774	666	2,380	29.8
Shaquille O'Neal, L.A. Lakers	74	813	499	2,125	28.7
Kobe Bryant, L.A. Lakers	68	701	475	1,938	28.5
Vince Carter, Toronto	75	762	384	2,070	27.6
Chris Webber, Sacramento	70	786	324	1,898	27.1
Tracy McGrady, Orlando	77	788	430	2,065	26.8
Paul Pierce, Boston	82	687	550	2,071	25.3
Antawn Jamison, Golden State	82	800	382	2,044	24.9
Stephon Marbury, New Jersey	67	563	362	1,598	23.9

Rebounding	G.	Off.	Def.	Tot.	Avg.
D. Mutombo, Philadelphia	75	307	708	1,015	13.5
Ben Wallace, Detroit	80	303	749	1,052	13.1
Shaquille O'Neal, L.A. Lakers	74	291	649	940	12.7
Tim Duncan, San Antonio	82	259	738	997	12.2
Antonio McDyess, Denver	70	240	605	845	12.1
Kevin Garnett, Minnesota	81	219	702	921	11.4
Chris Webber, Sacramento	70	179	598	777	11.1
Shawn Marion, Phoenix	79	220	628	848	10.7
Antonio Davis, Toronto	78	274	513	787	10.1
Elton Brand, L.A. Clippers	74	285	461	746	10.1

NBA champions—Los Angeles Lakers
(defeated Philadelphia 76ers, 4 games to 1)

*Made play-offs

play-offs. Philadelphia edged Toronto 4 games to 3 with a one-point win in game 7 in the Eastern Conference semifinals. The Sixers then defeated Milwaukee 4 games to 3 in the conference finals.

In the finals, the Lakers looked vulnerable at first when Philadelphia captured game 1 in Los Angeles in overtime. The Lakers bounced back, however, taking the next four games—three of which were played in Philadelphia—to win the title. O'Neal secured his second straight finals MVP award, after scoring 29 points and grabbing 13 rebounds in the final game on June 15.

The 76ers did not take the championship, but they became the first team in NBA history to capture four of the league's six major regular-season awards: Coach Larry Brown, who led the Sixers to the team's most wins since 1985, easily captured Coach of the Year honors; Allen Iverson won the regular-season Most Valuable Player (MVP) award; Aaron McKie captured the Sixth Man award; and Dikembe Mutombo, who joined the team in February, was named the NBA's top defender. The All-NBA first team was composed of San Antonio's Tim Duncan, Sacramento's Chris Webber, Los Angeles's O'Neal, and Phoenix's Jason Kidd. Orlando's Mike Miller was named the league's top rookie.

Professional women. Lisa Leslie, who was named MVP of the regular season, the WNBA All-Star game, and the finals, led the Los Angeles Sparks to a two-game sweep over the Charlotte Sting for the title. Leslie led the Sparks to a 82-54 rout of the Sting in the clinching game on September 1, collecting 24 points, 13 rebounds, 6 assists, and a title-game record 7 blocked shots. The Sparks finished the season with a record of 34 wins and 5 losses. Dan Hughes of the Cleveland Rockers won WNBA Coach of the Year hon-

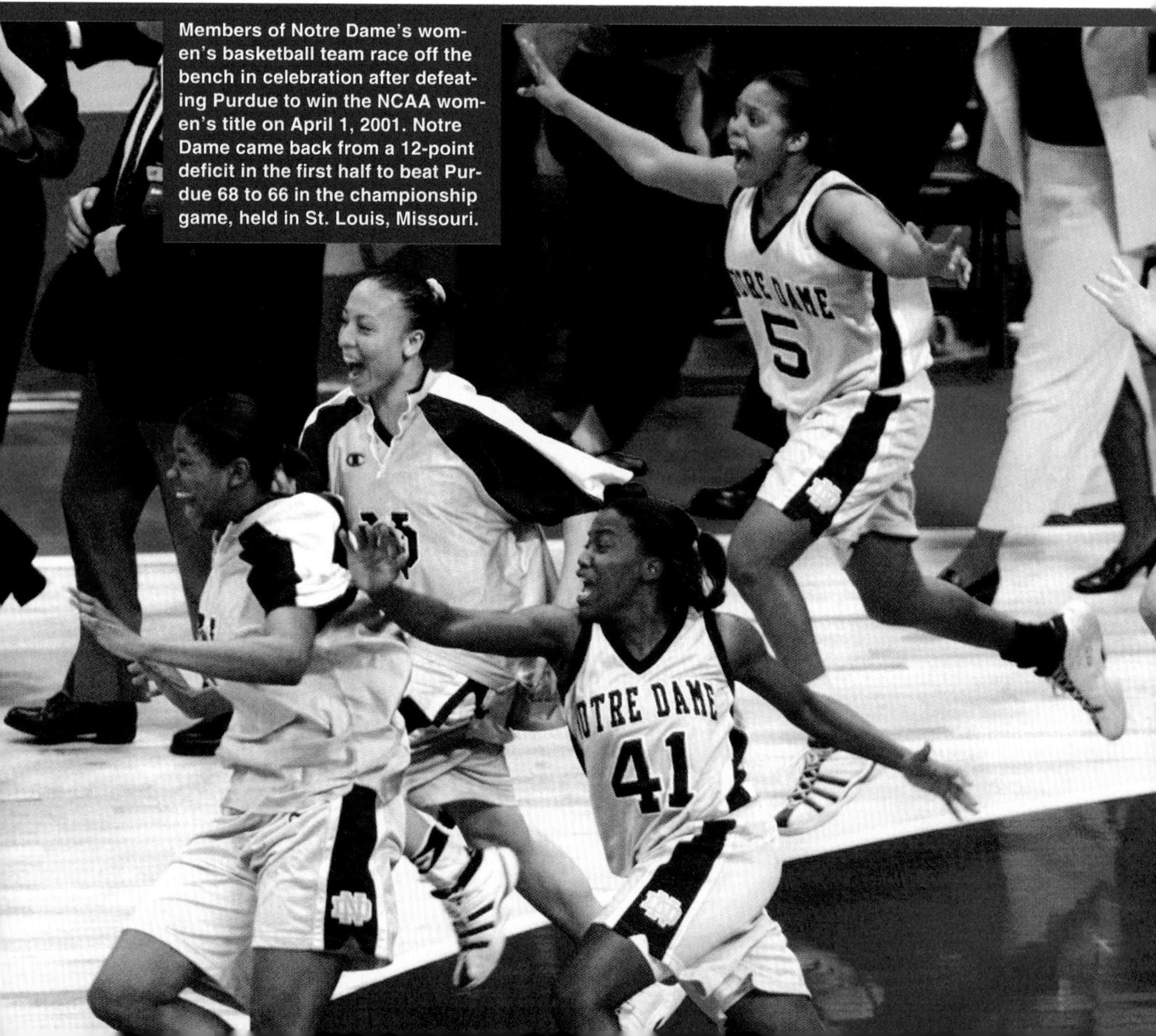

Members of Notre Dame's women's basketball team race off the bench in celebration after defeating Purdue to win the NCAA women's title on April 1, 2001. Notre Dame came back from a 12-point deficit in the first half to beat Purdue 68 to 66 in the championship game, held in St. Louis, Missouri.

ors, and Jackie Stiles of the Portland Fire won the Rookie of the Year award.

College men. On April 2, the Duke University Blue Devils defeated the University of Arizona Wildcats 82-72 in the NCAA championship game in Minneapolis, Minnesota. The Blue Devils were the first top-ranked team to capture the men's title since the 1995 UCLA Bruins squad. Duke forward Shane Battier, the national player of the year, played all 40 minutes, scoring 18 points, grabbing 11 rebounds, and dishing out 6 assists. Battier won 131 games in his four years at Duke, tying the mark set by Wayne Turner of Kentucky (1996-99). The title was the third for Duke under Coach Mike Krzyzewski, but the team's first since winning back-to-back titles in 1991 and 1992.

To reach the final, top-seeded Duke had overcome a 22-point deficit against the University of Maryland (College Park) in the national semifinal on March 31, 2001, to win 95-84. Arizona, which was a number two seed, reached the championship game by defeating top-seeded University of Illinois (Urbana-Champaign) in the Elite Eight and then blasting top-seeded Michigan State University (East Lansing) 80-61 in the other national semifinal.

The NCAA expanded the tournament field for the first time since 1985, adding a 65th team. Northwestern State University (Natchitoches, Louisiana) defeated Winthrop University (Rock Hill, South Carolina) 71-67 for the chance to play Illinois in the first round.

College women. Notre Dame rallied from a 12-point deficit in the first half to topple Purdue 68-66 and win the NCAA women's tournament on April 1, 2001, in St. Louis, Missouri. Notre Dame's Ruth Riley—a unanimous All-American and the national player of the year—hit a game-tying basket in the final minute. She then hit two free throws with 5.8 seconds left to give the Irish (34-2) the title. To reach the final game, Notre Dame had rallied from a 16-point deficit to beat the University of Connecticut in their national semifinal game. Purdue (31-7) reached the title game by beating Southwest Missouri State in the national semifinals.

Coaching carousel. In March 2001, Bob Knight, the former Indiana University coach who was fired amid scandal in 2000, was hired as head coach of Texas Tech University in Lubbock. Knight had been fired from Indiana University after an alleged altercation with a student.

Rick Pitino returned to college basketball in March 2001 as head coach of the University of Louisville Cardinals. Pitino had quit as head coach of the Boston Celtics in the NBA in early January. In 1996, Pitino had led the University of Kentucky to a national title. ☐ Michael Kates

The 2000-2001 college basketball season

College tournament champions

NCAA	(Men)	Division I:	Duke
		Division II:	Kentucky Wesleyan
		Division III:	Catholic University of America
	(Women)	Division I:	Notre Dame
		Division II:	Cal State Polytechnic
		Division III:	Washington (Missouri)
NAIA	(Men)	Division I:	Faulkner (Alabama)
		Division II:	Northwestern (Iowa)
	(Women)	Division I:	Oklahoma City
		Division II:	Northwestern (Iowa)
NIT	(Men)	Tulsa	

Men's college champions

Conference	School
America East	Hofstra*
Atlantic 10	St. Joseph's
	Temple (tournament)
Atlantic Coast	Duke*–North Carolina (tie)
Big 12	Iowa State
	Oklahoma (tournament)
Big East	
East Division	Boston College*
West Division	Notre Dame
Big Sky	Cal State Northridge*
Big South	Radford
	Winthrop (tournament)
Big Ten	Illinois–Michigan State (tie)
	Iowa (tournament)
Big West	University of California at Irvine
	Utah State (tournament)
Colonial	Richmond
	George Mason (tournament)
Conference USA	Charlotte (tournament)
American Division	Cincinnati
National Division	Southern Mississippi
Ivy League	Princeton†
Metro Atlantic	Iona*–Siena–Niagara (tie)
Mid-American	
East Division	Kent State*
West Division	Central Michigan
Mid-Continent	Southern Utah*–Valparaiso (tie)
Mid-Eastern	Hampton*–South Carolina State (tie)
Midwestern	Butler*
Missouri Valley	Creighton
	Indiana State (tournament)
Mountain West	Brigham Young*–Wyoming–Utah (tie)
Northeast	St. Francis (New York)
	Monmouth (tournament)
Ohio Valley	Tennessee Tech
	Eastern Illinois (tournament)
Pacific 10	Stanford†
Patriot League	Holy Cross*
Southeastern	
Eastern Division	Kentucky*–Florida (tie)
Western Division	Mississippi
Southern	UNC Greensboro (tournament)
North Division	East Tennessee State
South Division	Charleston
Southland	McNeese State
	Northwestern State (tournament)
Southwestern	Alabama State*
Sun Belt	
East Division	Western Kentucky*
West Division	South Alabama
Trans America	Georgia State*
West Coast	Gonzaga*
Western Athletic	Fresno State
	Hawaii (tournament)

*Regular season and conference tournament champion.
†No tournament played.
Sources: National Collegiate Athletic Association (NCAA); National Association of Intercollegiate Athletics (NAIA); National Invitation Tournament (NIT); Conference Web sites.

The collision of two trains in the Belgian village of Pecrot in March 2001 jackknifes commuter cars, killing eight people. The accident was attributed to one of the drivers ignoring a traffic signal.

Belarus. Aleksandr Lukashenko won reelection as president of Belarus by an overwhelming margin on Sept. 9, 2001. According to the state election commission, the president received more than 75 percent of the vote. Lukashenko initially became president in 1994. His term was extended by a 1996 referendum.

European observers denounced the election, citing widespread irregularities in the balloting. The United States Department of State dismissed the vote as meaningless. Brushing aside allegations of vote fraud and intimidation, Lukashenko declared his victory elegant, asserting, "Our elections don't need any recognition."

During the campaign, opponents of Lukashenko released a videotaped confession of a former secret police officer who claimed that Lukashenko ordered the abduction and murder of several political opponents. Lukashenko denied the charges, but police agencies later converged on independent media outlets in what observers characterized as a thinly veiled intimidation campaign. Lukashenko, in his Sept. 20, 2001, inaugural address, reaffirmed his support for reunification with Russia. He also vowed not to launch any "shock" economic reforms. Economists estimated that the average income in Belarus in 2001 was about $100 per month. ☐ Steven L. Solnick

See also **Europe; Russia.**

Belgium. The Belgian national airline, Sabena SA of Brussels, became one of the first victims of the 2001 global crisis in the aviation industry when it ceased operations in November. Sabena collapsed because of its dependence on Swissair, the Swiss national airline, which itself sought court protection from creditors in October.

The Belgian government had sold 49.5 percent of Sabena to Swissair in 1995 in an effort to save Sabena, which had accumulated close to $2 billion in debts. In 2000, the government agreed to sell Swissair a further 35.5 percent stake. Swissair backed out of the agreement in mid-2001, however, because of its own mounting losses. In July, Swissair, together with the Belgian government, agreed to invest $367 million in Sabena and to scale back the airline's operations. However, the Swiss company reneged on that agreement when its financial problems became acute after the terrorist attacks on the United States on September 11. The attacks depressed air traffic around the world. Sabena began liquidation proceedings in November, making it the first national airline in Europe to go out of business. The government and leading Belgian companies agreed to invest $179 million in Delta Air Transport, a Sabena subsidiary, which operated a much-reduced service using some of Sabena's planes and staff.

European Union presidency. Belgium led efforts to reform the governing institutions of the European Union (EU) when it held the rotating presidency of the EU during the second half of 2001. At a summit meeting in the Brussels suburb of Laeken in December, EU leaders agreed to hold a constitutional convention. Convention delegates were to propose changes to EU bodies and voting procedures to ensure that the bloc could continue to make effective decisions when it admits as many as a dozen new members from Eastern and Southern Europe in coming years. The constitutional changes were to be agreed upon by 2004, when the first new members from Eastern Europe were expected to join the EU.

Constitutional reform. The national parliament approved a new round of changes to the Belgian constitution in June 2001, giving more power to the country's three regions: Dutch-speaking Flanders in the north; French-speaking Wallonia in the south; and the capital region of Brussels. The changes gave the regions greater tax-raising authority and responsibility for agriculture and trade promotion. ☐ Tom Buerkle

See also **Aviation; Europe.**

Belize. See **Latin America.**

Benin. See **Africa.**

Bhutan. See **Asia.**

Biology. Evidence of a possible "sixth sense" in humans was reported by psychologist Martha McClintock and neurobiologist Suma Jacob of the University of Chicago in July 2001. McClintock published brain-scan images indicating that airborne chemical substances called pheromones influence human behavior. Scientists have long known that pheromones are released by various insects and mammals to influence the behavior of other members of their species—for example, by warning of danger or provoking a sexual response. Although researchers had previously discovered evidence that humans also produce pheromones, these substances were not known to affect human behavior.

McClintock's team swiped tiny amounts of androstadienone—a chemical compound found in male sweat, blood, hair, and semen—under the noses of several female volunteers. The researchers added clove oil to the compound to mask any possible odor. Brain scans of the women taken while they were working at computers revealed increased activity in areas of the brain associated with emotion, attention, vision, and smell. This indicated to the researchers that the androstadienone produced an airborne chemical signal—a pheromone—that affected brain activity and processing of information in the female volunteers.

McClintock said humans may unconsciously produce a variety of pheromones that influence psychological states, including emotion, attention, and memory, in other people. She added that more research was needed to prove that humans really do exchange these chemical social signals.

Two elephant species in Africa. Genetic studies reported in August suggest that African elephants living in forests belong to a different species than those living in savannas. A team from the National Cancer Institute in Frederick, Maryland, and the Mpala Research Center in Kenya examined *deoxyribonucleic acid* (DNA, the molecule that genes are made of) from both types of elephants. The scientists concluded that the genes of the forest and savanna elephant varieties are so different that the varieties should be considered different species.

The scientists added that there are also a number of physical differences between the two types of elephants. The savanna elephant, or *Loxodonta africana*—the name previously used for both elephant types—has large, ragged ears and curving tusks. The forest elephant, which the researchers renamed *Loxodonta cyclotis,* is smaller than the savanna elephant and has rounded ears and straighter tusks.

Forest elephants made up no more than one-third of the approximately 500,000 African elephants thought to exist in 2001, according to researchers. Conservationists noted that forest elephants are threatened by demand for their hard, pinkish ivory tusks.

Flamingos related to grebes. The closest living relative of the long-legged, graceful flamingo is the grebe, a squat, short-legged bird, according to a July report by two groups of scientists. Researchers at Pennsylvania State University in University Park and the University of Wisconsin at Madison reached their surprising conclusion by comparing the DNA of several species of birds. They said the genes of flamingos are more similar to the genes of grebes than to any other bird they studied, despite the fact that the birds show no outward resemblance to each other.

The results suggested to the researchers that such physical features as long legs and webbed feet—long used by biologists to group birds into family trees—may not be reliable indicators of relationships. Such traits may have evolved independently at different times in several different bird lines.

Bird brains recognize mom. An April study demonstrated that the brains of some birds are "hardwired" to recognize the sound of their mother's voice. The finding helped explain how some birds are able to respond to their mothers' calls immediately after hatching.

Neurobiologist Evan Balaban of the City University of New York suspected that a maternal recognition system might be located in a small region in the brains of birds that seemed to have no other function. To test this idea, Balaban surgically transplanted this region from the brains of *embryonic* (still-in-the-egg) quails into the same spot in embryonic chickens. The eggs hatched in a sound-proof incubator. After hatching, the altered chicks were exposed to recordings of both chicken and quail calls. The researchers reported that the chicks responded much more strongly to quail calls than to chicken calls.

The transplant could not be performed in the opposite direction because a quail's brain is too small to contain the chicken-brain section. However, the scientists planned to conduct other experiments to discover more about this sound-perception region. They hoped these experiments would shed light on the evolution of learning processes in birds and other animals.

Ant gender control. Queen ants regulate the proportion of males and females in colonies by controlling the gender of the eggs they lay, according to an August report by biologists led by Laurent Keller of the University of Lausanne in Switzerland. *Entomologists* (insect experts) previously believed that worker ants controlled the proportion of the two genders by starving or killing unwanted male *larvae* (immature insects).

The biologists raised 24 colonies of fire ants in the laboratory. Each colony included a queen, the only ant in a colony that lays eggs. Eleven of the colonies consisted mostly of males, and 13 contained mainly females. The researchers switched the queens of predominantly male colonies with the queens of predominantly female colonies. Within a matter of weeks, the colonies that had been dominated by males became dominated by females and vice versa. This indicated that it was the queens themselves who controlled the sex ratio of the colonies.

The biologists proposed that queen ants maintain control over sex ratios by regulating the number of eggs that they fertilize with *sperm,* male sex cells, stored inside the queen's body. Fertilized eggs develop into female worker ants, while unfertilized eggs grow into males.

Salt-tolerant tomato. Researchers at the University of California at Davis announced in August that they had genetically modified a tomato plant so that it could grow in salty conditions. The researchers reported that the modified plant grew in a solution of sodium chloride, or table salt, in the laboratory, drawing salt out of the solution and storing it in its leaves. They believed this breakthrough might open large areas of infertile soil to the growing of tomatoes and other cash crops.

Irrigation water tends to deposit tiny amounts of salt in the soil. Over time, the salt builds up until the soil becomes too salty for crops to grow. Scientists estimate that salt has ruined as much as a third of all irrigated land worldwide. The UC Davis research team designed the salt-tolerant tomato to extract salt from ruined farmland so that other crops could grow there.

In 1999, the research team added an active version of a normally inactive plant gene to the weed *Arabidopsis thaliana* to make the weed salt-tolerant. The gene is the blueprint for a protein that transports sodium from the environment into sacs inside plant cells. This protects the cells from salt damage. The team achieved the same feat with tomato plants in 2001. The tomatoes were able to grow in a laboratory solution containing four times the amount of salt normally fatal to agricultural crops. The scientists noted that the taste of the tomatoes was not affected.

The researchers said that field tests of the genetically modified tomato would be necessary to further demonstrate the salt-extracting properties of the tomato as well as to look for such commercially important traits as uniform ripening. They also said they planned to conduct similar experiments with other crops.

☐ Thomas H. Maugh II

See also **Agriculture; Conservation.**

Boating. New Zealand's Grant Dalton sailed around the world in a stunning 62 days to win the inaugural Millennium Race in 2001, and Britain's Ellen MacArthur became the youngest person to sail around the world solo.

Millennium Race. Dalton and his 12-person crew aboard the catamaran *Club Med* won the inaugural Millennium Race on March 3. The team completed the voyage in 62 days, finishing more than 1,000 miles (1,600 kilometers) ahead of their nearest competitor. Although Dalton shattered the around-the-world mark, set by France's Olivier de Kersauson in 1997, by more than nine days, he could not claim the world record because the race did not begin and end in the same harbor. The race, featuring five of the fastest sailboats ever made, began in Barcelona, Spain, on Dec. 31, 2000, and ended in Marseille, France.

Vendee Globe. On Feb. 11, 2001, Ellen MacArthur, 24, broke two world records, becoming the youngest person and the fastest woman to complete the Vendee Globe around-the-world solo sailing race, which began and ended in Les Sables d'Olonne, France. MacArthur completed the 24,000-mile (38,600-kilometer) journey in 94 days, 4 hours, and 30 minutes aboard her 60-foot (18-meter) yacht *Kingfisher.* Despite her feat, she finished the race second to Michel Desjoyeaux of France. Desjoyeaux set a new world solo record

The crew of the J-class yacht *Shamrock V* fights the choppy waters of the Solent, the channel between England and the Isle of Wight, in August 2001 during the Jubilee Regatta at Cowes, England, celebrating the 150th anniversary of the America's Cup.

with his time of 93 days, 3 hours, 57 minutes, and 32 seconds aboard *PRB.*

World championships. Australians John Forbes and Darren Bundock won the Tornado World Championships on February 18, at Richards Bay, South Africa. Fernando Leon and Luis Doreste, both of Spain, won Group A and B, respectively, in the IMS Offshore World Championship in Valencia, Spain, on July 8. Christoph Skolaut, of Austria, won the Yngling World Championship regatta July 21 in Newport, Rhode Island. Robert Scheidt, of Brazil, won the Laser World Championship on August 8 in Cork, Ireland. Jonathan and Charlie McKee, of the United States, won the 49er World Championship on September 22 in Malcesine, Italy.

America's Cup Jubilee. In August, yachting enthusiasts celebrated the America's Cup Jubilee, the 150th anniversary of the America's Cup, in Cowes, England. More than 2,000 sailors aboard 205 yachts participated. The Italian *Prada Challenge* team defeated Britain's *GBR Challenge* by six seconds to win the Louis Vuitton Trophy.

Powerboats. Michael Hanson piloted *Tubby's Grilled Subs* to victory in the Gold Cup race on July 15 in Detroit. It was Hanson's third win in the American Powerboat Association's Unlimited Hydroplanes category and his first Gold Cup.

☐ Michael Kates

Bolivia. See **Latin America.**

Books. See **Literature American; Literature, world; Literature for children.**

Bosnia-Herzegovina. On Feb. 22, 2001, members of the federal parliament of Bosnia-Herzegovina formed the nation's first nonnationalist government since the Dayton Accords established how Bosnia would be governed. The Dayton Accords, a 1995 agreement to end a civil war that began in 1992, divided Bosnia into two parts—one under a Muslim-Croat federation, and the other part ruled by Bosnian Serbs. The Alliance for Change, a coalition of parties advocating a unified, multiethnic country, took control of the government in 2001 under a new prime minister, Bozidar Matic. In a speech before parliament, Matic declared that he would represent all the people of Bosnia.

Matic formed the new government after nearly three months of political deadlock, during which Bosnia had no functioning government. The breakdown took place after none of the three main nationalist parties—the Muslim SDA, the Croat HDZ, and the Serb SDS—captured enough seats in parliamentary elections held in November 2000 to form a new government.

Matic's government embraced a program of judicial, economic, and administrative reform. Wolfgang Petritsch, the international community's High Representative in Bosnia (an office created by the Dayton Accords), welcomed Bosnia's first nonnationalist government as a step toward democracy and integration into Europe.

Split-up threatened. In March 2001, Croatian hardliners among the Bosnian leadership called for the creation of a separate Croatian state in Bosnia. Ante Jelavic, the Croat representative on Bosnia's joint presidency, endorsed the proposal. In response, High Representative Petritsch removed Jelavic from the presidency.

Croatian soldiers responded to the removal of Jelavic by leaving the Muslim-Croat federation army, and eventually, the majority of the 7,500 Bosnian Croats in the Muslim-Croat joint army deserted. The attempt to create a new state failed when leaders of neighboring Croatia rejected the separatist movement, and Bosnian federal officials brought legal charges against the separatist leaders. By late May, approximately 3,000 of the Bosnian Croat soldiers who had deserted had returned to the Muslim-Croat army.

Economy. In 2001, Bosnia remained the second poorest country in Europe, after Albania. Unemployment remained at more than 50 percent throughout the year. At an October economic conference held in Bucharest, Romania, international donors pledged more than $2 billion for infrastructure development in Balkan countries, with the majority earmarked for Bosnia.

☐ Sharon L. Wolchik

See also **Croatia; Europe.**

Botswana. See **Africa.**

Bowling. The bowling world mourned the August 2001 death of its all-time leading men's champion, Earl Anthony. On the lanes, three bowlers, Parker Bohn, III, Jason Couch, and Walter Ray Williams, Jr., battled for the 2001 Professional Bowlers Association (PBA) Player of the Year Award. In the Professional Women's Bowling Association (PWBA), Carolyn Dorin-Ballard of North Richland Hills, Texas, appeared to be headed for Player of the Year honors after being runner-up four times.

PBA. In December, in a heated battle for top player honors, Parker Bohn, III, of Jackson, New Jersey, led in points (234,185) and earnings ($140,300). Bohn's scoring average of 222.04 was just behind that of Jason Couch of Clermont, Florida, who was averaging 222.41. Couch ranked second in points and fourth in earnings. Walter Ray Williams, Jr., of Ocala, Florida, ranked third in points, second in earnings, and fifth in scoring average.

On February 4, Williams captured the PBA National Championship in Toledo, Ohio, routing Jeff Lizzi of Sandusky, Ohio, 258-204. It was Williams's third career major, adding to his victories at the 1998 U.S. Open and 1994 Tournament Players Championship.

On Nov. 11, 2001, Williams throttled Mike Machuga of Erie, Pennsylvania, 247-194 to win the Greater Cincinnati Classic for his 34th career title. Williams's victory tied him with PBA Hall of Fame bowler Mark Roth for the second-most PBA titles, just seven behind the leader, Earl Anthony.

PWBA. Carolyn Dorin-Ballard won her seventh title of the season on November 10 in Las Vegas, Nevada, tying the record set by Patty Costello in 1976. Dorin-Ballard defeated Michelle Feldman of Skaneateles, New York, 280-258 in the title match of the Brunswick Women's World Open.

Dorin-Ballard, a four-time runner-up for PWBA Player of the Year, appeared poised to finally take that honor by leading the tour in titles (7), earnings ($125,670), and average (215.13).

Seniors. Bob Glass became only the third Senior Tour player to win four titles in one year when he captured the Hammond (Indiana) Senior Open on Oct. 26, 2001. Glass, of Lawrence, Kansas, defeated Charlie Tapp of Kalamazoo, Michigan, 233-232 to take the title.

Anthony dies. Earl Anthony, six-time PBA bowler of the year and the all-time leader in professional titles with 41, died August 14. Anthony, 63, had been the first player to earn more than $1 million on the PBA tour.

Milestone. In May, James Hylton, an amateur bowler from Keizer, Oregon, bowled the fifth perfect 900 series in the 106-year history of the American Bowling Congress.

☐ Michael Kates

Hasim Rahman shows off the heavyweight championship belts he won after defeating Lennox Lewis on April 23 in South Africa. In a rematch in November, Lewis defeated Rahman.

World champion boxers

World Boxing Association

Division	Champion	Country	Date won
Heavyweight	John Ruiz	Puerto Rico	3/01
	Evander Holyfield	U.S.A.	8/00
Light heavyweight	Roy Jones Jr.	U.S.A.	7/98
	Lou del Valle	U.S.A.	9/97
Middleweight	Bernard Hopkins	U.S.A.	9/01
	William Joppy	U.S.A.	1/98
Welterweight	Andrew Lewis	Guyana	2/01
Lightweight	Raul Balbi	Argentina	10/01
	Julien Lorcy	France	7/00
Featherweight	Derrick Gainer	U.S.A.	9/00
	Fred Norwood	U.S.A.	5/99
Bantamweight	Eidy Moya	Venezuela	10/01
Flyweight	Eric Morel	Puerto Rico	8/00
	S. Pisnurachank	Thailand	9/99

World Boxing Council

Division	Champion	Country	Date won
Heavyweight	Lennox Lewis	United Kingdom	11/01
	Hasim Rahman	U.S.A.	4/01
Light heavyweight	Roy Jones Jr.	U.S.A.	8/97
Middleweight	Bernard Hopkins	U.S.A.	9/01
	Keith Holmes	U.S.A.	4/99
Welterweight	Shane Mosley	U.S.A.	6/00
	Oscar de la Hoya	U.S.A.	3/00
Lightweight	Jose Luis Castillo	Mexico	11/99
	Stevie Johnston	U.S.A.	2/99
Featherweight	Erik Morales	Mexico	2/01
	Guty Espadas	Mexico	4/00
Bantamweight	Veeraphol Nakhonluang	Thailand	12/98
	Joichiro Tatsuyoshi	Japan	11/97
Flyweight	Wonjongkam Pongsaklek	Thailand	3/01
	Malcolm Tunacao	Philippines	5/00

Boxing. Two surprising upsets stunned boxing fans in 2001. Bernard Hopkins defeated Felix Trinidad to unify the middleweight titles, and Hasim Rahman knocked out champion Lennox Lewis to capture a pair of heavyweight titles.

In the fight between Hopkins and Trinidad on September 29 in New York City, Hopkins, who had not lost a bout since 1993, defended his middleweight title for the 14th time, tying the record set by Carlos Monzon in 1977. He led on all three judges' cards when he hit Trinidad with a devastating right midway through the 12th and final round. At that point, Trinidad's trainer stopped the fight. With the win, Hopkins became the undisputed middleweight champion, unifying the World Boxing Association (WBA) title, which had been held by Trinidad, with Hopkins's own International Boxing Federation (IBF) and World Boxing Council (WBC) middleweight titles.

Heavyweights. On April 21, 2001, in Brakpan, South Africa, Hasim Rahman knocked out then-heavyweight champion Lennox Lewis near the end of the fifth round. The surprise victory gave Rahman the WBC and IBF heavyweight titles. It was Lewis's first loss since 1994. After the fight, Lewis demanded a rematch, but Rahman was not interested. In June 2001, a U.S. District Judge ruled that Rahman had to either give Lewis a rematch or not fight for 18 months.

After intense negotiations between the two camps, a fight was slated for November 17. In that fight, held in Las Vegas, Nevada, Lewis regained his heavyweight crown by knocking out Rahman in the fourth round. Lewis's victory meant that his next bout would be with Mike Tyson, who retained his spot as the mandatory top WBC challenger by beating Brian Nielsen by a technical knockout in Copenhagen, Denmark, on October 13.

John Ruiz beat Evander Holyfield on March 3 in Las Vegas to capture the WBA heavyweight crown. A rematch scheduled for late November 2001 in Beijing was postponed because of the September 11 terrorist attacks on the United States.

Milestone. Oscar de la Hoya joined Sugar Ray Leonard and Thomas Hearns as the only champions to win titles in five weight divisions when he beat Javier Castillejo for the WBC super-welterweight title on June 23 in Las Vegas.

Deaths. Light-heavyweight Beethavean Scottland died on July 2 from head injuries he received during a bout with George Jones on June 26.

Eddie Futch, 90, a trainer who worked with 20 world champions including heavyweights Larry Holmes, Joe Frazier, Riddick Bowe, Michael Spinks, and Trevor Berbick, died on October 10.

☐ Michael Kates

Brazil. A global economic slowdown, shortages of energy, and a world glut of coffee combined to drive Brazil's economy into recession in mid-2001. The economic downturn was worsened by a financial crisis in Argentina, Brazil's most important South American trading partner.

Energy crisis. In June, Brazilian authorities imposed the rationing of electric power for six months. Government officials said the move was prompted by several years of below-average rainfall, which had dried up the watersheds of hydroelectric dams. Approximately 90 percent of all of Brazil's electricity is generated from water power. The rationing required Brazilians to reduce power consumption by 20 percent or face rolling blackouts that would cause unscheduled power interruptions across the country.

In order to save electricity, lights on city streets and in parks were dimmed throughout Brazil, and nighttime public events, including soccer games, were canceled. Many Brazilian businesses, especially such heavy energy users as the iron alloy, cement, and aluminum industries, were forced to make major cuts in production.

Foreign investment and trade. Uncertainties about Brazil's economy caused foreign investment to fall from $21 billion in the first eight months of 2000 to $14 billion in the same period of 2001. The export earnings of Brazil, the world's largest coffee producer, suffered in 2001 from severely depressed coffee prices, which fell to 30-year lows. In October, Brazilian and Argentine officials agreed to temporary trade safeguards to maintain their country's balance of trade and protect Mercosur, a trading bloc of several South American countries.

Financial assistance. To shore up the Brazilian economy and guard against the troubles ravaging Argentina, the International Monetary Fund, a United Nations-affiliated organization that provides credit to countries experiencing economic difficulties, granted Brazil $15 billion in credit in August. To qualify for the credit, Brazilian officials agreed to reduce spending by $2.5 billion over the next 18 months.

Equal rights for women. Brazil's Congress, after 26 years of debate, passed a legal code in August that granted women equal rights with men. Feminist groups in Brazil said the most significant advance in the code was the abolition of the traditional concept of "paternal power," which had long provided fathers with unrestricted legal rights to make all family decisions. The new law granted these rights to both men and women on an equal basis.

Drugs and crime. In July, General Alberto Cardoso, Brazil's national security minister, attributed 70 percent to 80 percent of all violent crimes in Brazil to illicit drugs. Law enforcement officials noted that neighborhoods in several Brazilian cities had been turned into urban battlefields ruled by "drug commands," groups of young, armed men who dealt in drugs and fought for turf with other groups. These groups sponsored "samba parties," where cocaine was openly sold. The officials said criminal activity had increased in direct proportion to the availability of *crack* (a relatively inexpensive form of cocaine that is smoked).

AIDS patent victory. The United States government in June withdrew a complaint against Brazil for violating U.S. patents of anti-AIDS medications. A Brazilian law permits government-run laboratories to produce copies of expensive AIDS drugs and market them at lower prices than the original versions. The U.S. move came after Brazil agreed to provide advance notice whenever it believed that emergency situations required a violation of U.S. drug patents. Brazil also agreed to establish a joint panel with the United States to address the AIDS drug issue.

☐ Nathan A. Haverstock

See also **Argentina; Energy supply: A Special Report; Latin America; Latin America: A Special Report.**

British Columbia. See **Canadian provinces.**

Brunei. See **Asia.**

Building and construction. The most significant event in building and construction during 2001 was actually an act of destruction—the September 11 terrorist attack that leveled the World Trade Center's twin towers in New York City. In the attack, terrorists flew hijacked airliners into the World Trade Center's 110-story north and south towers. Both buildings subsequently collapsed.

The World Trade Center towers were built using two main support systems: a central core made of structural steel and an outer wall made of steel columns placed every 22 inches (55.8 centimeters). These two systems shared the tremendous weight of the buildings.

The buildings were designed to withstand the impact of an airplane but not of airplanes as large as the Boeing 767. Tremendously hot fires fed by jet fuel weakened the structural steel. As the steel columns buckled, the floors they supported fell onto the floors below in a progressive "pancake" collapse.

Construction of the World Trade Center towers began in 1966. They had been the world's tallest structures upon their completion in 1972. The north tower, which was slightly taller than the south, was 1,368 feet (417 meters) in height. It was surpassed in height by the Sears Tower in Chicago in 1973.

Milwaukee Art Museum. On Oct. 11, 2001, officials of the Milwaukee Art Museum in Wisconsin unfurled a movable sunscreen, the final piece of a $75-million, 142,000-square-foot (13,200-square-meter) addition. The sunscreen, designed to keep the museum in shade, is highlighted by a 200-foot (61-meter) spanned wing. The screen can be raised or lowered and has 36 pairs of fins ranging in length from 24 to 105 feet (7 to 32 meters). The well-known Spanish-born architect, engineer, and designer Santiago Calatrava designed the addition.

Calatrava's striking design features a single-story glass, concrete, and steel-vaulted gallery space and lecture hall that links the original museum building to a reception hall. The 90-foot-(27-meter-) high glass reception hall, which overlooks Lake Michigan, is shaded by the movable screen. The screen is supported by an angled mast that also supports a cable-stayed pedestrian bridge that provides access to the museum from one of Milwaukee's major thoroughfares.

Calatrava is renowned for his *asymmetrical* (unevenly proportioned) cable-stayed bridges. He originally proposed a carbon fiber design for the fins. But after prototype testing raised concern about the connection between carbon steel fins and rotating steel spines, the museum switched to a steel design. The change saved millions of

Miller Park in Milwaukee—the new home of the Milwaukee Brewers baseball team—opens on March 30, 2001. The $400-million stadium, which seats 43,000 people, features a seven-panel retractable roof that opens and closes like a fan in 10 minutes.

dollars, officials said, but also added weight. To compensate for the heavier design, the sunscreen was programmed to automatically close when wind gusts exceed 24 miles (39 kilometers) per hour for three seconds or more. Despite its size, the screen can fold up in less than three minutes.

Tower of Pisa repairs. The Leaning Tower of Pisa in Italy, closed to tourists since 1990 while repairs to the building were made, reopened on Dec. 15, 2001. The cathedral bell tower, which is 180-feet- (54.8-meters-) tall, was begun in 1173 and was completed between 1360 and 1370. By the time the tower was completed, the soft, sandy soil under the tower's southern foundation had caused it to lean. At one point, it leaned more than 14 feet (4.2 meters) out of line. In the latest series of repairs carried out on the tower, engineers installed lead counterweights and removed the firmer soil under the northern foundation in an attempt to stabilize the structure. As a result of the repairs, the tilt of the tower was returned to about what it had been in 1838.

I-15 improvements. On May 14, 2001, the Utah Department of Transportation opened all major lanes of Interstate 15 after a $1.6-billion improvement program was completed months ahead of schedule. Utah transportation officials renamed the improved stretch of road the "21st Century Freeway."

The improvements to I-15, a major interstate highway that runs through Salt Lake City, began in 1997 and were completed just in time to accommodate increased traffic for the 2002 Winter Olympic Games to be held in February 2002 in Salt Lake City. Officials project that 1.7 million people will visit Salt Lake City during the Games.

Working on a fast schedule, contractors transformed 17 miles (27 kilometers) of interstate into a 12-lane superhighway with nine new interchanges, 142 bridges, and three major intersections. The contractors qualified for $50 million in bonus awards by finishing five months early.

The I-15 construction project made use of an innovative design and construction method. Most public works projects in the United States involve paying a design firm to provide a set of plans, then allowing contractors to compete for the project, with the work routinely going to the lowest bidder. This process can be slow and unwieldy. Because of the time constraints of the I-15 project, officials used a single-step process, putting a single team in charge of design and construction. Officials said that this approach, along with several road-building methods developed during the project, including the use of new materials to protect utility lines, would gain acceptance in the future. ☐ Andrew Wright

See also **Architecture; Italy; Terrorism; Terrorism: A Special Feature**, p. 38.

Bulgaria.

Bulgaria. In June 2001, the National Movement for Simeon II, a political party established by the former king of Bulgaria, Simeon Saxe-Coburg-Gotha, won a landslide victory in parliamentary elections that left the party only one seat short of a majority. The Simeon II party quickly formed a coalition government with the ethnic Turkish Movement for Rights and Freedoms, which had garnered less than 8 percent of the votes in the parliamentary election.

In November, Georgi Parvanov, leader of Bulgaria's Socialist Party, defeated Petar Stoyanov, an ally of Saxe-Coburg-Gotha, for the presidency. The presidency is a largely ceremonial position.

Bulgaria's *gross national product* (the total value of the goods and services produced by a nation during a specific period) grew at a rate of about 5 percent for the second year in a row. The rate of unemployment declined from 18 percent in 2000 to 16.7 percent in mid-2001.

☐ Sharon L. Wolchik

See also **Europe; People in the news** (Saxe-Coburg-Gotha, Simeon).

Burkina Faso. See **Africa.**

Burma. See **Myanmar.**

Burundi. See **Africa.**

Bus. See **Transportation.**

Business. See **Bank; Economics; Labor and employment; Manufacturing.**

Cabinet, U.S. In 2001, the U.S. Senate supported most of President George W. Bush's nominees for Cabinet positions and approved the majority of appointments early in the year.

The Senate's only serious challenge to a Bush nominee involved Linda Chavez, his choice for secretary of labor. President Bush was forced to name a new nominee after the news media reported that Chavez had given room, board, and spending money, but no salary to an illegal immigrant from Guatemala in the 1990's. Chavez withdrew her name from consideration on Jan. 9, 2001.

On January 11, President Bush nominated Elaine Chao for labor secretary. Chao was a former president and chief executive officer of the United Way of America; a former director of the Peace Corps; and a former deputy secretary of transportation in the administration of President George H. W. Bush. The Senate confirmed Chao on January 29.

Some senators criticized the president's choice for attorney general, John Ashcroft, a Republican who served as governor of Missouri from 1985 to 1993 and as a U.S. senator from 1995 to 2001. However, the Senate voted 58 to 42 to confirm the nomination on February 1.

Other nominees. On January 20, the Senate confirmed Colin L. Powell as secretary of state, making him the first African American to hold the position. From 1989 to 1993, Powell served as chair-

Mineta, the only Democrat in President Bush's Cabinet, had served as commerce secretary in the administration of President Bill Clinton. ☐ Geoffrey A. Campbell

See also **People in the news** (See related Cabinet members); **Terrorism: A Special Feature,** p. 38; **United States, Government of the; United States, President of the.**

California. See **Los Angeles; San Francisco; State government.**

United States Secretary of State Colin L. Powell and Saudi Foreign Minister Saud al-Faisal meet in Washington, D.C., in September 2001 to discuss U.S.-Arab relations after the terrorist attacks on the United States on September 11. Foreign affairs experts lauded Powell's contribution to building a global coalition in support of the U.S.-led war against terrorism.

man of the Joint Chiefs of Staff, the highest U.S. military advisory group.

The Senate in January 2001 also confirmed Paul O'Neill, former chairman of aluminum manufacturer Alcoa, Inc., of Pittsburgh, Pennsylania, as secretary of the treasury; Donald Rumsfeld as secretary of defense, a post he also held during the administration of President Gerald R. Ford; former Houston schools superintendent Rod Paige as secretary of education; Donald Evans, a Texas oil executive, as secretary of commerce; Spencer Abraham, a former senator from Michigan, as secretary of energy; and Ann Veneman, a California agriculture official, as secretary of agriculture.

The Senate also confirmed Wisconsin Governor Tommy Thompson as secretary of health and human services; Gale Norton, former Colorado state attorney general, as secretary of the interior; Mel Martinez, chairman of Orange County, Florida, as secretary of housing and urban development; Anthony Principi, a former acting secretary of veterans affairs, as secretary of veterans affairs; and Norman Mineta as secretary of transportation.

Cambodia. The Cambodian government established a court to try leaders of the Khmer Rouge in 2001. The Khmer Rouge was a Communist regime that ruled Cambodia from 1975 to 1979 and was responsible for the deaths of more than 1.5 million people during that time.

Placing leaders of the Khmer Rouge on trial had been a political issue in Cambodia for years. Prime Minister Hun Sen, a former member of the Khmer Rouge, long resisted Western pressure for an international tribunal. He insisted that Cambodia alone should handle the trials. China, which backed the Khmer Rouge regime, also opposed outside involvement. To ensure world standards of justice, Western nations that provide essential aid to Cambodia sought United Nations (UN) involvement in any trial of Khmer Rouge members.

Under UN pressure, the Cambodian parliament in August 2001 passed a law to create an international tribunal. Under the law, local judges would outnumber foreign judges, but at least one international jurist would have to agree with any decision. Cambodian political experts speculated that few Khmer Rouge leaders would ever reach trial.

Cambodian farmers had a successful rice harvest in 2001, while the nation's exports—mostly garments made in foreign-sponsored factories—continued to grow. However, Cambodia's economy remained dependent on foreign aid, which totalled nearly $500 million in 2001. ☐ Henry S. Bradsher

See also **Asia.**

Canada

For Canadians, much of 2001 was a period of general prosperity. The centrist Liberal Party, triumphant after a third general election victory in 2000, dominated Canada's national political scene. Prime Minister Jean Chretien's political opponents remained badly divided, and he and his party reaped the political benefits of a long spell of prosperity. However, the terrorist attacks on the United States on Sept. 11, 2001, transformed Canada, shattering the tranquility of the previous eight months. Uncertainty darkened the prospect of continued economic growth, and national security rose higher among government priorities.

Relations with the United States. Canada watched cautiously as the Republican administration of President George W. Bush took office in January 2001. Bush had made it plain that Mexico, not Canada, ranked as his top foreign-relations priority. Canadians were disturbed by Bush administration predictions that U.S. trade with Mexico would exceed U.S. trade with Canada within a decade. Canada sells more than 80 percent of its exports to the United States. On February 5, Chretien met with Bush in Washington, D.C., to lay the basis for a good working relationship.

Canadian officials also worried about the tendency of the Bush administration to follow an independent path in international affairs. Traditionally, Canada, as a smaller nation, has preferred to work in cooperation with other countries in attempting to solve world problems. Of particular concern were U.S. plans to abandon a 1972 missile treaty with the former Soviet Union in favor of a U.S. missile defense system. Canadian officials were also troubled by Bush's coolness toward a multilateral agreement discouraging the trafficking in small arms and an agreement establishing an international criminal court.

Response to terrorist attacks. These concerns were put aside following the terrorist attacks in New York City and outside Washington, D.C., on Sept. 11, 2001. Canada offered immediate assistance. Within hours, airline flights destined for the United States had been diverted to Canada. At least 200 flights carrying 31,000 passengers landed in Canada over the next few days. A memorial service for victims of the attacks, held on Parliament Hill in Ottawa, Canada's capital, drew 100,000 Canadians who expressed their solidarity with the United States in its hour of crisis.

In a September 20 speech on terrorism before the Congress of the United States, Bush failed to list Canada among America's allies. However, in a meeting with Chretien three days later, Bush said that he regarded Canada as "a brother" who did not need to be singled out for praise.

Security concerns. After the attacks, Canada moved to tighten immigration procedures and security arrangements. But Canadian officials emphasized that they did not see the need to harmonize Canada's immigration and customs regulations with those of the United States. The 5,500-mile (8,900-kilometer) border between the two countries was impossible to seal. Compared with the U.S.-Mexican frontier, the U.S.-Canadian border was lightly patrolled on both sides. Canadian officials argued that border checks would burden the flow of goods—valued at over $1 billion a day—between the two countries.

Nevertheless, on October 15 the Liberals proposed spending $250 million for new security and antiterrorism measures, including tightening border controls and improving airport security. (All amounts are in Canadian dollars.) The government also planned to issue new identification cards for recent immigrants. The Liberals introduced legislation that would authorize "preventive arrests" of people the police believed were about to carry out a terrorist act. The bill also increased jail sentences for terrorism-related crimes.

Problems among conservatives. The Canadian Alliance, a newly formed conservative party, experienced a leadership crisis in 2001. Preston Manning, of Alberta, formed the Canadian Alliance in 2000 to unite conservatives and strengthen opposition to the national Liberal government. Manning persuaded the members of the Reform Party, a largely regional party of the West that he had founded, to integrate into a new organization, the Canadian Reform Conservative Alliance. When Manning called for a vote to determine leadership of the Alliance, he lost to Stockwell Day, then provincial treasurer of Alberta. Under Day's leadership, the Alliance won 66 seats in Parliament in the 2000 election and became the official opposition.

Tens of thousands of people attend a memorial service outside the Canadian Parliament building in Ottawa, the capital, on Sept. 14, 2001, in remembrance of the victims of the September 11 terrorist attacks on the United States.

In early 2001, some members of the Alliance began expressing dissatisfaction with Day's leadership. In January, Day's political judgment came under attack following revelations that taxpayers in Alberta would have to pay $800,000 to settle a court case involving a letter Day wrote to a newspaper in 1999. In the letter, Day, then a member of Parliament, had criticized an Albertan lawyer for representing a man accused of possessing child pornography. In March 2001, Day apologized to the lawyer and announced that he would take out a $60,000 mortgage on his house to help pay damages in the case.

In April, Day's reputation suffered additional damage because of his alleged involvement in efforts by several Alliance officials to hire a private detective to spy on the Liberals. One day after acknowledging that he had been introduced to the investigator, Day denied ever meeting him.

On April 24, three senior Alliance officials resigned their posts within the party, announcing that they had lost confidence in Day's leadership. Deborah Grey, the Alliance's deputy leader and chairman of the party's *caucus* (members' group in Parliament), was one of the defectors. By July, 12 members had left the Alliance's caucus. The

The Bank of Canada introduced new $10 bills in 2001 that pay tribute to Sir John A. Macdonald, Canada's first prime minister (top), and to the theme of remembrance and peacekeeping (right).

dissidents claimed that instead of listening to the caucus, Day relied on a small group of advisers who were out of touch with party members.

In an effort to deal with the discontent, the governing body of the Alliance advanced the party's next leadership convention, scheduled for March 2002, by one month. On July 17, 2001, Day announced that he would step down as party leader at least 90 days before the convention, though he did not rule out the possibility that he would run again for the leadership.

Despite Day's action, 12 of the 13 dissident members of the Alliance formed a new caucus called the Democratic Representative Caucus in July. The members of the new caucus denied their group was a separate political party. Political analysts in Canada noted that a majority of the dissidents had been Manning supporters.

By summer 2001, bickering within the Alliance had severely damaged the party's standing with the country's voters. According to an opinion poll released in late June, the Alliance had the support of only 6 percent of voters nationwide, while support for the Liberals had climbed to 60 percent.

Day finally put an end to Alliance quarrels by issuing an ultimatum to the 12 dissidents: Return to the party and accept his leadership by September 10 or be expelled. Four of the rebels rejoined the Alliance. The other eight individuals announced they would cooperate with the Progressive Conservative Party (PCP) to form the first opposition coalition in Parliament in Canada's history. The eight former Alliance members acknowledged Joe Clark, leader of the PCP, as head of the new coalition. The new conservative group held 20 seats, giving Clark a stronger voice in Parliament.

Chretien under fire. In February, opposition leaders in Parliament mounted a spirited attack on the personal conduct of the prime minister. They accused Chretien of a conflict of interest for speaking to the head of a federal development bank about a personal property transaction in Chretien's home district of Shawinigan, Quebec.

In November 2000, the federal ethics counselor had cleared Chretien of wrongdoing in the affair. The opposition criticized the finding, noting that the prime minister had appointed the counselor. They also criticized the Liberals for failing to keep a 1993 election promise to make the ethics counselor an officer of Parliament.

On Feb. 13, 2001, the opposition raised a motion of no-confidence in the government. It was defeated, 145 to 122. On February 19, the Royal Canadian Mounted Police reported that it would not conduct a formal inquiry into Chretien's role in the loan transaction because it had uncovered no evidence of illegal activity. Although the opposition renewed its call for an investigation in April, criticism of Chretien subsided as the issue failed to arouse popular interest.

Problems for the BQ. The Bloc Quebecois (BQ), the party in the House of Commons that advocates independence for Quebec, also experienced problems in 2001. Although the BQ held a solid core of 38 of Quebec's 75 parliamentary seats, the party faced declining support in its home province. The number of Quebeckers favoring independence dropped to 40 percent in 2001, according to public opinion polls. In addition, in by-elections held on October 1, Liberal candidates took two seats in French-speaking districts from the Parti Quebecois (PQ), the separatist party in Quebec's National Assembly. One of the seats, in the nationalist Lac St. Jean district north of Quebec City, had been held by Lucien Bouchard, former leader of the PQ, who resigned the seat in January. Although local issues often influence by-elections, the results represented a hard blow to the separatist cause.

Medical marijuana. Canada in July became the first country to allow its citizens to grow, possess, and smoke marijuana for medical reasons. The new law allows people who are terminally ill to grow their own marijuana or obtain the drug from a designated supplier or the government to ease their symptoms. To become eligible for the program, a patient must obtain a physician's statement that marijuana is the only drug that will relieve the patient's symptoms. The federal government harvested its first crop of so-called "medical marijuana" from an abandoned copper mine in northern Manitoba in August. The government expected to make marijuana available to approved recipients in early 2002.

Health care worries. The cost and accessibility of Canada's public health system continued to cause concerns in 2001. The system is funded by the provincial and federal governments but administered by the provinces. Despite federal grants, health care remained the largest single item in provincial budgets. Health care workers in many provinces complained of overwork and low salaries. In April, the federal government asked Roy Romanow, the respected, recently retired premier of Saskatchewan, to conduct a thorough inquiry into the costs and operations of Canada's public health system.

In 2000, the federal government had agreed to give the provinces and territories $23.4 billion in health and education grants for the next five years. In August 2001, provincial and territorial premiers demanded an additional $7 billion in federal health care grants. Led by Ontario Premier Mike Harris, the leaders called on the federal government to boost health care grants from 14 percent to 18 percent of costs, the amount provided before budget cuts were imposed in 1994.

Economy. Canada's economy enjoyed strong growth during the first quarter, with a 2-percent increase in the gross domestic product (GDP). (The GDP is the total value of goods and services produced in a country in a given period.) During the second quarter, the GDP rose only 0.4 percent. Economists blamed the slowdown on Canada's dependence upon the faltering U.S. economy, which particularly affected exports of automobiles and information technology.

The consumer price index, which had risen to 3.9 percent in May because of soaring energy costs, dropped to 2.6 percent in July and held steady through the rest of 2001. The unemployment rate remained steady at 7 percent for the first half of the year but began to rise as the economy slowed.

Budget. Finance Minister Paul Martin issued an federal budget on December 10 after previously assuring Canadians that there was no need for a fiscal statement in 2001. The terrorist attacks on September 11, together with an economic downturn at mid-year, changed conditions drastically.

Federal spending in Canada
Estimated budget for fiscal 2001-2002*

Department or agency	Millions of dollars†
Agriculture and agri-food	2,168
Canada customs and revenue agency	2,841
Canadian heritage	3,031
Citizenship and immigration	901
Environment	634
Finance	68,998
Fisheries and oceans	1,310
Foreign affairs and international trade	3,518
Governor general	16
Health	2,739
Human resources development	28,169
Indian affairs and northern development	5,012
Industry	4,570
Justice	1,092
National defence	11,403
Natural resources	870
Parliament	355
Privy Council	239
Public works and government services	4,183
Solicitor general	3,190
Transport	960
Treasury board	2,076
Veterans affairs	2,104
Total	**150,379**

* April 1, 2001, to March 31, 2002.
† Canadian dollars; $1 = U.S. $0.64 as of Oct. 12, 2001.

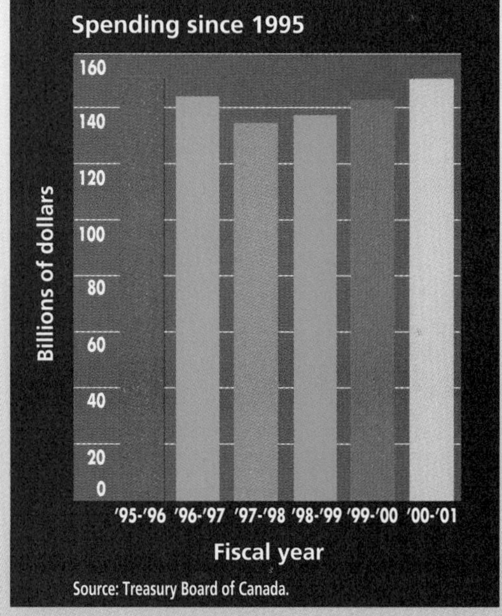

Source: Treasury Board of Canada.

Members of the Canadian House of Commons

The House of Commons of the first session of the 37th Parliament convened on Jan. 29, 2001. As of Oct. 12, 2001, the House of Commons consisted of the following members: 172 Liberal Party, 58 Canadian Alliance, 38 Bloc Québécois, 13 New Democratic Party, 12 Progressive Conservative Party, and 8 Independents. This table shows each legislator and party affiliation. An asterisk (*) denotes those who served in the 36th Parliament.

Alberta
Diane Ablonczy, C.A.*
Rob Anders, C.A.*
Leon E. Benoit, C.A.*
Rick Casson, C.A.
David Chatters, C.A.*
Joe Clark, P.C.
Ken Epp, C.A.*
Peter Goldring, C.A.*
Deborah Grey, Ind.*
Art Hanger, C.A.*
Grant Hill, C.A.*
Rahim Jaffer, C.A.*
Dale Johnston, C.A.*
Jason Kenney, C.A.*
David Kilgour, Lib.*
Preston Manning, C.A.*
Anne McLellan, Lib.*
Rob Merrifield, C.A.
Bob Mills, C.A.*
Deepak Obhrai, C.A.*
Charlie Penson, C.A.*
James Rajotte, C.A.
Monte Solberg, C.A.*
Kevin Sorenson, C.A.
Myron Thompson, C.A.*
John Williams, C.A.*

British Columbia
Jim Abbott, C.A.*
David Anderson, Lib.*
Andy Burton, C.A.*
Chuck Cadman, C.A.*
John Cummins, C.A.*
Libby Davies, N.D.P.*
Stockwell Day, C.A.
Herb Dhaliwal, Lib.*
John Duncan, C.A.*
Reed Elley, C.A.*
Paul Forseth, C.A.*
Hedy Fry, Lib.*
Jim Gouk, C.A.*
Gurmant Grewal, C.A.*
Richard Harris, C.A.*
Jay Hill, Ind.*
Betty Hinton, C.A.
Sophia Leung, Lib.*
Gary Lunn, Ind.*
James Lunney, C.A.
Keith Martin, C.A.*
Philip Mayfield, C.A.*
Grant McNally, Ind.*
Val Meredith, Ind.*
James Moore, C.A.
Stephen Owen, Lib.
Joe Peschisolido, C.A.
John Reynolds, C.A.*
Svend Robinson, N.D.P.*
Werner Schmidt, C.A.*
Darrel Stinson, C.A.*
Chuck Strahl, Ind.*
Randy White, C.A.*
Ted White, C.A.*

Manitoba
Reg Alcock, Lib.*
Bill Blaikie, N.D.P.*
Rick Borotsik, P.C.*
Bev Desjarlais, N.D.P.*
Ronald Duhamel, Lib.*
John Harvard, Lib.*
Howard Hilstrom, C.A.*
Inky Mark, Ind.*
Pat Martin, N.D.P.*
Anita Neville, Lib.
Rey Pagtakhan, Lib.*
Brian Pallister, C.A.
Vic Toews, C.A.
Judy Wasylycia-Leis, N.D.P.*

New Brunswick
Claudette Bradshaw, Lib.*
Jeannot Castonguay, Lib.
Yvon Godin, N.D.P.*
John Herron, P.C.*
Charles Hubbard, Lib.*
Dominic LeBlanc, Lib.
Andy Savoy, Lib.
Andy Scott, Lib.*
Greg Thompson, P.C.*
Elsie Wayne, P.C.*

Newfoundland
George Baker, Lib.*
Gerry Byrne, Lib.*
Norman Doyle, P.C.*
Loyola Hearn, P.C.
Bill Matthews, Lib.*
Lawrence D. O'Brien, Lib.*
Brian Tobin, Lib.

Northwest Territories
Ethel Blondin-Andrew, Lib.*

Nova Scotia
Scott Brison, P.C.*
Bill Casey, P.C.*
Rodger Cuzner, Lib.
Mark Eyking, Lib.
Gerald Keddy, P.C.*
Wendy Lill, N.D.P.*
Peter MacKay, P.C.*
Alexa McDonough, N.D.P.*
Geoff Regan, Lib.
Peter Stoffer, N.D.P.*
Robert Thibault, Lib.

Nunavut
Nancy Karetak-Lindell, Lib.*

Ontario
Peter Adams, Lib.*
Sarkis Assadourian, Lib.*
Jean Augustine, Lib.*
Sue Barnes, Lib.*
Colleen Beaumier, Lib.*
Réginald Bélair, Lib.*
Mauril Bélanger, Lib.*
Eugène Bellemare, Lib.*
Carolyn Bennett, Lib.*
Maurizio Bevilacqua, Lib.*
Ray Bonin, Lib.*
Paul Bonwick, Lib.*
Don Boudria, Lib.*
Bonnie Brown, Lib.*
John Bryden, Lib.*
Sarmite Bulte, Lib.*
Charles Caccia, Lib.*
Murray Calder, Lib.*
John Cannis, Lib.*
Elinor Caplan, Lib.*
Aileen Carroll, Lib.*
Marlene Catterall, Lib.*
Brenda Chamberlain, Lib.*
David M. Collenette, Lib.*
Joe Comartin, N.D.P.
Joe Comuzzi, Lib.*
Sheila Copps, Lib.*
Roy Cullen, Lib.*
Paul DeVillers, Lib.*
Stan Dromisky, Lib.*
Art C. Eggleton, Lib.*
John Finlay, Lib.*
Joe Fontana, Lib.*
Cheryl Gallant, C.A.
Roger Gallaway, Lib.*
John Godfrey, Lib.*
Bill Graham, Lib.*
Herb Gray, Lib.*
Ivan Grose, Lib.*
Albina Guarnieri, Lib.*
Mac Harb, Lib.*
Tony Ianno, Lib.*
Ovid Jackson, Lib.*
Joe Jordan, Lib.*
Jim Karygiannis, Lib.*
Stan Keyes, Lib.*
Bob Kilger, Lib.*
Gar Knutson, Lib.*
Karen Kraft Sloan, Lib.*
Walt Lastewka, Lib.*
Derek Lee, Lib.*
Judi Longfield, Lib.*
Paul H. Macklin, Lib.
Steve Mahoney, Lib.*
Gurbax Malhi, Lib.*
John Maloney, Lib.*
John Manley, Lib.*
Diane Marleau, Lib.*
John McCallum, Lib.
Larry McCormick, Lib.*
John McKay, Lib.*
Dan McTeague, Lib.*
Peter Milliken, Lib.*
Dennis Mills, Lib.*
Maria Minna, Lib.*
Andy Mitchell, Lib.*
Lynn Myers, Lib.*
Robert Nault, Lib.*
Pat O'Brien, Lib.*
John O'Reilly, Lib.*
Carolyn Parrish, Lib.*
Janko Peric, Lib.*
Jim Peterson, Lib.*
Beth Phinney, Lib.*
Jerry Pickard, Lib.*
Gary Pillitteri, Lib.*
David Pratt, Lib.*
Carmen Provenzano, Lib.*
Karen Redman, Lib.*
Julian Reed, Lib.*
Scott Reid, C.A.
John Richardson, Lib.*
Allan Rock, Lib.*
Benoît Serré, Lib.*
Judy Sgro, Lib.*
Alex Shepherd, Lib.*
Bob Speller, Lib.*
Brent St. Denis, Lib.*
Paul Steckle, Lib.*
Jane Stewart, Lib.*
Paul Szabo, Lib.*
Andrew Telegdi, Lib.*
Tony Tirabassi, Lib.
Alan Tonks, Lib.
Paddy Torsney, Lib.*
Rose-Marie Ur, Lib.*
Tony Valeri, Lib.*
Lyle Vanclief, Lib.*
Joseph Volpe, Lib.*
Tom Wappel, Lib.*
Susan Whelan, Lib.*
Bryon Wilfert, Lib.*
Bob Wood, Lib.*

Prince Edward Island
Wayne Easter, Lib.*
Lawrence MacAulay, Lib.*
Joe McGuire, Lib.*
Shawn Murphy, Lib.*

Quebec
Carole-Marie Allard, Lib.
Mark Assad, Lib.*
Gérard Asselin, B.Q.*
André Bachand, P.C.*
Claude Bachand, B.Q.*
Eleni Bakopanos, Lib.*
Michel Bellehumeur, B.Q.*
Stéphane Bergeron, B.Q.*
Robert Bertrand, Lib.*
Bernard Bigras, B.Q.*
Gérard Binet, Lib.
Diane Bourgeois, B.Q.
Pierre Brien, B.Q.*
Serge Cardin, B.Q.*
Jean-Guy Carignan, Lib.
Martin Cauchon, Lib.*
Yvon Charbonneau, Lib.*
Jean Chrétien, Lib.*
Denis Coderre, Lib.•
Irwin Cotler, Lib.•
Paul Crête, B.Q.*
Madeleine Dalphond-Guiral, B.Q.*
Odina Desrochers, B.Q.*
Stéphane Dion, Lib.*
Nick Discepola, Lib.*
Claude Drouin, Lib.*
Antoine Dubé, B.Q.*
Gilles Duceppe, B.Q.*
Claude Duplain, Lib.
Georges Farrah, Lib.
Raymonde Folco, Lib.*

Ghislain Fournier, B.Q.*
Alfonso Gagliano, Lib.*
Christiane Gagnon, B.Q.*
Marcel Gagnon, B.Q.
Michel Gauthier, B.Q.*
Jocelyne Girard-Bujold, B.Q.*
Monique Guay, B.Q.*
Michel Guimond, B.Q.*
André Harvey, Lib*.
Marlene Jennings, Lib.*
Mario Laframboise, B.Q.
Francine Lalonde, B.Q.*
Robert Lanctôt, B.Q.
Raymond Lavigne, Lib.*
Ghislain Lebel, B.Q.*
Clifford Lincoln, Lib.*
Yvan Loubier, B.Q.*
Richard Marceau, B.Q.*
Serge Marcil, Lib.
Paul Martin, Lib.*
Réal Ménard, B.Q.*
Gilbert Normand, Lib.*
Pierre Paquette, B.Q.
Denis Paradis, Lib.*
Bernard Patry, Lib.*
Gilles-A. Perron, B.Q.*
Pierre Pettigrew, Lib.*
Pauline Picard, B.Q.*
Louis Plamondon, B.Q.*
David Price, Lib.*
Marcel Proulx, Lib.*
Lucienne Robillard, Lib.*
Yves Rocheleau, B.Q.*
Jean-Yves Roy, B.Q.
Jacques Saada, Lib.*
Benoît Sauvageau, B.Q.*
Hélène Scherrer, Lib.
Caroline St-Hilaire, B.Q.*
Diane St-Jacques, Lib.*
Guy St-Julien, Lib.*
Yolande Thibeault, Lib.*
Stéphan Tremblay, B.Q.*
Suzanne Tremblay, B.Q.*
Pierrette Venne, B.Q.*

Saskatchewan
David Anderson, C.A.
Roy Bailey, C.A.*
Garry Breitkreuz, C.A.*
Brian Fitzpatrick, C.A.
Ralph E. Goodale, Lib.*
Rick Laliberte, Lib.*
Lorne Nystrom, N.D.P.*
Jim Pankiw, Ind.*
Dick Proctor, N.D.P.*
Gerry Ritz, C.A.*
Carol Skelton, C.A.
Larry Spencer, C.A.
Maurice Vellacott, C.A.*
Lynne Yelich, C.A.

Yukon Territory
Larry Bagnell, Lib.

The Ministry of Canada*

Jean Chrétien—prime minister
Herbert Eser Gray—deputy prime minister
David Michael Collenette—minister of transport
David Anderson—minister of the environment
Ralph Goodale—minister of natural resources and minister responsible for the Canadian Wheat Board
Brian Tobin—minister of industry
Sheila Copps—minister of Canadian heritage
John Manley—minister of foreign affairs
Paul Martin—minister of finance
Arthur Eggleton—minister of national defence
Anne McLellan—minister of justice; attorney general of Canada
Allan Rock—minister of health
Lawrence MacAulay—solicitor general of Canada
Alfonso Gagliano—minister of public works and government services
Lucienne Robillard—president of the Treasury Board; minister responsible for infrastructure
Martin Cauchon—minister of national revenue; secretary of state (Economic Development Agency of Canada for the Regions of Quebec)
Jane Stewart—minister of human resources development
Stéphane Dion—president of the Queen's Privy Council for Canada; minister of intergovernmental affairs
Pierre Pettigrew—minister for international trade
Don Boudria—leader of the government in the House of Commons
Lyle Vanclief—minister of agriculture and Agri-Food
Herb Dhaliwal—minister of fisheries and oceans
Ronald Duhamel—minister of veterans affairs; secretary of state (Western economic diversification/Francophonie)
Claudette Bradshaw—minister of labour
Robert Daniel Nault—minister of Indian affairs and Northern development
Maria Minna—minister for international cooperation
Elinor Caplan—minister of citizenship and immigration
Sharon Carstairs—leader of the government in the Senate
Robert G. Thibault—minister of state (Atlantic Canada Opportunities Agency)
Ethel Blondin-Andrew—secretary of state (children and youth)
Hedy Fry—secretary of state (multiculturalism/status of women)
David Kilgour—secretary of state (Latin America and Africa)
James Scott Peterson—secretary of state (international financial institutions)
Andrew Mitchell—secretary of state (rural development/federal economic development initiative for Northern Ontario)
Gilbert Normand—secretary of state (science, research, and development)
Denis Coderre—secretary of state (amateur sport)
Rey Pagtakhan—secretary of state (Asia-Pacific)

*As of Dec. 31, 2001.

Premiers of Canadian provinces

Province	Premier
Alberta	Ralph Klein
British Columbia	Gordon Campbell
Manitoba	Gary Doer
New Brunswick	Bernard Lord
Newfoundland	Roger Grimes
Nova Scotia	John Hamm
Ontario	Mike Harris
Prince Edward Island	Patrick George Binns
Quebec	Bernard Landry
Saskatchewan	Lorne Albert Cal

Government leaders of territories

Northwest Territories	Stephen Kakfwi
Nunavut	Paul Okalik
Yukon Territory	Patricia Jane Duncan

Saskatchewan Indians give Prince Charles of the United Kingdom a new name—Kisikawpisim Kamiyowahpahmikroot—meaning "The sun watches over you in a good way," during the prince's visit to Canada's Wanuskewin Park in April 2001.

The Chretien government announced in December that it would spend an additional $12 billion over the next five years. The bulk of these funds would be devoted to improving security at borders, airports, and aboard commercial airliners. A charge would be levied on air travelers to help cover the cost of more stringent airport security. Efficient procedures and new infrastructure would be provided for easing the massive flow of traffic, estimated to be worth $1.3 billion a day, across the Canadian-U.S. border. Continued congestion at border crossings would harm the economies of both countries.

The new expenditures would wipe out the 2001 surplus that Martin had predicted. However, the minister pledged balanced budgets for the next three years, abandoning his commitment to reduce debt. He estimated that the economy would begin to revive by the second quarter of 2002, leading to an anticipated 1.1-percent increase in the 2002 GDP.

Summit of the Americas. Canada hosted the Summit of the Americas in Quebec City from April 20 to April 22, 2001. Thirty-four nations from the Western Hemisphere—all countries except Cuba—attended. Conference delegates agreed that only countries with democratic governments would be permitted to participate in the Free Trade Area of the Americas (FTAA). Scheduled to go into effect in December 2005, the FTAA would be a free trade zone that would include the 34 democratic countries of the Western Hemisphere.

At least 25,000 demonstrators gathered in Quebec to protest the FTAA. They argued that the FTAA would strengthen international business at the expense of workers and the environment. Outside a perimeter fence that protected the delegates, the protesters held parallel sessions to discuss issues raised in the conference.

Alberta for G8 meeting. In an effort to minimize the kind of disruptions that had occurred at other international economic meetings, Chretien announced in July 2001 that Canada would host the 2002 summit of the Group of Eight (G8) at an isolated ski resort. The G8 is an informal organization of eight major industrialized countries. At the 2001 meeting of the G8 in Genoa, Italy, numerous demonstrators protested *globalization*—the trend toward increased business, cultural, and governmental interaction across international borders. Chretien said Canada would hold the meeting at Kananaskis, a tiny Rocky Mountain resort about 50 miles (80 kilometers) west of Calgary, Alberta.

Kyoto Protocol meeting. In July 2001, Canadian delegates attended a conference on the Kyoto Protocol held in Bonn, Germany. The protocol is an international agreement to cut the rate at which carbon dioxide and five other gases are released into the atmosphere. The gases contribute to global warming. U.S. President George

W. Bush rejected the agreement in March.

At the Bonn meeting, delegates from 179 countries worked to devise a formula under which countries could cut their carbon dioxide emissions. Canada argued that it should receive credit for its large forests, which absorb carbon dioxide.

The delegates agreed to work towards a 5-percent cut in emissions by 2012, using the total emission levels of all industrialized countries in 1990 as a base. Canadian officials hoped to ratify the Kyoto Protocol in 2002. ☐ David M. L. Farr

See also **Canada, Prime Minister of; Canadian provinces; Canadian territories; Montreal; Terrorism: A Special Feature**, p. 38; **Toronto.**

2001 Canadian population estimates

Province and territory populations

Alberta	3,035,500
British Columbia	4,099,800
Manitoba	1,153,200
New Brunswick	758,900
Newfoundland and Labrador	536,800
Northwest Territories	43,100
Nova Scotia	942,800
Nunavut	28,400
Ontario	11,823,000
Prince Edward Island	140,200
Quebec	7,395,800
Saskatchewan	1,021,500
Yukon Territory	30,300
Canada	31,009,300

City and metropolitan area populations

	Metropolitan area	City
Toronto, Ont.	4,838,700	2,618,200
Montreal, Que.	3,513,700	1,054,500
Vancouver, B.C.	2,069,900	591,900
Ottawa-Hull	1,094,100	
Ottawa, Ont.		347,600
Hull, Que.		67,100
Calgary, Alta.	981,200	839,700
Edmonton, Alta.	960,400	632,500
Quebec, Que.	691,100	174,200
Winnipeg, Man.	682,200	624,600
Hamilton, Ont.	678,900	335,800
Kitchener, Ont.	428,600	192,000
London, Ont.	424,100	340,500
St. Catharines-Niagara Falls	391,500	
St. Catharines, Ont.		133,800
Niagara Falls, Ont.		79,100
Halifax, N.S.	359,600	119,100
Victoria, B.C.	318,100	78,000
Windsor, Ont.	308,800	210,400
Oshawa, Ont.	303,400	151,100
Saskatoon, Sask.	234,300	201,100
Regina, Sask.	201,000	182,200
St. John's, Nfld.	174,700	103,300
Chicoutimi-Jonquière	158,200	
Chicoutimi, Que.		62,900
Jonquière, Que.		56,400
Sudbury, Ont.	154,900	93,700
Sherbrooke, Que.	153,300	80,400
Trois-Rivières, Que.	141,700	49,800
Saint John, N.B.	127,600	72,400
Thunder Bay, Ont.	125,500	114,200

Source: World Book estimates based on data from Statistics Canada.

Canada, Prime Minister of. Prime Minister Jean Chretien faced criticism early in 2001 stemming from allegations that he intervened in securing a bank loan for a hotel in Quebec during the 1990's. A friend of the prime minister owned the hotel. On Feb. 19, 2001, Royal Canadian Mounted Police officials announced that they had uncovered no evidence of illegal activity on Chretien's part and declined to conduct a formal inquiry into his role in the loan transaction between the owner of the hotel and the Business Development Bank of Canada.

Meeting with Bush. Chretien traveled to Washington, D.C., in February to become the first foreign leader to meet with United States President George W. Bush after the president's inauguration. Chretien and Bush discussed a series of topics, including trade, national and international energy policy, and various national security issues.

Funding for the arts. In May, Chretien announced a three-year government plan to contribute $560 million to Canadian art and culture programs. Chretien said that the program was the largest government investment in the arts since the 1960's. ☐ David M. L. Farr

See also **Canada; Canadian provinces; Canadian territories; Terrorism: A Special Feature**, p. 38.

Canadian provinces. Strong growth in Canada's national economy benefited the country's provinces in 2001. An economic downturn in the second half of the year, however, reduced provincial revenues and curtailed some planned spending. Although Ontario, Canada's largest province, remained the country's engine of economic development, dynamic expansion also occurred in the energy-rich provinces of Alberta and Newfoundland.

Canada's national health care system continued to preoccupy provincial governments, which administer and supply most of the system's funding. In April, the federal government asked a respected provincial leader, Roy Romanow of Saskatchewan, to conduct an inquiry into the operations and finances of the health system.

Alberta. Premier Ralph Klein's Progressive Conservative Party (PCP) government, awash in dramatically higher revenues from oil and gas sales, distributed benefits to Albertans on a generous scale in 2001. On January 30, Klein announced that homeowners' credits for the purchase of natural gas would triple to $150 a month. (All amounts are in Canadian dollars.) This assistance, which ran from January 1 to April 30, also applied to businesses and farmers.

On February 5, provincial Treasurer Steve West predicted that booming energy revenues would boost the provincial budget surplus to $7.3 billion. West announced that $5.6 billion of the projected windfall would be used to reduce the province's $12.5-billion debt.

Spending jumped by 24 percent in Alberta's $4.1-billion budget for fiscal year 2001-2002 (April 1, 2001, to March 31, 2002), presented on April 24, 2001, by Finance Minister Patricia Nelson. Much of the additional spending was earmarked for health care, education, and transportation, generally for one-time projects.

Buoyed by Alberta's healthy finances, Klein held provincial elections on March 12. During his eight years in office, Klein had made it a priority to reduce spending. Albertans gave Klein his third consecutive victory, continuing the PCP's 30-year domination of Alberta's government. The PCP won 74 of 83 seats in the provincial legislature and 62 percent of the popular vote. The Liberal Party lost half its seats in the legislature, dropping from 15 to 7.

British Columbia. The Liberal Party, out of office since 1952, routed the New Democratic Party (NDP) in provincial elections held on May 16, 2001. The Liberals' victory ended the NDP's 10-year control of British Columbia's government. Political analysts attributed the NDP's collapse to inept management of provincial finances, costly subsidies for a failed ferry service, and a stagnant economy since 1992. Political scandal also drove two NDP premiers from office.

Public opinion surveys conducted just before the election revealed that the NDP had the backing of only 17 percent of voters. Despite efforts by Premier Ujjal Dosanjh to shore up support for his beleaguered government, voters slashed the party's representation in the legislature from 39 to 2 seats, both held by women. The Liberals, headed by former Vancouver Mayor Gordon Campbell, won the remaining 77 seats.

The new premier announced on his first day in office, June 6, 2001, a 25-percent reduction in the provincial portion of the personal income tax. The cut, which began immediately, was to extend over the next two years.

Campbell also moved swiftly to review government operations. However, government spending continued to rise. On August 9, the government gave 33,000 provincial nurses and health care workers a 23.5-percent salary increase over three years, making them among the best-paid caregivers in Canada. The action followed seven months of unsuccessful negotiations with health care unions, which angrily criticized the settlement.

Manitoba enjoyed strong economic growth during 2001. Economists cited the export of electricity from the province's hydroelectric power plants as a profitable mainstay of the economy. The provincial budget, introduced on April 10, forecast a surplus of $46 million. The NDP government of Premier Gary Doer increased spending on health care and education and included funds in the budget for improving the floodway around Winnipeg, the provincial capital. The floodway had proved useful in the disastrous flood of 1997. Personal income taxes were reduced for the second year under a three-year plan, introduced in 2000, which called for a total reduction of 10.5 percent. Homeowners also saw a modest reduction in property taxes in 2001.

An abandoned copper mine near remote Flin Flon, about 360 miles (575 kilometers) north of Winnipeg, became the site of Canada's first legal marijuana farm in 2001. A crop of marijuana was cultivated for medical use at the *hydroponics* (soilless) farm in August. The farm was established under a federal plan to make the drug available to ease the symptoms of terminally ill patients by February 2002.

New Brunswick faced unrest among health care workers in 2001. From January 8 to January 10, about 1,300 provincial physicians walked off the job after the government rejected their demands for a 30-percent salary increase over three years. The physicians contended that the 12-percent raise offered by the PCP government of Premier Bernard Lord was insufficient to remedy a severe shortage of doctors in the province. On April 18, the Lord government announced a new $40-million fee arrangement that boosted physicians' salaries by $50,000 a year.

Despite modest economic growth and strains on government spending, the Lord government brought in an optimistic budget on March 27. The budget, which projected a $34.4-million surplus, included a measure that dropped about 15,000 low-income workers from the tax rolls.

Newfoundland Labrador. On October 30, the lower house of Parliament approved an amendment to the Canadian constitution to formally change the province's name from Newfoundland to Newfoundland and Labrador. Canada's easternmost province consists of the island of Newfoundland, where more than 90 percent of the population lives, and the coast of Labrador, a part of the Canadian mainland.

Roger Grimes, a former health minister, won a convention election as the leader of Newfoundland's governing Liberal Party on February 3. Grimes succeeded Premier Brian Tobin, who resigned in October 2000 to become the federal minister of industry. The Liberals held 30 of 48 seats in the provincial legislature.

On his first day in office, the new premier angered some legislators by reversing the Tobin administration's demand that Inco Limited of Toronto, one of the world's largest nickel-min-

Quebec Premier Lucien Bouchard of the governing Parti Quebecois announces his resignation in January 2001. Bouchard acknowledged his unhappiness over his inability to increase public support for Quebec independence.

ing companies, process all the nickel ore mined from Labrador's Voisey's Bay at a smelter to be built in Newfoundland. Inco, which in 1996 paid $4.3 billion for the right to exploit the bay's rich reserves, argued that it should not be forced to build and operate an unprofitable smelter. In March 2001, Grimes revealed that he had met with Inco representatives to discuss reopening negotiations on the project, which had collapsed in January 2000.

In March 2001, Grimes announced a tentative deal under which Inco would be allowed to process some of the Voisey ore outside Newfoundland. The Voisey's Bay discussions created anxiety among Newfoundlanders, who feared the province would not reap the full benefits of the project. Negotiations continued through 2001.

Newfoundland, Canada's poorest province, made a significant recovery in 2001 following the collapse of its historic cod fishery in the early 1990's. The 1998 expiration of a government income-support program had also devastated fishers and fishery plant workers. By 2001, the province had added new sources of revenue—two major offshore oil projects. Hibernia was brought into production in 1997, and Terra Nova's massive $2.7-billion oil platform was launched in August 2001.

The budget, released by the Liberals on March 22, offered a bright picture of the province's economic growth. In 2000, for the third consecutive year, the economy had expanded by 5 percent. Finance Minister Joan Marie Aylward, however, predicted lower revenues for fiscal year 2001-2002. Positive economic news included Newfoundland's lowest unemployment rate since 1990 and a record number of tourists, drawn by the province's scenic and historic attractions.

On April 1, 2001, two unions representing 19,000 public employees staged the largest strike in Newfoundland's history. The strike followed a breakdown in talks between the unions, which wanted a 15-percent increase in wages and pensions over three years, and the government, which offered 13 percent. Later in April, the union voted to accept the government's offer.

Nova Scotia. A dispute over salaries and protests against an antistrike law rocked Nova Scotia's health care industry in 2001. On June 27, hundreds of nurses and other health care workers threatened to resign unless the provincial government rescinded a new law repealing their right to strike. The workers also demanded a wage increase of 25 percent over three years. Pleading financial problems, the PCP government of Premier John Hamm offered 10 percent over the same period. The dispute went to an arbitrator on August 3. On August 13, the arbitrator awarded the nurses a 17-percent salary increase. Other health care workers received a 7.5-percent salary increase plus a signing bonus.

The province's 2001-2002 budget, introduced on March 29, 2001, emphasized new spending instead of the cost cutting that in 2000 had caused widespread labor protests. The Hamm government offered an additional $100 million in expenditures in 2001, mainly for health care, rural roads, and colleges. The budget projected a $91-million increase in Nova Scotia's overall debt of $11.5-billion.

Ontario. Jim Flaherty, in his first budget since being appointed finance minister in February, announced Ontario's third consecutive balanced budget on May 9. The $63-billion budget recorded a surplus of $3.1 billion. It also included the final phase of the PCP government's promised 20-percent cut in personal income taxes. However, this cut was delayed until 2002 because of a slowdown of the economy. Flaherty also announced reductions in corporate taxes.

The centerpiece of the 2001-2002 budget was a tax credit for parents with children attending private or religious schools. The credit, the first established in any province, was scheduled to increase yearly. It would provide up to 50 percent (or $3,500) in tuition costs by 2006. An estimated 100,000 Ontario children were enrolled in schools outside the public education system.

Prince Edward Island. The United States on May 2001, lifted a six-month ban on potatoes from Prince Edward Island. The ban had been imposed after the discovery of the potato wart virus in a single potato field in 2000. The virus, which disfigures the potato, has no harmful effect on human beings. The ban cost the province, which sells about 10 percent of its potato crop to the United States, an estimated $50 million. While the ban was in effect, potato farmers received $30 million in federal and provincial aid. On August 1, 2001, the United States lifted all restrictions except for potatoes from 25 fields near the contaminated field.

Despite the resumption of shipments, the potato industry on Prince Edward Island remained crippled. Agricultural experts predicted that a severe summer drought would cut the potato crop by about half.

Despite the province's slow economic growth, Treasurer Patricia Mella presented a budget with a small surplus on March 29. Since first winning election in 1996, the PCP government of Patrick Binns had worked to lower the provincial debt.

Quebec. A change in leadership threw the governing Parti Quebecois (PQ), committed to the separation of Quebec from Canada, into upheaval in 2001. Deep divisions within the party surfaced, especially over the government-mandated use of the French language.

In a move that surprised Quebeckers, Premier Lucien Bouchard announced his resignation on January 11. Bernard Landry, the deputy head of the government, was the only likely successor. Landry, a founding member of the PQ, had served four Quebec premiers and had been minister of finance since 1994. Landry was sworn in as Quebec's 28th premier on March 8, 2001. As premier, he remained a separatist with a sound grasp of Quebec's economic position and policies needed to promote growth.

Landry's financial goals were carried forward in the first budget of his administration, delivered by new Finance Minister Pauline Marois on March 29. A three-year program of personal income tax cuts, promised in Landry's last budget, offered tax reductions of 16 to 24 percent, depending on income. Even with the tax cuts, Quebec remained the most heavily taxed province in Canada. Marcois earmarked a predicted surplus of $2.6 billion for strengthening health and social services, promoting economic growth in regions outside financially robust Montreal, and making a modest payback of Quebec's $102-billion public debt.

Saskatchewan gained a new premier on January 27 when Lorne Calvert, a clergyman and political veteran, was chosen to replace Roy Romanow as head of the governing NDP. Romanow had resigned in September 2000. The NDP, with 29 members, held a slender majority in the provincial legislature with the support of two Liberal members.

On March 30, 2001, Finance Minister Eric Cline presented the NDP's first budget under Calvert. For the eighth straight year, the government recorded a balanced budget. Cline offered more than $370 million in new spending, while predicting a $2.6-million surplus on revenues of $6 billion.

On June 26, Calvert's governing coalition faced a no-confidence vote on a budget measure. It was sponsored by the conservative Saskatchewan Party, which had captured many rural seats in the 1999 election. The coalition survived the challenge by a narrow vote of 28 to 26. ☐ David M. L. Farr

See also **Canada; Canadian territories; Montreal; Toronto.**

Canadian territories. Yukon and the Northwest Territories in 2001 remained locked in an intense competition for the construction of a multibillion-dollar pipeline to transport Alaskan and Canadian natural gas from the Arctic to the rest of North America. In 2001, the three-year-old government of Nunavut continued to experience growing pains as Nunavut leaders attempted to administer the vast, sparsely settled region.

Northwest Territories. Diamonds provided a powerful spur to economic growth in the Territories, which expected to reap $30 million in income—4 percent of total budget revenues—from diamond mining and processing in 2001. (All amounts in Canadian dollars.) Output at the Ekati mine, which produced about 250,000 carats per month in 2001, pushed Canada to fifth place among the world's diamond-producing nations after only three years of operation. Construction continued on the $500-million Diavik mine, Canada's second diamond mine, which engineers expected to begin operating in 2003. Both mines are located at Lac de Gras, northeast of Yellowknife, the territorial capital. In 2001, Yellowknife also boasted three plants for cutting and polishing diamonds.

De Beers Canada, a subsidiary of the giant South African-based diamond conglomerate, continued construction in 2001 on Canada's first underground diamond mine. The $300-million mine, located in Snap Lake, about 140 miles (220 kilometers) northeast of Yellowknife, is the first De Beers mine to be developed outside of southern Africa.

In 2001, revenue from tourism in the Territories continued to grow. The aurora borealis, or northern lights, in particular, became an increasingly popular attraction for Japanese tourists, whose culture emphasizes a quest for beauty and an appreciation of natural wonders. In 2001, about 10,000 visitors from Japan arrived in Yellowknife, where the aurora appears an average of 243 nights a year.

The territorial government of Premier Stephen Kakfwi continued to lobby in 2001 for a natural gas pipeline through the Territories. The proposed pipeline would run under the Beaufort Sea from Alaska to the MacKenzie River Delta, then continue aboveground along the MacKenzie River Valley to connect with pipelines in northern Alberta. The project requires the approval of native groups living along the proposed route. Backers estimated the pipeline would cost $3 billion and take three years to complete. An estimated 56 trillion cubic feet (158,500 cubic meters) of natural gas lies along Canada's Arctic coast.

Yukon in 2001 continued to push a rival pipeline proposal—a 4,350-mile (2,700-kilometer) pipeline that would begin on Alaska's northern coast, follow the Alaska Highway south, then cut across Yukon to Alberta. In addition to being more direct, Yukon's proposed pipeline promised lower servicing costs. The estimated construction cost, however, exceeded $11.5 billion.

Yukon, the smallest of Canada's territories in size and population, experienced disappointing economic growth during 2001. The budget, introduced on February 22 by Premier Patricia Duncan, predicted a deficit of $24.1 million on expenditures of $535.5 million. Duncan's government planned to make up the deficit with funds from a previously accumulated surplus. Because Yukon derives a smaller share of budget revenues from the federal government than other territories, it must raise more of its funds from local taxation.

Yukon officials believed transferring oil and gas earnings from the federal government to the territorial government would boost the territory's revenue base and relieve its budgetary problems. Federal and territorial negotiators hoped to resolve this issue in 2002.

Nunavut, homeland for Canada's Inuit people, continued to face formidable social challenges in 2001. The territory has a population of about 27,700 people living in 26 communities scattered over 770,000 square miles (2.2 million square kilometers) of Arctic terrain. At least 85 percent of the residents are Inuit. There are no permanent roads between settlements. As a result, travelers and companies shipping goods must rely mainly on air transport. The high transportation costs helped give Nunavut Canada's highest cost of living. Unemployment ranged from 20 to 40 percent in 2001. Housing, most of it provided by the state, remained in desperately short supply.

The cost of administering and providing services to the inhabitants of Nunavut continued to be a pressing burden for Nunavut's government in 2001. The territorial budget, introduced on February 27, revealed a deficit of $12 million on expenditures of $679.5 million. The shortfall was to be made up from an existing surplus. Nunavut received 98 percent of its revenue from federal grants. This support came to $21,500 for each inhabitant, the highest level of per capita support in any jurisdiction in Canada.

In 2001, the government of Nunavut demanded additional funds from the federal government, claiming that it could not balance its budget in the face of crushing responsibilities. During a visit to Nunavut in March, Finance Minister Paul Martin promised to study the territory's financial problems. He also noted that grants from the federal government would remain unchanged for the next three years. ☐ David M. L. Farr

See also **Canada**.

Cape Verde. See **Africa**.

Census. The United States Census Bureau reported in April 2001 that the population of the United States reached 281,421,906 people in 2000, an increase of 32.7 million people between 1990 and 2000. The increase was the largest in any single decade since the Census Bureau began collecting data in 1790. The 10-year increase exceeded the growth spurt that took place between 1950 and 1960 at the peak of the *baby boom* (the large group of people born in the United States from 1946 to 1964).

According to the 2000 Census, the population in all 50 states increased for the first time in 100 years. Officials said that growth came at a faster rate than had been projected. The population grew by 19.7 percent in the West; by 17.3 percent in the South; 7.9 percent in the Midwest; and 5.5 percent in the Northeast.

The Census Bureau reported that the population center of the United States moved to Edgar Springs, Missouri, approximately 40 miles (64 kilometers) southwest of DeSoto, Missouri, which was the population center after the 1990 census. The bureau defines a population center "as the place where an imaginary, flat, weightless, and rigid map of the United States would balance perfectly if all 281,421,906 residents were of identical weight."

Minority growth. Census data revealed that the Hispanic population in the United States increased by about 60 percent, from 22.4 million persons in 1990 to 35.3 million people in 2000. The number of African Americans in the United States rose roughly 16 percent to 34.7 million people in 2000, up from 30 million people in 1990. Although the nation's population in 2000 was still predominantly white, the census revealed that Hispanic Americans, for the first time, had surpassed African Americans as the nation's largest minority.

The 2000 census also allowed respondents for the first time to select more than one ethnic group from six racial categories to identify themselves. This option created a possible 63 choices. Nearly 7 million U.S. citizens—approximately 2.4 percent of the population—identified themselves as belonging to more than one race on their 2000 census forms.

Census data released in May 2001 revealed that the number of people of Mexican ancestry in the United States grew 53 percent during the 1990's, spurring much of the almost 13 million increase in the number of the nation's Hispanics between 1990 and 2000. Mexicans made up the largest Hispanic group in the United States, with 20.6 million people.

Living standards. The U.S. standard of living increased dramatically during the 1990's, the Census Bureau reported in August 2001. The bureau compiled the data from a survey of 700,000 respondents conducted along with the 2000 census. According to the bureau, family income, home size, and car ownership all increased between 1990 and 2000.

Nuclear families. According to the 2000 census, fewer than 25 percent of all U.S. households were made up of married couples with children. The Census Bureau reported in May 2001 that the number of married couples with children fell to 23.5 percent of all households in 2000, down from 25.6 percent in 1990 and 45 percent in 1960. Analysts said that the number of families headed by women with children grew five times faster during the 1990's than the number of families composed of married couples with children. In addition, the number of unmarried couples in the United States increased from 3.1 million in 1990 to 5.5 million in 2000.

Median age. The median age of the U.S. population in 2000 rose to 35.3 years, the highest age ever recorded by the Census Bureau. The median age is the age at which half of the population is older and half of the population is younger. The bureau attributed the higher median age, which stood at 32.9 years in 1990, to the aging of the baby boom generation.

☐ Geoffrey A. Campbell

See also **City; United States, Government of the: A Special Report.**

Chemistry. In February 2001, researchers at the University of Illinois at Urbana-Champaign reported that they had developed a type of plastic that can seal itself when cracked. Materials engineer Scott R. White said that when the *polymer composite* (plastic made of long chains of molecules) they designed begins to form tiny fractures under pressure, the fractures seal themselves before they grow into large cracks.

The composite material developed by the researchers contains microscopic capsules filled with molecules called dicyclopentadiene. The microcapsules are evenly distributed in the plastic alongside *catalysts,* substances that cause chemical reactions while themselves remaining unchanged. When a fracture begins to form in the plastic, the nearby microcapsules rupture, spilling the dicyclopentadiene into the crack. Once in the crack, the dicyclopentadiene comes into contact with a catalyst, which causes the molecules to link together into long polymer chains that seal the crack.

The engineers noted that their technique could be applied to the manufacture of many other polymer composites, materials that are used in a wide variety of products. Eventually, self-sealing composites might be used in cell phones, door panels of cars, frames of eyeglasses, implanted medical devices, parts of satellites, and deep-ocean sensors. The engineers speculated that other brittle materials, including glass and ceramics, could also be designed to self seal.

Dangerous drug interactions. The chemical structure of a substance that determines how the body responds to drugs was described in June by researchers at the University of North Carolina (UNC) at Chapel Hill and at GlaxoSmithKline, a drug company in Triangle Park, North Carolina. The description explained how pregnane X receptor, or PXR, a liver *enzyme* (a protein substance that influences chemical reactions), is able to bind with and regulate the activity of a wide variety of drugs. The research also shed light on why some drugs become ineffective or even harmful when used in combination with other drugs.

PXR's natural function is to help break down potentially harmful drugs and toxins in the liver. However, PXR also interacts with a number of medications, including cyclosporine, a drug used after tissue transplants to suppress the immune system; the anticancer drug taxol; contraceptives; and antidepressants. Reactions with PXR can cause these drugs to lose their effectiveness when patients take them while using other drugs. For example, when a woman using an oral contraceptive also takes the antidepressant St. John's wort, the antidepressant may activate PXR, which then breaks down the contraceptive.

To help them understand how PXR reacts with drugs, a team led by Matthew R. Redinbo, a molecular biology researcher at UNC, studied PXR with X-ray crystallography. In this procedure, X rays are passed through a specially prepared substance, which then spreads out the rays into a particular geometric pattern. The pattern reveals the molecular structure of the substance. This procedure showed that PXR has an unusually large cavity with five chemically active sites. The large cavity allows PXR to bind with many different substances. This capability explained why PXR can interact with so many different drugs.

The researchers said knowledge of the structure of PXR may lead to the development of computer simulations that clarify how drugs interact with PXR. This, in turn, would allow drug makers to screen new drugs for dangerous interactions.

Cosmic component of life. A key component of living cells may have come to Earth from space billions of years ago, according to a January report by chemist Louis J. Allamandola of the National Aeronautics and Space Administration's Ames Research Center in Mountain View, California, and colleagues at the University of California at Santa Cruz. Allamandola's group announced that a laboratory mixture of water, methanol, ammonia, and carbon monoxide gives rise to *vesicles,* bubblelike structures resembling the membranes of cells. A variety of complex vesicles formed when the scientists exposed the chemical mixture, which is known to exist in *interstellar* (between stars) clouds, to a high vacuum, extreme cold, and ultraviolet radiation—conditions like those in space.

All living cells have a type of protective housing, such as a cell membrane or cell wall, that separates the cell from its environment. The housing keeps chemicals in cells in close contact with each other, allowing reactions essential to life to take place. Cellular membranes also control the flow of nutrients into cells and waste products out of cells. In addition, cell membranes help control the flow of energy into cells.

The scientists demonstrated that the vesicles they created acted like cell membranes in a number of ways. For example, some of the vesicles converted ultraviolet light into visible light, an energy source that is essential for life.

The researchers said their experiment indicated that membranelike structures may have formed in space and fallen onto a young Earth with interplanetary dust or meteorites. On the warm and wet conditions of Earth, the membranes may have "kick-started" the creation of life. The research supported a theory called *panspermia,* which states that life on Earth may have originated in space. □ Peter J. Andrews

See also **Medicine.**

Chess. The Federation Internationale des Echecs (FIDE), the governing body of international chess, held its championship qualification tournament in Moscow from Nov. 25 to Dec. 14, 2001. In the event, held in the Kremlin, defending champion Viswanathan Anand of India, Vassily Ivanchuk of Ukraine, Peter Suidler of Russia, and Rusian Ponomarior of Ukraine were fighting for two slots in an 8-game match to be held in mid-January 2002 to decide the title.

Drug testing. In July 2001, FIDE began drug-testing on top chess players to lend credence to its effort to qualify chess for the Olympic Games. Caffeine is on the list of banned substances, along with amphetamines and some prescription drugs.

Major tournaments. Vladimir Kramnik continued to reign as the second Brain Games world chess champion by virtue of his defeat of Garry Kasparov in 2000. Kasparov, however, retained his number-one world ranking. Kramnik is number two, and Anand is ranked number three. In December 2001, Kramnik and Kasparov played a series of nontitle matches in Moscow for a prize of $500,000. Kasparov won the speed matches, which were the only decisive matches.

In March, chess teams from the United States and China competed with each other for the first time. The competition, which was held in Seattle, was designed so that the top six players of each country faced each other in one game a day for four days. In addition, each team fielded two leading women and two junior players to compete against each other. China won the event 21-19, mainly with the help of strong play by its junior players.

Other tournaments. Almost every chess player in the United States had an opportunity to qualify for the 2001-2002 U.S. Championship because of a new format that made it easier to participate. In the championship, to be held in Seattle in January 2002, men and women were to play in the same championship for the first time.

Young champions. In February, Hikaru Nakamura, of White Plains, New York, became at 13 years old the youngest international master. Bobby Fischer had previously held that distinction. Nakamura also won the U.S. Junior (under 20 years old) championship in July.

In August, Peter Acs of Hungary bested the 92-player field at the boys' World Junior (under age 20) Championship in Athens. Humpy Koneru of India overpowered a 62-player field to become the girls' World Junior Champion.

Hall of Fame. The World Chess Hall of Fame, the new official museum for both the FIDE and the U.S. Chess Federation, opened on December 16 in Miami, Florida. ☐ Al Lawrence

Chicago. Chicago's population in 2001 reflected a decade of changes that produced the city's first growth spurt in 50 years and a dramatic shift in its ethnic makeup. Data from the 2000 census, released on March 14, 2001, revealed that during the 1990's, the city's population had risen by about 4 percent, to 2.9 million residents. The population increase was powered by a 38-percent rise in the number of Hispanic residents. The city's Asian population rose by 26 percent.

In contrast, the number of non-Hispanic white Chicagoans fell by 14 percent between 1990 and 2000; and the number of African Americans declined by nearly 2 percent. According to 2000 census figures, non-Hispanic blacks made up 36 percent of Chicago's population; non-Hispanic whites constituted 31 percent; Hispanics accounted for 26 percent; and Asians made up 4 percent of Chicago's population.

Wacker Drive. A $200-million reconstruction effort shut down historic but crumbling Wacker Drive in February. The double-decker street, which opened in 1926, runs along the Chicago River on the north and west sides of the Loop, the city's central business district. The drive was expected to reopen in November 2002.

School system shakeup. Paul Vallas, chief executive officer of the Chicago Public Schools, resigned under pressure from Chicago Mayor Richard M. Daley in June 2001. Vallas had headed Daley's school-reform efforts since 1995. However, a study of Chicago schools, released on March 9, 2001, revealed that despite efforts to improve teaching skills, poor instruction plagued more than half the city's high schools. Elementary math and high school reading scores also had dropped.

Seeking to reverse what he called a "period of stagnation," Daley named Arne Duncan, a deputy school official, as Vallas's replacement. Daley also named Michael W. Scott, a business executive, as the new president of the Chicago Board of Education. He replaced Gery Chico, who resigned on May 24.

Business. The Boeing Co., the aerospace manufacturer that had been headquartered in Seattle, moved its headquarters to downtown Chicago in September. Chicago and Illinois officials offered the company $60 million in tax breaks over 20 years as an incentive to relocate.

Sears, Roebuck and Co. of Hoffman Estates, Illinois, opened a 250,000-square-foot (23,000-square-meter) department store at the corner of State and Madison streets, the city's historic retail center, in May. The company had closed its original Loop department store in 1983.

Soldier Field dispute. The Chicago Plan Commission on March 15, 2001, approved a highly controversial makeover of Soldier Field, the lakefront stadium that is home to the Chicago Bears of the National Football League. Renovation plans called for the stadium to be replaced with a 61,500-seat bowl, complete with skyboxes, all set inside the colonnades of the original Soldier Field, built in 1924. A segment of the renovation plan called for adding approximately 17 acres (7 hectares) of green space around the stadium by replacing some of the existing parking lots with two garages, including an underground garage. The entire project was scheduled to be finished in September 2003.

Chicago architectural critics blasted the design of the new stadium, and the Friends of the Parks, an advocacy group, filed lawsuits against city and state agencies involved in the project. The suits contended that the new stadium would violate a city ordinance protecting the lakefront against development and that the plan commission had failed to review the stadium proposal properly.

City and Bears officials backed off a plan to attach the name of a corporate sponsor to Soldier Field in the wake of the terrorist attacks on Sept. 11, 2001. Several veteran organizations opposed altering the name of a memorial to U.S. military veterans. ☐ Harold Henderson

See also **Census; City; United States, Government of the: A Special Report.**

Children's books. See **Literature for children.**

Chinese police patrol Tiananmen Square in Beijing in January with fire extinguishers after five members of Falun Gong spiritual movement set themselves on fire to protest the government's crackdown.

Chile. The Chilean government struggled to create more jobs as unemployment hovered around 10 percent through much of 2001. In May, President Ricardo Lagos Escobar unveiled a program to generate as many as 150,000 new jobs. Doubts about the economy caused Chileans to deposit an estimated $1.5 billion in safe havens abroad between January and April. This represented a 75-percent increase in such deposits compared with 2000.

In June 2001, the Chilean government announced that it would purchase 12 F-16 fighter jets from Lockheed Martin Aeronautics Company in Marietta, Georgia, for an estimated $650 million. The decision drew criticism from Chile's Roman Catholic bishops, who urged the government to invest more money in the country's many social needs. Officials in Peru also condemned the purchase, claiming it would upset the balance of power in the region.

A Chilean appeals court ruled in July that former President Augusto Pinochet Ugarte was not well enough to stand trial on charges of human rights abuses committed during his 1973-1990 dictatorship. The decision seemed to end any possibility that the enfeebled 85-year-old retired general would ever be put on trial. □ Nathan A. Haverstock

See also **Latin America.**

China. Chinese President Jiang Zemin met with United States President George W. Bush in Shanghai in October 2001. Jiang voiced his support of the U.S.-led war on terrorism that was triggered by the September 11 terrorist attacks on the United States.

Despite China's pledge of support to the United States, relations between the two countries were troubled in 2001. In April, a U.S. Navy EP-3 plane flying over international waters to monitor Chinese military communications collided with a Chinese jet fighter that was shadowing the American aircraft. The Chinese plane crashed, and its pilot was lost at sea. The damaged U.S. plane made an emergency landing at a military base on China's Hainan Island after the crew destroyed some of their secret equipment and materials gathered during the mission.

The collision resulted in a tense confrontation between Chinese and U.S. officials. China accused the United States of spying and blamed the collision on the crew of the American plane. U.S. officials denied responsibility, saying the Chinese pilot's reckless flying caused the collision.

Chinese officials allowed the 24 men and women of the U.S. crew to return to the United States after holding them for 11 days. However, China refused to allow the U.S. plane to be repaired and flown home. Chinese officials insisted that the plane be dismantled and removed in a cargo aircraft. The U.S. plane left Hainan in pieces in July.

China subsequently billed the United States $1 million for expenses in caring for and feeding the United States crew and for storing the damaged U.S. aircraft. The Bush administration offered China $34,500 in compensation. The United States had already resumed *reconnaissance flights* (aircraft equipped with electronic sensing devices to collect information about enemy forces) off China's coast on May 7 without incident.

U.S. Secretary of State Colin Powell visited China in July. He agreed that specialists from the two countries needed to discuss disputes such as U.S. reconnaissance flights and human rights in China. President Jiang said in August that the two countries "share a positive desire for a good relationship." However, Chinese officials remained unhappy with the United States because of U.S. arms sales to Taiwan. In April, President Bush had announced that if Taiwan came under attack from China, he would order U.S. forces to defend the island, which China regards as a renegade province. Bush administration officials later attempted to soften the president's commitment.

Russian pacts. Russian President Vladimir Putin visited Shanghai in June to join President Jiang and the leaders of Kazakhstan, Tajikistan, Kyrgyzstan, and Uzbekistan in the formation of the Shanghai Cooperation Organization. The group was organized to counter Islamic militancy.

In July, President Jiang visited Moscow to sign a Treaty of Good Neighborly Friendship and Cooperation with Putin. According to Chinese and Russian officials, the agreement was not a military alliance but rather was designed to foster closer economic, security, and cultural ties.

Olympic win. In July, the International Olympic Committee, meeting in Moscow, selected Beijing as the site for the 2008 Summer Olympic games. The choice was greeted with enthusiasm in China. Critics of the choice pointed to China's record on human rights and warned that the Chinese government might try to repress domestic dissidents during the games to hide any hint of opposition to Communist rule.

Human rights abuses. Amnesty International, an independent worldwide human rights organization based in London, reported in February 2001 that torture and abuse of detainees and prisoners remained widespread in China. The U.S. State Department later announced that the human rights situation in China had worsened between 2000 and 2001.

In April, Chinese officials launched what they called "strike hard," a campaign to repress public unrest and prevent crime. From April through June, the Chinese government reportedly carried out 1,781 executions. According to Amnesty International figures, China executed more people in three months than all other countries had executed in the previous three years.

In July, China released three Chinese-born U.S. academics who had been accused of spying. They were among a number of scholars whom Chinese officials had arrested amid tightened controls over visits to China by academic researchers. Some scholars were accused of espionage for working with what Chinese officials called sensitive internal information. The scholars insisted that the materials were unclassified.

Security forces in China also tried to limit the circulation of unauthorized news and opinions in 2001. Experts on Chinese politics suggested that these cases and others involving U.S. citizens of Chinese origin indicated that the government was making a strong effort to prevent any questioning of Communist Party control in China.

Falun Gong. Chinese authorities continued to put pressure on members of Falun Gong in 2001. Falun Gong is a spiritual movement that combines exercises, meditation, and breathing techniques with religious ideas from Buddhism and Taoism. Falun Gong leaders claimed in 1999 to have 70 million members, and the Communist Party continued to consider Falun Gong a threat to the party's role as the sole representative of the public.

More than 50,000 Falun Gong members had been imprisoned since 1999, according to Falun Gong leaders. The leaders also reported that some of those arrested were confined to psychiatric hospitals. In June 2001, the Falun Gong also claimed that at least 15 members had been tortured to death in a reeducation camp. Chinese officials denied the accusation.

Growing public disconent. A research group within the Communist Party issued a warning in May that public discontent in China was growing as a result of widening social and economic inequality and government corruption. The group called corruption "the main fuse worsening conflicts between officials and the masses" and reported that public protests were becoming more frequent and violent.

The report cited disparities in income as a leading factor in riots and group protests. In April, farmers in Yuntang, a village in Shanxi Province refused to pay what they called "illegal" and "impossibly high" local taxes. The taxes of farmers had increased more than the taxes of city residents, though city incomes rose faster. Police responded to the protest by attacking the farmers, killing two men and wounding 18 others. Fearing additional trouble, the Chinese Ministry of Public Security ordered that additional antiriot police units be moved into the province.

President Jiang vowed in 2001 to fight rampant corruption, which many officials said under-

Chinese youths celebrate in Beijing in July 2001 after the International Olympic Committee voted to make the Chinese capital host of the 2008 Olympic Games. Beijing was selected despite international protests over China's human rights record.

mined Communist Party support. According to official estimates, 40 percent of all goods produced in China are substandard because of administrative and employee theft; 15 to 20 percent of the cost of an average building project is lost on bribery, fraud, or shoddy work; and corrupt officials and workers "skim off" as much as 13 to 17 percent of China's *annual gross domestic product* (the value of all goods and services produced in a country in a given year).

Anniversary. The 80th anniversary of the founding of China's Communist party was observed by the government on July 1. In his anniversary speech, Jiang insisted that Communist Party rule was essential to China. Without it, the country would "sink into a chaotic abyss," he said. However, he also opened the way for private businessmen, who in 2001 led the country's economic growth, to join the party. Jiang declared that entrepreneurs were helping to build "socialism with Chinese characteristics." Critics responded that the party was becoming simply a vehicle for exercising power without a Marxist ideological foundation. Party members argued that party leaders were only allowing capitalists into the party to prevent a challenge from alternate political groupings of businessmen.

A series of explosions in March leveled four state-owned apartment buildings in Shijiazhuang, killing 108 people. The man blamed for the attack reportedly sought revenge on relatives. He and two accomplices were executed in April for the attacks. In July, an unemployed man blew up 69 villagers, also reportedly for revenge. Later in July, a house in which cheap, illegal explosives were being manufactured exploded, killing 47 people.

In March, an explosion at a rural school in Shanxi Province killed 38 elementary school students and 4 adults. Officials initially blamed the blast on a deranged suicide bomber but later conceded that the explosion was an accident. School authorities had set up a fireworks factory in the school and used the children as forced laborers.

Continued growth. Figures from the November 2000 government census, published in 2001, revealed that China's population stood at 1.265 billion people. The population had increased 11.6 percent since the last census in 1990.

In September 2001, China posted a growth rate of 7 percent. In 2000, the growth rate had been 8 percent. Economists agreed that China's admission to the World Trade Organization (WTO) would open new opportunities. China joined the WTO on November 11, ending years of negotiations. The WTO is a United Nations affiliated organization that arbitrates trade disputes among member nations. ☐ Henry S. Bradsher

See also **Asia; Armed Forces; Olympic Games; Terrorism: A Special Feature**, p. 38; **Russia.**

City. According to the 2000 Census, published in 2001, the population of cities in the United States grew twice as rapidly in the 1990's as it did in the 1980's. More than three-fourths of U.S. cities—urban centers with more than 10,000 residents—reported increases in population during the 1990's. The cities of the Sun Belt—in states such as California, Florida, Texas, Arizona, and Nevada—grew the fastest, while the so-called Rust Belt cities—such as Detroit; Cleveland, Ohio; and Pittsburgh, Pennsylvania—continued to decline as their industrial base grew outdated.

The loss of population from Rust Belt cities slowed, however, during the 1990's. The nation's older cities lost only 6.2 percent of their populations, compared with 10.4 percent in the 1980's. In addition, New York City, Atlanta, Chicago, and Boston increased their populations. Urban affairs analysts proposed that the booming urban economies of the 1990's, as well as a drop in urban crime rates, had drawn people back to the cities.

Immigration also played a role. Cities that turned around decades of population decline attracted immigrants. New York City's population, for example, grew 9.4 percent in the 1990's, to more than 8 million people. While part of that increase was attributed to people moving back to the city from the suburbs, much of the rise was attributed to Hispanic and Asian immigration. In New York City in the 1990's, the white population fell, the African American population remained stable, but the Hispanic and Asian populations rose. Nationally, the Hispanic population alone increased by 60 percent in the 1990's.

According to census data, minorities constituted the majority of the population in 48 of 100 of the largest U.S. cities by 2000, up from 30 cities in 1990. Moreover, 70 percent of the nation's largest cities lost more than 2 million white residents in the 1990's. In the same cities, Hispanic populations increased by 43 percent, resulting in 3.8 million new Hispanic residents.

Suburbs. The growth of suburbs, which had dominated U.S. demographics since World War II (1939-1945), began to slow in the 1990's, according to the 2000 Census. The suburbs that ring America's major cities grew increasingly dense in the 1990's, reaching their physical limits of growth. In some of the fastest growing areas of the United States, suburbs reached the density levels of the city they surrounded.

Overall, the U.S. population in 2000 had become 12 percent more urban than that of 1990, because of both an increase in city populations and the rise of suburbs to urban-level population density. The census and economic studies released in 2001 also showed that the vast majority of jobs created during the 1990's were in metropolitan areas. Such areas accounted for 80 per-

50 largest cities in the United States

Rank	City	Population*
1.	New York, N.Y.	8,083,556
2.	Los Angeles, Calif.	3,716,989
3.	Chicago, Ill.	2,907,600
4.	Houston, Tex.	1,992,313
5.	Philadelphia, Pa.	1,511,025
6.	Phoenix, Ariz.	1,366,357
7.	San Diego, Calif.	1,235,879
8.	Dallas, Tex.	1,209,974
9.	San Antonio, Tex.	1,170,172
10.	Detroit, Mich.	944,135
11.	San Jose, Calif.	907,830
12.	Indianapolis, Ind.	797,232
13.	San Francisco, Calif.	782,403
14.	Jacksonville, Fla.	747,240
15.	Columbus, Ohio	720,292
16.	Austin, Tex.	683,481
17.	Memphis, Tenn.	654,326
18.	Baltimore, Md.	643,666
19.	Milwaukee, Wis.	593,989
20.	Boston, Mass.	590,673
21.	Nashville, Tenn.	576,502
22.	El Paso, Tex.	568,960
23.	Washington, D.C.	568,798
24.	Seattle, Wash.	568,501
25.	Denver, Colo.	564,952
26.	Charlotte, N.C.	560,622
27.	Fort Worth, Tex.	545,121
28.	Portland, Ore.	540,233
29.	Las Vegas, Nev.	519,197
30.	Oklahoma City, Okla.	513,117
31.	Tucson, Ariz.	496,482
32.	New Orleans, La.	483,462
33.	Cleveland, Ohio	475,820
34.	Long Beach, Calif.	464,983
35.	Albuquerque, N. Mex.	456,054
36.	Kansas City, Mo.	442,207
37.	Fresno, Calif.	436,504
38.	Virginia Beach, Va.	428,744
39.	Atlanta, Ga.	418,848
40.	Mesa, Ariz.	411,279
41.	Sacramento, Calif.	411,170
42.	Oakland, Calif.	402,400
43.	Omaha, Nebr.	396,286
44.	Tulsa, Okla.	395,800
45.	Minneapolis, Minn.	384,110
46.	Honolulu, Hawaii	372,289
47.	Colorado Springs, Colo.	371,139
48.	Miami, Fla.	362,869
49.	Wichita, Kan.	348,829
50.	St. Louis, Mo.	343,941

*2001 World Book estimates based on data from the U.S. Census Bureau.

50 largest metropolitan areas in the United States

Rank	Metropolitan area*	Population†
1.	Los Angeles-Long Beach, Calif.	9,589,781
2.	New York City, N.Y.	9,398,063
3.	Chicago, Ill.	8,368,732
4.	Philadelphia, Pa.-N.J.	5,119,294
5.	Washington, D.C.-Md.-Va.-W.Va.	5,004,877
6.	Detroit, Mich.	4,459,761
7.	Houston, Tex.	4,285,429
8.	Atlanta, Ga.	4,272,163
9.	Dallas, Tex.	3,630,030
10.	Boston, Mass.	3,425,567
11.	Phoenix-Mesa, Ariz.	3,399,186
12.	Riverside-San Bernadino, Calif.	3,338,470
13.	Minneapolis-St. Paul, Minn.-Wis.	3,018,979
14.	Orange County, Calif.	2,897,807
15.	San Diego, Calif.	2,849,287
16.	Nassau-Suffolk, N.Y.	2,769,060
17.	St. Louis, Mo.-Ill.	2,615,323
18.	Baltimore, Md.	2,571,376
19.	Seattle-Bellevue-Everett, Wash.	2,460,011
20.	Tampa-St. Petersburg-Clearwater, Fla.	2,434,093
21.	Oakland, Calif.	2,428,206
22.	Pittsburgh, Pa.	2,355,157
23.	Miami, Fla.	2,290,092
24.	Cleveland-Lorain-Elyria, Ohio	2,255,823
25.	Denver, Colo.	2,172,560
26.	Newark, N.J.	2,045,390
27.	Portland, Ore.-Vancouver, Wash.	1,969,028
28.	Kansas City, Mo.-Kan.	1,797,730
29.	Fort Worth-Arlington, Tex.	1,745,361
30.	San Francisco, Calif.	1,745,032
31.	San Jose, Calif.	1,703,449
32.	Orlando, Fla.	1,700,969
33.	Las Vegas, Nev.-Ariz.	1,693,503
34.	Fort Lauderdale, Fla.	1,670,572
35.	Sacramento, Calif.	1,663,203
36.	Cincinnati, Ohio-Ky.-Ind.	1,659,402
37.	Indianapolis, Ind.	1,633,849
38.	San Antonio, Tex.	1,624,549
39.	Norfolk-Virginia Beach-Newport News, Va.	1,583,353
40.	Columbus, Ohio	1,562,489
41.	Charlotte-Gastonia, N.C.-Rock Hill, S.C.	1,542,772
42.	Milwaukee-Waukesha, Wis.	1,507,945
43.	Bergen-Passaic, N.J.	1,383,328
44.	Salt Lake City-Ogden, Ut.	1,366,462
45.	New Orleans, La.	1,343,211
46.	Austin-San Marcos, Tex.	1,309,377
47.	Greensboro-Winston-Salem-High Point, N.C.	1,275,538
48.	Nashville, Tenn.	1,262,094
49.	Raleigh-Durham-Chapel Hill, N.C.	1,234,152
50.	Providence-Fall River-Warwick, R.I.-Mass.	1,194,318

*The U.S. Bureau of the Census defines a metropolitan area as a large population nucleus with adjacent communities having a high degree of economic and social integration.

†2001 World Book estimates based on data from the U.S. Census Bureau.

50 largest urban centers in the world

Rank	Urban center	Population
1.	Tokyo, Japan	26,444,000
2.	Mumbai, India	18,599,000
3.	Mexico City, Mexico	18,194,000
4.	Sao Paulo, Brazil	17,963,000
5.	New York City, U.S.	16,697,000
6.	Lagos, Nigeria	14,039,000
7.	Los Angeles, U.S.	13,228,000
8.	Calcutta, India	13,152,000
9.	Shanghai, China	12,931,000
10.	Dhaka, Bangladesh	12,861,000
11.	Buenos Aires, Argentina	12,687,000
12.	Karachi, Pakistan	12,209,000
13.	Delhi, India	12,022,000
14.	Jakarta, Indonesia	11,408,000
15.	Manila, Philippines	11,169,000
16.	Osaka, Japan	11,013,000
17.	Beijing, China	10,878,000
18.	Cairo, Egypt	10,752,000
19.	Rio de Janeiro, Brazil	10,668,000
20.	Seoul, Republic of Korea	9,888,000
21.	Istanbul, Turkey	9,704,000
22.	Paris, France	9,633,000
23.	Moscow, Russia	9,327,000
24.	Tianjin, China	9,218,000
25.	London, U.K.	7,640,000
26.	Lima, Peru	7,584,000
27.	Bangkok, Thailand	7,433,000
28.	Tehran, Iran	7,284,000
29.	Hyderabad, India	7,086,000
30.	Hong Kong, China	7,004,000
31.	Chicago, U.S.	6,978,000
32.	Madras, India	6,789,000
33.	Essen, Germany	6,546,000
34.	Taipei, Taiwan	6,518,000
35.	Bogota, Colombia	6,409,000
36.	Lahore, Pakistan	6,260,000
37.	Bangalore, India	5,709,000
38.	Santiago, Chile	5,621,000
39.	Chongqing, China	5,557,000
40.	Wuhan, China	5,312,000
41.	Kinshasa, Congo	5,261,000
42.	St. Petersburg, Russia	5,134,000
43.	Baghdad, Iraq	4,917,000
44.	Shenyang, China	4,860,000
45.	Toronto, Canada	4,704,000
46.	Ho Chi Minh City, Vietnam	4,686,000
47.	Philadelphia, U.S.	4,424,000
48.	Yangon, Myanmar	4,295,000
49.	Ahmedabad, India	4,255,000
50.	Milan, Italy	4,251,000

Source: 2001 estimates based on data from the United Nations.

cent of U.S. economic growth in the 1990's.

Census undercount. City officials were concerned in 2001 about how undercounts would affect the federal funding their cities received over the next 10 years. The U.S. Census Bureau estimated that between 0.6 percent and 1.2 percent of the U.S. population had not been counted in the 2000 census. The majority of those missed were minorities and immigrants, the vast majority of whom lived in cities.

The Census Bureau had considered using a statistical adjustment known as "sampling" to correct the undercount, but in October, the federal government announced that it would use only the raw census data in its disbursement of federal aid. The U.S. Conference of Mayors estimated that this decision would cost cities hundreds of millions of dollars in education, social services, transportation, and housing funds over the next 10 years.

New York City and Chicago, which both experienced increases in population, had campaigned against undercounting. Both city governments believed that their populations had been undercounted in the 1990 census. New York City officials convinced the Census Bureau to add 370,000 names to the roles of people to be surveyed by checking post office mailing lists. New York City workers also mounted publicity campaigns to encourage immigrants to fill out census forms.

Urban transportation. In 2000, for the third year in a row, nationwide use of public transportation grew faster than road use, according to a survey reported in April 2001 by the American Public Transportation Association, a nonprofit organization located in Washington, D.C. Ridership on subways, buses, and commuter rail lines increased by 3.5 percent in 2000, or 9.4 billion rides.

Nevertheless, people still made more than 1 trillion trips by car in 2000, causing congestion in urban areas. According to the 2001 Urban Mobility Study, released in May by the Transportation Institute at Texas A&M University in College Station, the average rush hour in a major U.S. city lasted almost three hours twice a day in 1999, compared with one-and-a-half hours twice a day in 1982. The study estimated that such delays cost the 68 studied urban areas $78 billion in lost work hours and gas consumption in 2000.

The analysts warned that building new roads merely slows the growth of congestion and suggested that regional transportation plans must combine road building with improved public transport, more efficient use of existing systems, and better-informed citizens.

City economies. The National League of Cities (NLC), a Washington, D.C.-based organization that seeks to improve the quality of life in

U.S. cities, reported in July 2001 that many city officials were concerned about their city's economy. Of the 325 cities surveyed—each with a population of more than 10,000 people—44 percent indicated concern with their financial situation, up from 27 percent in 2000.

In the wake of the Sept. 11, 2001, terrorist attacks on the United States, city finances were taxed even further. Most cities rushed to improve their emergency plans; to increase the cooperation among health, medical, and emergency services; and to expand their police forces. City economies, moreover, were heavily hit by the economic downturn that followed the terrorist attacks in September. In November, city governments estimated that revenues would decline by 4 percent in the last quarter of 2001, a loss of more than $11 billion. In addition, the new security measures were expected to add $1.5 billion to the financial burdens of cities in 2002.

Most expensive cities. In 2001, Tokyo, Moscow, and Hong Kong were the world's most expensive cities in which to live, according to a report published in July by William M. Mercer Consulting Group of New York City. Seven of the world's 10 most expensive cities were in Asia. However, the gap between the most and least expensive cities narrowed by almost 20 percent in 2001.

The Mercer group annually ranks about 150 cities throughout the world by comparing the city-by-city rents and the costs of over 200 goods and services. The company assigns each city a numerical rating, comparing it with New York City, which is assigned a rating of 100. In 2001, the decline in the cost of living in many non-Western cities was attributed to the growing availability of Western goods and services throughout the world and to the strength of the U.S. dollar against world currencies.

The dollar's strength pushed New York City to 8th place on the list of most expensive cities, from 13th in 2000; Tokyo (134) was only a third more expensive than New York City, compared with two-thirds in 2000. Other U.S. cities also rose: San Francisco (84.4) to 19 from 33; Chicago (84.3) to 20 from 38; and Los Angeles (83.4) to 24 from 36. Overall, 14 of the world's 50 most expensive cities were in the United States.

Moscow (132.4), St. Petersburg (106.5), and London (92.9) were Europe's most expensive cities. Following Tokyo and Hong Kong (130), Asia's other most expensive cities were Beijing (124.4), Osaka, Japan (116.7), and Shanghai (11.4.3). The Middle East was led by Tel Aviv (85) in 18th place and Beirut (83.8) in 21st; South America, by Buenos Aires (83.6) in 23rd place.

☐ Robert Messenger

Civil rights. See **Human rights.**

Classical music. North American symphony orchestras, once the mainstay of the cultural life of their cities and communities, faced serious challenges in 2001 that forced them to reexamine their relevance to culture and society. Rising budget deficits, falling attendance, declining record sales, and cutbacks in classical recording and radio broadcasting came as major financial blows to orchestras in Chicago; Los Angeles; Philadelphia; St. Louis, Missouri; Miami, Florida; and Toronto and Calgary in Canada, among others.

Some cultural critics maintained that orchestras were clinging to old-fashioned European art-music traditions that were out of step with modern American life. Other critics took a more positive view of the situation, calling the problems faced by orchestras a "wake-up call" that should inspire them to redefine their musical mission more broadly and reach out more vigorously to a society that had grown more ethnically and culturally diverse since the 1970's.

***Klinghoffer* canceled.** After the Sept. 11, 2001, terrorist attacks on the United States, the Boston Symphony Orchestra canceled plans to perform choruses from U.S. composer John Adams's opera *The Death of Klinghoffer,* which had been scheduled for late November and early December. The opera is about the 1984 hijacking of the cruise ship *Achille Lauro* and the murder of wheelchair-bound U.S. passenger Leon Klinghoffer by Palestinian terrorists. The orchestra management said it dropped the Adams pieces to "err on the side of being sensitive" in the wake of the September 2001 terrorist attacks. One of the singers in the chorus had lost her husband in the attacks.

Musical chairs. Many of the world's leading symphony orchestras appointed new directors in 2001. In October, the Boston Symphony Orchestra named James Levine as its 14th music director. Levine, the artistic director of New York City's Metropolitan Opera, was the first U.S.-born music director in the orchestra's 121-year history. He was scheduled to begin his tenure in 2004, succeeding Seiji Ozawa, whose 29-year tenure was the longest of any music director in the orchestra's history.

In January 2001, the New York Philharmonic appointed U.S. conductor Lorin Maazel as music director. Maazel was to follow Kurt Masur to the podium in 2002. German maestro Christoph Eschenbach signed on in November 2001 to succeed Wolfgang Sawallisch as music director of the Philadelphia Orchestra in 2003. In September 2001, the Berlin Philharmonic Orchestra announced the appointment of British conductor Sir Simon Rattle as its artistic director. He was scheduled to succeed Italian conductor Claudio Abbado in 2002.

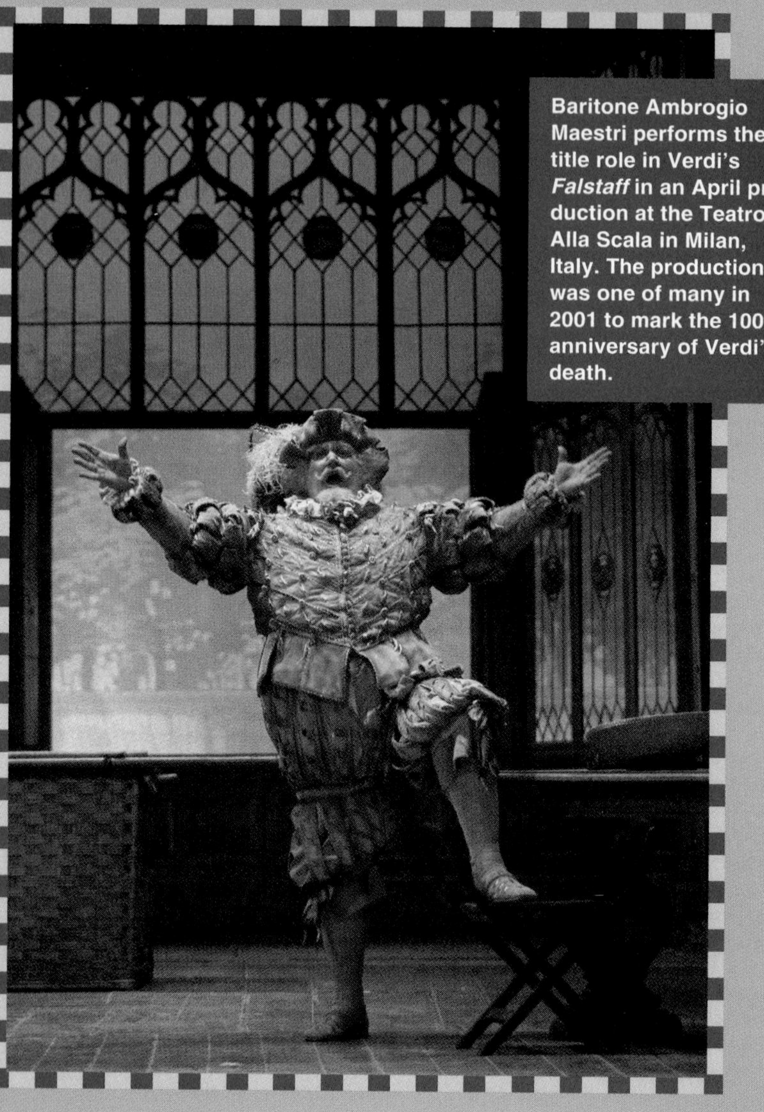
Baritone Ambrogio Maestri performs the title role in Verdi's *Falstaff* in an April production at the Teatro Alla Scala in Milan, Italy. The production was one of many in 2001 to mark the 100th anniversary of Verdi's death.

Verdi anniversary. In January 2001, the music world observed the 100th anniversary of the death of composer Giuseppe Verdi. The great master of Italian opera, who was born in 1813, composed such beloved stage works as *Aida, La Traviata, A Masked Ball, Otello,* and *Falstaff.* Verdi was honored in 2001 with numerous publications, conferences, and recordings, as well as new productions of his 27 operas by theaters around the world.

Wagner in Israel. Conductor Daniel Barenboim stirred up controversy in July by performing music by the German composer Richard Wagner (1813-1883) in Israel. Since Israel was founded in 1948, a taboo has existed about performing Wagner's music in the nation. Many Israelis associate Wagner's music with Adolf Hitler, dictator of Germany during World War II (1939-1945) and the *Holocaust* (the systematic murder of millions of Jews and others by Nazis during World War II). Wagner was Hitler's favorite composer. Barenboim, who is Jewish, played the overture to Wagner's opera *Tristan und Isolde* as an encore in a concert with the Berlin Staatskapelle at the Israel Festival in Jerusalem. Although some audience members angrily protested the music and walked out of the concert hall, most of the audience stayed and gave the performers a standing ovation.

Grawemeyer Award. U.S. composer Aaron Jay Kernis received the 2002 Grawemeyer Award for Music Composition for the revised version of his work for cello and orchestra, *Colored Field.* The award carries the greatest dollar amount—$200,000—of any in the classical music field.

New orchestral and vocal music. A host of U.S. composers had premieres in 2001. In September, cellist Yo-Yo Ma gave the world premiere of Elliott Carter's *Cello Concerto,* with the Chicago Symphony Orchestra under Daniel Barenboim's direction. In March, Ma played the first performance of Richard Danielpour's cello concerto, *Through the Ancient Valley,* with Kurt Masur conducting the New York Philharmonic. Yet another cello concerto, by Tobias Picker, made its debut in August in London, courtesy of soloist Paul Watkins and the BBC Symphony Orchestra, conducted by David Robertson.

Yan Pascal Tortelier led the Minnesota Orchestra in the premiere of John Harbison's *Partita,* a concerto for orchestra, in March. Joan Tower's percussion concerto, *Strike Zones,* had its premiere in October with Evelyn Glennie as soloist and Leonard Slatkin conducting the National Symphony Orchestra. Also in October, John Adams conducted the Netherlands Radio Philharmonic in his latest work, *Guide to Strange Places.* In May, David Del Tredici's *Gay Life,* a cycle of six songs for baritone and orchestra, was premiered by the San Francisco Symphony, with William Sharp as soloist and Michael Tilson Thomas conducting.

New operas. Tobias Picker's *Therese Raquin,* an adaptation of the tragic novel by French author Emile Zola, had its world premiere by the Dallas Opera in November. Also in November, the New York City Opera gave the premiere of *Lilith,* an adaptation by composer Deborah Drattell and librettist David Steven Cohen of the Cabala, a mystic Jewish interpretation of the Scriptures.

Notable deaths. American violinist Isaac Stern, 81, died in September 2001. Stern was a cultural icon and one of the greatest violinists of his time. In 1960, Stern led efforts to save New York City's Carnegie Hall from demolition. The celebrated Italian conductor Giuseppe Sinopoli, 54, died in April 2001 after suffering a heart attack during a performance of Verdi's *Aida* in Berlin. Iannis Xenakis, the Greek-French composer and engineer who composed highly complex works using computers and mathematical probability systems, died in February at age 78. ☐ John von Rhein

See also **Popular music; Terrorism: A Special Feature,** p. 38.

Clothing. See **Fashion.**

Coal. See **Energy supply.**

Grammy Award winners in 2001

Classical Album, *Shostakovich: The String Quartets;* Emerson String Quartet.

Orchestral Performance, *Mahler: Symphony No. 10;* Berlin Philharmonic Orchestra; Sir Simon Rattle, conductor.

Opera Recording, *Busoni: Doktor Faust;* Dietrich Henschel, Kim Begley, Eva Jenis, singers; Kent Nagano, conductor.

Choral Performance, *Penderecki: Credo;* Oregon Bach Festival Chorus and Orchestra; Helmuth Rilling, conductor.

Instrumental Soloist with Orchestra, *Maw: Violin Concerto;* Joshua Bell, violin; London Philharmonic Orchestra; Sir Roger Norrington, conductor.

Instrumental Soloist without Orchestra, *Dreams Of A World (Works Of Lauro, Ruiz-Pipo, Duarte, Etc.);* Sharon Isbin, guitar.

Chamber Music Performance, *Shostakovich: The String Quartets;* Emerson String Quartet.

Small Ensemble Performance, *Shadow Dances (Stravinsky Miniatures—Tango; Suite No. 1; Octet, Etc.);* Orpheus Chamber Orchestra.

Classical Vocal Performance, *The Vivaldi Album (Dell'aura al sussurrar; Alma oppressa, Etc.);* Cecilia Bartoli, mezzo soprano.

Classical Contemporary Composition, *Crumb: Star-Child;* George Crumb, composer; Warsaw Philharmonic Orchestra and Choir.

Classical Crossover Album, *Appalachian Journey (1B; Misty Moonlight Waltz; Indecision, Etc.);* Yo-Yo Ma, cello; Edgar Meyer, double bass; Mark O'Connor, violin; Alison Krauss, fiddle and vocals; James Taylor, vocals.

Colombia. Many Colombians lost hope in 2001 that negotiations begun by Colombian President Andres Pastrana Arango in 1998 would end the 37-year-old civil war with leftist rebels. "There now seems to be a new belief in military solutions," noted Jan Egeland, the United Nations special envoy to Colombia, in August 2001.

Prisoner release. On June 28, the Revolutionary Armed Forces of Colombia (FARC), the major rebel group battling the government, released 242 soldiers and police whom they had captured. Some of those released had been held for more than three years. The prisoner release was the largest ever made by the rebels. Despite this gesture, fighting continued between FARC and government forces.

Killings continue. On October 8, Luis Alfred Colmenares, a Colombian congressman, was murdered in his car by gunmen on motorcycles in Bogota, the capital. Colmenares was the fourth member of Congress slain since December 2000.

The body of Consuelo Araujo, Colombia's former minister of culture, was found near the northern town of Valledupar on Sept. 29, 2001. Araujo, who had been kidnapped by FARC, was shot to death. FARC was also holding four members of Congress hostage.

In total, more than 1,000 Colombians were killed during 2001. Government officials blamed most of the killings on the rebels or the United Self-Defense Forces of Colombia, a paramilitary group.

Irish bomb experts. In August, Colombian authorities arrested three explosive experts with ties to the Irish Republican Army, a militant oganization that has long sought to unite Northern Ireland with Ireland. According to the authorities, the three men had spent the previous month in a Switzerland-sized territory controlled by FARC in southern Colombia, where they taught bombing techniques to the Colombian rebels.

Oil pipeline bombed. In mid-2001, the Colombian army, newly equipped with U.S-supplied transport aircraft and helicopter gunships, launched a series of coordinated attacks against rebel forces throughout Colombia. One of the largest of these operations involved the rapid deployment of 2,000 elite battalions in the northern, oil-rich province of Arauco. In the first eight months of 2001, rebels operating in Arauco bombed an oil pipeline owned by Occidental Petroleum of Los Angeles 119 times, spilling nearly 220,000 barrels of oil and causing the company some $400 million in losses.

Drug kingpins captured. The Colombian army captured Ney Machado, one of Brazil's most wanted drug traffickers, in February after pursuing him in a remote region of the Amazon jungle. The capture was part of a counternarcotics operation by the military near the borders of Brazil and Venezuela. Documents captured with Machado described a recent transaction in which FARC rebels had provided a shipment of cocaine to traffickers in exchange for more than 2,750 machine guns, rifles, and pistols. In April, Colombian forces in the counternarcotics operation captured Luiz Fernando da Costa, who was reportedly Brazil's biggest cocaine dealer.

Tough new laws. President Pastrana signed legislation in August granting the armed forces and police broad new powers in prosecuting crime and terrorism. Under the legislation, suspects can be held indefinitely on unspecified charges without recourse to the courts. The law also gave military commanders authority over civilian officials in zones of conflict and limited the power of civilian officials to investigate crimes allegedly committed by police or military personnel. ☐ Nathan A. Haverstock

See also **Brazil; Latin America; Latin America: A Special Report; Northern Ireland.**

Colorado. See **State government.**

Common Market. See **Europe.**

Commonwealth of Independent States. See **Asia; Azerbaijan; Belarus; Georgia; Kazakhstan; Russia; Ukraine.**

Comoros. See **Africa.**

Computers. Apple Computer, Inc., of Cupertino, California, began selling the Mac OS X for its Macintosh computers in March 2001. The *operating system* (OS, the master control program that coordinates a computer's activities) was based on Unix OS, which has long been used in scientific and business fields because of its power and *stability* (resistance to freezing and crashing).

New windows. Microsoft Corporation of Redmond, Washington, introduced two new versions of its popular Windows OS in October. Windows XP Home Edition was intended for home computers, while Windows XP Professional Edition was designed for businesses of all sizes.

New domains. The United States Department of Commerce announced in June that two additions to the Internet domain system could begin to be used. Domains are the last part of an Internet address, such as .com and .gov. The new domains, .biz (for businesses) and .info (for such informational pages as product promotion), were the first of seven new domains scheduled to be activated in 2001 and 2002. The other domains were .name (for personal Web pages); .pro (for professionals), .aero (for the air transport industry); .coop (for cooperative organizations); and .museum (for museums).

Pixie dust. The IBM Corporation of Armonk, New York, announced in May 2001 that it had begun mass producing hard disk drives using a new magnetic coating. IBM said the new technology would quadruple the data-storage capacity of hard drives in personal computers by 2003.

The technology was expected to lead to smaller hard drives that store much more data in personal computers, entertainment devices, and other electronic gear. IBM designed the drives to meet the growing demands of consumers who want to store large files, such as digital music, photographs, and video, on their computers.

IBM developed the hard drives by sandwiching a three-atom-thick layer of the metallic element ruthenium between two magnetic layers. The microscopic size of the ruthenium layer led IBM scientists to dub the metal "pixie dust."

No breakup for Microsoft. In June 2001, the U.S. Court of Appeals for the District of Columbia overturned a lower court's ruling that Microsoft Corporation be split into two companies for anticompetitive business practices. In November, the U.S. Department of Justice and Microsoft settled their antitrust dispute by agreeing to restrictions on some of Microsoft's business practices and independent monitoring of the company for at least five years. However, several states continued to pursue legal action against Microsoft. ☐ Michael Woods

See also **Courts; Internet.**

Congo (Kinshasa). On Jan. 16, 2001, a presidential bodyguard assassinated President Laurent Kabila at the presidential palace in the capital, Kinshasa. Palace guards then shot and killed the assassin, Rashidi Kasereka. President Kabila had seized power in May 1997 from dictator Mobutu Sese Seko. Experts on Congo political affairs speculated that senior military officers may have plotted the assassination. On Jan. 26, 2001, the slain leader's son, Joseph Kabila, succeeded his father as president after being chosen by government ministers.

Efforts to end Congo's civil war continued in 2001, but peace remained elusive. The civil war, which began in August 1998, pitted government troops—backed by Angolan, Namibian, and Zimbabwean forces—against rebel factions supported by Rwanda and Uganda. Amnesty International, a London-based human rights organization, estimated that 2.5 million people had died from war-related causes in the region between August 1998 and 2001.

In late March 2001, the United Nations (UN) sent troops into Congo to protect UN observers monitoring a shaky three-month-old cease-fire. The UN mission eventually exceeded 2,500 people, including unarmed observers. In the much fought-over, mineral-rich eastern Congo, the UN attempted to establish a buffer zone between

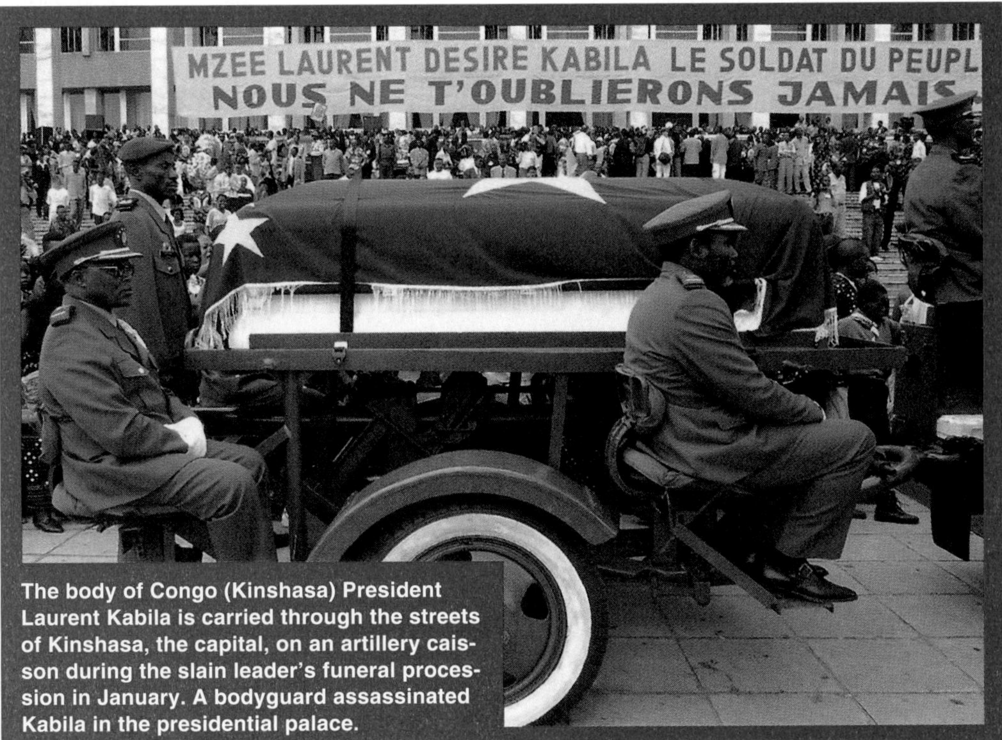

The body of Congo (Kinshasa) President Laurent Kabila is carried through the streets of Kinshasa, the capital, on an artillery caisson during the slain leader's funeral procession in January. A bodyguard assassinated Kabila in the presidential palace.

progovernment troops and rebel forces. Factions involved in the civil war gathered in Addis Ababa, Ethiopia's capital, in October for peace talks. The conference broke down, however, when Joseph Kabila declined to participate. In November, the UN Security Council unanimously approved a resolution to begin to implement the next phase of the peace process—the gradual withdrawal of foreign troops and disarmament of local armed groups.

Red Cross killings. Six aid workers from the International Committee of the Red Cross, an organization headquartered in Geneva, Switzerland, that protects war victims during conflicts between nations, were found murdered in April near the Congo-Uganda frontier. Ugandan troops discovered the bodies while on patrol. Red Cross officials said they had no knowledge about who the attackers might be.

Child soldiers. The United Nations Children's Fund (UNICEF), an agency of the UN that aids children in over 100 countries, announced in June that Joseph Kabila had launched a national campaign to end the recruitment of child soldiers in Congo. UNICEF officials estimated that between 8,000 and 12,000 *kadogos* (little ones) were serving in Congo's armed forces and various rebel groups in 2001. ☐ Simon Baynham

See also **Africa; Uganda.**

Congress of the United States.

The U.S. Congress reacted quickly to terrorist attacks on the United States on Sept. 11, 2001, by passing measures designed to strengthen national security and bolster an already weak economy. Political observers said that the quick passage of the legislation showed a new cooperation between Democrats and Republicans that had not been seen in years. Debate was hampered in October when the House of Representatives closed the House chambers for decontamination after a letter containing anthrax spores (an inactive form of the bacteria) was opened inside an office.

Terrorist attacks. Terrorists hijacked four commercial airliners in flight over the eastern United States on September 11, crashing two of the aircraft into the twin towers of the World Trade Center in New York City and a third into the Pentagon Building, the headquarters of the U.S. Department of Defense, outside Washington, D.C. The fourth airliner crashed into a field in western Pennsylvania. The attack killed thousands of people.

On September 12, the U.S. Senate approved a resolution condemning the terrorist attacks and offering condolences to the families and friends of the victims. The resolution also expressed the belief of the vast majority of the members of Congress that the attacks struck not only at the people of America, but at symbols and structures of the nation's economic and military strength, and that the United States had a right under international law to respond. The House approved the bill on September 13. President George W. Bush signed the legislation on September 18.

Death benefits. Congress on September 13 unanimously approved legislation to speed the payment of death and disability payments to beneficiaries of those killed or injured as a result of the September 11 terrorist attacks. The legislation was signed by the president on September 18. It required that the Bureau of Justice Assistance authorize payment to beneficiaries of public safety officers within 30 days of receiving certification of death or disability. The bureau is a federal agency that supports local strategies to achieve safe communities.

Retaliation authorized. On September 14, the U.S. Senate voted 98 to 0 to authorize the president to use "necessary and appropriate force" in retaliating against terrorists. The House passed the use-of-force resolution by a 420-to-1 margin. Signed by President Bush on September 18, the legislation authorized the president to use force against any nation, organization, or person that he determined had planned, authorized, committed, or aided in the terrorist attacks. The measure also allowed President Bush to use force against any person or nation that harbored terrorists.

Disaster assistance. On September 14, Congress voted to approve a $40-billion emergency aid package for the states hit by the terrorist attacks. The Senate approved the spending measure by a vote of 96 to 0. The House approved it by a vote of 422 to 0. The legislation provided more money for disaster assistance, funding for antiterrorism programs, and general assistance for the recovery efforts in New York City and at the Pentagon.

Antiterrorism legislation. The House on October 24 voted 356 to 66 in favor of a sweeping measure to combat terrorism, including enhanced powers for law enforcement agencies. The Senate approved the legislation on October 25 by a 98-to-1 vote. The president signed it into law on October 26. The legislation expanded the federal government's ability to conduct electronic surveillance, allowed government officials to share grand jury information, and permitted the government to detain immigrants without charging them with a crime.

Airline bailout. The terrorist attacks severely damaged the economy of the airline industry. Immediately following the attacks, federal officials halted all air travel in the United States. Commercial flights were grounded for several days, which cost airlines millions of dollars in lost revenue. To bolster the reeling airline industry, Congress on September 21 approved a $15-billion relief package for the airline carriers. The 356-to-54 House vote in favor of the rescue plan came hours after the Senate approved the same bill in a 96-to-1 vote.

Under the legislation, which the president signed on September 22, the U.S. aviation industry received a total of $5 billion in compensation for the grounding of the commercial air system. The airlines also received $10 billion in loan guarantees. The measure limited the liability of American Airlines of Fort Worth, Texas, and United Airlines of Elk Grove Township, Illinois—the two carriers whose jets were hijacked and crashed—to the maximum of their insurance coverage. Lawmakers acted quickly because of concerns that commercial airlines, which were struggling financially even before the terrorist attacks, were in imminent danger of financial collapse.

Airline security. Although Congress responded rapidly on many fronts in the nation's war against terrorism, lawmakers were divided over the best way to ensure the safety of commercial air travel. On November 16, the House and the Senate passed legislation designed to improve airport security in the wake of the September 11 terrorist attacks. The bill created a new division—the Transportation Safety Administration—within the Department of Transportation (DOT) and required that the DOT hire 28,000 employees to conduct security screening of travelers and baggage at the nation's airports. After three years, airports will have the option of requesting that security screening be turned over to private contractors. The measure also required that cockpit doors be fortified against attack and allowed pilots to carry guns.

The legislation was a compromise worked out by House and Senate negotiators to end a long political battle over what role the federal government should play in aviation security. Republican leaders in the House had argued that airport security should remain in the hands of private contractors. President Bush signed the legislation on November 19.

Taxes. In May, Congress approved broad tax-cut legislation that included a measure under which U.S. taxpayers received tax rebates of up to $600. The tax cut was the first major reduction enacted since the administration of President Ronald Reagan in 1981. President Bush signed the legislation into law on June 7, 2001.

Congress began to examine other tax issues as a means of invigorating the economy in the aftermath of the September terrorist attacks. In October, the House in a narrow 216-to-214 vote approved a $100-billion tax cut plan that included $70 billion in tax reductions for corporations. The

Members of the United States Senate

The Senate of the second session of the 107th Congress consisted of 50 Democrats, 49 Republicans, and 1 Independent when it convened on Jan. 23, 2002. The first date in each listing shows when the senator's term began. The second date in each listing shows when the senator's term expires.

State	Term
Alabama	
Richard C. Shelby, R.	1987-2005
Jeff Sessions, R.	1997-2003
Alaska	
Theodore F. Stevens, R.	1968-2003
Frank H. Murkowski, R.	1981-2005
Arizona	
John McCain III, R.	1987-2005
Jon Kyl, R.	1995-2007
Arkansas	
Tim Hutchinson, R.	1997-2003
Blanche Lambert Lincoln, D.	1999-2005
California	
Dianne Feinstein, D.	1992-2007
Barbara Boxer, D.	1993-2005
Colorado	
Ben N. Campbell, R.	1993-2005
Wayne Allard, R.	1997-2003
Connecticut	
Christopher J. Dodd, D.	1981-2005
Joseph I. Lieberman, D.	1989-2007
Delaware	
Joseph R. Biden, Jr., D.	1973-2003
Thomas Carper, D.	2001-2007
Florida	
Bob Graham, D.	1987-2005
Bill Nelson, D.	2001-2007
Georgia	
Max Cleland, D.	1997-2003
Zell Miller, D.	2000-2005
Hawaii	
Daniel K. Inouye, D.	1963-2005
Daniel K. Akaka, D.	1990-2007
Idaho	
Larry E. Craig, R.	1991-2003
Mike Crapo, R.	1999-2005
Illinois	
Richard J. Durbin, D.	1997-2003
Peter Fitzgerald, R.	1999-2005
Indiana	
Richard G. Lugar, R.	1977-2007
Evan Bayh, D.	1999-2005
Iowa	
Charles E. Grassley, R.	1981-2005
Tom Harkin, D.	1985-2003
Kansas	
Sam Brownback, R.	1996-2005
Pat Roberts, R.	1997-2003
Kentucky	
Mitch McConnell, R.	1985-2003
Jim Bunning, R.	1999-2005

State	Term
Louisiana	
John B. Breaux, D.	1987-2005
Mary L. Landrieu, D.	1997-2003
Maine	
Olympia Snowe, R.	1995-2007
Susan M. Collins, R.	1997-2003
Maryland	
Paul S. Sarbanes, D.	1977-2007
Barbara A. Mikulski, D.	1987-2005
Massachusetts	
Edward M. Kennedy, D.	1962-2007
John F. Kerry, D.	1985-2003
Michigan	
Carl Levin, D.	1979-2003
Debbie Stabenow, D.	2001-2007
Minnesota	
Paul D. Wellstone, D.	1991-2003
Mark Dayton, D.	2001-2007
Mississippi	
Thad Cochran, R.	1978-2003
Trent Lott, R.	1989-2007
Missouri	
Christopher S. (Kit) Bond, R.	1987-2005
Jean Carnahan, D.	2001-2003
Montana	
Max Baucus, D.	1978-2003
Conrad Burns, R.	1989-2007
Nebraska	
Chuck Hagel, R.	1997-2003
Ben Nelson, D.	2001-2007
Nevada	
Harry M. Reid, D.	1987-2005
John Ensign, R.	2001-2007
New Hampshire	
Robert C. Smith, R.	1990-2003
Judd Gregg, R.	1993-2005
New Jersey	
Robert G. Torricelli, D.	1997-2003
Jon S. Corzine, D.	2001-2007
New Mexico	
Pete V. Domenici, R.	1973-2003
Jeff Bingaman, D.	1983-2007
New York	
Charles E. Schumer, D.	1999-2005
Hillary Rodham Clinton, D.	2001-2007
North Carolina	
Jesse A. Helms, R.	1973-2003
John Edwards, D.	1999-2005
North Dakota	
Kent Conrad, D.	1987-2007
Byron L. Dorgan, D.	1992-2005

State	Term
Ohio	
Mike DeWine, R.	1995-2007
George V. Voinovich, R.	1999-2005
Oklahoma	
Don Nickles, R.	1981-2005
James M. Inhofe, R.	1994-2003
Oregon	
Ron Wyden, D.	1996-2005
Gordon Smith, R.	1997-2003
Pennsylvania	
Arlen Specter, R.	1981-2005
Rick Santorum, R.	1995-2007
Rhode Island	
Jack Reed, D.	1997-2003
Lincoln D. Chafee, R.	1999-2007
South Carolina	
Strom Thurmond, R.	1955-2003
Ernest F. Hollings, D.	1966-2005
South Dakota	
Thomas A. Daschle, D.	1987-2005
Tim Johnson, D.	1997-2003
Tennessee	
Fred Thompson, R.	1994-2003
Bill Frist, R.	1995-2007
Texas	
Phil Gramm, R.	1985-2003
Kay Bailey Hutchison, R.	1993-2007
Utah	
Orrin G. Hatch, R.	1977-2007
Robert F. Bennett, R.	1993-2005
Vermont	
Patrick J. Leahy, D.	1975-2005
James M. Jeffords, I.	1989-2007
Virginia	
John W. Warner, R.	1979-2003
George F. Allen, R.	2001-2007
Washington	
Patty Murray, D.	1993-2005
Maria Cantwell, D.	2001-2007
West Virginia	
Robert C. Byrd, D.	1959-2007
John D. Rockefeller IV, D.	1985-2003
Wisconsin	
Herbert Kohl, D.	1989-2007
Russell D. Feingold, D.	1993-2005
Wyoming	
Craig Thomas, R.	1995-2007
Mike Enzi, R.	1997-2003

Members of the United States House of Representatives

The House of Representatives of the second session of the 107th Congress consisted of 211 Democrats, 220 Republicans, and 2 Independents (not including representatives from American Samoa, the District of Columbia, Guam, Puerto Rico, and the Virgin Islands) when it convened on Jan. 22, 2002. This table shows congressional district, legislator, and party affiliation. Asterisk (*) denotes those who served in the 106th Congress; dagger (†) denotes "at large."

Alabama
1. Sonny Callahan, R.*
2. Terry Everett, R.*
3. Bob Riley, R.*
4. Robert Aderholt, R.*
5. Bud Cramer, D.*
6. Spencer Bachus, R.*
7. Earl Hilliard, D.*

Alaska
†Donald E. Young, R.*

Arizona
1. Jeff Flake, R.
2. Ed Pastor, D.*
3. Bob Stump, R.*
4. John Shadegg, R.*
5. Jim Kolbe, R.*
6. J. D. Hayworth, R.*

Arkansas
1. Marion Berry, D.*
2. Vic Snyder, D.*
3. John Boozman, R.
4. Mike Ross, D.

California
1. Mike Thompson, D.*
2. Wally Herger, R.*
3. Douglas Ose, R.*
4. John Doolittle, R.*
5. Robert T. Matsui, D.*
6. Lynn Woolsey, D.*
7. George E. Miller, D.*
8. Nancy Pelosi, D.*
9. Barbara Lee, D.*
10. Ellen Tauscher, D.*
11. Richard Pombo, R.*
12. Tom Lantos, D.*
13. Fortney H. (Peter) Stark, D.*
14. Anna Eshoo, D.*
15. Mike Honda, D.
16. Zoe Lofgren, D.*
17. Sam Farr, D.*
18. Gary Condit, D.*
19. George Radanovich, R.*
20. Calvin Dooley, D.*
21. William M. Thomas, R.*
22. Lois Capps, D.*
23. Elton Gallegly, R.*
24. Brad Sherman, D.*
25. Howard McKeon, R.*
26. Howard L. Berman, D.*
27. Adam Schiff, D.
28. David Dreier, R.*
29. Henry A. Waxman, D.*
30. Xavier Becerra, D.*
31. Hilda Solis, D.
32. Diane E. Watson, D.
33. Lucille Roybal-Allard, D.*
34. Grace Napolitano, D.*
35. Maxine Waters, D.*
36. Jane Harman, D.
37. Juanita Millender-McDonald, D.*
38. Steve Horn, R.*
39. Edward Royce, R.*
40. Jerry Lewis, R.*
41. Gary Miller, R.*
42. Joe Baca, D.*
43. Kenneth Calvert, R.*
44. Mary Bono, R.*
45. Dana Rohrabacher, R.*
46. Loretta Sanchez, D.*
47. C. Christopher Cox, R.*
48. Darrell Issa, R.
49. Susan Davis, D.
50. Bob Filner, D.*
51. Randy (Duke) Cunningham, R.*
52. Duncan L. Hunter, R.*

Colorado
1. Diana DeGette, D.*
2. Mark Udall, D.*
3. Scott McInnis, R.*
4. Bob Schaffer, R.*
5. Joel Hefley, R.*
6. Tom Tancredo, R.*

Connecticut
1. John Larson, D.*
2. Rob Simmons, R.
3. Rosa DeLauro, D.*
4. Christopher Shays, R.*
5. James H. Maloney, D.*
6. Nancy L. Johnson, R.*

Delaware
†Michael Castle, R.*

Florida
1. Jeff Miller, R.
2. Allen Boyd, D.*
3. Corrine Brown, D.*
4. Ander Crenshaw, R.
5. Karen Thurman, D.*
6. Clifford B. Stearns, R.*
7. John Mica, R.*
8. Ric Keller, R.
9. Michael Bilirakis, R.*
10. C. W. Bill Young, R.*
11. Jim Davis, D.*
12. Adam Putnam, R.
13. Dan Miller, R.*
14. Porter J. Goss, R.*
15. Dave Weldon, R.*
16. Mark Foley, R.*
17. Carrie Meek, D.*
18. Ileana Ros-Lehtinen, R.*
19. Robert Wexler, D.*
20. Peter Deutsch, D.*
21. Lincoln Diaz-Balart, R.*
22. E. Clay Shaw, Jr., R.*
23. Alcee Hastings, D.*

Georgia
1. Jack Kingston, R.*
2. Sanford Bishop, Jr., D.*
3. Mac Collins, R.*
4. Cynthia A. McKinney, D.*
5. John Lewis, D.*
6. Johnny Isakson, R.*
7. Bob Barr, R.*
8. Saxby Chambliss, R.*
9. Nathan Deal, R.*
10. Charlie Norwood, R.*
11. John Linder, R.*

Hawaii
1. Neil Abercrombie, D.*
2. Patsy T. Mink, D.*

Idaho
1. Butch Otter, R.
2. Mike Simpson, R.*

Illinois
1. Bobby Rush, D.*
2. Jesse L. Jackson, Jr., D.*
3. William O. Lipinski, D.*
4. Luis Gutierrez, D.*
5. Rod R. Blagojevich, D.*
6. Henry J. Hyde, R.*
7. Danny Davis, D.*
8. Philip M. Crane, R.*
9. Janice Schakowsky, D.*
10. Mark Kirk, R.
11. Gerald Weller, R.*
12. Jerry F. Costello, D.*
13. Judy Biggert, R.*
14. J. Dennis Hastert, R.*
15. Timothy Johnson, R.
16. Donald Manzullo, R.*
17. Lane A. Evans, D.*
18. Ray LaHood, R.*
19. David Phelps, D.*
20. John Shimkus, R.*

Indiana
1. Peter J. Visclosky, D.*
2. Mike Pence, R.
3. Tim Roemer, D.*
4. Mark Souder, R.*
5. Steve Buyer, R.*
6. Danny L. Burton, R.*
7. Brian Kerns, R.
8. John Hostettler, R.*
9. Baron Hill, D.*
10. Julia M. Carson, D.*

Iowa
1. Jim Leach, R.*
2. Jim Nussle, R.*
3. Leonard Boswell, D.*
4. Greg Ganske, R.*
5. Tom Latham, R.*

Kansas
1. Jerry Moran, R.*
2. Jim Ryun, R.*
3. Dennis Moore, D.*
4. Todd Tiahrt, R.*

Kentucky
1. Edward Whitfield, R.*
2. Ron Lewis, R.*
3. Anne Northup, R.*
4. Kenneth Lucas, D.*
5. Harold (Hal) Rogers, R.*
6. Ernie Fletcher, R.*

Louisiana
1. David Vitter, R.*
2. William J. Jefferson, D.*
3. W. J. (Billy) Tauzin, R.*
4. Jim McCrery, R.*
5. John Cooksey, R.*
6. Richard Hugh Baker, R.*
7. Chris John, D.*

Maine
1. Thomas Allen, D.*
2. John Baldacci, D.*

Maryland
1. Wayne T. Gilchrest, R.*
2. Robert Ehrlich, Jr., R.*
3. Benjamin L. Cardin, D.*
4. Albert Wynn, D.*
5. Steny H. Hoyer, D.*
6. Roscoe Bartlett, R.*
7. Elijah Cummings, D.*
8. Constance A. Morella, R.*

Massachusetts
1. John W. Olver, D.*
2. Richard E. Neal, D.*
3. James McGovern, D.*
4. Barney Frank, D.*
5. Martin Meehan, D.*
6. John Tierney, D.*
7. Edward J. Markey, D.*
8. Michael Capuano, D.*
9. Stephen F. Lynch, D.
10. William Delahunt, D.*

Michigan
1. Bart Stupak, D.*
2. Peter Hoekstra, R.*
3. Vernon Ehlers, R.*
4. Dave Camp, R.*
5. James Barcia, D.*
6. Frederick S. Upton, R.*
7. Nick Smith, R.*
8. Mike Rogers, R.
9. Dale E. Kildee, D.*
10. David E. Bonior, D.*
11. Joseph Knollenberg, R.*
12. Sander M. Levin, D.*
13. Lynn Rivers, D.*
14. John Conyers, Jr., D.*
15. Carolyn Kilpatrick, D.*
16. John D. Dingell, D.*

Minnesota
1. Gil Gutknecht, R.*
2. Mark Kennedy, R.
3. Jim Ramstad, R.*
4. Betty McCollum, D.

5. Martin O. Sabo, D.*
6. William P. Luther, D.*
7. Collin C. Peterson, D.*
8. James L. Oberstar, D.*

Mississippi
1. Roger Wicker, R.*
2. Bennie Thompson, D.*
3. Charles Pickering, R.*
4. Ronnie Shows, D.*
5. Gene Taylor, D.*

Missouri
1. William Clay, D.*
2. Todd Akin, R.
3. Richard A. Gephardt, D.*
4. Ike Skelton, D.*
5. Karen McCarthy, D.*
6. Samuel Graves, R.
7. Roy Blunt, R.*
8. Jo Ann Emerson, R.*
9. Kenny Hulshof, R.*

Montana
†Dennis Rehberg, R.

Nebraska
1. Doug Bereuter, R.*
2. Lee Terry, R.*
3. Tom Osborne, R.

Nevada
1. Shelley Berkley, D.*
2. Jim Gibbons, R.*

New Hampshire
1. John E. Sununu, R.*
2. Charles Bass, R.*

New Jersey
1. Robert E. Andrews, D.*
2. Frank LoBiondo, R.*
3. H. James Saxton, R.*
4. Christopher H. Smith, R.*
5. Marge Roukema, R.*
6. Frank Pallone, Jr., D.*
7. Mike Ferguson, R.
8. William Pascrell, Jr., D.*
9. Steven Rothman, D.*
10. Donald M. Payne, D.*
11. Rodney Frelinghuysen, R.*
12. Rush Holt, D.
13. Robert Menendez, D.*

New Mexico
1. Heather Wilson, R.*
2. Joe Skeen, R.*
3. Thomas Udall, D.*

New York
1. Felix Grucci, Jr., R.
2. Steve Israel, D.
3. Peter King, R.*
4. Carolyn McCarthy, D.*
5. Gary L. Ackerman, D.*
6. Gregory Meeks, D.*
7. Joseph Crowley, D.*
8. Jerrold Nadler, D.*
9. Anthony Weiner, D.*
10. Edolphus Towns, D.*
11. Major R. Owens, D.*
12. Nydia Velazquez, D.*
13. Vito J. Fossella, R.*
14. Carolyn Maloney, D.*
15. Charles B. Rangel, D.*
16. Jose E. Serrano, D.*
17. Eliot L. Engel, D.*
18. Nita M. Lowey, D.*
19. Sue Kelly, R.*
20. Benjamin A. Gilman, R.*
21. Michael R. McNulty, D.*
22. John Sweeney, R.*
23. Sherwood L. Boehlert, R.*
24. John McHugh, R.*
25. James Walsh, R.*
26. Maurice Hinchey, D.*
27. Thomas Reynolds, R.*
28. Louise M. Slaughter, D.*
29. John J. LaFalce, D.*
30. Jack Quinn, R.*
31. Amo Houghton, R.*

North Carolina
1. Eva Clayton, D.*
2. Bob Etheridge, D.*
3. Walter Jones, Jr., R.*
4. David Price, D.*
5. Richard Burr, R.*
6. Howard Coble, R.*
7. Mike McIntyre, D.*
8. Robin Hayes, R.*
9. Sue Myrick, R.*
10. Cass Ballenger, R.*
11. Charles H. Taylor, R.*
12. Melvin Watt, D.*

North Dakota
†Earl Pomeroy, D.*

Ohio
1. Steve Chabot, R.*
2. Rob Portman, R.*
3. Tony P. Hall, D.*
4. Michael G. Oxley, R.*
5. Paul E. Gillmor, R.*
6. Ted Strickland, D.*
7. David L. Hobson, R.*
8. John A. Boehner, R.*
9. Marcy Kaptur, D.*
10. Dennis Kucinich, D.*
11. Stephanie Jones, D.*
12. Pat Tiberi, R.
13. Sherrod Brown, D.*
14. Thomas C. Sawyer, D.*
15. Deborah Pryce, R.*
16. Ralph Regula, R.*
17. James A. Traficant, Jr., D.*
18. Bob Ney, R.*
19. Steven LaTourette, R.*

Oklahoma
1. Steve Largent, R.*
2. Brad Carson, D.
3. Wes Watkins, R.*
4. J. C. Watts, Jr., R.*
5. Ernest Jim Istook, R.*
6. Frank Lucas, R.*

Oregon
1. David Wu, D.*
2. Greg Walden, R.*
3. Earl Blumenauer, D.*
4. Peter A. DeFazio, D.*
5. Darlene Hooley, D.*

Pennsylvania
1. Robert Brady, D.*
2. Chaka Fattah, D.*
3. Robert A. Borski, Jr., D.*
4. Melissa Hart, R.
5. John Peterson, R.*
6. Tim Holden, D.*
7. W. Curtis Weldon, R.*
8. Jim Greenwood, R.*
9. Bill Shuster, R.
10. Donald Sherwood, R.
11. Paul E. Kanjorski, D.*
12. John P. Murtha, D.*
13. Joseph Hoeffel, D.
14. William J. Coyne, D.*
15. Patrick Toomey, R.
16. Joseph Pitts, R.*
17. George W. Gekas, R.*
18. Michael Doyle, D.*
19. Todd Platts, R.
20. Frank Mascara, D.*
21. Philip English, R.*

Rhode Island
1. Patrick Kennedy, D.*
2. James Langevin, D.

South Carolina
1. Henry Brown, R.
2. Joe Wilson, R.
3. Lindsey Graham, R.*
4. James DeMint, R.*
5. John M. Spratt, Jr., D.*
6. James Clyburn, D.*

South Dakota
†John Thune, R.*

Tennessee
1. William Jenkins, R.*
2. John J. Duncan, Jr., R.*
3. Zach Wamp, R.*
4. Van Hilleary, R.*
5. Bob Clement, D.*
6. Bart Gordon, D.*
7. Ed Bryant, R.*
8. John S. Tanner, D.*
9. Harold E. Ford, Jr., D.*

Texas
1. Max Sandlin, D.*
2. Jim Turner, D.*
3. Sam Johnson, R.*
4. Ralph M. Hall, D.*
5. Pete Sessions, R.*
6. Joe Barton, R.*
7. John Culberson, R.
8. Kevin Brady, R.*
9. Nick Lampson, D.*
10. Lloyd Doggett, D.*
11. Chet Edwards, D.*
12. Kay Granger, R.*
13. Mac Thornberry, R.*
14. Ron Paul, R.*
15. Ruben Hinojosa, D.*
16. Silvestre Reyes, D.*
17. Charles W. Stenholm, D.*
18. Sheila Jackson Lee, D.*
19. Larry Combest, R.*
20. Charlie Gonzalez, D.*
21. Lamar S. Smith, R.*
22. Tom DeLay, R.*
23. Henry Bonilla, R.*
24. Martin Frost, D.*
25. Ken Bentsen, D.*
26. Richard K. Armey, R.*
27. Solomon P. Ortiz, D.*
28. Ciro Rodriguez, D.*
29. Gene Green, D.*
30. Eddie Bernice Johnson, D.*

Utah
1. James V. Hansen, R.*
2. Jim Matheson, D.
3. Christopher Cannon, R.*

Vermont
†Bernard Sanders, Ind.*

Virginia
1. Jo Ann Davis, R.
2. Edward Schrock, R.
3. Robert Scott, D.*
4. J. Randy Forbes, R.
5. Virgil Goode, Jr., Ind.*
6. Robert Goodlatte, R.*
7. Eric Cantor, R.
8. James P. Moran, Jr., D.*
9. Rick C. Boucher, D.*
10. Frank R. Wolf, R.*
11. Tom Davis, R.*

Washington
1. Jay Inslee, D.*
2. Rick Larsen, D.
3. Brian Baird, D.*
4. Doc Hastings, R.*
5. George Nethercutt, Jr., R.*
6. Norman D. Dicks, D.*
7. Jim McDermott, D.*
8. Jennifer Dunn, R.*
9. Adam Smith, D.*

West Virginia
1. Alan B. Mollohan, D.*
2. Shelley Moore Capito, R.
3. Nick J. Rahall II, D.*

Wisconsin
1. Paul Ryan, R.*
2. Tammy Baldwin, D.*
3. Ron Kind, D.*
4. Gerald D. Kleczka, D.*
5. Thomas Barrett, D.*
6. Thomas E. Petri, R.*
7. David R. Obey, D.*
8. Mark Green, R.*
9. F. James Sensenbrenner, Jr., R.*

Wyoming
†Barbara Cubin, R.*

Nonvoting representatives

American Samoa
Eni F. H. Faleomavaega, D.*

District of Columbia
Eleanor Holmes Norton, D.*

Guam
Robert Underwood, D.*

Puerto Rico
Anibal Acevedo-Vila, D.

Virgin Islands
Donna Christian-Christensen, D.

legislation also reduced the tax rate on *capital gains* (the tax imposed on the sale of assets such as stocks, bonds, and real estate) and provided approximately $12 billion to state governments to extend unemployment insurance and health benefits to employees left without jobs as a result of the terrorist attacks. At the end of 2001, the Senate had not acted on the measure.

Funding measures. Congress in 2001 failed to pass any of the required 13 spending bills prior to the beginning of fiscal year 2002, which began on Oct. 1, 2001. The budget process was hampered by the terrorist attacks and by plans for an economic stimulus package. In October, economists warned that the cost of the government's response to the terrorist attacks could eliminate the estimated $52-billion surplus predicted for the end of fiscal year 2002. Combined with the stalled economy, some experts said that the spending could create a deficit in the federal budget.

Anthrax scare. A letter sent to U.S. Senator Thomas A. Daschle (D., South Dakota), the Senate majority leader, tested positive for anthrax spores in October. Anthrax is a potentially fatal infectious disease that is caused by the bacterium *Bacillus anthracis.* Anthrax can be treated with antibiotics, but infected individuals must begin taking the drugs before symptoms appear.

The letter, opened by aides to Daschle in his office in the Hart Senate Office Building on October 15, contained a powdery substance. Tests on the powder indicated the presence of anthrax spores. As a precaution, police closed Daschle's office and shut down the Capitol mail delivery system. Public tours of the Capitol were also suspended.

On October 17, Speaker of the House Dennis Hastert (R., Illinois) announced that the House of Representatives would close so that half of the Capitol could be swept for the presence of anthrax. Hastert made the announcement after health officials confirmed that anthrax spores were found in a Senate mailroom in the Dirksen Office Building and that more than 30 people who work for Daschle in the Hart Senate Office Building had tested positive for exposure. The Hart Senate Office Building is across the street from the Capitol. Senate leaders opted not to close the Senate chamber in the Capitol.

On November 20, Federal Bureau of Investigation (FBI) agents reported that a sealed letter sent to Senator Patrick J. Leahy (D., Vermont) was contaminated with a highly refined form of anthrax. Investigators theorized that the same person who mailed the anthrax-tainted letter to Daschle probably sent the letter to Leahy. Both letters were postmarked October 9 in Trenton, New Jersey. The FBI found the Leahy letter on

U.S. Senator Thomas Daschle (D., South Dakota) (left), the new Senate majority leader, greets Senator Trent Lott (R., Mississippi), the outgoing majority leader, after Democrats assumed control of the Senate in June.

November 16 in a huge stack of unopened mail that had been held by postal authorities since the discovery of the letter to Daschle.

Control over the Senate shifted to the Democratic Party in June for the first time since 1995. The shift followed an announcement on May 24, 2001, by Senator James M. Jeffords of Vermont that he was leaving the Republican Party and would become an independent aligned with the Democrats. The move reduced the number of Senate seats held by the Republicans from 50 to 49, shifting control to the Democrats. The Republicans had maintained control through the tie-breaking vote of Republican Vice President Richard Cheney. Daschle replaced Trent Lott (R., Mississippi) as majority leader, and Democrats moved into the chairmanships of key committees.

Democratic leadership. House Democrats elected Representative Nancy Pelosi (D., California) *minority whip* (assistant leader) in October. Pelosi, who replaced Representative David Bonior of Michigan as whip, was the first woman in U.S. history to be elected to a position of leadership in either the House or Senate.

New memorials. Congress cleared the last obstacles to a World War II (1939-1945) memorial in May 2001 when the House approved a Senate-amended measure that ended lawsuits and procedural problems that had held up the beginning of construction. The measure, signed into law on May 28, also included provisions to insulate construction of the memorial from judicial challenge. The memorial, to be constructed between the Lincoln Memorial and the Washington Monument in Washington, D.C., was to consist of a circle of granite pillars representing the states and two four-story arches to signify victory in Europe and Asia. Some groups, including some veterans organizations, argued that the design was too grandiose and would clutter the view on the National Mall between the Lincoln Monument and the Washington Memorial.

In October, the Senate gave final approval to a plan that authorized the Adams Memorial Foundation to establish a memorial honoring President John Adams, his wife, Abigail Adams, and their son, President John Quincy Adams. The House approved the legislation in June, and President Bush signed it on November 5. The legislation allows the memorial to be constructed on federal land in the District of Columbia. The design and location of the memorial had not been determined by the end of 2001.

☐ Geoffrey A. Campbell

See also **Armed forces; Democratic Party; Education; Republican Party; Taxation; Terrorism: A Special Feature,** p. 38; **United States, Government of the; United States, President of the.**

Connecticut. See **State government.**

Conservation. United States President George W. Bush moved in early 2001 to reverse a number of conservation initiatives proposed by his predecessor, Bill Clinton, in the waning days of his administration. He also sought to open Alaska's Arctic National Wildlife Refuge (ANWR, pronounced "anwar') to oil exploration. President Bush later backed away from some of his earlier decisions and proposed new regulations to protect national parks from air pollution.

National monuments. Before Clinton left office in January, he designated several new national monuments covering a total of more than 1 million acres (405,000 hectares) of federal lands in Western states. The designations protected the lands from such potentially damaging activities as vehicle use, mining, and oil drilling. After taking office, Bush ordered a freeze on the designations, pending a review by his Cabinet. In February, Secretary of the Interior Gale Norton announced that the administration would allow the designations to stand. However, she promised state officials that the Bush administration would manage the lands to cause minimum disruption on neighboring landowners and local governments.

National forests. In March, President Bush suspended Clinton-era rules that banned new roads and logging in some 60 million acres (24 million hectares) of national forests. In May, Bush said his administration would revise the rules to allow local officials and landowners to have greater say in decisions affecting forests in their regions and to clarify what activities would be banned in the forests.

The Arctic National Wildlife Refuge, in northwestern Alaska, became the focus of a heated environmental debate after President Bush unveiled a national energy policy in May that called for opening part of ANWR to oil drilling. ANWR is a protected wilderness region for birds, polar bears, and other animals. The refuge covers some 20 million acres (8 million hectares). However, 1.5 million acres (607,500 hectares) of the coastal plain along the Arctic Ocean was excluded from full wilderness protection. The U.S. Department of Energy estimated the plain may sit on 5.7 billion to 16 billion gallons (21.6 billion to 60 billion liters) of oil, though only about 71 million gallons (270 million liters) could be recovered using existing technology. Conservationists claimed this supply would last only a few months.

President Bush contended that without an increase in the U.S. production of oil, natural gas, and nuclear energy, energy shortages would "undermine our economy, our standard of living, and our national security." Many members of the U.S. Congress and the oil industry agreed that drilling in ANWR would decrease U.S. dependence on foreign oil, reduce energy costs for American consumers, and create new jobs. The oil industry also contended that modern drilling technology is safe in environmentally sensitive areas.

Conservation groups responded that any drilling operation would probably be much larger and more harmful than that described by the administration. They also contended that drilling would disturb the large herds of caribou that annually migrate to ANWR's coastal plain to calve. Furthermore, conservationists worried that oil spills would cause irreparable harm to the fragile Arctic ecosystem.

In August, the U.S. House of Representatives approved an energy bill that authorized drilling for gas and oil in ANWR. The U.S. Senate had not acted on the legislation by the end of 2001.

Protecting parks. In June, Christine Todd Whitman, the head of the Environmental Protection Agency (EPA), proposed new regulations to cut emissions from coal-fired power plants that were built between 1962 and 1977. According to EPA officials, these plants were the primary source of dense haze that blanketed many national parks and wilderness areas, including Great Smoky Mountains National Park in Tennessee and Acadia National Park in Maine. The new regulations were nearly identical to rules proposed by the Clinton administration.

During a visit to Everglades National Park in Florida in June 2001, President Bush committed his administration to a 40-year project, proposed by former President Clinton, to restore the park's natural ecosystem. Bush requested $219 million for the $8-billion project for fiscal year 2002 (Oct. 1, 2001, to Sept. 30, 2002)—a 30-percent increase over the allotment for fiscal year 2001.

Endangered species agreement. The U.S. Fish and Wildlife Service (USFWS) announced in August an agreement with environmental groups under which the agency would speed up action to protect 29 critically endangered plant and animal species. In return, the environmental organizations agreed to drop legal efforts to force the government to immediately place additional species on the Endangered Species List.

In April, the Interior Department had proposed suspending for at least one year the right of citizens to take the USFWS to court to compel the agency to add new species to the list. Private citizens have initiated most of the efforts to expand the list. Interior Department officials said the moratorium was necessary to allow the overburdened USFWS to deal with a backlog of cases concerning more than 400 species.

Condor ups and downs. The USFWS's project to establish endangered California condors in the wild made limited progress in 2001. In May, project scientists reported finding the first intact condor eggs in the wild since the release of the first captive-bred condors in 1992. The two eggs were found in the Los Padres National Forest near Santa Barbara, California. They had been laid in a single nest by two adult females who had apparently mated with the same male and then took turns incubating the eggs.

Biologists monitoring the nest became concerned that the birds were not incubating the eggs as much as necessary. Upon inspecting the eggs, the scientists concluded that one *embryo* (unhatched bird) was dead, and the other was deformed. They removed the faulty eggs and, in order to give the condors experience in nurturing young, substituted a healthy egg laid by a captive condor at the Los Angeles Zoo. A few days after that egg hatched, however, the chick was found dead. The biologists believed it was killed by one of the adult female condors.

Despite the setback, the biologists were pleased to see that captive-reared condors had finally begun to breed in the wild. As of December 2001, there were 54 California condors in the wild, 17 in field pens waiting release, and 112 in captivity, according to the Peregrine Fund, a conservation organization in Boise, Idaho.

Good news about gorillas. The population of mountain gorillas at Volcano National Park, a wildlife refuge that lies in parts of Rwanda, Congo (Kinshasa), and Uganda, increased from 324 in 1989 to 358 in 2001, according to a March report by park researchers. Conservationists had feared that the gorilla population might have decreased during this period because of an ongoing civil war and *poaching* (illegal killing of wildlife) in all three African countries. However, funding by international conservation organizations made it possible for the park to hire several rangers to protect the gorillas from attacks by rebels and poachers. Park scientists said there were some 300 additional mountain gorillas in the Bwindi Impenetrable Forest in Uganda.

Saving an African Eden. A German-owned logging company announced in July that it would voluntarily transfer its lease on a 100-square-mile (260-square-kilometer) plot of rain forest and swampland to the government of Congo (Brazzaville). The government added the area, called the Goualogo Triangle, to the neighboring Nouabale-Ndoki National Park. Officials for the company, Congolaise Industrielle des Bois, said they decided to give up the land without compensation when a survey of the tract revealed an amazing diversity of wildlife, including chimpanzees, gorillas, colobus monkeys, elephants, and forest antelopes. ☐ Eugene J. Walter, Jr.

See also **Environmental pollution.**

Costa Rica. See **Latin America.**

Courts. On May 29, 2001, a federal jury in New York City found four men guilty of charges connected to the 1998 bombing of two United States embassies in Tanzania and Kenya. The terrorist attacks left 224 people dead and thousands more injured. The jury found the four men—Mohamed Rashed Daoud al-'Owhali of Saudi Arabia; Khalfan Khamis Mohamed of Tanzania; Wadih El-Hage, a naturalized U.S. citizen born in Lebanon; and Mohamed Sadeek Odeh of Jordan—guilty on charges of conspiracy to kill Americans, conspiracy to kill U.S. government employees, using weapons of mass destruction, and destroying U.S. government properties. They also found al-'Owhali and Mohamed guilty of murder. On Oct. 18, 2001, U.S. District Judge Leonard Sand sentenced the four men to life in prison without parole.

Federal authorities believed that all of the men were disciples of Osama bin Laden, a Saudi-born exile. Bin Laden was believed to have planned the 1998 embassy attacks and the Sept. 11, 2001, terrorist attacks on the United States.

Microsoft breakup. The U.S. Circuit Court of Appeals for the District of Columbia on June 28 upheld a lower court's decision that computer software giant Microsoft Corporation of Redmond, Washington, violated antitrust laws designed to prevent business from monopolizing its industry. However, the appeals court reversed the decision of U.S. District Judge Thomas Penfield Jackson, who had ordered Microsoft officials to break the corporation into smaller companies.

In 2000, Jackson had ordered that the company be divided into two separate companies—one dedicated to Microsoft's Windows *operating system* (master control program) and another company dedicated to *applications software* (programs for all the specific uses of computers), such as Microsoft Office and the Internet Explorer Web browser. The appeals court concluded that Jackson was biased against the software maker.

Attorneys representing Microsoft appealed the ruling to the U.S. Supreme Court. On Sept. 6, 2001, officials with the U.S. Department of Justice announced that the government would stop trying to break up Microsoft into smaller companies. However, the government maintained that the company had broken the law by requiring computer makers who used the Windows 95 operating system to also install Microsoft's Internet Explorer browser software. In October, Supreme Court justices announced that they would not hear the Microsoft appeal.

In November, Microsoft and federal officials reached an agreement to settle the case. Microsoft officials agreed to a series of business restrictions upheld by an independent panel of computer experts.

Nine of the 18 states involved in the litigation, however, refused to back the agreement. On November 9, U.S. District Judge Colleen Kollar-Kotelly set a March 2002 hearing date to determine what sanctions should be imposed against Microsoft on behalf of those states.

Smoking verdict. A jury in Los Angeles on June 6, 2001, found that a smoker with terminal lung cancer was entitled to billions of dollars from cigarette maker Philip Morris Inc. of Richmond, Virginia, for its role in causing his illness. The jury found that the tobacco company should pay Richard Boeken $5.5 million in compensation and $3 billion in punitive damages. Jurors said that Philip Morris engaged in fraud and negligence by producing a defective product and failing to warn smokers of the health risks of smoking. Boeken began smoking before tobacco manufacturers placed warning labels on their products. The verdict was the largest in a single lawsuit against a cigarette company. However, the judge in the case determined that the punitive damage award was too large and on August 15 lowered the amount to $100 million.

McVeigh trial. U.S. Attorney General John Ashcroft in May 2001 postponed the execution of Timothy J. McVeigh, who was convicted of the 1995 bombing of the Alfred J. Murrah Federal Building in Oklahoma City, Oklahoma, which killed 168 people. The postponement of the May 16, 2001, execution came after Federal Bureau of Investigation (FBI) officials discovered that hundreds of reports had not been turned over to defense lawyers during McVeigh's trial in 1997. U.S. District Judge Richard Matsch rejected an appeal filed by McVeigh's attorneys, ruling on June 7, 2001, that the newly found documents would not have made a difference in the outcome of the trial. McVeigh was executed on June 11. He was the first federal inmate to be put to death since 1963.

Parody controversy. U.S. District Judge Charles A. Pannell, Jr., issued an injunction in April 2001 against the publication of a novel that parodied Margaret Mitchell's 1936 novel, *Gone With the Wind. The Wind Done Gone,* written by Alice Randall, revisits Mitchell's Civil War (1861-1865) story through the eyes of a slave. Pannell ruled that Randall plagiarized from Mitchell's work and stopped the book's publication.

In May 2001, the 11th U.S. Circuit Court of Appeals in Atlanta, Georgia, lifted the injunction. The three-judge panel determined that the injunction was an "extraordinary and drastic remedy" that violated the U.S. Constitution's First Amendment guarantee against prior restraint. ☐ Geoffrey A. Campbell

See also **Computers; Supreme Court of the United States; Terrorism; Terrorism: A Special Feature,** p. 38; **United States, Government of the.**

Cricket. International Cricket Council (ICC) officials continued in 2001 to investigate allegations of match-fixing and corruption in professional cricket. In May 2001, the ICC released the report of the Anti-Corruption Unit, headed by former British police chief Sir Paul Condon. The official report indicated that the corruption of international cricketers by the illegal betting industry had begun as early as the 1970's, when expanded television coverage increased the popularity of cricket. This, in turn, made illegal betting more lucrative and attractive.

The report was critical of the ICC and local cricket boards for not doing enough to halt illegal activities sooner. The Anti-Corruption Unit proposed several new security measures to reduce illegal activities, such as restricting access to players during international matches. The report contained no fresh allegations against individuals. However, in August 2001, several leading players who had been accused of taking money for supplying information to an Indian *bookmaker* (a person who makes a living accepting bets), were cleared after the bookmaker failed to supply evidence to support his allegations.

Test cricket. Fans enjoyed some exceptionally exciting international cricket in 2001. In January, Australia, the leading test match-playing country, wrapped up its defeat of the West Indies 5-0. In March, Australia set a new record of 16 straight test victories with its defeat of India. However, later in that same month, India stormed back with an astonishing victory over Australia after following on, 274 runs behind. In its second innings, India scored 657-7 declared, leaving Australia with 384 runs to win. But India bowled out Australia for 212, winning the match by 171 runs. India then went on to win the third and final test by two wickets. Harbhajan Singh, the young off-spinner for India, played a major role in India's success, taking 31 wickets at an average of 17.03.

England's 2001 summer cricket season started out well, with a victory over Pakistan in the first of a two-match series. However, Pakistan took the second match to draw the series 1-1. In the battle for the Ashes, Australia overwhelmed England, winning by 4 tests to 1. Glenn McGrath and Shane Warne were Australia's leading bowlers during the Ashes series. McGrath's 32 wickets raised his test match wicket aggregate to 358. Warne, who took 31 wickets, lifted his aggregate to 407. Steve and Mark Waugh headed the batting averages.

Bangladesh, the newest test-match-playing country, played its second test-match series in April 2001 against Zimbabwe. Zimbabwe easily took down the inexperienced Bangladesh team in the two-match series. In the Asia Test Championship, a test-match competition scheduled to run between August 2001 and February 2002, Bangladesh again lost by large margins to both Pakistan and Sri Lanka. However, batsman Mohammed Ashraful proved to be a bright spot for Bangladesh. Ashraful became the youngest player ever to score a century on his test debut. There was some debate over Ashraful's age. According to his passport, he was just under 17, but cricket officials claimed he was over 17.

Courtney Walsh, the great West Indies bowler, announced his retirement after the final game of the test series against South Africa. Walsh left cricket but not before taking his test match aggregate of wickets to a record 519. India's Kapil Dev was second on the list with 434.

The use of television replays to question decisions made by umpires proved highly controversial during the 2001 cricket season. Many cricket lovers believed that the use of this technology undermined the authority of the umpires, who have traditionally made all rulings on the conduct of the game.

World Test Championship. In February, the ICC approved the World Test Championship, a new championship system whereby all 10 test-match-playing countries play each other at home and away once every five years. The new system was to replace the unofficial grading of teams, which had been done in the past. Each series was required to include at least two tests. Sides were to get two points for a series win and one point for a draw. The results of all these series were to count toward the World Championship, which was to operate on a roll-over basis, with the most recent result replacing the equivalent in the table. The ICC instituted the new system in the hopes of reviving fan interest in the five-day game, which had lost popularity to the one-day game in some parts of the world.

One-day cricket. In July, 22 teams competed in a one-day tournament for the ICC Trophy in Toronto, Canada. Both the Netherlands and Namibia teams qualified to participate in the 2003 World Cup by taking the first two places in the final Super League stage. Canada defeated Scotland in a play-off for a third World Cup place. These three teams joined Kenya, a non-test-match country, which had already qualified. The United States finished seventh in the eight-nation Super League, with two victories and five defeats.

A legend dies. Australian Sir Donald Bradman, whom most authorities rated as the greatest cricketer of the last century, died on Feb. 25, 2001. In his 52 test matches for Australia, Bradman scored 6,996 runs at an average of 99.94, an achievement that no other player has ever come close to breaking. ☐ Keith Lye

Crime. The U.S. Federal Bureau of Investigation (FBI) reported in its Uniform Crime Report in June 2001 that crime fell nationwide by 0.2 percent in 2000, the last year for which statistics were available. It was the ninth consecutive time that crime had fallen in the United States from the year before. From 1991 to 2000, overall crime decreased 22 percent. Law enforcement officials, however, said that the large decreases in the crime rate may be leveling off, as the drop in 2000 was the smallest during these years.

According to the FBI report, violent crime—which includes murder, rape, robbery, and aggravated assault—fell by 0.1 percent. Property crime—which includes motor vehicle theft, larceny, and burglary—fell by 0.3 percent. The murder rate decreased nationwide by less than one-tenth of 1 percent, compared with 1999. Burglary decreased by 2.4 percent; robbery decreased by 0.4 percent; assault decreased by 0.1 percent; rape increased by 0.9 percent; larceny increased by 0.2 percent; and car theft increased by 1.2 percent.

Crime was slightly down in U.S. cities—0.1 percent—but it fell 1.8 percent in the suburbs. Crime in large cities fell in 2000, but in cities with less than 25,000 people, it rose noticeably. Rural areas experienced a small increase of 0.5 percent. Regionally, the West was the only part of the United States where crime rose in 2000, with a 1-percent increase. Crime fell 0.1 percent in the South, 0.6 percent in the Midwest, and 2 percent in the Northeast. The FBI estimated that 11.6 million crimes were reported in 2000.

Conflicting figures. Shortly after the FBI issued its report, the U.S. Bureau of Justice Statistics published its own figures showing a 15 percent decrease in crime in 2000. The National Crime Victimization Survey (NCVS) was based on a nationwide poll of 160,000 people who were asked if they were the victims of any crimes in 2000.

The results of the NCVS, which has been published since 1973, have typically agreed with the FBI's numbers. The report for 2000, however, showed that violent crime had dropped by 14.9 percent, rape or sexual assault by 29.4 percent, robbery by 11.1 percent, assault by 14.2 percent, and personal theft by 33.3 percent. U.S. Justice officials estimated there were 26 million crimes in 2000, down from 28.8 million in 1999. By comparison, 44 million crimes were reported in 1973 when the survey was first published.

The two reports were so different because of major differences in the way the FBI and the Bureau of Justice gathered data. The FBI report only tracked the seven major violent crimes, which excluded a crime like simple assault, which is an attack on another person without a weapon. Most importantly, the FBI report was based on crimes reported to the police, and some criminologists estimated that more than half of the crimes in the United States go unreported. The NCVS is an attempt to track all forms of crime—though homicide cannot be included in the survey as its victims are unavailable for interview. Criminologists believe that a large nationwide drop in simple assault and minor property crime drove down the violent crime rate in the NCVS. When the Department of Justice compared the two surveys on just the serious crimes covered in the FBI report, the results were much closer.

Post-September 11. Crime rates took some puzzling turns in the wake of the Sept. 11, 2001, terrorist attacks in New York City and near Washington, D.C. The reaction in those two cities was completely opposite. Crime rose in Washington, D.C., but dropped in New York City. In the first eight months of 2001, Washington, D.C., had enjoyed its lowest homicide rate since 1987 and overall crime plummeted by 24 percent. After Sept. 11, 2001, however, crime rates jumped dramatically. City officials denied the increase was related to police officers spending less time on patrol and more time guarding public buildings. In New York City, the crime rate during the week of the attack on the World Trade Center towers fell 34 percent from the same week a year earlier. Criminologists were surprised at the development, since the New York City police force was so heavily involved in the massive clean-up efforts. The daily number of total arrests fell by almost 50 percent. The decrease in crime was part of a trend for the city, in which crime fell overall in each quarter of 2001.

Anthrax investigation. In October 2001, law enforcement officials began investigating a series of letters mailed to government offices and media outlets in Washington, D.C., New York City, and Boca Raton, Florida, that contained spores of the dangerous anthrax bacterium.

Prison populations. In August, the U.S. Department of Justice reported that after 30 years of constant growth, the number of people incarcerated in U.S. prisons appeared to be leveling off. The state prison population actually declined in the second half of 2000, though it was up 1.3 percent for the whole year, the lowest annual rate of increase since 1972. Over the past 30 years, the U.S. prison population increased 500 percent. It grew by more than 6 percent annually during the 1990's, when crime rates plunged across the country. At the end of 2000, there were slightly more than 1.3 million people incarcerated in prisons in the United States.

☐ Robert Messenger

See also **Medicine; New York City; Prison; Public health and safety; Terrorism; Terrorism: A Special Feature,** p. 38; **United States, Government of the; Washington, D.C.**

News bulletins flood the airwaves as helicopters hover over an ordinary suburban school. Frantic parents rush to the campus. Police officers, weapons at the ready, move into position. Television cameras zoom in on weeping students. Ambulances whisk away bleeding victims on stretchers.

Such images, etched into our minds in April 1999 by the massacre of 12 students and a teacher at Columbine High School in Littleton, Colorado, have become eerily familiar. In a single month in the spring of 2001, three school shootings grabbed

By Dianne Hales

JUVENILE VIOLENCE

Most experts agreed that while juvenile violence in the United States increased dramatically during the early 1990's, public perception of the violence exceeded its true scope by 2001.

national attention. On March 5, a 15-year-old boy opened fire in a bathroom at his high school in Santee, California, killing 2 students and wounding 13 other people. Two days later, a 14-year-old girl at a Roman Catholic school in Williamsport, Pennsylvania, shot an eighth-grade classmate in the cafeteria. On March 22, an 18-year-old wounded 5 students and teachers at a high school in El Cajon, California. Throughout the month, school officials and police departments across the country reported dozens of threats or plots by and against teen-agers.

High school students Eric Harris (opposite page, left) and Dylan Klebold stalk the Columbine High School cafeteria in Littleton, Colorado, on April 20, 1999. The pair shot and killed 12 students and a teacher.

What is juvenile violence?

When experts use the term "juvenile violence," they are usually referring to one of four types of violent crimes committed by youths aged 10 to 17:

criminal homicide—the willful killing of one human being by another;

robbery—taking or attempting to take anything of value from a person or persons by force, threat of force, violence, or putting the victim in fear;

aggravated assault—an unlawful attack by one person upon another in which the offender uses a weapon or displays it in a threatening manner or the victim suffers severe bodily injury, such as broken bones, loss of teeth, possible internal injury, severe laceration, or loss of consciousness;

forcible rape—having sexual intercourse with a person against the person's will or in a situation where the victim is unable to give consent because of temporary or permanent mental or physical incapacity or because of youth.

Sources: *Youth Violence: A Report of the Surgeon General.* 2001. U.S. Department of Justice, Federal Bureau of Investigation, 2000.

Why are there suddenly so many shootings? Are today's young people more violent than youths of the past? Are our schools becoming more dangerous?

For the most part, the answer is "no." According to United States government statistics, the number of *juveniles* (young people between the ages of 10 and 17) arrested for violent crimes—murder, rape, robbery, and aggravated assault—actually has decreased since the mid-1990's. The Office of Juvenile Justice and Delinquency Prevention, a division of the U.S. Justice Department, reported that in 1999 juveniles accounted for only 16 percent of all violent crime arrests. Violent crime by juveniles fell by 36 percent from 1994 to 1999. Juvenile arrests for murder, which peaked in 1993, declined by 68 percent by 1999, reaching the lowest level since the 1960's. Despite such high-profile school shootings as the Columbine High School massacre, fewer than 1 percent of teens killed are murdered at school, at school functions, or while traveling to or from school, according to data collected by the Centers for Disease Control and Prevention in Atlanta (CDC) and the U.S. Departments of Justice and Education.

The U.S. Surgeon General's study on teen violence

Teen violence nevertheless remains "an ongoing, startlingly pervasive problem," according to a 2001 report on youth violence published by the Office of the Surgeon General. "Even though youth violence is less lethal today than it was in 1993, the percentage of adolescents involved in violent behavior remains alarmingly high. . . [Y]oung people in every community are involved in violence, whether the community is a small town or a central city, a neatly groomed suburb or an isolated rural region."

In 2000, the National Center for Injury Prevention and Control, an agency of the CDC located in Atlanta, Georgia, reported that murder rates for young people in the United States remained the highest in the world. The murder rate for 15-to-24-year-old males is 10 times higher in the United States than in Canada; 15 times higher than in Australia; and 28 times higher than in France or Germany. Homicide is the second leading cause of death (after accidents) for young Americans between the ages of 15 and 24. American teen-agers are more likely to die of gunshot wounds than of all natural causes combined. Despite the overall

The author:
Dianne Hales is a free-lance writer.

drop in teen homicides, the rise in mass murders by teen-agers in the mid- and late 1990's renewed public concern about teen violence.

Experts offer a host of explanations for the continuing violence in the lives of American adolescents: the breakdown of families; the media; easy access to guns; bullying and harassment in schools; undiagnosed mental disorders; and abuse of alcohol and drugs. However, experts no longer view teen violence as inevitable, untreatable, and destined to increase, as many believed in the 1980's. As David Satcher, the surgeon general, reported in 2001, "We possess the knowledge and tools needed to reduce or even prevent much of the most serious youth violence."

The history of teen violence

Teen violence in what is today the United States is hardly new. American colonial records from as early as the 1600's document criminal acts of aggression by adolescent boys and girls. At that time, juvenile offenders were treated as adults and punished in the same ways that adults were punished, by serving time in prison or by being executed. In the early 1640's, a court in the Massachusetts Bay Colony ordered a 16-year-old boy to be hanged. He was the first child to be legally executed in what would become the United States.

Adolescent gangs have plagued U.S. cities through much of the nation's history. As immigrants began crowding into cities in the 1800's, teen-agers often formed gangs to protect themselves from victimization and to gain power and status. In the Five Points section of New York City, a group of 8- to 13-year-olds formed the Forty Little Thieves around 1850. The gang members served as decoys and lookouts for older criminals and committed their own crimes as well. In Chicago, two gangs—the Irishers and the Bohemians—carried on a war with guns, knives, and clubs

Juvenile violence with no apparent motive is not a new phenomenon of U.S. culture. A newspaper engraving (below, left) illustrates a true incident in which young girls drowned a 6-year-old in a well in Patterson, New Jersey, in 1868. In 1995, two children dropped a 5-year-old boy to his death from the 14th floor of a Chicago public housing development (below, right).

Police officers arrest Neal Simonetti in 1942 after the juvenile shot and killed his teacher at a Brooklyn, New York, high school (above, left). In 2001, 14-year-old Nathaniel Brazill (above, right) leaves a Florida courthouse after being convicted of murdering his English teacher.

from 1881 until 1905. Much of the violence took place in classrooms and on the streets around the school that members of both gangs attended.

When juveniles broke the law in the late 1800's, they entered a criminal justice system that had evolved from one based strictly on punishment to one that allowed rehabilitation at a judge's discretion. Institutions called houses of refuge, or reform schools, attempted to treat abused, abandoned, and criminal youths that judges felt could be deterred from a life of crime. Serious juvenile offenders, however, were still sent to adult prisons or jails.

The beginnings of the juvenile justice system

In 1899, officials in Cook County, Illinois, which includes Chicago, established the first juvenile court in the nation. Over the next 50 years, virtually all states established similar institutions. Unlike adult criminal courts, the juvenile courts focused primarily on the best interests of the child. Youths sentenced in a juvenile court—regardless of how violent a crime they had committed—were generally confined only until they reached the age of 18 or 21.

Incidents of teen crime increased dramatically in the 1960's and 1970's. In part, the rise was due to the increase in the number of teen-agers present in the population because of the baby boom (the rise in births in the United States that occurred after World War II ended in 1945). Lawmakers responded to the growing problem by allowing youths in most states to once again be prosecuted in adult criminal courts if the seriousness of the crime or the past history of the child seemed to indicate that rehabilitation would not prove effective.

All forms of teen violence, by gangs and by individuals, exploded throughout the United States between 1983 and 1993. Arrest rates for serious violent crimes jumped by 70 percent

Members of a New York City gang (above, left) loiter on a street corner in the 1940's. Gangs in U.S. cities date back to at least the early 1800's. In 1988, members of the Los Angeles Diamond Street gang stand before graffiti marking their territory and flash their gang sign (above, right).

among adolescents. The number of young killers increased by 168 percent. Agencies at all levels of government searched for reasons behind the teen violence. Three major factors emerged: a rise in drug traffic; an increase in gang activity; and easy access to weapons, particularly firearms. Use of *crack* (a relatively inexpensive form of cocaine that can be smoked) surged in the 1980's. The numbers of teen gangs increased, and the gangs spread from larger cities to smaller towns and rural areas. Cheaper, larger-caliber guns flooded gun markets in the 1980's and made their way onto the streets. Because the law frequently allowed lighter sentencing for adolescents who committed crimes, drug dealers recruited teen-age gang members—who routinely carried and used guns—as distributors.

Police forces responded to the epidemic of teen violence by intensifying their efforts to crack down on drug traffic and illegal gun purchases. Neighborhoods organized to clear out crack houses and drug runners. The U.S. Congress and many state legislatures passed new gun control laws between 1992 and 1997. Judges and prosecuting attorneys began channeling children as young as 10 out of the juvenile justice system and into adult criminal courts.

The tide began to turn in 1994. The number of teens arrested for serious violent crimes declined dramatically. In the late 1990's, fewer young people carried guns and used guns to commit crimes, according to federal statistics. By 1999, overall arrest rates for adolescents were the lowest in that decade—though still 15 percent higher than in 1983.

The rise in school shootings

Beginning in the mid-1990's, a terrifying new trend in teen violence emerged: mass murders, or the killing of at least three victims on the same occasion. "We've seen an increase in this phenomenon despite a progressive decline in other forms of teen violence," reported J. Reid Meloy, a psychologist at the University

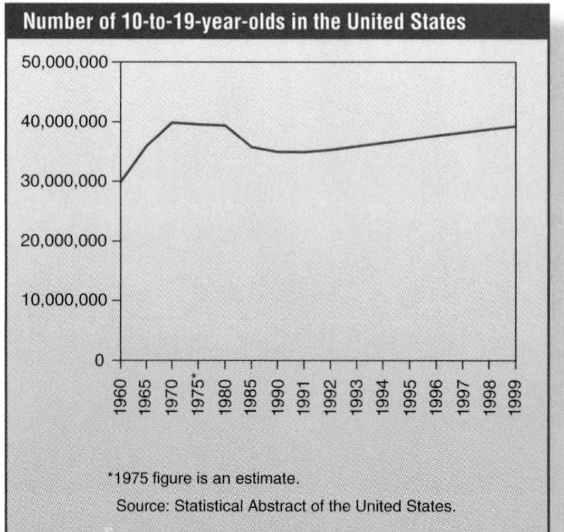

The number of juveniles in the U.S. population remained relatively stable from the 1960's through the 1990's, except for a period between 1970 and 1980, when the majority of *baby boomers* were teenagers. (Baby boomers are people who were born during a period of rising births after the end of World War II in 1945.) Criminologists have theorized that the incidence of teen violence increases when the number of 10-to-19-year-olds in the population rises.

of California in San Diego who has studied adolescent mass murderers. The most highly publicized of these killing sprees occurred on school grounds. From 1996 to 2000, according to a *New York Times* survey, 18 separate school shootings left a total of 39 people dead.

Who are these young killers?

Many people think they know what types of teens cause trouble: children who were abused or neglected; children who were raised in urban poverty; and children who have been aggressive toward other youngsters since early childhood.

Many different studies, however, have shown that none of these factors definitively predisposes a child toward violence. Not all teen-agers involved in violent crime were victimized as children. Many violent teens showed no early signs of aggressive behavior. Although male teens—particularly those from minority groups—are arrested for violent crimes in numbers out of proportion to their presence in the general population, researchers have found that life circumstances, such as neglect or poverty, are not good predictors of whether a child will become violent.

Living in a small community rather than a large city does not protect teens from violent crime either. Although the overall rate of youth homicide fell in the late 1990's, it increased among small-town and rural teens, just as the number of gangs and gang members in smaller communities increased. By the late 1990's, some 2,550 cities, towns, and villages and 1,150 counties in the United States reported problems with gangs—a rise of more than 800 percent from 1970. "[N]o longer can any of us outside inner-city areas believe that we and our children are immune to lethal youth violence," says James Garbarino, a psychologist at Cornell University in Ithaca, New York, and author of *Lost Boys* [1999] and numerous other studies of teen violence. "[A]lmost every teen-ager in America goes to school with a kid who is troubled enough to become the next killer, and chances are that kid has access to the weapons necessary to do so."

Even the teens involved in most school shootings do not conform to stereotypes about "bad boys." Most such shooters are middle-class males raised in small towns or suburbs. "Classroom avengers," as Meloy and other researchers have called them, typically show no outward signs of violence. Considered outcasts or loners by their peers, they often immerse themselves in violent fantasies and video games. Rather than acting impulsively—another assumption many people mistakenly make—they deliberately and methodically plan their acts of vengeance.

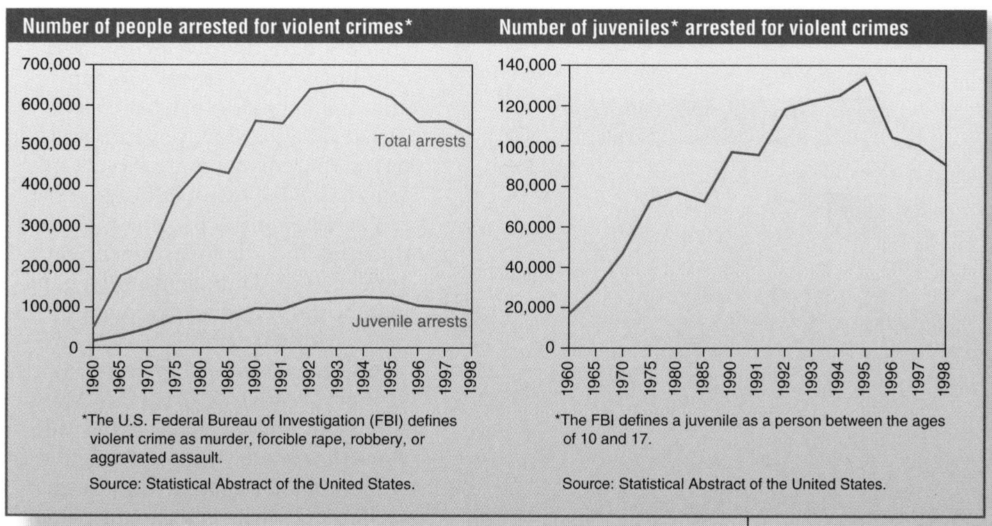

Juveniles commit far fewer violent crimes than adults (above, left), despite public perception to the contrary. Juvenile arrests for violent crimes soared between 1985 and 1995 (above, right), during a period of rising gang membership and gun and drug usage among teen-agers.

Risk factors for violence

So what are the factors that can predict whether a particular child is likely to become violent? Experts have debated whether violent youths are born or made—that is, whether they are aggressive from birth or whether they "learn" violent behavior as they grow—since the 1800's.

Most children who are aggressive or have behavioral disorders early in life do not become serious violent offenders. However, some offenders follow the "early onset" path and commit their first serious violent act before puberty. In studies reported by a number of researchers between 1986 and 1999, between 20 and 45 percent of boys who committed serious violent offenses by ages 16 or 17 had first exhibited violent behavior in childhood. A higher percentage of female serious violent offenders—45 to 69 percent—did the same. Early-onset offenders commit more crimes, and more serious crimes, in adolescence and are more likely to remain violent throughout their lives.

Teens who develop "late-onset" violence—the majority of male adolescent offenders—do not become violent until puberty, at about age 13. As children, they show few or no signs of problem behavior, aggression, or behavioral disorders. As teen-agers, their offenses tend to be less frequent and less serious. Most give up their violent behavior as they reach adulthood.

Certain *risk factors* (influences) increase the likelihood of both patterns of teen violence. Some risk factors, such as being born male, are biological. Statistics consistently confirm that boys are much more likely to be the perpetrators and the victims of violent acts. However, most risk factors come from a child's environment or ability to respond to his or her environment. Children of violent parents who become violent themselves are more likely to have learned this behavior than to have inherited a tendency to act this way.

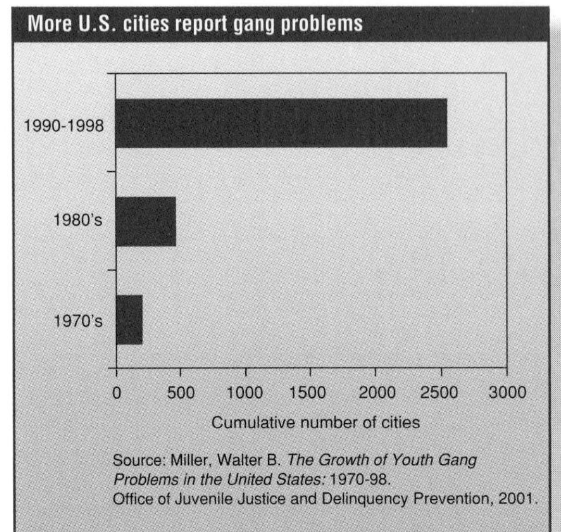

The number of U.S. cities plagued by serious gang problems surged dramatically in the 1990's.

The strongest risk factors during childhood are involvement in serious, but not necessarily violent, criminal behavior; substance use; physical aggression; poverty; and having parents who are violent or criminal. Risk factors during adolescence, when peers become more influential, include involvement with antisocial or delinquent peers; gang membership; and involvement in other criminal acts.

Some risk factors are more subtle, says psychologist Garbarino. Many American families have changed in ways that leave youngsters highly vulnerable to negative influences. As parents work, relocate, divorce, or remarry, children may lose their emotional bearings. Psychologists estimate that 1 in 10 teen-agers suffers from a mental illness or a neurological problem, such as attention deficit hyperactivity disorder (ADHD), severe enough to cause impairment. (ADHD is a condition in which the child finds it difficult to concentrate on a task and may behave in ways that disrupt classrooms and family life.) Fewer than 1 in 5 of these children receives treatment.

Subtle risk factors

Teens with psychiatric or neurologic disorders are not the only youths struggling to study and learn, form healthy relationships, or simply make it through the school day. According to a federal survey of 15,686 public and private school students published in the *Journal of the American Medical Association* in April 2001, nearly 1 of every 3 U.S. children in 6th through 10th grades is bullied. Verbal and physical harassment can create deep-seated humiliation and emotional pain. Several school shootings, including those at high schools in Columbine and Santee, were committed by boys who had been bullied or ostracized.

The intense media attention focused on these shooters may in itself increase the likelihood of violence by inspiring "copycats." "Some adolescents are particularly prone to the desire to have the kind of instantaneous and intense notoriety and attention that are in stark contrast to the reality of their lives, which often are bleak and alienated and isolated," says psychologist Meloy.

Depictions of violence on television, in films, and in video games also have an impact. The American Medical Association, American Psychiatric Association, American Academy of Child Psychiatry, and American Psychological Association have all expressed concern that continual exposure to violent entertainment makes violence appear normal and acceptable. According to the Lion and Lamb Project, an organization that lobbies against violent entertainment, a long-range study that followed 875 children

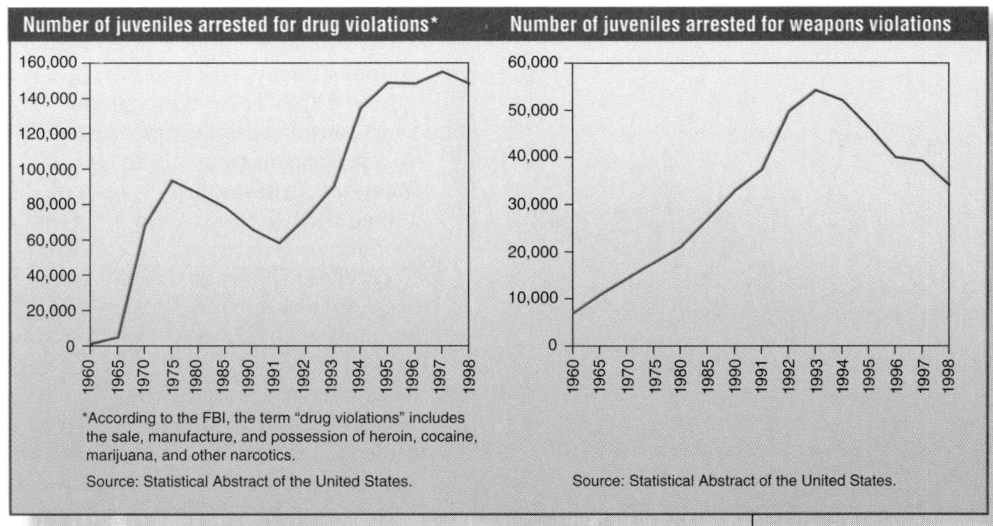

*According to the FBI, the term "drug violations" includes the sale, manufacture, and possession of heroin, cocaine, marijuana, and other narcotics.

Source: Statistical Abstract of the United States.

Source: Statistical Abstract of the United States.

The number of juveniles arrested for drug violations (above, left) fell during the 1980's, when government agencies waged a campaign against illegal drug usage. The arrest rate rose again in the 1990's. Juvenile arrests for weapons violations began to fall in the mid-1990's (above, right), when federal and state legislatures passed stronger gun ownership laws, and the justice system began a stronger crackdown on offenders.

showed that early viewing of violent TV programs is related to later aggression, including violent crimes, spousal abuse, and child abuse.

Drug or alcohol abuse add to the risk. In numerous analyses, school violence has been linked with alcohol and marijuana and with the availability of illegal drugs on school property. In one study of teen mass murders, the majority of the killers used a variety of legal and illegal drugs as well as alcohol, not necessarily at the time of a shooting, but in the weeks and months leading up to it.

Experts believe the most significant factor contributing to teen violence is the availability of guns. Although fewer teens reported carrying guns in the late 1990's than had in the 1980's, firearms

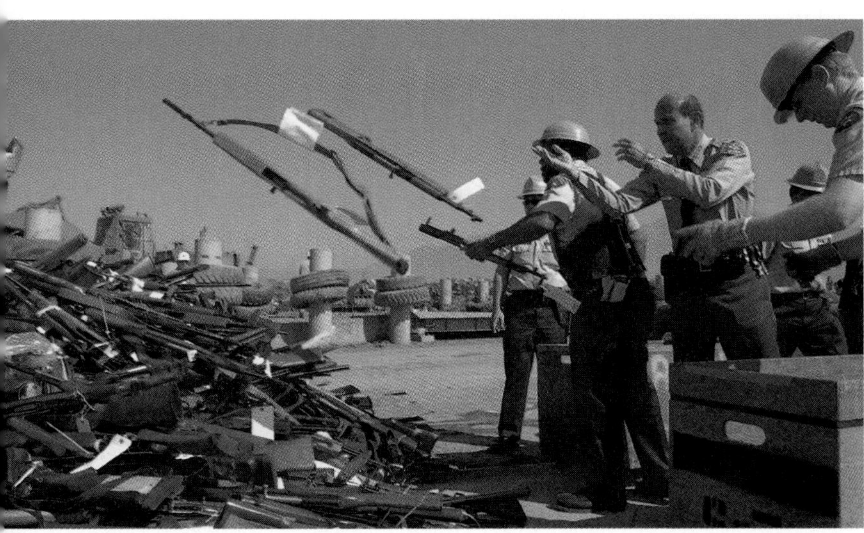

Law enforcement officers in Los Angeles (left) unload confiscated guns into a pile at a steel company lot, where the weapons were later melted down for use in various construction projects.

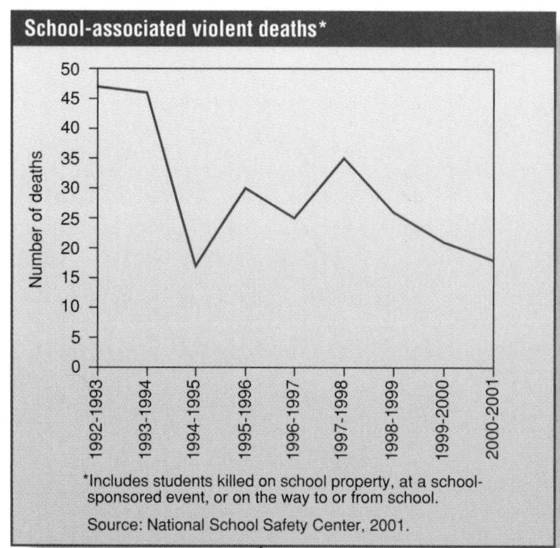

During the 1990's, the number of school shootings in the United States—which make up less than 1 percent of teens killed—actually declined.

remained in wide use. According to CDC statistics, about 1 in 20 high school students reported having a gun in 1999. Teens who commit mass murders are far more likely to use firearms than any other weapons. In several cases, they obtained their firearms from a parent's or relative's house. Some school shooters have reported a long-standing fascination with firearms and spent much of their lives immersed in gun culture.

Experts agree that being "at risk" does not doom any child to a life of violence. There is no single underlying trigger for teen violence. However, the more risk factors that a child experiences, the greater the chance of violent behavior. According to the surgeon general's report, a 10-year-old exposed to 6 or more risk factors is 10 times as likely to be violent by age 18 as a 10-year-old exposed to only one risk factor.

Factors that decrease violence

Psychologists and criminologists also have identified factors and approaches that can decrease the likelihood of violence—as well as approaches that do not work. During the 1980's, many experts considered the prospect of halting teen violence to be bleak. The only option seemed to be putting dangerous teens behind bars by sentencing them in adult courts. According to the surgeon general's report, research over the past 20 years has shown that such an approach is not effective. Teens tried and sentenced

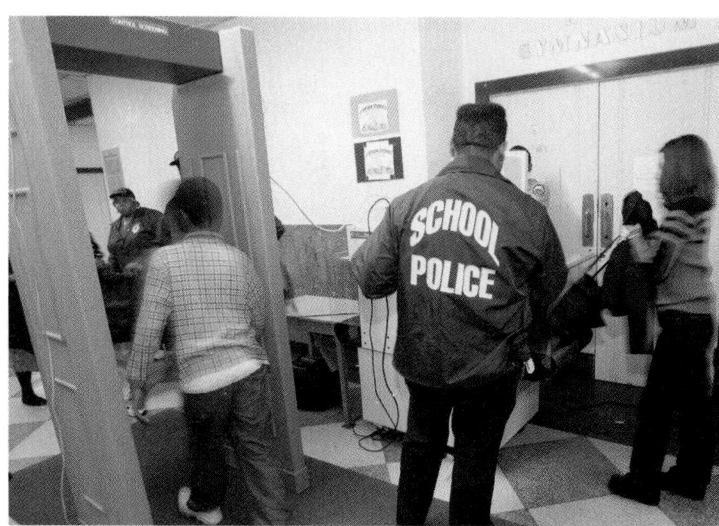

In October 1999, Philadelphia students enter their high school through a metal detector that screens for weapons. Many schools adopted such safety measures after several highly publicized school shootings.

in adult courts are more likely to engage in further criminal behavior than those who remain in the juvenile justice system. Boot camps, which are modeled on military training, or shock programs such as Scared Straight, in which teens visit prisons and attend lectures given by prisoners, also have not yielded good results.

The most promising approaches, according to the surgeon general, are those that focus on prevention rather than punishment. One such program, called Multidimensional Treatment Foster Care, places young offenders with couples specifically trained to work with violent teens. The couples have round-the-clock access to expert support for help in solving problems as they occur. The teaching of problem-solving and conflict-management techniques to students and clamping down on bullying in schools have also proven to be effective.

The surgeon general's report also noted that certain organizations are showing promising results. S.A.V.E. (Students Against Violence Everywhere) asks teens to pledge that they will respect others and oppose physical or verbal abuse based on race, religion, or gender. Members of Youth Crime Watch train teens to watch out for each other and make anonymous reports when they learn about possible trouble.

There are a number of less tangible factors that help prevent teen violence. Regardless of income or environment, youngsters who feel connected to their parents—or to a teacher or community leader—are less likely to behave violently. A commitment to school, recognition for performance in various mainstream activities, and supportive friends who are involved in conventional activities are all important factors.

"The most hopeful thing," says Meloy, "is that all these efforts are enhancing communication both among teens and between teens and adults. Everyone is paying more attention to teenagers' emotional states, and that's what will lead to the greatest benefits." While America's schools and streets have become less dangerous for teen-agers, most experts agree that the nation still faces the challenge of making those schools and streets truly safe and free of violence. ■■■

Risk factors for violent criminal behavior*

When violent behavior begins before puberty (ages 6 to 11)

- involvement in serious, but not violent, criminal offenses
- substance use
- being male
- poverty
- antisocial parents
- physical aggressiveness
- hyperactivity
- weak social ties
- harsh, lax, or inconsistent parental discipline
- antisocial behavior
- exposure to television violence
- poor attitude toward and performance in school

When violent behavior begins after puberty (ages 12 to 14)

- weak ties to conventional peers
- ties to antisocial or delinquent peers
- belonging to a gang
- involvement in serious, but not violent, criminal offenses
- restlessness
- poor parental supervision, inconsistent discipline, and low parental involvement
- aggression (in males only)
- being male
- poor attitude toward and performance in school

*Listed in descending order of importance.
Source: Youth Violence: A Report of the Surgeon General. 2001.

Croatia. The prosecution of suspected war criminals developed into a major political issue in 2001 after Croatia's governing coalition cooperated with the United Nations International Criminal Tribunal for the Former Yugoslavia in apprehending alleged war criminals.

In February, Croatian authorities issued an arrest warrant for former General Mirko Norac for war crimes alleged to have been committed in the central Croatian town of Gospic in 1991. On Feb. 11, 2001, approximately 100,000 Croatians in Split, a coastal city, staged public protests against the investigation. Angered over the government's cooperation with the tribunal, the protesters called for early elections in an effort to bring down the politically moderate government. Following the protests, members of the Croatian Democratic Union, the former governing coalition in Parliament, demanded that the government end its cooperation with the tribunal.

On February 21, Norac surrendered to police after government officials announced that Croatian authorities, not the tribunal, would investigate the charges against him. However, Croatian justice officials repeatedly postponed the trial against Norac and four codefendants due to various legal and technical issues. In July, Prime Minister Ivica Racan's ruling coalition survived a no-confidence vote in parliament. The vote had been called in response to the government's cooperation with the war crimes tribunal.

European relations. The president of Croatia, Stjepan Mesic, and the president of Yugoslavia, Vojislav Kostunica—meeting in June at a conference of central and southeastern European leaders—announced in Stressa, Italy, that their countries had no interest in occupying Bosnian territory. Both presidents expressed their support for the Dayton Accords, a 1995 agreement to end the civil war in Bosnia that began in 1992. Mesic and Kostunica also called for the full normalization of relations between Croatia and Yugoslavia.

In July 2001, the governments of Croatia and Slovenia approved a border agreement. Croatia granted Slovenia the right to use territorial waters near Piran Bay, which allows Slovenia full access to the Adriatic Sea.

Croatia and officials of the European Union (EU) signed a stabilization and association agreement in late October. Croatian officials expressed hope that the agreement was a first step toward eventual EU membership.

Economy. Croatia's economy grew at a rate of 4.2 percent in the first half of 2001. Unemployment remained steady at approximately 21 percent. ☐ Sharon Wolchik

See also **Bosnia-Herzegovina; Europe; Yugoslavia.**

Cuba. Cuban President Fidel Castro marked his 75th birthday on Aug. 13, 2001, amid mounting concern over his health and the future of Cuba after his death. In June, Castro nearly collapsed from heat exhaustion during a long outdoor speech in Havana, the capital. Castro later told reporters that he expected his 70-year-old brother, Raul, Cuba's defense minister, to succeed him upon his death.

Rocky U.S.-Cuba relations. In a May Day speech, Castro lashed out at the United States and the Free Trade Area of the Americas (FTAA), a proposed free-trade zone encompassing the entire Western Hemisphere. All countries in the hemisphere except Cuba agreed to create the FTAA by 2005 at an April 2001 summit meeting in Quebec City, Canada. Castro warned that the United States would use the FTAA to control every institution in Latin America, ranging from airlines and banks to pizza parlors.

In July, U.S. President George W. Bush ordered stricter enforcement of the U.S. trade *embargo* (restriction on commerce) against Cuba, enacted in 1960. Bush said the U.S. government would crack down on unauthorized travel to Cuba; enforce limits on *remittances* (sending of money) from Cubans living in the United States; and increase support for prodemocracy activists in Cuba.

Cuban spies in U.S. On September 21, U.S. authorities charged Ana Belen Montes, an expert on Cuba at the U.S. Defense Intelligence Agency, with spying for the Castro government for at least five years. Montes entered a plea of no contest to the indictment. On June 8, a federal court in Miami convicted five Cubans of spying for Castro's government. One member of the spy group was also convicted of conspiracy to commit murder in connection with a 1996 incident in which a Cuban fighter jet downed an anti-Castro organization's plane, killing four Americans.

Terrorist attacks set back tourism. Cuba's economy suffered a major setback when tourism to the island declined following the terrorist attacks on the United States on Sept. 11, 2001. According to Cuba's tourism ministry, one-third of the 36,000 hotel rooms in Cuba were vacant in late October, and 20 of 225 hotels had closed. Cuba relies on tourism as a major source of foreign exchange.

Hurricane Michelle left five people dead and caused millions of dollars worth of damage in Cuba on November 4. The U.S. government authorized U.S. companies to sell food and medicine to Cuba to help Cubans recover from Michelle. It was the first such sale allowed in the history of the U.S. embargo. ☐ Nathan A. Haverstock

See also **Latin America; Terrorism: A Special Feature,** p. 38; **United States, Government of the.**

Cyprus. See **Middle East.**

Czech Republic. Protests in the Czech Republic over the highly unpopular appointment of a new director of Czech state television escalated in early 2001 into the largest street demonstrations in Prague, the capital, since the 1989 revolution that brought down the Communist government. Protesting journalists, who occupied the state TV newsroom in a sit-down strike, charged that the new director, Jiri Hodac, intended to run the news facility for the benefit of the Czech Republic's two largest political parties. The two parties have shared power since 1998.

The political crisis ended in mid-January 2001, when Hodac resigned as director. The Czech parliament later passed a reform measure to depoliticize the Czech Television Council, which oversees state television.

Supersonic jet controversy. In January, the Czech government asked aerospace companies to bid on the manufacture of 24 to 36 supersonic jet fighters for the Czech Air Force. In May, the government of the United States, protesting certain conditions of the bid process, barred U.S. manufacturers from submitting estimates. In a June meeting with his Czech counterpart, U.S. Defense Secretary Donald Rumsfeld urged the Czech government to postpone plans to buy the jets. Rumsfeld expressed concerns that the cost of the jets would interfere with ongoing reforms of the Czech Army, particularly the equipping of ground forces. Some North Atlantic Treaty Organization (NATO) officials echoed Rumsfeld's concerns.

Relations with the European Union. Officials of the European Union (EU) continued to view the Czech Republic as a candidate for early admission to the EU. At a June 2001 summit in Gothenberg, Sweden, EU officials set a timetable for qualifying nations to complete negotiations in late 2002 and gain full EU membership in time for parliamentary elections in 2004. However, officials with the European Parliament, an advisory body of the EU, warned the Czech government against continuing its heavy deficit spending. The Czech Republic's budget deficit grew from 1.8 percent of *gross domestic product* (GDP—the value of all goods and services produced in a country in a given period) in 1999 to an estimated 9.4 percent in 2001.

Economy. The Czech Republic's GDP grew by 3.5 percent in the first half of 2001. However, EU economists predicted that growth would slow in late 2001, due to the global economic downturn. In 2001, the rate of inflation climbed to 5.9 percent, compared with 3.9 percent in late 2000. Unemployment remained constant at 8.5 percent, according to figures released in August 2001.

☐ Sharon L. Wolchik

See also **Europe**.

More than 50,000 people crowd Wenceslas Square in Prague, capital of the Czech Republic, to support striking television journalists in January. They claimed the appointment of a new director of state television was politically motivated.

Dallas. The United States Census Bureau released population statistics on March 12, 2001, showing that Hispanics had became the largest ethnic group in Dallas. In 2000, Hispanics made up 36 percent of city residents, compared with about 21 percent in 1990. The shift in the city's ethnic majority intensified the pressure to increase Hispanic representation in city government and on the Dallas school board. In 2001, the 15-member Dallas City Council had two Hispanic members. The Census Bureau also reported that 35 percent of Dallas's population in 2000 was white, a 14-percent drop from 1990. The number of African Americans had grown since 1990 by about 5 percent, to 26 percent. Dallas's total population rose by 18 percent between 1990 and 2000, allowing the city to regain from San Antonio the position of second most populous city in Texas, after Houston.

City government. In October 2001, the mayor and other members of the city council began receiving annual salaries for the first time. In May, city voters had approved a referendum to pay the mayor $60,000 and city council members $37,500 yearly. In eight previous referendums, voters had refused to raise the mayor's and councilors' pay above $50 per meeting.

Ron Kirk, Dallas's first African American mayor, resigned on November 7 to run for the U.S. Senate in the 2002 Democratic primary. First elected mayor in 1995, Kirk helped pass the largest bond issue in Dallas's history and brought $600 million in new economic development to southern Dallas.

In June and August 2001, six former top-ranking Dallas police administrators who claimed they had been illegally demoted won settlements totaling at least $6 million from the Dallas city government. The six were among nine police executives who had sued the city after incoming Dallas Police Chief Terrell Bolton, the first African American to head the department, had replaced them with lower-ranking officers. Bolton, who contended the new administrators were more loyal to his policies, had argued for the right to appoint his own executive team. Many council members supported Bolton's position, saying that they had approved the settlements to avoid additional legal fees.

Revitalization coordinator. In August, a development group composed of business and city officials chose the Madison Retail Group of Washington, D.C., to coordinate a major effort to revitalize downtown Dallas. In May, the Boeing Company, a major aerospace developer and manufacturer, had cited a lack of downtown retail development as one reason for its decision to move its corporate headquarters from Seattle to Chicago, rather than to Dallas.

Love Field plan. On April 11, the city council approved a plan for Love Field, Dallas's municipal airport, that resolved a long-running dispute with nearby Fort Worth, Texas. In 1998, Fort Worth took legal action to block expansion of Love Field, arguing that growth at Love would threaten business at the Dallas/Fort Worth International Airport, a larger, newer airport located between the two cities. The new plan called for transforming Love Field into a regional airport; limiting expansion to 32 gates from the current 29; and the demolition of one concourse.

New arena. The American Airlines Center, located on the northwest edge of downtown Dallas, opened to the public on July 28, 2001, with a sold-out concert by the Eagles, a rock group. The city and the owners of the Dallas Mavericks professional basketball team and the Dallas Stars professional hockey team jointly financed the $421-million arena. Both teams will play home games there. American Airlines paid $195 million for naming rights to the arena.

Aikman retires. Quarterback Troy Aikman, who led the Dallas Cowboys to three Super Bowl victories during a 12-year career, was released from the team's roster on March 7. Aikman had spent most of his final season off the field because of injuries. □ Henry Tatum

See also **Census; City.**

Dance. The American Ballet Theatre (ABT) soared artistically in 2001 under the direction of Kevin McKenzie. Backstage, however, the company fell into a shambles. About 30 of the company's 40 staff members resigned or were fired during 2000 and 2001. Executive director Louis G. Spisto resigned under pressure in July 2001. In October, the ABT appointed Wallace Chappell as its new executive director.

The ABT continued to perform a primarily classical program during its travels in 2001. However, the company also staged major new productions featuring choreographers from modern dance. *Black Tuesday* by Paul Taylor premiered in April during the ABT's run at the Kennedy Center for the Performing Arts in Washington, D.C. Set to songs from the *Great Depression* (a worldwide business slump of the 1930's), this suite of dances presented an assemblage of down-and-out characters spiced with Taylor's characteristic ironic sense of humor.

Mark Morris, who in recent years had made as many works for ballet troupes as for his own Mark Morris Dance Company, created *Gong*, which the ABT premiered in May 2001 at the beginning of the group's engagement at the Metropolitan Opera House in New York City. The title reflected a Balinese influence on the music, written by the late Canadian composer

Colin McPhee. Morris's choreography fused the formal qualities of Southeast Asian dance with ballet language.

The ABT's most anticipated 2001 premier, however, received generally negative reviews. *The Pied Piper*, first seen in May and billed as a dance stage technological breakthrough, used film projections and digitally animated puppets with choreography by former Paul Taylor dancer David Parsons.

The Mark Morris Dance Company celebrated its 20th anniversary in 2001 with a three-week season in March at the Brooklyn Academy of Music (BAM) in New York City, where it performed 16 of Morris's works. The group moved into its first permanent home in March, a new building designed for the company across the street from the BAM.

Morris's creative output was as strong as ever through the 2001 season. In addition to *Gong* for the ABT, he choreographed *A Garden* for the San Francisco Ballet. Set to Richard Strauss's *Tanzsuite*, it premiered in February at the War Memorial Opera House in San Francisco. Morris's own group premiered his *V*, set to the Schumann piano and string quintet in E flat, in October at the Sadler's Wells Theatre in London.

New York City Ballet choreographer-in-residence Christopher Wheeldon created two new works in 2001 that premiered at the New York State Theater in New York City's Lincoln Center for the Performing Arts. His spare *Polyphonia*, set to music by Gyorgy Ligeti, opened in January. *Variations Serieuses*, a comedy set to music by Felix Mendelssohn, followed in May. The piece offered an inside look at the ballet world, featuring a temperamental star and her aspiring understudy; a stage manager dreaming of being a dancer; and other stock theater figures. Ian Falconer's set showed the audience the ballet from the perspective of the wings, with the footlights on one side of the stage and the backdrop on the other. New York City Ballet artistic director Peter Martins also created two new ballets, *Quartet for Strings* and *Viva Verdi* with scores by Giuseppe Verdi. The troupe premiered both pieces in Parma, Italy, in September during a festival honoring the composer's l00th birthday.

Australian dance figured prominently among dance attractions in the United States during 2001. The Australian Dance Theatre presented Garry Stewart's *Birdbrain*, a new take on *Swan Lake*. Instead of tutus, the swans wore T-shirts, and the dance language included break-dancing and gymnastics as well as classical ballet. The Australian Dance Theatre performed in October in Toronto, Ottawa, and New York City. A group that founder Gideon Obarzanek called Chunky Move appeared in Ann Arbor, Michigan, and at the Next Wave Festival at the BAM. Chunky Move performed *Crumpled*, a series of calculated collisions, and *Corrupted 2,* whose title alluded to electronic data, with choreography full of abrupt stops, starts, and other "mistakes."

A third company from Australia, the Bangarra Dance Theatre, was inspired by the continent's Aboriginal cultures. Stephen Page's *Corroboree* was the company's main production in 2001. The title referred to a meeting ground where Aboriginal people engage in ritual, dance, and song. Bangarra's U.S. tour began in October in Princeton, New Jersey, and ended in November in Torrance, California.

The ancient court and folk dances of Cambodia inspired a program—*Dance, the Spirit of Cambodia*, a project of the Royal University of Fine Arts in Phnom Penh—which toured in North America in 2001. The very existence of the ensemble was noteworthy, since an estimated 90 percent of all Cambodian artists perished during the Khmer Rouge regime in the mid-1970's. (The Khmer Rouge were Cambodian Communists who took over the country and were responsible for the deaths of over 1 million people.) Some of the company's dances were based on carved figures at Angkor Wat, a temple complex constructed in the 1100's. Other dances related stories featuring whimsical animals and all-too-human deities. The ensemble's tour began at the Center for the Arts Theater at Wesleyan University in Middletown, Connecticut, in August 2001 and ended at the Kennedy Center in September.

England's Royal Ballet's visit to the United States was of special interest because of its emphasis on the ballets of the late Sir Frederick Ashton, whom most critics consider one of the greatest choreographers of the 1900's. Appearing in June 2001 at the Kennedy Center, the troupe danced three full ballets by Ashton and assorted *pas de deux* (dances for two performers). One of these duets, *Soupirs*, had been created for British stars Anthony Dowell and Antoinette Sibley near the ends of their careers. They danced it again in a surprise appearance. The Royal Ballet performed *Swan Lake* at the Wang Center in Boston later in June.

In Boston. The Boston Ballet announced the appointment of Mikko Nissinen as the company's new artistic director in September, following the hasty departure of Maina Gielgud. Boston's Dance Umbrella, an important organization that presented modern dance in New England, folded in April for financial reasons.

Houston Ballet. Ben Stevenson resigned as the director of the Houston Ballet in February after leading the company for 25 years. He later agreed to stay on as coartistic director with Trinidad Vives.

☐ Nancy Goldner

Deaths

in 2001 included those listed below, who were Americans unless otherwise indicated.

Aaliyah (Aaliyah Haughton) (1979–August 25), rhythm-and-blues singer whose hits included "Try Again" and "Are You That Somebody."

Adams, Douglas (1952–May 11), British author who wrote *The Hitchhiker's Guide to the Galaxy* and the BBC science-fiction series "Doctor Who."

Adler, Larry (1914–August 7), harmonica player who introduced the instrument to the concert hall.

Adler, Mortimer (1902–June 28), educator, philosopher, and author who created the Great Books program to champion the teaching of classic texts.

Alzana, the Great (Harold Davis) (1918–February 16), English-born circus acrobat who was billed as "the greatest and most foolhardy high-wire artist who ever lived."

Ammons, A. R. (1926–February 25), poet who won National Book Awards in 1972 and 1993.

Anastasi, Anne (1908–May 4), psychologist whose groundbreaking 1954 textbook *Psychological Testing* revolutionized standardized testing.

Anderson, Poul (1926–July 31), physics-trained author of the scrupulously correct science-fiction novels *Tau Zero* (1970), *A Midsummer Tempest* (1974), and *The Boat of a Million Years* (1989).

Jack Lemmon, actor

Anthony, Earl (1938–August 14), pro bowler who won 41 professional titles, was named Professional Bowling Association bowler of the year six times, and was the first to exceed $1 million in winnings.

Arkoff, Samuel Z. (1918–September 16), cofounder of American International Pictures who produced classic B movies of the 1960's: the Vincent Price films based on Edgar Allan Poe stories and the Annette Funicello-Frankie Avalon beach series.

Ash, Mary Kay (1918–November 22), businesswoman who founded the Mary Kay Inc. cosmetics empire.

Atkins, Chet (Chester Burton Atkins) (1924–June 30), guitarist and record producer who changed the sound of country music in the 1950's and 1960's, which contributed to moving country music into mainstream popular culture.

Balthus (Balthasar Klossowski) (1908–February 18), French painter who was best known for his mysterious portraits and landscapes.

Barnard, Christiaan (1922–September 2), South African surgeon who in 1967 performed the first human heart transplant.

Birendra Bir Bikram Shah Dev (1945–June 1), king of Nepal who was murdered by his son.

Boudreau, Lou (1917–August 10), Hall of Fame shortstop who helped lead the Cleveland Indians to a World Series championship in 1948.

Bradman, Sir Donald (1908–February 25), Australian cricketer who dominated the sport between 1928 and 1948 and was rated the greatest player in the history of cricket.

Broun, Heywood Hale (1918–September 5), sports writer and television commentator who was known for his droll sense of humor and outlandish sport jackets.

Brown, Les (1912–January 4), orchestra leader whose Band of Renown was one of the last surviving big bands of the swing era.

Buhl, Bob (1928–February 16), right-hander who was one of three Milwaukee Braves star pitchers of the 1957 World Series.

Carle, Frankie (Francis Carlone) (1903–March 10), "wizard of the keyboard" and big band leader who composed "Sunrise Serenade."

Cavanna, Betty (Elizabeth Cavanna Harrison) (1909–August 13), author of more than 80 books for young people, including mysteries and romance novels highly popular with teen-age girls.

Chavis, Boozoo (Wilson Anthony Chavis) (1931?–May 5), bandleader and king of button-accordion zydeco music who recorded the hit "Paper in My Shoe" (1954).

Chisolm, J. Julian (1921–June 27), physician who is credited with saving hundreds of lives with his chelation treatment for removing lead from the blood in severe poisoning.

Clermont, Nicolas (1942–April 13), Canadian filmmaker who produced *Bethune: The Making of a Hero* (1990), *This Is My Father* (1998), and *Eye of the Beholder* (1999).

Coca, Imogene (1908–June 2), comedian who helped forge television's "golden age" in the early 1950's playing opposite Sid Caesar in "Your Show of Shows."

Como, Perry (Pierino Como) (1912–May 12), popular singer and television personality who was as well known for his relaxed, low-keyed manner as for his rich voice.

Cram, Donald J. (1919–June 17), chemist who shared the 1987 Nobel Prize in chemistry for synthesizing molecules that mimicked the way enzymes function within living organisms.

Dagmar (Virginia Ruth Egnor) (1922?–October 9), voluptuous "not-so-dumb blond" TV star.

Davidsen, Arthur (1944–July 19), astrophysicist whose research at Johns Hopkins University contributed to human understanding of the composition and density of intergalactic space.

Dale Evans, actress, singer, and composer

Anthony Quinn, actor

Donald Cram, chemist

Eddie Mathews, baseball player

DeCamp, Rosemary (1910–February 20), character actress who most often played mothers, including James Cagney's in *Yankee Doodle Dandy* (1942) and Marlo Thomas's on the TV sitcom "That Girl."

De Cordova, Fred (1910–September 15), producer of such television series as "The Jack Benny Show" and "The Tonight Show" with Johnny Carson.

de Valois, Dame Ninette (Erdis Stannus) (1898–March 8), English dancer and choreographer who founded the Royal Ballet.

Dionne, Yvonne (1934–June 23), one of the Dionne quintuplets—the first surviving quintuplets and the center of a Depression-era media circus.

Donahue, Troy (1936–September 2), film actor and teen heartthrob who appeared in *A Summer Place* (1959) and *Parish* (1961).

Donovan, Carrie (1928–November 12), highly accessorized fashion editor (*The New York Times, Vogue,* and *Harper's Bazaar*) who found fame representing the retail chain Old Navy.

Earnhardt, Dale (1951–February 18), stock car racing legend who won 76 races in his Nascar Winston Cup career. Earnhardt was killed on the last turn of the last lap of the Daytona 500.

Evans, Dale (1912–February 7), actress who appeared in dozens of films with her husband Roy Rogers and composer of "Happy Trails to You" and "The Bible Tells Me So."

Evans, Rowland (1921–March 23), conservative political columnist who with partner Robert Novak wrote "Inside Report" and appeared on the television program "Evans and Novak."

Foster, Willie (1921–May 20), harmonica player who earned international renown as a blues musician, playing with such greats as Muddy Waters.

Francis, Arlene (Arlene Francis Kazanjian) (1907–May 31), actress and television personality who served as a panelist on the television game show "What's My Line" from 1950 to 1975.

Freeman, Kathleen (1919–August 23), veteran character actress who appeared in more than 100 films, including *Singin' in the Rain* (1952), *The Nutty Professor* (1963), and *The Blues Brothers* (1980).

Gebel-Williams, Gunther (1934–July 19), German-born animal trainer who was the number-one attraction at the Ringling Bros. and Barnum & Bailey Circus in the 1970's and 1980's.

Gombrich, E. H. (1909–November 3), Austrian-born English art historian who was best known for his book *The Story of Art*, which was translated into 23 languages and sold millions of copies.

Goring, Percy (1894–July 27), British army engineer who was the last known survivor of Britain's catastrophic World War I Gallipoli campaign in 1915.

Graham, Katharine (1917–July 17), former publisher of *The Washington Post* who led the *Post* during the era of the Pentagon Papers and Watergate and transformed the newspaper from a provincial Washington, D.C., publication into a national institution.

Greco, Jose (1918–January 1), Italian-born, American dancer who popularized Spanish dance, particularly flamenco.

Greer, Jane (1924–August 24), actress called the "queen of film noir" for her roles in such films as *Out of the Past* (1947) *and The Big Steal* (1949).

Haley, Jack, Jr. (1933–April 21), award-winning producer who was best known for nostalgic documentaries, including *That's Entertainment* (1974).

Hanna, William (1910–March 22), animator who, with his partner, Joseph Barbera, created dozens of cartoon figures, including Tom and Jerry, the Flintstones, the Jetsons, and Yogi Bear.

Harrison, George (1943–November 29), Beatles lead guitarist who composed "Something," "Here Comes the Sun," and "While My Guitar Gently Weeps"; led the group's spiritual quest into Eastern philosophy; and created the concept of the charity rock concert with his benefit to aid refugees in Bangladesh.

Hartford, John (1937–June 4), bluegrass musician and country music composer who wrote the 1967 hit "Gentle on My Mind."

Henderson, Joe (1937–June 30), innovative jazz saxophonist of the post-bebop era who composed "Isotope" and "Black Narcissus."

Herblock (Herbert Lawrence Block) (1909–October 7) Pulitzer Prize-winning journalist considered the dean of American political cartoonists who coined the term "McCarthyism" to describe Senator Joseph McCarthy's political tactics during the "red scare" of the early 1950's.

Hewett, Christopher (1921–August 3), British actor who appeared in the film comedies *The Lavender Hill Mob* (1951) and *The Producers* (1968) and played the title role of the television series "Mr. Belvedere."

Hewlett, William (1913–January 12), engineer and Hewlett-Packard cofounder who was regarded as one of the pioneers of Silicon Valley and the computer age.

Hillegass, Clifton Keith (1918?–May 5), creator and publisher of Cliffs Notes, the study guides that Hillegass originally published as "Cliff's Notes."

Hooker, John Lee (1917–June 21), blues guitarist and singer—"I'm in the Mood" (1951) and "Boom Boom" (1962)—whose eclectic, one-chord boogies provided a foundation for rock music.

Horwich, Frances R. (1908–July 22), educator who became known as Miss Frances as the host of the long-running children's television program "Ding Dong School," which premiered in 1952.

Hoyle, Sir Fred (1915–August 20), English astrophysicist who was awarded the Nobel Prize for explaining how the heavier elements were formed. Hoyle also coined the term "big bang" in the 1940's to ridicule the theory that the universe originated in a massive explosion.

Hume, Paul (1916?–November 26), *Washington Post* music critic who became a focus of presidential ire when he panned the singing voice of Harry Truman's daughter, Margaret, in 1950.

Hunter, Rita (1933–April 29), British soprano who won international fame in the 1970's for her performances in Wagner's Ring Cycle.

John Lewis, jazz pianist

Chet Atkins, guitarist

Ingstad, Helge (1899–March 29), Norwegian adventurer and novelist who identified the site in Newfoundland where Vikings landed some 500 years before Columbus.

Jansson, Tove (1914–June 27), Finnish author and illustrator of the Moomins children's books, which were translated into 30 languages.

Johnson, J. J. (1924–February 4), influential jazz trombonist who played with some of the finest musicians of the post-World War II era, including Miles Davis and Charlie Parker.

Johnson, Johnnie (1915–January 30), English fighter pilot of World War II who earned the title "great ace" for shooting down 38 German planes while completing some 700 missions.

Jones, Etta (1928–October 16), jazz singer who was best known for her 1960 recording of "Don't Go to Strangers."

Kabila, Laurent (1939–January 16), president of the Democratic Republic of Congo who drove dictator Mobutu Sese Seko from power in 1997.

Kael, Pauline (1919–September 3), provocative and highly influential film critic whose reviews appeared in *The New Yorker* for 24 years.

Karnilova, Maria (1920–April 20), ballerina with the American Ballet Theatre who won a Tony Award

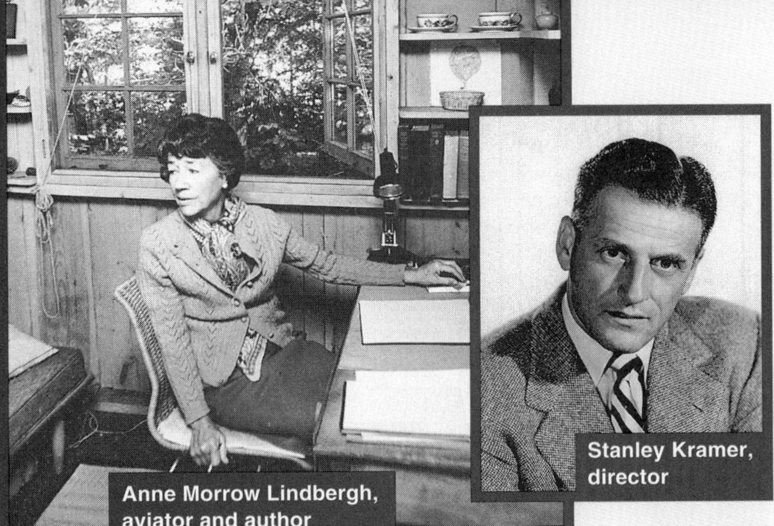

Anne Morrow Lindbergh, aviator and author

Stanley Kramer, director

Eudora Welty, writer

for her performance as Golde in the Broadway musical *Fiddler on the Roof* (1964).

Kesey, Ken (1935–November 10), author of *One Flew Over the Cuckoo's Nest* (1962) and *Sometimes a Great Notion* (1964) who was also the subject of Tom Wolfe's *The Electric Kool-Aid Acid Test* (1968).

Ketcham, Hank (1920–June 1), cartoonist who created "Dennis the Menace" in 1951.

Knowles, John (1926–November 29), author whose coming-of-age novel *A Separate Peace* became an instant classic when it was published in 1960.

Kramer, Stanley (1913–February 19), producer and director whose films, including *High Noon* (1952), *Judgment at Nuremberg* (1961), and *Guess Who's Coming to Dinner* (1967), examined a variety of social issues.

Lapidus, Morris (1902–January 18), architect who was best known as the designer of such glitzy and extravagant hotels as the Fountainebleau and Eden Roc in Miami Beach, Florida.

Lemmon, Jack (John Uhler Lemmon III) (1925–June 27), Academy Award-winning stage, screen, and television actor whose versatility ranged from comedy—*Some Like It Hot* (1959), *The Apartment* (1960), and *The Odd Couple* (1968)—to drama—*Days of Wine and Roses* (1962), *Save the Tiger* (1973), and *Long Day's Journey into Night* (1986).

Leswick, Tony (1923–July 1), hockey winger for the New York Rangers, Detroit Red Wings, and Chicago Blackhawks whose goal in overtime in game 7 won the 1954 Stanley Cup championship for the Red Wings.

Lewis, John (1920–March 29), pianist, composer, and arranger who was the musical director of the Modern Jazz Quartet and a leader of the "cool jazz" movement of the 1950's.

Lindbergh, Anne Morrow (1906–February 7), aviator wife of Charles Lindbergh and author who wrote 13 books, including the 1955 best seller *Gift from the Sea.*

Livingston, Jay (1915–October 17), Hollywood composer and lyricist who with partner Ray Evans wrote Academy Award-winning "Buttons and Bows" (1948), and "Que Sera, Sera" (1956).

Ludlum, Robert (1927–March 12), prolific novelist who was best known for his Jason Bourne series of thrillers involving international intrigue.

Perry Como, singer

Ann Sothern, actress

Mansfield, Mike (1903–October 5), Montana senator who served as majority leader longer than any senator in history (1961-1977).

Masters, William H. (1915–February 16), physician who with Virginia E. Johnson revolutionized research in human sexuality and wrote the 1966 best seller *Human Sexual Response.*

Mathews, Eddie (1933–February 18), Hall of Fame third baseman who hit 512 home runs and who was the only member of the Braves to remain with the team as it moved from Boston to Milwaukee to Atlanta.

McCarty, Theodore (1910?–April 1), Gibson Guitar Co. president who designed the iconic Les Paul, Flying V, and Firebird electric guitars.

McCorkle, Susannah (1946–May 19), cabaret jazz-pop singer noted for her pure style.

Mordecai Richler, Canadian author

Katherine Graham, publisher

Isaac Stern, violinist

McGuire, Dorothy (1918–September 13), actress who appeared in such films as *A Tree Grows in Brooklyn* (1945), *Gentlemen's Agreement* (1947), and *Friendly Persuasion* (1956).

McKay, John (1923–June 10), football coach who led the University of Southern California to four national championships and five Rose Bowl victories.

McVeigh, Timothy (1968–June 11), the man convicted and executed for the 1995 bombing of the Murrah Federal Building in Oklahoma City, Oklahoma, which killed 168 people.

Moon, Robert Aurand (1917–April 10), career postal employee who created the U.S. Postal Service's ZIP code system in 1963.

Moore, Jo-Jo (Joseph Moore) (1908–April 1), All-Star outfielder who helped lead the New York Giants to three National League championships in the 1930's.

Narayan, R. K. (1906–May 13), novelist whose stories of small-town life, written in English, were among the first by an Indian author to reach an international audience.

O'Connor, Carroll (1924–June 21), film and television actor whose portrayal of Archie Bunker on television's "All in the Family" made the strangely lovable bigot emblematic of the social turmoil of the 1970's.

Painter, John (1888–March 1), oldest American veteran. Painter drove horse-drawn ammunition caissons in France during World War I.

Parker, Eddie (1931–February 2), pool player known as "Fast Eddie" whose life inspired the book and film *The Hustler.*

Patri, Stella Nicole (1896–March 31), last known survivor of the 1906 San Francisco earthquake.

Phillips, John (1935–March 18), singer and Mamas and the Papas founder who wrote "California Dreamin'," "Monday Monday," and "San Francisco (Be Sure to Wear Some Flowers in Your Hair)."

Prieste, Hal (1896-April 19), oldest U.S. Olympian who won the bronze medal in platform diving at the 1920 games in Antwerp, Belgium.

Quinn, Anthony (Rudolph Oaxaca) (1915–June 3), Mexican American actor who appeared in more than 200 films and received Academy Awards for best supporting actor for *Viva Zapata* (1952) and *Lust for Life* (1956) but was best known for his portrayal of *Zorba the Greek* (1964).

Richler, Mordecai (1931–July 3), Canadian author who created vivid portraits of Montreal's Jewish community in such novels as *The Apprenticeship of Duddy Kravitz* (1959), *St. Urbain's Horseman* (1971), and *Barney's Version* (1997).

Richter, Mischa (1910–March 23), Ukrainian-born artist whose drawings and cartoons were featured in *The New Yorker* and other magazines for more than 50 years.

Ripley, S. Dillon (1913–March 12), biologist who

Actress Imogene Coca, with actor Sid Caesar

added eight new museums and launched *Smithsonian* magazine during his tenure (1964-1984) as head of the Smithsonian Institution.

Ritchie, Michael (1938–April 16), movie and television director who was best known for the films *Downhill Racer* (1969) and *The Candidate* (1972).

Rogers, William P. (1913–January 2), lawyer who served in the Eisenhower Cabinet as attorney general (1957-1961) and in the Nixon Cabinet as secretary of state (1969-1973).

Rutherford, Maud Russell (1897–March 8), singer and dancer who introduced the Charleston, the 1920's dance craze, to Broadway in the 1922 musical *Liza.*

Schultes, Richard E. (1915–April 10), botanist and preeminent authority on medicinal and hallucinogenic plants for whom more than 120 newly discovered species were named.

Secombe, Sir Harry (1921–April 11), English comedian whose tenor voice and antics on the "Goon Show" radio program made him one of Britain's most beloved entertainers.

Shull, Clifford G. (1915–March 31), physicist who was awarded the Nobel Prize in physics in 1994 for neutron scattering—bouncing neutrons off molecules to investigate molecular structure.

Sinopoli, Giuseppe (1946–April 20), Italian composer and conductor of the Romantic and modern repertory who collapsed and died while conducting Verdi's *Aida* in Berlin.

Sothern, Ann (Harriet Lake) (1909–March 15), film actress who starred in the "Maisie" series, *Lady Be Good* and *Panama Hattie,* and two early TV series, "Private Secretary" and "The Ann Sothern Show."

Slaughter, Frank (1908–May 17), author of best-selling novels who typically wrote about his own original profession, medicine.

Snow, Sebastian (1929–April 20), British amateur explorer and eccentric who helped confirm the source of the Amazon River in 1951.

Spence, Floyd (1928–August 16), Republican congressman from South Carolina's 2nd Congressional District who advocated smaller government and increased military spending.

Spence, Hartzell (1908–May 9), founder and executive editor of *Yank* magazine who is credited with inventing the word "pinup" to describe the pictures of bathing-suit-clad movie stars he published during World War II.

Stanley, Kim (1925–August 20), acclaimed actress who stared on Broadway in William Inge's *Picnic* (1955) and *Bus Stop* (1955) and in such films as *The Goddess* (1958), *Seance on a Wet Afternoon* (1964), and *Frances* (1982).

Stargell, Willie (1940–April 9), Hall of Fame home run hitter who helped lead the Pittsburgh Pirates to World Series championships in 1971 and 1979.

Stern, Isaac (1920–September 22), concert violinist who was considered one of the great instrumentalists of his era and the man who saved New York City's Carnegie Hall from the wrecking ball.

Stringer, Korey (1974–August 1), Minnesota Vikings' offensive tackle who died after suffering heat stroke on the opening day of training camp.

Sutton, Margaret (Rachel Beebe Sutton) (1903–June 21), author of one of the most successful girls' series ever published, the 38 Judy Bolton mysteries.

Stassen, Harold E. (1907–March 4), former governor of Minnesota and perennial candidate for the Republican presidential nomination in 1948, 1952, 1956, 1960, 1964, 1968, 1972, 1976, and 1988.

Tillotson, Neil (1899?–October 17), resident of Dixville Notch, New Hampshire, who cast the first ballot in presidential primaries and elections from the early 1960's until 2000.

Walston, Ray (1917–January 1), character actor best known for his Tony Award-winning performance as the devil in *Damn Yankees* (1955) and as Uncle Martin in the 1960's television comedy "My Favorite Martian."

Welty, Eudora (1909–July 23), novelist—*The Optimist's Daughter* (1972)—and master of the short story—"The Robber Bridegroom" (1942)—whom literary critics ranked among the preeminent American authors of her time.

Wilson, Justin (1904?–September 5), Cajun chef and author of cookbooks who hosted several public television cooking shows.

Wing, Toby (Martha Virginia Wing) (1915–March 23), platinum-blond star of the 1930's who appeared in more than 35 films, including *42nd Street*, before marrying aviator Dick Merrill.

Woodcock, Leonard (1911–January 16), president of the United Automobile Workers who as envoy to China negotiated the historic reestablishment of diplomatic relations between the United States and China in 1979.

Woodling, Gene (1922–June 2), left fielder and left-handed batter who helped the New York Yankees win five consecutive World Series between 1949 and 1953.

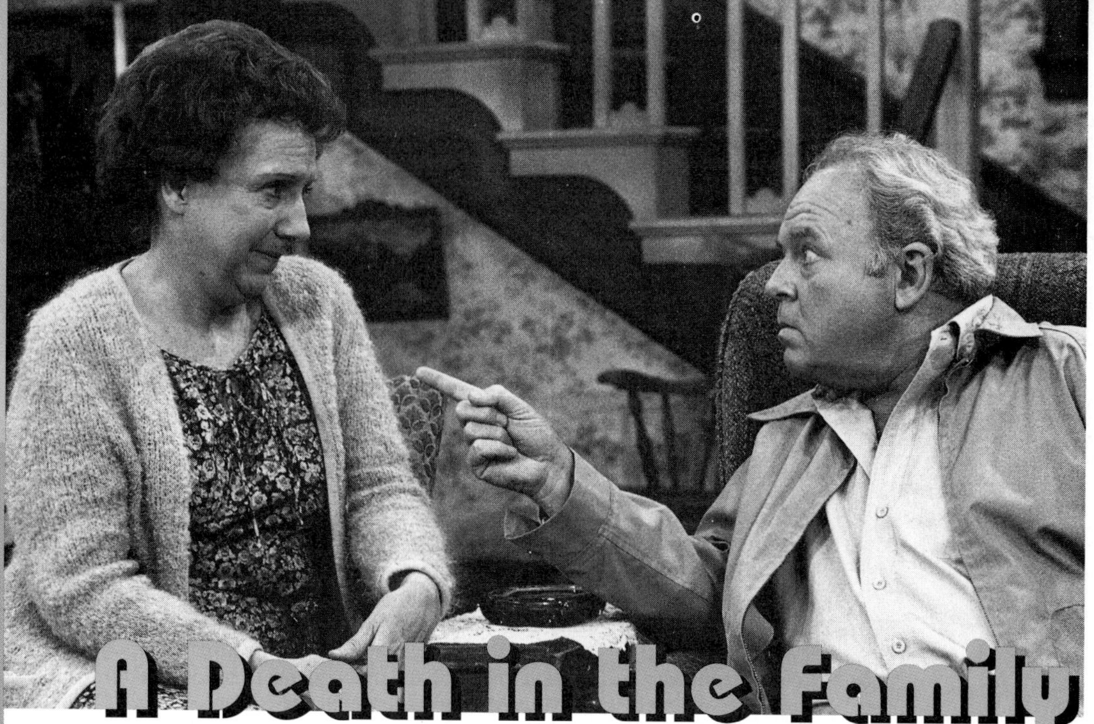

A Death in the Family

By Tim Frystak

Actor Carroll O'Connor's portrayal of Archie Bunker reflected the turmoil of America in the 1970's.

Television actor Carroll O'Connor died on June 21, 2001, at age 76. Although his acting career spanned nearly 50 years and included roles in films and the Broadway stage, O'Connor was best known as Archie Bunker, a working-class "everyman" who was the central character of the 1970's situation comedy (sitcom) "All in the Family." His portrayal of the narrow-minded Archie Bunker as a bigoted yet sympathetic figure evolved into an emblem of the social turmoil of the 1960's and 1970's.

Carroll O'Connor was born on Aug. 2, 1924, in New York City. His father was an attorney, and his mother was a teacher. In 1941, O'Connor enrolled at Wake Forest College, which is now Wake Forest University, in Winston-Salem, North Carolina. He dropped out after the United States entered World War II (1939-1945) to enroll in the United States Merchant Marine Academy. O'Connor eventually left the academy and joined the National Maritime Union, where he served as a civilian seaman.

O'Connor admitted in his 1998 autobiography that after the war, his life was relatively aimless. He returned to New York City in 1946 and returned to college in 1947 at the University of Montana in Missoula. In 1950, a restless O'Connor enrolled in University College Dublin, the main branch of Ireland's National University, where he studied Irish history and English literature and where he obtained a degree in 1952. O'Connor initially was drawn to acting while in Dublin, where he managed to find work in a series of professional stage productions.

Upon his return to the United States in 1954, O'Connor had trouble finding work as an actor and instead taught in the New York City public school system for several years. In the late 1950's, O'Connor landed roles in off-Broadway plays, films, and a number of television series.

In 1971, O'Connor accepted the role of Archie Bunker in "All in the Family." The series also starred Jean Stapleton as Edith Bunker, Archie Bunker's traditional, but strong-willed, wife; Sally Struthers as Gloria, their daughter; and Rob Reiner as Michael Stivic, Gloria's husband, a liberal college student living with his in-laws. They engaged in arguments that mirrored the society around them. Most focused on political extremes, with the narrow-minded Archie clashing with his daughter and son-in-law. The character of Edith Bunker, characterized as a "dingbat" by her husband, offered a "centralist" view and a moral middle that more often than not provided the message in the story line.

"All in the Family" was one of the first sitcoms to address such controversial social issues as gender equality, racism, religious tolerance, and the Vietnam War (1957-1975). It tapped into the angst and anger rampant in the United States in the early 1970's, an era of enormous upheaval. The series aired at a time when the U.S. economy was changing; when the nation's citizens were strongly divided over the U.S. involvement in the Vietnam War; when the drive for equality that began with African Americans in the 1960's had spread to other groups.

Archie Bunker, as played by Carroll O'Connor (opposite page, right) delivers orders to his hapless wife, Edith Bunker, as played by Jean Stapleton, in "All in the Family."

It also reflected conflict within families. Americans who had lived through the *Great Depression* (a worldwide business slump of the 1930's) and survived the hardships of World War II found themselves in a generation gap with their own offspring—members of the *baby boom generation* (the large group of people born in the United States from 1946 to 1964).

Archie Bunker's bigotry was a mirror in which the American public saw glimpses of its own intolerance. The humorous way in which O'Connor's portrayal was presented made that mirror acceptable to the public. By seeing pieces of themselves in Archie Bunker, the American public was able to view its own weaknesses and fears, especially the fear of the unknown that the country faced at the time. Seeing their own intolerances on screen enabled them to reflect on their own beliefs.

"All in the Family" went off the air in 1979. For several years after the series ended, O'Connor found it difficult to escape from the shadow of Archie Bunker. However, he was also unwilling to step away from the icon he had created. From 1979 to 1983, O'Connor re-created the role in a revamped sitcom titled "Archie Bunker's Place." The series was unable to muster the same critical or viewer loyalty as the original.

In the late 1980's, O'Connor found new success playing a character who was the opposite of Archie Bunker. From 1988 to 1994, O'Connor starred as Bill Gillespie, a liberal-minded police chief in a Mississippi town on the television drama "In the Heat of the Night."

Personal tragedy marred the final years of O'Connor's life. In 1995, his adopted son, Hugh, committed suicide after a long battle with alcohol and drug addiction. For the remainder of the 1990's, O'Connor became an outspoken crusader against drugs.

In his 1998 autobiography, *I Think I'm Outta Here,* O'Connor wrote that as he got older, he found himself talking less because he was merely repeating the same tales he had told throughout his career. "Why do I say the same things over and over?" O'Connor wrote. "Because I have never changed my opinions about anything." It seemed an ironic statement from someone who taught a generation of Americans how to change. ■■■

The author:
Tim Frystak is a senior editor on *The Year Book.*

Democratic Party. The Democratic Party scored several victories in November 2001 elections, including taking gubernatorial races in New Jersey and Virginia. Democrats also made inroads in mayoral races, winning 32 of 34 major mayoral campaigns. Following the terrorist attacks on the United States on September 11, Democrats joined Republicans to present a united front during the nation's war on terrorism.

Senate control. The Democratic Party regained control of the U.S. Senate on June 6, 2001, for the first time since 1995. The shift followed an announcement on May 24, 2001, by Senator James M. Jeffords of Vermont that he was leaving the Republican Party and would become an independent aligned with the Democrats. The move reduced the number of Senate seats held by the Republicans from 50 to 49, shifting control to the Democrats. Senator Tom Daschle (D., South Dakota) replaced Senator Trent Lott (R., Mississippi) as majority leader, and Democrats moved into the chairmanships of key Senate committees.

Democratic leadership. Democrats elected Representative Nancy Pelosi (D., California) the House *minority whip* (assistant leader) in October. In a 118 to 95 vote, Pelosi defeated Representative Steny Hoyer of Maryland to replace Representative David Bonior of Michigan as whip. Bonior was to step down from the position in 2002 to concentrate on his race for governor of Michigan.

Pelosi became the first woman in U.S. history to be elected to a position of leadership in the U.S. Congress. Political experts explained that the vote represented a significant move by Democratic Party members who had resisted changing their leadership structure since losing control of the House to the Republican Party in 1994.

Terrorist attacks. Members of the Democratic Party united with members of the Republican Party in a U.S.-led war against terrorism following the Sept. 11, 2001, terrorist attacks on the World Trade Center in New York City and the Pentagon Building outside Washington, D.C. In the days following the attacks, Democratic and Republican congressional leaders praised each other's statesmanship and voiced joint support of President George W. Bush.

Gubernatorial races. In the Virginia election for governor on November 6, Democrat Mark Warner defeated Republican Mark Earley with 52 percent of the vote. Warner was to succeed Republican Governor James Gilmore, III, who was prohibited by term limits from seeking reelection.

In New Jersey, Democrat Jim McGreevey won 56 percent of the vote to defeat Republican Bret Schundler. McGreevey was to replace Acting Gov-

U.S. Representative David Bonior (D. Michigan hands Representative Nancy Pelosi (D. California) a whip after she was elected House minority whip in October. Pelosi was the first woman ever to be elected to a position of leadership in the U.S. Congress.

ernor Donald DiFrancesco, who came to office in early 2001 when Christine Todd Whitman resigned to head the Environmental Protection Agency. DiFrancesco did not run for governor on his own.

Mayoral elections. Democratic candidates also scored major victories in several cities in 2001. In June, a Democrat captured the mayoral race in Los Angeles, a seat that the Republican Party had held since 1993. The party was assured of victory when Democrats James K. Hahn, the city attorney, and Antonio R. Villaraigosa, a former state Assembly member, both outpolled Republican Steve Soboroff in the April 2001 primary. Hahn defeated Villaraigosa in a runoff election on June 5 to succeed two-term Republican Mayor Richard Riordan, who was prohibited from running by term limits.

The Democratic Party suffered a major defeat in New York City on November 6, when Republican candidate Michael Bloomberg, a billionaire who founded a financial information services company, defeated Democrat candidate Mark Green, the city's public advocate, in the race to succeed Rudolph Giuliani as mayor. Bloomberg won 50 percent of the vote compared with Green's 47 percent. Bloomberg had trailed Green in opinion polls for much of the campaign until Giuliani backed Bloomberg for the post.

After the elections, Democratic National Committee Chairman Terry McAuliffe said that the 2001 elections demonstrated "an embrace of the strong fiscal stewardship offered by the Democratic Party." McAuliffe said that the Democratic Party would seek to increase gains among gubernatorial ranks in 2002, when 36 states are scheduled to hold elections for governor. Of those 36 offices, 23 were held by Republicans in 2001. Party leaders also planned to make an intense effort to widen the party's narrow majority in the Senate and retake the majority in the U.S. House.

Campaign finance. The Democratic Party raised $70 million and spent $48.5 million between January 1 and June 30, according to the Center for Responsive Politics, a Washington, D.C.-based research group that tracks political contributions. During the same period, the Republican Party raised $143.3 million and spent $101.7 million. The center based its totals on summaries reported by the national party committees to the Federal Election Commission.

☐ Geoffrey A. Campbell

See also **Congress of the United States; Elections; Los Angeles; New York City; People in the news** (Whitman, Christine Todd); **Republican Party; State government; Terrorism: A Special Feature,** p. 38; **United States, Government of the.**

Denmark moved sharply to the political right in 2001 as Danes voted to end nine years of Social Democratic rule and elected a new center-right government. The election was the first in Western Europe since the September 11 terrorist attacks on the United States, and the campaign was dominated by competing proposals to restrict immigration.

Prime Minister Poul Nyrup Rasmussen, whose Social Democratic Party had slumped in the polls, sought to capitalize on a spurt in popularity after September 11 by calling for an election on November 21, four months ahead of schedule. His government had responded to the attacks by promising strong support for the U.S. campaign against terrorism. During the campaign, however, center and right-wing parties made gains by promising to get tough on immigration. The Liberal Party, the main conservative party, pledged to restrict welfare payments to immigrants, by requiring people to live in Denmark for seven years before receiving full benefits.

The Liberals won 56 seats in the Folketing, the Danish parliament, up from 42 seats in the previous parliament. The Social Democrats won 52 seats, down from 63 seats previously. Large gains were also made by the right-wing Danish People's Party, which had gained support during the 1990's with an anti-immigrant platform. The party won 22 seats in parliament, up from 13 seats.

The Liberal leader, Anders Fogh Rasmussen, who was not related to Poul Rasmussen, vowed to keep the Danish People's Party out of his government. He formed a coalition with the more moderate Conservative People's Party, which had won 16 seats. However, the coalition only controlled a minority of seats in the parliament and was dependent on the support of the Danish People's Party on many issues.

Economy. Denmark's economy slowed significantly in 2001 as the country was affected by the worldwide slowdown. The European Commission, the executive arm of the EU, projected that Denmark's economic output would grow by 1.3 percent in 2001, down from 3.2 percent in 2000.

Airline cartel. Scandinavian Airline Systems (SAS), the Nordic airline owned by the governments of Denmark, Sweden, and Norway, and Maersk Air, a Danish carrier, were found guilty in July 2001 of violating EU competition rules by agreeing to split major Danish domestic and international routes and fix fares. The European Commission fined SAS $35 million and Maersk, $12 million. The deputy chief executive and the entire board of directors at SAS later resigned, as did the chairman and chief executive of Maersk.

☐ Tom Buerkle

See also **Europe.**

Dinosaur. See **Paleontology.**

Disabled. The Educational Testing Service (ETS) announced in February 2001 that it would stop flagging the test results of students with disabilities who had been given special accommodations—such as extra time—during tests. The ETS administers such standardized tests as the Graduate Record Examination, which is used to screen graduate school applicants, and the Test of English as a Foreign Language.

The new policy, which went into effect in October, was the result of a lawsuit filed in 1999 by a physically disabled man who charged that his application for admission to several business schools had been rejected because of it was flagged. As part of the settlement, the College Board, the organization that owns the SAT, a major college admissions test, agreed to review its own flagging policies by March 2002.

The United States Supreme Court ruled in February 2001 that state employees may not sue to recover money damages from their states for their employers' failure to comply with the Americans with Disabilities Act (ADA). A majority of Supreme Court justices determined that the federal disability law does not supersede states' immunity from being sued in federal court. Disability advocates criticized the ruling for limiting the scope of the ADA. □ Kristina Vaicikonis

See also **Supreme Court of the United States.**

Disasters. The deadliest disaster of 2001 was an earthquake in India in January that killed more than 14,000 people. Disasters that resulted in 25 or more deaths include the following:

Aircraft crashes

May 16—Turkey. A military cargo plane crashes shortly after takeoff from the city of Diyarbakir in southern Turkey, killing 34 members of Turkey's Special Forces.

July 3—Irkutsk, Siberia. All 136 passengers and 9 crew members aboard a Russian Avia Tu-154 airplane en route to Vladivostok are killed as the plane crashes near the city of Irkutsk.

October 4—Russia. At least 78 passengers and crew members aboard a Sibir Airlines flight from Tel Aviv to the Siberian city Novosibirsk are killed when the plane is hit by a missile during routine Ukrainian military exercises on the Crimean peninsula and falls into the Black Sea.

October 8—Milan, Italy. At least 118 people are killed when a Scandinavian Airlines System's MD-87 slams into a baggage terminal at the Linate Airport, after colliding with a small private jet that strayed onto the runway in heavy fog.

November 12—New York City. American Airlines Flight 587, en route from New York City to Santo Domingo in the Dominican Republic, crashes into a residential neighborhood in Queens minutes after takeoff. All 260 people aboard the plane and 5 people on the ground are killed.

Blizzards and cold

January 9—Northeast Asia. Blizzards that began on January 1 in northeast China, Japan, and North and South Korea leave more than 30 people dead and thousands of others stranded. More than 600,000 animals die in the snow, decimating the area's nomadic herding economy.

January 29—Afghanistan. At least 110 people, most of them children, die during a freezing night in a refugee camp in western Afghanistan. About 80,000 refugees had moved to the camp to escape war and the worst drought in 30 years.

Earthquakes

January 13—El Salvador. A 7.6-magnitude earthquake centered along El Salvador's Pacific coast kills more than 800 people and leaves tens of thousands homeless in and around San Salvador, the capital. Some 500 aftershocks follow the quake.

January 26—India. A 7.9-magnitude earthquake kills more than 14,000 people and injures 166,000 others in the state of Gujarat in northwest India.

February 13—El Salvador. At least 350 people are killed when a 6.6-magnitude earthquake strikes about 15 miles (24 kilometers) southeast of San Salvador. Among those killed are rescue workers aiding victims of a quake that had occurred in the same area on January 13.

June 23—Peru. An earthquake of 8.1 magnitude rocks southern Peru, killing at least 100 people and injuring 1,300 others. The epicenter is under the Pacific Ocean, about 120 miles (190 kilometers) west of the coastal city of Arequipa.

Explosions and fires

March 6—China. An explosion in a village school in Shanxi province kills at least 40 people, most of them children. Villagers insist that school authorities had set up a firecracker factory in the school, using the children as forced labor.

July 16—China. More than 40 people are killed, many of them buried alive, when illegally stored homemade explosives blow up in a house in the village of Mafang in northwest China.

August 6—India. Twenty-five people in a facility for the mentally ill in Erwady, in the southern state of Tamil Nadu, die in a fire that broke out in the palm-thatched shed in which they were housed. Police officers indicate that many of the patients had been chained to their beds or to pillars.

August 18—the Philippines. More than 70 people are killed when a fire sweeps through a hotel in Manila, the capital. Many of the victims were unable to escape the blaze because burglar-proof bars blocked the windows.

September 1—Tokyo. Forty-four people die when a gas explosion ignites a fire in a video mah-jongg gambling parlor.

September 21—Toulouse, France. Twenty-nine people are killed and more than 1,100 others are injured when unstable chemicals explode, blasting a crater 50 feet (15 meters) deep and 165 feet (50 meters) wide under a chemical plant warehouse.

December 29—Lima, Peru. At least 275 people are killed when a fireworks explosion sparks a blaze that spreads through a four-block shopping area in downtown Lima, the capital.

Mine disasters

May 16—China. More than 500 coal miners die in 62 accidents over a six-week period between April 1 and May 16. According to Chinese authorities, most of the accidents occurred in small mines as a result of gas explosions.

May 18—China. Thirty-nine convicts from a prison in Sichuan province drown when the coal shaft they are working in floods. On the same day, a gypsum mine in the southern region of Guangxi collapses, burying 29 miners 650 feet (200 meters) below ground.

June 22—China. An explosion in an illegal coal mine near the city of Xuzhou in Jiangsu province kills at least 38 miners. Officials had closed the mine in mid-June because of safety concerns.

July 17—China. Eighty-one workers die when illegal blasting sends torrents of water through a tin mine about 150 miles (240 kilometers) north of Nanning, the capital of the Guangxi region. Five days later, 92 miners are killed in a coal mine explosion in eastern Jiangsu province.

November 22—Colombia. At least 100 people are killed when a wall collapses at the Pescadero open-pit gold mine at Irra, west of Bogota, the capital. Several of the victims are children who eked out a living scavenging at the mine.

Shipwrecks

January 1—Turkey. At least 50 people drown when part of a cargo ship sinks after the vessel breaks apart during a storm along Turkey's southern Mediterranean coast. Most of the victims are illegal immigrants locked in a cargo hold.

October 19—Indian Ocean. More than 350 people are killed when a small wooden ship overloaded with passengers sinks off the coast of Indonesia. Most of the victims were refugees from the Middle East who had paid to be smuggled into Australia.

Storms and floods

February 2—Mozambique. Days of heavy rain cause massive flooding of the Zambezi River, leaving more than 100 people dead and forcing up to 225,000 people from their houses.

February 11—Java. Local officials announce that more than 130 people were killed in floods and mudslides in the Banten province of West Java during the week of February 4. Many of the victims were miners who died in a landslide at a gold mine in the village of Lebak Situ.

June 13—Ecuador. Days of heavy rains in Ecuador's Andes Mountains trigger a landslide of mud and rock that buries 31 people who had taken refuge in a shack some 30 miles (48 kilometers) east of Quito, the capital. The victims were motorists stranded in the mountains when an earlier avalanche blocked the highway.

June 24—Southeastern China. Typhoon Chebi leaves at least 70 people dead and more than 80 people missing in the province of Fujian. Most of the victims lived in Fuzhou, the provincial capital. Before hitting mainland China, the typhoon crossed southern Taiwan with heavy rains and winds of 75 miles (120 kilometers) per hour, killing 9 people.

July 2 to 4—Vietnam. At least 30 people die in floods unleashed by Typhoon Durian in Thai Nuguyen province, north of Hanoi. The floods were triggered by more than 17 inches (44 centimeters) of rain that fell in a 48-hour period.

July 4 to 5—the Philippines. More than 160 people are killed—most of them in landslides—when Typhoon Utor hits the Philippines. One million people are displaced by the storm.

July 15—South Korea. At least 45 people are killed and 34,000 houses are flooded when torrential rains inundate Seoul, the capital, and surrounding areas. Up to 12.2 inches (31.1 centimeters) of rain fell overnight, less than one month after South Korea's worst drought in 90 years.

July 22—India. More than 100 people in the eastern state of Orissa die in floods caused by monsoon rains that have raised local rivers to flood level. More than 500,000 people are marooned on high ground, depending on emergency airdrops for food.

July 23—Pakistan. At least 200 people drown when rains trigger flash floods that destroy dozens of houses and other structures. In Islamabad, the capital, 24 inches (61 centimeters) of rain fall in less than 24 hours, Pakistan's heaviest downpour in 100 years of record keeping.

August 1—Indonesia. Heavy rains on the island of Nias trigger flash floods and landslides that leave at least 60 people dead. Authorities blame the flooding on uncontrolled logging that has stripped mountainsides of vegetation.

August 12—Iran. Officials in Tehran, the capital, confirm that an estimated 200 people were killed in flash floods and mudslides triggered by a series of severe rainstorms. The storms, which began on August 10, ended three years of severe drought in the region. Officials described the flooding as the worst in 200 years.

September 18—Taipei, Taiwan. More than 80 people drown, are buried in landslides, or are electrocuted by downed power lines when Typhoon Nari inundates the western coast of Taiwan with rain for more than 50 hours.

October 10—North Korea. More than 80 people are killed and tens of thousands are left homeless when torrential rain and tidal waves strike the eastern coast of North Korea over a period of two days.

October 21—India. Government officials report the deaths of at least 73 people in massive flooding in the town of Kurnool, located 100 miles (160 kilometers) south of Hyderabad in the southern state of Adhra Pradesh.

November 7-9—the Philippines. As many as 300 people are killed when Typhoon Lingling strikes the central and southern regions of the Philippines. The storm produces wind gusts of up to 56 miles (90 kilometers) per hour and triggers flash floods and landslides. Lingling moves on to central Vietnam, where it kills at least 20 people and leaves thousands of others homeless.

November 10—Algeria. More than 24 hours of heavy rainfall and violent winds trigger flooding and mudslides, killing more than 700 people.

Train wrecks

June 22—Southwestern India. At least 57 people are killed and 300 others wounded when a mail train traveling from Mangalore to Chennai derails on a bridge spanning the Kadalundi River in the state of Kerala, plunging the three final cars 100 feet (30 meters) into the river.

September 2—Indonesia. A passenger train slams into a locomotive approximately 125 miles (201 kilometers) east of Jakarta, the capital, killing at least 40 people and injuring 60 others.

Other disasters

March 4—Portugal. In the worst traffic accident in Portuguese history, 58 people are killed when a 116-year-old bridge collapses into the Douro River.

March 5—Saudi Arabia. At least 35 people are crushed among 2 million Muslim pilgrims during the ritual stoning of Satan on the third day of the hajj, the annual journey to Mecca.

May 9—Accra, Ghana. At least 125 people are killed in a stampede at the end of a soccer match in Accra, the capital of Ghana. The stampede was triggered when police fired tear gas into a crowd of rioting soccer fans.

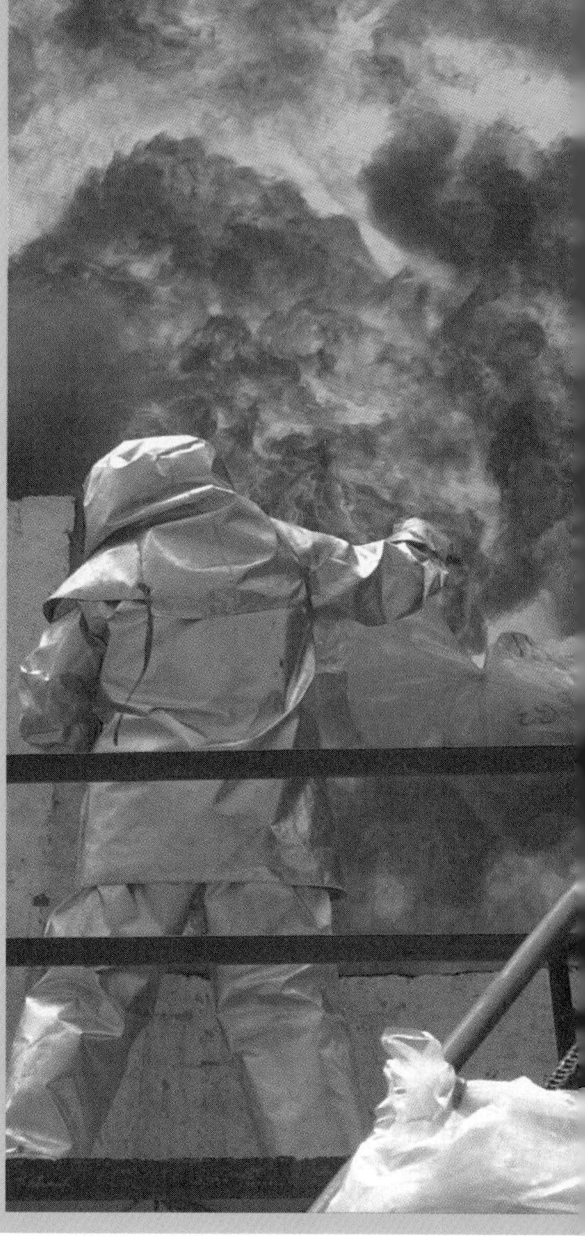

Drug abuse.. The number of Americans using illegal drugs in 2000 rose slightly to 14 million people, according to the National Household Survey on Drug Abuse (NHSDA) released in October 2001. The survey is an annual report on illegal drug use prepared by the Substance Abuse and Mental Health Services Administration (SAMHSA), part of the U.S. National Institutes of Health (NIH), a government agency. The previous annual survey had reported that 13.8 million Americans were illicit drug users in 1999. The NHSDA defines an illicit drug user as a person who has used illegal drugs at least once in the month prior to the survey.

Illicit drug use by 12 and 13 year olds fell from 3.9 percent in 1999 to 3.0 percent in 2000.

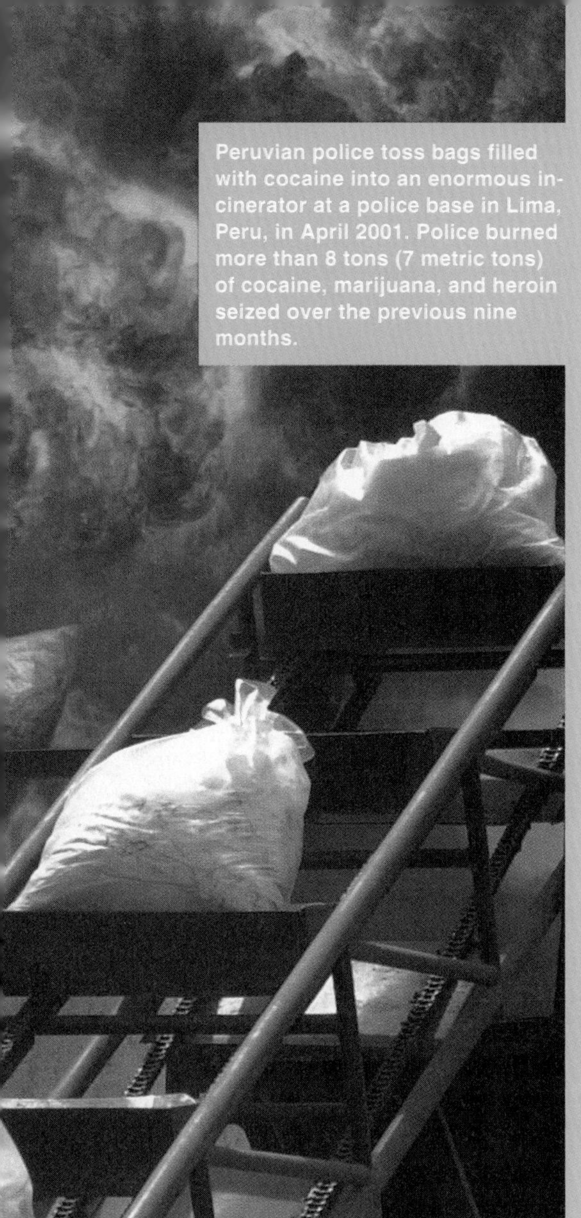

Peruvian police toss bags filled with cocaine into an enormous incinerator at a police base in Lima, Peru, in April 2001. Police burned more than 8 tons (7 metric tons) of cocaine, marijuana, and heroin seized over the previous nine months.

Among all youths aged 12 to 17, the rate of illicit drug use remained nearly stable at 9.7 percent in 2000, as compared with the 1999 figure of 9.8 percent.

Tobacco use declined among two categories of youths, according to the NHSDA. Among youths aged 12 to 17, the rate of cigarette use declined from 14.9 percent in 1999 to 13.4 percent in 2000. For young adults between the ages of 18 and 25, the rate fell from 39.7 percent in 1999 to 38.3 percent in 2000.

Ecstasy. A powerful stimulant that produces feelings of euphoria was used by an increasing number of teen-age drug users in 2001. The drug, MDMA, an illegal substance commonly known as "ecstasy," had become associated with "rave culture," a youth cultural phenomenon that involved all-night dance parties and "techno music."

An annual survey of drug use among high-school students published by the U.S. government in December 2000 reported that ecstasy use among 12th-graders increased from 5.6 percent in 1999 to 8.2 percent in 2000. A study released by the Maryland Department of Education in October 2001 showed a similar sharp rise among high school seniors in that state.

Ecstasy's side effects included increased heart rate and blood pressure, confusion, depression, and involuntary teeth clenching. Studies of the effects of ecstasy on animals indicated that high doses of the drug may be *neurotoxic* (harmful to the nervous system). Users also risked taking impure ecstasy mixed with toxic substances.

Ritalin. Rising prescription rates and potential for drug abuse prompted some states in 2001 to review laws regulating Ritalin, a commonly prescribed stimulant that is effective in treating attention-deficit/hyperactivity disorder (ADHD). In prescribed oral doses, Ritalin calms ADHD sufferers and helps them concentrate. When crushed and injected, however, the drug produces effects similar to those of cocaine. ☐ David C. Lewis

See also **Drugs.**

Drugs. High doses of zinc and antioxidants may slow vision loss in patients with serious age-related macular degeneration (AMD), the National Eye Institute (NEI), a United States government research agency, reported in October 2001. Antioxidants are a group of chemical compounds that may prevent certain types of cell damage. The body naturally produces some antioxidants. Fruits and vegetables are excellent sources of other antioxidants, including vitamins C and E and beta-carotene.

AMD is the leading cause of vision loss and blindness in Americans aged 65 and over. The disease cuts off the circulation of blood in the *macula,* the center of the *retina* (inner layer of eyeball). A person with AMD gradually loses central vision but retains *peripheral* (side) vision.

The study, which involved 4,757 AMD patients at 11 U.S. medical centers, evaluated the benefits of a combination of vitamins C and E, beta-carotene, and zinc. Researchers reported that the combination of substances slowed the development of AMD in about 25 percent of patients in advanced stages of AMD and in about 19 percent of patients in intermediate stages. The treatment had no apparent benefit on people with early AMD.

Paul A. Sieving, director of the NEI, hailed the study for confirming the first effective treatment for patients in the intermediate and advanced stages of AMD. He emphasized, however, that the treatment does not cure AMD.

Crohn's disease drug. A drug for treating some patients with mild to moderate Crohn's disease won approval from the U.S. Food and Drug Administration (FDA) in October. Crohn's disease is a chronic inflammation of digestive organs. The inflammation usually extends into the muscles and other tissues surrounding these organs. Symptoms of Crohn's disease include vomiting, diarrhea, and fever.

Marketed under the brand name Entocort EC, the new drug benefits patients with inflammation in specific sections of the small and large intestines. Because the drug works directly in the intestines, it causes fewer side effects than do standard Crohn's medications, which are absorbed by other parts of the body.

Acne drug warning. In August, the FDA issued a public warning about a popular acne drug called Acutane. The FDA called on physicians, pharmacists, and patients to ensure that women taking Acutane, which is prescribed to treat a severe form of acne, do not become pregnant. Taken during pregnancy, Acutane can cause serious birth defects.

The FDA recommended that female patients should have two negative pregnancy tests before starting the drug. The agency also advised physicians to give their female patients only a one-month supply of Acutane and to renew the prescription only after further negative pregnancy tests.

Baycol withdrawn. Reports linking numerous cases of a life-threatening muscle disease—rhabdomyolysis—with Baycol, a drug used to lower blood cholesterol levels, led Baycol's manufacturer, Bayer AG of Germany, to recall the drug in August. In patients with rhabdomyolysis, muscle tissue breaks down, leading to pain, weakness, fever, and sometimes kidney failure.

The FDA said 31 deaths in the United States, and more than 20 in other countries, were linked to Baycol, or cerivastatin. Researchers found that Baycol was most likely to cause the disease when taken with another cholesterol-lowering drug called Lopid, or gemfibrozil.

Glaucoma drugs. Two new drugs to treat glaucoma won FDA approval in March. Glaucoma is a serious eye condition that affects about 3 million people in the United States. The disease causes fluid to build up inside the eye, creating abnormally high pressure that can damage the optic nerve. The new drugs, Lumigan and Travatan, are intended for patients who do not respond to existing glaucoma medications. They said that the new drugs might help many patients avoid surgery to correct the condition.

Cancer fighters. In January, the FDA approved the use of the anticancer drug Femara as an initial treatment for advanced breast cancer that has metastasized, or spread, to other body organs. Femara was approved in 1997 for use only in women who did not respond to tamoxifen, the standard therapy for such patients. New clinical trials, however, showed that Femara was more effective than tamoxifen in delaying the progression of advanced breast cancer. Femara slowed the progression by an average of 9.4 months, compared with 6 months for tamoxifen.

A new medicine for chronic myelogenous leukemia (CML) became available in May 2001 under a special FDA procedure that makes life-saving drugs quickly available to patients. CML is a rare form of cancer in which too many white blood cells are produced. The excess white blood cells attack *bone marrow*, a substance in bone that produces red blood cells and other blood components. The FDA approved the drug, marketed under the brand name Gleevec, just three months after its manufacturer, Novartis Pharmaceuticals Corporation of East Hanover, New Jersey, submitted an application. Gleevec blocks the action of an enzyme that causes the fast growth of white blood cells. ☐ Michael Woods

See also **AIDS; Drug abuse; Health care issues; Medicine.**

Eastern Orthodox Churches.

The Greek Orthodox Church elected Metropolitan Irineos I as Patriarch of Jerusalem in August 2001. The Israeli government, to whom the Greek Orthodox Patriarchate of Jerusalem had submitted a list of 15 candidates for approval in July, initially disqualified five of the candidates, including Irineos, citing "security considerations" and "interests in Jerusalem." Israel later withdrew its objections under pressure from the church.

Archbishop of Athens Christodoulos continued in 2001 to lead the Greek Orthodox Church's effort to restore religious designations to Greek government identity cards. The government had removed the designations in 2000, citing the need to conform to European Union standards for the protection of privacy. A church-sponsored petition drive garnered over 3 million signatures calling for a referendum on the subject, but in August 2001, the Greek government refused the request.

Orthodox Churches in the United States. The General Assembly of the Orthodox Christian Archdiocese of North America voted in July to ask the Patriarchate of Antioch, its mother church in Syria, for *autonomy* (self-government). The new status, if granted, would allow the archdiocese greater independence, but not complete separation, from the Syrian church.

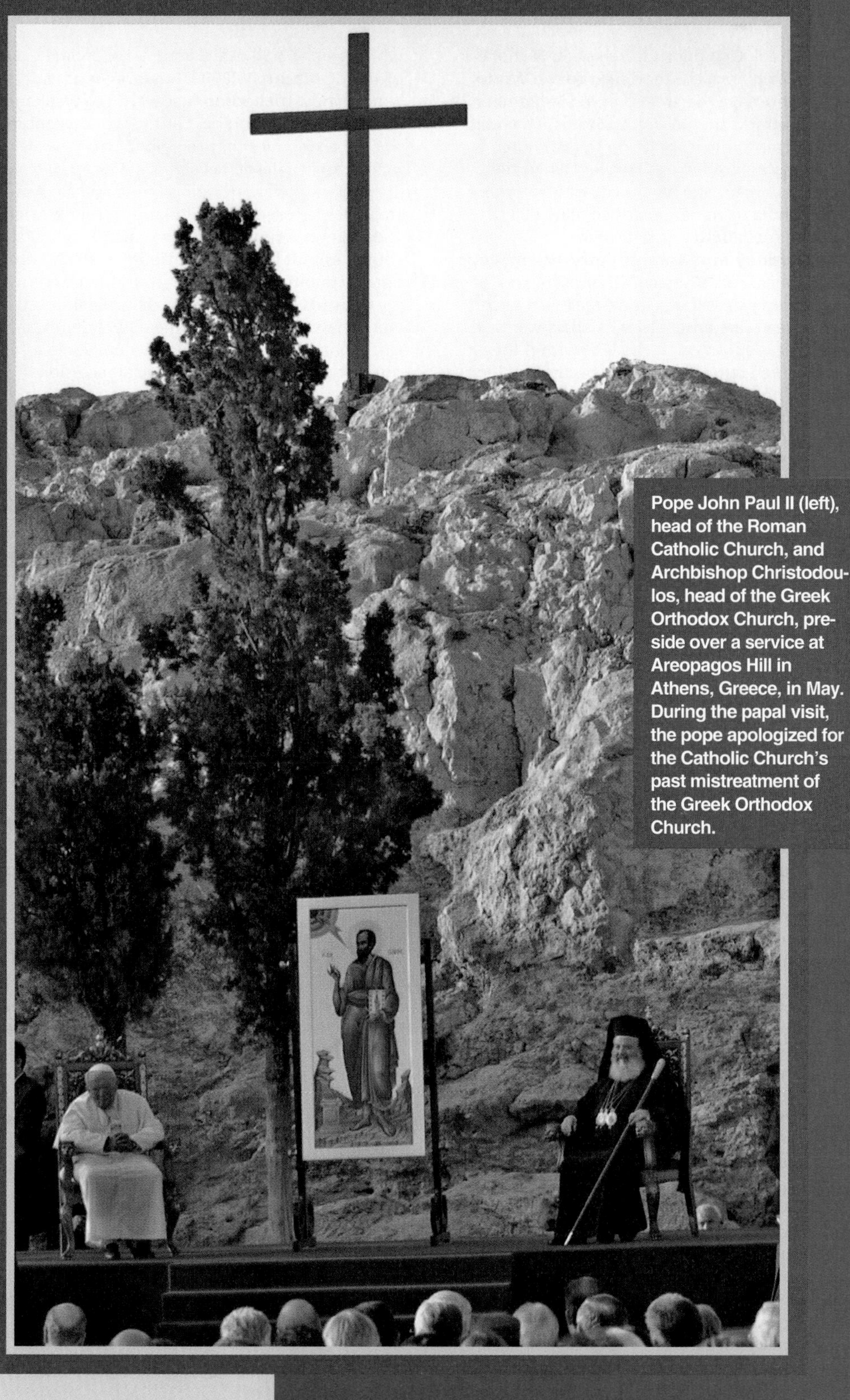

Pope John Paul II (left), head of the Roman Catholic Church, and Archbishop Christodoulos, head of the Greek Orthodox Church, preside over a service at Areopagos Hill in Athens, Greece, in May. During the papal visit, the pope apologized for the Catholic Church's past mistreatment of the Greek Orthodox Church.

The Greek Orthodox Church of St. Nicholas in New York City, which stood next to the World Trade Center, was destroyed in the September 11 terrorist attacks on the United States. The relics of three saints and icons given to the church by Czar Nicholas II of Russia were lost when the church collapsed. The Italian city of Bari, where Saint Nicholas is buried, pledged $500,000 toward the rebuilding of the church.

Orthodoxy and Roman Catholicism. Pope John Paul II of the Roman Catholic Church visited Greece in May. Although the Greek Orthodox Church had reluctantly given its approval for the papal visit, opposition to the visit within the Greek church remained strong, because of long-standing hostilities between the two churches. During the visit, John Paul apologized for the Catholic Church's past mistreatment of the Orthodox Church. Archbishop Christodoulos expressed gratitude to the pope for a "brief but fruitful visit."

Citing deep rifts between the Russian Orthodox Church and Roman Catholicism, Patriarch of Moscow Alexei II strongly opposed the pope's visit to Ukraine in June. The Moscow Patriarchate also expressed regret that the pope did not seek Alexei's blessing for his September visit to Kazakhstan. ☐ Stanley Samuel Harakas

See also **Roman Catholic Church.**

Economics. The global economy weakened significantly in 2001, as key industrial nations slumped for much of the year and were further jolted as the result of the September 11 terrorist attacks on the United States. The U.S. economy sank into recession in 2001 for the first time in 10 years. Japan slipped into its fourth recession since 1990, and economic growth declined to recession levels in many emerging-market nations.

Most of the world's regions were already experiencing economic weakness before the Sept. 11, 2001, terrorist attacks. The attacks curbed normal business operations across numerous industries, which sharply worsened the slide already underway in commercial activity, and made it clear that the huge U.S. economy was suffering its first downturn since the recession of 1990-1991. Although overall output of goods and services worldwide continued to grow in 2001, analysts warned that enough nations were suffering downturns that the global economy in 2001 could turn in its worst performance since the recessions of the early 1980's.

Economic conditions in 2001 were in some ways worse than the shocks of the 1998 financial crisis, which began in Asia and eventually struck fragile economies around the world. In 1998, the U.S. economy continued to surge and the economies of many European nations remained strong, which helped pull other national economies out of the downturn. In 2001, however, most advanced industrial economies were too weakened to act as growth engines for the world economy.

The economies that remained strong were mainly among large developing nations or smaller industrial ones, including China, Russia, Australia, India, Greece, and Ireland. Weakness pervaded Latin America and some of the same Asian countries that had been buffeted in 1993. European economies slowed but continued to grow.

Growth estimates and risks. Economists were sharply divided over the actual depth of the economic slowdown worldwide. Some argued that an even broader global recession could develop in 2002, which could surpass the problems of the early 1980's. Others countered that the U.S. Federal Reserve's (Fed) yearlong monetary policy to lower interest rates, along with similar action in other global regions and a sharp fall in fuel prices, had already laid the basis for a solid recovery in 2002. The Fed is an independent government agency that oversees U.S. banks. Many economists said it might be well into 2002 before anyone could gauge how much worldwide output of goods and services had weakened in 2001.

The International Monetary Fund—a United Nations affiliate agency that provides policy advice and financial aid to countries needing help—estimated on November 15 that worldwide output minus inflation would grow by 2.4 percent for all of 2001, which was sharply below the 4.7- percent growth of 2000. The IMF also warned in October 2001 that growth in gross domestic product (GDP)—the value of all goods and services produced by a country in a given period—was slowing worldwide. IMF economists noted that "downside risks have been further exacerbated by the terrorist attack...."

The emerging slowdown was already evident toward the end of 2000, the year of the collapse of many of the "new economy" companies that had propelled the huge stock market gains of the late 1990's. In 2001, markets continued to decline as bad news poured in from economic indicators and about corporate earnings. In the first and second quarters, fuel costs soared, business investment spending dropped, and consumer demand cooled.

The downturn in the important U.S. manufacturing sector began in the second half of 2000. It was matched to varying degrees in many other nations. At the end of 2000, the Fed warned that the U.S. economy had weakened abruptly. Earlier in the year, however, the Fed and other world central banks had hiked interest rates to slow down what they saw as overly fast economic growth in North America and Europe. Observers correctly interpreted the Fed's end-of-year warning to mean it was about to reverse that policy.

Efforts to stimulate the U.S. economy. The Fed cut interest rates 11 times in 2001, beginning with a half-point cut on January 3. By December 11, it had dropped short-term interest charges to their lowest levels since July 1961. The European Central Bank (ECB) refrained from cutting its interest rates until mid-2001.

Early in 2001, the U.S. Congress passed a large multiyear tax cut. During the summer of 2001, the U.S. Treasury sent out tax rebates to boost consumer spending. Despite these attempts to stimulate the U.S. economy, it underwent a dramatic slowdown. Gross domestic product grew only 1.3 percent in the first quarter of 2001 and nearly stalled in the second quarter at just 0.3 percent. In 2000, GDP increased by 4 percent.

Effects of terrorist attacks. Commerce of all types was disrupted by the terrorist attacks of Sept. 11, 2001. The impact on the U.S. economy sent shock waves around the world. The U.S. aviation system went through an unprecedented shutdown after the attacks, and demand for air travel shriveled when airports reopened. Other industries also were profoundly affected by the attacks—entertainment, hotels, retailers, insurance, factories, and cargo operations. New security measures added costs to a wide range of activities, squeezing profits for many companies. As employers tightened belts, layoffs soared. U.S. GDP fell 1.1 percent in the third quarter.

In November 2001, the National Bureau of Economic Research (NBER), a Cambridge, Massachusetts-based panel of economists that studies U.S. business cycles, officially ruled that the U.S. economy had been in recession since March. The NBER confirmed that the terrorist attacks worsened the economy. The NBER evaluated four criteria before deciding that the U.S. economy was in recession: industrial production, employment, personal income, and wholesale/retail trade.

The year 2001 had begun with the merger in January of Time-Warner Inc. of New York City and America Online, Inc., of Dulles, Virginia. The year ended with the collapse of the energy trading giant Enron Corporation of Houston. Enron became the largest U.S. company ever to file for bankruptcy.

Bright spots? Although markets plunged following the September terrorist attacks, the losses were largely recovered by early November. Oil prices fell sharply as global demand ebbed. Some economists speculated that energy cost savings might provide some of the fuel for an economic recovery. □ John D. Boyd

See also **International trade; Manufacturing.**

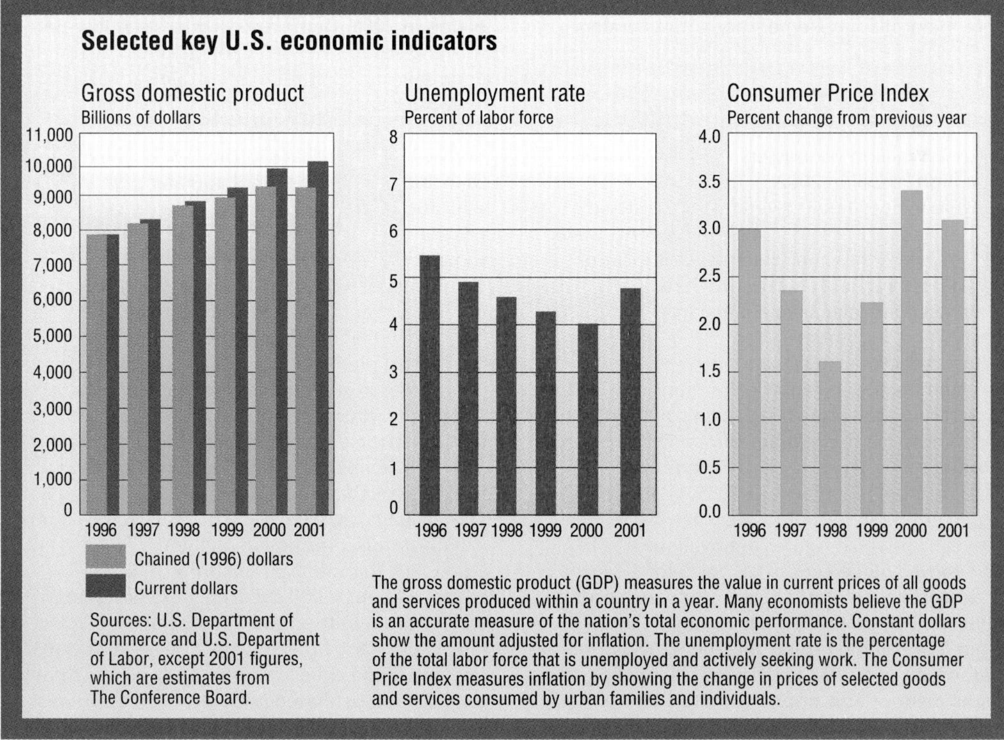

Ecuador. In June 2001, the Ecuadoran government approved the plans of an international *consortium* (group of companies) to build a pipeline linking oil fields in Ecuador's interior to a port on the Pacific coast. Techint, an engineering and construction firm in Argentina, was contracted to oversee construction of the $1.1-billion pipeline, which was designed to carry some 450,000 barrels of oil per day. Ecuadoran President Gustavo Noboa Bejarano predicted that the pipeline, scheduled to be operating by 2003, would reenergize the country's economy by providing tens of thousands of jobs in construction and other fields.

On June 22, 2001, Ecuadoran police arrested 57 members of a gang alleged to have kidnapped 10 foreign oil workers in Ecuador in October 2000. One of the captives, Ronald Sander of the United States, was found slain on a jungle road in January 2001. Seven other hostages—from the United States, Argentina, Chile, and New Zealand—were released on March 1 after oil companies reportedly paid a ransom of $13 million. (Two French captives had escaped soon after being kidnapped.) The ringleader of the gang, Gerardo Herrera, was a former member of a small Colombian guerrilla group.

☐ Nathan A. Haverstock

See also **Latin America.**

Education. About 53.1 million students were in enrolled in elementary and secondary schools in the United States in autumn 2001. Children enrolled in private schools accounted for about 10 percent of all school-aged children. U.S. Department of Education officials estimated that about 2.8 million youngsters would graduate from high school in 2002.

College enrollments were also at historic highs in 2001. About 15.3 million students were attending colleges and universities. Education officials estimated that a record 1.2 million students would receive bachelor's degrees during the 2001-2002 academic year.

In a trend that the Department of Education has been unable to explain, the number of women entering and graduating from college continued to outpace the number of men. Women accounted for 57 percent of all college students in 2001, up from 52 percent in 1985. Women earned 56 percent of all bachelor's degrees in 1997, the last year for which figures are available. In 1971, men earned 56 percent of all bachelor's degrees.

Spending on public elementary and secondary schools by all levels of government totaled about $345 billion during the 2001-2002 school year, or about $7,487 per student, according to Department of Education estimates. The United States spends about 7 percent of its *gross domestic product* (the value of all goods and services produced in the country in a year) on education.

Congressional action. President George W. Bush declared education to be one of his highest domestic priorities during his 2000 campaign. Only days after taking office on Jan. 20, 2001, he sent the U.S. Congress his education plan, called "No Child Left Behind." After nearly a year of debate, Congress passed an education bill in December containing many of the president's ideas.

Among other things, the compromise legislation required the states to give yearly math and reading tests to all students in grades three through eight. Each state was to write its own tests and was required to ensure that all children pass both yearly tests within 12 years. Schools that failed to meet yearly progress goals were to be given extra help by their districts and states, but they would also lose some independence. For example, if a school did not meet its progress goals for three years, some of the federal funds it receives would be split among parents, who could use the money for tutoring or extra services for the children. The legislation greatly expanded the federal government's role in education, which had long been a state and local responsibility in the United States.

As part of the compromise, Congress agreed to raise federal aid to kindergarten through 12th grade education to over $22 billion in the 2002-2003 federal budget year, an increase from $18.4 billion in 2001. Democrats argued that low-performing schools need the extra funds for training and new curricula if they are to improve.

Vouchers. The Democratic majority in the U.S. Senate repeatedly refused during its negotiations with Republicans in the U.S. House in 2001 to include a private-school voucher plan in the education bill. Vouchers allow children to attend private school at taxpayer expense. Although some voters—including a growing number of parents whose children attend low-performing inner-city schools—support the idea, others are wary of vouchers, fearing they will take money away from public schools. Because many private schools are affiliated with a church, people are also afraid vouchers will violate the separation of church and state stipulated in the Constitution.

In September, the U.S. Supreme Court stepped into the voucher debate by agreeing, during its 2001-2002 term, to review a Cleveland, Ohio, program that offers vouchers to low-income parents who want to send their children to private schools. About 4,000 children were enrolled in the program in the 1999-2000 school year, the latest for which figures were available. About 96 percent of the children used the vouchers to attend schools affiliated with a church. Supporters and opponents of vouchers had asked the court to hear the Cleveland case so that the question of the constitutionality of vouchers could be settled.

The practice of issuing vouchers continued to spread in 2001, as Florida passed legislation that allowed the parents of disabled or special-education students to enroll the children in private schools that meet their needs. The law required the state to pay the tuition, regardless of the parents' income. An estimated 3,800 youngsters were enrolled in the program during the 2001-2002 school year.

Charter schools continued to gain support in 2001. Many parents and educators believe that the schools, which are publicly funded but operate outside of school-district supervision, allow educators more freedom to experiment with new approaches to education. The Center for Education Reform, a Washington, D.C., organization that tracks charter schools, reported that there were 2,063 charter schools enrolling 519,000 students in 34 states at the start of the 2001 academic year. Although many of the schools proved to be very successful, others were hampered by a lack of start-up money and by opposition from legislators and teachers' groups.

Home schooling also continued to grow in popularity. According to a Department of Education report on home schooling released in August, 850,000 children aged 5 to 17—about 1.7 percent of all students—were home-schooled in 1999, the latest year for which figures were available. In 1990, education officials estimated that up to 350,000 children were being home-schooled.

Test scores. Student math scores on the National Assessment of Educational Progress (NAEP) inched up in 2001, compared with scores reported in 1990. Nevertheless, the results of the majority of U.S. students fell below the test's definition of being competent in the subject. Only 19 percent of 12th-graders scored high enough to be considered proficient in math in 2001. Almost three-quarters of 4th- and 8th-graders scored below proficient levels. The NAEP is a federally administered achievement test given to a statistically reliable sampling of 4th-, 8th-, and 12th-graders across the nation.

Scores on the 2001 SAT, a college admissions test owned by the College Board, a nonprofit organization located in New York City, barely budged from scores in 2000. Verbal scores rose by one point to an average 506, while mathematics scores remained flat at 514 out of a possible 800 points each. On the ACT, a college-entrance exam owned by the nonprofit ACT organization of Iowa City, Iowa, the average composite score was 21 out of a possible 36 points for the fifth straight year. ☐ June Kronholz

See also **People in the news** (Paige, Rod); **State government.**

Egypt.

Egyptian President Hosni Mubarak resisted pressure from the United States to join a "war on terrorism" following terrorist attacks on the United States on Sept. 11, 2001. Mubarak feared he would fuel Muslim-Christian strife in Egypt if he supported U.S. military strikes against Afghanistan's ruling Taliban, which began in early October. The United States accused the Taliban of harboring Saudi-born millionaire Osama bin Laden, the head of the Islamic terrorist network al-Qaida, whose members were believed to be responsible for the September terrorist attacks.

Terrorism's "most wanted." The U.S. government in October placed several Egyptians, including Ayman al-Zawahiri and Mohammed Atef, on its "most wanted" list of terrorists. Zawahiri and Atef were both thought to be possible successors of Osama bin Laden.

Zawahiri headed Egypt's militant Islamic Jihad for most of the 1990's. In 1998, he formed an alliance with bin Laden known as The Islamic Front for Fighting Crusaders and Jews, which called for a "holy war" against the United States. In 1999, an Egyptian military court sentenced Zawahiri to death in absentia for the 1995 bombing of the Egyptian embassy in Pakistan. Egyptian authorities believed that Zawahiri was also involved in the massacre of Western tourists in Luxor, Egypt, in 1997. In the 1980's, Zawahiri spent three years in prison for complicity in the 1981 assassination of Egyptian President Anwar el-Sadat.

Atef, whose daughter had married one of bin Laden's sons, was considered to be al-Qaida's military chief. He was killed in the U.S. military strikes on Afghanistan in November 2001.

Action against extremists. In October, Mubarak ordered that more than 250 detained Islamic extremists be tried in military courts. At least 13,000 other suspected extremists remained jailed in 2001. Since 1992, Islamic extremists in Egypt have conducted a series of attacks on Western tourists, Egyptian police, and Coptic Christians that have resulted in the deaths of more than 1,200 people. Militants attempted to assassinate Mubarak in 1995.

Democracy activist sentenced. In May 2001, Egypt's Supreme Security Court sentenced prodemocracy activist Saad Eddin Ibrahim to seven years in prison for spreading information harmful to Egypt and accepting foreign donations for his research center. International human rights groups condemned the sentence. Some Egyptian analysts believed that the government moved against Ibrahim, an Egyptian American sociology professor, because his center studied such politically sensitive issues as election fraud and Muslim-Christian relations. ☐ Christine Helms

See also **Israel; Middle East; Terrorism; Terrorism: A Special Feature,** p. 38.

Elections. The Democratic Party took two gubernatorial offices from the Republican Party in 2001; voters in several major U.S. cities elected new mayors during the year; and a review, published in November, of disqualified ballots in the 2000 presidential election revealed that George W. Bush would have won the presidency even if the Florida recount had gone forward.

Gubernatorial races. In off-year elections on Nov. 6, 2001, Democratic candidates in New Jersey and Virginia defeated their Republican challengers in races for governor. The Republican Party had controlled both governorships for eight years.

James McGreevey defeated Bret Schundler for New Jersey's top elected post. McGreevey, the mayor of Woodbridge, took 56 percent of the vote to defeat Schundler, the former mayor of Jersey City. McGreevey was to replace Acting Governor Donald DiFrancesco, who replaced Christine Todd Whitman. Whitman resigned to become head of the Environmental Protection Agency. DiFrancesco, a Republican, opted not to seek a full term in the post.

In Virginia, Mark Warner, who narrowly lost a race for the U.S. Senate in 1996, defeated Mark Earley, a former state attorney general. Warner had 52 percent of the vote. He was to succeed Republican Governor James Gilmore III, who was prohibited by term limits from seeking reelection.

Mayoral races. City Attorney James K. Hahn won 54 percent of the vote in the race for mayor of Los Angeles on June 5, 2001. Hahn, a Democrat, defeated Antonio R. Villaraigosa, a former California State Assembly member, to succeed two-term Mayor Richard J. Riordan. Riordan was prohibited by law from running for a third term.

In New York City on November 6, Republican Michael Bloomberg, founder of a financial information services company, defeated Democrat Mark Green, the city's public advocate, in the race to succeed Rudolph W. Giuliani as mayor. Bloomberg won 50 percent of the vote compared with 47 percent of the vote for Green.

In the wake of the terrorist attacks on the World Trade Center in New York City on September 11, many New Yorkers had encouraged Giuliani to attempt to seek a third term as mayor despite term limits. Giuliani had received a groundswell of support for his handling of events following the attacks. On October 3, Giuliani, a Republican, announced that he would not seek reelection as a candidate for the Conservative Party because he did not want to cause division in the city.

Other mayoral elections. On November 6 in Atlanta, Georgia, voters elected City Administrator Shirley Franklin as Atlanta's first woman mayor. Voters in Cleveland, Ohio, also elected their first woman mayor, Jane Campbell.

In Detroit, voters chose Michigan House Minority Leader Kwame Kilpatrick to succeed Mayor Dennis Archer, who decided not to seek reelection. Voters in Austin, Texas, elected Gus Garcia as the city's first Hispanic mayor. Eddie A. Perez became the first Hispanic mayor of Hartford, Connecticut. In Miami, Mayor Joe Carollo lost a bid for reelection on November 6. In a November 13 runoff election in Miami, Manuel A. Diaz, an attorney, defeated Maurice Ferre, a former mayor.

Election review. In November, a review of some 175,000 disqualified Florida ballots from the 2000 presidential election revealed that George W. Bush won the popular vote in Florida by a slim margin over Al Gore, who was then vice president. The bipartisan review was commissioned by a group of eight news organizations and conducted by the National Opinion Research Center at the University of Chicago. Bush, who received fewer popular votes nationwide than Gore, won the presidency in the Electoral College, where he tallied 271 votes, including all of Florida's 25 votes. He needed 270 votes to win. The study suggested, however, that more Floridians attempted to vote for Gore than for Bush. The review turned up statistical evidence that supported the claims of many minority and elderly voters that confusing ballots caused them to spoil their ballots by voting for more than one presidential candidate.

In June 2001, the U.S. Civil Rights Commission, a federal agency that works to guarantee civil rights, reported that many African American voters in Florida had their ballots discounted because of design problems. A separate report, prepared by Democrats on the U.S. House of Representatives' Government Reform Committee and released in July, found a similar trend nationwide.

Reform proposals. The National Task Force on Election Reform, a group composed of state and local election administrators, issued a report in July calling for a stronger federal role in elections and in establishing national standards for elections equipment. The task force also recommended uniform standards for counting ballots.

On July 31, the task force, co-chaired by former presidents Jimmy Carter and Gerald R. Ford, recommended that Congress enact legislation to hold presidential and congressional elections on a national holiday to help bolster voter turnout. The commission also recommended that the federal government establish a voting equipment system standard and provide extra money to help states improve voting equipment.

☐ Geoffrey A. Campbell

See also **Congress of the United States; Democratic Party; Los Angeles; Miami; New York City; Republican Party; State government; United States, Government of the.**

Electronics. In August 2001, the Consumer Electronics Association (CEA), a New York City-based trade group, predicted the electronics industry would sell a record $95.6 billion worth of consumer electronics products in 2001. The group cited increased demand for DVD players, digital cameras, and other devices for the projected 6-percent increase over the $90.1 billion sales in 2000.

Officials with the CEA said, however, that the rate of increase in sales would be slower than the 10-percent growth rate achieved in 2000. The officials said an economic slowdown that caused consumers to delay purchasing some electronic products was to blame for the decreased growth.

Xbox versus GameCube. Consumers had two choices for the newest in-home video game systems in 2001, with the release in November of both the Xbox Video Game System from Microsoft Corp. of Redmond, Washington, and the GameCube from Nintendo Company Limited of Kyoto, Japan.

Unlike most existing video game systems, which used only one microprocessor, the Xbox used two—a 733-MHz Pentium chip and a separate graphics chip. As a result, the Xbox was nearly as powerful as most home computers. The Xbox also featured an 8-gigabyte hard drive and an Ethernet port to enable users to plug the device into high-speed Internet connections. The Xbox had a retail price of $299.

Nintendo's GameCube offered four-person play and was also compatible with Nintendo's handheld video game GameBoy Advance. The compatibility enabled owners of GameBoys to plug into the GameCube, which was being sold for a retail price of $199.

PDA phone. In October 2001, officials with Samsung Telecommunications of Dallas officially introduced the SPH 1300, a new cellular telephone combining features of cell phones with those of popular handheld computers known as personal digital assistants, or PDA's. The $500 phone contained the popular Palm operating system used in PDA's made by Palm Inc. of Santa Clara, California, and other companies. The SPH 1300 enabled users to instantly dial telephone numbers in their address books and send and read electronic mail, in addition to performing other tasks, such as electronic scheduling.

Smart Pan. In January, Digital Cookware, Inc., of Woodridge, Illinois, introduced the Smart Pan, the first programmable digital skillet. The pan features a digital display that signals when food is finished cooking. Consumers indicate the kind of food being prepared, and the handle of the $90 pan flashes and beeps after it reaches the proper cooking temperature. The Smart Pan signals again when the food is done. The pan was available in 10-inch (25-centimeter) and 12-inch (30-centimeter) sizes.

Web appliance. In 2000, the public showed little interest in Internet appliances—devices other than traditional desktop computers that can be connected to the Internet. Nevertheless, in June 2001, Sony Corp. of Tokyo released the eVilla Entertainment Center, a simple Web appliance that consumers could use to send and receive e-mail and access the Internet to shop or read news reports. The eVilla could also be used to play multimedia content such as video and audio clips.

In addition to the $500 purchase price, eVilla users had to agree to purchase service from an Internet Service Provider (ISP) for a monthly fee. The device does not have a hard drive for storing data, but users could make use of 10 megabytes of online storage made available from their ISP.

Back seat safety. In January, Donnelly Corp. of Holland, Michigan, introduced the VideoMirror BabyVue, the first in-vehicle monitoring system. The device enables drivers to check on children sitting in the back seat without turning around. The system uses a small adjustable mini-camera in the rear of the vehicle to transmit images to a swiveling video screen placed under the rearview mirror. The system cost $500.

☐ Michael Woods

See also **Internet; Toys and games.**

El Salvador. Two earthquakes struck populous suburban communities near San Salvador, El Salvador's capital, on Jan. 13, 2001, and February 13. The tremors left approximately 1,150 people dead and 1.2 million people—about one-sixth of El Salvador's population—homeless.

United States President George W. Bush, in a March meeting with Salvadoran President Francisco Flores Perez, pledged to provide a two-year package consisting of relief and reconstruction aid to El Salvador. The aid was to total $52 million in 2001 and approximately the same amount in 2002. Bush also agreed to permit as many as 150,000 Salvadorans living illegally in the United States to remain in the United States for as long as 18 months. This move allowed the Salvadorans to earn extra money to send to their friends and family in El Salvador.

On Jan. 1, 2001, El Salvador adopted the U.S. dollar as an official currency to be used together with the colon, the country's existing currency. Salvadorans converted their holdings of the colon at the fixed rate of 8.75 to the dollar.

☐ Nathan A. Haverstock

See also **Disasters; Latin America.**

Employment. See **Economics; Labor and employment.**

Endangered species. See **Biology; Conservation.**

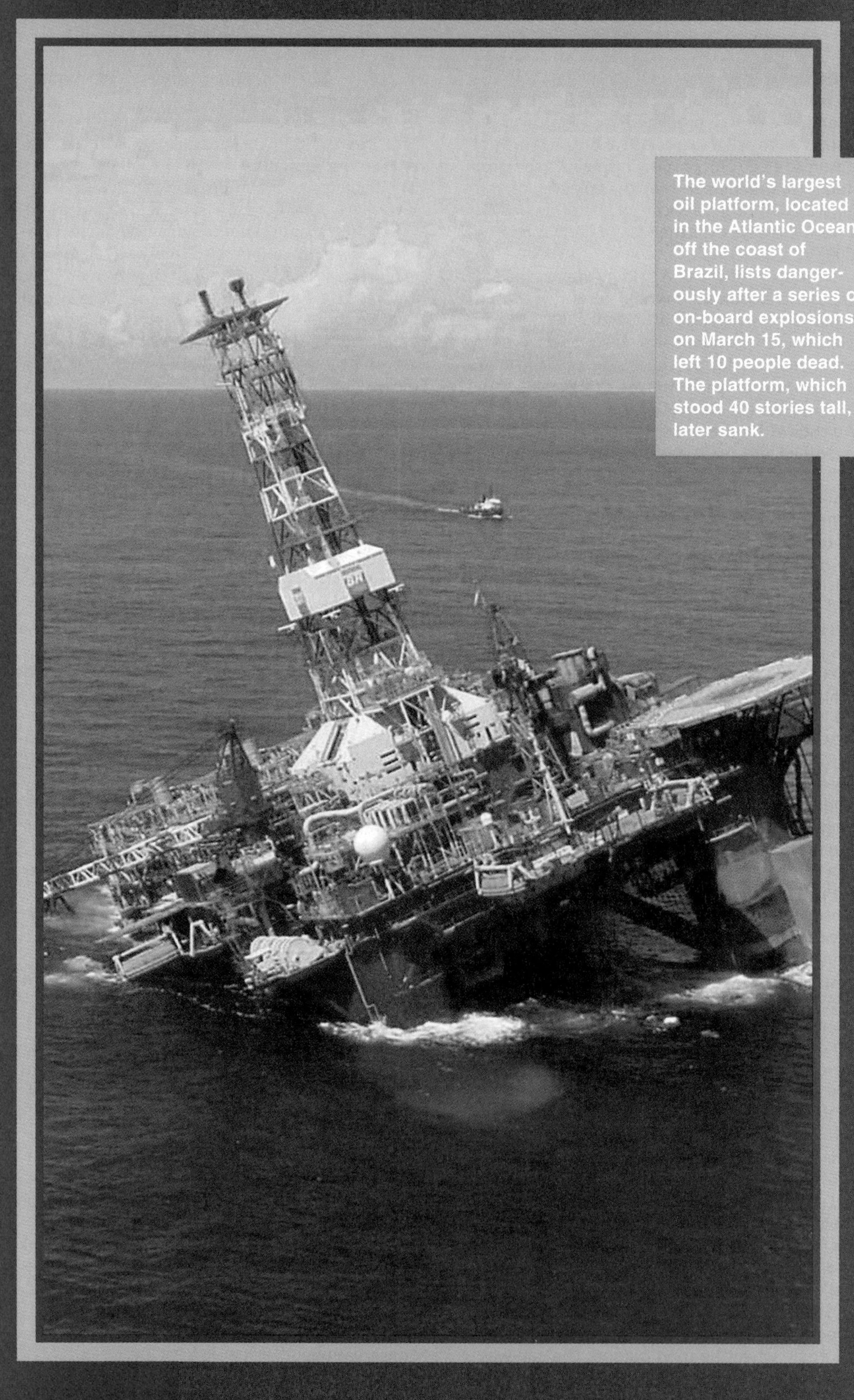

The world's largest oil platform, located in the Atlantic Ocean off the coast of Brazil, lists dangerously after a series of on-board explosions on March 15, which left 10 people dead. The platform, which stood 40 stories tall, later sank.

Energy supply. An energy crisis in the early months of 2001 threatened to cause widespread fuel shortages and power outages but eased during the second half of the year. The reason for the scarcity-to-glut swing in fuel and electricity supplies was a surprising, if temporary, easing of world demand for energy as global economies weakened.

In early 2001, the United States faced its worst energy shock since the 1970's. California experienced blackouts and power shortages; the use of electricity and fuels, particularly natural gas and gasoline, was surging; and demand for crude oil was rising around the world. As a result, fuel costs were at the highest levels in 10 years.

Increased prices. The price of crude oil, which had increased to more than $35 a barrel late in 2000—30 percent above the price one year before—appeared to be headed even higher in early 2001 as oil exporters reduced output. The escalating cost of crude oil could be seen in gasoline prices, which reached $2 a gallon in some areas in early 2001. Many energy analysts predicted prices would increase further.

Natural gas prices also surged, peaking at $10 per 1,000 cubic feet in early 2001, and contributed to the rising cost of electricity. Most newly constructed power plants burned natural gas, rather than coal, to generate electricity.

Recession. Before summer 2001, the energy picture changed as the United States went into a recession that affected world economies. The rise in 2001 energy use that experts had predicted failed to materialize. In September, terrorist attacks on the United States further depressed the U.S. economy, as well as demand for energy. As a result, fuel prices fell to the lowest levels since 1998. The cost of natural gas dropped to $2 per thousand cubic feet by summer 2001. Gasoline prices, which were predicted to reach $3 a gallon in some areas, settled at less than one-half that amount. By November, some service stations were selling gasoline at less than $1 a gallon.

The global cost of crude oil fell despite efforts by the Organization of Petroleum Exporting Countries (OPEC), a group of 11 oil-producing nations, to inflate prices by reducing production. The cost of crude oil spiked higher briefly in the wake of the terrorist attacks on the United States on September 11. But by the end of 2001, the price of oil stood at about $20 a barrel, from a low of $17 a barrel. A barrel of oil contains 42 gallons (159 liters) and holds the energy equivalent of some 6,000 cubic feet (169.9 cubic meters) of gas.

World oil demand contracted by an estimated 750,000 barrels a day in the third quarter of 2001, the International Energy Agency (IEA) reported in November 2001. Still, the Paris-based agency representing the world's major oil consuming nations estimated 2001 oil demand at 76 million barrels a day, up slightly from the 2000 daily average. The IEA estimated that oil demand would rise to 76.6 million barrels a day in 2002 as global economies recover.

U.S. oil demand averaged 19.7 million barrels a day through November 2001, some 100,000 barrels a day higher than in 2000, according to the Energy Information Administration (EIA), an arm of the U.S. Department of Energy. The EIA reported that consumption of motor gasoline remained strong in 2001, averaging 8.6 million barrels a day through November.

In 2001, the United States imported more than 50 percent of the oil it used. Much of the imported oil came from the Middle East. Uncertainties about that source of oil in the aftermath of the September terrorist attacks prompted U.S. officials to take steps to ensure adequate U.S. oil supplies in 2001.

In November, U.S. President George W. Bush directed Spencer Abraham, the secretary of energy, to increase the *strategic petroleum reserve* (oil stockpiled in the U.S. for emergency use) to its capacity, 700 million barrels. Officials reported that the increased oil in the nation's emergency stockpile was intended to strengthen the U.S. capability to respond to potential oil supply disruptions.

Natural gas. In the first nine months of 2001, according to the EIA, Americans burned 16.49 trillion cubic feet (471.14 billion cubic meters) of natural gas, down from 16.67 trillion cubic feet (476.28 billion cubic meters) during the same period in 2000. Despite the reduction, EIA officials projected increased natural gas consumption of nearly 1 percent a year through 2020. Use of natural gas for electricity generation was expected to be the fastest-growing sector.

Electricity demand and rates, which also had skyrocketed in early 2001, slumped later in the year. Total electric retail sales were up slightly, however, according to the EIA, to a total of 1.97 trillion kilowatt hours in the first seven months of 2001, from 1.94 trillion kilowatt hours during the same period in 2000.

Coal accounted for more than one-half of the nation's output of electricity in 2001. Through the first nine months of 2001, according to the EIA, coal production reached 856,228 tons (776,600 metric tons), up from 806,173 tons (731,200 metric tons) in the first nine months of 2000. Production in 2001 was nearly 5 percent above 2000 production, according to the EIA. Although coal is abundant and relatively cheap in the United States, it is the only fossil fuel whose price did not decline in 2001. ☐ James Tanner

See also **Energy Supply: A Special Report.**

Engineering. See **Building and construction.**

England. See **United Kingdom.**

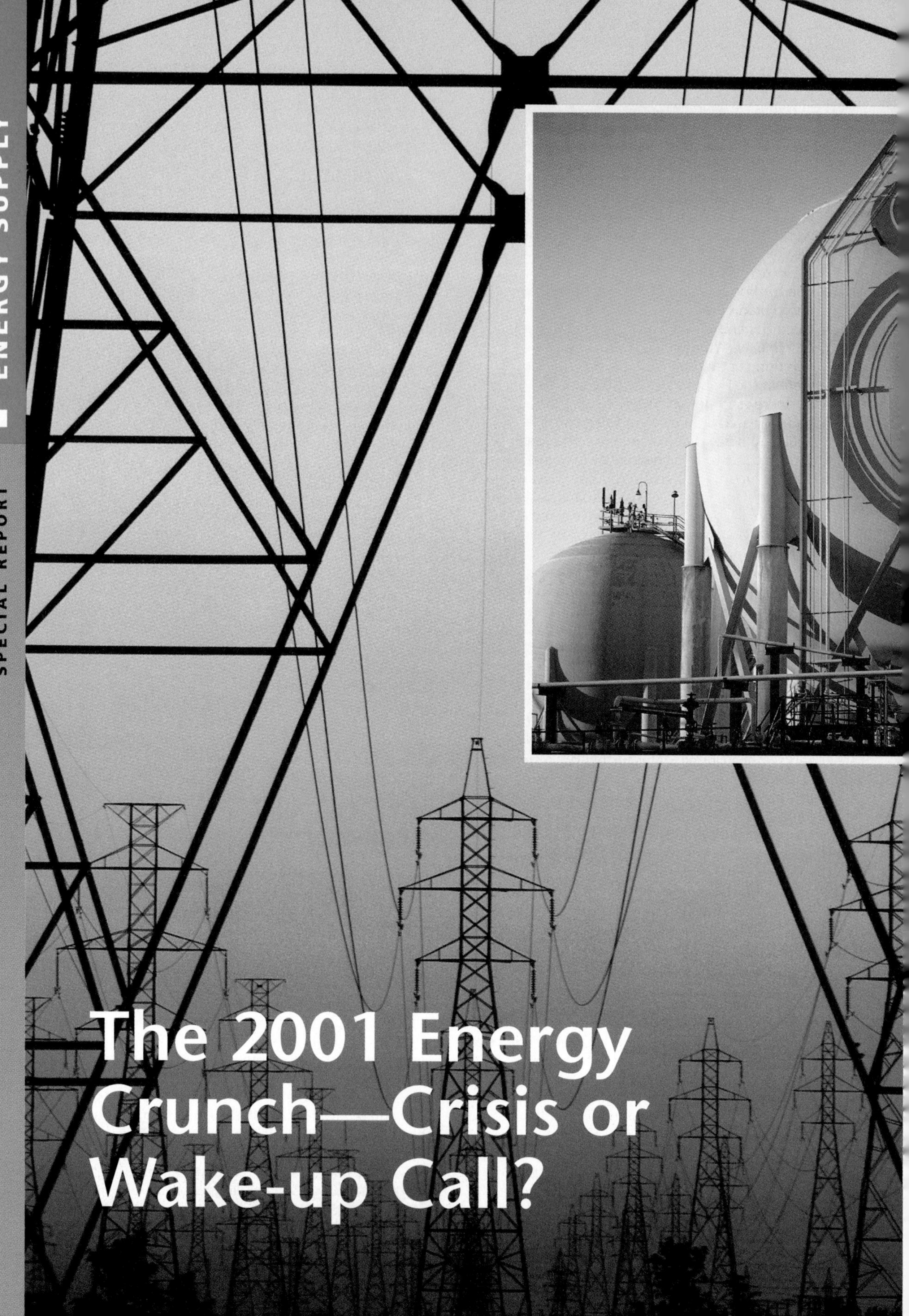

The 2001 Energy Crunch—Crisis or Wake-up Call?

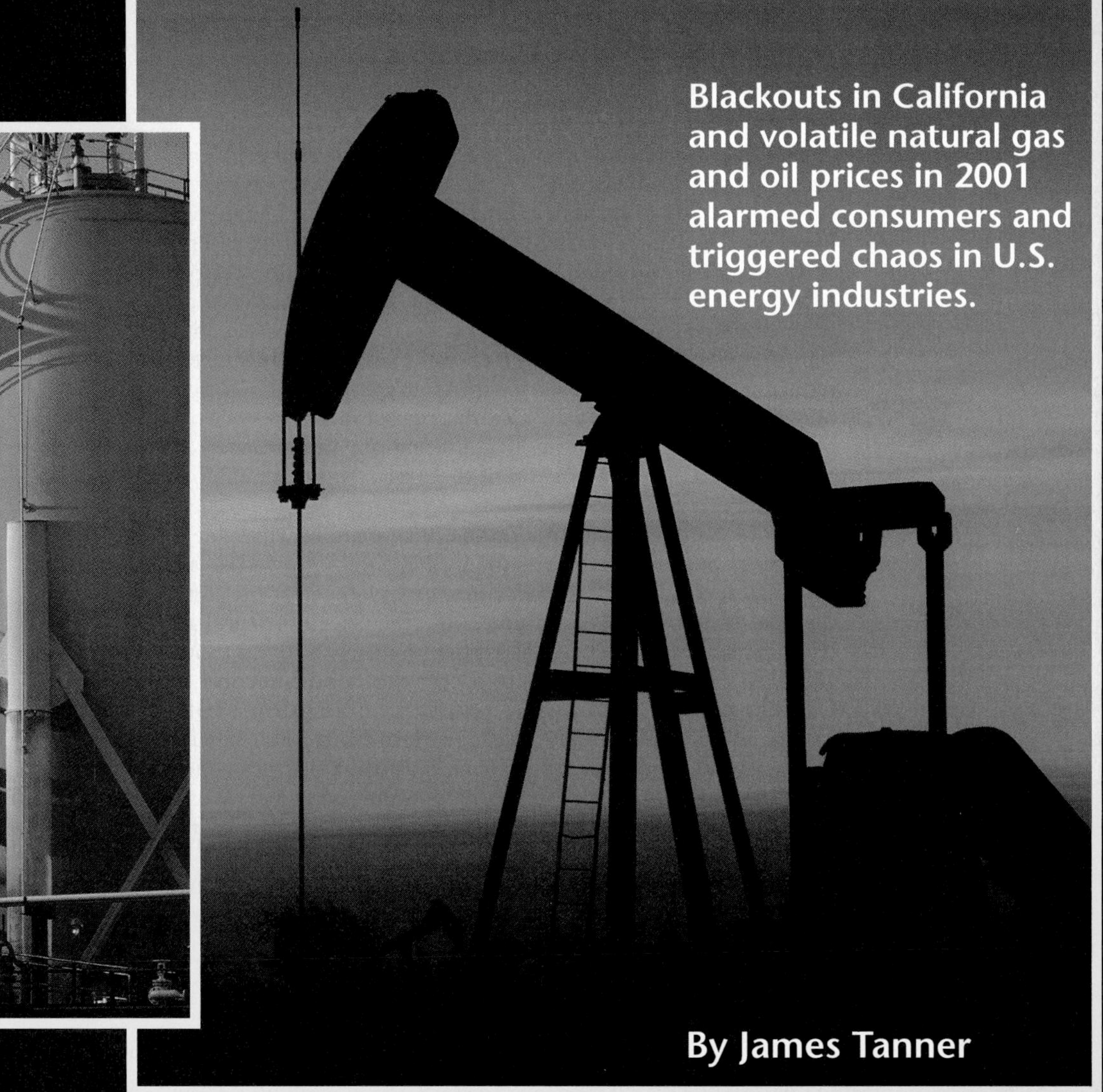

Blackouts in California and volatile natural gas and oil prices in 2001 alarmed consumers and triggered chaos in U.S. energy industries.

By James Tanner

California's power industry slid into chaos. The wholesale price of electricity jumped by more than 1,000 percent between January 2000 and January 2001. In March 2001, the state's two main utility companies ordered rolling blackouts that shut down industries and left millions of people without electricity in areas stretching from San Francisco to Los Angeles. One of the state's two largest electric utility companies declared bankruptcy, and the California Public Utilities Commission passed the largest rate hike in California history, boosting the price the public paid for electricity by up to 46 percent.

Energy problems spread beyond California's borders as the price of natural gas and gasoline increased dramatically across the nation. Natural gas—the source of heat in most houses in the United States—nearly doubled in price between January 2000 and June 2001. In spring 2001, U.S. gasoline prices jumped from an average of about $1.40 a gallon to about $1.60 a gallon. In parts of the Midwest, including Chicago, a gallon of regular unleaded gasoline rose to at least $2.

Alarmed by the economic dangers posed for the United States by surging fuel and electricity costs, the administration of President George W. Bush launched a new national energy strategy in May 2001. Noting that the nation faced the most serious energy problems since the energy shocks of the 1970's, the Bush administration proposed a multifaceted energy plan. The plan suggested reducing government regulations; encouraging the production of oil, gas, and nuclear power; introducing tax incentives to both boost coal output and promote conservation; and allowing oil companies to drill in a portion of the Arctic National Wildlife Refuge in Alaska.

Before Congress could act on the Bush plan, however, demand for energy began to decline as the U.S. economy slowed down. The high fuel costs that some economists blamed for the slowdown also declined. By late June 2001, the price of natural gas had dropped by almost two-thirds, from nearly $10 per thousand cubic feet (28.3 cubic meters) to $3 per thousand cubic feet. Gasoline prices settled down to an average of less than $1.50 a gallon, and electricity prices in the western United States fell to the lowest level in more than a year. California officials actually boasted of a surprising, if temporary, surplus of power. Was the crisis over, as some skeptics claimed? Or was it just beginning, as the authors of the Bush energy program suggested?

The latest energy shock, whether short-lived or just beginning, raised troubling questions: Did the nation have a sufficient number of power plants to generate the electricity needed in California and elsewhere once the economy rebounds and demand for electricity accelerates again? Was there enough natural gas—the preferred fuel for most new electric power plants—to keep power facilities running and still meet other energy requirements? Would the worldwide production of oil keep up with demand if consumption continued to climb as it had in recent years?

Forces affecting the energy market

The 2000-2001 energy shock, like the energy crises of the 1970's, was the result of a number of complex factors, including a sharp increase in the demand for electricity. The growing use of computers and the popularity of the Internet—along with the electronic technology needed to feed its popularity—was seen as driving the energy-use increase in the 1990's. However, demand for electricity was on the rise even before the era of the desktop computer. Annual consumption of electricity in the United States stood at 1 trillion kilowatt-hours, and a kilowatt-hour is the work done by one kilowatt in an hour, in 1965. (One kilowatt is 1,000 watts.) By 1980 annual use had surpassed 2 trillion kilowatt-hours. It climbed to 3 trillion kilowatt-hours by the mid-1990's. In 2000, annual demand for electric power topped 3.6 trillion kilowatt-hours a year. (It takes 1 kilowatt-hour of electric energy to keep a 100-watt light bulb burning for 10 hours.)

The U.S. electric power industry did not keep up with con-

The author:
James Tanner is a former energy news editor for *The Wall Street Journal.*

Energy production versus consumption in the United States

The United States produces far less oil than it consumes, making the nation dependent on foreign imports of oil, particularly from the Organization of Petroleum Exporting Countries (OPEC). Most of the natural gas consumed domestically is produced in the United States or imported from Canada.

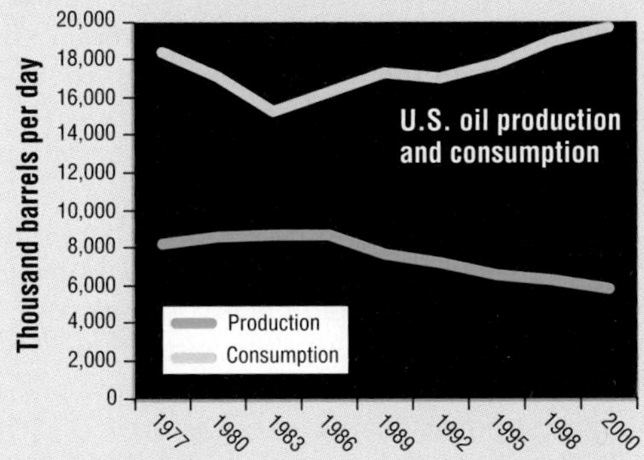

U.S. natural gas production and consumption

Trillion cubic feet

25
20
15
10
5
0

1980 1990 1992 1993 1994 1995 1996 1997 1998

Production
Consumption

Source: Department of Energy, Energy Information Administration.

sumer demand by building a sufficient number of new power plants during this period. There were two primary reasons: first, plants are expensive to build; second, they are unpopular with neighbors, primarily because they can be a source of pollution and are often perceived as dangerous.

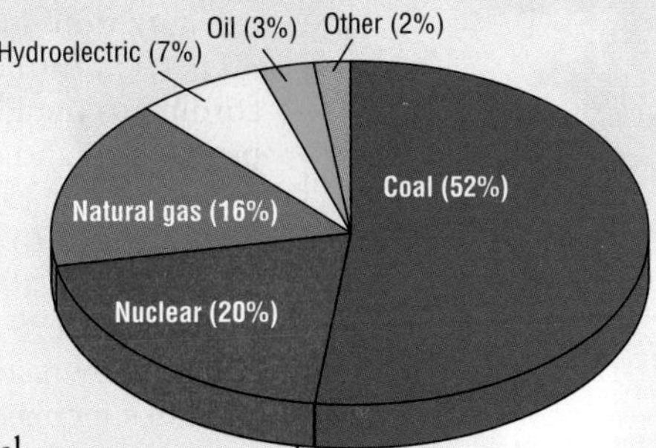

In 2001, coal remained the primary energy source for the generation of electricity. However, the use of natural gas to produce electricity continued to increase rapidly, particularly in California.

Coal-fired power plants

In 2001, 52 percent of all U.S. power plants generated electricity by burning coal, which is plentiful and cheap but dirty. Federal law prohibits the burning of medium- or high-sulfur coals to generate electricity in power plants built after 1971, unless the plants are equipped with scrubbers. These are devices that absorb sulfur dioxide fumes as they pass through the plant's smokestacks. The expense of installing scrubbers and other so-called "clean-coal" technology, coupled with widespread opposition to the burning of coal from environmental groups, discouraged utility companies from constructing new plants that used coal to produce electricity.

Coal is an abundant source of energy. The Energy Information Administration (EIA) at the U.S. Department of Energy estimates that U.S. coal reserves will last more than 250 years at current levels of production. However, coal is an unpopular source of energy because of pollution problems. EIA officials projected that the percentage of electricity generated from the burning of coal will decline to 44 percent by 2020.

Nuclear power plants

Nuclear power plants are even less popular with the public than coal-burning plants because of the risk of radioactivity being released as the result of an accident. A potentially devastating accident occurred in 1979, when mechanical and human failures resulted in the destruction of a nuclear reactor core at the Three Mile Island nuclear power plant in Pennsylvania. Although scientists and technicians prevented large amounts of radioactivity from being released, no nuclear power facilities have been built in the United States since the accident. The 104 nuclear power plants that remained in operation in the United States after the accident generated 20 percent of the nation's electricity in 2000.

The growing demand for natural gas

Meanwhile, natural gas used to generate electricity gained in popularity during the 1990's. It burned cleaner than either coal or oil and was considered by many to be safer than nuclear power. By 2000, natural gas generated 16 percent of all electricity in the United States. In California, the percentage was even higher. Three of the state's five largest power plants were gas-fired.

Between 1990 and 2000, total U.S. demand for natural gas—for home heating, electricity generation, and all other uses—grew by 22 percent. In 2000, the country consumed 22.8 trillion cubic feet of natural gas—nearly 25 percent of the nation's total energy consumption. In California, natural gas provided approximately 30 percent of the total amount of energy consumed in 2000. According to the EIA, U.S. natural gas reserves—at current levels of production and consumption—will last only about 66 years. However, the EIA also projected that natural gas consumption will continue to rise and will likely be used to generate as much as 36 percent of all U.S. electricity by 2020.

Between 1991 and 2000, a period when demand for natural gas grew by nearly 20 percent, natural gas production in the United States increased only slightly, by less than 300 billion cubic

Recoverable U.S. reserves of petroleum, natural gas, and coal

Petroleum	
Consumption:	19.5 million barrels per day in 2000
U.S. Reserve:	21.8 billion barrels
Years left:	77 years of recoverable reserves left at current rates of production
Natural Gas	
Consumption:	22.8 trillion cubic feet in 2000
U.S. Reserve:	167.4 trillion cubic feet
Years left:	66 years of recoverable reserves left at current rates of production
Coal	
Consumption:	1,079.7 million short tons
U.S.Reserve:	502.7 billion short tons
Years left:	250+ years of recoverable reserves left at current rates of production

Source: Department of Energy, Energy Information Administration.

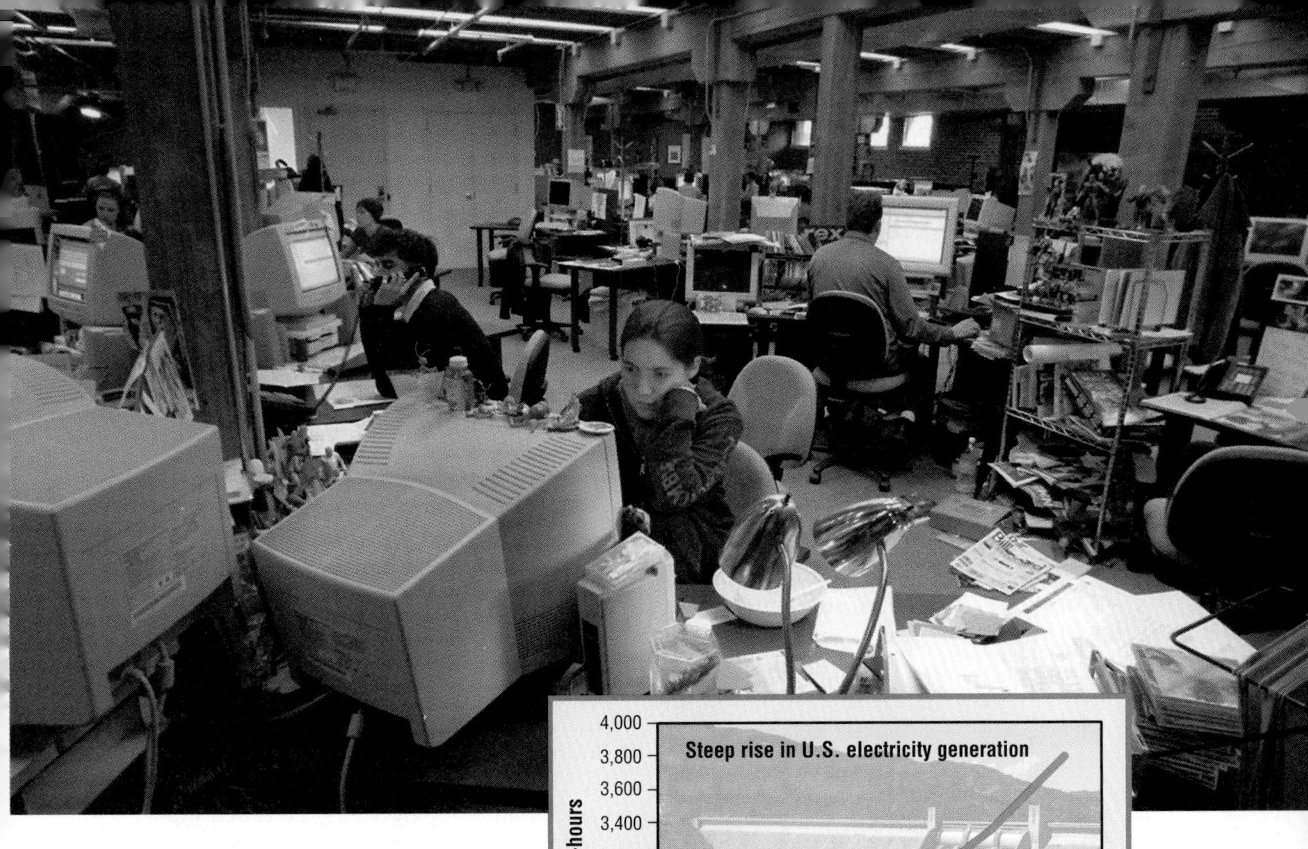

The rapid adoption of the computer by U.S. businesses and in American households combined with the rapid rise of the Internet helped fuel the steep rise in the consumption of electricity in the United States in the 1990's.

feet annually. According to industry officials, the price of natural gas was low during much of the 1990's, limiting the profits earned by natural gas producers. To compensate, the natural gas companies cut costs by decreasing investments in exploration and production by as much as 50 percent. With few new sources, by 2000, demand for natural gas had overwhelmed supply. For a while, increasing imports from Canada and withdrawing natural gas from storage helped meet demand, and prices remained stable. However, colder-than-normal weather during the winter of 2000-2001 greatly reduced inventories, driving up prices. In California, the state in which electrical generation was most dependent on natural gas, demand exceeded the capacity of the pipelines that transported gas into the state. This sent natural gas prices sharply higher, driving up the wholesale price of electricity in California and home-heating costs across much of the country.

The California energy crisis

An insufficient number of generating facilities and high natural gas prices were responsible for only a portion of California's energy problems in 2001. California utilities purchased electricity from companies in the Pacific Northwest, where electricity generated by hydroelectric plants is generally cheap and plentiful. (A hydroelectric plant uses water that is stored in a reservoir behind a dam and converts the energy of falling water into electric energy.) However, a drought in the Pacific Northwest in 2000 and 2001 resulted in low water levels in reservoirs. The water shortages severely cut the amount of power that could be generated in the region's hydroelectric plants, putting even more pressure on California's natural gas-fired power plants.

California's energy crisis also was driven by a factor that had nothing to do with supply and demand. In 1996, the California legislature deregulated the state's electric utilities with the idea that increased competition would drive down price. (Traditionally, electric utilities in the United States operated as regional monopolies overseen by a state board, which regulated retail prices and company profits.) After deregulation, a number of California's utility companies sold off their power plants and switched from generating electricity to distributing electricity. The utility companies bought electricity from electric power producing companies and then sold and distributed it to their electricity customers over transmission lines.

Critics of California's deregulation legislation pointed out that the law required utilities to buy power on the open market at market prices but barred the utilities from passing increases on to customers until 2002. When demand for electricity exceeded supply in 2000 and 2001, the price of electric power went higher and higher. The utilities soon ran out of money. When the corporations that now owned the generating plants refused to sell the utility companies electricity on credit, the utility companies were forced to institute rolling blackouts.

Factors that drive the price of oil

While California had its hands full with electricity problems, a crisis was brewing in the oil industry that sharply pushed up the price of gasoline in the United States. Gasoline, other fuels, and even plastics are made from crude oil, which is pumped out of the ground and shipped to refineries for processing. The nationwide jump in the price of gasoline in early 2001 involved three interrelated factors—the growing demand for the fuel in the United States; the worldwide supply of oil in relation to demand; and the influence of the Organization of Petroleum Exporting Countries (OPEC), an association of 11 oil-producing nations—Algeria, Indonesia, Iran, Iraq, Kuwait, Libya, Nigeria, Qatar, Saudi Arabia, United Arab Emirates, and Venezuela.

World demand for oil grew at rates of 1 percent to 2 percent annually during the 1990's, reaching 75.5 million barrels a day in 2000. Despite the global economic slowdown, demand continued to climb to 76 million barrels a day in 2001. These record levels of consumption strained the capacity of oil fields and refineries alike.

In 2001, OPEC produced nearly 40 percent of the world's oil. Holding nearly three-fourths of the world's known reserves, the OPEC nations exercise a great deal of power over the world's petroleum supplies. OPEC was founded in 1960 to wrest control of oil prices from U.S. and European oil companies. In the 1970's,

Energy consumption on the home-front

Americans use a lot more electricity than they think they do. While most people conscientiously turn off lights, electric light actually accounts for a small fraction of domestic consumption of electricity. In many households, the entire heating and cooling systems are powered by electricity, and most modern households contain an extraordinary array of appliances: home entertainment centers with televisions, VCR's, and stereos; kitchens with dishwashers, microwaves, and coffee makers; washing machines and dryers; bathrooms with hair dryers and electric toothbrushes; and the home office with its computer, printer, and fax. The result is incredible convenience and an incredible increase in electricity usage. In 1949, U.S. households consumed 1.1 trillion kilowatt-hours of electricity. In 2000, domestic usage hit 67 billion kilowatt-hours.

In 1975, the amount of electricity used to power small appliances was so little that electric companies listed the appliances as "miscellaneous" when compiling consumption statistics. By 1998, "miscellaneous" consumption had skyrocketed. Some of the worst offenders were small appliances—computers, microwaves, televisions, and VCR's—that have electric clocks that continuously draw power even when the appliance itself is not in use. In 2000, the "miscellaneous" appliances accounted for 20 percent of all domestic consumption, and most of the time, they were not even in use!

The average monthly cost for a family of four people to operate various household appliances is based on an electric rate of 7.5 cents per kilowatt-hour.

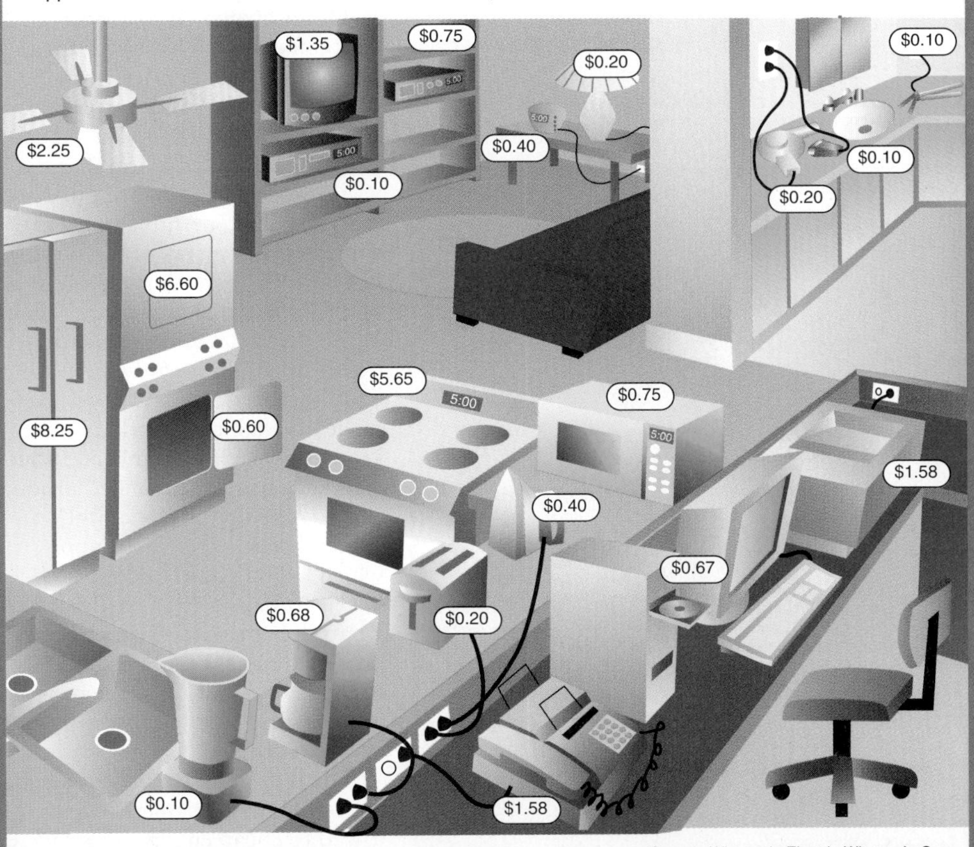

Source: Wisconsin Electric-Wisconsin Gas.

The fuel efficiency of various 2001 vehicles

Small cars	miles per gallon
Dodge Neon	24 city/31 highway
Nissan Sentra	26 city/33 highway
Toyota Corolla	29 city/33 highway
Family Sedan	
Dodge Stratus	20 city/30 highway
Nissan Maxima	19 city/26 highway
Toyota Camry	20 city/ 27 highway
Mini-vans	
Ford Windstar	18 city/24 highway
Honda Odyssey	18 city/25 highway
Nissan Quest	17 city/23 highway
Sports-Utility Vehicles	
Ford Expedition	14 city/18 highway
Nissan Xterra	15 city/19 highway
Toyota 4Runner	17 city/20 highway

U.S. Department of Energy; U.S. Environmental Protection Agency

many of the OPEC nations pushed the oil companies out of their countries by nationalizing oil operations within their borders. Production surged to a peak of more than 30 million barrels a day as OPEC gained a monopoly over oil markets. In fact, OPEC is often blamed for the energy crisis that followed, but an Arab oil *embargo* (restriction on commerce) that began in 1973, not OPEC, triggered the first energy crisis.

Past energy crises

In October 1973, the oil-producing countries of the Middle East and North Africa, including OPEC's seven Arab member nations, halted shipments of crude oil to the United States and other countries that supported Israel, during a conflict between the Arab nations and Israel. The embargo triggered the first energy crisis in the United States. However, OPEC's non-Arab members continued to ship oil. The embargo lasted only until March 1974, but this was long enough for the leaders of oil-consuming nations to panic. Western traders and refiners bid up the price of oil, while their governments rushed to enact rules on energy use.

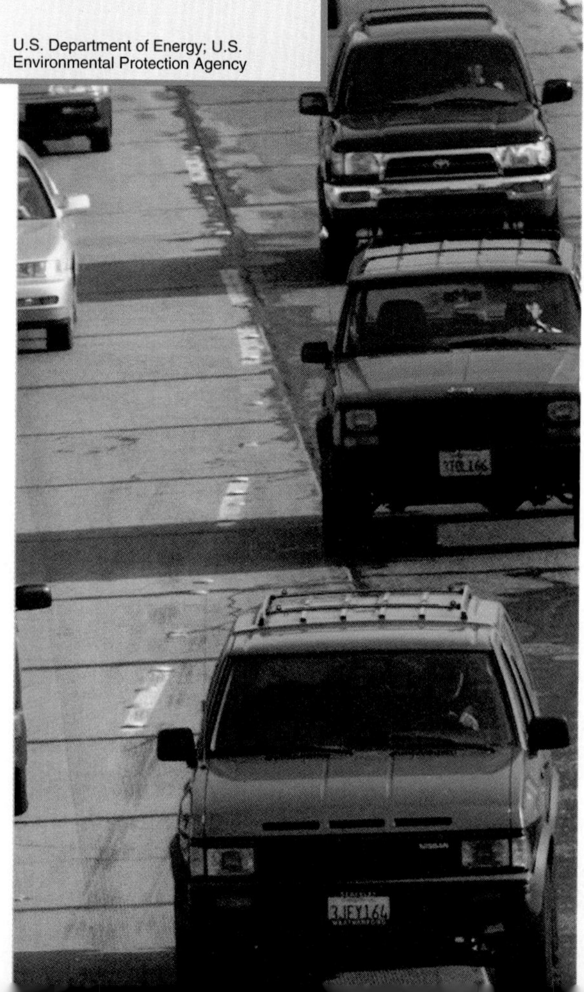

Of far greater consequence, the Arab oil embargo led to the quadrupling of petroleum prices from $3 a barrel to nearly $12 a barrel between 1973 and 1974. The oil embargo also sparked alarm that the world was running out of oil. Those fears faded after Arab nations resumed oil shipments to the West. But in 1979, a revolution in Iran brought on the second energy shock of the decade. During the revolution, Iranian oil output—as much as 6 million barrels a day—was no longer available on world oil markets. Other OPEC members, including Saudi Arabia, expanded production to take up the slack. Still, demand was higher than supply, which led oil prices to double between 1978 and 1981 to about $24 a barrel. Some oil industry analysts predicted prices would reach $100 a barrel before 2000. But the response to the crisis actually caused oil prices to drop.

The leap in oil prices sent alarming signals to consumers accustomed to cheap energy. There were efforts to improve energy efficiency of buildings and businesses, houses and appliances, and cars and planes. The search for oil fields outside OPEC accelerated. A pipeline about 800 miles (1,300 kilometers) long was built in Alaska to transport crude oil from the giant Prudhoe Bay field, which was discovered in 1968. New oil fields were developed in the North Sea and other non-OPEC regions. Even war and political turmoil in the Middle East during the 1980's had little lasting effect on oil supplies or prices in the United States.

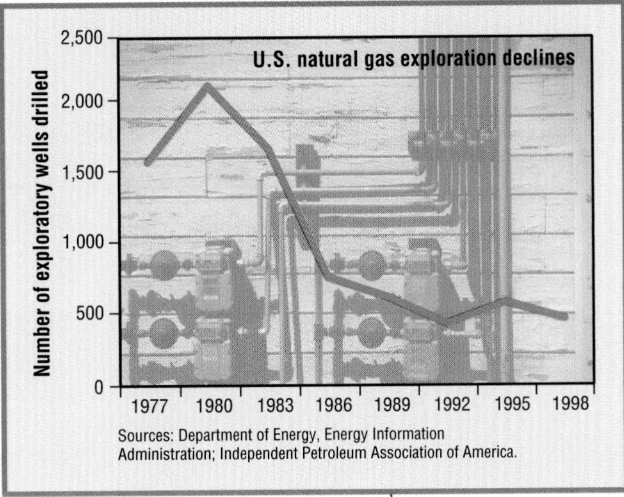

Exploration for natural gas in the United States declined during the 1980's and 1990's, as falling profits prompted energy companies to cut costs by decreasing investments in exploration and production.

OPEC's influence faded in the early 1990's, largely because of an oversupply of oil on world markets. In addition, exporters made a big mistake in the late 1990's when they increased oil output further on the eve of an economic crash in Asia, which had been importing increasing volumes of oil. As a result of the overproduction, world oil prices fell. In 1998, the price of crude oil dropped to $10 a barrel, its lowest price in 70 years, after adjustments for inflation. OPEC revenues plunged, and many oil companies, suffering from a lack of capital, quit drilling.

At service stations in the United States, gasoline prices dipped below $1 a gallon. Some economists claimed that gasoline had fallen to its lowest level in history, when inflation and federal and state taxes were accounted for. Sports-utility vehicles (SUV's) that could go only a few miles on a gallon of gasoline soared in popularity. Wasteful use of energy, combined with an economic boom in the United States and other nations, and a lackluster search for new oil supplies, set the stage for another energy crisis.

The 2001 energy shock

It began when Mexico, another major oil-producing country, prodded OPEC to restrict output in an effort to push up sagging prices. In the past, OPEC had tried to restrict oil output but without much success. Individual OPEC countries always restored production output. This time, to the surprise of analysts, OPEC nations set restricted output quotas and stuck to them. The strategy proved successful, leading to a 1999 increase in crude oil prices that accelerated in 2000. The strategy also led to talk of possible oil shortages. Worried that the high prices would reduce oil demand again, OPEC backed off and began increasing output. Nevertheless, the price of crude oil surged beyond $35 a barrel late in the year. By 2001, with the growth in world oil demand showing signs of slowing, OPEC again reversed itself. It cut production several times to maintain a target price of $25 a barrel. While some analysts were skeptical that OPEC could manage world oil

OPEC nations and top importers of OPEC oil

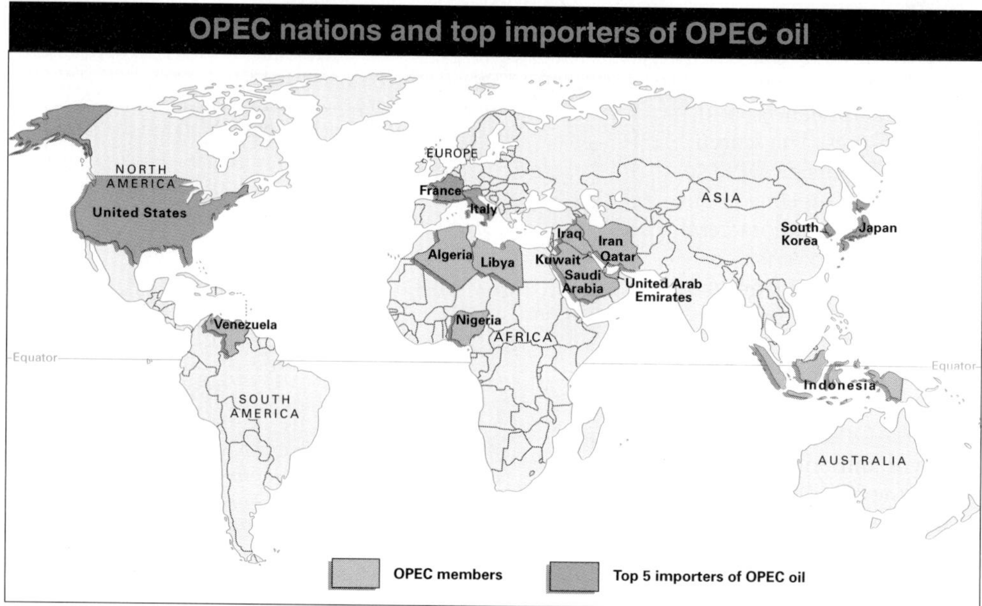

The 11 nations of OPEC supply 40 percent of the world's oil. Most of OPEC's production is consumed by a small number of industrialized nations, particularly the United States, which consumes fully one-quarter of the world's oil output.

markets for long, oil exporters clearly intended to try, and few analysts could foresee oil prices ever dropping back to $10 a barrel.

U.S. dependence on foreign oil

Americans are OPEC's best customers. With 4.5 percent of the world's population, the United States in 2001 consumed one-fourth of the world's oil output, close to 20 million barrels a day. Although Americans complained about high pump prices in the spring of 2001, U.S. motorists burned an average of 8.4 million barrels of oil a day in the first five months of the year—nearly 200,000 barrels a day more than in the first five months of 2000.

Despite Americans' rate of usage, industry analysts believed the world had enough oil to meet the fuel needs of the United States and other nations for 30 to 40 years at current consumption rates even if no new oil fields were found. Experts estimated that the world's proven reserves of petroleum exceed 1 trillion barrels. Proven reserves consist of oil that oil companies can economically recover from known underground deposits with current technology at current prices. According to EIA estimates of recoverable reserves of oil, there is possibly enough petroleum within the United States to provide for current rates of production for 77 years.

In the United States, however, the combination of rising oil demand and falling production has resulted in increased dependence on imported oil. Between 1918 and 1999, the United States produced 180 billion barrels of crude oil, more than any other country. Domestic crude oil production peaked in 1970 at 9.6 million barrels a day. Except for brief periods, domestic production has been on a decline since, mainly because many U.S. fields are exhausted. While the discovery of oil by companies drilling in the deepwater region of the Gulf of Mexico have helped to offset declines in other oil fields, domestic oil production in 2001 averaged only 5.9 million barrels a day, significantly less than demand.

In 1973, the United States consumed an average of 17.3 million barrels of oil a day, nearly 40 percent of which was imported. In 2000, the United States consumed 19.5 million barrels of oil a day, 54 percent of which was imported, according to the U.S. Department of Energy. In addition, the United States does not have enough refining capacity to process all of the petroleum products it uses and, therefore, must import gasoline and other fuels that are refined from oil.

Lessons of the 2001 oil shock

A number of lessons can be drawn from the 2001 energy shock, regardless of whether it was short-lived or the tip of an iceberg. First, say experts, the existing *power grids* (a complex network of power distribution lines that provide electricity to businesses and homes) in the United States are inadequate, antiquated, and filled with bottlenecks. New power plants need to be built and the power grids need to be modernized and expanded. Construction of several new power plants began in 2001. Whether these would be completed in time to supply the nation's power needs during the next period of economic expansion depended on how quickly the U.S. economy recovers from a slowdown that began in 2000. Also, California's electricity crisis highlighted possible dangers in the hasty deregulation of an industry as vital as electricity, according to some economists and political observers. In 2001, 24 of the 50 states were in the process of deregulating public utilities.

Second, experts agree that the United States needs to become less dependent on imported oil. In 2001, the U.S. continued to import more than one-half of all the oil consumed. Much of that oil was imported from OPEC's Arab nations. This source could dry up quickly if renewed conflict in the Middle East were to alter economic and diplomatic ties in the region. While the United States still has large reserves of oil, it could take months if not years to make those reserves fully operational.

Another lesson learned, according to many experts, is that U.S. natural gas and oil companies need to increase domestic drilling. The high oil and natural gas prices encouraged companies to increase drilling. In June 2001, there were 1,270 rotary rigs drilling in the United States, compared with 878 rotary rigs in June 2000.

Finally, many experts believed that U.S. consumers needed a renewed sense of conservation. Unplugging appliances, turning off lights, putting on a sweater when it's chilly rather than bumping up the heat, and abandoning gasoline guzzling SUV's can all contribute to lowering demand for energy. A new national energy policy that stressed conservation and the development of new energy sources, as well as the development of existing resources, could be an important step toward guarding the national interest against future energy shocks. ■■■

Environmental pollution. Environmental protection policies in the United States underwent a major change with the swearing in of a new president, George W. Bush, in January 2001. President Bush supported some of the initiatives of his predecessor, Bill Clinton, such as greatly reducing the emissions created by diesel-powered buses and trucks and the protection of tens of thousands of acres of wetlands. However, President Bush acted to reverse others, such as U.S. participation in a landmark global climate treaty and rules that would have placed one-third of national forests off-limits to most development.

Kyoto Protocol. In November, representatives from 165 countries, meeting in Morocco, agreed on rules for the implementation of the Kyoto Protocol, the 1997 treaty requiring industrialized nations to reduce the emissions of gases that cause global warming. The agreement reached in Morocco set the stage for *ratification* (approval) of the treaty. In order to go into effect, 55 countries must ratify the Kyoto Protocol, including countries responsible for producing more than 50 percent of the *greenhouse gases* (gases, such as those generated from the burning of fossil fuels, blamed for the gradual warming of Earth's climate).

However, the United States, which emits about one-fourth of the world's greenhouse gases, was absent from the voting. President Bush had rejected the Kyoto treaty in March 2001, citing the failure of treaty organizers to include developing countries, such as China and India, and concern that complying with the treaty would weaken the U.S. economy.

If formally ratified by the required number of countries, the treaty could take effect as early as 2002. The final treaty requires industrialized nations to reduce emissions of greenhouse gases between 2008 and 2012 to an average of 5.2 percent below 1990 levels. The agreement permits countries to receive credits for reducing emissions through such means as protecting trees, which absorb carbon dioxide. It also includes a system for countries to buy and sell emission credits.

Hudson River cleanup. In November 2001, the U.S. Environmental Protection Agency (EPA) officially ordered General Electric Company (GE), of Fairfield, Connecticut, to begin a nearly $500-million project to dredge dangerous chemicals called polychlorinated biphenyls (PCB's) from a stretch of the Hudson River in New York State. The order came after more than 20 years of research and disputes over the potential dangers presented by the PCB's, which have been linked to cancer in humans and animals.

GE dumped an estimated 1.1 million pounds (500,000 kilograms) of PCB's into the Hudson River north of Albany, New York, from the 1940's until 1977, when dumping was banned. Under the EPA's order, which was similar to a proposal the agency had made in August 2001, GE must dredge a 40-mile (64-kilometer) section of river bottom to remove about 150,000 pounds (68,000 kilograms) of the PCB's. Environmentalists expect the project to be one of the most complex environmental cleanups in history.

GE officials had sharply criticized the EPA's original proposal and had launched a publicity campaign to prevent the agency from proceeding. Company officials and others contended that the river was cleaning itself by slowly burying the chemicals in the river mud and that dredging would only stir up the PCB's and harm the environment. However, many environmentalists welcomed the effort as a way to bring the river back to life. Because of the pollution in the Hudson, New York State health officials had been warning residents for years to avoid eating fish caught in the river.

Hybrid automobiles. In May, a task force headed by Vice President Dick Cheney recommended providing tax credits to people who buy vehicles powered by fuels other than gasoline. The tax credits, which the task force suggested should be implemented in 2002, would encourage people to buy alternative-fuel vehicles to reduce air pollution.

Such vehicles include "hybrid" cars, which are powered by a combination of gasoline and electricity, and fuel-cell vehicles, which generate power by chemical reactions. In 2001, fuel-cell cars were not yet available, but hybrid cars, especially popular models such as the Toyota Prius and Honda Insight, enjoyed growing consumer interest. These vehicles use less gasoline than traditional cars, averaging about 60 miles (97 kilometers) per gallon. Several car manufacturers in 2001 indicated that they would speed production of hybrid cars due to increased demand.

Mercury warning. In January, the U.S. Food and Drug Administration (FDA) issued a warning that pregnant women and those who might become pregnant should not eat several types of fish because of a concern that they may contain high levels of mercury that may be harmful to unborn babies. Shark, swordfish, king mackerel, and tilefish were included on the FDA list. Mercury is a hazardous chemical element that occurs naturally and is also released into the environment by coal-fired power plants and other industries. Other major sources of mercury include discarded batteries, light switches, and fluorescent lights. Mercury has been shown to damage the brain and kidneys of a developing fetus. Fish ingest mercury when it collects on the bottoms of lakes and rivers.

The oil tanker *Jessica* lists to one side after running aground in the Galapagos Islands in January 2001. More than 160,000 gallons (606,000 liters) of crude oil were spilled, threatening endangered wildlife.

Trans-Alaska pipeline spill. On Oct. 4, 2001, a gunman using a high-powered rifle pierced the Trans-Alaska pipeline, causing one of the worst oil spills since the pipeline went into operation in 1977. The pipeline, among the world's longest at 800 miles (1,290 kilometers), was ruptured at a point before a long uphill climb. When the spill was discovered and the pipeline was temporarily shut down, hundreds of thousands of pounds of oil flowed down the hill to the rupture. The high pressure of the oil caused it to spray as far as 75 feet (23 meters) from the bullet hole.

Daniel Carson Lewis, of Livengood, Alaska, was arrested and charged with felony assault, weapons misconduct, criminal mischief, and driving while intoxicated. The pipeline was brought back into service after only three days. However, more than 285,600 gallons (1 million liters) of oil had already spilled, covering more than two acres (0.8 hectares) of pristine spruce forest. Despite the damage, the Alaska Department of Environmental Conservation reported that no animals had been directly harmed by the oil.

The Trans-Alaska pipeline carries more than 1 million barrels a day—about 17 percent of U.S. oil output—from Prudhoe Bay on the Arctic Ocean to Valdez, on the coast of Alaska. Oil companies that supply the pipeline were asked to cut production by 95 percent after the incident. The spill was the worst since 1978, when an unknown assailant detonated a bomb at the pipeline, spilling 670,000 gallons (2.5 million liters) of oil.

Exxon *Valdez* ruling. In November 2001, a federal appeals court in San Francisco overturned the $5.3-billion punitive damage judgment that the Exxon Corporation (now Exxon Mobil Corp. of Irving, Texas) had been ordered to pay in 1994 for environmental damage caused by a 1989 oil spill in Alaska. The spill had occurred when the Exxon oil tanker *Valdez* ran aground on a reef, spilling 11 million gallons (41.6 liters) of crude oil into Prince William Sound and damaging more than 1,500 miles (2,400 kilometers) of coastline. The 1994 ruling had ordered Exxon to pay thousands of commercial fishermen, Alaska natives, and other groups harmed by the spill.

In its November 2001 decision, the panel ruled that the $5-billion award had been excessive. The court ordered that another judge should review the case and determine a smaller award to be paid to the groups affected by the spill.

☐ Andrew Hoffman

See also **Conservation; Energy supply: A Special Report; Global warming: A Special Report.**

Equatorial Guinea. See **Africa.**

Eritrea. See **Africa.**

Estonia. See **Europe.**

Ethiopia. See **Africa.**

Europe

A deepening economic downturn and a campaign against terrorism following terrorist attacks on the United States on September 11 dominated Europe in 2001. The attacks dealt a blow to consumer and business confidence in Europe, worsening the slowdown of European economies. European countries offered political and military support for the U.S.-led campaign and cracked down on terrorist cells inside their own countries.

European-U.S. relations. Prior to the September 11 attacks, European government leaders found themselves in conflict with the new U.S. administration of President George W. Bush over a number of issues. Most European governments protested the Bush administration's decision to withdraw U.S. support for the Kyoto Protocol, an international treaty intended to limit the emission of carbon dioxide and other so-called greenhouse gases that contribute to global warming. Europeans also expressed concern about U.S. plans for a missile defense system that would violate the U.S.-Russian Antiballistic Missile (ABM) Treaty. Leaders of the 15 European Union (EU) nations met with Bush on the eve of their summit meeting in Goteborg, Sweden, in June in an effort to defuse tensions over policy differences. The meeting was the first that any U.S. president had had with all EU leaders. Nevertheless, President Bush announced on December 13 that the United States would withdraw from the ABM treaty in 2002.

European governments quickly offered support for the U.S.-led campaign against terrorism after the Sept. 11, 2001, attacks. Leaders of the EU endorsed U.S. retaliation for the attacks at a specially convened summit meeting on September 21 in Brussels, Belgium. In early October, the United Kingdom and France sent troops to assist the U.S. military effort in Afghanistan against the Taliban government, which harbored Osama bin Laden, an exiled Saudi-born millionaire whom U.S. intelligence officers accused of masterminding the attacks. Leaders of the allied force in Afghanistan also sought the leaders of bin Laden's al-Qaida ("The Base" in Arabic) terrorist network. Germany offered to provide troops in November, after Chancellor Gerhard Schroeder won a vote of confidence in parliament over the issue.

European governments also cooperated with the United States in cracking down on alleged terrorists in Europe after investigators discovered that some of the hijackers who carried out the attacks on September 11 had lived in Germany. Others had links to people living in various European countries. Dozens of suspects were arrested in Germany, Spain, France, and other EU countries. European governments also agreed to freeze bank accounts held by people and groups that were cited by the United States as having links to terrorists.

Differences among EU members over the future of the antiterrorism campaign arose late in the year. Many European governments opposed the idea of extending the military campaign to countries beyond Afghanistan, such as Iraq. Several small European countries also protested when Prime Minister Tony Blair of the United Kingdom, President Jacques Chirac of France, and Chancellor Schroeder of Germany held a private meeting just before the start of an EU summit meeting in Belgium in October to discuss their military cooperation with the United States. The leaders of the smaller EU countries argued that the private meeting undermined EU efforts to develop defense cooperation among member countries.

Economy. Economic growth slowed dramatical-

Coins and bills of the euro, the common European currency, went into circulation on Jan. 1, 2002. The coins replaced the individual currencies of 12 of 15 member nations of the European Union.

Thousands of mourners gather outside Saint Paul's Cathedral in London on September 14 for a memorial service for victims of the terrorist attacks against the United States on September 11.

ly in 2001 because Europe was heavily affected by the recession in the United States. During the late 1990's, many European companies had forged closer economic ties with the United States by buying U.S. firms. This made the European firms vulnerable to the recession that began in the United States in March 2001. Unlike the United States, where the government passed a major tax cut in 2001 in an effort to stimulate the economy, major European countries—including Germany, France, and Italy—were constrained from taking action by EU rules requiring that countries using the euro, the common currency, maintain low budget deficits.

The European Commission (EC), the executive agency of the EU, forecast in November that economic growth in the bloc would slow to 1.7 percent in 2001, down from 3.3 percent in 2000. Unemployment, which had been declining for several years, edged up late in 2001. Earlier in the year, unemployment had dropped below 8 percent for the first time since the early 1980's.

European businesses came under intense pressure in 2001 as the economy slowed and the September 11 terrorist attacks dampened travel. Airlines suffered the most. Switzerland's national airline, Swissair, was pushed into bankruptcy in October. The Swiss government and a group of Swiss corporations and banks salvaged a small portion of Swissair by investing $2.5 billion in its low-cost, regional airline subsidiary, Crossair. Swissair's bankruptcy triggered the collapse of the Belgian carrier Sabena. Swissair owned 49.5 percent of Sabena, which began liquidation proceedings in November. The Belgian government and major Belgian companies invested

Facts in brief on European countries

Country	Population	Government	Monetary unit*	Foreign trade (million U.S.$) Exports†	Imports†
Albania	3,152,000	President Rexhep Mejdani; Prime Minister Ilir Meta	lek (141.30 = $1)	261	1,091
Andorra	69,000	Co-sovereigns bishop of Urgel, Spain, and the president of France; Prime Minister Marc Forne Molne	French franc & Spanish peseta	58	1,077
Austria	8,255,000	President Thomas Klestil; Chancellor Wolfgang Schuessel	schilling (14.98 = $1)	63,696	68,414
Belarus	10,175,000	President Aleksandr Lukashenko	ruble (1,486.00 = $1)	7,380	8,477
Belgium	10,165,000	King Albert II; Prime Minister Guy Verhofstadt	franc (43.93 = $1)	185,639	172,460
Bosnia-Herzegovina	3,890,000	Chairman of the collective presidency Jozo Krizanovic	marka (2.13 = $1)	950	2,450
Bulgaria	8,128,000	President Georgi Parvanov; Prime Minister Simeon Saxe-Coburg-Gotha	lev (2.12 = $1)	4,810	6,492
Croatia	4,460,000	President Stjepan Mesic	kuna (8.16 = $1)	4,432	7,923
Czech Republic	10,215,000	President Vaclav Havel; Prime Minister Milos Zeman	koruna (36.63 = $1)	29,059	32,240
Denmark	5,307,000	Queen Margrethe II; Prime Minister Anders Fogh Rasmussen	krone (8.09 = $1)	48,574	44,164
Estonia	1,368,000	President Arnold Ruutel; Prime Minister Mart Laar	kroon (17.04 = $1)	3,132	4,241
Finland	5,193,000	President Tarja Halonen; Prime Minister Paavo Lipponen	markka (6.47 = $1)	44,533	32,610
France	59,411,000	President Jacques Chirac; Prime Minister Lionel Jospin	franc (7.14 = $1)	295,015	300,970
Germany	82,286,000	President Johannes Rau; Chancellor Gerhard Schroeder	mark (2.13 = $1)	549,686	497,902
Greece	10,647,000	President Konstandinos Stephanopoulos; Prime Minister Konstandinos Simitis	drachma (370.97 = $1)	9,815	25,433
Hungary	9,956,000	President Ferenc Madl; Prime Minister Viktor Orban	forint (279.72 = $1)	28,012	31,951
Iceland	286,000	President Olafur Grimsson; Prime Minister David Oddsson	krona (102.13 = $1)	1,895	2,591
Ireland	3,811,000	President Mary McAleese; Prime Minister Bertie Ahern	pound (punt) (0.86 = $1)	76,874	50,553
Italy	57,092,000	President Carlo Azeglio Ciampi; Prime Minister Silvio Berlusconi	lira (2,108.42 = $1)	238,310 (includes San Marino)	236,671
Latvia	2,305,000	President Vaira Vike-Freiberga; Prime Minister Andris Berzins	lat (0.62 = $1)	1,867	3,187
Liechtenstein	34,000	Prince Hans Adam II; Prime Minister Otmar Hasler	Swiss franc	2,470	917

$179 million in Delta Air Transport, a Sabena subsidiary, and continued to operate a skeleton service using some of Sabena's planes and staff.

Europe's telecommunications companies also suffered a major industry shakeout in 2001. Telephone operating companies had agreed to spend more than $100 billion in 2000 to buy licenses to provide third-generation services, which were designed to deliver high-speed Internet access to mobile handsets. However, doubts about the technology and the potential demand for services grew in 2001, and companies struggled to finance the cost of the licenses. British Telecommunications Plc of the United Kingdom spun off its mobile telephone subsidiary to shareholders and sold off other assets to reduce debt. KPN N.V. of the Netherlands and Finland's Sonera Oyj also sold assets and effectively abandoned their plans to build pan-European businesses.

Telephone equipment makers suffered a sharp drop in orders as a result of the global slowdown in technology industries. Alcatel S.A. of France posted a first-half loss of $2.7 billion and cut 14,000 jobs after its attempt to acquire Lucent

Country	Population	Government	Monetary unit*	Foreign trade (million U.S.$) Exports†	Imports†
Lithuania	3,647,000	President Valdas Adamkus; Prime Minister Algirdas Mikolas Brazauskas	litas (4.00 = $1)	3,810	5,457
Luxembourg	438,000	Grand Duke Henri; Prime Minister Jean-Claude Juncker	franc (43.90 = $1)	7,899	10,254
Macedonia	2,048,000	President Boris Trajkovski	denar (64.76 = $1)	1,192	1,796
Malta	394,000	President Guido De Marco; Prime Minister Eddie Fenech Adami	lira (0.44 = $1)	2,337	3,417
Moldova	4,383,000	President Vladimir Voronin; Prime Minister Vasile Tarlev	leu (12.87 = $1)	465	567
Monaco	35,000	Prince Rainier III	French franc	no statistics available	
Netherlands	15,849,000	Queen Beatrix; Prime Minister Wim Kok	guilder (2.40 = $1)	208,916	196,340
Norway	4,505,000	King Harald V; Prime Minister Kjell Magne Bondevik	krone (8.77 = $1)	57,519	32,655
Poland	38,835,000	President Aleksander Kwasniewski; Prime Minister Jerzy Buzek	zloty (4.15 = $1)	31,651	48,940
Portugal	9,863,000	President Jorge Sampaio; Prime Minister Antonio Guterres**	escudo (218.31 = $1)	23,314	38,257
Romania	22,171,000	President Ion Iliescu; Prime Minister Adrian Nastase	leu (30,740.00 = $1)	10,367	13,055
Russia	146,376,000	President Vladimir Putin	ruble (29.51 = $1)	104,836	49,125
San Marino	28,000	2 captains regent appointed by Grand Council every 6 months	Italian lira	238,310	236,671 (includes Italy)
Slovakia	5,404,000	President Rudolf Schuster; Prime Minister Mikulas Dzurinda	koruna (47.39 = $1)	11,803	13,316
Slovenia	1,982,000	President Milan Kucan; Prime Minister Janez Drnovsek	tolar (239.61 = $1)	8,733	10,107
Spain	39,567,000	King Juan Carlos I; President of the Government (Prime Minister) Jose Maria Aznar	peseta (181.18 = $1)	113,348	152,900
Sweden	8,947,000	King Carl XVI Gustaf; Prime Minister Goran Persson	krona (10.59 = $1)	154,182	128,942
Switzerland	7,445,000	President Kaspar Villiger	franc (1.62 = $1)	74,876	76,082
Turkey	68,509,000	President Ahmet Necdet Sezer; Prime Minister Bulent Ecevit	lira (1,600,000.00 = $1)	26,572	53,499
Ukraine	50,083,000	President Leonid Kuchma	hryvna (5.35 = $1)	11,582	11,846
United Kingdom	58,959,000	Queen Elizabeth II; Prime Minister Tony Blair	pound (0.68 = $1)	281,551	334,367
Yugoslavia	10,655,000	President Vojislav Kostunica; Prime Minister Dragisa Pesic	new dinar (64.88 = $1)	1,500	3,300

*Exchange rates as of Oct. 5, 2001, or latest available data. †Latest available data.
**Guterres resigned Dec. 17, 2001. A new prime minister was to be elected in 2002.

Technologies Inc. of Murray Hill, New Jersey, failed in May. L.M. Ericsson AB of Sweden pulled out of the business of making mobile handsets and cut more than 12,000 jobs.

Interest-rate policy. European political leaders tangled with officials of the European Central Bank over interest-rate policy as the economy slowed. Several prime ministers and finance ministers criticized the central bank for not cutting interest rates aggressively to stimulate growth, as the Federal Reserve, the central bank of the United States, did 11 times in 2001. ECB officials at first refused to bow to pressure. However, the bank cut interest rates more aggressively in the autumn as inflation eased and the economy slowed after the September 11 terrorist attacks.

The euro remained relatively weak throughout 2001. EU officials hoped that the value of the currency would rise in 2002 after euro notes and coins went into circulation in the 12 participating countries.

EU enlargement. The EU moved a step closer to accepting new members in 2001. At a summit meeting in Goteborg, Sweden, on June 15 and

June 16, EU leaders declared that plans to expand the EU into Eastern Europe were irreversible, and the EU was committed to admitting new members by 2004. The EC, which handles membership negotiations for the EU, announced in November 2001 that most candidate countries had made significant progress in meeting EU entry criteria. These include installation of a democratic government, respect for the rights of minorities, and a market-oriented economy. The EC stated that as many as 10 of the 12 candidate countries—Poland, Hungary, the Czech Republic, Slovakia, Slovenia, Estonia, Latvia, Lithuania, Cyprus, and Malta—could join the EU in 2004 if they maintained the current pace of reform. Romania and Bulgaria were deemed unprepared for early membership.

The leaders of EU governments remained divided at the end of 2001 on how to amend governing rules and institutions to ensure that a larger union can still make effective decisions. In April, German Chancellor Schroeder suggested a radical restructuring of the EU into a more centralized federal government, similar to Germany's. Schroeder proposed increasing the power of the European Parliament and the European Commission. In May, Prime Minister Lionel Jospin of France launched a counterproposal. He called for closer cooperation on tax rates, policing, and other issues but insisted that authority over such policies be kept firmly in the hands of national governments. At a summit meeting in the Brussels suburb of Laeken in December, EU leaders agreed to set up a political convention to prepare ideas for reforming the bloc's structure.

Violent demonstrations by antiglobalization protesters marred European political meetings in 2001. A demonstration at the Goteborg summit in June turned violent, and police shot three protesters. Violence also broke out at the Group of Eight summit meeting in Genoa, Italy, in July. One person was killed and more than 100 others were injured as several thousand protesters and anarchists battled with police on the city's streets.

Right-leaning politics. The political pendulum swung to the right in Europe in 2001 as voters in several countries elected conservative governments. In May, Italian voters chose a conservative government led by media mogul Silvio Berlusconi, ending five years of rule by the center-left Olive Tree alliance. In the autumn, voters in Norway and Denmark elected conservative governments as the countries' once-dominant Social Democratic parties suffered their worst results in decades. In Portugal, Prime Minister Antonio Guteres resigned in December, after his ruling Socialist Party suffered a heavy defeat in local elections.

British voters bucked the trend. In June, the Labour Party won a landslide reelection victory over the opposition Conservative Party.

Balkan unrest. Former Yugoslav President Slobodan Milosevic was arrested in June 2001 and transferred to The Hague, the Netherlands, to face trial before the United Nations International War Criminal Tribunal for Yugoslavia. The tribunal indicted Milosevic for various war crimes allegedly committed during conflicts in the Balkans in the 1990's, including *genocide* (the systematic extermination of a racial or cultural group) carried out against Muslim and Croatian civilians in Bosnia-Herzegovina. Milosevic was to go on trial in 2002. Milosevic fought the proceedings, claiming the tribunal was illegitimate and biased.

Western governments intervened in 2001 to contain ethnic violence in the former Yugoslav republic of Macedonia. Rebels from the country's ethnic Albanian minority began attacking Macedonian security forces in February to press their demands for equal rights with the country's Slav majority. The EU brokered an agreement between the two sides in August. The North Atlantic Treaty Organization (NATO) sent troops to Macedonia to supervise the surrender of the rebels' weapons. Later in 2001, a smaller NATO force provided security for an international team of civilian observers who monitored the agreement. ☐ Tom Buerkle

See also various European country articles; **Aviation; Economics; Terrorism: A Special Feature,** p. 38; **United Nations; Yugoslavia.**

Fashion. The age of informality continued in 2001 with people looking for clothing that was not extravagant, but comfortable, easy to wear, and requiring little upkeep. A typical casual outfit for a young woman in 2001 consisted of a T-shirt—possibly decorated with a logo or some sequins—and fitted jeans—dipped in an acid wash to give them a unique texture or low-slung and belted at hip level. If going out to dinner, the young woman might have added a pair of high-heeled shoes. Young men's casual clothing in 2001 was not very different, though sneakers took the place of the heels. Men did not usually opt for suits in 2001, unless they were dressing for job interviews or for work in offices where suits were still required.

Fabrics. See-through or at least translucent materials became popular in 2001. Clothing made with stretch yarns was also in demand for blouses, pants, and other items, since it fit snugly and held its shape. New developments in fabrics that helped keep the body warm or cool spurred interest in fashion. Leather continued to find acceptance in skirts and tops as well as jackets, appearing in supple finishes and soft colors.

Accessories, such as cellular phones and personal digital assistants, many of which were carried in their own cases or compartments in handbags and briefcases, were part of the fashion look

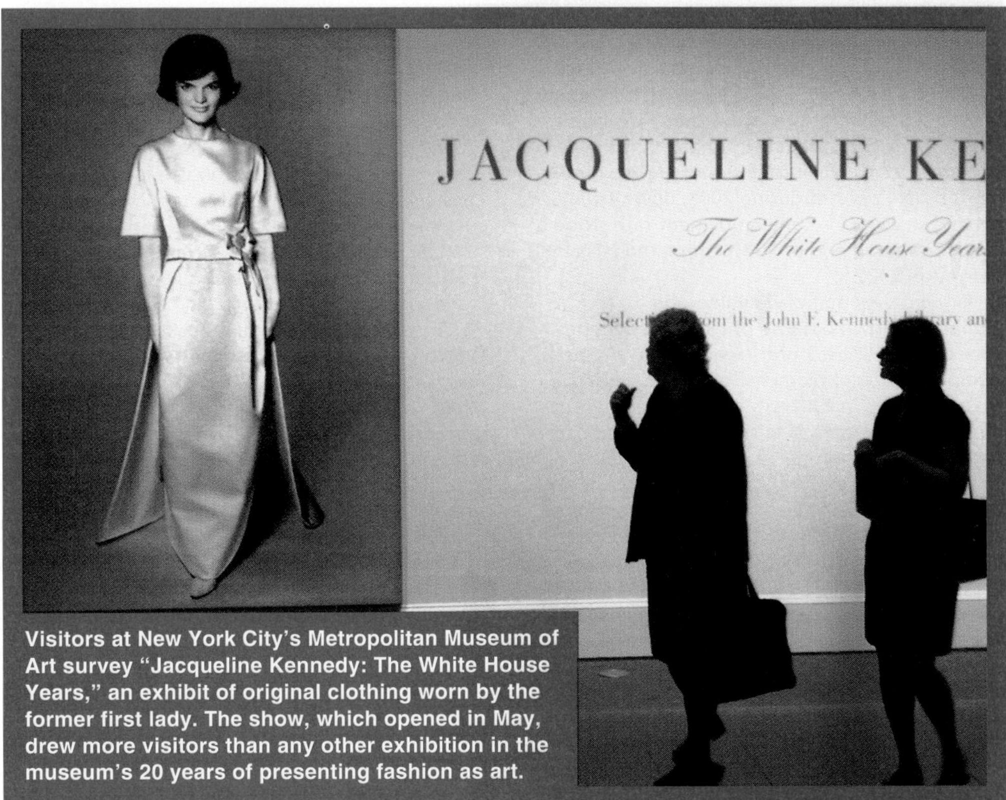

Visitors at New York City's Metropolitan Museum of Art survey "Jacqueline Kennedy: The White House Years," an exhibit of original clothing worn by the former first lady. The show, which opened in May, drew more visitors than any other exhibition in the museum's 20 years of presenting fashion as art.

in 2001. So were sunglasses and decorated socks.

Entertainment figures continued to be a source of fashion guidance and inspiration. On television, in magazines, and in newspaper reports of ceremonies such as the Academy Awards, celebrities' clothing was emphasized. Actresses such as Gwyneth Paltrow, Nicole Kidman, Renee Zellweger, and Angelina Jolie displaced supermodels, such as Linda Evangelista and Iman, who had once held the public eye. The clothes these entertainers wore were provided by the best-known names in fashion. One popular movie star and musical artist, Jennifer Lopez, introduced her own clothing line.

September 11. Even before the terrorist attacks on the United States on Sept. 11, 2001, the fashion industry had been searching for ways to deal with the sluggish economy, primarily through expansion into overseas markets and new product categories. After the attacks, consumer paralysis set in and clothing sales dropped dramatically, though a noticeable resurgence was underway by early October.

After air traffic was shut down in response to the terrorist attacks, designers on both sides of the Atlantic were forced to cancel or reschedule fashion shows, many of which had been planned for mid-September. As alternatives, some designers offered "virtual" fashion shows via big-screen relay, while others presented their collections online, on CD-ROM's, or in books.

Fashion retrospective. From May through July 2001, the Metropolitan Museum of Art in New York City drew 650,000 visitors to "Jacqueline Kennedy: The White House Years," an exhibition featuring some 80 original outfits Jacqueline Kennedy wore at state events in the early 1960's. One of the most popular first ladies in United States history, Jacqueline Kennedy, the wife of President John F. Kennedy, was famous for her fashionable clothing and sense of style. In addition to suits, dresses, and coats, the exhibition presented accessories and original documents, such as photographs, letters, and campaign memorabilia. People waited in line as long as three hours to see the enormously popular show, which attracted the largest number of visitors in the museum's 20-year history of fashion presentations. In September 2001, the exhibition moved to the John F. Kennedy Library in Boston.

Mademoiselle, the iconic women's fashion magazine, folded in October in the face of the economic slowdown, competition from other women's magazines, and a decline in advertising. Founded in 1935, the magazine had long been a major source of fashion information for women. ☐ Bernadine Morris

See also **Magazine.**

Finland suffered from the global economic slowdown during 2001, as the country's economy slowed significantly late in the year. Finland's central bank forecast in September that the country's economic output would grow by little more than 1 percent during 2001, down from 5.7 percent in 2000. The unemployment rate stood at 9 percent at the end of 2001, compared with 8.9 percent in 2000.

Finland's economy was vulnerable to the global slowdown because of its heavy dependence on trade. The country was also hit by the slump in the technology sector, which caused sharp cutbacks in Finland's mobile telephone industry and the many small Internet-related companies that had sprung up during the 1990's.

Nokia Oyj, the country's largest company and the world's biggest maker of mobile telephones, cut some 4,700 jobs by October 2001, as growth in the mobile phone industry slowed dramatically. Nokia's stock price plunged by more than 20 percent on June 12, when the company issued a warning of lower earnings. Nokia makes up nearly 75 percent of the value of the country's entire stock market, and the plunge caused a record one-day decline of 16 percent on the Helsinki Stock Exchange.

Sonera Oyj, Finland's main telephone company, struggled to reduce debts it had run up in an effort to build a European-wide mobile telephone network. The company announced in October that it would cut 1,000 jobs, or 9 percent of its work force.

Government reforms. The deteriorating economy forced the Social Democratic government of Prime Minister Paavo Lipponen to abandon the idea of increasing social welfare spending, which it had discussed early in the year. Instead, the government promised late in 2001 to introduce measures to curb state pension spending by discouraging people from taking early retirement. The government also announced plans in August to reduce income and social security taxes in 2002, in hopes that the cuts would help to revive growth.

Doping scandal. Finland suffered a major sports scandal in 2001, when six members of the country's cross-country ski team tested positive for performance-enhancing drugs at the World Nordic Skiing Championships at the Finnish town of Lahti in February. The six skiers were barred from international competition for two years, and the team forfeited four medals, including the gold medal in the men's 40-kilometer relay. The head of the Finnish Ski Association resigned, and three of the country's top coaches were dismissed and banned for life from the sport for their roles in the scandal. ☐ Tom Buerkle

See also **Economics; Europe**.

Food. Many grocery and food manufacturing companies offered donations of products and money to victims of the terrorist attacks on the World Trade Center in New York City and on the Pentagon Building outside Washington, D.C., on Sept. 11, 2001. By late September, member companies of the Grocery Manufacturers of America, a trade association based in Washington, D.C., had contributed at least $70 million to disaster relief organizations and funds.

The Coca-Cola Company of Atlanta split a $12-million corporate donation between the American Red Cross and local relief organizations in New York City and Washington, D.C. Coca-Cola also provided beverages to relief groups in those cities. Other companies, such as Wild Oats Markets, Inc., a nationwide chain of natural food markets based in Boulder, Colorado, donated a percentage of their sales for a day to relief funds. H.E. Butt Grocery Company, a Texas grocery store chain based in San Antonio, was one of many businesses that added donations from customers to their own contributions. Del Monte Foods of San Francisco and Uncle Ben's of Vernon, California, donated food or beverages to rescue and relief workers. Kal Kan Foods, Inc., also of Vernon, provided dog food to the search-and-rescue dogs working at the World Trade Center site.

Food safety. The attacks on September 11 and the discovery in October of letters containing anthrax *spores* (an inactive stage of the bacteria) raised concerns about bioterrorism threats to the U.S. food supply. Bioterrorism is the use of biological or chemical agents to carry out terrorist activities. Some experts also renewed calls for improvements in the government's food safety inspection system. In October, a top official with the General Accounting Office, the investigative arm of Congress, called the current inspection system a "patchwork structure" that provides "reason to doubt our ability to detect and fully respond to an organized bioterrorist attack."

In 2001, the U.S. Department of Agriculture and the Food and Drug Administration shared primary inspection duties for the U.S. food supply, though another 13 federal agencies also had restricted areas of responsibility. Senator Richard J. Durbin (D., Illinois) introduced legislation in October to create an independent agency to protect U.S. food supplies.

Online grocery shopping. The shakeout in the online grocery industry continued in 2001. In July, financial difficulties forced the shutdowns of Webvan Group, Incorporated, of Foster City, California, and HomeRuns.com of Burlington, Massachusetts.

Convenience stores enjoyed record sales in 2000 (the latest year for which figures were available), according to a May 2001 report by the Na-

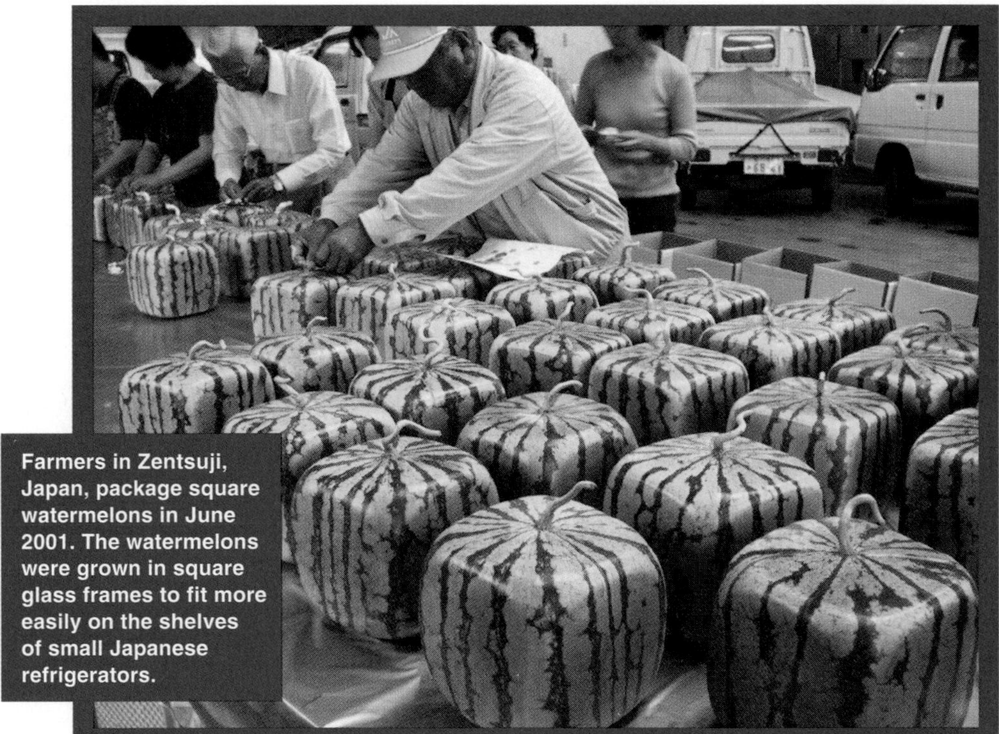

Farmers in Zentsuji, Japan, package square watermelons in June 2001. The watermelons were grown in square glass frames to fit more easily on the shelves of small Japanese refrigerators.

tional Association of Convenience Stores (NACS), a trade group based in Alexandria, Virginia. NACS reported that sales at the 119,751 convenience stores in the United States rose to $269.4 billion, up 15.1 percent from 1999 sales. Food accounted for 13.3 percent of sales. In 2000, 78 percent of U.S. convenience stores had fuel pumps, which provided 61.4 percent of sales.

Convenience stores in 2001 increasingly expanded their food offerings to include freshly prepared meals, fresh meat and produce, and other items commonly found in supermarkets. This tactic represented, in part, a reaction to the growing number of supermarket chains installing gasoline pumps at their stores.

Self-checkout. Food retailers' use of computerized systems that allow customers to scan, package, and pay for purchases on their own using credit cards grew in 2001. The Kroger Co. of Cincinnati installed its 5,000th U-Scan unit in May. Advocates of self-checkout systems argued that the systems improved service by allowing consumers to avoid waiting in checkout lines.

Supercenters. Traditional supermarkets faced increased competition from huge supercenters in 2001. Wal-Mart Stores opened its 1,000th supercenter in St. Roberts, Missouri, in August. ☐ Robert C. Gatty

See also **Agriculture**.

Football. The University of Miami Hurricanes won their first national football championship since 1991 by beating the University of Nebraska (Lincoln) 37-14 in the Rose Bowl on Jan. 3, 2002. In the National Football League (NFL), the Baltimore Ravens beat the New York Giants in the Super Bowl on Jan. 28, 2001. The deaths of several football players before and during the 2001 season cast a shadow on the sport.

Deaths. Football fans in 2001 were stunned by the deaths of several college and professional football players during or shortly after preseason practices. Devaughn Darling of Florida State University in Tallahassee died on Feb. 26, 2001, after a workout. An autopsy revealed that he may have died because of a preexisting condition. On July 25, Eraste Autin, an incoming freshman at the University of Florida (Gainesville), died of complications from heatstroke, nearly a week after collapsing following a workout. In the NFL, Minnesota Vikings offensive lineman Korey Stringer died August 1 from multiple organ failure due to heatstroke suffered the previous day during practice. Two days after Stringer died, Rashidi Wheeler of Northwestern University in Evanston, Illinois, died from a bronchial asthma attack that occurred during a practice drill. The deaths forced football coaches across the country to reevaluate training methods.

College. On Jan. 3, 2002, the Miami Hurricanes easily defeated the Nebraska Cornhuskers 37-14 to take the Bowl Championship Series (BCS) title. Miami's victory made the team the undisputed national champion, averting a potential split championship that could have occurred had Nebraska won. The title could have been split because the University of Oregon Ducks, which were ranked higher than Nebraska in the polls of media and coaches, could have been voted champions in those polls had Nebraska won.

BCS under fire. In 2001, the National Collegiate Athletic Association modified its BCS formula, which it adopted in 1998 to determine the best teams. The new system took into account victories over top-15 teams in addition to polls of journalists and coaches, strength-of-schedule formulas, and eight computer rankings. However, many fans questioned whether Nebraska deserved a shot at the national title when the team did not even win its own conference, the Big 12.

The controversy was fueled by several upsets at the end of the season. The University of Colorado (Boulder) came on strong and upset top-ranked Nebraska on Nov. 23, 2001, and then upset third-ranked University of Texas (Austin) the next weekend to win the Big 12 conference. Nebraska's loss appeared to ruin the team's chances for a national title. Instead, the advantage went to the University of Tennessee (Knoxville), which on December 1 pulled off a huge upset of second-ranked University of Florida (Gainesville).

Tennessee's title hopes were dashed after being upset by 21st-ranked Louisiana State on December 8. This allowed Nebraska to slip into second place in the final BCS standings and into the title game. Despite being ranked ahead of Nebraska in both the coaches' and media polls, Colorado was third in the BCS, mainly because the team had lost twice. Nebraska had only one loss.

The University of Oregon lost only one game during the regular season and was ranked second in both the coaches' and media polls, but came in fourth in the BCS rankings. Although Oregon had not played as tough a schedule as Nebraska, fans believed the team deserved a shot at the title.

Coaching record. On October 27, Pennsylvania State University coach Joe Paterno broke Paul "Bear" Bryant's record for Division I victories, notching his 324th career win.

Heisman Trophy. On Dec. 8, 2001, Nebraska quarterback Eric Crouch won the Heisman Trophy in one of the closest votes in the history of the award. Crouch beat University of Florida (Gainesville) quarterback Rex Grossman by 62 votes.

NFL. In the 2000-2001 season, the Baltimore Ravens rode one of the most dominating defenses in NFL history to a 34-7 victory over the New York Giants in Super Bowl XXXV on January 28 in Tampa, Florida. The Ravens, which went 12-4 in the regular season and qualified for the play-offs as a wild-card team, set NFL records for fewest points allowed (165) and fewest yards allowed (970) in a 16-game season. The Tennessee Titans finished the regular season with the league's best record at 13-3. St. Louis's Marshall Faulk, who set an NFL record with 26 nonpassing touchdowns in the 2000-2001 season, was named the most valuable player of the league.

In Super Bowl XXXV, Baltimore allowed just 152 yards, collected four sacks, and forced five turnovers. Ravens linebacker Ray Lewis was named the game's most valuable player. The Ravens became the third wild-card team to win a Super Bowl, joining the 1997-1998 Denver Broncos and the 1980-1981 Oakland Raiders.

In the American Football Conference (AFC) wild-card play-offs, Miami edged Indianapolis 23-17 in overtime on Dec. 30, 2000, while Baltimore toppled Denver 21-3 on December 31. Oakland blanked Miami 27-0 on Jan. 6, 2001, while Baltimore scored two fourth-quarter touchdowns to beat Tennessee 24-10 on January 7. In the AFC title game on January 14 in Oakland, California, Baltimore beat the Raiders 16-3.

In the National Football Conference (NFC) wild-card play-offs, New Orleans ousted the defending champion St. Louis Rams 31-28 on Dec. 30, 2000, while Philadelphia beat Tampa Bay 21-3 on December 31. The following weekend, the New York Giants beat Philadelphia 20-10, and Minnesota crushed New Orleans 34-16. In the NFC title game on Jan. 14, 2001, in East Rutherford, New Jersey, the Giants beat Minnesota 41-0.

2001-2002 season. The Chicago Bears were among the surprise teams of the 2001 regular season, mainly due to the aggressiveness of their defense. Linebacker Brian Urlacher led the Bears defense, which played a critical role in three midseason victories. The Bears won two of those games in overtime on interception returns for touchdowns and won the third when Tampa Bay missed a field goal at the end of regulation that would have sent the game into overtime.

On September 13, NFL officials made the unprecedented decision to postpone the second week of its season because terrorists had attacked the United States on September 11. The games were rescheduled at the end of the regular season, and the play-offs were pushed back one week.

Milestones. On September 23, Dallas Cowboys running back Emmitt Smith rushed for 85 yards, giving him 15,291 career yards and making him the second all-time leading rusher in NFL history. Only Walter Payton, who ran for 16,726 career yards, had more career yards than Smith.

On November 11, St. Louis Rams quarterback

2001 National Football League final standings

American Conference

East Division	W.	L.	T.	Pct.
New England Patriots*	11	5	0	.688
Miami Dolphins*	11	5	0	.688
New York Jets*	10	6	0	.625
Indianapolis Colts	6	10	0	.375
Buffalo Bills	3	13	0	.188
Central Division				
Pittsburgh Steelers*	13	3	0	.812
Baltimore Ravens*	10	6	0	.625
Cleveland Browns	7	9	0	.438
Tennessee Titans	7	9	0	.438
Jacksonville Jaguars	6	10	0	.375
Cincinnati Bengals	6	10	0	.375
West Division				
Oakland Raiders*	10	6	0	.625
Seattle Seahawks	9	7	0	.562
Denver Broncos	8	8	0	.500
Kansas City Chiefs	6	10	0	.375
San Diego Chargers	5	11	0	.312

*Made play-offs

Team statistics

Leading offenses (yards gained)	Total	Per game
Indianapolis	5,955	372.2
Pittsburgh	5,887	367.9
Kansas City	5,673	354.6
Oakland	5,361	335.1
Tennessee	5,354	334.5

Leading defenses	Avg. points against	Yards per game
Pittsburgh	13.2	258.6
Baltimore	16.6	277.9
Miami	18.1	288.0
Denver	21.2	298.4
Cincinnati	19.3	302.0

Individual statistics

Leading scorers, touchdowns	TD's	Rush	Rec.	Ret.	Pts.
Shaun Alexander, Seattle	16	14	2	0	96
Marvin Harrison, Indianapolis	15	0	15	0	90
Corey Dillon, Cincinnati	13	10	3	0	78
Antowain Smith, New England	13	12	1	0	78
Rod Smith, Denver	11	0	11	0	68

Leading kickers	PAT made/att.	FG made/att.	Longest FG	Pts.
Jason Elam, Denver	31/31	31/36	50	124
Matt Stover, Baltimore	25/25	30/35	49	115
Kris Brown, Pittsburgh	34/37	30/44	55	124
Mike Vanderjagt, Indianapolis	41/42	28/34	52	125

Leading quarterbacks	Att.	Comp.	Yds.	TD's	Int.
Rich Gannon, Oakland	549	361	3,828	27	9
Steve McNair, Tennessee	431	264	3,350	21	12
Tom Brady, New England	413	264	2,843	18	12
Peyton Manning, Indianapolis	547	343	4,131	26	23
Mark Brunell, Jacksonville	473	289	3,309	19	13

Leading receivers	Passes caught	Rec. yards	Avg. gain	TD's
Marvin Harrison, Indianapolis	109	1,524	14.0	15
Jimmy Smith, Jacksonville	112	1,373	12.3	8
Rod Smith, Denver	113	1,343	11.9	11
Troy Brown, New England	101	1,199	11.9	5

Leading rushers	Rushes	Yards	Avg.	TD's
Priest Holmes, Kansas City	327	1,555	4.8	8
Curtis Martin, New York Jets	333	1,513	4.5	10
Shaun Alexander, Seattle	309	1,318	4.3	14
Corey Dillon, Cincinnati	340	1,315	3.9	10

Leading punters	Punts	Yards	Avg.	Longest
Shane Lechler, Oakland	73	3,375	46.2	65
Tom Rouen, Denver	81	3,668	45.3	64
Hunter Smith, Indianapolis	68	3,023	44.5	65
Jeff Feagles, Seattle	85	3,730	43.9	68

National Conference

East Division	W.	L.	T.	Pct.
Philadelphia Eagles*	11	5	0	.688
Washington Redskins	8	8	0	.500
New York Giants	7	9	0	.438
Arizona Cardinals	7	9	0	.438
Dallas Cowboys	5	11	0	.312
Central Division				
Chicago Bears*	13	3	0	.812
Green Bay Packers*	12	4	0	.750
Tampa Bay Buccaneers*	9	7	0	.562
Minnesota Vikings	5	11	0	.312
Detroit Lions	2	14	0	.125
West Division				
St. Louis Rams*	14	2	0	.875
San Francisco 49ers*	12	4	0	.750
New Orleans Saints	7	9	0	.438
Atlanta Falcons	7	9	0	.438
Carolina Panthers	1	15	0	.062

*Made play-offs

Team statistics

Leading offenses (yards gained)	Total	Per game
St. Louis	6,690	418.1
San Francisco	5,689	355.6
Green Bay	5,463	341.4
New York	5,335	333.4
New Orleans	5,226	326.6

Leading defenses	Avg. points against	Yards per game
St. Louis	17.1	279.4
Dallas	21.1	287.4
Tampa Bay	17.5	290.8
Philadelphia	13.0	293.8
Washington	18.9	302.9

Individual statistics

Leading scorers, touchdowns	TD's	Rush	Rec.	Ret.	Pts.
Marshall Faulk, St. Louis	21	12	9	0	128
Terrell Owens, San Francisco	16	0	16	0	96
Mike Alstott, Tampa Bay	11	10	1	0	70
Ahman Green, Green Bay	11	9	2	0	66

Leading kickers	PAT made/att.	FG made/att.	Longest FG	Pts.
Jay Feely, Atlanta	28/28	29/37	55	115
John Carney, New Orleans	32/32	27/31	50	113
David Akers, Philadelphia	37/38	26/31	50	115
Brett Conway, Washington	22/22	26/33	55	100

Leading quarterbacks	Att.	Comp.	Yds.	TD's	Int.
Kurt Warner, St. Louis	546	375	4,830	36	22
Jeff Garcia, San Francisco	504	316	3,538	32	12
Brett Favre, Green Bay	510	314	3,921	32	15
Donovan McNabb, Philadelphia	493	285	3,233	25	12
Chris Chandler, Atlanta	365	223	2,847	16	14

Leading receivers	Passes caught	Rec. yards	Avg. gain	TD's
David Boston, Arizona	98	1,598	16.3	8
Terrell Owens, San Francisco	93	1,412	15.2	16
Torry Holt, St. Louis	81	1,363	16.8	7
Keyshawn Johnson, Tampa Bay	106	1,266	11.9	1

Leading rushers	Rushes	Yards	Avg.	TD's
Stephen Davis, Washington	356	1,432	4.0	5
Ahman Green, Green Bay	304	1,387	4.6	9
Marshall Faulk, St. Louis	260	1,382	5.3	12
Ricky Williams, New Orleans	313	1,245	4.0	6

Leading punters	Punts	Yards	Avg.	Longest
Todd Sauerbrun, Carolina	93	4,419	47.5	73
Mitch Berger, Minnesota	47	2,046	43.5	67
Sean Landeta, Philadelphia	97	4,221	43.5	64
John Jett, Detroit	58	2,512	43.3	62

The 2001 college football season

National champions

NCAA Div. I-A*	Miami	37	Nebraska	14
NCAA Div. I-AA	Montana	13	Furman	6
NCAA Div. II	North Dakota	17	Grand Valley State	14
NCAA Div. III	Mt. Union	30	Bridgewater	27
NAIA	Georgetown	49	Sioux Falls	27

Bowl Championship Series games

Bowl	Result			
Rose*	Miami	37	Nebraska	14
Orange	Florida	56	Maryland	23
Fiesta	Oregon	38	Colorado	16
Sugar	Louisiana State	47	Illinois	34

Other bowl games

Alamo	Iowa	19	Texas Tech	16
Citrus	Tennessee	45	Michigan	17
Cotton	Oklahoma	10	Arkansas	3
Gator	Florida State	30	Virginia Tech	17
Holiday	Texas	47	Washington	43
Humanitarian	Clemson	49	Louisiana Tech	24
Independence	Alabama	14	Iowa State	13
Insight.com	Syracuse	26	Kansas State	3
Las Vegas	Utah	10	USC	6
Liberty	Louisville	28	Brigham Young	10
Mobile (GMAC)	Marshall	64	East Carolina	61
Motor City	Toledo	23	Cincinnati	16
Music City	Boston College	20	Georgia	16
New Orleans	Colorado State	45	North Texas	20
Outback	South Carolina	31	Ohio State	28
Peach	North Carolina	16	Auburn	10
Seattle	Georgia Tech	24	Stanford	14
Silicon Valley	Michigan State	44	Fresno State	35
Sun	Washington State	33	Purdue	27
Tangerine	Pittsburgh	34	N.C. State	19

*Championship decided in the Rose Bowl on Jan. 3, 2002.

Conference Champions

NCAA Division I-A

Conference	School
Atlantic Coast	Maryland
Big 12	Colorado
Big East	Miami
Big Ten	Illinois
Conference USA	Louisville
Mid-American	Toledo
Mountain West	Brigham Young
Pacific 10	Oregon
Southeastern	Louisiana State
Sun Belt	North Texas—Middle Tennessee State (tie)
Western Athletic	Louisiana Tech

NCAA Division I-AA

Conference	School
Atlantic 10	Maine—Hofstra—Villanova—William&Mary (tie)
Big Sky	Montana
Gateway	Northern Iowa
Ivy League	Harvard
Metro Atlantic	Duquesne
Mid-Eastern	Florida A&M
Northeast	Sacred Heart
Ohio Valley	Eastern Illinois
Patriot	Lehigh
Pioneer	Dayton
Southern	Georgia Southern—Furman (tie)
Southland	Sam Houston State—McNeese State (tie)
Southwestern	Grambling State

All-America team (as chosen by the Associated Press)

Offense

Quarterback—Rex Grossman, Florida
Running backs—Luke Staley, BYU; Travis Stephens, Tennessee
Wide receivers—Jabar Gaffney, Florida; Josh Reed, Louisiana State
Tight end—Dan Graham, Colorado
Center—LeCharles Bentley, Ohio State
Other linemen—Mike Pearson, Florida; Bryant McKinnie, Miami-Florida; Toniu Fonoti, Nebraska; Andre Gurode, Colorado
All-purpose player—Eric Crouch, Nebraska
Place-kicker—David Duval, Auburn

Defense

Linemen—Alex Brown, Florida; Julius Peppers, North Carolina; Dwight Freeney, Syracuse; John Henderson, Tennessee
Linebackers—Rocky Calmus, Oklahoma; Levar Fisher, North Carolina; E.J. Henderson, Maryland; Robert Thomas, UCLA
Backs—Roy Williams, Oklahoma; Edward Reed, Miami-Florida; Quentin Jammer, Texas; Lamont Thompson, Washington State
Punter—Travis Dorsch, Purdue

Player awards

Heisman Trophy (best player)—Eric Crouch, Nebraska
Nagurski Trophy (best defensive player)—Roy Williams, Oklahoma
Lombardi Award (best lineman)—Julius Peppers, North Carolina

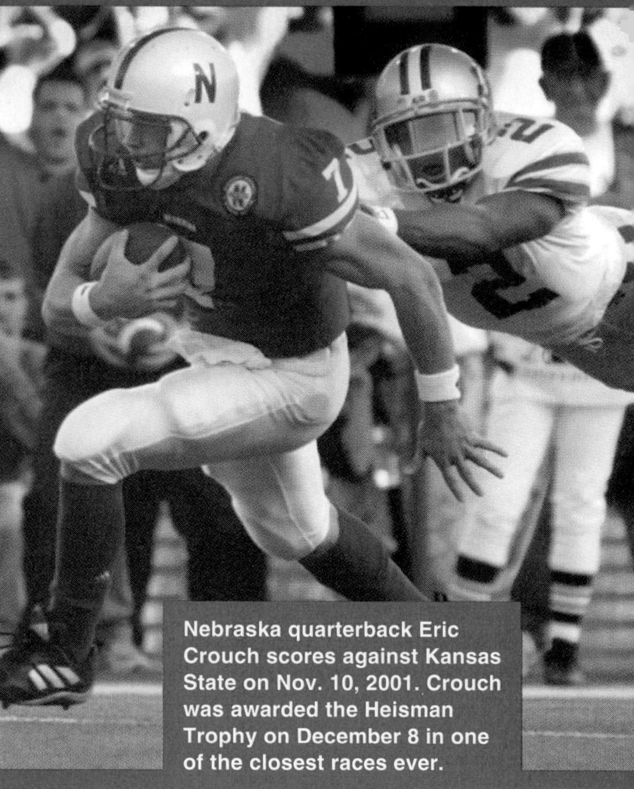

Nebraska quarterback Eric Crouch scores against Kansas State on Nov. 10, 2001. Crouch was awarded the Heisman Trophy on December 8 in one of the closest races ever.

Kurt Warner became the fastest player in NFL history to pass for 10,000 yards, reaching that mark after only 36 games, two fewer than Miami's Dan Marino. Also during the 2001 season, Baltimore's Shannon Sharpe set career records for receptions and receiving yards by a tight end.

Retirement. Quarterback Troy Aikman, who led the Dallas Cowboys to three Super Bowl titles in the mid-1990's, retired on April 9, 2001, after 12 seasons in the NFL. Aikman retired in part because of injuries. He had at least 10 concussions in his career, including 4 in his final 20 starts.

XFL. The Extreme Football League (XFL), which was launched as a joint project between the World Wrestling Federation (WWF) and NBC Sports, debuted in February 2001 but was disbanded later in the year because of miserable ratings and reviews. The XFL attempted to blend scantily clad cheerleaders and innovative camera angles with hard-nosed football. Poor ratings, including a broadcast in March that netted the lowest prime-time ratings ever on a major network, forced NBC to pull out in May. When WWF officials could not find another network that was interested in airing the XFL's second season, it folded the league. The failure of the XFL cost NBC an estimated $35 million and the WWF an estimated $47 million. ☐ Michael Kates

See also **Sports; Television.**

France. The French economy weakened in 2001, as a result of the worldwide economic slowdown. Economists projected that France's *gross domestic product* (GDP, the value of all goods and services produced in a year) would grow by only 2 percent in 2001, down from 3.1 percent in 2000. Unemployment, which had fallen below 9 percent early in 2001 for the first time since the 1980's, rose above 9 percent again in September 2001.

Many French companies reacted to the slowdown by cutting jobs. In March, the food company Danone S.A. announced it would close two cookie factories and lay off 570 workers. Marks & Spencer, a British-owned department store, said it would close its French stores, which employed 1,700 people. Unions protested the moves, and the government responded by passing a new labor law aimed at discouraging layoffs. The law, adopted by the National Assembly in June, gave workers' representatives the right to make counterproposals or demand arbitration if a company announced plans to lay off workers. Business groups said the law would hamper companies' efforts to remain profitable.

Political scandals. Allegations of corruption continued to dominate French politics in 2001. Magistrates looking into alleged illegal funds in Paris politics began an investigation of President Jacques Chirac early in the year, after discovering that he had paid cash for lavish overseas trips for himself and his family in the early 1990's, when he was the city's mayor. Chirac denied any wrongdoing. The investigation was halted in October 2001, when the country's highest court ruled that a French president could not be prosecuted or called as a witness while in office. The ruling cleared the way for Chirac to seek reelection in 2002.

Prime Minister Lionel Jospin, a Socialist who was expected to challenge Chirac in the presidential election, also faced embarrassing disclosures about his own past during 2001. A French newspaper reported in May that Jospin had belonged to a Trotskyist group in the 1960's and 1970's. The group, named after Leon Trotsky, a leader of the Communist revolution in Russia in 1918, espoused radical left-wing beliefs. Jospin acknowledged associating with Trotskyists in his youth but said he ended the ties before joining the Socialist Party.

Dominique Strauss-Kahn, a close ally of Jospin who resigned as finance minister in 1999 to fight corruption charges, was cleared by a Paris court in November 2001. Strauss-Kahn had been accused of forging documents to claim $85,000 in legal fees, but a court ruled that he had performed work for the fees.

Volunteers push a boat laden with emergency supplies through the streets of Abbeville in the Somme region of northern France in April. The area endured six weeks of the worst flooding recorded in more than 100 years.

One of the country's most notorious corruption cases ended on May 30, when Roland Dumas, a former foreign minister, was found guilty of illegally taking money from a state-owned oil company in the early 1990's. Dumas accepted money and gifts from his mistress, who in turn was paid more than $10 million by the oil company, Elf Aquitaine. Dumas was sentenced to six months in prison and fined $135,000.

Business. Two major French companies suffered serious setbacks as a result of failed merger attempts in 2001. Alcatel S.A., the country's largest maker of telecommunications equipment, proposed a $22-billion acquisition in May of Lucent Technologies of Murray Hill, New Jersey, a financially troubled rival. Alcatel hoped the deal would strengthen its U.S. presence and enable both companies to weather a sharp slowdown in the telecommunications industry. The deal collapsed when Lucent refused to cede control to Alcatel executives. In subsequent months, Alcatel announced that it would cut 33,000 jobs worldwide—30 percent of its work force—and expected to report a loss of $4.5 billion for 2001.

Schneider Electric S.A., France's largest maker of electrical equipment, agreed in January to buy its smaller French rival Legrand for $6.6 billion, only to have the European Commission veto the deal. The commission, which rules on antitrust issues in Europe, ruled in October that the merger would have created a monopoly in France.

A two-year-old battle for control of Gucci Group N.V. between two of France's richest businessmen, Francois Pinault and Bernard Arnault, ended in 2001. Pinault-Printemps-Redoute S.A., the retailing company owned by Pinault, agreed in September to take control of the Italian fashion company Gucci by buying a 20-percent stake owned by Arnault's LVMH Moet Hennessy Louis Vuitton S.A. The deal left Gucci and LVMH as the two biggest rivals in the global fashion industry.

Concorde returns. The supersonic airliner returned to passenger service in 2001, after being grounded for more than a year for safety modifications. An Air France Concorde flew from Paris to New York City on November 7, the airline's first passenger flight since an Air France Concorde crashed shortly after takeoff from Charles de Gaulle Airport in July 2000, killing 109 passengers and 4 people on the ground.

High-speed train. The national railway, SNCF, opened a new high-speed rail line in June 2001. The TGV Mediterranee reached a top speed of 185 miles (298 kilometers) per hour, allowing passengers to travel from Paris to the Mediterranean port of Marseille, a distance of nearly 466 miles (750 kilometers), in three hours.

☐ Tom Buerkle

See also **Europe.**

Gardening.

Simplicity was the keynote in home gardening in 2001. As Americans struggled with ever more hectic lives, more gardeners came to share the views of Tom Christopher and Marty Asher, who wrote in *The 20-Minute Gardener* that a plant that requires too much attention "should be in a nursing home, not your garden." Gardening retailers promoted "instant gardens," which eliminated sweat and dirt with arrangements of plants growing in pots of soilless mix, fertilizer, and polymer crystals that reduced watering chores. Sales of garden plants exceeded sales of seeds by 500 percent, with mature trees and large plants most in demand. Organic gardening became mainstream because it was easier.

The gardening industry. Retail growth in the gardening industry slowed in 2001 in the face of a gathering recession in the United States, and some well-established companies stumbled. *Big-box stores* (large-scale, mass market retailers), which had invested heavily in new gardening departments in recent years, continued to offer stiff competition to local garden centers. In 2001, these huge outlets also squeezed producers of garden plants, seeds, and equipment by cutting both orders and prices.

Foster & Gallagher, Inc. of Grand Rapids, Michigan, filed for bankruptcy on July 2, citing mass market competition as the cause. In September, Gardens Alive, a mail-order firm based in Lawrenceburg, Indiana, purchased Foster & Gallagher's horticultural business for $10.75 million. Two groups of investors rescued Stark Brothers Nurseries & Orchards Co., one of Foster & Gallagher's 21 domestic subsidiaries. The investors said they were determined to keep Stark Brothers, established in 1816 and one of Missouri's oldest companies, operating and to retain the company's staff of employees.

The Burpee Holding Company of Warminister, Pennsylvania, parent company of the familiar W. Atlee Burpee & Co. seed catalog, filed for bankruptcy in September 2001. The company cited the failure of its four-store retailing operation as a major reason for its financial difficulties.

Magazines. Falling advertising led two of the most prestigious U.S. garden magazines, prize-winning *Garden Design* and 97-year-old *Horticulture*, to hire new editors in chief. Rodale Inc. of Emmaus, Pennsylvania, slimmed down the popular, but unprofitable *Organic Gardening* and renamed it *OG*. Rodale also trimmed the magazine's circulation, sending nearly half its subscribers a new lifestyle magazine, *Organic Style*, aimed at readers interested in incorporating spiritual and environmental values into busy lives.

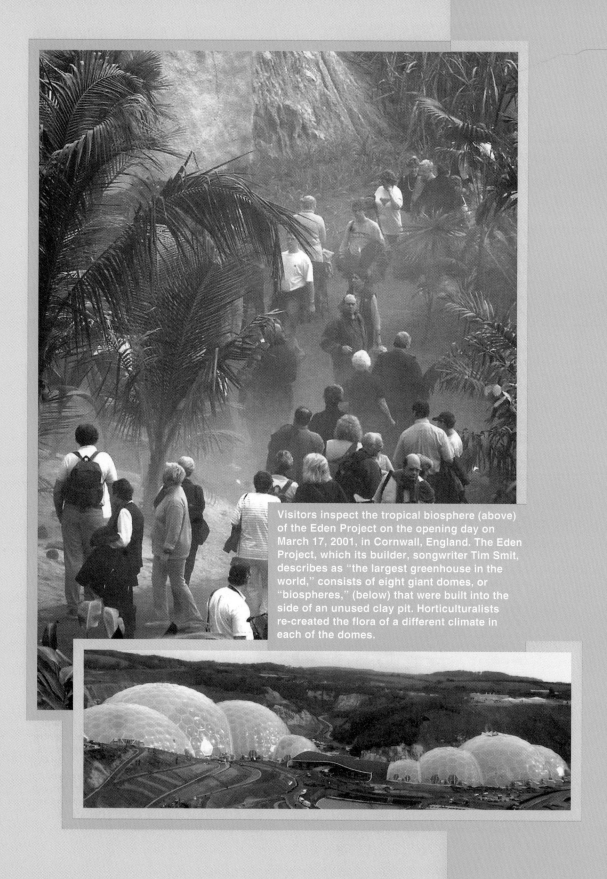

Visitors inspect the tropical biosphere (above) of the Eden Project on the opening day on March 17, 2001, in Cornwall, England. The Eden Project, which its builder, songwriter Tim Smit, describes as "the largest greenhouse in the world," consists of eight giant domes, or "biospheres," (below) that were built into the side of an unused clay pit. Horticulturalists re-created the flora of a different climate in each of the domes.

Botanical gardens. More than 7,000 people attended the opening on March 17 in Cornwall, England, of the Eden Project—a "living garden" under eight giant domes that constitute the world's largest greenhouse. The U.S. Botanic Garden reopened on December 11 after undergoing extensive renovations. Established in 1820, the garden consists of a conservatory, the Bartholdi Park, and a National Garden located on the Mall across from the U.S. Capitol in Washington, D.C.

Chicago v. beetles. Chicago began inoculating 23,000 trees with a new insecticide in April in a $2.1-million effort to battle Asian longhorned beetles. Workers injected the trees with imidacloprid, which had proven effective against the beetle. Since its arrival in Chicago in 1998, the beetle had destroyed 1,500 city trees. In 2000, forestry workers had tested the pesticide on 11,000 Chicago trees, none of which became infested in 2001.

Deaths. Self-taught botanist Rupert C. Barneby, who described and named 1,160 new plant species, died on December 5 at age 89 in New York City. Garden designer, lecturer, and writer Rosemary Verey died in London on May 31 at age 82. Her garden at Barnsley House in the English Cotswolds attracted 20,000 visitors annually.

☐ Carol M. Stocker

Gas and gasoline. See **Energy supply.**

Genetic engineering. See **Biology.**

Geology.

A massive earthquake struck western India on Jan. 26, 2001, killing about 14,000 people and causing $4.5 billion in property damage. Initially, government officials feared the death toll would reach as high as 50,000, but it was later discovered that many victims had been counted several times. Geologists with the United States Geological Survey calculated that the quake measured 7.7 on the Surface Wave scale, a scale used to measure earthquakes.

The quake—the most powerful to hit India in more than 50 years—was an intraplate earthquake, a rare type that occurs far from the boundaries where *tectonic plates* (large plates of Earth's crust) meet. Geophysicists reported that the Indian quake was caused by stress generated by the collision of the Indian and Asian plates.

Mount Etna fires up. Sicily's Mount Etna, which began erupting again in July 2001, may be developing into a more explosive volcano. In August, a team of scientists led by Pierre Schiano of the University of Blaise Pascal in France reported that Mount Etna—one of the most active volcanoes in Europe—may be changing from a relatively passive type of volcano into a more violent one. While past eruptions have included such spectacular features as fountains of lava and car-sized chunks of molten rock, Mount Etna has not been a particularly violent volcano.

Schiano's team studied lava expelled from the volcano as far back as 500,000 years to determine the volcano's composition. They found that, over time, Mount Etna—which formed over a mantle plume, or "hot spot," a place in the Earth's crust where lava rises from the Earth's interior toward the surface—has started to change into an "island arc" volcano, a more violent, explosive type of volcano. The eruptions of island arc volcanoes are triggered by the collision of tectonic plates.

The scientists suggested that partial melting caused by the collision of the European and African tectonic plates, which come into contact not far from Mount Etna, could be serving as the source of recent eruptions.

El Nino is growing up. In February 2001, a team of scientists led by Alexander Tudhope of the University of Edinburgh in Scotland reported that weather conditions on Earth were more severe than they were thousands of years ago. The scientists studied the chemical makeup of living and fossil corals from Papua New Guinea to learn more about the long-term history of a weather phenomenon known as the El Nino-Southern Oscillation (ENSO). ENSO events occur every 2 to 7 years when a pool of warm water in the western Pacific moves eastward.

Scientists know that the strongest ENSO events occurred in 1982-1983 and 1997-1998. Many were also convinced that Earth was experiencing a rise in temperature due to the production of greenhouse gases from human activities. Greenhouse gases, such as carbon dioxide, trap heat from sunlight that reflects from the Earth. Scientists have suggested that ENSO is getting stronger in response to global warming. However, scientists do not have weather data over a long enough period to be sure of a connection.

By examining the changes in the chemical composition of corals over time, the scientists discovered that ENSO events have occurred for at least 130,000 years. But they determined that those of the 20th century were the strongest of any period. This could mean that rising global temperatures could be linked to wide variations in global weather patterns.

Carbon dioxide and climate change. In May 2001, Greg Retallack of the University of Oregon reported that he had developed a method of measuring carbon dioxide in Earth's atmosphere that could resolve the question of carbon dioxide's role in Earth's climate. Scientists have become increasingly concerned about carbon dioxide because of its involvement in global warming. Retallack's method, which involved examining living and fossilized tree leaves, provided a new way of learning more about how carbon dioxide has affected Earth's climate over hundreds of millions of years.

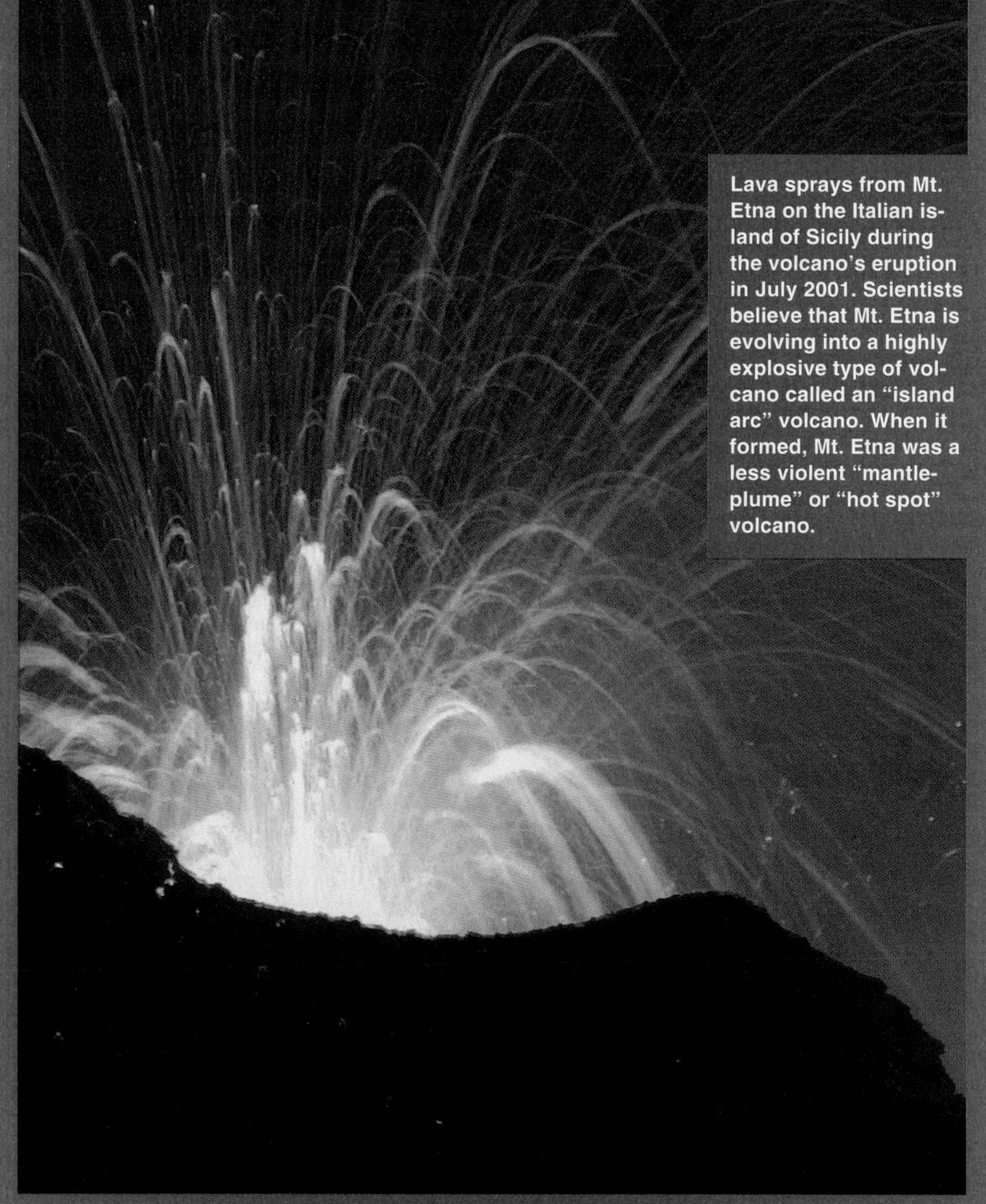

Lava sprays from Mt. Etna on the Italian island of Sicily during the volcano's eruption in July 2001. Scientists believe that Mt. Etna is evolving into a highly explosive type of volcano called an "island arc" volcano. When it formed, Mt. Etna was a less violent "mantle-plume" or "hot spot" volcano.

Retallack's measuring method involved studying the *stomata* (openings in leaves through which gas exchange occurs) of living and fossilized ginkgo trees. Scientists have long known that when carbon dioxide is plentiful, plants develop fewer stomata. Conversely, when carbon dioxide is scarce, plants develop more stomata. Retallack's method could be used to reconstruct the changes in the carbon dioxide levels going back more than 300 million years.

Before Retallack's method, scientists depended on other means of determining carbon dioxide levels, such as examining air pockets trapped in ice cores from polar regions. Using these methods, scientists found that ice ages often occurred during times of low carbon dioxide levels. Retallack's method generated the same result, and it can be used to determine carbon dioxide levels going back much further than other methods.

Ancient oceans. In January 2001, a team of scientists from the United States and the United Kingdom reported discovering a 4.4-billion-year-old mineral in Australia. The mineral, known as zircon, is the oldest ever found.

By analyzing the chemical composition of the zircon, the scientists concluded that it was part of an early continent. Other scientists found evidence that the mineral had also been in or near water. These findings could mean that the continents and oceans formed much earlier than had been previously thought.

☐ Henry T. Mullins

Georgia. Tensions between Russia and Georgia dramatically worsened in October 2001, when the Georgian government demanded that Russian peacekeepers leave Georgia's separatist province Abkhazia. Russian troops have maintained a cease-fire in Abkhazia since the end of Georgia's 1992-1993 civil war. The president of Georgia, Eduard Shevardnadze, threatened to withdraw from the Commonwealth of Independent States, the Russian-led security alliance uniting most of the Soviet Union's successor states.

A wave of violence in October 2001, which began when a United Nations helicopter was shot down over the disputed territory, triggered the confrontation. Bombing raids by unidentified aircraft and guerrilla raids followed. Russia accused Georgia's government of harboring guerrillas from Chechnya, a breakaway Russian republic that Russian officials claim is a haven for terrorists. Shevardnadze responded by accusing Russia of launching a campaign to "trigger the spread of military hostilities on to Georgian territory."

On November 2, Shevardnadze, under attack at home and abroad, dismissed his cabinet and accepted the resignation of the speaker of parliament. Shevardnadze then set about forming a new government. ☐ Steven L. Solnick

See also **Asia; Russia.**

Georgia. See **State government.**

Germany. Chancellor Gerhard Schroeder moved quickly in 2001 to offer German support for the campaign against terrorism in the wake of the attacks on the United States on September 11. Schroeder pledged to send German troops to assist U.S. forces in Afghanistan, the first time Germany had committed troops outside of Europe since World War II (1939-1945). The decision stirred controversy among members of Germany's Green Party, a traditionally pacifist group and the junior partner in the coalition government with Schroeder's Social Democrats. The majority of Green Party members opposed the U.S. military action in Afghanistan.

In order to win a clear mandate for his position, Schroeder in November 2001 turned a vote on the troop deployment in the Bundestag, the lower house of parliament, into a vote of confidence in his government. He won, however, by only two votes. Four Green parliamentarians voted against the measure, raising doubts that the party would remain in coalition with the Social Democrats after the next election in 2002.

Government scandals. A trial in early 2001 focused attention on the radical, left-wing political activities of Foreign Minister Joschka Fischer during the 1960's and 1970's. Fischer testified in January 2001 as a character witness for a radical-turned-terrorist who was prosecuted for three murders committed during a meeting of oil ministers from the Organization of Petroleum Exporting Countries in 1975. Fischer acknowledged having associated with several radicals who turned to terrorism but said he had never endorsed violence in support of left-wing objectives. Conservative opposition parties called for his resignation, saying Fischer's past links with terrorists made him unsuitable to serve as foreign minister. Fischer refused to step down and remained one of Germany's more popular politicians. German prosecutors in April 2001 dropped their investigation of Fischer, saying there was no evidence that he had lied about his past.

Helmut Kohl, the former chancellor, agreed in February to pay a $140,000 fine to settle a year-long investigation into his acceptance of $1 million in illegal, secret payments to the Christian Democratic Union (CDU) party while he was in power during the 1990's. Kohl had admitted accepting the payments but refused to disclose the donors, as required by law, saying he had given his word of honor to keep their names secret. The scandal damaged the popularity of the CDU.

Economy. The German economy stumbled to the verge of recession toward the end of 2001. The economy had been particularly affected by the economic slowdown in the United States, because many big German companies had invested heavily in that market. High energy prices early in the year also depressed consumer and business confidence. The government projected in October that Germany's *gross domestic product* (GDP, the value of all goods and services produced in a year) would grow by just 0.75 percent in 2001, down from a forecast of 2 percent in the spring and well below the 3 percent growth rate of 2000. Unemployment fell to 7.8 percent late in 2001 from 7.9 percent at the end of 2000.

The slowdown prompted business leaders and opposition politicians to demand an acceleration of tax cuts scheduled to take place in 2003 in an effort to revive growth. Finance Minister Hans Eichel refused, however, saying Germany needed to place a higher priority on efforts to reduce its budget deficit. The deficit was expected to rise to more than 2 percent of GDP in 2001, up from 0.8 percent in 2000, and close to the limit of 3 percent of GDP for countries using the euro.

Mergers. Allianz AG, Germany's largest insurance company, agreed to acquire Dresdner Bank AG, the country's third-largest bank, for $20.6 billion in April 2001. Dresdner had been vulnerable to a takeover since it failed to complete a merger with Deutsche Bank AG, Germany's largest bank, in 2000. Allianz hoped to use the Dresdner branch network to sell more insurance policies and other financial products to German consumers.

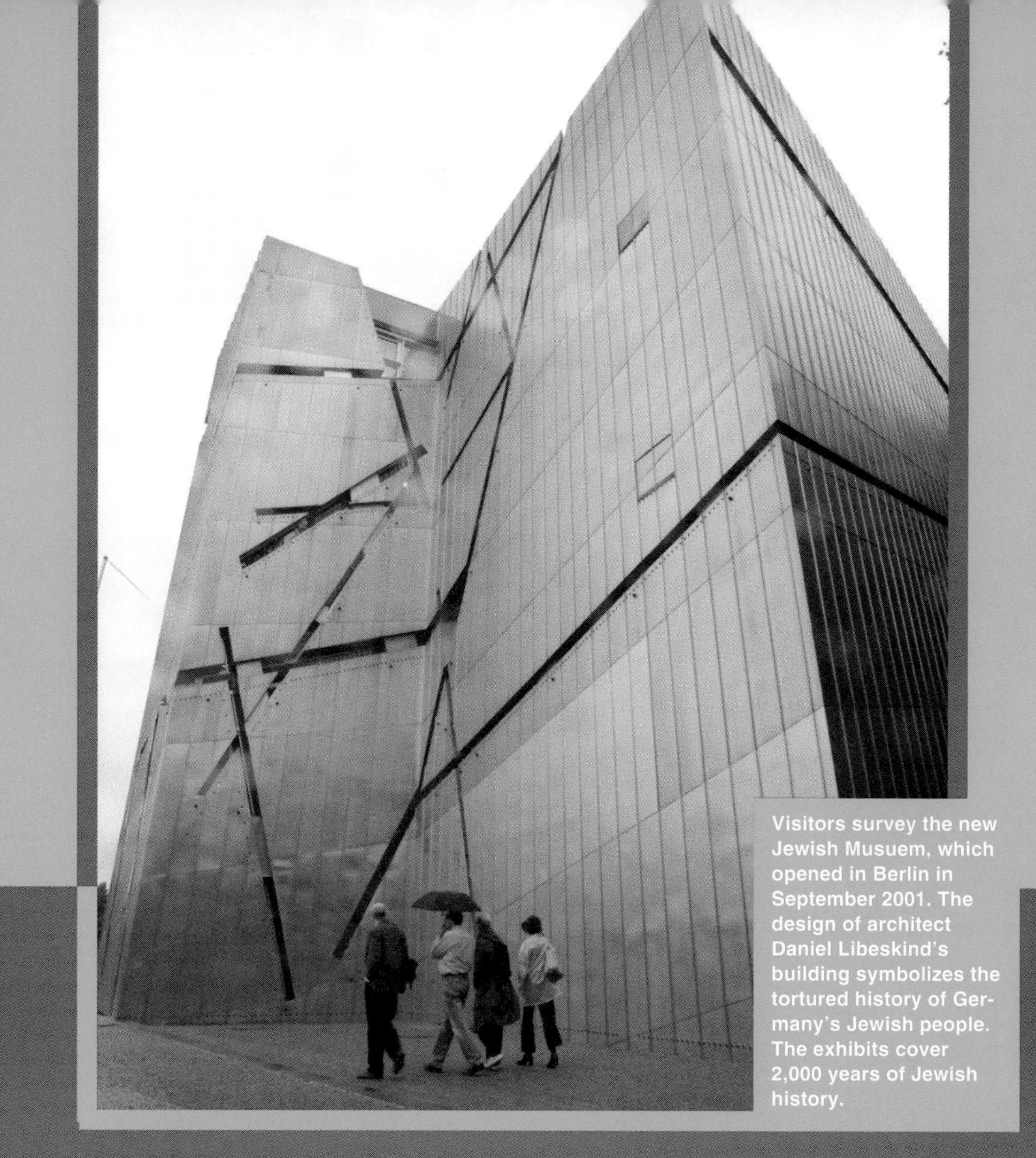

Visitors survey the new Jewish Musuem, which opened in Berlin in September 2001. The design of architect Daniel Libeskind's building symbolizes the tortured history of Germany's Jewish people. The exhibits cover 2,000 years of Jewish history.

In November 2001, Dresdner, Deutsche, and Commerzbank AG, Germany's fourth-largest bank, agreed to combine their mortgage lending subsidiaries into a separate bank. The new bank, named Eurohypo AG, became the largest German mortgage lender, with about $215 billion in outstanding loans. The merger was aimed at cutting costs and increasing competitiveness in the marketplace.

NATO role. In September, German troops took command of a NATO peacekeeping force in Macedonia. Germany provided 600 of the 1,000 troops, which had been deployed to safeguard civilian monitors of a peace agreement between the Macedonian government and ethnic Albanian rebels.

Slave labor payments. In June, a $4.5 billion fund contributed by German industry and the government began to make the first compensation payments as many as 1.5 million people who had been forced to work in Nazi concentration camps and ghettos. Most of the workers were non-Jews from central and Eastern Europe.

New chancellery. Gerhard Schroeder inaugurated a new chancellor's office and residence in Berlin in May. The ceremony completed the move of the federal government from Bonn in western Germany to Berlin, Germany's capital before the end of World War II. ☐ Tom Buerkle

See also **Europe; Macedonia; Terrorism: A Special Feature,** p. 38.

Ghana. See **Africa.**

WHAT WE KNOW ABOUT GLOBAL WARMING

By Ralph Cicerone

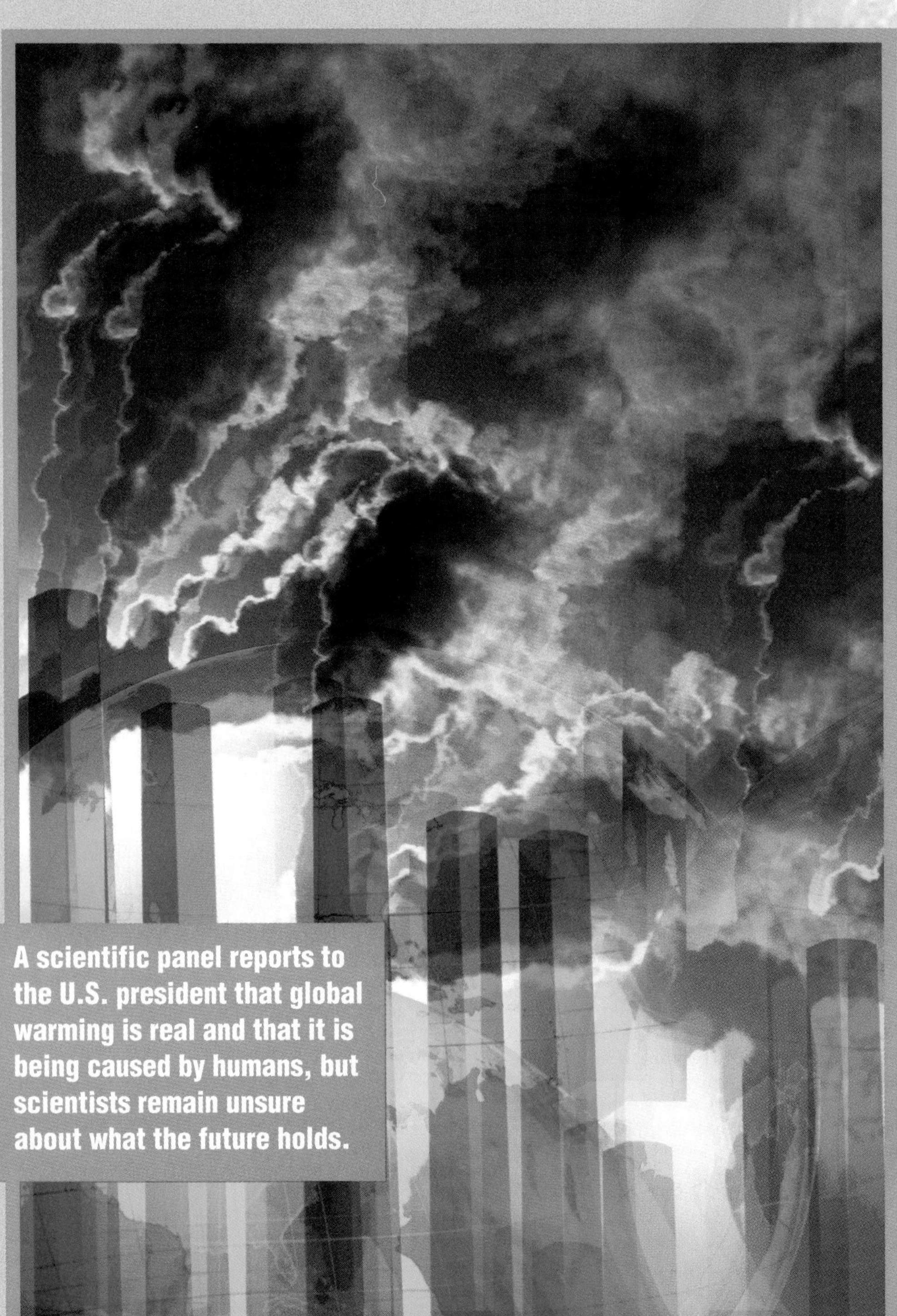

A scientific panel reports to the U.S. president that global warming is real and that it is being caused by humans, but scientists remain unsure about what the future holds.

In May 2001, United States President George W. Bush asked the National Academy of Sciences to summarize the current scientific understanding of global warming, and I was authorized to chair a committee to investigate the issue. The Committee on the Science of Climate Change, which included 11 climate scientists from various U.S. institutions, sought to clarify what is known and what remains unknown about global warming.

After reviewing the major scientific research on this subject, we reached a number of conclusions, which can be summed up in three statements: (1) Earth has become warmer during the past several decades; (2) the warming is likely due to human activities, mainly atmospheric changes caused by the burning of *fossil fuels* (coal, oil, gas, and wood); and (3) Earth will continue to warm, but we are not yet sure how fast temperatures will rise or how particular regions on Earth will be affected by climate change.

Evidence of present and past warm-ups

How do we know that Earth is warming up? Temperature records clearly show that Earth became warmer during the 1900's. Between 1900 and 2000, measurements made around the world indicate that the *globally averaged surface temperature* (the average of sea-surface temperatures and air temperatures over land) increased by between 0.7 and 1.4 °F (0.4 and 0.8 °C). Between 1980 and 2000, temperatures rose especially fast in both the Northern and Southern hemispheres—by between 0.45 and 0.7 °F (0.25 and 0.4 °C).

The present warming is well documented. But it is not the first time that the planet has gone through climate change. Scientists know of earlier climate changes from both historic and prehistoric records. The invention of the thermometer in the 1500's made it possible to measure actual temperatures, and scientists began to make regular recordings of air temperatures in the mid-1800's. Geologists and anthropologists, furthermore, have found evidence of earlier climate conditions. Some of these conditions were recorded by people in written histories or agricultural records. For prehistoric eras, modern scientists base estimates of temperature on "proxy" data derived from studies of tree rings, deposits left by glaciers, ocean coral formations, and sediments found in lake beds or at the bottom of the sea. Scientists can obtain such data by drilling *cores* (cylindrical samples) of sediment from the seafloor and cores of ice from polar regions and examining them for clues to past climate.

Little Ice Age and Medieval Warm Period

Proxy data provides evidence of both a Little Ice Age and a Medieval Warm Period within the past 1,000 years. In parts of the Northern Hemisphere, average temperatures were about 1.8 °F (1 °C) lower during the Little Ice Age, from about 1400 to 1800, than they were during most of the 1900's. Certain regions were colder than others. It was coldest in central Europe during the late 1600's, but people in Switzerland experienced their coldest weather from the 1560's through the 1570's. European glaciers

Greenhouse effect

Carbon dioxide, methane, and water vapor are gases that occur naturally in Earth's atmosphere. They allow sunlight to enter the atmosphere but trap some of the *infrared* (heat) rays from Earth's surface. This heat trapping makes Earth warm enough to support life. In this way, the gases act somewhat like greenhouse windows and are thus called greenhouse gases. The process by which greenhouse gases trap heat in Earth's atmosphere is called the greenhouse effect.

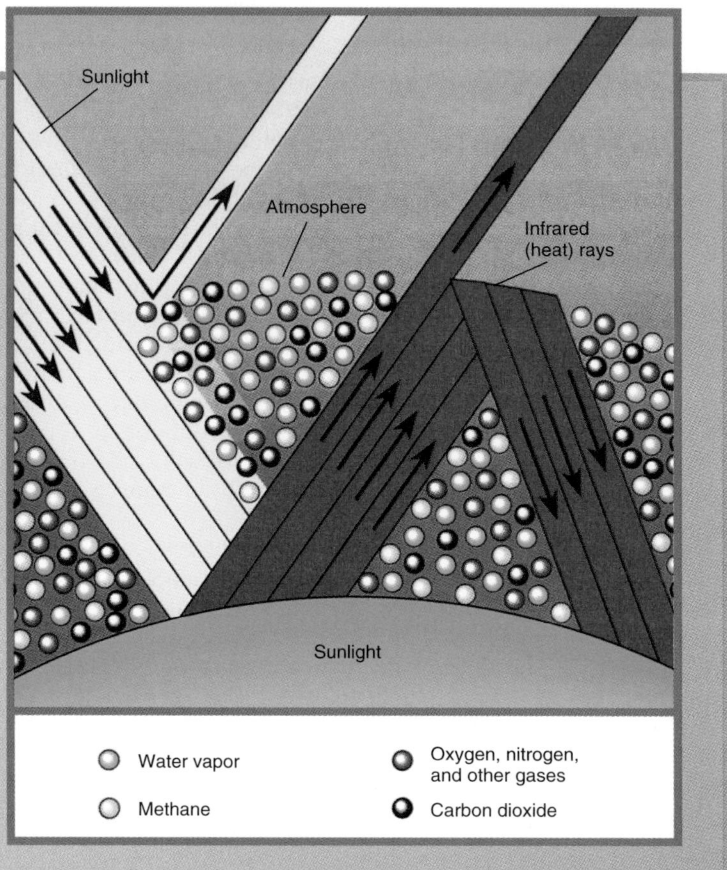

advanced noticeably, and some rivers and lakes froze over regularly during the Little Ice Age. The Thames River in London was frozen almost every winter until the early 1800's, allowing Londoners to hold annual "frost fairs" featuring skating, games, and entertainment on the river's ice. Scientists believe that temperatures south of the equator were warmer than those of the north during the Little Ice Age.

Prior to the Little Ice Age, a Medieval Warm Period occurred from about 1100 to 1300. Temperatures increased the most in regions around the north Atlantic Ocean. Grapes grew in England, and farming flourished in Scandinavia and Scotland. Scientists had previously thought that average temperatures in the Northern Hemisphere may have been between 1.8 and 3.6 °F (1 and 2 °C) above those of the later Little Ice Age. However, an examination of data from numerous ice cores and tree rings by climate expert Michael E. Mann of the University of Virginia in the late 1990's indicated that the Medieval Warm Period was cooler than previously believed. In fact, the new evidence revealed that average temperatures during the Medieval Warm Period—long considered a time of major climate change—were probably below those of 2000.

The author:
Ralph J. Cicerone is Aldrich Professor of Earth System Science and Chemistry, and Chancellor, at the University of California at Irvine.

Recurring ice ages

More drastic climate change occurred further back in time. Earth has gone through several *ice ages,* periods when average temperatures plummeted several degrees and ice sheets covered vast regions of land. Scientists have discovered geological and chemical evidence that ice ages have occurred approximately every 100,000 years during the last 900,000 years. The most recent ice age ended approximately 11,000 years ago.

The fact that there have been recurring warmer and colder periods in the past shows that there are natural variations in Earth's climate. These natural climate changes may be caused by the *oscillation* (back-and-forth movement) in the planet's axis of rotation and orbit. Earth is tilted on its axis, and this tilt results in the seasons as the planet moves around the sun. The angle of the tilt changes over time. As the angle varies, the amount of sunlight striking different parts of the planet varies with the tilt. Increasing tilt leads to greater differences between summer and winter temperatures. The shape of Earth's orbit also changes over time, so that, during certain periods, the planet's orbit is more *elliptical* (oval shaped) than during other periods. The more stretched the orbit, the more difference there is between seasons. Such seasonal changes can reduce the amount of solar energy striking the Northern Hemisphere during summer. This, in turn, may cause the annual growth and melting of polar ice to become imbalanced, leading to an ice age.

An enhanced greenhouse effect

Because changes in Earth's orbit and other natural variations have altered Earth's climate in the past, could the present warm-up also be caused by natural factors? This is unlikely. Scientific data collected over decades indicate that the present warm-up is related to an enhancement of the *greenhouse effect,* a process by which gases in the atmosphere trap heat energy, much like a greenhouse.

Energy flows to Earth from the sun, mostly in the form of visible light. Much of this energy is reflected back into space by the planet's cloud tops, snow, ice, and other light-colored surfaces. A greater amount, however, is absorbed by dark-colored surfaces, such as wet soil, vegetation, the ocean, and particles in the air and clouds. The absorbed energy warms these dark surfaces, which reemit the energy as infrared (IR) radiation, or heat. All objects that are warmer than their surroundings radiate IR energy. Earth, which is warm, loses heat as it moves through space, which is cold—just about balancing the incoming solar power. This balance determines Earth's temperature.

Not all of the IR radiation emitted by Earth's surface is lost to space. Some of it is intercepted by gases in the atmosphere known as greenhouse gases. Among these are carbon dioxide, methane, and water vapor. When these gases absorb the out-going radiation, they warm the air. The warmed air reemits more IR radiation, half of which is directed upward toward the upper atmosphere and half downward toward Earth's surface, which is further warmed.

Greenhouse gases

Human activities have increased the amount of various heat-trapping greenhouse gases in the atmosphere. Carbon dioxide is by far the most serious greenhouse gas.

Gas	Sources
Carbon dioxide	• Fossil fuel combustion • Deforestation
Methane	• Microbes in wetlands and rice paddies • Intestinal fermentation in cattle • Decomposition in landfills • Leaking and venting of oil and gas wells • Burning forests
Nitrous oxide	• Chemical processes in the soil and ocean • Fossil fuel combustion • Burning forests • Agricultural fertilizers
Halocarbons	• Industrial products, such as chlorofluorocarbon-based aerosol propellants, refrigerants, and solvents
Aerosol particles	• Fossil fuel combustion • Burning forests • Volcanoes
Ozone	• Chemical reactions between sunlight and pollutants from power plants and automobiles

Adapted from Intergovernmental Panel on Climate Change, 2001.

Carbon dioxide concentration

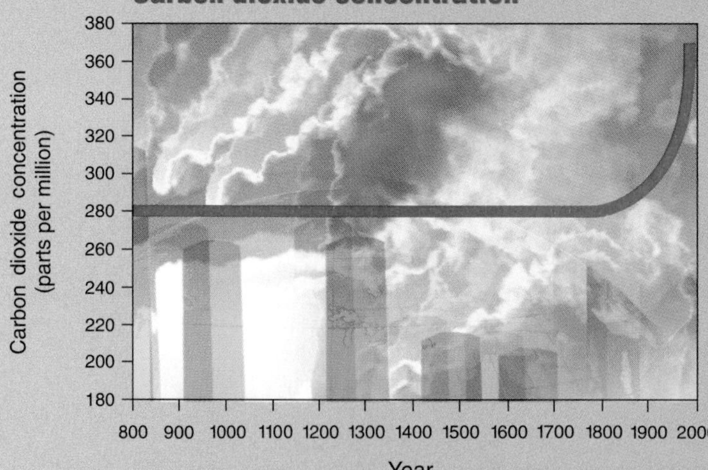

The concentration of carbon dioxide, a greenhouse gas generated by the burning of fossil fuels, began to increase in Earth's atmosphere during the Industrial Revolution in the mid-1800's. The increase has been greatest since the mid-1900's.

The greenhouse effect keeps Earth warmer than it would otherwise be. Throughout the planet's history, the greenhouse effect has prevented Earth from freezing and made life itself possible. We can see evidence of the power of the greenhouse effect on neighboring planets. Venus is much hotter than Earth because its thick, mainly carbon dioxide atmosphere is extremely good at trapping heat. Mars is a frozen planet because it has a very thin atmosphere without enough greenhouse gases to trap heat.

Carbon dioxide emissions

Large amounts of greenhouse gases are given off by a number of human activities. The most plentiful human-generated greenhouse gas is carbon dioxide, released by the burning of fossil fuels. Between 1957, when modern measurements began, and 2000, carbon dioxide concentrations in the atmosphere have increased by approximately 18 percent. At the beginning of the new millennium in 2000, the worldwide burning of fossil fuels injected about 6.6 billion tons (6 billion metric tons) of carbon, in the form of carbon dioxide, into the global atmosphere each year. Carbon dioxide emissions were increasing by about 1 to 2 percent per year. Approximately half of the carbon that is emitted ends up in the atmosphere, and half is absorbed by the ocean and plants.

The 20-year period between 1980 and 2000 during which temperatures rose by as much as 0.7 °F (0.4 °C) is especially important because, for the first time, scientists also measured the sun's output precisely. These measurements revealed that solar output did not change during this period. The rapid warming, therefore, must have been due to an increase in the atmospheric concentration of carbon dioxide and other greenhouse gases.

Certain land-use practices add to greenhouse gases. In the early 2000's, *deforestation* (cutting down trees) in the tropical rain forests injected 1.6 billion tons (1.5 billion metric tons) of carbon, in the form of carbon dioxide, into the atmosphere. Deforestation causes a build-up of carbon dioxide as a result of the burning of trees and the decomposition of dead organic matter by bacteria.

Other greenhouse gases

Carbon dioxide is by far the most important greenhouse gas, but human activities also generate other heat-trapping gases. For example, the atmospheric concentration of methane is increasing due to microbial activity in rice paddies and municipal landfills, intestinal fermentation in cattle, and the leaking and venting of oil and gas wells. Nitrous oxide, fluorocarbons, and ozone are other greenhouse gases produced through human activities.

Together, the greenhouse gases added to the atmosphere by humans trap the same amount of heat energy per square meter as is given off by a small Christmas-tree light bulb. While this does not seem like much, it equals about 1 percent of the solar energy absorbed every second by every square meter of Earth's surface. If the Sun's output of solar energy were to increase by 1 percent,

Earth would experience significant climate change. (The sun's energy output actually varies in a cycle by 0.1 percent over an 11 year period.) Therefore, if emissions from fossil fuels and other greenhouse-gas sources continue at their present rate, atmospheric concentrations of these gases will continue to grow, and the extra heating caused by the gases should alter Earth's climate.

Computer models predict the future

How will human input into the global climate system affect Earth in the future? Precise predictions were hampered in 2001 by the fact that scientists still had much to learn about the physics of climate and the ways in which biological systems respond to climate change. To better understand climate change, scientists use powerful computers capable of modeling, or simulating, such climate factors as sunlight, heat, *precipitation* (rain and snow), air currents, and ocean currents. Scientists program equations governing these factors into computer models to try to mimic the way Earth's climate works. They then add other factors to the model, such as a particular level of carbon dioxide, to see how these additions alter the model. In this way, the model tells researchers how the climate might change in the future.

Computer-model predictions of how climate might change yielded not one clear answer, but a range of possibilities. Yet, there were a number of outcomes that most scientists agreed upon. Most models predicted that global temperatures will continue to increase, with more hot days and higher maximum daytime temperatures over most land areas. Minimum daily nighttime temperatures were also expected to increase over most land areas. The computer models predicted that minimum daily temperatures will rise faster than the maximum temperatures. Scientists believed that faster *evaporation* (the conversion of a liquid into a gas through warming) will cause average amounts of precipitation around Earth to increase. Most models, however, predicted that global warming will result in less rain and increased risk of drought during summer in midcontinental regions. Melting ice sheets were expected to cause global average sea levels to rise between 4 inches and 2.9 feet (0.1 and 0.9 meters) by 2100, according to a range of model estimates.

Problems with model predictions

How accurate are climate changes predicted by computer models? Their accuracy depends on how well the models have been programmed to simulate the complex, dynamic processes of Earth's climate system. It is difficult to accurately model many important parts of the climate system, such as the degree to which cloud cover and cloud heights might change; the role that black soot particles in the air play in trapping heat; and the extent to which sulfate particles in the air (from the burning of sulfur-containing coal and oil) cool the ground. However, by combining a number of certainties and uncertainties, many scientists estimated that average global temperatures could increase by 2.7 to 9 °F (1.5 to 5 °C) by 2100.

Natural temperature variations

Records preserved in ice cores (right) and other evidence reveal that Earth's surface temperature has fluctuated throughout history. However, scientists disagree as to the exact temperature changes that occurred in the past and how widespread the changes were. Most scientists believe that the existing data best represents temperatures in the Northern Hemisphere.

Earth experienced a major warm-up after the end of the last Ice Age, approximately 11,000 years ago (upper graph). A number of cooler periods and warmer periods then followed. Before the present warm-up began in the mid-1800's, the Northern Hemisphere experienced a period of cooling called the Little Ice Age, which began around 1400.

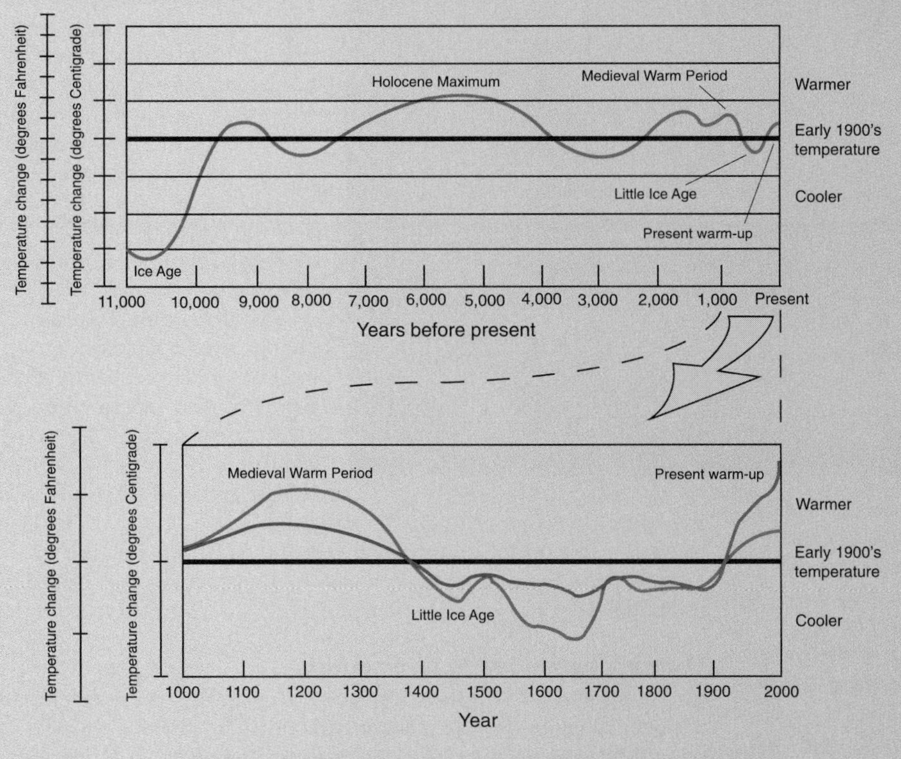

In 1990, the Intergovernmental Panel on Climate Change (IPCC) reported that the present warm-up did not seem to be as great as that of the Medieval Warm Period, which lasted from about 1100 to 1300 (lower graph). However, in 1999, climate expert Michael E. Mann of the University of Virginia concluded that present temperatures are higher than Medieval temperatures.

The glacier Qori Kalis in the Peruvian Andes melted substantially between 1983 and 2000. According to scientists at the Byrd Polar Research Center of Ohio State University, this melting provides a clear sign of global warming.

While computer models in 2001 were able to simulate changes in certain worldwide features of climate, such as average global temperatures, they were not able to make precise predictions for particular geographical regions. The climate for each region on Earth depends on many complex factors that scientists did not fully understand and computers could not yet model. Although a computer model may predict a rise in average global temperature, exactly how fast temperatures will rise and where they will rise the most remained unclear. It was also not clear in what season or by how much precipitation will increase in any given region on Earth. Moreover, scientists continued to question how climate change would affect the severeness of coastal flooding and the frequency of droughts, typhoons, and other extreme weather.

The impact that climate change might have on agriculture, society, and the environment also remained unclear. Some agricultural regions may profit by the longer growing season resulting from a warmer climate, but only if adequate rain falls to keep the soil moist. Some countries and ecosystems may be able to adapt to climate disruptions caused by global warming, but only if change does not come too fast.

Human behavior is important

Human behavior will have a major effect on the future of climate change. The greenhouse-gas emissions driving current climate change are the product of three factors dependent on human actions. The first is technological efficiency, in particular, the energy efficiency of such fuel-using technologies as electric power plants and automobiles; the second involves human consumption, for example, the number of cars purchased and driven; and the third factor is population—more people on the planet will cause more greenhouse gases to be emitted. Since none of these factors can be predicted with perfect accuracy, they add to the uncertainties in climate models.

Despite the uncertainties, scientists point to a number of actions that Americans could take that would not only limit greenhouse-gas emissions but also have economic side benefits. If Americans would use fossil fuels more efficiently, they would slow the growth of the global greenhouse effect. Greater fuel efficiency would also save money for Americans, decrease the trade imbalance of the United States with other nations, and lessen the U.S. dependence on foreign oil. The recycling of aluminum cans, paper, and other materials helps limit greenhouse-gas emissions by decreasing the volume of trash that must be buried in landfills or burned. It also helps conserve energy.

Working to limit global warming

Most of the scientific community supports international efforts to decrease greenhouse-gas emissions, such as the Kyoto Protocol, which set targets for carbon dioxide reductions. Some industrialized nations have ratified the Kyoto Protocol since 1997, but the U.S. government, citing economic concerns, withdrew from the agreement in 2001. Officials from the United States and some other countries were in favor of giving nations credit for carbon dioxide reductions by taking into account the amount of carbon that is naturally absorbed by plants and soil in forests and farms. However, most nations that lacked large areas of forests and farmland were opposed to this idea. Scientists note that such schemes will be effective only if it can be proven that the absorbed carbon is "locked up" in the plants or soil for long periods, preventing it from returning to the atmosphere. Scientists also stress that international efforts need to address the issues of energy efficiency, rates of consumption, and population growth. Some poorer countries, which use much less energy per person than the United States, are rapidly increasing their energy usage as their populations expand. Global warming is bound to quicken if such matters are not confronted.

The incredible complexity of Earth's climate demands that we intensify scientific research if we want to understand the changes that we are currently observing and accurately predict future changes. Meanwhile, we need to try to slow the rate of global warming in order to give researchers more time to predict changes before they actually happen.

Climate change will no doubt remain an important and controversial issue for a long time. While it has become clear that humans have the power to change the global climate, we are unlikely to be able to control the climate. The worldwide experiment that is underway bears close watching. ■■■

Additional reading:

National Academy Press, Climate Change Science, 2001
http://books.nap.edu/books/0309075742/html/

Golf. In April 2001, Eldrick "Tiger" Woods won the Professional Golfers' Association's (PGA) Masters tournament to become the first golfer to ever win four straight Grand Slam events. However, Woods's hot streak ended later in 2001, and golfers who had never before captured a major won all of the other majors. On the Senior PGA circuit, a tour for pros over 50 years old, four different men captured majors. On the Ladies Professional Golf Association (LPGA) tour, Karrie Webb took the U.S. Open and the LPGA Championship while Se Ri Pak won the British Open and Annika Sorenstam won the Nabisco Championship. The Ryder Cup, held between American and European players, was postponed until 2002 because of the Sept. 11, 2001, terrorist attacks.

PGA. On April 8, Tiger Woods became the first golfer to ever win four consecutive majors by taking the Masters at Augusta, Georgia. Woods finished at 16 under par, two shots short of the tournament record he set in 1997.

No player had ever won a true Grand Slam (winning all four majors in the same calendar year), but only Ben Hogan and Jack Nicklaus have come close, winning three in a row. In 1930, Bobby Jones had a comparable run to Woods's, winning the U.S. Open, U.S. Amateur, British Open, and British Amateur for an "amateur" Grand Slam. Later in the 2001 season, Woods struggled, failing to finish in the top 10 in five straight tournaments.

On June 18, Retief Goosen won the U.S. Open in Tulsa, Oklahoma, by two strokes in an 18-hole play-off with Mark Brooks. Goosen appeared to have had the title wrapped up the previous day, but he three-putted from 12 feet (3.6 meters) on the final hole to force the play-off.

David Duval won the British Open on July 22 at Lytham St. Annes, England. For the tournament, Duval shot a 10-under 274 to win by three shots over Niclas Fasth of Sweden.

In August, David Toms edged Phil Mickelson by one stroke to win the PGA Championship in Duluth, Georgia. On the final hole, Toms, holding a one-stroke lead, opted to lay up after he put his drive into the rough, rather than going for the green. Mickelson missed by inches his 20-foot (6-meter) birdie attempt that would have either forced a play-off or given him the win, and Toms drained his 12-foot (3.6-meter) par putt for the victory.

Senior PGA. On April 15, Doug Tewell shot a tournament record 10-under 62 to win the Tradition at Scottsdale, Arizona.

On May 27, Tom Watson beat Jim Thorpe by one stroke to win the Senior PGA Championship in Paramus, New Jersey.

On July 1, Bruce Fleisher parred his last 12

holes to take his first major, a one-stroke victory over Isao Aoki and Gil Morgan at the U.S. Senior Open in Peabody, Massachusetts.

On July 15, Allen Doyle topped Doug Tewell on the first play-off hole at the Senior Players' Championship in Dearborn, Michigan.

LPGA. On June 3, Karrie Webb became the seventh woman to win back-to-back Women's U.S. Opens. Webb beat Se Ri Pak by six strokes in the tournament, held in Southern Pines, North Carolina. On June 24, Webb, 26, became the youngest woman to complete a career Grand Slam by capturing the LPGA Championship in Wilmington, Delaware.

In August, Pak won the Women's British Open at Sunningdale, England, which replaced the Du Maurier Classic as a major. Pak shot a 6-under 66 on the final day for a two-stroke win.

On March 25, Annika Sorenstam won the Nabisco Championship at Rancho Mirage, California. It was her first major victory in five years.

Walker Cup. On August 12, Great Britain and Ireland defeated the United States 15-9 in the Walker Cup matches at Sea Island, Georgia. It was the first time that a non-U.S. team successfully defended the Walker Cup in the 79-year history of the amateur tournament. ☐ Michael Kates

See also **Sports.**

Great Britain. See **United Kingdom.**

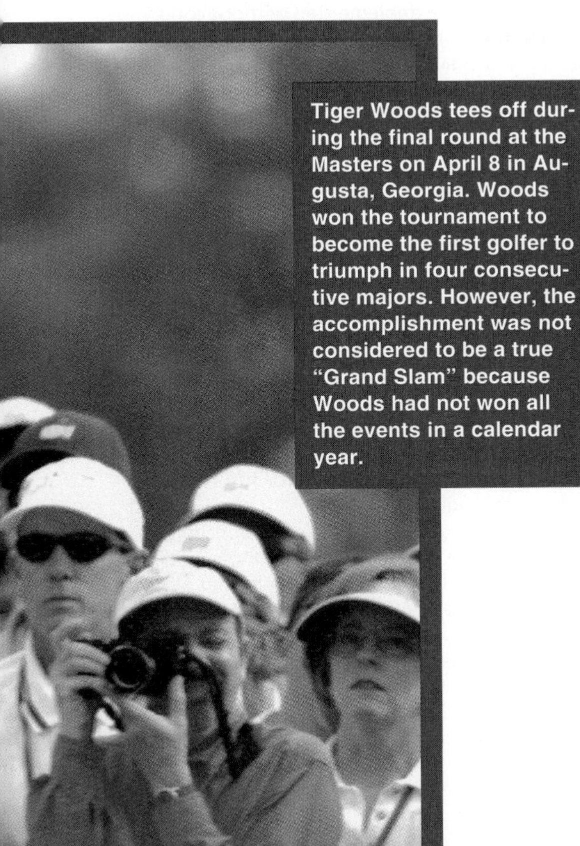

Tiger Woods tees off during the final round at the Masters on April 8 in Augusta, Georgia. Woods won the tournament to become the first golfer to triumph in four consecutive majors. However, the accomplishment was not considered to be a true "Grand Slam" because Woods had not won all the events in a calendar year.

Greece adopted the euro on Jan. 1, 2001, joining the 11 other European Union (EU) countries that use the single currency. The achievement culminated nearly a decade of efforts to end Greece's record of high inflation and government deficits and bring the country's economic performance in line with that of its EU partners.

The government of Prime Minister Costas Simitis, however, ran into economic and political difficulties as the year progressed. In April, the government announced plans to reform the costly state-financed pension system, a key element in its strategy to reduce the national debt and sustain a high rate of economic growth. The main reform would have raised the retirement age to 65 from 55, the age at which many Greek workers are currently eligible to retire. Unions, which opposed the measures, staged a series of one-day strikes that paralyzed the country and forced the government to postpone the reforms.

Simitis called a conference of his Socialist Party in October to seek renewed support for reform from party members. He was reelected as party leader by a wide margin on October 14. Nine days later, he reshuffled his Cabinet and demoted his main rival in the party, Akis Tsohatzopoulos, from defense minister to development minister. Tsohatzopoulos had argued that Greece could afford to relax its economic reform efforts after having adopted the euro.

Greece suffered from the economic slowdown that swept Europe in 2001. Economic output was expected to grow by 4.1 percent, down from 4.3 percent in 2000, and unemployment remained high at nearly 11 percent. The economy nevertheless grew faster than the EU average, which was expected to be about 1.6 percent.

Olympic preparations. In March 2001, the government appointed a new chief executive for the Athens organizing committee for the 2004 Olympic Games, amid growing concerns about delays in the construction of stadiums and transportation projects required for the event. Yannis Spanoudakis, a U.S. executive at Dow Chemical Company, replaced Petros Synadinos, who had resigned in December 2000.

At the end of March 2001, Athens opened a key part of the transportation infrastructure for the games—the new 2.2 billion euro ($2 billion) Eleftherios Venizelos Airport, located at Spata, 17 miles (27 kilometers) east of the capital. Nevertheless, the president of the International Olympic Committee, Jacques Rogge, warned Simitis during a visit to Athens in September to speed up construction because many sports facilities were far behind schedule. ☐ Tom Buerkle

See also **Europe; Olympic Games.**

Grenada. See **Latin America.**

Guatemala. On June 8, 2001, a three-judge tribunal in Guatemala gave three military officers 30-year prison sentences for the 1998 murder of Roman Catholic Bishop Juan Gerardi Conedera. Gerardi Conedera was slain after he publicly blamed the military for committing massacres during Guatemala's 36-year-long civil war, which ended in 1996.

On June 12, 2001, Guatemalan courts ordered investigations into accusations that two former presidents—Romeo Lucas Garcia and Efrain Rios Montt—directed massacres of Mayan Indians between 1978 and 1982. Rios Montt was the president of the Guatemalan Congress in 2001.

Barbara Ann Ford, a Roman Catholic nun from the United States, was shot to death in Guatemala City, the capital, in May. Ford had been in Guatemala for 22 years investigating human rights violations.

A law took effect in May that allowed Guatemalans to open bank accounts or request their paychecks in U.S. dollars. Government authorities hoped the legal circulation of U.S. currency in Guatemala would help attract international investment and check inflation.

☐ Nathan A. Haverstock

See also **Latin America.**

Guinea. See **Africa.**

Guyana. See **Latin America.**

Haiti. Jean-Bertrand Aristide was inaugurated as president of Haiti on Feb. 7, 2001. He previously had served as president in 1991 and again from 1994 to 1996. The day before the 2001 inauguration, a group of opposition parties called the Democratic Convergence formed an alternative government and staged a number of violent protests against Aristide's rule.

The Democratic Convergence accused Aristide of rigging legislative elections that were held in May 2000. The Organization of American States, a group of 35 American nations, condemned the 2000 elections as flawed and sought to mediate an agreement between Aristide and Convergence to hold new elections for parliament in 2002.

Sporadic violence flared in Haiti throughout 2001. On July 28, gunmen attacked two police installations near the Haitian capital of Port-au-Prince, killing three officers and wounding several others. On December 17, there was a similar assault on the National Palace, the presidential mansion. At least two policemen and two passersby were killed in the attack. In retribution, Aristide supporters torched the headquarters of Convergence and the Socialist Party, which they blamed for the assault. ☐ Nathan A. Haverstock

See also **Latin America.**

Harness racing. See **Horse racing.**

Hawaii. See **State government.**

Health care issues underwent a significant change of priorities after the Sept. 11, 2001, terrorist attacks on the United States. Before the attacks, Republicans and Democrats in the U.S. Congress were focused on the debate over how much the federal government should be involved in health care. After the attack, the government and the nation's health care system refocused on threats of biological terrorism.

Before the attacks, President George W. Bush promoted the health care priorities of his administration. They included changes in the Medicare program, which provides medical benefits for most seniors, and a drug discount plan for Medicare users.

Patients' rights. The new Senate leadership soon took up the issue of patients' rights in managed care plans. Despite the threat of a presidential veto, the Senate on June 29 passed a bill giving most patients the right to sue health plans in state court. On August 2, the House of Representatives passed a bill supported by President Bush that severely limited the rights of patients to sue their managed care plans. The two bills then went to a House-Senate conference committee. At the end of 2001, the committee had not yet crafted compromise legislation.

Drug discount plan. In mid-July, President Bush outlined his plan to offer Medicare patients pharmacy discount cards. The president said that the plan could be implemented without congressional approval by January 2002. Two pharmacy associations filed in federal court to stop the plan. On Sept. 6, 2001, they won a restraining order, effectively blocking the plan. The judge who issued the injunction lifted it in November to allow the Bush administration to revise the proposal. The administration said it would instead develop a new plan.

Stem cell research. The Bush administration faced a difficult political decision regarding federal funding of stem cell research. Stem cells are cells that have the ability to develop into a variety of cell types. Embryos created in fertility clinics are a primary source of stem cells, but harvesting such cells kills the embryos. Conservatives charged that the use of stem cells takes human life. Many researchers, however, viewed stem cell research as a promising avenue for future medical breakthroughs.

On August 9, President Bush announced a compromise. He said that federal funds could be used for research involving stem cells that already existed in about 60 "lines," or collections of living cells. Federal money could not be used, the president said, to create any new stem cell lines.

Cloning. In November, scientists with Advanced Cell Technology, Inc., headquartered in Worcester, Massachusetts, announced that they had created the first human embryos using a technique known as nuclear transfer. The scientists transferred genetic material from adult subjects into donated egg cells to create embryos that were *clones* (genetic duplicates) of the adults. The scientists hoped to use embryonic stem cells to make body tissues that would not be rejected by the subjects' immune systems. However, the embryos died shortly after being created. On November 26, President Bush condemned the cloning and called for federal laws to ban such activity.

After the attacks. Both Republicans and Democrats in Congress shifted national health priorities after September 11. The threat of biological terrorism emerged in early October when letters laced with anthrax spores (an inactive stage of bacteria) showed up at news media offices in Florida and New York City and at Senate offices in Washington, D.C. Anthrax is a potentially fatal disease that can be successfully treated with certain powerful antibiotics.

As the number of people exposed to anthrax grew, the Bush administration sought congressional funding to stockpile drugs to combat anthrax and vaccines to protect against smallpox virus, which could also be used by bioterrorists. ☐ Emily Friedman

See also **Medicine; Public health and safety.**

Hockey. The Colorado Avalanche toppled the defending champion New Jersey Devils to win the Stanley Cup in the 2000-2001 National Hockey League (NHL) season. Colorado beat New Jersey 4 games to 3, taking the title with a 3-1 victory on June 9 in Denver. The Avalanche rallied from a 3-games-to-2 deficit, the first to do so in a Stanley Cup final since the Montreal Canadiens did so against the Chicago Blackhawks in 1971.

Season. Colorado led the NHL in the regular season, posting 52 victories and 118 points over the 82-game schedule. New Jersey posted the best record in the Eastern Conference with 111 points, edging out divisional winners Ottawa, with 109 points, and Washington, with 96. Detroit, with 111 points, and Dallas, with 106 points, joined Colorado as Western Conference divisional winners.

Play-offs. Colorado reached the Stanley Cup finals by sweeping Vancouver in the first round 4 games to none and edging the Los Angeles Kings 4 games to 3 in the Western Conference semifinals. Colorado routed the St. Louis Blues 4 games to 1 in the conference final.

In the Eastern Conference, New Jersey beat Carolina 4 games to 2 in the first round, edged Toronto 4 games to 3 in the conference semifinal, and won the title by beating Pittsburgh 4 games to 1. The victory over Pittsburgh ended a brilliant

National Hockey League standings

Western Conference

Central Division	W.	L.	T.	Pts.
Detroit Red Wings*	49	20	9	111
St. Louis Blues*	43	22	12	103
Nashville Predators	34	36	9	80
Chicago Blackhawks	29	40	8	71
Columbus Blue Jackets	28	39	9	71
Northwest Division				
Colorado Avalanche*	52	16	10	118
Edmonton Oilers*	39	28	12	93
Vancouver Canucks*	36	28	11	90
Calgary Flames	27	36	15	73
Minnesota Wild	25	39	13	68
Pacific Division				
Dallas Stars*	48	24	8	106
San Jose Sharks*	40	27	12	95
Los Angeles Kings*	38	28	13	92
Phoenix Coyotes	35	27	17	90
Anaheim Mighty Ducks	25	41	11	66

Eastern Conference

Northeast Division	W.	L.	T.	Pts.
Ottawa Senators*	48	21	9	109
Buffalo Sabres*	46	30	5	98
Toronto Maple Leafs*	37	29	11	90
Boston Bruins	36	30	8	88
Montreal Canadiens	28	40	8	70
Atlantic Division				
New Jersey Devils*	48	19	12	111
Philadelphia Flyers*	43	25	11	100
Pittsburgh Penguins*	42	28	9	96
New York Rangers	33	43	5	72
New York Islanders	21	51	7	52
Southeast Division				
Washington Capitals*	41	27	10	96
Carolina Hurricanes*	38	32	9	88
Florida Panthers	22	38	13	66
Atlanta Thrashers	23	45	12	60
Tampa Bay Lightning	24	47	6	59

*Made play-offs

Stanley Cup champions—Colorado Avalanche
(defeated New Jersey Devils, 4 games to 3)

Leading scorers	Games	Goals	Assists	Pts.
Jaromir Jagr, Pittsburgh	81	52	69	121
Joe Sakic, Colorado	82	54	64	118
Patrik Elias, New Jersey	82	40	56	96
Alexei Kovalev, Pittsburgh	79	44	51	95
Jason Allison, Boston	82	36	59	95
Martin Straka, Pittsburgh	82	27	68	95

Leading goalies (26 or more games)	Games	Goals against	Avg.
Marty Turco, Dallas	26	40	1.90
Roman Cechmanek, Philadelphia	59	115	2.01
Manny Legace, Detroit	39	73	2.05
Dominik Hasek, Buffalo	67	137	2.11
Brent Johnson, St. Louis	31	63	2.17

Awards

Adams Award (coach of the year)—Bill Barber, Philadelphia
Calder Trophy (best rookie)—Evgeni Nabokov, San Jose
Hart Trophy (most valuable player)—Joe Sakic, Colorado
Jennings Trophy (team with fewest goals against)—Dominik Hasek, Buffalo
Lady Byng Trophy (sportsmanship)—Joe Sakic, Colorado
Masterton Trophy (perseverance, dedication to hockey)—Adam Graves, New York Rangers
Norris Trophy (best defenseman)—Nicklas Lidstrom, Detroit
Pearson Award (best player as voted by NHL players)—Joe Sakic, Colorado
Ross Trophy (leading scorer)—Jaromir Jagr, Pittsburgh
Selke Trophy (best defensive forward)—John Madden, New Jersey
Smythe Trophy (most valuable player in Stanley Cup)—Patrick Roy, Colorado
Vezina Trophy (best goalkeeper)—Dominik Hasek, Buffalo

run by the Penguins and star Mario Lemieux, who in 2000-2001 played his first full season after retiring in 1997 for health reasons.

Awards. Colorado's Joe Sakic took the Hart Trophy as the NHL's most valuable player (voted on by the media), the Lester B. Pearson Award as the top player (selected by fellow players), and the Lady Byng Trophy, which is awarded to the player who exhibits the best sportsmanship. Sakic scored 118 points while playing in every game in the regular season, was the top scorer in the play-offs, and served only 30 penalty minutes. Colorado's Patrick Roy received the Conn Smythe Trophy, which is awarded to the most valuable player in the play-offs.

World championships. The Czech Republic defeated Finland 3-2 on May 13 in Hanover, Germany, to become the first national team to win three men's hockey titles in a row since the former Soviet Union won five straight in 1983. The Canadian women's team beat the United States 3-2 on April 8 at Minneapolis, Minnesota, for the world title. It was the seventh straight time Canada had beaten the U.S. in the title game.

College. Boston College won its first hockey title in 52 years by edging defending champion North Dakota 3-2 on April 7 in Albany, New York.

☐ Michael Kates

Honduras. See **Latin America.**

Horse racing. The mysterious deaths of more than 500 thoroughbred foals, which were stillborn or died shortly after birth, rocked the thoroughbred horse industry in Kentucky in the spring of 2001. Similar deaths were also reported at horse farms in West Virginia and Ohio.

In May, scientists concluded that the foals had died when the mares carrying them had eaten grass poisoned by cyanide, which naturally occurs in the leaves of black cherry trees common in those areas. The scientists said that Eastern Tent caterpillars, which had recently invaded Kentucky, had eaten the black cherry leaves and excreted the cyanide on the grass where the horses fed. Kentucky officials estimated the value of the lost foals at more than $300 million.

Three-year-olds. On May 5, Monarchos, a 10.5-to-1 longshot, stunned the horse-racing world by running the second-fastest Kentucky Derby in history. Monarchos covered the 1¼-mile course at Churchill Downs in Louisville, Kentucky, in 1 minute 59.97 seconds. Only Secretariat, who posted 1:59.4 during the legendary horse's Triple Crown run in 1973, has run faster. Invisible Ink, a 55-to-1 longshot, finished second, nearly five lengths behind Monarchos.

Point Given, who had been favored to win the Kentucky Derby, was in charge for the rest of the Triple Crown season. On May 19, 2001, he won

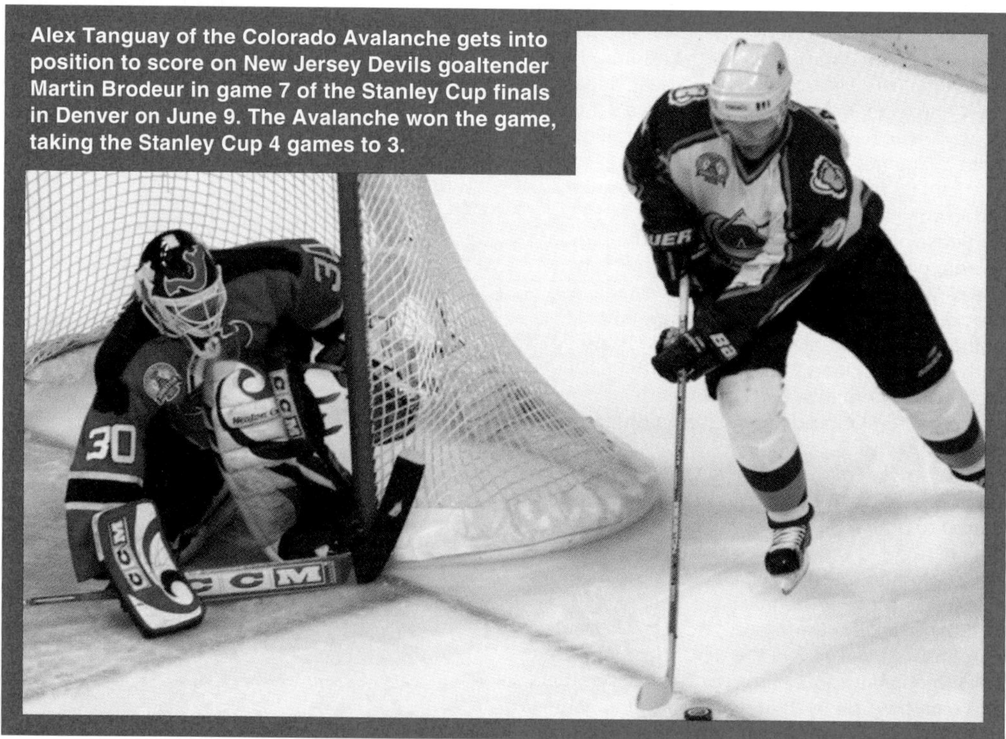

Alex Tanguay of the Colorado Avalanche gets into position to score on New Jersey Devils goaltender Martin Brodeur in game 7 of the Stanley Cup finals in Denver on June 9. The Avalanche won the game, taking the Stanley Cup 4 games to 3.

Point Given (center) hits the finish line to win the Preakness Stakes on May 19 at Baltimore's Pimlico Race Course by 2¼ lengths. He went on to win the Belmont Stakes on June 9 by 12¼ lengths.

Major horse races of 2001

Thoroughbred racing

Race	Winner	Value to Winner
Atto Mile (Canada)	Numerous Times	$600,000
Belmont Stakes	Point Given	$600,000
Blue Grass Stakes	Millennium Wind	$465,000
Breeders' Cup Classic	Tiznow	$2,080,000
Breeders' Cup Distaff	Unbridled Elaine	$1,227,200
Breeders' Cup Filly & Mare Turf	Banks Hill	$722,800
Breeders' Cup Juvenile	Johannesburg	$520,000
Breeders' Cup Juvenile Fillies	Tempera	$520,000
Breeders' Cup Mile	Val Royal	$592,800
Breeders' Cup Sprint	Squirtle Squirt	$520,000
Breeders' Cup Turf	Fantastic Light	$1,112,800
Canadian International Stakes	Mutamam	$570,704
Derby Stakes (United Kingdom)	Galileo	$570,704
Dubai World Cup (United Arab Emirates)	Captain Steve	$3,600,000
Haskell Invitational Handicap	Point Given	$900,000
Hollywood Gold Cup	Aptitude	$450,000
Irish Derby (Ireland)	Galileo	$551,430
Jockey Club Gold Cup	Aptitude	$600,000
Kentucky Derby	Monarchos	$812,000
Kentucky Oaks	Flute	$377,704
King George VI and Queen Elizabeth Diamond Stakes (United Kingdom)	Galileo	$620,136
Oaklawn Handicap	Traditionally	$600,000
Pacific Classic Stakes	Skimming	$600,000
Preakness Stakes	Point Given	$650,000
Prix de l'Arc de Triomphe (France)	Sakhee	$839,000
Santa Anita Derby	Point Given	$450,000
Santa Anita Handicap	Tiznow	$600,000
Spiral Stakes	Balto Star	$360,000
Stephen Foster Handicap	Guided Tour	$551,220
Travers Stakes	Point Given	$600,000

Harness racing

Race	Winner	Value to Winner
Cane Pace	Four Starzzz Shark	$172,847
Hambletonian	Scarlet Knight	$500,000
Kentucky Futurity	Chasing Tail	$138,000
Little Brown Jug	Bettor's Delight	$256,481
Meadowlands Pace	Real Desire	$504,750
Messenger Stakes	Bagel Beach Boy	$127,193
Woodrow Wilson	Allamerican Ingot	$350,000
Yonkers Trot	Banker Hall	$170,307

Sources: *The Blood Horse Magazine* and U.S. Trotting Association

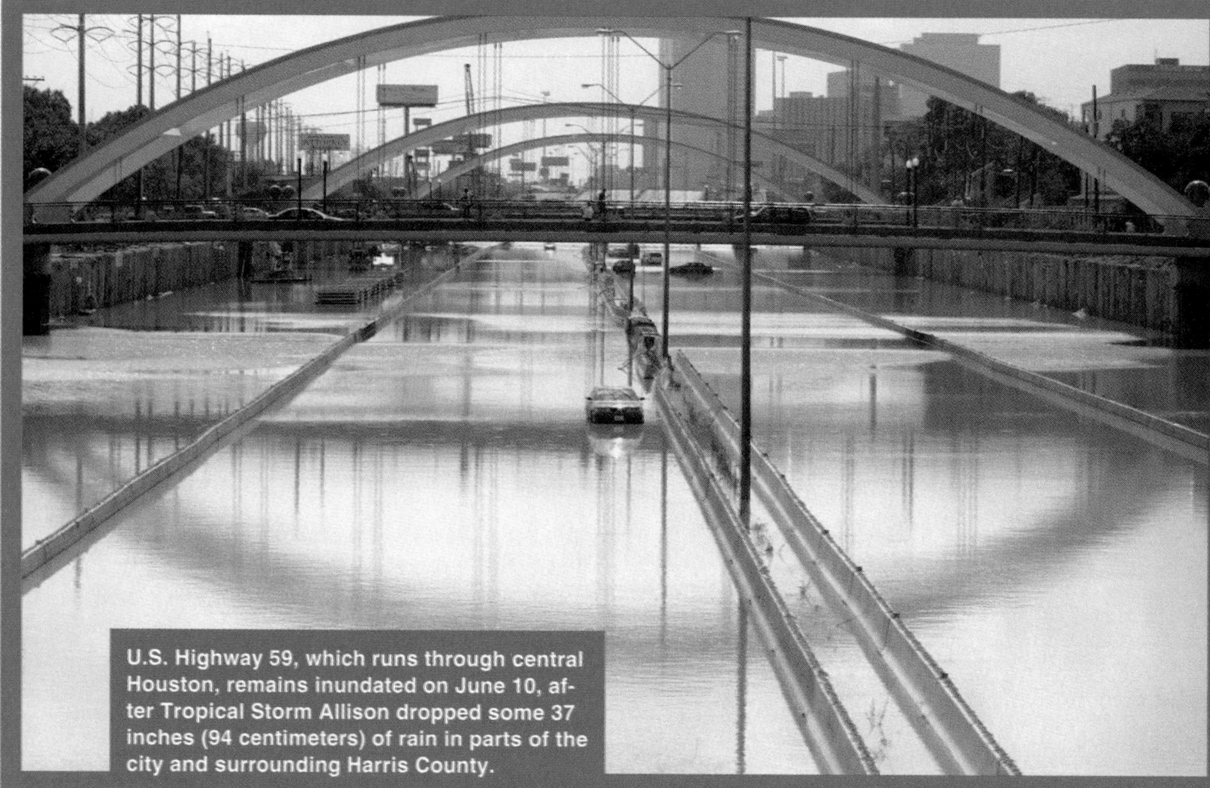

U.S. Highway 59, which runs through central Houston, remains inundated on June 10, after Tropical Storm Allison dropped some 37 inches (94 centimeters) of rain in parts of the city and surrounding Harris County.

the Preakness Stakes at Baltimore's Pimlico Race Course by 2¼ lengths over AP Valentine. On June 9, Point Given dominated the field in the Belmont Stakes, beating AP Valentine by 12¼ lengths at Belmont Park in Elmont, New York.

Harness racing. On August 4, Scarlet Knight held off Pegasus Spur to capture the $1-million Hambletonian at the Meadowlands Racetrack in East Rutherford, New Jersey. In the Pacing Triple Crown, Four Starzzz Shark won the Cane Pace on September 3 after Gunthatwonthewest broke stride about 50 yards (45 meters) short of the finish line; Bettor's Delight held off Real Desire by a length and a half to win the Little Brown Jug on September 20; and Bagel Beach Boy outdueled stablemate Exquisite Art to win the Messenger Stakes on October 27.

International. On March 24, Captain Steve won the biggest purse in thoroughbred racing, capturing the $3.6-million winner's share of the $6-million Dubai World Cup, held in the United Arab Emirates. Galileo, ridden by Irish jockey Michael Kinane, became the 14th horse to win both the Irish Derby and the English Derby, taking the Derby Stakes in England on June 9 and the Irish Derby three weeks later.

☐ Michael Kates

Hospital. See **Health care issues.**

Housing. See **Building and construction.**

Houston. Devastating floods in Houston and surrounding Harris County in June 2001 killed 23 people, destroyed at least 3,000 residences, and caused an estimated $5 billion in damage. From June 5 to June 9, the slow-moving remnants of Tropical Storm Allison dumped almost 37 inches (94 centimeters) of rain on parts of the county.

The Texas Medical Center was especially hard hit, with about $2 billion in damage. High water forced eight hospitals in the sprawling complex to declare internal emergencies. Two major research hospitals at the center lost a huge collection of laboratory specimens, at least 35,000 lab animals, and decades of research records.

Harris County's criminal courts were closed for several weeks after the storm flooded a new, $100-million criminal justice center in downtown Houston. The damage forced the county to scatter court operations around the city for several months. County officials expected to spend $16 million to repair the damage and secure the building against future floods.

In downtown Houston's theater district, the storm caused at least $27 million in damage to the Jesse H. Jones Hall for the Performing Arts, home of the Houston Symphony, and to the Gus S. Wortham Theater Center, home of the Houston Ballet and the Houston Grand Opera. The nationally known Alley Theatre suffered at least $7 million in damage. Nevertheless, all three facilities were in operation for their autumn seasons.

Houston's mayoral race attracted national attention in late 2001 when Republican candidate Orlando Sanchez, a Hispanic city councilman endorsed by U.S. President George W. Bush, came close to unseating incumbent Democratic Mayor Lee P. Brown, an African American who was running for a third term. Brown beat Sanchez by a margin of 52 percent to 48 percent in a runoff election on December 1.

New rail system. After more than a decade of public debate, the Metropolitan Transit Authority (Metro) broke ground in March for a 7.5-mile (12-kilometer) light-rail mass transit system. The $300-million line is to run from downtown Houston south through Hermann Park and the Medical Center to the Astrodome complex. Metro officials hoped to complete the project by 2004. Cars on the completed system will resemble trolleys rather than traditional commuter rail cars.

The groundbreaking followed years of political wrangling, including a successful effort by U. S. Representative Tom DeLay (R., Texas) of Sugar Land, southwest of Houston, to block federal funding for the project. He contended that the system would have almost no effect on regional traffic and pollution problems. As a result, Metro is to finance the project entirely with local funds.

Clean air plan. Houston won approval from the U.S. Environmental Protection Agency (EPA) in October 2001 for a five-year plan to clean the air in the metropolitan area. Houston ranks second worst among all U.S. cities in air pollution levels. Only Los Angeles has more severely polluted air. EPA officials expect the measures to reduce emissions of nitrogen oxide, one of the main components of smog, by 75 percent by 2007. The plan includes steep cuts in emissions from industrial plants, lower speed limits, and strict vehicle exhaust testing. Successful implementation would bring the region into compliance with the federal Clean Air Act of 1970 for the first time. Some of Houston's business leaders criticized the plan as too restrictive, while environmentalists argued that it was too weak. By the end of 2001, the plan faced at least 13 lawsuits.

New basketball arena. The Harris County-Houston Sports Authority began construction of a downtown basketball arena in August 2001. The $202-million arena is to have 18,500 seats for basketball and will be adaptable for hockey if the city can attract a franchise. Much of the building's cost, as well as that of an adjacent, $35-million parking garage, was to be financed with bonds approved by Houston voters in a 2000 referendum. ☐ Eric Berger

See also **City**.

Human rights.

On May 3, 2001, the members of the United Nations Economic and Social Council denied the United States a seat on the United Nations Human Rights Commission for the first time in the commission's 54-year history. The council oversees the Human Rights Commission and elects the commission's members. The United States was instrumental in founding the Human Rights Commission in 1947. Eleanor Roosevelt, the former first lady of the United States and the first U.S. delegate to the United Nations (UN), served as the first chairperson of the commission, which studies human rights issues and prepares recommendations and guidelines for guaranteeing such rights.

Human rights groups expressed concern about the council's action, noting that the United States had been forceful in bringing attention to human rights abuses throughout the world. Former U.S. Secretary of State Madeleine K. Albright characterized the omission as "beyond belief" in light of Sudan's membership on the commission. International human rights monitoring groups have accused the government of Sudan of numerous human rights abuses, including trafficking in slavery.

On May 30, 2001, Amnesty International USA, the New York City-based U.S. branch of the international human rights organization, criticized the recent human rights record of the United States, asserting that the country was no longer a world leader in championing human rights. The group accused the United States of overlooking human rights abuses for political reasons.

Church bombing conviction. An Alabama jury on May 1 convicted former Ku Klux Klan member Thomas E. Blanton, Jr., of murdering four African American girls in a 1963 church bombing in Birmingham. Blanton was sentenced to life in prison. The bombing at Birmingham's 16th Street Baptist Church was a key event of the civil rights era and gave momentum to passage of various civil rights laws.

Blanton's trial and conviction were delayed for nearly four decades because critical evidence—several audiotapes—was misplaced and long forgotten by the Federal Bureau of Investigation. Blanton was one of four suspects in the case: Robert Chambers was convicted in 1977 and sentenced to life in prison, where he died in 1985; Bobby Frank Cherry, who was indicted with Blanton, was found incompetent by a judge to stand trial; a fourth suspect died in 1994 without being charged.

War crimes. On Aug. 2, 2001, the International War Crimes Tribunal in the Hague, Netherlands, convicted Radislav Krstic, a Bosnian Serb general, of *genocide* (the deliberate and systematic mistreatment or extermination of a national, racial, political, religious, or cultural group). The tribunal concluded that Krstic played a leading role in the deliberate killing of more than 7,000 Muslim men near Srebrenica, in eastern Bosnia, in July 1995.

On June 28, 2001, Serbian government officials gave the tribunal custody of Slobodan Milosevic, former president of Yugoslavia. (Yugoslavia consists of two republics, Serbia and Montenegro.) The tribunal had indicted Milosevic in 1999 for crimes against humanity in Kosovo, a semiautonomous province of Serbia. As president of Yugoslavia, Milosevic had commanded military forces that killed thousands of ethnic Albanians in Kosovo and left more than 700,000 people homeless. In 2001, the War Crimes Tribunal indicted Milosevic for genocide. It also indicted 75 other Yugoslav officials for their actions during fighting in Bosnia and Croatia in the 1990's.

Execution ban. In 2001, officials in five U.S. states—Arizona, Connecticut, Florida, Missouri, and North Carolina—banned the execution of mentally retarded individuals, bringing the total number of states that ban the execution of the mental retarded to 18. In 2001, the law codes of 38 of the 50 states prescribed the death penalty for various crimes.

Federal death penalty. U.S. Attorney General John Ashcroft announced on June 6 that a Justice Department study had determined that there is no evidence to support the contention that African Americans and Hispanics are more likely to face the death penalty than white Americans. Ashcroft contended that African American and Hispanic defendants actually are less likely than white defendants to receive *capital punishment* (the death penalty) for committing a capital offense. Various U.S. legal experts responded that U.S. minorities are far more likely to be charged with capital crimes than whites.

The study, begun by former U.S. Attorney General Janet Reno, examined 973 cases in which the defendants were convicted of capital crimes between January 1995 and July 2000. Based on preliminary results of the study, Reno announced in late 2000 that she saw no reason to place a *moratorium* (a temporary halt) on federal executions, a position Ashcroft reaffirmed.

School admissions. On March 27, 2001, U.S. District Judge Bernard A. Friedman ruled that the use of race in determining the admissions policy at the University of Michigan in Ann Arbor was unconstitutional. Friedman rejected arguments made by attorneys representing the university that race was one of many factors used in admissions and said the university law school's admissions policy overemphasizes race to attain the equivalent of quotas of minority students.

Legal experts predicted the case would make its way to the U.S. Supreme Court, which in 1978 ruled that universities could consider race as a factor in selecting applicants.

Police brutality settlement. In July 2001, New York City and the Patrolmen's Benevolent Association, a police union, reached an $8.75-million settlement with Haitian immigrant Abner Louima in a police brutality case stemming from an attack on Louima in 1997 by members of the New York City police force. Juries in 1999 convicted two police officers of attacking Louima in a police station and convicted four other officers of participating in a cover-up of the attack. The settlement was the largest New York City has ever paid in a police brutality case.

Holocaust slave labor. The German parliament on May 30, 2001, approved $4.5 billion in compensation to the 1.5-million survivors of forced labor camps in Germany run by Nazis during World War II (1939-1945). Under the program, survivors were to receive up to $6,600. In July 2000, government and industry officials in Germany had agreed to establish a foundation to pay those survivors who had been forced to work as slaves or forced laborers.

☐ Geoffrey A. Campbell

See also **Courts; Crime; Germany; United Nations; Yugoslavia.**

Hungary. In June 2001, the Hungarian parliament passed a controversial law granting educational, social, and health benefits to ethnic Hungarians living outside of Hungary. The law makes identity cards available to Hungarians outside the country that enable them to work or study inside Hungary and to participate in social welfare programs sponsored by the Hungarian government.

More than 3 million ethnic Hungarians living in Croatia, Romania, Slovakia, Slovenia, Ukraine, and Yugoslavia qualified for the identity cards. According to experts on international affairs, many people in these countries viewed the new status law as a nationalistic threat to their country's sovereignty. The leaders of Slovakia and Romania, where the vast majority of ethnic Hungarians live, claimed that the status law set back relations between their countries and Hungary, which had been improving in recent years.

Hungary's new status law specifically excluded the Hungarian minority of Austria, about 70,000 people, from eligibility. Experts on Hungarian politics said application of the law to Austria—a member of the 15-nation European Union (EU) —could have violated EU rules and harmed Hungary's chances for early admission to the EU.

Prospects for fast-track EU admission. A September report issued by the European Parliament, an advisory body of the EU, expressed cautious optimism that Hungary would be able to meet EU requirements for membership on a fast-track schedule endorsed at the EU's June summit in Goteborg, Sweden. The schedule called for completion of membership negotiations by late 2002.

Individual EU officials praised Hungary for its progress toward a free-market economy. However, the European Parliament report expressed concern about Hungary's rate of inflation, which in 2001 was considerably higher than the inflation rates of the EU countries that have adopted the euro, the EU single currency. (Hungary's rate of inflation hit 10.8 percent in May but dropped to 8.7 percent in August.) The authors of the report also admonished Hungary to continue working toward integrating the country's *Roma* (gypsy) population.

Economic growth in Hungary dropped from 5.2 percent in 2000 to 4 percent in 2001. The rate of unemployment also dropped, with rates dipping below 6 percent in June.

Response to terrorism. Hungarian officials responded to the terrorist attacks on the United States on September 11 by tightening the country's own security. In southern Hungary, workers reinforced the Taszar military base by constructing 5-foot-high (1.5-meter) concrete walls around the entire complex.

☐ Sharon L. Wolchik

See also **Europe; Terrorism: A Special Feature,** p. 38.

Ice skating. At the 2001 World Figure Skating Championships in Vancouver, Canada, American Michelle Kwan claimed her fourth gold medal, and Russian Yevgeny Plushenko toppled his longtime rival, fellow Russian Alexie Yagudin. In other major competitions, Russian women swept the European championships for the third straight year, and Timothy Goebel captured his first U.S. national title.

World championships. On March 24 in Vancouver, Kwan became the first woman to win back-to-back golds since fellow American Kristi Yamaguchi did so in 1992. Kwan became the first woman since Katarina Witt of Germany in 1988 to take a fourth gold.

Irina Slutskaya, of Russia, landed a triple salchow-triple loop-double toe combination and attempted a triple lutz-triple loop-double toe combination in an effort to top Kwan. However, both jumps were flawed, and Slutskaya finished in second place. American Sarah Hughes finished third.

On March 22, 2001, Plushenko ended Alexei Yagudin's three-year run as world champion. Yagudin, struggling with a foot injury, failed to complete several triple jumps and finished second. American Todd Eldredge took third place. At age 29, he was the oldest skater to win a medal at the world championships since American Roger Turner did so in 1931 at the age of 30.

On March 21, 2001, Canadians Jamie Sale and David Pelletier scrambled from third to capture

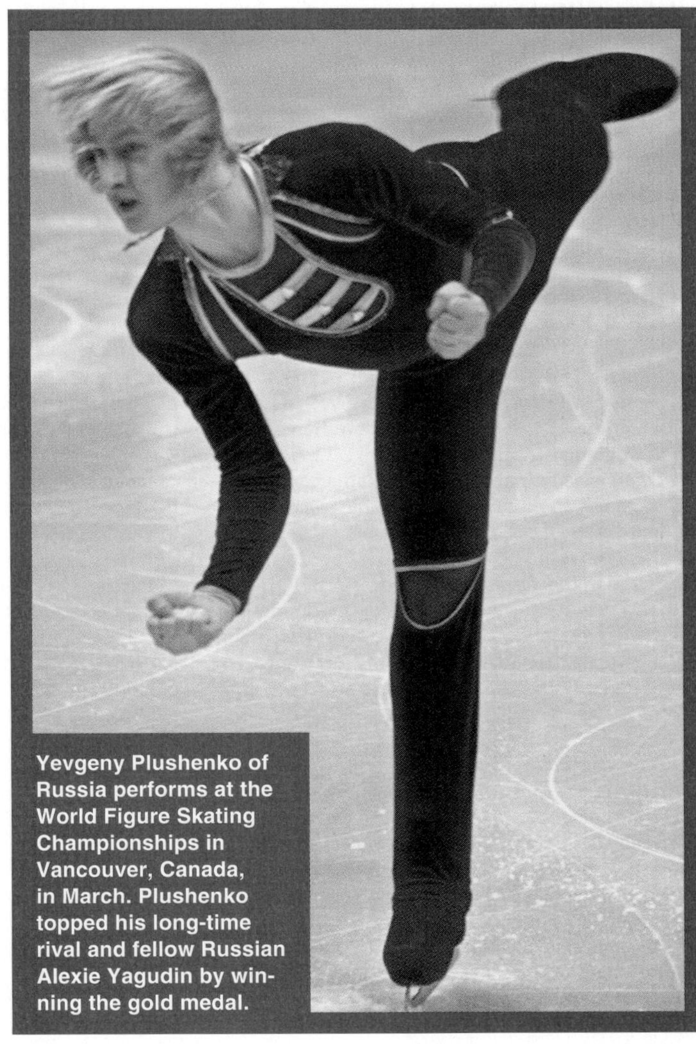

Yevgeny Plushenko of Russia performs at the World Figure Skating Championships in Vancouver, Canada, in March. Plushenko topped his long-time rival and fellow Russian Alexie Yagudin by winning the gold medal.

the pairs title, becoming the first Canadian pairs champions since 1993. Yelena Berezhnaya and Anton Sikharulidze of Russia took second, and Shen Xue and Hongbo Zhao of China took third.

European championships. On Jan. 24, 2001, in Bratislava, Slovakia, Berezhnaya and Sikharulidze recaptured the title that had been stripped from them in 2000 after Berezhnaya tested positive for a banned stimulant. In the men's competition on Jan. 25, 2001, Plushenko successfully defended his European title. On January 27, Russian women took all three medals. Slutskaya hit five triple jumps to win her fourth title, Maria Butyrskaya finished second, and Victoria Volchkova took third.

U.S. Championships. On January 20 in Boston, Timothy Goebel captured his first U.S. Figure Skating Championships title. Defending champion Michael Weiss plunged from first after the short program to finish fourth overall. Todd Eldredge, a five-time U.S. champion, took second place. Michelle Kwan captured her fourth consecutive women's title. Sarah Hughes placed second, and Angela Nikodinov finished third. Kyoko Ina and John Zimmerman successfully defended their pairs title. ☐ Michael Kates

Iceland. See **Europe.**

Idaho. See **State government.**

Illinois. See **Chicago; State government.**

Immigration and Naturalization Service (INS) Commissioner James W. Ziglar announced on Oct. 10, 2001, that INS officials would decide cases involving the families of victims of the September 11 terrorist attacks on the World Trade Center in New York City and on the Pentagon Building outside Washintgon, D.C. "in a compassionate manner." Ziglar became concerned about the families of the attack victims after hearing the story of a British woman who worried she would be deported after her husband died in the World Trade Center attack. Her husband was in the United States on a nonimmigrant work visa and had applied for another. Ziglar assured the families of victims that they would not face immediate deportation from the United States.

Border crossing cards. On October 1, the INS began enforcing a law that required new border crossing cards for Mexican nationals seeking entry into the United States. The cards, which resemble credit cards, included photos and machine-readable information. The cards, which were to remain valid for 10 years, were mandated by the Illegal Immigration Reform and Immigrant Responsibility Act of 1996. The U.S. Department of State and the INS received and processed more than 4 million applications for the new cards between April 1998 and September 2001.

Search and rescue improvements. In August, 32 members of the U.S. Border Patrol's Search, Trauma and Rescue team graduated from an intensive training program designed to improve the patrol's ability to provide assistance to migrants who become lost or injured while making illegal border crossings. The specialized training focused on teaching skills needed in search and rescue operations in remote border areas.

The graduates were to establish four new Border Patrol search and rescue teams in sectors in El Centro, California; Yuma, Arizona; Del Rio, Texas; and Marfa, Texas. The Border Patrol previously had search and rescue squads only in the San Diego, California, and Tucson, Arizona, border patrol sectors.

Immigration records online. In April, a new Web site allowed people to search an online database for information about ancestors who entered the United States through Ellis Island between 1892 and 1924. Ellis Island, located in New York Harbor, was a federal immigration station through which more than 12 million people passed. The Web site, www.ellisislandrecords.org, contained data compiled by the Statue of Liberty-Ellis Island Foundation, which runs the Ellis Island Immigration Museum, and representatives for The Church of Jesus Christ of Latter-day Saints. The database contains immigrants' names, their port of origin, age, nationality, hometown, and marital status. The Web site averaged 8 million requests per hour during the first day.

Supreme Court rulings. In two 5-to-4 rulings, the U.S. Supreme Court in 2001 gave new protections to immigrants facing deportation because they had committed crimes. On June 25, the justices ruled that legal immigrants who pleaded guilty to crimes before 1996 could not be deported automatically without being allowed to seek an appeal hearing. After the U.S. Congress strengthened immigration laws in 1996, the attorney general's office declined to allow such hearings. However, the justices determined that it was unfair to apply that policy to people convicted before 1996 because they might have pleaded guilty to try to block their deportation.

On June 28, 2001, the justices ruled that the INS could not keep convicted immigrants confined indefinitely once they served their sentences, even if there were no country to which to deport them. The justices concluded that aliens can be held for specific reasons, such as being suspected terrorists or national security threats, but those who have fulfilled their punishment must be released after a "reasonable time" to arrange for deportation. ☐ Geoffrey A. Campbell

See also **Terrorism: A Special Feature,** p. 38; **United States, Government of the.**

Income tax. See **Taxation.**

Pakistan's president General Pervez Musharraf scatters rose petals at Rajghat, the New Delhi memorial to the "father of the Indian nation," Mohandas K. Gandhi, as part of a state visit during which he and Indian Prime Minister A. B. Vajpayee began talks about the disputed Hamalayan state of Jammu and Kashmir.

India. Relations between India and Pakistan deteriorated in 2001. The two nuclear powers ended the year in a tense military standoff over the Himalayan state of Jammu and Kashmir—territory largely held by India but claimed by Pakistan since 1947. In 2001, Indian officials continued to accuse Pakistan of sponsoring terrorism in Kashmir in a guerrilla campaign that had been going on for years and had left more than 35,000 people dead, according to the Indian government.

President Pervez Musharraf of Pakistan announced upon his arrival in India for talks with Prime Minister Atal Behari Vajpayee in July 2001 that there could be no military solution to the Kashmir dispute. However, the talks quickly broke down over the wording of a joint statement, and clashes between Indian security forces and militants continued. In October, 38 people died when a suicide bomber detonated explosives in the Kashmir state assembly in Sringar.

Attack on Parliament. On December 13, five men attempted to shoot their way into India's Parliament building in New Delhi, the capital. The terrorists and nine other people died in the gun battle. India blamed the attack on two Islamic militant groups headquartered in Pakistan.

Demanding that Musharraf round up members of the two groups, Vajpayee withdrew the Indian ambassador to Pakistan. India also severed bus and train connections to Pakistan, banned Pakistani commercial flights over India, and began massing troops in Kashmir. Pakistan responded in kind, and both countries began a military buildup along their shared border. United States President George W. Bush and other world leaders urged India and Pakistan to avoid going to war.

Corruption. In 2001, an Internet news service filmed Indian politicians and army officers receiving or negotiating bribes to facilitate an arms deal. In March, the news story forced the president of Vajpayee's governing Bharatiya Janata Party (BJP) to resign. The minister of defense, a number of politicians, and three army generals were also forced to resign. Opposition political parties blocked parliamentary work for nine days while trying to discredit the BJP government. The former defense minister regained his post in October.

Another scandal in 2001 involved India's largest manager of mutual funds, the government-controlled Unit Trust of India (UTI), which was established in 1964 to raise funds for India's industrial development. UTI suspended operations in July 2001 after suffering major financial losses, leaving 20 million furious investors. Critics accused people in Vajpayee's office of maintaining close ties to UTI's disgraced boss, which raised questions about the prime minister's own integrity.

In response, 76-year-old Vajpayee threatened to resign on July 31. He withdrew the threat when the BJP rallied around him. The party's reluctance to lose Vajpayee's leadership stemmed from apprehension about the prime minister's likely successor, home minister Lal Krishna Advani. Advani was known as a Hindu nationalist hardliner.

State elections in five states in May shook Vajpayee's coalition. The Congress Party won control of two state legislatures and took control of two other legislatures in coalitions with other parties. The Communist Party extended its 24-year rule in West Bengal state.

In India's Tamil Nadu state, one-time movie star Jayaram Jayalalitha was banned from the May elections because she had been convicted of corruption while serving as chief minister—head of the state government—from 1991 to 1996. But she led her regional party back to power in coalition with the Congress Party despite the ban. In December 2001, the corruption conviction was overturned. This enabled her to return to politics after using political allies to run the state for her.

Internal unrest. In June, the government agreed on a cease-fire with a guerrilla group seeking independence for Nagaland, a state along India's eastern border with Myanmar (formerly known as Burma). The cease-fire was expanded to include Naga rebels in adjacent states, where residents feared that such a move might legitimize Nagaland's claims to their lands. After violent protests in Manipur state, which were put down by police gunfire that killed 15 people, the government limited the cease-fire to Nagaland.

Other separatist groups in northeastern India harassed authorities. In Tripura state, guerrillas seeking a separate tribal homeland killed 12 soldiers in March during the ambush of a convoy.

The "bandit queen," Phoolan Devi, a former outlaw leader who went from prison to serving in India's Parliament, was shot and killed in July. The murder apparently was in revenge for killings committed during her career in crime.

Hindu gathering. On January 24, a date that Hindu astrologers considered the most auspicious in nearly 140 years, Hindus gathered for a ritual washing away of sins in the Ganges River at Allahabad. Officials estimated that 15 to 30 million Hindus gathered for the ceremony, possibly the largest gathering of human beings in history.

India's total population topped 1 billion people in 2001, an increase of more than 180 million people since 1991.

Disasters. On India's Republic Day, Jan. 26, 2001, an earthquake struck Gujarat state in western India. The earthquake, which had a magnitude of 7.9, was the worst since 1947. More than 14,000 people were killed, and 192,000 buildings were damaged. Monsoon rains in eastern Orissa state in July 2001 triggered massive flooding that left 500,000 people homeless and more than 100 people dead. ☐ Henry S. Bradsher

See also **Asia; Geology; Pakistan.**

Indian, American. The number of people who identified themselves solely as American Indian by race rose to 2.4 million in 2000, according to preliminary reports released by the United States Census Bureau in early 2001. The figure represented an increase of 25 percent over 1990 figures. An additional 4.1 million people claimed some Indian ancestry in 2000, about 200 percent more than in 1990.

Tribal leaders attributed the increase to a higher birth rate, a greater interest in genealogy, a rise in cultural pride, and the fact that the Census Bureau does not require proof of tribal heritage by blood to count an individual as an American Indian. Census Bureau analysts cautioned that comparing figures from the 2000 census with those from 1990 was problematic, because the 2000 count was the first to give people the option of checking more than one category to describe their racial origin.

Indian trust funds. On Dec. 10, 2001, Secretary of Interior Gale Norton was placed on trial on charges of contempt of court. Norton was accused of lying about the efforts of the Bureau of Indian Affairs, a division of the Interior Department, in correcting more than 100 years of mismanagement of American Indian trust accounts.

The trust accounts had been created in 1887, when some reservations were divided up and plots of land were issued to more than 300,000 Native Americans. The lands could not be sold. Rather, the Bureau of Indian Affairs and other interior department agencies were to lease the lands, depositing funds from the sale of oil, timber, and other natural resources on the land into the accounts of the individual land owners.

In 1996, the Colorado-based Native American Rights Fund charged that more than $10 billion had been lost or stolen from the funds. The interior and treasury departments acknowledged mismanagement of the accounts. However, they contended that the losses amounted to hundreds of millions of dollars, not billions. In 1999, the interior department promised to revise its accounting procedures and correct its records by January 2001. However, problems with a new computer system and the destruction of documents pertaining to the case by treasury department officials hindered the process. In early December, a court-appointed investigator discovered that the government computer system on which trust information was stored was not secure, prompting the charges that the government had failed to comply with the 1999 mandate to correct its records.

Navajo code talkers. In July 2001, U.S. President George W. Bush honored 29 Native Americans who developed a code used by the U.S. Armed Forces during World War II (1939-1945). The code talkers, as they were called, were members of the U.S. Marine Corps. They used codes in

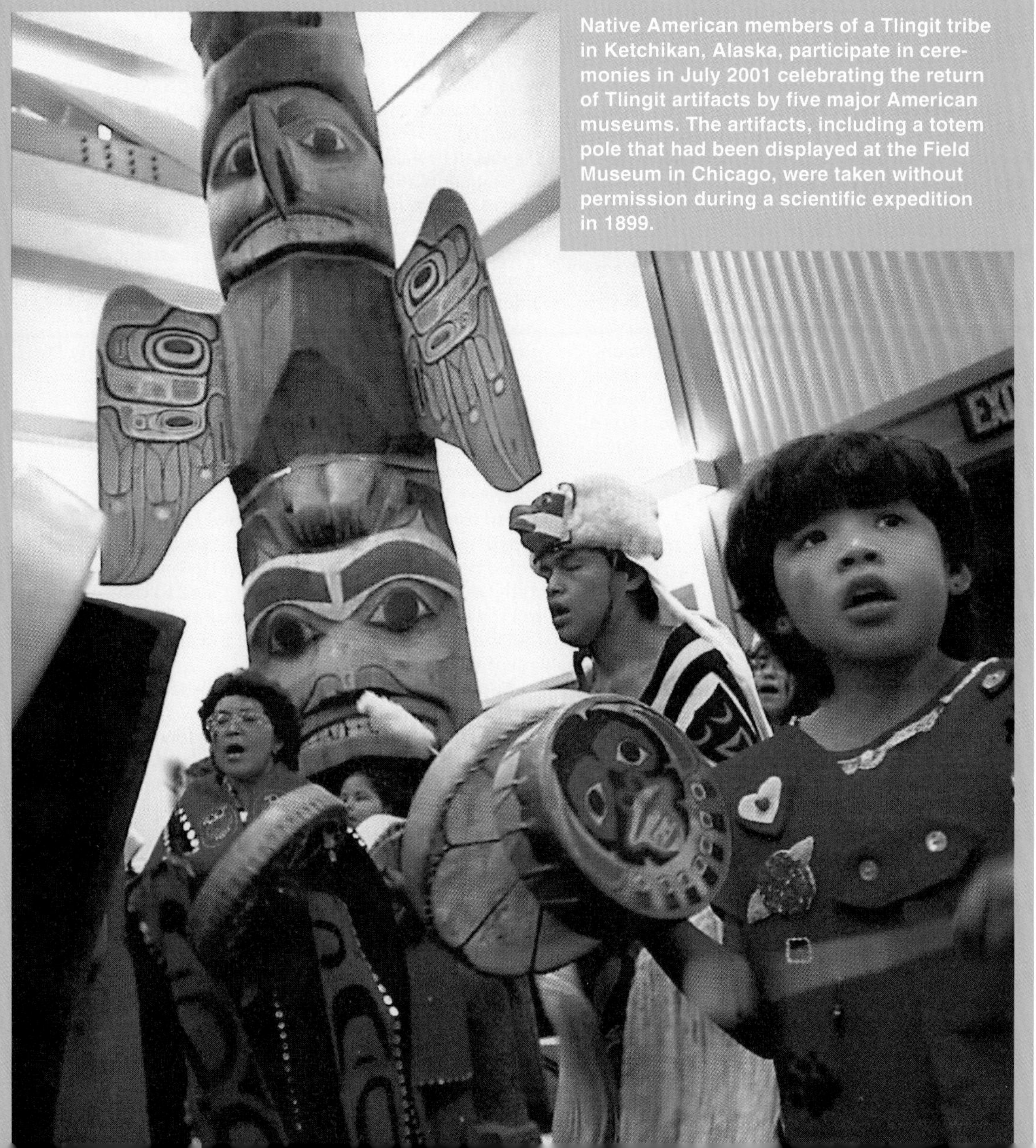

Native American members of a Tlingit tribe in Ketchikan, Alaska, participate in ceremonies in July 2001 celebrating the return of Tlingit artifacts by five major American museums. The artifacts, including a totem pole that had been displayed at the Field Museum in Chicago, were taken without permission during a scientific expedition in 1899.

their native Navajo language to send secret messages during the war in the Pacific. Because Navajo was an unwritten language unknown to most non-Navajo, the code was impossible for the Japanese to break. Bush presented the Medal of Honor to four of the five living code talkers and to the families of the 24 others.

Sacred objects returned. Five major U.S. museums returned various sacred artifacts to the Tlingit people of Alaska in July 2001. The objects had been taken without permission in 1899 and distributed to museums and universities throughout the United States. One of the most famous of the items was a totem pole that had been exhibited at the Field Museum in Chicago. The artifacts were returned under the terms of the Native American Graves Protection and Repatriation Act of 1990. According to the act, tribal people can petition for the return of human remains and sacred objects held by public institutions in the United States. In 2001, an estimated 200,000 items remained in public collections.

Connected. The last of 185 Bureau of Indian Affairs schools was connected to the Internet in August. The program allowed nearly 50,000 students and their families to access the World Wide Web. □ Kristina Vaicikonis

See also **People in the news** (Norton, Gale).

Indiana. See **State government.**

Indonesia. Vice President Megawati Sukarnoputri was sworn in as president of Indonesia on July 23, 2001. She succeeded Abdurrahman Wahid who was unanimously removed from office by the People's Consultative Assembly, Indonesia's highest government authority. The assembly acted after Wahid failed to account for his increasingly erratic actions and tried to illegally disband the body in order to block the group from voting for his removal from office.

Wahid, a nearly blind and partly infirm Islamic religious leader, was named president by the assembly in October 1999, even though Megawati, who was named vice president, had more followers in the assembly. Many Indonesians were soon disappointed in his ability to lead, citing his contradictory decisions and his neglect of domestic problems in favor of frequent travel abroad. Parliament, a lesser body than the assembly, voted on Feb. 1, 2001, and again on April 30 to censure Wahid for corruption and general incompetence. Finally in July, the leaders of the Indonesian army began to ignore his orders, and his removal became inevitable.

The new president, Megawati, is the daughter of Indonesia's first president, Sukarno. She entered politics when opponents of President Suharto (Sukarno's successor) sought to capitalize on the Sukarno name and regain leadership. Megawati, while actually saying little in public, quickly became popular. In 1993, she became head of the Democratic Party of Struggle. Despite Megawati's quiet approach to politics, she led her party in 1999 to win the largest block of seats in parliamentary elections.

President Megawati named her cabinet on Aug. 9, 2001, more than two weeks after she became president. Party leaders, squabbling over who should be assigned to the cabinet, caused the long delay. In the end, Megawati was widely praised for naming experienced professionals to key posts, especially those positions involving the economy. In her first major presidential speech, Megawati warned that it would take time for the country to recover from years of economic and political chaos.

Economy. Indonesia's economic output in 2001 was about 10 percent below what it had been before a financial crisis swept through East Asia in 1997. The country's foreign debts in 2001 were roughly equivalent to its annual *gross domestic product* (the value of all goods and services produced in a country in a given year), but Megawati promised to meet the nation's financial commitments and sought help from foreign creditors. In August, the International Monetary Fund (IMF)—a United Nations-affiliated organization, located in Washington, D.C., that provides credit to member nations—agreed to release money to Indonesia from a long-term loan program. The program was discontinued during Wahid's presidency because of allegations of human rights violations and government corruption.

Corruption. Megawati also promised to fight corruption, which most Indonesians believed to be rampant in the government. In August, she called on the army to reform itself. According to political observers, Indonesia's army leaders had long played too large a role in setting government policy and many people had worried that Megawati would be dominated by the military. However, she stated publically that she was determined to control the army saying, "We need a security force that is effective, highly disciplined, and under control of the government."

Separatism. After taking office, Megawati apologized to the people of two rebellious provinces, Aceh at the western tip of Indonesia and Irian Jaya at the eastern end. She expressed regret for years of human rights violations during military efforts to stop independence movements. Under Wahid, the army launched an offensive in Aceh in March 2001 that resulted in the deaths of nearly 1,000 people. Despite Megawati's apology, she called on the Aceh and Irian Jayan people to remain part of Indonesia and urged them to agree to more local autonomy.

In July, Parliament passed an autonomy plan

for Aceh. The plan gave the province 70 percent of the income from its oil, gas, and other mineral resources. In the past, the province kept only 5 percent of the income. In August, Megawati sent a delegation of officials to Aceh, but the rebels turned the group away. Inflamed by the discovery of graves of alleged victims of the Indonesian army, the rebels rejected the autonomy plan.

In Irian Jaya, also known as West Papua, rebels stepped up attacks in response to an increased army presence, according to the Human Rights Watch, a private humanitarian group based in New York City. In November, a leader of the Papuan independence movement, Theys Eluay, died under mysterious circumstances. He was mourned as a victim of Indonesian repression.

Other violence. In February, an Indonesian human rights commission reported that roughly 3,800 people had been killed during two years of fighting between Christians and Muslims in the Moluccas, formerly known as the Spice Islands. Local residents believed that the death toll could be as high as 20,000 people. The native Dayak people of Borneo renewed their attacks in February, on immigrants from the Indonesian islands of Madura. According to local citizens, the government had done little to stop previous attacks. ☐ Henry S. Bradsher

See also **Asia; Australia, Prime Minister of.**

International trade in goods and services lost momentum in 2001, as more and more nations fell into or near recession. The aftershocks of the terrorist attacks on the United States on September 11 further curtailed consumer demand and imposed new security screening that hampered the flow of goods.

Economists continued to lower their estimates of global output through the end of the year, but it was clear that international trade in 2001 was dramatically weaker than in 2000. Officials of the World Trade Organization (WTO)—the Geneva, Switzerland-based arbiter of trade disputes among member countries—estimated in October 2001 that worldwide merchandise trade volume would increase only 2 percent in 2001 after growing a robust 12 percent in 2000. They noted, however, that their projection was based largely on data for the first half of 2001 and might decline in later revisions. Economists at the International Monetary Fund (IMF), a United Nations-affiliated agency that provides credit to member nations, also said in October that a sharp decline in trade growth was underway.

Areas of strength and weakness. As many countries grappled with economic slowdown, China's export-driven economy continued to surge in 2001, with a growth rate of 7 percent or better, according to IMF estimates. Russia, on the rebound from economic crisis in 1998, experienced a 4-percent annual growth in 2001, according to the IMF. Moreover, Russia's new role as a top exporter of crude oil outside the Organization of Petroleum Exporting Countries (OPEC) made that nation a highly sought-after partner by industrial nations. OPEC is an association of 11 oil exporting nations.

Among the industrialized nations, Japan ended 2001 in recession, with its huge export sector in contraction. In the United States, what began as a mild recession in March 2001 had worsened sharply by the fourth quarter. The powerful U.S. economy had acted as an engine, pulling other countries back into growth in previous regional economic crises. Economists warned that the United States was too weak in 2001 to boost other economies.

Various European economies, including the dominant German economy, were also slipping into recession by late 2001. The economies of many other countries, from Mexico and Argentina in Latin America to Singapore and Taiwan in Asia, tipped downward in 2001, suppressing global trade.

Although crude oil prices soared during 2000, the price of that key commodity fell sharply in late 2001 as global demand slumped because of the economic downturn. OPEC considered cutting production to raise prices, but failed to do so. OPEC at first could not get non-OPEC nations, including Russia, Mexico, and Norway, to agree on similar cuts, though negotiations continued late in the year. United States President George W. Bush actively courted the leaders of Mexico and Russia, with the objective of reducing U.S. dependency on oil from the politically volatile Middle East.

WTO meeting. The WTO held its ministerial meeting in Doha, Qatar, in November, the organization's first such conference since violent street demonstrations broke up a 1999 meeting in Seattle. Protests were muted during the 2001 meeting in the wake of the September 11 attacks. Ministers formally approved the admission of China and Taiwan, ending years of negotiations.

Before the meeting's close, the WTO's 144 members agreed to launch a new three-year round of global talks to further lower trade barriers. Their plans called for new agreements by Jan. 1, 2005, to end agricultural subsidies and cut tariffs on imports.

G-8 meeting. The annual gathering of the Group of Eight (G-8) in Genoa, Italy, in July 2001 was anything but peaceful. The G-8 is an informal association of eight of the world's chief industrial nations—Canada, France, Germany, Italy, Japan, Russia, the United Kingdom, and the

Demonstrators march through the streets of Genoa, Italy, in July to protest trade and economic policies of the Group of Eight, an association of eight major industrial countries meeting in the city.

United States. Riots by thousands of protesters who had converged on the Italian port city left one person dead and hundreds of people injured.

New realities for NAFTA. The September terrorist attacks brought changes to the way partners in the North American Free Trade Agreement (NAFTA)—Canada, Mexico, and the United States—transacted business across their common borders. Before the attacks, the United States and Canada allowed freight to move across their borders with little delay for security checks. Policies for operating the U.S.-Mexican border appeared to be moving in the same direction in 2001, with President Bush pushing Congress to open that border by Jan. 1, 2002, to broad Mexican trucking operations in order to fulfill NAFTA terms.

However, after the attacks of Sept. 11, 2001, evidence that terrorists may have entered the United States through Canada raised serious security concerns about the U.S.-Canada border. The U.S. Congress passed measures to tighten border crossings, delaying cross-border shipping schedules. In December, Congress passed a bill that allowed Mexican trucks to haul cargo throughout the United States, once U.S. border security and new inspection procedures could be implemented.

Fast-track progress. On December 6, the U.S. House of Representatives by a single vote approved fast-track trade negotiating authority for President Bush. Senate leaders said a vote on fast-track authority would probably not come up in that chamber until early 2002. The Bush administration had requested fast-track authority, which would enable the president to negotiate trade agreements without consulting Congress. Under fast-track rules, Congress would have the power to accept or reject but not alter trade agreements negotiated by the administration.

In other trade developments, the U.S. government on Nov. 30, 2001, authorized the first direct sale in 41 years of U.S. food to Cuba. The bill was passed in response to widespread devastation in Cuba caused by Hurricane Michelle ear-lier in November. The U.S. government had maintained an embargo, or ban on trade, with Cuba since 1960. In December 2001, the UN General Assembly again urged the United States to end its embargo.

On November 28, Vietnam's National Assembly approved a historic pact that brought the country into normal trading status with the United States. The Clinton administration had negotiated the pact in 2000. ☐ John D. Boyd

See also **Economics; Manufacturing; Terrorism; Terrorism: A Special Feature,** p. 38.

Internet. In August 2001, Nielsen/NetRatings, a media research firm with headquarters in Milpitas, California, reported that the growth of the Internet was starting to slow down. Company officials said that the number of Americans gaining access to the Internet increased by 16 percent from July 2000 to July 2001. This was a significant drop from the 40-percent increase in Internet users during the same period a year earlier.

The company reported that the slowing growth might be due to the fact that many of the people who quickly adopt new technologies already have Internet access. Another factor could be that the slowing of the economy in 2001 caused people to postpone buying computers.

Computer attacks. Computer *crackers,* or *hackers* (people who illegally get into computer systems), unleashed several dangerous computer viruses onto the Internet in 2001. Two viruses—Nimda and Code Red—were especially troublesome. These were types of viruses known as "worms," which can make copies of themselves and spread from computer to computer, altering or deleting data.

In September, the Nimda worm began to spread, exploiting vulnerabilities in a popular mail software progam developed by Microsoft Corporation of Redmond, Washington. The worm infected more than 2 million computers. Once inside a victim's computer, Nimda made copies of itself and e-mailed them to addresses in the infected user's address book. By doing this millions of times, the worm clogged e-mail servers of many large corporations, causing enormous business losses.

Code Red, which was released in July, was similar to Nimda, but not as severe. Code Red infected more than 1 million computers worldwide and caused more than $2.4 billion in damage. Computer experts said users could protect themselves from such worms by installing software "patches," special programs that plug security holes. These patches were available for free from software vendors such as Microsoft.

Broadband stumbles. Despite its potential as a breakthrough Internet technology, the progress of broadband Internet access—which provides very high-speed Internet service—disappointed many customers and industry observers in 2001. Two of the leading providers of broadband Internet access to the home—Covad Communications Company of Santa Clara, California, and Excite@Home, Inc., of Redwood City, California, declared bankruptcy in 2001.

Covad offered Digital Subscriber Line (DSL) access to the Internet, which makes use of high-speed telephone lines. Excite@Home took a slightly different approach, providing its high-speed Internet connection through cable-television wiring. Both types of connection can transmit data up to 100 times faster than a system using traditional telephone lines.

Many people still considered broadband Internet connections to be a promising technology. An estimated 10 million customers signed up for broadband access in 2001, and experts saw potential for millions more. However, the financial difficulties of Covad and Excite@Home underscored the challenges involved in offering low-cost, high-speed Internet access to consumers.

Napster ruling. In February 2001, a federal appeals court in San Francisco shut down Napster, Inc., the controversial Redwood City, California, Internet file-sharing service. The service enabled users to trade digital music files for free. At its peak, about 50 million people were using Napster to trade compressed digital music files called MP3's. In December 1999, several major record companies sued Napster, arguing that the company was guilty of aiding in *copyright infringement* (improper use of legally protected material). The court ruled that Napster did infringe on the record companies' copyrights.

Despite the demise of Napster as a free file-sharing service, several similar technologies emerged to fill the void. Such services as Gnutella and Morpheus were different from Napster because they were shared among strings of users all across the Internet rather than using a central computer that could be shut down by a court order. This made them much more difficult to control. In addition, they enabled users to share digital movies and other types of files besides MP3's.

Controversial law. In July 2001, agents with the Federal Bureau of Investigation arrested Dmitry Sklyarov, a Russian computer programmer, for violating the Digital Millennium Copyright Act (DMCA). The DMCA was passed in 1998 to prevent people from making illegal copies of material that was protected by *copyright* (legal control of an author over his or her creations). Sklyarov had published a computer program that enabled users to defeat the built-in security protections to prevent the illegal copying of *electronic books* (books published in digital form and often downloaded from a Web site).

Critics of DMCA argued that it gives copyright holders too much control over their creations. Civil-rights proponents also claimed that DMCA prevents consumers from engaging in reasonable types of copying that the U.S. courts have always allowed. Such copying, known as "fair use," includes such things as taping a song from a compact disc (CD) that a person has legally purchased onto a cassette tape. ☐ Dave Wilson

See also **Internet: A Special Report.**

Iowa. See **State government.**

The Internet, Copyright, and You

By Doug Isenberg

Could unlimited Web access to media of all kinds spur individual creativity—or kill it?

Shawn Fanning, an 18-year-old college dropout from Massachusetts, was feverishly at work. A budding computer programmer, Fanning stayed awake for days at a time attempting to write a program that would make it easier for his friends to trade copies of digital music files over the Internet. He called his program Napster. That was in 1998. By 1999, Fanning had founded a company, Napster, Inc., of Redwood City, California, whose Web site—Napster.com—was attracting millions of investment dollars. At the height of the Web site's popularity, more than 50 million people were using Fanning's program to share hundreds of millions of song files, all for free. On its ride to the top, Napster shook the concept of *copyright law* (legal protection for original creations such as songs, novels, and motion pictures) to its very foundations and threw the music and motion picture industries into a panic.

While music lovers flocked to Napster because it offered a convenient and free way to download songs, many musicians and music publishing companies despised Napster, claiming they were losing billions of dollars in sales. In December 1999, 18 major record companies filed a lawsuit against Napster to put a stop to the sharing of digital music files. After a long legal fight, the U.S. Court of Appeals for the Ninth Circuit in San Francisco ordered Napster's file-sharing features shut down in early 2001, leaving the company's future in doubt.

The primary legal argument against Napster was that the program enabled people to copy and share music that was supposed to be protected by law from such copying. Such protection is known as copyright, the principle that a person who has an idea for a creative work and who puts that idea into a material form has certain rights to how that creation is used. Today, creations such as popular songs and motion pictures are worth millions of dollars. Because of this, the creators of these works and the corporations that often own the rights to the material have a great deal of incentive to protect them from illegal copying. The rise of the *Internet* (a global network of computers) in the 1990's made it possible for people to make flawless copies of copyrighted material, such as songs, photographs, and motion pictures, without paying the artists who created them. As a result, artists were more vulnerable to losing control over their works than at any time in history.

Lawmakers and the courts traditionally identified two reasons for creating copyright protections: (1) to reward authors for their hard work, and (2) to encourage them to create more works.

Most legal scholars agree that the first copyright law, the Statute of Anne, went into effect in 1710 during the reign of Queen Anne of Great Britain. The law stated that anyone who wanted to make copies of printed materials, such as books, had to have the author's permission. The law was passed to encourage the creation of printed materials so they would be more available to the public. The Statute of Anne made it possible for authors to be paid for their published work, which, in turn, would encourage them to create more works. The Statute of Anne granted authors control over their creations for 14 years after publication, with an option to renew the copyright for 14 more years if the author were still alive.

In the mid-1800's, British author Charles Dickens (above), lobbied in Great Britain and the United States for laws to protect the copyrights of authors. At the time, American publishers routinely sold copies of popular British books without paying royalties to their authors.

Early copyright laws

The United States followed England's lead in copyright protection in 1787, when the U.S. Constitution granted Congress the power to "promote the progress of science and the useful arts, by securing for limited times to authors and inventors the exclusive right to their respective writings and discoveries." The first U.S. copyright act was passed in 1790. Like the Statute of Anne, the law granted authors 14 years of protection for any "map, chart or book." Gradually, other works were added to this list, including public performances, dramatic compositions, photographs, paintings, drawings, and sculptures.

Despite these protections, *copyright infringement* (illegal use of copyrighted works) was a common problem from the very beginning. Most violations occurred when posters, books, and musical scores were printed and distributed without the permission of the authors. One especially thorny problem was that the laws that provided protection in one country were not enforced in others. In the mid-1800's, famed British author Charles Dickens was rarely paid *royalties* (payments to authors for sales of their copyrighted works) for copies of his books that were printed and sold in the United States, though these unauthorized copies sold quite briskly. As a result, Dickens lobbied on both sides of the Atlantic Ocean for international copyright agreements to protect authors.

In response to the complaints of Dickens and other authors, several European countries signed the Berne Convention in 1886, which bound its members to protect copyrighted works created in other member countries. While the United States did not join the Berne Convention, Congress did adopt the International Copyright Act of 1891, the first U.S. law establishing copyright agreements with other countries. The law was designed to protect the works of foreign authors, but it applied only to books manufactured in the United States.

Doug Isenberg is an attorney who practices intellectual property and Internet law and is the founder of gigalaw.com.

The U.S. Copyright Act of 1909 was perhaps the most important copyright law passed in the United States in the early 1900's. The 1909 law was prompted in part by a famous legal case concerning the "perforated music roll," a mechanism that enabled pianos to play music automatically. In 1908, White-Smith Publishing, a music publishing company, sued Apollo, a piano-roll manufacturer, claiming that Apollo's device violated copyrights because it played music copyrighted by White-Smith. The U.S. Supreme Court ruled that piano rolls did not constitute a "copy" of any music and, therefore, did not infringe on the copyrights of composers or publishers. However, lawmakers saw a need for protecting such copyrights and included provisions in later laws to ensure that composers and publishers were paid when their works were performed through such devices as piano rolls and phonographs.

Vera Lynn performs with an orchestra during a live radio program in 1945. To protect the copyrights of songwriters, composers, and music publishing companies, the American Society of Composers, Authors, and Publishers (ASCAP) and similar organizations began to monitor radio broadcasts to ensure that broadcasting companies paid royalties each time a copyrighted song aired.

The 1909 act was the largest revision of copyright law in the United States up to that time. It remained in effect for nearly 70 years. During that time, such new technological advances as commercial radio, motion pictures, television, and photocopying machines posed difficult challenges that threatened the copyrights of artists.

The U.S. Congress made another effort to modernize copyright law with the U.S. Copyright Act of 1976. The law, enacted in 1978, was prompted in part by new technologies, such as photocopy machines, which could be used to make high-quality copies of long works, such as books, easily and inexpensively. Publishing houses claimed that these machines threatened their copyrights and profits. The 1976 law addressed the problem posed by photocopy machines with an important concept called "fair use."

What can be copyrighted?

According to United States copyright law, the following types of works can be copyrighted:

- **literature**—novels and short stories
- **music**—written and performed
- **drama**—plays and screenplays
- **choreography**—dances
- **pictures**—photographs and diagrams
- **graphics**—illustrations
- **sculptures**
- **motion pictures/audio-visuals**—movies, documentaries
- **sound recordings**—albums, comedy routines
- **architectural works**—blue prints, building designs
- **computer programs**
- **computer chip designs**

Source: U.S. Copyright Office.

This doctrine, which had been developed by courts of law over generations of copyright disputes, allowed people to copy limited amounts of a copyrighted work under certain circumstances. In essence, people could copy small portions of a copyrighted work for their own use, as long as they did not try to profit from the copies.

Other new technologies that were developed during the 1970's and 1980's had a large impact on copyright law. The Betamax videocassette recorder (VCR) developed by Sony Corp. of Tokyo in the 1970's was the most famous of these new technologies. The VCR was capable of making copies of television broadcasts, which could be viewed later. When large numbers of consumers started to use VCR's to record motion pictures that were broadcast on television, motion picture studios sued Sony claiming the VCR made the *pirating* (illegal copying) of copyrighted motion pictures easy and inexpensive. After long deliberations, the U.S. Supreme Court in 1984 ruled that the Sony Betamax did not infringe on the copyrights held by the studios. The court declared that it was legal for people who owned VCR's to tape for their own personal use movies that were broadcast on television.

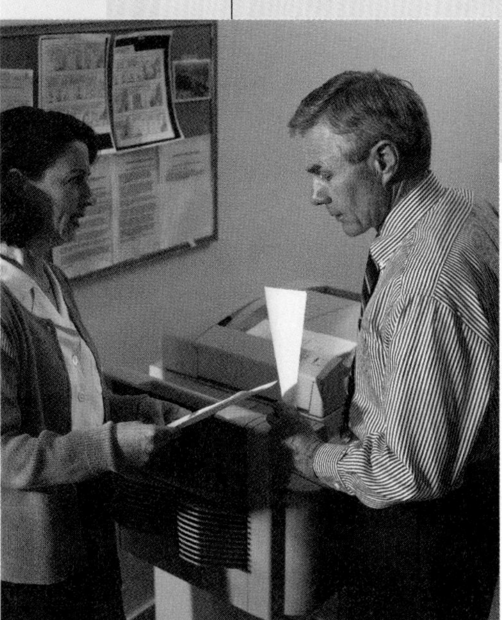

Photocopy machines capable of making high-quality copies of long works, such as books, threatened the copyrights held by authors and publishing companies. The U.S. Copyright Act of 1976 addressed that fear by formalizing the concept of "fair use," which limits the amount of material people can copy.

The Internet and copyright

In the mid-1990's, the explosion in the popularity of the Internet began to present new problems for copyright holders. The Internet made it much easier to make illegal copies of copyrighted material.

Information sent out and received over computer networks such as the Internet is *digital* (made up of binary digits). Digital files are a series of 1's and 0's that represent information, such as text documents, pictures, and songs. Digital files do not degrade in quality regardless of how many times they are copied. Before digital files, a person who wanted to copy a song had to obtain a physical version of the song, such as a vinyl record. The person then had to use a tape recorder to copy the song, resulting in a copy that was of slightly lesser quality than the original. To share the song with a friend, the person had to make a second copy and deliver the tape by hand or send it through the mail.

With the exploding popularity of the Internet beginning in the mid-1990's, someone could easily use their computer to convert all of the songs on a compact disc (CD) to compressed digital files called MP3's, a process known as "ripping." Then, the person could connect to the Internet and send these files to other users. The entire operation could take place without any of the participants leaving their computers, making illegal copying faster, easier, and less expensive than ever before.

In addition to the music industry, other industries whose main products were copyrighted works were also threatened by the ease of copying digital files. Software publishing companies pursued pirates who made illegal copies of their copyrighted software programs and distributed them. The motion picture industry feared that the growing popularity of high-speed Internet connections would make it easier for people to copy and share digital versions of motion pictures.

Congress responded to these concerns with the 1998 Digital Millennium Copyright Act (DMCA), a complex revision of the 1976 law. In order to encourage artists to post their creations on the Internet so their work was more accessible, the DMCA established new penalties for illegally bypassing restrictions on certain digital works. The law also incorporated several international treaties. While the entertainment industry and other businesses dependent on copyrights applauded the DMCA, critics complained that it severely limited the fair use of copyrighted material.

Napster goes online

Napster began operations in May 1999, just as the new digital copyright laws were going into effect. From the beginning, copyright holders considered Napster a major threat because it involved a new approach to computing known as peer-to-peer file sharing. When a Napster user searched for a song, the service compiled a list of other Napster users who had that song on their computers. The Napster software then set up a connection between the two computers, and the person searching for the song downloaded the MP3. Depending on the speed of each user's connection, the entire process took only a few minutes.

In December 1999, 18 major record companies filed suit against Napster claiming that it enabled Internet users to copy copyrighted sound recordings and unlawfully distribute them. Napster officials argued that since the service only connected the users' computers and did not provide the copyrighted songs to users itself, it was not violating copyright laws. However, in the

A government employee in Bangkok, Thailand, uses a steamroller to destroy "pirated," or illegally copied, compact discs and video tapes that had been confiscated by police. Copyright owners do not receive royalties from the sale of pirated copies of their works, a situation that discourages creative endeavor.

summer of 2000, a U.S. District Court judge ruled that Napster was to stop enabling its members to share copyrighted files. This decision was later reversed pending a final ruling, and Napster was allowed to continue operating. However, in February 2001, an appeals court ruled that Napster had to block users from sharing copyrighted songs. In 2001, Napster officials entered into agreements with several music publishers to obtain licensing rights for their song catalogs and was making plans to relaunch Napster as a subscription service in early 2002.

Copyright and civil liberties

Many industries include antipirating protections in their digital products to protect them from piracy. These protections include special computer codes that prevent CD players and similar devices from operating properly when a pirated disc is inserted. The DMCA included a clause that made it a crime to disable these protections. This law was tested in July 2001, when the Federal Bureau of Investigation (FBI) arrested Dmitry Sklyarov, a Russian computer programmer visiting the United States. Sklyarov had allegedly published a software program that made it possible to get around the built-in security protections of a device used to display *electronic books* (books published in digital form and often downloaded from a Web site). While free-speech advocates protested Sklyarov's arrest, claiming his civil rights were being violated, the FBI said Sklyarov had violated parts of the DMCA. Sklyarov faced up to five years in prison and a $500,000 fine.

In 2001, several industries were investigating new security measures to protect their intellectual property in cyberspace. A collection of music publishers and software makers formed the Secure Digital Music Initiative (SDMI) to try to forge a series of digital barriers to the copying of protected works. Computer codes known as "watermarks" were the main security feature of SDMI. These codes were attached to legitimate copies of protected works to identify them. Copies without these watermarks could not be used in devices such as CD players. However, in 2001, SDMI sponsored a contest to encourage *hackers* (computer users well-versed in breaking computer codes) to crack SDMI's security features. Several groups of hackers managed to disable the watermarks in only a few weeks, bringing the security of SDMI into serious question.

The battle lines were still being drawn in 2001 for the conflict between digital copyright holders and computer users wanting to download protected content for free. While Napster appeared to have been neutralized, similar technologies were evolving that could prove even more troublesome to copyright holders. One such technology, available through various services, including Gnutella, Aimster, LimeWire, and AudioGalaxy, enabled users to share MP3 files for free. Unlike Napster, however, these programs did not make use of a central computer. Instead, Gnutella software sent short messages over the Internet searching for other computers running Gnutella. When it found such computers,

Gnutella established a connection between them that enabled users to directly search the hard drives of other computers running Gnutella. Computer experts claimed that the lack of a central computer would make it extremely difficult for the music industry to stop these services. Also, unlike with Napster, users of these services could trade all types of digital files, not just MP3's.

The motion picture and music industries fought back to protect their intellectual property. Using sophisticated monitoring software, these groups attempted to identify copyrighted material being sent over the Internet. Once such files were traced, the industries contacted the user's Internet service provider (ISP). The ISP then threatened to cancel the individual's Internet account if he or she continued to share copyrighted content. This system, which was still experimental in 2001, could eventually be used to identify people who pirate copyrighted material. Entertainment companies expect that by using such a system, they could increase their profits.

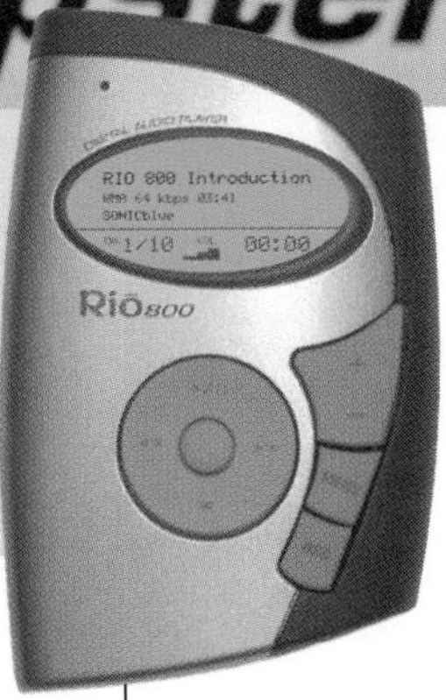

Protection versus privacy

However, privacy-rights groups, such as the Electronic Frontier Foundation (EFF), a San Francisco-based group dedicated to protecting people's online civil liberties, pointed out that this type of monitoring could be used to violate the privacy of Internet users. For example, they argue that law enforcement could use such a system to monitor the electronic correspondence of individuals without proper authorization from a court of law. Many Internet users felt they should be able to use the Internet to transmit any types of material they chose. They argued that the Internet should always be an open community where information is shared freely. Groups such as EFF feared that monitoring Internet users' activities for potential copyright infringement could one day lead to the erosion of other rights, such as free speech. Whether the actions of the entertainment industry would be considered a violation of people's rights to privacy online was a matter of debate in 2001 and will probably remain so for some time. ■ ■ ■

Napster's founder, Shawn Fanning, (top, right) speaks to reporters after a federal court shut down the file-sharing service. The court said Napster enabled the illegal copying of copyrighted music files that could be played on devices like the Rio 800 (above).

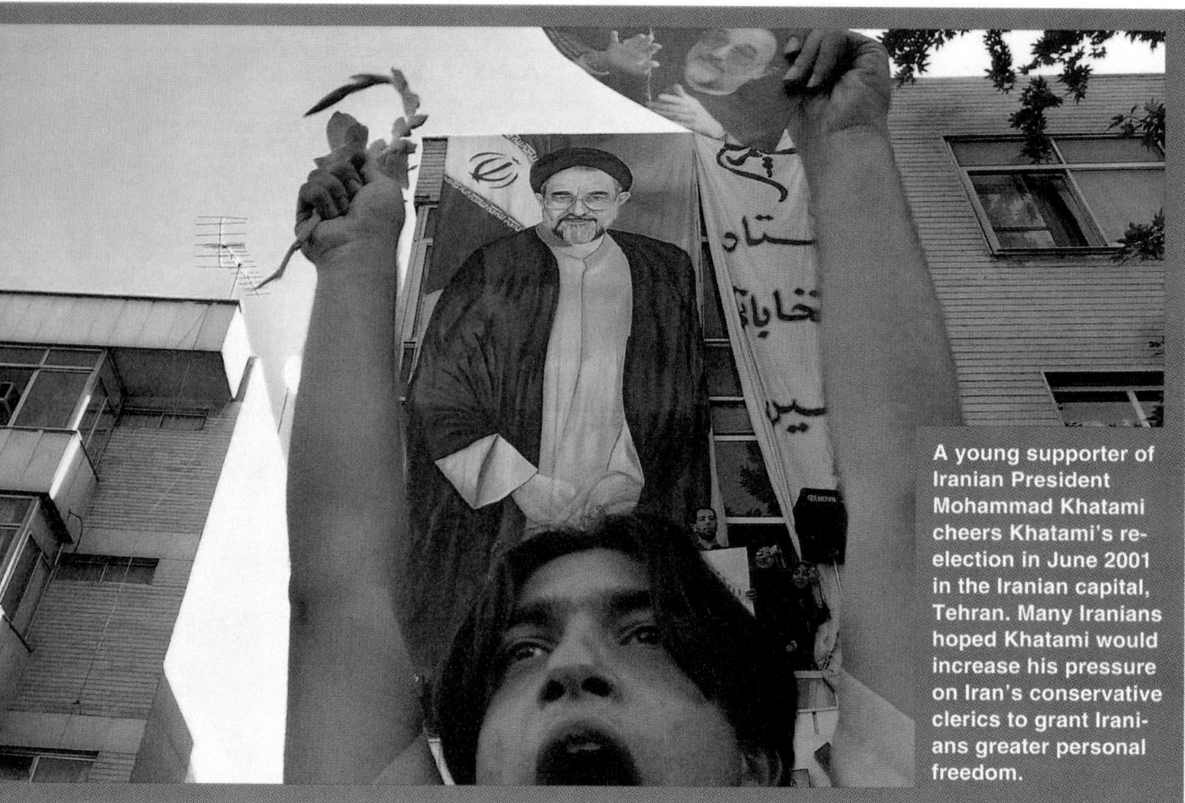

A young supporter of Iranian President Mohammad Khatami cheers Khatami's reelection in June 2001 in the Iranian capital, Tehran. Many Iranians hoped Khatami would increase his pressure on Iran's conservative clerics to grant Iranians greater personal freedom.

Iran. Reformist cleric Mohammad Khatami won a second four-year term as president on June 8, 2001, with 77 percent of the vote. Nonetheless, Iran's conservative clerics remained opposed to many of Khatami's plans to end Iran's economic and political isolation.

Parliamentary defeats. In August, Iran's proformist parliament refused to appoint religious conservatives to two vacancies on the 12-man Council of Guardians, a group that reviews parliamentary legislation. However, the Expediency Council, which resolves disputes between the parliament and the Council of Guardians, ruled that the parliament must fill the vacancies from names submitted by the head of the conservative judiciary, a man appointed by Ayatollah Ali Khamenei, Iran's supreme religious leader.

In June and December, the Council of Guardians rejected economic reform legislation that the parliament had passed in the hopes of attracting foreign investment. The council feared the legislation might lead to excessive foreign influence. In November, the Expediency Council rejected election law amendments passed by the parliament that would have reduced the power of the Council of Guardians to select candidates.

U.S. relations. President Khatami extended his condolences to the American people following the terrorist attacks on the United States on September 11. Supreme Leader Khamenei, however, rejected a role for Iran in a U.S.-led coalition against terrorism. In October, both Khatami and Khamenei condemned U.S. air strikes against Afghanistan. The United States accused Afghanistan's ruling Taliban of harboring the terrorist organizations responsible for the attacks.

Despite the condemnation, Iranian officials privately promised that Iranian forces would help rescue any U.S. military personnel who were shot down or otherwise in distress in Iran during the Afghanistan campaign. Iran also allowed international agencies to provide humanitarian relief to Afghanistan through a corridor in northeast Iran.

Some international affairs experts noted that the Afghanistan conflict might draw Iran and the United States closer, because both countries supported anti-Taliban Northern Alliance forces in Afghanistan. Iranian leaders accused the Taliban of warping the true meaning of Islam.

New trial. In August, Iran's Supreme Court ordered new trials for 15 former intelligence agents who had been convicted in January of slaying four opposition intellectuals in 1998. Reformers said government agents had killed 80 intellectuals during the 1990's. ☐ Christine Helms

See also **Afghanistan; Middle East; Terrorism: A Special Feature,** p. 38; **United States, Government of the.**

Iraq. In late November 2001, United States President George W. Bush urged Iraqi President Saddam Hussein to allow United Nations (UN) inspectors back into Iraq to determine if Iraq was developing weapons of mass destruction. Hussein had expelled UN inspectors in 1998. Iraqi officials responded by demanding that UN sanctions, imposed in 1990 after Iraqi forces invaded Kuwait, be lifted prior to any renewal of inspections.

Bush's statement led to increased speculation that the United States planned to expand its "war on terrorism" to include Iraqi targets. However, many nations, including the Muslim states of Saudi Arabia, Egypt, and Jordan, warned Bush that any attack on Iraq would undermine the U.S.-led coalition against terrorism. Bush had formed the coalition in the wake of the terrorist attacks on the United States on September 11.

Although the United States had long labeled Iraq as a country that sponsored terrorism, U.S. officials said they had uncovered no firm evidence linking Iraq to the September attacks. Suspicions about possible Iraqi involvement in the incidents had been raised by reports that one of the hijackers who flew two airliners into New York City's World Trade Center towers in September had met with an Iraqi intelligence officer. The Iraqi foreign ministry denied these reports.

Iraq was also suspected of being involved in bioterrorist attacks that resulted in the deaths from anthrax of five Americans in October and November. The outbreak was linked to letters containing anthrax *spores* (inactive stage of bacteria). Some experts noted that Iraq had produced anthrax bacteria in the past as part of a biological weapons program. In late 2001, investigators said the strain of anthrax found in the letters was a form that had been prodcued in the United States and that the most likely suspect was an American scientist acting alone.

UN sanctions. Iraq halted oil exports in June in protest against a proposed U.S.-British plan to alter the UN sanctions. The U.S.-British plan would have loosened restrictions on most civilian imports to Iraq but tightened controls on oil smuggling and imports that might be used by Iraq's military. The proposal was defeated in the UN Security Council in July due to opposition from Russia, which had strong commercial ties to Iraq, and several Middle Eastern countries, including Jordan, Turkey, and Syria. The Security Council then renewed the existing sanctions for a five-month period. In late November, the sanctions were renewed for a six-month period, but the Security Council agreed to negotiate revised sanction rules by June 2002. ☐ Christine Helms

See also **Middle East; Terrorism; Terrorism: A Special Feature,** p. 38; **United States, Government of the.**

Ireland. The Irish people showed signs of disenchantment with the European Union (EU) in 2001. In June, voters rejected a referendum on the Nice Treaty, which included guidelines for admitting Eastern European countries into the EU. (The treaty must be ratified by all 15 EU nations in order to go into effect.) The move shocked European leaders, who had long considered Ireland a nation that favored European unification. The result of the referendum was also a blow for *Taioseach* (Prime Måinister) Bertie Ahern and his Fianna Fail/Progressive Democrat coalition government. Ahern hinted that a second referendum might be necessary and insisted that Ireland remained fully committed to the EU.

New opposition leader. In February, John Bruton, who had led the opposition Fine Gael party for 10 years, resigned after a vote of no confidence from his party. He was replaced by the party's finance spokesman, Michael Noonan. The new leader banned corporate donations to the party in response to charges of corruption that had plagued Irish politics since the 1990's. Noonan's focus on social justice issues indicated a willingness to cooperate with Ireland's Labour Party toward the goal of forming a coalition for the next election, scheduled to be held in 2002.

Political corruption. Investigations into allegations of political corruption in Ireland continued in 2001. In January, Liam Lawlor, an independent member of the Dail (lower house of the legislature), was sentenced to three months in jail for refusing to cooperate with the Flood Tribunal, a panel investigating illegal payments to politicians. Lawlor had denied the tribunal access to his financial records. After Lawlor spent one week in prison, a judge suspended the remainder of his sentence. However, Lawlor's continued failure to comply with the tribunal's requests led to a second jail sentence in July. Lawlor, who had been forced to resign from Fianna Fail in June 2000, refused to resign from the Dail.

Economy. In February 2001, the finance ministers of 14 EU nations criticized the budget proposed by Ireland's finance minister, Charlie McGreevy, in late 2000. The ministers labeled the budget inflationary and a threat to the stability of the euro, the single European currency. McGreevy rejected the allegations, noting the drop of inflation in Ireland from 7.9 percent in November 2000 to 5.9 percent in January 2001. Economists forecast that Ireland's economic growth would slow to 6 percent in 2001, despite low unemployment, because of an economic slowdown throughout Europe and the United States. Ireland's economy was one of the strongest in Europe from 1995 to 2000, with an average growth rate of 8.4 percent. ☐ Rohan McWilliam

See also **Europe; Northern Ireland.**

Islam. Muslims were profoundly affected by the terrorist attacks on the United States on Sept. 11, 2001, which were committed by radical Islamic fundamentalists. In the attacks, hijackers flew two aircraft into the World Trade Center towers in New York City and a third airliner into the Pentagon Building outside Washington, D.C., killing thousands of people. Most American Muslims immediately condemned the attacks as incompatible with Islam. On September 27, a group of Islamic scholars in the United States issued a *fatwa* (religious opinion) approving the participation of U.S. Muslim military personnel in operations against other Muslims. The council noted that under Islamic law (Sharia), the terrorist attacks were crimes of *Hirabah* (waging war against society).

United States President George W. Bush went to considerable lengths to try and prevent those Muslims who had nothing to do with the attacks from being blamed. Bush invited Muslim religious leader Imam Muzammil Siddiqi to participate in a memorial service at the National Cathedral in Washington, D.C., on September 14. The president later visited the Islamic Center in Washington and met with American Muslims at the White House. American Muslims, however, did become occasional targets of harassment and assault in the weeks following the terrorist attacks.

The war on terrorism. President Bush declared a war on terrorism before a joint session of the U.S. Congress on September 20. The president demanded that the leaders of the Taliban, a hard-line Muslim militia that controlled most of Afghanistan, turn over exiled Saudi millionaire Osama bin Laden and members of bin Laden's Islamic terrorist organization, al-Qaida. U.S. intelligence agents had identified al-Qaida as being responsible for the attacks. In early October, after the Taliban refused Bush's demand, a U.S.-led coalition launched a massive military assault against the Taliban and al-Qaida in Afghanistan.

Bush also ordered that the assets of U.S. groups suspected of supporting terrorists be frozen. The U.S. Congress passed legislation in October restricting the activities of some Islamic banking and philanthropic organizations. In December, the U.S. Department of the Treasury froze the assets of the Holy Land Foundation for Relief and Development, one of the largest Islamic charities in the United States.

"The Mosque in America," a report released in April by the Hartford Institute for Religious Research in Connecticut found that the number of mosques in the United States increased 25 percent between 1993 and 2000. South Central Asians comprised 33 percent of American Muslims; African Americans made up 30 percent; and Arabs comprised 25 percent. ☐ A. Kevin Reinhart

See also **Terrorism: A Special Feature,** p. 38.

Israel. A series of attacks and counterattacks in Israel in 2001 plunged Israelis and Palestinians into turmoil that bordered on all-out war. On December 13, the cabinet of Israeli Prime Minister Ariel Sharon severed all contact with Yasir Arafat, leader of the Palestinian Authority (PA), after declaring him "no longer relevant." (The PA administers Palestinian territories in the West Bank and Gaza Strip.) The move came after Palestinian militants ambushed a bus in the West Bank on December 12, killing at least 10 Jewish settlers. On December 1 and December 2, Palestinian extremists had killed 26 Israelis in three suicide bombing attacks in the cities of Jerusalem and Haifa.

Sharon's election. In March, Sharon, a hard-line retired general and leader of the right-wing Likud Party, became Israel's fifth prime minister in less than six years. Sharon took 63 percent of the vote. His opponent, Prime Minister Ehud Barak, received 37 percent of the vote. Many Israelis blamed Barak, the Labor Party candidate, for being too willing to compromise during negotiations with Arafat in 2000 that, nonetheless, failed to produce a peace agreement.

Intifada. The Israeli and Palestinian populations became increasingly radicalized as a Palestinian uprising—or Intifada—which began in September 2000, escalated in 2001. Palestinian militants in the West Bank and Gaza killed Israeli settlers in drive-by shootings. This triggered Israeli military raids and the closing of Israel's borders with Palestinian areas, cutting many Palestinians off from their work. In June, Palestinian militants claimed responsibility for the bombing of a Tel Aviv nightclub that killed more than 20 Israelis. In August, the bombing of a pizzeria in Jerusalem killed another 15 people. The Israeli government responded by targeting leaders of Palestinian militant groups for assassination.

The Mitchell Report. In May, an international commission led by former U.S. Senator George Mitchell issued a framework for restarting peace talks. The commissioners urged Israeli authorities to freeze settlements in the West Bank and Gaza. They also urged Palestinian authorities to suppress terrorism. Prime Minister Sharon refused to halt construction of Israeli settlements, and Yasir Arafat failed to suppress Palestinian terrorists. By the end of 2001, Middle East experts had come to believe that Arafat was unwilling or unable to stop the violence.

Israeli investigators examine a bus that was blown up by an Arab suicide bomber in Haifa, Israel, on December 2. The suicide attack was one of three bombings that killed 26 Israelis in two days.

U.S. policy change. The terrorist attacks made by Islamic extremists on the United States on September 11 profoundly affected relations between the United States and the countries of the Middle East. After the attacks, U.S. President George W. Bush, attempting to gain Arab and Muslim support for an antiterrorism coalition, pressured Sharon to resume peace negotiations. Before the attacks, Arab leaders had criticized Bush for his reluctance to become more involved in the Arab-Israeli conflict. In November, Bush administration officials announced that the U.S. government envisioned Israel and a Palestinian nation existing side by side. Bush also sent U.S. envoys to Israel to try to revive a cease-fire.

Violence escalates. The suicide bombings on December 1 and 2 dealt a severe blow to any possibility of a cease-fire. The Islamic militant group Hamas claimed responsibility for the bombings in revenge for the November assassination of their leader by Israeli forces. Sharon held Arafat responsible for the attacks and launched a military assault on Palestinian targets, including Arafat's own headquarters. Arafat's security force rounded up more than 180 Palestinian militants and placed the Hamas spiritual leader under house arrest, but the violence continued.

The brink of war. Following the December 12 attack on Jewish settlers in the West Bank, Israeli forces increased their air strikes in Palestinian areas and arrested suspected Palestinian militants. A PA spokesman labeled the Israeli actions "an official declaration of war."

☐ Christine Helms

See also **Middle East; People in the news** (Sharon, Ariel); **Terrorism: A Special Feature,** p. 38.

Italy moved toward the political right in 2001 when voters returned Silvio Berlusconi, an Italian media tycoon, to power as prime minister in a sweeping election victory. The result marked a dramatic comeback for Berlusconi, who served briefly as prime minister in 1994 and then spent several years fighting criminal prosecution on charges of tax evasion.

Berlusconi ran on a platform promising significant cuts in income taxes, increased government spending on roads and other public works projects, and a large rise in payments to retirees under the state-run pension system. The campaign was also a personal referendum on Berlusconi, who pledged to bring to government the same dynamism and business acumen that had made him Italy's richest man. According to some sources, Berlusconi was worth an estimated $13 billion.

In the election on May 13, 2001, the House of Freedoms, a coalition of center-right parties led by Berlusconi's Forza Italia, won 368 seats in the Chamber of Deputies, a substantial majority in the 630-seat chamber. Berlusconi's coalition also won a majority in the Senate, the upper house of parliament. The center-left Olive Tree coalition led by former Rome mayor Francesco Rutelli won 242 seats in the Chamber of Deputies. The Olive Tree had offered similar promises of tax cuts and

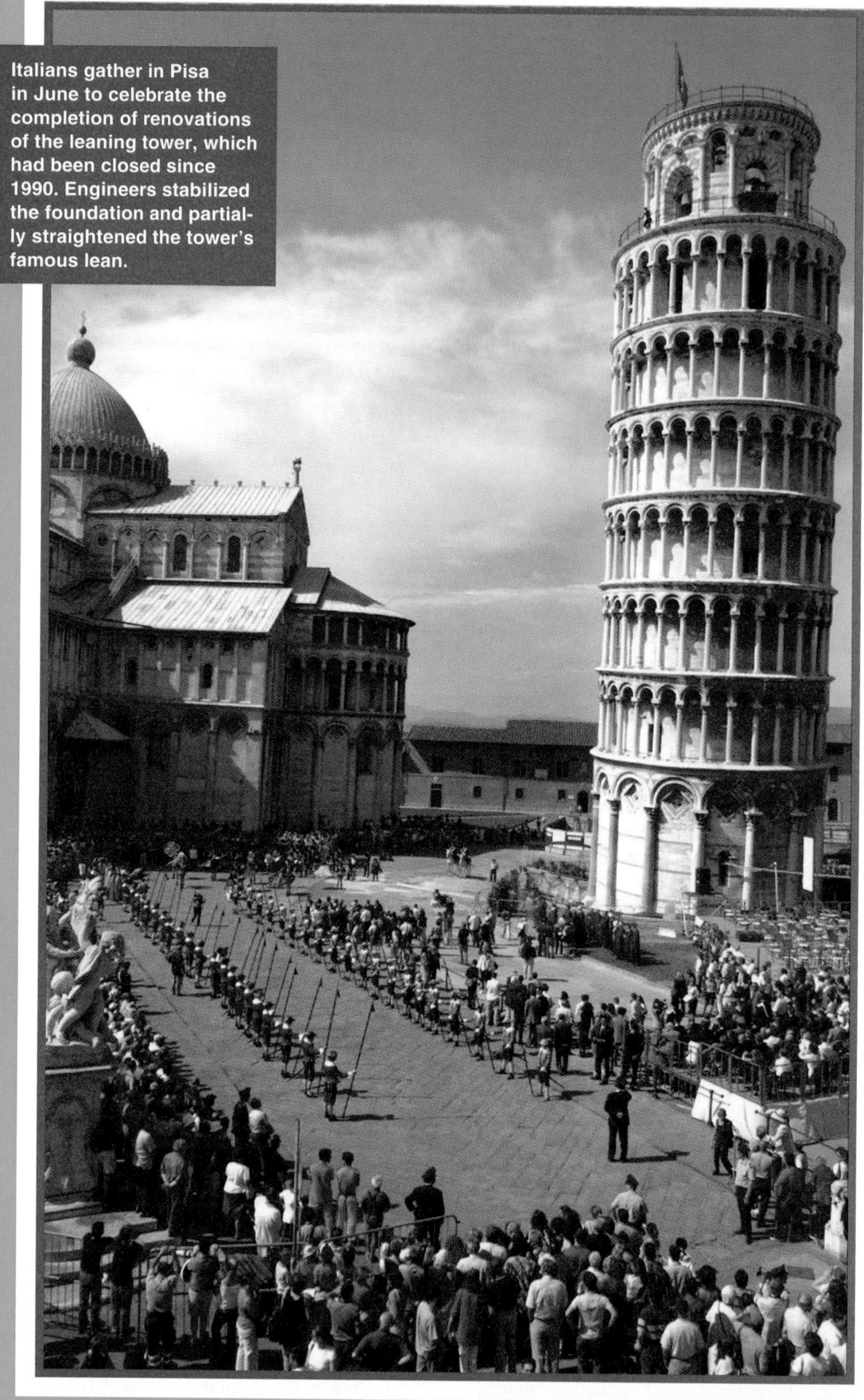

Italians gather in Pisa in June to celebrate the completion of renovations of the leaning tower, which had been closed since 1990. Engineers stabilized the foundation and partially straightened the tower's famous lean.

increased spending, but the coalition suffered from divisions among its members and a significant loss of popularity during the previous five years, when it governed Italy. Berlusconi was sworn in as prime minister on June 11, replacing Giuliano Amato of the Olive Tree.

Economic policy. Berlusconi's government launched a series of initiatives during its first 100 days in power designed to stimulate Italy's economy. The initiatives included the abolition of inheritance taxes, tax incentives for corporate investment, and measures making it easier for companies to hire and fire workers.

Berlusconi had to postpone his promises of income tax cuts and spending increases, however, because of a big rise in the government budget deficit. In late 2001, Finance Minister Giulio Tremonti said the deficit was likely to amount to at least 1.2 percent of Italy's *gross domestic product* (the total value of goods and services produced in a year), above the country's target of 0.8 percent. European Union rules require that countries using Europe's single currency, the euro, as Italy does, limit their deficits. The deficit reflected a broad economic slowdown in Italy, which reduced tax revenues and increased welfare spending. Government economists forecast that the country's growth rate would slow to less than 2 percent in 2001 from 2.9 percent in 2000 as a result of the global economic slowdown that began in the United States.

Foreign policy. Berlusconi promoted closer ties between Italy and the United States after taking power. In June 2001, he expressed his support for U.S. President George W. Bush's proposal to build a national missile defense system, a project that most European governments opposed. He also offered to contribute Italian troops to the U.S. campaign against the Taliban government in Afghanistan and the al-Qaida terrorist network of Osama bin Laden after the September 11 terrorist attacks on the United States.

Violent demonstrations by antiglobalization protesters marred a summit meeting of the Group of Eight leading industrial countries in July, which Italy hosted in Genoa. One person was killed and about 200 others were injured as several thousand protesters and anarchists battled with police on city streets on the opening day of the summit meeting on July 20.

The incident represented the most violent in a series of escalating protests that have marred international meetings since the gathering of the World Trade Organization in Seattle in 1999. As a result of the incident in Genoa, Berlusconi requested the postponement of a summit meeting of the United Nations' Food and Agriculture Organization, which had been scheduled to be held in Rome in November 2001.

Corporate mergers. Italian companies engaged in a fresh round of takeovers in 2001. In the biggest deal, the tire and cable company Pirelli SpA and its partner, the Edizione Holding, acquired control of the national telephone company, Telecom Italia SpA in July. Pirelli and Edizione paid $6.2 billion for a 23-percent stake in Olivetti SpA, which controlled Telecom Italia. The deal marked the second change of control for Telecom Italia in two years. (Olivetti had bought the telephone company in 1999.) The Pirelli deal also highlighted the complex web of ownership in corporate Italy, which allowed a company such as Pirelli to take over a much larger target—Telecom Italia—by using a chain of holding companies to buy a minority stake.

Also in July 2001, automaker Fiat SpA acquired Montedison SpA, one of Italy's largest energy companies, for $5 billion. Fiat teamed up with Electricite de France S.A., the state-owned French electric utility, to arrange the takeover. Electricite de France had sought to buy Montedison on its own but was rebuffed by Italian regulators, who did not want the French company to gain control of Italy's electricity industry.

☐ Tom Buerkle

See also **Europe.**

Ivory Coast. See **Cote d'Ivoire** in **Africa.**

Jamaica. See **West Indies.**

Japan. On April 26, 2001, the ruling Liberal Democratic Party (LDP) chose Junichiro Koizumi as prime minister. He had achieved wide popularity with party regulars by promising to be a dynamic reformer.

Koizumi succeeded Yoshiro Mori, an LDP politician whose year in office had been marked by controversy and scandal. Mori won a confidence vote in parliament in April, despite the fact that the LDP was pressuring him to resign and that an opinion poll showed that he had the support of only 9 percent of Japanese voters. A week after the vote, Mori moved up the date of the elections for LDP leadership from September to April. In doing so, Mori effectively resigned. Because the LDP was the largest political party, its president automatically became prime minister, and Mori knew he would not be elected party president.

Ryutaro Hashimoto, who had been prime minister from 1996 to 1998, was the favorite among LDP members of parliament. But in April 2001, 2.3 million rank-and-file LDP members voted overwhelmingly for Koizumi and his promises of reforms. With an election for the upper house of parliament looming, LDP members of parliament fell into line with what the people wanted and named Koizumi prime minister.

Reform. Koizumi, a career politician, said he would seek to change Japan's Constitution. Writ-

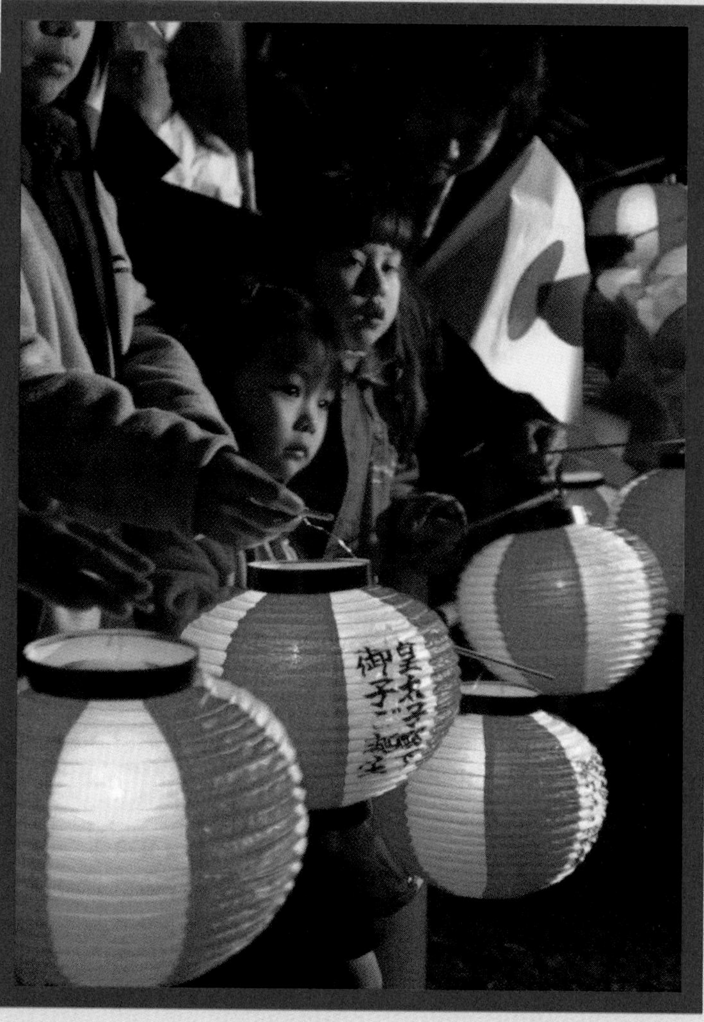

Japanese children gather at the Imperial Palace in Tokyo to celebrate the birth in early December of the first child of Crown Princess Masako and Crown Prince Naruhito. More than 80,000 people visited the palace after the royal birth to sign congratulatory books.

ten by leaders of the U.S. Army of Occupation after Japan's defeat in World War II (1939-1945), the Constitution prohibited the country from having armed forces. Koizumi said it was inaccurate to portray Japan's "self-defense forces" as anything but an army. The Constitution also established a parliamentary system to elect the prime minister. Koizumi sought to change the system to a popular election. In another step toward reform, Koizumi said he would slash government spending and allow heavily indebted businesses to collapse in order to free up investment capital. "Structural reform with nothing sacred" became Koizumi's motto.

The new prime minister quickly attained the popularity of a rock star, even though he warned the public that solutions to long-standing economic and social problems would be painful. Many people considered him a straightforward leader after decades of political doubletalk. The Japanese people lined up to buy posters showing Koizumi in dramatic poses, and by June, polls showed that an unprecedented 85 percent of the Japanese public supported the prime minister. His popularity, however, began to fall as economic problems persisted and Koizumi slowed his reform efforts.

Koizumi's cabinet choices included key economics ministers who sought reform, which broke the tradition of a cabinet mainly composed of representatives from LDP factions. However, Koizumi still faced the problem of how to reform the LDP. In 2001, the party remained tied to private industry, particularly the construction industry, which provided about 10 percent of the jobs in Japan. Political experts considered wasteful construction, with kickbacks for LDP politicians, a primary cause of Japan's massive public debt.

Koizumi named Makiko Tanaka, Japan's most famous woman politician, as foreign minister. The outspoken Tanaka was the daughter of a former prime minister. The popularity of her adversarial style quickly added to Koizumi's own public appeal, but she also got into disputes with him. Koizumi had to insist that Tanaka remove corrupt officials in the ministry. Tanaka then began to clean up corruption in the foreign ministry and impose accountability on its bureaucrats, who had long worked without effective political oversight.

Election. Political observers credited Koizumi's popularity, bolstered by Tanaka's own favorable rating, with turning around what was expected to be an LDP loss in July elections for the upper house of parliament. The LDP won 65 of the 121 contested seats in the 247-seat body, allowing it and two coalition partners to increase their majority.

Koizumi claimed the election was a mandate for his reform program. This put him on a collision course with LDP faction leaders who did not want to change the party's economic policies. The prime minister battled members of his own party to control the budget for the fiscal year beginning April 1, 2002, and to reform a banking system loaded with bad debts from the late 1980's.

Economic problems. Government figures released after the election in July 2001 showed industrial production during the previous 12 months was down by 15 percent, as more Japanese companies moved to China, where labor was cheaper. The day the government released these figures, the stock market closed at a 16-year low. Public spending continued to drop through the end of 2001, even though consumer prices were falling. Exports also slowed, mainly because of the weakened U.S. economy. Economists warned that reforms needed for long-term economic recovery would accelerate the economy's slide into recession.

In an effort to revive the economy, the Cabinet approved a budget cut of nearly $7.5 billion in August. The cuts were mostly in public works. Central bank officials subsequently moved to increase the supply of money to stimulate the economy.

In September, Japan's unemployment rate reached a record 5.3 percent, the highest since World War II. As the economy fell into recession, Koizumi called for a financial plan to help the unemployed. The plan conflicted with his promise to cut the national debt, making many people doubt his ability to resolve economic problems.

The 2000 census results, released in June 2001, revealed an aging population, raising concerns about how the government would support the elderly. Of Japan's 126.9 million people in 2000, 17.5 percent were aged 65 or older. Only 14.5 percent of the population were 15 years old or younger. Government officials worried that a declining birth rate would mean fewer workers to support the elderly, compounding economic problems.

War shrine. Koizumi, soon after becoming prime minister, promised that on August 15, the anniversary of Japan's surrender in World War II, he would visit the Yasukuni Shrine, which is dedicated to the 2.5 million Japanese who were killed in the war. Because of controversy over government officials honoring Japan's militaristic past, only one other prime minister—Yasuhiro Nakasoni in 1985—had made an official visit to the shrine. Both China and South Korea, which Japan occupied during the war, protested the planned visit. Koizumi tried to compromise by visiting the shrine two days before the anniversary, which did not satisfy either side.

Chinese and South Korean officials also objected to a new Japanese textbook that they said ignored many aspects of Japanese aggression during World War II. Few schools adopted the book.

Sub accident. In February 2001, Japan's relations with the United States were shaken when a U.S. Navy submarine collided with a Japanese fishing boat. Nine people were killed when the U.S.S. *Greenville* surfaced under the fishing boat off the coast of Hawaii. The United States paid for damages. The accident, however, renewed demands by many Japanese for stricter rules regarding the behavior of the 47,000 U.S. military personnel stationed in Japan.

Royal birth. A daughter was born in early December 2001 to Crown Prince Naruhito and Princess Masako. Naruhito's father, Emperor Akihito, named the baby Aiko Toshinomiya. The birth of the royal couple's first child was widely celebrated, and some Japanese commentators suggested changing a 1948 law that allowed only males to succeed to the Chrysanthemum throne.

Tragedies. In June 2001, a man stormed into an elementary school in Ikeda and began stabbing students and teachers. The man, who had a record of mental illness, killed eight children. He claimed he wanted to be arrested and executed.

In July, people leaving a fireworks display crowded onto a pedestrian bridge in Akashi. Overcrowding on the bridge triggered a stampede in which 10 people were killed and more than 90 others were injured. □ Henry S. Bradsher

See also **Armed forces; Asia; China.**

Jordan. King Abdullah II announced his support for United States President George W. Bush's call for a global "war on terrorism" following the Sept. 11, 2001, terrorist attacks on the United States. However, many Jordanians feared that growing animosity toward the United States in the Muslim world might lead to widespread unrest in Jordan.

Arab-Israeli conflict. In August, King Abdullah warned that Palestinian-Israeli violence threatened to grow into a wider Arab-Israeli conflict. Both Abdullah and Egypt's President Hosni Mubarak—leaders of the only two Arab states that had peace treaties with Israel in 2001—expressed frustration with the reluctance of President Bush to intervene in the conflict. After the September 11 attacks, the Bush administration increased its diplomatic involvement in the region.

Terrorism. In October, the Jordanian government amended laws to combat terrorism and enhance domestic security. The new laws broadened the definition of terrorism to include banking activities linked to terrorists and attacks against industrial or shipping targets. The laws authorized the death penalty for any acts resulting in deaths or involving weapons of mass destruction. The amendments also approved the closure of publications that incited unrest or undermined national unity.

In December, a Jordanian military court sentenced five terrorists to death for the 1994 assassination of a Jordanian diplomat in Beirut, the capital of Lebanon. Four of the five terrorists were sentenced in absentia—including Abu Nidal, founder of the radical Palestinian organization, Fatah-Revolutionary Council.

U.S. relations. The U.S. Congress passed the U.S.-Jordan Free Trade Agreement in September 2001. The legislation ended tariffs on two-way trade of virtually all industrial and agricultural goods within a 10-year period. Only Canada, Mexico, and Israel had similar agreements with the United States in 2001. Jordanian and U.S. officials hoped the agreement would create new jobs and investment opportunities in Jordan.

Iraq. In June, Jordanian officials rejected U.S. proposals to tighten United Nations (UN) trade sanctions against Iraq. The UN imposed the sanctions after Iraq's 1990 invasion of Kuwait. Many Jordanians blamed the United States for deteriorating humanitarian conditions in Iraq, Jordan's major trading partner. Jordan exported approximately $450 million in humanitarian goods to Iraq in 2001 in exchange for some 5.5 million tons (5 million metric tons) of crude oil and oil derivatives. ☐ Christine Helms

See also **Iraq; Israel; Middle East; Terrorism: A Special Feature,** p. 38.

Judaism. Israel remained the focus of Jewish life in 2001, however, tourism to Israel declined as a result of concern about violence and terrorism. Attacks on the World Trade Center in New York City and the Pentagon Building near Washington, D.C., on September 11 brought issues surrounding terrorism, Islamic fundamentalism, and the Israeli-Palestinian conflict to the forefront of international concern.

Israel. As an Arab uprising, which started in September 2000, continued in 2001, the death toll among Israelis and Palestinians mounted. There were terrorist attacks and clashes throughout the year, capped in December by Palestinian suicide bombings of a mall in Jerusalem and a bus in Haifa and a Palestinian ambush of a bus in the West Bank. As a result of the violence, tourism to Israel collapsed. The Union of American Hebrew Congregations, the synagogue body of Reform Jews, canceled its youth trips to Israel.

September 11. Jews were among the many who died in the September 11 attacks. Special synagogue services commemorated the victims, and, in the weeks that followed, some rabbis reported enhanced synagogue attendance, deeper commitments among their congregants to Jewish faith and service, and a heightened appreciation for the fragility of life. Jews expressed shock at anti-Semitic Internet postings that blamed Jews and the Mossad, Israel's secret service, for the September 11 violence, especially after these sentiments were echoed by some Arab media outlets. Jews also voiced concern over the revival on the Internet of a forged document known as the "Protocols of the Elders of Zion," which claimed to reveal a Jewish plan for world domination. Some Muslim organizations blamed Jews for fanning anti-Muslim feelings in the United States.

U.S. Jewish life was dominated by concern over Israel and fears connected with September 11. A pro-Israel rally scheduled in New York City for September 23 was canceled after the attacks.

Jewish educational institutions continued to open at a rapid rate during the year. But as the recession in the U.S. economy deepened, contributions to Jewish charities fell. Belt-tightening set in within Jewish organizations. B'nai B'rith, for example, sold its historic building in Washington, D.C., to relocate to more modest quarters.

There was a change of leadership in several U.S. Jewish organizations in 2001. Harvey Blitz was named president of the Union of Orthodox Jewish Congregations of America, a synagogue body of Orthodox Jews, and Rabbi David Ellenson became president of the (Reform) Hebrew Union (Reform) College-Jewish Institute of Religion, with branches in Cincinnati, New York City, Los Angeles, and Jerusalem. Norman Lamm, the president of Yeshiva University (Orthodox) in New York City, announced his retirement in 2001.

World. Tensions between the United Nations (UN) and Israel flared in 2001. In August, at the UN World Conference Against Racism in Durban, South Africa, delegates singled out Israel for condemnation. In response, the United States and Israel withdrew their delegations from the conference. In July, a long-time dispute was resolved when the UN permitted Israel to view evidence possessed by the UN that was related to the disappearance of three Israeli soldiers near the Lebanese border in October 2000.

Issues related to the *Holocaust* (the annihilation during World War II [1939-1945] of millions of Jews by the Nazis) continued to make news in 2001. A conflict over access to Vatican documents halted the work of Roman Catholic and Jewish historians impaneled to study the Vatican's role in World War II. In Poland, some Poles rejected evidence that citizens in the town of Jedwabne had murdered hundreds of local Jews during the Holocaust. There were efforts at reconciliation, including an apology from the Polish president. In September, the Jewish Museum of Berlin opened with exhibits highlighting two millennia of Jewish life in Germany.

☐ Jonathan D. Sarna and Jonathan J. Golden

See also **Germany; Israel; Middle East; Terrorism: A Special Feature,** p. 38.

Kazakhstan. President Nursultan Nazarbayev announced his support for the United States in its war against terrorists based in Afghanistan in the wake of the attacks on the United States on Sept. 11, 2001. Kazakhstan officials had expressed concern for some time about activities of the Islamic Movement of Uzbekistan, an extremist group with ties to Osama bin Laden, an exiled Saudi-born millionaire whom U.S. officials suspected masterminded the attacks on the United States. After September 11, Kazakhstan tightened border security and offered U.S. officials logistical support for military operations in Afghanistan.

In March, Kazakhstan's Tengiz oil field pumped the first Kazakhstan oil into the new Caspian pipeline, which terminates at the Russian port of Novorossiysk on the Black Sea. The first tanker was loaded in October. At full capacity, the pipeline was to transport 1.5 million barrels of oil a day.

Boosted by a strong oil sector and rising levels of foreign investment, Kazakhstan enjoyed its strongest year of economic growth since independence in 1991. The Kazakhstan finance ministry reported in November 2001 that the country's economy grew 13.7 percent in the first nine months of 2001. ☐ Steven L. Solnick

See also **Asia; Terrorism: A Special Feature,** p. 38.

Kentucky. See **State government.**

Kenya. President Daniel arap Moi's ruling Kenya African National Union (KANU) faced its worst economic crisis in 2001 since Moi came to office in 1978. According to figures released by the Central Bank of Kenya in February 2001, Kenya's economy declined by 0.3 percent in 2000, shrinking for the first time since Kenya gained independence from the United Kingdom in 1963. Nearly half of Kenya's people lived below the poverty line in 2000.

Corruption. In March 2001, President Moi dismissed Kenya's economic "dream team"—four senior civil servants headed by anthropologist and political leader Richard Leakey. Moi had appointed the team in response to pressure from international lending bodies such as the World Bank, a United Nations-affiliated organization that provides credit to member nations. Observers speculated that Leakey had angered the president by attacking corruption in Moi's government. The dismissals drew criticism from international donors who regarded Leakey's team as indispensable in restoring Kenya's economy.

In August, parliament threw out legislation to revive the Kenya Anti-Corruption Authority, effectively ending Moi's hope of receiving hundreds of millions of dollars in donor funds. The president's critics called the bill "a sham," claiming that its intent was to impress foreign investors rather than tackle graft.

Coalition. President Moi appointed National Development Party (NDP) leader Raila Odinga energy minister on June 11, forming the first coalition government in Kenya's history. Moi also appointed NDP legislator Awiti Adhu as minister of planning, giving Kenya's second-largest opposition party two posts in the 26-member Cabinet. The moves prompted speculation that a formal KANU/NDP merger might take place and that Moi was grooming Odinga for the presidency. Kenya's Constitution does not allow Moi to stay in office beyond 2002 elections.

Mysterious death. Tony Ndilinge, a KANU legislator whom Moi had fired from the Cabinet in 1999 for criticizing the government, was murdered in Nairobi, the capital, in August 2001. The murder refocused public attention on a number of other unresolved deaths, including the murder of Robert Ouko, a former foreign minister whose charred body was found in 1990.

On July 30, 2001, President Moi filed a lawsuit against Smith Hempstone, accusing the former U.S. ambassador of libel. Hempstone, who served in Nairobi from 1989 to 1993, had written in his memoirs, *Rogue Ambassador* (1997), that Moi participated in Ouko's murder and in attempts to hide the crime. ☐ Simon Baynham

See also **Africa.**

Korea, North. Efforts by the United States government to resume negotiations with North Korea on the issue of missiles and other armaments proved to be largely ineffective in 2001. Negotiations to limit North Korea's development and testing of long-range missiles and to halt sales of missiles to other countries were initiated during the administration of U.S. President Bill Clinton. President George W. Bush suspended the negotiations in 2001 until his administration could review U.S. policy toward North Korea. Bush claimed that North Korea's Communist government could not be trusted. The president later announced that he hoped talks would resume on limiting missile programs and would include discussions on North Korea's military. Most of North Korea's 1.1 million troops were concentrated near South Korea. In June, North Korean officials rejected any discussion regarding their conventional forces.

In July, Kim Chong-il, the leader of North Korea, announced a *moratorium* (suspension) until 2003 on the possible launch of long-range missiles. He denied that his country's missiles posed a threat to any country that respected North Korea's sovereignty. Observers interpreted this as North Korea's effort to discourage U.S. plans to build a missile defense system. The Bush administration had pointed to North Korea's missile program as a partial justification for the U.S. defense system.

Kim noted that his government would continue developing and selling missiles for other countries. Kim reiterated his pledge to suspend the launch of missiles in a joint declaration with Russian President Vladimir V. Putin during a visit to Moscow in 2001.

Relations with South Korea. In September, North Korean officials resumed cabinet-level talks with South Korea, which had broken off in December 2000. However, little real progress was made beyond visits between members of divided families and the construction of a railroad linkup between the north and the south.

Refugees. North Korea's relations with China were complicated in 2001 by China's refusal to care for the estimated 300,000 North Koreans who had crossed into China to avoid starvation. Since 1995, more than 220,000 people had died of famine-related causes in North Korea. Foreign observers blamed poor Communist management of agriculture for the tragedy, but drought, floods, and other natural disasters continued to cause famine in 2001.

Economy. A North Korean report released in May described an economy in collapse and a ruined health care system. Life expectancy in North Korea had dropped by more than six years since the famine of 1995. ☐ Henry S. Bradsher

See also **Asia; China; Korea, South.**

Korea, South.

President Kim Dae-jung's standing in political opinion polls fell sharply in 2001. One newspaper poll showed that only 19 percent of the people in South Korea supported him. Political experts regarded Kim, who was ineligible to run for reelection and was to leave office in February 2003, as increasingly ineffectual.

Kim's failing "sunshine policy" was the primary reason for his declining popularity. Kim won the Nobel Peace Prize in 2000 for his policy to improve relations with Communist North Korea. As a result, leaders in North and South Korea met for the first time since Korea was divided after World War II (1939-1945). The two leaders agreed on the need for reunification and reconciliation.

In March 2001, however, negotiations between the two countries fell apart when they failed to win the support of the United States. U.S. President George W. Bush said that he doubted North Korea would follow through on agreements. As a result, North Korea's leader, Kim Chong-il, refused to schedule a visit to South Korea.

In September, South Korea's National Assembly threatened Kim's sunshine policy further by giving a no-confidence vote to the minister for North-South unification, Lim Dong-won. Lim had been under attack by South Korean politicians for being "too easy" on the Communist North.

The no-confidence vote further weakened the

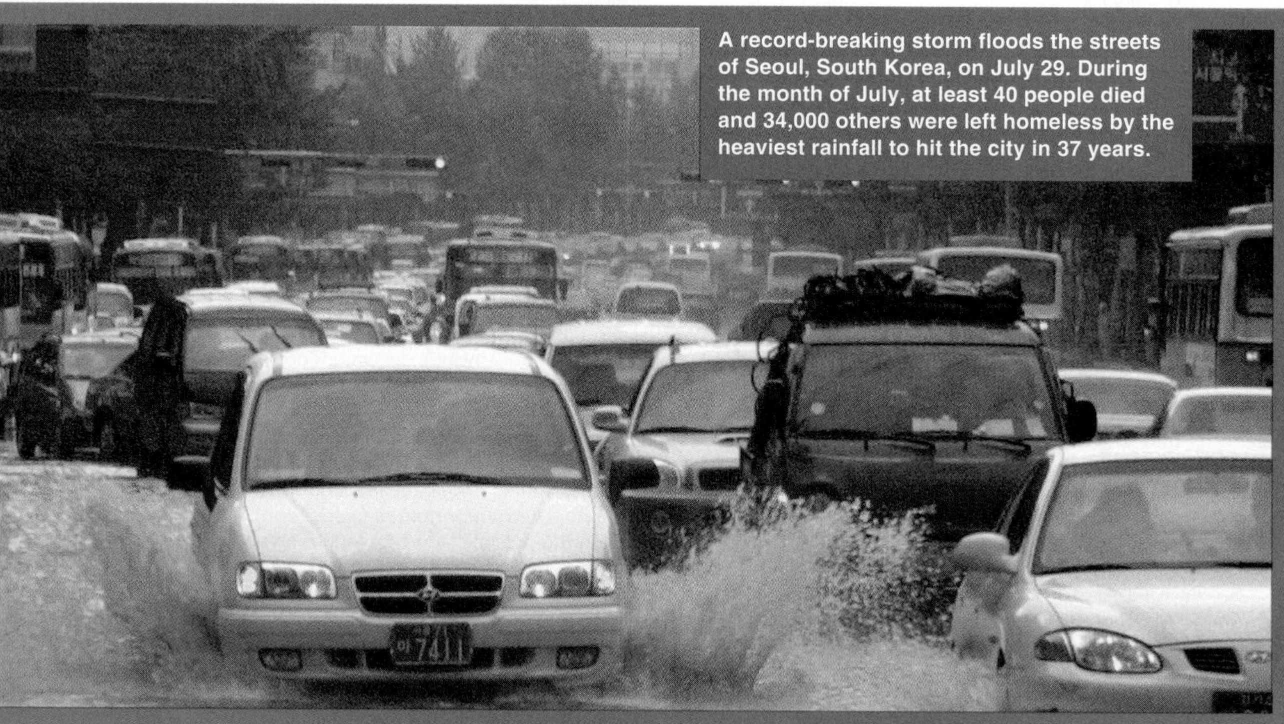

A record-breaking storm floods the streets of Seoul, South Korea, on July 29. During the month of July, at least 40 people died and 34,000 others were left homeless by the heaviest rainfall to hit the city in 37 years.

position that Kim's political party, the Millennium Democratic Party, held in the National Assembly (parliament). Kim was forced to reshuffle his cabinet in order to maintain his power. He named Lim a special adviser on security and reunification. North Korean officials then reopened talks with the south, but the talks broke down in November.

Failing reforms. Some critics accused Kim of spending too much time dealing with North Korea and too little time focusing on economic and social problems at home. Some economists claimed that Kim's reforms of the national medical insurance system left it nearly bankrupt. Critics also said that his education reforms, which sought to improve South Korean schools, did little but lower standards.

Economy. South Korean's economic worries of 2000 over inflation were replaced in 2001 by concern over economic growth. In September, the central bank warned that the economy might not reach the 3.8-percent growth targeted for the year.

Weather. In 2001, South Korea suffered the worst drought in nearly 90 years. During July, the heaviest rainfall in 37 years caused 40 deaths in and around the capital, Seoul, and left nearly 34,000 people homeless. ☐ Henry S. Bradsher

See also **Korea, North; Russia.**

Kuwait. See **Middle East.**

Kyrgyzstan. Islamic fundamentalists associated with the Islamic Movement of Uzbekistan staged border raids into Kyrgyzstan in July 2001 for the third year in a row. The guerrillas sought to establish an Islamic state in the Fergana Valley, where Kyrgyzstan borders Uzbekistan and Tajikistan. Concern over the growing Islamic fundamentalist threat prompted Kyrgyzstan President Askar Akayev to join the leaders of Uzbekistan, Kazakhstan, Tajikistan, Russia, and China at a June antiterrorism summit in Shanghai.

President Akayev voiced strong support for a U.S. military campaign against the Taliban regime in Afghanistan after terrorists attacked the United States on September 11. Akayev opened Kyrgyzstan's airspace to U.S. fighter planes involved in military operations and promised to share intelligence with the United States.

Political experts speculated that Akayev's cooperation with the U.S.-led international campaign against terrorism might silence criticism of his government's recent human rights record. International human rights groups had sharply criticized Akayev for allegedly harassing his political opponents and muzzling journalists since his reelection as president in 2000.

☐ Steven L. Solnick

See also **Afghanistan; Asia; Russia; Tajikistan; Terrorism: A Special Feature,** p. 38.

Labor and employment. A number of economists declared the economy of the United States, which had enjoyed a record-setting period of expansion from 1992 to 2001, to be in recession by the end of 2001. The National Bureau of Economic Research, a nonprofit group of economists, announced in November that the U.S. period of expansion had ended in March. Other economists, who defined a recession as two consecutive quarters of decline in economic activity, noted that the U.S. *gross domestic product* (GDP—the value of all goods and services produced in the country in a year) declined in the third quarter of 2001 for the first time since 1992. A decline in the fourth quarter would indicate a recession.

During the record economic expansion, employment soared from 118 million jobs in 1992 to almost 136 million jobs in the first quarter of 2001, according to the U.S. Bureau of Labor Statistics (BLS). Average annual unemployment fell from 7.5 percent in 1992 to 4 percent in 2000.

Terrorist attacks on the United States on Sept. 11, 2001, hammered at an already weakened economy. The attacks threw several industries into a steep decline. According to the BLS, the number of unemployed shot up by 1 million people in October and November, pushing the national rate of unemployment to 5.7 percent.

Unemployment rates for various demographic groups had fallen steadily throughout the 1990's. The drop stalled between July 2000 and June 2001 and began to rise in the second half of 2001. For men aged 20 years and older, the unemployment rate rose from 4.3 percent to 5.3 percent in November. For women in the same age group, the rate rose from 4.4 percent to 4.9 percent. The unemployment rate for teen-agers rose from 14.7 percent to 15.9 percent. For white workers, the unemployment rate rose from 4.3 percent to 4.8 percent in November; for African American workers, from 8.7 percent to 10.1 percent; and for workers of Hispanic origin, from 6.4 percent to 7.6 percent.

The Employment Cost Index—a BLS statistical measure of changes in wages, salaries, and benefits for all civilian workers—rose 4.1 percent from September 2000 to September 2001, compared with a rise of 4.3 percent for the same period a year earlier. The Consumer Price Index, a measure of changes in the prices of goods and services purchased in the United States, continued to rise at the low rates that prevailed in the 1990's.

Newspapers. The *Seattle Times* and the Pacific Northwest Newspaper Guild announced on Jan. 8, 2001, an agreement ending a seven-week strike. Guild members ratified the contract one week later. The pact provided wage increases of $3.30 an hour over the course of six years, as well as increases in the employer's health care contributions. The terms of the agreement were similar to those accepted by the guild in December 2000 at the *Seattle Post-Intelligencer* newspaper.

Telecommunications industry. In February 2001, SBC Communications of San Antonio and the Communication Workers of America (CWA) agreed to a contract covering some 120,000 workers in 13 states. CWA members approved the contract in March. The agreement included a 12.25-percent wage increase over three years, reduced mandatory overtime for technicians and service representatives, and provided a supplemental payment of $25 per week for employees who use bilingual skills on the job.

In September, members of the CWA ratified an agreement with BellSouth Corp., the telecommunications firm based in Atlanta, Georgia. The pact increased wages by 13 percent over three years for 56,000 employees, including customer service workers, telephone operators, and technicians.

Air travel industry. Faced with a number of critical contract negotiations in the air travel industry in 2001, U.S. President George W. Bush indicated early in the year that the federal government would take immediate action if strikes in the industry threatened the fragile U.S. economy. On March 9, President Bush acted on his promise, when negotiations between the Aircraft Mechanics Fraternal Association and Northwest Airlines, Inc., of St. Paul, Minnesota, broke down. President Bush signed an executive order creating a Presidential Emergency Board, a move that put off the possibility of a strike for 60 days while the board attempted to mediate the dispute. On May 9, union members approved a contract. Under the terms of the agreement, the union's 8,200 mechanics would receive an average pay increase of 24.4 percent over four years, while some 1,500 cleaners and custodians in the union would receive a 13-percent pay increase over four years.

In June, members of the Air Line Pilots Association approved a contract with Delta Air Lines Incorporated of Atlanta that increased most pilots' pay by between 24 percent and 39 percent over five years. The contract made Delta Air Lines pilots the best paid in the air travel industry. Pay for pilots at Delta Express, a lower-cost subsidiary of Delta Air Lines, also increased, though it remained about 10 percent lower than that of other pilots.

American Airlines Inc. of Dallas bargained with several unions during 2001. In late August, the airline and the Transport Workers Union (TWU) announced tentative agreement on seven contracts covering 16,000 ground workers. Wage increases varied by occupation, with all employees to receive 3-percent raises in the second and third years of the contract. In October, TWU members overwhelmingly ratified the contracts, covering fleet service workers, dispatchers, stock clerks, meteorologists, instructors, simulation technicians, and technical specialists, in October.

American Airlines also reached agreement with the Association of Professional Flight Attendants (APFA) in early July, just as a 30-day cooling-off period was about to expire. On September 12, members of the APFA ratified the six-year contract, which provided a pay increase of more than 25 percent over the life of the contract for 23,000 workers.

Following the September 11 terrorist attacks, President Bush signed into law a bill that provided assistance to faltering airlines. The bill pledged $5 billion in cash and $10 billion in loan guarantees. Despite the federal aid, a steep fall in ticket sales because of passengers' safety concerns caused the airlines, already in economic difficulties because of the worldwide economic downturn, to announce layoffs of approximately 100,000 workers.

Automobile manufacturing industry. The United Automobile Workers (UAW) and Mitsubishi Motor Manufacturing of America, of Southfield, Michigan, reached agreement in late August on a four-year contract after a three-day strike at Mitsubishi's Normal, Illinois, plant. The pact provided a $1,350 ratification bonus and 3-percent wage increases in 2003 for 2,700 workers. Wage increases in the last two years of the pact were dependent upon negotiated increases between Daimler-Chrysler Corporation of Auburn Hills, Michigan, and the UAW. DaimlerChrysler and Mitsubishi Motors operate the Normal facility as a joint venture.

Early in 2001, the UAW and General Motors Corporation of Detroit reached a "shelf agreement," a pact that is to go into effect at a later, unspecified date. The agreement was intended to ensure automobile production at the Lordstown, Ohio, plant beyond 2004, saving the jobs of almost 5,000 workers. Union members ratified the agreement on Jan. 12, 2001.

Steel industry. Members of the United Steelworkers of America tried in 2001 to keep the steelmaking plants of bankrupt Ohio manufacturer LTV Corp. running. In August, the union, which represents 9,000 workers at LTV, ratified a four-and-a-half-year contract with the firm that included significant cost-saving measures to enable the company to get a loan under the federal emergency steel loan guarantee program. Nevertheless, in November, LTV indicated doubt that the company could cut its costs enough to qualify for the loan and petitioned a bankruptcy court for permission to close its mills in Ohio, Indiana, and Illinois, eliminating 7,500 jobs. Union members responded by negotiating a contract with

Changes in the United States labor force

	2000	2001*
Civilian labor force	140,866,000	141,697,000
Total employment	135,215,000	135,326,000
Unemployment	5,652,000	6,370,000
Unemployment rate	4.0%	4.5%
Change in real weekly earnings of production and nonsupervisory workers (nonfarm business sector)†	+0.3%	+0.4%
Change in output per employee hour (nonfarm business sector)	+3.0%	+1.7%

*All 2001 data are through the third quarter of 2001 (preliminary data).

†Real weekly earnings are adjusted for inflation by using constant 1982 dollars.

Sources: U.S. Bureau of Labor Statistics; Joint Economic Committee, U.S. Congress.

LTV's creditors to further cut costs, including wage cuts, delayed pay increases, and health care reductions that would save the firm up to $350 million over four years. In December, LTV agreed to keep its mills in working condition until February 2002, while it continued to look for a buyer. Nevertheless, the court allowed the steelmaker to stop production until a final decision was made, leading to the layoffs of thousands of workers.

Union membership. In January 2001, the BLS reported that the total number of union members in the United States had declined in 2000, dipping by 219,000 to 16.3 million. The figure represented 13.5 percent of the total work force. In 1999, union membership equaled 13.9 percent of the work force.

At the end of March 2001, the United Brotherhood of Carpenters and Joiners, the main national carpenters' union, severed its affiliation with the American Federation of Labor-Congress of Industrial Organizations (AFL-CIO). The 500,000-member carpenters' union cited differences over the direction of the labor movement as the reason for the split.

In mid-April, the Independent Association of Continental Pilots voted to merge their 7,000-member union with the Air Line Pilots Association, which represents 67,000 members at 67 airlines in the United States and Canada. The agreement went into effect in June.

The International Brotherhood of Teamsters took an important step in 2001 to end federal supervision of the union. The supervision had been imposed in 1989, when some Teamster officials were suspected of having ties to organized crime. In June 2001, delegates at the annual Teamsters' convention approved amendments to the union constitution that mandated direct election of union officials by the membership. Prior to 1989, union officials were elected by the union's board.

Work stoppages. The BLS reported in February 2001 that work stoppages involving 1,000 workers or more reached a six-year high of 39 in 2000, up from an all-time low of 17 in 1999. The stoppages involved 394,000 employees and cost 20 million lost workdays. The rise was caused almost entirely by a strike of 135,000 actors in radio and television commercials in early 2000.

Federal government. On Jan. 2, 2001, President Bush nominated Linda Chavez, a former head of the U.S. Commission on Civil Rights, to be secretary of labor. Chavez withdrew her nomination a week later amid allegations that she had employed an illegal immigrant as a domestic worker. Two days later, President Bush nominated Elaine Chao, a fellow of the Heritage Foundation, a conservative think tank in Washington, D.C., and a former head of the United Way of America, to be secretary. The Senate confirmed Chao's nomination January 29.

International unemployment. Unemployment stood at 6.8 percent in October 2001 in 25 countries of the Organization for Economic Cooperation and Development (OECD). The figure represented a slight increase from 6.2 percent in October 2000. In the OECD's "major seven" countries (the United States, Canada, Japan, France, Germany, Spain, and the United Kingdom), unemployment rose from 5.6 percent in October 2000 to 6.3 percent in October 2001.

Unemployment in Europe fell slightly from 8.5 percent in October 2000 to 8.4 percent in October 2001, continuing a decline from a high of 9.7 percent in 1998. In the European Union, composed of 15 western European nations, unemployment fell from 7.9 percent in October 2000 to 7.7 percent in October 2001, also continuing a downward trend from 9.9 percent in 1998. Unemployment rates in the United States (5.7 percent in November 2001) and in Japan (5.3 percent in September) remained below the collective rates for all of Europe. The lowest rates reported by OECD were in the Netherlands (2.5 percent) and Luxembourg (2.4 percent).

☐ Robert W. Fisher

See also **Cabinet, U.S.; Economics; Motion pictures; People in the news** (Chao, Elaine); **Television; Terrorism: A Special Feature,** p. 38.

Latin America

A downturn in the world economy in 2001 had a severe impact on Latin America. The region's economic growth rate slowed to an average of 1 to 2 percent for the year, according to estimates released in September by the Economic Commission for Latin America and the Caribbean, a United Nations agency based in Santiago, Chile. The unemployment rate was approximately 9 percent for the region as a whole but much higher in such countries as Argentina and Brazil.

The recession that overtook the United States economy in 2001 led to many problems for Latin America's business sector. The value of shares traded in Latin American stock markets plunged as sources of foreign investment, which had buoyed the area's economies in the past, dried up. Lackluster foreign demand owing to surplus worldwide agricultural production hurt major agricultural producers, such as Brazil. A global coffee glut in 2001 caused the price of coffee in international markets to fall to a 30-year low. "Latin America is entering one of the most difficult periods it has faced in many decades," said the president of the Inter-American Development Bank, a Latin American lending institution based in Washington, D.C., in November.

Tourism suffered in Caribbean countries and Mexico following terrorist attacks on the United States on September 11. As a result, thousands of Latin Americans found themselves out of work. The airline trade journal *AvNews Latin America & Caribbean* estimated that Latin American airlines lost $1 billion in 2001.

The war on terrorism. After the September terrorist attacks, the governments of all Latin American nations—even Cuba—voiced support for the U.S.-led war on terrorism. On September 21, the foreign ministers of the Organization of American States (OAS), an association of 35 American nations, resolved to "pursue, capture, prosecute, and punish . . . the perpetrators, organizers, and sponsors of these terrorist acts." U.S. Secretary of State Colin Powell called for a strengthening of the OAS committee on terrorism. He also noted that the U.S. government considered drug traffickers, such as those in Colombia, to be terrorists.

Latin American law authorities moved quickly to apprehend suspected members of Islamic terrorist groups. Authorities took several suspects into custody in Buenos Aires, the capital of Argentina, where Arab terrorists had destroyed the Israeli embassy in 1992 and a Jewish cultural center in 1994. Brazilian authorities also apprehended terrorist suspects wanted in the United States.

Cocaine eradication in Colombia. Latin American governments lent their support to U.S. military efforts to eradicate cocaine in Colombia in 2001. The governments of Ecuador, El Salvador, and Honduras all permitted the modernization and use of military bases in their countries as part of the U.S. strategy to choke off drug smuggling. In May, the Dutch parliament ratified a treaty permitting U.S. aircraft to fly drug surveillance and interdiction missions out of bases on the Dutch colonies of Aruba and Curacao, small islands in the Caribbean.

Quebec City summit. Leaders of every country in the Western Hemisphere but Cuba met in Quebec City, Canada, in April for the third Summit of the Americas. The chiefs of state—with the exception of Venezuela's President Hugo Chavez Frias—agreed to set a deadline of January 2005 for the conclusion of negotiations to create the Free Trade Area of the Americas (FTAA), a hemisphere-wide free trade zone. Negotiations to create the FTAA began in the early 1990's. Chavez said he would not sign the accord unless he first had the approval of the Venezuelan legislature or people. Brazil's President Fernando Henrique Cardoso warned that unless the FTAA accord barred nations from imposing nontariff barriers to support domestic industries, the accord would be "irrelevant." Cardoso's remark was prompted by skepticism that the United States would allow such Brazilian exports as steel and shoes to enter the U.S. market duty free.

Leaders at the Quebec summit agreed to release a previously secret draft of the FTAA agreement so that environmentalists, labor unions, and other opponents of the FTAA could review the accord for the first time. Tens of thousands of protesters demonstrated against the FTAA during the Quebec City meeting.

Also at the meeting, officials from the Inter-American Development Bank and the World Bank, a UN-affiliated lending organization, committed $20 billion to strengthen democracy in Latin America. Some of this money was to be used for helping developing nations compete in free trade with wealthy countries.

Bringing former leaders to justice. A number of Latin American governments in 2001 moved to bring former leaders to justice for crimes committed during their administrations. In June, courts in Guatemala ordered investigations into human rights violations by two former presidents, Romeo Lucas Garcia and Efrain Rios Montt.

Peruvian authorities tried in vain to convince Japan to *extradite* (turn over) former Peruvian President Alberto Fujimori. Fujimori, who had fled to Japan in November 2000, was wanted in Peru on charges of murder and corruption. Vladimiro L. Montesinos, Fujimori's spymaster, was apprehended by Venezuelan authorities in June 2001 and extradited to Peru to face more than 150 charges of corruption.

Paraguayan officials were unsuccessful in their attempt to have Brazilian authorities hand over General Lino Cesar Oviedo, former chief of the Paraguayan armed forces. Oviedo was wanted on charges that he had helped organize the 1999 assassination of Vice President Luis Maria Argana.

In Argentina, former President Carlos Saul Menem was charged in July 2001 with participating in a conspiracy to smuggle arms to Ecuador and Croatia between 1991 and 1995. Former Argentine dictator Jorge Rafael Videla was indicted in July 2001 for conspiring to abduct and kill left-wing political opponents in the 1970's and 1980's.

New Bolivian president. Bolivian President Hugo Banzer Suarez, 75, resigned on Aug. 6, 2001. He was suffering from advanced cancer. Suarez

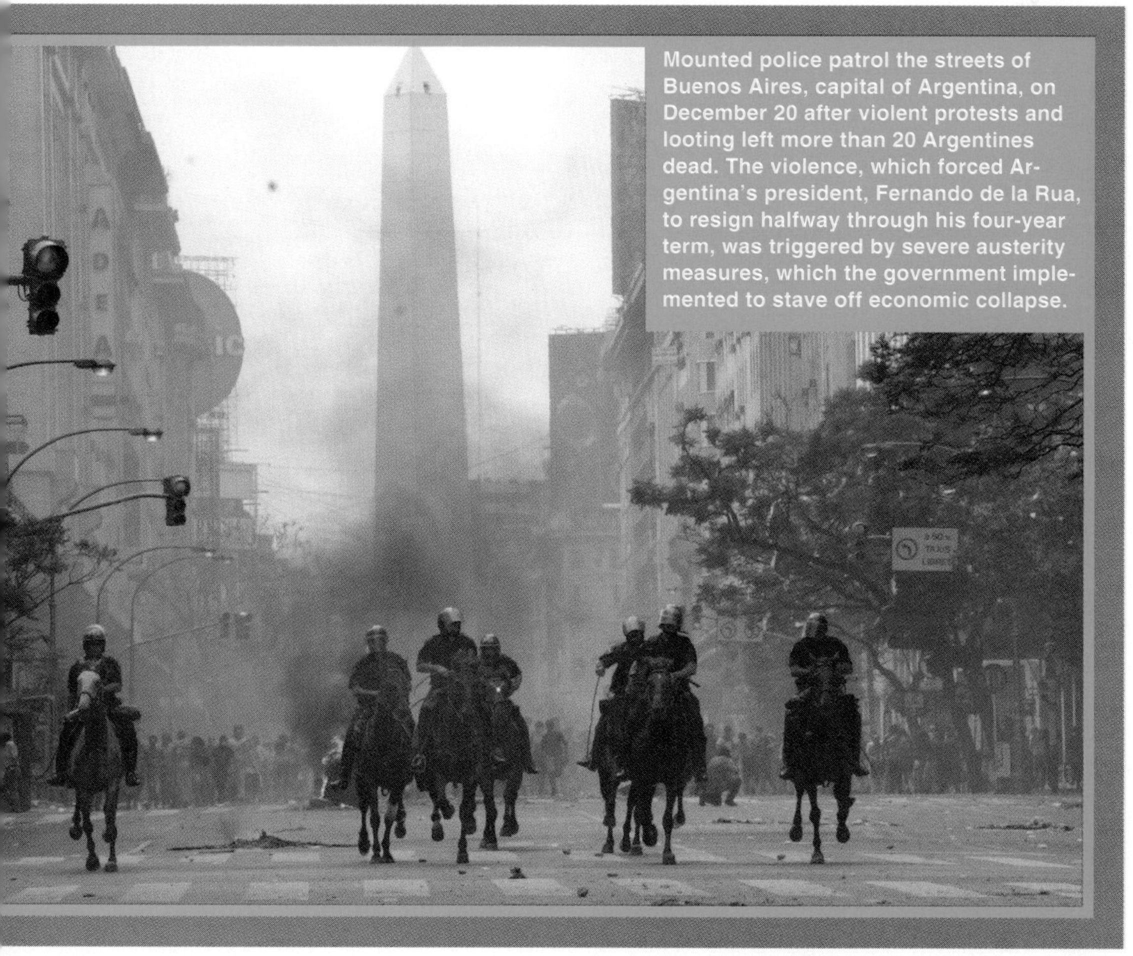

Mounted police patrol the streets of Buenos Aires, capital of Argentina, on December 20 after violent protests and looting left more than 20 Argentines dead. The violence, which forced Argentina's president, Fernando de la Rua, to resign halfway through his four-year term, was triggered by severe austerity measures, which the government implemented to stave off economic collapse.

Facts in brief on Latin America

Country	Population	Government	Monetary unit*	Foreign trade (million U.S.$) Exports†	Imports†
Antigua and Barbuda	69,000	Governor General James B. Carlisle; Prime Minister Lester Bird	dollar (2.67 = $1)	38	414
Argentina	37,919,000	President Eduardo Duhalde **	peso (1.00 = $1)	26,298	25,149
Bahamas	317,000	Governor General Orville Turnquest; Prime Minister Hubert Ingraham	dollar (0.99 = $1)	400	1,421
Barbados	272,000	Governor General Sir Clifford Husbands; Prime Minister Owen Arthur	dollar (1.99 = $1)	272	1,156
Belize	251,000	Governor General Sir Colville Young; Prime Minister Said Wilbert Musa	dollar (1.97 = $1)	210	480
Bolivia	8,691,000	President Jorge Fernando Quiroga Ramirez	boliviano (6.75 = $1)	1,051	1,755
Brazil	174,222,000	President Fernando Henrique Cardoso	real (2.78 = $1)	55,086	58,532
Chile	15,572,000	President Ricardo Lagos Escobar	peso (538.19 = $1)	18,158	18,107
Colombia	43,755,000	President Andres Pastrana Arango	peso (2,326.00 = $1)	13,040	11,539
Costa Rica	4,188,000	President Miguel Angel Rodriguez	colon (334.90 = $1)	5,865	6,372
Cuba	11,268,000	President Fidel Castro	peso (1.00 = $1)	1,800	3,400
Dominica	71,000	President Vernon Shaw; Prime Minister Pierre Charles	dollar (2.67 = $1)	53	147
Dominican Republic	8,740,000	President Rafael Hipolito Mejia Dominguez	peso (16.40 = $1)	966	6,416
Ecuador	13,090,000	President Gustavo Noboa Bejarano	U.S. dollar	4,853	3,484
El Salvador	6,507,000	President Francisco Flores Perez	colon (8.75 = $1)	1,342	3,796
Grenada	95,000	Governor General Daniel Williams; Prime Minister Keith Mitchell	dollar (2.67 = $1)	27	200
Guatemala	11,980,000	President Alfonso Antonio Portillo Cabrera	quetzal (8.03 = $1)	2,696	4,791
Guyana	872,000	President Bharrat Jagdeo	dollar (180.50 = $1)	643	629
Haiti	8,136,000	President Jean-Bertrand Aristide; Prime Minister Jean-Marie Antoine Polynice Cherestal	gourde (24.75 = $1)	165	1,041
Honduras	6,812,000	President Carlos Roberto Flores Facusse	lempira (15.63 = $1)	1,322	2,885
Jamaica	2,628,000	Governor General Sir Howard Cooke; Prime Minister P. J. Patterson	dollar (45.55 = $1)	1,296	3,216
Mexico	101,709,000	President Vicente Fox Quesada	new peso (9.56 = $1)	136,391	141,975
Nicaragua	5,350,000	President Arnoldo Aleman Lacayo	gold cordoba (13.70 = $1)	545	1,862
Panama	2,938,000	President Mireya Elisa Moscoso	balboa (1.00 = $1)	859	3,379
Paraguay	5,770,000	President Luis Gonzalez Macchi	guarani (4,530.00 = $1)	741	1,725
Peru	26,490,000	President Alejandro Toledo Prime Minister Roberto Danino	new sol (3.48 = $1)	7,002	8,797
Puerto Rico	3,930,000	Governor Sila Maria Calderon	U.S. dollar	38,500	27,000
St. Kitts and Nevis	38,000	Governor General Cuthbert Montraville Sebastian; Prime Minister Denzil Douglas	dollar (2.67 = $1)	53	152
St. Lucia	158,000	Governor General Perlette Louisy; Prime Minister Kenny Anthony	dollar (2.67 = $1)	68	319
St. Vincent and the Grenadines	116,000	Governor General Sir Charles James Antrobus; Prime Minister Ralph Gonsalves	dollar (2.67 = $1)	47	163
Suriname	421,000	President Runaldo Ronald Venetiaan	guilder (981.00 = $1)	435	551
Trinidad and Tobago	1,309,000	President Arthur Napoleon Raymond Robinson; Prime Minister Basdeo Panday	dollar (6.06 = $1)	2,803	2,740
Uruguay	3,384,000	President Jorge Batlle	peso (14.08 = $1)	2,295	3,466
Venezuela	25,058,000	President Hugo Chavez Frias	bolivar (742.50 = $1)	20,870	13,829

*Exchange rates as of Oct. 5, 2001, or latest available data. †Latest available data.
** Appointed Jan. 1, 2002, as the fourth president since the resignation of Fernando de la Rua on Dec. 20, 2001.

had spent much of his term fending off charges of human rights violations.

Vice President Jorge Fernando Quiroga Ramirez was sworn into office to complete Suarez's term, which was to end in August 2002. Quiroga was an industrial engineer with business experience at the International Business Machines Corporation, headquartered in Armonk, New York. He had also worked for the World Bank. Quiroga assumed office at a time of rising social tensions and high unemployment in Bolivia. He pledged to wage a war against poverty.

Hondurans elect president. In November 2001, Hondurans elected Ricardo Maduro, 54, of the National Party as their next president. Maduro took approximately 53 percent of the vote, compared with 44 percent for Rafael Pineda of the ruling Liberal Party. Maduro, a businessman and newcomer to politics, had pledged to crack down on crime during the campaign. Maduro's son had been killed by gunmen in 1997.

Drought and poverty. A severe drought left almost 1.5 million subsistence farmers in Central America with little to eat in 2001. Bean and corn fields in poor areas of Nicaragua, Honduras, El Salvador, and Guatemala were hit the hardest. More than 700,000 people in these areas lost at least half of their crops because of the drought. In the vicinity of Choluteca, Honduras, farmers lost 92 percent of their normal harvest. Many children, forced to live on a diet of bananas and mangoes, suffered from serious protein deficiency.

In June, President Vicente Fox Quesada of Mexico called for "a great alliance" aimed at improving life within the drought-stricken zones, as well as within nine states of Mexico where poverty was widespread. Fox proposed the alliance at a meeting of Central American presidents in San Salvador, capital of El Salvador. The presidents at the meeting agreed on a program to promote tourism, trade, education, environmental protection, and planning for disaster relief.

Remittances from the United States. *Remittances* (money sent from one person to another) by Latin Americans living in the United States to family and friends in Latin America will total $300 billion between 2001 and 2011, according to estimates by the Inter-American Development Bank. In Haiti, Nicaragua, El Salvador, and the Dominican Republic, remittances from the United States accounted for more than 10 percent of those nations' *gross domestic product* (the value of all goods and services produced in a nation in a given period). In Mexico, remittances from Mexicans living in the United States amounted to roughly $8 billion in 2001, ranking third as a source of national revenue after tourism and oil exports.

Amazon environmentalist murdered. In August, Ademir Federicci, an outspoken labor and environmental leader in Brazil, was murdered in his house in Altamira, Brazil. The slaying triggered widespread public outrage. Earlier in the year, Federicci had made accusations of corruption against the Superintendency for the Development of the Amazon, a government agency that funds development projects in Brazil's Amazon region. The damaging charges led to the abolition of the agency.

The official investigation into Federicci's death lasted just two days and concluded that Federicci had been killed by a petty thief. However, Federicci's wife charged that the investigation was a cover-up. She said her husband had struggled inside the house with an intruder, while he was shot by someone standing outside the window.

Free cigarettes for children. In 1999 and 2000, U.S. tobacco companies offered free cigarettes to 11 percent of the children aged 13 to 15 in Latin America, according to an August 2001 report by the World Health Organization, a UN organization based in Geneva, Switzerland, and the U.S. Centers for Disease Control and Prevention in Atlanta, Georgia. The cigarettes were dispensed on the streets of Latin American cities by youths wearing clothing adorned with cigarette company logos. The campaign succeeded in making many young teens regular smokers, noted the report.

Nobel Prize. In October, V. S. Naipaul, an author who was born in Trinidad to parents of Indian descent, was awarded the Nobel Prize in literature by the Royal Swedish Academy of Sciences. The Academy recognized Naipaul for both his nonfiction and fiction works that "compel us to see the presence of suppressed histories." In several of his works, Naipaul describes how various legacies of colonial rule have affected Trinidad and other former British colonies in Latin America.

Abuse of foreign domestics. Human Rights Watch, a human rights organization based in New York City, released a report in June that blamed the U.S. government for doing little to protect the rights of foreigners working in the United States as domestic servants. The majority of these foreign domestics were from Latin America. According to the report, many domestics employed by diplomats in Washington, D.C., were being held in virtual captivity for their services. As the report put it, "some of the world's most disadvantaged workers (are) held captive by some of the world's most powerful employers." Human Rights Watch found that the servants worked on an average of 14 hours a day and received a median wage of only $2.14 per hour. ☐ Nathan A. Haverstock

See also the various Latin American countries; **Latin America: A Special Report; Literature, world; Nobel Prizes.**

Latvia. See **Europe.**

Law. See **Courts; Human rights; Supreme Court of the United States; United States, Government of the.**

Drugs, Guns, and Money: The Conflict in Colombia

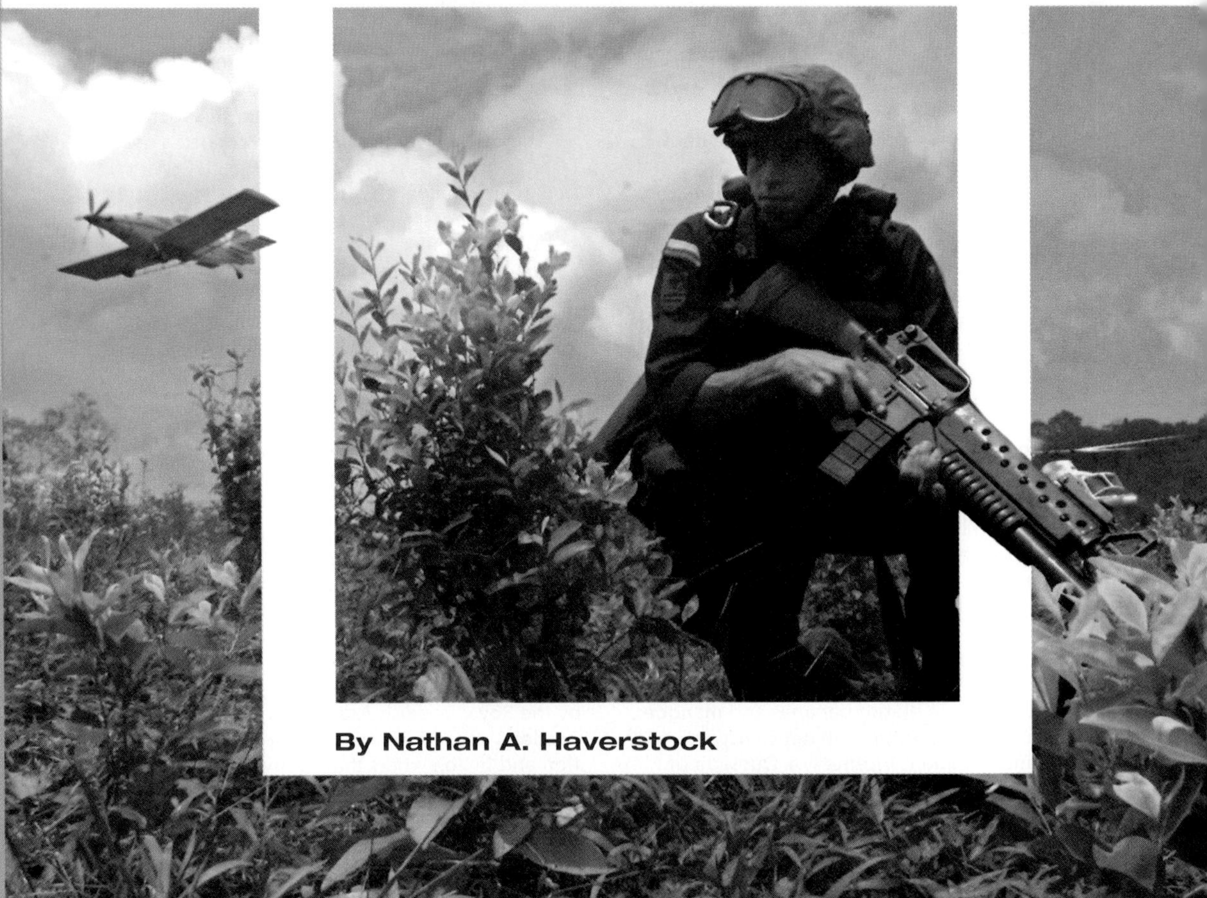

By Nathan A. Haverstock

Worldwide trafficking in cocaine continues to fuel terrorism, civil war, political corruption, and a host of other problems in Colombia.

The *Svesda Maru,* a fishing trawler, was sighted off Mexico's Pacific coast some 1,500 miles (2,400 kilometers) south of San Diego on May 3, 2001. But the trawler was carrying few fish and little fishing equipment. The United States Coast Guard boarded the *Svesda Maru* and discovered 13 tons (12 metric tons) of cocaine, worth an estimated $1.6 billion on the streets of U.S. cities. The seizure of the cocaine, which most probably originated in Colombia, was the largest maritime drug bust in U.S. history and part of a massive effort to stop the flow of cocaine from Colombia.

By 2001, the coca fields of Colombia had become the source of more than 80 percent of the cocaine that entered the United States—home to more than 5 million cocaine users and the main market for the drug.

In addition, Colombia supplied cocaine to an expanding international market in Europe and elsewhere. The seemingly insatiable appetite for cocaine in wealthy, industrialized nations fueled a host of social and economic problems in poverty-stricken Colombia, including a decades-long civil war, urban terrorism, murder, kidnappings, political corruption, and the flight of educated people from the country. These growing problems prompted the governments of both Colombia and the United States to dramatically step up their war on cocaine as the 21st century began.

The beginnings of trouble

Troubled times began in Colombia before cocaine was a problem. Historians trace the roots of Colombia's crisis to April 1948, when Jorge Eliecer Gaitan, the front runner for the presidency, was assassinated. His murder led to two decades of nationwide turmoil—called "La Violencia" (The Violence) by Colombians—and resulted in the deaths of some 200,000 people. The upheaval was especially vicious in rural areas, where stark social and economic inequalities had long been ignored by the government. In an attempt to end the violence, Colombia's military, led by Lieutenant General Gustavo Rojas Pinilla, seized power in 1953. However, Rojas's regime proved so brutal that his fellow officers removed him in response to public outrage in 1957.

In December 1957, Colombian voters overwhelmingly approved a plan mandating that the two major political parties—the Liberals and Conservatives—share power for 16 years. Alberto Lleras Camargo, the chief architect of the plan, became president in 1958 and headed the first in a series of National Front coalition governments. He launched ambitious programs of agricultural reform, education, and economic and social development. Lleras Camargo's efforts proved to be too little and too late. Civil unrest continued to smolder throughout Colombia.

In the mid-1960's, two revolutionary groups, the Revolutionary Armed Forces of Colombia (FARC) and the National Liberation Army (ELN), developed in remote, sparsely populated regions of the country. Both groups supported the establishment of a Communist government through revolution. For nearly two decades, FARC and ELN forces, acting like outlaw gangs, emerged periodically from jungle hideaways to seize temporary control of small isolated settlements and demand food and money. They also frequently resorted to kidnapping to raise ransom money to support their cause.

Drug trafficking becomes big business

In the early 1980's, the rebels discovered a much more lucrative source of income—drug trafficking. By that time, Colombia-based drug *cartels* (large groups of firms that dominate a business) were making huge profits by controlling the cultivation of coca shrubs; the processing of coca leaves into cocaine; and the sale and distribution of the illegal drug overseas, particularly in the United States. In the mid-1980's, the thriving cartel based in the city of Medellin offered to pay off Colombia's $13-billion foreign debt in exchange for *amnesty* (pardon) and a guarantee that their traffickers would not be turned over to the United States for trial on drug charges. The Colombian government rejected the cartel's offer.

As the drug business expanded, Colombian and U.S. law enforcement agencies worked closely together to hunt down several notorious drug kingpins, including Medellin cartel leader Pablo Escobar Gaviria, who was killed in 1993. In response to the crackdown, the besieged cartels mounted a campaign of urban terrorism, planting hundreds of bombs that killed or maimed innocent bystanders. To protect their drug trafficking operations, the cartels made huge payoffs to rebel groups, who, in turn, agreed to safeguard the traffickers and the coca fields. The rebels used the payoff money to buy arms, increase their forces, and carry out such terrorist acts as the assassinations of government officials.

U.S. involvement increases

In April 1986, U.S. President Ronald Reagan declared the flow of drugs across U.S. borders a national security threat and authorized the use of U.S. military forces in the war on drugs in Latin America. The decision to use the military in antidrug operations was prompted by a surge in the U.S. consumption of crack, an inexpensive form of cocaine that is smoked in a pipe. The widespread availability of crack sent drug-related crime and murder rates to record heights in cities across the United States in the mid-1980's. Shortly after the presidential directive, U.S. military aircraft began patrolling the skies over Central America and the Caribbean Sea to detect ships or aircraft that might be smuggling drugs. The aircraft reported sightings to law enforcement agencies, which moved in to seize the drugs and apprehend the traffickers.

Trafficking in cocaine, heroin, and other drugs soared to even greater heights in Colombia during the 1990's despite some U.S. and Colombian successes in seizing drugs and arresting drug kingpins. As Colombia's drug cartels became wealthier, they formed multinational links with organized crime elements in other countries. The cartels' vast resources enabled them to corrupt the whole fabric of Colombian society, including the government. In September 1994, Joe Toft, the newly retired chief of the U.S. Drug Enforcement Agency office in Bogota, the Colombian capital, described Colombia as a "narco-democracy," that is, a country controlled by the trade in narcotics. Toft said in a Colombian television interview, "I believe not a single Colombian institution has escaped infiltration by drug traffickers."

The author:
Nathan A. Haverstock is an affiliate scholar at Oberlin College in Oberlin, Ohio, and the author of several books about Latin America, including *South America—Then and Now: A Journalist's Memoir.*

Corruption discredits government

Hard evidence of Toft's allegation surfaced during the presidential term of Ernesto Samper Pizano, who served from 1994 to 1998. Colombians learned shortly after Samper's inauguration that their new president had knowingly accepted a campaign contribution of some $6 million from the Cali drug cartel. In response, the U.S. State Department revoked President Samper's visa to travel to the United States.

During Samper's administration, violence escalated throughout Colombia as the rebel armies found willing recruits for their struggle against the thoroughly discredited government. By the time Samper left office, rebel forces effectively controlled nearly half of Colombia's territory.

Negotiations fail to end violence

Samper's successor, President Andres Pastrana Arango, sought a compromise with the rebels shortly after taking office. In 1998, he opened peace talks with the government's main adversary, FARC leader Manuel Marulanda Velez, who commanded an armed force of 15,000 to 18,000 men and women. To pave the way for a negotiated settlement, Pastrana *ceded* (handed over) to FARC complete control of an area in southern Colombia that was equivalent in size to Switzerland. The zone, about 16,000 square miles (41,400 square kilometers), consisted of some 200 scattered settlements in areas where the government had never exerted much control. FARC, within the new territory, established its own system of governance and began to administer local courts, schools, and welfare programs. To the dismay of government officials who hoped the creation of the zone might lead to peace, FARC used the territory to continue building up its forces and to launch antigovernment attacks.

President Pastrana also opened peace negotiations with Colombia's second largest rebel force, the 5,000-member ELN. However, these negotiations, like the peace efforts with FARC, did little to curtail the violence. The ELN remained dedicated to ultranationalist principles similar to those of Cuban President Fidel Castro. ELN rebels attacked the installations of many foreign-owned businesses, which they blamed for Colombia's woes. In 1996, the British Petroleum Corporation (BP) signed a three-year agreement with Colombia's Ministry of Defense, which required elite government battalions to protect BP's 550-mile- (885-kilometer-) long oil pipeline in eastern Colombia. After the agreement expired, the ELN and FARC repeatedly bombed the BP pipeline, as well as a pipeline owned by Occidental Petroleum.

FARC and ELN rebels caused further turmoil by kidnapping employees of foreign oil companies and holding them for ransom. By 2000, Colombia led

Colombia's drug-linked history

Mid-1960's
Leftist revolutionaries form the Revolutionary Armed Forces of Colombia (FARC) and the National Liberation Army (ELN).

1984
Colombian police make the largest drug seizure in history—13.8 tons (12.5 metric tons) of cocaine.

1986
The popularity of crack cocaine drives U.S. cocaine imports up 500 percent over the amount imported in 1980.

United States President Ronald Reagan authorizes the use of the U.S. military in the war against drugs in Latin America.

1987
Carlos Lehder Rivas, a leader of the Medellin drug cartel, is arrested and extradited to the United States.

1993
Colombian police kill Medellin drug cartel leader Pablo Escobar Gaviria in a shootout.

1996
The United States revokes the visa of Colombian President Ernesto Samper Pizano, who accepted major campaign contributions from the Cali drug cartel.

1998
The Colombian government cedes a 16,000-square-mile (38,850-square-kilometer) zone in southern Colombia to FARC.

1999
Thirteen million people demonstrate throughout Colombia for peace.

2000
U.S. President Bill Clinton approves $1.3 billion, mostly in military aid, to help Colombia fight drugs under Plan Colombia.

2001
U.S. President George W. Bush proposes the Andean Regional Initiative, to provide more than $700 million in antidrug assistance to Colombia and six other nations in Latin America.

the world in kidnappings. In that year, 3,706 people were taken hostage. Many of the captured individuals were neither rich nor foreigners, but poor Colombians whom the rebels hoped to recruit into their ranks.

Paramilitary forces add to trouble

To counter the continuing threat from the revolutionary left, Colombia's wealthy aristocracy supported the formation in the late 1990's of the United Self-Defense Forces of Colombia (AUC), a right-wing paramilitary force that numbered about 8,000. The AUC quickly achieved notoriety by using "death squads" to murder Colombians suspected of being enemies of capitalism, including leaders of trade unions. Critics accused the AUC of working as a *surrogate* (substitute) for the Colombian army. In February 2001, Pastrana blamed the AUC for 70 percent of all the massacres in Colombia in 2000, which resulted in the deaths of more than 1,000 civilians. The U.S. State Department in September 2001 added the AUC to its list of terrorist organizations, a list that had long included the ELN and FARC.

In early 2001, the AUC blocked a government plan to cede control of a 1,500-square-mile (3,880-square-kilometer) zone in

Cocaine corridors

Cocaine enters the United States through three major routes from Colombia, Peru, and Bolivia, where it is grown and produced. Cocaine is also shipped to Europe.

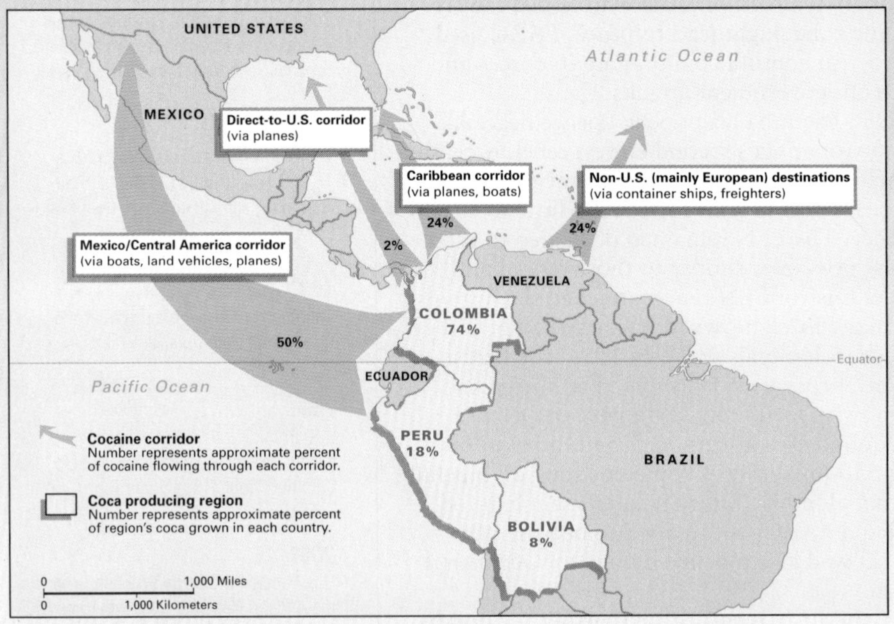

Based on 2000 data from the White House Office of National Drug Control Policy, the United States Department of State, and the United Nations Office for Drug Control and Crime Prevention.

north-central Colombia to the ELN. The zone was near Occidental Petroleum's oil installations, which the AUC and the Colombian military feared might fall into rebel hands. During several weeks of fighting, the AUC dislodged the ELN and its sympathizers from the region. This led to a breakdown in negotiations between the ELN and government.

By the late 1990's, Colombians, weary of decades of violence and turmoil, cried out for peace. On Oct. 24, 1999, 13 million Colombians took to the streets of cities and towns throughout the country to demonstrate for an end to the violence. By then, many other Colombians had lost all hope of peace and had fled

Growing coca

The amount of coca grown in Colombia has climbed steadily since the mid-1980's.

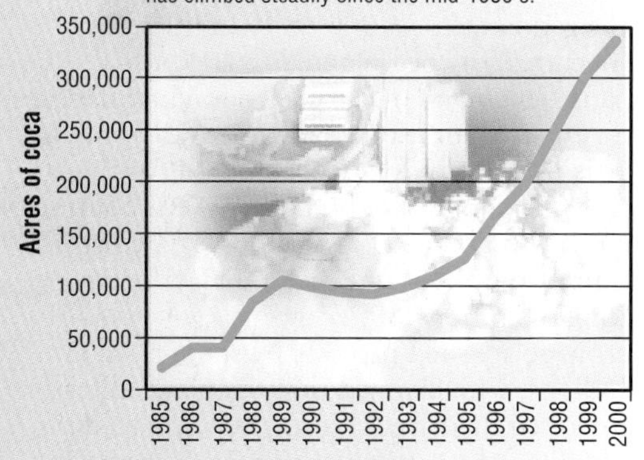

Cocaine users in the United States

The number of hardcore users of cocaine remained stable in the United States throughout the 1990's. The number of occasional users declined in the late 1990's.

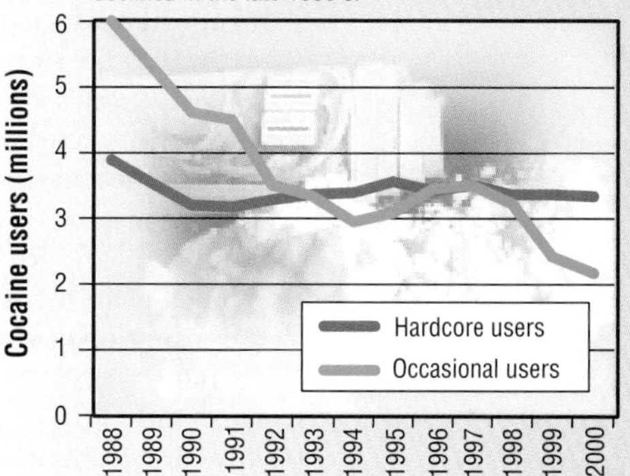

Age and cocaine use

The percentage of Americans aged 18 to 25 who had used cocaine increased sharply during the 1970's and then declined. However, the percentage of persons aged 26 and older who had used cocaine rose in the 1980's and continued to increase.

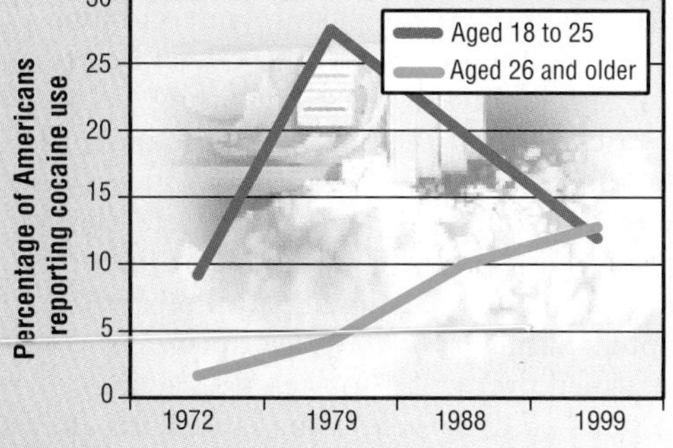

U.S. and European cocaine consumption

While cocaine consumption leveled off in the United States during the mid-1990's, it increased in certain other parts of the world, including Europe.

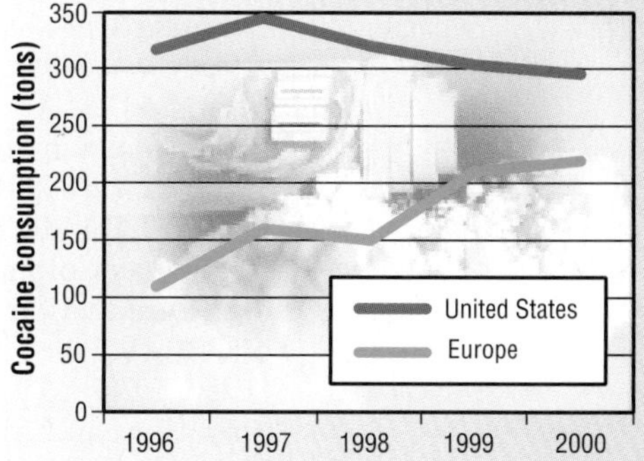

Sources: White House Office of National Drug Control Policy, United Nations Office for Drug Control and Crime Prevention.

the country. Between 1996 and early 2001, more than 1 million Colombians, including most of the nation's best educated citizens, left their homeland.

Plan Colombia goes into action

To cope with an increasingly desperate situation, President Pastrana's government developed Plan Colombia, a five-year, $7.5-billion program to promote social welfare and economic growth and eliminate drug trafficking. United States President Bill Clinton pledged $1.3 billion toward Plan Colombia in July 2000. Most of the U.S. money supported military efforts to eliminate the cultivation of coca. In December 2000, the first phase of a large-scale aerial offensive to eradicate the coca crop began in the Guamues Valley of Putumayo. Putumayo, a province on the Ecuadoran border, was then the source of about one-third of the Colombian crop. For six weeks, single-engine aircraft called crop dusters sprayed the fields with an *herbicide* (plant-killing compound). Other spraying operations followed. By August 2001, authorities estimated that they had sprayed 138,000 acres (55,900 hectares) of the estimated 336,000 to 402,000 acres (136,000 to 163,000 hectares) of coca planted in Colombia.

Although Colombians flew many of the coca-spraying planes, U.S. pilots working for DynCorporation of Reston, Virginia, also flew some missions. This private company began flying antinarcotics missions over Colombia in 1998 under a five-year contract with the U.S. government. On numerous occasions, DynCorp planes were hit by gunfire from rebel and paramilitary forces guarding drug trafficking operations.

The spraying of herbicide sparked protests by some farm families and Colombian Indians, who claimed that the plant killer threatened their health, killed their legal crops, and damaged the environment. In March 2001, the governors of four Colombian provinces exposed to the herbicide traveled to Washington, D.C., to demand an end to the spraying. The U.S. government maintained that the spraying was safe.

U.S. military deeply entangled

The U.S.-Colombian antidrug effort was headquartered at the Larandia army base, situated amid rolling pastureland and jungle-covered hills in southern Colombia. Some 100 Green Berets from the U.S. Army's 7th Special Forces began schooling Colombian soldiers in antinarcotics work at the Larandia base in April 1999. In May 2001, a number of senior U.S. military officers were at Larandia to see 698 Colombian soldiers complete their training as Colombia's third elite antidrug battalion. At the time of the graduation ceremony, these U.S.-trained battalions relied on 33 U.S. Huey helicopters dating from the Vietnam War (1957-1975) to provide armed protection for aerial spraying operations and conduct raids on drug-processing labs. Later in 2001, the United States supplied the battalions with 16 Blackhawk helicopters, which are much larger and more powerful than the Huey helicopters. The Blackhawks enabled the Colom-

Colombians (above) wait outside the U.S. embassy in the capital, Bogota, to apply for visas to travel to the United States in late 2000. More than 1 million Colombians have fled their homeland since 1996.
In May 2001, a truck filled with farmworkers (left), who had been kidnapped by paramilitary forces, rolls past government soldiers. Militia and rebel forces kidnapped thousands of Colombians in 2000 and 2001.

bian antidrug units to range farther and strike several targets at the same time.

In support of the war on drugs in Colombia, the United States was modernizing a military airfield in northern Ecuador, near the Colombian border, in 2001. The facility was to accommodate surveillance jets and house 150 to 250 U.S. military personnel when fully operational in 2002. El Salvador and Honduras also approved U.S. plans to prepare air bases for fighting drug trafficking.

Fears of a widening conflict

As the elements of the U.S. antidrug strategy were put in place in Latin America, some U.S. political leaders warned that the United States was being drawn into another Vietnam. They noted that Colombia—like Vietnam during the 1960's—was in the throes of a hard-to-solve, many-sided civil war in which friends and foes were hard to tell apart.

A villager walks through a field of coca plants that have been destroyed by the aerial spraying of an *herbicide* (plant-killing compound) in early 2001 (right). Colombian and U.S. forces began a major aerial offensive to eradicate coca in December 2000.

In 1998, Colombian President Andres Pastrana gave the Revolutionary Armed Forces of Colombia (FARC), Colombia's largest rebel group, control of an area in southern Colombia the size of Switzerland (below). Negotiations to grant the National Liberation Army (ELN), a smaller rebel group, its own zone in northern Colombia collapsed in 2001.

Worries of a growing conflict were shared by some of Colombia's neighbors. Officials in Bolivia and Peru expressed concern that the antidrug campaign in Colombia might lead to a resurgence in coca production in their countries, both of which had recently made large cuts in coca cultivation through stricter law enforcement and by providing farmers with financial incentives to grow alternative crops. In another troubling development, Colombian drug traffickers and leftist rebels were reportedly forging alliances with political dissidents in Ecuador and Venezuela. This put at risk the safe flow of oil from the region—a risk that posed a threat to U.S. national security.

In April 2001, U.S. President George W. Bush addressed some of these concerns by proposing the Andean Regional Initiative. The proposal, costing more than $700 million, was designed to help Colombia, Bolivia, Peru, Ecuador, Venezuela, Brazil, and Panama cope with disruptions caused by the drug offensive in Colombia. The initiative included funds for strengthening borders and promoting the cultivation of legal drugs.

Cocaine problem spreads

Support for the U.S.-Colombian drug effort increased in Latin America and Europe in 2000 and 2001 as many nations began to realize that they too had cocaine problems. An estimated 900,000 Brazilians, for example, used cocaine in 2001, according to a United Nations report.

U.S. special forces help train Colombian antidrug battalions at the Larandia army base in Colombia in May 2001. The training was part of Plan Colombia, a joint U.S.-Colombian program to wipe out drugs and promote social welfare and economic growth in Colombia.

Brazilian officials noted that the growing availability of crack was leading to an upsurge in urban crime, similar to what occurred in the United States during the 1980's. Statistics showing increasing cocaine consumption in Europe helped persuade the European Union (EU) to pledge more than $290 million to Plan Colombia. According to Europol, the EU's police agency, about 220 tons (200 metric tons) of cocaine were shipped from South America to Europe in 2000. This was double the amount entering Europe in 1996 and approached the approximately 300 tons (272 metric tons) of cocaine consumed in the United States in 2000.

National elections scheduled for May 2002 were expected to serve as a referendum on how Colombians felt about Plan Colombia's progress and the increasing U.S. presence in their country. Regardless of the poll results, Colombia's efforts to deal with the tragedies of drug trafficking, civil war, terrorism, and corruption were sure to continue. Meanwhile, a reduction in the demand for cocaine by the rest of the world—especially the United States—would go a long way toward helping Colombia solve these problems.

Additional reading:

Safford, Frank, and Palacios, Marco. *Colombia: Fragmented Land, Divided Society.* Oxford University Press, 2001.

Sanchez G., Gonzalo, and Meertens, Donny. *Bandits, Peasants, and Politics: The Case of "La Violencia" in Colombia.* University of Texas Press, 2001.

Lebanon. Demands by the United States government that Lebanese authorities prosecute or *extradite* (turn over) alleged terrorists living in Lebanon raised sensitive political issues in 2001. Lebanese officials denounced the terrorist attacks on the United States on September 11 but urged U.S. officials to distinguish between terrorists and "freedom fighters."

Hezbollah. In October, the U.S. State Department included Lebanon's Shiite Muslim Hezbollah (The Party of God) on a list of foreign terrorist organizations. The Lebanese government, however, resisted U.S. pressure to freeze the assets of the pro-Iranian Hezbollah, which held 12 seats in the 128-member Lebanese parliament. Hezbollah gained enormous popularity in 2000 after the guerrilla resistance movement it spearheaded successfully pressured Israel to withdraw troops from southern Lebanon, land Israeli forces had occupied since 1978. During 2001, Hezbollah-backed guerrillas continued their campaign to force Israeli troops to withdraw from Shebaa Farms, the last contested border region claimed by both Lebanon and Israel.

Most-wanted terrorists. U.S. officials announced in October the creation of a most-wanted-terrorists list, which included the names of three Lebanese suspects. A U.S. court had indicted the Lebanese men in 1985 on charges related to the hijacking of TWA Flight 847, in which a U.S. Navy diver was murdered. The United States contended that one of the men had also been responsible for the 1983 bombing of the U.S. Marine Corps barracks in Beirut, Lebanon's capital.

Lebanese authorities refused to apprehend the alleged terrorists because Lebanese law granted *amnesty* (pardon) for any crimes committed during the country's 1975-1990 civil war. However, Lebanese officials reportedly agreed to share intelligence information with the United States about terrorists linked to Osama bin Laden, the Saudi-born millionaire accused of orchestrating the September 2001 attacks. The United States listed Asbat al-Ansar, an organization active in Palestinian refugee camps in Lebanon, as a group allied with bin Laden.

Fatwa. Sheikh Mohammad Fadlallah, the spiritual leader of Lebanon's Shiite Muslims, said in September that he was "horrified" by the terrorist attacks on the United States. Nonetheless, he issued a *fatwa* (religious decree) prohibiting Muslims from giving any help to the United States "against any Muslim state or entity." Fadlallah also warned that the U.S. military response to the attacks would lead to "an increase in terrorism worldwide." ☐ Christine Helms

See also **Israel; Middle East; Syria; Terrorism; Terrorism: A Special Feature,** p. 38.

Lesotho. See **Africa.**

Library. The United States Senate voted in July 2001 to confirm President George W. Bush's nominee, Robert S. Martin, professor and interim director of the Texas Woman's University School of Library and Information Studies, as director of the Institute of Museum and Library Services (IMLS). An independent federal agency based in Washington, D.C., the IMLS administers federal library and museum programs.

The Campaign for America's Libraries. First Lady Laura Bush celebrated National Library Week in April 2001 by inaugurating "@ your library, The Campaign for America's Libraries," a five-year educational initiative sponsored by the American Library Association (ALA). The ALA planned to use the "@ your library" campaign to increase public awareness of libraries through local library programs and alliances with the media, businesses, and other organizations. During National Library Week, libraries in all 50 U.S. states introduced the effort through events that showcased new and traditional library services.

The Children's Internet Protection Act, which mandated that libraries receiving federal funding must equip public computers with Internet filters, went into effect in April 2001. Internet filters are software programs designed to prevent people from viewing Web sites with content that is considered objectionable, such as pornography. Libraries were expected to install the necessary software by 2003 or risk the loss of federal funding. The ALA and the American Civil Liberties Union filed suit in federal court against the United States in March 2001, challenging the constitutionality of the law on the grounds that it violated First Amendment guarantees of free speech. The case was scheduled to proceed to trial in February 2002. In October 2001, the San Francisco Board of Supervisors voted unanimously to bar the use of filters on city library computers accessed by adults and teen-agers.

Library of Congress news. The only known surviving copy of a 1507 map that was the first to designate the New World as "America" was purchased by the Library of Congress (LC) in July 2001. The LC agreed to pay $10 million for the map, the largest sum it had ever paid for a single item.

In August 2001, U.S. State Department spokesman Richard Boucher announced that former Secretary of State Henry Kissinger had agreed to give the department access to 10,000 pages of transcripts that were being held at the LC. The transcripts were of telephone conversations Kissinger had while secretary of state between 1973 and 1976. Kissinger had given copies of the transcripts to the LC in 1976, stipulating that the transcripts could not be made public until five years after his death. Boucher said that the transcripts would be made available to the public through Freedom of Information Act requests after personal information was removed from them.

The Bibliotecha Alexandrina in Alexandria, Egypt, opened in October 2001 for a trial period, under the directorship of Ismail Serageldin, former vice president of the World Bank. The new library was designed as a reconstruction of the ancient world's most famous library, which was founded in the 330's B.C. by Alexander the Great. Egyptian public libraries in 2001 were subject to raids by government censors, who had been urged by Egyptian President Hosni Mubarak to remove works deemed offensive to Islam. A senior official at the Bibliotecha Alexandrina said he did not expect materials there to be censored, since the library was funded by international organizations, including UNESCO, a United Nations agency. The library's official opening was scheduled for April 2002.

Library practices examined. Nicholson Baker's *Double Fold: Libraries and the Assault on Paper*, published in spring 2001, questioned the viability of digital and microfilm storage and criticized library policies that had resulted in the destruction of large quantities of printed materials. The book provoked controversy and debate in the library community. ☐ Nancy R. John

See also **Literature for children; Literature, American; Literature, world**.

Libya. Libyan leader Muammar Muhammad al-Qadhafi, who had been shunned during most of the 1990's as a supporter of terrorism, labeled the Sept. 11, 2001, terrorist attacks on the United States "horrifying." Prior to the attacks, Qadhafi had announced that he wished to normalize Libya's relations with the United States.

International outreach. Qadhafi made several moves in 2001 to improve Libya's relations with other countries. In January, France praised Libya for participating in a conference in Portugal in which Western Mediterranean nations pledged to boost trade between rich and poor countries. In October, Qadhafi secured the release of a Chinese hostage held by Muslim rebels in the Philippines by agreeing to provide humanitarian aid to the rebels. Qadhafi also provided drought relief to Kenya and pledged to relieve fuel shortages in Ghana and Zimbabwe in 2001.

Pan Am bombing trial. A Scottish court in the Netherlands convicted Libyan intelligence officer Abdelbaset Ali Mohmed al-Megrahi in January for his role in the 1988 bombing of Pan Am Flight 103, which resulted in the deaths of 270 people. The court acquitted a co-defendant, Lamen Khalifa Fhimah, who was a Libyan airlines manager. In August 2001, the court granted Megrahi the right to appeal the sentence.

United Nations sanctions, which were imposed on Libya in 1992 as punishment for its alleged role in the 1988 bombing, had been temporarily suspended in 1999 after Qadhafi turned over the two Libyans for trial. The sanctions were not expected to be permanently lifted until Megrahi's case was settled.

Berlin disco trial. In November 2001, a German court convicted a former Libyan diplomat and three other individuals in the 1986 bombing of a West Berlin disco. The bombing killed two U.S. soldiers and a Turkish woman. The court ruled that Libya bore "a considerable portion of the responsibility for the attack," but the judge said the prosecution failed to prove that Qadhafi ordered the bombing.

The U.S. Congress in August 2001 extended for five years the Iran-Libya Sanctions Act, a law passed in 1996 to deter foreign investment in nations accused of sponsoring terrorism. The extension reduced the amount the United States would allow a foreign company to annually invest in Libya—from $40 million to $20 million—before imposing sanctions against the company. However, the law allowed the U.S. president to waive the sanctions. ☐ Christine Helms

See also **Africa; Middle East; Netherlands; Terrorism; Terrorism: A Special Feature,** p. 38.

Liechtenstein. See **Europe**.

Literature, American. An author's scorn for television publicity for his new book widened the rift between publishing and electronic media in 2001. Jonathan Franzen became embroiled in controversy after the Oprah Winfrey book club chose his highly praised novel *The Corrections* as one of its selections.

The book, which won the National Book Award for fiction in November, tells the story of the Lambert family as Enid, the matriarch, tries to bring everyone together for a traditional Midwestern Christmas. Enid is in denial about her husband's worsening Parkinson disease and the problems of her three children. *The Corrections,* which covers 50 years of the family's history, ruthlessly dissects familial relationships while commenting on world events.

Although *The Corrections* debuted on many best-sellers' lists, its selection by Winfrey's book club in September was expected to raise its profile even higher. Franzen, however, objected to having a book club sticker placed on the novel's cover. He contended that the sticker might label his work as a woman's book, making men hesitant to read it. Franzen also claimed that appearing on Winfrey's television talk show would be out of keeping with his place in "the high-art literary tradition."

The controversy divided the publishing

world, with many writers and media commentators ridiculing Franzen's statements. Winfrey withdrew the invitation to Franzen to appear on her show, offered to all authors of book club selections.

Other nominees. In addition to *The Corrections,* four other books were nominated for the 2001 National Book Award for fiction. Jennifer Egan's second novel, *Look at Me,* tells parallel stories of two women from Rockford, Illinois—a fashion model with a shattered face and a plain, unhappy teen-ager having an affair with a high-school teacher. Egan uses the fashion world, the Internet, and teen-age traumas to examine questions of identity in an image-driven age. In *Among the Missing,* a collection of short stories, Dan Chaon focuses on the everyday existence of people living on the fringes of society.

Louise Erdrich's *The Last Report on the Miracles at Little No Horse* is her sixth novel to deal with the life of the Ojibwa in North Dakota. It tells the story of a benevolent priest with a secret, who is debating his involvement in an investigation of a nun's possible sainthood. Susan Straight's *Highwire Moon* opens with a young Mexican immigrant losing her daughter as she is being deported from the United States. The novel relates the mother's and daughter's search for each other 15 years later.

Notable novels. Walter Kirn's *Up in the Air* tells the story of Ryan Bingham, a corporate consultant who tries to collect 1 million frequent flier miles before losing his job. Kirn uses Bingham's quest to examine corporate culture. Colson Whitehead's *John Henry Days* is a complex novel that lyrically retells the story of American folk hero John Henry and contrasts his life with that of a modern African American journalist.

Richard Russo's *Empire Falls* is a panoramic and compassionate portrait of a failing mill town in Maine, leavened by Russo's marvelous comedy. *The Body Artist,* Don DeLillo's first work since his 1997 epic bestseller *Underworld*, is a haunting and spare ghost story set mostly in the mind of a young woman artist.

Short story collections. Eighty-six-year-old Saul Bellow, renowned for his novels, published a selection of his shorter fiction in 2001. *Collected Stories* displays the author's mastery of the short form. *The Collected Stories of Richard Yates* presents this accomplished and grim writer's exploration of his favorite themes—the loneliness and bitterness of modern life. Yates, who died in 1992, ranks as one of the strongest influences on contemporary American short-story writing.

Jonathan Franzen's *The Corrections,* winner of the 2001 National Book Award for fiction, is an exploration of relationships in a dysfunctional family. Franzen's reluctance to allow the novel to be associated with Oprah Winfrey's book club sparked a heated public controversy.

Don Lee's debut collection, *Yellow*, focuses on the joys and fears of Asian Americans attempting to fit into U.S. society in a California town. The biting, topical stories of Ann Beattie's *Perfect Recall* depict American families confronting long-denied truths and facing the challenges of sudden success or sudden failure.

The National Book Award in nonfiction went to Andrew Solomon's *The Noonday Demon: An Atlas of Depression*. In this cultural study, Solomon presents a factual description of depression, its history, treatments, and imaginative responses to it, while narrating his own experiences with the disorder.

Other Book Award nominees included Marie Arana's memoir about learning to bridge the gulf between her father's aristocratic Peruvian family and her mother's woodsy Wyoming family, *American Chica: Two Worlds, One Childhood*; David James Duncan's lovesong to Montana's Snake River and examination of Northwestern ecological practices, *My Story As Told By Water*; Nina Bernstein's account of a landmark foster care case, *The Lost Children of Wilder: The Epic Struggle to Change Foster Care;* and Jan Tomasz Gross's frightening story of atrocities by ordinary Poles during the Holocaust, *Neighbors: The Destruction of the Jewish Community of Jedwabne, Poland.*

Notable biographies appeared in abundance in 2001. David McCullough's surprise best seller of the summer, *John Adams*, is a comprehensive account of the second U.S. president, whose reputation had grown in recent years. Edmund Morris's *Theodore Rex* is the second volume in his biography of Theodore Roosevelt. It narrates Roosevelt's presidency and manages to draw a full portrait of a complex and active man.

Jean Edward Smith's *Grant* reevaluates Ulysses S. Grant's failures and successes as a soldier, general, and U.S. president. It challenges the prevalent historical judgment that Grant's presidency was a failure. Gary Giddins's *Bing Crosby: A Pocketful of Dreams*, the first of two volumes, is a nuanced portrait of the famed singer and of a musical era.

Two major literary biographies were published in 2001—Nancy Milford's *Oh, Savage Beauty: The Life of Edna St. Vincent Millay* and Alfred Habegger's *My Wars Are Laid Away in Books: The Life of Emily Dickinson*. Milford narrates the life of one of the most scandalous and successful poets in American history, while Habegger presents a careful look at how Dickinson's quiet life and adventurous poetry fit together.

Other nonfiction books that made a splash in 2001 were Laura Hillenbrand's *Seabiscuit: An American Legend;* Louis Menand's *The Metaphysical Club*; and Nicholson Baker's *Double Fold: Libraries and the Assault on Paper.* Hillenbrand's sparkling chronicle of the champion race horse's career in the 1930's and 1940's became one of the first horse racing books to find a national audience. *The Metaphysical Club* is a history of the origin of the philosophical school of pragmatism and a luminous portrait of American intellectual life in the late 1800's. *Double Fold* is Baker's impassioned attack on the way libraries have adapted to the electronic world. Its accusation that librarians are betraying their calling caused much controversy.

Authors. Arthur Miller received the National Book Foundation's 2001 Medal for Distinguished Contribution to American Literature. His plays, novels, essays, and screenplays are a running social commentary on the plight of the average American in the second half of the 20th century.

American literature lost one of its most distinctive and distinguished voices in July with the death of Eudora Welty at the age of 92. Her work, especially her short stories, immersed readers in the Southern mindset.

☐ Robert Messenger

See also **Literature for children; Poetry.**

Literature, world. Vidiadhar Surajprasad (V. S.) Naipaul, a British citizen who was born in Trinidad in 1932, won the 2001 Nobel Prize for literature. The Swedish Nobel Academy praised him "for having united perceptive narrative and incorruptible scrutiny in works that compel us to see the presence of suppressed histories." Naipaul, whose parents were emigrants from East India, often wrote about the conflict between colony and empire, the postcolonial world, and the cultural confusion of the Third World. These themes personally affected the author, who was raised in Trinidad, educated at Oxford University in England as a scholarship student, and knighted by Queen Elizabeth II in 1990.

Frequently representing the role of outsider in both worlds, he wrote numerous short stories and novels on the subject but is also known for travel writing, memoirs, and essays. His best-known novels included *A House for Mr. Biswas* (1961), believed to be about the author's father; *A Bend in the River* (1979), which deals with modern Africa and is often compared with Joseph Conrad's *Heart of Darkness* (1902); and *The Enigma of Arrival* (1987), which is commonly considered autobiographical, about an Indian writer born in Trinidad and educated at Oxford who travels extensively and settles in a cottage on the grounds of a decayed manor house in Wiltshire, England. His novel *Half a Life,* about an Indian expatriate who is unable to come to terms with himself, was published in 2001.

Chinese literature. The clash of ruler and ruled was a theme that ran through Chinese literature in 2001. Chinese writer Wei Hui's 1999 novel *Shanghai Baby,* translated into English in 2001, is a tale of Coco, a beautiful Shanghai novelist involved with wild experiments with sex and drugs. The book was banned in China, where copies were burned by the authorities. Expatriates of China focused on the repressive Chinese government in their fiction in 2001. Dai Sijie's *Balzac and the Little Chinese Seamstress,* first written in French and published in France in 2000, also was translated into English in 2001. It is a fabulist depiction of the violence of China's Cultural Revolution, which occurred between 1966 and 1976. In the novel, two city youths sent to a mountain village to be reeducated by working in mines are "liberated" by the discovery of a hidden cache of forbidden foreign novels. *Lili: A Novel of Tiananmen,* published in 2001, was Annie Wang's first novel written in English. It explores the prodemocracy uprising of 1989 in China. Geling Yan, who has lived in the United States since 1989, published an English translation of her novel *The Lost Daughter of Happiness,* originally written in Chinese, in April 2001. It is the story of a famous Chinese prostitute named Fusang, who is taken from south China to San Francisco in the 1800's.

The United Kingdom, Ireland, and Canada. *White Teeth* by the Jamaican-British author Zadie Smith won the Whitbread Best First Novel Prize in January 2001. The 24-year-old Smith fashioned a hyperkinetic narrative about the lives of three families in contemporary London. Matthew Neale's *English Passengers* won the Whitbread Best Book of the Year Award, the top honor of the prestigious annual awards for works published in the United Kingdom and Ireland. The story, which had already received the Whitbread Best Novel Award, tells of a vicar's hunt for the Garden of Eden in the 1850's in Tasmania.

Literary heavyweight Peter Carey won the 2001 Booker Prize for Fiction for his novel *True History of the Kelly Gang.* (The Booker Prize recognizes writers from the Commonwealth and other former British colonies.) The story was written in the style of a confession in letters to an estranged daughter by Australian outlaw Ned Kelly. The attention generated by the award increased the public's already strong interest in Kelly—Australia's most famous bushranger—and in Carey's archival material. Historians disagreed about whether Kelly was a villain or a victim. Carey, who had already won a Booker Prize in 1988 for his novel *Oscar and Lucinda,* became only the second author to win the prize twice. Other nominees on the 2001 short list for the prize were Ian McEwan for *Atonement*; Rachel Seiffert for *The Dark Room;* Ali Smith for *Hotel World*; Andrew Miller for *Oxygen;* and David Mitchell for *Number9dream.* Other well-received books by British writers in 2001 included *How to Be Good* by Nick Hornby; *On Green Dolphin Street* by Sebastian Faulks; and *Landor's Tower* by Iain Sinclair. British-Indian author Salman Rushdie released *Fury* in September. Divided into three parts, the novel has as its hero a brilliant man exiled from his homeland, lonely but in search of solitude and chased by fury. Also in 2001, Canadian luminary Alice Munro offered another book of her stories, *Hateship, Friendship, Courtship, Loveship, Marriage.*

Continental writers. Russian-born writer Andrei Makine, who lives in France, published an English translation of *Requiem for a Lost Empire* in 2001. Makine's novel, originally written in French, is about the history of Russia. Popular German author Bernhard Schlink, best known for *The Reader* (1997), released an English translation of his book of stories *Flights of Love* in October 2001. In these stories, Schlink addresses difficult emotional, political, and moral situations without pomposity. Ger-

Almost any job can lead to the White House. Presidents have been lawyers, teachers, farmers, sailors, engineers, surveyors, mayors, governors, congressmen, senators, and ambassadors. (Harry Truman owned a men's shop. Andrew Johnson was a tailor. Ronald Reagan was a movie actor!)

man-British author W. G. Sebald published an English translation of his fourth novel, *Austerlitz*, in 2001. Written in four segments, it is a fictional meditation on architecture and the displacing effects of war.

African literature. Two white South African writers offered political and fictional twists on colony and empire in 2001. Nadine Gordimer published *The Pickup*, a novel about a white South African woman who falls in love with an illegal immigrant, an Arab auto mechanic, and returns with him to his native country, where the roles of power are reversed. In September, novelist and two-time Booker Prize winner J. M. Coetzee published *Stranger Shores*, a collection of 29 essays on writers, writing, photography, and other subjects. Coetzee's essays ranged from the general—as in "What Is a Classic?"—to numerous pieces on individual writers, especially contemporary ones.

Latin American literature. Chilean-born writer Isabel Allende published an English translation of *Portrait in Sepia* in October 2001. The novel rounded out her trilogy that began with *House of the Spirits* (1987) and continued with *Daughter of Fortune* (1999). Peruvian politician and novelist Mario Vargas Llosa's *The Feast of the Goat*, about the last days of Rafael Trujillo's regime in the Dominican Republic, was published in an English translation in November 2001. Also in translation, *Our Lady of the Circus*, by Mexican writer David Toscana, appeared in September. It tells the story of a group of circus performers who break away from their troupe to settle in an abandoned town and lead ordinary lives. The tale ends on a note of bitter irony when the circus they have left reappears.

Translations of past writers. Reginald Gibbons offered *Bakkhai*, a new translation of ancient Greek dramatist Euripides' play *Bacchae*. *Bakkhai* premiered at the University of Texas at Dallas in February 2001. *The Complete Works of Isaac Babel*, edited by Babel's daughter Nathalie, with translations by Peter Constantine and an introduction by Cynthia Ozick, was published in November 2001. Babel, a Jewish writer from Odessa, Ukraine, was executed at age 46 by the Soviets. Hungarian author Sandor Marai's *Embers*, published in 1942, was made available in September 2001 in English in a translation by Carol Brown Janeway from an earlier German translation of the original Hungarian. The story, set on a vast estate, peaks with the confrontation of two people who had been involved in an adulterous triangle for 40 years. ☐ Brian Bouldrey

See also **Literature, American; Literature for children; Nobel Prizes; Poetry.**

Illustrator David Small won the 2001 Caldecott Medal for his caricatures of U.S. presidents in *So You Want to Be President?*—a fun look at the history of the presidency.

Literature for children.

Fantasies, picture books, and nonfiction were especially popular with young readers in 2001. Some of the outstanding books of 2001 included the following:

Picture books. *The Spider Weaver: A Legend of Kente Cloth* by Margaret Musgrove, illustrated by Julia Cairns (Blue Sky/Scholastic). Two Ashanti weavers find an extraordinary web and learn how to weave an intricately designed cloth from its maker. Ages 4 to 8.

The Three Pigs by David Wiesner (Clarion). The craziness begins when the wolf huffs and puffs and blows the first little pig right out of the story frame. All ages.

The Singing Hat by Tohby Riddle (Farrar Straus Giroux). When Colin Jenkins falls asleep under a tree, he wakes with a bird in a nest on his head. His decision not to disturb the bird triggers many complications. Ages 4 to 8.

The Journey by Sarah Stewart, illustrated by David Small (Farrar Straus Giroux). The diary of a young Amish girl's visit to a big city reveals her impressions against a backdrop of loving memories of her Amish home. Ages 5 to 8.

Milo's Hat Trick by Jon Agee (MDC/Hyperion). Milo goes in search of a rabbit when he gets one last chance to fix his horrible magician's act. Ages 5 to 8.

Baloney (Henry P.) by Jon Scieszka, illustrated by Lane Smith (Viking). A young alien who is late for school uses many different languages to concoct a far-out excuse about a trip through the galaxy. All ages.

Larky Mavis by Brock Cole (Farrar Straus Giroux). Old Mavis finds a peanut with a tiny, odd baby inside, which villagers want to take away until something magical happens. Ages 4 to 8.

The School Trip by Tjibbe Veldkamp, illustrated by Philip Hopman (Front Street/Lemniscaat). Davy, a bit hesitant about going to school, secretly builds his own school on wheels. All ages.

Petite Rouge: A Cajun Red Riding Hood by Mike Artell, illustrated by Jim Harris (Dial). A duck named Petite Rouge and her cat outsmart a big, bad alligator in this tale told in Cajun dialect verse. Ages 5 and up.

The Tin Forest by Helen Ward, illustrated by Wayne Anderson (Dutton). An old man living beside a junkyard dreams of a lush forest, which he slowly recreates out of tin. All ages.

Zigazak! A Magical Hanukkah Night by Eric A. Kimmel, illustrated by Jon Goodell (Doubleday). Only a wise rabbi can put things right when two devils wreak havoc on the village of Brisk during Hanukkah. Ages 5 to 8.

Fiction. *Witness* by Karen Hesse (Scholastic). Eleven narrators describe in free verse real events in a small Vermont town in 1924 when the townspeople fall under the influence of the Ku Klux Klan. Ages 7 to 11.

Dancing in Cadillac Light by Kimberly Willis Holt (Putnam). The lives of Jaynelle and her family in a small town in Texas in 1968 are changed forever when their widowed Grandpap moves in. Ages 9 to 12.

Moonpie and Ivy by Barbara O'Connor (Farrar Straus Giroux). Twelve-year-old Pearl struggles to fit in after her mom deserts her at her Aunt Ivy's farmhouse in Georgia. Ages 12 and up.

Benno's Bear by N. F. Zucker (Dutton). Eleven-year-old pickpocket Benno's mistake lands his father in jail and the boy's beloved dancing bear in a zoo. Ages 10 and up.

Fair Weather by Richard Peck (Dial). Three farm children and their irrepressible grandfather accept rich Aunt Euterpe's invitation to attend the World's Columbian Exposition in Chicago in 1893. Ages 10 and up.

The Land by Mildred D. Taylor (Phyllis Fogelman/Penguin Putnam). Paul-Edward Logan, son of a white plantation-owner father and a black slave mother, struggles to be independent and own his own land in a prequel to *Roll of Thunder, Hear My Cry.* Ages 12 and up.

Coram Boy by Jamila Gavin (Farrar Straus Giroux). Simple-minded Meshak saves an infant from Meshak's father, a man who disposes of orphan children in England in the 1700's. *Coram Boy* was named British 2000 Whitbread Children's Book of the Year. Ages 12 and up.

Fantasy. *Heaven Eyes* by David Almond (Delacorte). In this surreal, haunting story, three orphans run away on a raft and land in the Black Midden, an area of old, abandoned warehouses. Ages 10 and up.

The Girl on Evangeline Beach by Anne Carter (Stoddart Kids). Sixteen-year-old Michael travels back in time to 1755 to aid Marie, an Acadian girl, without changing history. Ages 12 and up.

The Gawgon and The Boy by Lloyd Alexander (Dutton). David (the boy), in poor health, is tutored by his difficult Aunt Annie who is full of surprises. Ages 9 to 12.

Treasure at the Heart of the Tanglewood by Meredith Ann Pierce (Viking). The arrival of a knight in search of treasure changes everything for Brown Hannah, who brews a special tea from flowers she grows in her hair. Ages 12 and up.

Arthur: The Seeing Stone by Kevin Crossley-Holland (Arthur A. Levine/Scholastic). The life of a young English boy in the 1100's parallels that of his namesake, the famous King Arthur, in Book I of a planned trilogy. Ages 12 and up.

Poetry. *Pocketful of Poems* by Nikki Grimes, illustrated by Javaka Steptoe (Clarion). Words in Tiana's pocket inspire poems that capture love for the power of words. All ages.

Carver: A Life in Poems by Marilyn Nelson (Front Street). Highlights of the life of George Washington Carver are described in poems and historical photos. Ages 10 and up.

Some from the Moon Some from the Sun: Poems and Songs for Everyone by Margot Zemach (Farrar Straus Giroux). Fine watercolors by a Caldecott-winning illustrator add new luster to nursery rhymes. All ages.

Big, Bad and a Little Bit Scary: Poems that Bite Back by Wade Zahares (Viking). Stunning illustrations accompany a collection of humorous and dramatic animal poems by Ogden Nash, Eve Merriam, and others. Ages 5 and up.

Weave Little Stars into My Sleep: Native American Lullabies selected by Neil Philip, with photographs by Edward S. Curtis (Clarion). Curtis's century-old photographs of Native Americans bring songs from a variety of native peoples to life. All ages.

Informational books. *Spiders and Their Web Sites* by Margery Facklam, illustrated by Alan Male (Little, Brown). Chilling illustrations accompany detailed information about spiders. All ages.

What's That Bug? by Nan Froman, illustrated

by Julian Mulock (Little, Brown). Striking illustrations accompany engaging descriptions of insect families. Ages 8 to 12.

The Kid Who Invented the Trampoline: More Surprising Stories about Inventions by Don L. Wulffson (Dutton). Fifty fascinating stories of inventions, including Graham crackers, Post-it Notes, false teeth, parking meters, and disposable diapers. Ages 8 and up.

In the Days of the Vaqueros: America's First True Cowboys by Russell Freedman (Clarion). How Native Mexican riders of the 1500's passed their skills along to future generations, including the American cowboy. Ages 10 and up.

The Dinosaurs of Waterhouse Hawkins by Barbara Kerley, illustrated by Brian Selznick (Scholastic). Intricate drawings illustrate the story of Hawkins, a British artist of the 1800's who was the first to sketch and build huge models of dinosaurs. All ages.

The 2001 Newbery Medal was awarded to Richard Peck for *A Year Down Yonder.* The award is given by the American Library Association (ALA) for "the most distinguished contribution to children's literature" published the previous year. The ALA's Caldecott Medal for "the most distinguished American picture book" was awarded to David Small for *So You Want to Be President?* ☐ Marilyn Fain Apseloff

Los Angeles. James K. Hahn defeated fellow Democrat Antonio Villaraigosa in a runoff election for mayor on June 5, 2001, ending Villaraigosa's hope of becoming the city's first Hispanic mayor since 1872. Hahn, the Los Angeles city attorney since 1985, took office on July 2, 2001.

Villaraigosa, a former speaker of the State Assembly, had outpolled Hahn in a nonpartisan primary in April, in which neither candidate won a majority. Although Villaraigosa benefited from a record turnout by Hispanic voters, Hahn won with strong support from African Americans and non-Hispanic whites.

Hahn succeeded two-term Republican Mayor Richard Riordan, who was barred by law from running again. In November, Riordan entered the 2002 race for governor of California.

Economy. Los Angeles's diverse economy, which includes both manufacturing and service industries, helped buffer the city against the economic effects of a national recession and the terrorist attacks on the United States on Sept. 11, 2001. The city also boasted stable electricity rates and supplies. In contrast to the sharp increases in unemployment in northern California, the jobless rate in Los Angeles County rose slowly, from 5.2 percent in May to 5.9 percent in October.

James K. Hahn accepts the congratulations of supporters after winning a runoff race for mayor of Los Angeles in June 2001. Hahn defeated fellow Democrat Antonio Villaraigosa, who had hoped to become the city's first Hispanic mayor since 1872.

Nevertheless, the Los Angeles Economic Development Corporation (LAEDC), a nonprofit regional business group, predicted in November that the county's unemployment rate would average 6.4 percent in 2002. The organization forecast continuing job losses in Los Angeles's manufacturing, communications, transportation, and public utility industries. The LAEDC blamed the decline on the collapse of many technology companies, a slowdown in film production, and a sharp drop in international trade passing through the five-county Los Angeles Customs District. In 2001, the value of exports out of the district was expected to total $78.8 million, an increase of 1.5 percent, compared to a 16.5 percent increase in 2000.

Film industry slump. Employment in Los Angeles's film industry dropped in September 2001 to its lowest level since June 1997. Although the national recession played a part, production cutbacks ranked as the chief factor. Uncertainties over threatened strikes by writers and actors during the summer of 2001 had led production studios and television networks to stockpile films in 2000 and early 2001.

In June, the Writers Guild of America ratified a three-year, $41-million deal with the Alliance of Motion Picture and Television Producers. In August, the Screen Actors Guild and the American Federation of Television and Radio Artists approved a three-year agreement with producers that boosted members' pay by 6.5-percent.

Housing. The number of new housing units in Los Angeles, especially multiunit dwellings, continued to trail population growth. Rents in Los Angeles rose faster than average wages in the area, according to an October report issued by the National Low Income Housing Coalition, an advocacy group based in Washington, D.C. The Housing Authority of Los Angeles reported in October that because of higher rents, the number of low-income residents who were able to find housing using federal rent subsidies dropped from 90 percent in 1999 to 41 percent in 2001.

Alameda extension. A 35-mile (56-kilometer) extension of the Alameda Corridor received $153 million from the California Transportation Commission in July. Scheduled for completion in 2002, the Alameda Corridor is a high-speed rail line that was designed to carry containerized cargo from the Ports of Los Angeles and Long Beach to railheads in downtown Los Angeles. The Alameda Corridor East project, which will cost an estimated $912 million, was to extend the line east to Pomona. ☐ Margaret A. Kilgore

See also **City; Motion pictures; Television.**

Louisiana. See **State government.**

Luxembourg. See **Europe.**

Macedonia. Fighting broke out in Macedonia between ethnic Albanian rebels and Macedonian government troops early in 2001. The rebels, calling themselves the National Liberation Army (NLA), moved into mountain villages in February along a 20-mile (32-kilometer) swath of Macedonia's northern border with Kosovo, where many of the rebels were based. Kosovo is a semiautonomous province of Serbia with an ethnic-Albanian majority. The fighting threatened to destabilize Macedonia, a multiethnic country with a Slavic Christian majority and an ethnic Albanian, Islamic minority. In early March 2001, North Atlantic Treaty Organization (NATO) officials dispatched a small number of troops from a peacekeeping force in Kosovo to assist Macedonian government troops with border patrols.

Representatives of the European Union (EU) also arrived in Macedonia's capital, Skopje, in March to encourage the government to address ethnic Albanian demands, which included amending the constitution to grant ethnic Albanians equal legal status with the Slavic majority.

In May, the Macedonian parliament formed a unity government—a coalition of six parties that represented both ethnic Albanian and Slavic Macedonians. The coalition was created to end the fighting. However, Ljubco Georgievski, an outspoken Macedonian nationalist, remained prime minister.

The fighting escalated in June when NLA rebels occupied Aracinovo, a Skopje suburb. NATO troops later disarmed the rebels in Aracinovo and moved them to a town farther from the capital but returned their weapons at the end of the operation. Slavs in Skopje responded with riots and attacked several foreigners, including two British Broadcasting Company (BBC) journalists.

EU and NATO officials persuaded the rebels and the government to accept a cease-fire on July 5, but the cease-fire collapsed in late July when heavy fighting erupted in Tetovo, a town in northwest Macedonia, that had been the scene of earlier fighting. However, Macedonia's political parties continued intense negotiations at the urging of EU and NATO officials.

Peace agreement. On August 13, political parties representing Macedonia's two main ethnic groups signed a peace agreement guaranteeing expanded political rights to the ethnic Albanian minority. The agreement called for greater Albanian participation in police forces, the granting of official status to the Albanian language, and constitutional guarantees of Albanian equality. It also required NLA rebels to give up their weapons.

On August 22, some 3,500 NATO troops began arriving in Macedonia to collect weapons from NLA guerrillas. The operation was successfully completed by late September. NATO then made preparations to replace the arms-collecting mission with a small German-led security force of about 1,000 troops to protect international monitors in Macedonia.

In October, the Macedonian government granted amnesty to all Albanian rebels who had not committed war crimes. Macedonian nationalist hardliners in parliament, however, blocked passage of 15 constitutional amendments granting full rights to ethnic Albanians. EU and NATO officials urged passage of the amendments, which were key elements in the August peace plan.

War costs. In October, military experts estimated that the fighting in Macedonia had resulted in the destruction of about 5,500 houses and the dislocation of about 70,000 people. The Macedonian vice prime minister said that the country would need more than $50 million to rebuild.

EU accord. On April 9, Macedonia signed a stabilization and association agreement with the EU that had been negotiated in late 2000. EU officials reported that the agreement would make Macedonia eligible for about $36 million in aid for various projects and up to $72 million in budgetary aid during 2001. The EU offered Macedonia an additional $40 million in late 2001 for reconstruction aid, contingent upon implementation of the peace terms. ☐ Sharon L. Wolchik

See also **Europe; Yugoslavia.**

Macedonian government troops shell enclaves of ethnic Albanian rebels in the hills above the city of Tetovo in March. The rebellion in Macedonia in 2001 dislocated as many as 70,000 people before the two sides agreed to a cease-fire in August.

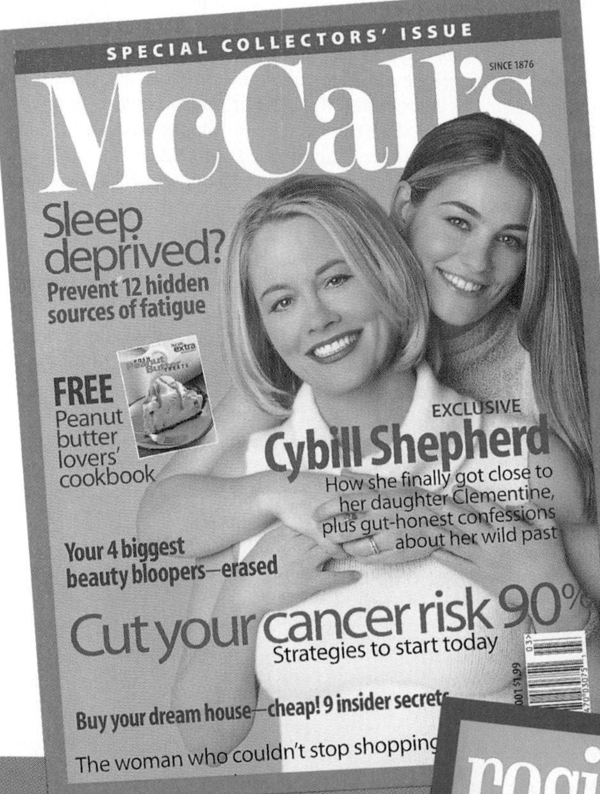

In April, Gruner & Jahr USA Publishing renamed the 125-year-old *McCall's* magazine *Rosie, The Magazine* for television host Rosie O'Donnell. The last *McCall's* cover (above) featured Cybill Shepherd and her daughter. O'Donnell and actress Fran Drescher highlighted the first issue of *Rosie.*

Magazine. The circulation and advertising revenues of a variety of magazines declined in 2001. The Magazine Publishers of America (MPA), a trade group headquartered in New York City, reported that the number of advertisement pages published in consumer magazines between January and August decreased about 11 percent compared with the same period in 2000. As a result, advertising revenues declined 3.5 percent during the first eight months of 2001, according to the MPA report. *Folio*, a magazine industry publication, reported in June that the number of advertisement pages in business-to-business magazines, which are devoted to an industry or specialty, fell nearly 8 percent in the first two months of 2001 compared with 2000.

Circulation among 76 of the 200 biggest consumer magazines fell in the first half of 2001 compared with the same period in 2000, according to an August 2001 report by the Audit Bureau of Circulations (ABC), an independent auditing firm in Schaumburg, Illinois. The circulation of *TV Guide*, a publication dependent on supermarket sales, fell by about 13 percent in the first six months of 2001. Similarly, the circulation of *Teen* declined by 10.8 percent. *Teen* is a monthly magazine published by New York City-based Emap USA that had previously exemplified the success of magazines aimed at teen-aged girls.

Publications fail. A number of popular magazines failed in 2001 amid a deteriorating economy. In

October, Conde Nast Publications of New York City announced that the 66-year-old magazine *Mademoiselle* would cease publication. The company cited a shrinking advertising market. *The Industry Standard*, a three-year-old Internet weekly, ceased publication in August after its advertisement pages fell by 75 percent between January and July, compared with the same period in 2000. *George*, the political magazine launched by John F. Kennedy, Jr., in 1995, ended its run with the February/March 2001 issue. Hachette Filipacchi Magazines had continued to print the magazine after Kennedy's death in 1999, despite declining circulation and revenue.

Women's magazines in 2001 increasingly became identified with celebrities. In April, Gruner & Jahr USA Publishing renamed the 125-year-old *McCall's* magazine *Rosie, The Magazine* after the television host Rosie O'Donnell. Television host Oprah Winfrey proved a successful magazine partner for Hearst Magazines in 2001. *O, The Oprah Magazine* nearly doubled its circulation to 2.8 million people after just 13 months of publication.

Terror. The nation's largest news magazines, *Time, Newsweek,* and *U.S. News & World Report*, all published special issues without advertisements after the September 11 terrorist attacks on the United States—an unprecedented reaction to a current event. ☐ Mark Fitzgerald

Malawi. See **Africa.**

Malaysia. Finance Minister Daim Zainuddin resigned in June 2001, amid reports of differences with Prime Minister Mahathir bin Mohammed. The change came as support weakened for the United Malays National Organization (UMNO), the party that has kept Mahathir in office since July 1981, longer than any other elected leader in Asia.

Daim, a wealthy UMNO powerbroker, served as finance minister from 1984 to 1991, when he stepped down. He returned to the job in 1999 after Mahathir ousted his deputy and heir apparent, Anwar Ibrahim. Daim's resignation in 2001 came after he had been fiercely criticized for using public money to help businesses in financial trouble. The criticism was part of broader complaints about UMNO members using government resources for political gains.

Corruption. At UMNO's annual congress meeting in June, Mahathir blamed party members for failing to eliminate corruption within the government. Yet, in January he had publicly stated that government leaders might be the source of corruption. The 75-year-old prime minister said that UMNO leaders may be too old and need to step down for a new generation. However, Mahathir showed no signs of relinquishing control.

Opposition. In April, Malaysian officials arrested 10 opposition leaders on suspicion that they were planning antigovernment demonstrations. Most of the people arrested had ties to the National Justice Party, which had been formed to support Anwar. The opposition leaders were held without trial, a move that was criticized by the government-created Human Rights Commission as a violation of human rights. Mahathir responded that public order was also a human right.

Extension on economic policy. In April, Prime Minister Mahathir announced a 10-year extension of the New Development Policy, which UMNO established in 1971 as the New Economic Policy to ease racial tensions by providing a balance of wealth among racial groups. By 1999, Malay Muslims owned nearly a 20-percent share in Malaysian corporations, up from a 2.4-percent share in 1971. Malay Muslims comprise 58 percent of the nation's 22 million people. Mahathir hoped the 10-year extension on the policy would raise Malay share to 30 percent—the original goal of the 1971 policy. Many Malays felt, however, that the quotas mostly helped wealthy businessmen who supported UMNO. Support for UMNO among Malays waned in 2001. ☐ Henry S. Bradsher

See also **Asia.**

Maldives. See **Asia.**

Mali. See **Africa.**

Malta. See **Europe.**

Manitoba. See **Canadian provinces.**

Manufacturing. The manufacturing sector of the U.S. economy contracted throughout 2001, continuing a painful trend that began late in 2000. Although the broader economy hovered near recession levels for much of 2001, manufacturing appeared to be edging toward a mild recovery in the summer of 2001. However, the terrorist attacks on the United States in September had a harsh economic impact, sharply cutting into overall demand. Most analysts anticipated that the economy would take a while to rebound and that 2002 would be another weak year.

Weakness that began early in 2000 with cutbacks by many high-technology firms spread by late 2000 to other manufacturing sectors, setting off a broad decline in factory output. That weakness spread further in 2001 to embrace all forms of manufacturing, from computers and heavy manufacturing to business equipment and consumer staples, such as clothing.

Ripple effects spread through service industries, triggering more layoffs, which cut into demand in a classic recessionary pattern. A pullback in consumer spending undermined production of new vehicles, while a slowdown in goods shipments from factories to retail stores cut into demand for trucking services.

Manufacturing trend. As the impact of the September 11 attacks magnified existing problems already in the economy, executives who managed supplies of raw materials for many of the top U.S. manufacturers reported that the contraction worsened dramatically during October. That month, a closely watched monthly index of manufacturing strength, published by the National Association of Purchasing Management (NAPM), sank to a reading of 39.8 percent, its lowest in 15 months. A reading under 50 percent indicates the sector is contracting. The NAPM index first sank below that level in August 2000.

Before the attacks, the NAPM gauge had been weakest in the first months of 2001 but was showing new strength during the summer. The NAPM index had descended to 41.2 percent in January, then rose and fell before climbing to a peak for the year of 47.9 percent in August. At that point, industry experts suggested that the index might soon turn positive, as the effects of lower interest rates and tax rebates helped spur new demand by companies and individuals.

However, with much of the economy halted for several days following the September 11 attacks and then operating at a reduced pace afterward, the NAPM index slid to 47.0 percent for September before plunging the next month.

Norbert Ore, a NAPM spokesperson, said that the October declines in production and new orders were "among the largest in the history of our report," which began in the Great Depression year of 1931. The Great Depression was a worldwide business slump of the 1930's. The index rebounded to 44.5 percent in November 2001, but it still was not clear when the manufacturing sector would really be strong again.

Industrial output. Government figures confirmed the downward economic trend and showed an even more dramatic drop after the terrorist attacks. The Federal Reserve (Fed)—an independent government agency that oversees the U.S. banking system—reported on November 16 that October's total industrial production by factories, mines, and utilities had fallen 1.1 percent after a 1-percent decline in September, the worst two-month drop since the recession of 1981-1982. Total output in October 2001 was down 6.3 percent from 2000. According to the government figures, the October 2001 drop was the largest in 13 consecutive months of decline, the longest industrial contraction since the Depression.

Manufacturing output fell 1.2 percent in October 2001 to a level 7.3 percent below October 2000. The decline was mainly in durable goods, such as business equipment, but also included declines in various types of consumer goods.

The new production figures brought the nation's capacity utilization level down to 74.8 percent of the total available. This meant that more than a quarter of available industrial capacity in the United States was going unused. Capacity usage was already weaker than in the recession of 1990-1991. Meanwhile, more companies were shrinking their capacity by closing factories across North America, including Canada and Mexico.

Employment. The U.S. Labor Department reported that through November 2001, factory employment had fallen for 16 consecutive months to wipe out 1.4 million manufacturing jobs in the United States. For factory workers who kept their jobs, the amount of hours they could work was steadily trimmed. An index of factory production workers' total weekly hours declined 12.6 percent between July 2000 and July 2001.

Companies and sectors. By late 2001, prices in an ailing world economy were declining for a wide range of raw materials and manufactured products alike. Price drops showed up in industries as varied as crude oil, coffee, computer chips, aluminum, and steel. Automobile manufacturers cut prices or offered zero-interest loans, and cellular phone services gave away telephones. Some industries, however, could not link product giveaways to profitable services.

Buffeted by the U.S. recession and competition from cheaper imports, more than 25 U.S. steel companies operated under bankruptcy laws in 2001. On October 15, Bethlehem Steel of Bethlehem, Pennsylvania, the third largest U.S. steelmaker, filed for bankruptcy protection. By year's end, LTV Corp. of Cleveland, Ohio, the nation's fourth largest steelmaker, was moving toward liquidation while industry leader USX Corporation of Pittsburgh began talks aimed at absorbing several other major steelmakers, consolidating U.S. steelmakers against foreign competition.

Some U.S. companies sought to reorganize in other ways. Computer manufacturing giants Hewlett Packard of Palo Alto, California, and Compaq of Houston announced plants to merge, as did oil producers Phillips Petroleum of Bartlesville, Oklahoma, and Conoco of Houston. U.S. manufacturers General Electric of Bridgeport, Connecticut, and Honeywell of Minneapolis, Minnesota, tried to merge in 2001, but European opposition killed the effort.

Microsoft settlement. Computer software giant Microsoft Corporation of Redmond, Washington, agreed in November to settle an antitrust lawsuit with the Bush administration on terms that allowed Microsoft to avoid being broken into two companies because of alleged monopolistic practices. The attorneys general of several states at year's end, however, refused to accept the remedies proposed in the national settlement.

☐ John D. Boyd

See also **Economics.**

Maryland. See **State government.**

Massachusetts. See **State government.**

Mauritius. On Feb. 25, 2001, Finance Minister Paul Berenger was reelected leader of the Militant Mauritian Movement (MMM), the second largest party in the ruling coalition led by Prime Minister Sir Anerood Jugnauth's Militant Socialist Movement (MSM). The alliance came to power following the election defeat of former Prime Minister Navinchandra Ramgoolam in September 2000. An agreement between MMM and MSM called for Berenger to serve as prime minister for the final two years of the five-year term.

On May 6, 2001, the tiny Republican Movement withdrew its support from the MSM/MMM alliance, claiming that there was insufficient communication between the coalition's party leaders. However, the defection was too small to endanger the ruling coalition.

Chagos developments. In 2001, many of the 3,000 exiled islanders from the British Indian Ocean Territory, a 65-island group also known as the Chagos Islands, said that they wanted to return to their original home, 1,200 miles (1,930 kilometers) to the northeast of Mauritius. In the late 1960's, the British government relocated most of the Chagossians, also called the Ilois, to Mauritius, a British colony until 1968. The evacuation had been made to allow for a United States military base on the largest Chagos island, Diego Garcia.

In November 2000, the British High Court stated that the Ilois had been illegally evicted. The court ordered that they be allowed to return, except to Diego Garcia, which was, under a 1966 agreement, leased to the U.S. government until at least 2016.

Diego Garcia became important to the United States and its allies as a forward base during the Persian Gulf War (1999). The base was of similar strategic importance in 2001 during the U.S. military campaign in Afghanistan following terrorist attacks on the United States on September 11.

Prospects for the Ilois. During 2001, the British Foreign Office began to encourage the idea of tourism on the Chagos islands, suggesting that investors might partner with the returning Ilois people to create economic opportunity. Describing the archipelago as "one of the most unspoilt areas of the world," officials at the British Foreign Office insisted that luxury resort development and eco-tourism needed to be environmentally and socially sustainable.

The status of the Chagos natives became more complicated in March 2001 when a group of the islanders staged a demonstration at Britain's embassy in Port Louis, the Mauritian capital, to demand British citizenship. Mauritius, which disputes Britain's claim to the Chagos Islands, opposed the demands. ☐ Simon Baynham

See **Africa; United Kingdom.**

Medicine. In October 2001, dozens of people in the United States were exposed to bacterium *Bacillus antracis*, which causes antrax. Anthrax is a noncontagious, but potentially fatal, infectious disease that can attack people's lungs, skin, and internal organs. By the end of 2001, five people had died from the disease, which authorities said was being spread through the U.S. mail by an unknown assailant or assailants. Letters containing a very pure form of anthrax specially prepared to easily enter the lungs were sent to several major media outlets, to two members of Congress, contaminating U.S. government offices. Thousands of people who may have come into contact with anthrax were given antibiotics.

Stem cells. U.S. President George W. Bush announced in August that he would permit federal funding for research using human embryonic stem cells. These cells can develop into nearly any kind of cell in the human body. Scientists think that stem cells could eventually be used to replace organ tissues damaged by disease or injury.

Research using embryonic stem cells is controversial because extracting the cells from embryos kills the embryos. The use of federal funding for research on human embryos had been banned in 1995. However, in 2000, President Bill Clinton declared that researchers could use federal funds as long as they got the stem cells from private labs.

President Bush, however, announced in 2001 that federal funds could only be used for stem cell research done with about 60 existing "lines," or colonies, of stem cells already growing in laboratories. Under Bush's policy, no federal funds could be spent on research that involved destroying embryos. However, many scientists expressed concern that some of the existing stem cell lines might not be suitable for research.

Cloning milestone. In November, scientists with Advanced Cell Technology, Inc., of Worcester, Massachusetts, announced they had created the first human embryos using a cloning technique known as nuclear transfer. The technique involved transferring genetic material from adults into donated egg cells to create embryos that were *clones* (genetic duplicates) of the adults. The scientists hoped to use stem cells from the embryos to make body tissues that would not be rejected by a patient's immune system. The embryos died shortly after being created.

New artificial heart. On July 2, surgeons from the University of Louisville implanted the first self-contained artificial heart into a human recipient at Jewish Hospital in Louisville, Kentucky. The device, called the AbioCor Implantable Replacement Heart, consisted of an electrically powered pumping unit weighing about 2 pounds (1 kilogram). The pump was powered by a battery that could be recharged by another battery worn around the patient's waist. A device attached to the patient's skin transmitted the charge to the internal battery, eliminating wires. The battery makes the device entirely self-contained. Before the invention of the AbioCor heart, manufactured by Abiomed, Inc., of Danvers, Massachusetts, artificial hearts included as much as 300 pounds (136 kilograms) of equipment.

The patient, one of five initially cleared by the U.S. Food and Drug Administration (FDA) to receive the experimental device, had suffered severe heart damage. Although surgeons had only expected the patient to live for about two months, he lived a fairly active life with the implanted device for nearly five months before dying on November 30.

Cholesterol guidelines. Scientists with the National Cholesterol Education Program (NCEP), a federal research program investigating cholesterol, announced new medical guidelines in May 2001 that were expected to greatly increase the number of people taking cholesterol-lowering drugs. Cholesterol is a fatty substance in the blood that is vital to health. However, too much cholesterol can cause coronary heart disease, which kills about 500,000 Americans annually.

The NCEP scientists redefined the levels of cholesterol that are considered healthy. If physicians follow the guidelines, the number of Americans taking cholesterol-lowering drugs could triple to more than 36 million. NCEP scientists recommended that adults over age 20 have their cholesterol tested every five years. These tests should check for total cholesterol, low density lipoprotein cholesterol (LDL), high density lipoprotein cholesterol (HDL), and triglycerides.

LDL is a type of cholesterol that can lodge in blood vessels, forming blockages that can lead to heart attacks. HDL is a type of cholesterol that scientists think removes excess cholesterol from the blood. Triglycerides are fatty substances in the blood that increase the risk of heart disease.

Heart damage. In June, scientists at the New York Medical College in Valhalla challenged the long-standing belief that heart damage is permanent. The scientists reported evidence that heart muscle cells damaged in a heart attack can return to a healthy condition.

The researchers studied muscle cells taken from the hearts of 13 people who had died of heart attacks. They found evidence that heart muscle cells can repair the damage that occurs when a heart attack cuts off their blood supply. The finding could lead to new ways of encouraging regeneration of heart muscle cells.

☐ Michael Woods

See also **Health care issues; Public health and safety; Terrorism: A Special Feature**, p. 38.

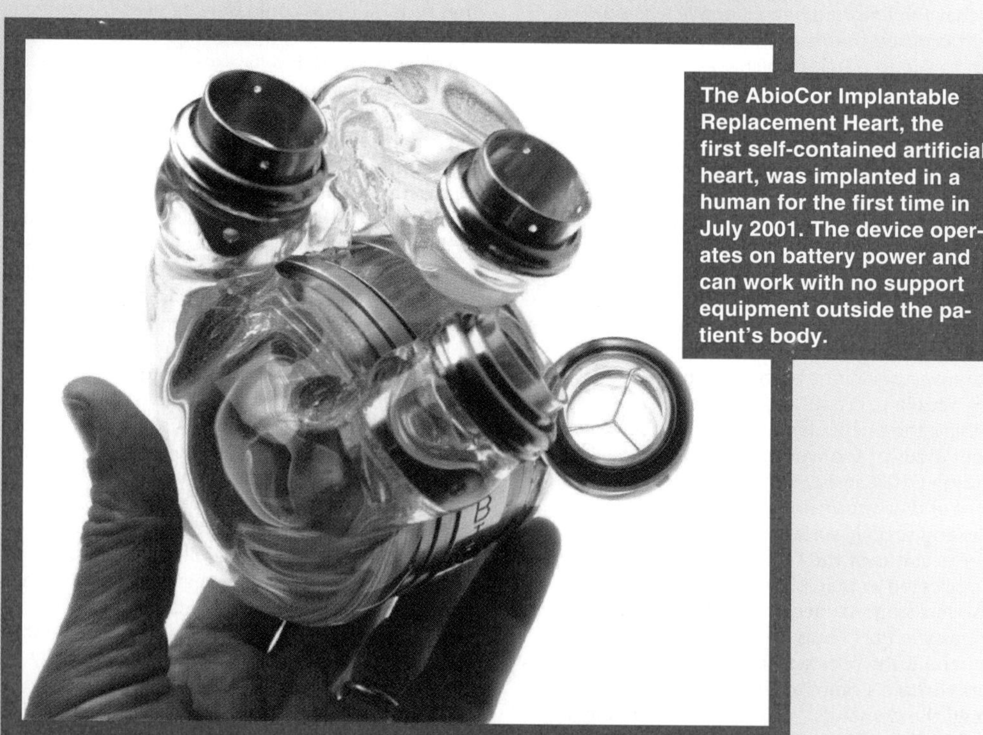

The AbioCor Implantable Replacement Heart, the first self-contained artificial heart, was implanted in a human for the first time in July 2001. The device operates on battery power and can work with no support equipment outside the patient's body.

Mental health. On Jan. 3, 2001, U.S. Surgeon General David Satcher issued a report calling for a national action agenda on children's mental health. The report, the result of collaboration among the U.S. departments of education, justice, and health and human services, cited statistics showing that 1 in 10 children and adolescents suffer from mental illness. Only 20 percent of those afflicted get needed treatment, according to the report. When left untreated, children with mental disorders often fail to perform well in school and social situations, and they may be subject to higher risk for other problems.

The surgeon general outlined a national action agenda that identified goals for improving mental health care. Several of the goals involved promoting public awareness of children's mental health issues, reducing the stigma associated with mental illness, adopting new scientific findings about the prevention and treatment of childhood mental illness, and putting greater emphasis on early diagnosis and treatment.

Childhood anxiety. Medication is effective in treating anxiety disorders in children and adolescents, the National Institute of Mental Health (NIMH) announced in April 2001 after the first major study on the topic. NIMH is part of the National Institutes of Health (NIH) in Bethesda, Maryland. Anxiety disorders, which involve excessive worry about everyday tasks, affect about 13 percent of children and adolescents,

The study tested the effects of fluvoxamine, sold under the brand name Luvox, in 128 children and adolescents. It is one of a group of medicines called selective serotonin reuptake inhibitors used to treat clinical depression and anxiety in adults. Symptoms improved in 76 percent of children given the drug, compared with 29 percent of those given a pill with no medicine. Prior to publication of the study, physicians who prescribed medications, such as Luvox, for children had no scientific evidence that they were effective.

Early detection. Newborn infants with abnormal levels of certain blood proteins may have an increased risk of developing autism, mental retardation, and cerebral palsy later in life, scientists reported in January. The scientists were with the National Institute of Neurological Disorders and Stroke, an agency of the NIH, and several other institutions.

Physicians usually cannot diagnose such mental conditions until a child is older and symptoms already have appeared. Researchers said the discovery could permit early detection of children at a high risk for mental problems, opening the possibility for early treatment or even prevention.

In the study, researchers analyzed frozen samples of blood taken years ago from newborn infants in California who later developed mental disorders. They compared the samples with blood from infants who did not develop mental illness. Individuals who developed mental disorders had elevated levels of proteins called nerve growth factors that stimulate growth of nerve tissue in the brain. The researchers suspected that the high levels disrupt normal development of the brain.

Dad's age. Older fathers are more likely to have children with schizophrenia, researchers from New York University, Columbia University in New York City, and the Israel Ministry of Health reported in April 2001. Schizophrenia, which affects about 2.2 million people in the United States, is a severe form of mental illness. Data for the study came from two Israeli databases involving more than 90,000 people.

The researchers found that the risk of having a schizophrenic child increased steadily with the father's age. Men aged 45-49 were twice as likely to have children with schizophrenia as men under age 25. For men over age 50, the risk tripled.

Genetic mutations, or changes in genes, that are passed from father to children may be responsible for the high risk. Researchers explained that the cells that become sperm divide hundreds of times during a man's lifetime, with each division opening the door to a genetic mutation. Older men have had more cell divisions and, therefore, more chance for mutations.

Workplace stress. Two studies published in April 2001 in the *Journal of Occupational Health Psychology* found that modern workplace realities—concern over job security and working long, stressful hours—can lead to increased injuries and illness among employees.

In the first study, psychologists at Washington State University in Vancouver studied 237 employees of a large food processing company that had reorganized operations and laid off workers. Employees who were worried about losing their jobs were less concerned about following safety rules. They had higher levels of workplace accidents and injuries involving the hand, wrist, and arm. Researchers involved in the study said employees may have felt pressured to cut corners on safety to keep their production numbers up.

The second study involved more than 2,000 employees at different companies around the country. Psychologists from the University of California at Los Angeles and the University of Northern Iowa in Cedar Falls analyzed how each individual's job affected physical and mental health. Employees who worked frequent overtime shifts and the night shift were most likely to feel that work undermined their health, the study showed. Researchers said companies might hire temporary help to avoid requiring employees to work constant overtime. □ Michael Woods

See also **Drugs; Medicine**.

Mexico. President Vicente Fox Quesada traveled to the United States in September 2001 to meet with U.S. President George W. Bush and address a joint session of the U.S. Congress. Fox called upon the Congress to end a requirement that Mexico be subject to U.S. economic sanctions unless it can prove each year that it is cracking down on drug trafficking. He also urged the lawmakers to open U.S. highways to unrestricted access by Mexican trucks—a move that U.S. officials had previously agreed to under the North American Free Trade Agreement (NAFTA) but later delayed. In December, the U.S. Congress passed legislation allowing Mexican trucks to haul cargo throughout the United States provided the trucks had passed safety requirements.

Illegal immigration. Although President Bush supported Fox on both the drug trafficking and trucking issues, Bush refused to commit himself to Fox's timetable for resolving the politically sensitive issue of Mexican illegal immigration. The two leaders reached a compromise agreement establishing a joint U.S.-Mexican committee to study how to best grant legal status to some of the estimated 3.5 million Mexicans who work illegally in the United States.

Zapatistas. In February and March 2001, 24 leaders of the Zapatista National Liberation Army (EZLN) undertook a 12-state truck-and-bus tour of Mexico to promote the cause of greater rights for Mexico's *indigenous* (native) people. The rebel group, based in the southern state of Chiapas, had staged a brief but bloody revolt against the government in 1994. On March 11, 2001, the EZLN caravan arrived in Mexico City, the capital, where a crowd of some 100,000 people gathered in the city's Zocalo Plaza to hear the EZLN's leader, Subcommander Marcos, deliver a speech. Marcos, wearing his trademark black woolen ski mask to conceal his identity, called for "democracy, liberty, and justice" for Mexican Indians.

On March 28, several of the Zapatista leaders spoke on the floor of the Mexican Congress to support proposed constitutional amendments based on accords reached between the previous presidential administration and the Zapatistas in 1996. President Fox endorsed the Indian rights amendments, which had been stalled in the Congress ever since, shortly after he took office in December 2000.

Congress finally passed the amendments in April 2001, granting "preferential use" of natural resources to Mexico's indigenous populations. The laws also gave Mexican Indians the right to choose local leaders according to tribal customs.

EZLN leaders, claiming that Congress had altered the wording of the amendments from that of the original 1996 accords, quickly rejected the

A crowd of some 100,000 people gather in Mexico City's Zocalo Plaza on March 11, 2001, to hear a speech by Subcommander Marcos, the leader of the Zapatista National Liberation Army, a Mexican rebel group. Marcos called for greater rights for Mexican Indians.

measures. They claimed the amendments actually diluted Indian *autonomy* (self-rule) and granted state governments too much control over indigenous affairs. The EZLN also refused to renew talks with the government aimed at resolving their differences.

Fugitive governor arrested. Mexican authorities in May 2001 arrested Mario Villanueva Madrid, the former governor of the state of Quintana Roo. Villanueva had been a fugitive for two years, charged with drug smuggling. He was captured in the resort city of Cancun and sent to a maximum security prison to await trial. In June, authorities apprehended former federal police officer Alcides Ramon Magana, Villanueva's suspected confederate in crime, in the southern town of Villahermosa.

Following the arrest of Villanueva and Magana, a U.S. grand jury in New York City unsealed an indictment alleging that both men conspired to smuggle 200 tons (180 metric tons) of cocaine through the Yucatan Peninsula to the United States between 1994 and 1996, when Villanueva was governor. The U.S. government asked Mexican authorities to *extradite* (hand over) Villanueva and Magana to the United States to face these charges. □ Nathan A. Haverstock

See also **Latin America; Latin America: A Special Report; Transportation.**

Miami. Manny Diaz, a 47-year-old attorney and political independent, was elected mayor on Nov. 13, 2001, winning 55 percent of the vote. Former Mayor Maurice Ferre received 45 percent of the vote. Joe Carollo, the mayor serving at the time of the election, had lost in an earlier round of balloting. In 2000, Diaz represented the Miami relatives of Elian Gonzalez, a 6-year-old survivor of the sinking of a boat carrying Cuban refugees, in their unsuccessful attempt to prevent the United States from returning the boy to Cuba.

Mayor in jail. Mayor Carollo spent the night of Feb. 7, 2001, in jail after police arrested him at his house on a misdemeanor charge of battery. According to police, Carollo hit his wife in the head with a cardboard box. The couple was in the process of divorcing. Carollo was released on a $1,500 bond. Miami-Dade County prosecutors dismissed the charge after the mayor completed a family counseling program, surrendered his firearms, and agreed to avoid his wife.

Miami police scandal. Federal prosecutors in September charged 13 Miami police officers with planting guns at crime scenes to justify fatal shootings by police. The indictments stemmed from a 10-month federal and internal police investigation into four police shootings of crime suspects between 1995 and 1997. Police officers had claimed that the suspects were armed.

Prosecutors were drawn into the investigation after six Miami officers fired several bullets into a 73-year-old African American man in 1996. Five of these officers were indicted in March 2001 on various charges, including conspiracy to violate the man's civil rights.

Split among Cuban exiles. In July and August, more than 20 members of the 170-member directors' board of the Cuban American National Foundation resigned in protest. The Miami-based foundation is the largest organization of Cuban exiles—Cubans who fled to Miami after the 1959 Cuban revolution brought Fidel Castro to power—and their descendants. The departed board members, who included some of the group's founders, complained that the foundation had become "too soft" on Cuban issues. They were especially critical of the foundation's 38-year-old chairman, Jorge Mas Santos, whom they accused of being too tolerant of Castro.

The resignations brought to light a growing generational split among Miami's Cuban-American community. Many older Cuban-Americans, with memories of Castro's revolution, continued to call for the overthrow of the Cuban dictator. Younger Cuban-Americans, many of whom had never been to Cuba, tended to favor a less confrontational approach to Castro's regime.

Tower of freedom. On May 19, 2001, Mas Santos helped rededicate the Freedom Tower, a landmark building in which more than half-a-million Cuban exiles were welcomed into the United States between 1962 and 1974. The tower was to be converted into a museum by 2002.

Census 2000. Miami-Dade County had the highest percentage of Hispanics of any large county in the United States, according to the results of the 2000 United States Census. The Census Bureau reported that Miami-Dade County's more than 1 million Hispanics made up 57 percent of the county's population in 2000, up from 49 percent in 1990.

According to the census, the African American population in Miami declined 18 percent between 1990 and 2000. Community leaders explained the decrease by noting that many blacks abandoned deteriorating, crime-ridden Miami neighborhoods during the 1990's and moved to North Miami Beach and unincorporated areas north of Miami. The census revealed that these moves were part of a population shift in Miami away from the troubled inner city and toward immigrant and working class neighborhoods, such as Little Havana and Flagami, and upper class areas, such as the bayside Brickell district.
□ Alfred J. Smuskiewicz

See also **City; Census; Cuba; United States, Government of the: A Special Report.**

Michigan. See **Detroit; State government.**

Middle East

Two unprecedented crises confronted the Middle East in 2001. On September 11, Islamic militants attacked the United States in the deadliest act of terrorism in U.S. history, killing thousands of people. United States President George W. Bush subsequently challenged Arab and other Muslim nations to join a U.S.-led global "war on terrorism" or risk isolation. As this crisis unfolded throughout the rest of the year, attacks by Palestinian extremists against Israelis provoked a major Israeli military assault against Palestinian targets, raising the specter of war in the Middle East.

War on terrorism. In a coordinated series of attacks on September 11, terrorists hijacked four civilian airliners, crashing two of them into the World Trade Center towers in New York City and one into the Pentagon Building outside Washington, D.C. A fourth hijacked plane crashed in a field in Pennsylvania. U.S. investigators identified Osama bin Laden, the Saudi-born leader of the Islamic terrorist network al-Qaida ("The Base" in Arabic), as the chief suspect in the attacks.

On October 7, the United States and the United Kingdom, with widespread international backing, launched a massive military assault against Afghanistan's ruling Taliban, which had given bin Laden *asylum* (refuge) in 1996 after he was expelled from Sudan. The Taliban had refused demands by the United States and the United Nations (UN) to turn over bin Laden for trial. President Bush vowed in September 2001 to not only wage war against terrorists but against any nation that harbored terrorists.

Arab and Islamic concerns. Most Arab and Islamic leaders condemned the Sept. 11, 2001, terrorist attacks. However, they feared that many Muslims in the Middle East viewed the U.S.-led antiterrorism campaign as a war against Islam and that this view would fuel anti-Americanism and Islamic extremism. The leaders urged the United States to distinguish between the terrorists responsible for the September 11 attacks and organizations such as Hamas, a militant Palestinian group, and Hezbollah, an Islamic group credited with forcing Israeli troops out of Lebanon in 2000. Many Arabs viewed these groups as "freedom fighters" against Israel.

Despite these concerns, the U.S. State Department included Hamas and Hezbollah on a list of organizations suspected of supporting terrorism. U.S. officials warned countries and financial institutions to freeze the assets of groups on the list or face retaliatory action against their own assets in the United States.

Sympathy for bin Laden. Arab and Islamic leaders also feared that the U.S. military attacks against Afghanistan would foster greater sympathy for bin Laden, whose message had attracted a growing number of disaffected Middle Easterners since the early 1990's. Bin Laden's message was threefold. He opposed the Arab-Israeli peace process; he condemned the presence of U.S. military troops in Saudi Arabia, where Islam's holiest sites are located; and he condemned UN sanctions that were imposed against Iraq after Iraq's 1990 invasion of Kuwait. Muslims of many nationalities agreed with bin Laden's ideas though not necessarily with his methods.

Detention of Arabs. Arab-American and civil rights organizations objected to the detention by U.S. authorities of hundreds of people, many believed to be Arabs, for questioning after Sept. 11, 2001. A coalition of these organizations sued the U.S. Department of Justice in December to force the department to release more information on the detainees. Law enforcement authorities in Europe, Latin America, and elsewhere also arrested many Arabs and Muslims suspected of belonging to al-Qaida or other terrorist organizations.

U.S. educational institutions reported that some of their Middle Eastern students left the United States in fear of anti-Arab and anti-Muslim prejudice. President Bush had repeatedly warned Americans against such prejudice.

Indictment. In December, the U.S. Department of Justice announced the first U.S. indictment in connection with the September 11 terrorist attacks. Federal prosecutors alleged that Zacarias Moussaoui, a French citizen of Moroccan descent who had been detained in the United States on immigration violations since August, was an active participant in the conspiracy to attack the World Trade Center and Pentagon Building.

The brink of war. Israeli Prime Minister Ariel Sharon severed contact with Palestinian Authority (PA) leader Yasir Arafat on December 13, and the Middle East was plunged into new turmoil as Israelis and Palestinians approached the brink of war. (The PA administers Palestinian territories in the West Bank and Gaza Strip.) The crisis began when three Arab suicide bombers killed 26 people in the

In August 2001, Palestinians in the West Bank town of Ram Allah protest the Israeli assassination of Mustafa Zubari, leader of the Popular Front for the Liberation of Palestine (PFLP). The assassination was part of a new Israeli policy of killing leaders of Palestinian militant organizations.

Israeli cities of Jerusalem and Haifa on December 1 and 2. On December 12, Palestinian militants attacked a bus filled with Jewish settlers in the West Bank, killing at least 10 of the Israelis. Hamas, which had vowed revenge for the November assassination by Israeli forces of its military leader, claimed responsibility for the attacks.

On December 3, Prime Minister Sharon publicly blamed Yasir Arafat for the suicide bombings. Sharon vowed to wage an antiterrorism campaign in Israel similar to the worldwide effort begun by the United States. Israeli forces on December 3 launched the first strikes of a military assault on Palestinian targets, including such symbols of Arafat's leadership as his headquarters in the West Bank town of Ram Allah. On December 13, the Israeli cabinet declared Arafat "no longer relevant" as it severed relations with the PA. The Israeli military also stepped up its attacks on PA sites.

A number of European leaders expressed fear that hostilities might engulf other countries in the region if the Israeli assault was intended to remove Arafat and the PA from power. Israeli officials, however, denied any intention to topple Arafat.

Palestinian reaction. After the suicide bombings in early December, the PA declared martial law and banned public demonstrations in the West Bank and Gaza. Arafat also ordered the detention of more than 180 suspected Islamic militants and placed Hamas spiritual leader Sheik Ahmed Yassin under house arrest. Following the December 12 attack, Arafat vowed to close the offices of Hamas and Islamic Jihad, another Arab extremist organization. Palestinian protests and clashes with Israelis continued despite the clampdown.

Many experts on the Middle East questioned Arafat's ability and willingness to repress anti-Israeli militancy. Polls showed that Palestinians were increasingly critical of Arafat's leadership and overwhelmingly supported the *Intifada,* or

Facts in brief on Middle Eastern countries

Country	Population	Government	Monetary unit*	Foreign trade (million U.S.$) Exports†	Imports†
Bahrain	636,000	Amir Hamad bin Isa Al Khalifa; Prime Minister Khalifa bin Salman Al Khalifa	dinar (0.38 = $1)	5,710	4,612
Cyprus	798,000	President Glafcos Clerides; (Turkish Republic of Northern Cyprus: President Rauf R. Denktash)	pound (0.63 = $1)	953	3,846
Egypt	70,818,000	President Hosni Mubarak; Prime Minister Atef Mohammed Obeid	pound (4.26 = $1)	4,691	14,010
Iran	69,049,000	Supreme Leader Ayatollah Ali Hoseini-Khamenei; President Mohammed Khatami-Ardakani	rial (1,750.00 = $1)	25,000	15,000
Iraq	24,451,000	President Saddam Hussein	dinar (0.31 = $1)	21,800	13,800
Israel	6,425,000	President Moshe Katzav; Prime Minister Ariel Sharon	new shekel (4.36 = $1)	31,338	3,769
Jordan	6,639,000	King Abdullah II; Prime Minister Ali Abu al-Ragheb	dinar (0.71 = $1)	1,832	3,717
Kuwait	2,062,000	Amir Jabir al-Ahmad al-Jabir Al Sabah; Prime Minister & Crown Prince Saad al-Abdallah al-Salim Al Sabah	dinar (0.30 = $1)	12,218	7,617
Lebanon	3,373,000	President Emile Lahoud Prime Minister Rafiq Hariri	pound (1,513.75 = $1)	714	6,228
Oman	2,711,000	Sultan Qaboos bin Said Al Said	rial (0.38 = $1)	11,100	4,500
Qatar	617,000	Amir Hamad bin Khalifa Al Thani; Prime Minister Abdallah bin Khalifa Al Thani	riyal (3.64 = $1)	9,800	3,800
Saudi Arabia	22,910,000	King & Prime Minister Fahd bin Abd al-Aziz Al Saud	riyal (3.75 = $1)	50,760	28,010
Sudan	30,742,000	President Umar Hasan Ahmad al-Bashir	dinar (258.70 = $1) pound (2,587.00 = $1)	616	1,988
Syria	16,928,000	President Bashar al-Assad; Prime Minister Muhammad Mustafa Miru	pound (52.68 = $1)	19,259	16,706
Turkey	68,509,000	President Ahmet Necdet Sezer; Prime Minister Bulent Ecevit	lira (1,600,000.00 = $1)	26,572	53,499
United Arab Emirates	2,522,000	President Zayid bin Sultan Al Nuhayyan; Prime Minister Maktum bin Rashid al-Maktum	dirham (3.67 = $1)	46,000	34,000
Yemen	19,391,000	President Ali Abdallah Salih; Prime Minister Abd al-Qadir Ba Jamal	rial (172.11 = $1)	2,438	2,006

*Exchange rates as of Oct. 5, 2001, or latest available data.
†Latest available data.

uprising against Israel, which began in September 2000. There was also an upsurge in support for Hamas.

United States. In early- and mid-2001, many Arab leaders criticized President Bush for adopting a "hands-off" policy in the Arab-Israeli conflict. Bush maintained that the United States could not impose peace on unwilling parties. Bush stepped up U.S. involvement in the conflict after the September 11 terrorist attacks, when Arab leaders argued that continued violence in Israel and the Palestinian territories threatened the U.S.-led coalition against terrorism. In November, the Bush administration called upon Israel to freeze settlements in Palestinian territories and urged Palestinian authorities to suppress terrorism. Also in November, President Bush declared his support for a Palestinian state during a UN address and sent U.S. envoys to the region. ☐ Christine Helms

See also **Terrorism; Terrorism: A Special Feature,** p. 38; various Middle Eastern country articles.

Minnesota. See **State government.**
Mississippi. See **State government.**
Missouri. See **State government.**
Mongolia. See **Asia.**
Montana. See **State government.**

Montreal on Nov. 4, 2001, came one step closer to becoming "one island, one city," with the election of Gerald Tremblay as mayor. Tremblay became head of Canada's newest and second-largest megacity when the legislated merger of 28 municipalities on Montreal Island went into effect on Jan. 1, 2002. Tremblay defeated two-term Mayor Pierre Bourque, who came under heavy criticism by suburban officials for proposing the merger. In his acceptance speech, however, Tremblay said he remained committed to the success of the new megacity.

Elected officials from many of the municipalities that became boroughs under Bill 171 legally challenged the Quebec government law that enforced the merger. The matter went to the Supreme Court of Canada, where the nine justices on Dec. 7, 2001, unanimously upheld the rights of provincial governments to merge and abolish municipalities. The towns, all of which were officially bilingual, had argued that the merger endangered the availability of services in English. Companion legislation to the merger law made it more difficult for municipalities to obtain official recognition as a bilingual community.

Business news. The Canadian National Railway Company announced on July 23 that it would eliminate about 245 jobs at its Montreal headquarters by the end of 2002 as part of cost-cutting measures. The downsizing would leave about 3,100 workers at various operation sites throughout the city.

Sports. Montreal's Circuit Gilles Villeneuve will join automobile racetracks in Toronto and Vancouver as a host for the Molson Indy from 2002 to 2006, Championship Auto Racing Teams Inc. (CART) announced on Jan. 18, 2001. The first Molson Indy Montreal, one race in CART's FedEx Championship Series, was scheduled for Aug. 25, 2002.

The majority ownership of the Montreal Canadiens of the National Hockey League (NHL) passed from Molson Incorporated, a Montreal-based brewing company, to Colorado businessman George N. Gillett, Jr., in January 2001. The NHL board of governors unanimously approved the $275-million deal on June 19. (Amount is in Canadian dollars.) The deal gave Gillett an 80.1-percent controlling interest in the team as well as complete ownership of the Molson Centre, the team's arena. Gillett said he would keep the team in Montreal.

Gang trials. In March, Quebec officials announced the construction of a special fortified courthouse near the Bordeaux jail in Montreal's north end. The bunker-courthouse was to accommodate the trials of some of the 125 members and associates of the Hell's Angels biker gang arrested in a massive Quebec-wide raid on March 28. The police operation, the largest against criminal biker gangs in Canadian history, involved at least 2,000 law enforcement officers from national, provincial, and local police agencies. The suspects faced a variety of charges, including drug trafficking and murder.

Crime. Boxer Davey Hilton of the Fighting Hiltons boxing family was convicted in March of sexually assaulting two adolescent sisters. Hilton's conviction led the World Boxing Council on May 1 to strip the super-middleweight champion of his title. On May 9, Hilton received a seven-year prison sentence.

A Montreal high-school student known as Mafiaboy was sentenced on September 11 to eight months in a youth detention center for temporarily shutting down five major Web sites—CNN, Yahoo, e-Bay, Dell, and Amazon—in 2000. In January 2001, the 17-year-old pleaded guilty to 58 charges, including denial-of-service attacks and illegally accessing a computer.

☐ Mike King

See also **Canada; Canadian provinces; City; Hockey.**

Morocco. See **Middle East.**

Motion pictures. Most movie critics and fans agreed that filmmaking quality suffered during 2001 even though box-office receipts enabled most of the year's films to show a profit. The summer months featured some of the weakest offerings in recent years. In the autumn and winter, however, audiences flocked to theaters to see some highly anticipated releases. Throughout the year, many audiences in European and Asian countries made movies from their native lands a top priority. Terrorist attacks in the United States in September affected the movie industry, forcing some companies to hold off releasing major films.

The threat of a strike by film actors loomed over the industry during the first six months of 2001. Many filmmakers rapidly completed their projects to avoid any potential delays. In July, members of the Screen Actors Guild, a union that represents film and television actors, reached an agreement on a new three-year contract with the major film studios, averting a strike. However, many of the films finished in a rush reflected that haste and were released to indifferent reactions.

Summer season. The lack of quality films was particularly noticeable during the summer months of 2001. Many studios released a series of outlandish yet shallow special-effects spectacles. Although these films opened to strong figures during their first weekends in theaters, their

Julia Roberts (above) portrays a law office employee in the true story *Erin Brockovich,* for which she received the Academy Award for best actress in 2001.

Academy Award-winning films in 2001 investigated corrupt business practices and urban drug trafficking and recreated the Colosseum in ancient Rome.

Benicio Del Toro (below, left) appears with Jacob Vargas in *Traffic,* an episodic film that explores illicit drug trade between the United States and Mexico. Del Toro received the Academy Award for best supporting actor in 2001.

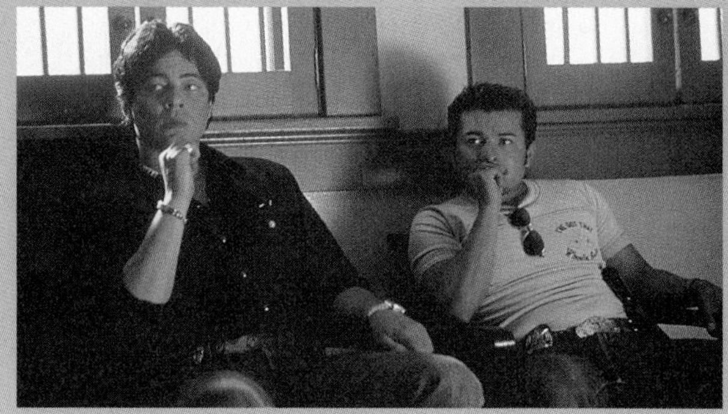

gross generally dropped 50 percent during their second weeks. These one-week sensations included sequels such as *American Pie 2, Jurassic Park III, Rush Hour 2,* and *The Mummy Returns.* In nonsequel features, Angelina Jolie made a physically impressive action heroine in *Lara Croft: Tomb Raider.* Based on a popular video game, the film was sabotaged by a weak screenplay.

The animated film *Shrek* was the summer's biggest success. The film, which featured the voices of Mike Myers, Eddie Murphy, Cameron Diaz, and John Lithgow, attracted diverse audiences with a message that beings should not be judged merely by their appearance.

Big-budget disappointments. *A.I. Artificial Intelligence,* an intellectual science-fiction fable directed by Steven Spielberg, was a major disappointment in 2001. Spielberg had been a staple of summer box-office magic, with such warm-weather blockbusters as *Raiders of the Lost Ark* (1981) and *Saving Private Ryan* (1998).

A.I. Artificial Intelligence starred child actor Haley Joel Osment as a manufactured boy seeking stability and love. The film had been planned by Stanley Kubrick, who directed such landmark films as *2001: A Space Odyssey* (1968). Following Kubrick's death in 1999, however, his family and business associates urged Spielberg to direct the film. Although the two directors were friends, their emotional approaches to their craft were very different, with Kubrick's as clinical as Spielberg's could be sentimental. The consensus of both moviegoers and critics was that a Spielberg/Kubrick merger was not an artistically happy union.

Tim Burton, who put unconventional spins on such films as *Batman* (1989) and *Sleepy Hollow* (1999), released a "reimagined" version of *Planet of the Apes* in 2001. Fans of the original 1968 science-fiction classic, which starred Charlton Heston

Russell Crowe fights a fellow gladiator to the death in the ancient Roman Colosseum in *Gladiator,* for which he won the Academy Award for best actor in 2001. *Gladiator,* directed by Ridley Scott, was named best picture of 2001.

Academy Award winners in 2001

The following winners of the 2000 Academy Awards were announced in March 2001:

Best Picture, *Gladiator*
Best Actor, Russell Crowe, *Gladiator*
Best Actress, Julia Roberts, *Erin Brockovich*
Best Supporting Actor, Benicio Del Toro, *Traffic*
Best Supporting Actress, Marcia Gay Harden, *Pollock*
Best Director, Steven Soderbergh, *Traffic*
Best Original Screenplay, Cameron Crowe, *Almost Famous*
Best Screenplay Adaptation, Stephen Gaghan, *Traffic*
Best Cinematography, Peter Pau, *Crouching Tiger, Hidden Dragon*
Best Film Editing, Stephen Mirrione, *Traffic*
Best Original Score, Tan Dun, *Crouching Tiger, Hidden Dragon*
Best Original Song, Bob Dylan, "Things Have Changed" from *Wonder Boys*
Best Foreign-Language Film, *Crouching Tiger, Hidden Dragon* (Taiwan)
Best Art Direction, Tim Yip, *Crouching Tiger, Hidden Dragon*
Best Costume Design, Janty Yates, *Gladiator*
Best Sound, Scott Millan, Bob Beemer, and Ken Weston, *Gladiator*
Best Sound Editing, Jon Johnson, *U-571*
Best Makeup, Rick Baker and Gail Ryan, *Dr. Seuss' "How the Grinch Stole Christmas"*
Best Visual Effects, *Gladiator*
Best Animated Short Film, *Father and Daughter*
Best Live-Action Short Film, *Quiero Ser (I Want to Be)*
Best Feature Documentary, *Into the Arms of Strangers: Stories of the Kindertransport*
Best Short Subject Documentary, *Big Mama*

and Roddy McDowell, considered the new version, starring Mark Wahlberg and Helena Bonham Carter, as lacking any of the flourishes that enriched Burton's best work.

Captain Corelli's Mandolin, the film version of Louis De Bernieres' 1994 novel, *Corelli's Mandolin,* proved to be another jarring disappointment of the summer season. The novel's appeal was on several levels—mystical, psychological, and romantic. The movie was a simple wartime romance played with a lack of conviction by its stars, Nicolas Cage and Penelope Cruz.

Pearl Harbor, a World War II (1939-1945) drama that some critics expected to be the summer's biggest financial success, failed to live up to the heavy hype it received. The film's lengthy action sequence recreating the Japanese attack on the U.S. Pacific Fleet based in Pearl Harbor, Hawaii, on Dec. 7, 1941, won praise for its intensity and high energy. However, audiences were bored by the standard romantic triangle, featuring stars Ben Affleck, Josh Hartnett, and Kate Beckinsale. Many servicemen criticized the dramatization of certain events and historical inaccuracies portrayed in the film. *Pearl Harbor* drew largely unfavorable reviews in the United States. Ironically, Japanese critics were more positive.

Early in 2001, Anthony Hopkins recreated his role as cannibalistic serial killer Hannibal Lecter in *Hannibal,* a sequel to *The Silence of the Lambs* (1991). *Hannibal,* which also starred Julianne Moore, opened to lukewarm reviews, which were especially critical for excessive violence, but strong box office returns worldwide.

Successful endeavors. Film actress Nicole Kidman scored two late-summer successes in 2001. Critics welcomed her performance in *The Others,* a low-key ghost story that solidly and quietly built suspense. Kidman also won praise for her role as a glamorous singer and prostitute in Paris in the 1800's in the extravagant musical *Moulin Rouge.*

Audiences welcomed the return of movie veteran Julie Andrews, the star of such films as *Mary Poppins* (1964), back to the screen in 2001. Andrews won praise for her performance as the queen of a small European country in *The Princess Diaries,* about an awkward teen-aged girl who discovers that she is heir to the throne.

Small budget hits. Many audiences preferred small budget films to their big budget counterparts in 2001. *In the Bedroom* featured superb performances from Sissy Spacek and Tom Wilkinson as bereaved parents coming to terms with their son's violent death. *The Business of Strangers* pit veteran actress Stockard Channing against Julia Stiles as corporate rivals.

Two films that tried to capture the life of alienated teen-agers scored mixed reviews. *Ghost World,* starring Thora Birch, was not unlike a graphic, but admirable novel. However, *Prozac Nation,* starring Christina Ricci, greatly suffered from the unsympathetic stridency of its main character.

Total revenue. Even though critics considered most offerings from major film studios to be poor, audiences were still willing to pay for the diversion that films offered. Film receipts in 2001 totaled \$3.06 billion between Memorial Day and Labor Day.

Year-end hopes. Director Steven Soderbergh, who scored acclaim in 2000 for his films *Erin Brockovich* and *Traffic,* repeated his success in 2001 with the star-studded film *Ocean's Eleven.* A remake of the 1960 movie of the same name, *Ocean's Eleven* starred Don Cheadle, George Clooney, Matt Damon, Andy Garcia, Brad Pitt, and Julia Roberts in a story of a gang of 11 criminal associates plotting to rob a string of casinos in Las Vegas, Nevada.

Other strong features released near the end of 2001 were delivered by David Lynch and Joel and Ethan Coen. Lynch's *Mulholland Drive* represented a return to the surreal worlds explored by the director in *Blue Velvet* (1986) and *Twin Peaks: Fire Walk with Me* (1992). *Mulholland Drive* told of three seemingly unrelated characters involved with the Los Angeles movie scene. But the characters are connected in unforeseen ways, as the film eventually deals with identity-switching and time-traveling.

The Coen Brothers' *The Man Who Wasn't There* starred Billy Bob Thornton in an atypical role as a quiet barber whose attempts to blackmail his unfaithful wife's lover lead to murder. Critics praised Thornton for a splendid performance as a defeated soul who finally acquires some wisdom about his misbegotten life. The film was aided by Roger Deakins's brilliant black-and-white cinematography, which echoed such earlier film noirs as *The Postman Always Rings Twice* (1946) while enhancing the art of black-and-white cinematography.

Family fare. Studio executives in late 2001 capitalized on the success of two well-known novels. *Harry Potter and the Sorcerer's Stone,* featuring characters from the J. K. Rowling novels, received praise from audiences and critics. Some fans purchased tickets a week in advance to watch the adventures of an orphan boy and his classmates at an English boarding school for wizards. *Harry Potter* grossed $31.3 million in its first day of release in November, the highest single-day take ever. *The Lord of the Rings: The Fellowship of the Ring,* the first of three scheduled films based on the J. R. R. Tolkien novels, also captured the family market during the year-end holiday season.

International films. *Amelie,* a sentimental French film about a young woman who overcomes a sad childhood to bring joy to herself and those around her, became one of the most well-received films in the United States and overseas in 2001.

Singapore's list of successful films was topped by *Return to Pontiniak*, an interpretation of an ancient Malay supernatural folktale. Animation ruled the film scene in Japan, spotlighted by such feature-length cartoons as *Detective Conan,* which was based on a popular television series.

South Korea contributed to the motion pictures industry with the release of *Friend,* which in 2001 became the top-grossing Korean film. The movie followed four friends from childhood to young adulthood, when two of the men become members of rival gangs.

Terrorism and Hollywood. The September 11 terrorist attacks on the World Trade Center in New York City and the Pentagon Building outside Washington, D.C., also affected Hollywood. Several studios postponed the release of films that featured terrorism and espionage as central themes. Warner Brothers postponed the scheduled release of the action drama *Collateral Damage,* starring Arnold Schwarzenegger, in which a terrorist bombs a Los Angeles skyscraper. Touchstone Pictures postponed the release date of Tim Allen's comedy *Big Trouble,* which contained a scene featuring a bomb onboard an airplane.

Many film critics hoped that the tragedy of the terrorist attacks would lead filmmakers to attempt introspective, character-driven screenplays rather than the explosive special-effects action carnivals that had been the focus of most U.S. studios.

☐ Philip Wuntch

See also **Terrorism: A Special Feature,** p. 38; **People in the news** (Crowe, Russell; Roberts, Julia).

Mozambique. See **Africa.**

Music. See **Classical music; Popular music.**

Myanmar. In 2001, the military rulers of Myanmar, formerly Burma, held talks with Aung San Suu Kyi, leader of the National League for Democracy (NLD). The NLD won 82 percent of the vote in 1990 parliamentary elections, but the military refused to give up power. The government disclosed that in October 2000 negotiations had begun with Aung San Suu Kyii, who for years had attempted to assert the NLD's political rights.

In January 2001, Lieutenant General Khin Nyunt, a government official, met Aung San Suu Kyi at her residence, where she had been under house arrest since September 2000. The talks focused on the release of NLD leaders and other political prisoners. The government later released prisoners but gave no sign of yielding power.

The talks between the government and Aung San Suu Kyii coincided with United Nations (UN) special envoy Razali Ismail's efforts to ease political tensions in Myanmar and economic pressure from abroad. In 2001, the World Bank, which provides loans to countries for development, described Myanmar as "trapped in abject poverty." UN agencies reported in August that the country was on the brink of a disaster brought on by rapidly spreading HIV infection, widespread childhood malnutrition, and high mortality rates among infants and mothers. ☐ Henry S. Bradsher

See also **Asia.**

Nepal. King Birendra Bir Bikram Shah Dev and most of the royal family were fatally shot during a palace dinner on June 1, 2001. His brother, Gyanendra Bir Bikram Shah Dev, became king on June 4.

According to a government inquiry, Birendra's eldest son, 29-year-old Crown Prince Dipendra, had been drinking the night of the shooting. He was upset that his mother, Queen Aiswarya, refused to accept his choice of a bride. The two reportedly argued during dinner.

According to the accounts of survivors, Dipendra left the table, armed himself, returned to the dinner table, and began shooting. He fatally wounded his parents and seven other relatives before shooting himself. Dipendra, in a coma and on life support in a hospital, became king after his father's death. He died on June 4 without regaining consciousness.

Gyanendra Bir Bikram Shah Dev is crowned king of Nepal on June 4, 2001, in the courtyard of an ancient palace in Kathmandu, the capital. Gyanendra succeeded his nephew, Dipendra, who had murdered his father, Birendra, before shooting himself on June 1.

Gyanendra succeeded to the throne. Gyanendra was a wealthy businessman noted for conservation work. Nepal's king has exercised little formal power since the constitution was changed in 1990. However, Nepal's Hindu majority reveres the king as a reincarnation of deity.

Confusion. Conflicting early reports on the shooting caused public suspicion. While serving as *regent* (a person who rules when a monarch is unfit) before Dipendra's death, Gyanendra issued a statement that the accidental firing of a gun had caused the deaths. Gyanendra later explained his statement as an attempt to avoid placing blame on Dipendra while he was king. Some people suspected a conspiracy involving Gyanendra.

In October, 53-year-old Gyanendra named his only son, Paras, as his successor. Paras was known for a wild lifestyle. The 30-year-old Paras had been involved in two vehicular homicides but was not prosecuted in either case.

Maoist rebels expanded their efforts to establish a Communist government after the royal massacre with increased attacks on remote provincial police stations. Since 1996, such attacks had left some 2,000 people dead and about 4,000 guerrillas in control of seven poverty-stricken districts in Nepal's western Himalaya.

Prime Minister Girija Prasad Koirala was blamed for the rebel successes as well as for failing to protect the royal family. The 78-year-old premier resigned on July 19, 2001, and was succeeded by Sher Bahadur Deuba. Upon taking office, Deuba said that ending the Maoist rebellion was his top priority.

Brief cease-fire. The Maoists, who had hated Koirala, quickly agreed to a cease-fire once Deuba became prime minister. The two sides began talks in August. But on November 23, the Maoists broke the cease-fire with attacks on provincial police stations that left some 80 people dead. King Gyanendra declared an emergency and ordered the army to help the police. In the following two weeks, about 250 Maoists and and 80 soldiers were killed. ☐ Henry S. Bradsher

See also **Asia.**

Netherlands. Prime Minister Wim Kok announced in August 2001 that he would retire after the next general election, scheduled for May 2002. Kok, head of the Labor party, had led the Dutch government since 1994 and remained the country's most popular politician. His economic policies—which combined strict control of government spending, restraint on union wage demands, and measures to reduce unemployment—were credited with giving the Netherlands one of the strongest economic growth rates in Europe.

Kok chose Ad Melkert, the Labor Party's parliamentary leader, as his successor as party leader. Melkert faced a challenge from the Liberal Party, a coalition partner. The opposition Christian Democratic Party, which had governed the Netherlands from the end of World War II in 1945 until 1994, chose Jan-Peter Balkenende, a professor of economics, as its leader in October 2001.

Economic growth slowed significantly during 2001, as the Netherlands felt the impact of the worldwide economic slowdown. The government forecast in November that economic output would grow by 1.5 percent in 2001, down from 4 percent over the previous three years. The government also predicted a rise in unemployment for the first time in nearly a decade, though the jobless rate remained one of the lowest in Europe, at less than 3 percent.

Social policies. On April 1, the mayor of Amsterdam performed a civil marriage ceremony for four homosexual couples, the first such ceremony in the world. Parliament had adopted a law in 2000 giving homosexuals the same rights to marry, adopt children, and divorce as heterosexuals. On April 10, 2001, the parliament adopted a law allowing medically assisted suicide, legalizing a procedure the country had tolerated informally since 1993. The government hoped the new law would enable authorities to enforce strict rules for mercy killings.

Lockerbie verdicts. In January 2001, a jury in the Netherlands found Libyan intelligence officer Abdelbaset Ali Mohmed al-Megrahi guilty of the 1988 bombing of Pan Am Flight 103 over Lockerbie, Scotland. The bombing resulted in the deaths of 270 people. Al-Megrahi had been tried under Scottish law but at a special court set up in a former U.S. military base in the Netherlands. Al-Megrahi appealed the decision. A second Libyan defendant was found not guilty. ☐ Tom Buerkle

See also **Europe**.

Nevada. See **State government**.

New Brunswick. See **Canadian provinces**.

New Hampshire. See **State government**.

New Jersey. See **State government**.

New Mexico. See **State government**.

New York. See **State government**.

Thousands of people demonstrate at The Hague in the Netherlands in April as the Dutch parliament debates legalizing medically assisted suicide under certain conditions. The parliament passed the law later in April, making the Netherlands the world's first country to legalize euthanasia.

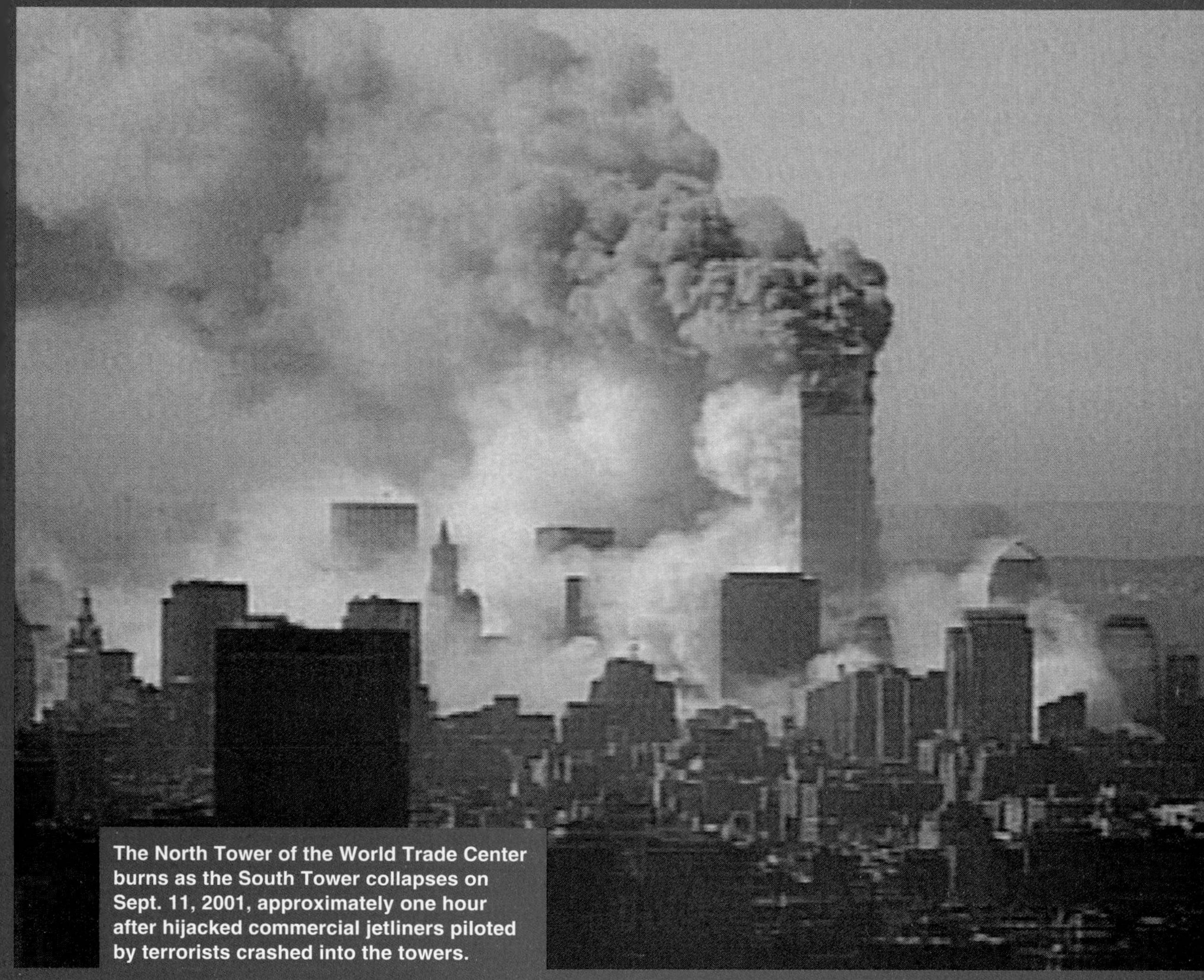

The North Tower of the World Trade Center burns as the South Tower collapses on Sept. 11, 2001, approximately one hour after hijacked commercial jetliners piloted by terrorists crashed into the towers.

New York City suffered a shocking terrorist attack on Sept. 11, 2001, that left thousands of people dead and the towers of the World Trade Center reduced to rubble. The twin towers had defined the city's downtown skyline for almost 30 years. The attacks also damaged or destroyed hundreds of businesses and devastated the city's tourism industry, which cut into tax revenues. The assault on the Trade Center was part of a coordinated strike against the United States in which terrorists hijacked four commercial jetliners.

The attacks in New York City began when American Airlines Flight 11 crashed into the Trade Center's 110-story North Tower shortly before 9 a.m. Eastern Daylight Time. Less than 20 minutes later, a second plane, United Airlines Flight 175, slammed into the South Tower. The exploding aircraft ignited massive fires, fed by jet fuel, that weakened the buildings' steel frameworks, causing them to collapse. The 47-story 7 World Trade Center also collapsed after tanks of diesel fuel inside the structure caught fire. The other buildings in the World Trade Center complex and many surrounding buildings also suffered severe damage.

Fire and police deaths. The Fire Department of New York City lost more than 300 firefighters in the disaster, a number exceeding the total of all firefighters killed in the line of duty in New York City in the previous 135 years. Most of the firefighters died when the towers collapsed. The New York City Police Department lost 23 officers as a result of the attacks. More than 70 civilian employees and security officers employed by the Port Authority of New York and New Jersey were also killed.

Economic impact. New York City's economy nose-dived following the attacks. City officials estimated the total monetary losses of the disaster at $80 billion to $100 billion. The city lost an estimated 125,000 jobs, 79,000 of them in October, in the largest one-month drop in city history. The attacks also cost the city an estimated $357.2 million in hotel, restaurant, and retail revenues between September 11 and early November. City officials predicted that declining tax revenues would create a shortfall of from $4 billion to $6 billion in the next city budget.

Anthrax scare. A bioterrorist attack on the United States in October claimed the life of one New York City woman and left a number of other New Yorkers infected with anthrax, a potentially fatal bacterial disease. Concerns about bioterrorism arose in early October after a 63-year-old man died from inhalation anthrax in Boca Raton, Florida. He apparently contracted the disease from anthrax *spores* (an inactive stage of the bacteria) sent in an envelope through the mail.

Later in October, an employee of NBC News in New York City developed a *cutaneous* (skin) form of anthrax. The woman had opened a letter addressed to news anchor Tom Brokaw containing a white powder. A CBS employee in New York City, who was an employee in the office of news anchor Dan Rather, also tested positive for the cutaneous form of anthrax, as did the child of a producer at ABC. In all three cases, the victims recovered after taking an antibiotic.

By the end of 2001, five people had died of inhalation anthrax in the eastern United States. Investigators believed that the anthrax had been manufactured in a U.S.-government labratory and speculated that the bioterrorist was likely an American scientist acting alone.

New mayor. Republican businessman Michael R. Bloomberg narrowly defeated Democratic candidate Mark Green, New York City public advocate, in an election for mayor of New York City on November 6. Bloomberg, who succeeded Rudolph W. Giuliani, spent a record $68.9 million of his own money on the campaign.

Airbus crash. An American Airlines jet bound for the Dominican Republic slammed into the Belle Harbor neighborhood of Queens, a borough of New York City, on November 12. The crash killed all 260 people on board the Airbus A-300 and 5 people on the ground. It destroyed or damaged a number of houses. □ Owen Moritz

See also **Aviation; City; Health care issues; Public health and safety; Republican Party; Terrorism; Terrorism: A Special Feature,** p. 38.

New Zealand.

Members of New Zealand's National Party, seeking new leadership after poor popularity polls, voted out party leader Jenny Shipley in October 2001. Shipley had served as New Zealand's first woman prime minister from 1997 to 1999 but had led the party to parliamentary defeat in 1999 elections. Finance spokesman Bill English succeeded her as party leader.

Economy. New Zealand's economy performed better than economists had predicted during the first half of 2001 with growth reaching 2.3 percent. Between August 2000 and August 2001, New Zealand's exports exceeded $32.6 billion (all amounts in New Zealand dollars), an increase of 21.6 percent over 2000. However, economists expected the slowdown of the global economy to impede New Zealand's economic growth in the fourth quarter.

Business confidence, which had risen as the Labour-led coalition government sought to improve relations with the commercial sector, fell in 2001, as the world economy weakened. New Zealand's economy also was affected by an electricity shortage, brought on by low lake levels, which fed hydroelectric power plants. In July, the government called for a 10-percent drop in electric consumption to avoid blackouts.

Aviation. The airline Qantas New Zealand collapsed in April with debts of almost $130 million. In September, the New Zealand national carrier, Air New Zealand, ran into financial trouble when its Australian subsidiary folded. However, the New Zealand government provided a $1-billion rescue package, which gave the government a majority stake in the airline.

Defense. In May, Prime Minister Helen Clark announced that the Royal New Zealand Air Force (RNZAF) was scrapping its combat strike capability. The move was expected to save $400 million over the next five years. The decision, which followed the cancellation in 2000 of an order for F-16 fighters, led to a public campaign to restore the RNZAF's combat capability.

Genetic engineering. In October, the government announced that research and development in genetic engineering (GE) would proceed, but there would be a two-year ban on commercial release of genetically engineered goods. Members of the Green Party, which takes an independent stand in Parliament, had opposed the GE research.

Yatchtsman killed. Renowned yachtsman Sir Peter Blake was killed by bandits who boarded his environmental research yacht, *Seamaster*, near Macapa on the Amazon River in Brazil on December 5. Blake, one of the world's leading yachtsmen, won the America's Cup in 1995 and 2000. He also won round-the-world races in 1990 and 1994.

□ Gavin Ellis

Newfoundland.

See **Canadian provinces.**

News bytes

Selected news from 2001:

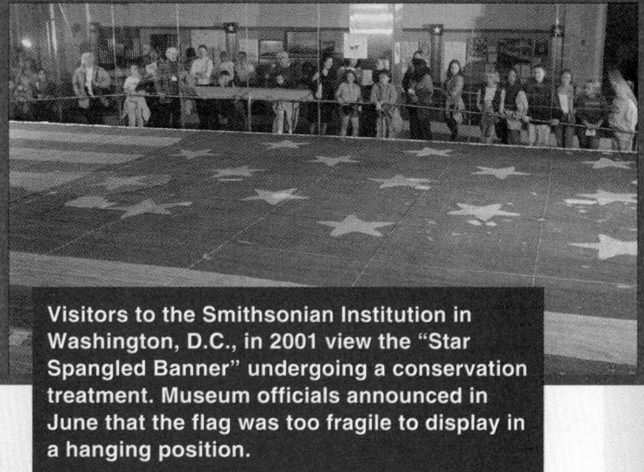

Visitors to the Smithsonian Institution in Washington, D.C., in 2001 view the "Star Spangled Banner" undergoing a conservation treatment. Museum officials announced in June that the flag was too fragile to display in a hanging position.

Flag conservation. Officials at the Smithsonian Institution's National Museum of American History in Washington, D.C., announced in June 2001 that the flag that inspired Francis Scott Key to write the "Star-Spangled Banner" in 1814 was too fragile to be displayed in a hanging position. In 1998, museum conservators, curators, and other specialists had moved the flag to a laboratory to begin a conservation project to clean and stabilize the fabric. The conservators discovered that the 30-foot by 34-foot (9-meter by 10-meter) flag was in worse condition than originally thought.

Officials believed that the flag may survive another 500 years if displayed in a controlled environment. In late 2001, museum officials announced plans to construct a special room within the museum in which they would display the flag at a 30-degree angle to ease stress on the fabric. The museum was scheduled to complete the conservation project in 2002, but officials expected it would take several more years to construct the new display room in the museum.

Gilbert Stuart's famed 1796 Landsdowne portrait of George Washington was purchased by the Smithsonian Institution in March with $20 million donated by the Donald W. Reynolds Foundation of Las Vegas, Nevada. The English owner of the painting, which had been on loan to the National Portrait Gallery in Washington, D.C., since 1968, had planned to sell the portrait at auction.

Abraham Lincoln artifact displayed. One of five flags that decorated President Abraham Lincoln's box at Ford's Theatre in Washington, D.C., the night that he was assassinated on April 14, 1865, was placed on display on July 5, 2001, at the Connecticut Historical Society in Hartford. A librarian at the historical society discovered the Treasury Guard flag in 1998 among other Civil War (1861-1865) relics in a basement at the society's headquarters. The librarian was searching for props for a lecture. The society later confirmed the historical significance of the flag, which has 13 stripes, with a painted eagle and 35 stars on a field of blue. The flag was donated to the society in the 1920's. Historians believe that it hung to the left of the president in the theater box. After examining period illustrations, a number of Civil War historians concluded that the flag appeared to be the one that Lincoln grasped after being shot by actor John Wilkes Booth.

In July, Susan Schoelwer, director of collections at the Connecticut Historical Society in Hartford (left), announces the discovery of a flag that decorated the presidential box at Ford's Theatre the night of Abraham Lincoln's assassination in 1865.

Medal of Honor. In January 2001, President Bill Clinton posthumously awarded the Medal of Honor to President Theodore Roosevelt for leading an uphill charge at the Battle of San Juan Hill during the Spanish-American War (1898). The Medal of Honor is the highest military honor awarded by the United States.

In July 1898, Roosevelt, as commander of the

First United States Volunteer Cavalry, also known as the "Rough Riders," led an attack against Spanish forces surrounding Santiago, Cuba, and was the first person to reach the enemy trenches. Roosevelt later served as president of the United States from 1901 to 1909. Roosevelt's descendants donated the medal to the White House for display in the Roosevelt Room.

Record week on Mount Everest. Good weather conditions supported a record 37 climbers who reached the peak of Mount Everest in May 2001. Mount Everest, the world's highest mountain, rises 29,035 feet (8,850 meters) above sea level in the Himalayas on Nepal's border with Tibet, an area that is controlled by China.

On May 25, Erik Weihenmayer became the first blind person to climb to the top of Mount Everest. A team of *Sherpas* guides and other climbers accompanied Weihenmayer on his trek. Weihenmayer followed the sound of bells tied to the jackets of his climbing mates and guides to climb Everest.

On the same day, 64-year-old Sherman Bull became the oldest person to conquer Everest. He was accompanied by his son, Brad Bull, and a Nepalese guide. The Bulls were the first father-and-son team to reach the mountain top.

On May 22, a 15-year-old Nepalese boy, Temba Tsheri, became the youngest person to reach the summit. He had lost five of his fingers to frostbite in a previous attempt that failed in 2000.

Sir Edmund Hillary of New Zealand and Nepalese mountaineer Tenzing Norgay were the first people to reach the summit of Mount Everest. Since their initial climb in 1953, more than 1,000 people have completed the climb, facing such challenges as avalanches, dehydration, depression, extreme weather conditions, frostbite, infections, hypothermia, and lack of oxygen.

Ride on the wild side. The HyperSonic XLC, the world's first compressed-air roller coaster, went into operation on March 24, 2001, at Kings Dominion theme park in Doswell, Virginia. The HyperSonic XLC contains no curls, twists, or loops. Rather, a blast of air sends riders straight up a 165-foot (50-meter) high steel tower and back down. The 45-second ride moves passengers from 0 to 80 miles (0 to 128 kilometers) per hour in less than two seconds.

It's Howdy Doody time. U.S. District Judge Christopher Droney ruled in January 2001 that a museum in Detroit was the rightful owner of the original Howdy Doody puppet. The puppet was used on "The Howdy Doody Show," the first nationally broadcast children's television show in the United States, from 1947 to 1960.

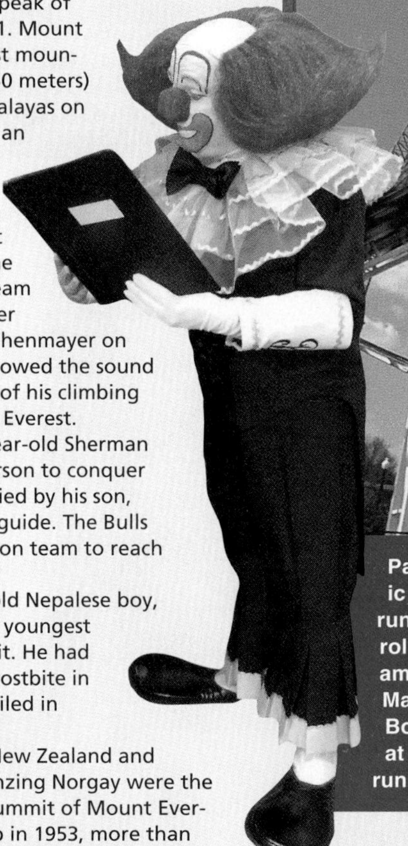

The puppet was the subject of a custody battle between the family of Rufus Rose, Howdy Doody's off-camera puppeteer, and the Detroit Institute of Arts. Judge Droney ruled that Rose, who died in 1975, and the NBC television network had made a clear contractual agreement in 1967 to donate the original Howdy Doody to the museum. Rose's family had argued that the puppeteer had only considered donating the Howdy Doody puppet to the museum. The family claimed that the freckle-faced puppet, which became a popular-culture icon, might not have been the original. The judge dis-

Passengers aboard the HyperSonic XLC (above) enjoy the inaugural run of the first compressed-air roller coaster at Kings Dominion amusement park in Virginia in March. Joey D'Auria (left) portrays Bozo the Clown in Chicago in July at the final taping of the longest running children's television show.

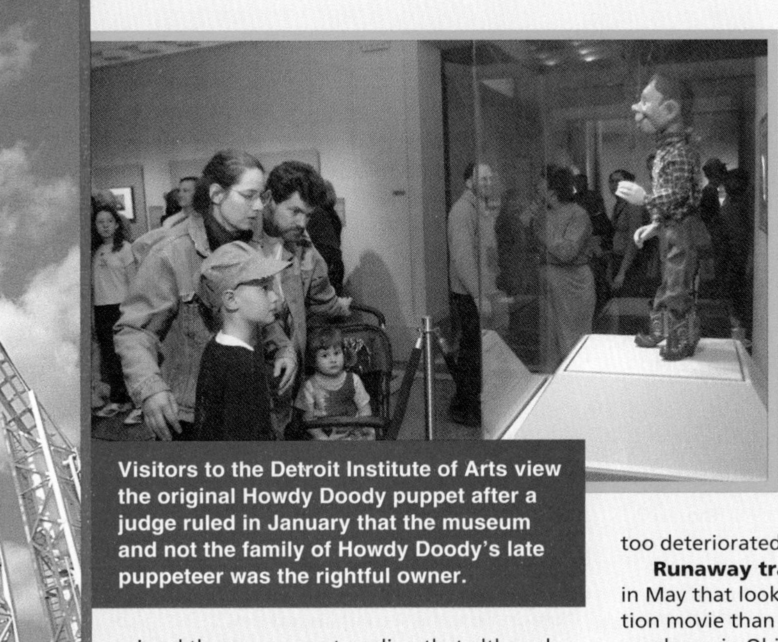

Visitors to the Detroit Institute of Arts view the original Howdy Doody puppet after a judge ruled in January that the museum and not the family of Howdy Doody's late puppeteer was the rightful owner.

missed these arguments, ruling that although several duplicate Howdy Doody puppets had been created during the course of the television program, the puppet in question was authentic and that the Detroit Institute of Arts was the rightful owner.

***Monitor* engine raised.** On July 16, 2001, crews raised the steam engine of the U.S.S. *Monitor* from the Atlantic Ocean, approximately 16 miles (26 kilometers) south of Cape Hatteras, off the coast of North Carolina. The *Monitor,* an ironclad ship built by the Union during the Civil War (1861-1865), sank in 1863 while being towed in a storm. The *Monitor* revolutionized naval warfare when it battled another ironclad, the Confederate C.S.S. *Virginia,* to a draw in 1862.

A search team found the *Monitor* in 1974. Work crews in 2001, using a crane onboard a barge, raised the *Monitor's* 30-ton (27-metric ton) engine from more than 200 feet (60 meters) below the water's surface. The U.S. Navy and the National Oceanic and Atmospheric Administration (NOAA), a federal agency that works to improve knowledge and use of the environment, jointly paid for the recovery operation. NOAA officials plan to restore the engine over the course of the next 10 years. It will be displayed at the Mariners' Museum in Newport News, Virginia. The rest of the ship was too deteriorated to be raised to the surface.

Runaway train rescue. In a dramatic rescue in May that looked more like a scene from an action movie than an event in real life, a railroad employee in Ohio leaped on board a runaway, unmanned train that was loaded with a hazardous material.

The locomotive was pulling 47 cars, two of which carried concentrated molten phenol, a hazardous liquid that can burn human skin on contact. The engineer left the locomotive unattended in a train yard near Toledo, Ohio. Investigators said that though the locomotive's brake was set, the throttle was left sufficiently open to overcome brake resistance and start the train moving.

The train rolled for more than 65 miles (105 kilometers) through four Ohio counties at ap-

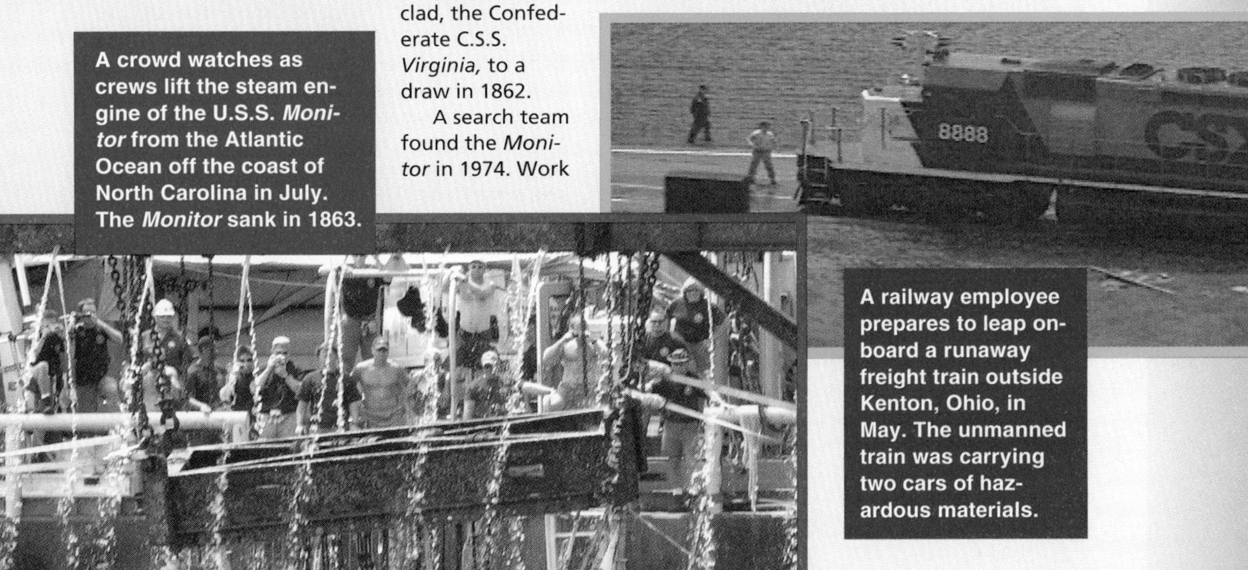

A crowd watches as crews lift the steam engine of the U.S.S. *Monitor* from the Atlantic Ocean off the coast of North Carolina in July. The *Monitor* sank in 1863.

A railway employee prepares to leap onboard a runaway freight train outside Kenton, Ohio, in May. The unmanned train was carrying two cars of hazardous materials.

proximately 45 miles (72 kilometers) per hour before two linked locomotives were able to link onto its last car and apply their brakes. The engines slowed the runaway train to about 15 miles (24 kilometers) per hour just outside the town of Kenton, Ohio, enabling Jon Hosfeld, a 31-year railroad veteran, to grab a handrail at the front of the engine and swing aboard to stop the train.

FDR Memorial. A bronze statue of President Franklin Delano Roosevelt seated in a wheelchair was unveiled on Jan. 10, 2001, at the Franklin Delano Roosevelt Memorial in Washington, D.C. The design of the original memorial, which was dedicated in 1997, sparked controversy among disability-rights activists because it failed to depict Roosevelt, who was disabled by polio in 1921, in a wheelchair. Roosevelt discouraged photographers from taking pictures of him in a wheelchair. The activists argued that the character traits Roosevelt developed in coping with his disability contributed significantly to his abilities as a leader during the national crises of the *Great Depression* (a worldwide business slump of the 1930's) and World War II (1939-1945). Advocates for the disabled praised the addition of the statue to the presidential memorial. They said that portraying Roosevelt in a wheelchair paid tribute to the president and to the successes of all people with disabilities.

☐ Tim Frystak

President Bill Clinton, with Franklin D. Roosevelt's grandchildren, Anna and James Roosevelt, attends the unveiling in January of a new statue at the Roosevelt Memorial in Washington, D.C. The controversial statue portrays the former president in a wheelchair.

Newspaper. The Supreme Court of the United States ruled on June 25, 2001, that publishers infringed on the copyrights of free-lance writers by reproducing their articles in electronic databases and on CD-ROM discs without permission from the authors. The free-lance authors who brought the lawsuit claimed that newspapers and magazines could owe thousands of contributors between $2.5 billion and $600 billion for reproducing or reselling articles written before 1995. Following the ruling, publishers told free-lance writers that affected articles would be removed from electronic databases unless the writers agreed to let the articles remain in archives for no additional compensation.

Advertising revenue declines. Newspaper publishers struggled with falling profits in 2001 following steep declines in classified advertising, an important source of revenue for newspapers. The steepest declines were in help-wanted advertisements, which were affected by a weak economy. The San Jose, California-based Knight-Ridder Corporation, the second-largest newspaper publisher in the United States, reported in May that help-wanted advertising at its newspapers had declined 26 percent in the first five months of 2001, compared with the same period in 2000. Officials at *The Washington Post* reported that their help-wanted ad revenue declined 31.5 percent in the first five months of 2001, compared with the same period in 2000.

Newspaper circulation. Figures released in October 2001 by the Audit Bureau of Circulations, an industry trade group located in Schaumburg, Illinois, revealed that most major newspapers in the United States increased their weekday circulation but lost sales on Sundays during a six-month period ending in September 2001. Seven of the top 10 U.S. newspapers showed weekday circulation gains, while only 3 of the top 10 Sunday U.S. newspapers increased circulation. The average weekday circulation of *USA Today,* the best-selling newspaper in the United States, declined 0.7 percent to 2,249,933 copies. *The New York Times,* the highest-selling Sunday newspaper, sustained a 0.8 percent decrease in sales. The paper's average Sunday circulation totaled 1,668,650 copies.

Newspaper closing. Officials at Cox Newspapers Inc. in Atlanta, Georgia, announced in October that they would stop publishing their afternoon newspaper, the *Atlanta Journal,* in November. The *Journal* was to be merged with its larger morning edition counterpart, the *Atlanta Constitution.* The company cited declining circulation and increased production and delivery costs.

☐ Mark Fitzgerald

See also **Economics; Supreme Court of the United States.**

Nicaragua. Enrique Bolanos, a former vice president and the candidate of the ruling Liberal Constitutionalist Party, was elected president of Nicaragua on Nov. 4, 2001. Bolanos defeated Daniel Ortega Saavedra, a former president. Bolanos received 54 percent of the vote to Ortega's 45 percent. Bolanos promised to create jobs, rebuild the economy, and fight corruption.

Ortega's new image. Bolanos, 73, was a businessman who had studied industrial engineering in the United States. His businesses were confiscated on three occasions by the Marxist government headed by Ortega from 1979 to 1990. During the 2001 campaign, Ortega abandoned his former Marxist principles and pledged that, if elected, he would respect property rights and embrace free market economics.

Coffee crisis. Nicaragua's economy was badly hurt in 2001 when world coffee prices plunged to less than half their 1999 levels. Approximately 16,000 people in the El Tuma-La Dalia coffee-growing region were unemployed in August 2001. To make their plight known, 500 workers from the region erected a shantytown in the provincial capital of Matagalpa. Economists blamed the low prices on a global glut of coffee.

☐ Nathan A. Haverstock

See also **Latin America.**

Niger. See **Africa.**

Nigeria. Analysts and foreign diplomats credited President Olusegun Obasanjo in 2001—two years into his elected four-year term—with bringing stability to Nigeria. Obasanjo's election in 1999 ended 15 years of military rule in Nigeria. However, the country had made little economic progress under the People's Democratic Party (PDP), according to the International Monetary Fund (IMF), a United Nations-affiliated organization that provides credit to member nations.

In August 2001, the IMF issued a critical assessment of Nigeria's economy in its annual report on the country. Mismanagement and corruption undermined Nigeria's economic performance. Although Nigeria was the world's sixth largest producer of crude oil in 2001, shortages continued at the country's gasoline pumps. In June, Obasanjo dismissed eight ministers from his economic reform team, alleging corruption and incompetence.

Military heads "retire." In April, Obasanjo dismissed chiefs of Nigeria's army, navy, and air force in a shakeup of the armed forces. According to a government press release, Lieutenant-General Victor Malu, Vice-Admiral Victor Ombu, and Air Marshal Ibrahim Alfa retired voluntarily. Political observers suggested that President Obasanjo had fired the men to rid the armed forces of people who remained loyal to the former military rulers.

Violence between Muslims and Christians flared again in Nigeria in 2001. In July, violent confrontations between Muslims and Christians in the northern state of Baluchi resulted in the deaths of 400 people. In early September, clashes between Christian and Muslim youths left at least 165 people dead and more than 1,000 others injured in the city of Jos in central Nigeria. Further violence rocked the northern city of Kano in October, leaving some 200 people dead.

Religious tensions had increased in Nigeria since the late 1990's, when many northern and central states introduced *Sharia* (Islamic religious law) into their law codes. The escalating violence in 2001 prompted some political analysts to speculate that Nigeria might split apart between the predominantly Muslim north and the mainly Christian south.

Space program. In July 2001, Nigeria established a National Space Research and Development Agency with a $100-million startup budget. The agency aimed to launch Nigeria's own satellite by 2005. The World Bank, a United Nations organization that provides loans to countries for development, described the project as "inappropriate" in a country where two-thirds of the population were living on less than $1 a day in 2001.

☐ Simon Baynham

See also **Africa.**

Nobel Prizes in literature, peace, the sciences, and economics were awarded in October 2001 by the Norwegian Storting (parliament) in Oslo and by the Royal Swedish Academy of Sciences, the Karolinska Institute, and the Swedish Academy of Literature in Stockholm. Each prize was worth about $943,000.

The 2001 Nobel Prize for literature was awarded to British writer V. S. Naipaul, who was born and raised on the island of Trinidad in the West Indies. Naipaul, whose family came to Trinidad from India, often explores themes of identity in postcolonial cultures. Critics have declared him one of the most important writers of the postcolonial experience.

Vidiadhar Surajprasad Naipaul's works include both fiction and nonfiction and are often autobiographical. He first gained recognition in 1961 with *A House for Mr. Biswas,* a novel about Indian immigrants in the Caribbean. *Beyond Belief* (1998) describes his travels in Indonesia, Iran, Pakistan, and Malaysia and expresses a highly critical view of the conversion of non-Arabic peoples to Islamic fundamentalism.

The 2001 Nobel Peace Prize was awarded jointly to the United Nations (UN) and Kofi Annan, the international organization's secretary-general, "for their work for a better organized and more peaceful world." The Nobel Committee praised Annan for his leadership on issues ranging from the AIDS crisis in Africa to the international campaign against terrorism in the wake of the Sept. 11, 2001, attacks on the United States. The committee also cited Annan's administrative skills in effectively managing the UN's "modest resources."

The 2001 Nobel Prize for physiology or medicine went to Leland H. Hartwell, of the Fred Hutchinson Cancer Research Center in Seattle, and R. Timothy Hunt and Paul M. Nurse, of the London-based Imperial Cancer Research Fund. The researchers were honored for their description of the cell cycle, a process by which a living cell grows, duplicates its genetic material, and divides into two daughter cells. Their work led to a greater understanding of how the process can lead to cancer.

Hartwell, in studies of yeast cell division, discovered more than 100 genes involved in regulating the cell cycle, including the "start" gene, which begins the process. Nurse, who studied a different type of yeast, identified a gene that controls cell division and discovered that the gene is also present in human cells. Hunt uncovered the process by which molecules called cyclins regulate phases of the cycle.

The 2001 Nobel Prize for economics was awarded to Joseph E. Stiglitz of Columbia University in New York City, George A. Akerlof of the University of California at Berkeley, and A. Michael Spence of Stanford University in Stanford, California. These economists challenged the widely held view that markets are completely self-regulating mechanisms that are usually better left alone. The three argued that markets operate on the basis of information, and if information is absent or inaccurate, markets can go badly astray. In their view, a proper role for government is to rectify inequality of information between sellers and buyers. The Nobel Committee made special mention of the work of Joseph Stiglitz, noting that his contributions "have transformed the way economists think about the working of markets."

The 2001 Nobel Prize for chemistry was awarded to retired chemist William S. Knowles of St. Louis, Missouri; K. Barry Sharpless of the Scripps Research Institute in La Jolla, California; and Ryoji Noyori of Nagoya University in Japan. The scientists developed techniques for controlling the outcomes of chemical reactions involved in the production of many drugs.

Many molecules come in two forms that are mirror images of each other. The two mirror forms can produce starkly different results. For example, a molecule in the drug thalidomide controls nausea in pregnant women. However, its mirror form—which was also in the drug when it was first produced in the 1950's—causes severe birth defects. Knowles, Sharpless, and Noyori developed methods of reliably producing the desired form of a molecule. Medications that have resulted from the researchers' discoveries include L-dopa for Parkinson disease, beta-blocker heart medications, and anti-inflammatory drugs.

The 2001 Nobel Prize for physics was awarded to U.S. physicists Carl E. Wieman of the University of Colorado at Boulder and Eric A. Cornell of the National Institutes of Standards and Technology in Boulder; and to German-born Wolfgang Ketterle of the Massachusetts Institute of Technology in Cambridge. In 1995, Wieman and Cornell produced an artificial state of matter, called the Bose-Einstein condensate, named for the physicists who had predicted its existence in the 1920's—Albert Einstein and Satyendra Nath Bose. Ketterle confirmed and extended Wieman's and Cornell's work.

In a Bose-Einstein condensate, atoms in a supercooled clump form a single wavelike entity similar to a laser beam. However, while laser beams are based on particles of light, a Bose-Einstein condensate is based on particles of matter. Some scientists believe the discovery may lead to such developments as ultrafast, ultratiny computing devices. ☐ Robert N. Knight

See also **Literature, world; United Nations.**

Northern Ireland. The peace process between Roman Catholics and Protestants in Northern Ireland remained in disarray for much of 2001. However, the two groups achieved a major breakthrough in October when the Irish Republican Army (IRA)—a military organization dedicated to uniting the independent country of Ireland with Northern Ireland—agreed to dispose of some of its weapons.

Throughout 2001, the Northern Ireland Assembly, a parliament created by the Good Friday peace agreement of 1998, attempted to implement the terms of the agreement. The Assembly was made up of representatives from all political parties under the leadership of First (Prime) Minister David Trimble of the Protestant Ulster Unionist Party. Sinn Fein, the political wing of the IRA, demanded reform of the Protestant-dominated Royal Ulster Constabulary and the reduction of a British military presence. The Ulster Unionists, who favored the continuation of the union of Northern Ireland with Great Britain, complained that the IRA had failed to *decommission* (remove from service) its weapons. Trimble came under repeated pressure from his own party not to cooperate with Sinn Fein until the IRA had begun to disarm.

David Trimble resigned from his position as first minister of Northern Ireland on July 1 because of the continued refusal of the IRA to abandon its weapons. Trimble insisted that the IRA's decision to allow an international inspection of its armories did not represent sufficient progress in the disarmament process. John Reid, the secretary for Northern Ireland in the government of the United Kingdom, chose to suspend Northern Ireland's government for two periods of six weeks each (to allow time for further negotiations), rather than to call for new elections to the Assembly that might result in greater representation for extremist parties.

IRA issues. In August, three members of the IRA were arrested in Colombia, where they were accused of training rebel forces in the use of explosives. The arrests led to allegations that the IRA had still not renounced violence. Terrorist attack on the United States on September 11, which led to global outrage against all forms of terrorism, put further pressure on the IRA. Gerry Adams, president of Sinn Fein, and Martin McGuiness, the party's chief negotiator, revealed in October that they had urged the IRA to disarm in order to salvage the peace process.

On October 23, the IRA reported that it had decided to put its arms "beyond use." The international decommissioning organization led by Canadian General Jean de Chastelain confirmed that the group had begun to dispose of its weapons. The move was generally regarded as a breakthrough in the peace process. Trimble expressed his satisfaction with the IRA's peaceful intentions and agreed that his party could share power with Sinn Fein once more. The British government began to reduce its military presence in Northern Ireland, dismantling a number of army watchtowers.

New government. Trimble's return to power was initially frustrated when he failed to obtain a majority vote in favor of his reelection on November 2. Two members of his own party voted against him, denying him the majority required in the Northern Ireland Assembly. The situation was resolved when the centrist Alliance party allowed three of its members to temporarily redesignate themselves as Unionists to vote Trimble back into power on November 6.

Hume retires. On September 17, John Hume, leader of the moderate Catholic Social Democratic and Labour party and a recipient of the 1998 Nobel Peace Prize for his role in negotiating the Good Friday agreement, announced his retirement from politics. Hume was replaced by Mark Durkan, who became deputy first minister in the reformed Northern Ireland government on November 6. ☐ Rohan McWilliam

See also **Ireland; United Kingdom.**

Northwest Territories. See **Canadian territories.**

Parents and police shield schoolgirls being pelted with bottles and nails as they pass through a Protestant neighborhood in Belfast, Northern Ireland, on their way to a Roman Catholic school in September.

Norway. Voters dismissed Norway's Labour government in an election on Sept. 10, 2001, and returned Kjell Magne Bondevik to power at the head of a center-right coalition. During the campaign, Bondevik, a Lutheran minister, promised to use more of Norway's oil wealth to finance tax cuts and higher government spending on social services, education, and the environment.

Bondevik's Christian Democratic Party won only 12 percent of the vote, down from 14 percent in the previous parliamentary election in 1997. The Conservative Party's share of the vote rose to 21 percent, from 14 percent in 1997. Nevertheless, Bondevik, because of his strong personal popularity, was able to form a government. He became prime minister on Oct. 19, 2001. Bondevik formed a three-party coalition with his Christian Democrats, the Conservatives, and the Liberal Party, which won 4 percent of the vote.

Bondevik led the same three parties in a coalition government from 1997 to 2000. Like its predecessor, the new coalition was a minority government and controlled only 62 seats in the 165-seat parliament. Bondevik's position was helped, however, by a collapse in support for the Labour Party, which had dominated Norwegian politics for more than 70 years. Labour's share of the vote declined to 24 percent from 35 percent. The election result reflected voter disenchantment with the high taxes and poor quality of social services during Labour's rule.

Norway's economy was less affected by the global slowdown of 2001 than were the economies of most other European countries. Norway's North Sea oil and gas industry, which makes up a large part of the country's *gross domestic product* (the value of all goods and services produced in a year), remained strong because of high oil prices in early 2001. The government forecast that the economy would grow by 1.7 percent in 2001, down from 3.4 percent in 2000 but equal to the average of the European Union nations. To improve Norway's oil production, the government sold an 18-percent stake in Statoil, the country's largest state-owned oil company, in June 2001 for $3 billion (3.27 billion euros).

Royal wedding. Norwegians thronged the streets of Oslo, the capital, on August 25 to celebrate the marriage of Crown Prince Haakon, son of King Harald V and heir to the throne, to Mette-Marit Tjessem Hoiby. The relationship had stirred controversy because Tjessem Hoiby was the mother of a four-year-old child. Her popularity soared, however, after she apologized for her former "wild life." ☐ Tom Buerkle

See also **Europe.**

Nova Scotia. See **Canadian provinces.**

Nuclear energy. See **Energy supply.**

Nutrition. See **Food.**

Ocean. Evidence mounted in 2001 that global warming is being caused by the burning of *fossil fuels* (coal, oil, gas, and wood), and dire predictions were made about the toll that global warming may take on the ocean. In addition, a hidden world was discovered inside coral reefs, and fossils revealed that whales are related to pigs.

Ocean warming. Much of the evidence of global warming has come from measurements of increasing air temperatures. However, oceanographer Sydney Levitus of the National Oceanic and Atmospheric Administration in Silver Spring, Maryland, has reported that the upper 9,800 feet (3,000 meters) of the world's oceans also warmed considerably between 1955 and 1996. In 2001, Levitus and Tim Barnett, a climate scientist at Scripps Institution of Oceanography in La Jolla, California, used computer simulations of the climate to test whether this ocean warming was caused by natural climate variations or *greenhouse gases,* gases that absorb heat in the atmosphere and direct it downward toward Earth. The burning of fossil fuels emits large amounts of the greenhouse gas carbon dioxide.

In April 2001, the scientists reported that the computer simulations produced the observed increase in ocean warming only when the computers were programmed to factor in greenhouse gas emissions. This implied that the increasing warmth of the sea is being caused by greenhouse gases generated by human activities.

Endangered coral reefs. Nearly all of the world's coral reefs may die by 2050 if ocean warming continues at the current rate, marine biologist Rupert Ormond of Glasgow University in Scotland reported in September 2001. Since the early 1990's, scientists have documented a widespread destruction of coral reefs resulting from *bleaching,* a process in which corals turn white. Bleached corals often die from disease or storm damage. Evidence indicates that bleaching may be caused by increased water temperatures. Ormand combined the measured rate of ocean warming with the observed rate of coral reef loss and projected these rates into the future. Marine scientists noted that several other factors besides ocean warming, including overfishing and pollution, threaten coral reefs.

Hidden reef community. In October 2001, an international team of scientists led by marine ecologist Claudio Richter of the Center for Tropical Marine Ecology in Germany reported the discovery of a previously unknown community of organisms inside coral reefs. Divers with the team used *endoscopes* (tubelike instruments with a camera on the tip) to examine the interior of deep crevices in coral reefs at nine sites in the Red Sea, which separates the Arabian Peninsula and northeastern Africa. They discovered more than 370 types of sponges living in the crevices, in addition to various other *filter-feeding* (feeding on small debris suspended in the water) species. According to Richter, the sponges inside reef crevices may excrete minerals that provide nutrients for organisms on the outside of reefs.

Land ancestors of whales. New descriptions of four species of whale ancestors in 2001 confirmed that whales are descended from land mammals related to modern pigs and cows. Paleontologist Philip D. Gingerich reported in September the discovery in Pakistan of 47-million-year-old fossils of two species. One of the species, a sea-lion-sized creature named *Rodhocetus balochistanensis,* had forefeet with hooflike nails and hind feet with webbed toes. Paleontologist Johannes Thewissen of Northeastern Ohio Universities College of Medicine in Rootstown published a description in September of 50-million-year-old fossils of two whale ancestors from Pakistan. These creatures—one the size of a wolf, the other the size of a fox—had long, spindly legs. All four of the species had ankle bones similar to those found in *even-toed ungulates,* a group of hoofed animals that includes pigs, cows, and hippopotamuses. ☐ Christina S. Johnson

See also **Global warming: A Special Report.**

Ohio. See **State government.**

Oklahoma. See **State government.**

Olympic Games. On July 13, 2001, the International Olympic Committee (IOC) awarded the 2008 Summer Games to Beijing, China. The IOC selected Beijing over Toronto, Paris, and Istanbul. The games will be the first held in China. The selection of China was controversial because of China's human rights record. IOC members voiced the hope that their selection of Beijing would accelerate human rights reforms in China.

Election. On July 16, 2001, the IOC selected Belgium's Jacques Rogge to replace Juan Antonio Samaranch as IOC president. Samaranch had served in the office for 21 years. Rogge, an orthopedic surgeon who became an IOC member in 1991, was chosen over Un Yong Kim of South Korea and Richard Pound of Canada.

Pound, who negotiated various Olympics television sponsorship deals, resigned after the vote but later decided to remain as head of the World Anti-Doping Agency. Kim, who in 1999 was reprimanded for misusing his influence in a scandal involving the selection of Salt Lake City, Utah, as host city of the 2002 Winter Games, refused to attend the ceremony during which Rogge's selection was announced. ☐ Michael Kates

Oman. See **Middle East.**

Ontario. See **Canadian provinces.**

Opera. See **Classical music.**

Oregon. See **State government.**

Pacific Islands. The South Pacific Forum, an organization that promotes cooperation among small, independent Pacific nations, Australia, and New Zealand, observed its 30th anniversary in 2001. Delegates at an August meeting in Nauru discussed two major issues: plans to develop a free-trade zone to include all the Forum nations; and the failure of Australia and the United States to ratify the Kyoto Protocol. The protocol is a 1997 international agreement to reduce fossil fuel emissions, which are blamed for global warming. Officials of many island countries believe their nations are at risk of flooding from rising sea levels expected to be caused by global warming.

Fiji citizens elected a new parliament in August 2001 to replace the military-backed interim government that had been in place since July 2000. The interim government, made up entirely of ethnic Fijians, had assumed power after a *coup* (overthrow) ousted Prime Minister Mahendra Chaudhry, who was of Indian descent.

The United Fiji Party, led by interim Prime Minister Laisenia Qarase and representing ethnic Fijians, won a parliamentary majority of 31 seats. The Fiji Labour Party, supported by mostly Indo-Fijians, took 27 seats. George Speight of the Conservative Alliance Party won a seat despite facing treason charges for leading the 2000 coup. Qarase formed a coalition government.

Solomon Islands. Citizens elected a new parliament on Dec. 5, 2001. The island had undergone a change of power in June 2000, when an armed group of Malaita islanders ousted Bartholomew Ulufa'alu as prime minister and installed Mannaseh Sogavare. In 2001, several political parties, including Sogavare's People's Progressive Party, contested 50 parliamentary seats up for election. The People's Alliance Party won 20 seats; Ulufa'alu's Solomon Islands Alliance for Change party won 12 seats. The People's Progressive Party lost seats. On December 17, the parliament named Sir Allan Kemakeza of the People's Alliance Party prime minister.

Papua New Guinea ministers signed an agreement in August with leaders of Bougainville Island granting the Bougainville people greater political and administrative control over their own affairs. The agreement allowed the Bougainville government to have various powers, such as local taxation, that existed nowhere else in Papua New Guinea. The agreement also authorized a referendum, to be held in 10 to 15 years, that would offer Bougainvilleans the chance to vote for independence. Bougainvilleans began armed conflict against the Papua New Guinea government in 1988.

Vanuatu. In April 2001, the Vanuatu parliament removed Prime Minister Barak Sope in a no-

Facts in brief on Pacific Island countries

Country	Population	Government	Monetary unit*	Foreign trade (million U.S.$) Exports†	Imports†
Australia	19,231,000	Governor General Peter Hollingworth; Prime Minister John Howard	dollar (1.97 = $1)	63,877	71,537
Fiji	840,000	President Josefa Iloilo; Prime Minister Laisenia Qarase	dollar (2.30 = $1)	510	721
Kiribati	85,000	President Teburoro Tito	Australian dollar	7	33
Marshall Islands	68,000	President Kessai Note	U.S. dollar	28	58
Micronesia, Federated States of	124,000	President Leo A. Falcam	U.S. dollar	73	168
Nauru	12,000	President Rene Harris	Australian dollar	25	21
New Zealand	3,930,000	Governor General Dame Silvia Cartwright; Prime Minister Helen Clark	dollar (2.41 = $1)	13,267	13,906
Palau	20,000	President Tommy Remengesau, Jr.	U.S. dollar	14	126
Papua New Guinea	5,015,000	Governor General Sir Silas Atopare; Prime Minister Sir Mekere Morauta	kina (3.53 = $1)	2,100	1,000
Samoa	187,000	Head of State Malietoa Tanumafili II; Prime Minister Tuila'epa Sailele Malielegaoi	tala (3.52 = $1)	14	106
Solomon Islands	470,000	Governor General Sir John Lapli; Prime Minister Sir Allan Kemakeza	dollar (5.37 = $1)	165	152
Tonga	100,000	King Taufa'ahau Tupou IV; Prime Minister Lavaka ata Ulukalala	pa'anga (2.21 = $1)	12	73
Tuvalu	13,000	Governor General Sir Tomasi Puapua; Prime Minister Koloa Talake	Australian dollar	1	4
Vanuatu	199,000	President Father John Bani; Prime Minister Edward Natapei	vatu (147.90 = $1)	26	10

*Exchange rates as of Oct. 5, 2001, or latest available data.
†Latest available data.

confidence vote. Political differences prevented Sope from holding his five-party parliamentary coalition together. Edward Natapei, whose Vanua'aku Party had led Vanuatu to independence in 1980, replaced Sope as prime minister.

During 2001, Vanuatu issued several licenses to companies in Australia to establish Internet Web sites for online gambling. The Vanuatu government received a percentage of profits from the gambling operations, in addition to license fees.

Samoa. In March elections, the ruling Human Rights Protection Party suffered a sharp loss of public support when its total number of parliamentary seats fell from 38 to 28. The party formed a coalition with independent parliamentarians to keep Tuila'epa Sailele Malielegaoi in office as prime minister.

The Samoan tourist industry benefited from unrest in other Pacific Island nations in 2001 because tourists chose to visit Samoa rather than such other tumultuous destinations as Fiji and the Solomon Islands. Australians, who make up a large part of the tourism market in the region, were warned by their government to stay away from Fiji and the Solomon Islands because of political unrest. Tourists poured an estimated $4 million into the Samoan economy in 2001.

Tuvalu. In December, Prime Minister Faimalaga Luk lost a no-confidence vote. The parliament elected Koloa Talake prime minister by secret ballot on December 13. Talake's government will hold power until a general election in 2002.

☐ Eugene Ogan

See also **Australia; Global warming: A Special Report; New Zealand.**

Painting. See **Art.**

Pakistan. A United States-led military campaign in Afghanistan, which began on Oct. 7, 2001, brought both trouble and benefits to Pakistan. The campaign was part of a "war against terrorism" in response to terrorist attacks on the United States on September 11. The United States accused the radical Islamic Taliban regime in Afghanistan of harboring a terrorist network involved in the attacks. The offensive triggered disorder when militant Pakistani supporters of the Taliban staged demonstrations. The Pakistani government managed to control the agitation by arresting various Islamic fundamentalist leaders. The U.S. bombing in Afghanistan also set off the migration of thousands of Afghan refugees, seeking safety in Pakistan. Pakistani President Pervez Musharraf sided with the West against the Taliban in the wake of the September 11 terrorist attacks, and the U.S. government promised new aid and lifted sanctions imposed on Pakistan for conducting nuclear tests in 1998.

Policy change. Musharraf's decision to support the United States was a major policy change for Pakistan, whose support for the Taliban had enabled the group to seize most of Afghanistan. After the Sept. 11, 2001, attacks, the United States told Musharraf to cooperate or be treated as a terrorist nation. Musharraf defied his domestic critics and gave the United States use of Pakistani military bases and granted U.S. warplanes the right to fly over Pakistani territory.

President Musharraf assumed the title of president on June 20, after pushing a figurehead president, Rafiq Tarar, from office. Musharraf had called himself "chief executive" after seizing power in a military *coup* (takeover) in October 1999. In October 2001, he extended his term as chief of staff of the army.

Confrontation. India blamed Pakistan for a suicide attack on India's Parliament on December 13 and demanded that Musharraf shut down Islamic groups supporting militants in Jammu and Kashmir, which is claimed by both countries. Pakistan arrested some Islamic leaders. At the end of 2001, India and Pakistan had massed troops along their shared border.

Economy. Pakistan carried out several reforms in 2001 to strengthen the economy. Ignoring public protests, the government imposed a general sales tax on retail trade, pursued tax evaders with measures that yielded an extra $785 million in revenue, and cut subsidies for energy. These efforts helped Pakistan avoid default on foreign debts. International lending agencies responded to the new measures by relaxing terms that had been imposed when previous governments had failed to deal with economic problems. ☐ Henry S. Bradsher

See also **Afghanistan; Armed forces; Asia; India**.

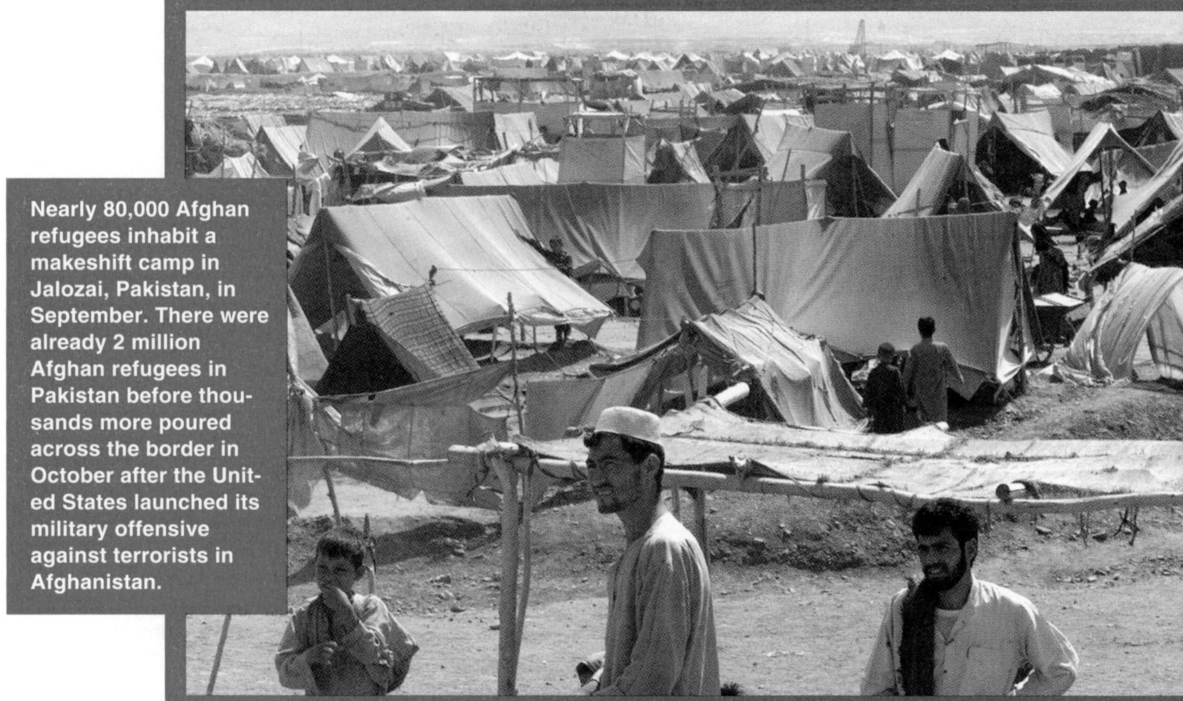

Nearly 80,000 Afghan refugees inhabit a makeshift camp in Jalozai, Pakistan, in September. There were already 2 million Afghan refugees in Pakistan before thousands more poured across the border in October after the United States launched its military offensive against terrorists in Afghanistan.

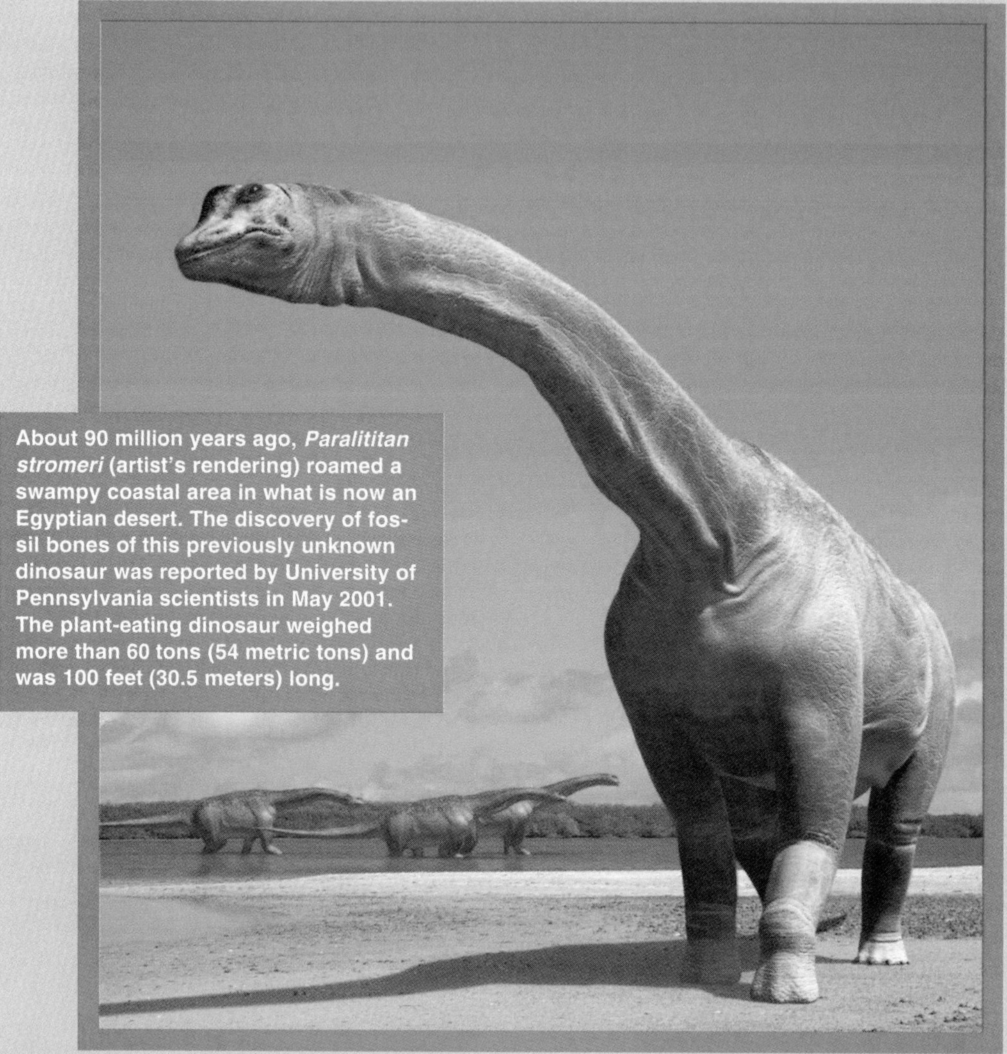

About 90 million years ago, *Paralititan stromeri* (artist's rendering) roamed a swampy coastal area in what is now an Egyptian desert. The discovery of fossil bones of this previously unknown dinosaur was reported by University of Pennsylvania scientists in May 2001. The plant-eating dinosaur weighed more than 60 tons (54 metric tons) and was 100 feet (30.5 meters) long.

Paleontology. A fossil described in July 2001 supported the view that some advanced types of animals evolved before the *Cambrian explosion,* a time approximately 540 million years ago when most major groups of modern animals first appeared in the fossil record. Paleontologist David Siveter of the University of Leicester in England and his colleagues said they had found a fossilized *crustacean,* an evolutionarily advanced group of animal that includes modern lobsters and crabs, that lived early in the Cambrian Period (544 million to 505 million years ago). The finding implied that such complex animals must have had highly evolved ancestors in late Precambrian time more than 544 million years ago.

Although the fossil record of most *phyla* (major groups) of animals begins during the Cambrian explosion, many paleontologists and biologists have long suspected that at least some of the phyla represented by Cambrian fossils have Precambrian origins. However, few complex animal fossils had ever been found in early Cambrian or late Precambrian rock.

Siveter's team discovered the small crustacean fossil in Early Cambrian rock in Shropshire, England. The fossil revealed that the creature had a two-part, unhinged shell and several pairs of two-branched *appendages* (body parts such as limbs and antennae). These features clearly identified the animal as a member of the class Crustacea, which is within the phylum Arthropoda, a group that also includes spiders and insects.

The fossil extended the known record of crustaceans back several million years. It also suggested that the Cambrian explosion was not as "explosive" as previously thought, because at least some advanced animal phyla must have existed prior to Cambrian time. The paleontologists said they hoped to find even earlier fossils of crustaceans and other complex animals.

Mollusk reconstruction. In March 2001, British researchers described their use of a computerized technique for producing highly detailed, three-dimensional (3-D) images of ancient fossil animals. This technique has helped paleontologists see intricate features of extinct animals previously hidden from view.

Mark Sutton of the Earth Sciences Department at the University of Oxford in England and colleagues discovered well-preserved fossils of a *mollusk* (a group of animals that includes shelled creatures, such as clams and snails) in a 425-million-year-old volcanic ash bed near Herefordshire, England. However, the scientists were unable to extract the fragile fossils from the rock in which they were embedded. Instead, the researchers ground away the rock and fossil one thin layer at a time while photographing each "slice." They then used a computer to combine the photographs of all the slices into a single 3-D image on a computer screen. The scientists could rotate the image on the screen to view it from any angle or zoom in for close-ups.

The technique enabled the researchers to analyze the oldest-known specimen of a primitive wormlike mollusk called an aplacophoran. These animals had a series of small plates and spines that the scientists could see in rich detail in the 3-D images. The images provided clues to the early evolution of mollusks.

Dinosaur noses. Long-held beliefs about dinosaur snouts are incorrect, according to an August report by evolutionary biologist Lawrence Witmer of Ohio University in Athens. Most museum reconstructions of dinosaurs show the nostrils far back on the snout or high up on the head. However, Witmer determined that the nostrils were probably located near the front of the snout.

Witmer examined the nostrils of various species of the two living animal groups most closely related to dinosaurs—birds and crocodiles. He noticed that most members of these groups have the soft tissue of the nostrils in front of, or even with, the nasal openings in the skull. Because dinosaurs, birds, and crocodiles are thought to share a common ancestor, Witmer reasoned that dinosaurs also had this type of nasal arrangement. To back up this idea, Witmer noted that modern animals have lots of blood vessels that leave pits and grooves on the skull beneath the nostrils. Witmer then found similar markings on the front end of the nasal openings in several dinosaur skulls.

Witmer said that having the nostrils in the front of the snout would have allowed air to flow more efficiently through the nasal passages. Moreover, he added, a frontal position for the nostrils would mean that dinosaurs had a more acute sense of smell than previously believed, because the nostrils would have been able to collect odor-causing chemicals directly in front of the snout.

Owl-like dinosaur? A small dinosaur that lived during the Cretaceous Period (145 to 65 million years ago) may have had eating habits similar to an owl, according to a February report by paleontologists Jose Sanz of the Universidad Autonoma de Madrid in Spain and Luis Chiappe of the Natural History Museum of Los Angeles County in California. The scientists discovered a small, early Cretaceous fossil "pellet" containing bird bones marked by pitting and etching. The pellet appeared to have been regurgitated by a predatory animal—in the same way that an owl swallows its prey whole and then regurgitates the indigestible bones in a pellet. The pitting and etching suggested that the fossil bones had been partially digested. The scientists proposed that the fossil pellet was produced by a small dinosaur that fed on nestling birds. ☐ Carlton E. Brett

Panama. In June 2001, the United States and other industrialized nations removed Panama from a "blacklist" of noncooperative nations in the fight against money laundering. The move came after Panama overhauled its banking rules, enabling it to investigate an estimated 25 cases of money-laundering. The overhaul also allowed the government to quickly assist the United States in searching for funds linked to terrorist networks following the September 11 terrorist attacks on the United States. However, the removal from the blacklist failed to reverse the move of foreign-owned banks out of Panama.

The Panama Canal Authority, the government agency in charge of managing the Panama Canal, approved plans in 2001 to widen the Gaillard, or Culebra, Cut of the canal and deepen Gatun Lake, a man-made reservoir. The improvements, scheduled to be completed by 2009, will increase the volume of water in the lake and canal and help prevent interruptions in traffic during the dry season. ☐ Nathan A. Haverstock

See also **Bank; Latin America; Terrorism: A Special Feature,** p. 38.

Papua New Guinea. See **Asia; Pacific Islands.**

Paraguay. See **Latin America.**

Pennsylvania. See **Philadelphia; State government.**

People in the news

in 2001 included those listed below, who were all Americans unless otherwise indicated.

Abraham, Spencer (1952-), was selected by United States President George W. Bush to serve as secretary of energy and was confirmed by the U. S. Senate on Jan. 21, 2001. Abraham had served one term in the Senate, representing Michigan, but was defeated for reelection in 2000 by Democrat Debbie Stabenow.

As a Senate Republican, Abraham had cosponsored legislation in 1999 to abolish the Department of Energy. As head of that department, he voiced strong support for the Bush administration's energy policy of aggressively seeking new domestic energy sources.

Edward Spencer Abraham was born in East Lansing, Michigan, on June 12, 1952. His family had immigrated to the United States from Lebanon. In 1974, Abraham earned a bachelor's degree from Michigan State University. In 1979, he earned a law degree from Harvard Law School in Cambridge, Massachusetts. Abraham served on the faculty of Thomas M. Cooley School of Law in Lansing, Michigan, from 1981 to 1983 and later worked in a Detroit law firm. In 1994, Abraham won election to the Senate.

See also **Cabinet, U.S; Energy supply.**

Ashcroft, John (1942-), was selected by President George W. Bush to be United States attorney general, and the U.S. Senate confirmed his appointment on Feb. 1, 2001. Various civil rights, women's, and liberal policy groups opposed the nomination, citing Ashcroft's sponsorship of antiabortion legislation and other conservative measures during his term representing Missouri in the U.S. Senate. They also cited Ashcroft's successful 1999 effort to block the appointment of Ronnie White, an African American member of the Missouri Supreme Court, to a federal judgeship. Ashcroft responded that he had opposed White on the basis of the judge's rulings, which he described as "procriminal."

U.S. Attorney General John Ashcroft

Attorney General Ashcroft became more prominent in the Bush administration after the Sept. 11, 2001, terrorist attacks on the World Trade Center in New York City and the Pentagon Building in Arlington, Virginia. As head of the U.S. Department of Justice, the attorney general oversees investigation and prosecution of federal criminals, including terrorists, and also enforces immigration laws.

John David Ashcroft was born on May 9, 1942, in Chicago but grew up in Springfield, Missouri. He graduated from Yale University in New Haven, Connecticut, and from the University of Chicago Law School. After returning to Missouri, he entered politics. Ashcroft was elected governor of Missouri in 1984 and served two terms in that office. In 1994, Ashcroft won election to the U.S. Senate. In 2000, he was defeated for reelection by Missouri's Democratic governor, Mel Carnahan, who had been killed in a plane accident during the election campaign. Carnahan's widow, Jean Carnahan, was appointed to fill the seat.

See also **Cabinet, U.S.; United States, Government of the.**

Bin Laden, Osama (1957?-), a Saudi-born millionaire and Islamic fundamentalist, was suspected of orchestrating terrorist attacks on the World Trade Center in New York City and the Pentagon in Arlington, Virginia, on Sept. 11, 2001. The attacks, which began with the hijacking of four commercial jets en route from East Coast cities to California, killed more than 3,000 people and caused billions of dollars in damage. Bin Laden was also suspected of masterminding attacks on U.S. embassies in Kenya and Tanzania in August 1998, as well as an attack on the U.S. Navy destroyer U.S.S. *Cole* in October 2000 while the ship was in port at Aden, Yemen.

Bin Laden operated at the center of al-Qaida ("The Base" in Arabic), an international terrorist network. He and other al-Qaida members supported radical fundamentalist Islam and strongly opposed U.S. policies in the Middle East, particularly the presence of U.S. troops in Saudi Arabia. In 1996, bin Laden transferred his headquarters to Afghanistan, where he controlled al-Quida activities. The Taliban, the ruling regime in Afghanistan, shielded bin Laden from arrest by international authorities.

Osama bin Laden was born in Riyadh, Saudi Arabia. His family had accumulated considerable wealth in the construction business. Bin Laden attended King Abdul Aziz University in Jidda, Saudi Arabia. In 1979, he joined a group of Islamic guerrillas fighting a *jihad* (holy war) against Soviet troops who had invaded Afghanistan. Bin Laden recruited Muslim fighters from around the world for the war and fought in several battles himself. In 1989, he returned to Saudi Arabia.

Bin Laden strongly opposed the Saudi government's 1990 decision to allow U.S. troops into Saudi Arabia during the Persian Gulf War (1991). The Saudi government pressured bin Laden to leave the country in 1991 because of his activities. He fled to Sudan. In 1994, he was stripped of Saudi citizenship and was disowned by his family because of his extremist views of Islam. In 1996, Sudan expelled bin Laden, and he moved to Afghanistan.

See also **Afghanistan; Islam; Middle East; Terrorism; Terrorism: A Special Feature,** p. 38; **United States, Government of.**

Chao, Elaine (1953-), was nominated by President George W. Bush as secretary of labor and confirmed by the U.S. Senate on Jan. 29, 2001. The president's previous choice for the labor post, Linda Chavez, withdrew her nomination after news sources alleged that she had hired an illegal immigrant to do housework.

Elaine Chao was born in Taiwan in 1953. Her parents, originally from China, had fled the mainland after the Communists under Mao Zedong took control of China in 1949. The Chao family later immigrated to New York City. Chao studied at Mount Holyoke College in South Hadley, Massachusetts, and at Harvard Business School in Cambridge, Massachusetts.

During Ronald Reagan's administration, Chao worked as a White House Fellow. (White House fellows are selected to serve for a year as special assistants to White House staff and Cabinet officers.) In that position she met Secretary of Transportation Elizabeth Dole, who later hired Chao for a position in the U.S. Department of Transportation. Chao eventually rose to the position of deputy secretary in the department. In 1991, fPresident George H. W. Bush appointed Chao director of the Peace Corps. From 1992 to 1996, she headed the United Way of America, a national service association with headquarters in Alexandria, Virginia. Chao is married to U.S. Senator Mitch McConnell (R., Kentucky).

See also **Cabinet, U.S.**

Actors Julia Roberts and Russell Crowe

Crowe, Russell (1964-), received the Academy Award for best actor on March 25, 2001, for his performance in the 2000 blockbuster film *Gladiator.* In *Gladiator,* Crowe played a betrayed Roman general forced into the life of a gladiator by the corrupt son of the emperor.

Russell Ira Crowe was born in Wellington, New Zealand, on April 7, 1964. When Crowe was 4 years old, his family moved to Australia. His acting career began at the age of 6, when he appeared on an episode of "Spyforce," an Australian television series. He also appeared as an extra in several films. In 1978, the Crowe family moved back to New Zealand.

When Crowe was 18 years old, he returned to Australia to resume his acting career. He performed in stage musicals including *Grease, The Rocky Horror Show,* and *Blood Brothers.* In 1990, Crowe received his major film role in the Australian movie *The Crossing.* Crowe made his American film debut in the 1995 Western *The Quick and the Dead.* He also delivered strong film performances in *Romper Stomper* (1992), *Virtuosity* (1995), *Rough Magic* (1995), *L.A. Confidential* (1997), and *The Insider* (1999), for which he received an Academy Award nomination.

See also **Motion pictures.**

Evans, Don (1946-), was sworn in as U.S. secretary of commerce on Feb. 5, 2001, after being confirmed by the U.S. Senate. Before joining the Cabinet of President George W. Bush, Evans was chief executive of Tom Brown, Inc., a Denver oil and gas company.

Evans, a close personal friend of the president, played key political roles throughout Bush's career. Evans served as chief fundraiser for Bush's unsuccessful 1978 Texas congressional race. Evans also chaired the 1994 campaign that resulted in Bush's election as governor of Texas and Bush's successful 1998 campaign for governor. As chairman of the Bush 2000 presidential campaign, Evans directed a fundraising effort that netted a record $100 million. Evans declared his support for the Bush administration's goals of tax reduction, free trade promotion, and expansion of domestic energy production.

Donald Louis Evans was born in Houston on July 27, 1946. After attending the University of Texas in Austin, he entered the oil business in

Midland, Texas, where he met George W. Bush. As Texas governor, Bush appointed Evans to the Texas Board of Regents, the body that runs the state's university system.

See also **Cabinet, U.S.**

Koizumi, Junichiro (1942-), became prime minister of Japan on April 26, 2001, when he was elected by the Diet, Japan's parliament. A few days earlier, Koizumi had been selected as leader of the ruling Liberal Democratic Party (LDP), which has governed Japan for all but a few months since 1955. Koizumi replaced Yoshiro Mori, who had only been in office for one year.

After becoming prime minister, Koizumi's affinity for youth-oriented styles, devotion to rock music, and flare for American-style "straight talk" quickly made him a cultural phenomenon. Koizumi-inspired products, such as "Koizumi chewing gum" and compact discs of the prime minister's favorite pop music, sold briskly in Japanese stores.

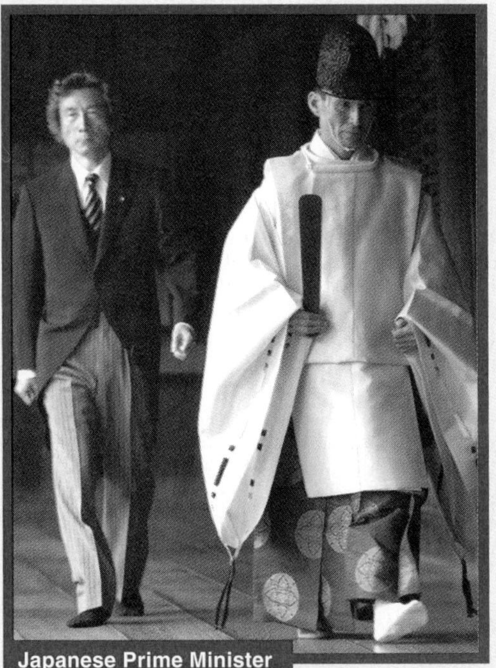
Japanese Prime Minister Junichiro Koizumi (left)

Koizumi embraced a reformist economic program and promised short-term pain in addressing Japan's economic woes. The country's economic problems included a government debt that was 120 percent of *gross domestic product* (the total goods and services produced in one period), and a banking industry that some economists estimated held trillions of dollars in bad debts in 2001. Japan's economy—the world's second largest—had been mired in recession since the early 1990's. By July 2001, the nation's unemployment rate was 5 percent, the highest since World War II (1939-1945). Koizumi proposed slashing government spending and ending subsidies to failing companies.

Campaigning on the slogan "Kaeyo!" which means "Let's change," Koizumi led the LDP to a landslide victory in 2001 parliamentary elections. Political experts interpreted the election results as a green light from voters for Koizumi's economic agenda.

Junichiro Koizumi was born on Jan. 8, 1942, in Yokosuka, Japan. He was raised in a political family. His father and grandfather were both members of parliament. Koizumi studied economics in London in the late 1960's. He was elected to the Diet in 1972.

See also **Japan.**

Macapagal-Arroyo, Gloria (1947-), became president of the Philippines on Jan. 20, 2001, after President Joseph Estrada was forced from office. Macapagal-Arroyo served as vice president of the Philippines under Estrada. The new president faced a daunting number of problems, including a seriously ailing economy and continuing violence inspired by a Muslim separatist group in the southern Philippines.

Gloria Macapagal was born on April 5, 1947. Her father, Diosdado Macapagal, served as president of the Philippines from 1961 to 1965. Gloria studied economics at Georgetown University in Washington, D.C., and earned a doctorate in economics from the University of the Philippines. After marrying Jose Miguel Tuason Arroyo, she adopted the name Macapagal-Arroyo.

In the mid-1980's, Macapagal-Arroyo served in former President Corazon Aquino's Cabinet as undersecretary of trade and industry. In 1992, she won election to the Philippine Senate and was reelected in 1995. Philippine voters elected her vice president in 1998.

See also **Philippines.**

Martinez, Mel (1946-), was selected by President Bush in 2001 to head the Department of Housing and Urban Development. The U.S. Senate confirmed Martinez's nomination on January 24.

Mel Martinez was born in Sagua La Grande, Cuba, on Oct. 23, 1946. In 1962, he fled Cuba as part of a Roman Catholic humanitarian effort called "Pedro Pan" (Peter Pan). Martinez was one of 14,000 children who were brought to the United States and placed in foster homes. In 1966, he reunited with his family in Orlando, Florida.

After earning a law degree from Florida State

University in Orlando in 1973, Martinez began practicing law. He chaired the Orlando Housing Authority between 1984 and 1986. In 1998, he was elected chairman of Orange County Commission, the local governing body of Orange County. Martinez also served as a cochair for the Bush 2000 presidential campaign in Florida.

See also **Cabinet, U.S.**

Mueller, Robert (1944-), was nominated by President George W. Bush in June 2001 to direct the Federal Bureau of Investigation (FBI). He was confirmed by the U.S. Senate in August.

Prior to becoming director of the FBI, Mueller served as U.S. attorney for the northern district of California. Earlier in his career with the U.S. Department of Justice, Mueller led the prosecution in several high-profile cases, including the 1992 convictions of New York City crime boss John Gotti and former Panamanian dictator Manuel Noriega. Mueller also led the investigation into the bombing of Pan Am Flight 103 over Lockerbie, Scotland, in 1988.

Mueller assumed his position at the FBI at a challenging time. The agency's reputation had been tarnished when convicted Oklahoma City bomber Timothy McVeigh's execution was delayed after the FBI revealed that the department had failed to turn over documents in the federal case against McVeigh. FBI officials were also left reeling when FBI agent Robert Hanssen was arrested on charges of spying for the Soviet Union, and then Russia, over a period of more than 15 years.

Mueller and the FBI confronted a formidable new challenge after the terrorist attacks on the United States on Sept. 11, 2001, and the discovery in October that a series of letters containing anthrax spores had contaminated federal offices, including those in the U.S. Capitol. In the months following the attacks, FBI agents investigated the crimes and sought to uncover possible new terrorist plots.

Robert Swan Mueller, III, was born on Aug. 7, 1944, in New York City. He grew up in Philadelphia. Mueller graduated from Princeton University in Princeton, New Jersey, in 1966 and served in the U.S. Army in Vietnam for three years, winning a Purple Heart and a Bronze Star. In 1973, Mueller began practicing criminal law after earning a law degree from the University of Virginia in Charlottesville.

Norton, Gale (1954-), U.S. President George W. Bush's choice for secretary of the interior, was confirmed by the U.S. Senate on Jan. 30, 2001. The Sierra Club and other environmental organizations had opposed her nomination, claiming that as attorney general of Colorado in the 1990's, Norton had failed to prosecute industries illegally polluting the environment. The groups also decried her ties to the Mountain States Legal Foundation, a conservative group that champions the rights of private property owners in legal disputes regarding federal environmental regulations. A number of other groups representing timber, mining, energy, and livestock interests strongly supported Norton's appointment.

Gale Ann Norton was born in Wichita, Kansas, on March 11, 1954. She was raised and educated in Colorado. After earning a law degree at the University of Denver, she worked for James Watt—later U.S. secretary of the interior in the Ronald Reagan administration—at the Mountain States Legal Foundation in Denver. In 1984, Norton worked for the Reagan administration in the agriculture and interior departments. Norton returned to Colorado in 1990 and won election as the state's first female attorney general. She served two four-year terms.

See also **Cabinet, U.S.**

O'Neill, Paul (1935-), was chosen by President Geroge W. Bush to be U.S. secretary of the treasury and was confirmed by the U.S. Senate on Jan. 20, 2001. O'Neill had been chairman and chief executive officer of the giant aluminum manufacturer, Alcoa Inc., of Pittsburgh, Pennsylvania, from 1987 to 2000.

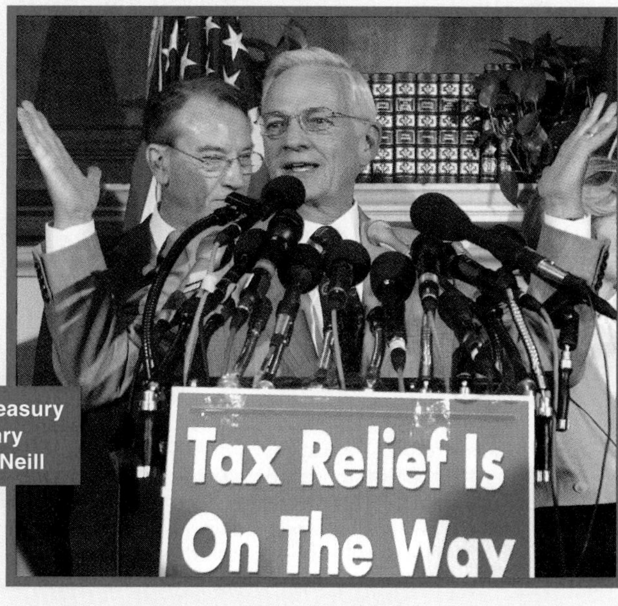

U.S. Treasury Secretary Paul O'Neill

Earlier in his career, O'Neill had spent more than 10 years working for the federal government. In 1967, he served in the Office of Management and Budget, where he was the agency's deputy director from 1974 to 1977. In the mid-1970's, O'Neill worked closely with two members of President Gerald Ford's administration—Chief of Staff Dick Cheney and Defense Secretary Donald Rumsfeld. O'Neill left government work for private industry in 1977, when he joined the International Paper Company of Purchase, New York. He served as president of International Paper from 1985 to 1987.

Paul Henry O'Neill was born in St. Louis, Missouri, on Dec. 4, 1935. He graduated from Fresno State College in Fresno, California, in 1960 and earned a master's degree in public administration from Indiana University in Bloomington.

See also **Cabinet, U.S.**

Paige, Rod (1935-), was selected by President George W. Bush to serve as secretary of education and was confirmed by the U.S. Senate on Jan. 20, 2001. Paige had served since 1994 as superintendent of the Houston city school district, the nation's seventh largest, with 212,000 students and a budget of $1.3 billion.

Paige was widely credited with improving student test scores and reducing the dropout rate in the Houston school system. He embraced standardized testing, teacher and principal accountability, and the establishment of *charter schools* (publicly funded schools that operate outside of school-district supervision and provide special educational services or programs).

National Security Adviser Condoleezza Rice

Paige's critics claimed that charter schools diverted resources from general public schools and that standardized testing discriminated against students from non-English speaking backgrounds. Nevertheless, Paige forged a broad coalition—including the head of the Houston teachers' union—to carry out his program of reform. In 1998, Houston voters passed a $678-million school bond package—the largest ever in Texas—sponsored by Paige.

Roderick Paige, Jr., was born on June 17, 1935, and grew up in the southern Mississippi town of Monticello. He began his career in education, working as a college football coach and administrator. In 1971, Paige joined the faculty of Texas Southern University in Houston. He first won election to the Houston school board in 1989.

See also **Cabinet, U.S.; Education.**

Principi, Anthony (1944-), was selected by President George W. Bush to be secretary of veterans affairs and was confirmed by the U.S. Senate on Jan. 23, 2001. Principi joined Department of Veterans Affairs with extensive experience working in the federal government on behalf of veterans. During the George H. W. Bush administration, Principi served as deputy secretary of veterans affairs and as acting secretary. During the Reagan administration, Principi served as chief counsel to the Senate Committee on Veterans Affairs. In 1996. Principi headed a special bipartisan committee established by the U.S. Congress to evaluate veterans' benefits. Experts expected Principi, in his position as secretary of veterans affairs, to push for broad expansion of veteran benefits.

Anthony J. Principi was born on April 16, 1944. His father was an emigrant from Argentina. Principi grew up in New York City and attended the U.S. Naval Academy in Annapolis, Maryland. After graduating in 1967, he served in the Vietnam War (1957-1975) and won a Bronze Star and a Navy Combat Action medal. Principi's wife is also a veteran, and two of their children have served in the military.

See also **Cabinet, U.S.**

Rice, Condoleezza (1954-), was selected by U.S. President George W. Bush to be national security adviser in 2001. Rice, who had served as Bush's top foreign policy adviser during the presidential campaign, assumed what foreign affairs experts described as a pivotal role in foreign policymaking in the Bush administration.

Condoleezza Rice was born in Birmingham, Alabama, on Nov. 14, 1954, and grew up in the South during the turbulent era of the civil rights movement. Rice's mother, Angelena, was a pianist who was inspired by the Italian musical term *con dolcezza* (to be performed sweetly) to name her daughter Condoleezza. Family members shortened the name to "Condi."

Rice studied political science at the University of Denver in Colorado, where she earned a doctoral degree. In 1981, Rice joined the political science faculty at Stanford University in Stanford, California. Rice was introduced to government service during the George H. W. Bush administration, in which she served as special assistant for national security from 1989 to 1991.

See also **Cabinet, U.S.**

Ridge, Tom (1945-), was selected by President George W. Bush to head the newly created office of homeland security shortly after the terrorist attacks on the United States on Sept. 11, 2001. The president announced the appointment on September 20, during an address before a joint session of Congress to rally the nation. As director of the new Cabinet-level post, Ridge, a two-term Pennsylvania governor, took on the task of coordinating antiterrorist operations among 40 federal agencies.

Thomas Joseph Ridge was born on Aug. 26, 1945, in Munhall, Pennsylvania, and grew up in Erie, Pennsylvania. He graduated from Harvard University in Cambridge, Massachusetts, with a degree in government in 1967. Ridge served with the U.S. Army in the Vietnam War (1957-1975) from 1968 to 1970, winning a Bronze Star for heroism in battle. After his military service, Ridge earned a law degree in 1972 at the Dickinson Law School in Carlisle, Pennsylvania, and began practicing law in Erie.

Ridge became active in Republican politics and participated in George H. W. Bush's 1980 presidential campaign. Ridge met the candidate's eldest son—future President George W. Bush—during the campaign. In 1982, Ridge was elected to the U.S. Congress, where he served four terms and earned a reputation as an independent-minded Republican.

Ridge was narrowly elected governor of Pennsylvania in 1992. He supported tax cuts, welfare reform, and a tough stance on crime. During his two terms as governor, Ridge signed more than 100 death warrants for criminals convicted of capital crimes. The Pennsylvania governor supported charter schools, school vouchers, and standardized testing. In 1996, Ridge easily won reelection as governor.

See also **Terrorism: A Special Feature,** p. 38.

Ripken, Cal, Jr. (1960-), announced in June 2001 that he would retire from baseball at the end of the 2001 season. At the time of his retirement, Ripken held the record for the most consecutive games played by a Major League Baseball player. In September 1995, Ripken broke Lou Gehrig's previous record of playing in 2,130 consecutive games. Ripken's consecutive-game streak began on May 30, 1982, and ended at 2,632 games on Sept. 20, 1998.

Ripken played his entire major league career, which began in 1981, with the Baltimore Orioles. In 1982, he was named the American League's Rookie of the Year. He was named American League Most Valuable Player in both 1983 and 1991. In 2000, Ripken became only the seventh player in major league history to tally 3,000 hits and 400 home runs during his career.

Calvin Edward Ripken, Jr., was born on Aug. 24, 1960, in Havre de Grace, Maryland. His father, Cal Ripken, Sr., was a major league baseball manager and coach. Cal, Jr., went directly into professional baseball from high school. He was drafted by Baltimore and played in the minor leagues from 1978 to 1981.

See also **Baseball.**

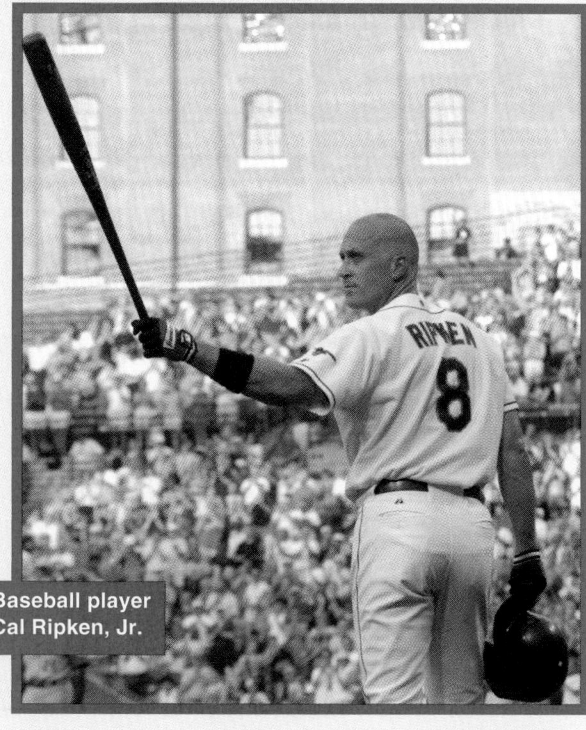

Baseball player Cal Ripken, Jr.

Roberts, Julia (1967-), received the Academy Award for best actress on March 25, 2001, for her performance in the 2000 film *Erin Brockovich.* Roberts had previously been nominated for a supporting role in *Steel Magnolias* (1989) and for her leading role in *Pretty Woman* (1990). These films had helped to establish Roberts as one of the most popular motion picture stars in Hollywood. The National Association of Theatre Owners voted Roberts

Female Star of the Year in 1991.

Julia Fiona Roberts was born on Oct. 28, 1967, in Smyrna, Georgia. She began acting at a theater in Atlanta run by her parents and made her film debut in 1986 opposite her brother, Eric Roberts, in *Blood Red.* The movie was released in the United States in 1989.

Julia Roberts has appeared in *Mystic Pizza* (1988), *Sleeping with the Enemy* (1991), *Hook* (1991), *The Pelican Brief* (1993), *Something to Talk About* (1995), *My Best Friend's Wedding* (1997), *Stepmom* (1998), *Notting Hill* (1999), *Runaway Bride* (1999), *The Mexican* (2001), and *America's Sweethearts* (2001), among other films. In 2001, she was the leading female box office draw in the United States.

See also **Motion pictures.**

Rumsfeld, Donald (1932-), was nominated by U.S. President George W. Bush to be secretary of defense and confirmed by the U.S. Senate on Jan. 20, 2001. Rumsfeld had served in the same post during Gerald Ford's administration in the mid-1970's.

Rumsfeld opposed U.S. involvement in United Nations peacekeeping missions. He advocated rapid development of an antimissile defense system in the United States. Many defense experts believed that the selection of Rumsfeld as defense secretary signaled President Bush's intention to overhaul U.S. foreign policy. However, the U.S.-led war in Afghanistan that followed the terrorist attacks on the United States on Sept. 11, 2001, drastically changed those policies. Rumsfeld, as secretary of defense, assumed a leading role in the Bush Cabinet in the war on terrorism.

Donald Henry Rumsfeld was born in Chicago on July 9, 1932, and was raised in the north shore suburb of Winnetka, Illinois. Rumsfeld graduated from Princeton University, in Princeton, New Jersey, in 1954 and served in the U.S. Navy as a aviator and flight instructor from 1954 to 1957. After leaving the Navy, he returned to the Chicago area and in 1962 won election, running as a Republican, to the U.S. House of Representatives. He served four terms in Congress before resigning in 1969 to serve in the administration of President Richard M. Nixon. Rumsfeld subsequently served in a variety of roles in the administrations of presidents Nixon, Ford, and Ronald Reagan. In 1996, he served as national chairman of Robert Dole's presidential campaign.

See also **Cabinet, U.S.; Terrorism: A Special Feature,** p. 38.

Saxe-Coburg-Gotha, Simeon (1937-), became prime minister of Bulgaria in July 2001 after his political party, the National Movement for Simeon II, swept parliamentary elections in June. The new prime minister was formerly King Simeon II of Bulgaria. He asked simply to be addressed as "Mr. Saxe-Coburg."

As prime minister, Saxe-Coburg promised to address the entrenched poverty and political corruption that had hobbled Bulgaria since the collapse of Communism in 1989. He also promised to improve Bulgarians' standard of living and embraced the

U.S. Defense Secretary Donald Rumsfeld

goals of joining the North Atlantic Treaty Organization and the European Union.

Saxe-Coburg-Gotha was born in 1937 to King Boris III and Queen Giovanna. He became King Simeon II at the age of 6, on the death of his father in 1943. The Communist regime that came to power in Bulgaria at the end of World War II deposed the young monarch in 1946 and exiled him. Simeon settled in Spain and later became a successful business executive. He returned to Bulgaria in 1996.

See also **Bulgaria.**

Sharon, Ariel (1928-), became prime minister of Israel in March 2001 after a landslide election victory by his party, the conservative Likud. Sharon defeated Prime Minister Ehud Barak of the Labor Party, who had been discredited by his failure to reach a peace agreement with Palestinian leader Yasir Arafat and by a Palestinian uprising that started in September 2000. Sharon's own highly publicized September 2000 visit to Jerusalem's Temple Mount—a holy site to both Jews and Muslims—had helped spark the uprising.

After the election, Prime Minister Sharon appointed a unity cabinet consisting of members from Likud, Labor, and other parties. The Sharon government insisted that the violence end before peace negotiations with the Palestinians resumed. Violence continued, however, with terrorist attacks on Israel and Israeli military crackdowns in Palestinian territories.

Ariel Sharon was born on a Jewish *kibbutz* (cooperative farming settlement) near Tel Aviv. As a youth, he joined an underground Jewish defense force. After the creation of Israel in 1948, he served in the Israeli defense forces, rising to the rank of major general in 1967. Sharon had fought in all four major Arab-Israeli wars since 1948.

In 1973, Sharon won election to the Knesset, Israel's parliament. He became defense minister in 1981 and directed Israel's June 1982 invasion of Lebanon, undertaken to eliminate Palestine Liberation Organization forces that had attacked northern Israel. In September 1982, members of the Lebanese militia in Israeli-controlled territory criticized Sharon for failing to stop a massacre of Palestinian civilians. Sharon, under pressure, resigned as defense minister in February 1983. He remained in the Knesset, however, and was selected as head of the Likud in 1999.

See also **Israel; Middle East.**

Thompson, Tommy (1941-), was chosen by U.S. President George W. Bush to be secretary of health and human services, and his appointment was confirmed by the U.S. Senate on Jan. 24, 2001.

Thompson served four terms as governor of Wisconsin, beginning in 1987. As governor of Wisconsin, Thompson had gained national attention for his sponsorship of several innovative state programs. In 1990, he signed into law the first school-voucher program in the United States. The program made scholarships available to some children of low-income families in Milwaukee, Wisconsin, allowing them to attend private schools.

Thompson's Wisconsin Works program, widely known as "W-2," served as a model for the federal welfare reform legislation passed by the U.S. Congress in 1996. Thompson also championed programs to extend health insurance to low-income families and to help disabled people enter the work force.

Tommy George Thompson was born on Nov. 19, 1941, in Elroy, Wisconsin. He earned a law degree at the University of Wisconsin–Madison in 1966. Thompson entered public service as a representative in the Wisconsin State Assembly in 1966. He became Assembly minority speaker in 1981.

See also **Cabinet, U.S.**

Veneman, Ann (1949-), U.S. President George W. Bush's choice for secretary of agriculture, was confirmed by the U.S. Senate on Jan. 20, 2001. Veneman became the first woman to head the U.S. Department of Agriculture (USDA).

Ann Veneman, a native of California, served in the administration of George H. W. Bush. As a member of the USDA Foreign Agricultural Service, she participated in the Uruguay Round of negotiations for GATT (General Agreement on Tariffs and Trade) in the late 1980's. From 1991 to 1993, Veneman served as deputy secretary of agriculture. Veneman headed the California Department of Food and Agriculture from 1995 to 1999 during the administration of Republican Governor Pete Wilson.

Between periods of government service, Veneman represented such agricultural companies as the multinational Dole Food Company, Inc., as a *lobbyist* (a person who tries to influence legislation) in Washington, D.C. She has also served on the board of directors of Calgene, Inc., a biotechnology company in Davis, California.

Ann M. Veneman was born in Modesto, California, on June 29, 1949, and grew up on a Central Valley peach farm. She earned her undergraduate degree from the University of California at Davis and a master's degree in public policy, as well as a law degree, from the University of California at Berkeley.

See also **Cabinet, U.S.**

Whitman, Christine Todd (1946-), was selected by U.S. President George W. Bush to administer the Environmental Protection Agency (EPA) and was confirmed by the U.S. Senate on Jan. 31, 2001. Whitman had been governor of New Jersey since 1994.

The EPA became a focus of controversy early in Bush's term. As administrator, Whitman had expressed support for the Kyoto Accords (an international treaty to reduce greenhouse gases such as carbon dioxide). However, when President Bush said in March 2001 that the United States would not be bound by the limits of the Kyoto accords, the policy placed Whitman in the position of having to defend the administration's stance. Environmentalists protested Bush's decision, as well as the administration's decision to table the implementation of new federal standards on arsenic levels in drinking water. The standards had been put in place in the final days of the administration of President Bill Clinton.

Christine Todd Whitman was born on Sept. 26, 1946, in New York City. She grew up in Hunterdon County, New Jersey, and attended Wheaton College in Norton, Massachusetts. In the 1980's, Whitman served as a *freeholder* (county commissioner) of Somerset County and as chairperson of the New Jersey Board of Public Utilities. She ran for the U.S. Senate in 1990 but lost narrowly to Senator Bill Bradley. In 1993, Whitman ran for governor of New Jersey on a tax-cutting platform and defeated incumbent Democratic governor Jim Florio. She won reelection in 1997.

See also **Conservation.**

☐ Robert Knight

Peru. Alejandro Toledo, leader of the Peru Posible Party, was sworn to a five-year term as president on July 28, 2001. Toledo had risen from poverty to become a college professor and an official with the World Bank, a United Nations-affiliated organization that finances development projects in member nations. Toledo was also Peru's first democratically elected president of Peruvian Indian ancestry. Indians comprise approximately half the population in Peru.

Toledo's inauguration followed a period of political turmoil. Former President Alberto Fujimori was forced to resign in November 2000 and then fled to Japan to escape charges of murder and corruption. Toledo, who was elected in June 2001, pledged to end corruption, restore democracy to Peru, and revive the economy.

Efforts to extradite Fujimori. In 2001, Peruvian authorities attempted unsuccessfully to persuade the Japanese government to *extradite* (turn over) Fujimori to Peru to stand trial. Fujimori held both Japanese and Peruvian citizenship, and Japan's constitution prohibits the extradition of nationals.

Peruvian President Alejandro Toledo takes part in a traditional Inca ceremony in July 2001 at the Inca ruins of Machu Picchu, which date from the 1400's. Toledo was Peru's first democratically elected president of Peruvian Indian ancestry.

Spymaster apprehended. Following an intensive international manhunt, Venezuelan authorities in June apprehended Vladimiro L. Montesinos, Peru's former chief of intelligence and Fujimori's top aide, and extradited him to Peru for trial. Montesinos fled Peru in September 2000 after Peruvian television stations began broadcasting a series of videotapes showing him apparently paying bribes to political, business, and military leaders. Montesinos was charged with bribing these officials to support the Fujimori administration. He was also accused of laundering drug money and using Fujimori's presidential jet to smuggle drugs and traffic in arms with a Colombian rebel group.

Peruvian authorities arrested more than a dozen generals and admirals seen accepting bribes on the tapes. They were charged with accepting payoffs from drug traffickers, taking kickbacks on the purchase of overpriced and obsolete Soviet-era fighter jets, and leading paramilitary death squads. The Peruvian military discharged more than 70 officers in 2001 in an attempt to cleanse the armed forces of corruption.

Missionary plane shot down. A Peruvian air force jet mistakenly shot down a small aircraft carrying U.S. missionaries on April 20 after the Peruvian crew was advised by the crew of a U.S. surveillance plane that the aircraft might be transporting narcotics. Two members of a missionary family, a mother and her infant daughter, were killed in the attack. Villagers rescued the injured pilot and the woman's husband and son after the plane crash-landed in a remote area near the Colombian and Brazilian borders.

In August, a joint U.S.-Peruvian inquiry concluded that the plane was shot down due to a series of procedural errors and misunderstandings between the U.S. and Peruvian crews while carrying out their mission of drug interdiction.

Berenson sentenced. In June, a civilian court in Peru sentenced Lori Berenson, a U.S. citizen, to 20 years in prison for collaborating with terrorists who tried to take hostage the entire Peruvian Congress in 1995. Berenson had already served more than five years of this sentence because of her conviction on the same charge by a military tribunal in 1996.

Deadly fire. More than 275 people were killed by a massive fire in downtown Lima, the capital, on Dec. 29, 2001. Authorities said the blaze was sparked by a fireworks explosion.

Earliest city in the Americas. A Peruvian-U.S. archeological team reported in April that they had dated the ruins of an ancient city in western Peru to 2627 B.C. The date was the earliest of any known city in the Americas. Researchers at Peru's National University of San Marcos and institutions in the United States said the site, called Caral, had been known since 1905 but never accurately dated. The ruins are dominated by the remains of six large, stone platform mounds, which were used for ceremonies.

☐ Nathan A. Haverstock

See also **Disasters; Japan; Latin America.**

Petroleum and gas. See **Energy supply.**

Philadelphia. Pennsylvania Governor Mark Schweiker and Philadelphia Mayor John F. Street agreed at the end of 2001 on a state takeover plan for the city's academically deficient and debt-ridden public school system. A new School Reform Commission, made up of three representatives appointed by the governor and two representatives appointed by the mayor, took control of the system on December 22, despite widespread objections by many of Philadelphia's political, educational, and civic leaders. The governor appointed James E. Nevels, head of a Pennsylvania financial services company and a former member of one of Pennsylvania's school district boards, to serve as chairman of the commission.

According to the plan, the commission was to consider the possibility of contracting with private companies to work in partnership with local community groups to manage the schools. Governor Schweiker used a report by Edison Schools, Inc., a for-profit operator of schools, as the basis for a proposal that called for the state to hire Edison to manage 45 schools in the city. About half of Philadelphia's 211,000 public school students score at the lowest levels on state reading and math tests. In addition, the district's $216-million budget deficit for the 2001-2002 school year was expected to reach $1.5 billion by 2006.

Mayor Street and other officials adamantly opposed *privatizing* the school system (giving a private company control over school operations). Under Schweiker's plan, community groups, working in partnership with Edison, would control the system's worst schools. The plan would also target some schools for curriculum changes and additional teacher training. In addition, the governor proposed that the state and city each contribute $75 million annually to the school system for five years.

Einhorn returned. Convicted murderer and long-time fugitive Ira Einhorn returned to Philadelphia from France in July 2001 and began serving the life sentence imposed on him in 1993 for the 1977 murder of his girlfriend, Holly Maddux. A prominent leader in the counterculture or hippie movement of the mid- and late 1960's, Einhorn fled the United States in 1981 to avoid trial but was tried *in absentia* (while absent). Authorities in France, where Einhorn was hiding, refused to extradite him to the United States until the Pennsylvania legislature passed a law granting Einhorn a second trial. On Sept. 12, 2001, he formally requested a new trial.

X Games. ESPN, a cable sports network, brought its X Games—champion competitions in skateboarding, in-line skating, BMX bike riding, and other alternative sports—to Philadelphia from August 17 to August 22. The event generated about $40 million in economic benefits for the city. In return, the city gave the X Games about $1-million worth of sanitation and police services and warehouse space. The network announced that 234,950 people attended the games, which were free to spectators. ESPN planned to hold the games in Philadelphia again in 2002, when it expected to open a 50,000-square-foot (4,600-square-meter) skatepark at the edge of the city.

Hospital error. Laboratory errors that resulted in the deaths of three people led the Pennsylvania Department of Health to impose a fine of $447,500 on a Philadelphia hospital, Saint Agnes Medical Center, on Oct. 24, 2001. In June and July, the hospital had reported faulty blood test results for 932 patients taking a powerful blood thinner. The three patients died from brain hemorrhages caused by overdoses of the drug. The hospital resumed testing after the state approved procedural changes.

New venues. The glass-encased Kimmel Center for the Performing Arts, Philadelphia's new $265-million concert hall, opened on December 14. The hall is the new home of the Philadelphia Orchestra and other performing groups. In June, the Philadelphia Eagles professional football team broke ground for a new 66,000-seat, $395-million stadium, scheduled to open in 2003. ☐ Howard S. Shapiro

See also **City**.

Philippines. Public demonstrations forced Joseph Estrada from the office of president in 2001. Estrada, who was impeached in November 2000, stood trial in early 2001 before the Philippine Senate on corruption charges. The Senate dissolved the proceedings in January, however, when some senators refused to admit key evidence against Estrada. Protests broke out in the capital, Manila, following the end of the trial.

On January 19, the military withdrew support for Estrada, after several days of protests. Estrada was forced to sneak out of the Presidential Palace under cover of darkness. The Supreme Court then declared the office of president to be vacant.

On January 20, Vice President Gloria Macapagal-Arroyo was sworn in as president. Macapagal-Arroyo, daughter of a former Philippine president, was elected vice president in 1998 with a larger popular vote than Estrada, who ran for president on a separate ticket. As scandals began to engulf Estrada, Macapagal-Arroyo distanced herself from him, and Estrada's opposition rallied around her.

After Macapagal-Arroyo was sworn in as president, Estrada said that he had not officially resigned but that he had only temporarily vacated the presidency. The Supreme Court ruled that Macapagal-Arroyo's government was legitimate.

Estrada was arrested in April 2001 on charges of corruption based on evidence disclosed during the impeachment proceedings. His supporters staged violent protests following the arrest.

Estrada had always been popular with poor Filipinos who, according to political observers, feared that Macapagal-Arroyo represented a return to rule by the country's elite. In May, nearly 20,000 protesters marched on the presidential palace. Macapagal-Arroyo declared the Philippines in a "state of rebellion" and arrested 11 opposition politicians on charges of inciting violence. Macapagal-Arroyo lifted the rebellion order on May 6.

In July, Estrada was charged with accepting $76 million in bribes and kickbacks while in office. If found guilty, he faced the death penalty, though few political observers expected him to be sentenced to death. During court proceedings, Estrada refused to enter a plea, and the judges recorded a "not guilty" plea for him. The trial was expected to last for months.

Elections. In May, the Philippines experienced its most violent election in more than 10 years. At least 100 people were killed when protests broke out during the campaign. Voters selected 13 of the 24 Senate seats, all 262 seats in the House of Representatives, and more than 17,000 local officials. Despite the violence, Macapagal-Arroyo's supporters won 8 of the 13 Senate seats, giving Macapagal-Arroyo a Senate majority. The vote was widely perceived as a public endorsement of

Vice President Gloria Macapagal-Arroyo is sworn in as the 14th president of the Republic of the Philippines on Jan. 20, 2001. Macapagal-Arroyo took office after Joseph Estrada was forced out of the presidency.

Arroyo's new government. However, several of the politicians arrested in the May uprisings were also elected to office.

Rebels. On February 20, Macapagal-Arroyo announced a unilateral cease-fire with the Moro Islamic Liberation Front (MILF), the main Muslim group seeking an independent state in the southern Philippines. The MILF agreed in April to halt its guerrilla attacks. This led to a cease-fire agreement signed in Malaysia on August 7 that was intended to end 30 years of Muslim rebellion.

However, voters in predominantly Christian areas of the south rejected being included in an autonomous zone. The zone was created under a 1996 agreement that ended the rebellion of another Muslim group, the Moro National Liberation Front (MNLF). In November 2001, MNLF rebels launched a new uprising on Jolo Island, reneging on the 1996 peace agreement.

Kidnapping. Another rebel Muslim group fighting for a separate state used kidnapping for ransom in 2001 to collect money for its cause. Abu Sayyaf, which consisted of an estimated 1,200 former MNLF guerrillas, threatened to behead a U.S. citizen, Jeffrey C. Schilling, whom Abu Sayyaf members had kidnapped in 2000. In April 2001, Macapagal-Arroyo's troops stormed a jungle hideout and freed Schilling. The move went against the philosophy of Estrada's government, which endorsed paying ransom in exchange for hostages.

In May, Abu Sayyaf members retaliated with a raid on a resort on Palawan Island. The group abducted 20 people, including three U.S. citizens. After Macapagal-Arroyo refused to negotiate their return, Abu Sayyaf members beheaded one of the Americans.

In July, Macapagal-Arroyo created a National Anticrime Commission to fight against groups that kidnap people for ransom. After 100 alleged Abu Sayyaf members and supporters were arrested, the group retaliated again. Abu Sayyaf members raided villages and beheaded 10 Christians.

Economy. After taking office, Macapagal-Arroyo sought to stimulate the Philippine economy and improve living standards. In July, she unveiled a plan that created at least 1 million jobs as part of an agricultural modernization plan. The plan also included the annual distribution of 494,000 acres (200,000 hectares) of land to landless farmers. In 2001, the wealthiest 5 percent of Filipinos owned nearly nine-tenths of all the land in the nation.

Natural disasters. The country's most famous volcano, Mayon, began erupting in June and continued to be active for months. The threat forced thousands of people to flee their residences. Typhoon Utor killed at least 120 people in July, and in November, Typhoon Lingling killed nearly 300 people. ☐ Henry S. Bradsher

See also **Asia.**

Physics. A team of scientists from Canada, the United Kingdom, and the United States announced in June 2001 that they may have solved one of the great mysteries in physics. The scientists, working at the Sudbury Neutrino Observatory (SNO), located at the bottom of a nickel mine near Sudbury, Canada, reported that they had found evidence that could solve a long-time problem of how the sun radiates energy. The scientists found evidence that tiny particles of matter known as neutrinos may have a tiny amount of *mass* (weight).

Ghostly particles. Neutrinos are particles of matter that have no electric charge. There are three types of neutrinos: the electron-neutrino (or e-neutrino), the mu-neutrino, and the tau-neutrino. Neutrinos interact with other types of matter so rarely that they can pass through Earth without striking a single atom.

Since the 1950's, scientists have been interested in e-neutrinos, which are produced in vast quantities in the core of the sun. Scientists trying to learn about the inner workings of the sun theorized the number of e-neutrinos being emitted.

Despite their tiny size and lack of electrical charge, neutrinos can be detected by the debris they leave behind on the rare occasions when they collide with atoms. Scientists running the first neutrino detectors in the 1960's found less than half the e-neutrinos predicted by the theories of solar power production. Scientists realized that either the theories were wrong or something was happening to the e-neutrinos between the sun and the Earth.

Since most neutrino detectors could only find e-neutrinos, some scientists suggested that the e-neutrinos were oscillating, or changing into one of the other two types of neutrino, which the detectors were not able to detect. According to the laws of physics, such a change would require that the particle have at least some mass.

A new detector. The Sudbury Neutrino Observatory (SNO), which began collecting data in 1999, is more than 1 mile (1.6 kilometers) under the Earth's surface in a Canadian nickel mine. Only neutrinos can penetrate to this depth, so the detector is protected from false alarms caused by other particles that strike Earth. The key component of the observatory is a vessel containing 1,100 tons (1,000 metric tons) of deuterium oxide, or "heavy water." Deuterium is a special type of hydrogen that contains a neutron and a proton in the nucleus. Normally, hydrogen nuclei contain only a proton. The presence of the neutron in deuterium permits interactions that scientists can use to identify neutrinos.

The heavy water is immersed in a tank filled with 7,700 tons (7,000 metric tons) of ordinary water, which shields out background radiation and also serves as an additional neutrino detector. The tanks are surrounded by nearly 10,000 special sensors that can detect when a neutrino strikes the nucleus of a water molecule.

Each day, SNO detects about 10 of the nearly 100 trillion neutrinos that pass through it. The SNO researchers found that they were only detecting about 35 percent of the expected number of e-neutrino interactions. However, by analyzing the reactions in the ordinary water molecules, scientists found that the total number of neutrino interactions closely matched the predicted rate. This provided evidence that the number of neutrinos predicted by theory was correct, that neutrinos may have mass, and that the e-neutrinos were, indeed, changing into mu-neutrinos, tau-neutrinos, or both types.

Future research. To learn more about how neutrinos change into other types of neutrinos, physicists planned to use particle accelerators that produce intense beams of different types of neutrinos that can be shot through the Earth toward underground detectors hundreds or thousands of miles away. By analyzing the rates at which various types of neutrinos oscillate, scientists may be able to measure the masses of the three types of neutrinos.

☐ Robert H. March

Poetry. Billy Collins, named Poet Laureate of the United States in June 2001, assumed his duties in October. In a time of cultural upheaval, Collins, the 11th U.S. Poet Laureate, filled the role of statesman as well as poet and spokesperson for poets in America. He planned to encourage high-school teachers in the United States to read a poem every day to students for the sheer enjoyment of the words, not for analysis or study.

In September, Collins published his seventh book of poetry, *Sailing Alone Around the Room*, new and collected poems that invoked joy and pleasure rather than philosophical ideas. Seeing everything from a piano to the dawn as a living entity, Collins showed readers his love of make-believe. However, there is also gravity in his work, even in the whimsy of the "what if?" scenario of "I Go Back to the House for a Book," in which he imagined another version of himself, one who, because he wants to get to a doctor's appointment on time, does not return to get a book: "I am doomed to follow/my perfect double/only bumped an inch into the future, and not nearly as well-versed as I in the love poems of Ovid."

Pulitzer Prize. In April 2001, the Pulitzer Prize for poetry went to Stephen Dunn for *Different Hours*, his 11th published collection of poetry. Although Dunn had a reputation for writing simply, he also was known for his intimate portraits of both the internal workings and external appearances of relationships between people. He worked to sort out moral qualities, such as good and evil, from qualities that seemed inherent and morally neutral.

National Book Award. Alan Dugan was named winner of the National Book Award in November 2001 for *Poems Seven: New and Complete Poetry*, a compendium of works produced over his 40-year career. Another nominee for the award was Agha Shahid Ali for *Rooms Are Never Finished*, a story about his mother's death and his journey with her body back to her homeland in India. Wanda Coleman was nominated for *Mercurochrome: New Poems*. Many of the poems were angry critiques of American culture. Nominee Cornelius Eady explored the challenges African American men face living in the United States in *Brutal Imagination*. Gail Mazur was nominated for *They Can't Take That Away From Me*, poems that look at life's passion and pain.

Short takes. Lyric poets with an intellectual edge offered several new collections in 2001. Mark Doty, famous for his shimmering water songs, published his new volume, *Source*, in December. Louise Gluck published *The Seven Ages,* her second book of lyric poetry in two years, in March.

In August, former U.S. Poet Laureate Maya Angelou published *Still I Rise,* in which her short, powerful poem written in the 1970's is paired with illustrations by Mexican artist Diego Rivera: "You may write me down in history/With your bitter, twisted lies,/You may trod me in the very dirt/But still, like dust, I'll rise." The radical prolific feminist poet Adrienne Rich offered *Fox: Poems 1998-2000* in October, in which she again combined intense introspection with attention to an unjust society: "On the bare slope where we were driven/ The most personal feelings became historical."

Seamus Heaney, winner of the Nobel Prize in literature in 1995, offered *Electric Light*, in which many of the poems were reflections on his rural boyhood. His figures of speech often combined elements of earth and nature with human beings themselves: "A captivating brightness held and opened/And the utter mountain mirrored in the lake/Entered us like a wedge knocked sweetly home/Into core timber."

Worldly Hopes, a collection of poems by A. R. Ammons, was reissued after the poet's death in February 2001. *Collected Poems*, a volume representing the career in poetry of James Merrill, who died in 1995, was also published in February 2001.

☐ Brian Bouldrey

See also **Literature, American; Pulitzer Prizes.**

Poland. Parliamentary elections on Sept. 23, 2001, resulted in a new governing coalition in Poland. The Democratic Left Alliance, which had governed from 1993 to 1997, won about 40 percent of the vote. Lacking a parliamentary majority, the Democratic Left Alliance forged a governing coalition with the Polish Peasants Party in early October 2001. The new prime minister, Leszek Miller, then assembled a cabinet.

Miller, despite leading a party that is the successor to Poland's former Communist Party, embraced market reforms. He also pledged greater cooperation with the European Union (EU), which had cited Poland as a leading candidate for early admission to the EU in 2004. Poland in 2001 lagged behind other candidate nations in completing negotiating *chapters* (agreements on specific policies) with the EU.

Poland's economy, long one of Eastern Europe's strongest, slowed markedly in 2001. Unemployment rose from 13.5 percent in early 2000 to 16 percent in mid-2001. The country's output, according to EU estimates, dropped from 5.6 percent in 2000 to less than 1 percent in 2001. However, inflation eased from about 10 percent in 2000 to 5.1 percent in August 2001.

□ Sharon L. Wolchik

See also **Europe**.

Pollution. See **Environmental pollution**.

Popular music. Two top-selling young sensations released new albums in 2001 but failed to match the record-breaking sales of their earlier albums. 'N SYNC released its third album, *Celebrity,* in July, which sold 1.8 million copies in the first week. However, sales were sharply down from the 2.4 million copies sold in the first week following the release of *No Strings Attached* in 2000. In November 2001, Britney Spears released her third album, titled *Britney.* The album sold 746,000 copies in its first week of release and featured more provocative songs than her 1999 release, *Oops!...I Did It Again,* which sold 1.3 million copies in its first week.

Some music critics argued that the declining sales were the result of artists releasing too many albums in quick succession. The acts released a flood of recordings so that they would not lose the spotlight to someone else. However, some audiences indicated they would prefer an artistically pleasing album to the hype surrounding each new release.

Industry experts, however, noted that record sales overall declined in 2001. On average, the sales of new releases fell more than 6 percent by the end of 2001, compared with sales in 2000. *Celebrity* was the only release in 2001 that sold more than 1 million copies in its debut week, compared with five albums that topped the 1 million

Grammy Award winners in 2001

Record of the Year, "Beautiful Day," U2

Album of the Year, "Two Against Nature," Steely Dan

Song of the Year, "Beautiful Day," U2

New Artist, Shelby Lynne

Pop Vocal Performance, Female, "I Try," Macy Gray

Pop Vocal Performance, Male, "She Walks This Earth," Sting

Pop Performance by a Duo or Group, "Cousin Depree," Steely Dan

Traditional Pop Vocal Album, "Both Sides Now," Joni Mitchell

Pop Instrumental Performance, "Caravan," Brian Setzer Orchestra

Rock Vocal Performance, Female, "There Goes The Neighborhood," Sheryl Crow

Rock Vocal Performance, Male, "Again," Lenny Kravitz

Rock Performance by a Duo or Group with Vocal, "Beautiful Day," U2

Hard Rock Performance, "Guerrilla Radio," Rage Against The Machine

Metal Performance, "Elite," Deftones

Rock Instrumental Performance, "The Call of Ktulu," Metallica with the San Francisco Symphony Orchestra

Rock Song, "With Arms Wide Open," Scott Stapp and Mark Tremonti

Alternative Music Album, "Kid A," Radiohead

Rhythm-and-Blues Vocal Performance, Female, "He Wasn't Man Enough," Toni Braxton

Rhythm-and-Blues Vocal Performance, Male, "Untitled (How Does It Feel)," D'Angelo

Rhythm-and-Blues Performance by a Duo or Group with Vocal, "Say My Name," Destiny's Child

Rhythm-and-Blues Song, "Say My Name," LaShawn Daniels, Fred Jerkins III, Rodney Jerkins, Beyonce Knowles, LeToya Luckett, LaTavia Roberson, and Kelendria Rowland

Rap Solo Performance, "The Real Slim Shady," Eminem

Rap Performance by a Duo or Group, "Forgot About Dre," Dr. Dre featuring Eminem

Rap Album, "The Marshall Mathers LP," Eminem

New Age Album, "Thinking of You," Kitaro

Contemporary Jazz Album, "Outbound," Bela Fleck & The Flecktones

Jazz Vocal Album, "In The Moment — Live In Concert," Dianne Reeves

Jazz Instrumental, Solo, "(Go) Get It," Pat Metheny

Jazz Instrumental Album, Individual or Group, "Contemporary Jazz," Branford Marsalis Quartet

Large Jazz Ensemble Album, "52nd Street Themes," Joe Lovano

Latin Jazz Performance, "Live At The Village Vanguard," Chucho Valdes

Country Album, "Breathe," Faith Hill

Country Vocal Performance, Female, "Breathe," Faith Hill

Country Vocal Performance, Male, "Solitary Man," Johnny Cash

Country Performance by a Duo or Group with Vocal, "Cherokee Maiden," Asleep At The Wheel

Country Vocal Collaboration, "Let's Make Love," Faith Hill and Tim McGraw

Country Instrumental Performance, "Leaving Cottondale," Alison Brown with Bela Fleck

Bluegrass Album, "The Grass Is Blue," Dolly Parton

Country Song, "I Hope You Dance," Mark D. Sanders and Tia Sillers

All Things Must Pass

George Harrison, 1943-2001

George Harrison, a cofounder and the lead guitarist of the Beatles, the most popular and influential group in the history of popular music, died on Nov. 29, 2001. The cause of death was cancer. He was 58 years old.

Harrison was born in Liverpool, England, on Feb. 25, 1943, the youngest of four children. He received his first guitar when he was 13 and displayed considerably more interest in music than in school. In 1958, classmate Paul McCartney invited him to audition for the Quarrymen, a band that included John Lennon, who renamed the band the Beatles in 1960. The youngest member of the group, Harrison became known as "the quiet Beatle."

Although Lennon and McCartney were the group's dominant songwriters, Harrison contributed some of the Beatles's most beloved songs, including "While My Guitar Gently Weeps," "Here Comes the Sun," and "Something," which Frank Sinatra called his favorite Beatles' song. Harrison became interested in Indian music in 1965 and popularized the sitar, an Indian string instrument, after incorporating it into the Beatles's song "Norwegian Wood."

After the Beatles disbanded in 1970, Harrison embarked on a sporadically successful solo career. Critics consider his first solo album, the three-record set *All Things Must Pass,* as one of the best by a former Beatle. It spawned Harrison's biggest hit, "My Sweet Lord." However, the song became the subject of a lawsuit because of its similarity to the Chiffons 1963 hit "He's So Fine." Harrison was found guilty of "unconscious plagiarism."

Harrison reflected on his years with the Beatles in two songs. "All Those Years Ago," a tribute to Lennon, who was murdered in 1980, appeared on Harrison's 1981 album, *Somewhere in England.* "When We Was Fab," a bittersweet recollection of Beatlemania, was featured on his acclaimed 1987 album, *Cloud Nine.*

Harrison's legacy extends beyond music. In 1971, he organized the first benefit rock concert, "The Concert for Bangladesh," and recruited some of the biggest names in rock to perform, including fellow former Beatle Ringo Starr and guitarist Eric Clapton. Harrison also branched out into films. He cofounded the production company Handmade Films, which produced *The Life of Brian* (1979), a comedy starring the comedy troupe Monty Python, and *Time Bandits* (1981). He published an autobiography, *I Me Mine,* in 1980.

George Harrison was uncomfortable with his rock idol status. "I asked to be successful," he once said. "I never asked to be famous." He will be remembered as more than just an influential guitarist. For him, music was the soundtrack to a spiritual journey, as reflected in his post-Beatles songs "Living in the Material World" and "Give Me Love."

■ Donald Liebenson

mark in 2000. The experts attributed declining sales to a sluggish U.S. economy; concern over terrorist attacks against the United States on September 11; and Web sites such as Napster, which had allowed users to exchange music stored on their computers for free.

Country music. The soundtrack to the film *O Brother, Where Art Thou?* became country music's most unlikely success story in 2001. Although most mainstream country music radio stations ignored the soundtrack's collection of traditional bluegrass music, it became the best-selling album of the year.

Garth Brooks, one of the best-selling solo artists of all time, released *Scarecrow* in November. *Scarecrow* was Brooks's first recording of new country songs in four years and his first release since his 1999 pop concept album, *Garth Brooks in . . . the Life of Chris Gaines,* which critics blasted.

Traditional country music in 2001 also received a boost from Brad Paisley's single "Too Country," from his album *Part II,* and the critically acclaimed bluegrass albums *Little Sparrow* by Dolly Parton, and *Mountain Soul* by Patty Loveless.

Jazz. Filmmaker Ken Burns's documentary, "Jazz," which was broadcast in January 2001 on Public Broadcasting System (PBS) stations, revitalized interest in mainstream jazz music. A number of albums released in association with the program dominated the jazz charts, including a five-CD soundtrack and an anthology featuring artists who appeared in the documentary.

Michael Jackson, the self-proclaimed "King of Pop," made a heavily hyped comeback in 2001. The comeback included the release of *Invincible* in October, Jackson's first studio album to contain all new material since 1991. *Invincible,* which reportedly cost $30 million to make, debuted at the top of the charts but dropped to third place after only three weeks. In September 2001, Jackson hosted two concerts in Madison Square Garden in New York City, which he organized as a tribute to himself.

Keys to success. Pianist, singer, and songwriter Alicia Keys was one of popular music's biggest breakout stars in 2001. Her debut album, *Songs in A Minor,* was released to overwhelmingly positive reviews in June. The album contained the popular single "Fallin'." Both fans and critics applauded her vocal ability and classical piano style.

Napster settlement. In February 2001, Napster, Inc., a Redwood City, California, company that enabled registered users to copy music for free over the Internet, offered to pay record companies $1 billion over five years for the right to include copyrighted music in a redesigned, fee-based version of its network. Several major record companies sued Napster in 1999, arguing that the company committed *copyright infringement* (improper use of legally protected material).

On Feb. 12, 2001, the 9th U.S. Circuit Court of Appeals in San Francisco ruled that Napster must stop the exchange of copyrighted music. In March, U.S. District Judge Marilyn Hall Patel also ruled that recording companies can block the use of copyright-protected songs on Napster. On September 24, the company reached a preliminary settlement with the National Music Publishers Association, located in New York City, and agreed to pay $26 million for past unauthorized use of music and an additional $10 million toward future royalties.

Tribute concerts. On September 21, musicians joined a roster of actors to raise money for the families of victims of the September 11 terrorist attacks. Sheryl Crow, Billy Joel, Alicia Keys, Willie Nelson, Paul Simon, Bruce Springsteen, and Neil Young were among the artists appearing on "America: A Tribute to Heroes." The two-hour telethon, which aired simultaneously on 30 television networks and cable stations, raised more than $200 million in pledges.

On October 20, various artists, including Eric Clapton, Billy Joel, and Paul McCartney performed at "The Concert for New York City" at Madison Square Garden. McCartney, who helped organize the concert, debuted a new song—"Freedom"—that was written following the terrorist attacks. In the militant song, McCartney sings "I will fight for, the right to live in freedom." The six-hour concert raised approximately $14 million for victims of the September 11 attacks and millions of dollars more in pledges.

A second fund-raising concert, "United We Stand: What More Can I Give?" raised about $2 million through ticket sales. The Backstreet Boys, James Brown, Mariah Carey, Destiny's Child, and Michael Jackson were among the performers at the concert at RFK Stadium in Washington, D.C., on October 21.

Several artists in late 2001 released reflective songs in the wake of the tragedy, including the country music songs "Where Were You (When the World Stopped Turning)" by Alan Jackson and "Where the Stars and Stripes and the Eagle Fly" by Aaron Tippin. ☐ Donald Liebenson

See also **Internet: A Special Report; Television; Terrorism: A Special Feature,** p. 38.

Population. The United Nations (UN) released revised estimates of the world's population on Feb. 28, 2001. The report, "World Population Prospects: The 2000 Revision," put the 2000 global population at 6.1 billion people and projected that the world's population would grow annually by 77 million people through 2005. Joseph Chamie, head of the UN Population Division, noted that the UN had in 1953 made a remarkably accurate projection of the world's 2000 population, 6.2 billion people.

According to UN statistics, half of the world population growth rate of 1.2 percent takes place in six countries: India, China, Pakistan, Nigeria, Bangladesh, and Indonesia. Annual population growth in India—about 16.2 million people—accounts for 21 percent of the 77 million additional people on Earth each year. India's population is currently slightly more than 1 billion.

Unequal growth. High population growth rates were becoming more concentrated in the poorer nations, the report noted. By 2050, the population of the world's 48 poorest countries will grow threefold, from 658 million in 2000 to 1.8 billion in 2050. The population of most developed nations, which account for about one-fifth of the world's countries, will be smaller in 2050. According to UN estimates, the populations of Japan and Germany will be 14 percent smaller in 2050 than in 2000; the populations of Italy and Hungary will be 25 percent smaller; the population of Ukraine will be 40 percent smaller; and the population of Russia will be 28 percent smaller.

The populations of some developed nations, including Canada, Australia, and the United States, will increase. By 2050, Canada's population will be 33 percent larger; Australia's population will be 38 percent larger; and the population of the United States will be 40 percent larger. By 2050, the United States will have nearly 400 million people, according to the report.

Immigration. According to the UN report, the worldwide human migration will increase in the 2000's, particularly immigration to developed regions, such as North America and Europe. UN officials estimated that 2 million immigrants will move to developed regions every year for the next 50 years. The United States annually takes in an estimated 1 million immigrants.

Aging population. While the world's population is growing larger, it is also aging. According to UN estimates, the number of people 60 years or older will triple by 2050, from 606 million in 2000 to nearly 2 billion by midcentury. The number of 80 year olds was expected to increase by 500 percent, from 69 million in 2000 to 379 million in 2050. ☐ J. Tuyet Nguyen

See also **Census; City.**

Portugal. Prime Minister Antonio Guterres resigned after six years in power in late 2001, after his ruling Socialist Party suffered a heavy defeat in local elections. The resignation culminated a year of political difficulties for the Socialists as Portugal's once-booming economy slowed dramatically.

The center-right opposition Social Democratic Party swept local elections on December 16 and won control of the cities of Lisbon and Oporto, previously held by Guterres's Socialists. The defeat was the first suffered by the Socialists since 1993. Guterres took responsibility and resigned on Dec. 17, 2001. President Jorge Sampaio called for a national election in 2002, more than one year ahead of schedule.

Guterres's market-oriented economic policies fostered years of strong growth and Portugal's admission into the bloc of European Union countries that adopted the euro in 1999. However, his popularity waned in 2001 as the country suffered its worst economic slowdown in more than a decade. The slowdown crushed hopes that the country could rise rapidly to the same level of wealth as its Western European neighbors.

Economy. According to the European Commission (EC), the executive agency of the 15-nation European Union, Portugal's economic output was expected to grow by 1.7 percent in 2001. The

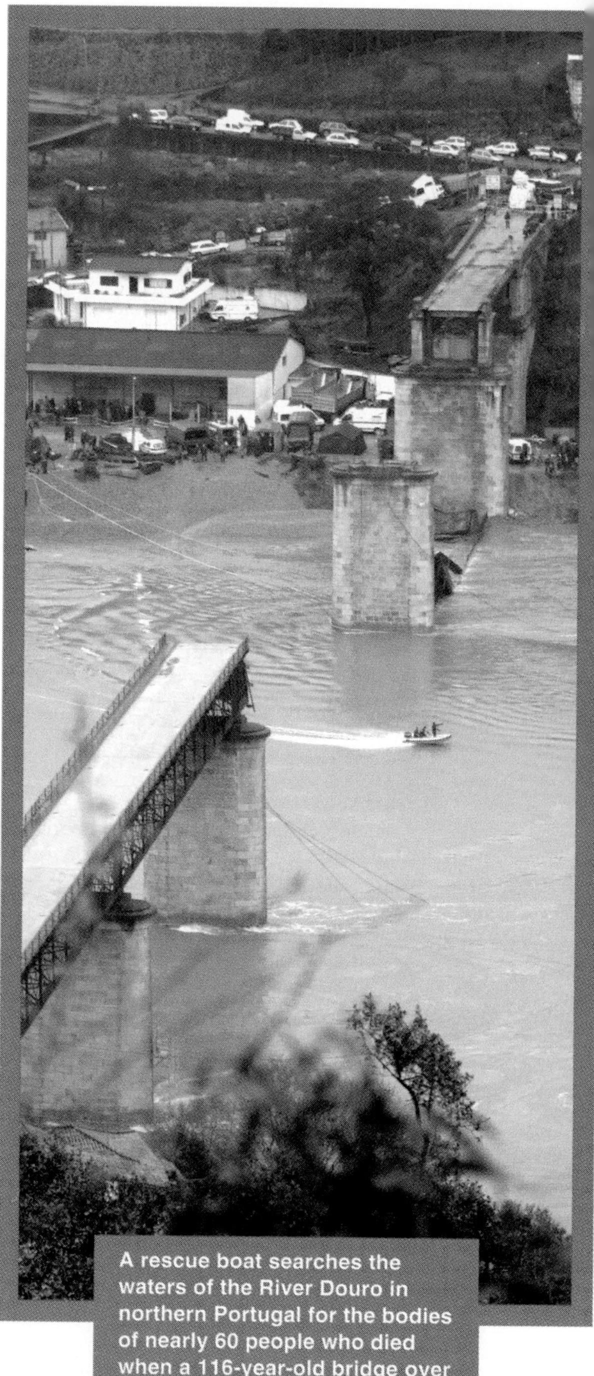

A rescue boat searches the waters of the River Douro in northern Portugal for the bodies of nearly 60 people who died when a 116-year-old bridge over the river collapsed in March. The road accident was the worst in the country's history and drew attention to the poor condition of Portugal's roadways.

figure was a drop from the 3.4-percent growth of 2000. The worsening economy caused the government deficit to widen to 2 percent of GDP. The EC, which enforces European Union rules requiring countries that use the euro to maintain low budget deficits, pressured the Portuguese government to limit deficit spending. In June 2001, the government announced it would cut spending by 750 million euros ($640 million) for the remainder of 2001 and limit spending growth over the next four years.

TAP-Air Portugal, the national airline, struggled to find financial backing after Swissair reneged on a commitment to buy a 34-percent stake in the airline. Swissair had agreed to the deal in February 2000 but backed out in February 2001 and declared bankruptcy in October.

Bridge collapse. A bridge over the River Douro in northern Portugal collapsed on March 4, causing the deaths of nearly 60 people. The collapse of the 116-year-old structure drew attention to the poor state of the country's roads and prompted the resignation of Public Works Minister Jorge Coelho. ☐ Tom Buerkle

See also **Europe; Switzerland.**

President of the United States. See **United States, President of the.**

Prince Edward Island. See **Canadian provinces.**

Prison. The United States Department of Justice reported in mid-2001 that there were 1.38 million offenders under federal or state jurisdiction in 2000, an increase of 1.3 percent from 1999 but less than the average growth of 6 percent recorded during the 1990's. The Justice Department report revealed that the number of women in prison increased 1.2 percent in 2000, to approximately 91,000 people. The number of men rose 1.3 percent to 1.2 million inmates.

In March 2001, the Justice Department reported that the inmate population in federal prisons in 2000 increased 9.3 percent. The number of inmates under state jurisdiction rose 1.5 percent—the smallest annual growth since 1971.

Local jails, which held people who awaited trial or served sentences of one year of less, contained approximately 687,000 inmates in 2000. Ten percent of those offenders were supervised outside jail facilities in such programs as community service, work release, weekend reporting, and electronic monitoring.

State prisons reported that they were between full capacity and 15 percent above capacity at the end of 2000. The 99 federal prisons in the United States reported that they were operating at 31 percent above capacity.

Racial disparity. In December 2000, there were 3,400 African American male inmates in federal and state prisons for every 100,000 African American men in the general population of the United States. There were 1,200 Hispanic male inmates per 100,000 Hispanic men and 449 white male inmates in prison for every 100,000 white men.

Death row inmates. Between January and mid-November 2001, prison officials executed 26 people in the United States, compared with 85 people in 2000. The number of executions carried out in the United States has declined annually since 1999, when 98 executions were carried out, which was the highest number of executions carried out in any year since 1951. In May 2001, 3,726 prisoners awaited execution in U.S. prisons.

In June 2001, Timothy J. McVeigh and Juan Raul Garza were executed under the federal death penalty. The executions were the first since 1963 by the federal government, as opposed to executions carried out by state governments. McVeigh was convicted for carrying out the 1995 bombing of the Alfred J. Murrah Federal Building in Oklahoma City, Oklahoma, which killed 168 people. Garza was sentenced to death in 1993 in Texas for murdering or ordering the murders of three drug traffickers in an effort to gain control of a drug distribution network. ☐ Brian Bouldrey

See also **Crime.**

Prizes. See **Nobel Prizes; Pulitzer Prizes.**

Protestantism. Protestants in 2001 were divided in their response to a proposal by United States President George W. Bush that involved establishing a federal Office of Faith-Based and Community Initiatives. The office was to grant federal funds, with some restrictions, to religious groups providing social services. The proposal led to much debate concerning civil rights and the separation of church and state.

Many Evangelical Protestants, including conservative editor Marvin Olasky of *World* magazine, noted several potential problems. A primary concern was that the office would prohibit religious organizations that accepted federal funds from considering religion in their hiring practices. Some religious organizations also expressed concerns that the acceptance of federal money might prevent staff members from advocating their religious beliefs. Many African American Protestant churches with limited funds, however, welcomed the proposal.

The U.S. House of Representatives approved legislation in July to fund the office. The Senate had yet to pass legislation on the issue by the end of 2001.

Stem cell research. Medical research involving human *embryonic stem cells* (cells that can develop into most any kind of tissue) was another major issue that divided Protestants in 2001. In

August, President Bush announced that he would allow federal funding of research on stem cell lines that had previously been created for reproductive purposes, but he would not allow federal funding to create new cell lines.

President Bush's decision "deeply disappointed us," said Southern Baptist Convention spokesperson Richard Land, who was opposed to all research involving embryonic stem cells. However, televangelist Jerry Falwell was among many Protestants who supported Bush's decision. The United Church of Christ, on the other hand, favored even greater federal support for stem cell research, noting that such research might lead to cures for many diseases.

Homosexuality. The General Assembly of the Presbyterian Church (U.S.A.) voted in June to give *presbyteries* (local Presbyterian governing bodies) the option of ordaining homosexuals. A minority of presbyteries voiced strong opposition to such a move. More than 170 presbyteries were scheduled to vote on the measure by spring 2002. Many Presbyterians feared the issue might split the church into two *synods* (governing bodies overseeing presbyteries).

The Evangelical Lutheran Church in America voted at its August 2001 convention in Indianapolis, Indiana, to undertake a four-year study of homosexuality. Church leaders expected the study to lead to a report recommending whether gay clergy should be ordained and whether homosexual unions should be blessed.

The Anglican Church of Canada announced in May that it was on the verge of bankruptcy as a result of lawsuits brought by thousands of *indigenous* (native) Canadians. Some 7,000 people claimed they had been sexually abused by priests and teachers at government-owned schools administered by the church prior to 1970. In October 2001, the Canadian government offered to pay 70 percent of validated claims, though the church asked for additional government aid.

In July, the Anglican Church passed full communion measures with the Evangelical Lutheran Church in Canada. The measures allowed for recognition of each other's clergy and sacraments.

Evangelical leader resigns. The National Association of Evangelicals, comprising 50 conservative Protestant denominations, pressured its president, Kevin Mannoia, to resign in June. Mannoia was criticized for having advocated policies friendly to some faiths that belonged to the more liberal National Council of Churches, an interdenominational organization headquartered in New York City. Mannoia's critics also voiced concern about a drastic decline in the association's finances. ☐ Martin E. Marty

See also **Health care issues; Medicine.**

Psychology. See **Mental health.**

Public health and safety. Public health officials responded to the terrorist attacks on the United States on Sept. 11, 2001, with new precautions to protect the public from *bioterrorism,* the use of biological agents in acts of terrorism. Concerns about bioterrorism arose in early October after a 63-year-old man died from inhalation anthrax in Boca Raton, Florida. He apparently contracted the disease from anthrax *spores* (an inactive stage of bacteria) sent in an envelope through the mail to the tabloid newspaper office where he worked.

Anthrax illness occurs in two main forms: inhalation and skin. The inhalation form, arising from infection of the lungs, is the most life-threatening. The skin form, in which sores erupt on the skin, is less serious. Anthrax can be treated with antibiotics, but infected individuals must begin taking the drugs before symptoms appear.

Later in October and November, letters containing anthrax spores showed up at news media offices in New York City and at the Washington, D.C., offices of U.S. Senate Majority Leader Tom Daschle (D., South Dakota) and Senator Patrick Leahy (D., Vermont). Anthrax contamination forced the closing and decontamination of several businesses, post offices, and government buildings. Health officials began stockpiling antibiotics for combating anthrax and treated thousands of individuals, many of them government employees exposed to the anthrax spores.

By the end of 2001, five people had died of inhalation anthrax, all in the eastern United States. Investigators by the end of 2001 had not determined whether the anthrax letters were directly related to the September 11 terrorist attacks.

Smallpox fears. The anthrax mailings raised fears that terrorists might use other biological agents, including the smallpox virus, in future attacks. In 1980, officials of the World Health Organization, a United Nations agency, had declared smallpox eradicated, but frozen samples of the virus were known to be kept in two laboratories—one in the United States and the other in Russia. After the anthrax outbreaks, U.S. government officials announced plans to resume production of smallpox vaccine. Unlike anthrax, smallpox has no effective treatment other than vaccination.

Traffic deaths increased in 2000 after declining to a record low in 1999. The National Highway Traffic Safety Administration (NHTSA) announced in March 2001 that 41,800 people died in highway crashes in 2000, compared with 41,611 in 1999. The number of people killed in alcohol-related car crashes increased to 16,068 in 2000 from 15,786 in 1999.

Backyard accidents. Since 1990, more children have died in accidents on backyard play equipment than on public playgrounds, a study by the U.S.

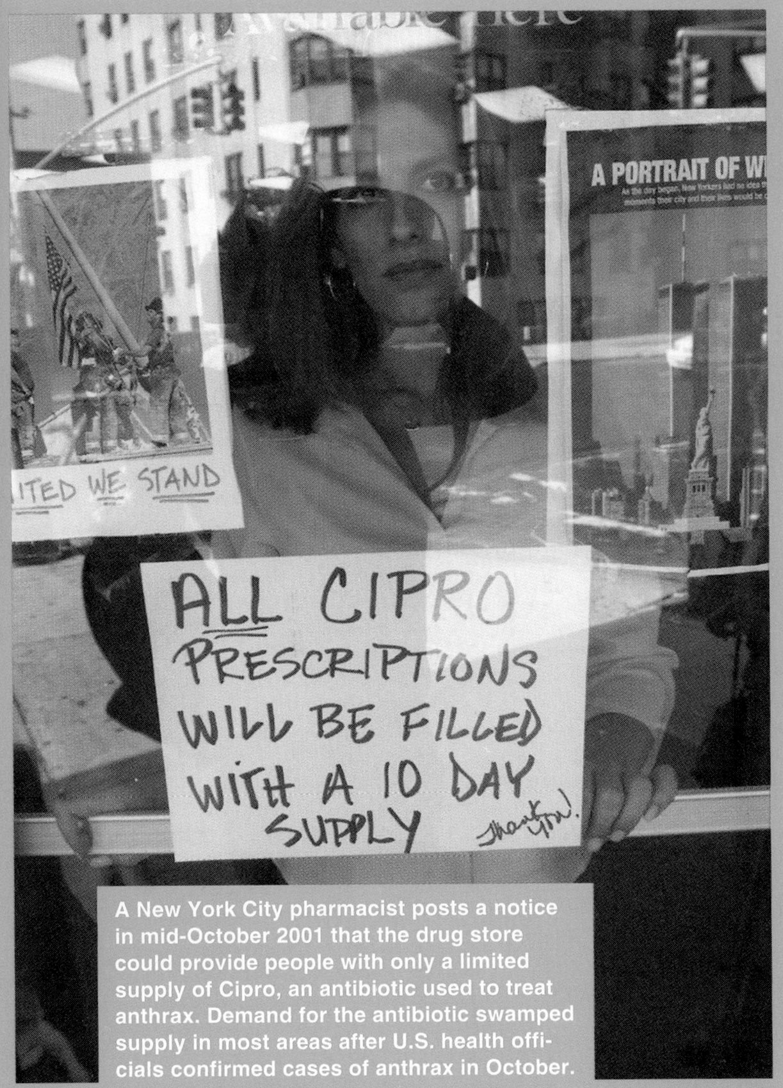

A New York City pharmacist posts a notice in mid-October 2001 that the drug store could provide people with only a limited supply of Cipro, an antibiotic used to treat anthrax. Demand for the antibiotic swamped supply in most areas after U.S. health officials confirmed cases of anthrax in October.

Consumer Product Safety Commission (CPSC) reported in August 2001. The study found that 90 of the 147 playground deaths since 1990 occurred on home playgrounds. Unintentional hangings accounted for most of the deaths.

Stroller recall. In June 2001, the CPSC announced the largest recall of baby strollers in history. CPSC said Century, Inc., of Macedonia, Ohio, was recalling about 650,000 strollers sold from December 1996 to March 2001. Century received 681 reports of problems, including a defect that could cause the stroller to collapse while in use, throwing the child to the ground. About 250 children were reported injured in the strollers, some with severe head injuries.

Causes of death. Heart disease and cancer remained the leading causes of death in the United States in 1999, despite continuing declines in deaths from both conditions, the U.S. Centers for Disease Control and Prevention (CDC) in Atlanta, Georgia, reported in June 2001. The two diseases still accounted for more than half of all deaths. The data was compiled by analyzing death certificates recorded in the United States in 1999, the most recent year for which such data was available.

The five leading causes of death, in order, were heart disease, cancer, stroke, chronic respiratory diseases, and accidents, unchanged from 1998. ☐ Michael Woods

See also **Health care issues; Medicine.**

Puerto Rico. Sila Maria Calderon of the Popular Democratic Party became Puerto Rico's first woman governor on Jan. 2, 2001. Calderon, a former mayor of San Juan, the capital, pledged to fight political corruption and provide more assistance to poor families. She also vowed to force the United States Navy to stop using the small island of Vieques, off Puerto Rico's east coast, as a target range for live bombing practice. The Navy had conducted training exercises on Vieques for almost 60 years.

Vieques protests. On April 24, the Calderon administration filed an emergency request with the U.S. District Court in Washington, D.C., to block a new round of military exercises on Vieques. The Puerto Rican government argued that the exercises damaged the ecology of Vieques and threatened the health of the 9,000 people who lived on the small island. The court denied the request on April 26, citing a lack of evidence to support the claims.

The court's decision sparked large protests on Vieques and in San Juan. By the end of April, more than 180 protesters had been arrested for trespassing on federal property. The protesters breached fences around the exercise area and entered the Navy firing range, forcing a brief suspension of military maneuvers. Smaller protests erupted in June.

Several prominent political figures were arrested and jailed during the protests—U.S. Representative Luis Gutierrez (D., Illinois); the Reverend Al Sharpton, a civil rights activist from New York City; Jacqueline Jackson, wife of civil rights leader Jesse Jackson; New York City Councilman Adolfo Carrion, Jr.; New York State Assemblyman Jose Rivera; and Bronx County Democratic Party Chairman Roberto Ramirez.

Bombing to end. In June, President George W. Bush announced that the use of Vieques for Navy bombing practice would end in May 2003. Bush's decision failed to satisfy most critics, who demanded an immediate end to all military exercises on Vieques. Bush responded that the Navy would need time to find an alternate location for its exercises.

Unemployment. The U.S. Department of Labor released figures in April showing that the unemployment rate in Puerto Rico had risen dramatically during the first quarter of 2001 to 11.2 percent. In some rural areas, the unemployment rate was as high as 20 percent. In a big blow to the town of Yabucoa in eastern Puerto Rico, Sunoco, Inc., an oil company based in Philadelphia, announced in March that it would close its Yabucoa refinery in May. The shut-down cost 220 people their jobs. ☐ Nathan A. Haverstock

See also **Latin America.**

Pulitzer Prizes in journalism, letters, drama, and music were awarded on April 16, 2001, by Columbia University in New York City on the recommendation of the Pulitzer Prize Board.

Journalism. *The* (Portland) *Oregonian* won the public service award for coverage of the United States Immigration and Naturalization Service's treatment of foreign nationals. Tom Hallman, Jr., of *The Oregonian* received the best feature prize for his profile of a disfigured teenager. Coverage of the raid by federal agents involving Elian Gonzalez won awards for breaking news for *The Miami Herald* staff and for breaking news photography for Alan Diaz of the Associated Press. David Willman of the *Los Angeles Times* won the investigative reporting award for an expose of the U.S. Food and Drug Administration's approval of unsafe drugs.

David Cay Johnston of *The New York Times* won the beat reporting prize for his articles on inequities in the U.S. tax code. The staff of *The New York Times* received the national reporting prize for a series on race in America. The staff of the *Chicago Tribune* won the explanatory reporting prize for a story about the air traffic system in the United States. The international reporting prize went to Paul Salopek of the *Chicago Tribune* for reports on Africa. Ian Johnson of *The Wall Street Journal* won a second award for international reporting for stories about the Chinese government's suppression of the Falun Gong spiritual movement.

Dorothy Rabinowitz of *The Wall Street Journal* was awarded the commentary prize for essays on American society. Gail Caldwell of *The Boston Globe* won the criticism prize for observations on contemporary life and literature. The editorial writing prize went to David Moats of the *Rutland* (Vermont) *Herald* for editorials on civil unions for gay couples. Matt Rainey of *The Star-Ledger* (Newark, New Jersey) won the feature photography prize for photographs of college students burned in a fire. The editorial cartooning prize went to Ann Telnaes of Tribune Media Services.

Letters, drama, and music. Michael Chabon won the fiction prize for his novel *The Amazing Adventures of Kavalier & Clay*. The history prize went to Joseph J. Ellis for *Founding Brothers*. David Levering Lewis received the biography prize for *W. E. B. DuBois*. Stephen Dunn won the poetry prize for his collection *Different Hours*. The general nonfiction prize was awarded to Herbert P. Bix for the biography *Hirohito and the Making of Modern Japan*. David Auburn won the drama prize for *Proof*. The music prize went to John Corigliano for *Symphony No. 2 for String Orchestra*. ☐ Brian Bouldrey

Quebec. See **Canadian provinces.**

Radio. Satellite radio, the radio industry's equivalent of cable television, finally became available to consumers on Sept. 25, 2001, when XM Satellite Radio Inc. of Washington, D.C., began broadcasting its digital signal in San Diego and Dallas-Ft. Worth. By November, the service was available nationwide.

Satellite radio is similar to cable television in that subscribers pay a fee to receive more choices of formats. XM subscribers paid $9.99 per month to receive 100 radio stations. The stations were beamed from XM's headquarters to two satellites in orbit around Earth: "Rock," which was launched in March, and "Roll," which was launched in May. The satellites were in geostationary orbit, a type of orbit in which satellites hover about 22,300 miles (35,900 kilometers) above Earth. The satellites follow the equator, so they are always over the same point on Earth.

The signal, broadcast by satellites, covered the entire continental United States so that subscribers could listen to their favorite stations in their cars without driving out of range. Hundreds of repeater stations throughout the country reinforced the signal so that it was not interrupted by tall buildings or tunnels.

Although XM was the first company to actually deliver programming to listeners, another company, Sirius Satellite Radio, Inc., of New York City, had put three satellites into Earth orbit in 2000. Sirius officials announced in November 2001 that they would launch their service on Feb. 14, 2002, in Houston, Phoenix, and Denver. Sirius's service was similar to XM's, but Sirius subscribers were expected to pay $12.95 per month to receive 100 channels, 60 of them commercial free.

In addition to the monthly fee, satellite radio subscribers had to purchase special receivers for between $250 and $1,000. The receivers were being produced by major electronics companies, such as Sony Corporation of Tokyo and Pioneer Electronics of Long Beach, California.

Internet radio. Beginning in April, several companies that owned radio stations stopped broadcasting on the Internet. The companies had been "streaming" their programming, or simultaneously broadcasting into the air and onto the Internet. The companies suspended this practice because of a conflict with the American Federation of Television and Radio Artists (AFTRA), a union representing actors who voice radio ads. AFTRA officials claimed that their contracts included additional fees if commercials were aired on the Internet.

Compounding the conflict with AFTRA, on Aug. 1, 2001, U.S. District Judge Berle Schiller in the Eastern District of Pennsylvania ruled that radio stations had to pay royalty fees for songs that they streamed over the Internet. Schiller's ruling came in a case brought in early 2000 by the Recording Industry Association of America (RIAA), an industry group representing record labels and recording studios. The RIAA had argued that radio stations were paying a single royalty fee to play copyrighted music over the airwaves, but in essence were using the song twice when they streamed their content over the Internet. Radio analysts expected a decision on the amount of that royalty fee to be reached in early 2002.

LPFM tuned out. In August 2001, the Federal Communications Commission released a list of approved low-power FM's (LPFM), radio stations equipped with low-power transmitters with a range of no more than 3.5 miles (5.6 kilometers). The list of more than 300 stations was much smaller than had originally been planned because of strict rules that had been passed by the U.S. Congress in late 2000. The rules significantly limited the power of LPFM's, which had been initiated during the Clinton administration to improve access to public airwaves. Critics of LPFM's, led by the National Association of Broadcasters, claimed that the stations would create interference with commercial radio stations. ☐ Greg Paeth

Railroad. See **Transportation.**

Religion. See **Islam; Protestantism; Roman Catholic Church.**

Republican Party. The Republican Party lost its majority in the United States Senate and lost two important gubernatorial races in 2001. Republicans in the U.S. Senate and the House of Representatives backed massive tax-cut legisla-

United States President George W. Bush and First Lady Laura Bush call it a night at 11:40 p.m. at one of the inaugural balls Republicans staged in January to celebrate the return of the GOP (Grand Old Party) to power.

tion in 2001. In the aftermath of terrorist attacks on the United States in September, Republicans joined with Democrats to back President George W. Bush and the U.S.-led war against terrorism.

Senate control. The Republican Party lost its majority in the Senate when Senator James M. Jeffords of Vermont announced on May 24 that he was leaving the party to become an independent aligned with the Democratic Party. Jeffords maintained that the Republican Party (or GOP for Grand Old Party) had become increasingly conservative. Jeffords's decision to leave the GOP reduced the number of Senate seats held by the Republicans from 50 to 49, shifting control to the Democrats. The Senate had been split equally, 50 Republicans to 50 Democrats, with Republican Vice President Dick Cheney's tie-breaking vote giving control of the Senate to the Republicans. After the realignment in May, Senator Trent Lott of Mississippi stepped down from Senate majority leader to minority leader.

Gubernatorial elections. The GOP on November 6 lost gubernatorial elections in New Jersey and Virginia after eight years of Republican control. In Virginia, Democrat Mark Warner defeated Republican Mark Earley to succeed Governor James Gilmore, III, who was prohibited by term limits from running again. In New Jersey, Democrat Jim McGreevey defeated Bret Shundler to replace Acting Governor Donald DiFrancesco. DiFrancesco had succeeded Christine Todd Whitman, who resigned in 2001 to head the Environmental Protection Agency.

Gilmore, chairman of the Republican National Committee, downplayed the losses and predicted that in 2002 voters "will be looking for Republican leadership on fighting the war on terrorism, turning our economy around, and keeping Americans and their families safe." Gilmore said that the Republican Party was well positioned to expand its majority in the House and to regain control of the Senate.

New York City mayor. Voters in New York City elected billionaire businessman Michael Bloomberg, founder of a financial information services company, mayor on Nov. 6, 2001, succeeding Republican Rudolph Giuliani. Bloomberg became the fourth Republican mayor of New York in the last 100 years. Some political experts claimed that Bloomberg had been a lifelong Democrat until he began running for the Republican nomination. He spent an estimated $68.9 million of his own money on the campaign.

Approval ratings. Although Republicans lost key elections in 2001, President Bush enjoyed phenomenally high approval ratings. Bush's approval rating rose from 51 percent in early September to 88 percent in October. In late October, his approval ratings stood at 98 percent among Republicans, 88 percent among independents, and 80 percent among Democrats.

Terrorist attacks. Republicans and Democrats alike praised the president's resolve following terrorist attacks on the World Trade Center in New York City and the Pentagon Building outside Washington, D.C., on September 11. Congressional leaders from both parties also praised each other's statesmanship and voiced joint support of the war on terrorism.

Tax cuts. Republican Congressional leaders successfully steered tax cuts sought by President Bush through the U.S. Congress in 2001, passing the legislation on May 26. The president signed the first broad U.S. tax cut since 1981 on June 7, 2001. The president said that the package would reduce taxes by an estimated $1.35 trillion over 10 years.

On October 12, the House Ways and Means Committee approved a $100-billion tax break plan that included $70 billion in tax breaks for corporations. The plan, led by the House Republican leadership, also provided $13 billion in tax rebates to 30 million workers whose incomes were too low to entitle them to the Bush administration's rebates passed in June. The House passed the legislation in October, but the Senate had not yet acted on it by the end of 2001.

Campaign finance. The Republican Party raised $143.3 million and spent $101.7 million between January 1 and June 30, according to the Center for Responsive Politics, a Washington, D.C.-based research group that tracks political contributions. The Democratic Party raised $70 million and spent $48.5 million during the same period. The center based its totals on summaries reported by the national party committees to the Federal Election Commission.

GOP national chairman. In late November, Virginia Governor James Gilmore announced that he would resign as the chairman of the Republican National Committee in January 2002. Political experts said that the resignation stemmed from concern by Republican Party leaders over the gubernatorial losses in Virginia and New Jersey in 2001. Gilmore cited demands on his time and his family for his departure from the position but did not mention conflicts between himself and members of the Republican Party. On December 5, Bush selected Marc Racicot, the former governor of Montana, as the new chairman. ☐ Geoffrey A. Campbell

See also **Congress of the United States; Democratic Party; Elections; New York City; People in the news** (Whitman, Christine Todd); **State government; Taxation; Terrorism: A Special Feature,** p. 38; **United States, Government of the; United States, President of the.**

Roman Catholic Church. Pope John Paul II marked the end of Jubilee 2000 by closing the Holy Door at St. Peter's Basilica on Jan. 6, 2001. According to Vatican officials, 30 million pilgrims visited Rome during the yearlong celebration, which included 34 major events. More than 1.5 million people attended general audiences with the pope. Jubilee 2000 marked the 2,000th anniversary of the birth of Jesus Christ.

New cardinals appointed. In February 2001, Pope John Paul II elevated 44 clergymen to the Sacred College of Cardinals, the group responsible for advising the pope and for electing a new pontiff in the event of the death of a pope. The pope named three new American cardinals: theologian Avery Robert Dulles, 82, of Fordham University in New York City; Archbishop Edward Michael Egan, 68, of New York City; and Archbishop Theodore Edgar McCarrick, 70, of Washington, D.C. It was the sixth time John Paul II had appointed new cardinals during his papacy. With these appointments, John Paul had chosen more than 87 percent of all living cardinals. The appointments brought the number of cardinals to 185, although only 135 were under the age of 80, the cutoff age for papal electors.

Catholic bishops approve directives. U.S. Catholic bishops took steps in 2001 to bring Catholic hospitals and universities into line with official Catholic teaching sanctioned by the pope and church leaders at the Vatican. At the annual spring meeting of the National Conference of

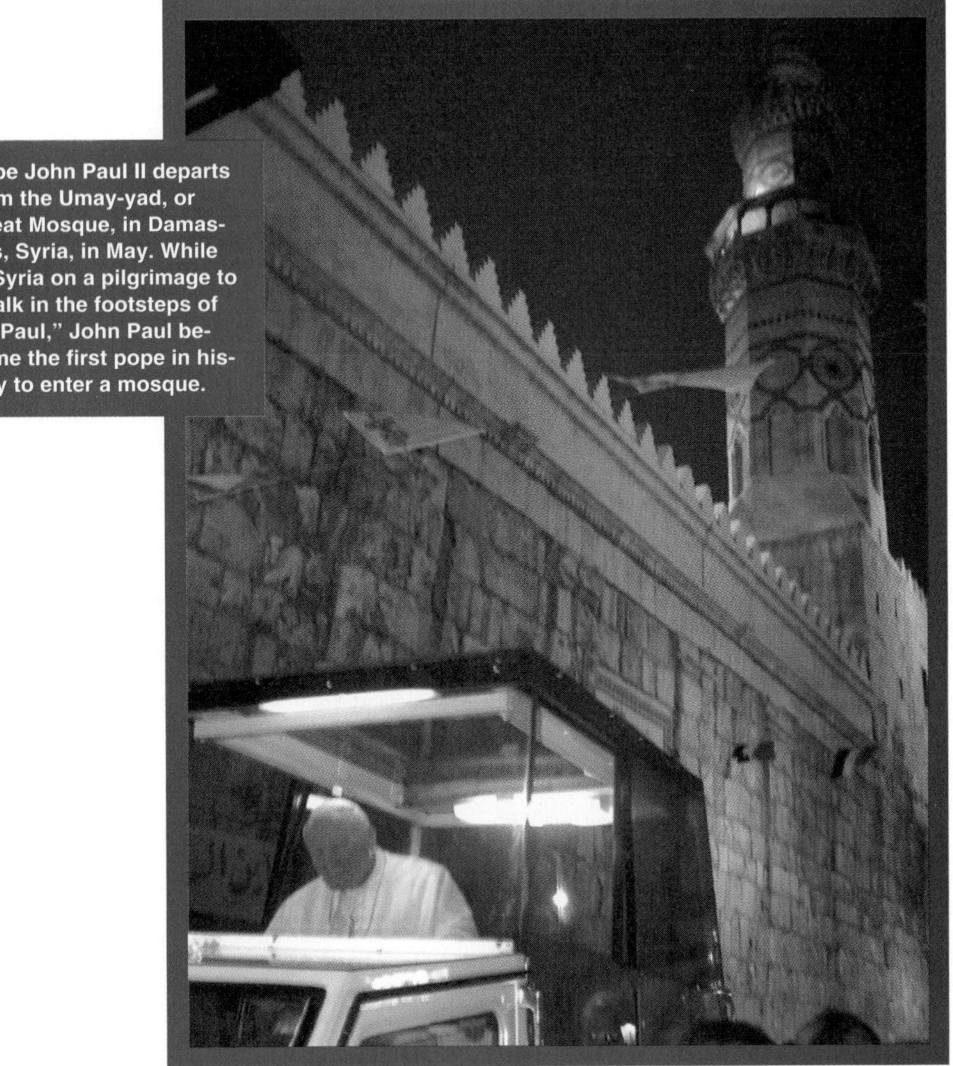

Pope John Paul II departs from the Umay-yad, or Great Mosque, in Damascus, Syria, in May. While in Syria on a pilgrimage to "walk in the footsteps of St. Paul," John Paul became the first pope in history to enter a mosque.

Catholic Bishops in Atlanta, Georgia, in June, the bishops approved directives prohibiting Catholic hospitals from directly offering or cooperating with institutions that perform sterilization, abortion, or *euthanasia* (mercy killing), which the bishops categorized as intrinsically immoral. The bishops also adopted rules requiring that theologians at Catholic universities seek ecclesiastical approval from a local bishop in order to ensure that their teachings agree with official doctrine. Both directives generated controversy among professionals in the affected groups.

The academic community feared threats to academic freedom and possible litigation by theologians removed from their posts because they had failed to seek or had been denied authorization.

American nun speaks on ordination. Defying Vatican orders, Benedictine sister Joan Chittister spoke out in favor of women's ordination at the first international conference of Women's Ordination Worldwide in June in Dublin, Ireland. Chittister's superior, Sister Christine Vladimiroff, prioress of the Benedictine Sisters of Erie, Pennsylvania, ignored a directive from the Vatican that she forbid Chittister to attend the meeting.

Supported by the vast majority of the active Erie nuns, Chittister addressed 370 participants at the conference amid fears that she and Vladimiroff would be expelled from their order or from the church. The Vatican, which prohibits the ordination of women, announced a week later that it would not punish the nuns for their stance.

Papal journeys. In spite of frail health, John Paul II made a pilgrimage in May to "walk in the footsteps of St. Paul" to Greece, Syria, and Malta. Although hundreds of Greek Orthodox protesters denounced the visit, the pope issued a joint statement with Greek Orthodox Archbishop Christodoulos condemning all violence and fanaticism in the name of religion and calling for unity among Christians. In Syria, the pope visited the Umayyad, or Great Mosque, where he appealed for peace in the Middle East in an address to Muslims in the courtyard.

In June, the pope went to Ukraine on a mission of "peace and reconciliation." The Russian Orthodox Church opposed the visit.

The pope visited Kazakhstan and Armenia in late September, despite tensions in central Asia following the terrorist attacks on the United States on September 11. In Kazakhstan, he offered a message of peace and tolerance to Muslims and Orthodox Christians, as well as to the country's small group of Roman Catholics.

☐ Thomas C. Fox

See also **Eastern Orthodox Churches; Terrorism: A Special Feature**, p. 38.

Romania. The government of Prime Minister Adrian Nastase launched a large-scale program to privatize unprofitable state-owned companies in 2001 with an announcement in February that five major state-owned companies were for sale. In October, the World Bank (WB), a United Nations agency that provides loans to member nations, agreed to lend Romania $300 million with the stipulation that the government sell off an additional 60 state-owned companies. The WB, which had granted Romania $50 million in July to finance the retraining of unemployed Romanian workers, promised an additional $1 billion in loans over three years if Romania would continue its policy of privatization.

In October, Nastase signed a military cooperation agreement with United States Secretary of State Colin Powell. The agreement gave the North Atlantic Treaty Organization (NATO) the right to move troops across Romanian territory. Nastase repeated the Romanian government's desire to be admitted to NATO in 2002.

Romania's economy grew by 4.8 percent in the first quarter of 2001. The inflation rate slowed from 41 percent in 2000 to 32 percent in mid-2001. The rate of unemployment stood at 8.4 percent in July. ☐ Sharon L. Wolchik

See also **Europe**.

Rowing. See **Sports**.

Rugby football. Australia retained its position at the top of the world game in Rugby Union in 2001 by winning the Southern Hemisphere Tri-Nations Series for the second consecutive year and beating the British Lions in a three-match Test Series. England retained the European Six-Nations Championship Title. In Rugby League, Australia also continued to dominate the 13-a-side game by defeating the United Kingdom in a three-Test Series.

International Rugby Union (RU). Australia, the 1999 World Cup holder, again won the Tri-Nations Series. The sixth annual competition was played on a home-and-away basis between New Zealand, South Africa, and Australia in July and August 2001. On September 1 in Sydney, the Australians scored a try in the dying seconds to narrowly defeat New Zealand 29-26. Australia also retained the Bledisloe Cup—an annual two-match Series contested by New Zealand and Australia—which is determined during the Tri-Nations competition. Australia won both games.

Australia also defeated the British Lions—a touring team made up of players from England, Ireland, Scotland, and Wales—in a three-Test Series. Australia won the deciding match on July 14 in Sydney 29-23 on two late penalty goals. England was eventually crowned Lloyds TSB European Six-Nations Champions despite suffering an unexpected defeat at the hands of Ireland on October 20 in a match that was delayed until autumn because of a serious outbreak of foot-and-mouth disease in the United Kingdom. Because of the defeat, England was denied the Grand Slam (victory against all five European opponents) for the third consecutive season.

In the Super 12 Series, a competition between 12 teams from the 3 Southern Hemisphere countries, ACT Brumbies of Australia defeated Natal Sharks of South Africa 36-6 in the final in Sydney on May 26. On July 8, Fiji beat Samoa 28-17 to take the Epson Cup in the Pacific Rim Series.

England defeated Australia 21-15 on November 10 in what has become a varied annual series of International matches played in Europe during November and December. England went on to dismantle Romania with a record score of 134-0 and beat South Africa 29-9. France defeated South Africa 20-10 in Paris on November 10 and Australia14-13 in Marseille on November 17. Scotland defeated Tonga 43-20 in Edinburgh but lost to Argentina 16-25 and to New Zealand 6-37.

New Zealand defeated Ireland 40-29 in Dublin on November 17. Wales, having lost to Argentina 16-30 in Cardiff, Wales, on November 10, defeated Tonga 51-7 on November 17 but was beaten by Australia 13-21 on November 25.

New Zealand defeated Australia 31-5 in Cardiff, Wales, to become the new World Champions in the Official World Series Seven-a-Side Tournament, which is played at 10 tournaments in various countries throughout the year.

National competitions. Leicester (England) defeated Stade Francais (France) 34-30 in Paris on May 19 in the Heineken European Cup Final. Harlequins (England) beat Narbonne (France) 42-33 at Twickenham on May 20 in the final of the European Shield (for teams not qualified for the Heineken Cup).

In England, Leicester once again became Champions of the Allied Dunbar Premier Division. In the Tetleys Bitter Cup final at Twickenham on February 24, Newcastle Falcons defeated Harlequins 30-27. Yorkshire won the County Championship 47-17 over Cornwall at Twickenham on May 26.

In Scotland, Hawick won the BT Premier League. In the final of the BT Cellnet Cup on April 1, Boroughmuir defeated Melrose 39-15.

In Ireland, Dungannon beat Cork Constitution 46-12 in the AIB League Final on May 21.

In Wales, Swansea won the new Welsh/Scottish League, and Newport won the Principality Cup at Cardiff

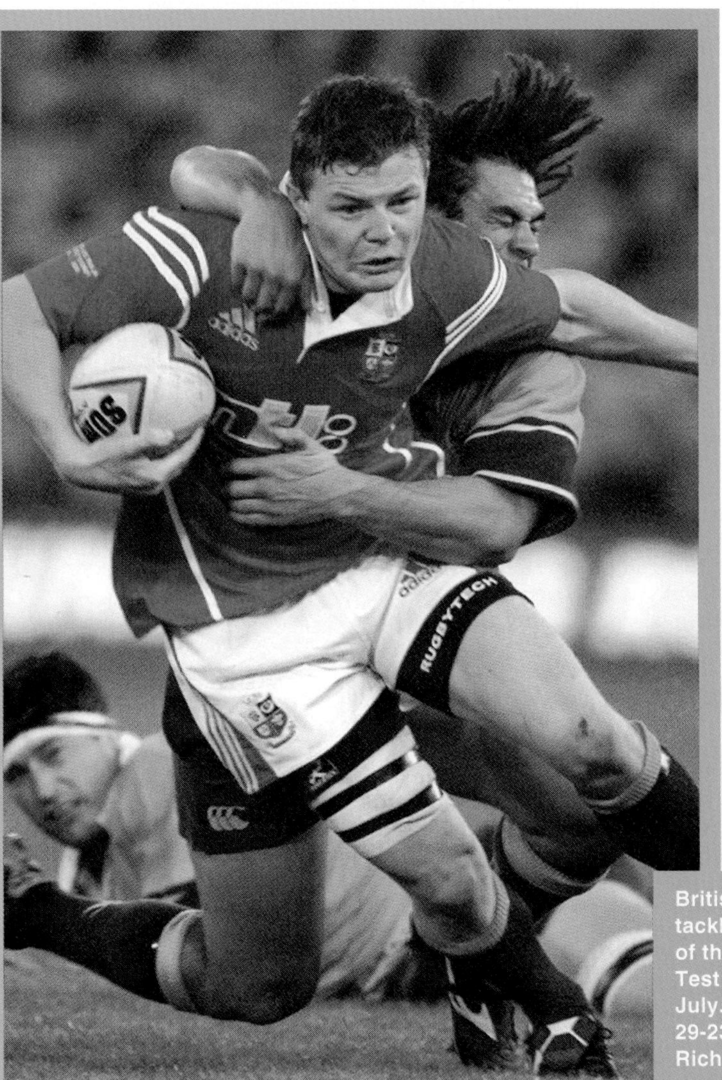

British Lions center Brian O'Driscoll is tackled from behind by George Smith of the Australia Wallabies during a Test match in Sydney, Australia, in July. The Wallabies defeated the Lions 29-23 to take the series and the Tom Richards Cup.

13-8 over Neath on May 12. In France, Toulouse beat Montferand 34-22 on June 9 to take the Club Championship final.

In Italy, Benetton Treviso defeated Calvisano 33-13 in a similar championship final on June 2.

In South Africa, Western Province defeated the Natal Sharks 29-24 on October 27, completing their bid for the Bankfin Currie Cup. In the Vodacom Cup final in May, Blue Bulls beat Boland Cavaliers 42-24.

In New Zealand, Canterbury prevailed over Otago 30-19 on November 3 to win the Air New Zealand National Provincial Championship First Division final. On August 4, NSW Country defeated Perth Gold 39-19 after five rounds to take the Australian Rugby Shield.

International Rugby League. In 2001, Australia once again reaffirmed its position as the leading rugby league nation by defeating Great Britain 2-1 in the United Kingdom in a three-match Test Series. Great Britain had defeated France 42-12 in a preliminary match on October 26 in Agen and scored an impressive victory of 20-12 at Huddersfield in the first Test on November 11. But Australia rallied to overcome Great Britain in convincing style in the remaining two Tests—40-12 at Bolton on November 17 and 28-8 at Wigan on November 24.

☐ David Duckham

Russia in 2001 enjoyed one of its most prosperous years since the collapse of the Soviet Union in 1991. The Russian economy was strong, and tensions with the United States over U.S. President George W. Bush's plans to build a missile defense system gave way to a warm new strategic partnership after the terrorist attacks on the United States on Sept. 11, 2001. President Vladimir Putin profited from both developments, ending 2001 as the most popular Russian leader in recent memory.

Russian-U.S. relations. In January 2001, Russian officials confronted a new U.S. administration led by President Bush. During his election campaign, Bush had criticized President Bill Clinton for attempting "nation building" in Russia and the other former Soviet states. Bush signaled his intention to devote less time and energy to relations with Russia, and he supported a plan to test an antiballistic missile shield. Such tests are prohibited by the 1972 Antiballistic Missile (ABM) treaty between the United States and the former Soviet Union. Russia, as the major successor state to the Soviet Union, maintains treaties negotiated by the Soviet government.

Throughout the first half of 2001, Putin and other Russian officials argued that the ABM treaty remained a key element of the strategic system that has prevented a nuclear exchange since World War II (1939-1945). According to the treaty, neither the United States nor Russia may deploy any system designed to defend against incoming nuclear missiles. The treaty also severely restricts any testing of such a system. Cold War-era diplomats had designed the treaty to preserve *deterrence,* a policy in which both the Soviet Union and the United States held the power to devastate the other, thereby deterring either nation from using its nuclear weapons. (The Cold War was a period of intense rivalry between Communist and non-Communist nations, led by the Soviet Union and the United States, respectively.)

After his inauguration, Bush announced that the United States was prepared to withdraw from the ABM Treaty unless Russia consented to U.S. testing of a new antimissile system. During the spring of 2001, Putin visited Europe and Asia to rally opposition to the Bush administration's plan.

First meeting. On June 16, Bush and Putin met for the first time in Ljubljana, Slovenia. Bush later said of Putin, "I looked the man in the eye. I found him to be very straightforward and trustworthy." For his part, Putin said that he also trusted Bush and that "Russia and the United States are not enemies, they do not threaten each other, and they could be fully good allies." The two presidents met again in Genoa, Italy, on July 22 and pledged to work to increase American investment in Russia and to find a solution to their disagreement over the ABM Treaty.

After the terrorist attacks on the United States on September 11, Putin was the first world leader to offer President Bush his condolences and assistance. In response to Bush's report that U.S. armed forces around the globe were going on high alert, Putin ordered Russian forces to *stand down* (revert to low alert), to avoid any confrontations between the two countries.

Putin also claimed that the al-Qaida terrorist network, which U.S. intelligence officials believed had carried out the attacks on the United States, had also supported terrorists in the breakaway Russian province of Chechnya. In September 1999, the Russian government had blamed Chechnya-based terrorists for the coordinated series of attacks on apartment buildings that killed hundreds of people in Moscow and other Russian cities. Putin argued in 2001 that the United States and Russia were united by their struggle against a common foe, just as they had been during World War II.

In the weeks following the attacks on September 11, Putin firmly committed Russia to supporting the U.S. campaign against the Taliban regime in Afghanistan, which Western governments accused of harboring terrorists. On September 24, Putin announced the opening of Russian and central Asian airspace for "humanitarian" missions

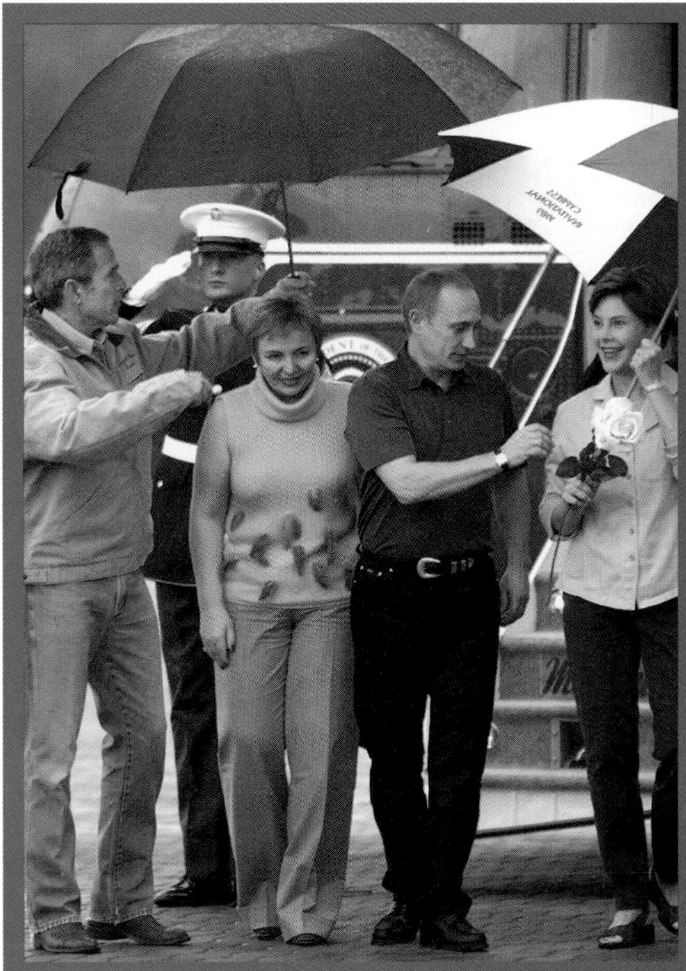

United States President George W. Bush (left) and First Lady Laura Bush (right) greet Russian President Vladimir Putin and his wife, Lyudmila Putin, on their arrival to the Bush's ranch near Crawford, Texas, in November 2001.

and expanded support for the anti-Taliban Northern Alliance in Afghanistan. He also pledged cooperation with Western intelligence agencies. U.S. and other Western officials warmly welcomed the Russians' offer to share intelligence. In the Soviet war in Afghanistan during the 1980's, Russians had gained invaluable knowledge about the country. By the end of October 2001, Putin had agreed to allow U.S. and British military forces to use Russian military bases in Tajikistan to conduct operations in neighboring Afghanistan.

Relations with NATO. Putin continued to align Russia more closely with the United States and Western Europe. On September 25, he visited Germany, where he had spent much of the 1980's as an intelligence agent for the Soviet KGB. In Berlin, he addressed the Bundestag (the lower house of Germany's parliament) in German, restating his support for the U.S.-led antiterrorism effort. In the same speech, he suggested that Russia might explore the possibility of membership in NATO. He repeated this message during a visit to the European Union (EU) headquarters in Brussels, Belgium, on Oct. 1, 2001, and to President Bush in Shanghai on October 21.

Putin's U.S. visit. The culmination of the new U.S.-Russian strategic partnership came during Putin's visit to Washington, D.C., and to President Bush's Texas ranch in early November. Bush and Putin announced they would reduce their countries' stockpiles of strategic nuclear arms from 6,000 to approximately 2,000 over the next 10 years. However, Putin failed to secure a commitment from Bush to formalize the arms reductions in a treaty. Bush said that a treaty would be needlessly time consuming and adversarial.

Both presidents maintained their longstanding positions on the ABM treaty. Putin claimed that the treaty was essential while Bush argued that it was a useless relic of the Cold War. Putin declared that the disagreement would not threaten the emerging new partnership between the two former adversaries. On December 13, President Bush announced that the United States would withdraw from the treaty by June 2002.

Freedom of the press. The new mood of cooperation between the United States and Russia brought a swift end to U.S. criticism of Russian policy toward private media outlets. In January 2001, business executive and former Putin supporter Boris Berezovsky was forced to sell his 49-percent stake in ORT, the nation's largest national television network. The sale effectively ended independent oversight of the network. In October 2001, Berezovsky was barred from returning to Russia after authorities issued a warrant for his arrest on charges of corruption.

Seizure of NTV. In April, the government-controlled natural gas monopoly, Gazprom, seized control of NTV, Russia's only remaining independent national television network. Gazprom had loaned NTV millions of dollars during the 1990's. In 2001, Gazprom claimed NTV—along with the rest of Media-Most, the media empire of which NTV was a part—as settlement for nonpayment of that debt. Meanwhile, government agents arrested senior executives at Media-Most on charges of financial mismanagement, tax evasion, and corruption. The Russian government also negotiated with Spain—unsuccessfully—to surrender Media-Most chairman Vladimir Gusinsky to Russian officials for criminal prosecution.

Many NTV journalists refused to work under the network's new management and moved to a smaller Moscow-based station called TV6. In October, Moscow tax authorities moved to liquidate TV6 as well for nonpayment of taxes. By the end of 2001, all major broadcast outlets in Russia were in the hands of the government.

Economic growth. Buoyed by high oil prices and growing consumer demand, the Russian economy enjoyed its second year of strong growth in 2001. Gross domestic product (GDP), the value of goods and services produced in a given period, grew at an estimated rate of 5.5 percent. As a result, the Russian government, which had defaulted on its international loans in August 1998, was able to meet all of its debt obligations without having to ask for rescheduling of payments. In addition, Putin successfully pushed through a broad range of economic reforms. These included new protections for shareholders and a land code permitting land sales for the first time since the establishment of Communism after the Bolshevik Revolution of 1917. Putin's economic reform program helped attract foreign investment and drive Russian stock prices sharply upward during 2001.

In 2001, Russia increased its output of oil by 8.1 percent. By year's end, Russia was producing 7.2 million barrels of oil a day, a level of production second only to Saudi Arabia. In September, Putin told Bush that Russia was capable of becoming an alternate source of oil to the West if Middle East oil were to become unavailable due to political instability in the area.

Chechnya. The Russian army remained bogged down in Chechnya, two full years after it invaded the secessionist territory in October 1999. In May 2001, Putin announced that Russian troops would again withdraw from Chechnya, as they had in 1996, leaving behind only a police force. The withdrawal was interrupted after less than a week, when a new round of violence erupted. Then, after the terrorist attacks on the United States in September 2001, U.S. and European officials, who

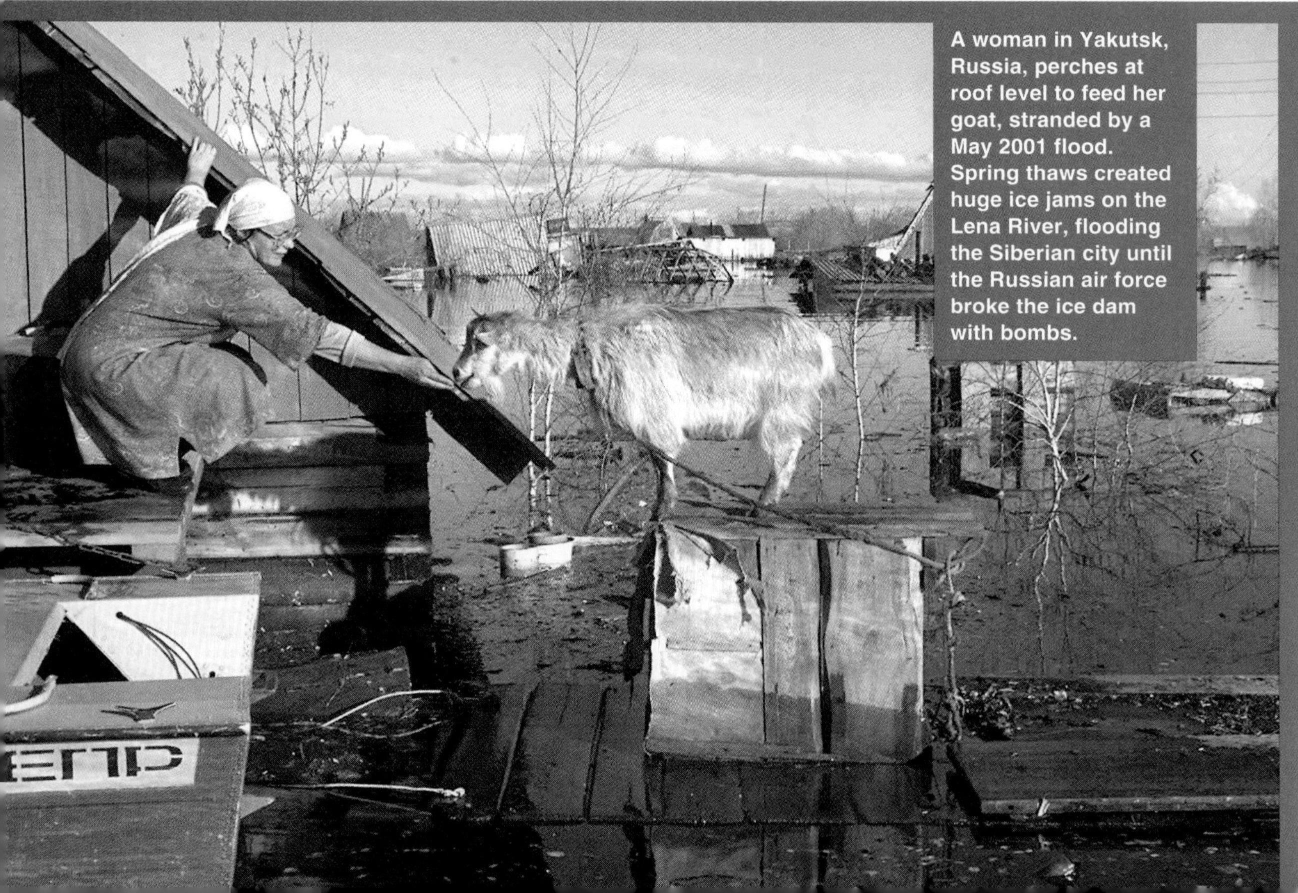

A woman in Yakutsk, Russia, perches at roof level to feed her goat, stranded by a May 2001 flood. Spring thaws created huge ice jams on the Lena River, flooding the Siberian city until the Russian air force broke the ice dam with bombs.

had previously characterized Russia's military campaign in Chechnya as "brutal," muted their criticisms as they began to plan antiterrorist campaigns.

Sibir airliner. On Oct. 4, 2001, a Sibir Airlines jetliner bound from Tel Aviv, Israel, to Novosibirsk, Russia, crashed into the Black Sea. All 78 passengers and crew died. After denying responsibility for over a week, the Ukrainian government finally admitted that its armed forces had accidentally shot down the commercial airliner while test-firing a ground-to-air missile.

Kursk. On October 8, the sunken Russian submarine *Kursk* was raised from the bottom of the Barents Sea by a Russian-Dutch salvage team. *Kursk*, one of Russia's newest nuclear submarines, sank just off the northern coast of Russia in August 2000. All 118 crew members died in the incident, which Russian naval officials initially blamed on a collision with a foreign submarine. U.S. authorities denied that any foreign submarines were near the *Kursk* when it sank. Instead, they speculated that a torpedo on board the ship may have exploded and torn apart its hull. The salvaged hull may help resolve the mystery of the sub's sinking. ☐ Steven L. Solnick

See also **Europe; Terrorism: A Special Feature, p. 38; Ukraine; United States; Government of the.**

Sailing. See **Boating.**

San Francisco in 2001 reeled from economic aftershocks caused by the terrorist attacks on the United States on September 11, as well as by the crash in 2000 of many of the area's high-tech companies. The terrorist attacks sent San Francisco's tourism industry, the city's number-one revenue producer, into a steep decline. In September 2001, hotel occupancy rates dropped to about 60 percent of capacity from about 90 percent in September 2000. Nearly 3,000 hotel and restaurant workers were laid off or had their hours reduced.

Many San Franciscans expressed delight when California Governor Gray Davis visited the city in October 2001 to announce a $5-million program to encourage Californians to vacation within the state. In early November, however, tourists all but disappeared from the city after Governor Davis warned the public of possible terrorist attacks on a number of the state's more prominent bridges, including San Francisco's famed Golden Gate Bridge. The slump in tourism, which earned the city about $474 million in 2000, led city officials to warn of a possible $100-million shortfall in the city's $5.2-billion budget by the end of 2001.

Rising unemployment. The continuing collapse of dot-com businesses and massive layoffs at larger, well-established technology companies in San Francisco and nearby Silicon Valley—the suburban Bay area center of high-tech businesses—brought the city's five-year economic boom to a halt. Dot-com companies are businesses that depend entirely on their Internet presence to sell products and services. The decline in the U.S. economy also contributed to the city's economic woes.

By September 2001, San Francisco's unemployment rate had climbed to a five-year high—5.5 percent, compared with 3.1 percent in September 2000. The jobless rate in Silicon Valley, where many San Franciscans work, jumped to 6.4 percent, compared with 1.6 percent the previous year. Many local businesses, especially those that had catered to high-tech employees, were forced to close their doors.

Office vacancy rates in downtown San Francisco jumped to 15.2 percent in September 2001—the highest since 1988—compared with about 2 percent a year earlier. Rents on vacant office space dropped by an average of 50 percent.

Housing market. Even San Francisco's notoriously expensive housing market cooled in 2001. The average rent for a two-bedroom apartment fell from $2,790 in December 2000 to $2,400 in June 2001. Nevertheless, an October report by the National Low Income Housing Coalition, a housing advocacy group based in Washington, D.C., ranked San Francisco as the least affordable metropolitan area in the United States. The California Budget Project, a nonprofit research group based in Sacramento, reported in September that a San Francisco family of four would need $61,600 a year to pay for such basic necessities as rent, utilities, and health care.

Energy crisis. San Francisco, along with other cities in California, suffered from acute energy shortages and skyrocketing energy costs after the Pacific Gas and Electric Company, the San Francisco-based firm that provides energy to most of northern and central California, declared bankruptcy in April 2001. To help conserve energy, the city imposed stiff fines for wasting, offered rewards for saving energy, and resorted to rolling brownouts in the spring and summer.

The energy crisis helped recharge efforts to establish a public power agency for San Francisco (an agency owned and operated by the city). However, San Francisco voters on November 6 narrowly rejected two measures to create a municipal agency to replace Pacific Gas and Electric. Utility companies and other businesses spent nearly $2 million to oppose the measures. Public power advocates vowed to continue their efforts. ☐ Brian Bouldrey

See also **City; Economy; Energy Supply: A Special Report.**

Saudi Arabia. Relations between Saudi Arabia and the United States became strained after the terrorist attacks on the United States on Sept. 11, 2001. In the attacks, 19 terrorists hijacked four commercial airliners. They flew two jets into the World Trade Center towers in New York City and one into the Pentagon Building near Washington, D.C. Another hijacked plane crashed southeast of Pittsburgh, Pennsylvania. Most of the men suspected of hijacking the planes were from Saudi Arabia.

The U.S. government blamed Osama bin Laden, a Saudi-born Islamic militant, for masterminding the attacks. Although the Saudis had revoked bin Laden's citizenship in 1994, a number of experts on terrorism believed that some Saudis continued to fund various Islamic groups linked to bin Laden's al-Qaida terrorist network. In addition, Saudi Arabia was one of three countries that, prior to the terrorist attacks, had recognized the Taliban leadership in Afghanistan, which provided refuge to bin Laden.

U.S. relations. Saudi authorities denounced the terrorist attacks, but they gave mixed signals about cooperating in a U.S.-led "war on terrorism." In late September 2001, the Saudi government announced that it would not permit U.S. forces based in Saudi Arabia to launch air strikes against Afghanistan. Yet, Saudi officials, in accord with U.S. wishes, agreed to sever diplomatic relations with the Taliban. In October, the Saudi government rebuffed U.S. criticism that it was acting too slowly to freeze the assets of Saudi nationals and organizations that the United States linked to terrorist groups.

Many experts on the Middle East believed that the Saudi ruling family was reluctant to embrace a U.S.-led antiterror coalition because it feared a backlash by Saudis opposed to U.S. policies in the Middle East. Many Saudis also supported bin Laden's call for the expulsion of U.S. military forces from bases in Saudi Arabia.

U.S. indictment. In June, the Saudi government criticized a U.S. grand jury indictment of 13 Saudis and 1 Lebanese for the 1996 bombing of U.S. Air Force barracks in Khobar, Saudi Arabia. The bombing killed 19 U.S. soldiers. The Saudi interior minister said that 11 of the suspects were imprisoned in Saudi Arabia but that Saudi Arabia would not *extradite* (surrender) them to the United States. International affairs experts believed the Saudis were angered that the indictment blamed Iran for inciting the bombing. In 2001, the Saudis were striving to improve relations with Iran. ☐ Christine Helms

See also **Iran; Middle East; Terrorism; Terrorism: A Special Feature,** p. 38.

School. See **Education.**

Senegal. See **Africa.**

Sierra Leone. Officials of Sierra Leone's government and leaders of the Revolutionary United Front (RUF) agreed on May 15, 2001, to take steps to end Sierra Leone's civil war, which began in 1991. Both sides accepted a cease-fire and agreed to begin a process of disarmament. The parties called on the United Nations (UN) peacekeeping mission in Sierra Leone, UNAMSIL, to oversee the disarmament process. The UN troops entered Sierra Leone in 1999. By late 2001, the UN had more than 17,500 soldiers in the country, making Sierra Leone the UN's largest peacekeeping mission. In addition, the United States, along with several West African nations, trained Ghanaian, Senegalese, and Nigerian troops in 2001 to bolster the UN forces.

Sierra Leone's government, headed by President Ahmed Tejan Kabbah, was democratically elected in 1996 but was overthrown in a military *coup* (takeover) in May 1997. In February 1998, Nigerian-led forces intervened and restored Kabbah to power. The RUF, which was formed in the early 1990's and had battled government forces in a seesaw civil war, was generally on the defensive by early 2001.

Child soldiers released. UNAMSIL officials reported on May 26 that about 1,500 progovernment soldiers and about 1,000 RUF rebels had given up their weapons in the cease-fire and that RUF units had released about 600 child soldiers. Oluyemi Adeniji, UN special envoy to Sierra Leone, declared that the release demonstrated "the commitment of the RUF to the total stoppage of this war."

International human rights groups had long condemned the RUF for abducting children to use as fighters. According to some estimates, as many as 8,000 children had been taken into RUF units since 1991. Human rights groups also accused the RUF of carrying out campaigns of intimidation and terror, such as amputating limbs, against civilians. According to UN sources, many of the child soldiers released by the RUF were addicted to illicit drugs.

Disarmament progress. By December 2001, UN monitors had disarmed nearly 37,000 rebels, and RUF units had released approximately 3,500 child fighters. Western diplomats and UN officials expressed hope that ongoing demobilization would bring permanent peace to Sierra Leone.

The continuing cease-fire paved the way for elections to take place in the first half of 2002. Presidential and parliamentary elections had been scheduled for early 2001, but the government postponed them, with UN backing, because of the unstable situation that had existed then. ☐ Simon Baynham

See also **Africa.**

Anja Paerson of Sweden negotiates a turn in the women's slalom competition at the World Alpine Ski Championships in St. Anton, Austria, in February. Paerson went on to win the event.

Singapore. The People's Action Party (PAP), which governed Singapore since its independence in 1965, won 82 out of the 84 seats in November 2001 parliamentary elections. PAP members took 75 percent of the votes, up from 65 percent in the last election in 1997.

Despite a strong election mandate, Prime Minister Chok Tong Goh warned of hard times ahead. Unemployment increased from 3.5 percent in 2000 to 4.5 percent in 2001. Singapore's economy fell by 3 percent in 2001, after the highest economic growth in Asia—9.9 percent—during 2000. Singapore's main export, electronics, was especially hard hit by declining demand abroad.

In an effort to revitalize Singapore's economy, Goh announced the formation of a committee to examine ways to restructure state-owned companies, which dominated Singapore's economy. Goh also wanted to liberalize the financial sector to create increased international competition.

In July 2001, the government announced a $1.3-billion spending plan to stimulate the economy. The plan included financing for infrastructure projects and rebates on property taxes. In October, after the economy did not improve significantly, the government reported it would put another $6.3 billion into the plan. ☐ Henry S. Bradsher

See also **Asia**.

Skating. See **Hockey; Ice skating; Sports.**

Skiing. In 2001, Croatia's Jana Kostelic became the second-youngest woman ever to win the overall World Cup title. Austrian Hermann Maier tied one of skiing's greatest records in the 2001 World Cup season before he was seriously injured in a motorcycle accident in August.

Kostelic captured the overall World Cup title on March 11, 2001, in Are, Sweden. Her victory, at age 19, made her the youngest woman to take that prize since Annemarie Moser-Proell of Austria did so in 1971 at the age of 17. Defending champion Renate Goetschl of Austria took second place.

Hermann Maier once again dominated the men's World Cup standings in 2001, winning the overall, downhill, Super-G, and giant slalom titles. His giant slalom victory on March 10 in Are, Sweden, tied Ingmar Stenmark's record of 13 victories in a World Cup season. Stenmark, of Sweden, set the mark in 1979.

Maier's overall title was his third in four years. His 1,618-point total was nearly double that of second-place finisher Stephan Eberharter of Austria, who had 875 points. Benjamin Raich of Austria completed the Austrian sweep of the men's events, taking the slalom title.

The World Alpine Championships, which are held every two years, took place from January 29 through Feb. 10, 2001, in St. Anton, Austria. American Daron Rahlves stunned Austrian favorites Maier and Eberharter with a Super-G run of 1 minute, 21.46 seconds, which was 0.08 second faster than Eberharter. Rahlves's title was the first captured by an American male since Steve Mahre took the giant slalom in 1982. In other Alpine events, France's Regine Cavagnoud won the women's Super-G; Germany's Martina Ertl won the women's combined; Norway's Kjetil-Andre Aamodt won the men's combined; and Sweden's Anja Paerson won the women's slalom.

Austrian skiers also enjoyed Alpine successes, with Mario Matt taking the men's slalom, Hannes Trinkl winning the downhill, and Michaela Dorfmeister taking the women's downhill. Swiss skiers Michael von Gruenigen and Sonja Nef won the giant slalom titles.

Nordic skiing. Bjarte Engen Vik of Norway successfully defended his Nordic combined world title in Lahti, Finland, on Feb. 16, 2001. Austria's Felix Gottwald won the World Cup overall Nordic combined title on March 9.

Maier injured. On August 24, Hermann Maier was seriously injured when his motorcycle struck a car that reportedly made an illegal turn near Radstadt, Austria. Maier broke his right leg in several places. Austrian ski officials doubted that Maier would recover in time to compete in the 2002 Winter Olympics. ☐ Michael Kates

Slovakia. Passage of a major administrative reform by Slovakia's parliament nearly broke up the ruling coalition of Prime Minister Mikulas Dzurinda in 2001. The reform, required as a condition for European Union (EU) membership, created eight regions that were to wield certain powers previously held by the national government. The Hungarian Coalition Party (SMK) threatened to leave Dzurinda's governing coalition when parliament passed part of the measure in July. The SMK claimed that the reform shut out Hungarians—Slovakia's largest ethnic minority—from regional governmental positions. In September, the parliament passed a compromise version agreeable to SMK.

Negotiations between Slovak and EU officials continued in 2001. In June, Slovakian officials closed two more negotiating *chapters* (agreements on specific policies) with the EU, bringing its total to 19. Among candidate nations, only Hungary, Cyprus, and Slovenia had completed more negotiating chapters by the end of 2001.

Slovakia's unemployment rate remained one of the highest in Europe in 2001. Over 18 percent of the work force was out of work, about the same percentage as in 2000. Inflation eased, however, from 12 percent in 2000 to 7.5 percent in 2001. ☐ Sharon L. Wolchik

See also **Europe.**

Soccer. Perennial power Brazil had a topsy-turvy season in 2001, nearly failing to qualify for the 2002 World Cup and being bumped from the top of the rankings of the Federation Internationale de Football Association (FIFA), the governing body of international soccer. The Major League Soccer (MLS) season was cut short by 10 games in 2001 because of the terrorist attacks on the United States on September 11. The Copa America tournament hosted by Colombia in July was canceled for fear of local terrorist activities, then rescheduled just five days before play was to began.

2002 World Cup. International soccer in 2001 focused on the qualifying tournaments for the 2002 World Cup to be held in South Korea and Japan beginning in May. In the South American zone, Brazil, which has four World Cup titles and is the only country to have played in every World Cup finals tournament, stunned the soccer world by losing six of its qualifying matches. They only clinched their World Cup finals berth by defeating Venezuela in its last qualifying match on Nov. 14, 2001. Argentina ran away with the group title, winning 13 matches and losing only one. Ecuador finished in second place.

In Europe, which was guaranteed at least 14 of the 32 World Cup finals slots, three-time champion Germany needed to win a play-off before qualifying. England had handed Germany a shocking 5-1 defeat in September in Munich. The Netherlands and the Czech Republic failed to qualify.

In the Football Confederation's final group of six, the United States qualified in third place, together with Costa Rica and Mexico.

In the Asian zone, host countries South Korea and Japan enjoyed automatic qualification for the finals. They were joined by China, which qualified for the first time, and Saudi Arabia. Iran lost in a play-off with Ireland. The five qualifiers from the African zone were South Africa, Cameroon, Nigeria, Senegal, and Tunisia. In the Oceania zone, Australia easily took the top spot, breaking World Cup scoring records by tallying 66 goals and giving up none in their four matches. However, Australia again failed to reach the World Cup, after losing a play-off to Uruguay on November 25.

Other championships. France, holder of the World Cup and European Championships, had another successful season. The French team won the FIFA Confederations Cup, defeating Japan 1-0 in the final at Yokohama, Japan, on June 10. On September 30, France defeated Nigeria 3-0 in the final of the Under-17 World Championship held in Trinidad and Tobago. Earlier in the tournament, France had lost to Nigeria 2-1 in the group phase. The United States, playing in the same group, failed to pick up a point in their three matches. French striker Florent Sinama Pongolle was voted player of the tournament, having scored a record nine goals in six matches.

On July 8 in Buenos Aires, Argentina defeated Ghana 3-0 to take the final of the World Youth Cup (20 and under). The United States finished second in its group to reach the second round but was then eliminated when it lost to the team from Egypt by a score of 2-0.

Real Madrid's Zinedine Zinane (left) maneuvers through the Valladolid defense during a Spanish league match in Madrid in September. In July, Real Madrid paid a record $64.5 million for the rights to sign Zinane.

Colombia hosted and won its first Copa America tournament in July 2001, defeating Mexico 1-0 in the final in Bogota. Colombia's centerback Ivan Cordoba scored the winner on a glancing header in the 65th minute. Mexico had two players sent off in the last 12 minutes.

The tournament, held every other year in South America, faced difficulties. In July, soccer officials had voted to move the tournament out of Colombia because of possible terrorism. Five days before the tournament was to begin, soccer officials voted to reinstate the tournament in Colombia. Because of the confusion and possible danger, Argentina and Canada withdrew from the tournament. Honduras, which had replaced Argentina, reached the last eight and knocked out Brazil before losing to Colombia in the semifinal. Colombia proved to be the team of the tournament, scoring 11 goals and allowing none in six games.

International club play. The Los Angeles Galaxy won the Football Confederation Champions Cup on January 21, defeating Olimpia of Honduras 3-2 in the final match at the Los Angeles Coliseum. Ezra Hendrickson scored two for the Galaxy, including the 78th-minute winner, and Cobi Jones scored one. Both finalists qualified for the second staging of FIFA's World Club Championship, which was scheduled for Spain in July and August. But the competition, which would have been FIFA's first venture into soccer at club level, was postponed until 2003 because of financial problems.

On May 23, 2001, Bayern Munich of Germany won its first European Champions title in 25 years in a very close match against Valencia of Spain. Bayern Munich defeated Valencia 5-4 in a shootout in the final in Milan.

Boca Juniors of Argentina successfully defended the Copa Libertadores on June 28, defeating Cruz Azul of Mexico on penalties in the final, which was held in Buenos Aires. Both teams had recorded 1-0 away victories to reach the final. By winning, Boca Juniors denied Cruz Azul in its bid to become the first Central American team to win the South American club championship.

Major League Soccer (MLS). On October 21, the San Jose Earthquakes defeated the Los Angeles Galaxy 2-1 on a thrilling overtime goal by Dwayne DeRosario to win their first MLS Cup title. Galaxy forward Luis Hernandez scored the first goal 21 minutes into the first period. However, the Earthquakes tied the game just before half-time when San Jose forward Landon Donovan pounced to slam a loose ball into the Galaxy's net.

San Jose's Dwayne DeRosario, an 85th-minute substitute, settled the game six minutes into the first overtime period when he curled in the winner. Los Angeles had finished two points ahead of San Jose in the Western Division in the regular season, which had been shortened because of the September 11 terrorist attacks on the United States. Ten games were canceled, and the final standings were determined on a points-per-game basis.

On October 28, exactly a week after losing in overtime to San Jose in the MLS Cup final, Los Angeles turned the tables and won on an overtime goal, defeating the New England Revolution 2-1 to capture the U.S. Open Cup. Two minutes into overtime, Los Angeles's Danny Califf headed in a feed from captain Cobi Jones in the final, held at Titan Stadium in Fullerton, California. New England had scored first on Wolde Harris's deflected free kick after 30 minutes. Los Angeles's Ezra Hendrickson knotted the game 40 minutes later when he floated a cross into the Revolution's net. New England's Jay Heaps was ejected with two minutes left in regulation play time for retaliating against a Galaxy player who had committed a foul.

Records and awards. On April 9, 2001, Australia set a world scoring record for an international soccer match when it beat Tonga 22-0 in a 2002 World Cup qualifying match. Two days later, Australia broke its own record with a 31-0 win over American Samoa. In that match, Australian striker Archie Thompson scored 13 goals, breaking the previous individual scoring record of 10 set in the 1908 Olympic Games. American Samoa, ranked last in the FIFA world rankings at the time, had lost its entire first team to passport irregularities and had been forced to field three 15-year-olds.

In May 2001, France replaced Brazil at the top of the FIFA world rankings. Brazil had owned the top spot for seven years. France was still at the top in the November rankings. The United States was ranked 20th, down two places from November 2000.

On July 9, Real Madrid of Spain paid a record $64.5-million transfer fee to sign French midfielder Zinedine Zidane from Juventus of Italy. Zidane had been named the 2000 FIFA World Player of the Year. The fee smashed the record that Real Madrid had set in 2000 when it had paid $54.4 million to Barcelona for Luis Figo. ☐ Norman Barrett

Social Security. Officials with the Social Security Administration (SSA) reported on March 19, 2001, that revenue surpluses for the Social Security program would continue until 2016, and the program would have adequate revenues until 2038. The 2001 report disclosed that Social Security ran a surplus of $153 billion in 2000 and ended the year with $1.049 trillion in assets. Officials expected to draw down the system's assets to pay benefits beginning in 2025.

New disability rules took effect Jan. 1, 2001, allowing more people with disabilities to work without jeopardizing government-provided cash benefits and health care coverage. As a result, Social Security disability beneficiaries could earn $740 per month and remain eligible for benefits.

Fraud alert. The SSA's Office of Inspector General (OIG) warned senior citizens in July to be wary of individuals or programs promising additional Social Security payments in exchange for personal information. OIG investigators found that more than 25,000 people had been tricked by fliers promising slavery reparations or extra Social Security benefits in exchange for personal information. Investigators warned that people could use such information to open fraudulent credit accounts. ☐ Geoffrey A. Campbell

See also **United States, Government of the.**

South Africa. President Thabo Mbeki and his ruling African National Congress (ANC) faced scandal, controversy, and political in-fighting in 2001. On February 9, Mbeki gave a state-of-the-nation speech that many observers described as "conciliatory." Promising economic reforms and striking a theme of reconciliation, Mbeki paid tribute to South Africans of all colors for their work in helping the country escape from "its painful past." Just days later, former president Nelson Mandela gave a newspaper interview in which he strongly rebuked high-ranking ANC officials for making prejudicial statements about South Africa's Indian racial minority. He called on the ANC and President Mbeki, in particular, to live up to the ANC's Freedom Charter. The charter states that South Africa belongs to all who live in it.

Alleged conspiracy. On April 24, Steve Tshwete, the government minister for safety and security, announced that prominent ANC members Cyril Ramaphosa, Mathews Phosa, and Tokyo Sexwale were under investigation in connection with an alleged plot to overthrow President Mbeki. Nelson Mandela and other powerful ANC figures promptly backed the accused men, rejecting allegations of conspiracy.

Two weeks later, President Mbeki cleared the three men of suspicion by declaring that he did not believe they were plotting against him. The episode fueled speculation in the South African media that the claims had been deliberately manufactured to discredit President Mbeki's political rivals.

A father and son mourn the deaths of 43 people who were crushed when thousands of soccer fans mobbed an already overcrowded stadium in Johannesburg, South Africa, on April 11.

Arms scandal. In early April, South African newspapers reported that as many as 30 ANC officials were under investigation for alleged corruption in dealings with foreign companies that had participated in a 1999 multibillion-dollar deal to modernize South Africa's armed forces. The allegations focused on several leading ANC figures, including chief whip Tony Yengeni and former defense minister Joe Modise. All of the individuals denied wrongdoing, but in October 2001, Yengeni was arrested and charged with corruption, forgery, and perjury for accepting a luxury car from one of the companies.

Political splitup. In late October, the Democratic Party (DP) and the New National Party (NNP) ended a political alliance forged in June 2000. The alliance had brought together the mainly white DP and the white and mixed-race NNP in opposition to the ANC, which is supported overwhelmingly by South Africa's black majority. The breakup of the alliance left the ANC without any serious political challenge in parliament.

Truth and Reconciliation Commission. On May 31, 2001, South Africa's Truth and Reconciliation Commission (TRC) officially closed its investigations. The commission had been established in 1995 by the ANC government led by Nelson Mandela to expose the crimes of *apartheid,* the system of rigid racial separation brutally enforced in the country from 1960 to 1994. In more than five years of proceedings, some 21,000 people came before the committee to speak either as victims or perpetrators. The committee granted more than 900 *amnesties* (pardons).

AIDS. South Africa's most celebrated AIDS victim, 12-year-old Nkosi Johnson, died of the disease on June 1, 2001. Johnson, who gained worldwide attention by chiding President Mbeki at the 13th International AIDS Conference in Durban in 2000, focused opposition to the AIDS policy of the Mbeki government. In 2000, President Mbeki had questioned whether the human immunodeficiency virus (HIV) causes AIDS, despite overwhelming scientific evidence that it does.

As a part of its AIDS stance, President Mbeki's government had refused to fund and implement a program to give anti-HIV medications to pregnant women. Medications such as AZT have been shown in medical studies to prevent HIV transmission from mothers to newborn infants between 50 and 70 percent of the time.

In 2001, South Africa had the world's largest HIV-positive population, with an estimated 4.7 million infected people. According to Treatment Action Campaign (TAC), an AIDS activist group in

South Africa, some 70,000 infants were born HIV-positive in South Africa in both 2000 and 2001. Hospitals in Johannesburg, South Africa's commercial capital, reported in 2001 that 75 percent of all pediatric deaths were AIDS-related.

Under mounting pressure, the Mbeki government promised in March to launch a nationwide program providing anti-HIV medications to pregnant women in state hospitals. But implementation of the program was repeatedly postponed. At the end of 2001, HIV-positive pregnant women were receiving the medications in some of the nation's hospitals but not in others.

In December, the High Court of Pretoria, South Africa's administrative capital, ruled that the government should provide all anti-HIV medications to all pregnant HIV-infected patients.

Deaths. Govan Mbeki, father of President Thabo Mbeki and a leading figure in South Africa's antiapartheid struggle, died on August 30, at age 91.

On September 2, Christiaan Barnard died at age 78. Barnard performed the world's first heart transplant operation in Johannesburg on Dec. 3, 1967.

Marike de Klerk, former wife of South Africa's last white president, was brutally murdered by a security guard on Dec. 3, 2001.

☐ Simon Baynham

See also **Africa; AIDS.**

Space exploration. The International Space Station remained the primary focus of human space flight in 2001. All flights of the United States space shuttle fleet and of Russian Soyuz spacecraft were devoted to construction and support operations on the station.

The Atlantis space shuttle, crewed by five NASA astronauts, took off for the station on February 7 with the $1.4-billion, U.S.-built Destiny laboratory module in the shuttle's cargo bay. Destiny, which is 28 feet (8.5 meters) long and 14 feet (4 meters) wide, was to be the only large laboratory on the station until Japanese and European labs were added in 2004.

On March 8, 2001, the Discovery space shuttle was launched with a crew of seven, including the second space station crew. When they arrived, Yuri V. Usachev of Russia and Susan B. Helms and James S. Voss of the United States replaced the first crew, which had been in orbit for four months. The shuttle carried an Italian-built module called Leonardo in its cargo bay. Leonardo was loaded with supplies and equipment needed for the station. On the return trip, Leonardo carried used items to be returned to Earth. During the mission, Helms and Voss set a record for the longest spacewalk—8 hours, 56 minutes.

On April 19, the Endeavour and a crew of seven—from the United States, Russia, Canada, and Italy—flew to the space station with a $1-billion remote manipulator system made in Canada and another Italian-built supply module, this one called Raffaello. The manipulator, known as Canadarm 2, was similar to the shuttle's robot arm but much more accurate and versatile. Canadarm 2 was attached to a mobile base, allowing it to be moved along the station's truss work and positioned where needed.

During the mission, the space station suffered significant computer problems. Controllers on the ground were forced to relay communications to the station crew through systems on the shuttle. After several days, astronauts and controllers were able to restore the critical systems.

On July 12, the Atlantis and five astronauts flew a mission to add an airlock module named Quest to the space station. The pressurized chamber was to be used by station crew members as they leave for and return from spacewalks. The airlock can be used with both U.S. and Russian space suits.

On August 10, the Discovery lifted off with a crew of seven, including the third space station crew—Frank Culbertson of the United States and Vladimir Dezhurov and Mikhail Tyurin of Russia. The shuttle carried the Leonardo module to the station with a new load of supplies and brought it back to Earth along with used equipment.

On December 5, the Endeavour was launched with a crew of seven, including the fourth station crew, Yuri I. Onufrienko of Russia and Daniel W. Bursch and Carl E. Walz of the United States. Endeavour's flight had been delayed for five days, while the station crew removed debris that prevented a Progress cargo ship from docking securely to the station. Endeavour carried the supply module Raffaello. Among the supplies were insulating blankets that astronauts installed over motors that help the station's energy-producing solar arrays track the sun, providing power for the station.

End of an era. In March 2001, Russia scuttled its Mir space station, an orbiting complex that

The solar-powered Helios aircraft soars above the Hawaiian Islands in July 2001 at a record-breaking altitude of 85,100 feet (26,000 meters). Helios, designed by engineers at the National Aeronautics and Space Administration (NASA), was used to test concepts that could be applied to an aircraft designed to fly in the thin atmosphere of Mars or the upper reaches of Earth's atmosphere.

had begun with a single module launched in 1986. NASA had long pressed its Russian counterparts to "de-orbit" Mir, because the U.S. agency's officials believed that the station was straining Russia's space resources and interfering with construction of the International Space Station. On March 23, a Progress cargo transport was used to slow Mir, allowing its orbit to descend until the station began to break up and burn. The station's wreckage crashed into the Pacific Ocean.

Chinese spacecraft. In 2001, China moved closer to launching humans into orbit. On January 10, the Shenzhou spacecraft was launched without a crew, atop a Long March 2F rocket, from the Jiuquan launch center in the Gobi Desert. The Shenzhou—whose name means "divine ship" in Chinese—closely resembles but appears somewhat larger than a Russian Soyuz spacecraft. A Shenzhou had flown for 21 hours late in 1999, also without a crew. But the 2001 flight lasted almost a week and completed 108 orbits of Earth. The return module landed in China's Inner Mongolia.

2001: A Mars Odyssey. A spacecraft launched to Mars on April 7 and named for Stanley Kubrick's 1968 film *2001: A Space Odyssey* reached the red planet in October 2001. Odyssey began examining the chemical elements that make up the surface and subsurface of Mars, looking especially for hydrogen, which would most likely be found in water ice.

Landing on an asteroid. On February 12, NASA's Near Earth Asteroid Rendezvous (NEAR) became the first spacecraft to land on a small planetary body. NEAR had spent four-and-a-half years flying around the inner solar system to reach Eros, a potato-shaped silicate asteroid 21 miles (33 kilometers) long and 8 miles (13 kilometers) wide.

In its year orbiting Eros, the spacecraft took 160,000 images and gathered millions of measurements of the asteroid, compiling a database of Eros, which scientists think resembles objects that were the building blocks of the planets.

At the end of its mission, controllers brought NEAR down to the surface of Eros—no small feat, since the asteroid has only 1/1000 the gravity of Earth and the spacecraft had not been designed to make landings. NEAR took scores of pictures as it descended and also sent back information about the chemical composition of Eros.

Space tourist. On April 28, American business executive Dennis Tito became the first person to travel in space as a tourist. Along with two Russian cosmonauts, he blasted off in a Soyuz spacecraft launched from Baykonur Cosmodrome in Kazakhstan. The Soyuz flew to the International Space Station, where the vehicle replaced another Soyuz kept at the station for emergency escapes. Tito reportedly paid the Russians $20 million for the trip.

New NASA chief. Daniel S. Goldin, who had served as head of NASA for nearly 10 years, retired in November 2001. Goldin had pressed the U.S. space agency to design less expensive spacecraft so that it could conduct more missions. Goldin was replaced by Sean O'Keefe, who had served as deputy director of the White House Office of Management and Budget in the first months of the George W. Bush administration.

☐ James R. Asker

See also **Astronomy; Space Exploration: A Special Report.**

Stepping Stone to the Final Frontier

By Alfred J. Smuskiewicz

A small orbiting outpost named Mir persevered through many problems to lead the way to a promising future of international cooperation in space.

The Russian space station, Mir, ended 15 years in orbit in March 2001, when it plunged into a remote area of the Pacific Ocean. With memories of a series of near-fatal accidents aboard Mir still vivid, many people thought it was high time the aging spacecraft was taken out of commission. In February 1997, a fire caused by the explosion of oxygen canisters filled Mir with smoke and threatened to burn through the aluminum hull; in March, oxygen generators on Mir broke down; and in April, a coolant leak caused the temperature in Mir to rise to 90 °F (32 °C). The worst accident happened in June 1997, when an unmanned cargo ship rammed into Mir, damaging a solar-power panel and gouging a hole into the station through which precious air rushed out. Fortunately, cosmonauts were able to repair the damage from these accidents without a loss of life. However, the incidents left a bad impression on much of the public, especially Americans, who were adjusting to the idea of U.S. astronauts working with Russian cosmonauts aboard Mir.

Scientists and engineers, however, noted that the frightening events of 1997 marked merely "one bad year out of fifteen," in the words of space-flight engineer James Oberg, an American expert on the Russian space program. According to Oberg, "Mir was a triumph that can be credited with many firsts in space." Mir was the first space station to be assembled in orbit. The lengthy stays of cosmonauts aboard Mir—the longest lasted 438 days—demonstrated how humans could live, work, and remain healthy in the *microgravity* (very low gravity) conditions of space for extended periods. The scientific and medical data obtained on Mir provided valuable information for planners of future human flights to Mars. Life aboard Mir also

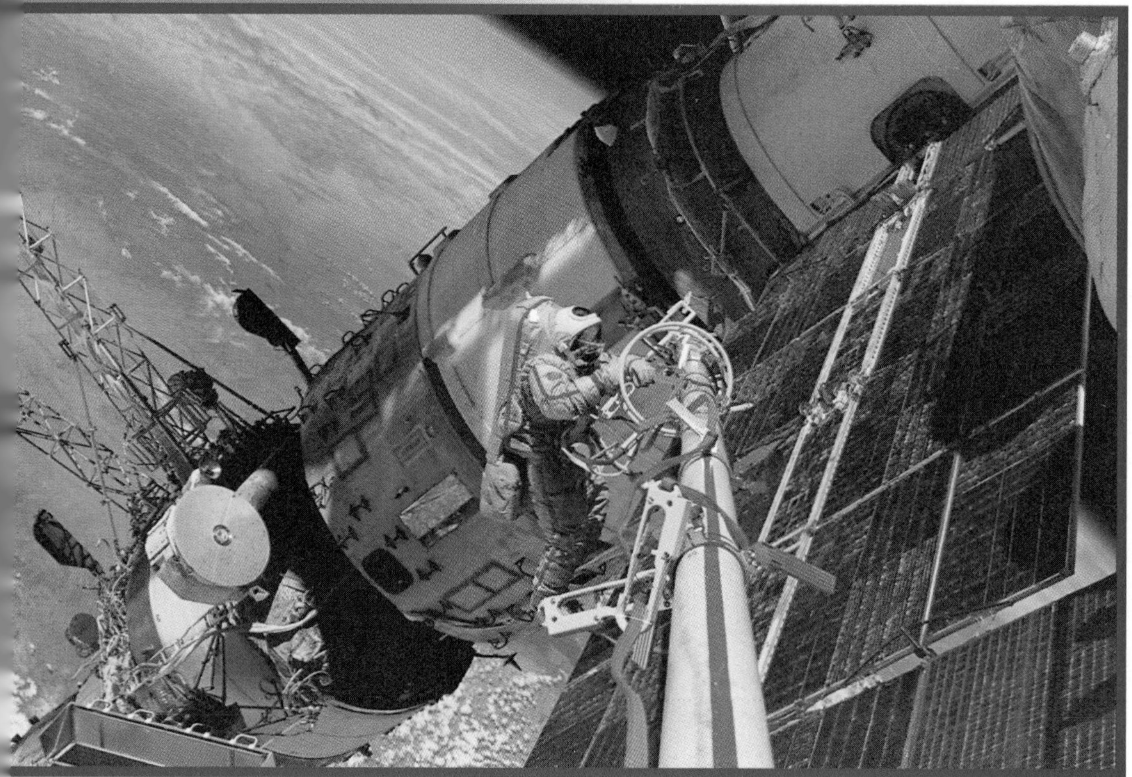

High above Earth, a Russian cosmonaut deploys scientific instruments outside Mir during an extravehicular activity in 1997. Cosmonauts and astronauts conducted thousands of scientific experiments aboard Mir.

generated a wealth of engineering information. The Russian craft served as an engineering test bed whose lessons were applied to the International Space Station (ISS), the 16-nation space platform under construction in orbit in 2001.

Mir, which means "peace" in Russian, was the pride of the Soviet space program when it was launched in 1986. For the Soviets, Mir was "an accomplishment on the level of the moon landing for the United States," according to Charles P. Vick, a space-policy analyst at the Federation of American Scientists, a scientific advocacy group in Washington, D.C. The station lasted 10 years beyond its expected lifespan, surviving the collapse of Communism and the breakup of the Soviet Union in December 1991. Cosmonaut Sergei Krikalev, who blasted off for Mir in May 1991, was stranded in space for several months while political turmoil wiped his Soviet homeland off the map. When Krikalev finally returned to Earth in March 1992, he landed in a changed homeland, named Russia, and a changed world.

Krikalev returned to a world in which the Cold War—the intense, decades-long rivalry between the Soviet Union and the United States—was a relic of the past. Gone was the "space race," the space-technology competition that Soviets and Americans had been engaged in since the Soviet Union launched Sputnik, the world's first artificial satellite, in 1957. Following the fall of the Soviet Union, Russia needed foreign investment to keep its space program afloat and boost its sagging economy. This led to a remarkable alliance between Russia and the United States. In 1993, Russia joined the U.S.-led ISS project. In 1995, U.S. astronauts, traveling aboard the U.S. space shuttle, began taking part in Mir missions. The unique cooperation between the former space rivals culminated in November 2000, when a team of two Russian cosmonauts and a U.S. astronaut became the first crew to live aboard the ISS.

The ISS was, in some respects, the offspring of Mir, which in turn descended from a long line of manned space stations placed in orbit by the Soviet Union. While American astronauts were planting the U.S. flag on the surface of the moon, the Soviets began shifting their resources toward maintaining the world's first permanent presence in Earth orbit. The Soviet Union launched its first space station, Salyut 1, in 1971. Six more Salyuts followed, the final one completing its mission in 1986. The longest-lasting Salyut operated four years and ten months.

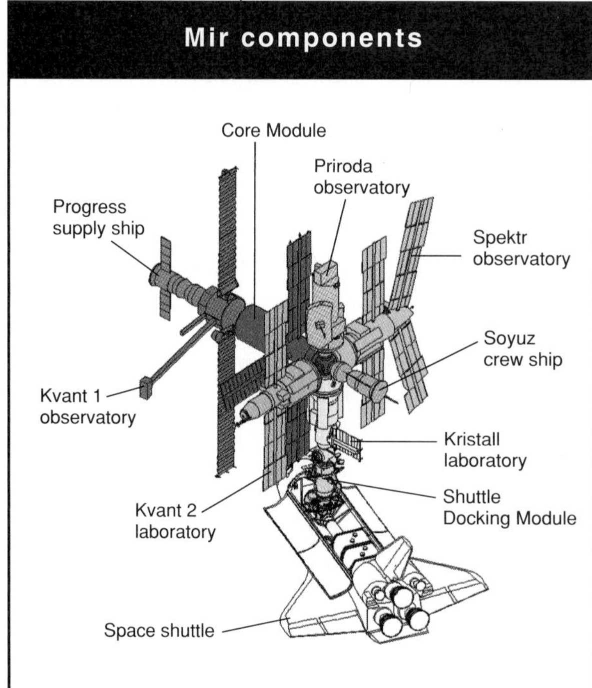

A "mutant dragonfly"

Mir was constructed from a number of individual units that were launched in several flights between 1986 and 1996. The first *module* (section) of Mir blasted off from the Baykonur Cosmodrome in the Soviet republic of Kazakhstan on Feb. 19, 1986. The finished station consisted of six modules arranged around a central Core Module. The Core Module, which was 49 feet (15 meters) long and 13 feet (4 meters) wide, served as the living quarters for the two-to-three-person crew, as well as the hub for life support, power, and temperature control. A module called Kvant 1, which contained an astrophysics observatory with telescopes and other instruments to observe galaxies and

Two cosmonauts exchange information about an engineering test aboard Mir in 1995 (left). Astronaut Shannon Lucid of the United States examines wheat plants growing in a Mir greenhouse during a joint U.S.-Russian mission in 1996 (above).

stars, was located at the rear of the Core Module. The front of the Core Module was joined to a round transfer node that had ports for four other modules: Kvant 2, Kristall, Spektr, and Priroda. Kvant 2 housed a scientific laboratory and such technical mechanisms as oxygen generators and a water recycling system, as well as an airlock through which cosmonauts passed to go outside for spacewalks. Kristall held a greenhouse and facilities for semiconductor experiments and was also used for storage. Spektr was a module with remote-sensing instruments, such as radar and infrared sensors, for observations of Earth's surface and atmosphere. Priroda also contained remote-sensing devices for Earth observation.

Mir included ports for the docking of Soyuz spacecraft, which delivered new members of the crew and took other crew members home, and Progress craft, unmanned vehicles that delivered supplies to the crew. A module for docking with the U.S. space shuttle was attached to Kristall in 1995.

When docked with Soyuz and Progress, Mir measured more than 107 feet (33 meters) long and 90 feet (27 meters) wide, making it the largest man-made object ever to orbit Earth. The interconnected segments of Mir, together with five pairs of solar panels, gave the station the appearance of a "mutant dragonfly" in the eyes of some observers. The awkward-looking but functional space station zipped around the planet every 90 minutes at an altitude of about 250 miles (402 kilometers).

The author:
Alfred J. Smuskiewicz is an assistant managing editor on *The Year Book*.

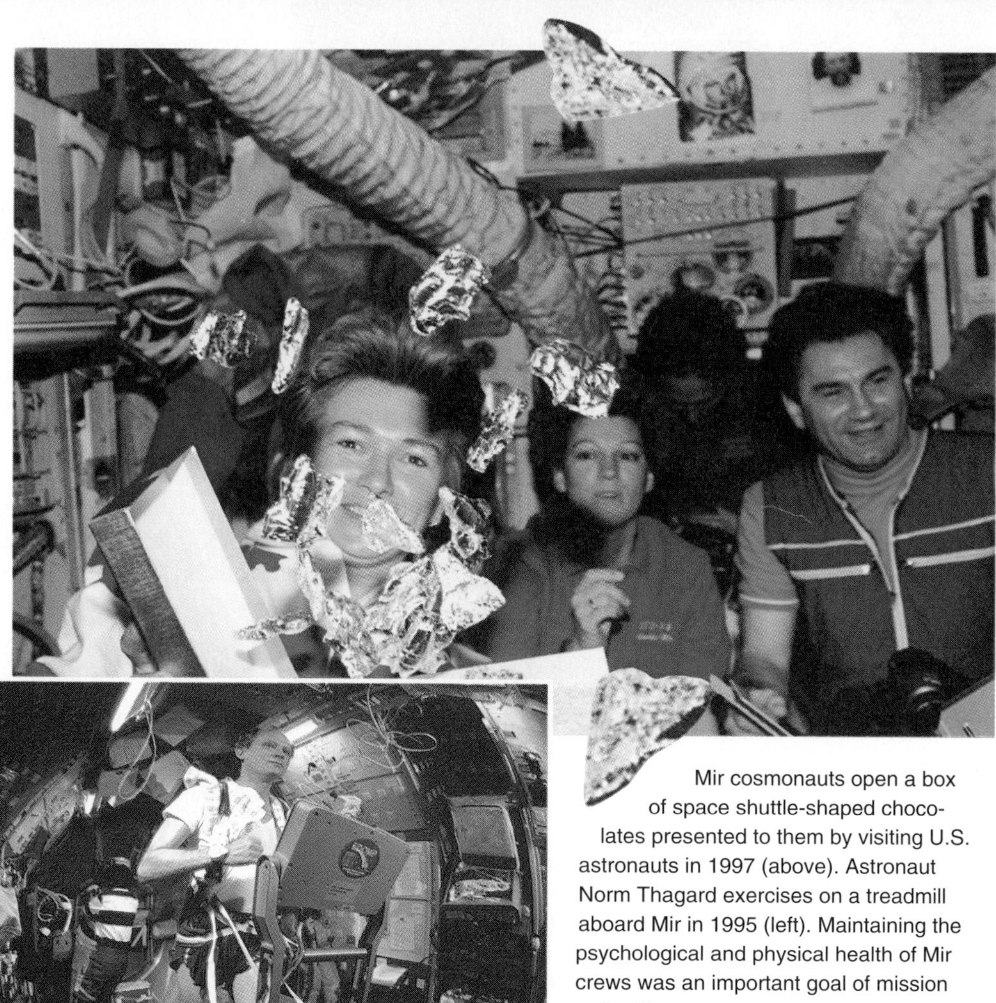

Mir cosmonauts open a box of space shuttle-shaped chocolates presented to them by visiting U.S. astronauts in 1997 (above). Astronaut Norm Thagard exercises on a treadmill aboard Mir in 1995 (left). Maintaining the psychological and physical health of Mir crews was an important goal of mission authorities.

Thousands of experiments

Mir, during its 15 years in space, hosted more than 100 cosmonauts and astronauts from a total of 12 different countries, including 7 astronauts from the United States. Mir's crew members maintained a busy work schedule, troubleshooting mechanical glitches, exercising to prevent muscle *atrophy* (wasting) in the microgravity environment, and conducting thousands of experiments. These experiments explored a wide spectrum of research topics, including biology, psychology, astronomy, space engineering, and even the possibility of turning the night into day.

Most of the biology experiments on Mir were designed to probe how long-term exposure to microgravity and the in-

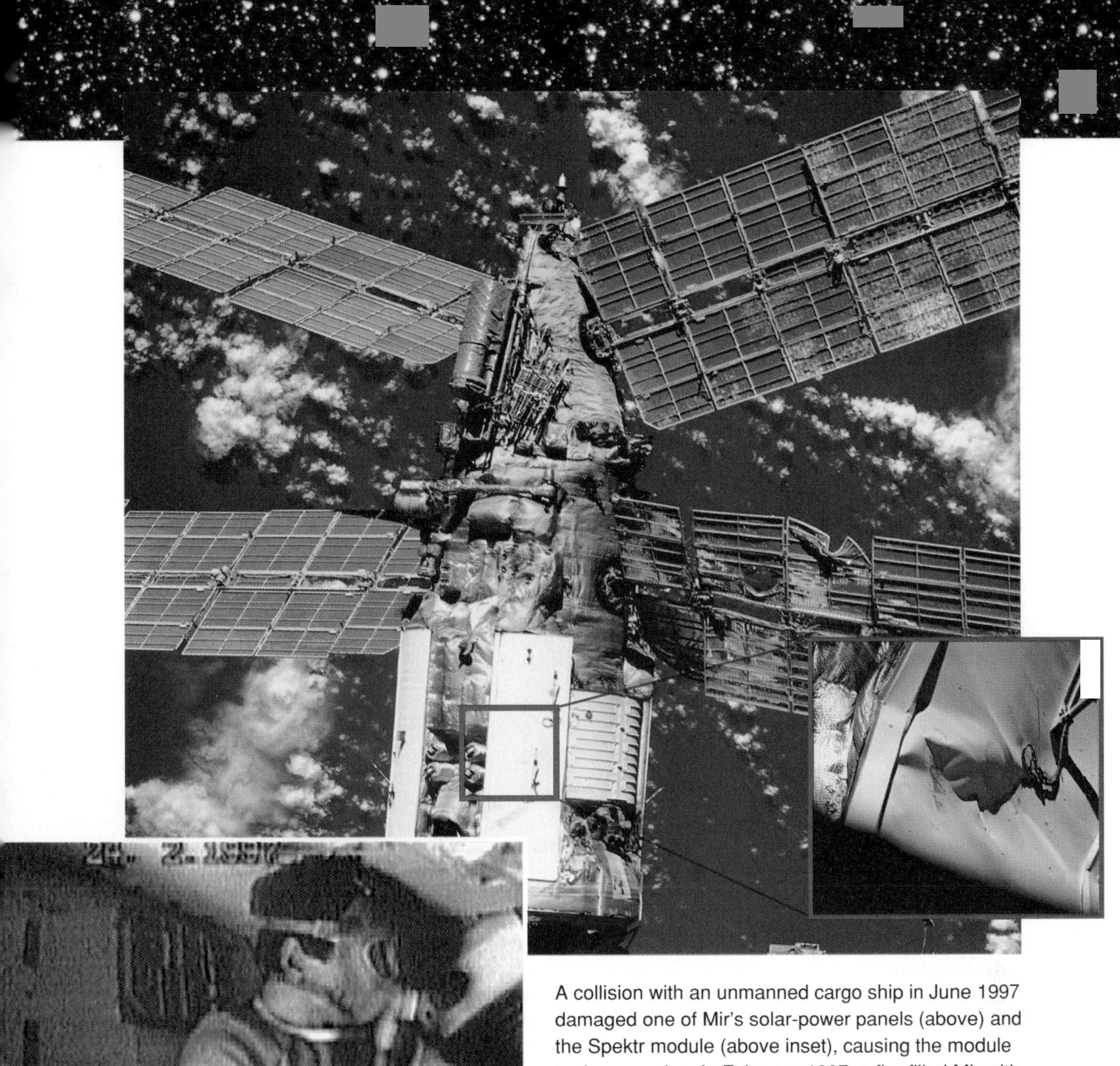

A collision with an unmanned cargo ship in June 1997 damaged one of Mir's solar-power panels (above) and the Spektr module (above inset), causing the module to depressurize. In February 1997, a fire filled Mir with smoke, requiring the crew, including visiting astronaut C. Michael Foale (left), to don gas masks.

creased radiation levels of space affect living organisms. Cosmonauts grew wheat and other plants in Mir greenhouses, proving that conditions in orbit do not harm *photosynthesis* (the food-making process of plants). These experiments demonstrated how plants might provide not only food but also oxygen during long space flights in the future.

The crew members of Mir acted as human research subjects, both in space and upon returning to Earth. Based on extensive medical examinations of the crew, Russian authorities devised special programs for exercise, sleep, and diet to keep cosmonauts in the best possible health.

Russian physicians also were concerned with the mental strain that long months aboard a small spacecraft would take

Fragments of Mir leave blazing trails as the station breaks up and falls to Earth on March 23, 2001, after Russian space officials directed the station to slow down and drop from orbit.

on the cosmic voyagers. Mir authorities gradually learned how to maintain the psychological well-being of the crews with such pleasures as regular video conversations with family, friends, and even celebrities; cargo ships bearing chocolates and other gifts; and schedules that allowed room for some improvisation and individual freedom in day-to-day duties.

Mir provided a platform for unique experiments in astronomy. Instruments aboard Mir measured the ratio of two forms of helium atoms, called helium-3 and helium-4, in *interstellar* (between the stars) space. These measurements provided astronomers with data—impossible to get on Earth—on the nature of the *big bang* (the hot, explosive event that is believed to have given rise to the universe).

Many of the experiments conducted aboard Mir had important benefits for space engineers. Experiments on the physics of fluid flow enabled engineers at the National Aeronautics and Space Administration (NASA) to design improved systems of ventilation and life support for future space missions, including the ISS. Solar-array research on Mir helped engineers perfect the array design for the ISS. Experience gained on Mir led to the development of transportable storage units for loading and unloading hardware in space. Swiveling foot platforms designed for ISS spacewalks owed their existence to various problems encountered by Mir cosmonauts when attempting to position themselves during difficult and dangerous work assignments outside Mir.

The most unusual experiment conducted by Mir cosmonauts took place in February 1999, when they tried to deploy an 80-foot- (24-meter-) wide disk of aluminum-coated plastic to reflect sunlight to Earth's surface. The Russians had hoped the experiment would prove the practicality of using giant, orbiting mirrors to shine light on sunless parts of the planet, such as Arctic cities during long, dark winters. The mirror, however, failed to unfurl properly.

The end of an era

As Mir became older and increasingly plagued by trouble, the station's crews had less and less time to conduct experiments. By 2000, the Russian space agency estimated that cosmonauts were spending more than 80 percent of their time repairing mechanical problems. At the same time, the Russian space agency was struggling to keep itself in business in the midst of a tight financial squeeze. To help make ends meet, Russian space officials in early 2000 accepted an offer from a private consortium based in the Netherlands to pay for the continued operation of Mir. The consortium, named MirCorp, planned to lease the station for commercial uses, including space tourism. NASA, however, fearing that this venture would divert scarce Russian resources away from the ISS, expressed strong opposition to the plan. So the Russians decided to end Mir's life and bring the station down to Earth.

The last two cosmonauts left Mir in June 2000 after a two-month mission. On March 23, 2001, a Progress cargo craft attached to Mir fired braking rockets to slow the station, allowing it to drop from orbit. As Mir fell through the atmosphere, it broke apart, leaving a trail of fiery debris that lit up the evening sky above the Pacific island of Fiji. Mir entered its watery grave in a blaze of glory. In eulogizing Mir, Russian mission control announced, "A whole historical stage in the exploration of space is over. . . mankind has still to assess Mir's contribution to science."

Mir's contributions—like those of the U.S. Apollo program that sent the first men to the moon—went far beyond science. Despite its share of trouble, Mir helped inspire the human spirit, highlighted the promise of space, and pointed the way to a future in which nations work together for something greater than themselves. ■■■

Spain experienced a rise in violence by separatists seeking independence for the northern Basque region throughout 2001. The separatist group ETA, whose initials stand for Basque Freedom and Homeland in the Basque language, killed several prominent people in shootings and bombings, including a Spanish army general, a senator from the Popular Party of Prime Minister Jose Maria Aznar, and a Basque regional judge. The attacks raised the number of people who have died in Spain of separatist violence to more than 35 since ETA broke a cease-fire agreement in December 1999. For the first time in 2001, ETA also targeted Spain's vital tourism industry by setting off bombs at several coastal resorts.

Some of the worst violence occurred just before Basque regional elections on May 13. Public revulsion over the killings led to a sharp drop in support for Euskal Herritarrok, the party viewed as the political arm of ETA, and a sharp increase in support for the more moderate Basque Nationalist Party, which seeks greater autonomy for the region through political means. The nationalists won 43 percent of the vote—their best result ever—and party leader Juan Jose Ibarretxe won a new term as regional president. Ibarretxe and Aznar held talks during the summer aimed at ending the violence. However, they made no progress as Aznar refused to agree to Basque demands for constitutional changes that would give the region greater autonomy.

Economy. Economic activity in Spain weakened in 2001, as the country felt the impact of the worldwide slowdown that spread from the United States. Output was expected to grow by 2.7 percent during the year, down from 4.1 percent in 2000 and the slowest since the mid-1990's. Nevertheless, the economy remained stronger than the economies of most of Spain's partners in the European Union.

Labor problems in Spain increased in 2001. Pilots staged a series of one-day strikes at the Spanish airline Iberia during the summer and disrupted air traffic. In June and July, hundreds of thousands of tourists were stranded on the resort islands of Majorca, Menorca, and Ibiza when bus drivers struck for higher pay.

Scandal. The Aznar government was shaken in 2001, following the collapse of Gescartera, a fund management company. The firm was accused of embezzling more than $90 million from investors. Pilar Valiente, an Aznar appointee, resigned as head of Spain's stock market regulatory agency, following allegations that the agency sought to block investigations of Gescartera. A deputy finance minister in the Aznar government, whose sister worked for the failed firm, also resigned. ☐ Tom Buerkle

See also **Europe; Soccer.**

Sports. The deaths of two high-profile athletes cast a pall on sports in 2001. Racing legend Dale Earnhardt died on February 18 in a crash on the final lap of the Daytona 500 at Daytona International Speedway in Daytona Beach, Florida. Korey Stringer, a member of the National Football League (NFL)'s Minnesota Vikings, collapsed during a preseason workout in August and died of complications from heat stroke.

Sports fans rejoiced in the return of superstar Michael Jordan to the National Basketball Association (NBA) after a three-season retirement. In Major League Baseball (MLB), Barry Bonds went on a season-long hot streak and broke the single-season home run record.

Eldrick "Tiger" Woods became the first professional golfer in the history of the Professional Golfers' Association (PGA) to win four straight major tournaments. In April, Woods captured the Masters to add to his victories in the U.S. Open, British Open, and PGA Championship in 2000. In cycling, Lance Armstrong won the Tour de France on July 29, 2001, to become the first American to win that event three consecutive times.

In professional team sports, the Baltimore Ravens won Super Bowl XXXV; the Los Angeles Lakers defended their NBA championship; and the Colorado Avalanche captured the Stanley Cup in the National Hockey League (NHL). In professional baseball, the upstart Arizona Diamondbacks won one of the most thrilling World Series in the history of Major League Baseball. The Seattle Mariners gave fans chills during the regular season by tying the all-time mark for wins.

Tragedies. Racing legend Dale Earnhardt, who won seven Winston Cup championships during his career, died on February 18 when his car hit the wall on the last lap of the Daytona 500. Earnhardt died from massive head injuries. The investigation into his death led to a push for improved safety devices for drivers.

The excitement of the upcoming college and professional football seasons was marred by the deaths of several football players during preseason workouts. Devaughn Darling, a linebacker for Florida State University in Tallahassee, collapsed and died on February 26 after a workout. Authorities said that Darling's death may have been caused in part by a preexisting medical condition.

On July 25, Eraste Autin, a freshman fullback at the University of Florida in Gainesville, died nearly a week after collapsing following an outdoor workout in 102 °F (38.8 °C) heat. An autopsy showed that Autin died from complications of heat stroke.

On August 1, Korey Stringer, an offensive lineman with the NFL's Minnesota Vikings, died from organ failure that was caused by heat stroke. The day before, Stringer had collapsed during a preseason practice. Stringer's death forced football coaches across the country to reevaluate their training methods during the summer.

Two days after Stringer died, tragedy struck again when Rashidi Wheeler, of Northwestern University in Evanston, Illinois, collapsed while running a practice drill on a mild day. Officials said Wheeler died from a severe bronchial asthma attack.

Terrorist attacks. The terrorist attacks on the World Trade Center in New York City and the Pentagon Building near Washington, D.C., on September 11 resulted in postponements and cancellations throughout the sports world. The NFL postponed games for the first time in the league's history, opting to add a week to the end of the season. As a result, the NFL pushed back the date of the Super Bowl one week. Major League Baseball officials decided to postpone games for six days, rescheduling the games to the end of the regular season. Most auto races were also postponed. All major college football games were either postponed or canceled, and Major League Soccer canceled the final week of the season. All professional golf tournaments were canceled, and the Ryder Cup, a golf event held every two years between European and American players, was postponed until 2002.

Home run record falls again. On Oct. 5, 2001, San Francisco Giants slugger Barry Bonds set a new major league home run record when he smacked his 71st homer of the season off Chan Ho Park of the Los Angeles Dodgers. Bonds broke Mark McGwire's home run record of 70 that had only stood since 1998. Bonds finished the 2001 season with 73 homers. Chicago Cubs slugger Sammy Sosa ended the 2001 season with 64 home runs, making him the first player to hit 60 or more in three seasons. McGwire retired at the end of the season because of injuries.

"His Airness" returns. Michael Jordan, who many observers considered the greatest player in the history of the NBA, announced on September 25 that he was returning to the court to play with the Washington Wizards. Jordan, who won six NBA titles in the 1990's with the Chicago Bulls before retiring in 1998, had been serving as part owner and president of basketball operations for the Wizards since January 2000.

Tiger falls to Earth. Eldrick "Tiger" Woods roared into the PGA season, becoming the first golfer ever to win four consecutive majors by taking the Masters in April 2001. Woods had been sizzling in 2000, scoring victories at the U.S. Open, British Open, and PGA Championship. Some observers did not concede that Woods's accomplishment was a true *Grand Slam* (winning all four majors in a season). Still, Woods's accomplishment was remarkable, as only two other golfers—Ben Hogan and Jack Nicklaus—had come even close by winning three majors in a row. Wood cooled off considerably the rest of the season and did not win another major tournament.

Lance's three-peat. Lance Armstrong made history on July 29, 2001, when he became the first American to win the Tour de France three consecutive times. Armstrong, who began the race well behind the leaders, made a sensational comeback in the most mountainous sections of the route. He covered the 2,151 miles (3,460 kilometers) in 86 hours, 17 minutes, and 28 seconds. Armstrong finished 6 minutes and 44 seconds ahead of his nearest rival, Jan Ullrich of Germany. The race marked another milestone in Armstrong's comeback from testicular cancer, which nearly killed him in 1996.

The record for most Tour victories is five, shared by four men: Belgium's Eddy Merckx, Spain's Miguel Indurain, and France's Jacques Anquetil and Bernard Hinault.

Hiking feat. On Oct. 27, 2001, Brian Robinson became the first person to hike the three longest scenic trails in the United States—the Pacific Crest, the Continental Divide, and the Appalachian—in less than one year. Robinson completed the 7,371-mile (11,862-kilometer) trek in 10 months. During his journey, Robinson consumed more than 6,000 calories each day.

Little League scandal. In 2001, the Little League World Series was rocked by one of the biggest scandals in its 54-year history. Officials discovered in August that the pitcher who had led a Bronx, New York, team to a third-place finish, was too old to play.

The pitcher, Danny Almonte from the Dominican Republic, had electrified fans with his skillful performances during the World Series in South Williamsport, Pennsylvania, including the first perfect game since 1957. However, on Aug. 27, 2001, the day after Japan's Tokyo Kitasuna team won the Little League World Series, Little League officials learned that Almonte was actually 14 years old and, therefore, ineligible. According to Little League rules, players must be 12 years old or younger. Almonte's perfect game was erased from the record books. In addition, Almonte's Little League team, the Rolando Paulino All-Stars, was stripped of its third-place finish.

Olympics scandal. On November 15, U.S. District Judge David Sam, a federal judge in the District of Utah, dismissed all charges against two Salt Lake City officials who prosecutors alleged had bribed officials of the International Olympic Committee in the city's bid to host the 2002 Winter Games. Sam ruled that prosecutors had improperly built their case against Tom Welch and

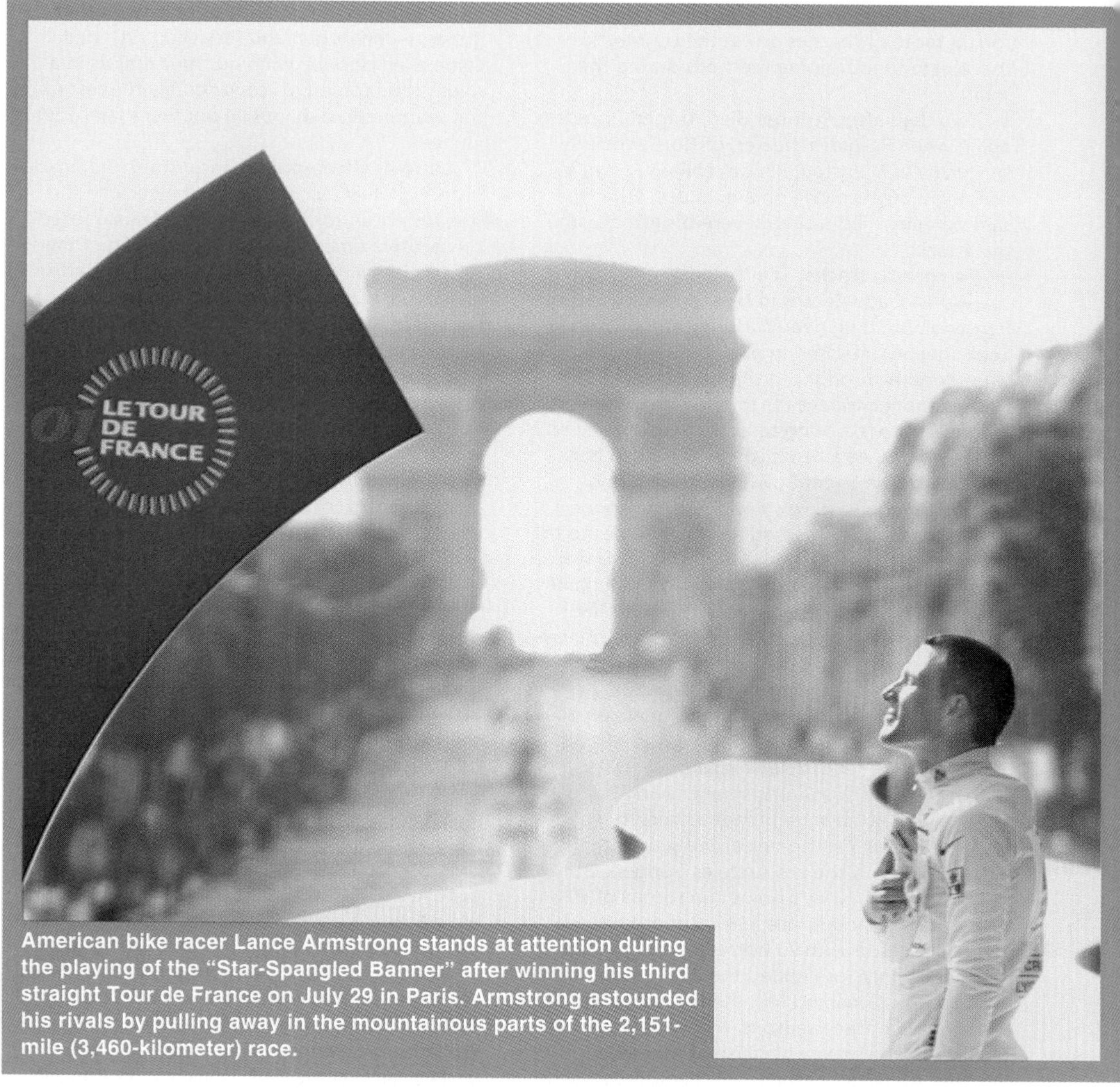

American bike racer Lance Armstrong stands at attention during the playing of the "Star-Spangled Banner" after winning his third straight Tour de France on July 29 in Paris. Armstrong astounded his rivals by pulling away in the mountainous parts of the 2,151-mile (3,460-kilometer) race.

Dave Johnson, who had led Salt Lake City's effort to land the games. In July, Judge Sam had thrown out four felony bribery counts against the pair.

Awards. American track star Marion Jones won the 2001 Jesse Owens International Trophy. The award goes to an athlete who promotes "understanding among people of all nations." In April, American wrestler Rulon Gardner won the James E. Sullivan Award. The award goes to the best amateur American athlete. During the 2000 Summer Olympics, Gardner had stunned the international sports community when he defeated Russia's Alexandre Kareline in the gold-medal match. Kareline had been heavily favored to win the match.

Among the winners in 2001 were—

Gymnastics. The Romanian women's gymnastics team took gold at the World Gymnastics Championships in Ghent, Belgium, on October 31. In the men's competition, the team from Belarus took the gold.

Handball. The French men's team defeated Sweden 28-25 to win the World Championship on February 4. In the women's competition, Russia defeated Norway 30-25 on December 16.

Rodeo. Cody Ohl won the All-Around World Champion Cowboy title in the National Finals Rodeo on December 16.

Rowing. Germany won its first-ever team trophy at the World Rowing Championships held from August 18 to August 26 in Lucerne, Switzerland. Germany captured a bronze medal in the final race—the men's eight—to squeak past Italy 70 points to 67. Germany won five golds, one silver, and two bronzes to Italy's two golds, three silvers, and three bronze medals.

In the Henley Royal Regatta on July 8 at Henley-on-Thames, England, Australian and British rowers each won five cup titles. In the race for the Ladies' Challenge Plate—the most exciting of the day—the team from Dartmouth College (Hanover, New Hampshir) took advantage of a late charge and outdueled the Princeton University from Princeton, New Jersey.

Sled-dog racing. Doug Swingley of Lincoln, Montana, won the Iditarod Trail Sled Dog Race on March 14 for the third straight year. Swingley and his dogs completed the 1,100-mile (1,770-kilometer) trip in 9 days, 19 hours, and 55 minutes. His time was 19 hours behind his record-setting pace in 2000. Several previous winners were among the competitors. It was Swingley's fourth Iditarod victory.

Soap Box Derby. Michael Flynn of Detroit won in the Masters division race held in Akron, Ohio, on July 28, 2001.

Speed skating. Monique Garbrecht-Enfeldt of Germany took the women's title and Michael Ireland of Canada took the men's crown at the World Sprint Championships, held in Germany.

Triathlon. Tim DeBoom of the United States won the men's Ironman Triathlon World Championship in Kailua-Kona, Hawaii, on October 6. Switzerland's Natascha Badmann took the women's title.

Weightlifting. Russians Vladimir Smortchkov and Albina Khomitch won the men's and women's gold medals, respectively, at the World Weightlifting Championships in Antalya, Turkey, in November.

Women's field hockey. Argentina defeated the Netherlands 3 to 2 to take the Champions Trophy in the final held on August 26 in Amstelveen, the Netherlands.

Other champions

Archery. World Indoor Archery Champions: men's compound, Morgan Lundin of Sweden; women's compound, Mary Zorn of the United States; men's team compound, Italy; women's team compound, United States.

Badminton. World Championships: men's singles, Hendrawan of Indonesia; women's singles, Gong Ruina of China; men's doubles, Tony Gunawan and Halim Haryanto of Indonesia; women's doubles, Huang Sui and Gao Ling of China; mixed doubles, Zhang Jun and Gao Ling of China.

Bobsledding. Men's four-man world champions: Christoph Langen, Markus Zimmerman, Sven Peter, and Alexander Metzger of Germany. Men's two-man world champions: Christoph Langen and Marco Jakobs.

Cross country. Men's world champion: Mohammed Mourhit of Belgium. Women's world champion: Gete Wami of Ethiopia.

Curling. Men's world champions: Sweden. Women's world champions: Canada.

Equestrian. World Cup Equestrian Final individual show jumping champion: Markus Fuchs of Switzerland. Dressage champion: Ulla Saltgeber of Germany.

Lacrosse. Men's National Collegiate Athletic Association (NCAA) champion: Princeton. Women's NCAA champion: Maryland.

Motorcycle racing. FIM Grand-Prix 500-cc champion: Valentino Rossi of Italy.

Taekwondo. World cup men's winners: lightweight, Hadi Saei Boneh Kohm, Iran; welterweight, Mahid Aflaki Khamsen, Iran; middleweight, Michael Borot, France; heavyweight, Pascal Gentil, France. World cup women's winners: lightweight, Selen Fernandez, Spain; welterweight, Lee Yung Min, Korea; middleweight, Chen Zhong, China; heavyweight, Jung Myoung Sook, Korea.

World Flatwater Championships. Team champion: Hungary. ☐ Michael Kates

See also **Automobile racing; Baseball; Basketball; Football; Golf; Hockey; Tennis.**

Sri Lanka.

Ranil Wickremesinghe became prime minister on Dec. 9, 2001, after his United National Party (UNP) and allies won control of parliament from the People's Alliance led by President Chandrika Kumaratunga. Kumaratunga had called for parliamentary elections after defections from her Sri Lanka Freedom Party (SLFP) caused her supporters to lose their weak majority in parliament in October. The previous election, just 14 months earlier, resulted in a divided parliament that accomplished little. Following the 2001 election, Kumaratunga remained president, with the power to overrule the cabinet formed by Wickremesinghe.

Two issues dominated the most violent election campaign in Sri Lankan history. The economy had fallen into the worst recession since Sri Lanka's independence from the United Kingdom in 1948. The second issue was how the government would deal with the civil war. Nearly 62,000 people have been killed in the war since the Liberation Tigers of Tamil Eelam (LTTE) began fighting for independence for the Tamil minority in northern and eastern Sri Lanka in 1983. During the election campaign, the UNP promised to revive the economy and hoped to renew peace talks with the LTTE, which had broken down under Kumaratunga.

A UNP-led group won 129 of the 225 seats in parliament, while the SLFP-led People's Alliance took only 77 seats. The alliance included a Marxist group, the People's Liberation Front (JVP), which had conducted Maoist guerrilla warfare against the government in the 1970's and 1980's. Political experts believed the JVP was responsible for the assassination of Kumaratunga's husband in 1988, though she blamed the UNP.

The civil war. In April 2001, the LTTE ended a unilateral cease-fire that it had proclaimed four months earlier. The group accused the Sri Lankan government of having intensified attacks during the cease-fire. Following the LTTE announcement, Sri Lanka's army launched a major offensive in the northeast. Despite heavy losses, the LTTE rebels forced Sri Lanka's military troops to retreat.

In July, suicide bombers attacked Sri Lanka's only international airport, near the capital, Colombo. In the attack, 13 rebels and 7 soldiers died. The attack shocked army leaders who regarded the airport as Sri Lanka's most heavily guarded government installation. The attack came on the 18th anniversary of riots between Tamil and Sinhalese ethnic groups that began the civil war.

Kumaratunga said the attacks caused $1 billion in losses, adding that the Sri Lankan economy would not recover as long as the civil war discouraged tourism and foreign investment. The airport attack also increased the cost of shipping goods, threatening essential trade. ☐ Henry S. Bradsher

See also **Asia**.

State government. State governments across the nation were forced to develop defensive plans of action in response to the terrorist attacks on the World Trade Center in New York City and the Pentagon Building in Arlington, Virginia, on Sept. 11, 2001. At the request of United States President George W. Bush, governors ordered National Guard units to provide security at major airports in their states.

In the wake of the attacks, the New York State legislature passed the nation's toughest antiterrorism laws, which Governor George Pataki signed on September 17. The legislation made it a felony to help terrorists with financial or other material support before an attack or to assist terrorists after they have struck.

By the end of 2001, every state had taken some type of action to tighten its security. The governors of eight states also named officials charged with overseeing antiterrorism efforts.

Fiscal concerns. The September 11 terrorist attacks further weakened state budgets, especially in those states reliant on the airline industry, travel, and tourism. In the weeks following the attacks, tens of thousands of people canceled or postponed scheduled vacations, adversely affecting the economies of a number of states, including California, Hawaii, Florida, and New York.

Many of the states had already experienced budget problems prior to September 11. Approximately one-third of the states dealt with budget shortfalls in the first six months of 2001, a sharp contrast to fiscal year 2000 when no state had a shortfall, according to a July 2001 report from the National Conference of State Legislatures (NCSL). The NCSL reported that tax cuts totaling $1.8 billion for all states in 2001 were far less than the record $9.9 billion in tax cuts made in 2000. The NCSL report covered 46 states. Legislatures in Massachusetts, New York, North Carolina, and Tennessee had not adopted budgets by the time the report was finished.

Lost sales tax. The 45 states that levy sales taxes lost an estimated $13.3 billion in 2001 from uncollected taxes on goods sold via Internet Web sites, according to a study by the Center for Business and Economic Research at the University of Tennessee in Knoxville. The study was commissioned by the Institute for State Studies, a nonprofit organization headquartered in Salt Lake City, Utah, which develops strategies to resolve public policy dilemmas resulting from new technology. Under a 1992 U.S. Supreme Court decision, states cannot collect taxes on mail order or Internet sales outside their jurisdiction.

Tax-cut loses. The National Governors' Association (NGA), a Washington, D.C.-based public policy organization, estimated that states would lose at least $50 billion by 2010 as the result of tax-cut legislation signed by President Bush in June 2001. The NGA reported that the $1.35-trillion tax cut would eliminate estate taxes that are linked to the federal levy in 40 states and reduce corresponding estate taxes in 10 other states.

Budget issues. Seven state legislatures were late in passing budgets by the end of their fiscal years, missing their statutory or constitutional deadlines. Officials in California, New York, Massachusetts, North Carolina, Oregon, Tennessee, and Wisconsin all missed deadlines.

The state legislature in North Carolina enacted a $14.5-billion budget on September 26, three months after the start of that state's fiscal year. Lawmakers agreed to a $620-million tax increase, including a half-cent sales tax increase, before ending the state's longest-ever legislative session.

Microsoft. In November, 9 of the 18 states involved in litigation against Microsoft Corporation of Redmond, Washington, refused to back an agreement between the company and U.S. officials to settle an antitrust lawsuit. Under the proposal, Microsoft officials had agreed to a series of business restrictions upheld by an independent panel of computer experts. U.S. District Judge Colleen Kollar-Kotelly on November 9 ordered a hearing in early 2002 to determine what sanctions should be imposed against Microsoft on behalf of those states.

Selected statistics on state governments

State	Resident population*	Governor†	Legislature† House (D)	House (R)	Senate (D)	Senate (R)	State tax revenue‡	Tax revenue per capita‡	Public school expenditure per pupil§
Alabama	4,447,100	Don Siegelman (D)	68	37	24	11	$ 15,501,000,000	$ 3,550	$ 4,950
Alaska	626,932	Tony Knowles (D)	13	27	6	14	7,313,000,000	11,800	8,830
Arizona	5,130,632	Jane Dee Hull (R)	24	36	15	15	15,122,000,000	3,160	4,510
Arkansas	2,673,400	Mike Huckabee (R)	70	30	27	8	10,361,000,000	4,060	5,540
California	33,871,648	Joseph Graham (Gray) Davis (D)	49	29	26	14	154,017,000,000	4,650	5,970
Colorado	4,301,261	Bill F. Owens (R)	27	38	18	17	14,158,000,000	3,490	5,280
Connecticut	3,405,565	John G. Rowland (R)	100	51	21	15	16,437,000,000	5,010	9,790
Delaware	783,600	Ruth Ann Minner (D)	15	26	13	8	4,540,000,000	6,030	8,020
Florida	15,982,378	Jeb Bush (R)	43	77	15	25	49,209,000,000	3,260	5,870
Georgia	8,186,453	Roy Barnes (D)	#105	74	32	24	27,639,000,000	3,550	5,950
Hawaii	1,211,537	Benjamin J. Cayetano (D)	32	19	22	3	6,646,000,000	5,610	6,260
Idaho	1,293,953	Dirk Kempthorne (R)	9	61	3	32	4,870,000,000	3,890	5,410
Illinois	12,419,293	George H. Ryan (R)	62	56	27	32	43,294,000,000	3,570	6,150
Indiana	6,080,485	Frank L. O'Bannon (D)	53	47	18	32	19,149,000,000	3,220	6,670
Iowa	2,926,324	Tom Vilsack (D)	44	56	20	30	11,629,000,000	4,050	6,010
Kansas	2,688,418	Bill Graves (R)	46	79	10	30	8,687,000,000	3,270	6,390
Kentucky	4,041,769	Paul E. Patton (D)	66	34	18	20	16,853,000,000	4,250	6,430
Louisiana	4,468,976	Murphy J. (Mike) Foster (R)	71	33	25	14	17,786,000,000	4,070	5,700
Maine	1,274,923	Angus S. King, Jr. (I)	#89	61	#17	17	5,888,000,000	4,700	7,620
Maryland	5,296,486	Parris N. Glendening (D)	106	35	34	13	19,613,000,000	3,790	7,170
Massachusetts	6,349,097	Jane Swift (R)	135	23	34	6	28,120,000,000	4,550	8,750
Michigan	9,938,444	John Engler (R)	52	57	15	23	46,724,000,000	4,740	7,450
Minnesota	4,919,479	Jesse Ventura (Reform)	65	69	#39	27	25,089,000,000	5,250	7,440
Mississippi	2,844,658	Ronnie Musgrove (D)	**86	33	#33	18	10,701,000,000	3,870	4,610
Missouri	5,595,211	Bob Holden (D)	86	74	16	18	19,505,000,000	3,570	5,850
Montana	902,195	Judy Martz (R)	42	58	19	31	3,725,000,000	4,220	6,130
Nebraska	1,711,263	Mike Johanns (R)	unicameral (49 nonpartisan)				5,576,000,000	3,350	6,000
Nevada	1,998,257	Kenny Guinn (R)	27	15	9	12	7,573,000,000	4,190	5,570
New Hampshire	1,235,786	Jeanne Shaheen (D)	††140	256	11	13	4,024,000,000	3,350	6,200
New Jersey	8,414,350	James E. McGreevey (D)	35	45	15	25	39,150,000,000	4,810	9,780
New Mexico	1,819,046	Gary E. Johnson (R)	42	28	24	18	8,757,000,000	5,030	5,860
New York	18,976,457	George E. Pataki (R)	99	51	25	36	102,242,000,000	5,620	9,800
North Carolina	8,049,313	Mike Easley (D)	62	58	35	15	34,064,000,000	4,450	5,720
North Dakota	642,200	John Hoeven (R)	29	69	17	32	2,936,000,000	4,630	4,510
Ohio	11,353,140	Robert Taft (R)	40	59	12	21	51,273,000,000	4,550	6,480
Oklahoma	3,450,654	Frank Keating (R)	52	49	30	18	11,935,000,000	3,550	5,630
Oregon	3,421,399	John Kitzhaber (D)	#27	32	14	16	15,666,000,000	4,720	8,610
Pennsylvania	12,281,054	Mark Schweiker (R)	99	104	20	28	49,482,000,000	4,130	7,240
Rhode Island	1,048,319	Lincoln C. Almond (R)	84	15	44	6	5,478,000,000	5,530	7,990
South Carolina	4,012,012	Jim Hodges (D)	54	70	22	24	14,566,000,000	3,750	6,110
South Dakota	754,844	William J. Janklow (R)	20	50	11	24	2,886,000,000	3,940	5,370
Tennessee	5,689,283	Don Sundquist (R)	58	41	18	15	16,904,000,000	3,080	5,390
Texas	20,851,820	Rick Perry (R)	78	72	15	16	71,649,000,000	3,570	6,090
Utah	2,233,169	Michael O. Leavitt (R)	24	51	9	20	8,742,000,000	4,100	4,040
Vermont	608,827	Howard Dean (D)	‡‡62	83	16	14	3,055,000,000	5,140	6,980
Virginia	7,078,515	Mark Warner (D)	#47	52	18	21	26,138,000,000	3,800	6,150
Washington	5,894,121	Gary Locke (D)	49	49	25	24	28,737,000,000	4,990	6,530
West Virginia	1,808,344	Bob Wise (D)	75	25	28	6	8,034,000,000	4,450	8,490
Wisconsin	5,363,675	Scott McCallum (R)	43	56	18	15	28,334,000,000	5,400	7,890
Wyoming	493,782	Jim Geringer (R)	14	46	10	20	3,092,000,000	6,450	6,910

*Source: U.S. Census Bureau
† As of December 2001. Source: National Governors' Association; National Conference of State Legislatures; state government officials
‡1999 figures.
§1999-2000 estimates for elementary and secondary students in fall enrollment
Source: National Education Association.

#One independent.
**Three independents.
††One libertarian.
‡‡One independent, four progressives.

Governors appointed to posts. In September 2001, President Bush named Pennsylvania Governor Tom Ridge director of the newly created Office of Homeland Security. In his new post, Ridge was to be responsible for coordinating defenses against and responses to terrorism in the United States. Ridge resigned as governor in October and was succeeded by his lieutenant governor, Mark Schweiker.

In January 2001, President Bush nominated two governors to positions within his administration. The president nominated New Jersey Governor Christine Todd Whitman as director of the Environmental Protection Agency and Wisconsin Governor Tommy Thompson as secretary of the U.S. Department of Health and Human Services.

New governors. New Jersey State Senate President Donald DiFrancesco succeeded Whitman in January as acting governor. He was to serve the remainder of her term, which was scheduled to end in January 2002. In Wisconsin, Lieutenant Governor Scott McCallum succeeded Thompson in February 2001 to serve Thompson's term through 2003.

In April 2001, Jane Swift succeeded Paul Cellucci as governor of Massachusetts. Swift, the state's lieutenant governor, was to serve the remainder of Cellucci's term, which was scheduled to end in January 2003. Cellucci had resigned the office to become U.S. ambassador to Canada.

On Nov. 6, 2001, voters in New Jersey and Virginia elected Democrats to succeed Republican governors in off-year elections. In New Jersey, Jim McGreevey, the mayor of Woodbridge, defeated Bret Schundler, the former mayor of Jersey City, in the gubernatorial race. McGreevey was to replace DiFrancesco, who opted not to seek a full term in the post. In Virginia, Mark Warner defeated Mark Earley for the state's top position. Warner was to succeed Republican Governor James Gilmore III, who was prohibited by term limits from seeking reelection.

Universal health care. Portland, Maine, voters in November approved a nonbinding resolution calling for universal health care in the state. Opponents claimed that government-mandated health care would result in longer waits and higher taxes.

Power shortages. Rolling blackouts and high prices during the first six months of 2001 forced California officials to take measures that effectively reversed its landmark law to deregulate electricity markets. In February, the California State Legislature approved a $10-billion plan authorizing the state to issue revenue bonds to raise money to buy electricity. The plan enabled California to purchase power through long-term contracts at prices lower than normally available on the market. California sold the electricity at cost to the state's two largest private utility companies. To further combat the crisis, the Federal Energy Regulatory Commission, a federal agency that regulates natural gas and oil pipelines and hydroelectric power plants, imposed price limits on electricity in 10 Western states on June 18.

Confederate flag controversies. Georgia Governor Roy Barnes signed legislation on February 7 to remove the Confederate battle emblem from prominence on the state flag. Critics of the previous flag design had argued that the Confederate emblem, which comprised two-thirds of the flag's design, represented slavery and racism. The redesigned flag reduced the size of the Confederate symbol and placed it as one of five smaller symbols at the bottom of a banner under the state seal.

Mississippi voters on April 17 decided to keep the design of the state flag, which displays the Confederate emblem in its upper left hand corner, rather than replace it with a new design.

☐ Elaine Stuart

See also **Energy supply; Energy supply: A Special Report; Health care issues; People in the news** (Ridge, Tom; Thompson, Tommy; Whitman, Christine Todd); **Supreme Court of the United States; Terrorism: A Special Feature,** page 38; **United States, Government of the; United States, President of the.**

Stocks and bonds. Terrorists attacked the United States on Sept. 11, 2001, profoundly affecting the heart of the global financial system. The attacks on the World Trade Center in New York City forced the New York Stock Exchange (NYSE) to stop trading for four days. The suspension was the longest since 1933, during the *Great Depression* (a worldwide business slump of the 1930's). When the NYSE reopened on Sept. 17, 2001, prices fell to their lowest levels since 1998 as investors worried about the economic consequences of the attacks.

Many economists said that the terrorist attacks damaged an already weakened U.S. economy, sending it into a recession. Economists had expressed concern over an economic downturn throughout 2001. To stimulate economic growth, the Federal Reserve System (the Fed)—the central bank of the United States—cut short-term interest rates 11 times in 2001. Three of the cuts came in the weeks following the terrorist attacks and left the rate at its lowest level in 40 years, which boosted prices of U.S. Treasury securities. Long-term rates also declined, prompting gains in bonds and bond mutual funds.

But for stock investors, the market slide in the wake of September 11 deepened a sell-off that began in March 2000. The sell-offs virtually guaranteed that major stock market indexes would

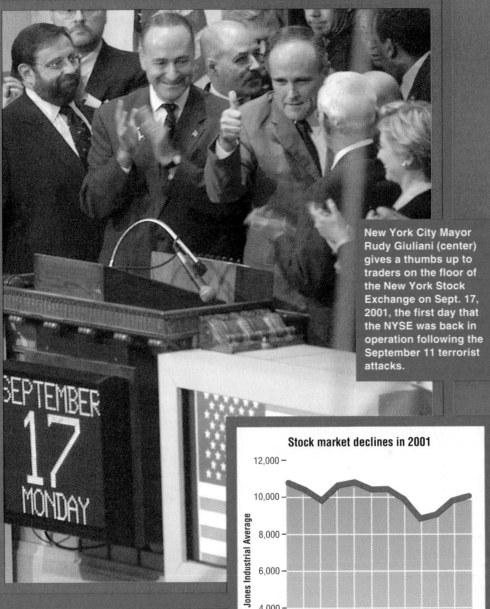

New York City Mayor Rudy Giuliani (center) gives a thumbs up to traders on the floor of the New York Stock Exchange on Sept. 17, 2001, the first day that the NYSE was back in operation following the September 11 terrorist attacks.

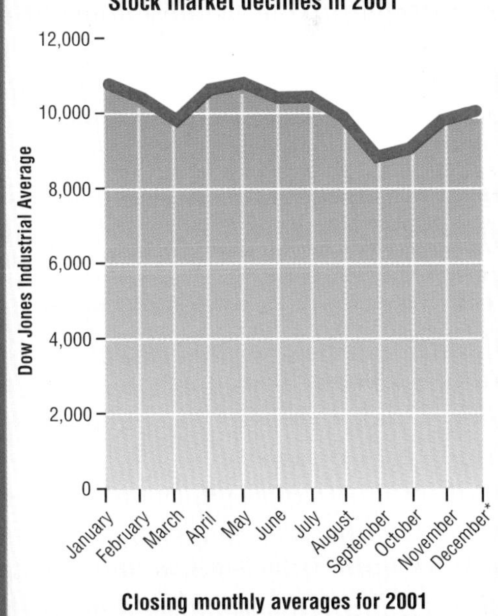

The Dow Jones Industrial Average suffered deep losses throughout 2001 and was down nearly 16 percent for the year. Analysts blamed the decline on a weak U.S. economy and consumer panic following the September 11 terrorist attacks on the United States.

post a second straight year of losses for the first time since 1974.

Through October 2001, the Dow Jones industrial average declined 15.9 percent to 9075.14. The Dow is a composite of the stock prices of 30 major companies traded on the NYSE and on the Nasdaq Stock Market, which is an electronic trading system linking stock brokers and dealers. The Nasdaq Composite Index, which consists of more than 3,000 stocks traded on the Nasdaq market, plunged 31.6 percent during the first nine months of the year. The Standard & Poor's 500 (S&P 500) index of 500 major companies was off 19.7 percent in the same period.

Consumer confidence. The terrorist attacks and their aftermath, including U.S. military action in Afghanistan, depressed consumer confidence and personal spending. Economists noted, however, that most world economies had been slumping well before September 11. Corporate net profits collapsed by more than 70 percent in the second and third quarters of 2001. As a result, stock prices eroded for much of the year. By November, major stock indexes rebounded to their preattack levels yet remained at three-year lows.

Winners and losers. Most major sectors of the stock market suffered major declines in 2001. However, the slide in computer technology stocks that began in 2000 lessened in 2001. Through October, semiconductor maker Intel Corporation of Santa Clara, California, was off 18.8 percent, to $24.42, after plunging 27 percent in 2000. Software developer Microsoft Corporation of Redmond, Washington, increased 34.1 percent, to $58.01, due in part to progress toward a settlement of antitrust charges filed against the company by the federal government.

Other stocks that had performed well in 2000 lost ground in 2001. The value of stocks of utilities and banks fell, damaged by the weakening economy and losses by credit card issuers. Through October 2001, the stock of Citigroup, a financial service firm headquartered in New York City, fell 10.8 percent, to $45.52.

The transportation sector experienced crises, especially among major airlines, including industry giant UAL of Elk Grove Township, Illinois, parent company of United Airlines, as air travel declined sharply after the attacks. UAL stock sank 67.3 percent, to $12.72, in the first nine months of 2001.

Major insurance companies also reported losses, despite the prospects for higher premium income in the postattack era. American International Group, located in New York City, fell 20.2 percent, to $78.60.

Health care stocks, including major pharmaceutical and biotechnological manufacturers, fared better than most stock market sectors. Analysts said that investors assumed that the federal government's antiterrorism campaign and efforts to boost the U.S. economy would divert any plans for new regulations on health care. As a result, stock in companies such as Abbott Laboratories, a pharmaceutical company headquartered in Abbott Park, Illinois, advanced. Abbot rose 9.4 percent, to $48.44, through October.

Consumer products held up fairly well, as investors sought safety in stocks that were less effected by recession. Procter and Gamble, based in Cincinnati, Ohio, was off 5.9 percent, to $73.78.

Enron. The stock market's attempt to recover from the terrorist attacks was complicated by the bankruptcy of one of the country's largest energy traders, Houston-based Enron Corporation. On October 16, the company announced an unexpected quarterly loss and disclosed a $1.2-billion reduction in shareholder's equity—the result of little-known partnerships the company had organized through its chief financial officer.

The disclosures destroyed Enron's credibility. Its stock fell to below $1 a share in November from $90.75 in August 2000. On Dec. 2, 2001, Enron became the largest U.S. company to ever file for bankruptcy protection. ☐ Bill Barnhart

See also **Economics; Labor and employment; Manufacturing; Terrorism: A Special Feature**, p. 38; **United States, Government of the.**

Sudan. President Umar al-Bashir made progress in ending Sudan's status as a "pariah among nations" during 2001. Most of the world's nations isolated Bashir's regime in the 1990's for its support of terrorism and human rights abuses.

United Nations. On Sept. 28, 2001, the United Nations (UN) Security Council voted to lift a ban against foreign travel by Sudanese officials. The UN had imposed the sanctions against Sudan in 1996 after Sudan allegedly granted *asylum* (sanctuary) to militants accused of trying to assassinate Egyptian President Hosni Mubarak. The militants were believed to have left Sudan.

U.S. relations. Sudanese officials condemned the terrorist attacks made by Islamic militants against the United States on Sept. 11, 2001. In the wake of the attacks, Sudan reportedly arrested some 30 suspected Islamic extremists; agreed to share counterterrorism intelligence with the United States; and vowed that Osama bin Laden, named by the United States as the mastermind behind the September attacks, would not be allowed back into Sudan. Bin Laden had lived in Sudan from 1991 to 1996.

In early September 2001, President Bashir cautiously welcomed the appointment by the United States of former U.S. Senator John C. Danforth as special envoy to mediate Sudan's 18-year-old civil war. The civil war pitted Sudan's mainly Arab and

Muslim northern government against black southerners, who practiced Christianity or traditional beliefs. The U.S. appointment came after Sudan agreed in July to discuss humanitarian issues with the European Union, and U.S. officials concluded that Sudan was cooperating in antiterrorism efforts. Danforth presented peace proposals to the government and rebels in November.

Gestures toward opposition. Bashir announced on October 1 that he would halt the trial of several activists from the National Democratic Alliance, an umbrella organization for opposition groups, who had been accused of plotting with the United States against the Sudanese government. Bashir also said he would drop charges against dissident Islamic leader Hassan al-Turabi and other officials of Turabi's Popular National Congress (PNC) on condition that they display "responsible" behavior. Bashir had arrested Turabi, his former ally, and 40 other PNC members in February, charging them with treason for reaching an accord with the Sudan People's Liberation Army, the largest rebel group.

In November, Bashir allowed Ahmed el-Mirghani, a former president and opposition figure, to return to Sudan from exile in Egypt.

☐ Christine Helms

See also **Middle East; Terrorism; Terrorism: A Special Feature,** p. 38; **United Nations.**

Supreme Court of the United States.

In 2001, the U.S. Supreme Court issued a significant ruling on the use of free-lance writers' work on the Internet and interpretations of the Americans with Disabilities Act. The justices also decided cases involving campaign finance, tobacco advertising, religious school clubs, and searches by police officers.

Copyright infringement. The court voted 7 to 2 on June 25 that publishers cannot reproduce the work of free-lance writers in an electronic database or on CD-ROM discs without the writers' permission. A group of free-lance writers who had filed a lawsuit against a group of newspaper and magazine publishers argued that while they had given consent for their work to be published in print form, the publishers committed copyright infringement when they reproduced the material in electronic forms without consent or additional compensation. Following the decision, publishers told free-lance writers that they would remove reproduced articles from electronic databases unless they received permission to use the material.

Americans with Disabilities Act. The court ruled on February 21 that state government employees cannot sue their employer under the Americans with Disabilities Act (ADA). The act requires employers to make reasonable accommodations for disabled workers. However, the court voted 5 to 4 that the act does not override states' rights under the Constitution from being sued in federal courts.

On May 29, the court voted 7 to 2 that professional golfer Casey Martin had the right under the ADA to use a golf cart while playing in Professional Golfers' Association (PGA) Tour events. PGA Tour officials had questioned Martin's use of a cart during tournaments, because of a circulatory disorder. PGA officials had argued that walking was an integral part of playing professional golf.

Under ADA requirements, public sites, such as the golf courses used in PGA tour events, must make reasonable modifications for disabled patrons unless it would "fundamentally alter" the nature of an activity. The justices concluded that, given the circumstances of Martin's health, allowing him to ride in a cart would not fundamentally alter the game.

Political spending. In a decision handed down on June 25, the court voted 5 to 4 that limiting the amount of money political parties spend on candidates for federal office does not violate the Constitution's guarantee of freedom of speech. The justices ruled that allowing unlimited spending would permit donors to bypass limits on individual contributions to campaigns for federal office set in a 1974 law. Under that law, individuals can contribute up to $1,000 per candidate per election. Political action committees can donate a maximum of $5,000.

Tobacco company victory. On June 28, 2001, the court ruled that states do not have the right to restrict outdoor tobacco advertisements near schools or public parks. The justices voted 5 to 4 that a Massachusetts law barring tobacco advertisements in store windows and within 1,000 feet (305 meters) of a playground, park, or school—on the theory that the ads could be seen by children—was too restrictive. The justices did not dispute that state government can establish programs to prevent children from smoking. However, the justices did decide that a 1965 federal law requiring health warnings on cigarette packages and limiting cigarette advertising prevents states from enacting separate laws restricting promotions for cigarettes, though not for cigars or smokeless tobacco.

Schools and religion. The court on June 11, 2001, ruled that all public schools, including elementary schools, must treat after-school religious activities on the same basis as any other after-school activity. In a 6-to-3 decision, the justices ruled that the school district of Milford, New York, had discriminated against an evangelical Christian organization when it refused to allow a club sponsored by the organization to meet after hours in an elementary school.

Police powers. The court issued several rulings affecting how much force police officers may use in certain situations. On February 20, the court ruled that police, under certain circumstances, may prevent suspects from entering the suspects' own residences until police can obtain a search warrant. By an 8-to-1 vote, the court ruled that such an action does not violate the U.S. Constitution's protection against unreasonable searches and seizures.

In a separate ruling handed down on June 11, the court voted 5 to 4 that police must obtain a warrant before searching a house from the outside using a thermal imaging device. A thermal imaging device registers heat escaping from a structure. The device enabled police to determine if marijuana was being grown under plant lights in a residence. The justices determined that as long as such specialized equipment was not in general public use, it required a search warrant.

In another law enforcement-related decision, the court ruled on March 21 that public hospitals must receive the consent of maternity patients before those patients may be screened for illegal drugs if the purpose is to report narcotics users to police. In a 6-to-3 decision, the court overturned a 1999 U.S. Court of Appeals ruling that an agreement between a public hospital in Charleston, South Carolina, and local police to test pregnant women for illegal drug use was justified by the "special needs" of stopping drug use by pregnant women and getting the women into treatment.

Free press. By a 6-to-3 vote handed down on May 21, 2001, the court determined that a federal wiretap law does not necessarily require punishment of the news media when the media publishes or broadcasts stories based on illegally taped phone conversations. The 1968 wiretap law bars people from taping another person's phone calls and from making illegally intercepted information available to the public. The justices ruled that the constitutional guarantee of freedom of the press protects the media when reporters do not take part in intercepting the call and that the information broadcast is of public importance.

English only? On April 24, the court ruled that individuals cannot sue states over laws that they consider to be racially or ethnically discriminatory. In a 5-to-4 decision, the justices ruled against a Mexican immigrant who had sued Alabama for refusing to give her a driver's license exam in any language besides English. The woman claimed that the practice discriminated against non-English speakers. The justices ruled that while the Civil Rights Act of 1964 prohibits government from discriminating based on national origin and allows individuals to sue for bias by the government, individuals cannot sue for the discriminatory effects of regulations.

Clean Air Act. In a unanimous ruling on Feb. 27, 2001, the court upheld the authority of the Environmental Protection Agency (EPA) to issue new rules for reducing smog and soot in the air. Business and industry groups had challenged standards the EPA adopted in 1997, arguing that the agency had not considered the costs of complying with the new regulations.

Microsoft decision. The justices announced in October 2001 that they would not hear an appeal by Microsoft Corporation of Redmond, Washington, to overturn a lower court's decision. Microsoft attorneys had requested the justices overturn a U.S. federal appeals court decision upholding an earlier verdict finding the software maker guilty of violating U.S. antitrust laws.

Unprecedented move. The justices met inside the U.S. Court of Appeals courthouse on October 29, marking the first time justices met outside the U.S. Supreme Court building since it opened in 1935. The move allowed health officials to test the Supreme Court building for anthrax, a potentially fatal bacterium.

☐ Geoffrey A. Campbell

See also **Courts; Immigration; Newspaper; Terrorism: A Special Feature,** p. 38.

Surgery. See **Medicine.**
Suriname. See **Latin America.**
Swaziland. See **Africa.**

Sweden held the rotating presidency of the European Union (EU) during the first half of 2001. During the country's term, the government of Prime Minister Goran Persson sought to strengthen the EU's commitment to accept new members from Eastern Europe. At a summit meeting in Goteborg, Sweden, on June 15 and June 16, EU leaders committed themselves to completing membership negotiations with several Eastern European countries in 2002, a move that would enable the nations to join the EU by 2004. The decision marked the first time the EU had set a clear timetable for enlargement and represented a significant achievement for Persson's government.

The EU leaders also pledged to ratify the Kyoto Protocol, aimed at limiting the emission of carbon dioxide and other gases believed to contribute to climate change, despite the decision by the United States to abandon the agreement. In an effort to ease trans-Atlantic tensions over the protocol and other issues, Persson hosted the first meeting between all 15 EU leaders and U.S. President George W. Bush in Goteborg.

The summit meeting was marred by the worst violence ever staged during an EU gathering. On June 15, 2001, a demonstration by 25,000 antiglobalization protesters exploded into violence. Swedish police responded with gunfire—the first time that live ammunition had ever been used against people protesting an EU meeting. Three protesters were shot.

The economy deteriorated during 2001, as Sweden suffered the effects of the worldwide slump that spread from the United States. Sweden's Central Bank forecast in October that economic output would grow by 1.3 percent in 2001, down from 3.6 percent in 2000. In September 2001, the government took advantage of a budget surplus and proposed to cut taxes by $4.2 billion in 2002 to stimulate a rebound in growth.

The economic slowdown hit L.M. Ericsson AB, a wireless equipment maker and one of Sweden's biggest companies, especially hard. Ericsson announced that it would stop making mobile telephone handsets and that it would cut its work force by at least 12,000 people because of weak demand for its telecommunications products.

The European Commission (EC) blocked an attempted $7.2-billion merger of two Swedish banks—Skandinaviska Enskilda Banken (SEB) and ForeningsSparbanken—in September 2001. Officials of the EC, which enforces antitrust rules in the EU, said a combined bank would control too much of the Swedish market. Critics of the decision claimed it would impair Swedish banks' ability to compete across Europe. ☐ Tom Buerkle

See also **Europe.**

Swimming.

Australia's Ian Thorpe dominated the 2001 World Swimming Championships by capturing an unprecedented six gold medals and setting three world records. A total of eight men's world records were set during the world championships, held in Fukuoka, Japan, from July 16 to July 29. However, the event was tarnished by an unreliable timekeeping system and the disqualification of three U.S. relay teams.

"Thorpedo" strikes. Thorpe, nicknamed the "Thorpedo," became the first swimmer to capture six golds at the World Championships, topping the five won by Americans Jim Montgomery in 1973 and Tracy Caulkins in 1978. Thorpe broke world records in the 200-, 400-, and 800-meter freestyle races and was a part of three winning relays. He won the 200 freestyle in 1:44.06, the 400 freestyle in 3:40.17, and the 800 freestyle in 7:39.16.

Eight men's world records fell at the world championships, including the 200-meter butterfly, in which American Michael Phelps broke his own world record with a time of 1:54.58. In the 1,500-meter freestyle, Australia's Grant Hackett broke the long-course record with a time of 14:34.56.

Inge de Bruijn of the Netherlands captured gold medals in the 50- and 100-meter freestyle and the 50-meter butterfly. Yana Klochkova of

Roman Sloudnov of Russia celebrates after breaking the world record in the 100-meter breaststroke on July 23 in Fukuoka, Japan. Sloudnov finished the race in 59.97 seconds.

Ukraine won both the 400-meter freestyle and individual medley.

Faulty relays. U.S teams were disqualified in three relays at the World Championships. In the most controversial race, the women's team lost a gold in the 800-meter freestyle relay, when a timing device indicated that a racer had entered the pool too early on an exchange. U.S. officials claimed the timing device was faulty, but an appeals committee awarded the gold to the British. The Australians had finished first but were disqualified when a team member entered the water in celebration before the race was over.

In the men's 400-meter medley relay, the U.S. team was stripped of its silver medal when a swimmer entered the pool early. The U.S. men also lost a bronze in the 400-meter freestyle relay after submitting an incorrect team roster.

Other world records. American Ed Moses set a new 50-meter men's breaststroke mark of 27.39 seconds on March 31 at the U.S. Swimming National Championships in Austin. Qi Hui of China set a new 200-meter women's breaststroke world record of 2:22.99 on April 13 in Hangzhou, China. Australian Grant Hackett shattered his own 1,500-meter short-course record by more than nine seconds with a time of 14:10.10 in Perth, Australia, in August. ☐ Michael Kates

Switzerland suffered the worst corporate bankruptcy in its history in 2001, when the national airline, Swissair, collapsed. In the late 1990's, Swissair attempted to expand by buying stakes in airlines in Belgium, France, and Portugal, but the strategy left the company $10.5 billion in debt and unable to compete with larger European airlines. A sharp drop in passenger traffic after the Sept. 11, 2001, terrorist attacks on the United States pushed the company into bankruptcy.

Swissair was forced to ground its fleet on October 2 and 3—stranding thousands of passengers around the world—after its banks refused to lend the company more money. The airline resumed flights after the Swiss government provided an emergency loan of $280 million. Three weeks later, the government and a group of the country's biggest corporations, led by Nestle S.A., agreed to salvage part of Swissair by investing $2.5 billion in its low-cost, regional airline subsidiary, Crossair. Crossair acquired some of Swissair's aircraft and international routes, while Swissair was to disappear after selling its remaining aircraft and other operations.

The Swiss economy slowed during 2001, as the economic slowdown in the United States spread to Europe, cutting Swiss exports. Economists predicted that the Swiss economy would grow by less than 2 percent in 2001, down from 3 percent in 2000.

Foreign relations. Swiss voters remained ambivalent in 2001 about closer ties with other countries. In a March 4 referendum, voters rejected a proposal calling for Switzerland to begin negotiations to join the European Union (EU). The result cast doubt on the government's plan to seek voters' approval for EU membership talks sometime after 2003. On June 10, 2001, voters approved a measure to allow Swiss troops to train with other armies and to carry weapons on international peacekeeping missions. Swiss troops had previously served as unarmed peacekeepers.

Tunnel fire. A fire broke out in the St. Gotthard road tunnel on October 24, killing 11 people, closing the tunnel, and disrupting traffic across Switzerland and beyond. The blaze erupted after two trucks collided in the tunnel, which is 10 miles (16 kilometers) long, a major artery through the Swiss Alps for traffic between Italy and northern Europe.

Massacre. A man involved in a legal dispute with authorities in the canton of Zug, near Zurich, opened fire on a meeting of the cantonal parliament on September 27, killing 14 people. The incident was the worst mass murder ever committed in Switzerland. ☐ Tom Buerkle

See also **Aviation; Europe.**

Syria withdrew 6,000 troops from government buildings and Christian neighborhoods in the Lebanese capital of Beirut in June 2001. Syrian officials said most of these troops returned to Syria, though some were redeployed elsewhere in Lebanon. Syrian troops entered Lebanon in 1976, during the Lebanese civil war (1975-1990), as part of peacekeeping forces sent by the Arab League, an organization of Middle Eastern and African nations. The Syrian troops numbered 35,000 at their height. After the June 2001 withdrawal, Syria still maintained more than 20,000 soldiers at various sites throughout Lebanon.

Many Middle East analysts believed Syria's withdrawal from Beirut may have been an attempt to ease growing criticism of the Syrian presence by Lebanese Christians and *Druse,* a secret religious group. This criticism intensified after Israel ended its military occupation of southern Lebanon in 2000. Some analysts also pointed out that the Syrian redeployment would reduce risks to Syrian troops from Israeli attacks.

Israel hits radar sites. Israeli planes bombed Syrian radar sites in Lebanon on April 16, 2001, and again on July 1. The bombings were in retaliation for attacks against Israeli soldiers by Islamic guerrillas belonging to the Lebanese Hezbollah (Party of God), which was backed by Syria and Iran. The strikes against the radar sites marked a

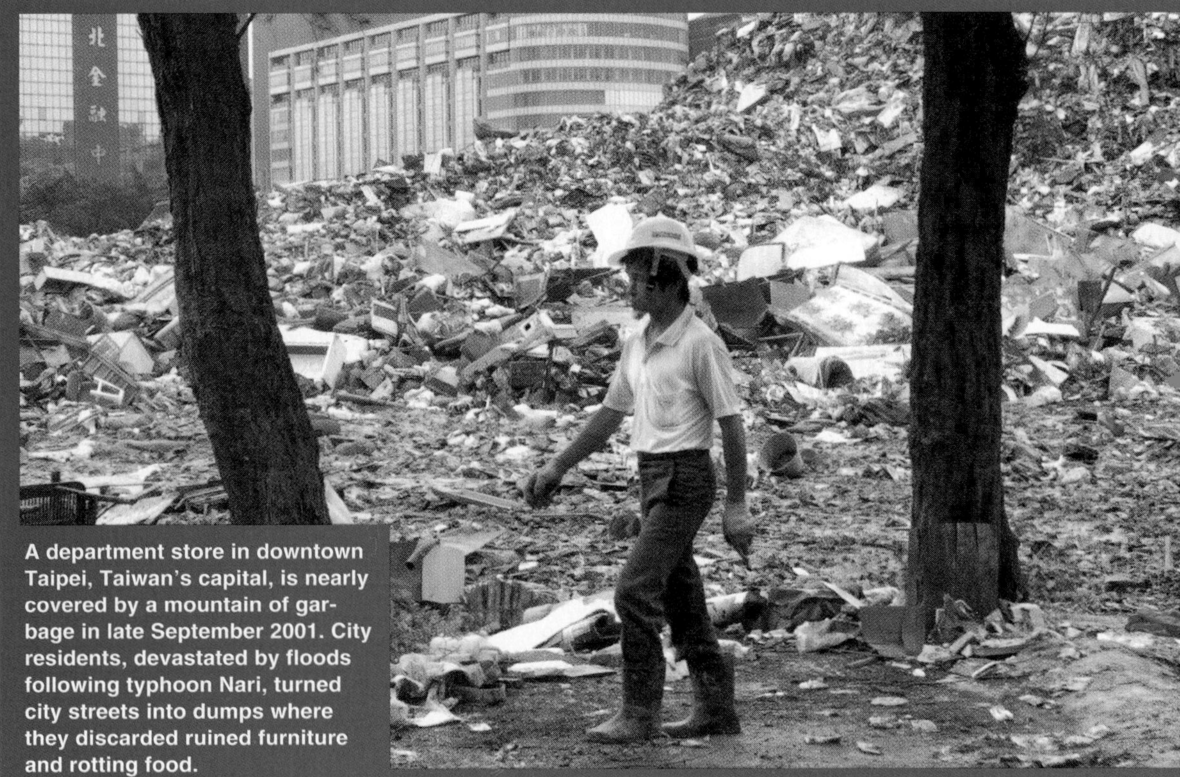

A department store in downtown Taipei, Taiwan's capital, is nearly covered by a mountain of garbage in late September 2001. City residents, devastated by floods following typhoon Nari, turned city streets into dumps where they discarded ruined furniture and rotting food.

shift in Israeli policy and raised fears of a widening Syrian-Israeli conflict. Israel had previously restricted its retaliatory attacks in Lebanon to Lebanese government and guerrilla targets.

United Nations seat. Syria won a two-year term on the 15-seat United Nations Security Council in October. The United States did not oppose Syria's bid for the seat despite the fact that the U.S. State Department classified Syria as a country that supports terrorism.

Assad condemns Afghan war. On October 31, Syrian President Bashar al-Assad condemned U.S. bombing raids on Afghanistan during a visit to Syria by British Prime Minister Tony Blair. Blair was hoping to shore up Islamic support for the U.S-led "war on terrorism." U.S. officials accused Afghanistan's ruling Taliban of harboring terrorists associated with the September 11 terrorist attacks on the United States.

Activists jailed. Syrian authorities arrested parliamentarian Riad Seif on September 6 after Sief hosted a political forum protesting the September 1 arrest of Riad Turk, a prominent opposition leader. Seif and Turk were among at least 10 Syrian political leaders, intellectuals, and human rights activists jailed between early August and late October. □ Christine Helms

See also **Israel; Lebanon; Middle East; Terrorism; Terrorism: A Special Feature,** p. 38.

Taiwan.

President Chen Shui-bian's Democratic Progressive Party (DPP) increased the number of seats it holds in the National Assembly in elections held on Dec. 1, 2001. The DPP won 87 seats, up from 66, but still short of a majority in the 225-seat house. The long-ruling Kuomintang (KMT), or Nationalist party, lost seats in the assembly, falling from 110 to 68 seats.

The elections were held after months of political gridlock that began with Chen's election as president in March 2000. The KMT, which held a majority in the assembly before the 2001 elections, continuously blocked Chen's plans.

In July, Chen expressed frustration with the political paralysis. He called for streamlining government and an anticorruption drive to improve interdepartmental cooperation. Chen also acknowledged that the government had failed to satisfy the expectations of voters.

Realignment. A political realignment began in June when KMT leaders launched talks with the government of China. Taiwan had split from China at the time of the Communist takeover in 1949, but China continued to claim Taiwan. In 2001, KMT leaders for the first time discussed reunification with Chinese Communist Party officials. This move alienated Chen's predecessor, Lee Teng-hui. As president, Lee had tried to distance the KMT party from reunification with China. After the meetings between the KMT and Chinese officials, Lee announced his support for Chen. Chen's DPP had long advocated independence for Taiwan.

In July, several of Lee's KMT supporters registered a new party, the Taiwan Solidarity Union (TSU), with a platform that fell just shy of Taiwanese independence. The KMT expelled Lee after he accused it of selling out to China. The TSU won 13 seats in the 2001 assembly election.

Defense. On April 24, U.S. officials announced that the United States would sell the government of Taiwan more weapons to protect itself from China. Officials in China were angered by the move. On April 25, U.S. President George W. Bush proclaimed that if China attacked Taiwan, he would order "whatever it took" to help Taiwan defend itself. Previous U.S. presidents had been deliberately vague about what the United States might do to protect Taiwan. Officials with the Bush administration later sought to limit the implications of President Bush's statement.

Economy. In 2001, Taiwan's economy fell into recession, and unemployment hit a record high of 5.17 percent. Economists expected the economy to improve after Taiwan was admitted in November to the World Trade Organization, a United Nations affiliate that reduces barriers to free trade.

☐ Henry S. Bradsher

See also **Asia; China.**

Tajikistan. In 2001, Tajikistan found itself used as a staging area for attacks on Afghanistan, more than 10 years after Soviet troops withdrew after the Soviet Union's failed war in Afghanistan. Soon after the September 11 terrorist attacks on the United States, President Emomali Rahmonov declared that U.S. forces could not use Tajikistan as a base for military action. However, Russian president Vladimir Putin, who strongly supported U.S. attacks on Afghanistan, pressured Rahmonov to reconsider.

In November, U.S. Defense Secretary Donald Rumsfeld visited Tajikistan to discuss cooperation in the war against terrorism. Soon afterward, U.S. advisers began inspecting potential bases for military operations.

A second year of drought claimed more than half of Tajikistan's wheat and bean crops in 2001. Officials from the Red Cross, an international organization that works to relieve human suffering, estimated that more than 1 million people in Tajikistan were at risk of starvation. Tajikistan remained the poorest of the post-Soviet nations, with the lowest per-capita gross domestic product—a measure of average individual wealth—of any of the former Soviet republics.

☐ Steven L. Solnick

See also **Afghanistan; Asia; Russia.**

Tanzania. See **Africa.**

President George W. Bush, surrounded by Republican Congressional leaders, signs into law on June 7, 2001, the first broad tax cut since 1981. President Bush said that the legislation would reduce U.S. taxes by $1.35 trillion over 10 years.

Taxation. United States President George W. Bush on June 7, 2001, signed tax-cut legislation that included an unusual rebate feature under which U.S. taxpayers received refunds on their taxes. The U.S. Congress passed the legislation on May 26, 2001. It was the first broad U.S. tax cut since 1981.

In the summer of 2001, taxpayers began to receive rebate checks on their taxes. Married couples received up to $600, while single taxpayers with at least $6,000 in taxable 2000 income received a maximum of $300. Among other provisions, the legislation was designed to lower by 3 percent the average income tax rate by 2006; eliminate the federal tax on estates by 2010; increase the tax credit to $1,000 per child from $500; and lower taxes for married couples. President Bush said that the package would reduce taxes by an estimated $1.35 trillion over 10 years. The president also said that future budget surpluses would cover the reduction in federal income caused by the tax cuts.

The tax legislation expires on Dec. 31, 2010, a provision legislators added because of Congressional rules governing spending more than a decade in the future. In order for the tax cut to remain in effect past 2010, additional legislation must be enacted by a future Congress and signed into law by a future president.

Terrorist attack aftermath. The Bush administration and members of Congress considered a number of additional tax cuts to stimulate the U.S. economy following the terrorist attacks on the World Trade Center in New York City and the Pentagon Building outside Washington, D.C., on Sept. 11, 2001.

On October 12, the House Ways and Means Committee approved a $100-billion tax break plan that included $70 billion in tax breaks for corporations. The plan, spearheaded by the House Republican leadership, provided $13 billion in tax rebates to 30 million workers whose incomes were too low to entitle them to the Bush administration's rebates passed in June. The proposed legislation also reduced the tax rate on *capital gains* (the tax imposed on the sale of assets such as stocks, bonds, and real estate) and provided approximately $12 billion to state governments to extend unemployment insurance and health benefits to employees left without jobs as a result of the terrorist attacks. The House passed the legislation on October 24, but the Senate did not act on it during 2001.

☐ Geoffrey A. Campbell

See also **Congress of the United States; Economics; Terrorism: A Special Feature**, p. 38; **United States, Government of the; United States, President of the.**

Telecommunications. The telecommunications industry suffered in 2001 after several years of skyrocketing growth. Even the sector's most stable companies experienced difficulties in the changing marketplace, including having to lay off tens of thousands of workers. The industry's dramatic reversal of fortune was tied in part to the economic slowdown in the United States and other countries in 2001. Another factor was the collapse of many Internet-related companies whose stock prices had been driven up in the late 1990's by overly optimistic visions of growth.

Dot-com fallout. In a domino effect that began early in 2001, Internet companies in financial trouble stopped paying Internet service providers and other vendors. These vendors, in turn, could not pay companies that delivered Internet connections to businesses and consumers. As a result, many young telecommunications service providers had to pull back expansion plans, file for bankruptcy, or go out of business.

Bankruptcy row. In January, NorthPoint Communications Inc. of San Francisco, a leading telecom, filed for bankruptcy. By the end of March, Northpoint had shut down its Digital Subscriber Line (DSL) business, which provided high-speed Internet connections over telephone lines. Two other leading DSL competitors, Rhythms NetConnections of Englewood, Colorado, and Covad Communications Company of Santa Clara, California, also filed for bankruptcy in 2001.

Large vendors suffer. In the wake of these bankruptcies, vendors that supplied switches, routers, cable, and other telecommunications infrastructure felt the pinch. Nortel Networks Corp. of Brampton, Ontario, posted a $19-billion loss in its second quarter and announced plans to cut 10,000 jobs. Lucent Technologies of Murray Hill, New Jersey, announced it was cutting about 20,000 jobs.

Large vendors suffered in two ways from the misfortunes of smaller telecoms. Many had extended credit to the expanding network operators in the form of equipment. When the upstarts failed, these debts became uncollectible. Also, with so much unused capacity available, surviving network operators sharply reduced equipment purchases, choosing instead to buy the equipment of failed companies at low prices.

Excess capacity also accelerated the drop in long distance rates, placing stress on companies like AT&T of New York City; WorldCom Group of Clinton, Mississippi; Sprint Corp. of Westwood, Kansas; Level 3 Communications of Broomfield, Colorado; and Global Crossing of Hampton, Bermuda.

AT&T sells cable unit. On December 19, AT&T sold its broadband unit, which included its cable-television and cable-Internet businesses, to

Comcast Corp., a large cable television firm based in Philadelphia. AT&T entertained offers from other major cable operators, including Cox Communications, Inc., of Atlanta, Georgia, and AOL Time Warner Inc. of New York City, but took Comcast's $72-billion offer, including stock and assumed debt. The new company was to be called AT&T Comcast Corporation. The acquisition, if approved by federal regulators, would make AT&T Comcast the biggest U.S. cable operator with 22 million subscribers.

Wireless provided the one bright spot among the generally dismal picture for the industry, as new customers continued to buy cellular phones and existing customers upgraded service. However, even this good news was not quite so good because the rate of growth had slowed from previous years, causing investors to balk.

Enhanced 911. In October, a deadline set by the Federal Communications Commission (FCC) for wireless companies to offer enhanced emergency services passed with few companies in compliance. The requirement was intended to make it possible for public safety officials to pinpoint the locations of wireless callers in the same way that landline callers are identified, enabling faster responses to emergencies. The FCC set a new deadline of Dec. 31, 2005. ☐ Jon Van

See also **Internet; Radio; Television.**

Television.

In 2001, two successful television series faced each other on Thursday nights, while a new football league was a ratings disaster on Saturdays. During the summer, studio executives dodged a possible actors' strike. Following terrorist attacks on the United States on September 11, celebrities joined forces in a telethon for the victims' families. The fall television season, the start of which was delayed by the terrorist attacks, finally brought with it some surprise hits and some even bigger surprise misses.

"Friends" versus "Survivor." In a bold programming strategy in January, CBS scheduled its reality-based series "Survivor: The Australian Outback" against NBC's comedy "Friends" on Thursday nights. NBC countered by adding 10 minutes to several episodes of the half-hour sitcom and filling the rest of the hour with new skits starring the cast of "Saturday Night Live." "Survivor: The Australian Outback" won the ratings battle with nearly 30 million viewers, compared with 22 million viewers for "Friends."

"The Weakest Link" proved to be a strong link for NBC during 2001. The program, based on a British game show, featured host Anne Robinson, who often ridiculed contestants. The phrase, "You are the weakest link; goodbye," which Robinson used to dismiss contestants, became an instant pop culture catch phrase.

The Extreme Football League, or XFL, a heavily hyped new football league, turned out to be one of the lowest-rated ventures in television history. NBC partnered with World Wrestling Federation head Vince McMahon to create the XFL, which debuted in February. The XFL had promised viewers "no-holds-barred football" and flamboyant personalities, but lackluster talent on the field doomed the league. In March, an XFL broadcast on NBC was the lowest prime-time program on a major network in broadcast history. The league disbanded in May.

Contract negotiations. Television and film actors threatened to strike during the first half of 2001, casting doubt on the start of the new fall television season. In July, representatives of the Screen Actors Guild and the American Federation of Television and Radio Artists—two unions that represent some 135,000 actors—reached an agreement on a new three-year contract. Under the new contract, actors received increased fees for appearing on screen; higher residuals from reruns broadcast on basic cable television stations; and increased salaries for guest-starring roles on programs.

Emmy Award winners in 2001

Comedy

Best Series: "Sex and the City"

Lead Actress: Patricia Heaton, "Everybody Loves Raymond"

Lead Actor: Eric McCormack, "Will & Grace"

Supporting Actress: Doris Roberts, "Everybody Loves Raymond"

Supporting Actor: Peter MacNicol, "Ally McBeal"

Drama

Best Series: "The West Wing"

Lead Actress: Edie Falco, "The Sopranos"

Lead Actor: James Gandolfini, "The Sopranos"

Supporting Actress: Allison Janney, "The West Wing"

Supporting Actor: Bradley Whitford, "The West Wing"

Other awards

Miniseries: *Anne Frank*

Variety, Music, or Comedy Series: "Late Show with David Letterman"

Made for Television Movie: *Wit*

Lead Actress in a Miniseries or Movie: Judy Davis, *Life with Judy Garland: Me and My Shadows*

Lead Actor in a Miniseries or Movie: Kenneth Branagh, *Conspiracy*

Supporting Actress in a Miniseries or Movie: Tammy Blanchard, *Life with Judy Garland: Me and My Shadows*

Supporting Actor in a Miniseries or Movie: Brian Cox, *Nuremberg*

"The West Wing," featuring (left to right) Richard Schiff, Allison Janney, Martin Sheen, John Spencer, and Rob Lowe, won the 2001 Emmy Award for outstanding drama series. Janney also won an Emmy for best supporting actress.

Edie Falco, Robert Iler, and James Gandolfini star in "The Sopranos." In 2001, Falco captured the Emmy Award for lead actress in a drama series. Gandolfini won the Emmy Award for lead actor in a drama series.

Terrorist attacks. Americans were riveted to their television sets following the September 11 terrorist attacks on the World Trade Center in New York City and the Pentagon Building near Washington, D.C. Almost all broadcast and cable networks suspended entertainment programming to cover the news. On September 11, approximately 105.5 million households tuned in to prime-time news coverage of the disaster.

Show of unity. On September 21, in an unprecedented show of unity, more than 30 television networks and cable stations simultaneously aired "America: A Tribute to Heroes," a two-hour telethon benefiting the families of victims of the September 11 terrorist attacks. A roster of actors and musicians—including Jim Carrey, George Clooney, Sheryl Crow, Tom Cruise, Tom Hanks, Billy Joel, Alicia Keys, Willie Nelson, Julia Roberts, Paul Simon, Bruce Springsteen, and Neil Young—raised more than $200 million in pledges.

Coping with the disaster. TV's late-night talk shows struggled with how to make people laugh after the September 11 attacks. "The Late Show" starring David Letterman, which originates in New York City, was the first to return. On September 17, Letterman, who is noted for his cynicism and sarcastic wit, was visibly moved as he talked about the attacks. Host Jay Leno of "The Tonight Show" began his first broadcast after the tragedy with an emotional speech.

Anthrax scares struck network news departments at all three major networks in October. Anthrax is a highly serious infectious disease caused by a bacterium. Concerns about exposure to the disease grew after an NBC employee, who had opened a letter addressed to news anchor Tom Brokaw that contained a white powder, tested positive for the *cutaneous* (skin) form of the disease. The powder later tested positive for anthrax. A week later, an employee of CBS News in New York City developed the cutaneous form of anthrax, as did the infant of a producer at ABC. Authorities said it was unclear how either the CBS employee or the child became exposed to anthrax. In all three cases, the victims recovered after being treated with an antibiotic.

Economic challenges. Television executives faced a number of economic challenges before and after the September 11 attacks. Before the tragedy, a decline in advertising sales forced networks to cut costs by scaling back the development of new programs to replace failed series. In the five days following the attacks, officials estimated that the networks lost approximately $190 million in revenues from broadcasting commercial free news coverage of the event.

The fall season. All major television networks postponed starting their fall seasons in the wake of the terrorist attacks. Several network executives feared audiences would be uninterested in new programs or returning favorites in light of the tragic events. By the time networks debuted new programming on September 24, many people were ready to embrace a diversion from the network news programs.

Hits and misses. Two acclaimed science-fiction series—both prequels to series that aired decades earlier—were among the most watched programs at the start of the new fall season. "Smallville," on the WB network, followed a teenage Clark Kent in his pre-Superman days. "Enterprise," which aired on UPN, revitalized the "Star Trek" franchise with adventures set a century before the original "Star Trek" series.

Many new dramas also received rave reviews. Critics and audiences welcomed Kiefer Sutherland in his TV series debut. Sutherland starred in the Fox network's critically acclaimed "24," about a counter-terrorist agent who has 24 hours to foil an assassination attempt. "The Education of Max Bickford," a CBS drama starring Richard Dreyfuss as a college professor having a midlife crisis, also drew large audiences and favorable reviews. Other new hits included "The Guardian," a CBS series about an attorney assigned to work at a children's service center; and "Crossing Jordan," an NBC drama about a medical examiner.

Several other popular and high profile television stars, however, could not lure viewers to their programs during the fall season. Jason Alexander was unable to muster success with "Bob Patterson." Alexander was a critical and ratings disappointment as a hapless motivational speaker on the ABC series. On NBC, chef Emeril Lagasse failed to serve up a hit with "Emeril," a fictionalized telling of Lagasse's life outside the kitchen. "The Ellen Show," which marked comedian Ellen DeGeneres's return to television on CBS, also got off to a poor start. Audiences seemed uninterested in DeGeneres's portrayal of a gay executive who moves back to her small hometown. Other quick cancellations during the fall season included the CBS series "Danny" starring Daniel Stern and the ABC series "What About Joan" starring Joan Cusack.

There goes the "Neighborhood." Public Broadcast System (PBS) stations on August 31 aired the last new episode of the children's program "Mister Rogers' Neighborhood." The program debuted in 1967. The final episode ended—as had all other episodes—with host Fred Rogers taking off his sneakers and cardigan sweater and promising viewers that he would be back. PBS stations were expected to continue airing reruns of the program. Rogers planned to create Web sites for children and parents. ☐ Donald Liebenson

See also **Football; Public health; Terrorism: A Special Feature,** p. 38.

Tennessee. See **State government.**

Top-rated U.S. television series

The following were among the most-watched television series for the 2000-2001 regular season, which ran from Oct. 2, 2000, to May 23, 2001.

1. "Survivor: The Australian Outback" (CBS)
2. "E.R." (NBC)
3. "Who Wants to Be a Millionaire?" (Wed.) (ABC)
4. "Friends" (NBC)
5. "Who Wants to Be a Millionaire?" (Sun.) (ABC)
6. "Everybody Loves Raymond" (CBS)
7. "Who Wants to Be a Millionaire?" (Tues.) (ABC)
8. "NFL Monday Night Football" (ABC)
9. "The Practice" (ABC)
10. "C.S.I." (CBS)
11. "Law and Order" (NBC)
12. "Will & Grace" (NBC)
13. (tie) "The West Wing" (NBC)
    "Who Wants to Be a Millionaire?" (Thurs.) (ABC)
15. "Temptation Island" (FOX)
16. "Becker" (CBS)
17. (tie) "60 Minutes" (CBS)
    "Frasier" (NBC)
19. "Just Shoot Me" (NBC)
20. "Who Wants to Be a Millionaire?" (Fri.) (ABC)

Tennis. Jennifer Capriati of the United States, whose career as a teen-age tennis star in the early 1990's faded after a series of personal problems, including allegations of shoplifting and drug abuse, roared back in 2001. Capriati captured the Australian Open in January and the French Open in June and rose to the number 1 ranking in mid-October.

In a historic U.S. Open women's championship match on September 8, Venus Williams defeated Serena Williams in the first Grand Slam final between sisters since 1884. In men's tennis, Pete Sampras failed to win a major championship for the first time in nine years, and Australian Patrick Rafter announced he would take time off to heal a sore shoulder. Some observers doubted he would return.

Australian Open. Capriati stunned the tennis world on Jan. 27, 2001, winning the Australian Open in Melbourne to take her first Grand Slam event. Capriati outslugged Switzerland's Martina Hingis, 6-4, 6-3 in the final. Seeded a distant 12th in the tournament, Capriati ousted defending champion Lindsay Davenport and four-time champ Monica Seles on her way to the final.

Patrick Rafter of Australia (right) congratulates Goran Ivanisevic of Croatia after Ivanisevic defeated Rafter in the Wimbledon men's singles final on July 8. Ivanisevic became the first wild-card player to win a Grand Slam event.

In the men's final, American Andre Agassi retained the championship by blasting 15th-seeded Arnaud Clement 6-4, 6-2, 6-2 on January 28. Clement, of France, had survived a grueling four-hour match to reach the final, while Agassi topped local hero Rafter. Venus and Serena Williams completed a career Grand Slam in women's doubles with a 6-2, 2-6, 6-4 win over Lindsay Davenport and Corina Morariu. Ellis Ferreira of South Africa teamed with Morariu to win the mixed doubles championship, and Todd Woodbridge and Jonas Bjorkman won the men's doubles title.

French Open. Capriati continued her hot streak, winning the French Open in Paris on June 9 over Belgium's Kim Clijsters. Capriati rallied from being one set down to win 1-6, 6-4, 12-10.

On June 10, Brazil's Gustavo Kuerten took the men's title 6-7 (3-7), 7-5, 6-2, 6-0 over Spain's Alex Corretja for his second straight French Open title and his third overall. Mahesh Bhupathi and Leander Paes of India won the men's doubles title; Virginia Ruano Pascual and Tomas Carbonell of Spain won the mixed doubles; and Ruano Pascual and Paola Suarez won the women's doubles title.

Wimbledon. Venus Williams overwhelmed Belgian Justine Henin 6-1, 3-6, 6-0 on July 8 to take her second women's Wimbledon crown. In the semifinals, Henin had ended Capriati's bid for a Grand Slam sweep.

In an emotional men's final, Croatia's Goran Ivanisevic surprised tennis fans by toppling Patrick Rafter 6-3, 3-6, 6-3, 2-6, 9-7 in front of a raucous, sold-out crowd. Ivanisevic, a former top-10 player participating in his fourth Wimbledon final, had slipped so far in the rankings that he only made the tournament as a wild-card entry. His victory made him the first wild-card player to win a Grand Slam event.

Americans Donald Johnson and Jared Palmer won the men's doubles title; Lisa Raymond of the United States and Rennae Stubbs of Australia took the women's doubles crown; and Leos Friedl of the Czech Republic and Daniela Hantuchova of Slovakia claimed the mixed doubles title.

U.S. Open. In the first Grand Slam finals match between sisters since 1884 when Maud Watson defeated her older sister, Lillian, at Wimbledon, Venus Williams easily dispatched her sister, Serena, 6-2, 6-4 on Sept. 8, 2001, to capture her second straight U.S. Open title. In the semifinals, Serena Williams had upset top-seeded Martina Hingis 6-3, 6-2, and Venus had defeated Capriati 6-4, 6-2.

In the men's final on September 9, Australia's Lleyton Hewitt, 20, upset Pete Sampras to become the youngest U.S. Open champion since 1989 when Sampras won at the age of 19. Hewitt defeated Sampras 7-6 (7-4), 6-1, 6-1.

In other matches, Wayne Black and Kevin Ullyett of Zimbabwe won in men's doubles; Raymond and Stubbs won in women's doubles; and Stubbs and Woodbridge won in mixed doubles.

☐ Michael Kates

Terrorism. On Sept. 11, 2001, 19 Islamic militants hijacked four airliners in the United States and flew two of them into the World Trade Center towers in New York City and one into the Pentagon Building outside Washington, D.C. A fourth plane crashed in a field in Pennsylvania. Approximately 3,000 people were estimated to have died in the attacks.

In response to the attacks, U.S. President George W. Bush declared a "war on terrorism" and launched a massive military assault in Afghanistan against the ruling Taliban militia, which was accused of harboring the terrorist organization responsible for the September attacks. That organization, a worldwide Islamic extremist network called al-Qaida, was headed by exiled Saudi-born millionaire Osama bin Laden.

President Bush warned that the United States would punish any terrorist group with "global reach" and any country that supported such groups. He urged all countries to join an antiterrorism coalition by cooperating in military efforts against terrorist groups; arresting terrorist suspects; freezing the financial assets of terrorists; or sharing intelligence information about terrorists.

Law enforcement authorities in the United States and other countries detained hundreds of people for questioning regarding the events of September 11. In December, the U.S. Department of Justice announced the first U.S. indictment in connection with these events. Prosecutors alleged that Zacarias Moussaoui, a French citizen of Moroccan descent who was in U.S. custody, was an active participant in the conspiracy to attack the World Trade Center and Pentagon Building.

Bioterrorism. In October and November, five people in the eastern United States died of the infectious disease anthrax after inhaling anthrax *spores* (an inactive stage of bacteria) that had been sent in envelopes through the mail. The first victim was an employee at a tabloid in Boca Raton, Florida, who had opened an anthrax-laden envelope. Additional letters showed up at news media offices in New York City and at the Washington, D.C., offices of U.S. Senate Majority Leader Tom Daschle (D., South Dakota) and Senator Patrick Leahy (D., Vermont). Investigators concluded that the anthrax in these letters likely contaminated other mail in mail-processing facilities.

At the end of 2001, investigators had not determined the source of the anthrax letters. However, they had discovered that the spores in the letters were of the Ames anthrax strain, a form of the bacteria that had been produced in U.S. government laboratories and laboratories under contract to the government. In November, the U.S. Federal Bureau of Investigation announced that the most likely suspect was a domestic terrorist.

The Middle East. Militant Palestinian organizations killed more than 160 Israelis during 2001. The militant groups Hamas, Islamic Jihad, and the Popular Front for the Liberation of Palestine claimed responsibility for most of the attacks. Israeli forces, in turn, struck targets in the Palestinian-controlled areas of the West Bank and Gaza Strip, killing or wounding hundreds of militants, demonstrators, and bystanders. More than 200 Israelis and more than 800 Palestinians were killed between the start of the Palestinian Intifada, or uprising against Israel, in September 2000 and the end of 2001.

Northern Ireland. The Irish Republican Army (IRA)—a military organization that had long sought to unite the independent country of Ireland with Northern Ireland, a part of the United Kingdom—began to dispose of its weapons in October. The disposal was in accordance with the 1998 Good Friday peace agreement.

In May 2001, the U.S. Department of State added the Real IRA, an IRA splinter group, to its official list of terrorist organizations. The Real IRA was opposed to the Good Friday peace agreement. ☐ Richard E. Rubenstein

See also **Afghanistan; Israel; Middle East; Northern Ireland; Terrorism: A Special Feature,** p. 38.

Texas. See **Dallas; Houston; State government.**

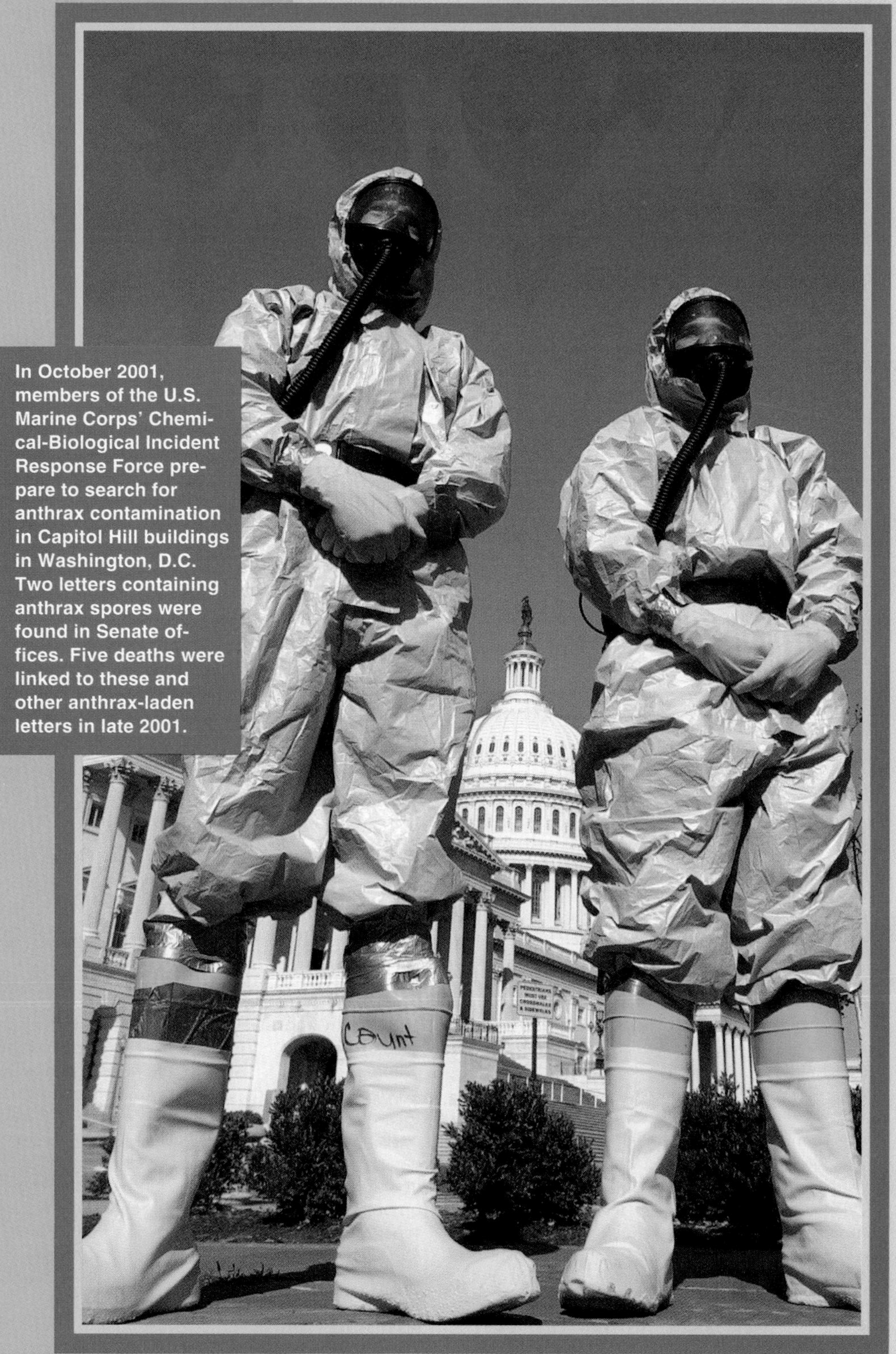

In October 2001, members of the U.S. Marine Corps' Chemical-Biological Incident Response Force prepare to search for anthrax contamination in Capitol Hill buildings in Washington, D.C. Two letters containing anthrax spores were found in Senate offices. Five deaths were linked to these and other anthrax-laden letters in late 2001.

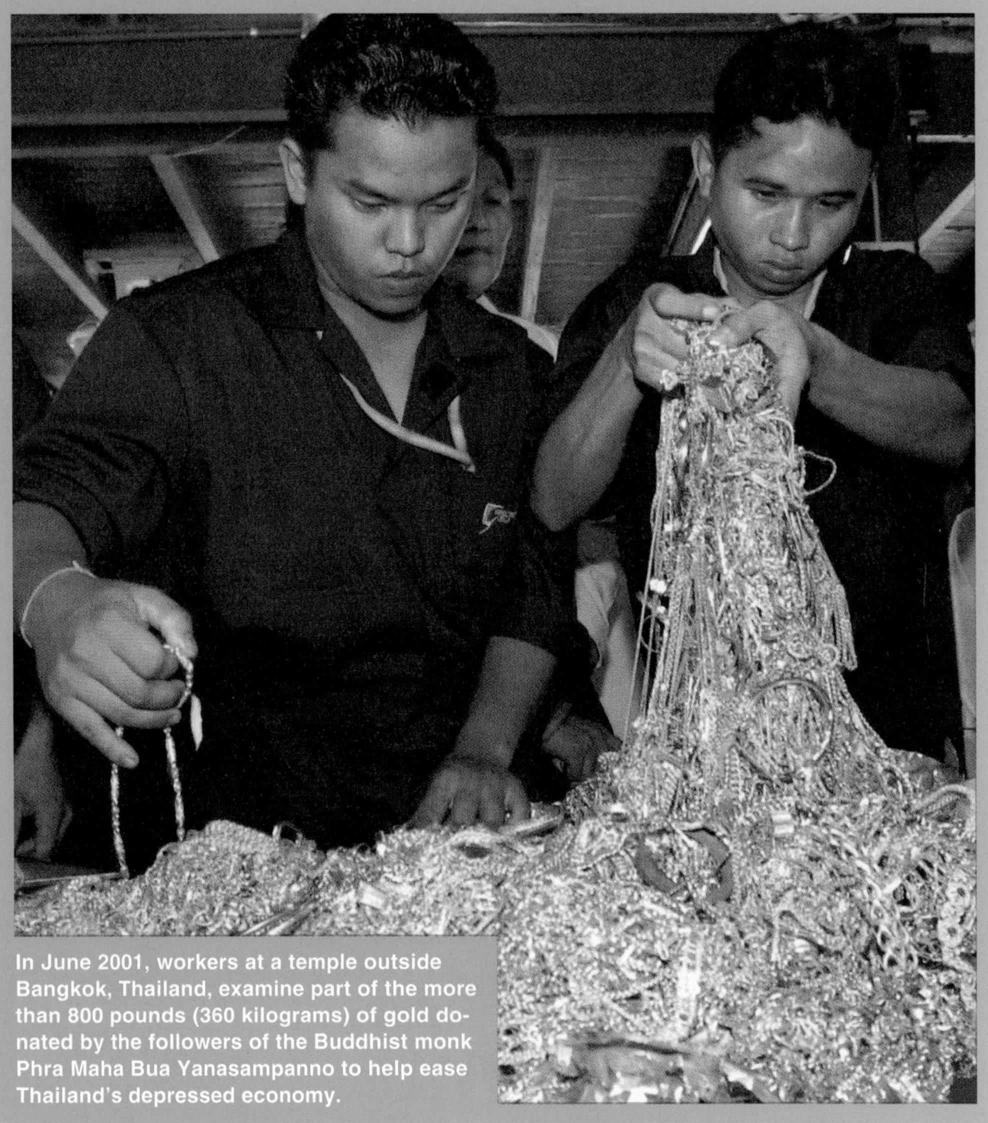

In June 2001, workers at a temple outside Bangkok, Thailand, examine part of the more than 800 pounds (360 kilograms) of gold donated by the followers of the Buddhist monk Phra Maha Bua Yanasampanno to help ease Thailand's depressed economy.

Thailand. Thaksin Chinnawat, a telecommunications billionaire, led his Thai Rak Thai party to victory in parliamentary elections in January 2001. The party, joined with two small coalition partners, won 325 out of 500 seats—the largest mandate in modern Thai history. Thaksin took office as prime minister in February.

The election was plagued by fraud despite being supervised by an anticorruption commission. In December 2000, the commission had indicted Thaksin for failing to declare millions of dollars of assets while serving as deputy prime minister in 1997. If convicted for failing to declare assets, Thaksin would have been removed from office and barred from politics for five years. In June 2001, he told the court that he had made an honest mistake and begged to be allowed to remain in office. In August, the court acquitted him by a vote of 8 to 7. Many Thai observers criticized the ruling as being based on politics rather than law.

Declining exports, especially of semiconductors, which accounted for 35 percent of Thai exports, weakened the economy in 2001. Thaksin had promised voters during the campaign that he would revive the ailing economy by shoring up banks, postponing farmers' debt payments for three years, organizing low-cost health care, and providing $23,000 in development money for each of Thailand's 70,000 villages. However, once in office, he moved slowly to fulfill his promises. ☐ Henry S. Bradsher

See also **Asia.**

Theater in 2001 was a year of feast and famine in New York City. In a season marked by the resounding success of Mel Brooks's *The Producers* on Broadway and a series of successful revivals of classic plays, including an all-star production of Anton Chekhov's *The Seagull*, the theater showed signs of excellent health. The destruction by terrorists of the World Trade Center towers in lower Manhattan on September 11, however, threw the New York theater world, like the city itself, into a state of shock from which it was still recovering at year's end.

The Producers, the musical comedy by Mel Brooks, based on his own 1968 movie, proved to be the biggest hit of 2001 as well as the biggest hit on Broadway in more than 25 years. Not since *A Chorus Line* (1975) had New York theater enjoyed such a popular, critical, and financial hit. *The Producers*, an unlikely farce about a pair of theatrical producers who succeed in spite of themselves with a show called *Springtime for Hitler*, received an unprecedented 15 Tony Award nominations in May 2001. Stephen Sondheim's *Company* had been the previous record-holder, with 14 nominations in 1971. In June 2001, *The Producers* won 12 Tony Awards, topping the previous record of 10 held by *Hello, Dolly!* (1964). *The Producers* largely overshadowed another musical based on a movie, *The Full Monty*, a critically successful show that in a different year might have taken the Tony for best musical. *The Producers* also received 11 Drama Desk Awards and 8 Outer Critics Circle Awards.

Rave reviews for its New York City premiere in April 2001 helped spur record-breaking sales for the musical. Despite the $100 price for the best seats, a Broadway high, the show continued to sell out months in advance. According to the show's backers, scarcity of tickets, combined with high demand, led to scalpers setting prices as high as $850 each for premium tickets. In what the show's producers described as a "war" on scalpers, they began offering 50 seats per show for $480 each.

Tony Awards. Although *The Producers* made a near sweep of the 2001 Tony Awards, several other productions were also honored. The Manhattan Theatre Club's production of David Auburn's Pulitzer Prize-winning drama *Proof*, a story about Catherine, a brooding young woman who may have written an important mathematical proof, won the award for Best Play. Mary-Louise Parker won the Award for leading actress in a play for her portrayal of Catherine. (In September, Parker was replaced by the actress Jennifer Jason Leigh, who also received critical acclaim.) The actors playing the poet A. E. Housman in Tom Stoppard's *The Invention of Love*—Richard Easton as the older Housman, and Robert Sean Leonard as the younger—won awards for leading actor and featured actor in a play, respectively.

Star-powered *Seagull*. The Joseph Papp Public Theater/New York Shakespeare Festival's production of Anton Chekhov's *The Seagull* at the outdoor Delacorte Theater in New York City's Central Park proved to be another hot ticket in 2001. The play, adapted by Tom Stoppard and directed by Mike Nichols, ran for five weeks in July and August and starred Meryl Streep, who had not appeared in a play in New York City for two decades. In addition to Streep, who played the aging actress Arkadina, the production featured a number of other Hollywood luminaries, including Kevin Kline, Christopher Walken, John Goodman, Natalie Portman, Philip Seymour Hoffman, and Marcia Gay Harden. While the production received mixed reviews, it was a clear popular success. As with all of the Public Theater's shows in Central Park, tickets for *The Seagull* were distributed free on a first-come, first-served basis on the day of each performance. Tickets were so coveted that numerous theatergoers camped out overnight at both the Delacorte in Central Park and the Public Theater downtown.

Trouble at the Public. Two of the Joseph Papp Public Theater's largest backers, Larry E. Condon and Dorothy Cullman, resigned from its board in October, shortly after the departure of Fran Reiter, the theater's executive director. Reiter, who had been hired less than a year before, was the financial counterpart to the theater's renowned producer and artistic director, George C. Wolfe. It was believed that Reiter, Condon, and Cullman departed over dissatisfaction with Wolfe's attitude toward finances. Wolfe, supported by the chairman of Public's board, Kenneth B. Lerer, said that the finances of the theater were sound and that his differences with Reiter resulted from a personality conflict.

In 2000 and 2001, the Public Theater enjoyed artistic success but ran into financial difficulty. While season memberships rose to 5,000 and the runs of five shows in the 2000-2001 season were extended, accountants projected a loss of $700,000 in 2002. The Public Theater's endowment, formerly $40 million, dwindled to about $23 million in 2001 because of the failure of two of its Broadway productions and the closing of its successful, long-running show *Bring In 'da Noise, Bring In 'da Funk*.

Revivals. A number of revivals of classic plays, on Broadway and off, compensated for the relative lack of new dramas on Broadway in 2001. The Brooklyn Academy of Music, a well-known venue for international and experimental work, presented two productions of Shakespeare's *Hamlet*, the first a pared-down version of the play directed by Peter Brook and titled *The Tragedy of Hamlet*, the second a production of Britain's Royal National Theatre. Several other classics succeeded on

Broadway in autumn 2001. Henrik Ibsen's *Hedda Gabler*, starring Kate Burton, and August Strindberg's *Dance of Death*, starring the acclaimed British actors Ian McKellen and Helen Mirren, were well received. A much-anticipated, star-filled Actors Studio production of Sophocles's *Oedipus Rex*, starring Al Pacino, continued its progress toward a staged production with several free, public readings of the play directed by Estelle Parsons and featuring Dianne Wiest. Other revivals in 2001 included a production of Michael Frayn's backstage farce *Noises Off*, starring Patti Lupone, and Clare Boothe Luce's *The Women*, starring Jennifer Tilly, Rue McClanahan, and Cynthia Nixon.

September 11. The hope of a banner year in New York theater was dashed in September by the drastic decrease in tourism that followed the September 11 terrorist attacks. Producers estimated that sales losses in the week following September 11 were between $3 million and $5 million. In the two weeks following the attacks, 5 of the 23 Broadway shows then running announced they were closing. A number of shows that had been scheduled to come to New York City either delayed or canceled their openings. Among these was the Roundabout Theater Company's revival of the Stephen Sondheim dark musical comedy *Assassins*, which was postponed indefinitely because its subject—people who have tried to assassinate U.S. presidents—was deemed inappropriate in light of recent events.

Although some wavering Broadway shows—including *The Phantom of the Opera*, *The Music Man*, and *Beauty and the Beast*—managed to get a second wind by November, six shows announced that

Matthew Broderick and Nathan Lane star in the Mel Brooks musical comedy *The Producers*, which opened in New York City on April 19 and quickly became the most popular Broadway production in 25 years.

they would close by January 2002 because of poor ticket sales. One of these was *By Jeeves,* written and directed by Alan Ayckbourn with music by Andrew Lloyd Webber, which had faced difficulty in October after two of its major backers pulled out in response to the Sept. 11, 2001, attacks.

Some shows succeeded in spite of this trend. The London musical hit *Mamma Mia!*, a drama centered around a pastiche of songs by the popular music group ABBA, successfully landed on Broadway in October and was expected to garner a number of Tony Award nominations in 2002.

Another musical that opened in autumn 2001 to rave reviews and strong ticket sales was the comedy satire *Urinetown*. The hit show was set in a future when water shortages have put an end to private bathrooms and people are obliged to pay to relieve themselves in public facilities controlled by a monopoly known as the "Urine Good Company."

☐ David Yezzi

Togo. See Africa.

Tony Award winners in 2001

Best Play, *Proof* by David Auburn
Best Musical, *The Producers*
Best Play Revival, *One Flew Over the Cuckoo's Nest*
Best Musical Revival, *42nd Street*
Leading Actor in a Play, Richard Eaton, *The Invention of Love*
Leading Actress in a Play, Mary-Louise Parker, *Proof*
Leading Actor in a Musical, Nathan Lane, *The Producers*
Leading Actress in a Musical, Christine Ebersole, *42nd Street*
Featured Actor in a Play, Robert Sean Leonard, *The Invention of Love*
Featured Actress in a Play, Viola Davis, *King Hedley II*
Featured Actor in a Musical, Gary Beach, *The Producers*
Featured Actress in a Musical, Cady Huffman, *The Producers*
Direction of a Play, Daniel Sullivan, *Proof*
Direction of a Musical, Susan Stroman, *The Producers*
Book of a Musical, Mel Brooks and Thomas Meehan, *The Producers*
Original Musical Score, Mel Brooks, *The Producers*
Orchestration, Doug Besterman, *The Producers*
Scenic Design, Robin Wagner, *The Producers*
Costume Design, William Ivey Long, *The Producers*
Lighting Design, Peter Kaczorowski, *The Producers*
Choreography, Susan Stroman, *The Producers*
Regional Theater, Victory Gardens Theater, Chicago
Special Theatrical Event, *Blast!*
Lifetime Achievement, Paul Gemignani, musical director
Tony Honors for Excellence in Theater, Betty Corwin and the Theater on Film and Tape Archive at the New York Public Library for the Performing Arts at Lincoln Center; the playwright workshop New Dramatists; and the annual reference Theater World

Toronto. A seven-year effort to convince the International Olympic Committee (IOC) to choose Toronto as the site for the 2008 Summer Olympic Games failed in 2001. At the IOC's general meeting in Moscow on July 13, Toronto placed second with 22 votes, after Beijing's 56 votes. On the day of the vote, Toronto officials had closed off the street in front of Union Station, the city's main rail terminal. Thousands attended a free pancake breakfast, intended as a kickoff to a street party celebrating Toronto's victory.

Waterfront development. Many Toronto residents consoled themselves with the hope that the unsuccessful Olympic effort would help the city achieve its long-cherished dream of redeveloping Toronto's decaying waterfront. In 2000, the federal and provincial governments had each promised $500 million to help finance a $12-billion renovation plan developed by Toronto-based financier Robert Fung. (All amounts are in Canadian dollars.) The City of Toronto had pledged an additional $500 million, mainly in land.

In March 2001, federal, provincial, and city officials announced the allocation of $300 million needed for the first phase of the $1.5-billion rejuvenation. The funds were earmarked for cleaning up polluted land along the waterfront and three other projects.

After the IOC vote, however, Toronto Mayor Mel Lastman expressed concerns about the cost of replacing the downtown section of the elevated Gardiner Expressway, a central element in Fung's plan, and asked city planners to review the proposal. On October 9, Paul Bedford, Toronto's chief planner, unveiled a revised plan that called for the construction of a $1.8-billion tunnel to replace the expressway. Lastman, however, also criticized the new plan for not including funding sources for the tunnel.

Nevertheless, on October 30, Lastman and other city officials celebrated when Ontario's deputy premier signed an interim agreement with Fung's Waterfront Development Corporation. The document gives the corporation authorization to open an office and begin work on the four projects announced in March. In November, the Toronto City Council's Economic Development and Parks Committee proposed establishing a museum and other cultural institutions and activities along the revitalized waterfront.

Moraine saved. The provincial government announced in November that it would freeze development on 50 percent of the Oak Ridges Moraine and severely limit growth on another 40 percent. The moraine is a 100-mile- (160-kilometer-) long ridge of glacial silt and gravel running through the region of Greater Toronto just north of the city. It absorbs rain and the spring runoff and feeds the headwaters of 30 rivers in the

Toronto region. Environmentalists feared that spreading development would damage the moraine's ability to absorb water. The provincial decision to protect the moraine came after a vigorous three-year campaign by environmentalists and several city and suburban politicians.

Urban transportation. In September, the provincial government announced a long-term plan to channel $3 billion into urban transportation and challenged the federal government to provide matching funding. Municipal and business leaders in Toronto welcomed the announcement, because the province had previously been reducing its contributions to transit.

The Ontario government also announced that all new transportation initiatives would be directed by the province itself. The decision left no responsibilities for the Greater Toronto Services Board (GTSB), a partnership of Toronto and 25 surrounding cities and 4 urban regions. The province had established the GTSB in 1998, giving it responsibility for operating commuter trains and buses in the Greater Toronto Area. After the province reassumed responsibility for funding commuter transportation, the GTSB announced that it would disband by the end of 2001.

☐ David Stein

See also **Canada; Canadian provinces; China; City; Montreal; Olympic Games.**

Toys and games.

The economic impact of the terrorist attacks on the United States on Sept. 11, 2001, reverberated throughout the U.S toy industry in 2001. Consumer confidence, which had a direct effect upon retail sales of all products including toys, plummeted to its lowest level in seven years during the month of October—just as the fourth quarter toy-buying season began. Many cautious consumers, still recovering from the aftermath of the terrorist acts, adopted a stay-close-to-home position and refrained from making unnecessary purchases. Adding to consumer concern was the rising unemployment rate. The result was a flat year in the $23-billion U.S. toy industry.

To the rescue. Following September 11 and through the 2001 holiday season, some of the biggest-selling toys were firefighter, police and emergency rescue vehicles, and related playthings. Action figures, such as G.I. Joe Search & Rescue Firefighter, from Hasbro Incorporated of Pawtucket, Rhode Island, and Rescue Hero Billy Blazes from the Fisher-Price unit of Mattel, Incorporated of El Segundo, California, were tops on many children's wish lists. Sales of a special edition of the Billy Blazes action figure, which came dressed in the official gear of the Fire Department of the City of New York (FDNY), were donated to a fire safety education fund. Retailers reported increased sales of such toys, especially for authentic licensed merchandise, such as the replica of a Fairfax County, Virginia, fire engine, made by Corgi U.S.A. of Chicago, Illinois. Fairfax County firefighters participated in rescue efforts at the Pentagon Building in Arlington, Virginia, on September 11. Code 3 Collectibles, a division of Funrise Toy Corporation of Woodland Hills, California, donated the proceeds of sales of its Fire Department of the City of New York vehicles to FDNY.

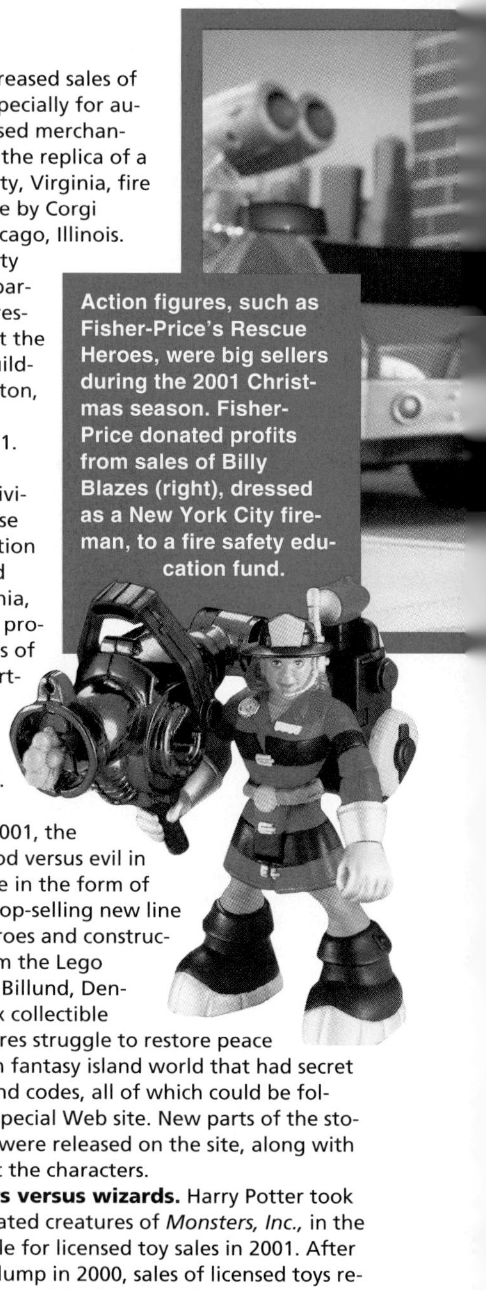

Action figures, such as Fisher-Price's Rescue Heroes, were big sellers during the 2001 Christmas season. Fisher-Price donated profits from sales of Billy Blazes (right), dressed as a New York City fireman, to a fire safety education fund.

Fantasy heroes. In 2001, the battle of good versus evil in toyland came in the form of Bionicles, a top-selling new line of action heroes and construction sets from the Lego Company of Billund, Denmark. The six collectible Bionicle figures struggle to restore peace in a war-torn fantasy island world that had secret languages and codes, all of which could be followed on a special Web site. New parts of the story and clues were released on the site, along with videos about the characters.

Monsters versus wizards. Harry Potter took on the animated creatures of *Monsters, Inc.,* in the toyland battle for licensed toy sales in 2001. After suffering a slump in 2000, sales of licensed toys rebounded, boosted by the November 2001 premiers of two major motion pictures. *Monsters, Inc.*, the Disney-Pixar animated feature, opened first, followed two weeks later by *Harry Potter and the Sorcerer's Stone*, the highly anticipated film based on the first volume of the best-selling book series by author J. K. Rowling. The success of the two box-office blockbusters fueled sales at retail stores as well, where consumers had the choice of several hundred Harry Potter licensed toys, including action figures, games, puzzles, trading cards, and construction sets.

Which box is best? In 2001, consumers had two new choices for which game player would sit on top of their television sets: Xbox from Microsoft Corporation of Redmond, Washington, or GameCube from Nintendo Company Limited of Kyoto, Japan. Xbox, computer software giant Microsoft's first venture into the video game industry, featured an internal hard drive, broadband Internet modem, and a DVD player, with a retail price of $299. A selection of 15 games was available for play on the new unit. Nintendo's GameCube retailed for $100 less at $199. The GameCube offered four-person play, the same as Xbox, and featured six games by the legendary game designer of the Donkey Kong and Super Mario Brothers video games. GameCube was also compatible with Nintendo's handheld video game, GameBoy Advance. The compatibility allowed GameBoy players to plug into the GameCube and play. Production problems for both systems, however, limited the games' availability in 2001.

☐ Diane Cardinale

Track and field. Zhanna Pintusevich-Block of Ukraine stunned the track world in August by defeating Marion Jones of the United States in the 100-meter sprint finals at the 2001 World Championships in Edmonton, Canada. The loss snapped Jones's string of 42 consecutive wins in 100-meter finals. Despite some fine performances during the World Championships, no world records fell, and 2001 may be best remembered for the retirement of three stellar performers: sprinters Michael Johnson of the United States and Donovan Bailey of Canada and pole-vaulter Sergei Bubka of Ukraine.

World Championships. On August 6, Pintusevich-Block toppled Jones in both the semifinal heat and in the final of the 100-meter sprint. Pintusevich-Block took the gold with a time of 10.82, 0.03 seconds faster than Jones. Until her loss in the semifinal, Jones had won 54 straight 100-meter competitions, 42 of which were in finals. Despite her loss at 100 meters, Jones claimed gold medals as the anchor of the 4x100-meter relay team and in the 200-meter dash, her first at that distance.

Charles Kamathi of Kenya broke another long winning streak at the World Championships, defeating the vaunted Ethiopian distance star Haile Gebrselassie in the 10,000-meter race. Gebrselassie had not lost at that distance since 1993. During his reign, he had set 12 world records in the event.

American Maurice Greene took his third straight 100-meter crown at the World Championships. Greene finished in 9.82 seconds, the third-fastest time in history. However, Greene injured his left leg during the race and was unable to defend his 200-meter title or serve as anchor of the 4x100-meter relay team.

Australia's Dmitriy Markov won the gold in the pole vault at 6.04 meters. However, Markov failed on three attempts to join Sergei Bubka as the only pole-vaulters to clear 6.1 meters.

Golden years. Michael Johnson ended his brilliant track and field career in 2001, having won five Olympic gold medals and nine World Championship titles. He also held world records at both the 200- and 400-meter distances. He concluded his competitive career with another gold, anchoring the winning U.S. 4x400-meter relay team at the Goodwill Games in Brisbane, Australia, on September 6.

Canada's Donovan Bailey, arguably his country's greatest sprinter, ran his final race on August 5 at the World Championships in Edmonton, Canada. During his career, Bailey won two Olympic gold medals, two World Championship gold medals, and for a time held the world record in the 100-meter sprint.

Sergei Bubka, who won six consecutive world

pole-vaulting titles and an Olympic gold medal and set world records 35 times, retired in February. Bubka still held the men's world indoor and outdoor records for the pole vault.

World records. Maurice Greene tied his own world record in the 60-meter dash on March 3 with a 6.39 in a semifinal heat at the USA Indoor Track and Field Championships in Atlanta, Georgia.

American pole-vaulter Stacy Dragila twice broke her own women's pole vault world record on June 9 at the U.S. Open in Palo Alto, California. Her new mark was 4.81 meters.

Catherine Ndereba of Kenya set a new world record in the women's marathon on October 7 in Chicago. She finished in 2 hours, 18 minutes, and 47 seconds.

Other records. Alan Webb, of Reston, Virginia, shattered Jim Ryun's 36-year-old national high school record for the mile at the Prefontaine Classic in Eugene, Oregon, on May 27. Webb, a senior in high school, finished with a time of 3 minutes 53.43 seconds, nearly two seconds better than Ryun's 1965 mark of 3 minutes 55.3 seconds.

On February 18 in New York City, Marla Runyan of the United States set a U.S. indoor record in the 5,000 meters, finishing in 15 minutes 7.33 seconds. She broke the previous mark by 15 seconds. In 2000, Runyan, who is legally blind, had become the first blind athlete to make a U.S. Olympic team. ☐ Michael Kates

See also **Sports**.

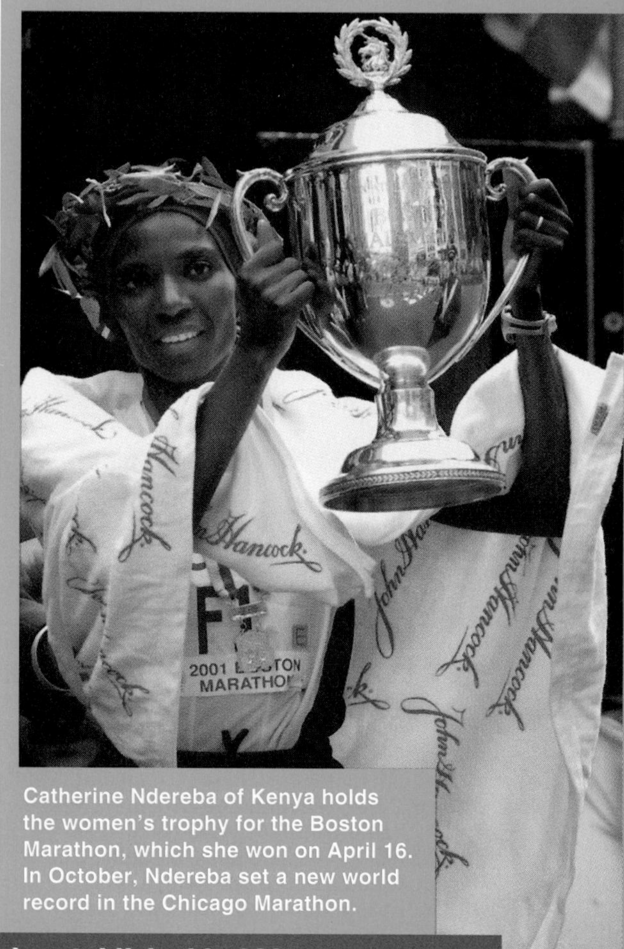

Catherine Ndereba of Kenya holds the women's trophy for the Boston Marathon, which she won on April 16. In October, Ndereba set a new world record in the Chicago Marathon.

World outdoor track and field records established in 2001

Event	Holder	Country	Where set	Date	Record
Men indoor					
60 meters	Maurice Greene	USA	Atlanta, Georgia	March 3	6.39
Women indoor					
Pole vault	Stacy Dragila	USA	Pocatello, Idaho	February 17	15' 5" 4.70 m
3,000 meters	Gabriela Szabo	Romania	Birmingham, England	February 18	8:32.88
Men outdoor					
3,000-meter steeplechase	Brahim Boulami	Morocco	Brussels, Belgium	August 24	7:55.28
Decathlon	Roman Sebrle	Czech Republic	Goetzis, Austria	May 27	9,026 points
Women outdoor					
3,000-meter steeplechase	Justyna Bak	Poland	Nice, France	July 9	9:25.31
Pole vault	Stacy Dragila	USA	Palo Alto, California	June 9	15' 9¼" (4.81 m)
Javelin throw	Osleidys Menendez	Cuba	Rethymno, Greece	July 1	234' 8" (71.54 m)*
20,000-meter walk	Olimpiada Ivanova	Russia	Brisbane, Australia	September 6	1:26:52.3
Marathon	Catherine Ndereba	Kenya	Chicago, Illinois	October 7	2:18.47**

m = meters
* = not yet ratified.
**= not recognized as a world record, but world best performance.
Source: International Amateur Athletic Federation (IAAF).

Transportation. The Federal Aviation Administration (FAA), a regulatory agency based in Washington, D.C., grounded all civilian air traffic in the United States on Sept. 11, 2001, for the first time in the nation's history. The action came after terrorists hijacked four U.S. passenger jets and flew two of the jets into the World Trade Center towers in New York City and one jet into the Pentagon Building, the headquarters of the U.S. Department of Defense, in Arlington, Virginia. The fourth jet crashed southeast of Pittsburgh, Pennsylvania. Thousands of people died as a result of the four plane crashes.

Although the FAA reopened U.S. air space on September 13, fears of more terrorist hijackings prevented many travelers from flying. Major airlines cut flights by approximately 20 percent and announced plans to lay off nearly 100,000 workers. The industry suffered through another catastrophe on November 12, when American Airlines Flight 587 crashed in a residential area of New York City, killing more than 260 people. Investigators said the crash was probably an accident unrelated to terrorist activity.

On November 19, President Bush signed legislation establishing a new federal agency to oversee air transportation security and requiring the Department of Transportation to hire some 28,000 employees to screen luggage and passengers at U.S. airports. The legislation also required other safety measures, including an increase in the number of federal air marshals aboard flights and stronger cockpit doors on planes.

Rail and bus ridership in the United States increased following the terrorist attacks as travelers sought a safer mode of transportation than airlines. Amtrak, a semipublic corporation that operates intercity passenger trains, and Greyhound Bus Lines upgraded security at their rail and bus facilities. However, travelers' fears intensified after a passenger aboard a Greyhound bus attacked the driver on October 3 near Manchester, Tennessee. The attack caused the bus to flip on its side, killing six passengers. Greyhound halted all its bus traffic for several hours until the Federal Bureau of Investigation concluded that the incident was not terrorist-related. On November 4, a struggle between a passenger and bus driver caused a Greyhound bus to crash south of Phoenix, Arizona, injuring more than 30 people.

Mexican trucks. An international arbitration panel ruled in February that the United States was in violation of the North American Free Trade Agreement (NAFTA) because U.S. officials restricted Mexican trucks from traveling beyond 20 miles (32 kilometers) of the U.S.-Mexico border. NAFTA, upon taking effect in 1994, created a free-trade zone in the United States, Mexico, and Canada. The agreement stipulated that Mexican trucks have full access to U.S. roads. In December 2001, the U.S. Congress passed legislation permitting Mexican trucks to haul cargo throughout the United States provided that the trucks pass rigorous safety and inspection requirements.

Rail mergers. In June, the Surface Transportation Board (STB), a Washington, D.C.-based agency that regulates some economic activities of railroads, lifted a 15-month ban on railroad mergers and issued new rules for mergers between large companies. The rules required railroad companies to show that proposed mergers would enhance competition and that plans were in place to prevent service disruptions during mergers. The STB had banned mergers due to concerns that they were squeezing out smaller companies and causing service disruptions.

The Canadian National Railway Company (CN) of Montreal and the Wisconsin Central Transportation Corporation (WC) of Chicago announced in September that the STB had approved CN's acquisition of WC. The merger provided CN with a rail link between Chicago and central and western Canada.

High-speed rails. Societe Nationale des Chemins de Fer, the national railway of France, extended its Paris-to-Lyon high-speed rail line to Marseille on the Mediterranean coast in June. The so-called TGV train made the journey of 466 miles (750 kilometers) in three hours. It reached a top speed of 185 miles (298 kilometers) per hour. The new link formed part of a larger network of high-speed trains in Western Europe.

In the United States, ridership on Amtrak's new Acela high-speed train serving Washington, D.C., New York City, and Boston was lower in 2001—the train's first full year of operation—than Amtrak officials had anticipated. Acela could reach its maximum speed of 150 miles (242 kilometers) per hour for only a short distance because it traveled on old track and used dated electrical equipment.

"It." In December, U.S. inventor Dean Kamen unveiled his highly anticipated personal transportation device, which had been the subject of wild rumors for months. The Segway Human Transporter, nicknamed "Ginger" or just "It," was a two-wheeled, battery-powered device for a single standing rider. A gyroscope mechanism enabled the speed and direction to be controlled by a rider's shifting weight. Although most of the public appeared to be underwhelmed by It, some government agencies and corporations planned to give the device field tests. ☐ Ian Savage

See also **Automobile; Aviation; Terrorism: A Special Feature,** p. 38.

Trinidad and Tobago. See **Latin America.**

Tunisia. See **Middle East.**

Turkey. Tens of thousands of protesters took to the streets of Turkish cities in April 2001 to call for the resignation of Prime Minister Bulent Ecevit. A 9-percent reduction in government spending, the loss of more than 400,000 jobs, and huge price increases had sparked the demonstrations.

Public unrest began in February, when a quarrel between Ecevit and Turkish President Ahmed Necdet Sezer over anticorruption measures triggered a loss of confidence in financial markets. By mid-April, the value of the lira, Turkey's currency, declined by nearly 50 percent.

In May, the International Monetary Fund, a United Nations-affiliated organization that provides credit to nations, and the World Bank, an international lending organization, offered Turkey emergency loans totaling $15.7 billion. However, the loans were provisional. The government had to undertake certain economic reforms, including restructuring the banking system, reducing public spending, and privatizing some state-owned industries.

Despite the reform efforts, the Turkish economy continued to slide in 2001. The terrorist attacks on the United States on September 11 triggered a 25-percent drop in Turkey's stock market. The Turkish ministry of economy estimated in September that Turkey's *gross national product* (the value of all goods and services produced in a country) would decline 7 percent in 2001.

Virtue banned. In June, Turkey's highest court banned the Islamic Virtue Party, charging that its activities undermined the government's *secular* (nonreligious) principles. However, the court allowed Virtue's 102 members to remain in the 550-seat parliament. Virtue's conservative members formed the Felicity Party in July. Moderate members formed the Justice and Development Party in August.

Turkish troops. Turkey's parliament voted in late October to allow some 90 members of the Turkish special forces to participate in U.S.-led military action in Afghanistan. U.S. forces began bombing Afghanistan in early October to destroy sites linked to al-Qaida, a terrorist network believed to be responsible for the September 11 attacks, and Afghanistan's ruling Taliban, which harbored al-Qaida's leader, Osama bin Laden.

Hunger strike. By November, more than 40 Turkish prisoners had died in hunger strikes that started in October 2000. The prisoners began the hunger strikes after authorities announced plans to transfer them from dormitory-style facilities to small cells. The prisoners said they feared that isolation in the cells would make them vulnerable to mistreatment by guards. ☐ Christine Helms

See also **Afghanistan; Armed forces; Middle East; Terrorism: A Special Feature,** p. 38.

Turkmenistan. See **Asia.**

Uganda. In 2001, Ugandan President Yoweri Museveni faced a real challenge to his leadership for the first time since his National Resistance Movement (NRM) seized power in 1986. Museveni won reelection to a new five-year term on March 12, 2001, with 69.3 percent of the vote. His chief opponent, Kizza Besigye, netted 27.8 percent, more than any other candidate to challenge the president, and charges of fraud and intimidation also marred Museveni's victory. Besigye claimed the vote had been rigged and demanded a new poll. Other opposition candidates accused the president of using troops to intimidate and attack his opponents. International monitors, however, declared the election generally fair and free. Violence during the election campaign left at least 12 people dead.

National Assembly elections on June 26 resulted in a parliament in which about 230 of the 282 members were pro-Museveni, according to political analysts. Since 1995, Uganda had operated under a "no-party" system that greatly restrained political parties and required candidates to campaign independently. Museveni's opponents claimed in 2001 that the system was little more than a one-party state designed to keep Museveni in office. The president's supporters countered that under Museveni, Uganda has experienced strong economic growth and achieved some success in improving public education and in fighting the AIDS epidemic.

Relations with neighbors. On April 29, President Museveni announced that Uganda would withdraw its armed forces from Congo (Kinshasa), but he gave no timetable for the retreat. Uganda had backed rebel groups against Congo's government since civil war broke out in August 1998. Ugandan troops remained on Congolese soil at the end of 2001.

Museveni visited Rwandan President Paul Kagame in Rwanda in July for discussions on improving relations between the two countries. Although both countries had supported Congolese rebels in the civil war, the Ugandan and Rwandan armies in Congo began fighting each other in mid-2000 in and around the city of Kisangani.

AIDS. The first meeting of the African Great Lakes AIDS conference took place in Entebbe, Uganda, in September 2001. The U.S.-based AIDS Foundation, the United Kingdom's Community Health and Information Network, and Uganda's Business Coalition on HIV/AIDS presented Museveni a joint award for his leadership in the fight against AIDS. Since the early 1990's, AIDS prevention programs in Uganda had lowered the infection rate among adults from about 14 percent of the total population to about 8 percent in 2000.

☐ Simon Baynham

See **Africa; AIDS; Congo (Kinshasa).**

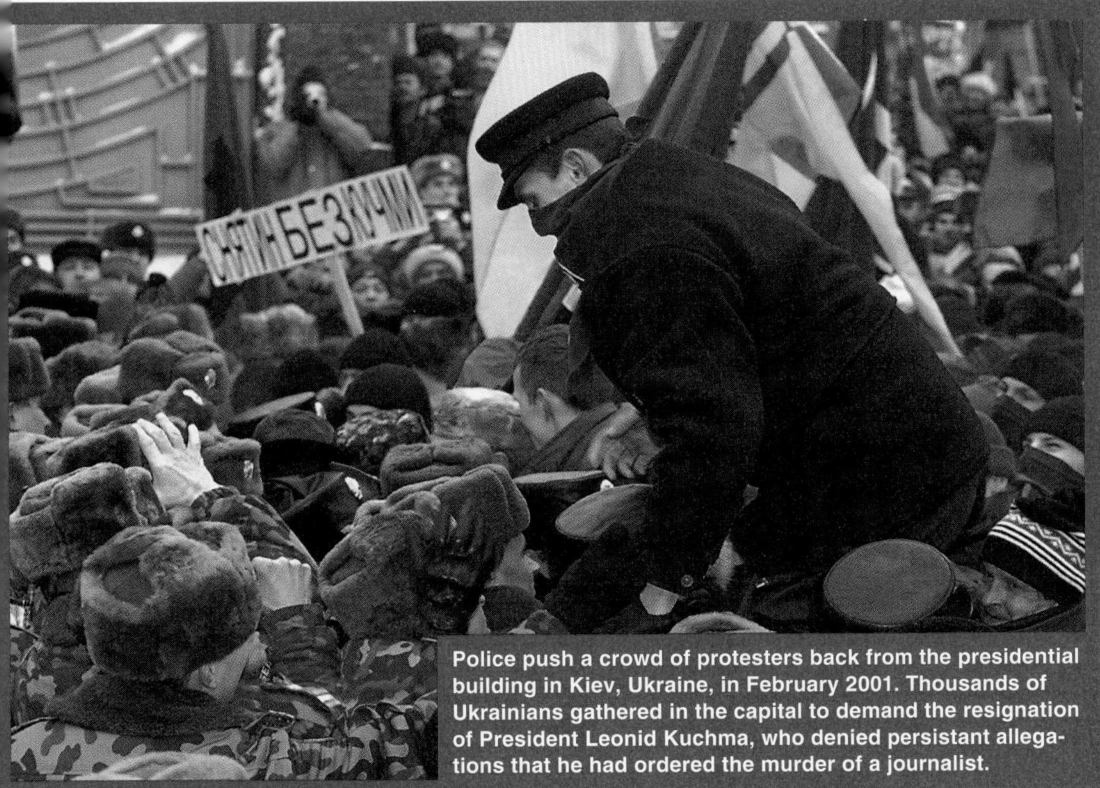

Police push a crowd of protesters back from the presidential building in Kiev, Ukraine, in February 2001. Thousands of Ukrainians gathered in the capital to demand the resignation of President Leonid Kuchma, who denied persistant allegations that he had ordered the murder of a journalist.

Ukraine. President Leonid Kuchma spent most of 2001 fighting accusations that he had ordered the death of an opposition journalist. Kuchma's voice was heard on tapes made secretly by his former bodyguard and released to the public in late 2000 by Socialist Party leader Oleksandr Moroz. On the tapes, Kuchma allegedly discusses with his aides how to silence Heorhy Gongadze, a journalist who had investigated corruption in Kuchma's administration. Gongadze disappeared in September 2000. Two months later, a headless corpse was found that was finally identified in May 2001 as Gongadze.

Demonstrators gathered in Kiev, the capital, in early 2001, demanding Kuchma's resignation, and opposition parties pressed for his impeachment. On May 15, Interior Minister Yuri Smyrnov announced that Gongadze had been murdered by two known criminals. He later retracted his statement, calling the announcement "premature." In September, the office of the prosecutor-general—the chief law enforcement officer in Ukraine—announced it would not investigate Kuchma's role in the disappearance of Gongadze.

New prime minister. In the midst of the political turmoil, the Rada (parliament) passed a no-confidence measure on April 26, forcing the resignation of Prime Minister Viktor Yushchenko. Yushchenko remained popular despite the scandal surrounding Kuchma, but his promarket reforms alienated both the Communist Party and powerful business interests. Kuchma nominated Anatoliy Kinakh, a trusted ally and former minister of industry, to replace Yushchenko. The Rada approved Kinakh on May 29.

Pope John Paul II began a four-day visit to Ukraine on June 23, the first papal visit to the country, whose Christian community is divided between Roman Catholicism and Ukrainian orthodoxy. The pope held masses before huge crowds and beatified 27 Ukrainians killed while Ukraine was a republic of the Soviet Union. Beatification is the final step before sainthood.

Downed airliner. On October 4, a Ukrainian surface-to-air missile mistakenly shot down a Russian passenger liner bound from Tel Aviv, Israel, to Novosibirsk, Russia. All 78 people on board—mostly Israelis and Russians—were killed when the plane crashed into the Black Sea. Ukrainian officials at first denied any responsibility, but President Kuchma finally admitted that a missile test had gone wrong. On October 24, Kuchma apologized to Russia and Israel and announced that Defense Minister Oleksandr Kuzmuk had resigned over the incident. ☐ Steven L. Solnick

See **Europe; Roman Catholic Church.**

United Arab Emirates. See **Middle East.**

United Kingdom

In June 2001, the Labour government of Prime Minister Tony Blair, which had been in power in the United Kingdom (UK) since 1997, was reelected with the largest majority ever recorded for a British party in its second term. Blair's personal popularity, as well as the buoyant economy, contributed to the historic victory—the first time that a Labour Party prime minister had won a full second term in office in the 100-year history of the party. Later in 2001, however, consumer confidence fell, as the number of unemployed workers began to rise. By November, unemployment had risen for a second straight month, amidst fears that Britain was experiencing the effects of a world-wide economic slowdown. The Bank of England repeatedly cut interest rates throughout 2001 to boost the economy. An outbreak of foot-and-mouth disease rocked both British agriculture and tourism, which took a second hit following terrorist attacks on the United States on September 11.

The general election campaign began on May 8, with the Labour Party ahead in the polls and the public's interest centered on the declining quality of public services. Labour's campaign focused on economic prudence, pledging to spend more on public services but also to request assistance from the private sector. The centrist Liberal Democrats promised tax increases as a way of delivering improvements in public services. Political experts criticized William Hague's Conservative Party for not addressing current problems with public services. Instead, the party pledged to introduce 8 billion pounds ($11.7 billion) in tax cuts while maintaining current levels of spending on health and education. The Conservatives also emphasized their opposition to British adoption of the euro, the single European currency, and claimed that the focus of their campaign was to save the pound as Britain's currency.

The results of the election on June 7 varied little from those of the 1997 election. The number of seats in the House of Commons (the lower house of Parliament) held by the Labour Party was reduced in 2001 from 419 to 413. The Conservatives picked up only one new seat, for a total of 166. The Liberal Democrats, led by Charles Kennedy, increased their representation from 46 to 52 seats, all of which were taken from the Conservatives. Labour's share of the vote fell from 44.4 percent in 1997 to 42 percent in 2001. Nevertheless, Labour held a majority of 167 seats in the 659-seat House of Commons.

The turnout of voters in the election—59 percent—was the lowest since 1918. Some commentators attributed the low turnout to the fact that many voters considered the campaign "dull" and Labour's victory predictable.

New cabinet. Blair reorganized his Cabinet immediately after being reelected. Robin Cook, the former foreign secretary, was demoted to leader of the House of Commons. Jack Straw, who had held the office of home secretary, replaced Cook as foreign secretary. David Blunkett, the former education secretary, replaced Straw at the home office. Blair broke up the Ministry of Environment, Transport, and the Regions, which had been headed by John Prescott, and Prescott was assigned the task of overseeing Labour's policy among the various government departments as deputy prime minister. More women were added to the Cabinet, with the appointments of Tessa Jowell as minister of culture, Patricia Hewitt as minister of trade and industry, and Estelle Morris as minister of education.

Conservatives. After the election, William Hague resigned as leader of the Conservative Party, acknowledging that he had failed to significantly improve the Conservatives' share of representation in the legislature. A number of contenders immediately arose for the position of party leader, including Kenneth Clarke, a former chancellor of the exchequer (finance minister); Michael Portillo, a former defense secretary; and Iain Duncan Smith, who was serving the party as shadow defense minister. (In the United Kingdom, the opposition party forms a "shadow" cabinet in which opposition party members occupy positions that mirror each post in the ruling party's Cabinet.)

Clarke had the most political experience, but

Visitors stroll through the Great Court of the British Museum after the final stage of its reconstruction—the opening of the North Portico—was completed in March. The newly enclosed courtyard offers visitors easy access to all parts of the museum for the first time in more than a century.

many party members considered him to be too pro-Europe in a party that had become increasingly critical of Britain's involvement with the European Union, especially Britain's participation in the euro. Portillo had been a rising star of the Conservative right under former prime ministers Margaret Thatcher and John Major, but his questioning of modern Conservative policy, as well as his admission of gay experiences in his youth, lost him votes among some former supporters. Duncan Smith had not previously held any major government post.

Portillo led in the first round of voting among Conservative members of Parliament (MP's) but was eliminated in the second round. Under rules drawn up by Hague, the final decision over the leadership position was voted on by the entire party membership. On Sept. 13, 2001, Duncan Smith won the vote as party leader and formed a shadow cabinet drawn mainly from the right wing of the party.

Budget. Chancellor of the Exchequer Gordon Brown presented his budget to the House of Commons on March 7. Brown projected that government revenues would exceed expenditures by more than 31 billion pounds ($46 billion) in 2001. However, he emphasized the need for economic prudence in 2002. He planned to reduce taxes for people of low income and to increase benefits to families, such as longer maternity leaves and an increase in the children's tax credit. The budget

Members of the British House of Commons

Queen Elizabeth II opened the 2001-2002 session of Parliament on June 20, 2001. As of November 23, the House of Commons consisted of the following members: 413 Labour Party, 164 Conservative Party, 54 Liberal Democrats, 6 Ulster Unionists, 6 Scottish National Party, 5 Plaid Cymru, 3 Social Democratic and Labour Party, 5 Ulster Democratic Unionist Party, 4 Sinn Fein, 1 Independent. In addition, the unaffiliated speaker and 3 deputies attend sessions but do not vote. This table shows each legislator and party affiliation. An asterisk (*) denotes those who served in the Parliament at some time before the 1997 general election.

A
Diane Abbott, Lab.*
Gerry Adams, S.F.*
Irene Adams, Lab.*
Nick Ainger, Lab.*
Bob Ainsworth, Lab.*
Peter Ainsworth, Con.*
Douglas Alexander, Lab.*
Richard Allan, L.Dem*
Graham Allen, Lab.*
David Amess, Con.*
Michael Ancram, Con.*
Donald Anderson, Lab.*
Janet Anderson, Lab.*
James Arbuthnot, Con.*
Hilary Armstrong, Lab.*
Candy Atherton, Lab.*
Charlotte Atkins, Lab.*
David Atkinson, Con.*
Peter Atkinson, Con.*
John Austin, Lab.*

B
Richard Bacon, Con.
Adrian Bailey, Lab.*
Vera Baird, Lab.
Norman Baker, L.Dem.
Tony Baldry, Con.*
Tony Banks, Lab.*
Gregory Barker, Con.
Harry Barnes, Lab.*
John Baron, Con.
John Barrett, L.Dem.
Kevin Barron, Lab.*
John Battle, Lab.*
Hugh Bayley, Lab.*
Nigel Beard, Lab.*
Margaret Beckett, Lab.*
Anne Begg, Lab.*
Roy Beggs, U.U.*
Alan Beith, L.Dem.*
Stuart Bell, Lab.*
Henry Bellingham, Con.
Hilary Benn, Lab.*
Andrew Bennett, Lab.*
Joe Benton, Lab.*
John Bercow, Con.*
Sir Paul Beresford, Con.*
Roger Berry, Lab.*
Harold Best, Lab.*
Clive Betts, Lab.*
Liz Blackman, Lab.*
Tony Blair, Lab.*
Hazel Blears, Lab.*
Bob Blizzard, Lab.*
David Blunkett, Lab.*
Crispin Blunt, Con.*
Paul Boateng, Lab.*
David Borrow, Lab.*
Tim Boswell, Con.*
Peter Bottomley, Con.*
Virginia Bottomley, Con.*
Keith Bradley, Lab.*
Peter Bradley, Lab.*
Ben Bradshaw, Lab.*
Graham Brady, Con.*
Tom Brake, L.Dem.*
Julian Brazier, Con.*
Colin Breed, L.Dem.*
Kevin Brennan, Lab.
Annette Brooke, L.Dem.
Gordon Brown, Lab.*
Nicholas Brown, Lab.*
Russell Brown, Lab.*
Desmond Browne, Lab.*
Angela Browning, Con.*
Malcolm Bruce, L.Dem.*
Chris Bryant, Lab.
Karen Buck, Lab.*
Richard Burden, Lab.*
Colin Burgon, Lab.*
John Burnett, L.Dem.*
Andy Burnham, Lab.
Simon Burns, Con.*
David Burnside, U.U.
Paul Burstow, L.Dem.*
Alistair Burt, Con.
John Butterfill, Con.*
Stephen Byers, Lab.*

C
Vincent Cable, L.Dem.*
Richard Caborn, Lab.*
David Cairns, Lab.
Patsy Calton, L.Dem.
David Cameron, Con.
Alan Campbell, Lab.*
Anne Campbell, Lab.*
Gregory Campbell, U.D.U.P.
Menzies Campbell, L.Dem.*
Ronnie Campbell, Lab.*
Ivor Caplin, Lab.*
Alistair Carmichael, L.Dem.*
Roger Casale, Lab*.
William Cash, Con.*
Martin Caton, Lab.*
Ian Cawsey, Lab.*
Colin Challen, Lab.
Ben Chapman, Lab.*
Sir Sydney Chapman, Con.*
David Chaytor, Lab.*
David Chidgey, L.Dem.*
Christopher Chope, Con.*
Michael Clapham, Lab.*
James Clappison, Con.*
Helen Clark, Lab.
Lynda Clark, Lab.*
Paul Clark, Lab.*
Charles Clarke, Lab.*
Kenneth Clarke, Con.*
Tom Clarke, Lab.*
Tony Clarke, Lab.*
David Clelland, Lab.*
Geoffrey Clifton-Brown, Con.*
Ann Clwyd, Lab.*
Vernon Coaker, Lab.*
Ann Coffey, Lab.*
Harry Cohen, Lab*
Iain Coleman, Lab.*
Tim Collins, Con.*
Tony Colman, Lab.*
Michael Connarty, Lab.*
Derek Conway, Con.
Frank Cook, Lab.*
Robin Cook, Lab.*
Yvette Cooper, Lab.*
Jeremy Corbyn, Lab.*
Sir Patrick Cormack, Con.*
Jean Corston, Lab.*
Brian Cotter, L.Dem.*
Jim Cousins, Lab.*
Tom Cox, Lab.*
James Cran, Con.*
Ross Cranston, Lab.*
David Crausby, Lab.*
Jon Cruddas, Lab.
Ann Cryer, Lab.*
John Cryer, Lab.*
John Cummings, Lab.*
Jack Cunningham, Lab.*
Jim Cunningham, Lab.*
Tony Cunningham, Lab.
David Curry, Con.*
Claire Curtis-Thomas, Lab.*

D
Paul Daisley, Lab.
Tam Dalyell, Lab.*
Alistair Darling, Lab.*
Edward Davey, L.Dem.*
Valerie Davey, Lab.*
Wayne David, Lab.
Ian Davidson, Lab.*
Denzil Davies, Lab.*
Geraint Davies, Lab.*
Quentin Davies, Con.*
David Davis, Con.*
Terry Davis, Lab.*
Hilton Dawson, Lab.*
Janet Dean, Lab.*
John Denham, Lab.*
Parmjit Dhanda, Lab.
Andrew Dismore, Lab.*
Jonathan Djanogly, Con.
Jim Dobbin, Lab.*
Frank Dobson, Lab.*
Nigel Dodds, U.D.U.P.
Pat Doherty, S.F.
Jeffrey Donaldson, U.U.*
Brian H. Donohoe, Lab.*
Frank Doran, Lab.*
Stephen Dorrell, Con.*
Sue Doughty, L.Dem.
Jim Dowd, Lab.*
David Drew, Lab.*
Julia Drown, Lab.*
Alan Duncan, Con.*
Peter Duncan, Con.
Iain Duncan Smith, Con.*
Gwyneth Dunwoody, Lab.*

E
Angela Eagle, Lab.*
Maria Eagle, Lab.*
Huw Edwards, Lab.*
Clive Efford, Lab.*
Louise Ellman, Lab.*
Jeff Ennis, Lab.*
Bill Etherington, Lab.*
Nigel Evans, Con.*
Annabelle Ewing, S.N.P.

F
Michael Fabricant, Con.*
Michael Fallon, Con.*
Paul Farrelly, Lab.
Frank Field, Lab.*
Mark Field, Con.
Mark Fisher, Lab.*
Jim Fitzpatrick, Lab.*
Lorna Fitzsimons, Lab.*
Howard Flight, Con.*
Caroline Flint, Lab.*
Adrian Flook, Con.
Paul Flynn, Lab.*
Barbara Follett, Lab.*
Eric Forth, Con.*
Derek Foster, Lab.*
Don Foster, L.Dem.*
Michael Foster, Lab.*
Michael Jabez Foster, Lab.*
George Foulkes, Lab.*
Liam Fox, Con.*
Hywel Francis, Lab.
Mark Francois, Con.

G
Roger Gale, Con.*
George Galloway, Lab.*
Mike Gapes, Lab.*
Barry Gardiner, Lab.*
Edward Garnier, Con.*
Andrew George, L.Dem.*
Bruce George, Lab.*
Neil Gerrard, Lab.*
Nick Gibb, Con.*
Ian Gibson, Lab.*
Sandra Gidley, L.Dem.*
Michelle Gildernew, S.F.
Cheryl Gillan, Con.*
Linda Gilroy, Lab.*
Roger Godsiff, Lab.*
Paul Goggins, Lab.*
Paul Goodman, Con.
James Gray, Con.*
Chris Grayling, Con.
Damian Green, Con.*
Mathew Green, L.Dem.
John Greenway, Con.*
Dominic Grieve, Con.*
Jane Griffiths, Lab.*
Nigel Griffiths, Lab.*
Win Griffiths, Lab.*
John Grogan, Lab.*
John Gummer, Con.*

H
William Hague, Con.*
Peter Hain, Lab.*
Mike Hall, Lab.*
Patrick Hall, Lab.*
David Hamilton, Lab.
Fabian Hamilton, Lab.*
Philip Hammond, Con.
Mike Hancock, L.Dem.*
David Hanson, Lab.*
Harriet Harman, Lab.*
Evan Harris, L.Dem.*
Tom Harris, Lab.
Nick Harvey, L.Dem.*
Sir Alan Haselhurst, Deputy*
Dai Havard, Lab.
Nick Hawkins, Con.*
John Hayes, Con.*
Sylvia Heal, Deputy*
Oliver Heald, Con.*
John Healey, Lab.*
David Heath, L.Dem.*
David Heathcoat-Amory, Con.*
Doug Henderson, Lab.*
Ivan Henderson, Lab.*
Mark Hendrick, Lab.*
Charles Hendry, Con.
Stephen Hepburn, Lab.*
John Heppell, Lab.*
Lady Sylvia Hermon, U.U.
Stephen Hesford, Lab.*
Patricia Hewitt, Lab.*
David Heyes, Lab.
Keith Hill, Lab.*
David Hinchliffe, Lab.*
Mark Hoban, Con.
Margaret Hodge, Lab.*
Kate Hoey, Lab.*
Douglas Hogg, Con.*
Paul Holmes, L.Dem.
Jimmy Hood, Lab.*
Geoffrey Hoon, Lab.*
Phil Hope, Lab.*
Kelvin Hopkins, Lab.*
John Horam, Con.*
Michael Howard, Con.*
Alan Howarth, Lab.*
George Howarth, Lab.*
Gerald Howarth, Con.*
Kim Howells, Lab.*
Lindsay Hoyle, Lab.*
Beverley Hughes, Lab.*
Kevin Hughes, Lab.*
Simon Hughes, L.Dem.*
Joan Humble, Lab.*
John Hume, S.D.L.P.*
Andrew Hunter, Con.*
Alan Hurst, Lab.*
John Hutton, Lab.*

I
Brian Iddon, Lab.*
Eric Illsley, Lab.*
Adam Ingram, Lab.*

J
Michael Jack, Con.*
Glenda Jackson, Lab.*
Helen Jackson, Lab.*
Robert Jackson, Con.*
David Jamieson, Lab.*
Bernard Jenkin, Con.*
Brian Jenkins, Lab.*

Alan Johnson, Lab.*
Boris Johnson, Con.
Melanie Johnson, Lab.*
Helen Jones, Lab.*
Jon Owen Jones, Lab.*
Kevan Jones, Lab.
Lynne Jones, Lab.*
Martyn Jones, Lab.*
Nigel Jones, L.Dem.*
Tessa Jowell, Lab.*
Eric Joyce, Lab.
K
Gerald Kaufman, Lab.*
Sally Keeble, Lab.*
Alan Keen, Lab.*
Ann Keen, Lab.*
Paul Keetch, L.Dem.*
Ruth Kelly, Lab.*
Fraser Kemp, Lab.*
Charles Kennedy, L.Dem.*
Jane Kennedy, Lab.*
Robert Key, Con.*
Piara S. Khabra, Lab.*
David Kidney, Lab.*
Peter Kilfoyle, Lab.*
Andy King, Lab.*
Oona King, Lab.*
Julie Kirkbride, Con.*
Archy Kirkwood, L.Dem.*
Greg Knight, Con.*
Jim Knight, Lab.
Ashok Kumar, Lab.*
L
Stephen Ladyman, Lab.*
Eleanor Laing, Con.*
Jacqui Lait, Con.*
Norman Lamb, L.Dem.
David Lammy, Lab.
Andrew Lansley, Con.*
Jackie Lawrence, Lab.*
David Laws, L.Dem.
Bob Laxton, Lab.*
Mark Lazarowicz, Lab.
Edward Leigh, Con.*
David Lepper, Lab.*
Christopher Leslie, Lab.*
Oliver Letwin, Con.*
Tom Levitt, Lab.*
Ivan Lewis, Lab.*
Julian Lewis, Con.*
Terry Lewis, Lab.*
Helen Liddell, Lab.*
Ian Liddell-Grainger, Con.
David Lidington, Con.*
Peter Lilley, Con.*
Martin Linton, Lab.*
Tony Lloyd, Lab.*
Elfyn Llwyd, P.C.*
Michael Lord, Deputy*
Tim Loughton, Con.*
Andrew Love, Lab.*
Ian Lucas, Lab.
Peter Luff, Con.*
Iain Luke, Lab.
John Lyons, Lab.
M
Thomas McAvoy, Lab.*
Stephen McCabe, Lab.*
Chris McCafferty, Lab.*
Ian McCartney, Lab.*
Siobhain McDonagh, Lab.*
Calum MacDonald, Lab.*
John McDonnell, Lab.*
John MacDougall, Lab.
John McFall, Lab.*
Eddie McGrady, S.D.L.P.*
Martin McGuinness, S.F.*
Anne McGuire, Lab.*
Anne McIntosh, Con.*
Shona McIsaac, Lab.*
Andrew Mackay, Con.*
Ann Mckechin, Lab.
Rosemary McKenna, Lab.*
Andrew Mackinlay, Lab.*
David Maclean, Con.*
Patrick McLoughlin, Con.*
Kevin McNamara, Lab.*
Tony McNulty, Lab.*
Denis MacShane, Lab.*
Fiona Mactaggart, Lab.*
Tony McWalter, Lab.*
John McWilliam, Lab.*
Khalid Mahmood, Lab.
Alice Mahon, Lab.*
Humfrey Malins, Con.*
Judy Mallaber, Lab.*
Seamus Mallon, S.D.L.P.*
Peter Mandelson, Lab.*
John Mann, Lab.
John Maples, Con.*
Rob Marris, Lab.
Gordon Marsden, Lab.*
Paul Marsden, Lab.*
David Marshall, Lab.*
Jim Marshall, Lab.*
Robert Marshall-Andrews, Lab.
Michael Martin, Speaker*
Eric Martlew, Lab.*
Michael Mates, Con.*
Francis Maude, Con.*
Sir Brian Mawhinney, Con.*
Theresa May, Con.*
Michael Meacher, Lab.*
Alan Meale, Lab.*
Patrick Mercer, Con.
Gillian Merron, Lab.*
Alun Michael, Lab.*
Alan Milburn, Lab.*
David Miliband, Lab.
Andrew Miller, Lab.*
Andrew Mitchell, Con.*
Austin Mitchell, Lab.*
Laura Moffatt, Lab.*
Chris Mole, Lab.
Lewis Moonie, Lab.*
Michael Moore, L.Dem.*
Margaret Moran, Lab.*
Julie Morgan, Lab.*
Elliot Morley, Lab.*
Estelle Morris, Lab.*
Malcolm Moss, Con.*
Kali Mountford, Lab.*
George Mudie, Lab.*
Chris Mullin, Lab.*
Meg Munn, Lab.
Denis Murphy, Lab.*
Jim Murphy, Lab.*
Paul Murphy, Lab.*
Andrew Murrison, Con.
N
Douglas Naysmith, Lab.*
Archie Norman, Con.*
Dan Norris, Lab.*
O
Mark Oaten, L.Dem.*
Bill O'Brien, Lab.*
Mike O'Brien, Lab.*
Stephen O'Brien, Con.*
Edward O'Hara, Lab.*
Bill Olner, Lab.*
Martin O'Neill, Lab.*
Lembit Opik, L.Dem.*
Diana Organ, Lab.*
George Osborne, Con.
Sandra Osborne, Lab.*
Richard Ottaway, Con.*
Albert Owen, Lab.
P
Richard Page, Con.*
James Paice, Con.*
Ian Paisley, U.D.U.P.*
Nick Palmer, Lab.*
Owen Paterson, Con.*
Ian Pearson, Lab.*
Linda Perham, Lab.*
Anne Picking, Lab.
Eric Pickles, Con.*
Colin Pickthall, Lab.*
Peter Pike, Lab.*
James Plaskitt, Lab.*
Kerry Pollard, Lab.*
Chris Pond, Lab.*
Greg Pope, Lab.*
Michael Portillo, Con.*
Stephen Pound, Lab.*
Sir Raymond Powell, Lab.*
Bridget Prentice, Lab.*
Gordon Prentice, Lab.*
John Prescott, Lab.*
Adam Price, P.C.
Dawn Primarolo, Lab.*
Mark Prisk, Con.
Gwyn Prosser, Lab.
John Pugh, L.Dem.
Ken Purchase, Lab.*
James Purnell, Lab.
Q
Joyce Quin, Lab.*
Lawrie Quinn, Lab.*
R
Bill Rammell, Lab.*
John Randall, Con.*
Syd Rapson, Lab.
Nick Raynsford, Lab.*
John Redwood, Con.*
Andy Reed, Lab.
Alan Reid, L.Dem.
John Reid, Lab.*
David Rendel, L.Dem.*
Andrew Robathan, Con.*
Angus Robertson, S.N.P.
Hugh Robertson, Con.
John Robertson, Lab.*
Laurence Robertson, Con.
Geoffrey Robinson, Lab.*
Iris Robinson, U.D.U.P.
Peter Robinson, U.D.U.P.*
Barbara Roche, Lab.*
Marion Roe, Con.*
Terry Rooney, Lab.*
Andrew Rosindell, Con.
Ernie Ross, Lab.*
Frank Roy, Lab.
Chris Ruane, Lab.
Joan Ruddock, Lab.*
David Ruffley, Con.
Bob Russell, L.Dem.
Christine Russell, Lab.
Joan Ryan, Lab.
S
Alex Salmond, S.N.P.*
Martin Salter, Lab.
Adrian Sanders, L.Dem.
Mohammad Sarwar, Lab.
Malcolm Savidge, Lab.
Phil Sawford, Lab.
Jonathan Sayeed, Con.*
Brian Sedgemore, Lab.*
Andrew Selous, Con.
Jonathan Shaw, Lab.
Barry Sheerman, Lab.*
Gillian Shephard, Con.*
Richard Shepherd, Con.*
Jim Sheridan, Lab.
Debra Shipley, Lab.
Clare Short, Lab.*
Mark Simmonds, Con.
Sion Simon, Lab.
Alan Simpson, Lab.*
Keith Simpson, Con.
Marsha Singh, Lab.*
Dennis Skinner, Lab.*
Andrew Smith, Lab*
Angela Smith, Lab.
Chris Smith, Lab.*
Geraldine Smith, Lab.
Jacqui Smith, Lab.
John Smith, Lab.*
Llew Smith, Lab.*
Sir Robert Smith, L.Dem.
Martin Smyth, U.U.*
Nicholas Soames, Con.*
Clive Soley, Lab.*
Helen Southworth, Lab.
John Spellar, Lab.*
Caroline Spelman, Con.
Sir Michael Spicer, Con.*
Bob Spink, Con.*
Richard Spring, Con.*
Rachel Squire, Lab.*
Sir John Stanley, Con.*
Phyllis Starkey, Lab.
Anthony Steen, Con.*
Gerry Steinberg, Lab.*
George Stevenson, Lab.*
David Stewart, Lab.
Ian Stewart, Lab.
Paul Stinchcombe, Lab.
Howard Stoate, Lab.
Gavin Strang, Lab.*
Jack Straw, Lab.*
Gary Streeter, Con.*
Graham Stringer, Lab.
Gisela Stuart, Lab.
Andrew Stunell, L.Dem.
Gerry Sutcliffe, Lab.*
Desmond Swayne, Con.
Hugo Swire, Con.
Robert Syms, Con.
T
Mark Tami, Lab.
Sir Peter Tapsell, Con.*
Ann Taylor, Lab.*
Dari Taylor, Lab.
David Taylor, Lab.
Ian Taylor, Con.*
John Taylor, Con.*
Matthew Taylor, L.Dem.*
Richard Taylor, Ind.
Sir Teddy Taylor, Con.*
Gareth Thomas, Lab.
Gareth R. Thomas, Lab.
Simon Thomas, P.C.
John Thurso, L.Dem.
Stephen Timms, Lab.*
Paddy Tipping, Lab.*
Mark Todd, Lab.
Jenny Tonge, L.Dem.
Don Touhig, Lab.*
David Tredinnick, Con.*
Michael Trend, Con.*
Jon Trickett, Lab.*
David Trimble, U.U.*
Paul Truswell, Lab.
Andrew Turner, Con.
Dennis Turner, Lab.*
Desmond Turner, Lab.
Neil Turner, Lab.*
Derek Twigg, Lab.
Stephen Twigg, Lab.
Paul Tyler, L.Dem.*
Bill Tynan, Lab.*
Andrew Tyrie, Con.
V
Keith Vaz, Lab.*
Peter Viggers, Con.*
Rudi Vis, Lab.
W
Joan Walley, Lab.*
Robert Walter, Con.
Claire Ward, Lab.
Robert Wareing, Lab.*
Nigel Waterson, Con.*
Angela Watkinson, Con.
Tom Watson, Lab.
Dave Watts, Lab.
Steven Webb, L.Dem.
Michael Weir, S.N.P.
Brian White, Lab.*
Alan Whitehead, Lab.
John Whittingdale, Con.*
Malcolm Wicks, Lab.*
Ann Widdecombe, Con.*
Bill Wiggin, Con.
John Wilkinson, Con.*
David Willetts, Con.*
Alan Williams, Lab.*
Betty Williams, Lab.
Hywel Williams, P.C.
Roger Williams, L.Dem.
Phil Willis, L.Dem.
Michael Wills, Lab.
David Wilshire, Con.*
Brian Wilson, Lab.*
David Winnick, Lab.*
Ann Winterton, Con.*
Nicholas Winterton, Con.*
Rosie Winterton, Lab.
Pete Wishart, S.N.P.
Mike Wood, Lab.
Shaun Woodward, Lab.
Phil Woolas, Lab.
Tony Worthington, Lab.*
James Wray, Lab.*
Anthony D. Wright, Lab.*
David Wright, Lab.
Tony Wright, Lab.
Derek Wyatt, Lab
Y
Tim Yeo, Con.*
Sir George Young, Con.*
Richard Younger-Ross, L.Dem

raised the national minimum wage by 11 percent, to 4.20 pounds ($6.17) per hour.

War on terrorism. Both the government and the British people reacted with great sympathy for the people of the United States after hearing news about the attacks on the World Trade Center in New York City and on the Pentagon Building near Washington, D.C., on September 11. Queen Elizabeth II ordered that the U.S. national anthem be played during the changing of the guard ceremony at Buckingham Palace on September 13 as a gesture of support.

Immediately after the attacks, Tony Blair pledged Britain's full support—including troops—for the U.S.-led war on terrorism and on the Taliban regime in Afghanistan, which U.S. intelligence sources suspected of harboring the planners of the attacks. He engaged in a world tour to build a coalition against Osama bin Laden, the exiled Saudi-born millionaire who was suspected of planning the attacks, and on bin Laden's al-Qaida terrorist network.

On October 7, British forces joined those of the United States in launching massive air strikes against Taliban targets within Afghanistan. By December 10, opposition forces in Afghanistan had taken control over most Taliban strongholds, though they continued to search for bin Laden. On December 19, the United Nations Security Council authorized the United Kingdom to lead an International Security Assistance Force that was to support Afghanistan's newly formed interim government.

Foot-and-mouth crisis. On February 20, British health authorities reported an outbreak of foot-and-mouth disease—a viral illness that is highly contagious among livestock—in Northumberland. The outbreak was the first in Great Britain since 1968. (Foot-and-mouth disease flared up briefly on the Isle of Wight in 1981.)

The government immediately banned the transport of sheep, hogs, cattle, and goats—all of which are susceptible to the disease—in an effort to contain the infection and embarked on a policy of mass slaughter of livestock. By September 2001, 3.8 million animals had been killed.

The disease took a significant toll on the British economy. The European Commission had banned exports of British livestock, and many farmers suffered not only a loss of income from the sale of animals, but also had to bear the expense of disposing of carcasses and sterilizing their property. The government offered partial compensation for the losses.

Tony Blair, who took charge of the fight against the disease, was forced to postpone local elections scheduled for May 3. Political experts had expected Blair to call a general election on the same day. By November, sufficient progress had been made in eradicating the disease for the government to announce that the condition of some parts of the countryside could be downgraded from "high risk" to "at risk."

Racial tensions. Violence between white and Asian Britons broke out in the spring and continued throughout 2001, sparking a national debate on race relations. The violence erupted in April in the northern cities of Bradford and Oldham, areas with high levels of poverty and unemployment and large Indian, Pakistani, and Bangladeshi communities. Asian youths reported being attacked by white youths and complained of mistreatment by the police. Members of the National Front and the British National Party—extreme right-wing organizations—staged rallies, which led to even worse rioting. Police arrested large numbers of people in Bradford and Oldham, as well as other northern towns, such as Leeds and Burnley.

The Cabinet of the United Kingdom*

Tony Blair—prime minister; first lord of the treasury; minister for the civil service

John Prescott—deputy prime minister; first secretary of state

Gordon Brown—chancellor of the exchequer

Robin Cook—president of the Privy Council and leader of the House of Commons

Lord Irvine of Lairg—lord chancellor

Jack Straw—secretary of state for foreign and Commonwealth affairs

David Blunkett—secretary of state for the home department

Margaret Beckett—secretary of state for environment, food and rural affairs

Clare Short—secretary of state for international development

Alistair Darling—secretary of state for work and pensions

Stephen Byers—secretary of state for transport, local government and the regions

Alan Milburn—secretary of state for health

John Reid—secretary of state for Northern Ireland

Paul Murphy—secretary of state for Wales

Geoff Hoon—secretary of state for defense

Andrew Smith—chief secretary to the treasury

Helen Liddell—secretary of state for Scotland

Lord Williams of Mostyn—lord privy seal; leader of the House of Lords

Patricia Hewitt—secretary of state for trade and industry

Estelle Morris—secretary of state for education and skills

Tessa Jowell—secretary of state for culture, media, and sport

Hilary Armstrong—parliamentary secretary to the treasury; chief whip of the House of Commons

Charles Clarke—minister without portfolio; chairman of the Labour Party

*As of Dec. 10, 2001.

A crane lowers the carcass of an animal infected with foot-and-mouth disease in preparation for incineration at a farm in northern England in February 2001. By September, 3.8 million animals had been destroyed in efforts to contain the disease.

Simon Hughes, a spokesman for the Liberal Democrats, Britain's third-largest political party, accused the Conservative Party of having stirred up the racial tension. On March 4, William Hague, then leader of the Conservatives, had called for limits on immigration and on the granting of political asylum. On March 27, the Conservative MP for Yorkshire East, John Townend, criticized the extent of immigration since the end of World War II in 1945, claiming it had undermined Britain's "homogeneous Anglo-Saxon society." Hague insisted that Townend retract the remarks but did not expel him from the party. Labour's Robin Cook gave a speech on April 19, 2001, in which he praised Britain's modern multicultural mix as a source of strength and celebrated the fact that the country's most popular dish was chicken tikka massala, a dish that combines Indian and Italian recipes.

Resignations. On January 24, Peter Mandleson, secretary of state for Northern Ireland and one of Blair's closest advisors, was forced to resign amid allegations that he had improperly tried to obtain a UK passport for an Indian business executive. Mandleson was subsequently cleared of the charges.

Scotland's first (prime) minister, Henry McLeish of the Scottish Labour Party, resigned on November 8, amid allegations that he had misreported office expenses. The Scottish Parliament elected Jack McConnell, leader of the Scottish Labour Party, to replace McLeish.

Blair's most trusted assistant, Anji Hunter, also resigned on November 8, from her position as director of political and government relations to accept a position as director of communications at British Petroleum. Lady Sally Morgan, who had held a position as minister of state in Blair's Cabinet, replaced Hunter.

Britain's railways, which had been privatized by the Conservative government of John Major in 1996, became the object of increasing criticism after the Hatfield rail crash of 2000 and the subsequent disruption of services. The crash, which resulted in the deaths of four people, was caused by a cracked rail. Railtrack, the company that maintained the track, subsequently declared bankruptcy. On Oct. 5, 2001, the government placed the company under the control of a British accounting firm.

Archer trial. On July 19, Lord Jeffrey Archer was sentenced to four years in prison for perjury and attempting to pervert the course of justice during a libel trial that had taken place in 1987. The novelist and former deputy chairman of the Conservative party had successfully sued the *Daily Star* newspaper over allegations that he had consorted with a prostitute in 1986. Archer had won damages of 500,000 pounds ($735,000). In 1999, Archer became the Conservative Party's candidate for mayor of London. During the election, Archer's friend, Ted Francis, announced that Archer had asked him to provide a false alibi during the 1987 trial. The accusation forced Archer to withdraw from the race and was instrumental in causing authorities to reopen the case. During the new trial, Archer's former secretary gave evidence that she had been asked to forge an appointment diary to prove Archer's story about his whereabouts. Archer did not speak in his own defense. The jury unanimously found him guilty.

Royal family. On Sept. 23, 2001, Prince William, grandson of Queen Elizabeth II, began his study of the history of art at St. Andrew's University in Scotland. The royal family had asked the press not to invade the prince's privacy while he was a student. The family was later embarrassed when it was revealed that Ardent Productions, the television company owned by Prince Edward, Queen Elizabeth's youngest son, had been secretly filming the prince for a documentary intended for U.S. television.

Prince Edward's wife, Sophie, embarrassed the royal family in April when she told a reporter disguised as a client that she used royal connections to help her clients. The reporter published the revelations. Sophie subsequently resigned as head of her public relations company RJH.

☐ Rohan McWilliam

See also **Europe; Terrorism: A Special Feature,** p. 38.

United Kingdom, Prime Minister of. In June 2001, Tony Blair became the first Labour Party prime minister to win a second full term in office, a feat that none of his predecessors had managed in the 100-year history of the party. Blair's opponents during his election campaign had criticized his proposals to improve public services by establishing partnerships with private companies to manage health, education, and transport services. Opponents also criticized the government for its reliance on "spin doctors," professionals who managed the presentation of government information and were unaccountable to Parliament.

Nevertheless, Blair's victory in the election was widely anticipated. He adopted a presidential style that seemed to be above party politics. However, he was disturbed during the election at the level of dissatisfaction with public services. Shortly after the election, he ordered ministers to find new ways to fund higher education, the government's most unpopular policy among young people.

Blair's international profile increased when he became a vocal supporter of the United States after the terrorist attacks on New York City and near Washington, D.C., on September 11. Blair pledged military assistance for the war in Afghanistan and engaged in a world tour to build a coalition against the al-Qaida network, which was suspected of staging the attacks. On September 20, Blair received a standing ovation from members of the U.S. Congress, when he attended an address by U.S. President George W. Bush on the proposed military action. ☐ Rohan McWilliam

Tony Blair, surrounded by his family, returns to 10 Downing Street, the official residence of the prime minister, in June after winning a second full term in office. Blair was the first Labour Party prime minister to ever be reelected to a second full term.

United Nations. In October 2001, the Norwegian Nobel Committee awarded the Nobel Peace Prize jointly to the United Nations (UN) and to Secretary-General Kofi Annan. The committee noted in its citation that the UN is at "the forefront of efforts to achieve peace and security in the world" as well as in mobilizing efforts to meet the world's economic, social, and environmental challenges. Annan received the prize for "bringing new life to the organization."

Special sessions. The UN General Assembly, which consists of representatives of 189 member nations, held two special sessions in 2001. One focused on the AIDS epidemic, while the other concentrated on the illicit trade of small arms. A third session, the World Summit on Children, was planned for September 19, but it was postponed because of the terrorist attacks on the United States on September 11.

From June 25 to June 27, the Assembly held discussions on the AIDS epidemic. UN representatives reported that an estimated 36 million people worldwide were living with AIDS in 2000. Twenty-five million of those people lived in sub-Saharan countries of Africa. Some 22 million people had died worldwide since the disease was first recognized in the early 1980's. An estimated 13 million children had lost one or both of their parents to the disease.

The Assembly issued a declaration calling for "strong leadership at all levels of society" to combat the disease on a global scale. The group called on governments to create national strategies and financing plans by 2003 to fight AIDS and to reduce by 25 percent the prevalence of the disease among people aged 15 to 24 in the most affected countries by 2005. The Assembly also approved the establishment of a Global Fund to which governments, private organizations, and individuals were asked to contribute a total of $10 billion a year to fight the epidemic.

From July 9 to July 20, 2001, the Assembly discussed ways to end the illicit trade in small arms and light weapons. UN representatives estimated that 500 million such weapons—60 percent of them illegal—were in circulation worldwide in 2000. Experts estimated that profits from the illicit trade in arms exceeded $1 billion a year. Many delegates were disappointed in the results of the meeting, when the Assembly adopted a nonbinding plan of action and failed to include compulsory provisions, such as a system of marking and tracing weapons. Countries with major weapons manufacturers, such as the United States and Russia, opposed measures that would limit individual gun ownership.

Secretary-General Kofi Annan. The General Assembly in June 2001 unanimously reelected Kofi Annan to a second five-year term, which began on Jan. 1, 2002. International affairs experts viewed Annan's unprecedented reelection six months before the expiration of his term as a reflection of the respect and support Annan enjoyed among rich and poor nations alike.

The UN General Assembly opened its 56th annual session on Sept. 12, 2001, a delay of one day caused by the terrorist attack on the World Trade Center in New York City. The Assembly elected South Korean Foreign Minister Han Seung-soo as president. Both the Assembly and the UN Security Council unanimously adopted resolutions condemning the acts of terrorism committed against the United States. On September 28, the group adopted international laws to fight terrorism. Member nations agreed to prohibit the financing of terrorists or terrorist organizations, freeze terrorists' assets and properties, deny them safe haven, prevent the movement of terrorists by tightening border controls, and share intelligence on terrorist activities.

Security Council. On October 8, the General Assembly elected five new members to the 15-member Security Council—Bulgaria, Cameroon, Guinea, Mexico, and Syria—to replace five outgoing countries. The new members began their two-year terms on Jan. 1, 2002. They joined Colombia, Ireland, Mauritius, Norway, and Singapore, and the five permanent members of the council—China, France, Russia, the United Kingdom, and the United States.

War crimes. The Serbian government surrendered former Yugoslav President Slobodan Milosevic to the UN International Criminal Tribunal at The Hague, the Netherlands, on June 28, 2001. Milosevic faced charges of war crimes and crimes against humanity committed in 1999 in the Serbian province of Kosovo while he was head of the Federal Republic of Yugoslavia. Later, additional charges were filed against Milosevic for crimes committed in 1991 and 1992 in Croatia and for *genocide* (the systematic murder of an ethnic group) committed between 1992 and 1995 in Bosnia-Herzegovina. Milosevic claimed that the court was "illegal."

On Aug. 2, 2001, the court found Bosnian Serb General Radislav Krstic guilty of genocide and sentenced him to 46 years in prison. Krstic commanded troops that were responsible for the deaths of an estimated 7,000 Bosnian Muslims at the town of Srebrenica in 1995.

U.S. dues. On Sept. 24, 2001, the U.S. House of Representatives voted to release $582 million to the UN, a major portion of the dues that the United States had owed the United Nations for more than a decade. The Senate had passed a similar bill in February. ☐ J. Tuyet Nguyen

See also **AIDS; Nobel Prizes; Terrorism: A Special Feature**, p. 38; **Yugoslavia.**

United States, Government of the. The United States launched a multipronged war on terrorism in 2001 in response to terrorist attacks made on September 11. Terrorists hijacked four commercial airliners in flight over the eastern United States. They crashed two of the jets into the twin towers of the World Trade Center in New York City and a third jet into the Pentagon Building, the headquarters of the U.S. Department of Defense, outside Washington, D.C. The fourth airliner crashed into a field in western Pennsylvania. The attacks killed thousands of people.

U.S. strikes back. On September 14, both the U.S. Senate and the U.S. House of Representatives overwhelmingly approved legislation authorizing U.S. President George W. Bush to use "necessary and appropriate force" in retaliating against terrorists. The measure also granted the president the authority to use force against any person or nation that harbored terrorists.

U.S intelligence officials suspected that Osama bin Laden, a Saudi-born millionaire and radical Muslim living in exile in Afghanistan, had masterminded the attacks. President Bush demanded that the Taliban regime in Afghanistan turn over bin Laden to the United States. Taliban leaders, who had harbored bin Laden since 1996, refused, claiming that U.S. officials offered no proof that he was connected to the attacks.

On Oct. 7, 2001, armed forces from the United States and the United Kingdom launched air strikes against the Taliban in Afghanistan and against bin Laden's terrorist network, al-Qaida ("The Base" in Arabic). Officials in the United States cautioned that the military campaign in Afghanistan and against terrorism worldwide would likely be a long battle.

U.S. bombers attacked Taliban military positions and targeted Kabul, the capital, and Qandahar (Kandahar), a Taliban stronghold in southern Afghanistan. On November 9, Northern Alliance forces, a group of anti-Taliban rebels, overwhelmed Taliban positions at Mazar-e Sharif, a strategically important Taliban stronghold in the north and entered the city. On November 13, the rebels took Kabul, the capital, after meeting little resistance from Taliban forces. By November 24, Taliban soldiers were pouring out of the besieged city of Qonduz (Kunduz), the Taliban's last stronghold in northern Afghanistan, to surrender to the Northern Alliance. The rebels captured Qonduz on November 25.

Leaders of the Taliban army surrendered Qandahar, the last Taliban-held city, on December 6. On December 10, officials with the U.S. Department of Defense announced that the Taliban had been defeated. Secretary of State Colin Powell announced on December 16 that al-Qaida had been destroyed in Afghanistan but that U.S. armed forces continued to search the mountains of Afghanistan's rugged Tora Bora region southeast of Jalalabad, where U.S. intelligence officials suspected bin Laden and al-Qaida leaders might be hiding.

The United States resumed an official diplomatic presence in Afghanistan on December 17 when the U.S. Embassy in Kabul was reopened for the first time since 1989.

The war at home. The U.S. government launched a domestic war on terrorism in the days following the attacks on Sept. 11, 2001. Federal and state officials detained foreign-born individuals who were in the country on expired visas; increased surveillance of suspected terrorists; and stepped up security at airports and in high-profile buildings. By the end of 2001, more than 600 people had been arrested or detained, and federal authorities continued the search for more than 200 other individuals.

Office of Homeland Security. In September, President Bush appointed Pennsylvania Governor Tom Ridge director of the Office of Homeland Security. The position, created in the aftermath of the September 11 attacks, was designed to help coordinate the government's antiterrorism efforts and ensure that information about terrorists and terrorism threats was shared among existing federal agencies. Ridge also was responsible for helping to develop a comprehensive national strategy to combat terrorism.

First charges. On December 11, Attorney General John Ashcroft announced the first federal indictments directly related to the terrorist attacks. Ashcroft said that Zacarias Moussaoui, a French citizen of Moroccan descent, had been charged with conspiring with bin Laden and al-Qaida to "murder thousands of people" on September 11. The multiple charges of conspiracy against Moussaoui alleged that he had engaged in the same preparation for murder as had the hijackers.

Federal law enforcement agents had arrested Moussaoui on August 17 on an alleged passport violation. Authorities believed that he may have been part of a broader plan to hijack other jets on September 11.

A continued threat. In the months following the terrorist attacks, officials with the Federal Bureau of Investigation (FBI) warned that they had reason to believe that additional terrorist attacks were being planned within the United States and against U.S. interests overseas. The FBI alerted all law enforcement agencies to be on high alert and asked citizens to notify authorities about any suspicious activities they had witnessed. The U.S. government also stepped up security at nuclear facilities.

Airline security. On September 13, officials with the U.S. Department of Justice ordered agents from the U.S. Marshals Service, U.S. Border Patrol, and U.S. Customs to provide added security at airports throughout the country. President Bush on September 27 asked governors to call up National Guard troops to patrol the nation's commercial airports.

The terrorist attacks sparked intense public debate on airline security in the United States. Some congressional leaders were divided over the best way to ensure the safety of commercial air travel and what role the federal government should play in aviation security. A number of Republican lawmakers maintained that airport security should remain in the hands of private contractors. Most Democrats and some Republicans felt that security guards should become federal employees.

The U.S. House and the Senate passed the airport security legislation on November 16. The bill created a new safety division within the Department of Transportation (DOT) and required that DOT hire 28,000 employees to conduct security screening of travelers and baggage at the nation's airports. The legislation also required that cockpit doors be fortified against attack and allowed commercial airline pilots to carry guns.

Assets frozen. President Bush authorized the U.S. Treasury Department on September 24 to freeze funds—held in U.S. banks—that federal officials believed might belong to terrorists. The order also gave the department the authority to freeze the U.S. assets of international financial institutions that officials believed did business with terrorists or terrorist organizations. By mid-October, treasury officials had frozen nearly $4 million in assets belonging to the Taliban and to bin Laden and his terrorist network. Treasury Department officials also worked to forge cooperation with other nations, which by mid-October had frozen more than $24 million in assets believed to be controlled by terrorist groups.

Anthrax scare. Health officials at the Centers for Disease Control and Prevention (CDC) in Atlanta, Georgia, along with state and local health officials, tried to calm public fears after five people in the eastern United States died of anthrax in October and November. Anthrax is a potentially fatal infectious disease that is caused by the bacterium *Bacillus anthracis.*

In October, an employee of a newspaper publishing company in Florida died of inhalation anthrax, and several other employees tested positive for exposure. A secretary in the New York City office of NBC network anchor Tom Brokaw was diagnosed with anthrax later in October. She had been exposed when she opened a letter addressed to Brokaw that was filled with a white power containing anthrax *spores* (an inactive stage of the bacteria).

Federal spending
United States budget for fiscal 2001*

	Billions of dollars
National defense	304.5
International affairs	16.5
General science, space, technology	20.7
Energy	–0.7
Natural resources and environment	23.7
Agriculture	28.3
Commerce and housing credit	5.8
Transportation	53.9
Community and regional development	12.8
Education, training, employment, and social services	62.9
Health	171.9
Social security	433.0
Medicare	217.4
Income security	263.3
Veterans' benefits and services	45.0
Administration of justice	29.8
General government	15.1
Interest	206.1
Undistributed offsetting receipts	–47.0
Total budget outlays	**1,863.0**

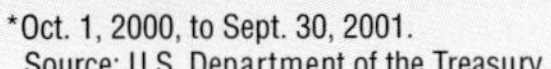
*Oct. 1, 2000, to Sept. 30, 2001.
Source: U.S. Department of the Treasury.

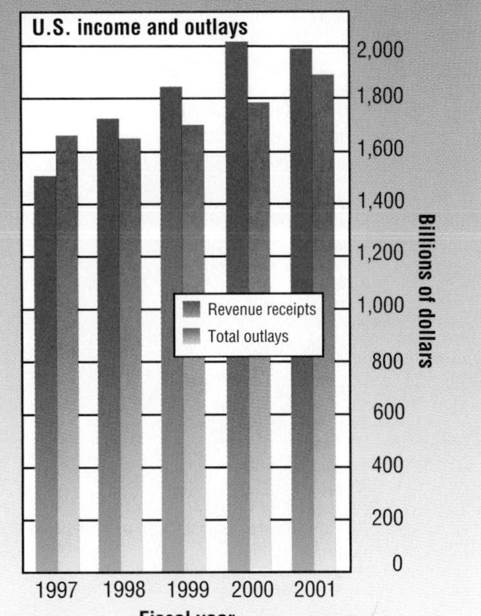

Source: U.S. Department of the Treasury.

Selected agencies and bureaus of the U.S. government*

Executive Office of the President
President, George W. Bush
Vice President, Richard B. Cheney
White House Chief of Staff, Andrew H Card, Jr.
Presidential Press Secretary, L. Ari Fleischer
Assistant to the President for Domestic Policy, Margaret La Montagne
Assistant to the President for Homeland Security, Tom Ridge
Assistant to the President for National Security Affairs, Condoleezza Rice
Assistant to the President for Science and Technology, John H. Marburger III
Council of Economic Advisers—R. Glenn Hubbard, Chair
Office of Management and Budget—Mitchell E. Daniels, Jr., Director
Office of National Drug Control Policy—John P. Walters, Director
U.S. Trade Representative, Robert B. Zoellick

Department of Agriculture
Secretary of Agriculture, Ann M. Veneman

Department of Commerce
Secretary of Commerce, Donald L. Evans
Bureau of Economic Analysis—J. Steven Landefeld, Director
Bureau of the Census—William G. Barron, Jr., Acting Director

Department of Defense
Secretary of Defense, Donald H. Rumsfeld
Secretary of the Air Force, James G. Roche
Secretary of the Army, Thomas E. White
Secretary of the Navy, Gordon R. England
Joint Chiefs of Staff—
General RIchard B. Myers, Chairman
General John P. Jumper, Chief of Staff, Air Force
General Eric K. Shinseki, Chief of Staff, Army
Admiral Vern Clark, Chief of Naval Operations
General James L. Jones, Jr., Commandant, Marine Corps

Department of Education
Secretary of Education, Roderick R. Paige

Department of Energy
Secretary of Energy, Spencer Abraham

Department of Health and Human Services
Secretary of Health and Human Services, Tommy G.Thompson
Office of Public Health and Science—Assistant Secretary†
Centers for Disease Control and Prevention—Jeffrey P. Koplan, Director
Food and Drug Administration—Commissioner†
National Institutes of Health—Ruth L. Kirschstein, Acting Director
Surgeon General of the United States, David Satcher

Department of Housing and Urban Development
Secretary of Housing and Urban Development, Mel Martinez

Department of the Interior
Secretary of the Interior, Gale A. Norton

Department of Justice
Attorney General, John Ashcroft
Bureau of Prisons—Kathleen Hawk Sawyer, Director
Drug Enforcement Administration—Asa Hutchinson, Administrator
Federal Bureau of Investigation—Robert S. Mueller III, Director
Immigration and Naturalization Service—James W. Ziglar, Commissioner
Solicitor General, Theodore B. Olson

Department of Labor
Secretary of Labor, Elaine L. Chao

Department of State
Secretary of State, Colin L. Powell
U.S. Ambassador to the United Nations, John D. Negroponte

Department of Transportation
Secretary of Transportation, Norman Y. Mineta
Federal Aviation Administration—Jane F. Garvey, Administrator
U.S. Coast Guard—Admiral James M. Loy, Commandant

Department of the Treasury
Secretary of the Treasury, Paul H. O'Neill
Internal Revenue Service—Charles O. Rossotti, Commissioner
Treasurer of the United States, Rasario Marin
U.S. Secret Service—Brian L. Stafford, Director
Office of Thrift Supervision—James E. Gilleran, Director

Department of Veterans Affairs
Acting Secretary of Veterans Affairs, Anthony J. Principi

Supreme Court of the United States
Chief Justice of the United States, William H. Rehnquist
Associate Justices—
John Paul Stevens
Sandra Day O'Connor
Antonin Scalia
Anthony M. Kennedy
David H. Souter
Clarence Thomas
Ruth Bader Ginsburg
Stephen G. Breyer

Congressional officials
President of the Senate pro tempore, Robert C. Byrd
Senate Majority Leader, Tom Daschle
Senate Minority Leader, Trent Lott
Speaker of the House, J. Dennis Hastert
House Majority Leader, Richard K. Armey
House Minority Leader, Richard A. Gephardt
Congressional Budget Office—Dan L. Crippen, Director
General Accounting Office—David M. Walker, Comptroller General of the United States
Library of Congress—James H. Billington, Librarian of Congress

Independent agencies
Central Intelligence Agency—George J. Tenet, Director
Commission on Civil Rights—Mary Frances Berry, Chairperson
Commission of Fine Arts—J. Carter Brown, Chairman
Consumer Product Safety Commission—Ann Winkelman Brown, Chairman
Corporation for National and Community Service—Leslie Lenkowsky, Chief Executive Officer
Environmental Protection Agency—Christine Todd Whitman, Administrator
Equal Employment Opportunity Commission—Cari M. Dominguez, Chair
Federal Communications Commission—Michael K. Powell, Chairman
Federal Deposit Insurance Corporation—Donald E. Powell, Chairman
Federal Election Commission—Danny Lee McDonald, Chairman
Federal Emergency Management Agency—Joe M. Allbaugh, Director
Federal Reserve System Board of Governors—Alan Greenspan, Chairman
Federal Trade Commission—Timothy J. Muris, Chairman
General Services Administration—Stephen A. Perry, Administrator
National Aeronautics and Space Administration—Administrator†
National Endowment for the Arts—Robert S. Martin, Chairman
National Endowment for the Humanities—Bruce Cole, Chairman
National Labor Relations Board—Peter J. Hurtgen, Chairman
National Railroad Passenger Corporation (Amtrak)—George D. Warrington, President & CEO
National Science Foundation—Rita R. Colwell, Director
National Transportation Safety Board—Carol Jones Carmody, Acting Chairperson
Nuclear Regulatory Commission—Richard A. Meserve, Chairman
Peace Corps—Charles R. Baouet III, Acting Director
Securities and Exchange Commission—Harvey Lloyd Pitt, Chairman
Selective Service System—Alfred V. Rascon
Small Business Administration—Hector V. Barreto, Jr., Administrator
Smithsonian Institution—Lawrence M. Small, Secretary
Social Security Administration—Jo Anne Barnhart, Commissioner
U.S. Postal Service—John E. Potter, Postmaster General

*As of Dec. 31, 2001. †Position vacant as of Dec. 31, 2001.

On October 22, federal health officials announced that two U.S. postal employees at the central mail processing center in Washington, D.C., had died of inhalation anthrax. The officials believed the two victims had been exposed when an anthrax-laden letter addressed to Senator Tom Daschle (D., South Dakota), the Senate majority leader, was processed in the main post office. Two additional postal employees were hospitalized after they were found to have inhaled anthrax spores. Traces of anthrax also were discovered at a U.S. Post Office sorting center near Capitol Hill and in the U.S. Senate and House mailrooms. FBI officials discovered a letter with anthrax spores addressed to Senator Patrick J. Leahy (D., Vermont) on November 16. The CDC issued guidelines in October on what people should do if they receive a suspicious-looking letter or package. The CDC, as well as the U.S. Postal Service, reported that people should be wary of envelopes and packages without a return address, containing excessive postage, that were discolored, or bound with an unusual amount of tape.

By the end of 2001, investigators had not uncovered who sent the anthrax-laden letters but concluded that the strain was the same form that had been produced in U.S. government laboratories and labs under contract to the government.

Legislation. Congress in May passed legislation cutting income taxes by $1.35 trillion over the next 10 years. In addition, most individual tax payers received a rebate of up to $300. The legislation also lowered the average income tax rate by 3 percent by 2006 and eliminated the federal tax on estates by 2010.

Federal budget. President Bush unveiled his first federal budget on April 9, 2001. The president proposed a $1.96-trillion budget for fiscal year 2002, which began Oct. 1, 2001. The budget was $104 billion larger than in fiscal year 2001. It outlined increased spending for education and defense and cuts in transportation and agriculture. Congress, preoccupied with emergency measures after the terrorist attacks on September 11, failed to pass any of the required 13 spending bills in 2001 prior to the beginning of fiscal year 2002.

In October 2001, economists warned that the cost of the government's response to the terrorist attacks could eliminate the estimated $52 billion surplus predicted for the end of fiscal year 2002.

☐ Geoffrey Campbell

See also **Afghanistan; Armed forces; Cabinet, U.S.; Congress of the United States; Democratic Party; Health care issues; Middle East; People in the news** (Ridge, Tom; Rumsfeld, Donald); **Public health; Republican Party; State government; Terrorism; Terrorism: A Special Feature,** p. 38; **United States, President of the.**

A United States Air Force special operations soldier stands guard near a helicopter in Khwaja Bahuaddin, Afghanistan, in November. U.S. armed forces and anti-Taliban forces in Afghanistan drove the ruling Taliban from power by the end of 2001.

The Changing Profile of America: The 2000 Census

U.S. Census Bureau data reveals a nation that is very different from the United States of 100 years before.

By Geoffrey A. Campbell

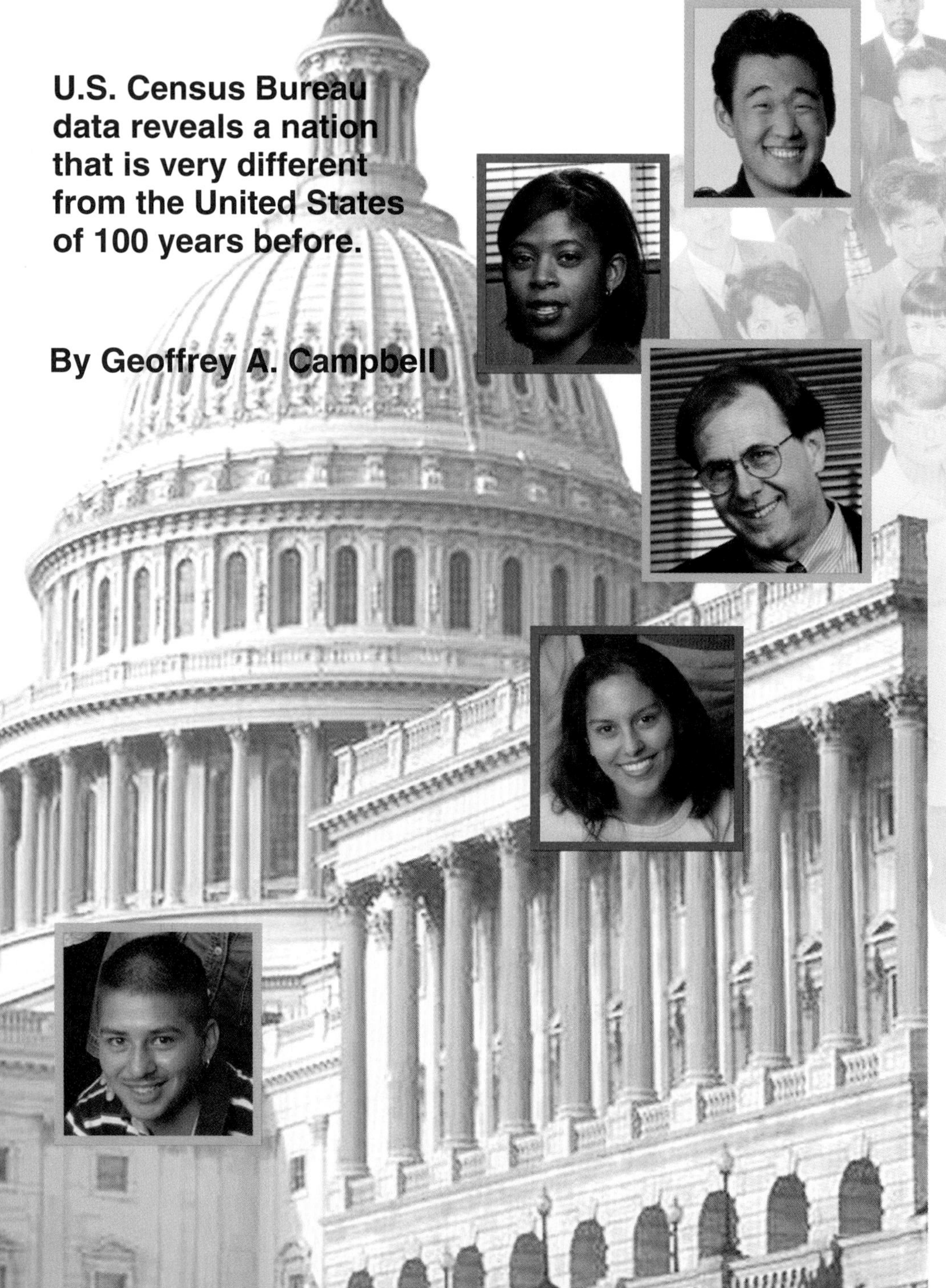

The United States has long prided itself upon being a "melting pot," a land in which people of various backgrounds, nationalities, and ethnicities have molded themselves into a united people. For much of the nation's history, the mix largely involved people from Europe along with Africans and Native Americans. The 2000 census, however, cast a spotlight on an America that was increasingly diverse, with people from many more cultures, nationalities, and ethnicities. The face of America has undergone radical change. The census, which is taken every 10 years, not only allows us to trace shifts in the U.S. population but also reveals other factors that contribute to the changing face of America.

The Founding Fathers of the United States, knowing that government officials would need up-to-date information about the population, wrote a clause into the U.S. Constitution mandating that the government establish a federal census to count the population every 10 years. The original intention was to determine the amount of taxation and congressional representation of each of the states. Population was to determine the number of representatives each state could send to the U.S. House of Representatives. As the population grew, representatives to Congress were to be *reapportioned* (fairly distributed) among all the states.

More than 200 years since the first official counting of the U.S. population, the census has come to serve an equally important purpose—documenting the changing face of the nation. Like a motion picture made up of tens of thousands of still pictures, the census provides social historians and policymakers with a highly detailed picture of the composition of the U.S. population.

Representing the nation

The U.S. government conducted the first *decennial* (every 10 years) census in 1790. In 1790, the House of Representatives had 106 representatives. By 1900, the House had increased in size to 391 members. Most members represented states on the East Coast and in the Midwest. Between 1900 and 2000, the House grew to 435 members, and regional representation changed dramatically. There was a major shift in the population from east to west and from north to south in just 100 years. In 1900, California had only 8 representatives. In 2000, it had 53 representatives, the largest total of any of the 50 states. Between 1900 and 2000, representation in the House from Utah and Washington state tripled. A decline in the relative populations of such Eastern States as New York and Pennsylvania resulted in a loss of House seats. Between 1900 and 2000, the number of representatives from New York state dropped from 37 to 31. The number from Pennsylvania declined from 32 to 21. The number of Texas's representatives, meanwhile, doubled from 16 in 1900 to 32 in 2000. The number of representatives from Florida grew from 3 to 25 during the same period.

The nation grows and changes

In 1790, the United States was a sparsely populated, rural nation. The official population of the United States was approximately 3.9 million people, slightly more than 50 percent of whom were white. Approximately 19 percent of the population was black, the majority of whom were slaves. It was an overwhelmingly agricultural land, with 95 percent of the population living on farms or in rural communities. Fewer than 30,000 people lived in the nation's largest city, Philadelphia. Fewer than 50,000 people lived in the cities that would later make up the five boroughs of New York City. Only two other U.S. cities—Boston and Baltimore—boasted more than 10,000 people in 1790.

The United States changed dramatically throughout the 1800's. By 1900, the U.S. population had grown to about 75.9 million people. Men then outnumbered women by about 38.8 million men to 37.1 million women. The median age of the population—the age at which half of the population is older and half of the population is younger—stood at 22.9 years. Whites comprised 87 percent of the population; blacks, 12 percent; and Native Americans, Asians, and Hispanics, less than 1 percent.

The 1900's bring great change

The United States in 1900 was still predominantly rural. Sixty percent of all U.S. residents lived on farms or in rural communities (defined by the Census Bureau as having fewer than 2,500 people). However, the seeds of change had already been planted, and throughout the 20th century, the United States became increasingly urbanized as Americans found employment outside of farms. In 1900, the U.S. work force consisted of 29 million people, about 40 percent of whom worked in agriculture. Twenty percent were employed in manufacturing; and 11 percent in the service industry, which ranged from highly skilled professions, such as doctors and lawyers, to housekeepers, janitors, and repair persons. In 1900, women made up only 18 percent of the work force, and 20 percent of all working women were employed in agriculture. More than 60 percent of working women in 1900 labored in manual and service jobs, including employment as household servants.

The U.S. population grew steadily throughout the 1900's, reaching 281,421,906 by 2000. A number of factors combined to account for the increase. Improvements in health care, for example, lengthened lives. In 1900, there were about 8 million people between the ages of 45 and 64 and only some 2 million people aged 65 and older. By 2000, there were 60 million people between the ages of 45 and 64 and 34 million aged 65 and older.

The *baby boom generation* (the large group of people born in the United States from 1946 to 1964) provided a major source of population increase. The increase was related to the fact that during World War II (1939-1945) and for two decades after, Americans married earlier than in previous generations. In 1940, 27.4 percent of all American males between 20 and 24 years old were married. By 1960, this number had jumped to 45.8 percent. For women, the increase was equally dramatic. In 1940, 51.3 percent

The author:
Geoffrey A. Campbell is a free-lance writer.

Shifts in Congressional representation

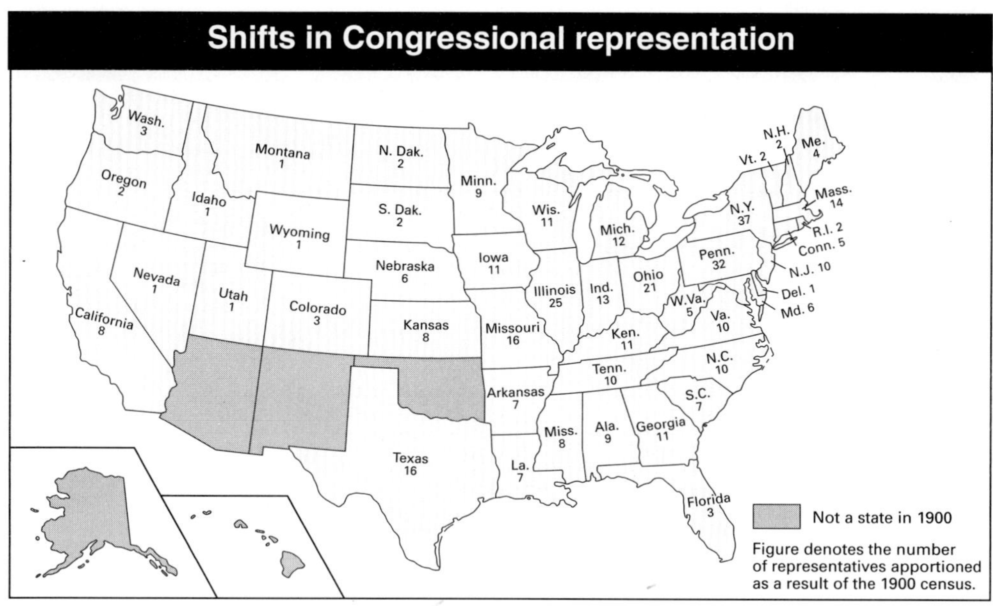

Figure denotes the number of representatives apportioned as a result of the 1900 census.

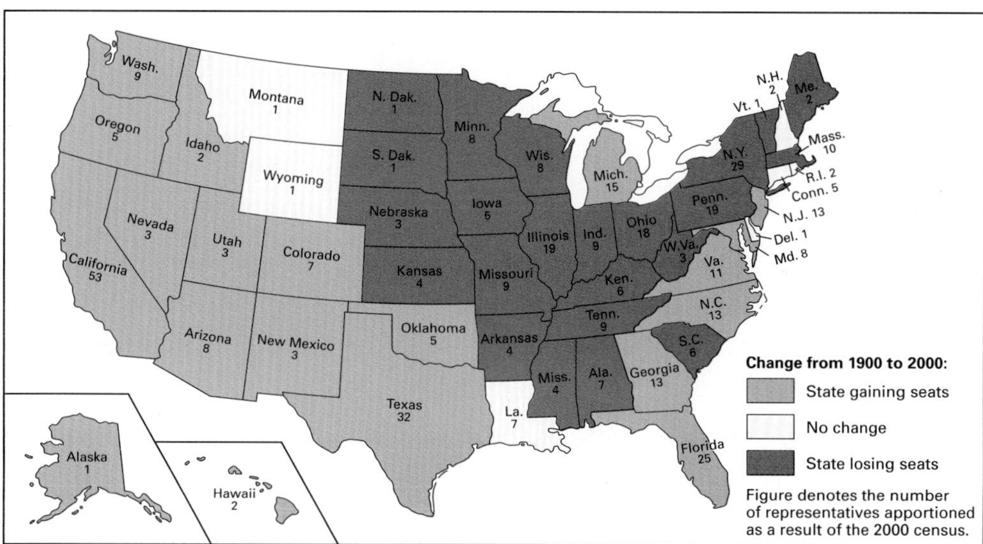

Figure denotes the number of representatives apportioned as a result of the 2000 census.

Throughout the 20th century, a shift in population from north to south and from east to west drastically changed the representation of the states in the the U.S. House of Representatives.

of women aged 20 to 24 were married; by 1960, 69.5 percent were married. *Demographers* (population experts) believe that this trend toward earlier marriages resulted in the baby boom, a wave that continues to have ripple effects through the nation's population.

The role of immigration

Immigration also played a major part in the nation's growing population. Early in the 20th century, the nation's ranks were swelled with immigrants, most of whom had come from Europe. By 1900, 13.6 percent of the nation's total population—

Who We Are

The changing profile of Americans

	1900	2000
Total population	75,994,575	281,421,906
Male	38,816,448	138,053,563
Female	37,178,127	143,368,343
Median age	22.9 years	35.3 years
Births per woman	4	2
Infant mortality*	165	7
Average life expectancy (men)	46 years	74 years
Average life expectancy (women)	48 years	79 years
High school graduates	6 percent	83 percent
College graduates	3 percent	25 percent
Total families	16.1 million	71.7 million
Married couple families	80 percent	52 percent
Average family size	4.7 people	3.14 people
Living alone	1 percent	26 percent
Average individual annual income	$8,360†	$40,816
Divorced men (not remarried)	1.1 percent	35 percent **
Divorced women (not remarried)	1.4 percent	25 percent **

* Deaths in the first year of life, per 1,000 births.
† Adjusted for inflation.
** Data is from 1998.

Source: U.S. Census Bureau.

10.3 million people—were foreign born. In 1900 alone, more than 114,000 people came to the United States from Austria-Hungary (which included parts of Austria, Hungary, Czechoslovakia, Poland, and Romania); 100,000 people came from Italy; and 90,000 people from Russia and the Baltic States.

Much smaller numbers of Asians entered the country over the same period due to restrictions in immigration. In the 1850's, Chinese men began arriving to take part in the California gold rush and help build the railways that linked the West with other regions of the country. In 1882, however, Congress passed the Chinese Exclusion Act, which severely limited further Chinese immigration. At roughly the same time, waves of Japanese men began to arrive in the United States, primarily to work in agriculture. However, in the early 1900's, both the United States and Japan restricted Japanese immigration, and the small Asian population in the United States became relatively stable.

From the 1920's to the 1970's, the growth of the foreign-born population slowed. In 1921, Congress set a ceiling on the number of Eastern Europeans allowed to enter the United States. The economic calamity of the *Great Depression* (a worldwide business slump of the 1930's) slowed immigration further, as did the outbreak of World War II. When the flow of immigrants to the United States resumed, the racial and ethnic makeup of the population began to change. In 1965, Congress reformed immigration laws, opening the nation's doors to immigrants from non-European nations. Soon after, the number of Asian and Latin American immigrants increased as the number of European immigrants shrank. In 1920, there were fewer than 500,000 immigrants from Mexico, ranking Mexico 10th as a source of immigrants. In 1990, there were more than 4.2 million Mexican immigrants, making Mexico the number-one source of immigrants to the United States.

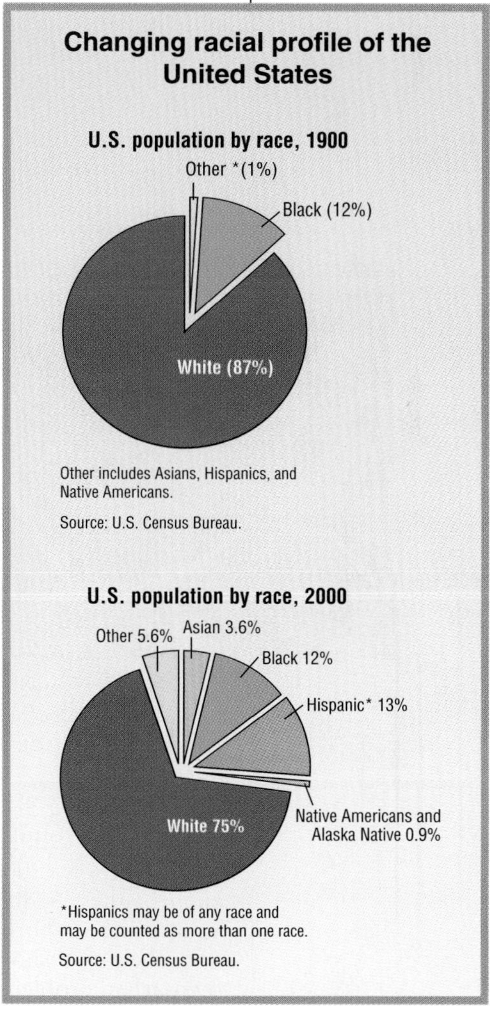

Shifts in immigration

Beginning in the 1970's, Asian immigration also increased. Between 1970 and 1990, nearly 1 million Chinese immigrants arrived in the United States along with another 1 million people from South Korea, Vietnam, and the Philippines. Like the earlier immigrants, many of the newcomers were attracted to the United States by greater economic possibilities and by the desire for greater political freedom. By 2000, Asians accounted for nearly 45 percent of all legal immigration in the United States.

The new influx of immigrants led to another surge in the percentage of the nation's foreign-born population. The 1970 census showed that the foreign-born population was 4.7 percent of the total U.S. population—approximately 9.6 million people. Later censuses revealed that, the U.S. foreign-born population climbed to 14.1 million in 1980 and 19.8 million in 1990. By 2000, the foreign-born population was 10.4 percent of the total U.S. population—28.4 million people—a slightly lesser percentage than in 1900.

The move toward an urban society

As the U.S. population increased in size, it continued to shift from rural to urban. In 1920, a little less than half of the U.S. population still lived in rural areas. Even in 1930, the urban population accounted for only 56.2 percent of the total. But the urbanization of the nation began in earnest after World War II and by 2000, the Census Bureau estimated that 80 percent of Americans lived in urban areas.

The migration from farms and small towns to cities and ultimately from cities to the suburbs changed the American landscape. Between 1900 and 2000, New York City more than doubled in size, from 3.4 million people to 8 million people. The population of Los Angeles grew from approximately 102,000 people in 1900 to 3.6 million in 2000. In Chicago, the population increased from 1.6 million people to 2.8 million.

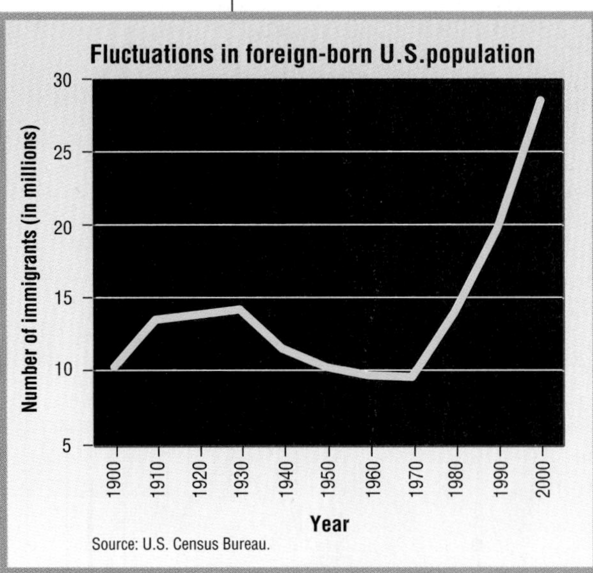

Source: U.S. Census Bureau.

Migration from rural areas had a drawing effect on small communities. Towns grew smaller; their industry and commerce dried up; and the population of many small communities aged as younger residents left to pursue the greater economic opportunities of urban America. Rural areas shrank as suburbs sprawled. In 1900, only 6 percent of the U.S. population lived in a suburb. By 2000, fully 50 percent of all Americans were suburbanites. As increasing numbers of Americans move to the suburbs, the suburbs themselves become increasingly urbanized, with their own shopping and dining establishments and their own urban problems, such as traffic and higher crime rates.

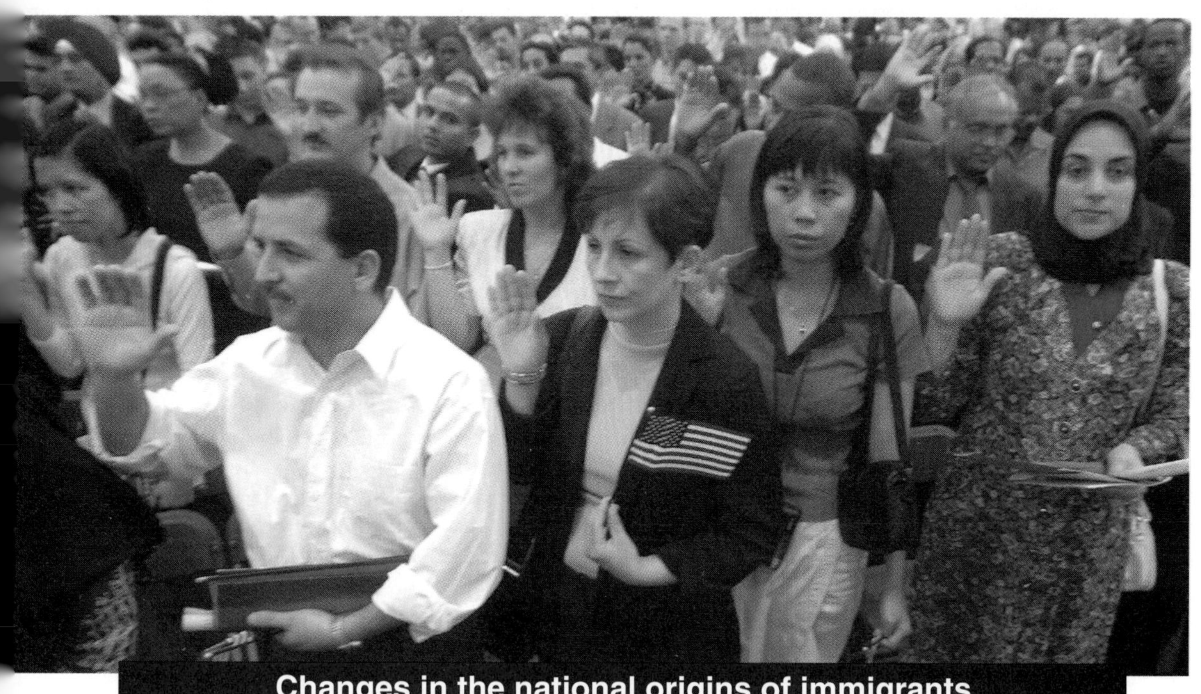

Changes in the national origins of immigrants

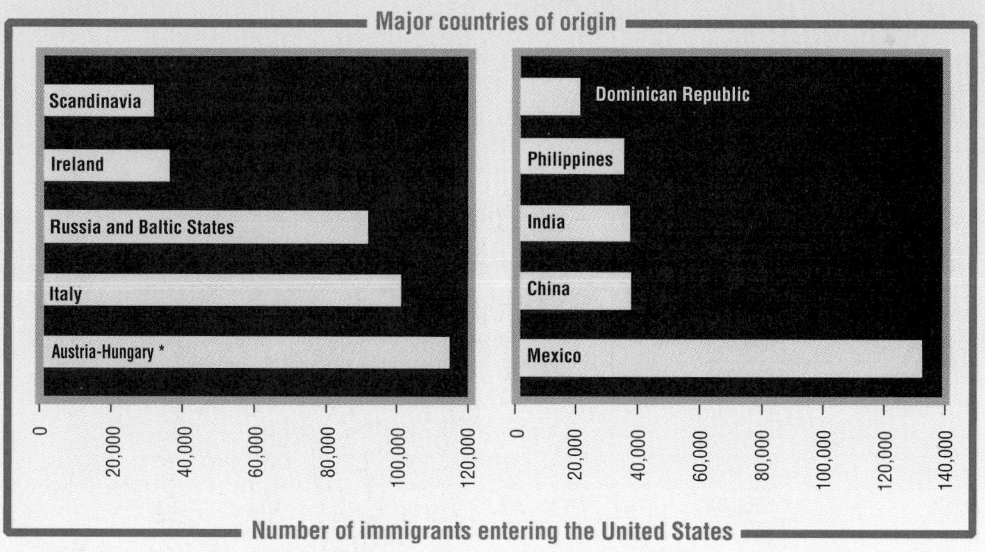

*Austria-Hungary included portions of what in 2000 were Austria, Hungary, Czech Republic, Slovakia, Poland, and Romania.

*Most recent data available.

Sources: U.S. Census Bureau; U.S. Immigration and Naturalization Services.

Where We Live

Population of the 20 largest U.S. cities in 1900

New York City	3,437,202
Chicago	1,698,575
Philadelphia	1,293,697
St. Louis	575,238
Boston	560,892
Baltimore	508,957
Cleveland	381,768
Buffalo	352,387
San Francisco	342,782
Cincinnati	325,902
Pittsburgh	321,616
New Orleans	287,104
Detroit	285,704
Milwaukee	285,315
Washington, D.C.	278,718
Newark	246,070
Jersey City	206,433
Louisville	204,731
Minneapolis	202,718
Providence	175,597

Population of the 20 largest U.S. cities in 2000

New York City	8,008,278
Los Angeles	3,694,820
Chicago	2,896,016
Houston	1,953,631
Philadelphia	1,517,550
Phoenix	1,321,045
San Diego	1,223,400
Dallas	1,188,580
San Antonio	1,144,646
Detroit	951,270
San Jose	894,943
Indianapolis	791,926
San Francisco	776,733
Jacksonville, Florida	735,617
Columbus	711,470
Austin	656,562
Baltimore	651,154
Memphis	650,100
Milwaukee	596,974
Boston	589,141

Source: U.S. Census Bureau.

To some extent, the nation's urbanization was inevitable. Technological advances made it possible for farmers to cultivate more land with fewer people at the same time that industrial might increased. Industry inevitably developed in urban areas where workers were readily available, and the allure of jobs in manufacturing drew more people into U.S. cities. In 1900, more than 80 percent of all nonfarm workers in the United States were employed as blue-collar workers in such physical labor jobs as steelmaking, auto building, and construction.

The shift toward a service economy

Urban areas also served as a beacon for more skilled workers. Eventually, the growth in the number of blue-collar jobs slowed in relation to the growth of white-collar, professional jobs. The number of people in white-collar jobs increased by 33 percent between 1950 and 1960, while the number of blue-collar jobs increased by just 15 percent.

In 2000, there were approximately 140.8 million people in the U.S. work force; 54 percent were men; 46 percent were women. According to U.S. Bureau of Labor Statistics, only 2 percent of

the total were employed in agriculture; 13 percent worked in manufacturing; and 34 percent were employed in the service industry, which had expanded to include such jobs as computer analysts and data processing services.

More than 8 million people were employed in management, more than 4 million people in business and finance, and 22.5 million people in office and administrative support. More than 7 million additional workers were employed in the teaching profession, with another 9 million in health care and health care support.

A nation grows older

Birth rates and the shift from a rural to urban society, along with dramatically improved health care, resulted in changes in the median age of the population. In 1820, a period in which the United States was both overwhelmingly rural and agricultural, the median age of the population was 16.7 years. The relatively low age indicated a high fertility rate. Couples had more children, spurred by demands for labor on the family farm.

The median age increased steadily through much of the 20th century. According to the 1900 census, the median age of the total population of more than 75 million people was 22.9 years. By the late 20th centu-

Where We Work

Changing profile of the work force

	1900	2000
Total work force	29 million	140.8 million
Male workers	82 percent	54 percent
Female workers	18 percent	46 percent
Average work week	59 hours	34.5 hours
Average hourly wage	$3.80*	$13.75

A shift in jobs

	1900	2000
Total number of jobs	29 million	140.8 million
Agricultural	40 percent	2 percent †
Construction	5 percent	5 percent
Manufacturing	20 percent	13 percent
Mining	2 percent	0.38 percent
Service **	11 percent	34 percent
Transportation	7 percent	5 percent

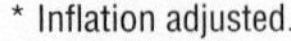

* Inflation adjusted.
† 1999 figures.
** Service industry includes repair services, entertainment, medical and legal professions, and computer and data processing services.

Sources: U.S. Bureau of Labor Statistics; U.S. Census Bureau.

ry, baby boomers began aging, pushing the median age up. In 2000, the median age of the U.S. population hit 35.3 years, the highest in U.S. history.

The new look of the nation

The nation's ethnic mix provided the greatest statistical difference between 1900 and 2000. The 2000 census offered citizens, for the first time, the opportunity to select more than one ethnic group from six racial categories. This option created a possible 63 choices. Nearly 7 million U.S. citizens—approximately 2.4 percent of population—identified themselves as belonging to more than one race on their 2000 census forms. The Census Bureau reported that 93 percent of the citizens who identified themselves as multiracial chose two races. Approximately 11 percent of multiracial Americans indicated that they were white and black; 13 percent indicated they were white and Asian; 16 percent indicated they were white and American Indian or Alaska Native; and 32 percent indicated they were white and some other race.

Of Americans indicating that they were of one race only, about 75 percent indicated they were white; 12 percent indicated they were black; and 13 percent indicated they were Hispanic—a historic shift in the population of the nation. Although the nation's population in 2000 was still predominantly white, the census revealed that Hispanic Americans, for the first time, had surpassed African Americans as the nation's largest minority. Approximately 3.5 percent of U.S. citizens indicated they were of Asian descent, a category that includes Asian Indians, Chinese, Filipinos, Japanese, Koreans, and Vietnamese.

The nation's scrapbook

Some historians have described the U.S. census as the nation's scrapbook or diary, offering a window on the nation at regular points in history. Although the data it provides are used in large measure to serve the needs of government and to make decisions about how money is spent and where it is spent, the 10-year census provides much more than mere numbers. The census demonstrates the nation's growth and increasingly diverse composition, revealing the changing nature of society, while at the same time offering a glimpse into how variables such as war and economic downturns affect the nation's growth. The United States in the early 2000's was remarkably different from the United States of the early 1900's. Just as the nation changed in the past 100 years, it is a certainty that even more changes can be expected when the Census Bureau undertakes its next count in 2010. ■■■

United States, President of the. President George W. Bush, who was sworn into office on Jan. 20, 2001, devoted the first months of his presidency to a new energy policy, tax cuts, and the creation of a missile defense system. His aims changed drastically after terrorists attacked the United States on September 11.

President Bush began promoting a new national energy policy in May. Pointing to the nation's dependency on foreign oil, he asked Congress for legislation that would provide U.S. companies with incentives to explore for new domestic sources of oil and gas.

The president signed legislation on June 7 that cut income taxes by $1.35 trillion by 2010. The tax cut was the largest since 1981.

In December 2001, President Bush announced that the United States would nullify the Antiballistic Missile (ABM) Treaty. The treaty, created in 1972 as a deterrent to nuclear war, restrained deployment of the types of missile systems that the U.S. military planned for the defense system.

Terrorist attacks. The focus of the Bush administration changed direction on Sept. 11, 2001, when terrorists attacked the World Trade Center in New York City and the Pentagon Building outside Washington, D.C. President Bush was in Sarasota, Florida, when he learned of the attacks. To ensure his safety, the Secret Service flew the president to a military base in Louisiana and then to the U.S. Strategic Command Center in Nebraska. When the president returned to the White House on the night of September 11, he urged the public to resume some sense of normalcy.

President Bush vowed to conduct a successful war on terrorism on September 20 during an address to a joint session of Congress. The president and members of his Cabinet met with a number of world leaders, building a coalition of allies. A series of meetings between President Bush and Russian President Vladimir Putin led to unprecedented Russian support of the U.S.-led war on terrorism.

Afghanistan action. On October 7, President Bush announced that the United States and the United Kingdom had launched airstrikes against the Taliban regime in Afghanistan, which refused to surrender Osama bin Laden, an exiled Saudi-born millionaire whom U.S. intelligence officials considered the main suspect behind the attacks on September 11. Officials with the U.S. Department of Defense announced the total defeat of the Taliban on December 10. Bin Laden's whereabouts remained unknown at the end of 2001.

☐ Geoffrey A. Campbell

See also **Afghanistan; Armed forces; Cabinet, U.S.; Congress of the United States; Middle East; Taxation; Terrorism: A Special Feature,** p. 38; **Transportation; United States, Government of the.**

Uzbekistan. The terrorist attacks on the United States on Sept. 11, 2001, changed Uzbekistan's relations with other nations, particularly with the United States. President Islam Karimov quickly offered his support to the U.S.-led war on terrorism in Afghanistan, primarily because Uzbekistan had its own troubles with an Islamic fundamentalist movement—the Islamic Movement of Uzbekistan (IMU). Karimov believed the IMU received support and training from the Taliban regime in Afghanistan and from Osama bin Laden. United States intelligence officers identified bin Laden as the leader of al-Qaida, a network of terrorists that was responsible for the terrorist attacks on September 11.

The first U.S. air and ground forces arrived in Uzbekistan in early October and were housed in former Soviet military bases. In return for the use of the base, the United States promised to increase investments in Uzbekistan and provide military assistance if Uzbekistan was attacked by IMU guerrillas.

U.S. Secretary of State Colin Powell visited Uzbekistan in December to cement the new relationship. He urged Karimov to speed up shipments of humanitarian supplies to Afghanistan.

☐ Steven L. Solnick

See also **Afghanistan; Russia; Terrorism; Terrorism: A Special Feature,** p. 38.

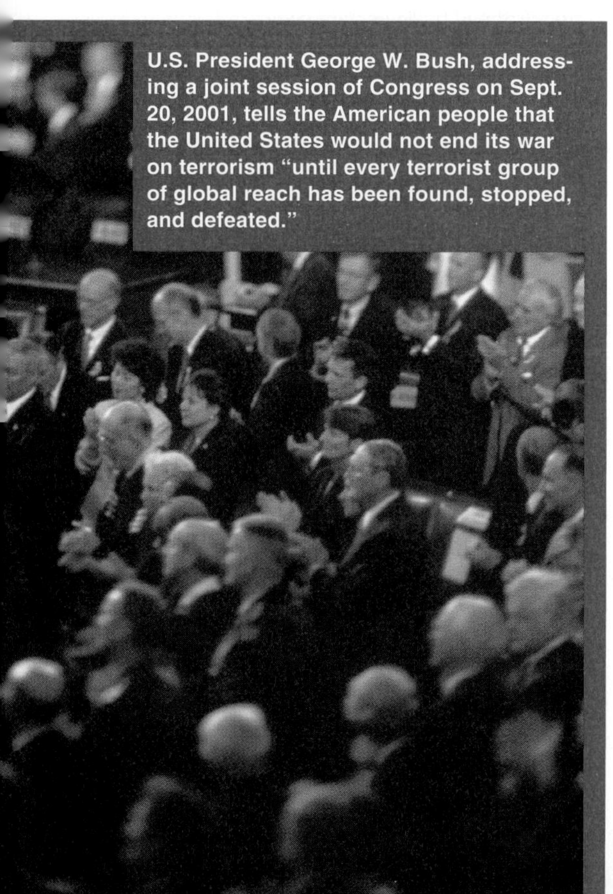

U.S. President George W. Bush, addressing a joint session of Congress on Sept. 20, 2001, tells the American people that the United States would not end its war on terrorism "until every terrorist group of global reach has been found, stopped, and defeated."

Venezuela. President Hugo Chavez Frias faced mounting opposition in 2001 as he sought to impose his populist, leftist agenda on Venezuela. During the year, teachers, oil workers, trade unionists, journalists, military officers, and business and cultural leaders all expressed fears over the increasingly repressive nature of Chavez's regime.

Work stoppage. The members of Venezuela's largest trade union joined businesses in a rare show of unity by supporting a day-long strike on December 10 to protest policies of Chavez. The strikers claimed that proposed new economic laws, particularly those affecting the oil and agrarian sectors, would scare away foreign investors, harm the economy, and threaten jobs.

Education plan. Thousands of teachers and parents marched in the capital, Caracas, in January to protest the National Education Project, Chavez's plan to expand government control of public education. Critics of the education project claimed that it was designed to promote Chavez's leftist ideology and reduce the influence of families and religious organizations over children. Civic groups were especially alarmed by a decree that allowed the ministry of education to fire principals and teachers who had received unfavorable reports from government-appointed supervisors. In February, Chavez led a large march of supporters of his plan in Caracas.

Military unrest. In February, Chavez appointed Jose Vicente Rangel, a left-wing journalist and former foreign affairs minister, as minister of defense. Many military leaders did not approve of the appointment of Rangel, the first civilian to head the armed forces since the 1920's. Rangel ordered the armed forces to perform activities that were previously the responsibilities of civilian agencies, including food distribution and the construction of clinics and schools.

National ID card. In January 2001, Chavez's administration awarded a $228-million contract to a group of businesses led by the Hyundai Corporation of South Korea to develop national electronic identification cards by 2003. The cards would enable government authorities to monitor the movements of all Venezuelans and transitory workers in the country. Many Venezuelans feared the government might use the identification system to violate their civil liberties.

Cultural revolution. Chavez fired several directors of Venezuelan artistic institutions in January 2001, including Sofia Imber, the widely admired 76-year-old head of the Caracas Museum of Contemporary Art. Chavez said he had fired the "elitist" directors as part of a populist "cultural revolution."

☐ Nathan A. Haverstock

See also **Latin America.**

Vermont. See **State government.**

Vietnam. Nong Duc Manh became secretary-general of the ruling Communist Party, Vietnam's most powerful position, on April 22, 2001. Manh, a Soviet-educated forester of the ethnic Tay minority, was Vietnam's first Communist leader who had not fought in Vietnam's wars with France and the United States between 1950 and 1975.

Manh became secretary-general with a reputation as a reformer, which he had earned as chairman of the National Assembly between 1992 and 2001. Many Communist Party members had considered Manh's predecessor, Le Kha Phieu, a hindrance to modernization because he had rejected economic reforms that his colleagues encouraged.

On January 29, riots broke out in Pleiku, capital of Gai Lai province, which later spread through two highland provinces. Observers in the Central Highlands attributed the unrest to land grievances by ethnic minorities angry over the land seizure by the ethnic Vietnamese majority. Residents also cited religious persecution as a possible cause for the protests. Many ethnic minorities in the highlands reportedly had converted to Protestantism.

Nguyen Van Thieu, leader of South Vietnam from 1965 to 1975, died on Sept. 29, 2001, in exile in the United States. Thieu had led South Vietnam during its unsuccessful war to avoid takeover by the Communist north. ☐ Henry S. Bradsher

See also **Asia.**

Washington, D.C., became a target of a terrorist attack on the United States on Sept. 11, 2001, when hijackers crashed a commercial jetliner into the Pentagon Building, the headquarters of the U.S. Department of Defense, which is located just outside the District in Arlington, Virginia. The attack killed 64 people on the plane and 125 in the building. The District came under attack again on October 15 when a letter containing anthrax *spores* (an inactive stage of the bacteria) was discovered in the Capitol Hill offices of Senator Majority Leader Tom Daschle (D., South Dakota). On November 16, a similar anthrax-laden letter was found in the offices of Senator Patrick Leahy (D., Vermont).

Preparedness. District officials and other observers agreed that Washington was unprepared for the attack on the Pentagon. The police, other city agencies, and the federal government acted without consulting one another. The city did not activate its emergency broadcast system, which would have provided official information to combat the rumors that swept the city. Shortly after the attack, government officials sent all 260,000 federal employees in the District home at one time, hopelessly snarling traffic.

A mayoral task force report on the city's performance on September 11, released in October, recommended the creation of a master emergency evacuation transportation plan to coordinate crisis responses by federal, city, and suburban agencies.

Economic news. Before September 11, Washington's economy had been improving. On March 2, Mayor Anthony Williams in his second "State of the District" address, contended that the District's economy was stronger than it had been in decades. He pointed to a $464-million budget surplus, upgraded *bond ratings* (eligibility to borrow money), and an increase in private investment in both downtown areas and city neighborhoods.

On October 1, the D.C. Financial Responsibility and Management Assistance Authority, commonly known as the control board, returned full governing powers to the mayor and city officials. In 1995, the U.S. Congress gave the newly created board almost total control over the nearly bankrupt city's finances. Since then, the city had repaid its federal loans, posted four straight balanced budgets, and met other financial requirements set by the federal legislation that established the board.

In the wake of the September 11 assault and the anthrax attacks, tourism—the District's largest industry after government—almost came to a halt. Hotel occupancy rates plummeted. In October, the number of visitors to the museums and other facilities operated by the Smithsonian Institution dropped by 44 percent compared with attendance in October 2000. The decline in tourism led to widespread layoffs in hotels, restaurants, and other tourism-related businesses.

Although tourism rebounded somewhat toward year's end, District officials projected a $100-million to $200-million budget shortfall. Washington also faced the need to increase security in all public venues and upgrade emergency services. In November 2001, Williams asked Congress to approve a $1-billion economic stimulus package for the District. He said 25 percent of that amount was needed immediately for emergency preparedness. The rest was to be used to replace lost revenues and alleviate chronic funding shortages for schools, hospitals, and police.

Crime. In the first eight months of 2001, Washington's homicide rate fell to its lowest level since 1987, with overall crime down by 24 percent. However, crime increased dramatically after Sept. 11, 2001. City officials maintained that the crime jump was not linked to the diversion of police officers from city patrols to security details around public buildings. ☐ Robert Messenger

See also **City; New York City; Public health and safety; Terrorism: A Special Feature,** p. 38; **United States, Government of the.**

Washington. See **State government.**
Water. See **Environmental pollution.**

Weather. Winter's deep chill eased in the United States at the start of 2001, after the coldest November-December period on record in 2000. In Chicago, the temperature rose above freezing on Jan. 5, 2001, ending a streak of 19 days of sub-freezing temperatures.

In the western United States, 2001 began with warm and dry weather. The arid heat and gusty winds fueled a brush fire near San Diego that burned 10,000 acres (4,000 hectares) and forced 500 residents to flee their houses on January 3. By late January, a shift in the weather pattern brought needed rain to southern California. After one of the driest early winters on record, a Pacific storm dumped 7 inches (18 centimeters) of rain in parts of Los Angeles County. Another vigorous storm pounded southern California on February 13, bringing winds of 75 miles (121 kilometers) per hour and 3 to 7 inches (8 to 18 centimeters) of rain to metropolitan Los Angeles. Seven feet (2.1 meters) of snow fell in the mountains east of the city.

Dry winter. By contrast, winter was the second driest on record in the Northwest. Snow packs measured on April 1 in the Columbia River Basin were the lowest on record. In the Southeast, Florida experienced its third-driest winter on record. The lack of rain, after several years of below average rainfall, produced the worst drought in 100 years. The dry conditions led to brush fires, which in February forced state officials to close the interstate highway connecting Tampa and Orlando for 10 days. Fires in Florida consumed more than 250,000 acres (102,000 hectares) between January and May.

Several winter storms brought heavy snow to parts of the Midwest and Northeast. On February 5 and February 6, a storm dumped snow from eastern Pennsylvania to New England, with over 3 feet (91 centimeters) of snow measured in New Hampshire. Another powerful storm blanketed parts of the Northeast on March 5 and March 6. One to three feet (30 to 91 centimeters) of snow fell from upstate New York to interior New England, while winds gusted to 97 miles (156 kilometers) per hour atop the summit of Mount Washington in New Hampshire. In the Midwest, the winter was the snowiest on record at Huron, South Dakota, where 89.5 inches (227 centimeters) fell. The cold and snow contributed to a new state record for consecutive days with snow cover in Iowa—141 days by March 28.

Spring rains. Heavy rain fell to parts of the upper Midwest in April. Minneapolis experienced its wettest April on record when 7 inches (18 centimeters) of precipitation fell. The heavy rain and melting snow caused water levels along the upper Mississippi River and many of its tributaries to rise to record levels. In April, the Red River of the North in North Dakota reached its highest level since the devastating 1997 flood, while in Iowa, the Mississippi River crested just short of its all-time record of 22.6 feet (6.8 meters), set in the summer of 1993. High river levels briefly closed over 400 miles (644 kilometers) of the Mississippi River to boat and barge traffic.

Tropical Storm Allison. A cluster of clouds that emerged off the west coast of Africa in late May 2001 and blew west across the Atlantic Ocean developed into Tropical Storm Allison in the western Gulf of Mexico. The storm barreled ashore near Houston late on June 5, with wind gusts of 60 miles (97 kilometers) per hour. Allison dropped more than 12 inches (30.48 centimeters) of rain in many areas along the Gulf Coast. Nearly 37 inches (94 centimeters) of rain were measured in a suburb of Houston before Allison wandered from eastern Texas up through the Southeast.

The storm produced more than 20 inches (51 centimeters) of rain in northeastern North Carolina between June 12 and 16. The remnants of Allison then combined with a cold front to drop heavy rain from Delaware to southern New England. More than 10 inches (25 centimeters) of rain fell near Philadelphia. During its two-week rampage, Allison became one of the most destructive tropical storms in U.S. history, causing more than $5 billion in damage. Fifty people died of storm-related causes. The rain dropped by Allison was enough to meet the water needs of the entire U.S. population for one year.

Summer heat and chill. July began with sizzling heat in the Southwest. On July 2, Phoenix reached a record 116 °F (46 °C), while the mercury at Death Valley, California, touched 126 °F (52 °C).

For the second straight year, midsummer was marked by persistent chill in the Mid-Atlantic states. In Virginia, Maryland, and Pennsylvania, the Julys of 2000 and 2001 ranked among the coolest since record-keeping began in 1895.

Below normal precipitation in the West during the winter of 2000 left timber and grasslands dried out and susceptible to wildfires. In August 2001, lightning-induced fires reached a peak at mid-month, when more than 500,000 acres (202,000 hectares) burned in 42 large fires.

Floods and snow. Heavy thunderstorms in the Midwest and East caused flash floods in Chicago on August 2 and in Washington, D.C., on August 11 and August 12. The floods in Washington damaged 1,500 houses, prompting the first request in history from the nation's capital for disaster relief. Tropical Storm Barry made landfall on the Florida panhandle on August 6, with wind gusts of 70 miles (113 kilometers) per hour and up to 9 inches (23 centimeters) of rain. After a

FOCUS ON WEATHER

Waves brought on by a severe winter storm threaten houses in Hull, Massachusetts, in March (above). The storm dropped more than 2 feet (0.6 meters) of snow on the Mid-Atlantic states and New England.

Floods, fires, and storms wreaked havoc across the United States in 2001.

Members of the National Guard erect an emergency dike on the Minnesota River at Granite Falls, Minnesota, in April (above). Heavy spring rain caused severe flooding along the Minnesota, Mississippi and St. Croix rivers and the Red River of the North.

Firefighters keep watch over a brush fire near Polk City, Florida, in February. The blaze had spread to 11,000 acres (4,400 hectares) by February 21 and forced the closing of Interstate Highway 4, which connects Tampa, Orlando, and Daytona Beach.

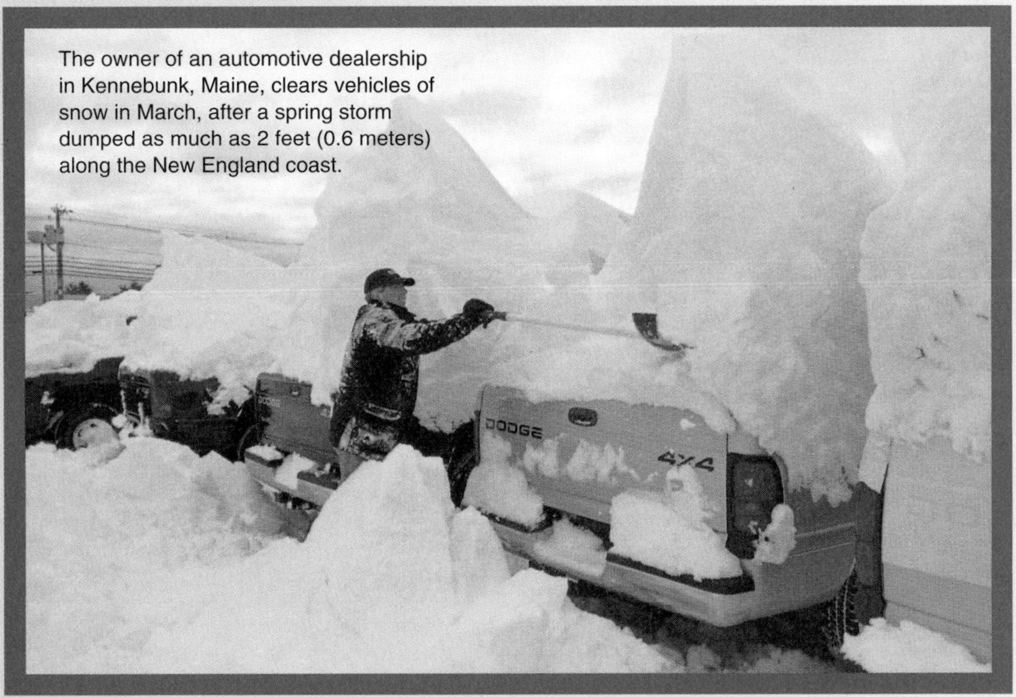

The owner of an automotive dealership in Kennebunk, Maine, clears vehicles of snow in March, after a spring storm dumped as much as 2 feet (0.6 meters) along the New England coast.

dry start to the snow season, a series of storms brought heavy snow to the Central Rockies in late November and early December with 135 inches (343 centimeters) measured at Snow Bird, Utah. In late December, Buffalo, New York, was pounded by a record 81.5 inches (207 centimeters) of snow.

Tropical Storm Gabrielle, bearing winds of more than 70 miles (113 kilometers) per hour, made landfall south of Tampa, Florida, on September 14. The storm moved across the peninsula into the Atlantic Ocean, dropping up to 11 inches (28 centimeters) of rain and leaving behind heavy flooding and minor wind damage.

A tornado associated with a cluster of severe thunderstorms tore through the campus of the University of Maryland in College Park on September 25 with winds of 200 miles (320 kilometers) per hour. The twister killed two students and prompted the evacuation of 3,000 residents.

Warm, dry autumn. November 2001 was the warmest across the Midwest and the second warmest of record nationally since record-keeping began in 1895. Autumn was also very dry along parts of the East Coast with Norfolk, Virginia, registering its driest November on record.

Around the world. Frequent blizzards and severe cold plagued parts of Asia in early 2001. In Inner Mongolia, a blizzard that lasted for three days beginning Dec. 31, 2000, followed by intense cold, threatened the lives of 60,000 herders and more than 220,000 cattle and sheep. In the Kemerovo region of Siberia, the temperature fell to -94 °F (-70 °C) in mid-January, setting a record for the lowest temperature ever recorded in Asia.

In Europe, unusually heavy rains brought severe spring flooding. The Tisza River reached its highest level in 100 years—25 feet (8 meters) above flood stage—at Zahony, Hungary, on March 16, 2001. More than 30,000 people were forced from their houses. The meteorological office of the United Kingdom reported that England and Wales received 51 inches (130 centimeters) of rain between April 1, 2000, and March 20, 2001—more than in any other year since record-keeping began in 1766.

In Asia, from mid-2000 to January 2001, more than 100,000 people were forced to flee from Afghanistan to Pakistan, in part because of the worst drought to affect the area in 30 years. In Central America, three months of drought during the summer rainy season resulted in the loss of as much as 80 percent of the grain crop, bringing hunger to 1.6 million people in Guatemala, El Salvador, Nicaragua, and Honduras. In Africa, Algeria suffered more than 24 hours of heavy rainfall on November 10, triggering flooding and mudslides that killed more than 700 people.

□ Fred Gadomski and Todd Miner

See also **Disasters; Houston.**

Weightlifting. See **Sports.**

Welfare. The Supreme Court of the United States on Feb. 28, 2001, ruled that the U.S. Congress had violated the First Amendment when it prohibited lawyers from the Legal Services Corporation, a federally funded organization based in Washington, D.C., from helping low-income people sue the government over welfare laws and regulations. Voting 5 to 4, the justices struck down a portion of the 1996 welfare reform law, under which Legal Services lawyers could help low-income people seek benefits but could not sue the government over the effects of the 1996 welfare law changes.

In the decision, Justice Anthony M. Kennedy wrote that even though the government paid them, Legal Services lawyers were not government spokespersons. As a result, the lawyers were not speaking on behalf of the government when they sued the government on behalf of their clients.

Stronger families. Tommy G. Thompson, secretary of the U.S. Department of Health and Human Services (HHS), reported on Aug. 21, 2001, that welfare reform enacted in 1996 had significantly helped families. According to HHS officials, the poverty rate had fallen, more former welfare recipients were working, and the number of people dependent on Temporary Assistance for Needy Families (TANF) had dropped.

Thompson reported that the poverty rate for individuals fell from 15.1 percent in 1993 to 11.8 percent in 1999, the lowest rate since 1979. Moreover, 3.8 percent of the total population in 1998 received more than half of their total income from TANF, food stamps, and Social Security, down from 5.8 percent in 1993. In addition, in an average month in 1998, 56 percent of TANF recipients lived in families with at least one family member working, up from 43 percent in 1993.

Early Head Start. Children definitely benefit from Early Head Start, a federal program that provided child and family development services to pregnant women and to children from birth to age 3, HHS officials reported in January 2001. Early Head Start began in 1995 as a complement to the Head Start program, which provides similar services to children ages 3 and 4.

According to the 2001 report, a preliminary evaluation showed that children in Early Head Start performed better in cognitive, language, and social-emotional development than nonparticipating children. Early Head Start children of 2 years of age used larger vocabularies and were able to speak in more complex sentences. In addition, parents of children in the program showed more positive parenting skills, used less physical punishment, and provided more opportunities for their children to learn at home.

□ Geoffrey A. Campbell

West Indies. The pace of economic and political cooperation among the countries and colonies of the Caribbean region picked up steam in 2001. In December, the 28 nations of the Association of Caribbean States (ACS) met in Venezuela, where they approved regional policies on air and sea transportation, programs to develop tourism, and plans to respond to natural disasters. The ACS, formed in 1994 and based in Trinidad and Tobago, works to increase cooperation among member nations. Members include the 15 countries in the Guyana-based Caribbean Community and Common Market (CARICOM), which is mainly concerned with economic integration, as well as other Latin American countries. French and Dutch colonies in the Caribbean have associate membership in the ACS.

CARICOM summit. At the 22nd summit meeting of CARICOM, held in July 2001 in Nassau, the capital of the Bahamas, political leaders agreed to remove restrictions on the movement of money, goods, and services within the Caribbean region. The leaders hailed the agreement as a significant step toward creating a single, integrated Caribbean market and economy.

At the summit, Mexican President Vicente Fox Quesada offered Mexico's help in resolving territorial disputes among Caribbean nations. One of the most difficult disputes involved a 10-acre (4-hectare) tract of rock called the Isle of Birds, which lies 350 miles (563 kilometers) north of Venezuela and 70 miles (113 kilometers) west of the island nation of Dominica. Venezuela maintained a military presence on the Isle of Birds and claimed the tiny island's rich deposits of *guano* (waste deposited by sea birds and bats), a substance that is valued as fertilizer. However, many Caribbean nations condemned Venezuela for seeking to enlarge its maritime territory at the expense of small Caribbean countries. CARICOM promised to continue efforts to resolve this and other territorial disagreements.

Jamaican violence. Gun battles between politically connected gangs and security forces resulted in the killing of 25 people in the Tivoli Gardens area of Jamaica's capital, Kingston, in early July. The violence erupted when police and soldiers entered the neighborhood to confiscate weapons used in some of the more than 300 murders committed in Jamaica earlier in the year. Tivoli Gardens was dominated by supporters of the opposition Jamaica Labour Party. Prime Minister P.J. Patterson, of the People's National Party, created a commission to propose steps to reduce the violence. ☐ Nathan A. Haverstock

See also **Latin America.**

West Virginia. See **State government.**

Wisconsin. See **State government.**

Wyoming. See **State government.**

Yugoslavia. Yugoslav authorities arrested former President Slobodan Milosevic in April 2001 and turned him over to the International Tribunal for War Crimes at The Hague, the Netherlands, in June. The tribunal indicted Milosevic for various war crimes allegedly committed during conflicts in the Balkans in the 1990's, including *genocide* (the systematic extermination of a racial or cultural group) carried out against Muslim and Croatian civilians in Bosnia-Herzegovina. Milosevic was to go on trial in 2002.

The European Union (EU) and the United States had pressured Yugoslav President Vojislav Kostunica to *extradite* (turn over) Milosevic to the tribunal by making economic aid contingent upon Milosevic's extradition. However, efforts to bring Milosevic and other Yugoslav officials accused of war crimes to justice were controversial. Yugoslav Prime Minister Zoran Zizic resigned in June 2001 to protest Milosevic's extradition.

Economic assistance. In January, U.S. President Bill Clinton lifted many of the economic sanctions imposed on Serbia in 1999. (Yugoslavia in 2001 consisted of two republics, Serbia and Montenegro.) The sanctions had been applied after Serbian troops entered the semi-independent Serbian province of Kosovo to put down a rebellion by ethnic Albanian separatists. A bombing campaign carried out by the North Atlantic Treaty Organization (NATO) in 1999 forced the Serbian troops to withdraw.

In March 2001, the International Monetary Fund, an organization that provides credit to member nations, agreed to provide Yugoslavia with a $260-million loan. In May, the World Bank, a United Nations (UN) agency that provides loans to countries for development, readmitted Yugoslavia, which had been expelled from the agency in 1993. In June 2001, Yugoslavia received pledges of nearly $1.3 billion in foreign aid at a World Bank and EU conference in Brussels, Belgium. In September, the UN lifted an arms embargo that was imposed on Yugoslavia in 1998, allowing the Yugoslav army to obtain military equipment from abroad.

Despite the international assistance that Yugoslavia received in 2001, economic conditions continued to be difficult for most Yugoslavs. At the end of 2001, unemployment stood at 35 percent. Inflation slowed during the first nine months of 2001 but remained over 30 percent.

Montenegro. In April, President Kostunica rejected a proposal from President Milo Djukanovic of Montenegro that Montenegro and Serbia become an alliance of independent countries, each with its own army and UN seat. Nevertheless, Djukanovic continued to press for independence in discussions with both Kostunica and Serbian Prime Minister Zoran Djindjic. In October,

Djukanovic announced that Montenegro would go ahead with a previously planned referendum on independence, most likely to be held in the spring of 2002. Western diplomats feared that Montenegro's moves toward independence would lead to renewed instability in the Balkans.

Kosovo. In January 2001, the UN Security Council condemned violence that erupted in the 3-mile- (5-kilometer-) wide buffer zone between Serbia proper and Kosovo when ethnic Albanian guerrillas attacked Serbian citizens and soldiers on the Serbian side of the zone. Also in January, NATO peacekeeping troops intervened in the ethnically divided town of Mitrovica in Kosovo to end rioting among young ethnic Albanians. In March, NATO allowed Serbian troops to reenter the buffer zone to suppress the Albanian guerrilla uprising. NATO tightened the border between Kosovo and Macedonia in mid-2001 to prevent ethnic Albanians from crossing into Macedonia and clashing with the Macedonian army.

The Democratic League of Kosovo, headed by moderate ethnic Albanian Ibrahim Rugova, led the voting for provincial assembly seats in November. ☐ Sharon L. Wolchik

See also **Europe; Macedonia.**

Yukon Territory. See **Canadian territories.**

Zambia. See **Africa.**

Zimbabwe.

President Robert Mugabe's ruling Zimbabwe African National Union-Patriotic Front (ZANU-PF) stepped up attacks in 2001 on its opposition, Morgan Tsvangirai's Movement for Democratic Change (MDC) and on Zimbabwe's judiciary and media. The targets of their attacks had been critical of ZANU-PF and of the pro-Mugabe "independence veterans"—armed squatters who claimed to be veterans of the pre-1980 guerrilla war against white rule in Zimbabwe. They invaded and looted some 1,700 farms owned by white farmers in 2000 and 2001, which disrupted agricultural production and resulted in food shortages.

Intimidation. On January 28, a bomb, which experts believed was planted by ZANU-PF agents, exploded in the printing plant of the independent *Daily News*, which opposed the government. On April 14, the Zimbabwe parliament passed legislation that gave Mugabe virtually unchallenged control over the nation's media.

In March, Mugabe's minister of justice refused to intervene when pro-Mugabe war veterans threatened Supreme Court Chief Justice Anthony Gubbay with physical harm. Gubbay, who had won high marks from judicial experts for preserving the independence of Zimbabwe's court system, resigned. President Mugabe filled the court vacancy with a close ZANU-PF associate.

The European Union (EU), the United States, and the Southern African Development Community—an association of 14 African nations—pressured Mugabe to halt political oppression and restore democratic principles. In May, Amnesty International, a London-based human rights group, issued a report that accused Mugabe's regime of widespread torture and murder. In November, EU officials discussed imposing sanctions against Zimbabwe after Mugabe refused to allow the EU permission to monitor the presidential election scheduled for 2002.

Abuja accord. In September 2001, Zimbabwean officials signed the Abuja accord, an agreement brokered in Abuja, Nigeria, by British officials, President Olusegun Obasanjo of Nigeria, and other African leaders. The accord obliged Mugabe to halt land occupations and implement a workable land reform program. The United Kingdom promised to partially fund the program. However, the invasions of farms and the assaults on both white owners and black farm workers continued, despite Mugabe's promises.

Economy. In November, Finance Minister Simba Makoni announced that 75 percent of Zimbabwe's people lived in poverty. Zimbabwe's rate of inflation exceeded 100 percent in 2001.

☐ Simon Baynham

See also **Africa.**

Zoology. See **Biology.**

Zoos.

"Texas Wild!" opened in June 2001 at the Fort Worth Zoo, featuring replicas of six Texas habitats that offer visitors a sampling of the state's remarkably diverse wildlife. The tour begins in the Hill Country of central Texas with a replica of an agricultural community of the 1890's. Multimedia and interactive displays showcase the region's plants and animals. A representation of state waterways spotlights the Guadalupe bass—the Texas state fish—and the Cagle's map turtle. A multimedia weather show generates rain, thunder, and wind to simulate the weather of central Texas.

"Texas Wild!" continues on the high plains and prairies of northwestern Texas. A tornado-battered house supplies a shady spot to view a black-tailed prairie dog town, which is shared by a burrowing owl. Next to the town is a pair of black-footed ferrets, prairie-dog predators.

Visitors then cross a bridge past an abandoned sawmill camp to piney woods and swamps typical of east Texas. River otters play in a clear spring, while alligators cruise a placid pond. Visitors see these animals both from above and below the water's surface. At the centerpiece of the display are black bears. Red wolves prowl a nearby woodland.

From east Texas, plank walkways lead to a weathered bait shack on Texas's Gulf Coast,

A baby Sumatran rhinoceros stands beside his mother one hour after he was born at the Cincinnati Zoo in Ohio in September 2001. The 72-pound (33-kilogram) male was the first Sumatran rhino born in captivity in 112 years.

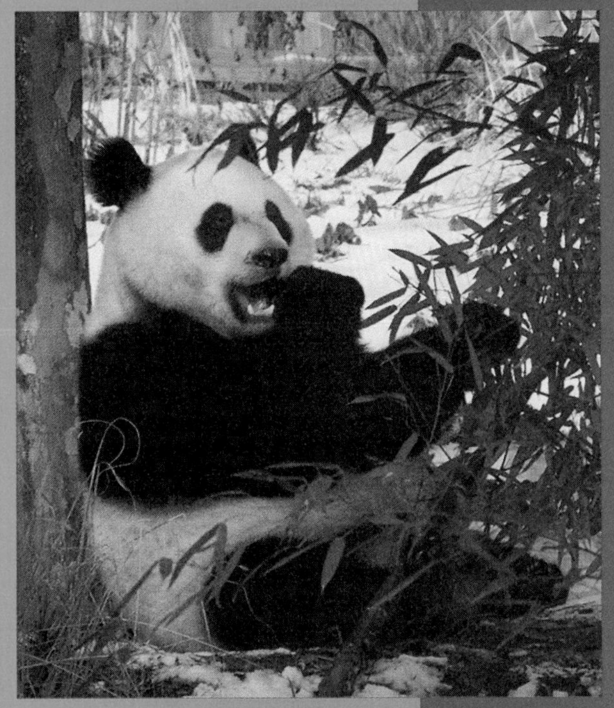

The giant panda Mei Xiang settles in at the National Zoo in Washington, D.C., soon after she and Tian Tian, a male panda, went on display in January 2001. The government of China loaned the pandas to the National Zoo for 10 years.

where the bottom of a fishing boat teems with a variety of fish. White and brown pelicans, roseate spoonbills, and other birds crowd the masts of a sunken shrimp boat.

The brush country of south Texas begins in a steep *arroyo* (normally dry stream channel) planted with mesquite, yucca, and prickly pear cactus and inhabited by jaguars, ocelots, mountain lions, bobcats, ringtail cats, and coatis. An aviary houses Texas birdlife—roadrunners, quail, doves, green jays, and birds of prey, such as the endangered Aplomado falcon.

An abandoned mine leads to the mountains and deserts of west Texas. Long-nose and Pallid bats share the exhibit with Western diamondback rattlesnakes, horned lizards, rare pecos pupfish, harvester ants, tarantulas, and scorpions.

Underwater predators. The Florida Aquarium in Tampa premiered "Sea Hunt," an exhibit of nearly 40 species of ocean predators, in May 2001. Zebra and black-tip sharks are among the nearly 200 animals on display. A giant Pacific octopus snuggles in a cave, while a cuttlefish nearby propels itself with swiftly moving tentacles. Wolf eels scour the sea-bottom for crabs and clams to crush with their powerful jaws. An anglerfish, which uses one of its fins as a lure, waits to snap open its huge mouth to suck in another fish. Lionfish, butterfly fish, moray eels, triggerfish, clownfish, and rockfish are among the other predators featured in the "Sea Hunt" exhibit.

Carolina rain forest. A troop of four gorillas—one male and three females—greeted the public when the Riverbanks Zoo and Botanical Garden in Columbia, South Carolina, opened "Ndoki Forest" in August. Designed to evoke a central African rain forest, the exhibit features thousands of trees, shrubs, and grasses. Open grassy areas allow ample room for the apes to romp or relax. Around a corner, African elephants bathe in a 3,000-square-foot (280-square-meter) pool beside a mudbank. Ndoki also features an artificial termite mound where burrowing animals called meerkats hunt for their food.

In February, the Riverbanks Zoo debuted a birdhouse that features three habitats. "Penguin Coast" spotlights African and rockhopper penguins and includes a model of a penguin nesting burrow through which children can crawl. In "Asian Trek," such birds as rhinoceros hornbills, fairy bluebirds, and Victoria crowned pigeons inhabit lush jungle settings. "Savannas" focuses on the grasslands of Africa and South America to demonstrate how animals in widely separated habitats, such as African bee-eaters and South American motmots, have developed in similar ways.

Swinging San Antonio. The San Antonio Zoo in Texas introduced "Gibbon Forest" in April. The Southeast Asian jungle habitat is dominated by huge trees. A limestone bluff encloses the rear and sides of the 35-foot- (11-meter-) high exhibit. A waterfall pours into a stream that flows into a pond, where Asian small-clawed otters dive. The exhibit includes a pair of white-handed gibbons, which are among the most acrobatic of all primates, and *muntjacs* (small forest deer).

Horses of different colors. In March, the National Aquarium in Baltimore premiered "Seahorses: Beyond Imagination." The exhibit spotlights 18 species, including yellow, tiger tail, potbellied, dwarf, and Pacific giant seahorses. Closely related weedy sea dragons and banded pipefish are also featured in the exhibit. Each species appears in a simulation of its native habitat, such as a Caribbean coral reef, the Chesapeake Bay sea floor, and a Tasmanian kelp bed.

Sumatran rhino born. A Sumatran rhinoceros, one of the rarest, most critically endangered animals, was born at the Cincinnati Zoo in Ohio in September. Named Andalas (the ancient name of Sumatra), the 72-pound (33-kilogram) male was the first of his species born in captivity in 112 years. Approximately 300 Sumatran rhinoceroses, the smallest species of rhinoceros, were alive in 2001—16 of them in captivity. □ Eugene J. Walter, Jr.

Zoo and aquarium attractions

Additional zoo and aquarium exhibit openings in 2001

Dickerson Park Zoo, Springfield, MO. "Diversity of Life," which opened in April, displays more than 50 species of reptiles, amphibians, and insects in three climate-themed halls: "Deserts and Dry Places," "Under the Canopy—Rainforest Life," and "The Ozarks."

Jacksonville Zoo, Jacksonville, FL. "Wild Florida," which opened in March, is a winding trek through wetlands with Florida panthers, red wolves, black bears, otters, bobcats, bald eagles, and alligators.

Minnesota Zoo, Apple Valley, MN. "Meerkats of the Kalahari," which opened in June, focuses on survival in a desert by a family of small burrowing animals called meerkats.

Monterey Bay Aquarium, Monterey, CA. Two endangered wildlife exhibits opened in May. "Saving Tunas, Turtles, and Sharks" examines how growing demand for seafood and destructive fishing methods are destroying ocean wildlife. "Saving Seahorses" exposes the many threats to seahorses.

North Carolina Zoo, Asheboro, NC. "Chimpanzee Habitat," which opened in May, replaced an older and smaller chimp exhibit. The new habitat features a 25-foot- (7.6-meter-) tall artificial tree in which the zoo's troop of 13 chimps climb and nest.

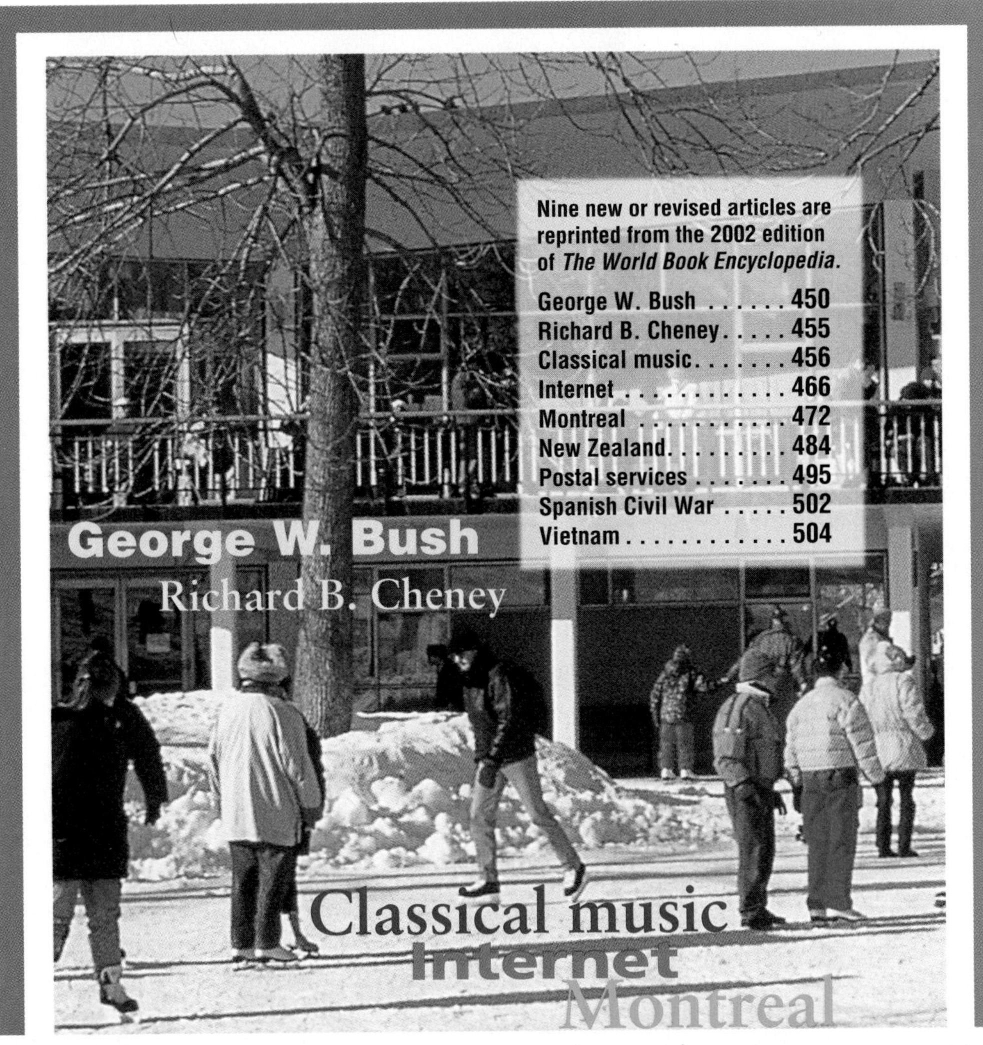

2001 WORLD BOOK SUPPLEMENT

New Zealand
Postal services
Spanish Civil War
Vietnam

43rd president of the United States 2001-

Clinton
42nd president
1993-2001
Democrat

Bush
43rd president
2001-
Republican

Richard B. Cheney
Vice president
2001-

© Bob Daemmrich, Corbis/Sygma

Bush, George Walker (1946-), was elected president of the United States in 2000 in one of the closest presidential elections in U.S. history. Bush, a Republican and the governor of Texas, received a smaller number of popular votes in the election than his Democratic opponent, Vice President Al Gore. But Bush received more votes in the Electoral College. However, the outcome was in doubt for weeks after the election. It was not clear which candidate had carried Florida, where the vote was extremely close. Delays resulted from recounts of Florida ballots and court challenges to the recounts. Five weeks after the election, following a decision by the U.S. Supreme Court to halt the recounts, Gore conceded the election to Bush.

Bush's election marked the second time in U.S. history that the son of a former president was elected president. Bush's father, George Herbert Walker Bush (1924-), served as president from 1989 to 1993. The only other father and son to be elected president were John Adams and John Quincy Adams, who held office from 1797 to 1801 and from 1825 to 1829, respectively.

Bush was elected president at a time of economic prosperity and low unemployment in the United States. Many Americans recognized that not everyone shared in the prosperity, however. They were concerned with high taxes and with the growing number of homeless people. They were also alarmed by the increase in violent crimes committed by children. Many were concerned about what they saw as a decline in moral values, particularly among the country's leaders.

During his presidential campaign, Bush emphasized what he called "compassionate conservatism." He proposed to cut taxes and to use the nation's prosperity to help those in need. He pointed to his record as governor of Texas, which included reducing taxes, initiating school reform, and strengthening the state's criminal justice system.

Bush enjoys outdoor activities, especially fishing, hunting, and playing golf. He also likes country music. He wrote an autobiography, *A Charge to Keep* (1999).

Bill Minutaglio, the contributor of this article, is the author of First Son: George W. Bush and the Bush Family Dynasty.

Early life

Family background. George Walker Bush was born on July 6, 1946, in New Haven, Connecticut. His parents were living in New Haven while his father was a student at Yale University.

Bush's father, George H. W. Bush, grew up in Connecticut. After achieving financial success as an oilman in Texas, he turned to politics. His father, Prescott Sheldon Bush, had been a U.S. senator from Connecticut. George H. W. Bush served in the U.S. House of Representatives from 1967 to 1971 as a Republican from Texas. During the 1970's, he served successively as U.S. ambassador to the United Nations, U.S. envoy to China, and head of the Central Intelligence Agency. He was vice president of the United States under President Ronald

Important dates in Bush's life

1946 (July 6) Born in New Haven, Connecticut.
1968 Graduated from Yale University.
1968-1970 Served in the Texas Air National Guard.
1975 Graduated from Harvard Business School.
1977 (Nov. 5) Married Laura Welch.
1994 Elected governor of Texas.
1998 Reelected governor of Texas.
2000 Elected president of the United States.

Reagan from 1981 to 1989. He was U.S. president from 1989 to 1993.

George Walker Bush's mother, Barbara Pierce Bush (1925-), grew up in New York. Her father was the publisher of *McCall's* and *Redbook* magazines.

Barbara Pierce was 16 years old and George Herbert Walker Bush was 17 when the two met at a Christmas dance in Greenwich, Connecticut, in 1941. They married in 1945 while Bush was on leave from active duty in the U.S. Navy during World War II.

George Walker Bush was the first of the couple's six children. The second child, born in 1949, was Pauline Robinson, called Robin. She died of leukemia in 1953 at the age of 3. Young George also had three brothers—John, called Jeb (1953-), Neil (1955-), and Marvin (1956-)—and another sister, Dorothy (1959-).

Boyhood. Bush grew up in Midland, in western Texas. His parents moved to the state from Connecticut when he was 2 years old. His father wanted to get involved in the booming oil business.

Bush was 7 years old when his little sister, Robin, died. He and his parents were grief-stricken. His parents later told friends that young George helped them deal with their sorrow. George tried to be cheerful and funny and make them laugh. As a child, he was known for his love of mischief and his joking remarks.

George Bush Presidential Library

Bush as a baby is held by his parents, Barbara Pierce Bush and George H. W. Bush. George W. Bush was born in New Haven, Connecticut, where his father was a student at Yale University.

George Bush Presidential Library

As an airman in the Texas Air National Guard, Bush learned to pilot an airplane. He entered the National Guard in 1968, during the Vietnam War, after he graduated from Yale University.

School life. Bush attended Sam Houston Elementary School in Midland, then went on to San Jacinto Junior High. He spent one year, seventh grade, at San Jacinto.

In 1959, the Bushes moved to Houston. For the next two years, George attended Kinkaid School, a private academy. He was a member of the football team, and he was remembered as making friends easily.

Bush spent his final years of high school at the exclusive preparatory school his father had attended, Phillips Academy in Andover, Massachusetts. His grades were average, but his lively personality and quick tongue won him attention. He played basketball and baseball and was the head football cheerleader in his senior year.

College and military service

In 1964, Bush began his studies at Yale University, the college his father had attended. He majored in history. Classmates found him friendly and fun-loving. He enjoyed parties and sports, especially rugby, and was elected president of his fraternity, Delta Kappa Epsilon. He also belonged to Yale's elite secret society, Skull & Bones.

In 1968, as Bush was finishing up at Yale, the United States was deeply divided over the country's involvement in the Vietnam War (1957-1975). Just before college graduation, Bush applied and was accepted as an airman in the Texas Air National Guard. His commitment included 53 weeks of full-time training to become a pilot. He graduated in December 1969. He then continued flight training on the F-102 jet fighter. Bush attempted to sign up for a program that rotated pilots to Vietnam but was not accepted. He was not eligible for the program because he had not logged enough flight hours.

Business school

Bush completed his active duty with the Texas Air National Guard in 1970. He graduated from flight training school with a rank of lieutenant. In 1973, he entered Harvard Business School, where he received an M.B.A. degree in 1975.

Bush later described the three years between completing active duty and entering business school as his "nomadic" period. He continued to fulfill his part-time commitment to the National Guard, but he did not find lasting, full-time employment. During this period, he applied for admission to law school but was not accepted. He was a management trainee with an agricultural firm. He worked on a political campaign in Alabama for a Republican candidate seeking a Senate seat. He also served as a counselor in a Houston program for disadvantaged youngsters.

Congressional candidate

Bush returned to Midland after graduating from Harvard Business School, and he began working in the oil business. In 1977, the congressional representative for the district that included Midland announced his retirement. Bush decided to seek the Republican nomination for the post.

Bush quickly assembled a campaign team, mostly made up of friends who volunteered to help him, and began raising funds. He campaigned tirelessly across the sprawling district. He won the nomination, but he lost the election to his Democratic opponent. The opponent, a native Texan, portrayed Bush as an "outsider." However, Bush received 47 percent of the vote in a district that had never elected a Republican to Congress.

Bush's family

In mid-1977, shortly after announcing his candidacy for Congress, Bush attended a cookout at the home of friends. There, he met Laura Welch (Nov. 4,1946-). The couple started dating, and they married about three months later, on Nov. 5, 1977. The newlyweds put off their honeymoon to focus on Bush's campaign for office.

Laura Welch Bush, a native Texan, grew up in Midland as an only child. Her father, Harold, was a building contractor, and her mother served as his bookkeeper. Laura was known as a reserved, quiet person who loved to read. She earned a bachelor's degree in education from Southern Methodist University and a master's degree in library science from the University of Texas at Austin. She was working as a librarian when she met Bush, and she had been a schoolteacher.

The Bushes had twin daughters, Barbara and Jenna. The children were born in 1981 and were named for their grandmothers.

George Bush Presidential Library

Bush's career in the oil business included forming his own oil exploration firm in the late 1970's. He merged the firm with another company in the early 1980's when petroleum prices fell.

George Bush Presidential Library

The young Bush family lived in Midland, Texas, while Bush worked in the oil business. Bush's family includes his wife, Laura Welch Bush, and their daughters, Barbara, *left,* and Jenna.

Business career

Oil exploration. In the late 1970's, Bush set up an oil exploration company, Arbusto Energy Incorporated, later called Bush Exploration Company. The company searched for potentially profitable oil and gas fields. After his election loss, Bush turned his energies to running his company.

In the early 1980's, oil prices fell, and many oil companies went out of business. Bush merged his company with another small oil firm, Spectrum 7 Energy Corporation. Bush became Spectrum's chief executive officer.

The downturn in the energy field continued, however, and Spectrum began to falter. In 1986, the struggling firm was taken over by Harken Oil and Gas, Incorporated, later known as Harken Energy Corporation. Bush received Harken stock for his Spectrum shares and became a member of Harken's board of directors.

In the late 1980's, Bush returned to politics. His father, then vice president of the United States, was campaigning for president in the 1988 election. The younger Bush and his family moved to Washington, D.C., to help manage his father's political campaign. After the election, which his father won, Bush and his family returned to Texas and settled in Dallas.

In 1990, Bush sold most of his shares in Harken at a profit shortly before the company declared huge losses. The timing of the sale later prompted charges that Bush had known about Harken's poor financial condition. Bush said he was not aware of the firm's financial difficulties when he sold his shares. An investigation into the matter by the Securities and Exchange Commission ended in 1993 with no charges brought against Bush. By the time Bush sold his Harken shares, he had already begun a new career. He was a part owner of a baseball team.

Baseball ownership. In late 1988, Bush learned that the Texas Rangers baseball team was for sale. The American League team was based in the nearby city of Arlington. Bush and a group of investors bought the team in 1989. Bush became a managing general partner of the team. He was an enthusiastic spectator at Ranger games, and he worked to promote the team and increase attendance. Bush helped win support for a controversial plan to have a new stadium built for the team. He was involved during the planning and construction stages of the new facility, called the Ballpark in Arlington. The stadium opened in April 1994. Later that year, Bush was elected to his first political office, and he stepped down from his post with the team.

Governor of Texas

Campaign. Bush's father lost his bid for reelection as president and left the White House in 1993. That year, the younger Bush announced his candidacy for governor of Texas. At the same time, his brother Jeb was campaigning for governor of Florida.

Bush's opponent was Ann W. Richards, the state's popular governor, who was seeking a second term. During the campaign, Richards said Bush was running on his family name. Bush made no personal attacks against Richards. Instead, he criticized the governor's record, and he focused on presenting his conservative views. He supported welfare reform. He called for *autonomy* (self-government) and increased state funding for public school districts. He stressed a need for stronger criminal laws, particularly against juvenile offenders. He promised reform of the Texas civil justice system, which was clogged with unimportant lawsuits. Bush won the election by a wide margin, receiving about 54 percent of the vote. His brother lost in Florida.

First term. As governor, Bush earned high approval ratings. He worked to get legislation passed on his proposed reforms. Bush's lieutenant governor was a Democrat, and Democrats controlled both houses of the Texas Legislature. But Bush became known for achieving success with a combination of personal charm and an ability to compromise. The lawmakers enacted legislation that put limits on welfare benefits, gave local school districts more authority, imposed stricter penalties on juvenile criminals, and placed limits on civil lawsuits.

AP/Wide World

Campaigning for governor of Texas, Bush talks with supporters. He won the Texas governorship by a wide margin in 1994 and was reelected by an even wider margin in 1998.

In 1997, Bush presented a plan to restructure the Texas tax system and increase state funding for schools. At the time, Texas schools were supported by local property taxes. Bush proposed reducing property taxes and increasing the state's role in financing education. To make up for the lower property taxes, he called for an increase in the state sales tax and for a new tax on fees of doctors, lawyers, and other professionals.

Bush's proposal for new taxes received much criticism, and it was not accepted. However, the members of the Legislature did reduce property taxes by increasing the amount of a home's value that was exempt from taxes. They used surplus funds in the state budget to make up for the decreased property taxes.

Reelection. Bush's popularity remained high throughout his term. In 1998, he ran for reelection. He defeated his opponent, Texas Land Commissioner Garry Mauro, by a wide margin. Bush received about 69 percent of the vote. He drew support not only from traditional Republicans but also from the state's Hispanic Americans, who often vote Democratic. Also in 1998, Bush's brother Jeb was elected governor of Florida.

During Bush's second term, the state increased school funding and continued to adopt educational reforms. The Legislature also approved the largest tax cuts in Texas history. Bush was criticized for not doing more to combat racism, poverty, and pollution.

Bush received national attention. Even before his second term began, he was spoken of as a possible candidate for the presidency in 2000.

Election as president

In June 1999, Bush announced that he would seek the Republican nomination for president. He faced several

© Reuters/Archive Photos

Bush and Richard B. Cheney, former U.S. secretary of defense, accept the Republican nomination for president and vice president at the Republican Party's 2000 convention in Philadelphia.

rivals, including Elizabeth Dole, former president of the American Red Cross; newspaper and magazine publisher Steve Forbes; Alan Keyes, a former State Department official; Arizona Senator John McCain, and former Vice President Dan Quayle.

The campaign. Early in Bush's presidential campaign, critics brought up events from his past. They questioned why he had been accepted in the Texas Air National Guard before others on a waiting list. They charged that Bush had gotten favorable treatment because his father was a congressman at the time. Bush said neither he nor his father had sought to influence his selection. Reporters asked Bush if he had used cocaine or other drugs in his youth, but Bush did not respond.

Senator McCain won the first of the primary elections, in New Hampshire in February 2000. By the time the March primaries ended, however, Bush had won enough delegates to secure the nomination.

At the Republican National Convention in Philadelphia in August 2000, Bush was named the Republican presidential nominee. At Bush's request, the delegates nominated Richard B. Cheney, a former congressman and U.S. secretary of defense, as their candidate for vice president. The Democrats nominated Vice President Al Gore for president and Senator Joseph I. Lieberman of Connecticut for vice president.

During the campaign, Bush labeled Gore "the candidate of the status quo." Bush emphasized what he called "compassionate conservatism." He said that the nation's prosperity must be extended to those still struggling to obtain decent living conditions. He pledged to cut taxes and to strengthen and preserve the nation's Social Security system. He stressed the need to improve the performance of the public schools and to rebuild the nation's military strength.

Gore argued that Bush lacked the experience to be president. He said Bush's proposal to use a federal budget surplus to make up for reduced taxes was risky. Gore also pointed to the danger, under Bush's plan, that the Social Security and Medicare programs would be left without sufficient funding.

The election was one of the tightest presidential contests in United States history. The outcome was in doubt for weeks after the election. It depended upon which candidate won the electoral votes of Florida, where the popular vote was very close. Florida election officials conducted a recount, and the results showed Bush ahead of Gore. But Gore asked for manual recounts in certain Florida counties. Bush challenged in court the need for those recounts. Five weeks after the election, a decision by the U.S. Supreme Court brought an end to the recounts. Gore then conceded the election, and Bush became the 43rd president of the United States.

Bush's administration

After taking office, Bush proposed legislation regarding a tax cut, education reform, and other issues that he had focused on during his presidential campaign. The Republican-controlled House passed much of this legislation, but Bush faced opposition in the Senate. The 2000 election had left the Senate evenly divided between Democrats and Republicans. However, in mid-2001, Senator James M. Jeffords of Vermont left the Republican Party to become an independent. As a result, control of the Senate shifted to the Democratic Party.

Bush and the nation faced a major crisis on Sept. 11, 2001, when the worst terrorist attack in U.S. history occurred. Terrorists in hijacked commercial airplanes crashed the planes into the two towers of the World Trade Center in New York City and into the Pentagon

Bush's election

Place of nominating convention	Philadelphia
Ballot on which nominated	1st
Democratic opponent	Al Gore
Electoral vote*	271 (Bush) to 266 (Gore)
Popular vote	50,996,039 (Gore) to 50,456,141 (Bush)
Age at inauguration	54

*For votes by states, see **Electoral College** (table).

Vice president and Cabinet

Vice president	* Richard B. Cheney
Secretary of state	* Colin L. Powell
Secretary of the treasury	Paul H. O'Neill
Secretary of defense	* Donald H. Rumsfeld
Attorney general	John D. Ashcroft
Secretary of the interior	Gale A. Norton
Secretary of agriculture	Ann M. Veneman
Secretary of commerce	Donald L. Evans
Secretary of labor	Elaine L. Chao
Secretary of health and human services	Tommy G. Thompson
Secretary of housing and urban development	Melquiades R. Martinez
Secretary of transportation	* Norman Y. Mineta
Secretary of energy	Spencer Abraham
Secretary of education	Roderick R. Paige
Secretary of veterans affairs	Anthony J. Principi

*Has a separate biography in *World Book.*

Building near Washington, D.C. Thousands of people died. On October 7, the United States began strikes against Afghanistan, the headquarters of the terrorists believed to be responsible for the attacks. Targets included airports, communication facilities, and suspected terrorist camps. Bill Minutaglio

See also **Bush, George Herbert Walker; Bush v. Gore; Election of 2000; President of the United States.**

Outline

I. Early life
- A. Family background
- B. Boyhood
- C. School life

II. College and military service

III. Business school

IV. Congressional candidate

V. Bush's family

VI. Business career
- A. Oil exploration
- B. Baseball ownership

VII. Governor of Texas
- A. Campaign
- B. First term
- C. Reelection

VIII. Election as president
- A. The campaign
- B. The election

IX. Bush's administration

Questions

How did Bush campaign against Vice President Al Gore?
What were some of Bush's achievements as governor of Texas?
Where did Bush do his military service during the Vietnam War?
What were the two most important industries Bush worked in before becoming governor of Texas?
Where did Bush grow up?
What did Bush mean by the phrase "compassionate conservatism"?
Before Bush, who was the only other son to follow his father as president of the United States?
What was the first political office Bush held?

Additional resources

Bush, George W. *A Charge to Keep.* Morrow, 1999.
Cohen, Daniel. *George W. Bush.* Millbrook, 2000.
Minutaglio, Bill. *First Son: George W. Bush and the Bush Family Dynasty.* Times Bks., 1999.

Cheney, *CHEE nee,* **Richard Bruce** (1941-), was elected vice president of the United States in 2000. He and his running mate, Texas Governor George W. Bush, defeated their Democratic opponents, Vice President Al Gore and Senator Joseph I. Lieberman, in an extremely close election.

© Reuters/Archive Photos

Richard B. Cheney

Cheney, a former U.S. representative from Wyoming, had served as secretary of defense under Bush's father, President George H. W. Bush, from 1989 to 1993. As secretary of defense, Cheney advised the president on military strategy against Iraq during the Persian Gulf War (1991). He also helped persuade other countries to join U.S.-led forces in the war.

Early life. Cheney was born in Lincoln, Nebraska. He moved with his parents to Casper, Wyoming, while still a boy. He entered Yale University on a scholarship but returned home after three semesters. He took a job with an electric company, working on power lines. He then attended the University of Wyoming, earning a B.A. in 1965 and an M.A. in 1966, both in political science.

In 1964, Cheney married Lynne Ann Vincent, a graduate student who went on to earn a Ph.D. in English literature. Lynne Cheney became a college teacher, novelist, and magazine editor. She headed the National Endowment for the Humanities from 1986 to 1993. The couple have two daughters, Elizabeth and Mary.

Career. The Cheneys moved to the Washington, D.C., area after Richard Cheney received a congressional fellowship in 1968. In 1969, Cheney joined the staff of Donald H. Rumsfeld, then director of the Office of Economic Opportunity. Cheney worked for Rumsfeld in various jobs until 1973. In 1974 and 1975, Cheney was a deputy assistant to President Gerald R. Ford. Cheney served as White House chief of staff under Ford from 1975 to 1977.

In 1978, Cheney won election to the U.S. House of Representatives as a Republican from Wyoming. He was reelected five times. As a representative, Cheney was known for his conservative political views. In 1988, he became the Republican *whip* (assistant leader) in the House. He also served on several House committees, including the Select Committee on Intelligence and a committee that investigated the sale of arms by the United States to Iran (see **Reagan, Ronald W.** [The Iran-contra affair]). Cheney gave up his House seat in 1989 after accepting the post of secretary of defense.

After Cheney completed his stint as defense secretary in 1993, he left government service and joined the boards of several corporations. In 1995, he became the president and chief executive officer of Halliburton Company, a Dallas-based oil-field services and construction firm. In July 2000, George W. Bush asked Cheney to be his running mate. Lee Thornton

© Ron Scherl, Stage/Image

Classical music can be performed by large groups of musicians, small groups, or soloists. Many composers have written their works to be played by symphony orchestras, sometimes accompanied by a chorus. Classical music is frequently performed in large, specially designed concert halls.

Classical music

Classical music is music composed chiefly for concerts, opera, ballet, and religious services. It includes music for solo instruments, groups of instruments, voices, and both instruments and voices.

The term *classical music* is used to contrast with *popular music,* which includes country music, jazz, and rock music. *Classical* also has other meanings. Especially if it is capitalized, *Classical* refers to a style of music that developed in the later 1700's. In addition, the term describes aspects of ancient Greek and Roman civilization.

Historically, classical music includes music composed from the Middle Ages to the present day. This article discusses the major types and styles of Western classical music, as well as its history. For information about other kinds of Western music, see such *World Book* articles as **Country music, Folk music, Jazz, Popular music,** and **Rock music.** For information on the basic elements of music and the music of other cultures, see **Music.**

Instrumental music

Three main types of instrumental music are (1) solo music, (2) chamber music, and (3) orchestral music.

Solo music is music for a single instrument. Solo music has been composed primarily for keyboard instruments, but also for wind and string instruments. Popular keyboard instruments since the 1600's have been the harpsichord, clavichord, organ, and piano. Wind instruments include the flute, clarinet, oboe, and horn. String instruments include the violin, cello, and guitar. Composers have written many works for solo wind or string instruments accompanied by piano.

Short solo pieces became popular in the 1800's, especially dances and *improvisatory* works. These improvisatory pieces sound as though they were made up by the musician during the performance, but they were well planned and written in musical notation. Soloists also played *characteristic pieces,* which expressed a mood and often had descriptive titles.

Chamber music is written for a small group of musicians, each instrument playing one part. Chamber music was originally intended for performance in a room smaller and more intimate than a concert hall. Chamber music is often identified by the number of instruments,

Daniel T. Politoske, the contributor of this article, is Professor of Music History at the University of Kansas.

such as a duo, trio, quartet, or quintet. These small ensembles are made up of string or wind instruments, or sometimes of mixed instruments. Chamber compositions are usually named according to the instruments required to play them. For example, a string quartet consists of four string instruments, typically two violins, a viola, and a cello. A *piano quintet* is made up of a piano and a string quartet.

Orchestral music is composed for small chamber orchestras and for large orchestras of 80 or more players. Small orchestras of the 1600's and 1700's consisted primarily of string instruments and harpsichord. As the orchestra grew in size in the 1700's and 1800's, it was organized into four sections—strings, woodwinds, brass, and percussion. For information on the instruments in each section, see **Orchestra** (The musicians).

The main types of orchestral music are (1) symphonies, (2) concertos, (3) overtures, (4) suites, (5) incidental music, and (6) symphonic poems.

Symphonies typically consist of four *movements* (large sections). A symphony commonly opens with an *allegro* (quick and bright) movement. The second movement is slow, and the third is moderately fast. The fourth movement returns to an allegro tempo.

Concertos. The solo concerto features one or more solo instruments, such as a piano or violin, with the accompaniment of an orchestra. The *concerto grosso* uses a small group of instruments playing in contrast to a larger string orchestra.

Overtures are orchestral pieces that open operas and oratorios. They are sometimes performed as individual concert pieces.

Suites originated in the pairing of dances during the 1500's. By the 1800's, a suite had become a series of connected instrumental movements. Many composers wrote suites for keyboard instruments and for orchestra.

Incidental music is written for use in plays. A famous example is the Norwegian composer Edvard Grieg's incidental music for *Peer Gynt* (1867), a play by the Norwegian playwright Henrik Ibsen.

Symphonic poems are one-movement compositions originated by the Hungarian composer Franz Liszt in the 1800's. Symphonic poems are inspired by subjects taken from literature, mythology, or history that are usually explained in the programs given to the audience.

Vocal music

The principal types of vocal music are (1) songs, (2) choral music, (3) operas, and (4) oratorios.

Songs are usually intended to be performed by a solo singer, sometimes accompanied by one or more instruments. Songs vary from simple folk songs to complex composed songs. Simple songs that use the same music for all stanzas of the text are called *strophic songs.* Most well-known patriotic songs are strophic songs. *Part songs* are written for two or more vocal lines, most often four or five. These multiple vocal lines are called *polyphonic.* A single vocal line is called *monophonic.*

Choral music is written for a chorus singing single-line music in unison or several vocal or instrumental parts. Most choral music is composed in parts for four voices. The voices have come to be known, from highest to lowest, as soprano, alto, tenor, and bass.

Operas are music dramas that combine solo and choral vocal music and instrumental music. They are staged like plays in which the dialogue is mostly or entirely sung. For more information on operas, see **Opera.**

Ken Firestone

A string quartet has two violinists, a viola player, and a cello player. It is one of the most common chamber music groups. Music written for such a group is also called a string quartet.

Oratorios, like operas, are dramatic works for soloists, chorus, and orchestra. Unlike operas, however, oratorios are presented in concert form without stage action, costumes, or scenery. The oratorio developed in Italy, as did opera, in the 1600's and soon spread to other countries. Most texts were based on religious themes. Probably the most famous oratorio is *Messiah* (1742) by the German composer George Frideric Handel. Two significant types of vocal music that resemble the oratorio are the *cantata* and *passion music.*

Classical music forms

Composers give form to their music by using the basic techniques of repetition and contrast of melodies, rhythms, and harmonies. Composers often vary all three during repetition of earlier material. The most important forms of classical music include *sectional form, rondo, variation, fugue, sonata,* and *free form.*

Sectional form. The basic sectional forms are *binary form* and *ternary form.* A composition in binary form has two sections. The first part typically begins in one key and then changes, or modulates, to another key. The second part begins in that key and then modulates back to the key in which the first part began. The two parts complement each other and are often repeated immediately after they are performed. A composition in ternary form has three sections: (1) a first section, (2) a contrasting second part, and (3) a repetition or varied presentation of the first section.

Rondo form is an extension of the ternary form. A first section, A, is followed by a contrasting B section, a repeat of the A section, another contrasting section, and a final A section. A five-part rondo follows the sequence A B A C A. A seven-part rondo is A B A C A B A. The composer usually changes the repetitions of the A and B materials from their first presentation for variety. The A material nearly always returns in the original key.

Variation form is also called *theme and variation* form. It consists of a principal melody called the *theme* and a number of subsequent variations on the theme with changes in rhythm, tempo, and key. Each variation is often the same or nearly the same length as the theme. In most compositions, each variation comes to a complete close before the next variation begins. An entire composition may take the form of a theme with variations, such as Johann Sebastian Bach's *Goldberg Variations* for harpsichord. A theme with variations may also make up a movement of a larger work, such as a symphony or a string quartet.

Fugue is a technique and form of composition in which a main melody is presented in turn by different voices or instruments. In the "exposition" section of the fugue, these melodies are presented as a "subject" and "answer." Then the subject returns in other closely related keys. The fugue often ends with the subject in the original key.

Sonata refers to a composition of several movements for keyboard or for keyboard and other instruments. Sonatas often consist of three or four movements and are often similar to the symphony in structure. The first movement is usually allegro. The second movement is slower and often songlike. A third movement is moderately fast, usually a minuet or a scherzo. The final movement is fast. Composers use the four-movement plan not only for sonatas but also for symphonies and chamber music. The concerto follows a three-movement plan.

An arrangement of movements in these compositions is called *sonata plan* or *sonata cycle.* The first movement of these works, and sometimes the second and fourth movements, are written in *sonata* form, sometimes called *sonata-allegro* form. This form is written in three basic sections: the *exposition,* the *development,* and the *recapitulation.*

Free form gives the composer the greatest freedom of all. It follows no standard pattern or structure, though themes and rhythms usually recur. Free-form compositions include *preludes, fantasias,* and *rhapsodies.* Composers of the 1900's explored a variety of free forms.

History

Early music. Historians know little about music in the earliest civilizations. Musicians and musical instruments appear in a number of ancient works of art. Few examples of music were written down, however, and so it is almost impossible to know how the music sounded.

The ancient Greeks had a highly developed knowledge of music and used music in many ways. They used instrumental and vocal music in drama, religious ceremonies, and athletic games. Greek composers based their music on scales called *modes* that resembled some aspects of the major and minor scales used today. Two important early Greek instruments were the *aulos,* a wind instrument, and the *kithara,* a string instrument. The early Romans learned much about music from the Greeks and, like the Greeks, used music in many aspects of their society.

The Middle Ages in music history extended from the A.D. 400's to the early 1400's. Most surviving music of the period was composed for church services, but some was *secular* (nonreligious) music.

Church music. The first medieval music was monophonic vocal music sung by a soloist or a choir singing in unison without accompaniment. This music, called *plainsong, plainchant,* or simply *chant,* was used in Christian religious services. This music developed from several sources, including early Jewish religious music.

Pope Gregory I, who reigned from 590 to 604, was probably responsible for collecting and organizing the chants used in Christian church services. Chant came to be called *Gregorian chant* in memory of the pope.

Chant and other music of the Middle Ages was based on a harmonic system of eight scales called *church modes.* The concept and names were borrowed from scales used in ancient Greek music. Monks composed chants throughout the Middle Ages as well as the Renaissance period. However, the names of very few composers of chant are known.

Early church music was monophonic. By the 800's, composers had begun taking the first steps toward polyphonic music by adding another vocal line to an existing chant. This music is called *organum* or, in the plural, *organa.* Two of the earliest composers known by name were creators of organa, the French composers Léonin and Pérotin, also known by their Latin names Leoninus and Perotinus. They worked as musicians in the Cathedral of Notre Dame in Paris in the late 1100's and early 1200's. Their organa represented some of the

Choral singing plays an important part in many works of classical music. This chorus is performing an oratorio written by the Austrian composer Wolfgang Amadeus Mozart in 1771. The composition also features major roles for vocal soloists. An orchestra accompanies the singers.

finest music of their time. Musical notation developed during the Middle Ages. Notation is a method of writing down music so it can be read and performed. The first notation consisted of a set of symbols, called *neumes,* placed near the words as a memory aid for melody. Later, neumes were arranged higher or lower to indicate pitch. Guido d'Arezzo, an Italian monk, contributed greatly to the development of notation in the 1000's. He gave notes individual names based on their relative positions in the scale, such as *ut* (later *do), re, mi,* and *fa.*

The *mass* and the *motet* were the main religious vocal compositions during the Middle Ages. The mass set to music the standard parts of the main Christian celebration known as the Mass. The motet was a shorter, unaccompanied vocal composition based on secular texts in the 1200's and then increasingly religious texts from the 1300's through the 1500's. The motet developed from organum and became the main type of composed polyphonic music of the 1200's. The *conductus* was another religious or secular Latin song of some importance during the 1100's and 1200's. The motet and conductus were probably intended for one singer per part.

Secular music was probably popular with people from all levels of society during the Middle Ages. Medieval songwriters based their texts on love and aspects of nature. In French-speaking areas, courtly poet-composers called *troubadours* and *trouvères* became famous for their songs in the 1100's and 1200's. In German-speaking countries, *Minnesingers* were the counterparts of the trouvères from the 1100's to the 1300's. Their songs had no written instrumental accompaniment, but musicians sometimes may have improvised accompaniments.

The music of the 1300's in France became known as the *Ars Nova* (new art). The name was the written description of music by Philippe de Vitry, a French composer and poet, about 1320. Ars Nova featured greater variety of rhythm and more independence in part writing. Vitry and his famous contemporary Guillaume de Machaut of France wrote motets with complex rhythmic organization. Machaut also composed monophonic and polyphonic chansons of high quality. His *Notre Dame Mass* was the first polyphonic setting of the parts of the Ordinary of the Mass. This work, his songs, and his motets set him apart as one of the first great composers in Western culture.

In England, significant musical activity took place in the 1400's with such composers as Leonel Power and John Dunstable. They, too, wrote motets, masses, and secular songs of high quality.

Music in Italian areas began to flourish in the middle to late 1300's. Many masses, motets, and Italian secular songs of high artistic merit were written. Francesco Landini was one of several leading Italian composers of that time.

A contemporary of Dunstable in France was Guillaume Dufay. He was a leading composer of masses and also wrote secular songs with French texts. Dufay's music had a great influence on performers and composers of the next generation in France and the Netherlands.

The Renaissance. In Western music, the transition to the Renaissance began in the early 1400's. The Renaissance style lasted through the 1500's. Most composers of the Renaissance began their careers as singers in cathedral or chapel choirs. They studied music and composition while they acquired general education. Gradually, secular music gained in importance.

The development of printing in the West during the 1400's had a major impact by making written music more available. The printing of music developed rapidly and soon replaced the older system of copying by hand.

Franco-Flemish music. Many developments in music occurred in Flanders, a region that included parts of what are now Belgium, the Netherlands, and northern France. Johannes Ockeghem and Jacob Obrecht, both born in Flanders, were two major Flemish composers at the end of the 1400's. They held positions as composer or musical director with royal and wealthy families in France and Italy.

Josquin Desprez was one of the greatest composers of the Renaissance. He was born in northern France but lived in Italy for many years. Desprez wrote masses, motets, and secular compositions during the late 1400's and early 1500's.

Many Franco-Flemish composers held important positions with the church and nobility in Italy. During the 1500's, young Italian composers studied with them and began to emerge as capable composers.

Italian music. Giovanni Palestrina, in particular, became a master of polyphonic music. He wrote about 250 motets and about 100 masses.

Italian vocal compositions called *madrigals* developed as a major type of secular polyphonic song in the 1500's. Costanzo Festa, Luca Marenzio, and Claudio Monteverdi wrote madrigals for three to five unaccompanied voices. Most madrigals dealt with romantic themes, using Italian poetry about love, nature, and mythology.

Music in other countries. At the end of the 1500's, the Italian madrigal spread to England, where it was adapted to English texts. Soon the madrigal became popular in England through the compositions of William Byrd, Thomas Morley, and others.

In France, the chanson thrived in the 1500's, with composers writing in a new style that featured quick, strong rhythms. The style is often called the *Parisian chanson.* Leading composers were Claudin de Sermisy and Clément Janequin.

Instrumental music. Composers also wrote instrumental music in the 1500's. Dances of many types flourished. Composers created new types of instrumental works from vocal forms. Two new types of instrumental music were the *canzona,* which developed from the French chanson, and the *ricercare,* which resembled the motet.

Orlando di Lasso and Philippe de Monte were the last Franco-Flemish master composers at the end of the 1500's. Lasso, also known by his Flemish name Roland de Lassus, composed almost 2,000 works, including masses, chansons, and motets. Monte also wrote more than 1,200 secular choral pieces.

The Reformation was a religious revolution that produced a number of new musical concepts in the second half of the 1500's. In Germany, the Reformation leader Martin Luther and his followers wanted worshippers to participate more actively in church services. They especially wanted people to sing more and in local languages instead of the traditional Latin. To meet these goals, composers created the *chorale,* a hymn with German words sung in unison by the congregation.

In Switzerland, Reformation leader John Calvin and his followers believed that only Biblical texts should be sung in church. They set to music poems from the Bible called Psalms, first in French and then in other languages as the Reformation spread to other countries.

Similar changes came about in the Church of England during the reign of King Henry VIII in the mid-1500's. A change to the use of English in church services was followed by development of the *Service* and the *anthem,* new types of liturgical music that gained prominence.

The Baroque period in Western music extended from the early 1600's through the mid-1700's, though its roots date from the late 1500's. During the Baroque period, new types of instrumental works developed, especially in Italy. These works included the sonata, concerto, suite, and fugue. New types of vocal music also emerged, such as *monody,* a song style with a single melodic line and chordal instrumental accompaniment. The longer and more complex cantata, opera, and oratorio also appeared.

Andrea Gabrieli and his nephew Giovanni were composers who worked as organists at St. Mark's Church in Venice, Italy. They both composed innovative works that influenced many Baroque composers. Giovanni became noted for his motets with instrumental accompaniment.

Baroque music was characterized by the use of chord-playing instruments, such as the harpsichord or organ, and low-pitched instruments, such as the viola de gamba or cello, to play the bass line. This group was called *basso continuo* or just *continuo.* Numbers were often added beneath notes in the bass line to show keyboard players the chords they should play.

Major Italian composers of the Baroque era included Giovanni Gabrieli, Claudio Monteverdi, Arcangelo Corelli, Alessandro Scarlatti, and Antonio Vivaldi. The major French composers of this period were Jean-Baptiste Lully and Jean-Philippe Rameau, both of whom were active in developing French opera. Writing for keyboard instruments became important in France. François Couperin and Nicolas de Grigny wrote major works for harpsichord and organ.

Music for harpsichord was highly regarded in England in the 1600's. William Byrd and Orlando Gibbons were major composers for the instrument. In the later 1600's, Henry Purcell excelled in composing for the stage. His opera *Dido and Aeneas* (1689) is one of the finest English works of the period.

German Baroque composers wrote nearly every type of music. Heinrich Schütz was especially gifted in writing sacred music. Georg Philipp Telemann wrote over 1,000 cantatas along with other vocal music.

Johann Sebastian Bach and George Frideric Handel brought German Baroque music to its peak. Bach excelled in works for organ and harpsichord, chamber music, concertos, cantatas, oratorios, motets, and masses. Handel is especially noted for his Italian operas and oratorios in English.

The Classical period. In the mid-1700's, a new musical style developed. Often referred to as *galant,* the style was elegant and graceful, emphasizing prominent melodies supported by light accompaniment. This style grew into the Classical style, which flourished into the

Highlights in the history of classical music

c. 3000 B.C. The Sumerians played music on harplike instruments.

c. 500 B.C. The Greeks began to develop systems of music theory.

A.D. 400's B.C. Western European composers started to create polyphonic music.

c. 800 Plain song became the chief music of Christian worship.

1100's and 1200's Composers in Paris introduced the earliest system for writing down rhythmic values.

(c) Loyola University Chicago: R. V. Schoder, SJ

The kithara was an important stringed instrument of ancient Greece. The Greeks believed that music played on the kithara had a calming effect on listeners.

Stock Montage

Guido d'Arezzo, *left,* an Italian monk, developed a revolutionary system of notation and method of sight-singing in the A.D. 1000's.

Granger Collection

Troubadours often performed for royalty during the 1100's and 1200's in southern France. These poet-musicians helped popularize nonreligious songs.

early 1800's. The Classical style was noted for its clarity, balance, and regularity. By the mid-1700's, these qualities could be heard in the sonata, chamber music, concerto, and symphony. During the Classical era, both instrumental and vocal music flourished. Opera became increasingly popular.

The major composers of instrumental music during the Classical period were Wolfgang Amadeus Mozart and Joseph Haydn of Austria and Ludwig van Beethoven of Germany. Each also wrote superb masses. In addition, Mozart was one of the greatest opera composers.

Many Classical composers wrote for the piano, which was invented in the early 1700's and became increasingly popular. Beethoven's piano sonatas rank among the masterpieces written for the instrument. The harpsichord declined in popularity in the late 1700's and was ignored until it was revived in the mid-1900's by composers and performers.

The Romantic era. In the early 1800's, music became more varied, intense, and expressive. The style of this music became known as Romantic. The Romantic style was not a revolt against the Classical style but an expansion of it. Beethoven's later works show his growth from the clarity and directness of the Classical style to an increasingly complex and emotional Romantic style.

Romantic composers favored short works for soloists or small performing groups, and large works for orchestra and choir, which increased greatly in size. Pieces for solo piano and solo songs with piano accompaniment were especially popular. Composers in German-speaking countries were inspired to write great songs due to the rising popularity of the piano and the availability of great poetry. Franz Schubert of Austria excelled at composing art songs—called *Lieder* in German. The songs reflect Schubert's skill and sensitivity in setting fine poetry to lyrical, easily sung melodies.

The piano's expressive and dramatic qualities made that instrument an ideal instrument to support a solo voice. Schubert and the German composer Robert Schumann were among the composers who wrote *song cycles,* collections of songs related by a theme in the texts and sometimes by repeated melodic material. Short piano pieces and dances and longer pieces, especially the sonata, became increasingly popular. People enjoyed piano music, either in solo performance or with other instruments. The piano became the most popular instrument, for both the virtuoso and the amateur. Masterpieces of piano music were composed by Beethoven, Schumann, Johannes Brahms, and Felix Mendelssohn of Germany; Schubert of Austria; Frédéric Chopin of Poland; and Franz Liszt of Hungary.

Longer compositions for large performing groups were also popular in the 1800's. These works were mainly symphonies, concertos, masses, and oratorios. The great symphony composers included Germany's Beethoven and Brahms; France's Hector Berlioz; and Austria's Schubert, Anton Bruckner, and Gustav Mahler. Concertos for solo piano or violin and orchestra were written for virtuoso performers. Operas became longer, more dramatic, and more romantic in the works of Richard Wagner in Germany and Giuseppe Verdi and Giacomo Puccini in Italy.

The hero was important in Romantic literature. In the same way, music lovers idolized the highly skilled

1300's — Guillaume de Machaut of France wrote the first polyphonic mass composed by a single person.

1597 — Jacopo Peri of Italy composed *Dafne,* probably the first opera.

1600's — The modern system of major and minor scales came into use.

1722 — Johann Sebastian Bach of Germany completed Book I of the *Well-Tempered Clavier.*

1722 — Jean-Philippe Rameau, a French music theorist, published *Treatise of Harmony.*

Detail of a relief sculpture (1431-1438) by Luca della Robbia (SCALA/Art Resource)

During the Renaissance period, choirs consisted entirely of male singers. This marble sculpture shows a choir of boys singing a psalm.

Detail of *Psalms of Penitence* (1565-1570), a miniature painting on parchment by Hans Mielich; Bayer. Staatsbibliothek, Munich, Germany

Chamber music flourished during the 1500's. This chamber orchestra featured composer Orlando di Lasso of Flanders at the keyboard.

Detail of a German engraving (1732) (Granger Collection)

Johann Sebastian Bach composed many masterpieces during the first half of the 1700's. He is shown here conducting a performance of chamber music.

soloist in Romantic music. Audiences thrilled to Chopin and Liszt as great pianists, and to the Italian composer-violinist Niccolò Paganini.

Romantic composers wrote the same types of music that had been favored in the Classical style. They also devised new types of short piano pieces, such as the *nocturne* and the *intermezzo.* The symphony developed along two paths. One was the *abstract* or *absolute symphony* that had purely musical content. The other was the *program symphony,* which explored a literary idea or presented a pictorial scene. The only larger work that was new in the Romantic era was the symphonic poem.

In the later 1800's, many European composers began to feature national elements in their music. They used folk songs, folk dances, and national legends and folk tales in operas and other music. This nationalistic trend continued well into the 1900's. Outstanding nationalistic composers included Edvard Grieg of Norway, Modest Mussorgsky of Russia, and Isaac Albéniz of Spain.

The 1900's. Composers of the 1900's developed many new styles of music. Some composers, such as Igor Stravinsky, explored several styles.

Impressionism. Claude Debussy in France developed a new style of music that came to be called Impressionism. This style expanded the limits of *tonality* (centering harmony around one pitch—C major) with unusual and rich harmonies, and different types of scales and chord progressions. Debussy was friends with many Impressionist painters and Symbolist poets of the later 1800's. His music, like their paintings and poems, emphasized impressions of moods, emotions, and atmospheric effects rather than realistic details.

Music in the early 1900's was a blend of the old and the new. Late Romantic styles continued in the works of many composers who used new and fresh harmonic approaches. Nationalism continued in the works of such composers as Ralph Vaughan Williams of England, Béla Bartók of Hungary, Charles Ives and Aaron Copland of the United States, and Sergei Prokofiev and Dimitri Shostakovich of Russia (later part of the Soviet Union). Bartók's piano and orchestra works rank among the most impressive works of the early 1900's.

Igor Stravinsky was a Russian-born composer who explored several styles and approaches to music. His early works were strongly nationalistic, such as his ballet *The Firebird* (1910), based on Russian fairy tales. Stravinsky's influential ballet *The Rite of Spring* (1913) portrays a fertility ritual. Although the music is fundamentally tonal, it abandons traditional harmonies to explore *dissonance.* Composers create dissonance by combining notes and chords that create harsh or restless sounds.

Neoclassicism blends characteristics of earlier music with distinctly modern traits. Stravinsky turned to Neoclassicism in many of his works, such as his ballet *Pulcinella* (1920). *Pulcinella* uses passages from the music of Giovanni Pergolesi, an Italian composer of the early 1700's, and adds Stravinsky's own orchestration and other personal touches. Other Neoclassical composers were Paul Hindemith in Germany and Béla Bartók.

Atonal music. By 1908, the German composer Arnold Schoenberg had become discontented with using tonality in his compositions. Schoenberg experimented with *atonal* music, which has no central key and is extremely dissonant.

1742 — *Messiah,* an oratorio by George Frideric Handel of Germany, was first performed.

1787 — Wolfgang Amadeus Mozart of Austria wrote the opera *Don Giovanni.*

1794 — The Austrian composer Joseph Haydn completed his "London" Symphonies.

Early 1800's — Ludwig van Beethoven of Germany composed many of his greatest works.

Detail of *Leopold Mozart with His Two Children* (about 1765), an oil painting on canvas by Louis Carrogis; Carnavalet Museum, Paris (Giraudon/Art Resource)

As a young boy, Mozart showed extraordinary musical talent. This painting portrays him playing the piano, accompanied by his father and sister.

Stock Montage

Beethoven's studio. Beethoven worked in this studio in his home during his final years. Although he became totally deaf, he continued to compose great music.

Granger Collection

Franz Schubert of Austria wrote brilliant piano solos, chamber music, and symphonies. Here he is sitting at the piano, *lower left,* in a friend's home.

In the 1920's, Schoenberg formulated a system of atonal music called *twelve-tone music* or *serialism.* All 12 notes of the scale get equal emphasis, with no notes dominating, as they do in major or minor keys. Twelve-tone music became the basis for most of Schoenberg's music in the 1930's and 1940's. Schoenberg's innovative works aroused protests from audiences and conservative composers and critics. However, serialism had a strong influence on other composers of the 1900's. This influence is seen mainly in the music of two of Schoenberg's students, Austrian composers Anton Webern and Alban Berg.

In the 1940's, Olivier Messiaen of France and Milton Babbitt of the United States independently developed *total serialism.* In this style, the composer arranges other aspects of the music in addition to pitch, such as rhythm and duration, in a certain order or series.

Experimental music. Many composers wrote for traditional instruments but used them in unorthodox ways to create new, fresh sounds. In the mid-1900's, Henry Cowell of the United States based several works on the music of Japan, India, and ancient Persia. Cowell also created new sounds with the piano by scraping, slapping, plucking, and sweeping the open strings with the hand.

John Cage of the United States developed one of the most inventive musical minds of the middle and late 1900's. As a young composer, he was influenced by the French-born composer Edgard Varèse, developing new styles and forms of percussion music. Cage became famous for his *prepared piano,* in which several strings were muted with pieces of wood, metal, rubber, or glass.

Cage also helped develop *aleatory,* or *chance, music,* in which all or part of the sounds depend on last minute choices by the performer. The composer provides only a general outline of the piece. The music leaves the performers largely free to create melodies and rhythms that vary with each performance.

Electronic music was explored by composers early in the 1900's. In electronic music, the composer uses electronic equipment to create sounds that have any desired pitch, loudness, tone, and duration. Pierre Schaeffer of France created a forerunner of electronic music that he called *musique concrète* about 1948. Schaeffer recorded natural sounds, such as instruments, voices, and noise, and then manipulated the recording to achieve the sound he desired. Although not truly electronic, this early work solved some of the problems for later composers working with electronically generated sounds.

Electronic music studios emerged in radio stations in Europe and then in universities in the United States in the 1950's. Some composers found that only electronic instruments, such as the synthesizer, provided the new sounds they desired. Other composers successfully combined traditional musical instruments with electronically generated sounds recorded on tape. Mario Davidovsky, an Argentine-born American composer, created many significant works in this way.

Third-stream music combined the harmonic qualities of classical music with the rhythmic and improvisational elements of jazz, blues, ragtime, and other forms of popular music. The American composer George Gershwin combined classical and popular forms in some of his compositions, but the term generally refers to music be-

The Polish-born composer Frédéric Chopin wrote outstanding compositions for solo piano.

Mid-1800's c.

Richard Wagner of Germany created operas that featured *leitmotifs* (recurrent themes).

Johannes Brahms of Germany composed brilliant symphonies in the style of Beethoven.

Late 1800's

A vivid musical style called Impressionism developed in France.

Granger Collection

Hector Berlioz ranked as the leading French musician of the Romantic period. He became famous throughout Europe as a composer, conductor, and music critic.

Bettmann Archive

The Ring of the Nibelung, a group of operas by Wagner, was first performed in its entirety in 1876. This painting shows a scene from that performance.

All-Union Association Vneshtorgizdat, Moscow

Swan Lake, one of the world's great ballets, premiered in Moscow in 1877. Peter Ilich Tchaikovsky of Russia composed the music for this ballet.

ginning in the 1950's. The American composer Gunther Schuller invented the term and created music in that style. Other composers of third-stream music included the Americans William Bolcom and John Lewis.

Minimalism began in the 1960's. Minimalist composers repeated melodies, rhythms, and harmonies with small, gradual changes. These repeated patterns often create a hypnotic effect. The American composers Steve Reich and Philip Glass became known for this style.

Classical music today

Many composers of the 1900's wrote challenging, often atonal, works without considering the taste of their audience. By the late 1900's and early 2000's, however, composers seemed increasingly interested in writing music to please their listeners. Leading practitioners of a return to tonality were the American composers John Adams and David Del Tredici. Adams began his career as a Minimalist and then turned away from that style. Del Tredici used folk music and rock music in many compositions.

John Corigliano of the United States won acclaim for his film scores as well as his orchestral works. The Americans Joan Tower and Ellen Taaffe Zwilich are two of the most successful women composers in history.

Daniel T. Politoske

Related articles in *World Book.* See the *Arts* section of the articles on various countries, such as **Mexico** (Arts). See also:

Biographies

For biographies of other persons relating to classical music, see the lists of *Related articles* at the end of **Hymn; Opera; Orchestra; Piano;** and **Violin.** See also:

American composers

Barber, Samuel
Bernstein, Leonard
Billings, William
Blitzstein, Marc
Bloch, Ernest
Cage, John
Carter, Elliott
Copland, Aaron
Cowell, Henry
Crumb, George
Dello Joio, Norman
Gershwin, George
Glass, Philip
Gottschalk, Louis M.
Gould, Morton
Grofé, Ferde
Hanson, Howard
Harris, Roy
Hovhaness, Alan
Ives, Charles E.
MacDowell, Edward Alexander
Menotti, Gian Carlo
Moore, Douglas S.
Piston, Walter
Schuman, William
Sessions, Roger
Still, William Grant
Thomson, Virgil
Varèse, Edgard
Zwilich, Ellen Taaffe

Austrian composers

Berg, Alban
Bruckner, Anton
Czerny, Karl
Haydn, Joseph
Kreisler, Fritz
Mahler, Gustav
Mozart, Wolfgang
Schoenberg, Arnold
Schubert, Franz P.
Strauss, Johann, Sr.
Strauss, Johann, Jr.
Webern, Anton

British composers

Britten, Benjamin
Byrd, William
Delius, Frederick
Dowland, John
Elgar, Sir Edward W.
Gibbons, Orlando
Holst, Gustav
Morley, Thomas
Purcell, Henry
Sullivan, Sir Arthur S.
Tallis, Thomas
Vaughan Williams, Ralph
Walton, Sir William

French composers

Berlioz, Hector
Bizet, Georges
Boulez, Pierre
Couperin, François
Debussy, Claude
Delibes, Léo
Dukas, Paul A.
Fauré, Gabriel U.

1920's — Arnold Schoenberg of Austria developed *serialism,* a method of composition based on all 12 notes of the scale.

1930's — Dimitri Shostakovich developed a sophisticated modern style of Russian music.

1958 — Edgard Varése, a French-born composer, produced *Poème Electronique,* the first major work of electronic music.

2000 — The American composer John Corigliano completed his Symphony No. 2 for string orchestra.

© Jack Vartoogian

The Firebird is a ballet composed by Russian-born Igor Stravinsky. The ballet was first performed in 1910. Stravinsky based the work on Russian folklore.

Stock Montage

Wozzeck, an opera by Alban Berg of Austria, caused a sensation at its premiere in 1925. This picture shows a performance in Germany in 1931.

© Ron Scherl, Stage/Image

Electronic music is composed with special electronic equipment. American composer John Coolidge Adams is creating music on an electronic keyboard.

Franck, César
Gounod, Charles
Honegger, Arthur
Ibert, Jacques
Lully, Jean-B.
Massenet, Jules
Messiaen, Olivier
Milhaud, Darius
Offenbach, Jacques
Poulenc, Francis
Rameau, Jean-Philippe
Ravel, Maurice
Saint-Saëns, Camille
Satie, Erik

German composers

Bach, Carl Philipp Emanuel
Bach, Johann Christian
Bach, Johann Sebastian
Beethoven, Ludwig van
Brahms, Johannes
Bruch, Max
Buxtehude, Dietrich
Gluck, Christoph Willibald
Handel, George Frideric
Henze, Hans Werner
Hindemith, Paul
Humperdinck, Engelbert
Mendelssohn, Felix
Meyerbeer, Giacomo
Orff, Carl
Schumann, Clara
Schumann, Robert
Stockhausen, Karlheinz
Strauss, Richard
Telemann, Georg Philipp
Wagner, Richard
Weber, Carl Maria von

Italian composers

Bellini, Vincenzo
Berio, Luciano
Boccherini, Luigi
Boito, Arrigo
Cherubini, Luigi
Clementi, Muzio
Corelli, Arcangelo
Dallapiccola, Luigi
Donizetti, Gaetano
Leoncavallo, Ruggiero
Mascagni, Pietro
Monteverdi, Claudio
Paganini, Niccolò
Palestrina, Giovanni
Pergolesi, Giovanni B.
Puccini, Giacomo
Respighi, Ottorino
Rossini, Gioacchino A.
Scarlatti, Alessandro
Scarlatti, Domenico
Tartini, Giuseppe
Verdi, Giuseppe
Vivaldi, Antonio

Russian composers

Borodin, Alexander
Glinka, Mikhail I.
Khachaturian, Aram I.
Mussorgsky, Modest
Prokofiev, Sergei S.
Rachmaninoff, Sergei V.
Rimsky-Korsakov, Nikolai
Rubinstein, Anton G.
Scriabin, Alexander
Shostakovich, Dimitri
Stravinsky, Igor
Tchaikovsky, Peter I.

Other composers

Albéniz, Isaac
Bartók, Béla
Chávez, Carlos
Chopin, Frédéric F.
Desprez, Josquin
Dvořák, Antonín
Falla, Manuel de
Ginastera, Alberto
Grainger, Percy A.
Grieg, Edvard
Janáček, Leoš
Kodály, Zoltán
Lasso, Orlando di
Liszt, Franz
Nielsen, Carl A.
Paderewski, Ignace J.
Penderecki, Krzysztof
Sibelius, Jean
Smetana, Bedřich
Villa-Lobos, Heitor

Elements of music

Counterpoint
Harmonics
Harmony
Key
Pitch
Rhythm
Sound
Tone

Instrumental musical forms

Concerto
Étude
Fantasia
Fugue
Intermezzo
March
Minuet
Overture
Rondo
Scherzo
Serenade
Sonata
Suite
Symphonic poem
Symphony
Variation
Waltz

Vocal music

Ballade
Barcarole
Bard
Canon
Cantata
Chorale
Hymn
Lieder
Madrigal
Meistersinger
Minnesinger
Minstrel
National anthem
Opera
Operetta
Oratorio
Passion music
Singing
Song
Troubadour
Trouvère
Voice

Other related articles

Aleatory music
American Society of Composers, Authors and Publishers
Ballet
Baroque (Baroque music)
Cecilia, Saint
Chamber music
Composer
Electronic music
Greece, Ancient (The arts)
Metronome
Music Clubs, National Federation of
Orchestra
Pulitzer Prizes (Music)
Romanticism (Romanticism in music)
Suzuki method
Treble
Tuning fork
Western frontier life in America (Music)

Outline

I. **Instrumental music**
  A. Solo music
  B. Chamber music
  C. Orchestral music
II. **Vocal music**
  A. Songs
  B. Choral music
  C. Operas
  D. Oratorios
III. **Classical music forms**
  A. Sectional form
  B. Rondo
  C. Variation
  D. Fugue
  E. Sonata
  F. Free form
IV. **History**

Questions

What was chant?
What are the main types of orchestral music?
What major new styles of music developed in the early 1900's?
What is chamber music?
What is the major difference between an opera and an oratorio?
Who were the major composers of instrumental music during the Classical era?
What are the main techniques that composers use to give structure to their music?
How is the sonata form arranged?
What is aleatory music? Electronic music?
What is a symphonic poem?

Additional resources

Cummings, David, ed. *Random House Encyclopedic Dictionary of Classical Music.* Random Hse., 1997.
Goulding, Phil G. *Classical Music: The 50 Greatest Composers and Their 1,000 Greatest Works.* 1992. Reprint. Fawcett, 1995.
Kendall, Alan. *The Chronicle of Classical Music.* 1994. Reprint. Thames & Hudson, 2000.
Kennedy, Michael. *The Oxford Dictionary of Music.* Rev. ed. Oxford, 1999.
Kramer, Lawrence. *Classical Music and Postmodern Knowledge.* Univ. of Calif. Pr., 1995.
Rosen, Charles. *The Classical Style: Haydn, Mozart, Beethoven.* 2nd ed. Norton, 1997.
Sadie, Stanley, ed. *The New Grove Dictionary of Music and Musicians.* 29 vols. 2nd. ed. Grove Pr., 2001.
Slonimsky, Nicolas. *The Great Composers and Their Works.* 2 vols. Ed. by Electra Yourke. Schirmer Bks., 2000.
Slonimsky, Nicolas, and Kuhn, L. D., eds. *Baker's Biographical Dictionary of Musicians.* 6 vols. 9th ed. Schirmer Bks., 2000.
Stanley, John. *Classical Music.* Reader's Digest, 1994.

© Peter Rogers, Getty Images

The Internet makes possible communication that reaches around the world. Individuals may use the Internet to exchange information, perform research, or even shop. At an Internet cafe, such as this one in Beijing, people pay a fee to use the establishment's Internet-ready computers.

Internet

Internet is a vast network of computers that connects many of the world's businesses, institutions, and individuals. The Internet, which is short for *interconnected network of networks,* links tens of thousands of smaller computer networks. It enables users of computers and other networked devices throughout the world to send and receive messages, share information in a variety of forms, and even play computer games with people thousands of miles or kilometers away. Computers linked to the Internet range from simple and inexpensive personal computers, often called *PC's,* to huge *mainframe* computers used by government institutions, educational institutions, and businesses. Other devices linked to the Internet include sophisticated telephones and televisions.

Computers and other devices require special hardware and software to connect to the Internet. Necessary hardware includes a *modem* or an *adapter.* A modem is a device that translates a computer's *digital* (numerical) information into signals that can be transmitted over telephone lines, over cable, or through the air as wireless communications (see **Modem**). An adapter links a computer to a high-speed communication system designed to carry data in digital form. Adapters are often called *modems,* though they are not true modems. Required software includes a communications program that allows the transmission and receipt of messages. Many computers and computing devices come with modems and communications software installed.

The Internet, often called simply the Net, began as a collection of text-only documents intended for scientists, universities, and some parts of government. But the development and rapid growth of the World Wide Web (also known as the Web) transformed the presentation of information on the Net. The Web is a worldwide system of interconnected computer files linked to one another on the Net. It enables the use of *multimedia*—which includes photographs, moving pictures, and sound as well as text. Multimedia presentations on the Web approach the visual quality of television and the *audio* (sound) quality of recorded music.

The Web consists of millions of *Web sites,* collections of information at specific electronic addresses. Web sites in turn contain *Web pages* that hold multimedia or text-only information. Web sites and their pages reside in computers connected to the Internet.

Uses of the Internet

Today, tens of millions of people and businesses use the Net and the Web daily. The major uses include communications, research, publishing, business transactions, and *push technology,* which employs the Web for the broadcast of video and audio programming.

Communications. Probably the most popular use of the Internet and the Web is sending and receiving electronic mail, usually called *e-mail.* The number of e-mail messages sent each year far exceeds the number of pieces of traditional mail carried by the world's postal systems.

Individuals, companies, and institutions have e-mail addresses that enable the sending and receipt of mail, just as a street address or post office box provides directions for traditional mail delivery. Users generally acquire e-mail addresses through an *Internet service provider* (ISP) or an *online service.* Both of these types of businesses provide access to the Internet. An ISP maintains its customers' e-mail addresses, routes e-mail and requests for Internet-based information to and from its users, and

Glossary of Internet terms

Bulletin board is an electronic message center. Most bulletin boards serve specific interest groups. They allow users to read messages left by others and to leave their own as well.
Chat room is a location on the Internet where users can discuss topics of common interest by sending typed messages back and forth. The messages appear as soon as they are typed.
Client is a user's computer.
Cookie is a piece of data placed on a client's hard drive by a server. It can be used for a variety of purposes. One such purpose would be to store a name and password so that a user would not have to enter this information every time he or she returned to the same Web site.
Download is to receive data or software over the Internet and store it so that it may be used later.
E-commerce is a term for business transactions that are carried out over the Internet.
E-mail, or electronic mail, is a way of sending a message over the Internet to another specific user or group of users.
Firewall is a combination of hardware and software that prevents a visitor to an organization's Web site from gaining access to other information stored on the organization's computer network, such as corporate records or employee information.
Home page is the starting page of a Web site. It generally includes tools and indexes to help visitors navigate through the rest of the site. In many ways, a home page functions as an electronic table of contents.
Hyperlink is a programmed connection from one Web site to another. It usually appears on a Web site as a highlighted or underlined word or phrase. When a user clicks a mouse on the passage, the client connects to the related Web site.
Hypertext markup language, or HTML, is the programming language most commonly used by the World Wide Web.
Hypertext transfer protocol, or HTTP, is the set of rules governing the transfer of files between a server and a client. HTTP electronically oversees the connection of clients to Web sites.
Internet service provider is a business that provides a client with the means to connect to the Internet and maintains exchanges of information between clients and servers.
Modem is a device that converts a computer's digital information to signals that can be transmitted over telephone lines, over cable, or through the air. It also converts signals it receives back to digital information.
Net is a common abbreviation for *Internet.*
Network is a communication system that links two or more computers.
Newsgroup, or *forum,* is an online discussion group in which participants with a common interest can exchange open messages.
Online service is a business that provides Internet access plus a wide range of exclusive content and features, such as chat rooms, games, and news reports.
Search engine is a program that allows a user to locate information on the Internet by typing in key words or phrases. The search engine then returns addresses of Web sites that most closely match the request.
Server, or host, is a computer that provides requested resources, such as information or software, to a client via a modem or network connection.
Surfing is the process of visiting a number of Web sites in rapid succession.
Uniform resource locator, or URL, is an electronic address that identifies a Web site.
Web browser, or simply *browser,* is a piece of software that allows a user to access Web sites.
Web site is a collection of information at a specific address on the World Wide Web.
World Wide Web is a worldwide system of interconnected computer files linked to one another on the Internet.

manages high-speed communications lines that quicken the transfer of data over the Internet. An online service resembles an ISP, but it provides a wide range of exclusive content in addition to Internet access. Most ISP's and online services allow customers to have several different e-mail addresses.

Many e-mail users attach illustrations, sound files, and even videos to their e-mails. An e-mail recipient whose computer system contains the required software can then view and listen to attachments as well as read the text message. Attachments may include charts and graphs, and even the text of entire books.

The Internet easily enables *multiple mailings,* the sending of the same e-mail to many addresses. Businesses advertise products and services via e-mail. *Newsgroups*—loose organizations of people who share a common interest—also use multiple mailings. They send their members copies of e-mail on the subject of interest. Members can respond to those e-mails and may introduce new topics.

Because much e-mail contains financial and other private information, most e-mail software includes *encryption technology*—programs that convert private e-mail into secret code for transmission. Similar software *decrypts* (translates back into readable language) the code when it reaches its intended destination.

Research. Much of the Internet resembles a vast library, containing as much information on every subject as might be held in tens of millions of books. Information may appear as files consisting only of text or as multimedia displays.

Special types of programs called *search engines* help people sort through the vast amounts of information on the Internet. Web users can choose from many search engines available on Web pages. A search engine allows a user to enter a topic for search, then finds Web pages that match that topic.

Because of the ease with which computers store information, and the speed with which computer users can access it, the Internet serves as a popular first stop for many people investigating a particular topic. A businessperson might search Internet resources for help in developing sales or product information. Students can access databases to find material related to homework assignments. Physicians can use the Net to compare medical treatments and to review advances in medical science. Scientists can share research data on the Net.

Publishing. Publishers increasingly use the Internet as a medium for presenting the contents of newspapers, magazines, and books. Because information on the Net is electronic, the publisher saves the costs of paper, printing, and distribution. More importantly, the publisher can update information almost instantly, making it possible to distribute far more current news than could be provided on paper.

Electronic versions of newspapers and magazines often contain more information than a paper publication could include. Web-based publications can also present interactive features. For example, a news story may contain *links* (interactive connections) to related stories or background information. If a reader wishes to explore the linked material, he or she simply clicks on a highlighted word to connect to a Web page containing that information.

The Internet also serves as a distribution system for *e-books* (electronic books). An e-book consists of digital files formatted so that when a reader *downloads* (transfers) them to a special handheld device—or to a computer

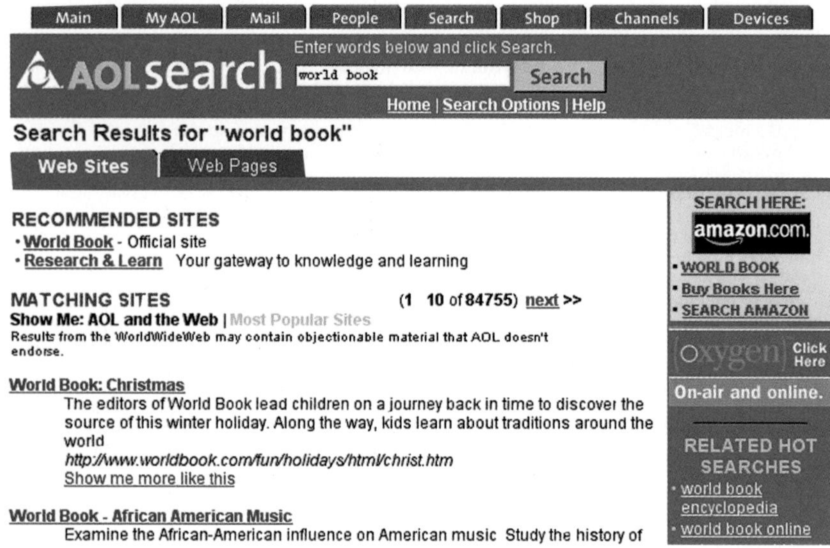

A search engine enables a user to locate Web sites related to a specified topic. The search engine returns results containing links that the user can select to connect to any of the Web sites.

with special software—the words and pictures appear much as they would on a printed page. A customer can buy e-books at the publisher's Web site or at a site owned by a bookstore. Some electronic library sites maintain collections of text-only e-books. These e-books can be viewed without special devices or software.

Business transactions. Many companies use the Internet to carry out business transactions commonly referred to as *e-commerce.* Retailers sell nearly every type of product over the Internet. Users generally pay for such purchases with credit cards. Software publishers view the Net as a convenient and inexpensive way to distribute their products. Over the Internet, users can buy new computer programs, sample programs before purchasing them, or receive upgrades to programs they already own. Music publishers sell copies of songs as downloadable digital files.

Transactions between companies and consumers are commonly known as B2C (business to consumer) transactions. Additionally, many companies use the Internet to engage in B2B (business to business) transactions. By linking together in a vast network, buyers and sellers can share information, keep track of inventories, assess needs, and compare products far more efficiently than they could using traditional business communications.

The Internet also has important uses within the financial community. Many banks and stockbrokers offer their customers software to make and track investments from their computer. Consumers can use similar software to pay many types of bills. Individuals can also file tax returns and pay taxes over the Internet. Economic transactions over the Internet use encryption technology to protect the privacy and security of the users.

A popular type of Internet business is the online auction. Online auctions enable people to post descriptions of items they wish to sell, along with a suggested opening bid. Visitors to the auction site may place a bid on any posted item. Consumer auction sites offer almost every imaginable type of item. But most forbid the sale of dangerous or illegal materials. Business auction sites, also called *trading exchanges,* have captured a large share of B2B transactions. Such sites may, for example, offer manufacturers the chance to bid on raw materials.

Push technology, also known as *Webcasting* or *Netcasting,* takes advantage of the ability of the Internet and the Web to deliver high-quality digital audio or video signals. Push technology enables producers to distribute their presentations to PC's and other devices capable of receiving and playing them.

Push technology programs have no fixed schedules. A producer can offer audio or video presentations to anyone who subscribes to them. The user might either download the entire video to his or her computer for later playback or play it in real time over the Internet. Real-time play is possible through a technology called *streaming.* Many radio stations stream their programming in real time so that people throughout the world may listen over the Web. Many also offer downloads of previous programming.

Television networks and movie producers often use push technology to promote their products and to present clips from programs and motion pictures. Some television producers have created programming specifically for the Web. Such programs are often called *Webisodes.*

Some television news organizations use the Web to post additional stories, constantly updating the news. They also offer extended versions of interviews and other features. Popular offerings include weather reports, global financial information, sports scores, and breaking news.

The Net is a popular showcase for short independent films. Many independent and amateur filmmakers create films using *digital video cameras,* which store video in digital format suitable for transmission over the Internet. They can then use special software to edit their films and to add professional-quality special effects.

Other uses. Yet another popular feature of the Net is *chat.* Using special software, users can gather in electronic "chat rooms" and send typed messages back and forth, discussing topics of common interest. The Internet also features many Web-based games with animation, sound effects, and music. Game players can challenge others in distant countries to tournaments.

The creation of personal Web pages is a particularly popular use of the Web. Individuals create and maintain these pages. Some people use their pages to share such information as personal interests or family history. Others use personal Web pages to promote particular ideas and theories. Most ISP's and online services provide space on a resource computer called a *server,* or *host,* for *hosting* (storing) Web pages for individuals. Many services include the use of this space within the subscription price. But some charge the individual separately for the use of server space.

Advertisers often place messages on frequently visited Web pages. Links join these messages electronically to the advertiser's own Web site. In effect, advertisers can invite Internet users to view commercials on their computer. Additionally, a user can supply the advertiser with his or her e-mail address to get further information, or such incentives as discount coupons.

How the Internet works

Computer networks enable computers to communicate and share information and resources. The simplest networks consist of a user's computer, known as the *client,* and a server. The client makes requests of the server, which, in turn, provides the requested resources, such as information or software. The Internet works in much the same way, on a far vaster scale. To connect to the Net, a user *logs on* by instructing his or her computer's communications software to contact the ISP or online service. To protect the user's security, this process usually requires a secret password.

The Internet was built around telephone connections that were, for the most part, the same as those used for voice communications. But the ever-increasing volume of Internet traffic, and the large size of video and sound files, require faster communications links. High-speed links, often called *broadband connections,* can deliver large amounts of information more quickly than traditional telephone lines can.

Among the most common broadband connections are (1) cable television connections, (2) fiber-optic telephone lines, (3) ISDN (integrated services digital network) and DSL (digital subscriber line), and (4) satellite connections. Cable television connections use the same cables that deliver television signals to carry Internet traffic. They require the use of a special cable modem. Fiber-optic telephone lines employ thin, high-capacity fibers to transmit vast amounts of information as patterns of light. ISDN and DSL use new technologies to increase the information-carrying capacity of traditional copper phone lines. Satellite connections use wireless communications with orbiting satellites. They enable people to use the Internet even in locations with no land-based communications lines.

Once connected to the ISP or online service, the user has several options. The user's communications software alone may provide access to such functions as e-mail and newsgroups. Most such software also includes a simple word processing program that enables a user to compose, revise, or read messages. A piece of software known as a *browser* enables a user to gain access to millions of Web sites. Each site has a separate electronic address,

© Brad Trent

Racks of routers enable an online service to direct the queries of millions of customers to the correct Internet addresses.

known as a *uniform resource locator* (URL). Many search engines and other programs throughout the Internet maintain and constantly update directories of addresses.

The addresses themselves are organized into various *top level domains* (major categories). In a URL, the top level domain takes the form of an extension of two or more letters, such as *.ca* for *Canada, .com* for *commercial, .edu* for *educational,* or *.museum* for *museum.* An organization called the Internet Corporation for Assigned Names and Numbers (ICANN) coordinates the assignment of top level domains. In the United States, a *domain name* includes a top level domain and a *second level domain.* In the domain name *worldbook.com,* for example, *worldbook* is the second level domain.

By typing an address, or by clicking on a link, a user transmits a request through the ISP or online service and onto the larger Internet. When the request arrives at the desired destination, the server responds by sending the user the requested information. This information is often in the form of a starting page called a *home page,* which often resembles the table of contents of a book or magazine. From a home page, the user can search for further information by using links to other pages within the same Web site or to other Web sites.

Most browsers include systems for *bookmarking* (recording) the addresses of favorite or frequently visited sites. A user who has bookmarked a site simply clicks on the appropriate bookmark to visit the site again.

Many individuals maintain personal Web sites under domain names that include their own names. Several companies register domain names. Many ISP's and online services also register domain names for their customers for an added charge.

Many files, especially illustration, motion-picture, and sound files, travel over the Internet in compressed form. One compression technique stores data that represent a less precise version of an image or sound than the original file does. Another technique saves space by removing image or sound data that are repeated, then merging all the repeated sections together into a separate file. When the original file is decompressed, the repeated sections return to their proper places.

Concerns about use of the Internet

The Internet and the Web have revealed only a fraction of their potential as tools for education, research, communications, news, and entertainment. Most people believe that the benefits of the Internet far outweigh its challenges. However, some people have serious concerns over the use of the Internet.

Concerns about material. Among concerns over use of the Internet are doubts about the accuracy and appropriateness of the material available on the Net. Much information posted on the Internet may be misleading, inaccurate, or even fraudulent. Many teachers teach their students how to evaluate the information they find on the Internet and identify which Web sites are reputable sources.

Many parents worry about violent or pornographic material available on the Net. Criminals may lurk in chat rooms, seeking to arrange face-to-face meetings with unsuspecting victims. Special programs known as *parental control software* can help parents restrict access to sites that may be unsuitable for children.

Security is an important concern for those who use the Internet. Mischievous programmers known as *hackers* often try to break into large computer systems. Some damage databases stored in these systems or attempt to steal information or electronic funds. Others may seek access to personal financial information. Many people feel concerned about the security and confidentiality of credit card numbers used to make purchases over the Internet. To protect themselves and their services from unwanted intruders, many ISP's and online services, corporations, and even individuals erect software and hardware barriers called *firewalls.* Such barriers seal off a server or other computer from intrusion.

Software itself can become a danger on the Internet. Programs known as *viruses, e-mail bombs, Trojan horses,* and *worms* have spread across the Internet and can cause damage to data on systems that receive them. Some of these programs have spread to computers around the world in a matter of hours. Many companies produce software designed to protect users from viruses and other such destructive programs. Most publishers of virus protection software update their programs when new types of viruses are detected. Customers can often download these updates over the Internet.

Legal issues. The distribution of e-books, digital music, and digital video poses important legal questions, particularly because digital files can be so easily *pirated*—that is, copied and distributed without permission or payment. Web users can e-mail copies of e-books and digital recordings anywhere. Unauthorized Web sites offer pirated e-books, recordings, or videos. Some Internet companies provide sites where people can share digital copies of music. At first, this sharing was free, and the traditional music industry claimed that the practice was illegal. Several music distributors participated in lawsuits against the companies. As a result, these companies have begun to charge customers for downloads and pay fees to music publishers.

Internet availability. As the Internet and Web have become more popular and powerful, concern has grown about equality of access to their resources. Computers are costly, as are ISP and online service subscriptions. To ensure more equal access to the Net, many public libraries and schools provide Internet-capable computers for individual use. In many cities around the world, establishments known as *Internet cafes* offer people the use of Internet-ready computers for a fee

WORLD BOOK diagram by Greg Maxson, Precision Graphics

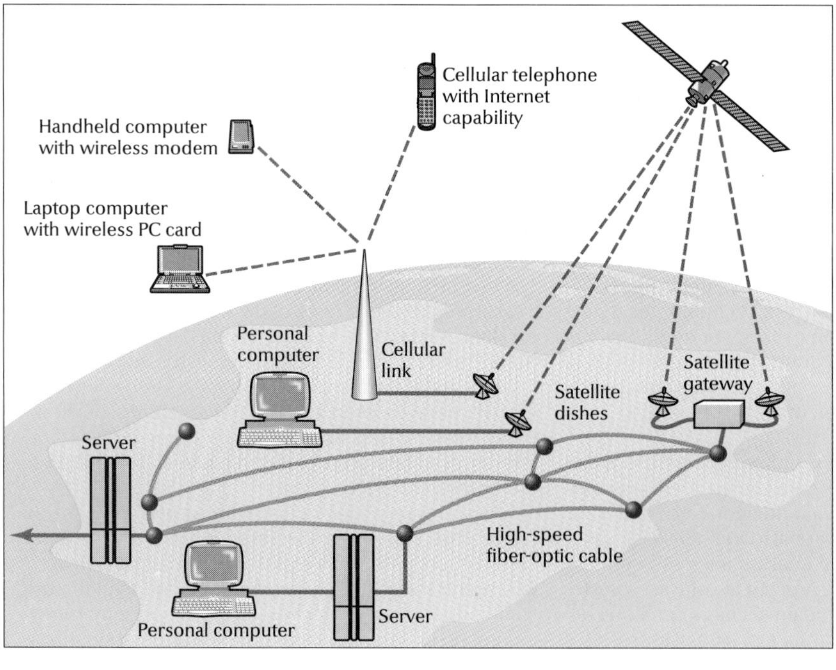

How the Internet works
A number of different types of equipment enable people to gain access to the Internet. High-speed communication lines, wireless transmitters, and satellites may all play a part in a single exchange of information between two computers via the Internet.

based on time of use. Such establishments are especially popular in areas of the world where many people do not have computers or even telephones.

History of the Internet

Early development. The Internet began to take shape in the late 1960's. The United States Department of Defense was concerned at the time about the possibility of devastating nuclear warfare. It began investigating means of linking computer installations together so that their ability to communicate might withstand a war. Through its Advanced Research Projects Agency (ARPA), the Defense Department initiated *ARPANet,* a network of university and military computers.

The network's operating *protocols* (rules) laid the groundwork for relatively fast and error-free computer-to-computer communications. Other networks adopted these protocols, which in turn evolved as new computer and communications technologies became available.

Throughout the 1970's, ARPANet grew at a slow but steady pace. Computers in other countries began to join the network. Other networks came into existence as well. These included Unix to Unix Copy (UUCP), which was established to serve users of the UNIX operating system, and the User's Network (USENET), a medium for posting text-based articles on a variety of subjects.

By 1981, just over 200 computers were connected to ARPANet. The U.S. military then divided the network into two organizations—ARPANet and a purely military network. During the 1980's, ARPANet was absorbed by NSFNET, a more advanced network developed by the National Science Foundation, an independent agency of the federal government. Soon, the collection of networks became known simply as the Internet.

One of the reasons for the slow growth of the early Internet was the difficulty of using the network. To access its information, users had to master a number of complex series of programming commands that required either memorization or frequent reference to special manuals.

The World Wide Web. The Internet's breakthrough to mass popularity occurred in 1991 with the arrival of the World Wide Web. The Web was developed by Tim Berners-Lee, a British computer scientist at the European Organization for Nuclear Research (CERN). One feature that helped popularize the Web was its ability to deliver multimedia.

The programming language that the Web used, called *hypertext markup language* (HTML), made it far easier to link information from computers throughout the world. This development effectively created an interactive index that enabled users to jump easily from the resources of one computer to another, effortlessly following an information trail around the world. The arrival of browsers in 1993 further simplified use of the Web and the Internet, and brought about staggering growth.

In the 1990's, many businesses were created on the Internet. Some were considered among the most valuable businesses in the world. But their values often rested in their potential, or the excitement people felt about this new way of doing business, and few actually made a profit. By 2000, many of these companies had gone out of business. Companies that operated traditional retail businesses in addition to ones on the Internet were, on the whole, more successful.

CERN

Tim Berners-Lee, a British computer scientist working at CERN, a European scientific research center, developed the World Wide Web. The Web opened the Internet to multimedia.

New technologies continue to increase the importance of the Internet. Handheld computers and Internet-capable cellular telephones take advantage of satellite communications to enable people to access the Internet from any location. Dedicated devices often called *Internet appliances* or *network computers* provide e-mail and Web browsing ability to people who do not require the greater capabilities of a PC. Manufacturers increasingly add computer features to television sets, and many of these sets provide Internet capabilities.

The Web has moved rapidly from inception to global acceptance. Most computer experts expect the Web to continue its rapid growth. New technologies will aid its growth by adding such features as spoken-word commands, instantaneous translation, and increased availability of historical and archival material. Keith Ferrell

Related articles in *World Book* include:

Auction
Berners-Lee, Tim
Communication (The development of the Internet)
Computer (Computer networks)
Distance learning
E-commerce
Electronic publishing
Etiquette (Internet etiquette)
Information retrieval
Medicine (Computers and electronic communication)
Online service
Web site
World Wide Web

Outline

I. Uses of the Internet
- A. Communications
- B. Research
- C. Publishing
- D. Business transactions
- E. Push technology
- F. Other uses

II. How the Internet works

III. Concerns about use of the Internet
- A. Concerns about material
- B. Security
- C. Legal issues
- D. Internet availability

IV. History of the Internet

Questions

What are some legal issues raised by the distribution of digital files over the Internet?
What is *multimedia?*
What is a *Web site?* A *Web page?*
How does the Internet aid television and movie producers?
How did the introduction of the World Wide Web increase the popularity of the Internet?
What are some ways in which the Internet benefits society?
How do *links* make it easy to move from Web page to Web page?
What is a *server?*
What role do telephone lines play in the Internet?
What is *e-commerce?*

© Ray Juno, Corbis Stock Market

Montreal is the second largest city in Canada, after Toronto, and one of the largest French-speaking cities in the world. Many modern office towers stand in downtown Montreal.

Montreal

Montreal, *MAHN tree AWL,* is the second largest city in Canada, after Toronto, and the largest city in the province of Quebec. Montreal is also one of the world's largest French-speaking cities. More than half of Montreal's people speak French as their first language.

Montreal is a major center of Canadian education, culture, business, and industry. Since the 1940's, Toronto has gradually replaced Montreal as Canada's most important economic center. However, Montreal remains more important than Toronto in higher education.

The city of Montreal lies on an island and is built around a mountain. The Island of Montreal sits in the St. Lawrence River, near where the St. Lawrence and Ottawa rivers meet in southern Quebec. A tree-covered mountain, Mount Royal, rises 763 feet (233 meters) in the island's center. This mountain gave the city its name.

The name *Montreal* can refer to the city itself or the broader metropolitan area. The broader area, known as Greater Montreal, includes the city of Montreal and surrounding suburbs.

Montreal is a modern metropolis with office towers, universities, a casino, luxury shopping areas, a subway, deluxe hotels, professional sports teams, major museums, and glittering nightlife. Residents take pride in making the best of the sometimes fierce winter weather. Montreal's National Hockey League team, the Canadiens, has had one of the most successful histories of any team in professional sports. The city also is known for the fashion sense of *les montrealaises* (the women of Montreal).

In 1535, the French explorer Jacques Cartier became the first European to reach the site that is now Montreal. Cartier climbed the mountain and named it Mont Réal (Royal Mountain, or Mount Royal). The first permanent European settlement on the site was established in 1642. That year, Paul de Chomedey, Sieur (Lord) de Maisonneuve—a former French Army officer—brought a small group of Roman Catholic missionaries and settlers to the island from France. The settlement was first called Ville-Marie (Mary's City) in honor of the Virgin Mary. But by the early 1700's, the town had become identified with the mountain and was called Montreal.

Today, Montreal faces challenges related to changes in its ethnic population. Many French-speaking people have moved to suburbs off the Island of Montreal, while many immigrants have moved into the city. As a result, there is social and political tension between people who welcome Montreal's growing ethnic diversity and people who wish to maintain the city's French character.

Tension also exists between Montreal and the rest of Quebec. Montreal has many immigrants, English speakers with ties to other Canadian provinces, and French Quebecers who also speak English. But the rest of Quebec remains deeply French in identity.

Montreal also faces problems common to other large cities. These problems include poverty, declining quality and availability of public services, drug abuse, criminal gangs, and pollution. However, Montreal has a reputation for being a safe, low-crime city.

The city

In 2000, the Quebec provincial legislature passed a law to combine the 28 municipalities on the Island of Montreal and some adjacent islands. This law, which was scheduled to take effect in 2002, provides for one

Brian Kappler, the contributor of this article, is Political Editor at The Gazette *in Montreal.*

city of Montreal stretching over the entire area. Unless noted otherwise, the information in this article refers to the city of Montreal before the planned merger.

The Island of Montreal is triangular, measuring about 32 miles (51 kilometers) long and 10 miles (16 kilometers) wide at its widest point. The city of Montreal occupies 68 of the 191 square miles (177 of the 495 square kilometers) that the island covers. Greater Montreal includes all of the Island of Montreal, Jésus Island to the north, several smaller islands, and parts of the Quebec mainland. The official Montreal metropolitan area covers 1,554 square miles (4,024 square kilometers).

The Montreal downtown area, called *le centre-ville* in French, lies between the St. Lawrence River and Mount Royal. A huge park covers the top of the mountain. The city's historic district, next to downtown and bordering the river, is called Vieux-Montréal (Old Montreal). Residential areas stretch away from downtown to the geographic north, south, and west.

Montrealers have an unusual way of describing directions on the Island of Montreal. For example, Boulevard St.-Laurent, one of Montreal's chief streets, is described by residents as running from south to north, away from the river. Geographically, however, this street runs more southeast to northwest. The lively, ethnic St.-Laurent divides east and west street addresses in Montreal.

Boulevard St.-Laurent was long considered the dividing line between the heavily *francophone* (French-speaking) east side and the more *anglophone* (English-speaking) west side. Geographically, the east and west side are more nearly the northern and southern parts of the city. During the 1980's and 1990's, Montreal saw increases in immigration, private-car travel, and *bilingualism* (ability to speak two languages). Today, as a result, English, French, and other languages can be heard anywhere on the Island of Montreal.

The St. Lawrence River and the Lachine Canal have historically been important commercial and industrial corridors. The canal, which crosses the southern part of the Island of Montreal, served as a detour around the river's Lachine Rapids. Since about 1940, however, changes in technology and transportation have reduced

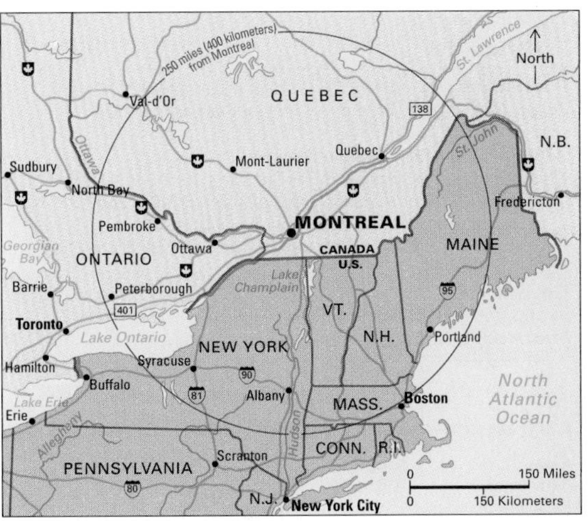

WORLD BOOK map

Montreal is in southern Quebec.

heavy industrial activity along the river and the canal. While the river remains an important route for cargo vessels, the canal is no longer in use for commercial shipping. Homes, stores, and recreational areas are replacing old industrial structures along the waterways.

Downtown Montreal has several streets with special characteristics. The wide Boulevard René-Lévesque (formerly Dorchester Boulevard) crosses the heart of downtown Montreal and is known for its skyscrapers. The city's best-known skyscraper, commonly called Place Ville Marie, is one of Montreal's most respected office centers. *Place* is the French word for *square.* The building rises 615 feet (187 meters) and is laid out in the shape of a cross. The height and shape of the building have made it a city landmark.

Rue Ste.-Catherine, a block away from Boulevard René-Lévesque, is noted for its shops, restaurants, and theaters. The fashionable Rue Sherbrooke, two blocks away from Rue Ste.-Catherine, attracts many visitors to its luxurious antique shops and art galleries. *Rue* is the

Vieux-Montréal (Old Montreal) is the city's historic district. Its streets are lined with many old stone buildings, charming stores and restaurants, and historic houses.

Facts in brief

Population: *City*—1,016,376. *Metropolitan area*—3,326,510.
Area: *City*—68 mi² (177 km²). *Metropolitan area*—1,554 mi² (4,024 km²).
Altitude: 187 ft (57m) above sea level.
Climate: *Average temperature*—January, 15 °F (-9 °C); July, 70 °F (21 °C). *Average annual precipitation* (rainfall, melted snow, and other forms of moisture)—40 in (102 cm). For information on the monthly weather in Montreal, see **Quebec** (Climate).
Government: Mayor-council. *Terms*—4 years for the mayor and the 51 council members.
Founded: 1642. Incorporated as a city in 1832.

Largest communities in the Montreal area

Name	Population	Name	Population
Montreal	1,016,376	Saint-Laurent	74,240
Laval	330,393	LaSalle	72,029
Longueuil	127,977	Saint-Leonard	71,327
Montreal-Nord	81,581	Brossard	65,927
Saint-Hubert	77,042	Verdun	59,714

Source: 1996 census.

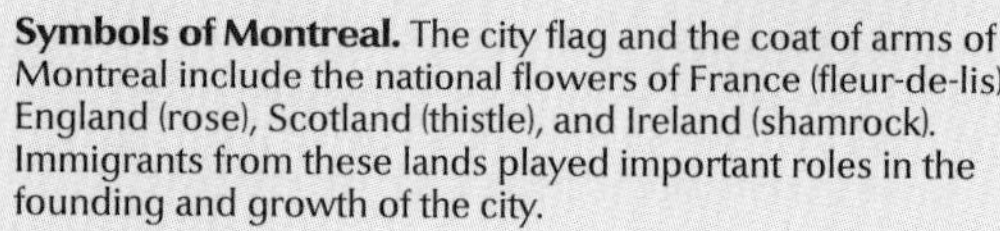

Symbols of Montreal. The city flag and the coat of arms of Montreal include the national flowers of France (fleur-de-lis), England (rose), Scotland (thistle), and Ireland (shamrock). Immigrants from these lands played important roles in the founding and growth of the city.

French word for *street.*

The city's harsh winter climate has led to the growth of the Cité Souterrain (Underground City). The Underground City is a network of passages beneath the downtown streets. Shops and restaurants line the passages, which link many public buildings and also provide access to several stations of the Métro, Montreal's subway.

© Thomas Kitchin, Tom Stack & Associates

The Cité Souterrain (Underground City) consists of stairways and passages beneath Montreal's downtown streets. Shops and restaurants line the passages, which link many public buildings.

Old Montreal borders the St. Lawrence River between Rue Berri and Rue McGill. Many of the old stone buildings of Old Montreal stand side by side with tall, modern structures. Charming restaurants, historic houses, and *boutiques* (small stores) line the area's narrow streets. Several of these streets are paved with cobblestones. Because Old Montreal has a European feel, producers often film movies and TV shows there. Old Montreal opens onto the Vieux-Port (Old Port), now a waterfront area of museums and other attractions.

Old Montreal has many reminders of Montreal's rich history. The city's oldest church, Notre-Dame-de-Bon-Secours, stands on Rue St.-Paul in Old Montreal. This Roman Catholic stone chapel was built in 1771 on the foundations of an earlier church. The St. Sulpice Seminary is on Rue Notre-Dame. Also known as the Vieux-

© Thomas Kitchin, Tom Stack & Associates

The Métro, Montreal's subway system, opened in 1966. Brightly colored mosaics decorate many Métro walls. The Métro has been called "the largest underground art gallery in the world."

Montreal

The small map shows the Montreal area. The large map shows downtown Montreal. Both maps show the boundary of the city of Montreal prior to Jan. 1, 2002.

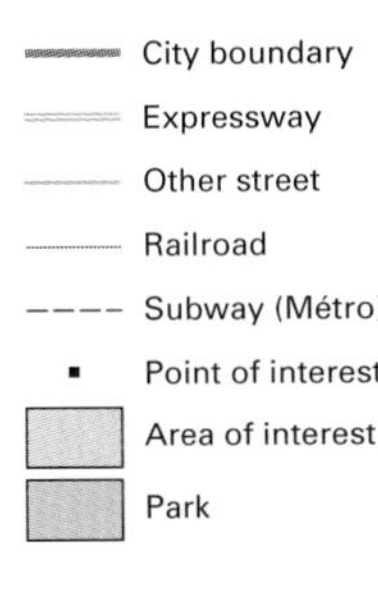

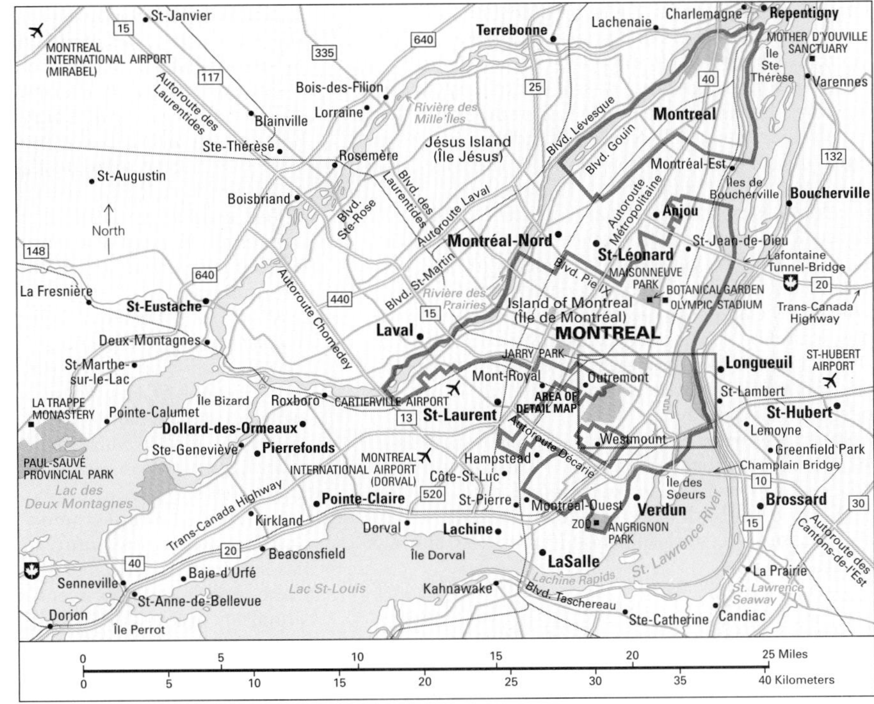

WORLD BOOK maps

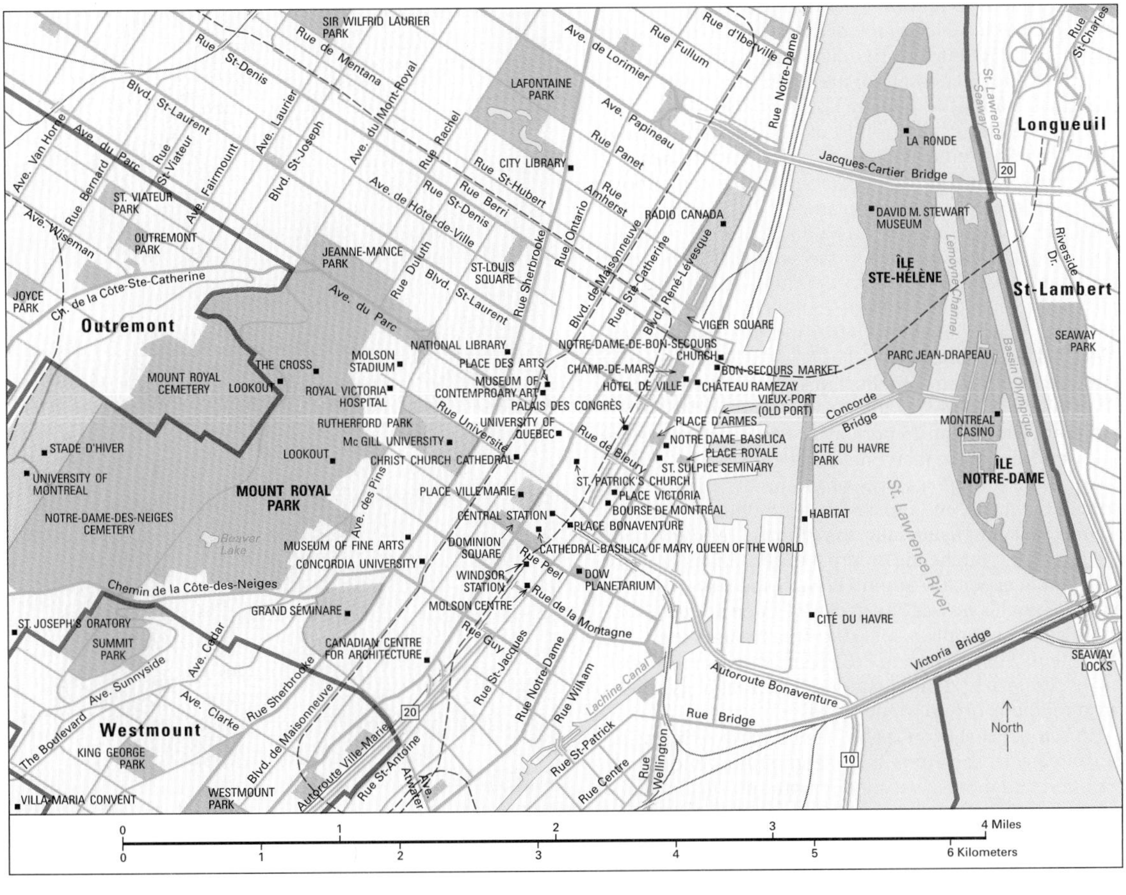

Séminaire (Old Seminary), it is the oldest building in Montreal. Ville-Marie's first priests opened it in 1685, and priests have lived in the building ever since.

Two historic squares are near the seminary. Across Rue Notre-Dame is Place d'Armes (Parade Ground). The first clash between Ville-Marie's founders and the Iroquois Indians took place there in 1644. The Maisonneuve Monument in the square honors the city's founder. Also near the seminary, on Rue St.-Paul, is Place Royale (Royal Square). This square was the site of Fort Montreal, built by Ville-Marie's pioneers in 1642.

Bank and insurance company offices border Place d'Armes. The area also has several government buildings, including courthouses and Montreal's Hôtel de Ville (City Hall). The city's large, modern Palais des Congrès (Convention Centre) stands where Old Montreal merges into downtown.

Metropolitan area. Greater Montreal is Canada's second largest urban area. Only the Toronto metropolitan area is larger. Laval, on Jésus Island, ranks as Montreal's largest suburb by population. Longueuil is the largest suburb on the south (geographic east) shore of the St. Lawrence.

People

Montrealers call themselves *francophone, anglophone,* or *allophone,* depending upon whether their main language is French, English, or another language. The Island of Montreal is more than half francophone. Signs posted throughout the city appear mainly in French, the official language of the province of Quebec. About half of Montreal's people speak both French and English. About 30 percent of the city's people speak only French, and about 13 percent speak only English.

Since the mid-1900's, hundreds of thousands of immigrants have settled in Montreal. Today, immigrants make up about a fourth of the city's people and almost a fifth of the metropolitan population.

Ethnic groups. More than half of Montreal's people have French ancestry. The city has well-established Italian, Greek, Jewish, and black communities. During the late 1900's, many people came to the city from South America, Africa, South Asia, Haiti and other parts of the West Indies, Lebanon and other Middle Eastern countries, China, Vietnam, and Portugal. Today, a stroller can often hear four or five languages on a single block in Montreal. More than 25 percent of Montrealers are descended from more than one ethnic group.

Religion. A large majority of Montreal's people are Roman Catholics, and most of the Catholics are of French descent. Historically, the Roman Catholic Church has strongly influenced Montreal public affairs and public opinion, especially among French speakers. However, the church's power has declined since about 1940. The majority of English-speaking Montrealers are Protestants. Anglicans and Presbyterians form the city's largest Protestant denominations. Jews make up another large religious group in Montreal.

Housing. Most Montrealers rent their dwellings. Because many leases expire at the end of June, Montrealers often find themselves moving into new living spaces on Canada Day, Canada's national day on July 1. Greater Montreal has a lower proportion of homeowners and a higher proportion of tenants than any other Canadian metropolitan area. However, rapid suburban growth since about 1970 has made home ownership more common, especially off the Island of Montreal.

Two- or three-story apartment buildings with outside staircases are a common sight in the city of Montreal. Buildings in this style, constructed chiefly during the 1920's and 1930's, were designed to make maximum use of inside space. Row houses—rows of similarly designed dwellings that share common walls—also are common in the city. Many row houses, especially on the east side, have winding exterior staircases, often in black wrought iron.

Montreal is the site of one of the world's most unusual apartment developments. This development, called Habitat, stands on Cité du Havre, a strip of land that extends into the St. Lawrence River. Designed by Canadian architect Moshe Safdie, Habitat consists of 158 apartments that look like a stack of concrete boxes. One apartment's roof serves as the terrace of another. See **Safdie, Moshe** (picture).

Montreal's city government strives to ensure decent housing, even in the poorest neighborhoods. The city has long had generous programs to help landlords make repairs and improvements. The city also spends a significant amount on "social housing," a local term de-

Barbara K. Deans

Balconies and outdoor staircases are a distinctive feature of many apartment buildings in the city. Montreal has a higher proportion of renters than any other Canadian metropolitan area.

scribing tax-supported rent for the poor.

Education. Until 1998, the public school system in Montreal was organized on the basis of language and religion. There were four kinds of schools within the public school system. They were: (1) Roman Catholic schools that taught entirely in English, (2) Roman Catholic, French-language schools, (3) Protestant, English-language schools, and (4) Protestant, French-language schools. But in 1998, school systems across Quebec were reorganized on the basis of language only. In Montreal, three school boards administer French-language schools, and two school boards administer English-language schools. Montreal also has numerous religious and nonreligious private schools.

Montreal is the home of two internationally known research universities, the University of Montreal and McGill University. Courses at the University of Montreal are taught in French, and courses at McGill are conducted in English. Montreal's other institutions of higher learning include Concordia University, an English-language university; and the University of Quebec at Montreal, which teaches in French. Specialized business and engineering schools also operate in Montreal.

Social problems. Montreal faces many familiar urban problems. One of these problems is poverty. Montreal ended the 1900's with a rapidly growing economy, and the city has a well-educated work force. But Montreal also attracts thousands of jobseekers from rural Quebec, some of whom lack necessary skills or training. As a result, many people live in Montreal with little income other than public assistance.

Beginning in the early 1970's, higher-income people, particularly francophones, began moving away from the Island of Montreal into off-island suburbs. As a result, lower-income people and immigrants became a higher proportion of Montreal's population.

In 1974, the Quebec government made French the official language of the province. In 1976, the Parti Québécois (PQ), which favors Quebec's independence from Canada, first gained control of the provincial legislature. The PQ has been in and out of power since then. These political developments have created tension between francophones and anglophones in Montreal and the rest of Quebec. Many English-speaking people, and some important companies that conduct business in English, have left Montreal and Quebec rather than switch to French.

Cultural life

Montreal is one of North America's leading cultural centers. It has outstanding dance, drama, and musical groups, and its art galleries and museums rank among the finest in Canada. The city is also known for its many beautiful churches and well-planned parks. Montreal's sports attractions include professional baseball, football, and hockey.

Each year, millions of tourists visit Montreal. Many restaurants in Montreal specialize in French cooking. Visitors can also find restaurants featuring a wide variety of other ethnic foods.

The arts. The world-famous Montreal Symphony Orchestra and the Montreal Metropolitan Orchestra make their home in the city. Other musical organizations in Montreal include I Musici, Musica Camerata Montreal, and the Montreal Baroque Orchestra. Montreal also has Les Grands Ballets Canadiens, a major ballet company; several jazz dance companies; and a number of French-language theater groups, including Le Théâtre du Nouveau Monde, Le Théâtre du Rideau Vert, and Le Théâtre Jean Duceppe. The Centaur Theatre features English-language productions.

Summer is "festival season" in Montreal. Cultural events, performances, and shows run almost nonstop from June through August, drawing thousands of people downtown. The major festivals include the International Jazz Festival, the World Film Festival, and the Just for Laughs/Juste pour Rire comedy festival.

Place des Arts at Rue Ste.-Catherine and Rue St.-Urbain is one of North America's finest centers for the performing arts. The center includes the Salle Wilfrid-Pelletier concert hall, which can seat 3,000 people. The center also houses the smaller Maisonneuve and Port-Royal theaters, both of which offer stage productions.

Libraries. The public library system in the city of Montreal consists of a main library and more than 20 branches. The system's most important books and other items are in French. But English-language collections and items in other languages are also available. Other libraries in Montreal include the Fraser-Hickson Library, the Jewish Public Library, the Quebec National Library, and the libraries of the city's four universities.

The Quebec government plans to build a major provincial library at Rue Berri and Boulevard de Maisonneuve. The new library is scheduled to open in 2003.

Museums. The downtown Musée des Beaux-Arts (Museum of Fine Arts) is Montreal's principal museum. It hosts major traveling exhibitions and also has a permanent collection of 25,000 objects. These items include major European works, Inuit art, other Canadian works, Asian and South American pieces, and collections of furniture, glass, lace, and silver. Founded in 1860, it is one of Canada's oldest museums.

The Centre Canadien d'Architecture (Canadian Centre for Architecture) includes a museum, library, and conference center focusing on architecture past and present. The city also has a Musée d'Art Contemporain (Museum of Contemporary Art) and a planetarium.

The Château Ramezay, in Old Montreal, dates from 1705. It was once the home of Claude de Ramezay, the second French governor of Montreal. The building has been a history museum since 1895. Other important history museums are the McCord Museum of Canadian History; the David M. Stewart Museum; and the Musée Pointe-à-Callière, which focuses on the city's early history and archaeological findings.

Churches. Montreal is famous for its more than 300 churches. Several are noted for their Gothic-style architecture. St. Patrick's Church, in downtown Montreal, serves English-speaking Roman Catholics. Basilique Notre-Dame (Notre Dame Basilica), in Old Montreal, is attended by French-speaking Catholics. This church has two towers, one of which houses a huge bell. This bell, called Le Gros Bourdon (the Great Bell), weighs 12 tons (11 metric tons). Notre Dame Basilica is also noted for its magnificently carved wooden interior.

Notre-Dame-de-Bon-Secours is a well-known chapel in Old Montreal. Some Montrealers call it the Sailors' Church. A statue of the Virgin Mary on the roof was

© Tourism Montreal

Ice skaters flock to Mount Royal Park in the winter.

© Guido Cozzi, Bruce Coleman Inc.

Place des Arts is one of the finest performing arts centers in North America. The center includes a concert hall that can seat 3,000 people.

once believed to perform miracles to help sailors.

The Basilique-Cathédrale Marie-Reine-du-Monde (Cathedral-Basilica of Mary, Queen of the World) stands in the heart of downtown Montreal. The designers of this church patterned it after St. Peter's Basilica in Vatican City. The church serves as the seat of the Catholic archdiocese of Montreal. The seat of the Anglican diocese, Christ Church Cathedral, is also downtown. St. Joseph's Oratory stands on the west slope of Mount Royal. Every year, hundreds of thousands of people visit this Roman Catholic shrine. The dome of the shrine is a major landmark.

Parks. Montreal has hundreds of parks and recreation areas. Mount Royal Park covers 494 acres (200 hectares) on the mountain. The park was designed by Frederick Law Olmsted, who designed New York City's Central Park. Mount Royal Park includes Beaver Lake, a popular spot for ice skating during the winter. Mount Royal also has lookout spots that offer visitors magnificent views of the Montreal area. An iron cross rises about 100 feet (30 meters) on the mountain's east side. The cross, illuminated at night, is a memorial to Ville-Marie's survival of a flood in 1642.

A world-class Jardin Botanique (Botanical Garden) lies in Montreal's east end near the Olympic Stadium. This vast attraction features gardens with various themes, including the Chinese Garden, the Japanese Garden, and the Rose Garden. Also on the Botanical Garden grounds is the Montreal Insectarium, which displays thousands of live and mounted insects.

© Rus Arnold

Basilique Notre-Dame (Notre Dame Basilica) is noted for its magnificent interior.

© Bernard Boutrit, Woodfin Camp, Inc.

The Musée d'Art Contemporain (Museum of Contemporary Art) has a permanent collection of about 6,000 works of art, including paintings and sculptures. The museum is popular with both children and adults.

Another large park, Parc Jean-Drapeau (formerly Parc des Îles), covers Île Ste.-Hélène and Île Notre-Dame. These two islands lie in the St. Lawrence River south (geographically east) of the Island of Montreal. Parc Jean-Drapeau includes numerous green spaces, the Montreal casino, and La Ronde amusement park, open during the summer months. La Ronde stands on the site of Expo 67, a world's fair held in Montreal in 1967.

Sports. The Montreal Canadiens of the National Hockey League have won more Stanley Cup championships than any other team in professional hockey. Montreal is also the home of the Montreal Expos baseball team of the National League and the Montreal Alouettes of the Canadian Football League.

Winter sports are a major attraction in the Montreal area. Cross-country skiers and tobogganers rush to Mount Royal after a snowfall. Downhill skiing is popular in the nearby Laurentian Mountains and Eastern Townships.

Economy

Montreal is one of Canada's chief transportation centers. It is the second most important Canadian city in finance and industry. Only Toronto is more important. In addition, Montreal lies in the most fertile and productive agricultural region of Quebec. As a result, the city has become a food-processing center.

Montreal's economy was once controlled by private companies that used English as the language of business. As a result, Montrealers needed a good knowledge of English to obtain a well-paying job. Since 1977, however, the Quebec government has required all companies that employ 50 or more people to use French as the language of business.

Transportation. The St. Lawrence River links Montreal with the Atlantic Ocean, about 1,000 miles (1,600 kilometers) to the northeast. The St. Lawrence Seaway extends shipping services about 1,300 miles (2,100 kilometers) inland. It makes Montreal a major stopover point for ships sailing between the Great Lakes and the Atlantic (see **Saint Lawrence Seaway**).

The Port of Montreal, also called Montreal Harbour, stretches 15 miles (24 kilometers) along the north (geographic west) bank of the St. Lawrence River. It serves oceangoing, coastal, and inland vessels and handles about 23 million tons (21 million metric tons) of cargo yearly. This amount includes about 2 $\frac{1}{5}$ million tons (2 million metric tons) of grain.

Montreal ranks as one of Canada's largest railroad centers. Canadian National Railway, a transcontinental rail line, has its headquarters in the city. This railroad carries freight east to the Atlantic seaboard and west to the Pacific Coast. Several railways connect Montreal and cities in the United States.

Major airlines use Montreal International Airport (Dorval), which lies in the western part of the Island of Montreal. Montreal International Airport (Mirabel), northwest of the island, handles mainly air freight. Air Canada, the nation's largest commercial airline, has its headquarters in the city. The International Civil Aviation Organization, a specialized agency of the United Nations, also has its headquarters there.

Several major highways serve Montreal. The Trans-Canada Highway, which runs from coast to coast, crosses the Island of Montreal. Nearly 20 railroad and highway bridges connect the island with Laval and the south (geographic east) shore of the St. Lawrence River.

A subway system called the Métro, buses, and commuter trains provide public transportation on the Island of Montreal. The Métro, which opened in 1966, was the first subway in the Western Hemisphere to use cars with rubber tires. Brightly colored mosaics and architectural designs decorate many Métro walls. Because of these decorations, the Métro has been called "the largest underground art gallery in the world."

Industry. Manufacturing is a leading source of employment in Greater Montreal. The more than 5,000 factories in the area employ about a fourth of its workers. These plants account for about two-thirds of Quebec's industrial production.

Greater Montreal's leading industries include the manufacture of aircraft and parts, the manufacture of telecommunications equipment, and food processing. The area's chief food products are beer, canned goods, and sugar.

Greater Montreal is also one of Canada's major centers for the manufacture of chemicals, clothing, and tobacco products. Pharmaceuticals are an important chemical product. Petroleum refineries in Montreal produce much of Canada's gasoline. Montreal's historic fur industry still thrives, as do newer firms that produce computer software and other high-technology products.

Trade and finance. Companies in Greater Montreal play an important role in Canada's international trade. Montreal's bilingual culture gives it special access to French and other European trade.

Companies engaging in wholesale and retail trade within Canada employ many people in Greater Montre-

Andre Pichette, Club de Hockey Canadien, Inc.

Hockey fans watch the Montreal Canadiens of the National Hockey League play. The Canadiens have had one of the most successful histories of any team in professional sports. Hockey is the most popular sport in Montreal and the rest of Canada.

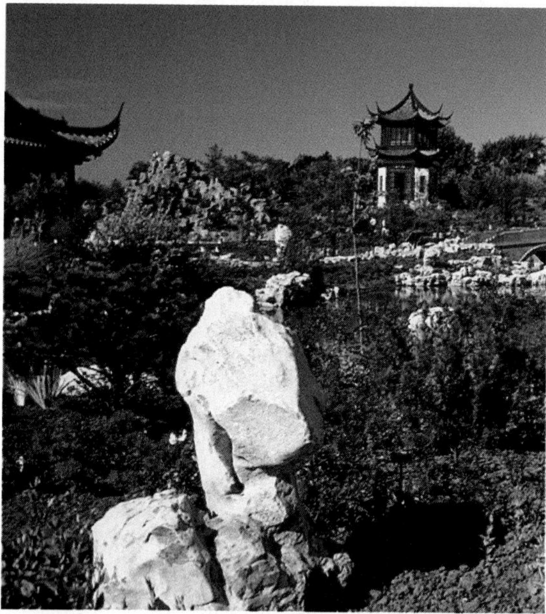

Montreal Botanical Garden

The Chinese Garden is one of several specialty theme gardens in Montreal's vast Jardin Botanique (Botanical Garden). The Jardin Botanique is among the most noted botanical gardens in the world. It also serves as the site of the Montreal Insectarium.

al. Wholesale companies sell goods to retail stores, while retail companies sell goods to consumers. Area retail stores include some of Canada's largest department stores. Place Bonaventure, in downtown Montreal, is one of the largest commercial buildings in the world. It has more than 3 million square feet (300,000 square meters) of space.

Montreal has branches of all of Canada's government-approved banks. Two of these banks, the Banque Nationale and Laurentian Bank, are based in Quebec. Banks, credit organizations, savings firms, and other financial companies in the area employ many people. Loans by these companies contribute to the growth of business and industry throughout Canada. The Bank of Montreal, founded in 1817, was the first bank in Canada.

The Montreal Exchange, Canada's first stock market, opened in the city in 1874. As a result of the reorganization of Canadian stock markets in 1999, major stock trading no longer takes place on the Montreal Exchange. The exchange, now called the Bourse de Montréal, instead specializes in the buying and selling of investment contracts called *derivatives.*

Communication. Four daily newspapers are published in Montreal. Three of the papers—*La Presse, Le Devoir,* and *Le Journal de Montréal*—are written in French. *The Gazette* is the only Montreal daily in English. *Le Journal de Montréal* has the largest circulation of any of Quebec's daily papers. *The Gazette,* founded in 1778, was the first newspaper published in Montreal.

Several radio and television stations broadcast from the city, about half of them in French and half in English. Station CFCF of Montreal was Canada's first radio station. It began broadcasting in 1919. Radio-Canada, the French-language network of the Canadian Broadcasting Corporation (CBC), is based in Montreal. More French-language TV programs are produced in Montreal than in any other city in the world except Paris. Television station CBFT, one of the first two Canadian stations, began broadcasting from Montreal in 1952. The other pioneer station was CBLT of Toronto.

Government

The city of Montreal has a mayor-council form of government. Voters elect the mayor and the 51 City Council members to four-year terms. The mayor acts as the administrative head of the city government. He or she supervises the various city departments. The City Council passes the city's ordinances. It also appoints and dismisses directors of city departments and adopts the annual city budget. The city of Montreal and other nearby municipalities receive some services from a metropolitan government called the Montreal Urban Community (MUC). These services include public transportation and police protection.

In 2000, the Quebec legislature passed a law to combine the 28 municipalities on the Island of Montreal and some adjacent islands. This law, which was scheduled to take effect in 2002, provides for one city of Montreal stretching over the entire area. The new city is to be divided into 27 *boroughs* (divisions) based partly on the boundaries of the former city of Montreal and its suburbs. The new City Council is to consist of a mayor and 72 city councilors, with each borough having at least one representative on the council. The new council is to replace the MUC.

More than 40 percent of the city of Montreal's revenue comes from taxes on property. The rest of the city's funds come from taxes on businesses, water, and amusements, and from aid given by the province.

Like most other big cities, Montreal has difficulty finding ways to pay for the rapidly rising costs of government services. The major problems faced by Montreal's government include building more low-cost housing and maintaining the city's *infrastructure* (public services and facilities).

History

Algonquin and Iroquois Indians lived in the Montreal region before European settlers arrived. The area's rivers and lakes provided the Indians with a plentiful supply of fish. The waterways also served as excellent transportation routes.

Exploration. In 1535, the French explorer Jacques Cartier sailed up the St. Lawrence River. The Lachine Rapids, geographically south of what is now Montreal, prevented Cartier from going farther by ship. He then explored the Island of Montreal and found the Iroquois village of Hochelaga at the foot of Mount Royal. Several thousand Indians lived in the village. Another famous French explorer, Samuel de Champlain, visited the site of Montreal in 1603 and 1611. By that time, the Iroquois had abandoned the site.

French settlement. In 1639, Jérôme Le Royer, Sieur de la Dauversière, a French tax collector, formed a company in Paris to establish a colony on the Island of Montreal. In 1641, the company sent a Roman Catholic missionary group to the island to convert the Indians to Christianity. The group, led by Paul de Chomedey, Sieur de Maisonneuve, arrived in 1642. The colonists built a fort at what is now Place Royale in Old Montreal and established the settlement of Ville-Marie.

Iroquois Indians attacked the colony, hoping to stop the profitable fur trade that the French had established with the Algonquin and Huron. The Algonquin and Huron were the chief rivals of the Iroquois. Despite the attacks, the colony prospered as a religious center and fur-trading post. The French and the Iroquois made peace in 1701.

By the early 1700's, Ville-Marie had become known as Montreal. It had a population of about 3,500 in 1710 and was the commercial heart of France's North American empire, called New France. Montreal's location on the St. Lawrence River made it an important center of trade. European goods passed through Montreal on the way to the North American west. Fur traders shipped pelts from Canada's interior to Europe by way of Montreal.

British settlement. British troops under General Jeffery Amherst captured Montreal in 1760, during the French and Indian War (1754-1763). The surrender of Montreal marked the end of the fighting in this war and led to the collapse of New France. The Treaty of Paris, signed in 1763, officially ended the French and Indian War and made Canada a British colony. A few English-speaking settlers then came to Montreal.

General Richard Montgomery's American forces occupied Montreal in November 1775, during the Revolutionary War in America (1775-1783). Benjamin Franklin and other American diplomats tried to gain French-

Lithograph (1843) by James Duncan; Public Archives of Canada

Montreal's waterfront district was the city's chief center of activity in the early 1800's, *shown here.* Today, the district is known as Old Montreal and has many historic sites.

Canadian support against the British. But their efforts failed, partly because most French Canadians regarded the war as just a quarrel between Britain (now the United Kingdom) and its colonies. In June 1776, the arrival of British troops forced the American soldiers to withdraw, and Montreal became a British possession again.

Fur traders in Montreal founded the North West Company as a rival to the Hudson's Bay Company fur trade. The new firm was first organized in the 1770's.

Montreal began to expand on the Island of Montreal in the late 1700's. English-speaking merchants began to establish businesses in Montreal during this period. They gradually gained control of the town's economy, in part because many French merchants had returned to France after British troops captured the city in 1760.

The early 1800's. By 1800, Montreal's population had reached 9,000. Canada's first steamboat, the *Accommodation,* sailed the St. Lawrence River from Montreal to the city of Quebec in 1809. In 1821, the Hudson's Bay Company bought the North West Company. The Hudson Bay area then became the chief market for furs, and Montreal declined as a fur-trading center.

The Lachine Canal, which crosses the southern edge of Montreal, opened in 1825. It provided a detour for small vessels around the river's Lachine Rapids and led to a sharp increase in trade and travel between Montreal and the Great Lakes. Shipping replaced fur trading as Montreal's chief industry, and Montreal grew in importance as a port.

In 1832, Montreal was incorporated as a city. From 1844 until 1849, it served as the capital of the Province of Canada. By 1850, the city's population had soared to about 50,000. For a short period, the majority of Montreal's population was English-speaking.

The growing city. Montreal continued to develop as a transportation center during the mid-1800's, when railways linked it to areas west of Toronto and to Portland, Maine. Investment by wealthy English-speaking merchants helped Montreal become a major industrial center during this period. Many industries were built along the Lachine Canal. Thousands of British immigrants, and French Canadians from other parts of Quebec, came to Montreal to find jobs in the new factories. By 1871, about 107,000 people lived in Montreal. About half of these people were of French ancestry.

The Canadian Pacific Railway Company, based in Montreal, completed Canada's first transcontinental railroad in 1885. The railroad attracted more industry and brought new prosperity to the city. By 1901, Montreal's population had risen to about 268,000. The *annexation* (addition) of several neighboring communities helped it reach about 468,000 by 1911.

The war issue. During World War I (1914-1918), Canada fought on the side of the Allies, which included France, the United Kingdom, and the United States. Some French Canadians in Montreal supported the government's policy and volunteered for the war, as did many of the city's English-speaking citizens. But many French Canadians, feeling little loyalty to the United Kingdom, took almost no interest in the war. In 1917, Canada's government introduced a military draft, also known as *conscription.* Many French Canadians opposed this policy.

During World War II (1939-1945), conscription again caused unrest among French Canadians. In 1940, Montreal Mayor Camillien Houde urged Montrealers to defy a Canadian government plan to register the country's men for possible military service. Houde charged that the registration would lead to a military draft for overseas service. Most French Canadians opposed a draft, and Canadian government leaders had pledged not to establish one. Federal authorities arrested Houde and kept him in a prison camp until 1944. Tensions increased when the Canadian government introduced a draft for overseas service in 1944.

The changing city. By the early 1950's, Montreal's

population had topped 1 million. During the late 1950's, the city entered a period of great economic growth. In 1958, a city development program enlarged Montreal Harbour. The opening of the St. Lawrence Seaway in 1959 attracted hundreds of industries.

During the 1960's, a construction boom in downtown Montreal gave the city a new skyline. Private developers tore down old structures throughout the area and replaced them with huge banks, hotels, and office buildings. Important downtown developments during this period included the Place Ville Marie and Place Victoria skyscrapers; Place Bonaventure, a trade mart; and Place des Arts, a cultural center. An underground shopping network was also constructed.

The city built new highways and a new subway, the Métro, to help serve visitors attending Expo 67, a world's fair held in Montreal in 1967. More than 50 million people attended the exhibition.

In 1975, the Montreal International Airport (Mirabel) opened. Montreal hosted the 1976 Summer Olympic Games. Construction for the event included housing for the athletes and a new sports stadium. Montreal officials began to rent the housing to the public in 1978. Jean Drapeau, the city's longest-serving mayor, held office from 1954 to 1957 and again from 1960 until 1986.

The separatist movement. In 1960, the Rassemblement pour l'Indépendence Nationale (Assembly for National Independence) was founded in Montreal. Its chief aim was to bring about the separation of Quebec from the rest of Canada and make the province an independent nation.

The Front de Libération du Québec (Quebec Liberation Front), a terrorist organization, began to use violence to promote separatism in 1963. At first, the FLQ attacked armories and other symbols of the federal government. The organization soon became involved in labor disputes. During the period from 1963 to 1968, the FLQ claimed responsibility for bombings and armed robberies in the Montreal area.

In October 1970, members of the FLQ kidnapped British Trade Commissioner James R. Cross and Quebec Labor Minister Pierre Laporte. Canadian Prime Minister Pierre Trudeau, a French Canadian born in Montreal, sent federal army troops to Montreal and other Quebec cities to guard government officials. The murder of Laporte later in the month increased tension in Montreal. Federal troops withdrew in January 1971, after police arrested four members of the FLQ and charged them with the kidnapping and murder of Laporte. Cross's kidnappers had released him after government officials guaranteed the kidnappers safe passage to Cuba.

In 1977, Quebec's government passed a law that required all companies with 50 or more employees to use French as the language of business. As a result, several major corporations based in Montreal that had primarily used English in the course of business left the city.

The late 1900's. In 1982, Montreal annexed the northern suburb of Pointe-aux-Trembles. This annexation increased the area of Montreal by about 10 percent. Development of downtown Montreal continued in the 1980's and 1990's. The Old Port area was developed for recreation and tourism during this period.

In the 1980's and 1990's, the focus of Montreal's economy changed greatly. Old manufacturing plants closed, and new high-technology companies moved into the city. Montreal's unemployment rate, which has often been high, dropped in the late 1990's as high-technology firms competed for skilled workers.

Recent developments. In 2000, the Quebec legislature passed Bill 170, a law to merge the 28 municipalities on the Island of Montreal and some adjacent islands. This law, which was scheduled to take effect in 2002, provides for one city of Montreal stretching over the entire area. Many suburban residents strongly opposed this merger. Some suburban governments challenged the law in court. Brian Kappler

Related articles in *World Book* include:

Biographies

Amherst, Lord Jeffery
Bourassa, Henri
Cartier, Jacques
La Vérendrye, Sieur de
Papineau, Louis Joseph
Trudeau, Pierre Elliott
Vanier, Georges-Philias

History

French and Indian wars
Hudson's Bay Company
North West Company
Revolutionary War in America

Other related articles

Laval
Ottawa River
Quebec (pictures)
Saint Lawrence River
Saint Lawrence Seaway

Outline

I. The city
- A. Downtown Montreal
- B. Old Montreal
- C. Metropolitan area

II. People
- A. Ethnic groups
- B. Religion
- C. Housing
- D. Education
- E. Social problems

III. Cultural life
- A. The arts
- B. Libraries
- C. Museums
- D. Churches
- E. Parks
- F. Sports

IV. Economy
- A. Transportation
- B. Industry
- C. Trade and finance
- D. Communication

V. Government

VI. History

Questions

What is the largest ethnic group in Montreal?
Why did the Iroquois Indians attack Ville-Marie in the 1600's?
Montreal's public school system is organized on what basis?
Who founded Montreal? When?
The design of the Cathedral-Basilica of Mary, Queen of the World, is patterned after what other church?
In what ways has the population of the city of Montreal changed since the 1970's?
What have been some of the consequences for Montreal of the French language law passed by the Quebec provincial legislature in 1974?
Why has the Métro been called the "world's largest underground art gallery"?
What is Habitat? Who designed it?
What is Montreal's Underground City?

© Steve Vidler, Leo de Wys

Downtown Auckland lies on the North Island on a strip of land between two harbors. Auckland is New Zealand's largest city. Its tallest landmark is the 1,076-foot (328-meter) Sky Tower, *center.*

New Zealand

New Zealand is an island country in the southwest Pacific Ocean. It lies about 1,000 miles (1,600 kilometers) southeast of Australia. New Zealand consists of two main islands—the North Island and the South Island—and a number of smaller islands. The country belongs to a large island group called Polynesia. Wellington is the capital of New Zealand, and Auckland is the largest city.

New Zealand was first settled by Polynesians from the eastern Pacific whose descendants are called the Maori. Many scholars think these Polynesians probably arrived about 1,000 years ago. British immigrants began settling in New Zealand during the early 1800's, and the country became part of the British Empire in 1840. Today, it is an independent member of the Commonwealth of Nations, an association of countries that replaced the empire.

New Zealand's current population represents many cultures. They include the Maori and other Polynesian groups; descendants of English, Irish, and other western European colonial settlers; and more recent immigrants from Asia, Africa, and eastern Europe.

Giselle M. Byrnes, the contributor of this article, is Lecturer in New Zealand History at Victoria University of Wellington.

New Zealand is a beautiful country of snow-capped mountains, green lowlands, beaches, and many lakes and waterfalls. No place is more than 80 miles (130 kilometers) from the coast, and most places have striking views of mountains or hills.

Government

New Zealand is a constitutional monarchy. Queen Elizabeth II of the United Kingdom is also Queen of New Zealand. She appoints a governor general, recommended by New Zealand's prime minister, to represent her. The governor general's main function is to arrange for the leader of the political party with the most support in Parliament to form a government. The governor general's consent is required before bills can become law, but this requirement is normally a formality. The legislature, prime minister, and Cabinet run the government.

The constitution. New Zealand has no formal written constitution. The country's unwritten constitution is a combination of *precedent* (tradition) and written material closely modeled on the constitutional practices of the United Kingdom. Written parts of New Zealand's constitution include Magna Carta, a 1215 document that put the king of England under the rule of law, and the

Habeas Corpus Act of 1679, which protects people from being imprisoned unjustly.

The legislature. New Zealand's Parliament consists of the monarch, represented by the governor general, and an elected House of Representatives, also called the Parliament. The House of Representatives consists of 120 members. Voters directly elect 67 of these members. Six of the directly elected seats are reserved for the Maori, though more Maori candidates can be elected. The rest of the House is chosen on the basis of *proportional representation.* Under this method, each political party that receives at least 5 percent of the popular vote gets a number of seats determined by the percentage of the vote it receives. A parliamentary election must be held every three years, but may be held sooner. All citizens 18 years of age or older can vote in a general election.

The prime minister and Cabinet. The leader of the political party that wins the most seats in a parliamentary election becomes prime minister. The leading party may also form a coalition government with other parties if it does not gain a majority in Parliament.

On the advice of the prime minister, the governor general appoints the Cabinet to run the various government departments. The Cabinet members, called *ministers,* are members of Parliament. The prime minister and the Cabinet are called the *Government.* The Government proposes most new legislation in Parliament. If Parliament votes in favor of the bill, it becomes law.

Political parties. There are about 30 registered political parties in New Zealand. The largest are the National Party and the Labour Party. There is no clear division between the policies of either party. Traditionally, the Labour Party has favored government control and public regulation of industry, whereas the National Party has favored free enterprise. Since 1984, however, both parties have adopted similar economic policies.

Local government. New Zealand has a *unitary* system of government, in which Parliament has the power to create and authorize local governments. The country has 12 regions, each with a regional council. Local government is further divided into territorial authorities, community boards, and special purpose authorities. The territorial authorities consist of city councils, district councils, and the council for the Chatham Islands.

Ombudsman is an official selected by Parliament to investigate complaints by citizens against government departments and related organizations. If an ombudsman believes a complaint is justified, he or she reports it to the department concerned along with any recommendation for action.

Courts. New Zealand's highest court is the Court of Appeal, which hears mainly cases that have been appealed from a lower court. Some decisions of the Court of Appeal, such as those involving large amounts of money, may be appealed to the Privy Council in the United Kingdom. The Privy Council is an honorary panel of advisers to the monarch (see **Privy Council**).

Below the Court of Appeal in New Zealand are the High Court and district courts. The High Court deals with major crimes, important civil claims, and appeals from lower courts. It also reviews administrative actions. District courts serve specific regions. Justices of the peace and community magistrates hear traffic and minor criminal charges. A number of courts also have special func-

Facts in brief

Capital: Wellington.
Official languages: English and Maori.
Area: 104,454 mi^2 (270,534 km^2). *North Island*—44,701 mi^2 (115,777 km^2); *South Island*—58,385 mi^2 (151,215 km^2); *Stewart Island*—674 mi^2 (1,746 km^2); *Chatham Islands*—372 mi^2 (963 km^2); other islands—322 mi^2 (837 km^2). *Coastline*—about 3,200 mi (5,150 km).
Elevation: *Highest*—Mount Cook, 12,316 ft (3,754 m) above sea level. *Lowest*—sea level along the coast.
Population: *Estimated 2002 population*—3,930,000; population density, 38 per mi^2 (15 per km^2); distribution, 85 percent urban, 15 percent rural. *1996 census*—3,618,303.
Chief products: *Agriculture*—apples, barley, beef, dairy products, hides, kiwi fruit, lamb, mutton, potatoes, wheat, wool. *Fishing industry*—blue grenadier (hoki). *Forestry*—Monterey pine. *Manufacturing*—beer, clothing, food products, footwear, machinery, paper, textiles, wood products. *Mining*—coal, gold, ironsand, limestone.
Anthems: "God Defend New Zealand" (national); "God Save the Queen" (royal).
Money: *Basic unit*—New Zealand dollar. One hundred cents equal one dollar.

New Zealand's flag, officially adopted in 1902, features the British Union Flag and four stars of the constellation Southern Cross against a royal blue background.

Coat of arms. Symbols on the shield represent the value of farming, mining, and trade to New Zealand. The crown represents the British monarch, who is also the monarch of New Zealand.

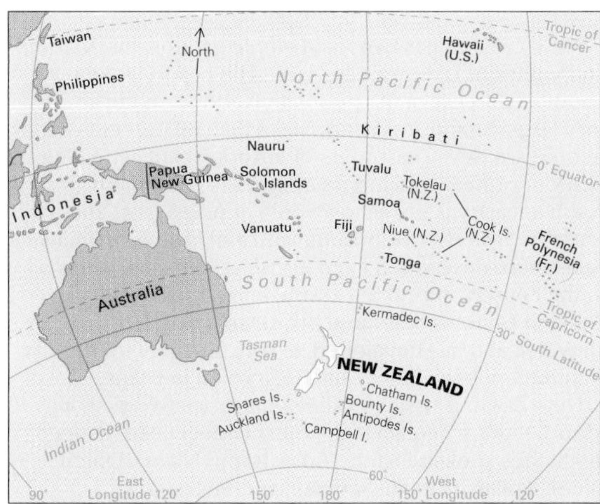

WORLD BOOK map

New Zealand, a country in the Pacific Ocean, lies about 1,000 miles (1,600 kilometers) southeast of Australia. New Zealand consists of the North Island, the South Island, and smaller islands.

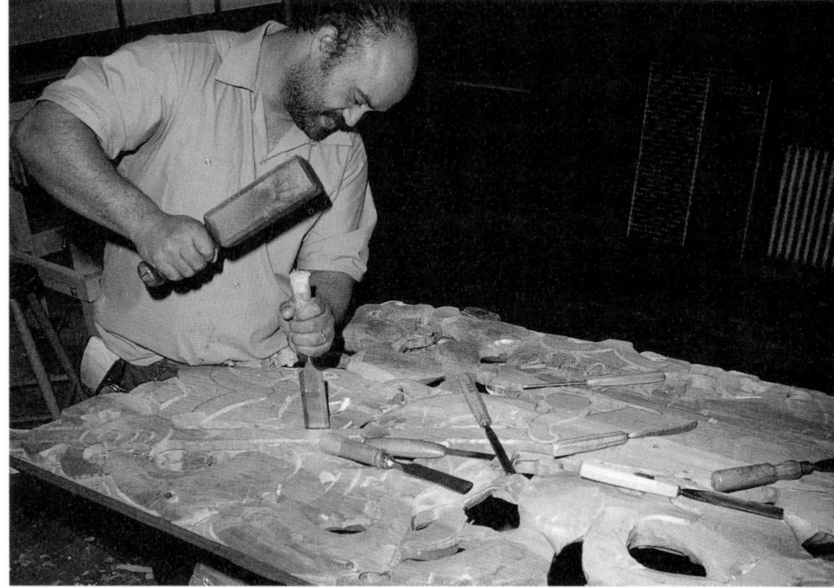

A Maori woodcarver works at the New Zealand Maori Arts and Crafts Institute in Rotorua. Modern Maori artists and craftspeople have incorporated traditional styles into their work.

tions, such as the employment court, family court, youth court, environment court, and Maori Land Court.

Armed forces of New Zealand are called the New Zealand Defence Force (NZDF). The NZDF consists of a navy, army, and air force, together with civilian employees. Military service is voluntary.

Overseas territories. New Zealand governs two overseas territories. They are Ross Dependency, a part of Antarctica; and Tokelau, an island group northeast of New Zealand. New Zealand formerly governed the Cook Islands and the island of Niue. The Cook Islands became self-governing in 1965 and Niue in 1974. But the people of these islands are still considered citizens of New Zealand, and the country still has some responsibility for the islands' defense and foreign affairs.

People

New Zealand has two main ethnic groups, the Maori and whites of European ancestry. The Maori make up about 15 percent of the population and form the country's largest minority group. More than 80 percent of the people are New Zealanders of European ancestry. The number of New Zealanders of other Pacific Island or Asian ancestry is growing. People of non-Maori ancestry are known as *Pakeha* (pronounced *PAH kee hah).* Many Pakeha are descended from British colonists who came to the country during the 1800's, and so many New Zealand customs resemble British customs. However, New Zealand has developed its own sense of identity as a country of both British and Polynesian heritage.

New Zealand has two official languages, English and Maori, though English is the most widely used. Other languages spoken include Cook Island Maori, Dutch, Greek, Italian, Niuean, Samoan, and Tongan.

Way of life

City life. New Zealand's cities offer a wide range of economic and social opportunities. City dwellers can work in New Zealand's business, communication, manufacturing, and shipping industries. Urban New Zealanders enjoy easy access to the fine arts, education, entertainment, and night life. New Zealand's cities are fairly uncrowded. Some city dwellers live in high-rise apartment buildings, but most own their own homes.

Rural life in New Zealand centers mainly around agricultural activities such as raising sheep and cattle and growing fruits, vegetables, and grain. Many people in the northern part of New Zealand's North Island raise dairy cattle. In other parts of North Island and on South Island, beef cattle and sheep are more common. Farmers produce large amounts of apples, kiwi fruit, and other fruits. Vineyards in the southern regions of North Island, the northern regions of South Island, and the eastern regions of both islands grow grapes and produce New Zealand wine.

Food and drink. New Zealand's cooking combines British traditions with foods grown in the country. Traditionally, New Zealanders have favored beef, mutton, and venison served as steaks, as sausages, or in meat pies. But vegetarianism is increasing in popularity. New Zealand's coastal waters offer an abundance of seafood. Dairy products such as milk, cheese, and ice cream are important foods. A favorite dish is a sweet meringue dessert called *pavlova.* Tea, coffee, beer, and wine are popular beverages.

Recreation. Sports and outdoor activities are important forms of recreation in New Zealand. New Zealanders enjoy Rugby Union, a form of rugby football generally regarded as the national sport. New Zealand's national Rugby Union football team is called the All Blacks. Cricket is another popular spectator sport. In the summer, New Zealand's mountainous terrain offers mountaineering, hiking, and climbing. In the winter, skiing and other snow sports are popular. New Zealand's coastal waters attract many boaters and surfers. Horse racing has always been a favored leisure activity.

Fishing and hunting are popular pastimes. Rainbow trout and brown trout abound in New Zealand's lakes and rivers. The North Island's warm coastal waters provide excellent line fishing and spear fishing. Boating offers the additional attraction of deep-sea fishing for marlin, shark, or tuna. The chief game birds for hunters are duck, swan, pheasant, quail, and geese.

Religion. The Anglican Church is the largest religious group in New Zealand. About 18 percent of the people are Anglicans. About 14 percent are Roman Catholics, and about 13 percent are Presbyterians. New Zealand society has become more *secular* (nonreligious), and a growing number of people have no religious affiliation.

Education. New Zealand has public schools funded by the state and private schools, most of which are church sponsored. All children from the ages of 6 to 16 must attend school, though most children begin at the age of 5. Students who live in isolated areas or who have special physical or psychological needs may receive instruction from The Correspondence School in Wellington. The school also serves adults and pupils who wish to study courses not offered at their local schools.

The country has eight universities. They are Massey University in Palmerstown North; Victoria University of Wellington; Lincoln University, near Christchurch; the University of Auckland; Auckland University of Technology; the University of Canterbury in Christchurch; the University of Otago in Dunedin; and the University of Waikato in Hamilton. A number of technical and professional institutions also offer degrees. Three institutions known as *wananga* provide technical and university-level programs for Maori students, with an emphasis on Maori culture and language.

Almost all of New Zealand's adult population can read and write. For the country's literacy rate, see **Literacy** (table: Literacy rates for selected countries).

The arts. New Zealand literature first gained widespread attention in the early and middle 1900's. Katherine Mansfield wrote sensitive short stories about her childhood in New Zealand. Sylvia Ashton-Warner is known for her fiction and autobiographical books that draw upon her experiences as a teacher in rural New Zealand. Keri Hulme won fame for her fiction and poetry that deal with the language and culture of the Maori. Other important New Zealand writers include James K. Baxter, Janet Frame, Ngaio Marsh, and Frank Sargeson.

Important New Zealand painters include Colin McCahon, Rita Angus, and Toss Woollaston. All three were leaders in introducing modern styles to New Zealand art in the 1900's. McCahon painted intense landscapes and religious scenes. Angus created vivid portraits and landscapes in both oil and water color. Woollaston painted landscapes as well as portraits of family and friends. The Maori have maintained a long tradition of folk art, especially carefully detailed woodcarvings and intricate, swirling tattoos. Modern Maori artists have incorporated traditional Maori styles into painting and sculpture.

In music, opera singer Kiri Te Kanawa won international acclaim as one of the finest sopranos of the later 1900's. The New Zealand Symphony Orchestra is internationally recognized. The Royal New Zealand Ballet, established in 1953, is the oldest professional dance company in the country. The New Zealand School of Dance and Te Kura Toi Whakaari o Aotearoa: New Zealand Drama School offer courses in the performing arts. There are many local theater and music groups.

New Zealand has many public museums and art galleries. New Zealand's national museum—Te Papa Tongarewa, Museum of New Zealand—opened in Wellington in 1998. The New Zealand Film Archive collects and preserves a national collection of New Zealand's motion-picture history. The New Zealand Historic Places Trust preserves archaeological sites, historic areas and buildings, and sites of special significance to the Maori.

AP/Wide World

Rugby Union football is widely popular in New Zealand and is regarded as the national sport. The country's national Rugby Union team is the All Blacks, shown here in black uniforms.

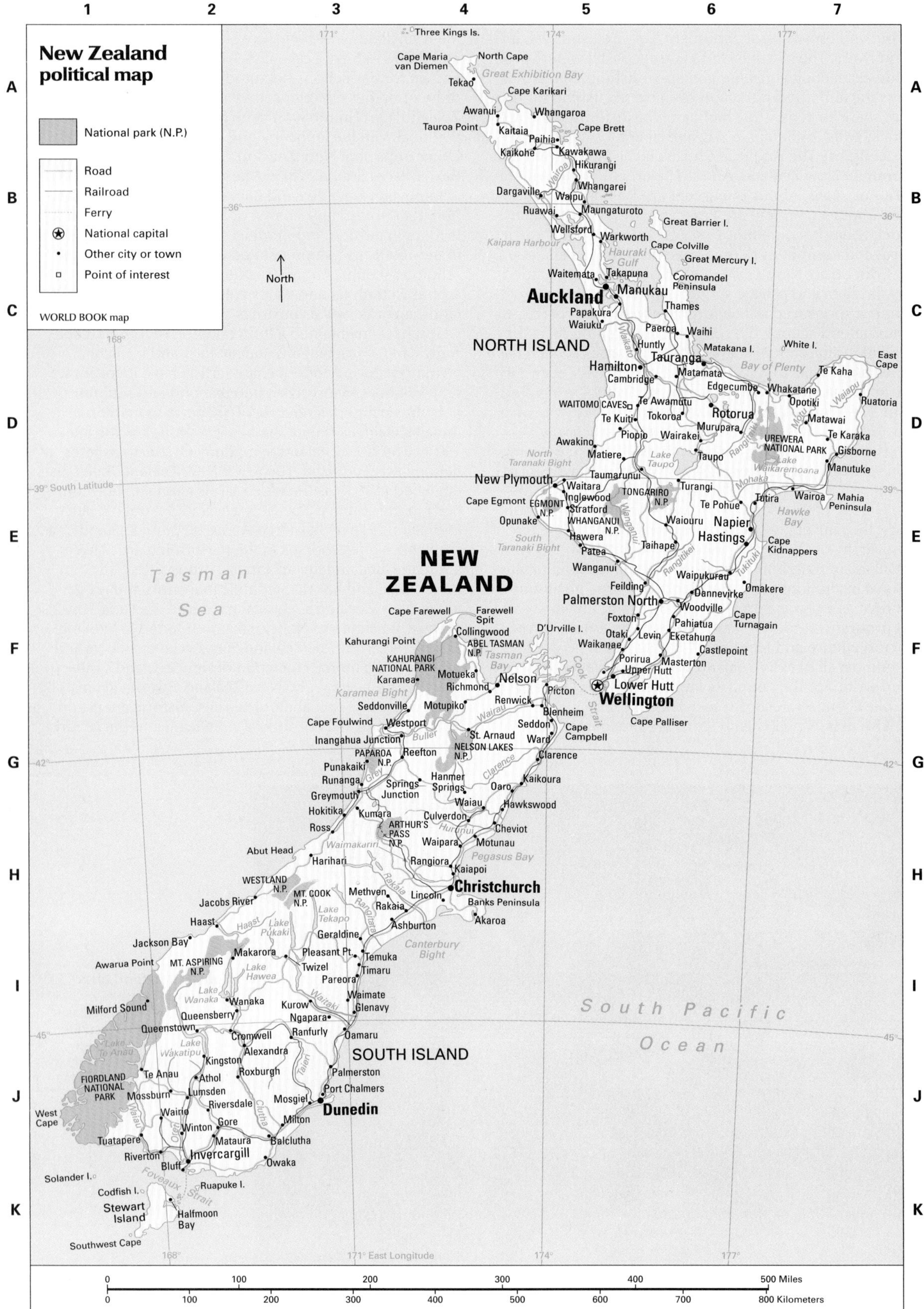
New Zealand political map
National park (N.P.)
Road
Railroad
Ferry
National capital
Other city or town
Point of interest
WORLD BOOK map
North
NEW ZEALAND
NORTH ISLAND
SOUTH ISLAND
Tasman Sea
South Pacific Ocean
Auckland
Wellington
Christchurch
Dunedin
Hamilton
Tauranga
Rotorua
Napier
Hastings
Nelson
Invercargill
Palmerston North
New Plymouth
Lower Hutt
Manukau
Three Kings Is.
North Cape
Cape Maria van Diemen
Great Exhibition Bay
Cape Karikari
Whangaroa
Cape Brett
Kaitaia
Kaikohe
Paihia
Kawakawa
Hikurangi
Whangarei
Dargaville
Waipu
Ruawai
Maungaturoto
Great Barrier I.
Wellsford
Warkworth
Kaipara Harbour
Hauraki Gulf
Cape Colville
Great Mercury I.
Waitemata
Takapuna
Coromandel Peninsula
Thames
Papakura
Waiuku
Paeroa
Waihi
Huntly
Matakana I.
White I.
East Cape
Bay of Plenty
Te Kaha
Cambridge
Matamata
Edgecumbe
Whakatane
Opotiki
Ruatoria
WAITOMO CAVES
Te Awamutu
Te Kuiti
Tokoroa
Murupara
Matawai
Te Karaka
UREWERA NATIONAL PARK
Gisborne
Manutuke
Piopio
Wairakei
Awakino
Matiere
Lake Taupo
Taupo
Lake Waikaremoana
North Taranaki Bight
Taumarunui
Waitara
Inglewood
TONGARIRO N.P.
Turangi
Tutira
Wairoa
Mahia Peninsula
Cape Egmont
EGMONT N.P.
Stratford
Te Pohue
Opunake
WHANGANUI N.P.
Waiouru
Hawke Bay
Hawera
South Taranaki Bight
Patea
Taihape
Cape Kidnappers
Wanganui
Waipukurau
Feilding
Dannevirke
Omakere
Woodville
Foxton
Pahiatua
Cape Turnagain
Otaki
Levin
Eketahuna
Waikanae
Castlepoint
Porirua
Masterton
Upper Hutt
Cape Palliser
Cape Farewell
Farewell Spit
Collingwood
D'Urville I.
Kahurangi Point
ABEL TASMAN N.P.
Tasman Bay
KAHURANGI NATIONAL PARK
Karamea
Motueka
Richmond
Picton
Cook Strait
Karamea Bight
Renwick
Blenheim
Seddonville
Motupiko
Seddon
Cape Foulwind
Westport
Cape Campbell
Buller
St. Arnaud
Ward
Inangahua Junction
NELSON LAKES N.P.
PAPAROA N.P.
Reefton
Clarence
Punakaiki
Runanga
Springs Junction
Hanmer Springs
Kaikoura
Greymouth
Oaro
Waiau
Hawkswood
Hokitika
Kumara
Culverdon
Ross
ARTHUR'S PASS N.P.
Cheviot
Waipara
Motunau
Abut Head
Waimakariri
Pegasus Bay
Harihari
Rangiora
Kaiapoi
WESTLAND N.P.
MT. COOK N.P.
Methven
Lincoln
Jacobs River
Rakaia
Banks Peninsula
Lake Tekapo
Akaroa
Haast
Lake Pukaki
Ashburton
Geraldine
Canterbury Bight
Jackson Bay
Makarora
Pleasant Pt.
Temuka
Awarua Point
MT. ASPIRING N.P.
Lake Hawea
Twizel
Timaru
Pareora
Lake Wanaka
Wanaka
Waitaki
Waimate
Milford Sound
Kurow
Glenavy
Queensberry
Ngapara
Queenstown
Ranfurly
Oamaru
Lake Te Anau
Lake Wakatipu
Cromwell
Alexandra
Kingston
Roxburgh
Palmerston
FIORDLAND NATIONAL PARK
Te Anau
Athol
Port Chalmers
Mossburn
Lumsden
Mosgiel
West Cape
Wairio
Riversdale
Milton
Winton
Gore
Clutha
Tuatapere
Mataura
Balclutha
Riverton
Owaka
Bluff
Solander I.
Foveaux Strait
Ruapuke I.
Codfish I.
Stewart Island
Halfmoon Bay
Southwest Cape
36°
39° South Latitude
42°
45°
168°
171°
171° East Longitude
174°
177°
0
100
200
300
400
500 Miles
500
600
700
800 Kilometers
1
2
3
4
5
6
7
A
B
C
D
E
F
G
H
I
J
K

New Zealand map index

Main islands

Map key	Island	Population	Area In mi²	Area In km²
C 5	**North Island**	2,795,800	44,701	115,777
J 3	**South Island**	918,300	58,385	151,215
K 1	**Stewart Island**	*	674	1,746

Cities and towns

City or town	Population	Map key
Alexandra		J 2
Ashburton	25,177	H 4
Ashhurst†		F 5
Auckland	345,768	C 5
Balclutha		J 3
Birkenhead†		C 5
Blenheim		G 5
Cambridge		D 5
Carterton†	6,812	F 6
Christchurch	309,028	H 4
Cromwell		I 2
Dannevirke		F 6
Dargaville		B 5
Devonport†		C 5
Dunedin	118,143	J 3
East Coast Bays†		C 5
Eastbourne†		F 5
Ellerslie†		C 5
Feilding		E 5
Gisborne	45,780	D 7
Glen Eden†		C 5
Gore	13,279	J 2
Green Island†		J 3
Greymouth		G 3
Halswell†		H 4
Hamilton	108,428	C 5
Hastings	66,280	E 6
Havelock North†		E 6
Henderson†		C 5
Heretaunga-Pinehaven†		F 5
Hokitika		G 3
Hornby†		H 4
Howick†		C 5
Huntly		C 5
Invercargill	53,209	K 2
Kaiapoi		H 4
Kaikohe		B 4
Kaitaia		A 4
Kapiti†	38,584	F 5
Kawerau†	7,829	D 6
Levin		F 5
Lower Hutt	95,872	F 5
Lyttelton†		H 4
Manukau	254,278	C 5
Marton†		E 6
Masterton	22,756	F 6
Matamata		D 6
Morrinsville†		C 6
Mosgiel		J 3
Motueka		F 4
Mount Albert†		C 5
Mount Eden†		C 5
Mount Maunganui†		C 6
Mount Roskill†		C 5
Mount Wellington†		C 5
Napier	53,462	E 6
Nelson	40,240	F 4
New Lynn†		C 5
New Plymouth	68,111	E 5
Ngaruawahia†		C 5
North Shore†	172,164	C 5
Northcote†		C 5
Oamaru		I 3
One Tree Hill†		C 5
Onehunga†		C 5
Opotiki	9,375	D 7
Otahuhu†		C 5
Otaki		F 5
Paeroa		C 6
Palmerston North	73,095	F 5
Papakura	39,627	C 5
Papatoetoe†		C 5
Petone†		F 5
Picton		F 5
Porirua	46,626	F 5
Port Chalmers		J 3
Pukekohe†		C 5
Putaruru†		D 6
Queenstown		I 2
Rangiora		H 4
Riccarton†		H 4
Richmond		F 4
Rotorua	64,509	D 6
St. Kilda†		J 3
Sockburn†		H 4
Southland†	30,562	K 1
Stratford	9,544	E 5
Takapuna		C 5
Taumarunui		D 5
Taupo	30,691	D 6
Tauranga	77,775	C 6
Tawa†		F 5
Te Awamutu		D 6
Te Kuiti		D 5
Te Puke†		D 6
Temuka		I 3
Thames		C 6
Timaru	42,631	I 3
Tokoroa		D 6
Turangi		E 6
Upper Hutt	36,716	F 5
Waihi		C 6
Waikanae		F 5
Wainuiomata†		F 5
Waipukurau		E 6
Wairoa	9,900	E 7
Waitakere†	155,565	C 5
Waitara		E 5
Waitemata		C 5
Waiuku		C 5
Wanganui	45,042	E 5
Wellington	157,646	F 5
Westport		G 3
Whakatane	33,125	D 7
Whangarei	66,748	B 5

*Population not reported separately; included in Southland District.
†Does not appear on the map; key shows general location.
Source: 1996 census; places without populations are unincorporated areas.

The land

New Zealand lies in the southwest Pacific Ocean. The North Island and the South Island are New Zealand's largest islands. They extend in a curve more than 1,000 miles (1,600 kilometers) long and cover about 99 percent of the country's total area. Cook Strait, which is about 16 miles (26 kilometers) wide at its narrowest point, separates the islands.

The North Island can be divided into three main land regions: (1) the Northern Peninsulas and Waikato Basin, (2) the Volcanic Region and Western Hill Country, and (3) the Eastern Hills.

The Northern Peninsulas and Waikato Basin occupy most of the northern part of the island. This region has forests, rich lowlands, and undeveloped hill country. In the lower lands, many farmers grow citrus or kiwi fruits or raise dairy cattle. Beef cattle and sheep are raised in the hill country. Long, sandy beaches line the west coast, and many inlets mark the east coast.

The Volcanic Region and Western Hill Country cover the western half of the island south of the Northern Peninsulas and Waikato Basin. Much of the region consists of volcanic rock. A large plateau covered with soft, yellow-brown soil made up of crushed *pumice*—the porous stone thrown off by volcanoes—rises along the eastern part of the region in the center of the island.

This region has several active volcanoes, including Mount Tongariro, and the highest peak on the island, 9,175-foot (2,797-meter) Mount Ruapehu. This region also has many hot springs and geysers.

The Eastern Hills occupy the eastern and southern parts of North Island. A mountain system runs through the region from East Cape to Cook Strait. The eastern slopes consist mainly of rugged hills. Ranchers use this land for grazing sheep and beef cattle. Lowlands along the east coast are used for growing vegetables and fruits. To the west of the mountains are lowlands and plains. Farmers raise dairy cattle, other livestock, and crops in this region.

The South Island has three main regions: (1) the Southern Alps and High Country, (2) the Canterbury Plains, and (3) the Otago Plateaus and Basins.

The Southern Alps and High Country cover most of the island. The highest peak in New Zealand, 12,316-foot (3,754-meter) Mount Cook, rises in the Southern Alps. The Maori name for Mount Cook is *Aoraki,* also spelled *Aorangi,* which is usually translated as *cloud piercer.* The Mount Cook region has some of New Zealand's

© Gerald Cubitt

Majestic Mount Cook, New Zealand's highest mountain, soars 12,316 feet (3,754 meters) on the South Island. Mount Cook and hundreds of other peaks attract many mountain climbers.

Physical features

Feature	Row	Column
Arthur's Pass	E	3
Banks Peninsula	F	4
Bay of Islands	A	4
Bay of Plenty	B	5
Bream Bay	A	4
Buller River	D	3
Canterbury Bight	F	3
Cape Brett	A	4
Cape Campbell	E	4
Cape Colville	B	5
Cape Egmont	C	4
Cape Farewell	D	3
Cape Foulwind	D	3
Cape Karikari	A	4
Cape Maria van Diemen	A	3
Cape Palliser	D	5
Clutha River	F	2
Cook Strait	D	4
Coromandel Peninsula	B	5
Doubtful Sound	F	1
D'Urville Island	D	4
East Cape	B	6
Firth of Thames	B	5
Foveaux Strait	G	2
Great Barrier Island	B	5
Great Exhibition Bay	A	4
Great Mercury Island	B	5
Grey River	E	3
Haast Pass	F	2
Hauraki Gulf	B	4
Hawke Bay	C	5
Hokianga Harbour	A	3
Kaikoura Peninsula	E	4
Kaipara Harbour	B	4
Kapiti Island	D	4
Karamea Bight	D	3
Lake Benmore	F	3
Lake Ellesmere	F	3
Lake Taupo	C	5
Lake Te Anau	F	2
Lake Wairarapa	D	4
Lake Wakatipu	F	2
Lewis Pass	E	3
Mahia Peninsula	C	6
Manukau Harbour	B	4
Matakana Island	B	5
Milford Sound	F	1
Mt. Aspiring	F	2
Mt. Cook	F	3
Mt. Egmont	C	4
Mt. Ngauruhoe	C	4
Mt. Ruapehu	C	5
Mt. Tapuaenuku	E	4
Mt. Tongariro	C	5
North Cape	A	4
North Island	B	4
North Taranaki Bight	C	4
Otago Peninsula	G	3
Pegasus Bay	E	4
Poverty Bay	C	6
Raglan Harbour	B	4
Rangitata River	F	3
Rangitikei River	D	5
Raupuke Island	G	2
Resolution Island	G	1
South Island	F	3
South Taranaki Bight	C	4
Southern Alps (mountains)	E	3
Southwest Cape	G	1
Stewart Island	G	2
Tasman Bay	D	4
Tasman Sea	D	2
Te Waewae Bay	G	1
Three Kings Islands	A	3
Waiau River	E	4
Waiau River	G	2
Waikato River	B	5
Wairau River	D	4
Waitaki River	F	3
Wanganui River	C	4
West Cape	G	1

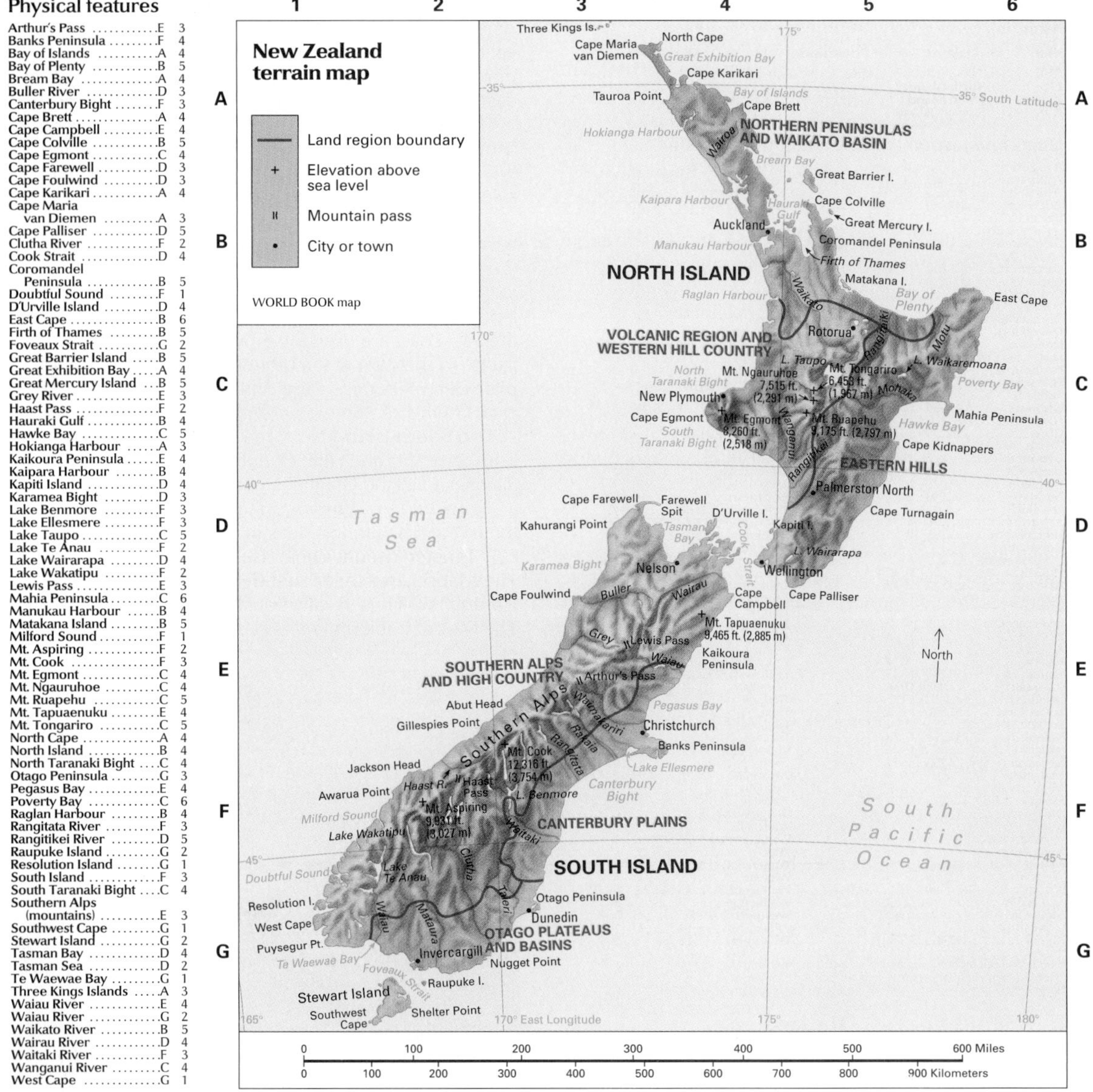

most spectacular scenery. Glaciers lie on mountain slopes high above thick, green forests. Sparkling lakes nestle in valleys throughout the regions.

The western slopes of the Southern Alps and High Country region are forested, rainy, and rugged. The eastern slopes are lower and much less rainy. Along the southwest coast, long inlets of the sea called *fiords* cut into the land, creating a jagged coastline. Forested mountains border many of the fiords.

The Canterbury Plains lie along the east-central coast of the South Island. They form New Zealand's largest area of flat or nearly flat land and make up the chief grain-growing region. The plains are laid out in a patchwork of fields on which farmers grow barley, fodder crops, oats, and wheat. The plains are also an important region for raising sheep.

The Otago Plateaus and Basins lie in the southeast corner of the South Island. The region has plains and rolling hills, where crops and livestock are raised.

Other islands. Stewart Island lies about 20 miles (32 kilometers) south of the South Island. Scrubby bushes cover most of the island. Most of the people earn their living by fishing and oyster gathering. The Chatham Islands lie about 530 miles (850 kilometers) east of the South Island. Most Chatham Islanders are Maori. Fishing and sheep farming are their main occupations.

Other islands and island groups are the Antipodes Islands, the Auckland Islands, the Bounty Islands, Campbell Island, the Kermadec Islands, the Snares Islands, Solander Island, and the Three Kings Islands. Of these, only Campbell Island has a permanent population.

Lakes, rivers, and waterfalls. New Zealand has

many rivers, lakes, and waterfalls. In the alpine regions of the South Island, mountain snows and glaciers feed many rivers. The North Island has New Zealand's longest river, the Waikato, flowing 264 miles (425 kilometers). The island also has the largest lake, Lake Taupo, which covers 234 square miles (606 square kilometers) and is a vacation area famous for trout fishing.

On both islands, the rivers rise in the mountains and flow down to the sea. Most of the rivers flow swiftly and are difficult to navigate. The Clutha River on the South Island carries the largest volume of water. The rapid flow of the rivers makes them important sources of hydroelectric power.

New Zealand has many waterfalls. Sutherland Falls tumbles 1,904 feet (580 meters) down a mountain near Milford Sound on the South Island.

Animal life. The islands of New Zealand were isolated for about 80 million years. As a result, the animal life is unique but limited in variety. There are many species of beetles, flies, and moths. The islands have several types of frogs, geckos, and skinks, and an ancient reptile called the tuatara. The only native land mammals are bats, but dolphins, seals, and whales live in the surrounding ocean. There are also many species of coastal and wetland birds. The flightless kiwi lives only in New Zealand. *Kiwi* has become a nickname for a New Zealander. The kea is a parrot noted for its playfulness.

Settlers introduced many animal species from other lands. The ancestors of the Maori introduced the dog and one type of rat to the islands. Europeans brought many other animals, including deer and rabbits, as well as cattle, pigs, and sheep. Small kangaroos called *wallabies* and brush-tailed possums came from Australia. The new species have depleted the native species to the extent that many are now severely endangered.

Plant life. About 7,000 years ago, rain forests covered most of what is now New Zealand. In the relatively dry Otago Plains in the south of the South Island, grasses and shrubs flourished. As the climate cooled, plant species sensitive to frost diminished, while more cold-tolerant species thrived, especially in upland areas. Low forests developed on the South Island. On the North Island, broadleaf and cone-bearing trees, such as the kauri, became more widespread. Beech forests grow on the cooler uplands of both islands. Since 1900, people have introduced many foreign trees into New Zealand.

Earthquakes. New Zealand has about 100 earthquakes every year that are strong enough to be felt. The country's most disastrous earthquake occurred near Hawke Bay in 1931. It killed 256 people and badly damaged the cities of Hastings and Napier.

Climate

The country has a mild, moist climate. New Zealand lies south of the equator, so its seasons are opposite those of the Northern Hemisphere. July is New Zealand's coldest month, and January and February are the warmest months. The country's mild climate results from ocean breezes that bring warmth in winter and cool temperatures in summer. Average summer temperatures range from about 59 °F (15 °C) to about 69 °F (20 °C), but summer temperatures occasionally rise above 90 °F (32 °C). Average winter temperatures range from about 35 °F (2 °C) to about 53 °F (12 °C).

Climate regions. On the North Island, the northern tip of the Northland Peninsula is warm and humid all year. The island's central plateau has hot, sunny weather in summer and sharp frosts with occasional snow in winter. Wellington lies exposed to the frequent gales of Cook Strait. On the South Island, the rainy west contrasts with the drier east. Southern New Zealand is cooler than northern New Zealand.

Rainfall. The mountains chiefly control the distribution of rainfall in New Zealand. Winds from the west carry moisture from the ocean. This moisture falls as rain on the western slopes of the mountain ranges. Almost the entire west coast of the South Island averages more than 80 inches (200 centimeters) of rain a year. Milford Sound, on the South Island, averages about 260 inches (660 centimeters) of rain each year. East of the mountains, the winds lose most of their moisture. Some eastern regions in the country average less than 20 inches (51 centimeters) of rain a year. Snow seldom falls in lowland areas, though some mountain peaks remain snow-capped all year.

Economy

For many years, New Zealand's economy depended on agriculture. Agriculture remains important, but changing domestic and international conditions have caused a shift in economic activity. Today, the main economic sector is service industries, which employ about 65 percent of the labor force. Service industries include retail trade, restaurants and hotels, finance, transportation, and community and social services. Nearly 25 percent of the labor force work in industry and construction, and about 10 percent work in agriculture.

Manufacturing. New Zealand's factories manufacture food, wine and beer, machinery, textiles, wood products, clothing, and footwear. These industries tend to be based in the larger commercial centers, especially Auckland. Since the mid-1900's, manufactured products have become an important export.

Agriculture. New Zealand's agriculture has centered on raising sheep and cattle to produce mutton, lamb, beef, wool, dairy products, and hides. Meat products are a profitable agricultural export. New Zealand is the world's largest producer of *crossbred wool*, a coarse type of wool from a sheep that is a cross of two breeds. Crossbred wool is used mainly in interior textiles, such as carpets, upholstery, bedding, and rugs. The major crops are apples, barley, kiwi fruit, potatoes, and wheat.

Mining. New Zealand contains a wide variety of minerals. The country is probably best known for its gold, but the mining industry also produces *ironsand* (sand containing iron ore), coal, limestone, and other mineral products.

Forestry. New Zealand's *indigenous* (native) forests grow mainly in the mountain regions, particularly on the west coast of the South Island. Less than 2 percent of New Zealand's total forest production is harvested from indigenous forests. More than 99 percent of the timber comes from planted forests, mostly the fast-growing Monterey pine. The logs are manufactured into plywood, wood pulp, veneer, and other wood products.

Fishing industry. New Zealand's exclusive economic fishing zone is one of the largest in the world, an area 15 times larger than the country's land mass. More than

© Superstock

Sheep are raised in many parts of New Zealand. These animals provide mutton, lamb, and wool. Many sheep are sold at auctions. New Zealand ranks as one of the world's most important sheep-producing countries.

1,000 species of marine fish live in these waters. About 10 percent of them have commercial value. Valuable commercial fish include blue grenadier (also called hoki), jack mackerels, snoek (also called barracouta), southern blue whiting, squid, orange roughy, and tuna.

Energy. New Zealand is self-sufficient in all forms of energy except oil. Water power provides about two-thirds of the nation's electric power. Underground steam in the North Island's volcanic area has become an increasingly important source of power. The country also produces a considerable quantity of natural gas.

International trade. New Zealand's biggest export and import partners are Australia, Japan, and the United States. The country also conducts trade with China, Germany, South Korea, Taiwan, and the United Kingdom. New Zealand's leading export is milk powder. Other important exports are aluminum, butter and cheese, fish, fruit and nuts, iron and steel, leather, machinery, meat, mineral fuels, paper, textiles, wood and wood products, and wool. The major imports include machinery, petroleum, plastics, textiles and textile articles, and vehicles.

Transportation. New Zealand has about 57,000 miles (92,000 kilometers) of streets and roads and about 3 million motor vehicles. The country also has an extensive rail system to carry both passengers and freight.

New Zealand has one of the highest ratios of aircraft to population in the world. Air New Zealand is the major domestic airline. New Zealand's largest international airports are in Auckland, Christchurch, and Wellington. While international air links have helped overcome the country's geographical isolation, New Zealand still relies heavily on sea transport for overseas trade. Auckland, the nation's chief seaport, overlooks a fine natural harbor in the northern part of the North Island.

Communication is one of the most rapidly growing sectors of the New Zealand economy. Television New Zealand operates two television channels, and offshore owners operate two others. There are also a number of local television broadcasters. Sky Television, a pay TV network, broadcasts to subscribers. Radio New Zealand Limited operates a radio network. Special broadcasts promote the Maori language and culture. New Zealand also has privately owned radio stations.

New Zealand has about 30 daily newspapers. The majority of the country's daily papers are owned by Independent Newspapers Limited and Wilson and Horton Limited. These two groups account for almost 90 percent of the country's daily newspaper circulation.

History

New Zealand's first settlers, the people who became known as the Maori, migrated from the islands of eastern Polynesia. They survived by fishing, hunting, and eventually farming. These people probably had established settlements along the coast by the A.D. 1000's. The Maori did not see themselves as one nation. Instead, they considered themselves members of their *hapu* (sub-tribe) and *iwi* (tribe). These groups jealously defended their territories. Wars among them were common.

Early European contact. In 1642, the Dutch explorer Abel Janszoon Tasman became the first European to sight New Zealand. The Maori attacked his boats, and Tasman left without going ashore. In 1769, the British explorer James Cook landed on New Zealand and claimed it for Britain (now the United Kingdom). Although Cook was cautious, he and his crew also had several violent clashes with Maori groups.

In the 1790's and early 1800's, the seals and whales in New Zealand's coastal waters attracted many American, Australian, and European hunters. Traders also came to buy flax and kauri timber from the Maori. Christian missionary groups targeted the Maori as possible converts. By the 1830's, these groups had begun to settle New Zealand. These settlers heavily relied on Maori tribes.

Before 1840, no legal government had authority over the settlers and traders who came to New Zealand. Warfare between Maori groups and disputes between missionary and trading settlements were common. In 1835, a group of Maori leaders called the Confederation of Chiefs of the United Tribes of New Zealand signed a declaration proclaiming the country's independence. The declaration requested the British monarch to act as the country's protector.

European colonization. Reports of lawless conditions and fear of competition from French and American settlers led the United Kingdom to declare New Zealand a colony. In 1840, the British negotiated the Treaty of Waitangi with the Maori. About 500 Maori chiefs eventually signed the treaty.

The Treaty of Waitangi was written in English and then translated into Maori. Problems with the translation of some important words have led to disputes over which rights the Maori kept and which they signed away. For example, in English the treaty proposed that the Maori hand over their sovereignty—that is, their right to rule themselves—in exchange for recognition of their ownership of the land and the right to be protected as British subjects. But in the Maori translation, the words used for *sovereignty* and *ownership* could be understood as giving the British limited powers to govern, rather than full sovereignty.

In the United Kingdom, the British colonial organizer Edward Gibbon Wakefield created the New Zealand Company. The company established settlements at Wellington and Wanganui in 1840, New Plymouth in 1841, and Nelson in 1842. Other groups founded settlements at Dunedin in 1848 and Christchurch in 1850.

The South Island began to prosper soon after the British claimed New Zealand as a colony. The island's rich grasslands provided good grazing for sheep imported from Australia, and soon the settlers began exporting wool. In 1861, prospectors discovered gold in Otago. Immigrants poured into the country, hoping to strike it rich. Few miners were successful, but many stayed to become farmers.

The New Zealand Wars. As the colonists' demand for Maori land grew, disputes over land ownership became more common and more violent. War broke out in 1860 when a group of Maori disputed the government's purchase of tribal land in the Taranaki region. Government forces seized a Maori fortification built on the disputed land near Waitara. The initial fighting in the Waitara region lasted about a year.

In July 1863, the British governor Sir George Grey ordered the invasion of the Waikato district, a Maori-occupied region on the North Island's western side. Grey had heard rumors that the Waikato Maori forces intended to attack Auckland. He was supported by the settlers who wanted to open up the Waikato's fertile grazing lands to British settlement. The wars continued until 1872.

In 1865, the colonial government created an agency called the Native Land Court to establish individual titles to land. The court defied the traditional Maori belief that land belonged to the entire tribe, not to individuals. By the end of the 1800's, settlers had taken most Maori land. The Maori were forced to withdraw into the harshest and most isolated regions of the country.

Depression and social reform. The expense of fighting the Maori, along with shrinking profits from South Island gold mines, took a severe toll on New Zealand's economy. Heavy government borrowing to support colonization and development projects also weakened the economy. In the late 1870's, the country entered an economic depression that lasted until the 1890's. In 1890, the Liberal Party won control of the government and remained in power for 21 years.

The Liberal Party represented the first stable nationwide political party in New Zealand's history. The party, under the leadership of Richard John Seddon from 1893 to 1906, carried out an extensive program of social reform. In 1893, New Zealand became the first country to give women full voting rights.

Dominion status. In the early 1900's, New Zealanders began to develop a sense of national identity. In 1907, the United Kingdom granted New Zealand's request to become a *dominion*, a self-governing country within the British Empire. New refrigeration methods developed in the late 1800's contributed to New Zealand's growing prosperity. These methods made it possible to export large quantities of butter, cheese, and meat.

During World War I (1914-1918), New Zealand sent about 100,000 troops to Europe to fight with the Allies against Germany. These soldiers suffered heavy casualties, with about 1 in 7 killed.

The Great Depression. New Zealand was hard-hit by the worldwide Great Depression that began in the late 1920's. Unemployment and desperate living conditions led to rioting against the government in the major cities. In 1935, the people elected a Labour Party government. The party increased public works projects, such as railway and road construction and forest planting, to put men to work. In 1938, the government set up a social security program that included health care for all citizens and special benefits for the aged, children, and widows.

World War II. In 1939, New Zealand followed the United Kingdom in declaring war on Germany. New Zealand troops fought beside British troops in Europe and the Middle East. When Japan entered the war in 1941, New Zealand began to fear a Japanese invasion. As British power declined in the Pacific, New Zealand increasingly relied on the United States. New Zealand fought beside the United States in the Pacific Islands.

During the war, New Zealand's domestic economy boomed. Manufacturing and farm production rose, and wages and prices stabilized. By the war's end in 1945, the country had climbed out of the Great Depression. The mid-1900's brought many years of prosperity.

International tensions developed between New Zealand and some of its overseas allies in the 1980's. In 1981, a tour by a South African rugby team caused controversy as many New Zealanders protested South Africa's policy of *apartheid* (racial segregation).

In 1984, Labour Party Prime Minister David Lange announced that New Zealand would ban ships carrying nuclear weapons or powered by nuclear reactors from entering its ports. This ban brought New Zealand into disagreement with the United States, a military ally. In 1986, the United States suspended its military duties to New Zealand under the ANZUS mutual defense treaty. The ANZUS treaty had been signed by Australia, New Zealand, and the United States in 1951. This suspension was partially lifted in 1999 to allow U.S. and New

Important dates in New Zealand

A.D. 1000's	Early Maori settlers lived in New Zealand.
1642	Abel Janszoon Tasman became the first European to sight New Zealand.
1769	James Cook landed on New Zealand and claimed it for Britain (now the United Kingdom).
1840	The British and Maori signed the Treaty of Waitangi, giving the British the right to govern New Zealand.
1860-1872	Settlers on the North Island fought the Maori in the New Zealand Wars.
1861	The New Zealand gold rush began.
1893	New Zealand became the first country to grant women the right to vote.
1907	New Zealand became a dominion within the British Empire.
1938	New Zealand set up a social security program that included health care for all citizens.
1984	New Zealand adopted a policy that banned nuclear weapons and nuclear-powered ships from its ports.
1997	Jenny Shipley became the first woman prime minister of New Zealand.

A drawing (1642) by Isaac Gilsemans from Abel Janszoon Tasman's Journal; Alexander Turnbull Library, Wellington, New Zealand

Maori in canoes attacked vessels of Dutch explorer Abel Janszoon Tasman along the New Zealand coast in 1642. Tasman and his crew had become the first Europeans to sight New Zealand.

Zealand troops to participate in joint United Nations (UN) peacekeeping operations.

New Zealand also strongly opposed France's testing of nuclear weapons in the South Pacific. In 1985, the environmental organization Greenpeace planned to use its ship *Rainbow Warrior* to protest French nuclear tests in the Pacific. But French agents bombed and sank the ship in Auckland Harbour. France apologized for sinking the ship in New Zealand's waters but prevented the agents from serving out their prison terms in New Zealand. In 1996, New Zealand cosponsored a UN resolution to ban nuclear weapons from the Southern Hemisphere.

Maori-Pakeha relations. Since the 1840's, the Maori had protested abuses of the Treaty of Waitangi. In 1975, the Maori showed their discontent with a march to Wellington. In 1975, the New Zealand government set up a panel called the Waitangi Tribunal to investigate tribal land claims and suggest possible settlements. The panel consists of half Maori and half Pakeha members appointed by the governor general.

In 1995, the government reached a historic settlement with a group of Maori known as the Tainui. The settlement included the return of land, money, and a formal apology. Since then, the government has made settlements with several other Maori groups.

Political changes. In 1993, New Zealand adopted a *mixed member proportional system* of electing members of Parliament. In this system, some chairs are reserved for elected legislators, while others are divided among the parties that receive 5 percent or more of the popular vote according to their share of the total votes cast. In the 1996 election, the first held under the new system, none of New Zealand's political parties won an outright majority. The number of seats held by third parties and Maoris increased dramatically. To obtain a majority, the National Party formed a coalition with the New Zealand First Party. The election showed that, under the new system, political parties would have to work together to accomplish their goals.

In 1997, Jenny Shipley became National Party leader as well as prime minister. Shipley was New Zealand's first woman prime minister. In elections held in 1999, a coalition of the Labour and Alliance parties won a majority of seats in Parliament. Helen Clark, the Labour Party's leader, became prime minister. Giselle M. Byrnes

Related articles in *World Book* include:

Biographies

Bolger, Jim
Clark, Helen Elizabeth
Hillary, Sir Edmund P.
Lange, David R.
Mansfield, Katherine
Marsh, Ngaio
Muldoon, Sir Robert
Shipley, Jenny
Tasman, Abel J.
Te Kanawa, Kiri

Cities

Auckland
Christchurch
Wellington

Other related articles

Bank (Australia and New Zealand)
Colombo Plan
Cook Islands
Maori
Moa
Mount Cook
National Park (New Zealand)
Pacific Islands
Ross Dependency
Southeast Asia Treaty Organization
Sutherland Falls
Television (In Australia and New Zealand)

Outline

I. Government
A. The constitution
B. The legislature
C. The prime minister and Cabinet
D. Political parties
E. Local government
F. Ombudsman
G. Courts
H. Armed forces
I. Overseas territories

II. People

III. Way of life
A. City life
B. Rural life
C Food and drink
D. Recreation
E. Religion
F. Education
G. The arts

IV. The land
A. The North Island
B. The South Island
C. Other islands
D. Lakes, rivers, and waterfalls
E. Animal life
F. Plant life
G. Earthquakes

V. Climate
A. Climate regions
B. Rainfall

VI. Economy
A. Manufacturing
B. Agriculture
C. Mining
D. Forestry
E. Fishing industry
F. Energy
G. International trade
H. Transportation
I.Communication

VII. History

Questions

What is an *ombudsman*?
When did Captain James Cook explore New Zealand?
What is the largest religious denomination in New Zealand?
Who was New Zealand's first woman prime minister?
What are New Zealand's most valuable commercial fish?
Where is Mount Cook?
How did the Maori and the English differ in their interpretations of the Treaty of Waitangi?
What are the two largest political parties in New Zealand?
Who were the first people to settle in New Zealand?
What are New Zealand's two overseas territories?

Additional resources

Jackson, William K., and McRobie, Alan. *Historical Dictionary of New Zealand.* Scarecrow, 1996.

King, Jane. *New Zealand Handbook.* 5th ed. Moon Pubns., 1999.

Nile, Richard, and Clerk, Christian. *Cultural Atlas of Australia, New Zealand, and the South Pacific.* Facts on File, 1996.

Sinclair, Keith, ed. *The Oxford Illustrated History of New Zealand.* 2nd ed. Oxford, 1996.

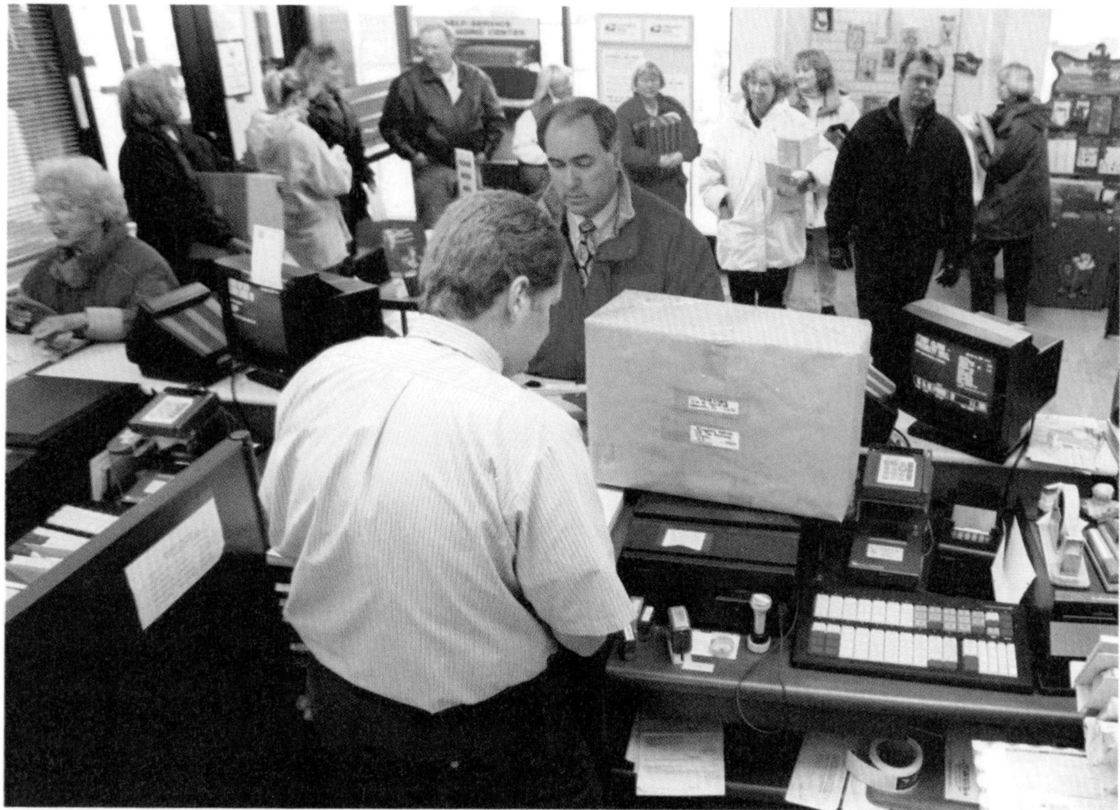

© Steve Warmowski, *Journal-Courier*/The Image Works

At a post office, customers buy stamps, envelopes, and other postal supplies, send money orders, and register packages to be mailed. Other postal services include the renting of post office boxes and the collection, sorting, and delivery of mail.

Postal services

Postal services, also called mail services, are the procedures involved in the collection, handling, and delivery of letters, messages, and packages. *Post offices* are places where mail is handled and postal materials and services are sold. The terms *postal service* and *post office* can also refer to a government agency that provides mail services. In the United States, the government agency that provides mail services is called the United States Postal Service. In the United Kingdom, it is called the Post Office. India Post provides similar services in India, as does An Post in Ireland. In Australia, the postal service is the Australian Postal Corporation, which operates under the name Australia Post; in Canada, it is the Canada Post Corporation, or Canada Post.

Mail is perhaps the one service of central government that touches nearly every citizen on almost a daily basis. Indeed, in many small towns, the post office is the only government building. By means of letters, people can share news and make plans with friends and relatives far away. Businesses send bills and receive payments through the mail. Most magazines and mail-order catalogs are delivered by mail.

Postal services have played a major role in the building of nations and the uniting of people throughout history. In ancient times, an extensive system of messenger routes served to knit the Roman Empire together. In Australia, Canada, and the United States, the postal services helped promote democracy by uniting citizens who were scattered over a vast continent. Until well into the 1900's, the postal services were the primary vehicle for communication and marketing.

The postal industry is big business. Postal agencies are large organizations, traditionally government-run, with many complicated managerial and economic concerns. The United States Postal Service, for example, is the country's largest single employer of civilian labor, with about 900,000 full- and part-time employees. About 80 percent of the costs of postal administrations go for payrolls and other labor expenses.

Mail service has long ranked as a vital public service, as well as a source of revenue for the government. Postal systems traditionally have an obligation of *universal postal service*—that is, a duty to deliver to every address in the country and to charge the same rate regardless of location and distance. Maintaining universal postal service would be difficult or impossible without government intervention. For this reason, most governments have provided national post offices with a legal

What happens to a letter

Mailing a letter to a friend is just the first step in a long, complicated process. Before your friend receives the letter, it will be handled by many people and numerous machines. The three main stages in the process are collection, sorting, and delivery.

© David R. Frazier

Mailboxes, also called *collection boxes,* are located alongside streets and inside buildings in many towns and cities. A person can mail a letter by dropping it into a mailbox.

© David R. Frazier

A postal employee called a *letter carrier* collects letters and packages from the mailbox. The carrier then transports the mail by truck to a nearby post office for sorting.

© David R. Frazier

Moving conveyor belts at a central mail-processing facility carry the mail to a machine called an *edger-feeder.* The edger-feeder separates items according to envelope size.

© David R. Frazier

A facer-canceler machine arranges the letters so they all face the same direction. It then prints lines over the stamps so they cannot be used again.

© David R. Frazier

A computerized optical character reader "reads" the address on each piece of mail. It then sprays a pattern of lines and bars called a *bar code* onto the envelope to indicate its destination.

U.S. Postal Service

A bar code sorter receives the mail after the optical character reader. The machine sorts the mail according to the destinations indicated by the bar codes.

U.S. Postal Service

A postal truck carries mail to other postal facilities nearer the mail's destination. Trucks may also take mail to airports, where it is then loaded onto airplanes.

U.S. Postal Service

Airmail is the fastest way to send letters and packages to distant places. Most mail going more than 200 miles (320 kilometers) travels by airplane.

© Consignia

At the destination airport, workers take the mail from the airplane and load it onto trucks. The trucks then carry the mail to local postal facilities for delivery.

© Consignia

At the postal facility, the mail is sorted and bundled for every delivery route served by the facility. Workers use mail carts to transport the bundled mail.

© Consignia

A special postal service vehicle departs from the local post office and carries the mail on its delivery route. Some letter carriers do not use vehicles and instead walk their entire routes.

© Consignia

A letter carrier delivers the mail to its final destination. Many carriers park their vehicle on every block along the route and make deliveries on foot.

monopoly, the right to be the only provider of certain types of mail service.

Although the post is an old and important institution, mail services worldwide have gone through great change. New electronic means of communication challenge the traditional role of mail for personal and business communication. In addition, the rise of private courier firms that provide shipping and delivery services has brought increased competition to the postal industry. The question of how to react to competition from new technologies and from private firms, while still upholding its universal service obligation, is a vital one for mail service today.

How mail is delivered

The sending of a letter or package is a long, complicated process. Many people and machines handle the mail before it reaches its destination. This section describes what happens to mail as it travels from the sender to the receiver.

Collection. A person can mail a letter by taking it to a post office, by dropping it into a mailbox, or by handing it to a postal worker. Senders place *postage stamps* on letters as proof that they have paid the mailing charges in advance. Many towns and cities maintain mailboxes, also called *collection boxes,* along many streets. Many large office towers and apartment buildings also have mailboxes. Postal employees called *letter carriers* take the letters and packages from the mailboxes to a nearby post office.

Sorting. Outgoing mail is first sorted at the *originating post office,* the postal facility near the sender. There, postal clerks put the newly collected mail into trays. They bundle packages separately. From the post office, the mail travels by truck to a central facility, sometimes called a *management sectional center.* These centers process nearly all the mail coming from or going to their regions.

Workers called *mail handlers* empty the trays of mail onto moving conveyor belts. The belts carry the mail to a machine called an *edger-feeder,* which separates the mail according to envelope size. The edger-feeder moves the letters into another machine known as a *facer-canceler.* Sensing devices in the facer-canceler find the stamp or facer identification mark on the envelope. These sensors enable the machine to arrange the letters so they all face the same way. The facer-canceler cancels stamps by printing black lines over them so they cannot be used again.

Mail then moves to computerized machines called *optical character readers.* These machines "read" the address on a letter and then spray a pattern of lines and bars known as a *bar code* onto the envelope. Machines called *bar code sorters* then read the codes and sort the mail according to region. Some businesses print their own bar codes on their outgoing mail; these precoded items skip the optical character readers and go directly to the bar code sorters.

If an optical character reader cannot read the address on a piece of mail, the rejected mail may be sent for *remote video encoding.* In this process, an image of the address is scanned and stored in a computer, where computer programs and operators attempt to read the address. If the process succeeds, an operator codes the item and sends it to the bar code sorter. If the process does not succeed, the address is read by a human being, and the mail is sorted accordingly.

Mail addressed to locations outside the region served by the central facility travels by truck, airplane, or train to other central facilities. The mail is then sorted mechanically or by hand into bundles for each delivery route served by the center. Finally, postal workers transport the mail to local post offices for delivery.

Delivery. At local post offices, letter carriers receive the mail for businesses and homes along their routes. They arrange the mail in the order in which they will deliver it by putting it into cases that have slots for each address. In some areas, letter carriers receive mail that has already been sorted by a bar code sorter. Some letter carriers walk their entire route. Most letter carriers, however, drive cars or special postal service vehicles.

The history of postal services

Ancient times. Many ancient civilizations, including the Chinese, Egyptians, Assyrians, and Persians, had well-organized mail systems. These early postal networks existed to help rulers govern empires that stretched over large areas. Generally, only government officials could use the postal system. There was little demand for public mail service because few people could read or write.

Nearly all ancient postal systems were *relay systems.* They consisted of runners or mounted couriers stationed at intervals along major roads. Messages relayed by these couriers traveled swiftly, sometimes more than 100 miles (160 kilometers) a day. In the 500's B.C., the Persian Empire, based in what is now Iran, developed an efficient relay system of mail delivery by couriers on horseback. Herodotus, a Greek historian of the 400's B.C., described the Persian messengers by writing, "Neither snow/ nor rain/ nor heat/ nor gloom of night stays these couriers from the swift completion of their appointed rounds." These words are inscribed on the central post office building in New York City.

The most highly organized mail system of ancient times was established by Augustus Caesar, who became the Roman emperor in 27 B.C. It was a relay system in which mounted couriers rode throughout the empire on a network of well-constructed roads. Along the roads, the Romans built relay stations called *posthouses.* There, messengers could rest, get fresh horses, or pass their messages to another courier. In the A.D. 200's, Roman couriers began to deliver a limited amount of private mail, as well as official messages.

The fall of the West Roman Empire in the A.D. 400's led to the collapse of the postal system. Rulers in some areas continued to use Roman roads and posthouses for their own postal services. But generally, organized communication ended throughout Western Europe.

Meanwhile, many civilizations in other areas of the world developed efficient postal systems. In North and South America, the Aztec and the Inca established networks of relay runners, who delivered messages and packages between major cities. In Asia, the Mongol leader Kublai Khan developed a highly organized postal relay system, with more than 10,000 postal stations, during the 1200's.

The growth of public mail systems. During the

1300's, the growth of international commerce led merchants and trading companies to establish their own courier services. Universities, religious groups, and *guilds* (organizations of skilled workers) also maintained mail service for their members. However, service was slow, expensive, and unreliable.

The invention of the printing press and the growth of education and learning during the 1400's increased the demand for postal services. Delivering mail became a profitable business, and private mail services sprang up in many areas. The Thurn and Taxis family organized one of the most famous private systems in the Holy Roman Empire, which covered what are now Austria, the Czech Republic, Germany, the Netherlands, Switzerland, and part of Italy. Generally, however, service remained costly and slow. In addition, mail services only delivered mail along major transportation routes.

The rise of strong centralized governments in Europe in the late 1400's and the 1500's led to the establishment of official postal services. In 1477, King Louis XI of France created a postal system of mounted couriers with regular schedules. By the end of the 15th century, the Thurn and Taxis family resurrected the old Roman postal system and began what would become a courier service connecting the monarchs of Europe. In the early 1500's, King Henry VIII of England organized a courier system in his own country.

During the early 1600's, many European governments established public postal systems. In 1627, the French government established post offices in major cities and regulated postal rates. Many countries passed laws giving the government the sole power to provide postal delivery. However, private mail services continued to operate in these countries, mostly along routes not covered by government postal systems.

The creation of the Penny Post. The development of mail service in England soon surpassed that on the European continent. In 1635, King Charles I, motivated largely by the need to raise money, became the first English monarch to offer mail services to his subjects. In 1680, a merchant named William Dockwra organized the London Penny Post, which delivered mail anywhere in London for a penny. Dockwra introduced the practice of postmarking letters to indicate when and where they had been mailed. The London Penny Post became so

Granger Collection

The Penny Black was the world's first postage stamp. The British Post Office issued the stamp, with a picture of Queen Victoria, in 1840.

The use of stagecoaches to deliver mail began in the 1700's and greatly improved the speed of postal services. This photo shows a mail coach in London in the 1800's.

Corbis/Bettmann

AP/Wide World

Private courier firms, such as Federal Express and the United Parcel Service, have taken much of the package shipment business away from government postal services.

successful that the government took control of the operation in 1682.

During the 1700's, a program to improve the condition of public roads in England greatly increased the speed at which mail traveled. In the late 1700's, the British government further improved postal service by sending mail on stagecoaches.

In 1837, a retired British schoolteacher named Rowland Hill wrote a pamphlet titled *Post Office Reform.* In it, he called for a uniform penny post, which would charge cheap, uniform postage rates, regardless of distance. At that time, the cost of sending a letter depended on how far it had to travel. Hill also proposed that postage should be paid in advance by the sender, with adhesive stamps to indicate payment. Previously, the letter carrier collected postage from the addressee unless postal officials had written "Paid" on the letter. In addition, Hill suggested the use of envelopes. Until that time, letters were merely folded and sealed with sealing wax. The British Post Office issued the first postage stamps in 1840 and later adopted many of Hill's other ideas. Following the introduction of the uniform penny post, the British system became the model for postal systems around the world.

During the middle and late 1800's, mail volumes increased dramatically. This expansion resulted in efforts to develop cooperation in postal communications between countries. In 1874, 22 countries attended an international postal conference in Bern, Switzerland, to organize and improve the flow of mail between nations. The conference established the General Postal Union, which began functioning in 1875. The name was later changed to the Universal Postal Union.

Postal service in the United States. The first official postal system in the American Colonies was established in 1639 in Boston. The Massachusetts Bay Colony gave a tavern owner named Richard Fairbanks the right to process mail to and from overseas locations. In 1691, King William III of England gave Thomas Neale, a colonial official, the sole right to provide postal services in the American Colonies. In 1707, the British government took control of Neale's system.

After the Revolutionary War in America (1775-1783) began, the Continental Congress named statesman and inventor Benjamin Franklin the first postmaster general of the United States. In 1789, after the nation had won its independence, Congress gave the federal government the sole power to provide postal services.

During the 1800's and early 1900's, postal services grew rapidly in the United States. In 1863, the U.S. Post Office Department began to provide free delivery in many cities. In 1918, airplanes began to carry mail regularly. In 1943, the department divided major cities into numbered postal zones. In 1971, Congress replaced the Post Office Department with the United States Postal Service, an independent agency in the executive branch of the government. For more information on the U.S. Postal Service, see **Postal Service, United States.**

Canadian mail service. The first organized postal service in Canada began in 1693, when Pedro da Silva transported letters between Montreal and Quebec City. At this time, most of Canada was controlled by either English or French colonists. In 1755, Canada's first government post office opened, under the administration of the British Post Office.

Canada took over responsibility for its postal services in 1851, and it created the Post Office as a department of the Canadian government in 1868. Canada won complete independence from the United Kingdom in 1931. The Canada Post Corporation Act, passed in 1981, created the Canada Post Corporation to operate the mail system.

Modern developments

Postal services in their modern form have resulted from a long line of advances, both cultural and technological. The introduction of steamboats, trains, automobiles, airplanes, and new machinery have been vital to the industry's growth since the 1800's. Since the mid-1900's, new developments have further improved the mail process in many ways, but they have also brought new challenges to the postal services.

Technological advancements. In the 1960's, many post offices began using high-speed equipment to perform much of the work previously done by hand. Since then, mail processing has gone through sustained technological innovation. The changes in technology in part stem from innovations in computers, telecommunications technology, and optical character reading.

A major application of these innovations has been the large-scale sorting of mail. Computerized machines, such as optical character readers and bar code sorters, enable post offices to quickly sort large amounts of mail with minimal costs. Many of these machines require fewer workers or less worker training, and some can be operated remotely.

Throughout this period of technological advancement, postal services had to contend with alternative methods of communication. Such innovations as the telegraph, telephone, and fax machine offered new, fast ways to share information. But although phone calls and faxes reduced the use of mail for certain types of communication, the demand for mail remained strong.

A new type of competition emerged in the 1990's, with the increased use of personal computers and the Internet. Computer users transmitted many messages that were once sent by mail by *e-mail* (electronic mail). In addition, many people began doing their shopping, banking, and business transactions over the Internet.

Competition from the Internet had a particularly great impact on traditional letter mail, known in the United States as First-Class Mail. This class of mail—used mainly for messages, invoices, and bills—is the class most easily replaced by electronic communication. The Internet also affected advertising mail, known in the United States as *standard mail,* as companies shifted some of their advertising to the World Wide Web. The demand for shipment of *parcels* (boxes and packages), on the other hand, grew with the rise of the Internet. This increased demand resulted, in part, because items purchased over the Internet still had to be shipped to the customer.

These changes have serious implications for the future funding of postal services and for the maintenance of universal service. If the demand for letter mail and advertising mail further decreases, as many experts expect, postal services worldwide may lose revenue and be forced to increase their rates and adjust their policies. Many postal systems, including the U.S. Postal Service, are themselves working to provide communication and bill payment by electronic means.

Competition and privatization. In addition to coming to terms with technological innovations like those just described, postal administrations face competition from private companies. For example, courier firms, such as the United Parcel Service, have taken much of the parcel business away from the United States Postal Service. Postal services are limited in their ability to raise parcel rates, because parcel shipment is not subject to the same monopoly protection that covers letter mail.

In addition, some private firms offer *presorting* services in competition with traditional mail services. Presorting refers to any sorting of mail that occurs before the postal service handles it. For example, a presorting company working for a newspaper or magazine, at least in the United States, may sort the mail and drop it off at the post office. Businesses find that they can afford presorting services, in part, because national post offices give a discount to mailers who presort their own mail.

Many people believe that mail delivery can function better as a competitive business than as a government monopoly. As a result, many countries have been *privatizing* their postal systems—that is, transferring certain operations and responsibilities from government agencies to privately owned companies. For instance, the Dutch Post Office is a private company with stock held both by the Netherlands government and by private individuals. Germany plans to privatize its post office, Deutsche Post, during the early 2000's. In other countries, a government postal administration may simply hire private firms to handle certain tasks.

Michael A. Crew and Paul R. Kleindorfer

Related articles in *World Book* include:

Airmail
Comstock Law
E-mail
Envelope
Fax machine
Franking and penalty privileges
Letter writing
Mail-order business
Money order
Parcel post
Pony express
Postal Service, United States
Postal Union, Universal
Rural delivery
Stamp
Stamp collecting
United Parcel Service
ZIP Code

Outline

I. **How mail is delivered**
   A. Collection
   B. Sorting
   C. Delivery
II. **The history of postal services**
III. **Modern developments**
   A. Technological advancements
   B. Competition and privatization

Questions

What are some of the machines post offices use to help them process mail more efficiently?
What were some of the innovations suggested by Rowland Hill?
What agency is the largest single employer of civilian labor in the United States?
What does it mean to have an obligation of universal postal service?
How has the Internet affected the demand for traditional letter mail? How has it affected the demand for shipment of parcels?
When did airmail service go into operation?
How did ancient relay systems work?
Who was the first postmaster general of the United States?
What is privatization?
How did the Thurn and Taxis family of Austria contribute to the development of mail service?

Additional resources

Level I

Bolick, Nancy O. *Mail Call! The History of the U.S. Postal Service.* Watts, 1994.
Burns, Peggy. *The Mail.* Thomson Learning, 1995.
Gibbons, Gail. *The Post Office Book: Mail and How It Moves.* Harper, 1986.
Kroll, Steven, *The Pony Express!* Scholastic, 1996.

Level II

John, Richard R. *Spreading the News: The American Postal System from Franklin to Morse.* Harvard Univ. Pr., 1996.
Stewart-Patterson, David. *Post Mortem: Why Canada's Mail Won't Move.* Macmillan, 1987.
Tierney, John T. *The U.S. Postal Service.* Auburn Hse., 1988.
Toch, Mark U. *Opportunities in Postal Service Careers.* VGM Career, 1992.

© Hulton Getty from Liaison

The Spanish Civil War pitted conservative rebels, called Nationalists, against Spain's elected Republican government. In this photo, Nationalist troops guard captured Republican soldiers.

Spanish Civil War (1936 to 1939) was fought between the forces of Spain's democratically elected, liberal government and conservative rebels. The war cost the lives of hundreds of thousands of Spaniards and set the stage for a dictatorship that lasted more than 35 years.

The conservative or *right-wing* forces that rebelled against the government were known as Nationalists. They included military leaders, parts of the Roman Catholic Church, groups that wanted Spain to become a monarchy again, and *fascists.* The fascists were members of a political party called the *Falange Española* (Spanish Phalanx). Like similar groups in Germany and Italy, the fascists wanted to set up a dictatorship.

The forces that fought on the side of the government were known as Republicans. They included a variety of liberal or *left-wing* groups, such as socialists, Communists, and *anarchists* (those who believe people should live without government).

Much of the world viewed the Spanish Civil War as a contest between democracy and fascism. It became a major source of concern for many nations, which believed that the outcome could determine the balance of power in Europe. Many people who felt strongly about the war held fund-raising rallies and publicized the international issues at stake in Spain's domestic conflict.

Background to the war. From 1923 to 1930, General Miguel Primo ruled Spain with the power of a dictator. King Alfonso XIII supported his government. By the end of Primo's time in power, the movement for a republican form of government had gained strength in Spain. Supporters of the movement included liberals, socialists, and other people who did not want a monarchy. The strength of popular support forced Alfonso to allow free elections. In April 1931, the people voted overwhelmingly for republican candidates in city elections. Following the elections, Alfonso left the country, though he refused to give up his claim to the throne. Republican leaders then took control of the government and established what became known as the Second Republic.

The left-wing alliance of republicans and socialists that ruled Spain between 1931 and 1933 attempted to transform Spain's social, economic, and political institutions. Some policies, including certain land reforms and the establishment of an eight-hour work day, threatened the upper classes who owned Spain's land and industries. The government tried to reduce the long-standing influence of the Roman Catholic Church in Spanish society and politics. The government also adopted controversial measures aimed at reforming the armed forces.

These reforms created opposition to the government among many Spaniards, especially conservatives. In parliamentary elections held in 1933, an alliance of moderate and right-wing parties gained control of the government. The new government tried to reverse the pro-gressive reforms of the earlier administration.

Elections held in February 1936 returned the liberals to power in an alliance of left-wing parties known as the Popular Front. In the late spring, a series of strikes, violent public demonstrations, and political assassinations caused most Spaniards to lose faith in the Popular Front.

Rebellion leads to civil war. On July 17, 1936, Spanish army units in Morocco launched a rebellion against the Spanish government. The revolt soon spread to Spain itself. The rebels hoped to overthrow the government quickly and to restore order in Spain. But Republican forces took up arms against the military. Within four days after the start of the uprising, the rebels controlled about a third of Spain. The Republicans controlled Spain's industrial centers and most of its densely populated towns and cities, including the capital, Madrid.

On both sides, a wave of terror and repression followed the military uprising. The Nationalists shot thousands of workers and Republican supporters living in areas under their control. In the Republican zone, thousands of civilians were executed by working-class groups fearful of a reaction from rebel supporters.

In some areas held by Republicans, workers belonging to anarchist and other left-wing organizations dismantled existing government institutions. They replaced them with agricultural and industrial *collectives*—that is, groups jointly owned by their workers—and with bodies known as *people's committees* that intended to rule on behalf of the working classes.

In late July 1936, the Nationalists set up a government in Burgos called the Junta de Defensa Nacional (Council of National Defense). In September, this group chose Francisco Franco to serve as head of both the armed forces and the Nationalist government. Franco and his advisers based the new government on fascist and conservative principles and created a prominent role in the government for the Roman Catholic Church. By the end of 1937, all the forces on the Nationalist side had joined together under Franco's leadership.

Foreign assistance. In August 1936, France, Germany, Italy, the United Kingdom, and other European countries agreed not to intervene in the war. The French and British in particular feared that interference by other countries in the Spanish conflict could cause the war to spread to the rest of Europe. As a result of the agreement, the United Kingdom and France—both supporters of the Republican government—did not provide it with aid. However, Germany's Nazi government and Italy's

Fascist government both violated the agreement. Germany provided military aid to the Nationalists in exchange for certain mining rights. Italy supplied military equipment and troops to help Franco's army.

The Soviet Union sent the Republicans food, clothing, and military equipment in exchange for most of Spain's gold reserves. No Soviet troops were sent, but the Soviet-led organization known as the Comintern recruited volunteers from around the world to fight for the Republicans in groups called the International Brigades.

Progress of the war. Early in the war, the Nationalists demonstrated superior military strength. By the first week of November 1936, rebel troops were closing in on Madrid, hoping to occupy the capital quickly. The determined resistance of the city's population, supported by newly organized units of the International Brigades and Republican troops, stopped the Nationalist advance. The Republicans also defeated the Nationalists at the Jarama River near Madrid in February 1937 and at Guadalajara in March. But they lost the coastal city of Málaga to the Nationalists on February 8.

With the Madrid front stalled, Franco decided to launch a major offensive in the north. As part of this operation, on April 26, 1937, bombers of the German Condor Legion attacked the small market town of Guernica. They destroyed much of the town center and killed over 1,500 civilians, according to most estimates. News of the bombing generated a storm of international protests and demonstrations, and the incident became known as a symbol of fascist brutality. The Spanish painter Pablo Picasso captured the terror of the bombing in his masterpiece *Guernica.* See **Picasso, Pablo** (illustration).

The Nationalists continued their northern assault. The city of Bilbao fell in June. A few months later, the Nationalists conquered the northern coastal areas and industrial regions that had been under Republican control. A major Nationalist offensive launched in the region of Aragon in March 1938 led farther into Republican territory. Franco's army pushed east through the region and reached the Mediterranean Sea by mid-April, cutting the Republican-controlled zone in two.

Franco's advance on Valencia was interrupted by the Republican army's last major offensive, the Battle of the Ebro. This battle, fought from July to November 1938, was the longest of the war. Despite early Republican gains, the Nationalists eventually halted the attack. The Republican defeat paved the way for the Nationalists' march on Catalonia in the northeast. By the end of January 1939, most of the region, including Barcelona, was in Nationalist hands. Republican troops and civilian supporters retreated toward the Spanish-French frontier.

Republican forces were plagued by disagreements among themselves throughout the war. By 1939, internal disputes had split the Republicans into two camps. The government of Juan Negrín, who had come to power in 1937, wanted to continue fighting. But an alliance of left-wing parties considered further resistance useless. In March, this group set up its own government in Madrid. Shortly afterward, Negrín's government collapsed.

As street fighting broke out between pro- and anti-Communist forces in Madrid and elsewhere, representatives of the new government sought in vain to negotiate a surrender with the Nationalists. On March 28, Franco's troops began entering the capital. The remaining Republican forces throughout Spain surrendered, and Franco announced on April 1 that the war was over.

Results of the war. The Spanish Civil War resulted in widespread destruction. Estimates of the numbers of people killed during the conflict vary. Many experts estimate that from 600,000 to 800,000 people died as a result of the war, including deaths caused by combat, bombing, execution, and starvation.

Following the war, Franco established a harsh right-wing dictatorship. Franco had thousands of Republican supporters executed and outlawed all political parties but his own. Spain did not return to democracy until after Franco's death in 1975. George R. Esenwein

See also **Franco, Francisco; Spain** (History [Civil war]).

The Spanish Civil War

The Nationalists quickly captured about a third of Spain. Republicans held most of the country's industrial areas and large cities, including Spain's capital, Madrid. The superior military strength of the Nationalists eventually triumphed.

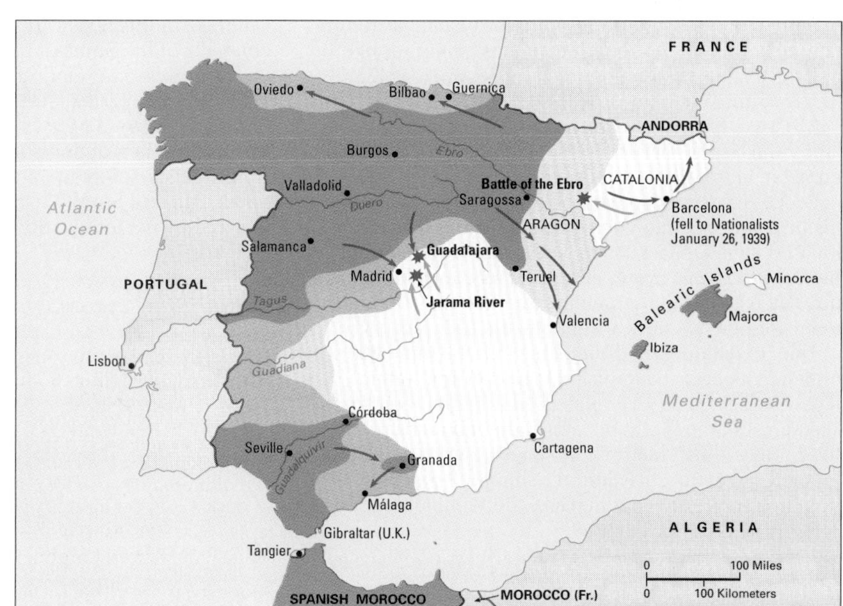

WORLD BOOK map

© Steve Raymer, CORBIS

The rice fields of Vietnam provide one of the primary foods of the Vietnamese people. Most of the people in Vietnam are farmers, and rice is the chief crop.

Vietnam

Vietnam, *VEE eht NAHM* or *VEE eht NAM,* is a country in Southeast Asia with its eastern coast on the South China Sea. Vietnam is bordered by China to the north and Laos and Cambodia to the west. The Gulf of Thailand lies to the southwest. Hanoi is the capital of Vietnam. Ho Chi Minh City, formerly named Saigon, is the largest city.

The population of Vietnam is concentrated in the Red River Delta in the north and the Mekong River Delta in the south. Central Vietnam is less heavily populated than either the north or the south because it has mountainous terrain. Although Vietnam has a number of ethnic groups, most of the people are classified as Kinh—that is, ethnic Vietnamese.

Most Vietnamese are farmers who live in small villages. Rice is the main crop. But manufacturing has become an increasingly important economic activity.

People have lived in what is now Vietnam since prehistoric times. Ethnic Vietnamese developed a culture in the Red River Delta 4,000 to 5,000 years ago. Through the centuries, this group expanded its control of what is now Vietnam. At the same time, the Vietnamese fought many foreign invaders, frequently the Chinese.

The French governed Vietnam from the mid-1800's until Japan occupied it during World War II. After Japan's defeat in 1945, France tried to regain control of Vietnam. But the Vietminh, a group headquartered in the north and headed by Vietnamese patriot and Communist leader Ho Chi Minh, resisted the French. In 1954, fighting between the French and the Vietminh ended with a French defeat in the Battle of Dien Bien Phu.

An international peace conference, held in Geneva, Switzerland, decided to divide Vietnam temporarily into two zones—Communist North Vietnam and non-Communist South Vietnam. Elections were supposed to be held to reunite the country, but they were continually postponed and never took place. In 1957, fighting broke out between revolutionaries in the South and the South Vietnamese government. The fighting eventually developed into the Vietnam War, which the Vietnamese call the American War. The United States became the chief ally of the South. It backed the South's war effort with supplies and hundreds of thousands of troops.

In 1973, the participants in the war agreed to a cease-fire, and the United States withdrew its last combat troops. But the fighting soon resumed. In April 1975, the Communists defeated South Vietnam. In 1976, they unified North and South Vietnam into a single nation, which they named the Socialist Republic of Vietnam.

Patricia M. Pelley, the contributor of this article, is Assistant Professor of History at Texas Tech University.

Facts in brief

Capital: Hanoi.
Official language: Vietnamese.
Area: 128,066 mi² (331,689 km²). *Greatest distances*—north-south, 1,030 mi (1,658 km); east-west, 380 mi (612 km). *Coastline*—2,140 mi (3,444 km).
Elevation: *Highest*—Fan Si Pan, 10,312 ft (3,143 m) above sea level. *Lowest*—sea level along the coast.
Population: *Estimated 2002 population*—79,387,000; population density, 620 per mi² (239 per km²), distribution, 76 percent rural, 24 percent urban. *1999 census*—76,324,753.
Chief products: *Agriculture*—rice. *Manufacturing*—cement, fertilizer, steel, shoes, textiles. *Mining*—coal.
Money: *Basic unit*—dong. One hundred xu equal one dong.

Government

According to the Vietnamese Constitution, which was adopted in 1980 and extensively revised in 1992, Vietnam is a socialist nation. It is governed by a single political party—the Communist Party of Vietnam (CPV). The party is the leading force in the state and society. Political power in Vietnam is based on the principle of *democratic centralism.* Under this principle, authority and power originate at the highest levels of the CPV and flow downward through a rigid political structure.

National level. The National Assembly is the highest legislative body in Vietnam. The 450 delegates to the Assembly are elected by the people to a maximum term of five years. No candidate can run for the Assembly without the approval of the Communist Party. All Vietnamese 18 years of age or older are allowed to vote.

Vietnam's highest government officials are the president and the prime minister. The National Assembly elects one of its own members to serve as president. The president directs members of the Assembly to appoint the vice president, prime minister, chief justice of the Supreme People's Court, and head of the Supreme People's Organ of Control. As head of state, the president acts as official representative of Vietnam, has overall command of the armed forces, and chairs the National Defense and Security Council. As chief executive, the prime minister manages the government, assisted by deputy prime ministers and cabinet ministers.

Local level. Vietnam is divided into 57 *tinh* (provinces) and four municipalities—Da Nang, Haiphong, Hanoi, and Ho Chi Minh City. Each tinh and municipality has a legislature called a People's Council and an executive body known as a People's Committee. The people elect the members of each People's Council, who then elect the members of the People's Committee.

Courts. The judicial system of Vietnam consists of two main divisions: the People's Courts and the People's Organs of Control. The People's Courts include the Supreme People's Court, local courts, and Military Tribunals. The People's Organs of Control monitor the bodies of government.

Armed forces of Vietnam consist of a *main force* and *paramilitary forces.* The main force includes an army of about 412,000 members and a small navy and air force. The paramilitary forces include local urban and rural militias and border defense forces. About 40,000 people serve in the paramilitary forces.

People

Ancestry. Vietnam has 54 ethnic groups. Over 85 percent of the people of Vietnam are Kinh—that is, ethnic Vietnamese—who are spread throughout the country. Minority ethnic groups live mainly in the mountain areas of the country. The largest groups are the Tay, who live to the north and northeast of the Red River Delta; and the Tai, who live in scattered villages in valleys of the Red and Black rivers, in the northwest and north-central interior. Other large minority groups include the Hmong, the Khmer, the Muong, and the Nung. A number of ethnic Chinese people, known as the Hoa, live mainly in the cities.

Language. Vietnamese is the most widely spoken language in Vietnam. However, minority peoples speak their own language and may have only limited knowledge of Vietnamese. In urban areas, English is the most widely spoken foreign language, but Chinese, French, and Russian are also spoken.

Way of life

Rural life. Most Vietnamese live in small villages in the countryside. Most rural Vietnamese are farmers who organize their lives around the cultivation of crops, especially rice. In general, the family and the village are the centers of social life in rural areas.

Houses in the villages vary. Some have tile roofs and walls made of clay or brick. Others have thatched roofs and walls made of woven bamboo. In the mountains and in areas that flood, many houses stand on stilts.

City life. Many villagers have migrated to the cities in search of jobs and a higher standard of living. However, urban development has not kept pace with immigration from the countryside. As a result, the cities of Vietnam are densely packed and face serious housing shortages. In many cases, two or three generations of a family share a one-room apartment.

Vietnam's cities bustle with traffic. Bicycles are a popular means of transportation. Cities also have numerous motor scooters and *cyclo taxis*—three-wheeled, pedaled cycles with a seat in front for carrying passengers.

Vietnam's flag and coat of arms feature a star that stands for Communism. The rice and the cogwheel on the coat of arms represent the importance of agriculture and industry to Vietnam. The flag was first officially adopted by Vietnamese Communists when they declared independence in 1945. The shape of the star was modified slightly in 1955.

WORLD BOOK map

Vietnam is in Southeast Asia, with its eastern coast on the South China Sea. It is also bordered by Cambodia, Laos, and China.

Cafes, food stands, and stalls that sell craftworks, books, clothing, and other items line many urban streets. Architecture in the cities ranges from simple wooden dwellings to elegant colonial villas built by the French to modern high-rise office and apartment buildings.

Urban Vietnamese work in a variety of occupations. For example, some are employed as public officials or work in factories, hotels, or restaurants. Others are merchants who own their own business.

Clothing. The Vietnamese typically wear lightweight clothing. Rural women wear loose-fitting dark pants and blouses that are often embroidered in brilliant colors. Conical hats called *non la* shield their faces from the sun. In cities, many girls and women wear the traditional *ao dai,* a long tunic worn with loose-fitting pants. However, a growing number of urban women now wear dresses and skirts. Rural and working-class men typically wear simple shirts and trousers. City men generally wear Western-style clothing.

Members of minority groups often dress in traditional costumes. For example, Hmong women wear blouses and skirts or baggy shorts, with embroidered belts and aprons or long vests. Some roll their hair into a turban, but most wrap their heads with a cloth. Hmong men wear skullcaps, loose trousers, shirts, and a long vest.

Food and drink. The national dish of Vietnam is a noodle soup called *pho.* This dish consists of long rice noodles and fresh vegetables in a broth with meat or seafood. Many Vietnamese also eat boiled rice with vegetables, *tofu* (soybean curd), seafood, chicken, pork, or duck. A fish sauce called *nuoc mam* is used as a seasoning in many dishes. People in central Vietnam often eat beans, corn, cassava, sweet potatoes, or other starchy foods instead of rice.

Green tea is the most popular beverage. Fruit and sugar cane juices, coconut milk, and soft drinks are widely available. In urban areas, cafes and restaurants serve local and imported beer, wine, and liquor. Coffee and long loaves of bread called *baguettes,* both of which were favorites of the French, are still popular in Vietnam.

Recreation. The Vietnamese, especially children, enjoy swimming in the country's many lakes and rivers, and in the sea. Vietnamese children also engage in lively games of soccer. Many people play chess or tennis. Competitions involving judo and the martial arts of tae kwon do and kung fu are also popular. Families who can afford to do so vacation at seaside resorts.

Religion. Most Vietnamese practice a combination of the Three Teachings—that is, Mahayana Buddhism, Confucianism, and Taoism. The country also has a small number of Christians and Muslims. In the south, a religion known as Cao Dai and the Hoa Hao Buddhist sect, both of which originated in Vietnam, have numerous followers. Some people, especially in villages, worship the spirits of animals, plants, and other parts of nature.

Education. Nearly all Vietnamese 15 years of age or older can read and write. For the literacy rate, see **Literacy** (table: Literacy rates). Children ages 6 through 10 are required to attend school. Schools of higher education in Vietnam include universities, agricultural colleges, technical institutes, and private business academies. The largest are Hanoi University of Technology, Vietnam National University, and Can Tho University. Vocational training is available to adults.

The arts. Traditional Vietnamese forms of art include woodblock printing, woodcarving, lacquerware, ceramics, jade carving, silk painting, and basketry. The Vietnamese are also known for their fine embroidery.

In 1925, the French opened the École des Beaux-Arts de l'Indochine (School of Fine Arts of Indochina) in Hanoi, and Vietnamese artists began to study European-style painting. They started using such materials as oil paints and canvas, painting portraits and scenes of everyday life, and adopting such styles as Cubism and Impressionism. In the late 1940's and early 1950's, a number of artists created works that focused on the resistance to French colonial rule. From the mid-1950's to the 1970's, Socialist Realist artists in the North created paintings that celebrated combat and glorified work.

After the reunification of Vietnam in the mid-1970's to the mid-1980's, art continued to serve mainly a social and political purpose. Since the mid-1980's, however, Vietnamese art has become more open, and paintings now include a variety of styles and subjects. The country's best-known artists include Bui Xuan Phai, known for his Hanoi street scenes; Nguyen Tu Nghiem, whose subjects come from mythology and folklore; Nguyen Sang, who creates paintings of village people; and Do Quang Em, noted for his realistic still lifes and portraits.

Traditional Vietnamese musical instruments include a variety of string, wind, and percussion instruments. Among them are the *dan nhi,* a two-stringed fiddle; the *dan tranh,* a 16-string zither; the *dan nguyet,* a long-

Vietnam map index

Provinces*

Province		
An Giang	J	2
Bac Can	A	3
Bac Giang	B	3
Bac Lieu	K	3
Bac Ninh	B	3
Ba Ria-Vung Tau	J	4
Ben Tre	J	3
Binh Dinh	E	3
Binh Duong	I	3
Binh Phuoc	I	3
Binh Thuan	I	4
Ca Mau	K	2
Can Tho	J	3
Cao Bang	A	3
Dac Lac	H	4
Da Nang	F	4
Dong Nai	I	3
Dong Thap	I	2
Gia Lai	G	4
Ha Giang	A	2
Ha Nam	B	3
Ha Tay	B	2
Ha Tinh	D	2
Hai Duong	B	3
Haiphong	B	3
Hanoi	B	3
Hoa Binh	B	2
Ho Chi Minh	J	3
Hung Yen	B	3
Khanh Hoa	H	5
Kien Giang	J	2
Kon Tum†	G	4
Lai Chau	A	1
Lam Dong	I	4
Lang Son	B	3
Lao Cai	A	1
Long An	I	3
Nam Dinh	C	3
Nghe An	D	2
Ninh Binh	C	3
Ninh Thuan	I	4
Phu Tho	B	2
Phu Yen	H	5
Quang Binh	E	3
Quang Nam	F	4
Quang Ngai	E	3
Quang Ninh	B	3
Quang Tri	E	3
Soc Trang	J	3
Son La	B	1
Tay Ninh	I	3
Thai Binh	C	3
Thai Nguyen	B	3
Thanh Hoa	C	2
Thua Thien-Hue	E	3
Tien Giang	J	3
Tra Vinh	J	3
Tuyen Quang	A	2
Vinh Long	J	3
Vinh Phuc	B	2
Yen Bai	A	1

Cities and towns

City or town	Population		
An Loc	15,276	I	3
Ap Phuoc Tuy*	16,419	I	3
Ba Ra		I	3
Ba Ria		J	3
Bac Can		A	3
Bac Giang	66,349	B	3
Bac Lieu	53,841	K	3
Bac Ninh	45,137	B	3
Bac Quang		A	2
Bao Ha		A	2
Bao Loc	17,774	I	4
Ben Cat		I	3
Ben Tre	65,424	J	3
Bien Hoa	313,868	I	3
Bien Son*	29,482	C	3
Bong Son		G	5
Buon Me Thuot	176,429	H	4
Ca Mau	67,484	K	2
Cam Pha	108,656	B	3
Cam Ranh	118,111	I	5
Can Tho	285,083	J	2
Cao Bang	30,917	A	3
Cao Lanh	16,482	J	3
Chau Doc	76,652	J	2
Cheo Reo	6,195	H	4
Con Son	3,143	K	3
Da Lat	116,139	I	4
Da Nang	370,670	F	4
Di Linh		I	4
Dien Bien Phu	124,596	B	1
Dong Ha	29,603	D	3
Dong Hoi	63,441	E	3
Gia Nghia	4,526	I	4
Go Cong	36,248	I	3
Ha Dong	81,632	B	3
Ha Giang		A	2
Ha Tien		J	2
Ha Tinh		D	3
Hai Duong	95,899	B	3
Haiphong	1,447,649	B	3
Ham Tan*	19,323	J	4
Hanoi	3,058,855	B	3

*Does not appear on map; key shows general location.
Sources: 1989 census for largest cities, 1979 census and official estimates (1970-1973) for other places.

Ho Chi Minh
City . . . . .3,934,395 . . J 3
Hoa Binh . . . . .54,850 . . B 2
Hoi An . . . . .64,714 . . F 4
Hong Gai . . . . . .115,312 . . B 3
Hue . . . . .362,696 . . E 4
Khanh An* . . . . K 20
Khiem
Cuong* . . . . .6,839 . . J 3
Kontum . . . . .67,616 . . G 4
Lang Son . . . . . . .38,127 . . B 3
Lao Cai . . . . .23,721 . . A 2
Loc Ninh . . . . I 3
Long
Xuyen . . . . . . .185,221 . . J 2
Moc Hoa . . . . .3,191 . . I 3
My Tho . . . . .149,330 . . J 3
Na Sam* . . . . B 3
Nam Dinh . . . . . .219,607 . . C 3
Nha Trang . . . . .263,637 . . H 5
Ninh Binh . . . . C 3
Phan Rang . . . . . .33,377 . . I 5
Phan Thiet . . . . . .93,219 . . I 4
Phu Giao . . . . I 3
Phu Quoc . . . . J 1
Phu Tho . . . . .39,719 . . B 2
Pleiku . . . . .92,470 . . G 4
Quang Ngai . . . . .14,119 . . F 4
Quang
Trach . . . . D 3
Quang Tri . . . . .458,000 . . E 3
Quang Yen* . . . . B 3
Qui Nhon . . . . . .202,230 . . G 5
Rach Gia . . . . . . .106,675 . . J 2
Sa Dec . . . . .73,104 . . J 2
Saigon, see
Ho Chi
Minh City
Soc Trang . . . . . .74,967 . . J 3
Son La . . . . .36,585 . . B 1
Son Tay* . . . . B 2
Song Cau . . . . H 5
Tam Ky . . . . .38,532 . . F 4
Tan An . . . . .43,364 . . J 3
Tay Ninh . . . . .32,151 . . I 3
Thai Binh . . . . . . .79,566 . . C 3
Thai
Nguyen . . . . .173,113 . . B 3
Thanh Hoa . . . . .114,928 . . C 3
Thu Dau
Moi . . . . .99,426 . . I 3
Tien Yen . . . . B 3
Tra Vinh . . . . .55,403 . . J 3
Tung Nghia* . . . .14,350 . . I 4
Tuy Hoa . . . . .63,667 . . H 5
Tuyen
Quang . . . . . . .38,998 . . B 2
Uong Bi . . . . .69,771 . . B 3
Vi Thanh* . . . . . . .20,694 . . J 2
Viet Tri . . . . .116,140 . . B 2
Vinh . . . . .174,830 . . D 3
Vinh Long . . . . . . .94,692 . . J 3
Vinh Yen . . . . .30,238 . . B 2
Vung Tau . . . . . . .88,978 . . J 4
Xuan Loc . . . . .25,071 . . I 4
Yen Bai . . . . .51,148 . . B 2

Physical features

Annamite
Range . . . . E 3
Ba River . . . . H 4
Bach Long
Vi Island . . . . C 4
Be River . . . . I 3
Black River . . . . B 2
Boung River . . . . F 4
Ca Mau
Peninsula . . . . J 2
Can River . . . . D 2
Cam Ranh Bay . . . . I 5
Cape Ron . . . . D 3
Central
Highlands . . . . H 4
Cham Island . . . . F 4
Chiang River . . . . D 3
Chu Yang Sin
(peak) . . . . H 4
Con Son
(islands) . . . . K 3
Dong Nai River . . . . I 3
Fan Si Pan (peak) . . . . A 1
Gam River . . . . A 2
Gulf of Thailand . . . . K 1
Gulf of Tonkin . . . . C 3
Khoai Island . . . . K 2
Krong River . . . . H 4
Lo River . . . . A 2
Ma River . . . . C 2
Me Island . . . . C 3
Mekong River
Delta . . . . J 3
Nam Du Islands . . . . J 2
Ngoc Linh (peak) . . . . F 4
Phu
Luong (peak) . . . . B 2
Phu Quoc Island . . . . J 1
Point Ca Mau . . . . K 2
Point Lay . . . . E 3
Re Island . . . . F 4
Red River . . . . B 2
Red River Delta . . . . C 3
South China Sea . . . . E 5
Tay Chang Pass . . . . B 1
Thap Muoi Plain . . . . J 3
Tho Chu Island . . . . K 1
Thu Bon River . . . . F 4
Thu Island . . . . J 4
Van Phong Bay . . . . H 4

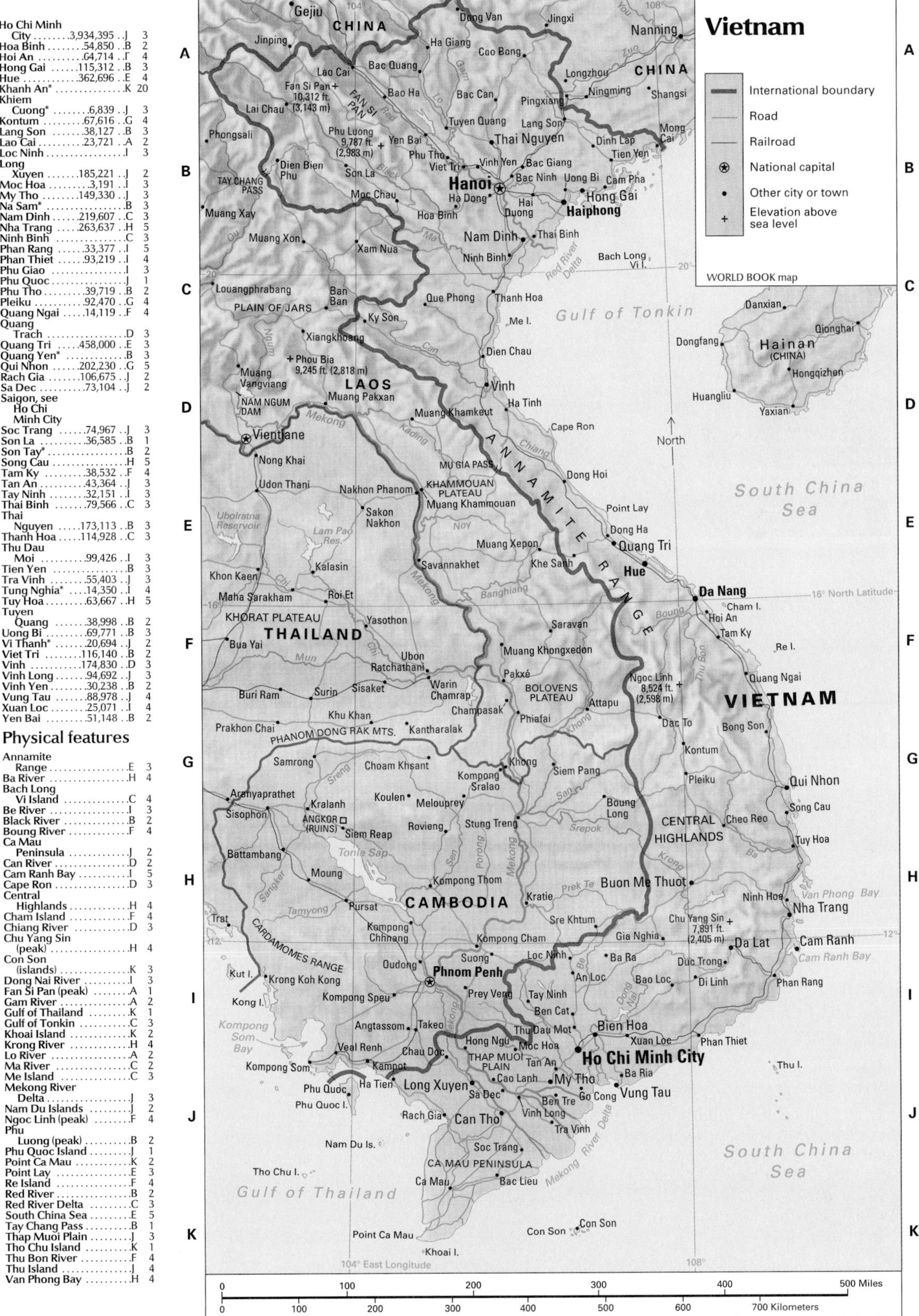

Traffic in Vietnam's cities fills the streets with many kinds of vehicles. This street in Ho Chi Minh City is crowded with bicycles, motor scooters, and cars. Two pedal-driven cyclo taxis, *foreground,* carry their passengers through the traffic.

necked lute; the *dan ty ba,* a pear-shaped lute; the *dan tam,* a three-stringed banjo; the *sao,* a bamboo flute; the *trong com,* a barrel-shaped drum; and the *chieng,* a gong.

Vietnam has a long tradition of oral literature. The nation's first great writer was Nguyen Trai, who lived in the late 1300's and early 1400's. He became famous as a pioneer of *chu nom*—a form of Vietnamese written in modified Chinese characters. Literature written in Vietnamese began to appear around the 1600's. *Truyen Kieu (The Tale of Kieu),* a long poem by Nguyen Du from the early 1800's, ranks as one of the greatest works in the Vietnamese language. Although a love story, the poem also reflects society's struggles during Nguyen Du's time.

Authors of the late 1900's and early 2000's include Duong Thu Huong, known for her novels *Paradise of the Blind* (1988) and *Novel Without a Name* (1991); Bao Ninh, whose most famous work is the novel *The Sorrow of War* (1991); and the short-story writer Nguyen Huy Thiep, some of whose works have been collected in *The General Retires and Other Stories* (1988).

The land

Vietnam occupies an S-shaped stretch of the rugged eastern Indochinese Peninsula. Four-fifths of the country is covered by hills, plateaus, and mountains. The coastline borders on the South China Sea and extends more than 2,100 miles (3,400 kilometers) from the Gulf of Tonkin to the Gulf of Thailand. Geographers divide Vietnam into three regions: northern, central, and southern.

Northern Vietnam extends from the border with China in the north to about Thanh Hoa in the south. This region is dominated by the Red River Delta, the most densely populated center of agricultural production in Vietnam. The triangular delta is the heartland of Vietnamese civilization, and the capital city of Hanoi is there.

Northern Vietnam also includes the mountains of the north and northwest. Vietnam's highest mountain is Fan Si Pan, also spelled Phan Xi Pang. It rises to 10,312 feet (3,143 meters) in northwestern Vietnam.

Central Vietnam is the most mountainous of the country's three regions. The Annamite Range, also known as the Truong Son mountains, dominates this area. The Central Highlands lie to the south. Poor soil makes farming difficult in central Vietnam. However, rich soil is available in the lowlands along the coast and on a few plateaus in the Central Highlands.

Southern Vietnam. The Mekong River in the southern part of Vietnam forms the country's largest network of agricultural plains. As a result, the Mekong Delta is often referred to as the "rice bowl" of Vietnam. Ho Chi Minh City, formerly named Saigon, is the region's major urban center and the country's economic hub.

Climate

Vietnam has a tropical climate with high humidity. Most of Vietnam has two seasons—a wet, hot summer and a drier, slightly cooler winter. *Monsoons* (seasonal winds) affect the weather throughout the year. The summer monsoon brings heavy rains from the southwest. The winter monsoon brings lighter rainfall from the northeast.

In Hanoi, in northern Vietnam, the average temperature is about 63 °F (17 °C) in January and about 85 °F (29 °C) in June. From May to October, the Red River Delta has high temperatures, heavy rains, and some typhoons, which sweep across the Gulf of Tonkin. Hanoi receives about 68 inches (173 centimeters) of rainfall a year.

In southern Vietnam, most rain falls in summer. The Ho Chi Minh City area receives about 70 inches (180 centimeters) of rain between May and October. From November through February, the weather is cooler with little rain. Average temperatures there range from about 79 °F (26 °C) in December to about 86 °F (30 °C) in April.

Central Vietnam has the greatest temperature range and includes the driest and the wettest regions of the country. Typhoons often strike the central coast. Mountain areas generally have lower temperatures and less rainfall than the delta regions and the coastal lowlands.

Economy

From 1976 to 1986, the state owned all banks and factories in Vietnam and controlled nearly every sector of the economy. During that period, the economy steadily declined. In 1986, however, Vietnamese leaders began adopting a series of far-reaching economic changes known as *doi moi* (renovation). These changes were designed to restore some economic power to the private sector. Under doi moi, for example, farmers who had satisfied their obligations to the state were allowed to produce for the market. Some state-run industries that had operated at a loss for a decade or more were dismantled. Vietnam also began to welcome foreign investment in the form of direct loans and joint ventures.

Agriculture is the leading economic activity in Vietnam. Rice is the chief crop. Most Vietnamese farmers practice wet-rice agriculture, in which rice is grown on irrigated paddies. This farming method requires much labor but produces high yields. Vietnamese farmers also cultivate cashews, a root crop called cassava, corn, peanuts, and sweet potatoes. Bananas, coconuts, melons, and other fruits are also grown. Many farmers raise animals, especially chickens, ducks, and hogs. Industrial crops, such as coffee, rubber, sugar cane, tea, and tobacco, are cultivated on large plantations.

Manufacturing. Textile production is the leading manufacturing industry in Vietnam. The country also produces cement, chemical fertilizers, glass, shoes, steel, and tires. Factories manufacture various household goods, including bicycles and televisions. Most of Vietnam's industrial development is in the south. Ho Chi Minh City has a number of high-tech industries.

Mining. Vietnam is rich in mineral resources. Its coal fields, most of which are in the north, have tremendous reserves. The country also has large deposits of chromite, copper, gold, iron ore, lead, phosphate, tin, and zinc. Bauxite, the basic ingredient of aluminum, is also mined. An abundance of limestone contributes to a thriving cement industry. Vast deposits of silica supply the basis for the manufacture of glass. The country also has extensive reserves of petroleum and natural gas, mainly offshore.

Fishing industry. With Vietnam's long coastline and many lakes and rivers, fishing has always played an important role in the economy. Vietnamese fishing crews catch a variety of fish and shellfish. Vietnam is rapidly becoming one of the world's leading producers of processed shrimp.

Service industries are those industries that provide services rather than produce manufactured goods or agricultural products. Many Vietnamese work in service industries as barbers, clerks, computer technicians, construction workers, drivers of cyclo taxis, hairdressers, housekeepers in hotels, and waiters in restaurants.

International trade. Vietnam's chief exports include clothing and textiles, coffee, fish and shellfish, petroleum, rice, rubber, shoes, and tea. Its main imports include cotton, fertilizer, machinery and equipment, motorcycles, petroleum products, and steel products. Vietnam's chief trading partners are Japan, Singapore, South Korea, and Taiwan.

Transportation and communication. Bicycles and motorcycles are popular forms of transportation in Vietnam. Many people also ride buses. The nation's rivers are widely used to transport goods and people. Vietnam has about 62,000 miles (100,000 kilometers) of roads, though only about a fourth of them are paved.

A railroad network connects the major cities of the Red River and Mekong deltas and cities along the coast. However, much of the system was damaged by bombs during the Vietnam War and remains in disrepair. Vietnam's chief ports include Da Nang, Haiphong, and Ho Chi Minh City. Hanoi and Ho Chi Minh City have international airports.

Several daily newspapers are published in Vietnam. The government controls all newspapers, magazines, and television and radio broadcasts.

History

People have lived in what is now Vietnam since prehistoric times. Archaeologists have discovered remains of a stone age culture dating back about 500,000 years in the province of Thanh Hoa. Agriculture developed in northern Vietnam more than 7,000 years ago.

About 5,000 years ago, a kingdom called Van Lang emerged in the Black and Red river valleys under the rule of the Hung kings. One of the most important cultures of Van Lang, the Dong Son civilization, flourished in the valleys of the Red and Ma rivers from about 800 to 300 B.C. This civilization is known mainly for its elaborately decorated bronze drums.

Nam Viet. In 258 B.C., a leader named An Duong

Important dates in Vietnam

111 B.C. The Chinese conquered Nam Viet, a kingdom in what is now northern Vietnam.

A.D. 939 China ended its rule over the Vietnamese, who then set up an independent state.

1802 Nguyen Anh united the country and called it Vietnam.

1860's-1880's France took control of Vietnam.

1940-1945 Japan controlled Vietnam during World War II.

1946 War began between France and the Vietminh.

1954 The Vietminh defeated the French. The Geneva Conference temporarily divided Vietnam into two zones.

1957 The Vietnam War began, as Communist-supported rebels began a revolt against the South Vietnamese government.

1973 United States participation in the Vietnam War ended.

1975 The Vietnam War ended on April 30 with the surrender of South Vietnam.

1976 The Communists unified North and South Vietnam into the Socialist Republic of Vietnam.

1986 Vietnam's Communist government introduced some free-market economic reforms.

1995 Vietnam joined the Association of Southeast Asian Nations.

The Indochina Peninsula in 1900

This map shows French Indochina, which included Cambodia, Laos, and Vietnam. France divided Vietnam into Tonkin, Annam, and Cochin China. Present-day Vietnam is shown in yellow.

WORLD BOOK map

founded the kingdom of Au Lac. In 207 B.C., an official of China's Qin dynasty named Zhao Tuo (Trieu Da in Vietnamese) founded the kingdom of Nam Viet. Nam Viet included Au Lac and several other kingdoms in what is now northern Vietnam. In 111 B.C., the Chinese Han dynasty conquered Nam Viet. Through the centuries, many Vietnamese resisted Chinese rule. But not until A.D. 939, as a result of a rebellion led by Ngo Quyen, did the Vietnamese gain independence.

Despite the centuries of Chinese occupation, many aspects of Vietnamese culture remained in place, but new patterns also emerged. Specifically, the rise of a mixed Chinese and Vietnamese ruling class ensured the lasting importance of Chinese writing, even though the Vietnamese continued to speak their own language. Chinese ideas of historical writing also had an enormous impact on how Vietnamese historians represented their past. Vietnamese officials sometimes adopted Chinese administrative practices. The Three Teachings—Mahayana Buddhism, Confucianism, and Taoism—are another legacy of Chinese rule.

Independence. After Ngo Quyen's death in 944, Vietnam was troubled by succession disputes and the competition of war lords. These troubles ended with the establishment of the Dinh dynasty in 968, though the dynasty lasted only 12 years. The succeeding dynasty, established in 980, lasted only until 1009. Two long-lasting dynasties, the Ly (1009-1225) and the Tran (1225-1400), stabilized politics.

In 1400, Ho Quy Ly seized the Vietnamese throne, and in 1407, the Ming Chinese invaded the country and took control. In 1428, Le Loi drove out the Chinese rulers and established the Le dynasty. Under the Le rulers, the Vietnamese empire continued the process of Nam Tien (Advance to the South). During the 1400's, for example, the Vietnamese conquered Champa, a rival kingdom in what is now central Vietnam.

In 1527, the Mac dynasty overthrew the Le dynasty, and, in 1540, was formally recognized by the Ming Chinese. Le forces regained control over central Vietnam in 1545 and northern Vietnam in 1592. However, Mac forces continued to fight against the Le for more than 35 years.

During the mid-1500's, Vietnamese politics became further fragmented as the Trinh and Nguyen families, the two clans closest to the Le court, drifted apart. By 1600, the country was effectively divided, and the Le kept control in name only. Even though the Ming Chinese had recognized the Le dynasty as ruler of Vietnam, the Trinh lords actually governed the north and the Nguyen lords were in charge of the south. In the 1600's, the rivalry between these two clans occasionally erupted into armed conflict.

The Nguyen lords continued their expansion to the south until 1771. That year, three brothers from the region of Tay Son in central Vietnam began a series of successful attacks against Nguyen rule. This upheaval, known as the Tay Son Rebellion, resulted in the collapse of Nguyen power in the south, Trinh power in the north, and, in 1788, the end of the Le dynasty. After defending Vietnam against an invasion of Qing Chinese troops in 1789, the Tay Son dynasty tried to consolidate its rule over all of what is now Vietnam.

In 1802, Nguyen Anh became the first emperor of the Nguyen dynasty. He took the reign name of Gia Long. He united the country and called it Vietnam. The Nguyen dynasty, Vietnam's last, established its capital in Hue. It formally ended in 1945.

French rule. In 1858, French warships captured the city of Da Nang. The French claimed that they were protecting Jesuit missionaries and Vietnamese who had converted to Roman Catholicism. By continuing the armed attacks and through diplomatic pressure, France succeeded in taking control of the southern part of Vietnam, known then as Cochin China, in the 1860's. In the 1880's, France took control of the northern (Tonkin) and central (Annam) parts of Vietnam. With the conquest of Cambodia in the 1860's and of Laos in the 1890's, French control of Indochina was complete.

The French were principally interested in Vietnam and the surrounding area as a base for trading with China. They also hoped to exploit the mineral wealth of Vietnam and to establish plantations for coffee, rubber, and tea. To help carry out these plans, the French built roads and railways linking the lowlands, the midlands, and the mountains. They also expanded port facilities.

Under French rule, the traditional Vietnamese ruling class withdrew from public life, and a new French-Vietnamese ruling class emerged. The romanized written version of Vietnamese known as *quoc ngu* also became more prominent in private and public affairs.

Through the years, Vietnamese resistance to French rule grew. Various nationalist associations and societies emerged, as did a number of political parties. These parties included the Vietnamese Nationalist Party, Indochinese Communist Party, and the New Vietnamese Revolutionary Party.

The August Revolution of 1945. In August 1940, during World War II (1939-1945), France's wartime Vichy government granted Japan permission to use northern

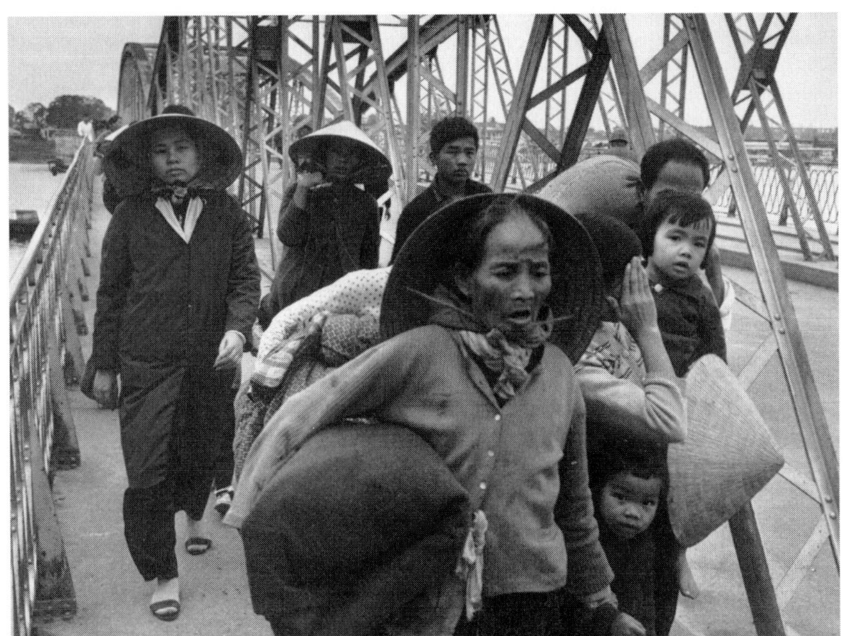

© Hulton/Archive

Vietnamese refugees flee fighting during the Vietnam War (1957-1975). The war caused enormous destruction and resulted in millions of deaths. Millions of Vietnamese became refugees.

Vietnam for military operations. When Japanese troops advanced into other Southeast Asian colonies of European powers, they took control over the colonial governments. In Vietnam, the Japanese at first allowed French officials to continue to carry out their administrative duties. In March 1945, however, the Japanese ousted the French officials.

Initially, most Vietnamese had welcomed the Japanese, expecting that they would free Vietnam from French rule. When it seemed that Japan was also a threat to their independence, however, many Vietnamese reconsidered their plans to join with the Japanese to fight the French. One result of such reconsideration was the creation of an organization called the Vietminh in 1941. Established by Ho Chi Minh and other leaders of the Indochinese Communist Party, the Vietminh was designed to encourage national unity and independence.

Japan agreed to surrender on Aug. 14, 1945. Within days, anticolonial activists in Vietnam staged the August Revolution. On September 2, Ho recited Vietnam's declaration of independence, in which he quoted directly from the American Declaration of Independence. Ho and other revolutionary leaders expected that the United States would support the new state—the Democratic Republic of Vietnam (DRV)—for a number of reasons. For instance, the United States had gained its own independence through a revolution. The United States had also criticized European colonialism for most of the 1900's. In addition, the Vietminh had cooperated with U.S. diplomatic and military personnel during World War II. However, the DRV never received U.S. support, mainly because of U.S. opposition to Communism.

The First Indochina War. After World War II, France tried to reclaim its former colonies in Southeast Asia. In 1946, war broke out between France and the Vietminh. Throughout the war, the French controlled cities in north and south Vietnam. The revolutionaries, based in the mountains of the north and northwest, controlled most of the countryside. Many southern Vietnamese rejected the idea of a Communist-dominated government and sided with the French. By mid-1949, the French had formed the Associated State of Vietnam to oppose the Vietminh. Bao Dai, the last of the Nguyen emperors, headed the government of the Associated State. The fighting in Vietnam ended in May 1954, when the Vietminh defeated the French garrison at Dien Bien Phu.

Fearing the growth of Communism, the United States began in 1948 to channel aid to the countries of Western Europe to help them rebuild after the devastation of World War II. The assistance provided by the Marshall Plan made it possible for France to rebuild and to continue fighting the war in Vietnam. Further expressing its support for the French attempt to reconquer Vietnam, the United States formally recognized the Associated State of Vietnam in 1950.

During the final stages of the First Indochina War, negotiators representing nine countries—Cambodia, China, France, Laos, the United Kingdom, the United States, the Soviet Union, the Democratic Republic of Vietnam, and the Associated State of Vietnam—assembled in Geneva, Switzerland. In July 1954, the representatives produced a series of agreements known as the Geneva Accords. One of these agreements provided that Vietnam be temporarily divided into northern and southern zones at the 17th parallel. Another agreement called for an election in 1956 to unify the country. Fearing that Ho Chi Minh would win such an election, however, southern Vietnamese, with U.S. support, refused to participate. The election was never held.

The Vietnam War began in 1957. It is sometimes called the Second Indochina War, and the Vietnamese know it as the American War. Communist-supported rebels in the South began a revolt against the government of Ngo Dinh Diem, who was backed by the United States. United States military and civilian advisers then rushed to aid South Vietnam. Through the years, South Vietnam received extensive assistance from the United States, including cash, military equipment, and more than 500,000 troops. Despite this aid, South Vietnam failed to shape itself into a popularly supported, non-Communist state. In April 1975, the People's Army of North Vietnam launched an offensive that resulted in the complete collapse of Southern power.

The Vietnam War caused enormous destruction. The United States dropped tons of chemicals on central Vietnam designed to clear the jungles and forests. Parts of the country remained barren of vegetation for many years afterwards. The U.S. forces also destroyed many rice fields and villages. The Vietnam War resulted in the deaths of millions of Vietnamese, many of them civilians. More than 58,000 American military personnel also lost their lives. For a detailed discussion of the war, see **Vietnam War.**

Postwar Vietnam. In April 1976, national elections determined the nearly 500 members of the new National Assembly for a reunited Vietnam. In July, the Socialist Republic of Vietnam was officially proclaimed. In the process of establishing a single state, leaders of the new government sought out supporters of the former South Vietnamese government. According to official sources, more than 1 million southerners were subjected to some form of "reeducation" in the political culture of the North. For most of these people, this process took several days or weeks. But thousands of others, viewed as greater threats, spent a decade or more in labor camps.

Following reunification, thousands of northerners resettled in the south. As a consequence, the northern dialect of Vietnamese is now regarded officially as standard Vietnamese. In addition, the government has taken thousands of Kinh from the deltas and relocated them in the highlands and mountains.

With the collapse of the Southern regime, many Vietnamese fled the country. They settled in the United States, Canada, and Australia, or joined earlier generations of exiles in Belgium and France. Following the government's nationalization of industries, tens of thousands of ethnic Chinese also left the country.

Many refugees left Vietnam in boats, risking drowning and pirate attacks in the South China Sea. These refugees became known as *boat people.* They went to other countries in Southeast Asia, where they stayed in refugee camps until they could be relocated. Many later moved to the United States. In the mid-1990's, the United Nations and countries that housed or helped pay for the camps closed nearly all of them. Most of the remaining refugees were sent back to Vietnam.

Invasion of Cambodia. In 1978, Vietnam invaded Cambodia. It replaced Cambodia's Khmer Rouge Communist government with a pro-Vietnamese Communist government. The Khmer Rouge and non-Communist groups then fought against the government and the Vietnamese forces in Cambodia. Vietnam gradually withdrew its troops in the 1980's, and the war ended in 1991.

Recent developments. In the late 1980's, the Vietnamese government began a program of economic restructuring known as *doi moi.* This program encouraged some forms of private enterprise and competition as well as foreign investment. In early July 1995, Vietnam and the United States established diplomatic ties. Later that month, Vietnam became a member of the Association of Southeast Asian Nations (ASEAN), a regional organization that promotes political, economic, cultural, and social cooperation among its members. In July 2000, Vietnam and the United States signed a trade agreement. This pact cleared the way for normal trade relations between the two countries for the first time since the Vietnam War. Patricia M. Pelley

Related articles in ***World Book*** include:

Association of Southeast Asian Nations
Da Nang
Dien Bien Phu, Battle of
Geneva Accords
Haiphong
Hanoi
Ho Chi Minh
Ho Chi Minh City
Hue
Indochina
Mekong River
Ngo Dinh Diem
Southeast Asia
Southeast Asia Treaty Organization
Vietnam War

Outline

I. Government
- A. National level
- B. Local level
- C. Courts
- D. Armed forces

II. People
- A. Ancestry
- B. Language

III. Way of life
- A. Rural life
- B. City life
- C. Clothing
- D. Food and drink
- E. Recreation.
- F. Religion
- G.Education
- H.The arts

IV. The land
- A. Northern Vietnam
- B. Central Vietnam
- C. Southern Vietnam

V. Climate

VI. Economy
- A. Agriculture
- B. Manufacturing
- C. Mining
- D. Fishing industry
- E. Service industries
- F. International trade
- G. Transportation and communication

VII. History

Questions

What area is the heartland of Vietnamese civilization?
What is considered the leading force in the state and society in Vietnam?
What are the Three Teachings?
What nation controlled Vietnam during World War II?
How did the opening of the École des Beaux Arts de l'Indochine affect Vietnamese art?
What was the importance of the Battle of Dien Bien Phu?
What is the chief crop of Vietnam?
What are the largest minority groups in Vietnam?
Why did Ho Chi Minh and other Vietnamese leaders expect the United States to support the Democratic Republic of Vietnam?
What is *pho? Nuoc mam? Doi moi?*

Additional resources

Cole, Wendy M. *Vietnam.* Rev. ed. Chelsea Hse., 1999. Younger readers.
Duiker, William J. *Historical Dictionary of Vietnam.* 2nd ed. Scarecrow, 1998.
Kamm, Henry. *Dragon Ascending: Vietnam and the Vietnamese.* Arcade, 1996.
Larimer, Tim, and Forbes, Andrew, eds. *Insight Guide: Vietnam.* Rev. ed. APA Pubns., 1998.
SarDesai, D. R. *Vietnam: Past and Present.* 3rd ed. Westview, 1998.

Index

How to use the index

This index covers the contents of the 2000, 2001, and 2002 editions.

Each index entry gives the edition year and the page number or page numbers—for example, **Chiapas.** This means that the information on this topic may be found on page 310 in the 2002 edition.

When there are many references to a topic, they are grouped alphabetically by clue words under the main topic. For example, the clue words under **Children** group the reference to that topic under several subtopics.

When a topic such as **CHINA** appears in all capital letters, this means that there is an Update article entitled China in at least one of the three volumes covered by this index. References to the topic in other articles may also appear after the topic name.

When only the first letter of a topic, such as **Cholesterol,** is capitalized, this means that there is no article entitled Cholesterol but that information on this topic may be found in the edition and on the pages listed.

The "see" and "see also" cross-references—for example, **Chrysler Corp.,** refer the reader to other entries in the index or to Update articles in the volumes covered by the index.

An entry followed by *WBE* refers to a new or revised *World Book Encyclopedia* article in the supplement section, as in **Classical music.** This means that a *World Book Encyclopedia* article on this topic begins on page 456 of the 2002 edition.

The indications (il.) or (ils.) mean that the reference on this page is to an illustration or illustrations only, as in **Clinton, Bill,** of the 2002 edition.

A

O

P

Q

R

S

T

U

V

W

X

Y

Z

Acknowledgments

The publishers acknowledge the following sources for illustrations. Credits read from top to bottom, left to right, on their respective pages. An asterisk (*) denotes illustrations and photographs created exclusively for this edition. All maps, charts, and diagrams were prepared by the staff unless otherwise noted.

6 © Reuters/Getty Images; AP/Wide World
7-9 AP/Wide World
10 AP/Wide World; © Getty Images
11 Goddard Space Flight Center from NOAA Goes-8 DATA/Hal Pierce/Fritz Hasler/NASA
12 AP/Wide World
15 © Agence France-Presse
16 © Reuters/Getty Images
19 AP/Wide World
20 © Karen Pike, Getty Images
23 © Gamma
25-29 AP/Wide World
31 © Agence France-Presse
32-35 AP/Wide World
36 © Rendering of planets by Sylvain Korzennik, Harvard University; photograph by Till Credner, Max Planck Institute for Aeronomy
38-42 AP/Wide World
43 © Reuters/Getty Images
45 © Gary Miller, *New York Post* from Rex Features
46 © Jim Lo Scalzo for *U.S. News & World Report*
49 AP/Wide World
50 © Agence France-Presse
53 © Koji Harada, Kyodo News International; © Agence France-Presse
54 AP/Wide World
62 © National Museums of Kenya, photo by Fred Spoor
64-65 AP/Wide World
66 Photo illustration: Christophe Valtin © Milwaukee Art Museum
68 Drawing of Frank Lloyd Wright © 2001 The Frank Lloyd Wright Foundation, Scottsdale, AZ; The Frank Lloyd Wright Foundation, Scottsdale, AZ
71 © Christian Korab
72-75 The Frank Lloyd Wright Foundation, Scottsdale, AZ
76-78 Steelcase Inc.
82 AP/Wide World
85 Adele Bloch-Bauer (1907) oil and gold on canvas by Gustav Klimt, Austrian Gallery, Vienna
86 AP/Wide World
90 NASA/Hubble Heritage Team
91 © Anglo Australian Observatory; NASA
93 © Agence France-Presse
98 Ford Motor Company
99 General Motors Corporation
100 AP/Wide World; © Agence France-Presse
102 © Steve Marcus, *Las Vegas Sun*
104 © Reuters/Getty Images
106 © Jed Jacobsohn, Allsport
108-110 AP/Wide World
112 © Getty Images
115 © Agence France-Presse
117 AP/Wide World
119 Milwaukee Brewers Baseball Club
121-123 AP/Wide World
124 Bank of Canada
128 Press Association Ltd.
131 AP/Wide World
137-139 © Reuters/Getty Images
144 © Andrea Tamoni, Teatro alla Scala
147 © Reuters/Getty Images
152 AP/Wide World
158 © Jefferson County SO from Getty Images
161 Granger Collection; AP/Wide World
162 Culver Pictures; AP/Wide World
163 Culver Pictures; AP/Wide World
167-171 AP/Wide World
174 © Hulton/Archive
175 © Hulton/Archive; Kobal Collection; © Hulton/Archive; AP/Wide World
176 © Mosaic Images from Corbis; © Hulton/Archive
177 © New York Times Co. from Hulton/Archive; AP/Wide World; © Philip Gould, Corbis; © Getty Images; © Hulton/Archive
178 © Hulton/Archive; © Lyn Sidaway, *The Gazette* (Montreal); © Getty Images
179 NBC from Globe Photos
180 Everett Collection
182-189 AP/Wide World
196 © Reuters/Getty Images
198-199 © Corbis
203 © Norbert von der Groeben, The Image Works; © Corbis
206 AP/Wide World
207-209 © Corbis
211 AP/Wide World
212 European Central Bank
213 © Getty Images
217 AP/Wide World
219 Kyodo News International
222-223 AP/Wide World
225 © Reuters/Getty Images
227-229 AP/Wide World
230 © Pictor/Alamy.com; NASA
232 WORLD BOOK illustration by JAK Graphics
234 © Corbis
237 © Morton Beebe, Corbis
238 © Lonnie G. Thompson, Byrd Polar Research Center
240 © Reuters/Getty Images
244 AP/Wide World
245-246 © Agence France-Presse
249 AP/Wide World
251 © Reuters/Getty Images
253 Alex Garcia © *Chicago Tribune*
256-258 AP/Wide World
260-261 © Hulton/Archive
262 © PhotoDisc, Inc.
263 AP/Wide World
265 AP/Wide World; © SONICblue Inc.
266 AP/Wide World
268-270 © Reuters/Getty Images
272-281 AP/Wide World
284 © Reuters/Getty Images
289 © PhotoDisc, Inc.
291-293 AP/Wide World
298 Illustration from *So You Want to Be President?* Text © 2000 by Judith St. George. Illustrations © 2000 by David Small. Printed with permission of Philomel Books, a division of Penguin Putnam Books for Young Readers. All rights reserved.
301-303 © Agence France-Presse
308 Abiomed, Inc.
310-312 AP/Wide World
316 © Columbia/Universal from Shooting Star; © Universal/Dreamworks from Shooting Star; © USA Films from Shooting Star
319 © Agence France-Presse
320-321 AP/Wide World
323 © Smithsonian Institution; AP/Wide World; AP/Wide World
324 AP/Wide World; © Paramount Parks
325 © Detroit Institute of Art; AP/Wide World; AP/Wide World
326 © Agence France-Presse
329 © Reuters/Getty Images
333 AP/Wide World
334 © Reuters/Getty Images
336-340 AP/Wide World
341 © Agence France-Presse
342 U.S. Dept. of Defense
344 © Getty Images
346-355 AP/Wide World
357 Peter Souza © *Chicago Tribune*
359 AP/Wide World
361 © Reuters/Getty Images
363 AP/Wide World
364 © Agence France-Presse
367-371 AP/Wide World
372 NASA
374 © Reuters/Getty Images
375-379 NASA
380 © Reuters/Getty Images
384-395 AP/Wide World
396 © Agence France-Presse
399 © Warner Bros. from Shooting Star; © HBO from Reuters/Getty Images
401 © Agence France-Presse
403-404 AP/Wide World
406 © Paul Kolnik
408-409 Fisher-Price, Inc.
410 © Reuters/Getty Images
413 AP/Wide World
414 Press Association Ltd.
419 © Reuters/Getty Images
420 © Getty Images
425 AP/Wide World
426 © PhotoDisc, Inc.
430 Brown Bros.
432 AP/Wide World
434 © Hulton/Archive
435 AP/Wide World
436 WORLD BOOK photo by Steven Spicer; Culver Pictures
438 © Jim Lo Scalzo, *U.S. News & World Report*
442 © Reuters/Getty Images; AP/Wide World
443 AP/Wide World
447 © David Jenike, Cincinnati Zoo; AP/Wide World
449 © Tourism Montreal